Elements of
Language
Fourth Course

Lee Odell

Richard Vacca

Renée Hobbs

Grammar, Usage, and Mechanics
Instructional Framework by

John E. Warriner

HOLT, RINEHART AND WINSTON
A Harcourt Education Company
Orlando • **Austin** • New York • San Diego • London

Printed in the United States of America

ISBN 0-03-079682-2

1 2 3 4 5   048   08 07 06

A STUDENT'S GUIDE FOR LANGUAGE ARTS SKILLS AND STRATEGIES AND COUNTDOWN TO TESTING

Language Arts Skills and Strategies

Throughout your school career, you've become familiar with the language arts skills and strategies that help you read, write, and create and analyze presentations or media messages. These skills not only help you do well in your classes and on state tests, but also help you communicate effectively with others.

For a list of the most common language arts skills and strategies, take a look at the chart on the next seven pages. This chart provides definitions with specific examples from *Elements of Language* for each skill and strategy. Use this list as a quick reference to the skills and strategies you will practice this year.

Countdown to Testing

One way to show that you know language arts skills and strategies is to take a test. In fact, many states require that students take standardized tests to show mastery of these language arts skills. To help you prepare for such a test, use the weekly Countdown to Testing activities that appear on pages S9–S32.

The Countdown to Testing section consists of 20 weeks of questions. During each week, you will answer one multiple-choice question each day. Here are a few important points to remember about the questions.

▶ Some of the questions refer to a passage, and if they do, the directions at the top of each page will direct you to the passage.
▶ Some of the questions include sentences or graphics you must analyze in order to answer the question.
▶ All of the questions have a page reference showing you where to go in your textbook to find more information about the skill or strategy the question covers.

By answering these questions in Countdown to Testing, you'll have more practice using language arts skills and strategies, and you'll be better prepared for standardized tests.

LANGUAGE ARTS SKILLS AND STRATEGIES

The following chart lists the four strands of language arts, plus the skills and strategies within these strands that are commonly addressed in language arts classrooms. Each skill or strategy appears in a yellow-tint box. To the right of each skill or strategy you'll find a specific example from your textbook.

READING

Comprehension

▶ **Identifying Main Idea and Details:** identifying the most important point or focus of a passage and the details that support or explain that focus	The **Reading Skill** on pages 61–62 gives instruction, examples, and practice on how to identify an implied main idea and details. The **Test-Taking Mini-Lesson** on page 65 gives instruction and examples on identifying main ideas on reading tests.
▶ **Making Inferences:** adding information you already know to textual information to draw a conclusion about something in the text or form a generalization about something outside the text.	The **Reading Skills** on pages 21–23, 132–134, and 172–173 give instruction, examples, and practice on making inferences, forming generalizations, and drawing conclusions, respectively. The **Test-Taking Mini-Lesson** on page 27 gives instruction on and examples of making inferences on reading tests.
▶ **Summarizing:** noting the most important ideas of a text using only as few words as possible	For instruction and examples on summarizing, see page 884.
▶ **Determining Author's Purpose:** noting the author's reason for writing—to inform, persuade, entertain, instruct, or express oneself	For instruction and examples on determining author's purpose and point of view, see page 876.
▶ **Distinguishing Fact and Opinion:** being able to tell the difference between information that can be proved (facts) and personal beliefs (opinions)	The **Reading Skill** on pages 255–257 gives instruction, examples, and practice on on how to tell the difference between facts and opinions. The **Test-Taking Mini-Lesson** on page 262 gives instruction and examples on identifying facts and opinions on reading tests.
▶ **Making Predictions:** the act of deciding what you think will happen next in a text	For instruction and examples on predicting, see page 882.
▶ **Identifying Causes and Effect:** noting the difference between causes (what makes something happen) and effects (what happens as a result of a causes)	The **Reading Skill** on pages 95–97 explains and gives instructions, practice, and examples for identifying cause and effect. The **Test-Taking Mini-Lesson** on page 103 gives instruction and examples on identifying implied cause and effect on reading tests. The **Critical Thinking Mini-Lesson** on page 108 gives instruction, examples, and practice on identifying false cause-and-effect statements.

▶ Identifying Point of View: determining an author's attitude about a subject

To help you understand author's point of view, see pages 876.

▶ Analyzing Text Structures: recognizing the organizational patterns authors use

The **Reading Focuses** on pages 62–63, 97–101, and 134–135 give instruction, examples, and practice for analyzing comparison-contrast, cause-effect and problem-solution text structures, respectively. For additional instruction, see pages 885–886.

▶ Paraphrasing: restating in your own words ideas you have read

The **Reading Focus** on pages 213–214 explains and gives instructions, examples, and practice for paraphrasing. For additional instruction, see page 882.

▶ Analyzing Persuasive Techniques: identifying methods authors use to persuade their readers

The **Reading Skill** on pages 300–302 explains and gives instructions, examples, and practice for identifying persuasive techniques. The **Reading Focus** on pages 257–260 explains and gives instructions, examples, and practice for identifying elements of persuasion.

▶ Taking Reading Tests: answering reading questions on standardized tests

For strategies and practice on answering multiple-choice questions and extended response questions, see pages 3–10 and 911–927. The **Test-Taking Mini-Lessons** on pages 27, 65, 103, 137, 177, 217, 262, and 305 give examples and instruction on how to answer test questions on a variety of reading skills.

Vocabulary

▶ Using Context Clues: determining meaning of words through the group of words or sentences surrounding the word

The **Vocabulary Mini-Lessons** on pages 64, 136, and 304 give instruction, examples, and practice on using context clues. The **Test-Taking Mini-Lesson** on page 217 gives instruction and examples on using context to understand specialized or technical terms. For additional instruction on and examples of context clues, see page 887.

▶ Analyzing Word Structure: looking at a word's root, prefix, or suffix to help figure out its meaning

The **Vocabulary Mini-Lessons** on pages 102 and 176 give instruction, examples, and practice on analyzing word structure. See pages 887–888 and 891–894 for additional instruction and examples.

▶ Using Multiple-Meaning Words: defining words with multiple meanings through context

The **Vocabulary Mini-Lesson** on page 26 gives step-by-step instruction, examples, and practice on understanding multiple-meaning words. See page 889 for additional instruction and examples.

▶ Understanding the Origins of English Words: studying how words came into the English language

To help you understand and study the history of English, see pages 861–865.

▶ Understanding Connotation and Denotation: understanding the difference between word associations and word definitions

The **Vocabulary Mini-Lesson** on page 261 gives step-by-step instruction, examples, and practice on connotation and denotation.

WRITING

Writing Strategies

▶ **Progressing through the Writing Process:** using the four stages of writing to create texts

See pages xxxiv–xxxv for instruction and examples on the writing process.

▶ **Considering Audience and Purpose:** choosing words and sentences to address the reason for writing a text and the people you are writing for

The prewriting stage of each of the **Writing Workshop** on pages 28, 66, 104, 138, 178, 218, 263, and 306 gives instruction and examples for how to consider audience and purpose.

▶ **Evaluating and Revising for Coherence and Unity:** improving the way details are connected

See pages 374–381 for instruction, examples and practice on unity and coherence.

▶ **Evaluating and Revising for Content and Organization:** assessing writing to improve the development and order of the ideas in a text

The evaluating and revising stage of each of the **Writing Workshop** on pages 42, 78, 114, 150, 188, 240, 276, and 321 gives instruction, examples, and practice on revising content and organization. See pages 376–380 and 392–393 for instruction, examples, and practice on how to elaborate in a text.

▶ **Evaluating and Revising for Conciseness and Clarity:** assessing writing to improve the precision of word choice and sentences in a text

The **Focus On** features on pages 44, 80, 116, 152, 190, 242, 278, and 323 give instruction, examples, and practice on revising sentences to improve word choice and sentence style. **Chapter 10** on pages 362–366 gives instruction, examples, and practice on improving conciseness and clarity.

Writing Applications

▶ **Writing Narrative Texts:** producing texts that tell a story

The **Connections to Literature** on pages 195–197 gives instruction, examples, and practice on how to use the writing process to create a short story.

▶ **Writing Expository Texts:** producing texts that explore or explain

The **Writing Workshops** on pages 66–84, 104–119, 138–156, and 218–245 give instruction, examples, and practice on how to use the writing process to create a comparison-contrast essay, a cause-and-effect explanation, a problem-analysis essay, and a research paper, respectively.

▶ **Writing Persuasive Texts:** producing texts to convince readers to think or act in a particular way

The **Writing Workshops** on pages 263–281 and 306–326 give instruction, examples, and practice on how to use the writing process to create a persuasive essay and a persuasive brochure, respectively.

▶ **Writing Expressive Texts:** producing texts to share feelings and thoughts

The **Writing Workshop** on pages 28–47 gives instruction, examples, and practice on how to use the writing process to create a personal reflection.

▶ **Writing Responses to Literature:** producing texts that respond to a piece of literature

The **Writing Workshop** on pages 178–194 gives instruction, examples, and practice on the process of writing a literary analysis. The **Connections to Literature** on page 157 gives instruction, examples, and practice on the process of writing an analysis of a literary character.

▶ **Writing Creative Texts:** producing texts that use language in an original and imaginative way

The **Connections to Literature** on pages 48–49 and 195–197 give instruction, examples, and practice on the process of writing a poem and a short story, respectively. The **Writing Mini-Lesson** on page 37 gives instruction, examples, and practice on using figurative language.

▶ **Writing Descriptive Texts:** using sensory details to support a dominant impression of a subject

The **Writing Workshop** on pages 28–47 gives instruction, examples, and practice on how to use descriptive detail to create a personal reflection.

▶ **Writing Correspondence:** using the correct format to write letters

For instruction and examples on writing letters, see pages 939–943 and 949–950.

▶ **Taking Writing Tests:** answering multiple-choice writing questions and responding to on-demand writing prompts

For strategies and practice on responding to writing tests, see pages 11–15 and 924–925. The **Test-Taking Mini-Lesson** on page 282 gives instruction and strategies for answering on-demand writing prompts.

Written Language Conventions

▶ **Proofreading for Correct Modifier Usage:** reading a final text to identify and correct errors in comparison and placement

Chapter 19, pages 612–635, gives instruction, examples, and practice on using modifiers correctly. The **Grammar Links** on pages 118 and 244 give instruction, examples, and practice on dangling and misplaced modifiers, respectively.

▶ **Proofreading for Correct Verb Usage:** reading a final text to identify and correct errors in tense, agreement, and form

Chapter 16, pages 510–531, and **Chapter 18,** pages 572–607, give instruction, examples, and practice on using verbs correctly. The **Grammar Link** on page 46 gives instruction, examples, and practice on subject-verb agreement.

▶ **Proofreading for Correct Pronoun Usage:** reading a final text to identify and correct errors in case and agreement

Chapter 16, pages 532–542, and **Chapter 17,** pages 546–571, give instruction, examples, and practice on using pronouns correctly.

▶ **Proofreading for Fragments and Run-On Sentences:** reading a final text to identify and correct errors in sentence structure

Chapter 9, pages 340–349, gives instruction, examples, and practice on correcting fragments and run-on sentences. The **Grammar Link** on page 155 gives instruction, examples, and practice on correcting sentence fragments.

▶ **Proofreading for Correct Spelling:** reading a final text to identify and correct errors in spelling	**Chapter 26,** pages 778–807, gives instruction, examples, and practice for spelling correctly.
▶ **Proofreading for Correct Punctuation:** reading a final text to identify and correct errors in punctuation	**Chapters 22–25** on pages 672–777 give instruction, examples, and practice on punctuating text correctly. The **Grammar Link** on page 193 gives instruction, examples, and practice on punctuating quotations.
▶ **Proofreading for Correct Capitalization:** reading a final text to identify and correct errors in capitalization	**Chapter 21,** pages 666–691, gives instruction, examples, and practice on using capital letters correctly.
▶ **Proofreading for Correct Manuscript Style:** reading a final text to identify and correct errors in indentation and spacing	For guidelines for manuscript style, see page 849.

Grammar

▶ **Understanding and Identifying the Parts of Speech:** recognizing the eight parts of speech	**Chapter 12,** pages 402–435, gives instruction, examples, and practice for identifying and using the eight parts of speech.
▶ **Understanding and Identifying the Parts of a Sentence:** recognizing subject, predicate, and complements of a sentence	**Chapter 13,** pages 436–465, gives instruction, examples, and practice for identifying and using the subject, predicate, and complements of a sentence.
▶ **Understanding and Identifying Phrases and Clauses:** recognizing phrases and clauses	**Chapters 14–15,** pages 466–509, give instruction, examples, and practice for identifying and using phrases and clauses.
▶ **Understanding and Identifying Sentence Structure:** recognizing kinds of sentences and the four basic sentence structures	**Chapter 13,** pages 459–462, and **Chapter 15,** pages 504–506, give instruction, examples, and practice on the classification of sentences and the four basic sentence structures, respectively.

SPEAKING AND LISTENING

Speaking and Listening Strategies

▶ **Understanding the Techniques of Clear and Distinct Speech:** studying the strategies of an effective speaker

For instruction and strategies for effective speaking, see pages 896–905.

▶ **Analyzing Oral Texts:** listening to an oral presentation in order to understand its message and purpose

For instruction and strategies for analyzing oral texts, see pages 907–910.

▶ **Understanding the Listening Process:** studying the skills involved in an effective listening process

For instruction and strategies for the listening process, see page 906.

Speaking and Listening Applications

▶ **Giving and Listening to an Informative Speech:** presenting and listening to a speech that explains

The **Focus on Speaking and Listening** on pages 158–161 gives instruction, examples and practice on giving and listening to an informative speech. For instruction and strategies for a formal speech, see pages 897–899.

▶ **Giving and Listening to a Persuasive Speech:** presenting and listening to a speech that presents a position

The **Focus on Speaking and Listening** on pages 279–280 gives instruction, examples and practice on presenting a persuasive speech. For instruction and strategies for a formal speech, see pages 897–899.

▶ **Giving and Listening to an Oral Interpretation:** presenting and listening to a story or a reading of a literary selection

The **Focus on Speaking and Listening** on pages 203–204 gives instruction on and practice in presenting and listening to an oral interpretation. Page 905 gives instruction and strategies for presenting an oral interpretation of a literary selection. Page 907 gives instruction and strategies for appreciative listening.

▶ **Participating in an Oral Discussion:** presenting and listening to discussions

For instruction and strategies for participating in a group discussion, see **Connections to Life,** pages 120–121, and pages 904–905.

▶ **Holding a Debate:** presenting a debate

For instruction on how to hold a debate, see pages 896–897.

▶ **Giving and Listening to an Extemporaneous Speech:** presenting and listening to an unplanned speech

For instruction and strategies for an impromptu speech, see page 899.

VIEWING AND REPRESENTING

Viewing and Representing Strategies

▶ **Understanding Electronic Media Terms:** studying terms used by the electronic media

See pages 928–935 for instruction on and examples of electronic media terms.

▶ **Understanding Print Media Terms:** studying terms used by the print media

See pages 936–938 for instruction on and examples of print media terms.

▶ **Understanding Type Styles, Visuals and Graphics, and Page Layout:** studying how writers use nonverbal elements such as font, graphics, and columns

The **Designing Your Writing** features on pages 45, 81, 117, 153, 191, 243, 279, and 324 give instruction on and examples of the effective use of type styles and graphic elements. Pages 849–860 give instruction on and examples of key concepts in document design including page layout.

▶ **Analyzing Print and Electronic Media Messages:** looking at print and electronic media in order to understand their messages and purpose.

The **Connections to Life** on pages 84–85, 246, and 327 give instruction and examples on critically viewing messages in the media. The **Focuses on Viewing and Representing** on pages 86–88, 122–124, 163–164, 198–202, 247–248, and 284–287 give instruction, examples, and practice for critiquing media messages.

Viewing and Representing Applications

▶ **Creating Print Media:** producing print media texts

The **Writing Workshop** on pages 306–326 gives instruction, examples, and practice for creating a persuasive brochure.

▶ **Creating Electronic Media:** producing electronic media texts

The **Designing Your Writing** on page 45 gives instruction and examples for designing a Web page. The **Focuses on Viewing and Representing** on pages 50–52 and 329–336 give instruction, examples, and practice for creating a video reflection and a documentary, respectively.

WEEK 1

DIRECTIONS Answer each question below on the day of the week assigned to it.

MONDAY

Read the first sentence below. Then choose the response in which the underlined word is used in the same way.

The winter decorations have been taken down, and there is a <u>spring</u> display in the store window.

A That lively man always seems to have a <u>spring</u> in his step.
B By summer we will have blooms from our <u>spring</u> planting.
C If that <u>spring</u> dries up, there will be no water for the horses.
D The animal was crouched and ready to <u>spring</u>.

Vocabulary Mini-Lesson, page 26

TUESDAY

The sentence below may contain an error. Select the <u>best</u> revision, or pick *D*.

Thrashing through the bushes, the terrified man spied a house on a hill in the distance.

A The terrified man thrashing through the bushes on a hill spied a house in the distance.
B The terrified man spied a house on a hill in the distance thrashing through the bushes.
C The terrified man spied a house thrashing through the bushes on a hill in the distance.
D correct as is

Chapter 19, page 628

WEDNESDAY

Dianna is writing a persuasive letter to her school board in hopes of persuading them to restore funding for music instruction. Dianna needs to think particularly about the concerns of board members who

A believe music is universal.
B have a solid background in music.
C don't think music is important for learning.
D want their own children to take music classes.

Writing Workshop, page 264

THURSDAY

Read the following sentence. Choose the response that fixes the underlined error. If there is no error, choose *D*.

My cousin will be competing in the <u>boston marathon</u> this year.

A Boston marathon   **C** boston Marathon
B Boston Marathon   **D** correct as is

Chapter 21, page 677

FRIDAY

Decide whether one of the underlined words is spelled wrong or whether there is *no mistake*.

A The college has five <u>libraries</u>.
B The term *sahara* is the Arabic word for "<u>desert</u>."
C Conflicts between nations are <u>regretable</u>.
D no mistake

Chapter 26, page 779

DIRECTIONS **Read the following short story.**

What Gave the Women the Strength to Go On?

1　Catherine looked ahead along the "Knife Edge" to the last two hundred yards to Baxter Peak. She shivered. An icy wind grabbed at the hood of her parka and nearly threw her off balance. Three inches of slick snow already covered the top of Mt. Katahdin, and more was falling. She glanced back quickly at her friend Michelle, who was groping along the narrow crest about twenty yards behind her.
10　There wouldn't be much daylight left on this cold autumn evening in north-central Maine.

　　Catherine looked ahead once again. The last stretch of the approximately 2,100-mile hiking trail could be underline perilous, even under the most favorable conditions. For a moment she wondered whether, after all these months of hiking, she and her best friend could make it.

　　The two friends had talked about hiking the Appalachian National Scenic Trail for
20　what seemed like forever. They had read about it, watched films about it, and talked with several "through hikers," those who had made the entire journey from northern Georgia to Maine. They had corresponded with a park ranger. Catherine had even dreamed about the adventure. They had decided that the best time would be right after graduation. Catherine remembered how they had worked at various part-time jobs for
30　nearly three years, saving every dime for the supplies they'd need for five months of wilderness hiking. Here they were, within an hour of their destination, and they had experienced few of the troubles that plagued many less-prepared hikers.

　　The thought warmed Catherine a little. She smiled back at Michelle and gave a "thumbs up" sign. She hoped that her face didn't betray any of the underline trepidation she was feeling
40　as she looked again along the Knife Edge.

　　She recalled more of the details about the past spring back in Texas as graduation approached. Both she and Michelle had felt nearly overwhelmed. Not only were they studying as hard as they could for final exams, but also they were studying trail maps, road maps, and the "specs" on camping gear. The walls of their rooms were covered with long sheets of paper containing
50　list after list: what items were most essential to carry; the locations of all the trail shelters; and the most nutritious foods to pack.

　　Catherine advanced one careful step at a time. She paused to check Michelle's progress. She could feel her confidence returning as she remembered how they had faced every challenge of the arduous journey together. Catherine almost laughed aloud as she thought about the terrible section in
60　Pennsylvania where they trudged for days on solid rock, their feet sore in spite of their sturdy, well-padded boots. She could still see the look of dismay on Michelle's face as they faced mile after mile of boulders.

　　As Michelle drew close enough that they could hear each other above the wind, Catherine heard her call. "I was just thinking about those boulders in Pennsylvania," Michelle yelled. "Nothing, I mean nothing,
70　could be worse than that!"

　　With a huge grin, Catherine called back, "That's exactly what I was thinking."

WEEK 2

DIRECTIONS The questions below refer to the story "What Gave the Women the Strength to Go On?" on page S10. Answer each question below on the day of the week assigned to it.

MONDAY

The word <u>perilous</u> in line 14 means

A visible.
B crowded.
C beautiful.
D dangerous.

Vocabulary Mini-Lesson, page 64

TUESDAY

Where does the story take place?

A Maine
B Georgia
C Pennsylvania
D Texas

Reading Workshop, page 24

WEDNESDAY

Which happened first chronologically?

A The girls graduated.
B The girls began planning their trip.
C The girls worked at various part-time jobs.
D The girls arrived at the formation known as "Knife Edge."

Reading Workshop, page 24

THURSDAY

Why did Catherine give Michelle a "thumbs up" sign?

A to congratulate her on their success
B to warn her of approaching danger
C to encourage her to go on
D to indicate she was not hurt

Test-Taking Mini-Lesson, page 27

FRIDAY

What is this passage <u>mainly</u> about?

A buying camping gear
B climbing a steep mountain
C the doubts of two young women
D completing a challenging outdoor adventure

Test-Taking Mini-Lesson, page 65

WEEK 3

DIRECTIONS The questions below refer to the story "What Gave the Women the Strength to Go On?" on page S10. Answer each question below on the day of the week assigned to it.

MONDAY

The word <u>trepidation</u> in line 39 means

A excitement.
B pain.
C fear.
D confidence.

Vocabulary Mini-Lesson, page 64

TUESDAY

To what do Catherine and Michelle <u>mainly</u> owe the fact that they have come this far on their journey?

A sheer luck
B thorough planning
C the help of a park ranger
D comfortable trails

Test-Taking Mini-Lesson, page 103

WEDNESDAY

From what point of view is the story narrated?

A first-person
B second-person
C third-person omniscient
D third-person limited

Connections to Literature, page 196

THURSDAY

From the passage, you can tell that Catherine and Michelle are <u>most</u> likely to

A have a serious accident.
B complete their long journey.
C give up and face defeat.
D get lost going home.

Test-Taking Mini-Lesson, page 27

FRIDAY

Why do Catherine and Michelle think back about their experience of crossing hard, rocky ground?

A because the experience was so amusing
B because no one believed they could do it
C because thinking about it renews their determination
D because they want to be sure to recall every detail

Test-Taking Mini-Lesson, page 103

WEEK 4

DIRECTIONS Answer each question below on the day of the week assigned to it.

MONDAY

There may be a problem in the structure of the word group below. Select the <u>best</u> revision, or choose D.

An epidemic that is believed to have been plague and killed up to half the population of Constantinople.

A Killing up to half the population of Constantinople, an epidemic that is believed to have been plague.
B An epidemic that is believed to have been plague struck Constantinople and killed half the population.
C To kill up to half the people of Constantinople, an epidemic that is believed to have been plague.
D correct as is

Chapter 9, page 342

TUESDAY

Read the following sentence. Choose the response that fixes the underlined error. If there is no error, choose D.

The <u>dog, that we adopted has</u> changed our lives.

A dog, that we adopted, has
B dog that we adopted has
C dog, that we adopted, has
D correct as is

Chapter 22, page 704

WEDNESDAY

Read the following sentence. Choose the response that fixes the underlined error. If there is no error, choose D.

The platypus, which has a bill like that of a duck and lays eggs, <u>are classified</u> as a mammal.

A were classified
B have been classified
C is classified
D correct as is

Chapter 16, page 512

THURSDAY

Choose the word that means the same, or about the same, as the underlined word.

I do not mind losing to a worthy <u>adversary</u>.

A opponent
B ruler
C relative
D champion

Quick Reference Handbook, page 887

FRIDAY

Read the following sentence. Choose the response that fixes the underlined error. If there is no error, choose D.

Although one candidate is the <u>better campaigner, no one can predict whom</u> the voters will choose.

A best campaigner, no one can predict who
B better campaigner, no one can predict who
C good campaigner, no one can predict whom
D correct as is

Chapter 17, page 558

WEEK 5

DIRECTIONS **Answer each question below on the day of the week assigned to it.**

MONDAY

Decide whether one of the underlined words is spelled wrong or whether there is *no mistake*.

A Two <u>sopranos</u> are needed to sing solos in the cantata.

B Various types of <u>grasses</u> are seen on the African plains.

C Justin suffered only <u>miner</u> injuries in the accident.

D no mistake

Chapter 26, page 779

TUESDAY

Read the following sentence. Choose the response that fixes the underlined error. If there is no error, choose *D*.

We are planning to <u>meet Uncle James</u> at the airport this evening.

A meet uncle James

B meet uncle james

C meet Uncle james

D correct as is

Chapter 21, page 682

WEDNESDAY

Read the first sentence below. Then choose the response in which the underlined word is used in the same way.

Who is the <u>authority</u> in charge here?

A You must ask an <u>authority</u> to sign this document.

B The court has final <u>authority</u> for that decision.

C We have it on good <u>authority</u> that the claim is false.

D Using reliable sources will lend <u>authority</u> to your report.

Vocabulary Mini-Lesson, page 26

THURSDAY

Read the following sentence. Choose the response that fixes the underlined error. If there is no error, choose *D*.

By this time tomorrow, the delegates <u>chose</u> their new president.

A had chosen

B will have chosen

C are choosing

D correct as is

Chapter 18, page 590

FRIDAY

Which of the following is a statement of opinion?

A My guidance counselor said that getting into college takes planning and effort.

B Many students take out loans to pay for college.

C Grants and scholarships are available to some students.

D Going to a good college is a matter of hard work.

Test-Taking Mini-Lesson, page 262

WEEK 6

DIRECTIONS **Answer each question below on the day of the week assigned to it.**

MONDAY

There may be a grammar problem in the sentence below. Select the best revision, or choose D.

Alarmed by the storm, the campers' equipment was hastily loaded into the truck.

A Alarmed by the storm, the campers hastily loaded their equipment into the truck.
B Alarmed by the storm, the campers loaded into the truck their equipment hastily.
C Alarmed by the storm, the equipment was hastily loaded by the campers into the truck.
D correct as is

Chapter 19, page 626

TUESDAY

Read the following sentence. Choose the response that fixes the underlined error. If there is no error, choose D.

Donating clothes and food to areas shelters <u>are one way our class plans</u> to help others in our community.

A is one way our class plans
B were one way our class plans
C was one way our class will plan
D correct as is

Chapter 16, page 512

WEDNESDAY

Choose the word that means the same, or about the same, as the underlined word.

He <u>squandered</u> his fortune and was left with nothing.

A discussed
B chose
C increased
D wasted

Vocabulary Mini-Lesson, page 136

THURSDAY

Read the following sentence. Choose the response that fixes the underlined error. If there is no error, choose D.

I can have my suitcase packed and ready to go at <u>a moments notice</u>.

A a moments' notice   **C** a moment's notice
B a moments's notice   **D** correct as is

Chapter 25, page 758

FRIDAY

Which of the following is most likely a valid statement of cause and effect?

A Warts are caused by touching toads.
B Both genetic and environmental factors shape our personalities.
C Thunder is the cause of lightning.
D The Boston Tea Party caused the Revolutionary War.

Critical-Thinking Mini-Lesson, page 108

WEEK 7

DIRECTIONS **Answer each question below on the day of the week assigned to it.**

MONDAY

Read the following sentence. Choose the response that fixes the underlined error. If there is no error, choose D.

Sandra Cisneros's first full-length work, <u>The house on Mango Street,</u> was published in 1984.

A *The house on mango street*
B *The House On Mango Street*
C *The House on Mango Street*
D correct as is

Chapter 21, page 683

TUESDAY

Decide whether one of the underlined words is spelled wrong or whether there is *no mistake.*

A City workers have built several new trails for <u>joggers</u>.
B The small <u>childs</u> squealed with delight at the clowns' antics.
C Michelle has a <u>lovely</u> voice but is afraid to sing in public.
D no mistake

Chapter 26, page 779

WEDNESDAY

There may be a grammatical problem in the word group below. Select the <u>best</u> revision, or choose D.

The young representative elected only recently in a close vote and national attention.

A Electing in a close vote the young representative who has attracted national attention.
B To elect the young representative only recently in a close vote attracting national attention.
C Elected only recently in a close vote, the young representative has already attracted national attention.
D correct as is

Chapter 9, page 342

THURSDAY

Which of the following is an example of either-or reasoning?

A The Civil War began over the issue of slavery.
B Overeating leads to diabetes.
C My opponent in the city council race is a bold-faced liar.
D Stores that provide plastic bags instead of paper do not care about the environment.

Critical-Thinking Mini-Lesson, page 270

FRIDAY

Read the first sentence below. Then choose the response in which the underlined word is used in the same way.

There were <u>scores</u> of people at the ballgame.

A He plans to settle some old <u>scores</u>.
B Did you get good <u>scores</u> on your exams?
C <u>Scores</u> of visitors lined up to enter the museum.
D She will bring the musical <u>scores</u> for the production.

Vocabulary Mini-Lesson, page 26

WEEK 8

DIRECTIONS **Answer each question below on the day of the week assigned to it.**

MONDAY

Read the following sentence. Choose the response that fixes the underlined error. If there is no error, choose *D*.

Both competitors feel that <u>they played well</u> during yesterday's tournament.

A they are playing good
B they played good
C they will have played well
D correct as is

Chapter 19, page 617

TUESDAY

Read the following sentence. Choose the response that fixes the underlined error. If there is no error, choose *D*.

My father always forgets where he <u>has lain</u> his car keys.

A had laid
B is lying
C has laid
D correct as is

Chapter 18, page 582

WEDNESDAY

Choose the word that means the same, or about the same, as the underlined word.

He is not to be trusted, because he <u>covets</u> everything we have.

A smothers
B repairs
C praises
D desires

Quick Reference Handbook, page 887

THURSDAY

Read the following sentence. Choose the response that fixes the underlined error. If there is no error, choose *D*.

Because he could not choose <u>one my brother has two majors business</u> and journalism.

A one; my brother has two majors . . . business
B one, my brother has two majors: business
C one my brother has two majors business
D correct as is

Chapter 22, page 708; Chapter 23, page 729

FRIDAY

What type of conflict is depicted in this drawing?

A internal
B external
C societal
D personality

Connections to Literature, page 195

Understanding Dyslexia

A   [1] Albert Einstein, who *Time* magazine named its person of the twentieth century, was a genius. [2] Surprisingly, he was a late talker and a poor student. [3] During his early schooling, teachers thought he was not very smart. [4] Ironically, he originally couldn't remember his times tables and was a complete failure at spelling. [5] Einstein, it turns out, was dyslexic. [6] Although dyslexia afflicts between 10 and 15 percent of the American population, most people know very little about it.

B   [7] Dyslexia is a language disorder. [8] The word *dyslexia* comes from two Greek words: *dys-*, meaning *difficult*, and *lexis*, meaning *word*. [9] Literally translated, *dyslexia* means *difficulty with words*. [10] Dyslexia may be a neurological condition, which means that it is caused by the way the brain functions. [11] Dyslexia often runs in families, leading researchers to believe it may be an inherited condition. [12] Other hereditary conditions include sickle-cell anemia and cystic fibrosis. [13] Researchers once thought that boys were four times as likely to have dyslexia as girls; the latest studies, however, show that girls are just as likely to be dyslexic as boys.

C   [14] Signs of dyslexia include difficulty in learning how to read and spell. [15] Confusing directions, such as right and left, is another symptom of dyslexia. [16] Many dyslexics cannot create rhymes. [17] Reversing letters, such as writing *a b* for *d* or reading *saw* for *was*, may also be a symptom.

D   [18] Dyslexics have trouble understanding the relationship between letters and sounds. [19] Reading the word *cat* involves identifying the letters, matching the letters to sounds, and blending the sounds together to make words. [20] The word *cat*, for example, is made up of three sounds: *kuh, aa,* and *tuh.* [21] Most people sound out the word so quickly that the process is automatic. [22] For dyslexics, this decoding process, however, is rarely automatic. [23] Thus, dyslexics often read at a slower rate than others.

E   [24] Because dyslexic children have difficulty learning to read, some people jump to the wrong conclusion that these children are not bright. [25] As the example of Einstein shows, dyslexia is not a sign of low intelligence.

F   [26] Some people mistakenly believe that dyslexics are lazy and that dyslexics just need to work harder. [27] Most dyslexic students, however, work incredibly hard but require a different kind of instruction. [28] Multisensory instruction is helpful; many dyslexics learn better by using visual aids, touch, and movement. [29] Students may also need instruction in phonics to help them match phonemes to letters more easily.

G   [30] Dyslexia can be a challenge to anyone, but it does not mean failure. [31] Just ask any of the accomplished and successful people who have learned how to live with dyslexia.

WEEK 9

DIRECTIONS The questions below refer to the student draft "Understanding Dyslexia" on page S18. Answer each question below on the day of the week assigned to it.

MONDAY

Read the following sentence. Choose the response that fixes the underlined error. If there is no error, choose D.

Albert Einstein, <u>who *Time* magazine named</u> its person of the twentieth century, was a genius.

A whom *Time* magazine named
B whom was named by *Time* magazine
C who "Time" magazine named
D correct as is

Chapter 17, page 558

TUESDAY

Which sentence destroys the unity of Paragraph B?

A 9
B 10
C 11
D 12

Chapter 11, page 374

WEDNESDAY

Read this sentence from the article.

"Ironically, he originally couldn't remember his times tables and was a complete failure at spelling."

The irony to which the writer refers is called

A verbal irony.
B dramatic irony.
C situational irony.
D unintended irony.

Writing Workshop, page 180

THURSDAY

Which of the following is the <u>best</u> order for the sequence of sentences in the middle of Paragraph D?

A 18, 22, 21, 20, 19
B 18, 20, 19, 21, 22
C 18, 22, 19, 21, 20
D correct as is

Chapter 11, page 374

FRIDAY

Read this sentence from the article.

"Dyslexia can be a challenge to anyone, but <u>it</u> does not mean failure."

To what does the word <u>it</u> refer?

A failure
B challenge
C dyslexia
D anyone

Chapter 11, page 375

WEEK 10

DIRECTIONS The questions below refer to the student draft "Understanding Dyslexia" on page S18. Answer each question below on the day of the week assigned to it.

MONDAY

Select the statement about dyslexia that is a hasty generalization based on inadequate evidence.

A Poor spellers and poor rhymers are dyslexic.
B Girls are just as likely to be dyslexic as boys are.
C Reversing letters may be a symptom of dyslexia.
D Some dyslexics struggle in school.

Critical-Thinking Mini-Lesson, page 270

TUESDAY

With which of the following words does <u>dyslexia</u> share a common ancestor?

A lexicon
B legend
C dysfunctional
D all of the above

Quick Reference Handbook, page 891

WEDNESDAY

The purpose of this report is <u>mainly</u> to

A educate general readers about dyslexia.
B persuade the audience to fund dyslexia research projects.
C give encouragement to people who have dyslexia.
D inform health educators about the symptoms of dyslexia.

Quick Reference Handbook, page 876

THURSDAY

Read this sentence from the report.

"Some people mistakenly believe that dyslexics are lazy and that <u>dyslexics</u> just need to work harder."

Which pronoun can replace the underlined word?

A their
B those
C they
D them

Chapter 16, page 532

FRIDAY

You can tell from the passage that <u>multisensory instruction</u> [Sentence 28] refers to instruction

A in phonics and phonemes.
B delivered through visuals, touch, or movement.
C delivered telepathically.
D in how to create sensory images in writing.

Vocabulary Mini-Lesson, page 217

DIRECTIONS **Read the following advertisement.**

Central Power and Light

1 Graduating from high school? Looking for a job? Do we have a bright future for you!

We're Central Power and Light. For more than fifty years, we have been providing the energy you need every day. We keep you warm in winter and cool in summer. Without us, your CD players, televisions, radios, and computers wouldn't work. In fact, without us, you might have trouble reading these words
10 because we are responsible for things as basic as the lights in your homes and classrooms.

We're quite a business. However, as important as electric and gas power are to our customers, we're more than just a utility company. We're also a good neighbor, working hard to help keep our environment as <u>pristine</u> as we possibly can while still keeping our rates low and our lives humming along.

It takes many people with a wide variety
20 of skills and interests to keep a company like ours in business. That's why we have more than one hundred job openings in several areas. Do any of these sound right for you?

- mechanic trainee
- word processor
- safety inspector trainee
- driver
- security guard
- customer service representative
30 - custodian
- maintenance worker
- accountant

We are always looking for new talent, and we offer a <u>host</u> of benefits.

- competitive salaries
- pension plan
- insurance
- tuition reimbursement
- company social events
40 - medical coverage
- pleasant working conditions
- continuing training classes
- convenient location

If you would like to talk with one of our employment counselors, we invite you to our job fair being held the week of May 3–May 7. Just drop in. You will be glad you came.

You've already made plans for college? No problem. Come and talk with us anyway.
50 We may have a position for you part time or during your summer break. If we don't have anything that suits your needs right now, keep us in mind for after graduation. We have many professional and managerial jobs requiring two- and four-year degrees, so you could end up working for us in the future. We'll still be here. In the meantime, we'll keep right on working for you.

WEEK 11

DIRECTIONS **The questions below refer to the advertisement for Central Power and Light on page S21. Answer each question below on the day of the week assigned to it.**

MONDAY

The word <u>pristine</u> in line 16 means

A busy.
B industrial.
C unspoiled.
D inexpensive.

Quick Reference Handbook, page 887

TUESDAY

The first three benefits listed in lines 35–43 are <u>best</u> described as

A social.
B educational.
C financial.
D health-related.

Reading Workshop, page 132

WEDNESDAY

According to the passage, what should an interested reader do?

A talk to a friend
B visit a school counselor
C attend a job fair
D consult his or her parents

Reading Workshop, page 60

THURSDAY

A reader who has already been accepted to college might be interested in this ad for all of the following <u>except</u> a

A scholarship.
B summer job.
C part-time job.
D future career.

Reading Workshop, page 60

FRIDAY

What is the main idea of this advertisement?

A the power company wants people to think it is doing a good job.
B The power company wants people to apply for jobs.
C The power company is raising rates.
D The power company wants new customers.

Test-Taking Mini-Lesson, page 65

WEEK 12

DIRECTIONS The questions below refer to the advertisement for Central Power and Light on page S21. Answer each question below on the day of the week assigned to it.

MONDAY

The word <u>host</u> in line 34 means a

A person who entertains.
B large number.
C plant organism.
D sacrament.

Vocabulary Workshop, page 26

TUESDAY

This advertisement is designed to appear in a place where it will be seen by

A teachers.
B high school seniors.
C power company workers.
D the general public.

Quick Reference Handbook, page 876

WEDNESDAY

Which is a fact from this passage?

A Central Power and Light is quite a business.
B Central Power and Light is also a good neighbor.
C Central Power and Light will be glad to talk to students.
D Central Power and Light has more than 100 job openings.

Test-Taking Mini-Lesson, page 255

THURSDAY

Read this passage from lines 15–17.

We're also a good neighbor, working hard to help keep our environment as pristine as we possibly can . . ."

What persuasive technique does it employ?

A name-calling
B glittering generality
C testimonial
D bandwagon

Reading Workshop, page 300

FRIDAY

Which of the following visual images would be <u>least</u> likely to accompany this advertisement?

A a light bulb
B a photo of a lush landscape
C a photo of a power plant's smokestack
D a diverse group of professionals working together

Writing Workshop, page 313

WEEK 13

DIRECTIONS **Answer each question below on the day of the week assigned to it.**

MONDAY

Read the first sentence below. Then choose the response in which the underlined word is used in the same way.

If we hurry we can see the 7:00 P.M. <u>feature</u> at the theater.

A I have been told that my nose is my best <u>feature</u>.

B The fashion collection will <u>feature</u> silks and wools.

C He wrote the <u>feature</u> story in the newspaper.

D What time does the next <u>feature</u> start?

Vocabulary Mini-Lesson, page 26

TUESDAY

Walter is writing a personal reflection about a formative experience. Instead of writing a traditional thesis statement in his introduction, Walter should hint at

A the figures of speech he will be using later.

B the reference sources he used.

C the structure of his essay.

D the meaning of the experience.

Writing Workshop, page 38

WEDNESDAY

Read the following sentence. Choose the response that fixes the underlined error. If there is no error, choose *D*.

The goal <u>is the same for both him and me</u>— to balance career with family obligations.

A are the same for both him and I

B is the same for both he and I

C are the same for both me and he

D correct as is

Chapter 16, page 512; Chapter 17, page 553

THURSDAY

Decide whether one of the underlined words is spelled wrong or whether there is *no mistake*.

A The ski slope on the left is intended for <u>beginners</u>.

B The weak lamps seemed barely to pierce the <u>darkness</u> of the cave.

C Bob's team will <u>forfiet</u> the game if they cannot find one more player.

D no mistake

Chapter 26, page 779

FRIDAY

Read the following sentence. Choose the response that fixes the underlined error. If there is no error, choose *D*.

My aunt is on the board of <u>the american dental association</u>.

A the American dental association

B the American Dental Association

C The American dental Association

D correct as is

Chapter 21, page 675

WEEK 14

DIRECTIONS **Answer each question below on the day of the week assigned to it.**

MONDAY

The sentence below may contain an error. Select the <u>best</u> revision, or pick D.

The travelers viewed remnants of Hadrian's Wall touring the English countryside.

A Touring the English countryside, remnants of Hadrian's Wall were viewed by the travelers.

B The travelers viewed remnants of Hadrian's Wall, which was touring the English countryside.

C While they were touring the English countryside, the travelers viewed remnants of Hadrian's Wall.

D correct as is

Chapter 19, page 628

TUESDAY

Read the following sentence. Choose the response that fixes the underlined error. If there is no error, choose D.

<u>"I wonder," Tajiro said whether</u> our relatives from Chicago will visit us in Japan this winter."

A "I wonder," Tajiro said, "whether

B "I wonder," Tajiro said "whether

C "I wonder Tajiro said, "whether

D correct as is

Chapter 24, page 743

WEDNESDAY

Choose the word or words that means the same, or about the same, as the underlined word.

The soldiers fought <u>valiantly</u> and won the battle.

A easily   **C** bravely
B haltingly   **D** narrowly

Quick Reference Handbook, page 887

THURSDAY

Read the following sentence. Choose the response that fixes the underlined error. If there is no error, choose D.

Mrs. Campbell, our drama teacher, generously gave <u>Jamal and I</u> another day to memorize our lines.

A myself and Jamal   **C** I and Jamal
B Jamal and me   **D** correct as is
                          Chapter 17, page 553

FRIDAY

The sentence below may contain an error. Select the <u>best</u> revision, or pick D.

A supervisor should be good at communicating, able to handle conflicts, and provide direction to subordinates.

A A supervisor should be able to communicate well, handle conflicts, and provide direction to subordinates.

B A supervisor should be able to communicate, able to handle conflicts, and providing direction to subordinates.

C A supervisor communicating, handling conflicts, and providing direction to subordinates

D correct as is

Chapter 10, page 362

WEEK 15

DIRECTIONS Answer each question below on the day of the week assigned to it.

MONDAY

Decide whether one of the underlined words is spelled wrong or whether there is *no mistake.*

A The diplomat has agreed to <u>intersede</u> to obtain the captive's release.

B Amino acids are the building blocks of <u>protein</u> molecules.

C You are required to obtain a <u>referral</u> from your primary-care physician.

D no mistake

Chapter 26, page 779

TUESDAY

Which of the following is a statement of fact?

A The city must do more to promote clean energy.

B Solar power is the only realistic alternative to fossil fuels.

C The city has created bicycle-only lanes throughout the municipality.

D Most people wouldn't use a light-rail or other rapid-transit system.

Test-Taking Mini-Lesson, page 262

WEDNESDAY

There may be a grammar problem in the word group below. Select the <u>best</u> revision, or choose *D.*

Enthralled by the works of Monet, the young artist, a frequent visitor to the museum.

A Enthralled by the works of Monet, the young artist was a frequent visitor to the museum.

B The young artist, a frequent visitor to the museum and enthralled by the works of Monet.

C Frequently visiting the museum, the young artist enthralled by the works of Monet.

D correct as is

Chapter 9, page 342

THURSDAY

Read the following sentence. Choose the response that fixes the underlined error. If there is no error, choose *D.*

Michelangelo, <u>an Italian painter, architect, and poet</u>, is best known for painting the ceiling of the Sistine Chapel in the Vatican.

A an Italian painter, Architect, and Poet

B an Italian painter, architect, and poet

C an Italian painter, Architect, and Poet

D correct as is

Chapter 21, page 669

FRIDAY

Read the following sentence. Choose the response that fixes the underlined error. If there is no error, choose *D.*

The workers, <u>her and Bob, tried frantically to complete their</u> last task of the day.

A she and Bob, tried frantically to complete his

B she and Bob, tried frantically to complete their

C her and Bob, tried frantically to complete its

D correct as is

Chapter 17, page 561

WEEK 16

DIRECTIONS **Answer each question below on the day of the week assigned to it.**

MONDAY

Read the following sentence. Choose the response that fixes the underlined error. If there is no error, choose *D*.

This is the <u>worstest</u> situation I have ever found myself in.

A more worser
B most worse
C worst
D correct as is

Chapter 19, page 623

TUESDAY

Read the following sentence. Choose the response that fixes the underlined error. If there is no error, choose *D*.

Singer Leontyne <u>Price, who studied at Julliard has</u> toured in opera productions all over the world.

A Price who studied at Julliard, has
B Price: who studied at Julliard, has
C Price, who studied at Julliard, has
D correct as is

Chapter 22, page 704

WEDNESDAY

Read the first sentence below. Then choose the response in which the underlined word is used in the same way.

As the <u>strain</u> of the work ended, his health improved.

A Do not <u>strain</u> my patience by teasing me.
B The constant <u>strain</u> of the deadlines was exhausting
C Be sure to <u>strain</u> the pineapple slices.
D He has to <u>strain</u> to hit the song's low notes.

Vocabulary Mini-Lesson, page 26

THURSDAY

Annette is writing a letter to the editor about the need to develop solar technology. In her opinion statement, she should clearly state the issue and

A her opinion on it.
B her sources of information.
C opposing arguments.
D the biases of the audience.

Writing Workshop, page 264

FRIDAY

Choose the response that correctly combines the two sentences below.

Vincent van Gogh created colorful, vibrant canvases. They stand in stark contrast to his dark and tragic life.

A Vincent van Gogh created colorful, vibrant canvases they stand in stark contrast to his dark and tragic life.
B Vincent van Gogh's colorful, vibrant canvases stand in stark contrast to his dark and tragic life.
C Standing in stark contrast to his dark and tragic life, Vincent van Gogh created colorful, vibrant canvases.
D Vincent van Gogh's colorful, vibrant canvases, in stark contrast to his dark and tragic life.

Chapter 10, page 353

WEEK 17

DIRECTIONS Answer each question below on the day of the week assigned to it.

MONDAY

Read the following sentence. Choose the response that fixes the underlined error. If there is no error, choose D.

"You can call <u>the league of women voters</u> to find out where to vote," Mrs. Ames advised us.

A the League of Women Voters
B the League Of Women Voters
C the League of women voters
D correct as is

Chapter 21, page 675

TUESDAY

Which type of logical fallacy is contained in the statement below?

She should win the Academy Award for Best Actress because she deserves it.

A attacking the person
B circular reasoning
C card stacking
D either-or reasoning

Critical-Thinking Mini-Lesson, page 315

WEDNESDAY

Choose the response that correctly combines the two sentences below.

Kendra wrote her report on Genghis Khan. Dana chose a different historical figure.

A Kendra wrote her report on Genghis Khan, but Dana chose a different historical figure.
B Kendra wrote her report on Genghis Khan, and Dana choosing a different historical figure.
C After Dana chose a different historical figure Kendra wrote her report on Genghis Khan.
D Kendra wrote her report on Genghis Khan, then Dana chose a different historical figure.

Chapter 10, page 358

THURSDAY

Decide whether one of the underlined words is spelled wrong or whether there is *no mistake*.

A One must be careful not to <u>overreact</u> in a frightening situation.
B The <u>thieves</u> turned out to be a pair of mischievous raccoons.
C <u>Navies</u> of several countries will be represented in the flotilla.
D no mistake

Chapter 26, page 779

FRIDAY

Choose the word or words that means the same, or about the same, as the underlined word.

We were <u>aghast</u> at his shameful behavior.

A surprised
B horrified
C annoyed
D irritated

Vocabulary Mini-Lesson, page 261

Analyzing a Nutrition Label

1 A nutrition label can tell you a lot of facts about a food product. An <u>agency</u> of the United States government defines what information must appear on a food label. It also strictly defines the meaning of terms such as "low fat." For example, if a food is labeled "low fat," it must have less than 3 g of fat per serving. If the daily total fat intake is 65 g and a nutrition label on a brand of milk states that the milk contains 8 percent of the daily intake of fat, can the milk be labeled "low fat"? To answer this you need to calculate 8 percent of 65 g or 65 g × 0.08 = 5.2 g. The milk cannot be labeled "low fat."

It helps if you know what certain phrases mean. If a label claims that the product is unsweetened or that there is no sugar added, it means no common table sugar (sucrose) has
10 been added. It does not mean there are no other sugars present. Honey, jam, and fruit juice all contain sugars other than sucrose. (Hint: many sugars such as fructose [fruit sugar] and lactose [milk sugar] end with the letters -*ose*.)

Look at the good label shown in Figure 1. Just below the label "Nutrition Facts," the size of a single serving is indicated. Notice that the total number of calories for one serving are listed, together with the number of those calories that come from fat. Below this the quantities of fats, carbohydrates, and proteins that make up a single serving are shown. Alongside of these appear <u>values</u> in
20 percent of the recommended daily intake of each type of <u>nutrient</u> found in a serving of the food. In this case, one serving provides 4 percent of the recommended daily fat intake and 9 percent of the recommended daily carbohydrate intake. Values for sodium and cholesterol are listed as well because many people must restrict their intake of these substances. Near the bottom of the nutrition statement is a listing of vitamins and minerals, again with values in percent of the recommended daily intake of each.

30 Remember that what you read in a "Nutrition Facts" label really *is* a set of facts. Read food advertisements carefully, and think critically about the promotional claims being made. Compare claims with the information you know to be true, and be an informed consumer.

Nutrition Facts

Serving Size 1 bar (37g)
Servings Per Container 8

Amount Per Serving

Calories 140	Calories from Fat 25
	% Daily Value*
Total Fat 2.5g	4%
Saturated Fat 0.5g	3%
Cholesterol 0mg	0%
Sodium 60mg	2%
Total Carbohydrate 27g	9%
Dietary Fiber 1g	4%
Sugars 14g	
Protein 1g	

Vitamin A 15%	Vitamin C 0%
Calcium 20%	Iron 20%
Thiamin 35%	Riboflavin 35%
Niacin 35%	Vitamin B6 40%

*Percent Daily Values are based on a 2,000 calorie diet. Your daily values may be higher or lower depending on your calorie needs:

	Calories:	2,000	2,500
Total Fat	Less than	65g	80g
Sat Fat	Less than	20g	25g
Cholesterol	Less than	300mg	300mg
Sodium	Less than	2,400mg	2,400mg
Total Carbohydrate		300g	375g
Dietary Fiber		25g	30g
Protein		50g	60g

Figure 1

WEEK 18

DIRECTIONS The questions below refer to the article "Analyzing a Nutrition Label" on page S29. Answer each question below on the day of the week assigned to it.

MONDAY

What does <u>agency</u> in line 1 mean?

A a group of concerned citizens
B an act of Congress
C an administrative division
D handbook of terms

Quick Reference Handbook, page 887

TUESDAY

What criterion must be met for a food to be labeled "low fat"?

A It must contain 8% of the daily intake of fat.
B It must have less than 3 grams of fat per serving.
C It must have less than 5.2 grams of fat per serving.
D It must be fat-free.

Reading Workshop, page 60

WEDNESDAY

What is the author's point of view toward nutrition labels?

A They are full of misleading or inaccurate information.
B They are a good antidote to food advertisers' inflated claims.
C They are so difficult to read as to be useless.
D They should be required on all food items.

Quick Reference Handbook, page 876

THURSDAY

What is the most likely meaning of the suffix <u>-ose</u>?

A enzyme
B fat
C honey
D sugar

Vocabulary Mini-Lesson, page 102

FRIDAY

What is the purpose of the table at the bottom of the "Nutrition Facts" label in Figure 1?

A It tells what the daily intake of various food components should be based on two diets.
B It gives the values of fat, protein, carbohydrates, and so on, for a single serving.
C It gives the values of fat, protein, carbohydrates, and so on, for the entire package.
D It tells how many calories are contained in each food component.

Quick Reference Handbook, page 880

WEEK 19

DIRECTIONS The questions below refer to the article "Analyzing a Nutrition Label" on page S29. Answer each question below on the day of the week assigned to it.

MONDAY

The purpose of this article is to

A use nutrition labels to teach mathematical concepts.
B warn consumers of how nutrition labels are deceptive.
C teach consumers the meaning of "low fat."
D educate consumers on how to read nutrition labels.

Quick Reference Handbook, page 876

TUESDAY

What is the meaning of <u>values</u> in line 19?

A amounts
B guiding principles
C measures
D monetary worth

Vocabulary Mini-Lesson, page 26

WEDNESDAY

You can tell from the article that <u>nutrient</u> in line 21 refers to

A vitamins and minerals.
B protein, fat, and carbohydrates.
C Percent Daily Values.
D sodium and cholesterol.

Vocabulary Mini-Lesson, page 136

THURSDAY

The "Nutrition Facts" label reveals all of the following <u>except</u>

A calories per serving.
B the significance of "Percent Daily Value."
C the meaning of "Saturated Fat."
D The amount of protein recommended in a 2000-calorie-per-day diet.

Reading Workshop, page 60

FRIDAY

You can tell from the food label that "Dietary Fiber and Sugars" are

A not good for you.
B types of carbohydrates.
C each 4% of the recommended daily value.
D types of fat.

Quick Reference Handbook, page 880

WEEK 20

DIRECTIONS **Answer each question below on the day of the week assigned to it.**

MONDAY

The word group below may contain an error. Select the best revision, or pick D.

Nervously reviewing their lines, the actors listened for their cues and prepared to take the stage.

A Prepared to take the stage, their lines were nervously reviewed by the actors listening for their cues.

B The actors listened for their cues and prepared to take the stage reviewing their lines nervously.

C The actors listening for their cues, preparing to take the stage, nervously reviewing their lines.

D correct as is

Chapter 19, page 628

TUESDAY

Choose the word that means the same, or about the same, as the underlined word.

Someone who is <u>induced</u> to do something is

A dictated   **C** persuaded
B employed   **D** discouraged

Vocabulary Mini-Lesson, page 176

WEDNESDAY

Which of the following types of graphics is <u>least</u> suitable for representing numerical data?

A pie chart   **C** bar graph
B line graph   **D** Venn diagram

Quick Reference Handbook, page 879

THURSDAY

Read the following sentence. Choose the response that fixes the underlined error. If there is no error, choose D.

The ostrich usually eats plants, but it also <u>will have eaten</u> turtles and lizards when they are available.

A eats
B had eaten
C ate
D correct as is

Chapter 18, page 590

FRIDAY

The word group below may contain an error. Select the <u>best</u> revision, or pick D.

The markings on the horse's side becoming noticeable only after the horse loses its winter coat.

A The markings on the horse's side become noticeable only after the horse loses its winter coat.

B To become noticeable after the horse loses its winter coat, the markings on its side.

C After the horse loses its winter coat, the markings on its side becoming noticeable.

D correct as is

Chapter 9, page 342

LEE ODELL helped establish the pedagogical framework for the composition strand of *Elements of Language*. In addition, he guided the development of the scope and sequence and pedagogical design of the Writing Workshops. Dr. Odell is Professor of Composition Theory and Research and, since 1996, Director of the Writing Program at Rensselaer Polytechnic Institute. He began his career teaching English in middle and high schools. More recently he has worked with teachers in grades K–12 to establish a program that involves students from all disciplines in writing across the curriculum and for communities outside their classrooms. Dr. Odell's most recent book (with Charles R. Cooper) is *Evaluating Writing: The Role of Teachers' Knowledge about Text, Learning, and Culture* (1999). Dr. Odell is Past Chair of the Conference on College Composition and Communication and of the NCTE's Assembly for Research.

RENÉE HOBBS helped develop the theoretical framework for the viewing and representing strand of *Elements of Language*. A national expert in media literacy, Dr. Hobbs guided the development of the scope and sequence; served as the authority on terminology, definitions, and pedagogy; and directed the planning for the video series. Dr. Hobbs is Associate Professor of Communication at Babson College in Wellesley, Massachusetts, and Director of the Media Literacy Project. Active in the field of media education, Dr. Hobbs has served as Director of the Institute on Media Education, Harvard Graduate School of Education; Director of the "Know TV" Project, Discovery Networks and Time Warner Cable; and Board Member, The New York Times Newspaper in Education Program. She works actively in staff development in school districts nationwide. Dr. Hobbs has contributed articles and chapters on media, technology, and education to many publications.

RICHARD VACCA helped establish the conceptual basis for the reading strand of *Elements of Language*. In addition, he guided the development of the pedagogical design and the scope and sequence of skills in the Reading Workshops. Dr. Vacca is Professor of Education at Kent State University. He recently completed a term as the forty-second President of the International Reading Association. Originally a middle school and high school teacher, Dr. Vacca served as the project director of the Cleveland Writing Demonstration Project for several years. He is the co-author of *Content Area Reading; Reading and Learning to Read;* and articles and chapters related to adolescents' literacy development. In 1989, Dr. Vacca received the College Reading Association's A. B. Herr Award for Outstanding Contributions to Reading Education. Currently, he is co-chair of the IRA's Commission on Adolescent Literacy.

JOHN E. WARRINER was a high school English teacher when he developed the original organizational structure for his classic *English Grammar and Composition* series. The approach pioneered by Mr. Warriner was distinctive, and the editorial staff of Holt, Rinehart and Winston have worked diligently to retain the unique qualities of his pedagogy. For the same reason, HRW continues to credit Mr. Warriner as an author of *Elements of Language* in recognition of his groundbreaking work. John Warriner also co-authored the *English Workshop* series and was editor of *Short Stories: Characters in Conflict*. Throughout his career, however, teaching remained Mr. Warriner's major interest, and he taught for thirty-two years in junior and senior high schools and in college.

Continued

Doris F. Frazier
East Millbrook Magnet Middle
    School
Raleigh, North Carolina

Shayne G. Goodrum
C. E. Jordan High School
Durham, North Carolina

Bonnie L. Hall
St. Ann School
Lansing, Illinois

Doris Ann Hall
Forest Meadow Junior High
    School
Dallas, Texas

James M. Harris
Mayfield High School
Mayfield Village, Ohio

Lynne Hoover
Fremont Ross High School
Fremont, Ohio

Patricia A. Humphreys
James Bowie High School
Austin, Texas

Jennifer L. Jones
Oliver Wendell Holmes Middle
    School
Dallas, Texas

Kathryn R. Jones
Murchison Middle School
Austin, Texas

Bonnie Just
Narbonne High School
Harbor City, California

Vincent Kimball
Patterson High School #405
Baltimore, Maryland

Nancy C. Long
MacArthur High School
Houston, Texas

Carol M. Mackey
Ft. Lauderdale Christian School
Ft. Lauderdale, Florida

Jan Jennings McCown
Johnston High School
Austin, Texas

Alice Kelly McCurdy
Rusk Middle School
Dallas, Texas

Elizabeth Morris
Northshore High School
Slidell, Louisiana

Victoria Reis
Western High School
Ft. Lauderdale, Florida

Dean Richardson
Scarborough High School
Houston, Texas

Susan M. Rogers
Freedom High School
Morganton, North Carolina

Sammy Rusk
North Mesquite High School
Mesquite, Texas

Carole B. San Miguel
James Bowie High School
Austin, Texas

Jane Saunders
William B. Travis High School
Austin, Texas

Gina Sawyer
Reed Middle School
Duncanville, Texas

Laura R. Schauermann
MacArthur High School
Houston, Texas

Stephen Shearer
MacArthur High School
Houston, Texas

Elizabeth Curry Smith
Tarpon Springs High School
Tarpon Springs, Florida

Jeannette M. Spain
Stephen F. Austin High School
Sugar Land, Texas

Carrie Speer
Northshore High School
Slidell, Louisiana

Trina Steffes
MacArthur High School
Houston, Texas

Andrea G. Freirich Stewart
Freedom High School
Morganton, North Carolina

Diana O. Torres
Johnston High School
Austin, Texas

Jan Voorhees
Whitesboro High School
Marcy, New York

Ann E. Walsh
Bedichek Middle School
Austin, Texas

Mary Jane Warden
Onahan School
Chicago, Illinois

Beth Westbrook
Covington Middle School
Austin, Texas

Char-Lene Wilkins
Morenci Area High School
Morenci, Michigan

CONTENTS IN BRIEF

PART 1 Communications **1**

    Taking Tests: Strategies and Practice 2
- **1** **Narration/Description:** Reflecting on Experiences 16
- **2** **Exposition:** Exploring Comparisons and Contrasts 54
- **3** **Exposition:** Examining Causes and Effects 90
- **4** **Exposition:** Analyzing Problems 126
- **5** **Exposition:** Analyzing a Short Story 166
- **6** **Exposition:** Sharing Research Results 206
- **7** **Persuasion:** Persuading Others 250
- **8** **Persuasion:** Using Persuasion in Advertising 294

PART 2 Sentences and Paragraphs **339**

- **9** Writing Complete Sentences 340
- **10** Writing Effective Sentences 352
- **11** Understanding Paragraphs and Compositions 370

PART 3 Grammar, Usage, and Mechanics **403**

Grammar
- **12** Parts of Speech Overview 404
- **13** The Parts of a Sentence 436
- **14** The Phrase 466
- **15** The Clause 490

Usage
- **16** Agreement 510
- **17** Using Pronouns Correctly 546
- **18** Using Verbs Correctly 572
- **19** Using Modifiers Correctly 612
- **20** A Glossary of Usage 636

Mechanics
- **21** Capitalization 666
- **22** Punctuation: End Marks and Commas 692
- **23** Punctuation: Semicolons and Colons 722
- **24** Punctuation: Italics, Quotation Marks, and Ellipsis Points 738
- **25** Punctuation: Apostrophes, Hyphens, Dashes, Parentheses, Brackets 756
- **26** Spelling 778
- **27** Correcting Common Errors 810

PART 4 Quick Reference Handbook **845**

PART 1   Communications 1

Taking Tests: Strategies and Practice 2
Taking Reading Tests 3
Taking Writing Tests 11

CHAPTER 1

Reflecting on Experiences 16

Connecting Reading and Writing 17

READING WORKSHOP: *A Personal Reflection* 18
  Preparing to Read 18
  READING SKILL ■ **Making Inferences**
  READING FOCUS ■ **Narrative and Descriptive Details**

Narration/
Description

  Reading Selection: from An American Childhood, Annie Dillard 19
  Vocabulary Mini-Lesson: *Using Multiple-Meaning Words* 26
  Test-Taking Mini-Lesson: *Answering Inference Questions*
    on Reading Tests 27

WRITING WORKSHOP: *A Personal Reflection* 28
  Prewriting 28
  Writing Mini-Lesson: *Using Figurative Language*

  Writing 38
  Framework for a Personal Reflection
  A Writer's Model: "Kicking Shyness" 39
  A Student's Model: "My Last Goodbye," Tabitha Henry 41

  Revising 42
  First Reading: *Content and Organization*
  Second Reading: *Style*
    Focus on Sentences: *Combining Sentences to Add Sentence Variety*

  Publishing 46
  Proofreading: Grammar Link—*Subject-Verb Agreement*
  Connections to Literature: *Writing a Free-Verse Poem*
    "Lost," Carl Sandburg 48

  Focus on Viewing and Representing
    Making a Video Reflection 50

  Choices: *Crossing the Curriculum: Social Studies • Literature • Careers •*
    Viewing and Representing 53

Exploring Comparisons and Contrasts

.... **54**

Informational Text

Exposition

Connecting Reading and Writing 55

READING WORKSHOP: *A Comparison-Contrast Article* 56
Preparing to Read 56
READING SKILL ■ Identifying Main Idea and Supporting Details
READING FOCUS ■ Comparison-Constrast Structure

Reading Selection: "Two Peoples Divided by Common Road Signs,"
Norman Berdichevsky from *Contemporary Review* 57
Vocabulary Mini-Lesson: *Comparison-Contrast Context Clues* ... 64
Test-Taking Mini-Lesson: *Main Idea* 65

WRITING WORKSHOP: *A Comparison-Contrast Essay* 66
Prewriting 66
Critical-Thinking Mini-Lesson: *Synthesizing Information to Form a Thesis*

Writing 74
Framework for a Comparison-Contrast Essay
A Writer's Model: "Movie? Video? What Is the Difference?" 75
A Student's Model: "Higher than Society," Adam Caputo 77

Revising 78
First Reading: *Content and Organization*
Second Reading: *Style*
Focus on Word Choice: *Avoiding Worn-out Adverbs*

Publishing 82
Proofreading: Grammar Link—*Using Comparative and Superlative Forms*
Connections to Life: *Distinguishing the Purposes of Media Forms* ... 84

Focus on Viewing and Representing
Comparing and Contrasting Media Coverage 86

Choices: *Careers • Literature • Speaking and Listening •*
Crossing the Curriculum: Science 89

Examining Causes and Effects

Examining Causes and Effects **90**

Connecting Reading and Writing 91

READING WORKSHOP: *A Cause-and-Effect Article* 92
   Preparing to Read 92
   READING SKILL ■ **Inferring Causes and Effects**
   READING FOCUS ■ **Cause-and-Effect Structure**

   Reading Selection: "Yellowstone Makes a Triumphant Return Ten
     Years After Fires," Bruce Babbitt from the
     Austin American-Statesman 93
   Vocabulary Mini-Lesson: *Suffixes* 102
   Test-Taking Mini-Lesson: *Inferring Causes and Effects* 103

WRITING WORKSHOP: *A Cause-and-Effect Explanation* ... 104
   Prewriting 104
   Critical-Thinking Mini-Lesson: *Oversimplification and
     False Cause and Effect*

   Writing 110
   Framework for a Cause-and-Effect Essay
   A Writer's Model: "School Daze" 111
   A Student's Model: "TV Baby Sitters: Help or Hindrance?"
     Gwen Miller 113

   Revising 114
   First Reading: *Content and Organization*
   Second Reading: *Style*
     Focus on Sentences: *Using Infinitives and Infinitive Phrases as Openers*

   Publishing 118
   Proofreading: Grammar Link—*Dangling Modifiers*
   Connections to Life: *Participating in Group Discussions* 120

Focus on Viewing and Representing
   Analyzing the Effects of TV 122

Choices: *Careers • Viewing and Representing • Crossing the
   Curriculum: Arts and Science • Literature* 125

Informational
Text

Exposition

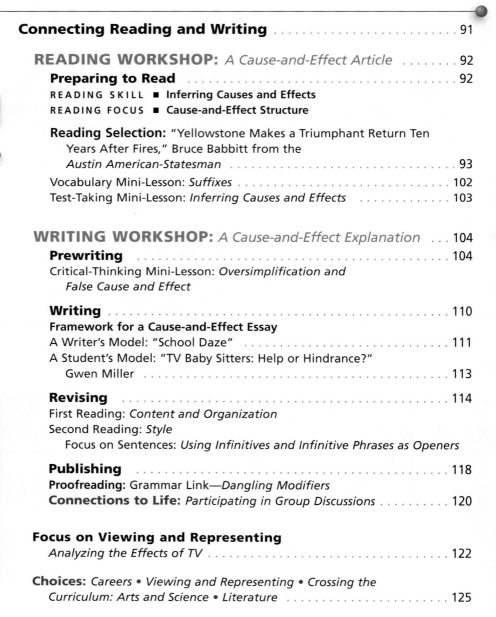

CHAPTER

4

Analyzing Problems 126

Connecting Reading and Writing 127

Informational Text

Exposition

READING WORKSHOP: *A Problem-Analysis Article* 128
Preparing to Read 128
READING SKILL ■ Making Generalizations
READING FOCUS ■ Problem-Solution Structure

Reading Selection: "Danger Beneath the Dash," Steven Levingston
from *Reader's Digest* 129
Vocabulary Mini-Lesson: *Context Clues: Definitions and Restatements* 136
Test-Taking Mini-Lesson: *Answering Logic Questions* 137

WRITING WORKSHOP: *A Problem-Analysis Essay* 138
Prewriting 138
Critical-Thinking Mini-Lesson: *Coordinating and Subordinating Ideas*

Writing 146
Framework for a Problem-Analysis Essay
A Writer's Model: "Licensed—but Safe?" 147
A Student's Model: "Athletes Trying to Be Too Perfect,"
David Thompson 149

Revising 150
First Reading: *Content and Organization*
Second Reading: *Style*
Focus on Word Choice: *Eliminating "Word Wasters"*

Publishing 155
Proofreading: Grammar Link—*Sentence Fragments*
Connections to Literature: *Analyzing the Problems*
of a Literary Character 157

Focus on Speaking and Listening
Giving an Informative Speech 158

Focus on Viewing and Representing
Recognizing News Genres 162

Choices: *Careers • Crossing the Curriculum: Literature • Speaking and*
Listening • Media and Technology 165

Analyzing a Short Story 166

Connecting Reading and Writing 167

READING WORKSHOP: *A Literary Analysis* 168
Preparing to Read 168
READING SKILL ▪ Drawing Conclusions
READING FOCUS ▪ Literary Elements

Reading Selection: from "An Introduction to Charles Dickens's
A Christmas Carol," John Irving from *You've Got to Read
This: Contemporary American Writers Introduce Stories that
Held Them in Awe* 169
Vocabulary Mini-Lesson: *Using Roots* 176
Test-Taking Mini-Lesson: *Literary Elements* 177

WRITING WORKSHOP: *A Literary Analysis* 178
Prewriting 178

Writing 184
Framework for a Literary Analysis
A Writer's Model: "Characterization in 'A Man Called Horse'" 185
A Student's Model: "Number One," Jeremy Schmidt 187

Revising 188
First Reading: *Content and Organization*
Second Reading: *Style*
Focus on Sentences: *Using Complex Sentences*
Writing Mini-Lesson: *Weaving Quotations into Your Essay*

Publishing 193
Proofreading: Grammar Link—*Using Quotation Marks in a Literary
Analysis*
Connections to Literature: *Writing a Short Story* 195

Focus on Viewing and Representing
Critiquing a Film 198

Focus on Speaking and Listening
Presenting an Oral Interpretation 203

Choices: *Literature • Careers • Media and Technology •
Viewing and Representing* 205

Informational
Text

Exposition

CHAPTER 6

Sharing Research Results 206

Connecting Reading and Writing 207

READING WORKSHOP: *A Research Article* 208
Preparing to Read 208
READING SKILL ■ Paraphrasing
READING FOCUS ■ Primary and Secondary Sources

Reading Selection: "The Art of Money," David Standish
from *Smithsonian* 209
Vocabulary Mini-Lesson: *Specialized and Technical Terms* 216
Test-Taking Mini-Lesson: *Using Context to Understand Specialized or
Technical Terms* 217

WRITING WORKSHOP: *A Research Paper* 218
Prewriting 218
Critical-Thinking Mini-Lesson: Evaluating Sources

Writing 232
Framework for a Research Paper
A Writer's Model: "The Rise of Radio" 233
A Student's Model: "An Indecisive Conclusion," Yen Co 236

Revising 240
First Reading: *Content and Organization*
Second Reading: *Style*
Focus on Sentences: *Varying Sentence Length*

Publishing 244
Proofreading: Grammar Link—*Correcting Misplaced Modifiers*
Connections to Life: *Research in the Media* 246

Focus on Viewing and Representing
Evaluating Web Sites 247

Choices: *Careers • Literature • Crossing the Curriculum: the Arts •
Media and Technology* 249

Informational Text

Exposition

Persuading Others 250

Connecting Reading and Writing 251

READING WORKSHOP: *A Persuasive Newspaper Article* ... 252
Preparing to Read 252
READING SKILL ■ **Distinguishing Facts from Opinions**
READING FOCUS ■ **Elements of Persuasion**

Reading Selection: "Force-Fed Television," Adam Hochschild
from *We the Media* 253
Vocabulary Mini-Lesson: *Understanding Connotations
and Denotations* 261
Test-Taking Mini-Lesson: *Fact-and-Opinion Questions* 262

WRITING WORKSHOP: *A Persuasive Essay* 263
Prewriting 263
Critical-Thinking Mini-Lesson: *Evaluating Your Reasoning*

Writing 272
Framework for a Persuasive Essay
A Writer's Model: "Do Something Good for the Earth" 273
A Student's Model: "Uniforms Reduce Problems," Katie Baker 275

Revising 276
First Reading: *Content and Organization*
Second Reading: *Style*
    Focus on Sentences: *Active and Passive Voice*

Publishing 280
Proofreading: Grammar Link—*Double Negatives*
Test-Taking Mini-Lesson: *Analyzing a Writing Prompt*
Connections to Life: *Writing Letters of Application* 283

Focus on Viewing and Representing
Analyzing Editorial Cartoons 284

Focus on Speaking and Listening
Giving a Persuasive Speech 288

Choices: *Careers • Literature • Media and Technology • Crossing the
Curriculum: Journalism • Art* 293

Using Persuasion in Advertising

.... **294**

Connecting Reading and Writing 295

READING WORKSHOP: *A Persuasive Brochure* 296
Preparing to Read 296
READING SKILL ■ Identifying Persuasive Techniques
READING FOCUS ■ Analyzing Persuasive Visual Elements

Reading Selection: "Adopt-A-Bison," The Nature Conservancy 297
Vocabulary Mini-Lesson: *Synonym and Antonym Context Clues* 304
Test-Taking Mini-Lesson: *Persuasive Devices* 305

WRITING WORKSHOP: *A Persuasive Brochure* 306
Prewriting 306
Critical-Thinking Mini-Lesson: *Evaluating Reasoning in Advertising*

Writing 316
Framework for a Persuasive Brochure
A Writer's Model: "Tech Teens" 316
A Student's Model: "Gourmet School Lunch," Jason Potterf 319

Revising 321
First Reading: *Content and Organization*
Second Reading: *Style*
   Focus on Word Choice: *Eliminating Clichés*

Publishing 325
Proofreading: Grammar Link—*Consistent Verb Tenses*
Connections to Life: *Analyzing Persuasion in the Media* 327

Focus on Viewing and Representing
   Creating a Documentary on Print Advertising 329

Choices: *Careers • Literature • Crossing the Curriculum: History •
   Media and Technology* 337

PART 2 **Sentences and Paragraphs** **338**

CHAPTER

9

Writing Complete Sentences **340**

SENTENCE FRAGMENTS 340
 Phrase Fragments 342
  Verbal Phrases 342
  Appositive Phrases 343
  Prepositional Phrases 343
 Subordinate Clause Fragments 344

RUN-ON SENTENCES 347
 Revising Run-on Sentences 348

REVIEW A: Correcting Fragments and Run-on Sentences 350

REVIEW B: Revising Fragments and Run-on Sentences 351

CHAPTER

10

Writing Effective Sentences **352**

COMBINING SENTENCES 352
 Inserting Words 353
 Inserting Phrases 355
  Prepositional Phrases 355
  Participial Phrases 355
  Appositive Phrases 355
 Using Compound Subjects and Verbs 357
 Creating a Compound Sentence 358
 Creating a Complex Sentence 359
  Adjective Clauses 359
  Adverb Clauses 359
  Noun Clauses 360

REVIEW A: Revising Sentences by Combining 361

REVIEW B: Revising a Paragraph by Combining Sentences 362

IMPROVING SENTENCE STYLE 362
 Using Parallel Structure 362
 Revising Stringy Sentences 363

Revising Wordy Sentences 365
Varying Sentence Beginnings 366
Varying Sentence Structure 368

REVIEW C: Writing a Paragraph Using a Variety of Sentence Structures . . . 369

CHAPTER 11

Understanding Paragraphs and Compositions 370

HOW PARAGRAPHS AND COMPOSITIONS FIT TOGETHER 370

THE PARTS OF A BODY PARAGRAPH 370
Putting the Parts Together 372

QUALITIES OF PARAGRAPHS 374
Unity 374
Coherence 374
Elaboration 376
Looking at the Qualities of Paragraphs 378

REVIEW A: Analyzing Paragraphs 381

PARAGRAPHS WITHIN COMPOSITIONS 382

WHAT MAKES A COMPOSITION? 382

THE INTRODUCTION 382
Catching the Reader's Interest 383
Techniques for Writing Introductions 383
Setting the Tone 385
The Thesis Statement 386
The Structure of Introductions 388

THE BODY 391
Unity 391
Coherence 391
Direct References 391
Transitional Expressions 392
Elaboration 392

THE CONCLUSION 393

USING A BASIC FRAMEWORK 397

A WRITER'S MODEL 398

REVIEW B: Writing an Informative Composition 400

Contents   **xvii**

PART 3 **Grammar, Usage, and Mechanics** **402**

Parts of Speech Overview
Identification and Function **404**

DIAGNOSTIC PREVIEW: Determining the Parts of Speech of Words 404

NOUNS 405
Common Nouns and Proper Nouns 406
Compound Nouns 406
Concrete Nouns and Abstract Nouns 407
Collective Nouns 407

PRONOUNS 408
Personal Pronouns 409
Reflexive and Intensive Pronouns 409
Demonstrative Pronouns 410
Interrogative Pronouns 410
Relative Pronouns 410
Indefinite Pronouns 411

ADJECTIVES 412
Articles 412
Pronoun or Adjective? 414
Noun or Adjective? 415

VERBS 417
Main Verbs and Helping Verbs 417
Action Verbs and Linking Verbs 418
Transitive Verbs and Intransitive Verbs 421

ADVERBS 422
Adverbs Modifying Verbs 422
Adverbs Modifying Adjectives 423
Adverbs Modifying Other Adverbs 424
Noun or Adverb? 424

PREPOSITIONS 426
Preposition or Adverb? 427

CONJUNCTIONS 428
Coordinating Conjunctions 428
Correlative Conjunctions 428

CHAPTER

12

INTERJECTIONS 429

DETERMINING PARTS OF SPEECH 430

CHAPTER REVIEW 433
    A. Identifying the Parts of Speech in Sentences
    B. Identifying the Parts of Speech in a Paragraph
    C. Identifying Pronouns in Sentences
    D. Identifying Words as Nouns, Pronouns, or Adjectives
    E. Classifying Nouns
    Writing Application: *Using Adjectives in a Poem* 435

The Parts of a Sentence
Subjects, Predicates, Complements **436**

CHAPTER

13

DIAGNOSTIC PREVIEW 436
    A. Identifying Subjects, Verbs, and Complements
    B. Classifying Sentences According to Purpose

WHAT IS A SENTENCE? 437

SUBJECTS AND PREDICATES 439
    The Subject 440
    The Predicate 441
    Finding the Subject 442
    Sentences Beginning with *There* or *Here* 446
    Sentences Asking Questions 446
    The Understood Subject 447
    Compound Subjects and Compound Verbs 447

COMPLEMENTS 450
    The Subject Complement 453
    The Object of a Verb 455

CLASSIFYING SENTENCES BY PURPOSE 459

CHAPTER REVIEW 463
    A. Identifying Subjects, Verbs, and Complements
    B. Identifying Subjects and Predicates
    C. Completing Sentences by Supplying Subjects and Verbs
    D. Identifying Predicate Nominatives and Predicate Adjectives
    E. Classifying Sentences as Declarative, Interrogative, Imperative, or
       Exclamatory
    Writing Application: *Using Varied Sentences in a Letter* 465

The Phrase

CHAPTER 14

Prepositional, Verbal, and Appositive Phrases **466**

DIAGNOSTIC PREVIEW: Identifying Prepositional, Verbal, and
    Appositive Phrases 466

WHAT IS A PHRASE? 467

PREPOSITIONAL PHRASES 467
    Adjective Phrases 468
    Adverb Phrases 469

VERBALS AND VERBAL PHRASES 472
    The Participle 472
    The Participial Phrase 473
    The Gerund 476
    The Gerund Phrase 478
    The Infinitive 479
    The Infinitive Phrase 480

APPOSITIVES AND APPOSITIVE PHRASES 483

CHAPTER REVIEW 487
    A. Sentences with Prepositional Phrases
    B. Identifying Participles and Participial Phrases
    C. Identifying Phrases in Sentences
    D. Identifying Phrases in a Paragraph
    Writing Application: *Using Phrases in a Newspaper Article* 489

The Clause

CHAPTER 15

Independent Clauses and Subordinate Clauses **490**

DIAGNOSTIC PREVIEW 490
    A. Identifying and Classifying Clauses
    B. Classifying Sentences According to Structure

WHAT IS A CLAUSE? 492

INDEPENDENT CLAUSES 492

SUBORDINATE CLAUSES 493
    Complements and Modifiers in Subordinate Clauses 494

USES OF SUBORDINATE CLAUSES 495
    The Adjective Clause 495
    Relative Pronouns 496

THE ADVERB CLAUSE 498
    Subordinating Conjunctions 498

THE NOUN CLAUSE 501

SENTENCES CLASSIFIED ACCORDING TO STRUCTURE 504

CHAPTER REVIEW 507
    A. Identifying and Classifying Clauses
    B. Identifying and Classifying Subordinate Clauses
    C. Classifying Sentences According to Structure
    Writing Application: *Writing a Paragraph* 509

Agreement
Subject and Verb, Pronoun and Antecedent **510**

DIAGNOSTIC PREVIEW 510
    A. Identifying Subject-Verb Agreement and
       Pronoun-Antecedent Agreement
    B. Identifying Subject-Verb Agreement and
       Pronoun-Antecedent Agreement

AGREEMENT OF SUBJECT AND VERB 512
    Indefinite Pronouns 516
    Compound Subjects 520
    Special Problems in Subject-Verb Agreement 522

AGREEMENT OF PRONOUN AND ANTECEDENT 532
    Indefinite Pronouns 533
    Compound Antecedents 535
    Special Problems in Pronoun-Antecedent Agreement. 536

CHAPTER REVIEW 543
    A. Identifying Subject-Verb and Pronoun-Antecedent Agreement
    B. Choosing Pronouns That Agree with Their Antecedents
    C. Identifying Subject-Verb Agreement and
       Pronoun-Antecedent Agreement
    Writing Application: *Using Agreement in a Letter* 545

Using Pronouns Correctly
Nominative, Objective, and Possessive Case; Clear Reference

CHAPTER 17 .... **546**

DIAGNOSTIC PREVIEW 546
   A. Proofreading Sentences for Correct Pronoun Forms
   B. Proofreading Sentences for Correct Forms and Uses

CASE FORMS OF PERSONAL PRONOUNS 547
   The Nominative Case 549
   The Objective Case 553
   The Possessive Case 556

SPECIAL PROBLEMS IN PRONOUN USAGE 558
   The Relative Pronouns *Who* and *Whom* 558
   Appositives 561
   Reflexive and Intensive Pronouns 564
   Pronouns in Incomplete Constructions 565

CLEAR PRONOUN REFERENCE 566

CHAPTER REVIEW 569
   A. Using Pronouns Correctly in Sentences
   B. Selecting Pronouns to Complete Sentences Correctly
   C. Proofreading Sentences for Correct Pronoun Usage
   Writing Application: *Using Pronouns Correctly in a Letter* 571

Using Verbs Correctly
Principal Parts, Tense, Voice, Mood

CHAPTER 18 .... **572**

DIAGNOSTIC PREVIEW 572
   A. Writing the Past and Past Participle Forms of Irregular Verbs
   B. Revising Sentences to Correct Problems in Verb Tense and Voice
   C. Determining Correct Uses of *Lie* and *Lay, Sit* and *Set,* and *Rise* and *Raise*

THE PRINCIPAL PARTS OF VERBS 574
   Regular Verbs 575
   Irregular Verbs 576

SIX TROUBLESOME VERBS 582
   Lie and *Lay* 582

Sit and *Set* 585
Rise and *Raise* 588

TENSE 590
Verb Conjugation 590
The Uses of the Tenses 594
Consistency of Tense 597

MODALS 599

ACTIVE VOICE AND PASSIVE VOICE 601
Using the Passive Voice 604

MOOD 606

CHAPTER REVIEW 608
A. Writing the Past or Past Participle Form of Verbs
B. Revising Verb Tense or Voice
C. Determining Correct Use of *Lie* and *Lay, Sit* and *Set,*
   and *Rise* and *Raise* in Sentences
D. Using the Different Tenses of Verbs
E. Choosing the Correct Forms of Verbs
Writing Application: *Using Verb Tense in an Essay* 611

The Granger Collection, New York.

Using Modifiers Correctly
Forms, Comparison, and Placement **612**

CHAPTER

19

DIAGNOSTIC PREVIEW 612
A. Revising Sentences to Correct Errors in the Use and
   Placement of Modifiers
B. Revising a Paragraph to Correct Errors in the Use and
   Placement of Modifiers

WHAT IS A MODIFIER? 614
One-Word Modifiers 614
Phrases Used as Modifiers 616
Clauses Used as Modifiers 617

EIGHT TROUBLESOME MODIFIERS 617
Bad and *Badly* 617
Good and *Well* 617
Slow and *Slowly* 618
Real and *Really* 618

COMPARISON OF MODIFIERS 620
   Regular Comparison 621
   Irregular Comparison 622
   Use of Comparative and Superlative Forms 623

DANGLING MODIFIERS 626

MISPLACED MODIFIERS 627
   Misplaced One-Word Modifiers 627
   Misplaced Phrase Modifiers 628
   Misplaced Clause Modifiers 630

CHAPTER REVIEW 633
   A. Correcting Errors in the Use of the Comparative and
      Superlative forms
   B. Revising Sentences by Correcting Dangling and
      Misplaced Modifiers
   C. Revising Sentences by Correcting Unclear Comparisons and
      Incorrect, Misplaced, and Dangling Modifiers
   Writing Application: *Using Comparison in a Consumer Guide.* 635

A Glossary of Usage

CHAPTER

20

Common Usage Problems **636**

DIAGNOSTIC PREVIEW 636
   A. Revising Errors in Usage
   B. Proofreading Paragraphs to Correct Usage Errors

ABOUT THE GLOSSARY 638

THE DOUBLE NEGATIVE 656

NONSEXIST LANGUAGE 659

CHAPTER REVIEW 661
   A. Revising Expressions by Correcting Errors in Usage
   B. Proofreading a Paragraph to Correct Usage Errors
   C. Identifying Standard Usage
   Writing Application: *Creating a Flier.* 665

Capitalization

CHAPTER

21

Standard Uses of Capitalization **666**

DIAGNOSTIC PREVIEW 666
   A. Capitalizing Sentences Correctly
   B. Capitalizing a Paragraph Correctly

USING CAPITAL LETTERS CORRECTLY 668
   Abbreviations 686

CHAPTER REVIEW 689
   A. Using Capitalization Correctly
   B. Capitalizing Words in a Paragraph Correctly
   C. Using Capitalization Correctly
   D. Correcting Sentences by Capitalizing Words
   Writing Application: *Writing a Guidebook* 691

Punctuation

CHAPTER

22

End Marks and Commas **692**

DIAGNOSTIC PREVIEW 692
   A. Correcting Sentences by Adding Periods, Question Marks,
      Exclamation Points, and Commas
   B. Correcting Paragraphs by Adding Periods, Question Marks,
      Exclamation Points, and Commas

END MARKS 694
   Abbreviations 696

COMMAS 700
   Items in a Series 700
   Independent Clauses 703
   Nonessential Clauses and Phrases 704
   Introductory Elements 707
   Interrupters 711
   Conventional Uses of Commas 714
   Unnecessary Commas 716

CHAPTER REVIEW 719
   A. Using End Marks
   B. Correcting Sentences by Adding Punctuation
   C. Correcting Paragraphs by Adding Punctuation
   Writing Application: *Using Commas in Instructions* 721

Punctuation

CHAPTER 23

Semicolons and Colons **722**

DIAGNOSTIC PREVIEW: Correcting Sentences by Adding Semicolons
    and Colons 722

SEMICOLONS 724

COLONS 729

CHAPTER REVIEW 733
    A. Correcting Sentences by Using Semicolons and Colons
    B. Correcting Sentences by Adding Colons
    C. Correcting Sentences by Adding Semicolons and Colons
    Writing Application: *Punctuating a Business Letter* 737

Punctuation

CHAPTER 24

Italics, Quotation Marks, and Ellipsis Points **738**

DIAGNOSTIC PREVIEW: Correcting Sentences by Adding Italics
    (Underlining), Quotation Marks, and Ellipsis Points 738

ITALICS 739

QUOTATION MARKS 743

ELLIPSIS POINTS 750

CHAPTER REVIEW 753
    A. Correcting Sentences by Adding Italics (Underlining)
       and Quotation Marks
    B. Correcting Sentences by Adding Italics (Underlining)
    C. Using Ellipsis Points Correctly
    Writing Application: *Writing an Interior Dialogue* 755

Punctuation

Apostrophes, Hyphens, Dashes, Parentheses, Brackets

CHAPTER

25

Apostrophes, Hyphens, Dashes, Parentheses, Brackets **756**

DIAGNOSTIC PREVIEW 756
   A. Correcting Sentences by Using Apostrophes and Hyphens
   B. Correcting Sentences by Using Dashes, Parentheses, and Brackets

APOSTROPHES 758
   Possessive Case 758
   Contractions 763
   Plurals 766

HYPHENS 767
   Word Division 767
   Compound Words 768

DASHES 770

PARENTHESES 770

BRACKETS 772

CHAPTER REVIEW 775
   A. Using Apostrophes and Hyphens Correctly
   B. Using Dashes, Brackets, and Parentheses Correctly
   C. Writing the Possessive Forms of Nouns
   D. Proofreading a Paragraph for Errors in Punctuation
   Writing Application: *Punctuating a Poem* 777

Spelling

Improving Your Spelling

CHAPTER

26

Improving Your Spelling **778**

DIAGNOSTIC PREVIEW: Correcting Misspelled and Misused Words
   and Numerals 778

GOOD SPELLING HABITS 779

SPELLING RULES 780
   ie and *ei* 780
   –cede,–ceed, and *–sede* 780
   Adding Prefixes 781

Adding Suffixes 782
Forming Plurals of Nouns 787
Writing Numbers 791

WORDS OFTEN CONFUSED 793

CHAPTER REVIEW 803
A. Proofreading Sentences to Correct Spelling Errors
B. Proofreading a Paragraph to Correct Spelling Errors
C. Distinguishing Between Words Often Confused
Writing Application: *Using Correct Spelling in an Application Letter* . . 805

SPELLING WORD LISTS 807

Correcting Common Errors
Key Language Skills Review **810**

GRAMMAR AND USAGE 811
Grammar and Usage Test: Section 1 827
Grammar and Usage Test: Section 2 830

MECHANICS 832
Mechanics Test: Section 1 840
Mechanics Test: Section 2 842

CHAPTER

27

PART 4 | **Quick Reference Handbook** **844**

THE DICTIONARY 846
Information About Words 846

DOCUMENT DESIGN 849
Manuscript Style 849
Desktop Publishing 849
Graphics 855

THE HISTORY OF ENGLISH: ORIGINS AND USES 861
The History of English 861
Varieties of American English 864

THE LIBRARY/MEDIA CENTER 866
Using Print and Electronic Sources 866

READING AND VOCABULARY 876
Reading 876
Vocabulary 887

SPEAKING AND LISTENING 896
Speaking 896
Listening 906

STUDYING AND TEST TAKING 911
Study Skills and Strategies 911
Test-Taking Skills and Strategies 915

VIEWING AND REPRESENTING 928
Media Terms 928

WRITING 939
Skills, Structures, and Techniques 939

GRAMMAR AT A GLANCE 960

Diagramming Appendix **986**

Index **1000**

Acknowledgments **1032**

Photography and Illustration Credits **1034**

MODELS

READING SELECTIONS

- Bruce Babbitt, **"Yellowstone Makes a Triumphant Return Ten Years After Fires,"** from *Austin American-Statesman*

- Norman Berdichevsky, **"Two Peoples Divided by Common Road Signs,"** from *Contemporary Review*

- Annie Dillard, ***An American Childhood***

- Adam Hochschild, **"Force-Fed Television,"** from *We the Media*

- John Irving, **"An Introduction to Charles Dickens's *A Christmas Carol*,"** from *You've Got to Read This*

- Steven Levingston, **"Danger Beneath the Dash,"** from *Reader's Digest*

- Norman Maclean, ***Young Men and Fire***

- The Nature Conservancy, **"Adopt-A-Bison"**

- David Standish, **"The Art of Money,"** from *Smithsonian*

WRITING MODELS

- Robert D. Ballard, ***Exploring the Titanic***

- Stephen Crane, **"The Bride Comes to Yellow Sky"**

- Ian Darragh, **"Prince Edward Island: A World Apart No More,"** *National Geographic*

- John L. Eliot, **"Snake Venom Strikes at Heart Attacks,"** *National Geographic*

- William Fleming, ***Arts and Ideas***

- Wendy M. Grossman, **"Access Denied,"** *Scientific American*

- Kim Hubbard, **"Review of *The Eat a Bug Cookbook*,"** *Discover*

- John Elkington, Julia Hailes, Douglas Hill, and Joel Makower, ***Going Green***

- Nicholas L. Johnson, **"Monitoring and Controlling Debris in Space,"** *Scientific American*

- Michael E. Long, **"The Vanishing Prairie Dog,"** *National Geographic*

MODELS

- Steve Nadis, **"Bug Zappers Miss Their Mark,"** *Omni* magazine Web site

- Carl Sandburg, **"Lost"**

- Paul Theroux, ***Riding the Iron Rooster***

- Mark Wheeler, **"Science Friction,"** *Discover*

- Harold M. Williams, **"Don't Ignore the Arts,"** *USA Today*

- Ethel Yari, **"Teenage Lincoln Sculptor,"** *American History*

STUDENT MODELS →

- Katie Baker, **"Uniforms Reduce Problems"**

- Adam Caputo, **"Higher than Society"**

- Yen Co, **"An Indecisive Conclusion"**

- Tabitha Henry, **"My Last Goodbye"**

- Gwen Miller, **"TV Baby Sitters: Help or Hindrance?"**

- Jason Potterf, **"Gourmet School Lunch"**

- Jeremy Schmidt, **"Number One"**

- David Thompson, **"Athletes Trying to Be Too Perfect"**

STUDENT'S OVERVIEW

Elements of Language is divided into four major parts.

PART 1   Communications

This section ties together the essential skills and strategies you use in all types of communication—reading, writing, listening, speaking, viewing, and representing.

Reading Workshops In these workshops, you read an article, a story, an editorial—a real-life example of a type of writing you will later compose on your own. In addition, these workshops help you practice the reading process through

- a Reading Skill and Reading Focus specific to each type of writing,

- Vocabulary Mini-Lessons to help you understand unfamiliar words, and

- Test-Taking Mini-Lessons targeting common reading objectives

Writing Workshops In these workshops, you brainstorm ideas and use the writing process to produce your own article, story, editorial—and more. These workshops also include

- Writing and Critical-Thinking Mini-Lessons to help you master important aspects of each type of writing

- an organizational framework and models to guide your writing

- evaluation charts with concrete steps for revising

- Connections to Literature and Connections to Life, activities that extend writing workshop skills and concepts to other areas of your life

- Test-Taking Mini-Lessons to help you respond to writing prompts for tests

Focus on Speaking and Listening
Focus on Viewing and Representing

This is your chance to sharpen your skills in presenting your ideas visually and orally and to learn how to take a more critical view of what you hear and see.

PART 2 Sentences and Paragraphs

Learn to construct clear and effective sentences and paragraphs—what parts to include, how to organize ideas, and how to write these essential parts of compositions with style.

PART 3 Grammar, Usage, and Mechanics

These are the basics that will help you make your writing correct and polished.

Grammar Discover the structure of language—the words, phrases, and clauses that are the building blocks of sentences.

Usage Learn the rules that govern how language is used in various social situations, including standard versus nonstandard and formal versus informal English.

Mechanics Master the nuts and bolts of correct written English, including capitalization, punctuation, and spelling.

PART 4 Quick Reference Handbook

Use this handy guide anytime you need concise tips to help you communicate more effectively—whether you need to find information in a variety of media, make sense of what you read, prepare for tests, or present your ideas in a published document, speech, or visual.

Elements of Language on the Internet

Put the communication strategies in *Elements of Language* to work by logging on to the Internet. At the *Elements of Language* Internet site, you can dissect the prose of professional writers, crack the codes of the advertising industry, and find out how your communication skills can help you in the real world.

As you move through *Elements of Language,* you will find the best online resources at **go.hrw.com.**

The Reading and Writing Processes

Do these situations sound familiar? While reading, you suddenly realize you have read the same sentences several times without gaining any meaning from them. While writing, you stare at the single sentence you have written, unable to think of anything else to write. When you find yourself stuck, step back and look at the processes of reading and writing.

Reading

The reading you do in high school requires you to think critically about information and ideas. In order to get the most from a text, prepare your mind for the task before you read, use effective strategies while you read, and take time to process the information after you read.

- **Before Reading** Get your mind in gear by considering your purpose for reading a particular piece of writing and by thinking about what you already know about the topic. Preview the text by skimming a bit and considering headings, graphics, and other features. Use this information to predict what the text will discuss and how challenging it will be to read.

- **While Reading** As you read, figure out the writer's main idea about the topic. Notice how the text is organized (by cause and effect or in order of importance, for example) to help you find support for that point. Connect the ideas to your own experiences when you can. If you get confused, slow down, re-read, or jot ideas in a graphic organizer.

- **After Reading** Confirm and extend your understanding of the text. Draw conclusions about the writer's point of view, and evaluate how well the writer communicated the message. Use ideas in the text to create a piece of art, to read more on a related topic, or to solve a problem.

Writing

A perfect text seldom springs fully formed from your mind; instead, you must plan your text before you write and work to improve it after drafting.

TIP Reading and writing are both recursive processes—that is, you can return to earlier steps when needed. For example, you might make new predictions while you are reading a text or you might develop additional support for ideas when you are revising a piece of writing.

- **Before Writing** First, choose a topic and a form of writing, such as a poem or an editorial. Decide who your readers will be and what you want the text to accomplish. Develop ideas based on your knowledge and on research. Organize the ideas, and jot down your main point.

- **While Writing** Grab attention and provide background information in an introduction. Elaborate your ideas to support your point, and organize them clearly. Then, wrap things up with a conclusion.

- **After Writing** To improve a draft, evaluate how clearly you expressed your ideas. Ask a peer to suggest areas that need work. Then, revise. Proofread to correct any mistakes. Share your finished work with others, and reflect on what you learned.

You may have noticed that the reading and writing processes involve similar strategies. The chart below summarizes these similarities.

The Reading and Writing Processes

Reading

Writing

Reading		Writing
■ Determine your purpose for reading. ■ Consider what you already know about the topic. ■ Preview the text to make predictions about what it will include.	Before	■ Identify your writing purpose and your audience. ■ Draw upon what you know about the topic, and do research to find out more. ■ Make notes or an outline to plan what the text will include.
■ Figure out the writer's main ideas. ■ Look for support for the main ideas. ■ Notice how the ideas in the text are organized.	While	■ Express your main ideas clearly. ■ Support them with details, facts, examples, or anecdotes. ■ Follow prewriting notes or an outline to organize your text so readers can easily follow your ideas.
■ Evaluate the text to decide how accurate it is and its overall quality. ■ Relate what you have read to the world around you by creating something, reading further, or applying ideas. ■ Reflect on what you have read.	After	■ Evaluate and revise your text. Use peer editors' comments to help improve your work. ■ Relate your writing to the world around you by publishing it. ■ Reflect on what you have written.

The Reading and Writing Workshops in this book provide valuable practice for strategies that will help you effectively use these related processes.

Communications

Taking Tests: Strategies
and Practice. 2

1 Narration/Description:
Reflecting on Experiences . . . 16

2 Exposition: Exploring
Comparisons and Contrasts . . 54

3 Exposition: Examining
Causes and Effects 90

4 Exposition: Analyzing
Problems 126

5 Exposition: Analyzing
a Short Story 166

6 Exposition: Sharing
Research Results. 206

7 Persuasion: Persuading
Others. 250

8 Persuasion: Using Persuasion
in Advertising 294

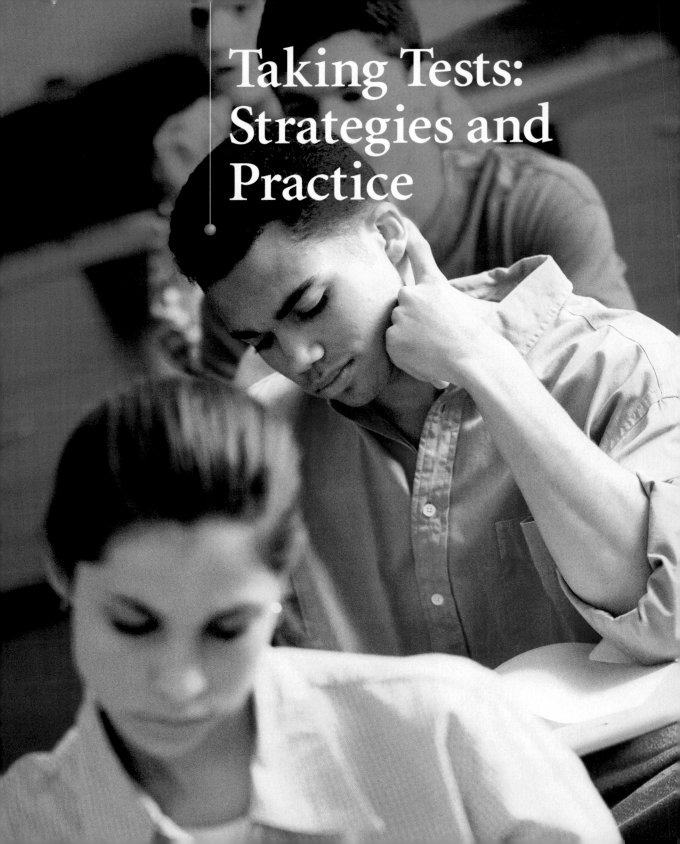

Taking Tests: Strategies and Practice

Taking Reading Tests

Perhaps once a year, you'll face a national or statewide standardized test of reading and writing. A standardized reading test contains brief **reading passages** followed by many **multiple-choice questions** and sometimes an open-ended **essay question.** The test is designed to evaluate the entire range of your reading skills.

THINKING IT THROUGH   Reading Test Strategies

▶ **STEP 1** **Pace yourself.** Skim the test to see how many questions there are, and estimate how long you can spend on each question. Check every five or ten minutes to see if you need to work faster.

▶ **STEP 2** **Read carefully.** Read the directions and any introduction to the reading passage. Then, focus your complete attention on the reading passage. If you can mark in the test booklet, underline key words.

▶ **STEP 3** **Make sure you understand the question.** Beware of words like *not* and *except,* which direct you to choose an answer that is false or opposite in some way. Watch out also for distractors—answers that are true but don't answer the question that's being asked. Never choose an answer until you've read *all* of the answer choices.

▶ **STEP 4** **Make educated guesses.** Eliminate answers you know are wrong. Then, make an educated, not a random, guess. Remember that your answer must depend entirely on information in the reading passage—not on any prior knowledge you may have about the topic.

▶ **STEP 5** **Keep on going.** Don't get stuck on a difficult question. Skip questions that baffle you and return to them later if you have time.

▶ **STEP 6** **Watch your bubbles.** Carefully match each question to the number on the answer sheet, and make sure you neatly bubble in the answer you intend. If you skip a question, don't lose your place.

▶ **STEP 7** **Check your work.** When you finish, go back and try answering questions you skipped the first time round. Give yourself time to check your answer sheet carefully, and be sure to erase any stray pencil marks.

TIP Know how the test is scored. If no points are taken off for wrong answers, then answer every question. If wrong answers count against you, answer (1) the questions you know and (2) those you can answer with an educated guess.

Read the following passages carefully. Then, choose the **best** answer to each question.

LAND OF THE GIANTS

by George Laycock

The giant cat with long teeth as sharp as daggers slid down the steep bank toward the water. It never suspected it was headed for serious trouble.

Waiting beneath the shallow water was a pool of black sticky tar (*la brea* in Spanish). From the instant the cat splashed in, it could not lift its feet. The harder it fought to get free, the tighter it was held, and gradually it disappeared into the blackness.

Its bones joined those of thousands of other animals buried in the La Brea Tar Pits, in what is today downtown Los Angeles, Calif.

More bones of ancient beasts lie buried in other places across the country. They are clues. They help scientists learn the secrets of extinct animals that once walked the earth where we live today.

Among the ice-age animals living here until about 11,000 years ago were unbelievable giants. There were powerful wolves, cats, elephants and sloths. There were giant bison, moose and a meat-eating bird that stood seven feet tall. There was even an amazing bear much larger than today's biggest grizzly bear.

Giant Short-Faced Bear: 11 Feet Tall—and Mean

This ancient bear would make the modern grizzly look like a runt. Because it had a face more like a bulldog than a bear, scientists call it the giant short-faced bear.

It stood about five feet high on all fours, and when it reared up on its hind feet it was 11 feet tall. Its long legs tell us that it was built for speed. It probably ate any animal it could outrun, including the camels and horses that once lived in North America.

Bones of the giant short-faced bear have been found from Alaska to Mexico and east to Virginia. The last of them died about 11,000 years ago.

Mammoths and Mastodons: The American Elephants

The giant bear's neighbors included early elephants called mammoths and mastodons. These were the largest of all the ice-age giants. One species stood 13 feet high. Mammoths and mastodons lived in most parts of North America.

The 10-foot-tall woolly mammoth wore a heavy shaggy coat of thick fur that protected it from the cold winds sweeping off the glaciers. Beneath its fur blanket was a thick layer of fat.

Modern scientists even know what the mammoths ate because, in frozen mammoths, they found stomachs full of leaves and grass. Hanging down from the mammoth's face were long curved tusks, which probably were used to sweep snow off the grass and bushes they ate.

Early people hunted these giant elephants for food, but this was risky business. Their weapons were rocks or spears they made from sticks and stones. Their best chance of bagging an elephant was to find one stuck in a swamp where it could not fight back.

Because adult mammoths and mastodons were so large, predators probably left them alone. They were too big, even for the fierce cat that scientists call Smilodon.

Saber-Toothed Cat: Surprise Attacker

Smilodon, the saber-toothed cat, was a bit smaller but heavier than today's African lion and had teeth so long they hung outside its mouth. These seven-inch-long teeth were stabbing tools. The giant cat's other weapon was a set of long sharp claws.

Smilodon was probably not a distance runner because its hind legs were short. But it must have been speedy on the short dash. It probably hunted from ambush. Hiding beside the trail, it waited for an unsuspecting horse, antelope, or camel to come close. Then it dashed out and took its victim by surprise.

Giant Ground Sloth: 18 Feet Long—And Very Slow

Among Smilodon's food items was the giant ground sloth. The sloth was a slugging bag of meat and bones too slow to even try running away.

Modern sloths living in South American jungles creep along upside-down in tall trees and grow to about two feet long. The giant version that moved into North America from the south was elephant-size and lived on the ground. The males, sometimes 18 feet long, weighed as much as three tons—6,000 pounds.

The sloth was tall enough to reach 15 feet up into the trees for fresh green leaves and twigs. Its bones have been discovered in Texas, Florida, and other states. It has been gone about 10,000 years.

Giant Beaver: A Champion Swimmer

One day more than 100 years ago, well diggers in Minneapolis, Minn., dug up part of a jawbone. Scientists said it came from an extinct giant beaver. Other bones of this ancient beast have been found from Alaska to New York to Florida. The giant beaver was as big as a black bear and weighed as much as 500 pounds.

But this beaver did not cut trees and build dams as the modern beaver does. It did not have the right kind of teeth for cutting wood. Instead it sloshed around in the swamps on the edges of lakes eating vegetation. It was probably clumsy on land but a champion swimmer. It became extinct about 9,000 years ago. No one is sure why.

Toward the end of the latest ice age 10,000 years ago, other animals also became extinct. Why so many in the parade of ice-age giants disappeared forever at this time is one of history's greatest mysteries.

Maybe, over thousands of years, the changing climate killed off their food plants. Theories are plentiful; answers are not. Whatever the reasons, we know they lived here long ago. Their bones tell us so.

1. **What is the article's main idea?**
   A. Scientists know almost nothing about extinct animals.
   B. Gigantic animals are unable to survive for very long.
   C. Many gigantic animals, now extinct, once lived in North America.
   D. During the ice age, many species lived together peacefully.
   E. Fossils of prehistoric creatures can be found in every U.S. state.

2. **In what way does the author organize ideas?**
   F. by cause and effect
   G. by logical categories
   H. in chronological order
   J. by problem and solution
   K. in order of importance

3. **From this article you can infer that**
   A. scientists are still researching why these animals died out
   B. another ice age could not occur in the future
   C. animals today are much smaller than their ancestors
   D. most discoveries of fossils are accidental
   E. bones of all of these animals have been found in the La Brea Tar Pits

4. **The writer uses subheads to indicate**
   F. his personal views
   G. his source of information
   H. a humorous fact about an animal
   J. a change in subject
   K. the start of each paragraph

5. You can infer that during the ice age mentioned in the article

   A. global warming melted the ice

   B. the climate was colder but not necessarily icy

   C. ice covered all of North America

   D. the Atlantic Ocean was frozen solid

   E. most animals were unable to survive the cold

6. How did the scientists discover the facts stated in the article?

   F. from written records

   G. from cave drawings

   H. from photographs

   J. from ancient stories and poems

   K. from animals' bones

7. "This ancient bear would make the modern grizzly look like a runt." A *runt* is

   A. a fierce predator

   B. a small creature

   C. a gentle giant

   D. an extinct animal

   E. a beautiful animal

8. The author's main purpose is to

   F. entertain the reader

   G. persuade the reader

   H. present factual information

   J. present both sides of a controversy

   K. explain a process

Write several paragraphs in response to **one** of the following questions:

9. A time machine is about to zap you back to the ice age in North America more than eleven thousand years ago. You'll land at the feet of one of the animals described in this article. Tell which animal you'd choose to meet up close, and why. Then, tell which animal you'd least like to meet, and why. Use details from the article to elaborate.

10. The same information may be communicated in different ways, depending on who the intended audience is. Use details from the article to decide who the intended audience for this piece is, and then explain how the information might be presented for another specific audience of your choice.

Digging the Past

by Jenny Lawrence

David Hurst Thomas is at the archaeological site of San Marcos, twenty miles south of Sante Fe, New Mexico. His job as an archaeologist is to understand the lives of people in the present and the past, including those who lived at San Marcos at least 800 years ago. Dave learns about these people by studying what they left behind, including ancient trash heaps called middens. The middens contain pottery and bones that tell him how people cooked and what they ate.

It is hard to believe that beneath these dry, grassy hills is a buried settlement called a pueblo. In it were a Spanish mission,[1] nine plazas, and twenty-two blocks of flat-roofed adobe[2] rooms. Some of these ancient "apartment buildings" were three stories high. San Marcos may be the largest ancient Indian pueblo in the United States. The area was probably settled about A.D. 1200, because it was near the Cerrillos Mountains, the only source of turquoise in New Mexico. This made San Marcos a very important center for trade. In the 1620s, Franciscan friars built a mission church, which was abandoned, along with the whole pueblo, after an Indian revolt in 1680.

---

1. **mission:** group of persons sent by a religious body to spread its religion, especially in a foreign land. California missions were founded by Catholics from Spain.

2. **adobe:** made of sun-dried bricks.

When Dave is not working at the San Marcos site, he is at the American Museum of Natural History, where he is curator of North American Archaeology and in charge of one of the world's largest collections of Native American artifacts.

Another Museum archaeologist, Nels Nelson, was the first to excavate at San Marcos. That was in 1915. His technique was to dig down into middens, carefully retrieve buried objects, and figure out how old they were according to how deep they were buried. He introduced this method, now called stratigraphy, to America.

More than eighty years later, Dave has returned to the hillside on which the Franciscan mission once stood. He knows what he's looking for before his excavation team begins to dig because they use high-tech machines to check out what's below the ground.

"We are doing a new kind of archaeology here," Dave says. "With Ground Penetrating Radar, we detected the adobe walls of the mission and sure enough, within two hours of starting to dig, the crew exposed these very walls. We also used magnetometry and soil resistivity—techniques that measured changes in the magnetic and water content of the soil and that showed us rock foundations and pits, metal tools, and clay pots.

"We even chart the ragweed that grows precisely over the buried outlines of the entire mission," he adds.

Digging trenches that follow that mission's walls, Dave and his team spend six weeks working to expose the west end of the church. When they leave, they will cover the excavation with dirt to protect the ruins. Eventually, Dave hopes to make use of remote-sensing satellites.[3] Then he will be able to see things without disturbing the site at all. Back in the Museum's laboratory in New York City, he and his wife, Lori, also an archaeologist, will analyze the glittering pieces of mica rock that people used as ornaments, fragments of the mission's bell, and other artifacts. Then they will return them to New Mexico's Maxwell Museum.

Dave is training Native American and Hispanic students from the area as archaeologists. They will help out next summer. "San Marcos's heritage," he explains, "is very much alive in New Mexico today."

---

3. **remote-sensing satellites:** satellites that can detect changes on and below the earth's surface caused by man-made building.

---

11. Archaeologists learn about past civilizations by studying

  A. written historical records

  B. buried buildings and artifacts

  C. living cultures related to ancient ones

  D. oral histories of people's ancestors

  E. present-day art in the area

12. The author speculates that San Marcos was located where it was to be near

  F. water

  G. a Spanish mission

  H. nine plazas

  J. ancient apartment buildings

  K. turquoise

continued

13. Why does the author mention magnetometry and Ground Penetrating Radar?
- **A.** to tell us something about modern archaeological techniques
- **B.** to make archaeology seem as important as physics
- **C.** to increase her credibility
- **D.** to help raise money for archaeologists
- **E.** to increase readers' vocabulary

14. Which of these is a modern midden?
- **F.** a history museum
- **G.** a book
- **H.** a computer
- **J.** a landfill
- **K.** a garbage disposal

15. Why does the author include quotations from David Hurst Thomas?
- **A.** to make the article sound scientific
- **B.** to show the source of her information
- **C.** to help Thomas become a more respected archaeologist
- **D.** to present opposing opinions on the topic
- **E.** to encourage students to help him during the summer

16. The technique of stratigraphy dates objects according to their
- **F.** condition
- **G.** materials
- **H.** purpose
- **J.** location
- **K.** shape

17. We can infer from this article that
- **A.** archaeology has not changed much during the past eight hundred years
- **B.** modern archaeology uses new equipment and techniques
- **C.** archaeologists study both animal and human life
- **D.** archaeologists prefer never to do any digging
- **E.** little training is needed to determine the importance of a find

Comparing the Passages

18. The first article cites only "scientists" as the source of its information. The second article
- **F.** does the same
- **G.** quotes a specific archaeologist
- **H.** cites a specific reference work
- **J.** cites the writer's personal research
- **K.** does not refer to any sources

Write several paragraphs in response to *one* of the following questions:

19. You can use only one of these articles as a source of information for a report on America's distant past. Which will you choose and why? Compare and contrast the two articles, considering style, organization, interest level, and credibility.

20. Construction workers are excavating a downtown site for a large office building. In doing so, they have unearthed some bones and other objects. What will happen next? Use details from both articles to support your points.

Taking Writing Tests

Writing tests come in two different formats:

- An **on-demand writing prompt** asks you to write a narrative, expository, or persuasive **essay** in a limited time.
- **Multiple-choice questions** test your knowledge of sentence construction and revision and paragraph content and organization.

There you are, facing a writing prompt you've never seen before, with less than an hour to produce a coherent, well-written essay. Not to worry. Use the following strategies for writing all types of essays. You'll find these steps comfortable and familiar—you know them already.

THINKING IT THROUGH   Writing Test Strategies

> **STEP 1** **Analyze the writing prompt.** Read it carefully, and analyze what you're being asked to do. Look for the key verbs (such as *analyze, argue, explain, summarize, discuss*) that define your specific writing task. (Before the test, review the chart of **key verbs that appear in essay questions,** page 916.) Consider all parts of the prompt. You'll lose points unless you address the entire writing task. Identify your audience.

> **STEP 2** **Plan what to say.** If you have forty-five minutes to write the essay, take about ten minutes for prewriting. On scratch paper, brainstorm ideas, make a rough outline or graphic organizer, and think about organization. Before you start writing, decide on your main idea statement and how you'll support it.

TIP Don't skip this prewriting step. Using prewriting strategies will result in a stronger, more interesting essay.

> **STEP 3** **Draft your essay.** Allow about two thirds of your time to draft your essay, making sure you address all parts of the prompt. Include a strong opening paragraph and a definite closing. Express your ideas as clearly as you can, and add relevant details to support and elaborate your main points.

> **STEP 4** **Edit and revise as you write, but leave some time to re-read your draft.** See if you can add transitions or combine sentences. If you add a word or sentence, insert it clearly and neatly.

> **STEP 5** **Proofread your essay.** Focus on finding and correcting any errors in grammar, usage, mechanics, and spelling. Your score depends in part on how well you follow these conventions of standard English.

Narrative Writing

Sample Writing Prompt *Choose an older person who has been a positive influence on your life. Tell about a single incident that involved you and that older person. Then, explain why this event was important to you.*

The prompt asks you to tell a story—an autobiographical incident. What else does it ask you to do? Use a story map to plan your essay.

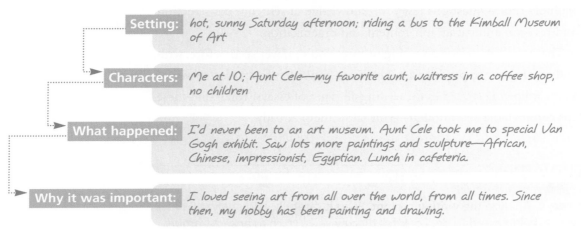

Setting: *hot, sunny Saturday afternoon; riding a bus to the Kimball Museum of Art*

Characters: *Me at 10; Aunt Cele—my favorite aunt, waitress in a coffee shop, no children*

What happened: *I'd never been to an art museum. Aunt Cele took me to special Van Gogh exhibit. Saw lots more paintings and sculpture—African, Chinese, impressionist, Egyptian. Lunch in cafeteria.*

Why it was important: *I loved seeing art from all over the world, from all times. Since then, my hobby has been painting and drawing.*

As you draft your autobiographical incident, give it an interest-catching beginning and a definite end. Include dialogue—always a good idea—to make readers feel as if they're standing at your side, listening. (See **punctuating dialogue,** pages 743–746.)

Expository Writing

Sample Writing Prompt *Think about a hobby or extracurricular activity you enjoy. Explain the essential information (rules, definitions, techniques) to help a reader unfamiliar with this activity understand it.*

Quickly choose your subject, and brainstorm its procedures, jargon, equipment—everything you'll need to explain to someone who knows nothing about your hobby or activity. Create a strong introduction that includes a main idea statement and a conclusion that brings your essay to a definite end.

Extra-curricular activity: debate club with Mr. Ulery—team debate (traditional, or formal, debate)

Procedures: research debate proposition, or resolution; identify key issues; gather evidence; prepare to argue either pro (affirmative) or con (negative); build argument; refute opposing arguments.

Define terms: three kinds of debate propositions (fact, value, policy); constructive speeches, rebuttal speeches; argument; brief

Tournaments: regional, state, national; required format and times

Equipment: huge file boxes for evidence; file folders; formal clothes

Persuasive Writing

Sample Writing Prompt *To save money, your school board is proposing eliminating either drivers education or several team sports. Write a letter to the school board to support the option you prefer, and back up your opinion with two or three strong reasons.*

Here's a cluster diagram by a student who favors keeping sports.

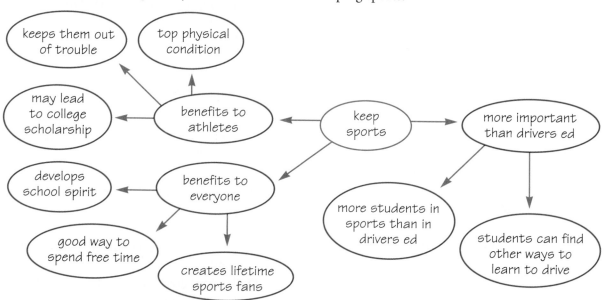

Draft an attention-getting introduction with a clear opinion statement. Arrange your reasons in order of importance, and elaborate each reason with facts, examples, anecdotes, or other kinds of evidence. End with a strong concluding paragraph.

Multiple-Choice Writing Questions

In some standardized tests, multiple-choice writing questions test your understanding of sentence and paragraph structure and the conventions of standard English (grammar, usage, punctuation, capitalization, and spelling). You may find questions like the ones below.

Read the following paragraph. Then, choose the best answer for each question.

(1) There are two essential elements of aerodynamics: lift and drag. (2) *Lift* is the force that gets a bird off the ground and keeps it in the air. (3) Lift, whether in animals or machines, is produced by air moving around and past an *airfoil*, such as a wing. (4) Airfoils produce lift as a byproduct of their shape.

(5) Physical laws ordain that the air flowing over the top of the wing must reach the back of the wing (the trailing edge) at the same time as air flowing under the wing. (6) The curvature of the wing forces air to travel farther across the top surface than across the bottom. (7) In order to travel the longer distance in the same amount of time, the air passing over the top of the wing must flow faster than the air flowing underneath the wing. (8) This faster-moving air results in lower air pressure above the wing than below. (9) The net result is lift, an upwardly directed force that, if strong enough, causes the bird to rise off the ground.

From *National Audubon Society: The Sibley Guide to Bird Life and Behavior* by David Allen Sibley. Copyright © 2001 by Chanticleer Press, Inc. Reprinted by permission of **Alfred A. Knopf, Inc., a division of Random House, Inc.**

1. Paragraph 2 has the organizational pattern of a
   A. problem-solution analysis
   B. comparison-contrast analysis
   C. cause-effect explanation
   D. logical argument
   E. personal narrative

2. Where should this sentence be added?
   The penguin is a flightless bird.

   F. after sentence 2
   G. after sentence 4
   H. after sentence 5
   J. after sentence 9
   K. nowhere; it destroys unity

3. Which sentence supports the following topic sentence?
   The second aerodynamic force affecting flight is *drag*, which reduces lift by slowing down the air moving over the wing.

   A. Most birds fly by flapping their wings.
   B. Hummingbirds move their wings in a figure-eight pattern.
   C. Lift and drag only affect wings with feathers.
   D. To slow down, birds adjust their wings to create more drag.
   E. Airplane wings and bird wings work in the same way.

4. From the context, you can guess that *aerodynamics* is the study of

   F. birds

   G. the forces involved in flight

   H. rockets and space vehicles

   J. barometric pressure and weather

   K. the earth's atmosphere

5. The word *farther* in sentence 6 is

   A. a noun

   B. a preposition

   C. a conjunction

   D. an adverb

   E. an adjective

6. Sentence 2 can be classified as

   F. a simple sentence

   G. a compound sentence

   H. a complex sentence

   J. a compound-complex sentence

   K. an interrogative sentence

7. What is the **best** transition to use to combine these two sentences?

   Birds' bones are very light. They are filled with air spaces.

   A. although

   B. because

   C. however

   D. until

   E. unless

8. Which word is misspelled?

   The shape and size of a <u>bird's</u> wings
                                     F

   <u>necessarily</u> <u>effect</u> <u>its</u> flight.   NO ERROR
     G   **H**   **J**   **K**

9. How would you correct this sentence?

   Young birds often look different from their parents; by a year most songbirds had acquired their adult plumage.

   A. Change the semicolon to a colon.

   B. Change the semicolon to a comma.

   C. Change *had* to *have*.

   D. Change *their* to *there*.

   E. Make no change; the sentence is correct.

10. Which source would most likely provide specific information about aerodynamics and human flight?

   F. a television program about birds

   G. an encyclopedia entry on airplanes

   H. instructions for operating a radio-controlled model airplane

   J. a biography of the Wright brothers

   K. a glossary of science terms

Reference Note

For more on preparing for reading and writing tests, see the **Test-Taking Mini-Lesson** in each Part 1 chapter and **Studying and Test Taking** on pages 911–927.

Reflecting on Experiences

Reading Workshop

Reading a Personal Reflection

Writing Workshop

Writing a Personal Reflection

Viewing and Representing

Making a Video Reflection

Personal Reflection

■ Driving down the street, you hear a song on the radio that makes you think of a summer weekend you spent at the beach.

■ Your older sister goes off to college. As you sit in her room, looking at her things, you remember when you both were much younger.

■ At a family reunion, a cousin says to you, "Boy, you sure have changed!" The remark makes you ask yourself, "How have I changed?"

> **Narration/ Description**

   When you take advantage of opportunities like these to examine events in your life that have shaped your unique personality, you are making a **personal reflection.** Personal reflection helps you know yourself better by making you think about who you are and how you got to be the way you are. Many people write down their personal reflections as autobiographical narratives, memoirs, journal entries, or diary entries. When you read personal reflections like these, you not only get to know the thoughts, feelings, and experiences of other people, but you also learn new ways of reexamining your life through the examples set by others.

YOUR TURN 1   Thinking About Personal Reflection

Working with a partner, look through magazines, newspapers, or Web pages for two examples of personal reflections. Write down what you liked about the reflections and what they told you about the author. Be prepared to share your findings with your classmates.

internet connect

go.
hrw
.com
GO TO: go.hrw.com
KEYWORD: EOLang 10-1

Reading a Personal Reflection

WHAT'S AHEAD?

In this section, you will read a personal reflection and learn how to

- **make inferences**
- **analyze narrative and descriptive details**

Have you ever had an experience that you thought was unimportant at the time, but that you later realized actually shaped your life? In the selection from *An American Childhood* that begins on the next page, Annie Dillard reflects on such a life-changing experience. As you read the selection, you may think of experiences or emotions you have had that are similar to the ones Dillard describes.

Sometimes the **significance,** or importance, of an experience is not immediately obvious. At other times, a small, insignificant experience can begin a series of events that cause major, life-altering changes.

Preparing to Read

READING SKILL ➤

Making Inferences An **inference** is an educated guess you make based on the facts presented to you and on your personal knowledge and experience. For example, as you enter a freeway ramp, you find that traffic is backed up. Since it is too early for rush hour, you infer that there must be an accident or perhaps road repairs up ahead. Inferences are also important to understanding what you read. When you read, you make inferences by taking the details that writers give and connecting them to your own knowledge and experience. A good narrative unfolds with your active participation as a reader, uncovering details and making personal connections. As you read the following passage from *An American Childhood*, see if you can recognize places where the writer expects you to connect the details she has provided with your own knowledge and experience.

READING FOCUS ➤

Narrative and Descriptive Details Writers of narratives mainly use two types of details to help the reader share their experiences. **Narrative details** specifically relate actions and events, while **descriptive details** describe important people, places, and objects. Be on the lookout for the details the writer has included in the following personal reflection.

As a student, Pulitzer Prize–winning writer Annie Dillard encountered a moth that changed her life. In this passage from her autobiography, *An American Childhood*, she examines that encounter and its significance. As you read, write down your answers to the numbered active-reading questions.

from

An American Childhood

BY **ANNIE DILLARD**

Everywhere, things snagged me. The visible world turned me curious to books; the books propelled me reeling back to the world.

1. How old do you think the writer was when this event occurred? What makes you think so?

At school I saw a searing sight. It turned me to books; it turned me to jelly; it turned me much later, I suppose, into an early version of a runaway, a scapegrace.[1] It was only a freshly hatched Polyphemus moth crippled because its mason jar[2] was too small.

The mason jar sat on the teacher's desk; the big moth emerged inside it. The moth had clawed a hole in its hot cocoon and crawled out, as if agonizingly, over the course of an hour, one leg at a time; we children watched around the desk, transfixed. After it emerged, the wet, mashed thing turned around walking on the green jar's bottom, then painstakingly climbed the twig with which the jar was furnished.

2. What details about the Polyphemus moth's appearance does the writer include?

There, at the twig's top, the moth shook its sodden clumps of wings. When it spread those wings—those beautiful wings—blood would fill their veins, and the birth fluids on the wings' frail

_____

1. **scapegrace:** a graceless, unprincipled person.
2. **mason jar:** a jar with a wide mouth and screw-on lid.

sheets would harden to make them tough as sails. But the moth could not spread its wide wings at all; the jar was too small. The wings could not fill, so they hardened while they were still crumpled from the cocoon. A smaller moth could have spread its wings to their utmost in that mason jar, but the Polyphemus moth was big. Its gold furred body was almost as big as a mouse. Its brown, yellow, pink, and blue wings would have extended six inches from tip to tip, if there had been no mason jar. It would have been big as a wren.

The teacher let the deformed creature go. We all left the classroom and paraded outside behind the teacher with pomp and circumstance. She bounced the moth from its jar and set it on the school's asphalt driveway. The moth set out walking. It could only heave the golden wrinkly clumps where its wings should have been; it could only crawl down the school driveway on its six frail legs. The moth crawled down the driveway toward the rest of Shadyside,[3] an area of fine houses, expensive apartments, and fashionable shops. It crawled down the driveway because its shriveled wings were glued shut. It crawled down the driveway toward Shadyside, one of the several sections of town where people like me were expected to settle after college, renting an apartment until they married one of the boys and bought a house. I watched it go.

I knew that this particular moth, the big walking moth, could not travel more than a few more yards before a bird or a cat began to eat it, or a car ran over it. Nevertheless, it was crawling with what seemed wonderful vigor, as if, I thought at the time, it was still excited from being born. I watched it go till the bell rang and I had to go in. I have told this story before, and may yet tell it again, to lay the moth's ghost, for I still see it crawl down the broad black driveway, and I still see its golden wing clumps heave.

3. What does this paragraph seem to reveal about the writer's attitude toward Shadyside?

4. Do you think the writer is correct about what will happen to the moth? What makes you think this?

---

3. Shadyside: The neighborhood in east Pittsburgh, Pennsylvania, where Dillard was raised.

Making Inferences

Playing Detective To spur your interest, writers often give clues about what they want you, as the reader, to understand. As a reader, you must play the part of a detective, piecing together the clues and relating them to your own experiences. When you carry out this process, you are **making inferences**—educated guesses based on information in the text and on your own knowledge and experience. Inference can be used to

- **draw conclusions:** to make judgments that are *specific to the text* that you are reading

    Example:
    A writer describes her experience viewing Halley's comet from the hood of her car. You conclude that this reflection must have taken place in 1986—the only time Halley's comet has passed the earth since automobiles were invented.

- **make generalizations:** to make judgments that *apply to the world in general* and not just the text you are reading

    Example:
    After reading that the dahlia got its name from an eighteenth-century botanist named Anders Dahl, the magnolia was named for Pierre Magnol, a French botanist, and the zinnia's name came from J. G. Zinn, a German botanist, you could make the generalization that flowers often get their names from scientists who work with the plants.

> **TIP** Good writers will sometimes **create suspense** by leading readers to make invalid inferences. They do this by withholding details, providing misleading information, or going against the expectations readers have developed from past knowledge and experience.

- **make predictions:** to foretell events

  Example:
  When a multiplex theater opens in the narrator's town, you predict that the single-screen theater her parents own will have trouble competing.

- **determine causes or effects:** to figure out the probable effect or the probable cause when only a cause or effect is stated

  Example:
  A writer tells about losing his dog and about his resulting sadness. He describes coming home to an open fence gate. You determine that someone might have left the gate open, and the dog ran out.

- **determine main idea:** to understand the unstated focus or key idea in a piece of writing

  Example:
  A passage of a memoir written by a World War I veteran describes a fear-filled night in the trenches during the Battle of the Somme. The narrator later wins a Congressional Medal of Honor. You determine that the main idea of the passage was that even heroes feel fear when faced with great challenges.

Although inference serves a variety of purposes, in every case the process of making inferences can be illustrated by the following equation.

details from the reading + **personal knowledge and experience** = **inference**

One difficulty with making inferences, however, is that your knowledge and experience may sometimes fail to match a writer's expectations. When there are cultural or educational differences between a writer and his or her readers, some readers are likely to have problems making inferences—whether they are reading Shakespeare or *The New York Times*. For example, a politician's memoir might describe her New York City childhood as "growing up in the shadow of Lady Liberty." The writer expects her readers to make the inference that "Lady Liberty" is the Statue of Liberty, a symbol of political freedom and democracy, and that living near the statue influenced her political dreams. A reader unfamiliar with the term "Lady Liberty" or the symbolism of the monument might not be able to make the inference that the writer intended.

Making Inferences

Watch how the three-step process of making an inference shown in the following Thinking It Through can be used to draw a reasonable conclusion from the following passage. These same steps can be applied to all types of inferences.

> When I returned home hours late, the only light that greeted me was the flickering television. The only sounds I heard were the TV's babble and my father's snores coming from his favorite chair.

▶ **STEP 1 Identify the details the writer has given.**

The narrator came home late. The TV is still on. No lights are on. The narrator's father is asleep in the chair.

▶ **STEP 2 Relate the details to your knowledge and experience.**

Normally people do not sleep in chairs with the TV on, except when exceptionally tired—maybe from staying up too late. My dad tends to fall asleep in front of the TV when he has stayed up too late. My dad sometimes waits up for me when I have been out too late.

▶ **STEP 3 Decide what you think the writer has left out and what you are being asked to infer.**

Based on the passage and my knowledge and experience, I conclude that the father may have fallen asleep while waiting for the narrator to return home.

YOUR TURN 2 Making Inferences

Using the Thinking It Through steps above, explain what conclusions you can infer about Annie Dillard's attitude toward the moth in the selection from *An American Childhood* on page 19. Pay close attention to the following key words.

- *would, would have, could have,* and *could not* in paragraph four
- *bounced, could, crawled, shriveled,* and *glued* in paragraph five

Write your answer on your own paper.

Narrative and Descriptive Details

The Spice of Life   Do you have a favorite food? If you had to eat that favorite food every day for the next two weeks, do you think you would still like it as much? No matter how good that food is, you would probably be ready for a little variety. As a reader, you probably have a similar desire for variety in what you read. For example, when you read a narrative, you probably want to see a variety of **narrative** and **descriptive details.**

Narrative details are the elements that provide a basic framework for specifying the **people, things, places,** and **events** of a narrative. They give an account of not only the **actions** but also the **thoughts and feelings** of those people involved, and often include **dialogue**—the exact words of the speakers. Narrative details answer the questions *Who? What? When?* and *Where?* The narrative details in *An American Childhood* include the school (place), the teacher and students (people), the deformed moth (thing), and Dillard's sympathetic reaction to the moth's plight (feelings).

Added to the simple framework of narrative details are **descriptive details,** which elaborate on or "flesh out" the framework. Just as a leafless tree in the winter is still a tree, a narrative without descriptive details is still a narrative—though very stark and bare. Three key kinds of descriptive details help a narrative come alive for the reader: **sensory details, factual details,** and **figurative details.**

- **Sensory details** appeal to the five senses: sight, hearing, taste, touch, and smell. These details bring you into the narrative through elements you recognize from your own experiences. They answer the questions *How does it look? How does it sound? How does it taste? How does it feel?* and *How does it smell?*

  Example:
  Its *brown, yellow, pink, and blue wings* would have extended six inches from tip to tip, if there had been no mason jar. [Details of *sight* are provided.]

- **Factual details** give the straightforward, objective aspects of the events, people, places, and objects in the narrative. They often involve names, dates, and numbers.

  Example:
  It was only a freshly hatched *Polyphemus* moth crippled because its *mason* jar was too small. [*Polyphemus* and *mason* tell us what kind of moth and what kind of jar are being discussed.]

- **Figurative details** use figures of speech to compare things in imaginative ways that prompt readers to look at the things differently. The three

TIP   Some details can be from more than one category. For example, the sentence "The lightning flashed around us like spears" tells what happened and to whom (both narrative details) and also illustrates what the lightning looked like (sensory detail) by using the simile *like spears* (figurative detail).

kinds of figurative details used most often are **simile, metaphor,** and **personification.** The following chart provides information that will help you recognize these details as you read.

Figure of Speech	How to Recognize	Example
Simile	uses the word *like* or *as* to compare two things	Maxwell's heart leapt **like a frightened cat** at the unexpected barks of the dog behind the fence. Explanation: The leaping feeling of his heart is compared to the leaping reaction of a frightened cat.
Metaphor	says that one thing *is* another thing; compares two things without using *like* or *as*	Mishka's **words were the shining ribbon on the wonderful gift** my day had been. Explanation: The girl's words enrich a wonderful day (which is compared to a gift).
Personification	gives animals or objects human characteristics	The **Colosseum proudly says,** "I was born of the Roman Empire; while I stand, the Romans shall not be forgotten." Explanation: An unliving thing cannot show pride or speak, but the writer imaginatively describes what the Colosseum would feel and say if it were alive.

YOUR TURN 3 Identifying Narrative and Descriptive Details

For each sentence below, identify the italicized word or phrase as either a narrative detail or a descriptive detail.

■ Label the narrative details as people, things, places, events, actions, or thoughts and feelings.

■ Label the descriptive details as sensory, factual, or figurative.

Write your answers on your own paper.

1. "... the birth fluids on the wings' frail sheets would harden to make them *tough as sails.*"

2. "A *smaller* moth could have spread its wings to their utmost in that mason jar. ..."

3. "Nevertheless, it was crawling with what seemed wonderful vigor, as if, I thought at the time, *it was still excited from being born.*"

4. "It *crawled down the driveway.* ..."

5. "After it emerged, the *wet, mashed* thing turned around walking on the *green* jar's bottom. ..."

Using Multiple-Meaning Words

When you read the selection from *An American Childhood*, you encountered several multiple-meaning words. **Multiple-meaning words** are words that have more than one meaning and (sometimes) different pronunciations.

(**Homographs** are words that are spelled the same but have different meanings and origins.) To determine the intended meaning of a multiple-meaning word in a sentence, follow the steps below.

THINKING IT THROUGH **Understanding Multiple-Meaning Words**

Take a look at the example sentence below and the steps following it.

Zane drank the orange juice with *relish*.

1. **Eliminate known meanings that will not work.** For example, if you think of *relish* as meaning only "chopped pickles," then either Zane has really odd tastes or you need to consider another meaning for the word.

2. **Use a dictionary to check the other meanings of the word.** Read the entire entry for that word. Most dictionaries define **homographs** in separate entries. Check to see if there is a second or even third entry that might match the intended meaning of the word.

    relish (rel´ish) *n.* [[ME *reles* < OFr *relais*, something remaining < *relaisser*: see RELEASE]] **1** distinctive or charac-

teristic flavor [a *relish* of garlic in the stew] **2** a trace or touch (*of* some quality); hint or suggestion [a *relish* of malice in his action] **3** an appetizing flavor; pleasing taste **4** *a)* pleasure; enjoyment; zest [to listen with *relish*] *b)* liking or craving [showing little *relish* for the task] **5** anything that gives pleasure, zest, or enjoyment; attractive quality **6** any of a variety of foods, as pickles, olives, piccalilli, raw vegetables, etc., served with a meal to add flavor or as an appetizer —*vt.* **1** [Now Rare] to give flavor **2** to enjoy; like —*vi.* **1** to taste or have the flavor (*of* something) **2** to have a pleasing taste

3. **Determine which meaning fits best within the context of the sentence.** For the sentence about Zane's drinking juice, meaning number 4 of *relish* works best. The main idea is that Zane drank the juice with *pleasure* or *enjoyment*.

PRACTICE

Use the steps above to determine the meanings of the italicized words in the following sentences. Write on your own paper.

1. After six perfect innings, the pitcher felt his energy *flag*.

2. Many people look back to the 1950s and wonder whatever happened to the "perfect" *nuclear* family.

3. The senator said he would *brook* no opposition to his proposed amendment.

4. Many religions specify holidays as a time to *fast*.

5. There was great debate before the group could decide on a *platform*.

Answering Inference Questions on Reading Tests

Reading tests often include questions that check your ability to make inferences from a reading passage. Here are a typical reading passage and inference test question.

> As a child, I watched my father grow old before his time. His hair grayed, and his skin grew rough and wrinkled. His walk slowed and became more purposeful with each passing day. Although I never saw him leave, each day I watched him return from the fields with the setting sun making him a scarecrow in silhouette. His eyes reflected only the flicker of our farm-house candlelight, but little light of their own. The father I had known before the hard times seemed to be drying up like the dusty fields he worked.

Which of the following statements about the narrator's father can you infer from the passage?

A. He is confused about his family's future.

B. He lost his job because of the economy.

C. He is a farmer whose hard work has affected him physically and emotionally.

D. He feels sorry for his child and wants to make things better for his family.

THINKING IT THROUGH **Answering Inference Questions**

Use the following steps to answer inference test questions like the one above.

1. **Skim the passage once for a general understanding; then, re-read it carefully.** Keep in mind that most of these questions are designed to measure your reading comprehension, not your reading speed.

2. **Locate key words and phrases in the answer choices that match similar words and phrases in the reading passage.** You may be able to eliminate some answers right away. Choices **A** and **D** discuss the father's feelings with *confused* and *feels sorry*. The reading passage does not say how the father feels. Choice **B** mentions *lost his job* and *the economy*, words that are not used in the reading passage. Choice **C** uses the words *farmer* and *hard work* along with the phrase *affected him*

physically. The reading passage does evoke images of a farm with the words *fields*, *farmhouse*, and *scarecrow*. The father also has undergone physical changes, as evidenced by the descriptions of his hair, skin, and walk. Choice **C** seems the most likely answer.

3. **Confirm your answer by considering your prior knowledge about the subject of the passage.** The image of dusty fields might remind you of pictures of farms in the Dust Bowl you may have seen when studying the Great Depression in history class. This knowledge, combined with the details from the passage, makes the inference in answer **C** a safe (and correct) choice.

Writing a Personal Reflection

WHAT'S AHEAD?

In this workshop, you will write a personal reflection. You will also learn how to

- **gather and organize details**
- **reflect on the meaning of an experience**
- **use figurative language**
- **combine sentences to add sentence variety**
- **check subject-verb agreement**

Imagine that you receive an application to a college you really want to attend. One section asks you to write a thousand-word essay about a life experience that has prompted you to study a particular subject. What will you write? How will you write it?

This kind of essay calls for writing a **personal reflection**—an autobiographical narrative reflecting on an experience in your life that has helped make you the person you are today. People write personal reflections to share their experiences and life lessons with others. Some writers are famous people, telling the stories of their private lives. Other writers are simply ordinary people with extraordinary tales to tell. Still others have ordinary tales to tell but an extraordinary ability to tell them. In this Writing Workshop, you will learn how to choose an important experience you have had and to write a personal reflection describing that experience in an interesting way.

Prewriting

Choose an Experience

Who Are You? To find an experience to use as the topic for a personal or autobiographical narrative, you should begin by exploring the experiences in your life that have made you who you are. You can think of the important experiences that have changed your life as **defining moments** because they have helped define your character. Follow the suggestions below to start thinking of experiences to write about in your personal reflection.

- **Look through old photo albums, diaries, and scrapbooks.** Take a few hours to look through them and stir up old memories. Write down notes about experiences they make you remember.

- **List your hobbies**—the things you like to do. Then, think about the experiences in your life that got you interested in these hobbies. What about those experiences made them meaningful to you?

- **Interview a parent, teacher, or friend** to see whether these people remember any experiences that they think were important in your life. You might also ask what they find interesting about you. Then, you can think about any experiences in your life that may have helped to make you interesting.

- **Carry a notebook** with you for a day or two. When you find yourself thinking of interesting experiences from your past, you will have a handy place to write them down.

When choosing an experience in your life to write about, there are three things you should keep in mind.

- **The experience should be one important to you.** If it is not very significant to you, you will have a hard time interesting your reader.

- **The experience should stand out clearly in your memory.** Make sure you can remember the major details of the experience—they will form the core of your personal reflection.

- **The experience should not be too personal or too private to share.** Others will be reading your narrative. Make sure your topic is one you are willing to share with them.

After you have brainstormed a list of possible experiences, choose three or four that are of special interest to you. Show the list to your friends, parents, or teachers and get their opinions on which one would be the most interesting for them to read. Once you have chosen one of the experiences from your list, you are ready to begin.

> **TIP** Do not reject an experience as a topic just because you do not immediately remember every single detail about it. Often, details from your memory will surface over time as you continue to think about past experiences.

Consider Purpose, Audience, Tone, and Voice

The Big Picture   To write an interesting personal reflection, you must have a clear idea of your **purpose, audience, tone,** and **voice.** These will be the main forces that influence the choices you make while planning, writing, and revising your work.

Purpose   The main **purpose** of a personal reflection is to express yourself. You examine an experience in your life and explore your thoughts and feelings about it. Unlike a diary or a journal entry, this is writing in which your purpose is also to write something that you can share with others. You must not only reach into yourself but also try to reach *out* to others.

Audience   It is especially important to have a specific **audience** in mind as you compose your personal reflection. That means you need to choose an appropriate audience *before* you begin writing. For example, if you are writing about an experience that involves a relative of yours, that relative might be an appropriate audience for your personal reflection. However, if you are writing an autobiographical narrative to send in with a college application, the choice is clear: Your audience is any college admissions counselor who might read the narrative. Before you begin writing, try listing everything you know about the audience for whom you plan to write. Here are some questions to help you form a clear mental image of your audience and what they will want to see in your personal reflection.

- Who might benefit from reading my personal reflection?
- What kinds of things will this audience be expecting to read?
- How are my audience's experiences similar to mine? How are they different?
- Which people and places will be familiar to my audience? Which will I need to explain better?
- Will they understand or disapprove if I use informal language?

Tone   **Tone** is the feeling or attitude you, the writer, convey about your topic. In a personal reflection, how you *feel* about the experience should come through clearly. For example, if the experience was funny, you should choose words and examples that are light and amusing—ones that give your narrative a humorous tone. Because personal expression is informal, you will also use first-person pronouns: *I, me, our,* and *we.*

Voice   Isn't it great that your friends recognize your voice when you telephone them? **Voice** in writing is the unique sound and rhythm of a writer's language. By letting your own voice show through in your writing, you make the reader know that there is a real person behind the words on the page. Trying to adopt the voice of someone else (for example, by using overblown, pretentious language) often is a mistake because it will make your writing sound insincere.

Gather Details

Putting the Pieces Together   Gathering details is like sorting pieces of a complicated jigsaw puzzle. You reach into a box that holds hundreds of brightly colored parts of a picture. Your task is to turn the pieces over and see which ones fit into the section of the picture you are working on—with that picture in mind at all times as you work. Similarly, you should keep in mind the "big picture" for your personal reflection while you work on connecting all of its particular details.

Events After you have selected your topic, brainstorm a list of events central to the telling of the narrative—events that you need to relate so readers will understand and share the experience with you. Include **narrative details,** which tell about specific actions and events. List the events **chronologically,** in the order that they happened. One writer created the list of events below when she began gathering details for her personal reflection.

TIP Sometimes meeting with a small group of your peers to discuss the events you are focusing on helps you remember details better. If you use this strategy, be sure to employ effective **listening strategies.**

- Ask clear questions.
- Respond appropriately to others' questions.
- Be an empathic listener by responding to feelings, not just to facts.

Events List

- I watched others practicing tae kwon do and imagined that I could do it, too.
- I met an instructor who taught me techniques.
- I practiced hard.
- I entered a competition.
- My mom and dad saw me compete for the very first time.

People and Places Next, make a list of people and places you will need to include in your narrative. Who, besides yourself, played a part in your experience? Where did the experience take place? Use **descriptive details** to paint a clear image of the experience. What did the people look like? What did they say? What did the place look like? What did you hear there? Notice that most of these questions deal with your senses. When you describe details of sight, hearing, smell, touch, and taste, you use **sensory details,** which many of your readers will be able to identify. Other descriptive details include **figurative language** (such as **similes** and **metaphors**) and **factual details.** Below is an example of a list that includes a mix of details.

People and Places List

- **Me**—shy, not very confident, age 13, physically unimpressive
- **People in the class**—graceful, like swaying trees
- **Gwen**—college student, strong and swift, friendly smile
- **Derek and Tamara**—brother (17) and sister (15), older, popular, smart
- **Mom and Dad**—protective, amazed at what I did, proud
- **YMCA**—pool, activity rooms, picnic place—really hot
- **Practice room**—both youths and adults, white uniforms, noisy

Thoughts and Feelings To make your reflection truly personal, you should let your reader know what you were thinking and how you felt during the experience. At times, this will appeal to similar thoughts and feelings your reader has had in other situations. At other times it will give readers an insight into thoughts and feelings with which they may not be familiar. Use actions, appearance, and dialogue to show externally what is going on with you internally. For example, to show that she was terrified of sparring, a writer might say that her knees were "like mashed potatoes." Here are some thoughts and feelings one writer wrote down while preparing a personal reflection.

> **Thoughts and Feelings List**
>
> - Envy—imagined being graceful, perfect techniques; afraid to join the group
> - Surprise and fear—knees shaking, needed a compliment
> - Accomplishment—Mom and Dad proud; photo in the newspaper; a good match

Reference Note

For more on **interviewing,** see page 910 in the Quick Reference Handbook.

TIP **Interviewing** other people who were involved in the experience will refresh your memory about details of the experience and give you different perspectives from which to view the experience.

Dialogue The final kind of detail is dialogue—another narrative detail. Because you are telling a story, you should use dialogue to add variety and to make the people in your narrative more real to your readers. Try to remember who said what, and use their own words. Keep in mind that **dialogue should fit the speaker and can be informal** (for example, it can include slang and sentence fragments). Here are a couple of pieces of dialogue one writer recorded.

KEY CONCEPT

DIALOGUE LIST	
What happened?	**What did they say?**
Gwen was encouraging.	"Why don't you come help me practice? I could teach you some other techniques."
Friends teased me.	"Here comes Jackie Chan!"

Put It All Together

Collect all your details and gather them in a chart like the one below.

Who or What	Details
Events	
I watched others practicing tae kwon do and imagined that I could do it, too.	Others practicing kicks, blocks, and stances
	I just watch, practice at home where no one can laugh at me
I met an instructor who taught me techniques.	Gwen offers to help; pretends that I am helping her
	I am scared; do it anyway because she is so friendly
I practiced hard.	Tough exercise; lots of sore muscles
	Eventually earn some belts
I entered a competition.	Confident; ready to show the world that I am good enough
My mom and dad saw me compete for the very first time.	They hear my name on loudspeaker
	See me in the ring
People	
Me	Shy, not very confident, age 13, physically unimpressive
People in the class	Graceful, like swaying trees
Gwen	College student, strong and swift, friendly smile
Derek and Tamara	Brother (17) and sister (15), older, popular, smart
Mom and Dad	Protective, amazed, proud
Places	
YMCA	Pool, activity rooms, picnic place—really hot
Practice room	Both youths and adults, white uniforms, noisy

(continued)

(continued)

Thoughts and Feelings	
Envy	Imagined being graceful, perfect techniques
	Afraid to join the group
Surprise and fear	Knees shaking, needed a compliment
Accomplishment	Mom and Dad proud; photo in the newspaper—a good match
Dialogue	
Gwen was encouraging.	"Why don't you come help me practice? I could teach you some other techniques."
Friends teased me.	"Here comes Jackie Chan!"

COMPUTER TIP

Try dimming your screen while you are brainstorming a list of details at a computer. Because you will not see any typing mistakes you make, you will be able to focus more on the details themselves rather than on your typing ability.

KEY CONCEPT

List as many details as you can remember. When you write your personal reflection, you will not necessarily use all of the details that you put in this chart, and you can always add other details as you write. Remember, the goal of collecting details is not to make your notes perfectly grammatical or flawlessly neat—it is to write your ideas down as they come to you. However, make sure they are clear enough so that you will understand the notes when you come back to them.

Reflect on the Meaning of Your Experience

That Was Then, This Is Now A personal reflection about an experience should convey the significance of the experience. **Your readers should clearly see a difference between the way you were before the experience and what you became after it.** Your narrative will not be a personal reflection if it does not include actual **reflections**—your thoughts and feelings—about the significance of the experience you describe.

Give background information early in your personal reflection. Readers will not be able to recognize the change in you if they do not know what you were like before the experience. Unlike thesis statements in many essays, your thesis statement, which directly states the significance of your experience, does not appear in your narrative's introduction. Instead, you only hint at the meaning of your experience through the details of your background information. For example, if your introduction says, "When I was fourteen, I never really cared about sea life. Until then, I had never seen a humpback whale," readers should sense that your reflection will be about how seeing a humpback whale changed your views on sea life. Save the direct statement of the significance of your experience for the conclusion of your narrative—after your readers have had a chance to share in your experience and possibly determine for themselves how it changed your life.

THINKING IT THROUGH — Interpreting Meaning

Use the following Thinking It Through steps to reflect on the meaning of your experience. One writer's responses are shown as an example.

STEP 1 Ask yourself if you were somehow different at the end of the experience. If so, what were you like at the beginning? How exactly did you change?

> In the beginning I was shy and not very confident. I didn't ever really do my own thing. By learning tae kwon do, I think I became more confident.

STEP 2 Ask yourself whether you learned something new about yourself. What was it?

> I never realized how much I was comparing myself to my brother and sister—like I was living in their shadows. I think I even unconsciously thought my parents didn't think I was anything special because I didn't have the achievements Derek and Tamara had.

STEP 3 Ask yourself if you learned something new about other people, human nature, or life in general. What was it?

> I learned that my parents were proud of me no matter what. I was the one who needed to accomplish something on my own to feel like a real person.

STEP 4 Write one or two sentences about the meaning of the experience. These will become the focus of your essay. You can use a simple sentence structure like one of these to get started:

- At first, I _____ , but afterward I _____ .

- I realized that _____ .

> At first, I was shy and lacked confidence, but afterward I was more self-assured. I realized that I had felt myself to be only a shadow of my older brother and sister, but now I had an accomplishment of my own to prove I was my own person.

Reference Note

For more on **chronological order,** see page 375.

Organize Your Details

Following the Leader   After listing the details of your experience, you need to put them in an order that will make the most sense to your readers. Commonly, **chronological order**—which shows the order in which the events occur over time—is the easiest for readers to follow. Another effective way of organizing a narrative is through the use of a **flashback.** In a flashback, the narrative starts in the middle or end, then "flashes back" to the beginning to relate the events leading up to that point. You should choose the order that best presents your personal reflection. The writer of the tae kwon do lesson ended up with the following arrangement.

Ordered Events List

1. Watched others practicing tae kwon do
2. Imagined I could do it
3. Met Gwen
4. Learned some techniques from Gwen
5. Joined the class
6. Practiced hard
7. Entered a competition; had a great match
8. Picture in the paper

TIP   When you write your personal reflection, you need to give your readers time signals to show the order of events. You can signal the passage of time with **transitional expressions.** These expressions include words such as *next, then, eventually, soon, until, the next day,* and so on. Readers rely on these clue words to be able to follow a narrative.

YOUR TURN 4   Planning Your Personal Reflection

Review this list of prewriting steps to ensure that you have everything ready to begin writing your personal reflection. You should

- choose an experience that was a defining moment in your life and that your audience will find interesting
- gather details that will make your reflection vivid and engaging
- reflect on the meaning of the experience
- organize the events in the experience so that it will make sense

Using Figurative Language

One important way of grabbing your readers' attention and creating interest in your personal reflection is to use **figurative language**—imaginative comparisons of something unfamiliar with something familiar. Using figurative language helps the reader to experience your events with you. These descriptions form memorable images that are clearer and more concrete.

Below are definitions and examples of three of the most common forms of figurative language.

If you do use figures of speech, you should be careful to avoid figures of speech that are **clichés**—tired and overused phrases. Clichés include similes such as "fog as thick as pea soup," metaphors such as "raining cats and dogs," and personification such as "raging blizzard" or "Old Man Winter." Clichés do not challenge readers to think of things in a new way and thus are not as fresh as figurative language should be.

A *simile* compares two things using *like* or *as*.	The smile spread across her face like autumn leaves across a crystal pond.
A *metaphor* says one thing *is* something else.	The smile was a lighthouse beacon illuminating the room.
Personification gives human characteristics to nonhuman things.	The smile knew it would make me look foolish, but it sprang forth regardless.

PRACTICE

Using the following chart, create five figures of speech by comparing one word in column **A** with one word in column **B**.

Then, use each new figure of speech in a sentence. Use each of the three different figures of speech at least once. Put your answers on your own paper.

Example:
child, stamp

The frightened child clung to his mother like a stamp to an envelope.

Column A	Column B
fog	sand
puppy	stamp
sailboat	leaf
bicycle	ball
child	tablecloth
canyon	river
music	book
pencil	paint

Writing

Personal Reflection

| Framework | Directions and Explanations |

Introduction

- Start with an interesting opener.
- Provide background information.
- Hint at the meaning of the experience.

Capture Your Readers' Interest   Include an interesting thought or image to grab your audience's attention.

Provide a Glimpse of You *Before* the Experience Give enough background information to provide an impression of what you were like prior to the experience.

No Mixed Signals   Give your readers a clue about why this experience was important.

Body

- Relate the events.
- Include details about people, places, thoughts, and feelings.

Watch the Clock   Structure your essay so that your readers can follow it easily. Use **transitional words** or phrases to signal chronological order. If you feel adventurous, provide flashbacks.

Solid as a Rock   Provide a solid basis of **narrative details** to help your readers see what happened. Write about people and places, but also describe thoughts and emotions.

A Large Palette and Beautiful Canvas   Use **descriptive details** to paint vivid images. Provide a variety of **sensory details**. Where appropriate, include **figurative language** to show things from a new perspective.

Conclusion

- Reflect on what the experience means to you.

Drive It Home   Let your readers know how you feel now. Use this portion of your narrative to reflect on how this experience changed you.

YOUR TURN 5 **Writing a First Draft**

Using the above guidelines, write the first draft of your personal reflection on an experience. For an example of an essay that follows the same guidelines, see the Writer's Model on the next page.

A Writer's Model

The following short essay, which is a final draft, closely follows the framework on the previous page.

Kicking Shyness

My whole way of looking at the world began to change around the time I turned thirteen. That May, my parents began taking the family to a local YMCA. We could swim, play softball, and visit with other families. Without admitting it to myself, I always seemed to live in the shadows of my older brother and sister. However, beginning with those hot summer days at the center, I started to lose track of what my brother and sister did—because for the first time in my life I was too busy doing my own thing.

After about a month, I found a tae kwan do class and was mesmerized as I watched men and women, boys and girls practice moves and spar with each other. The room was filled with swishing white uniforms and the roar of *ki-hop* yells. I imagined I was one of these people, timing my strokes perfectly, blocking so gracefully, sneaking in the winning point. In reality I spent weeks blending into the wall farthest from the others, shadowboxing at home behind locked doors, too afraid to join the others.

Then, after weeks of my watching, one day it happened. The *sabom-nim* (instructor), a college student named Gwen who moved as if gravity did not apply to her, called to me just as I was about to sneak out the door. "Hey, wallflower! Why don't you come help me practice some of my blocks?" she asked. I told her that I was not part of the class, but she insisted. "I promise I'll only block your moves. No counter-moves until you're ready—and I can teach you some other techniques, too." If Gwen had not been so friendly, I might have tried to escape. Instead, I found myself on the mats, outfitted in all the protective gear. My knees were like mashed potatoes, my heartbeat thundering in my head. There was no place to go but forward—head tucked safely behind my pads so that I could barely see. After a few minutes, though, I started to relax and enjoy myself. "See?" Gwen said afterward. "Once you've loosened up, you're a natural." That was the

(continued)

INTRODUCTION
Interesting opening

Background information

Hint at meaning

BODY
Event 1
Sensory details

Thoughts

Narrative detail

Event 2

Dialogue

Sensory detail
Figurative details

Actions show thoughts/feelings

right thing to say, then, because I needed praise.

Event 3
Narrative detail

That night, I convinced my parents to let me enroll in the class. I memorized all the moves: *ahre maggi* (down block), *guligi cha-gi* (hook kick), *poom sogi* (tiger stance), and so on. Believe me, this "natural" never worked so hard in her life. There is no doubt about it—tae kwon do is a tough, aerobic

Figurative detail
Dialogue

workout. Sometimes my muscles felt like limp noodles by the end of the day. My friends thought I was crazy. "Here comes Jackie Chan!" they would tease. Eventually, though, I was not

Narrative detail

just graceful but good enough to earn a yellow, then orange, and eventually a green belt.

Event 4

My mother still likes to tell the next part of this story. The following March, I had invited her, Dad, and my brother and sister to the center one Saturday for the spring tournaments— not telling them that I was competing. While they were looking for me on the

Narrative detail

Feelings

bench, they were surprised to hear my name blared over a loudspeaker. However, their shock was not over. Finally they

Narrative detail

noticed their younger daughter, poised confidently in the ring, waiting to spar in her first competition match. What a match it was! I didn't win, but I did get my picture in the newspaper (a

Thoughts/feelings

close-up of my determined face) and had the reward of my parents' amazed and proud faces.

CONCLUSION
Thoughts/feelings
Significance of experience

Looking back, I realize now that my parents did not need proof to think I was worth something—*I* did. I needed an accomplishment all my own, and tae kwon do was it. I learned confidence and greater respect for myself, not from winning, but from trying. From then on, I felt like a real person, not just a shadow.

A Student's Model

In the following reflection, Tabitha Henry of Weston High School in Cazenovia, Wisconsin, describes a personal experience that is familiar to many of us. Notice how she begins with background information that hints at what is to come.

My Last Goodbye

My life was perfect when I was twelve years old. I had a family, including my sister, Chrissy, and a little brother, Patrick, whom I loved greatly. Spring was coming, and I was excited about another summer with Grandma. She and I did a lot of things together. We used to talk to each other, go shopping, tell each other our secrets, and garden together. She was retiring this year, so that meant more time with her.

Then, on April 11, 1994, at 10:00 P.M., we were all going to bed when the phone rang. My mom answered; my uncle was calling to say that Grandpa had just taken Grandma to the hospital. . . .

My life fell apart that night. The next morning I was told that Grandma had had a heart attack and that she was gone. My heart stopped at that moment. I tried to be strong, but even my father cried. I just kept asking myself, "Why her?" I was so mad that I had not even gotten to say goodbye. I still thought that I could keep my feelings hidden until someone said of me, "This is the one that will miss her the most." I couldn't control my feelings anymore. I burst into tears. It finally hit me: She was gone forever. All I had left were memories in the garden—the hours we spent planting flowers and taking care of them. Although my aunt and I later tried to work the garden, it just was never the same.

I believe that my grandma is a star watching over me, just like she would be if she were still here. No one could ever fill that part of my heart that died with her. Still, my grandma would have wanted me to be strong and happy like her, even though there are good times and bad. My family and friends love me for who I am and support me for what I do, as I know my grandma would, too.

INTRODUCTION

Background information

Hint at what is to come

BODY
Event 1
Narrative detail

Event 2
Narrative detail

Dialogue

Thoughts/feelings
Figurative detail

CONCLUSION

Figurative detail

Significance of experience

Revising

Evaluate and Revise Your Draft

Taking a Second Look   Your task as a writer does not end with writing your first draft. You also need to evaluate and revise what you have written. You should work collaboratively with a peer to re-read each other's writing at least twice—first to focus on possible revisions of content and organization, and second to focus on style.

▶ **First Reading: Content and Organization**   By yourself or with a peer, use the following guidelines to evaluate and revise your personal reflection.

Personal Reflection: Content and Organization Guidelines for Peer and Self-Evaluation

Evaluation Questions	▶ Tips	▶ Revision Techniques
❶ Will the introduction grab the reader's attention? Does it provide background information and hint at the meaning of the experience?	**Circle** the sentences in the introduction that capture the reader's attention or provide background. **Bracket** the sentence or sentences that hint at the meaning of the experience. If there are no circles or brackets, revise.	**Replace** the opening sentences with one or two sentences that will grab the reader's attention. **Add** background or a hint of the meaning of the experience.
❷ Does the narrative include details that make the events, people, and places memorable?	**Underline** each sentence that begins a description of a separate event. **Double underline** each phrase or sentence that provides memorable details about each event. If there are no double underlines, revise.	**Add** memorable details or **elaborate** on existing details.
❸ Can the reader find descriptions of the writer's thoughts and feelings?	**Mark with a star** any sentences that describe thoughts and feelings. If you do not see any, revise.	**Add** or **elaborate** on details about your thoughts and feelings and those of other people in the narrative.
❹ Are the events of the narrative easy to follow? Are any events unnecessary to the experience?	**Number** the events in the narrative, looking for gaps. **Put an X** next to any event that does not seem to fit into the narrative.	**Reorder** the events in a way that will be clearer for the reader. **Cut** any events marked with an X.
❺ Does the conclusion state the significance or meaning of the experience?	**Highlight** any sentences that state why the experience was important to the writer. If there are none, revise.	**Add** one or two sentences to the conclusion that clearly state the significance or meaning of the experience.

ONE WRITER'S REVISIONS Here is how one writer used the content and organization chart to revise a section of the essay "Kicking Shyness," on page 39. After examining the changes, answer the questions following the paragraph.

like mashed potatoes, my heartbeat thundering in my head.
My knees were ~~shaking and my heart was pounding.~~ There

replace

was no place to go but forward—head tucked safely behind my

After a few minutes, though,
pads so that I could barely see. I started to relax and enjoy myself.

add

Analyzing the Revision Process

1. What do the changes in the first sentence add to the narrative?
2. Why did the writer insert *After a few minutes, though?*

PEER REVIEW

Ask a classmate to read your paper and to answer the following questions:

1. Did the narrative keep your interest? Why or why not?
2. What else would you like to know about the writer's experience?

YOUR TURN 6 Focusing on Content and Organization

Evaluate and revise the content and organization of your personal reflection using the guidelines on the previous page.

➤ **Second Reading: Style** During your second reading, you should focus on style. One stylistic change that will keep your readers interested in your narrative is to vary your sentence length. Uninterrupted stretches of long or short sentences make writing either drag on too long or sound choppy. **Sentence combining** is a way to improve sentence variety. You can use the style guidelines below to find and fix sentence monotony in your personal reflection.

Style Guidelines

Evaluation Question	▶ Tip	▶ Revision Technique
Is there a series of sentences that are the same length?	▶ **Put a jagged line** beneath sentences of five to seven words. If you find more than two short sentences in a row, revise.	▶ **Combine** sentences using participial phrases to add variety to sentence length.

Focus on Sentences

Reference Note

For more on **participial phrases,** see page 473.

Combining Sentences to Add Sentence Variety

You can add variety to sentences by reducing some sentences to **participial phrases** and then inserting them into other sentences. A participial phrase consists of a **participle,** a verb form (usually ending in *–ing* or *–ed*) that can be used as an adjective, and any complements or modifiers the participle may have. Short sentences with words that are repeated from the previous sentence are often the best to combine. In each of the following sentences, the participial phrase is underlined, the participle is in boldface, and the noun or pronoun it modifies is underlined twice.

Running through the trees, I sped toward the camp.

My brother, **rested** from an afternoon nap, waited for me there.

ONE WRITER'S REVISIONS The example below shows how the writer of the personal narrative on page 39 used the style guidelines to combine short sentences into a single sentence.

BEFORE REVISION

four sentences of similar length in a row

> I imagined I was one of these people. I timed my strokes perfectly. I was blocking so gracefully. I snuck in the winning point.

AFTER REVISION

three sentences reduced to participial phrases (in blue)

> I imagined I was one of these people, timing my strokes perfectly, blocking so gracefully, sneaking in the winning point.

Analyzing the Revision Process

1. How does reducing three sentences to participial phrases help the flow of the paragraph?

2. Do you think the sentence after the revision is too long or complicated? Why or why not?

YOUR TURN 7 Focusing on Style

Use the style guidelines on page 43 to revise any sentences in your essay that can be combined by using participial phrases. Remember to use sentences of *varying* length throughout your narrative—you do not need to eliminate *all* of your short sentences.

Designing Your Writing

Designing Your Web Page Uploading your personal reflection to the World Wide Web is a great way to reach an audience beyond your classroom and to incorporate visual elements into your narrative. However, creating an effective Web page takes more than just scanning or typing in your essay. Below are a few tips for designing your personal reflection Web page. Even if you do not have the technology to make a Web page, knowing about these basic design concerns will help you understand the choices Web designers make when creating the pages you see on the World Wide Web.

- **Limit the number of graphics you use.** Too many graphics make pages seem "busy" and cause them to take longer to download.

- **Keep your line lengths under two thirds of the page width.** Solid text across a screen can be difficult to read and hard on the eyes.

- **Try looking at your Web page on different computers,** especially ones with smaller screens, to see if all of your words fit on the page. Scrolling may be required if text runs off the right or bottom edge of the screen. Your readers will accept scrolling down the page only if the information in the top portion captures their interest.

- **Use strong visual contrasts.** Pages filled with solid blocks of text appear as a dull mass of words, as shown on the left below.

Dull, no visual focus   *Strong visual contrasts*

Publishing

Proofread Your Essay

Putting on the Polish   Have you ever read a piece of writing and found a typographical error or noticed that a word was omitted? When you run across errors of this kind, you become distracted—your attention focuses on the errors instead of the meaning of the writing. To avoid distracting your reader, work collaboratively to put the final polish on your writing by proofreading for errors. In your personal reflection, be especially careful to catch subject-verb agreement errors. Poor subject-verb agreement can leave a reader confused about the experience you are sharing.

Reference Note

For more on **subject-verb agreement with intervening phrases,** see page 513.

Grammar Link

Subject-Verb Agreement

Many sentences contain **intervening phrases,** phrases that separate a sentence's subject and verb. If a phrase comes between the subject and verb of a sentence, be sure that the verb agrees with the true subject and not with any nouns or pronouns within the phrase. A singular subject should have a singular verb, and a plural subject should have a plural verb.

Example:
Today my **brother,** together with his prize-winning dogs, **appears** in a special-interest story on the local news.

[The phrase *together with his prize-winning dogs* is an intervening phrase between the subject *brother* and the verb *appears.* The subject *brother* is singular, so the verb *appears* must be singular.]

Example:
The dogs with the black ears are sisters.

[The phrase *with the black ears* is an intervening phrase between the subject *dogs* and the verb *are*. The subject *dogs* is plural, so the verb *are* must be plural.]

PRACTICE

Identify the subject of each of the following sentences. Then, determine whether the verb (in italics) agrees in number with the subject. On your own paper, write *I* and the correct verb if the verb is incorrect. Write *C* if the verb is correct.

1. My mother, along with Mrs. Shapiro and Mr. Talbot, *run* a health fair at school every year.

2. The movies at the theater *were* all new that weekend.

3. Ms. Wyatt's class on movie icons *interest* many students.

4. The old mall, which was the first in town, *has* a renovated food court.

5. My grandfather on my mother's side of the family *tells* wonderful stories about his childhood in Mexico.

Publish Your Essay

Making the World a Little Smaller   By sharing your personal reflection with others, you can connect your experiences with those of your readers. Here are some suggested ways to have others read and respond to your narrative:

- If your reflection is about a time spent in a special place, such as a national park, check to see if that place has a Web site that welcomes visitor feedback. If so, submit your essay for posting.

- Ask your teacher to arrange a "cultural exchange" of personal reflections with a class in another part of the country or world. You can see the ways in which you are all similar or different.

- Put old photos of the experience in your reflection together with your personal reflection to create a family memento.

- Many magazines publish personal reflections that are entertaining or that will provide readers with examples of positive growth experiences. Ask your teacher or parents to help you submit your reflection to a topic-appropriate magazine.

Reflect on Your Essay

◄ PORTFOLIO

Looking Back, Looking Forward   Answering the following questions will help you think about what you have learned while writing your reflection and what you might do differently the next time you write one. If you include this essay in your portfolio, make sure to attach these responses to it.

- Which prewriting step did you find most difficult? Do you think it will be easier for you the next time you write a narrative? Why or why not?

- While writing your reflection, what new insights did you have into the experience you chose as a topic?

YOUR TURN 8   Proofreading, Publishing, and Reflecting

Before you share your personal reflection with an audience, be sure to

- correct any spelling, punctuation, or grammatical errors
- find ways to follow through on any publishing ideas you have
- answer the reflection questions above

Writing a Free-Verse Poem

Sometimes thoughts and feelings drawn to the surface when you reflect on an experience are more interesting to explore through verse rather than through prose.

One kind of poetry that is well suited to writing about feelings and images is **free verse.** Free-verse poems usually do not follow a regular pattern of rhythm or rhyme. Instead, words and lines are arranged according to natural speech patterns. In other words, line length is determined by natural **"breath rhythm"**—the line breaks coincide with natural pauses for breathing.

Learn from an Example The following free-verse poem describes a lonely harbor scene. Notice that the final word in each line is important to the meaning of the poem.

Lost
by Carl Sandburg

last word emphasized	Desolate and lone
	All night long on the lake
personification	Where fog trails and mist creeps,
imagery (sound)	The whistle of a boat
	Calls and cries unendingly,
	Like some lost child
	In tears and trouble
personification	Hunting the harbor's breast
	And the harbor's eyes.

Choosing a Topic You can write a free-verse poem on almost any topic. Here are some example topics that might work well:

- an item, activity, or person from your personal reflection
- a plant or animal that has interesting similarities to human beings
- sights, sounds, or smells that remind you of a friend or relative

Basic Elements Remember that free verse does not have a set rhythm or rhyme scheme. However, form is determined by the content of the poem.

- **Words that need special emphasis should be placed at the beginning or the ends of lines.** Key words should be placed on a line by themselves. Look at the last word on each line of "Lost."

- **A stream of words related in meaning should flow together in one line.** For example, "Where fog trails and mist creeps" is a description of the lake.

- **Line length is controlled to create a visual arrangement.** For example, the short lines of "Lost" might visually emphasize the loneliness of the scene, or the variation of line length could suggest waves.

Of course, free-verse poems should also contain some of the numbered items in the chart at the top of the next page.

1. **sensory details** of sight, hearing, touch, taste, and smell to create vivid images

2. **figurative language,** like the following examples, to give readers new perspectives on familiar things

   - **simile:** a comparison of two basically unalike things, using the words *like* or *as*
     Like some lost child

   - **metaphor:** a direct comparison of two things without using the words *like* or *as;* says that something *is* something else
     The moonlight rays are the eyelashes of night

   - **personification:** giving human characteristics to nonhuman things
     (T)he harbor's eyes

   (For more on **figurative language,** see page 37.)

3. **sound elements** to help create mood and evoke images; these include

   - **assonance:** the repetition of vowel sounds in words or syllables
     Like some lost child

   - **alliteration:** the repetition of the same consonant sound in words or syllables
     All night long on the lake

TIP When you revise your poem, read it aloud. Do the words and line breaks follow your natural speech patterns? If not, make some adjustments.

YOUR TURN 9 **Writing a Free-Verse Poem**

Choose a topic that interests you, and write your own free-verse poem about it. Pay attention to line breaks and word choice. Try to include sensory details and figurative language to make your poem more vivid and memorable.

PEANUTS reprinted by permission of United Feature Syndicate, Inc.

Making a Video Reflection

WHAT'S AHEAD?

In this section you will

■ plan a visual presentation
■ create a storyboard
■ tape a video reflection

Just as you may sometimes prefer verse as a way of expressing yourself, you may at other times choose to express yourself using images—photographs, film, or video. One good way to develop your skills as a visual storyteller is to create a **video reflection**—a short series of videotaped scenes that visually tell a narrative. You can use the experience from your personal reflection essay as the basis for a video reflection, or you can base it on some other personal experience.

Putting Words into Motion

Planning a Visual Presentation   If you have ever seen the film version of a book you have read, you know that filmmakers must choose which events, characters, dialogue, and scenes to include and which ones to omit. You, too, will have to decide what can go into your video reflection and what you must leave out. Use the steps below to plan.

■ Break the narrative into a list of essential events.
■ Determine the number of shots needed to illustrate each event.
■ Decide how each shot will look. A close-up shot of someone's face? A long shot of the setting?
■ Create a storyboard. (See the detailed instructions below.)

Every Picture Tells a Story   A vital part of creating a film or video is **storyboarding**—the process of sketching out scenes before filming or taping. A storyboard is a series of sketches that chronologically depicts important narrative events. These sketches will become separate "shots" in the finished film or video. A completed storyboard looks very much like the pages of a comic book, with dialogue and descriptions written below or beside the illustrations.

Here are some terms for describing transitions from shot to shot.

- **Cut**—instantaneous change from one scene to another
- **Dissolve**—scene slowly disappears as the next slowly appears
- **Fade-in**—scene begins as black, and then slowly appears
- **Fade-out**—scene slowly disappears to a black screen
- **Wipe**—scene slowly replaces the previous scene, usually through use of a line moving across the screen

An Example Storyboard   The following is a portion of the storyboard for a video presentation of the Writer's Model on page 39. Notice that the marginal notes give information that cannot be portrayed only with images. However, all of the information involves actions that will take place either on-screen or with camera and audio effects.

1 fade-in: long shot.
Girl in foreground; tae
kwon do class in back-
ground, moving in unison
sounds: "ki-hop" yells,
swishing of movements

2 close-up from front
girl's face; she looks long-
ingly at the class; after a
moment, closes eyes
sounds: same as last
fade-out

3 fade-in, effects indicate
a daydream; girl, confi-
dent, wearing headgear,
eyes straight ahead
takes three deep breaths
sound: breathing

4 still daydream
girl spars effortlessly
with opponent
sound: swish of movement
fade-out

5 fade-in, daydream
effect gone
sound: same as scene 1
girl looks down, sighs
fade-out

Roll the Tape   If you do not have the editing technology available to professionals, you will instead need to use **in-camera editing**—taping your reflection in exactly the same sequence you planned in your storyboard.

Make sure that all people involved in your production are familiar with the storyboard and their parts in the video reflection. Rehearse the sequence of actions and any dialogue several times in the days before you begin taping. Still, if mistakes happen, relax. If you are using in-camera editing, view each scene as soon as you finish taping it. You can always rewind the video and tape over a weak scene. If you have editing equipment, you can tape the scene several times and insert the best version into the final tape.

Basic Video Techniques   Here are a few tips to remember when preparing your video reflection.

■ **Give your reflection sound.** Dialogue and background sound effects help you relate thoughts, feelings, and elements that you cannot portray visually. Consider using a **voice-over,** offscreen narration to describe on-screen events or the thoughts of the narrator in a first-person reflection. Voice-overs can be directly input to the video as you tape using a microphone, or added later with editing equipment.

Keep in mind that unwanted noise may intrude on your audio. To avoid these distractions, add voice-over narration in a quiet room after the video has been shot. You add voice-overs by either using video editing equipment or simply taping the narration on an audiocassette to accompany your video. Just be careful to ensure that your audio and video stay in sync.

■ **Make lighting work for—not against—you.** Taping in natural sunlight works best for most home video recorders—but do not be afraid to test your camera's indoor capabilities.

■ **Use a tripod, or set your camera on a stable surface when taping.** No matter how steady you think your hand is, it will invariably move as you tape. Even the slightest movement can make the final videotape seem unsteady and sloppy.

YOUR TURN 10   **Creating a Video Reflection**

Create a storyboard for a five- to seven-minute video reflection (you may want to use a portion of the personal reflection you wrote in the Writing Workshop). Then, videotape your reflection using your storyboard as a guide. If you do not have access to a video camera, you may be able to present the narrative through a series of still photographs or drawings.

Choices

Choose one of the following activities to complete.

▶ **CROSSING THE CURRICULUM: SOCIAL STUDIES**

1. Snatched from the Headlines Choose a current event featured in a newspaper, magazine, TV, or Internet news source. Consider local, state, or national government decisions that have had a direct effect on you or your family. Produce a two-minute **audio commentary** on that news item, explaining how the event influenced you.

▶ **LITERATURE**

2. Join the Book Club Choose a book that has had special meaning to you, and submit a one-hundred-word **online review** to a book club or to a bookstore's customer comments section. Reading this book may have been a defining moment in your life, making you the person that you are today. Think of characters that you respect and have tried to emulate or ones that you despise and have tried hard not to be like. Consider books that have inspired you to reach for certain goals: playing a guitar, flying an airplane, or becoming a veterinarian. Include

passages from the book as details to show your reader why it was so important.

▶ **CAREERS**

3. You're Hired! Often, when interviewing, potential employers will ask you to tell about a time when you failed. Their interest is not in seeing what you did wrong, but rather how you handled it. Prepare a **two-minute oral response** to an interviewer's question about your failure and your reaction. Your response should show that you have used the failure as a chance for personal reflection to help you learn from your mistakes.

▶ **VIEWING AND REPRESENTING**

4. The Land That Time Forgot Imagine that one million years from now, archaeologists will unearth your house. Create **a message** for these archaeologists. Keep in mind that they will probably not understand our language, so you will have to communicate to them through **illustrations** only. Your pictures should show who you were, how you lived, and what was important to you.

PORTFOLIO

2

Exploring Comparisons and Contrasts

Reading Workshop

Reading a Comparison-Contrast Article

Writing Workshop

Writing a Comparison-Contrast Essay

Viewing and Representing

Comparing and Contrasting Media Coverage

Similarities and Differences

- Two creeks run through your community. You discover that one is polluted, while the other is clean. What differences in the environments that surround the creeks make one polluted and one not?

- You meet a new friend who shares your interest in snowboarding, and you swap stories. What similar snowboarding experiences have you had?

    In these situations, you **compare** and **contrast** things or ideas to get more information or to explain something to someone. When you compare two things, you look at their similarities. For instance, as you compare your snowboarding experiences with those of a friend, you may find out about similar experiences you have had. When you contrast two things, you look at their differences. As you contrast the environment around a clean creek with that around a polluted creek, you may discover differences in the two environments that explain why one is polluted and the other is not.

> **Informational Text**
>
> Exposition

YOUR TURN 1 — Comparing and Contrasting

How important is comparison and contrast in the real world? Consider the times when you have had to evaluate two things based on their similarities or differences. For instance, think about when you made decisions or judgments about two hobbies, experiences, products, or TV shows. Work with a partner to create a list of these instances, and be ready to share your list with the class.

internet connect

go.
hrw
.com

GO TO: go.hrw.com
KEYWORD: EOLang 10-2

Reading a Comparison-Contrast Article

WHAT'S AHEAD?

In this section, you will read a magazine article and learn how to

■ **identify the main idea and supporting details**

■ **analyze comparison-contrast structure**

Imagine hopping in a car and heading out to school on the wrong side of the road. How long would it be before you created a traffic jam, or worse? When Americans drive on British roads or when British people drive on American roads, they have to switch sides of the road and obey different driving rules. The article on the next page, "Two Peoples Divided by Common Road Signs," compares and contrasts American and British road systems and the frustration they bring to tourists.

Preparing to Read

READING SKILL

Main Idea and Supporting Details   To understand an article or other type of writing, you must first figure out its **main idea**—the message, opinion, or insight on which the writing is focused. Once you determine the main idea, you can look for **supporting details,** the information that develops and explains the main idea.

READING FOCUS

Comparison-Contrast Structure   Writers usually organize their discussion of comparison and contrast in one of two ways: the **block method** or the **point-by-point method.** Writers use the block method when they want to discuss all of the points about each subject separately. They use the point-by-point method to deal with both subjects at the same time, making a point about one subject, then following it with a comparable point about the other.

As you read "Two Peoples Divided by Common Road Signs," look for clues that will help you determine how the writer, Norman Berdichevsky, organized his discussion.

In the following satirical article, the writer makes frequent use of exaggeration and humor to point out some confusing differences between British and American (U.S.) road systems. As you read, write down answers to the active-reading questions.

from Contemporary Review

TWO PEOPLES DIVIDED

By Norman Berdichevsky

BY COMMON ROAD SIGNS

As an American in Britain, it is my firm belief that the confusion stemming from the two different road systems and their portrayal on maps is the single most irritating factor causing frustration, anger and a shrug of the shoulders accompanied by mutterings of . . . those crazy Brits (Americans)."

1. According to the writer, what causes anger and frustration among Americans driving in Britain and British tourists driving in America?

Squares versus Circles

It is not, as many might believe, the Left v. Right hand side of the road conundrum which is the source of the most awful aggravation, and cursing (swearing), but rather the totally opposing circulatory systems. Americans are "squares"—a condition which stems from the geometric

2. What aspects of driving in Britain and in America does this paragraph contrast?

lay-out based on the cardinal directions of the compass and lines of latitude and longitude on which North America was shaped (French Canada, Louisiana and the Spanish-Mexican land grant systems being the exceptions). The American systems of grids and rectangles stand in sharp contrast to the devious British who move in gyratory arcs, curves and circles frequently interrupted by dead ends leading nowhere. Put in simpler terms, this simply means that almost anywhere in North America, a motorist can, even without a map, make three consecutive right (or even left) turns and come back to where he started. In Britain, there is practically no chance of returning to one's starting point.

Roundabouts versus Grids

During many years of driving in the United States, I have encountered one roundabout (it was in Cape Cod, Massachusetts, and stands out in my memory as a freak occurrence). Along a stretch of a few miles of road in the UK [United Kingdom], I have often encountered a dozen or more roundabouts. This means that the chances of taking a wrong road in the UK as compared to the US are on the order of 12:1 (i.e., an American intersection of two roads meeting at right angles compared to a half a dozen roundabouts each of which contain four spin-offs). In America, [it would be difficult] to make an unwanted U-turn and go back on the same road but in the opposite direction, whereas this has frequently happened to me in the UK after driving round a roundabout and exiting by the same road I entered it (in spite of a Ph.D. in geography).

> **3. A roundabout is compared with an intersection of two roads. What is a roundabout?**

Traveling within a city also presents a nightmare of what Americans consider gross violations of the most elementary "rules of thumb" for finding an address. The American grid systems with few exceptions apply in cities everywhere and not just Manhattan so that a newcomer can easily orient himself in terms of numbered streets and lettered avenues. Washington D.C. is an "exotic" variation on this theme due to its diagonally trending avenues and pentagonal street pattern rather than the standard square. In Britain however, roads have names

> **4. What facts does the writer provide to show that British street addresses break American "rules of thumb"?**

which often change along commercial stretches (frequently called "Parades") and then return to their original name. This often results in Americans being convinced that they have already made a wrong turn somewhere along the line. Odd and even numbers which are always on the opposite sides of the street and close in numerical order in the US may be neither in British cities.

Street Names

Road signs with street names are often absent from major thoroughfares in British cities although every minor abutting street is prominently named. To add to the confusion, it is common practice for many streets to bear the same patronymic but be distinguished by a confusion of appendages, i.e. Wallace Road, Wallace Street, Wallace Avenue, Wallace Crescent, Wallace Close, Wallace Parade, Wallace Gardens, etc. Even more absurd is the existence of a dozen or more streets in the same city with exactly the same name! The most recent edition of the famous London *A to Z* (pronounced A to Zed) Street Atlas contains sixteen Essex Roads, thirteen Durham Roads, etc. in widely different parts of the city. One of the most helpful items for an American motorist to obtain is a map of London's postal zones (not obtainable in Post Offices). These practices have convinced me and other Americans that the British must have devised all this to intentionally thwart a German invasion

> **5. What does the writer imply about American road names?**

in 1940 and then forgot to restore helpful information.

Compass Points versus "Clockwise"

As far back as the novels of Sir Arthur Conan Doyle, an American character, the Mormon refugee in *A Study in Scarlet*, comments on his work in London as a cab driver (a horse-drawn cab that is): "The hardest job was to learn my way about, for I reckon that of all the mazes that ever were contrived, this city [London] is the most confusing." Nothing offends the American sensibility as much as coming to a divided highway without being clearly informed far in advance which lane turns East or West, North or South. Instead, the signs tell you the destinations of the next major towns—often three, four, or more bunched together on the sign. This creates problems of visibility and recognition as well as taxing one's memory even after a careful pre-journey perusal of the map. This is especially so in unfamiliar territory. On quite a few occasions, I found that the drivers or pedestrians I asked for help were really not speaking the same language as me because they spoke only of the "clockwise" and "anti-clockwise" (counter clockwise) flows of traffic rather than the points of the compass.

Many times I have approached a huge sign informing me of the approaching highway with its boldly emblazoned number but without having a clue as to how I should proceed to get to the same numbered highway leading in the opposite direction. In the United States, not a few drivers make good use of a compass mounted on the dashboard but I have yet to observe one anywhere inside an automobile in Britain.

"Get Out of the Way!" versus "Please Go First!"

Then there is the strange British preference to do major road works during rush hour traffic rather than on week-ends and late at night and the many urban roads too narrow for two cars to pass each other at the same time. Someone has to give way. Here too, there is room for maximum confusion for an American recently arrived in the UK. Courteous British drivers will flash their headlights which in the US would signify "Get out of the way. I have the right of way and even if I don't, I'm coming through now!" In Britain, this sign actually means the opposite—"Please go first!"

Although Britain is now the only European nation which drives on the left hand side of the road (Sweden went over to the right more than a decade ago), in most other respects, European and British driving habits, rules, and regulations coincide. If an American-British reunion were ever attempted, it would immediately founder on the absolute incompatibility of the square grid *v.* the roundabout. It's no wonder that at the Battle of Yorktown which ended the American Revolution in 1783, the British military band at the surrender ceremony played "The World Turned Upside Down."

6. What do the subheads tell you about the organization of this article?

Main Idea and Supporting Details

What's the Point?   When you read an article or essay, you want to make sure you get the point. Being able to identify the main idea of an article ensures that you get the point the writer is trying to make. The **main idea** of an article, also called the **thesis,** is the idea on which the entire piece is focused. In an article that is several paragraphs long, the main idea or thesis is sometimes sketched out in one or two sentences, often near the beginning of the piece. These one or two sentences, known as the **thesis statement,** declare the topic of the entire piece and the main idea about it. Some pieces of writing, however, lack a thesis statement and instead have an **implied main idea.** When this is the case, the reader must determine the main idea by examining and combining the details found in each paragraph.

Each paragraph in the piece focuses on a specific point, its own **paragraph main idea,** that helps complete the picture outlined by the thesis. The paragraph main idea often appears in a topic sentence, and **supporting details** make up the rest of each paragraph. Sensory details, facts or statistics, examples, or anecdotes are all details that can support the main idea of a paragraph.

The diagram on the next page shows how the thesis, the main idea of each paragraph, and the supporting details all relate to each other in a piece of writing.

TIP   An implied main idea is often found in narrative and descriptive writing.

Main Idea and Supporting Details

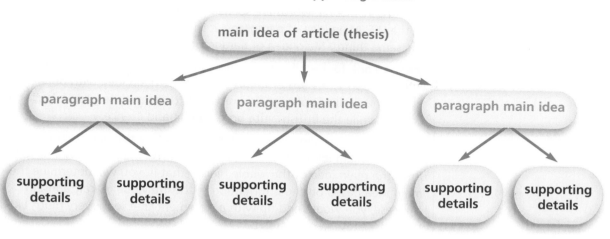

TIP Many essays and articles you read deal with only one subject. Comparison-contrast articles, however, always deal with at least two subjects. In professional writing, if one of the subjects is unfamiliar and the other is more familiar, a writer might **imply** details about the familiar subject because the writer assumes the reader already knows those details. For example, in a comparison of the two sports baseball and cricket, a writer might give all the details about cricket bats without fully describing the more familiar baseball bats.

THINKING IT THROUGH Identifying Main Idea and Supporting Details

You can use the following process to identify the main idea and supporting details of a reading selection. The examples below are based on an article titled "British English *vs.* U.S. English."

▶ **STEP 1 Read the piece and identify the subjects. Pay special attention to the title and to repeated words and phrases. Think about what the writer is addressing.** Based on the title, it would be reasonable to guess that Britain and the U.S. are probably the two subjects.

▶ **STEP 2 Look for a clearly stated thesis. A thesis statement often appears in the introduction or in the conclusion of a piece.** A piece of this kind might contain a thesis statement like this one: Although U.S. citizens and the British both speak English, there are differences in the ways they communicate.

▶ **STEP 3 If the writer does not include a thesis statement, follow steps 3–5. Re-read the selection. As you finish each paragraph, write a**

sentence that expresses the main idea of the paragraph. Main idea of paragraph 1: Some words are spelled differently in Britain than they are in the U.S. Main idea of paragraph 2: Different words are used to name the same things. Main idea of paragraph 3: Some words sound different.

▶ **STEP 4 Look for details that support the main idea of each paragraph.** In paragraph 1, the writer might support the main idea with details about the spellings of specific words: U.S. citizens write *gray, labor,* and *license,* while the British write *grey, labour,* and *licence.*

▶ **STEP 5 After looking at each paragraph, write a statement that combines the main ideas of *all* the paragraphs.** This means you will have to *infer* the main idea of the whole piece—that is, you will determine the main idea based on the information in the individual paragraphs. In this case, you would end up with a statement that looks very much like the thesis statement in step 2.

YOUR TURN 2 — Identifying Main Idea and Supporting Details

Use the Thinking It Through steps above to identify the overall main idea (or thesis) and the supporting details of "Two Peoples Divided by Common Road Signs." As you re-read the article, watch for implied details about American roads.

READING FOCUS ▶

Comparison-Contrast Structure

Recognize How It's Organized When you read a comparison-contrast essay, you can expect to find details about the two subjects organized with either the **block method** or the **point-by-point method.**

Writers use the block method to separate all of the points about one subject from all of the points about the other subject. This type of organization is called the block method because it presents all of the information about the first subject in a block of paragraphs and then presents all of the information about the second subject in a block of paragraphs.

Writers use the point-by-point method to group each point about the first subject with its corresponding point about the second subject. A point about the first subject is made in one or more sentences and then that point is followed by the corresponding point about the second subject. The writer will continue pairing up each subject until all of the points have been made.

In the following diagram, which illustrates the difference between the two methods, A is the first subject and B is the second subject.

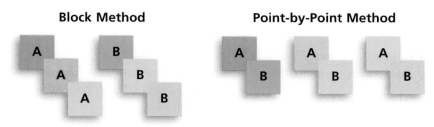

The following graphic organizers compare cricket with baseball. Look at the differences in how the two subjects are presented using the block method and the point-by-point method.

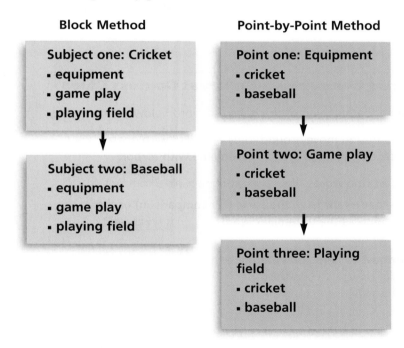

YOUR TURN 3   Analyzing Comparison-Contrast Structure

Analyze the structure of "Two Peoples Divided by Common Road Signs." First, decide which organizational method the writer uses; then, create a graphic organizer to list the differences between British and American road systems. Remember that details about American road systems may be implied because the writer assumes you are already familiar with them.

Comparison-Contrast Context Clues

When you encounter an unfamiliar word in a comparison-contrast piece, consider its **context,** or surrounding words. Look for nearby **comparison-contrast clue words** that signal a comparison (such as *like, similar, also,* and *as*) or a contrast (*however, but, contrast,* and *conversely*).

In a comparison, an unfamiliar word might have a meaning similar to a familiar word or phrase in the sentence.

British *car parks* are **like** U.S. parking lots. (*Like* signals a comparison between *car parks* and *parking lots.* A car park is probably the same as a parking lot.)

In a contrast, an unfamiliar word might have a meaning dissimilar to a familiar word.

The *lift* is faster, **but** I usually take the stairs. (*But* signals contrast between *lift* and *stairs.* A lift is probably the same as an elevator.)

THINKING IT THROUGH   **Using Comparison-Contrast Context Clues**

Look at the steps to determine the meaning of the italicized word below.

> When the orangutans are free to move around, they are filled with energy. When confined in their cages, however, they are overcome with *torpor.*

1. **Look for comparison-contrast clue words.** The word <u>however</u> signals a contrast.

2. **Look for a word or phrase that might have the same (for comparison) or the opposite (for contrast) meaning as the unfamiliar word.** The word <u>energy</u> is probably an opposite of the word <u>torpor</u>.

3. **Use the comparison or contrast to help you determine the unfamiliar word's meaning.** If <u>energy</u> is contrasted with <u>torpor</u>, then <u>torpor</u> probably means "a lack of energy" or "dullness."

PRACTICE

Use the steps above to find the meanings of the italicized words in the following sentences. Write your answers on your own paper.

1. Driving on the left side of the road is a *conundrum* for Americans. Roundabouts also are a point of confusion.

2. British and European drivers seem to get along; however, a union of British and American drivers would certainly *founder.*

3. American and British drivers may agree about gasoline prices, but the conflicting road systems are a large source of *discord.*

4. British streets may share a name but have a different *appendage,* like "street" or "road." U.S. streets have similar extensions.

Main Idea

Many reading tests feature questions that require you to identify the main idea of a reading passage. Below are a reading passage and a typical comprehension question that you might find on a reading test.

Many people think that bacteria and viruses are the same thing. After all, both are extremely small. They both can cause infectious diseases and are scientifically classified as microbes. However, even though they may seem similar, bacteria and viruses are very different.

Bacteria can live independently of host organisms and can reproduce without any outside aid. In fact, they can live in soil and thrive without any direct contact with other organisms.

Viruses, on the other hand, are completely inert or dormant outside a host organism. Viruses can reproduce only by using the machinery of a host cell's nucleus; they must hijack the cells of host organisms to make copies of themselves.

1. Which of the following best states the main idea of the third paragraph?

   A. Bacteria can reproduce on their own.

   B. Viruses and bacteria are almost the same.

   C. Viruses are dependent on a host organism.

   D. Viruses use cell machinery to reproduce.

THINKING IT THROUGH — **Answering Questions About Main Idea**

The following steps will help you identify the main idea on reading tests.

▶ **STEP 1 Read through the entire paragraph or passage.** Many tests include answer choices meant to catch those who only skim through a passage. Choice **A** is true, but it is stated in the second paragraph, not the third.

▶ **STEP 2 Look for a directly stated main idea—a sentence that all the other sentences support.** This is often the first sentence of a paragraph or passage. Choice **D** appears in the third paragraph, but it only supports the sentence that comes before it. Choice **C** is a restatement of the paragraph's main idea; the remaining paragraph sentences provide details that support that idea.

▶ **STEP 3 If the passage includes no directly stated main idea, try summarizing the paragraph or passage in your own words.** Read each sentence in the paragraph or passage, and try to come up with a summary that states the main idea that unites them. Then, look for an answer choice that matches this inferred main idea. The passage makes the point that bacteria and viruses are different. Choice **B** states the opposite. The correct answer has to be Choice **C**.

Writing a Comparison-Contrast Essay

Picture this situation: You have just moved to a new neighborhood and attended your first day at a new school. Your best friend at your old school is dying to know what your new school is like. Is your new science teacher as spirited as your last one? Are your classes still on block schedule? Are the graduation requirements similar? Does the new school offer the same extracurricular activities, or are there different ones? In an e-mail to your friend, you describe the similarities and differences between your new school and your old one. That is, you **compare and contrast** the two schools to help your friend more easily understand your ideas.

Comparing and contrasting are two natural ways you seek to understand the world around you. This understanding can help you to make informed decisions and sound judgments. In this Writing Workshop, you will have a chance to plan, organize, and write a comparison-contrast essay about two subjects that you choose on your own.

Prewriting

Choose Two Subjects

Pick and Choose   When you write a comparison-contrast essay, you focus on the similarities or the differences (or both) of two subjects in order to understand them better. To get started, you first must decide which two subjects you will compare and contrast.

- If you have ever wondered how two things are different or similar, you could compare and contrast them to find out. For example, you might wonder how the trumpet and the trombone are alike and different.

- Think about any time you have to make a choice between two things. If your family is thinking about buying a computer or a car, for instance, but can't decide between two models, you could compare and contrast the models to help make the choice clearer.

- Think about your hobbies and interests. If you are a fan of the *Star Wars* movies, you might compare and contrast the latest movie in the series with an earlier one. Similarly, if you are a sports enthusiast who likes both snowskiing and waterskiing, you might compare and contrast the two sports.

As you think of possible subjects, ask yourself the following questions to determine whether the subjects can be developed well in a comparison-contrast essay.

- **Do the subjects have something in common?** The subjects must have at least one basic similarity. For instance, you could compare watching movies on videotape to watching movies in theaters because both are ways to view a common form of entertainment—movies.

- **Do the subjects have significant differences?** The subjects you choose must be different enough to be interesting. For example, the differences in the cost, the convenience, and the experience of watching videos at home and seeing movies in theaters are significant enough to make for an interesting essay.

Remember to choose subjects that can be easily compared in a short essay. Comparing all forms of live entertainment with all forms of pre-recorded entertainment, for instance, would be too much to accomplish. However, comparing home video viewing with watching movies in theaters is manageable. After you have found two subjects that you think will work, jot them down in a notebook or journal.

TIP The word *compare* is sometimes used to mean "look at both similarities and differences, not just similarities." If a teacher asks you to compare two subjects, check to see if you should look for differences as well as similarities.

Consider Purpose, Audience, and Tone

Thinking of the Why, the Who, and the How   You will communicate more clearly with your audience if you are sure of why you are writing—that is, if you have your **purpose** clearly in mind. The main purpose of this comparison-contrast piece is to inform your readers about your subjects. To begin, you must first determine which aspects of your subjects you want to discuss: their similarities, their differences, or both. To do this, think about the focus of your paper.

- If your purpose were to show your readers how softball and baseball are alike, you would write an essay about their **similarities**.

TIP Comparison-contrast structure is often used only to present information about two subjects. However, it can be used for persuasive purposes—to convince you that one subject is better, or worse, than the other.

- If your purpose were to inform your readers about the differences between owning a cat and owning a dog, you would write an essay about **differences.**

- If your purpose were to explain to your readers how the Sahara and the Mojave deserts have both similar and different characteristics, you would write an essay about **both similarities and differences.**

In order for your writing to be as informative as it can be, you should carefully consider who your intended **audience** is—who your readers are. You must also consider what those readers already know about your subject so you can define terms and provide necessary background information. For example, suppose that you were planning to write an essay contrasting owning a cat and owning a dog. If you were writing for an audience of cat owners, you would include more details about owning a dog. Your readers would already be familiar with cat ownership—you would not have to include as many details about it.

To help you decide what kinds of information you should include for your readers, ask yourself the following questions.

- What do your readers already know about your two subjects?

- Is one subject more familiar to them than the other?

- What facts and information will your readers want to know about the two subjects?

Finally, you should decide on the **tone** of your writing, or how you will present your message. Tone is like the personality of your writing. Whether you are serious, funny, casual, or formal, your tone is created by the details, words, rhythms, and sounds of language that you choose. Writers of informative pieces, such as comparison-contrast essays, usually use a clear, authoritative tone because they want to sound knowledgeable about their subjects. You might decide, however, that a humorous tone is more fitting for your essay. For example, humor might be appropriate in an essay comparing and contrasting a satirical novel with its movie version. The tone you use depends on the purpose of your writing, on your intended audience, and on the subjects you are comparing and contrasting.

Gather Information and Determine Relevant Features

Get the Facts In order to discuss your two subjects seriously, you must gather information about them. Information you will want to gather includes definitions, facts, statistics, and descriptions of the distinct characteristics of each subject. Some of this information may come from your own knowledge or experience, but most often you will need to research information, even if only to support the claims you make based on what you know.

Where you get the information for your essay will depend on your two subjects. You might go to a library for books or articles written about the subjects. You might search the Internet for information as well, or interview people who are experts on the subjects. Once you have gathered the information that you will include in your comparison-contrast essay, you will begin to identify your two subjects' *relevant features*. **Relevant features are the important characteristics of your two subjects; they provide the main points for supporting your thesis.** These features are called *relevant* because they are important, or significant, to the understanding of the two subjects.

KEY CONCEPT

The relevant features you choose depend on your audience. If you are writing for the general public, you might contrast features of general interest. On the other hand, if your intended audience consists of experts or enthusiasts on your subjects, you might choose specific relevant features that would interest them more.

THINKING IT THROUGH

Discovering Relevant Features

Take the following steps to determine possible relevant features for your subjects. The chart that follows the steps shows how a student determined relevant features for an essay contrasting watching movies in the theater with watching videos at home.

▶ **STEP 1 Freewrite a list of the details of the two subjects you have chosen.** Try to list as many as possible. Note that a detail of one subject may trigger a corresponding detail of the other subject.

▶ **STEP 2 Label the items in your list.** For instance, if you have a detail that relates to a subject's cost, then label it "cost." Labeling the details you have discovered will help you organize and compare your details later. You can always go back and relabel an item if necessary.

▶ **STEP 3 Create a two-column chart like the one on the following page. Within each column, group all details with the same label, or details that seem to belong together. Cross out any details that do not have a corresponding detail in the other column.** The group labels, shown on the chart in boldface type, are the relevant features. The details are the specifics the essay will address.

RELEVANT FEATURES

Movies in theaters	Videotapes at home
Comfort • seating may be limited • people may block your view of the screen	**Comfort** • can sit where you want • usually no one will block your view
Cost • expensive tickets • snacks very expensive	**Cost** • rental price a few dollars • can eat whatever is in the house
Control • cannot rewind bits you miss • going to the restroom or snack bar, you miss out on the movie • chatty patrons are annoying	**Control** • can rewind, pause, and so on • easy to take restroom breaks and snack runs to the refrigerator • can talk during the movie or stop movie to chat
Movie quality • big screen; sharp sound	**Movie quality** • smaller screen size; poorer sound

From the chart you can see that the relevant features of the two subjects are comfort, cost, control, and movie quality.

Write a Thesis Statement

State Your Case You must state a thesis, or main idea, in the introduction of your comparison-contrast essay to let your readers know what to expect as they read. Your thesis statement should identify the subjects of your essay and alert your readers to the approach you will use—whether you will discuss mostly similarities, mostly differences, or both similarities and differences. For an example, look at the following thesis statement.

TIP When writing your essay, you may have to adjust your thesis a little to represent your essay's final focus better and to capture your readers' interest.

When deciding between watching a video at home or watching a movie in a theater, most people base their choices on differences in comfort, cost, control and quality.

CRITICAL THINKING

Synthesizing Information to Form a Thesis

Synthesizing information is a critical thinking skill that involves putting together parts into a unified whole. For example, you are synthesizing information when you draw conclusions about the similarities and differences between two subjects you have chosen as the subjects of a comparison-contrast essay. The conclusion you reach is your thesis.

THINKING IT THROUGH **Synthesizing Information**

Use the following steps to synthesize information and create a thesis statement about the subjects of your essay. The responses are based on the subjects baseball and cricket.

STEP 1 List the relevant features of each subject. The relevant features for baseball and cricket are equipment, game play, and playing field.

STEP 2 List details for each relevant feature. Then, determine which details are similarities and which are differences between the two subjects. Game play is different for baseball and cricket in that there are more innings played in baseball, but a baseball game is shorter. The playing field in baseball has four bases that make up a diamond-shaped running path, while the field in cricket is called the pitch and has two wickets that stand at each end. Lastly, only the wicketkeepers use gloves in cricket, and a cricket bat is flat-edged.

STEP 3 Write a sentence that states whether there are more similarities, more differences, or a balance of both, for your subjects. When it comes to the equipment, the playing field, and actual game play, there is little that would make someone confuse cricket with baseball.

PRACTICE

For each pair of subjects, use the steps above to synthesize information and create a thesis statement for a comparison-contrast essay.

1. News in newspapers; news on TV
2. Shopping in a mall; shopping online
3. Driving to school or work; taking the bus
4. Live music; recorded music (CDs, cassettes)
5. Video games; board games

Arrange Your Supporting Details

KEY CONCEPT

Get It Together! To support the main idea expressed in your thesis statement, **you can arrange the information you have gathered in one of two ways: the block method or the point-by-point method.**

Use the **block method** when you want to discuss all of the points about each subject separately. The block method presents all of the information about the first subject in a block of one or more paragraphs and then presents all of the information about the second subject in a block of paragraphs. Consider this method if you plan on discussing only a few features. The following diagram shows how the relevant features and supporting details on page 70 could be arranged according to the block method.

ORGANIZATION DIAGRAM

Block Method

Subject 1: Viewing videos at home

Feature 1: Comfort—choice of seating; no one blocks your view

Feature 2: Cost—a few dollars for tape rental; low-cost snacks

Feature 3: Control—can pause and rewind

Feature 4: Quality—smaller screen size; poorer sound

Subject 2: Seeing a movie in a theater

Feature 1: Comfort—seating may be limited, people may block view

Feature 2: Cost—several dollars admission per person; high prices for snacks

Feature 3: Control—no control of viewing (pause, stop, rewind)

Feature 4: Quality—big screen and sharp sound

TIP When you are organizing your ideas, you may come up with new ones. If so, include them where they seem to fit naturally.

Use the **point-by-point method** to deal with both subjects at the same time. With this method, you make a point about one subject and then follow it with a corresponding point about the second subject. Then, you continue pairing up each subject until all of the points have been made. This method is extremely helpful when comparing or contrasting subjects that are very similar or very different, because it is easier to see the similarities and differences when the points about each subject are discussed together. The diagram on the next page shows an example of the point-by-point method of organization.

ORGANIZATION DIAGRAM

Point-by-Point Method

Feature 1: Comfort

Subject 1: Video—choice of seating; no one blocks your view

Subject 2: Theater—seating may be limited; people may block view

Feature 2: Cost

Subject 1: Video—a few dollars for tape rental; low-cost snacks

Subject 2: Theater—several dollars admission per person; high prices for snacks

Feature 3: Control

Subject 1: Video—can pause and rewind

Subject 2: Theater—no control of viewing (pause, stop, rewind)

Feature 4: Quality

Subject 1: Video—smaller screen size; poorer sound

Subject 2: Theater—big screen and sharp sound

TIP In an essay that explores differences, you might begin with the one or two similarities the subjects have in common and then explore their differences. In the same way, you might explore similarities by beginning with the one or two differences between the subjects and then devoting most of your paper to exploring similarities.

YOUR TURN 4 Planning Your Comparison-Contrast Essay

Review the prewriting steps on the previous pages to be sure you have everything in place to plan your comparison-contrast essay.

- Choose two subjects that have enough differences or similarities to provide sufficient material for a comparison-contrast essay.

- Think about your purpose, your audience, and the tone of your essay.

- Gather information in order to discover the relevant features of your two subjects.

- Write a thesis statement that clearly identifies your two subjects and indicates the approach you plan to use.

- Arrange your information using either the block method or the point-by-point method.

**Writing**

Comparison-Contrast Essay

Framework	**Directions and Explanations**

Introduction
- Open with an attention getter.
- Give background information.
- Include a thesis statement.

Get Their Attention Make your readers eager to see what you have to say by starting with a "hook"—a high-interest opener that pulls readers into your essay.

Give Some Background If one or both of your subjects are unfamiliar to your readers, provide background information to help them understand the subjects.

Declare Your Thesis Include a clear thesis statement that identifies your subjects and indicates whether you will compare them, contrast them, or both.

Body
- Organize your information into multiple paragraphs using either the block method or the point-by-point method.

Inform Your Readers Present the information that supports your thesis, using either the block or point-by-point method. Use transitional words and phrases to connect and clarify ideas. Words and phrases like *also, similarly, both,* and *just as* signal a comparison. *By contrast, however, unlike,* and *on the other hand* signal a contrast.

Conclusion
- Connect your points back to your thesis.
- Leave your readers with something to remember.

Stress the Point Be sure your readers understand your main idea: Remind them how the points you have made in your body paragraphs support your thesis.

Wrap It Up Finish with an engaging fact or insight to leave your readers thinking about the points you have made about your subjects.

YOUR TURN 5 **Writing a First Draft**

Using the framework and the directions and explanations above as a guide, write the first draft of your comparison-contrast essay.

A Writer's Model

The following essay, which is a final draft, closely follows the framework on the previous page, using the point-by-point method to contrast watching movies in a theater with watching videos at home.

Movie? Video? What Is the Difference?

You and a couple of friends are trying to decide what to do on a Friday night. One friend asks, "Want to go to the movies?" The other chimes in with, "A movie? No way! How about a video?" As they argue back and forth you may be tempted to say, "Movie, video—who cares? What difference is there anyway?" When you stop to think about it, though, you will realize that there are very real differences in comfort, cost, control, and quality between watching movies and watching videos.

Comfort is one way that watching a video at home and watching a movie in a local theater differ. At home, you can stretch out on the sofa, curl up in a recliner, or even sprawl out on the floor as you watch. Also, when you enjoy a video at home, you can relax and talk with your friends. In a theater, you are confined to one seat—often behind someone who is so tall that you cannot see. If you happen to whisper a comment to a friend, you are likely to get a glare or a disgusted "Sh!" from someone else in the audience.

Another obvious difference between the two ways of watching a film relates to cost. You can rent a video to play at home for just a few dollars—no matter how many people watch it. Furthermore, you can buy inexpensive grocery-store snacks to enjoy with the video. Admission for a movie in a theater, on the other hand, can cost twice as much as a video rental—and that is the price for just one person. If the high prices for popcorn, drinks, and other snacks are added, the cost can really mount up.

An additional point to consider is control. Thanks to the VCR's versatility, viewers can stop a video if they need to leave the room, and then hit PLAY when they return—and not miss a single line of dialogue. If your attention is lagging or you are just too tired to finish a video, you can stop the tape and finish watching it the next day. At a theater, if a person

(continued)

INTRODUCTION
Attention getter

Thesis statement
(focus on differences)

BODY
Relevant feature 1:
Comfort

Videos

Theater

Relevant feature 2:
Cost

Videos

Theater

Relevant feature 3:
Control

Videos

Theater

(continued)

tries heading out to the concession stand for another bag of popcorn, he or she will be sure to miss the most dramatic part of the movie—with no way to rewind it and see what was missed. Since you have to pay the full admission price every time you see a movie at a theater, you will probably choose to sit through the entire movie in spite of lagging attention or tiredness.

When just the differences in comfort, cost, and control are considered, watching videos at home seems like the clear choice. So what, if anything, is better about watching a movie in a theater? That question can be answered in a single word: *quality*. A movie seen on a TV screen does not compare to the rich color and clarity of a movie seen on a big screen in a theater. Some may argue that home theater quality is getting better with large digital televisions, surround sound, and digital sound and video technology. Still, theater technology keeps improving on already excellent sound and projection quality, promising to continue surpassing home theater systems. For some people, the difference in quality far outweighs any other considerations.

When you think about comfort, cost, control, and quality, it is easy to see how friends could disagree about whether watching a movie at home or in a theater is better. Maybe one is not better than the other. Clearly, they both have their advantages. It is true—videos are cheaper and controllable, but would you want to see the latest action-packed movie on a TV set or on the big screen?

Relevant feature 4: Quality

Videos

Theater

CONCLUSION: Connection of support to thesis

MADE-FOR-TV MOVIE

In the following excerpt, Adam Caputo of Leesville Road High School in Raleigh, North Carolina, examines similarities and differences between characters in two of literature's most famous works.

Higher than Society

A massive gap of more than two millennia separates Creon of Sophocles' <u>Antigone</u> (442 B.C.) and Torvald Helmer of Henrik Ibsen's <u>A Doll's House</u> (A.D. 1879). Nevertheless, these characters share common hardship and suffering as they confront the omnipresent conflict between higher laws and the laws of society.

Both Creon and Torvald stubbornly view the human-created laws of society as the supreme law—superior to the higher laws of morality, conscience, and respect of the divine. Torvald displays this by forcing his wife Nora to be subordinate to him. He establishes his superiority by naming Nora with such words as <u>little,</u> <u>squirrel,</u> and <u>foolish.</u> These derogatory comments illustrate that Torvald feels he is superior to Nora, and that women should be subservient to their husbands—a common idea at the time. By controlling Nora like a child, Torvald follows society's law that women are inferior to men while breaking the higher law of equality for all. Similarly, King Creon supports his society's law when he punishes his niece Antigone. When Creon puts in place a law that anyone who buries Antigone's dead brother Polyneices (a traitor) would be stoned to death, Antigone, respecting the higher law of respect for the dead, defies Creon's edict. To establish that his law is supreme, Creon punishes Antigone with death. Through their actions, Creon and Torvald show parallel traits of stubbornness and disrespect for higher causes by overruling laws that are the keystones of life. These personality traits lead them further into conflict between higher laws and the laws of society.

Eventually, Torvald and Creon face peak moments of conflict between higher laws and the law of society. . . .

Thesis statement

Relevant feature 1

Relevant feature 2

Revising

Evaluate and Revise Your Draft

Check It Out Look at your draft to see which parts are working well and which parts you might change to make your writing even better. Read your entire essay at least twice. First, focus on content and organization; then, evaluate and revise sentence style.

➤ **First Reading: Content and Organization** Use the chart below to evaluate and revise your essay. Answer the questions in the left-hand column; then, use the tips to find possible places for revision. Finally, use the techniques in the right-hand column to guide you in revising your work.

Comparison-Contrast Essay: Content and Organization Guidelines for Peer and Self-Evaluation

Evaluation Questions	▶ Tips	▶ Revision Techniques
❶ Does the introduction grab your attention?	**Underline** the parts of the introduction designed to get readers interested. If you find none, revise.	**Add to** the introduction by including an interesting scenario, fact, or question about your subjects.
❷ Does the thesis statement clearly identify the subjects and the main idea of the essay?	**Circle** the subjects being discussed. **Highlight** the thesis statement. If the subjects and main idea are not clearly stated, revise.	**Add** a thesis that identifies the two subjects being discussed and tells whether the essay focuses on similarities, differences, or both.
❸ Does the essay fully develop relevant features of both subjects, and are there transitional words and phrases between the features?	**Put an A** next to points about the first subject. **Put a B** next to points about the second subject. If similar points are not made about both subjects, or if points are not clearly connected, revise.	**Add** points about one subject that correspond to those made about the other subject. **Elaborate** on points about a subject. **Add** transitional words or phrases between ideas.
❹ Is the body organized by the block method or by the point-by-point method?	**Look at each A and B you marked.** All the As should be in one part and all the Bs in another (block); or, each A should be followed by a B (point-by-point). If the organization does not follow either of these patterns, revise.	**Reorder** the ideas into either a block or point-by-point pattern.
❺ Is the conclusion effective?	**Double underline** the parts of the conclusion that restate or support the thesis. If you underline nothing, revise.	**Add** a restatement of your thesis, and **add** a statement that summarizes the information in your essay.

ONE WRITER'S REVISIONS The example below shows how one writer used the content and organization guidelines to revise part of the comparison-contrast essay on page 75. Look at the revisions carefully, and answer the questions that follow.

Another,
~~An~~obvious difference between the two ways of watching a   replace

film relates to cost. You can rent a video to play at home for just

a few dollars—no matter how many people watch it.

Furthermore,
∧Admission for a movie in a theater, on the other hand, can cost   add

twice as much as a video rental—and that is the price for just

one person. If the high prices for popcorn, drinks, and other

snacks are added, the cost can really mount up. You can buy   reorder

inexpensive grocery-store snacks to enjoy with the video.

Analyzing the Revision Process

1. How did changing the first word of this paragraph more effectively connect the paragraph to the one before it?
2. How did reordering the sentences enhance the writer's presentation of ideas?

YOUR TURN 6 Focusing on Content and Organization

Use the guidelines on the previous page and the sample revisions above to revise the content and organization of your essay.

PEER REVIEW

Ask someone in your class to read your essay and respond to the following questions:

1. How did the essay's organization make it easy (or difficult) to follow the writer's points?
2. Did you want more information about one of the subjects? If so, what did you want to know?

Second Reading: Style Now that you have revised your essay for content and organization, read it a second time and examine your sentence style. Look carefully at the adverbs you have used. Adverbs are an easy way to add emphasis to your points about similarities and differences—so easy, in fact, that many adverbs tend to be overused and worn-out. Use the style guidelines on the next page to help you eliminate overused adverbs. If you need more help, see the Focus on Word Choice on page 80.

Evaluation Question	▶ Tip	▶ Revision Technique
▶ Are worn-out adverbs used in the essay?	▶ **Highlight** worn-out adverbs, such as *very, really, awfully, rather, extremely,* and *somewhat.*	▶ **Replace** the overused adverbs with more precise words, or **delete** the adverbs.

Word Choice

| COMPUTER TIP

Do not use the grammar checker in your word-processing program as a substitute for stylistic editing. Grammar checkers can be helpful, but they cannot recognize many common style problems.

Avoiding Worn-out Adverbs

When you are drafting a comparison-contrast essay, it is natural to use adverbs because you are explaining the degree to which two subjects are alike or different. However, worn-out adverbs like *very, really,* and *somewhat* are imprecise. Eliminate imprecise adverbs by replacing them, and often the words they modify, with more precise words. For example, a more precise word for *very large* is *enormous.* Other times, the worn-out adverb is completely unnecessary in the sentence, in which case you can just delete it. In the phrase *extremely enormous,* for example, *extremely* is unnecessary because *enormous* itself is an extreme word.

ONE WRITER'S REVISIONS Here is how the writer of the essay on page 75 used the guidelines above to eliminate overused adverbs.

BEFORE REVISION

In a theater, you are confined to one seat— very often behind someone who is so extremely tall that you cannot see. If you happen to whisper a comment to a friend, you are really likely to get an awfully dirty look or a disgusted "Sh!" from someone else in the audience.

Overused adverbs are highlighted.

AFTER REVISION

delete
delete
delete, replace

In a theater, you are confined to one seat—often behind someone who is so tall that you cannot see. If you happen to whisper a comment to a friend, you are likely to get a glare or a disgusted "Sh!" from someone else in the audience.

Analyzing the Revision Process

1. Why did the writer delete the words "very" and "extremely"?
2. How does replacing "awfully dirty look" with "glare" improve the paragraph?
3. How is "likely" better than "really likely"?

 7 **Focusing on Style**

Use the style guidelines on the previous page to eliminate or replace overused adverbs in your essay. Use the sample revisions as a model.

Designing Your Writing

Subheads   Long essays that are not broken up into clearly labeled sections can sometimes be overwhelming for readers. Writers often make such essays more readable by introducing **subheads** into them. Subheads are words or short phrases that identify the topics of sections of a paper. They stand alone on the line above the section they identify.

Subheads benefit both the reader and the writer. Readers can focus better on a single paragraph or group of paragraphs, and they can easily move to the parts of the essay that they want to read. For the writer, subheads provide a succinct transition from one section to the next.

You might find it useful to add subheads to your comparison-contrast essay. If you use them, they should be flush with the left margin. For a point-by-point organization, you could label each paragraph with a subhead that names the main point you will discuss in that paragraph. With the block method, you could still use subheads, but you might use fewer—one for each subject. Here is how the writer of the Writer's Model might have used a subhead to identify the topic of a paragraph.

Cost

Another obvious difference between the two ways of watching a film relates to cost. You can rent a video to play at home for just a few dollars—no matter how many people watch it. Furthermore, you can buy inexpensive grocery-store snacks to enjoy with the video.

Publishing

Proofread Your Essay

Reference Note

For more information and practice on **comparative and superlative forms,** see page 623.

Double-Check Yourself Be sure your essay is free of grammar, spelling, and punctuation errors. Check for proper use of comparative and superlative forms of modifiers (adjectives and adverbs) because they are frequently used in comparison-contrast writing.

Grammar Link

Using Comparative and Superlative Forms

When you compare or contrast two subjects, you will often rely on **adjectives and adverbs** to make comparisons. These modifiers change form to show different degrees of comparison: **positive, comparative,** and **superlative.**

■ Most one-syllable modifiers form the comparative degree by adding *–er* and the superlative degree by adding *–est.*

  big   bigger   biggest

■ The same is true for most two-syllable modifiers, but they may also form the comparative degree by using *more* and the superlative degree by using *most.*

  quickly   more quickly   most quickly

■ Modifiers that have three or more syllables always use *more* and *most.*

  dramatic   more dramatic   most dramatic

■ The comparative and superlative forms of some modifiers are irregular.

  good   better   best

Use the **comparative degree** when comparing *two* items; use the **superlative degree** when comparing *more than two* items.

Comparative	Ala likes biology better than chemistry.
Superlative	Of all her classes, she likes math best.

Avoid double comparisons. A **double comparison** is one that uses both *–er* and *more* (or *less*) or *–est* and *most* (or *least*).

Incorrect	more louder, least brightest
Correct	louder, least bright

PRACTICE

Read each sentence below. Correct any incorrect modifiers. If the sentence is correct, write **C.** Write your answers on your own paper.

1. Juan thinks that writing with a computer is easier than writing with pencil and paper.
2. Of the two movies, this one is clearly the best.
3. Books are more better than movies because they make you imagine.
4. Newspapers give more in-depth information than television news shows.
5. Playing computer games for hours is badder than watching television all evening.

Publish Your Essay

Tell the World Here is a list of ideas for publishing your comparison-contrast essay.

- If your essay is about two subjects that are appropriate for a particular section of your school newspaper (sports, entertainment, and so on), try to get your paper published in the newspaper.

- If your essay is about two subjects that might interest other students (two movies or two CDs, for instance), post your paper where everyone in the class can read it. You might also make copies of your paper to pass out to class members.

- If you can find a Web site that deals with one or both of the subjects of your essay—and that publishes outside material—submit your essay to the site for publication.

TIP Remember to create a title for your essay. The title should give your readers a clue to your thesis. If you need help thinking of a title, look for the most memorable phrase in your essay.

PORTFOLIO

Reflect on Your Essay

Looking Back Think about and jot down answers to the following questions. Your answers will increase your awareness of what you have learned in this workshop.

- How easy or hard was it to identify the relevant features that supported your thesis? What might you try next time to refine your process?

- What new things did you learn about the subjects you compared or contrasted?

- What do you think is the most important revision you made to your writing? Why?

    If you put your essay in your portfolio, be sure to include your responses to the above questions.

YOUR TURN 8 Proofreading, Publishing, and Reflecting

Review each of the sections on this page and on the previous page. Before you hand in your comparison-contrast essay, be sure you have

- proofread your writing carefully
- considered how to publish your work
- answered the reflecting questions above

Connections to Life

Distinguishing the Purposes of Media Forms

Media Purposes Every day, you are surrounded by messages from various **media forms,** such as radio, television, newspapers, magazines, compact discs, and the Internet. Just as you have a purpose when you write, each media message you see or hear is created by someone with a purpose in mind. Using comparison-and-contrast techniques can help you analyze those messages and understand the purposes behind them as an important part of being an informed, active media consumer.

Media Genres In order to analyze media purposes, you must understand media *genres*. **Genres** are categories into which media products can be classified. For example, genres of television shows include news broadcasts, game shows, soap operas, and talk shows. Each genre generally has one primary purpose that it has been created to fulfill. The following chart describes four common purposes of media messages and gives examples of some media genres that fulfill these purposes.

MEDIA PURPOSES		
Purpose	**Explanation**	**Genres**
to inform	These messages primarily provide information.	• TV and radio news programs • news articles in newspapers • educational Web sites • magazine articles
to entertain	These messages use drama, comedy, or other means to engage an audience.	• movies • TV dramas and sitcoms (situation comedies) • comic books • novels
to advertise	These messages attempt to persuade an audience to buy something or take some sort of action.	• TV and radio commercials • banner advertisements on Web pages • billboards • movie previews
to teach	These messages show an audience how to do something, or they explain concepts or subjects of study.	• "how-to" TV shows and videos, such as those that teach how to cook or repair a car • textbooks, educational journals, magazines, and newspapers

Mixed Purposes Although we usually associate a media genre with one **primary purpose,** most genres also have at least one **secondary purpose.** For example, a TV commercial's primary purpose may be to advertise a product, but it may also try to entertain in order to keep the viewer's interest. A "how-to" video might teach how to repair a car's brakes and also give information on different kinds of brakes and how they work.

Sometimes it is hard to determine the primary purpose of a media genre because it may have a disguised purpose. Consider, for instance, the **infomercial.** Infomercials are advertisements (commercials) disguised as informational programs. Although they do always give a great deal of information about the product they advertise, infomercials are created with a single goal: to sell a product.

Another media genre with mixed or disguised purposes is the **infotainment program.** These programs can be highly informative and highly entertaining at the same time. An example of an infotainment program is a children's TV show that teaches science in a way that is entertaining and appealing to children.

A third media genre, the **docudrama,** presents factual or historical information in a dramatic format. The reenacted life story of a famous person, for instance, would be classified as a docudrama. Like the children's science show, docudramas are meant to be both informative and entertaining.

It's That Important The fact that most media genres have mixed purposes can make identifying a particular message's purpose difficult. However, identifying media purposes is a vital part of analyzing media. Knowing why a message was created helps you understand a message's intended effect on you, and it will allow you to evaluate whether the message accomplishes its purpose. In addition, a knowledge of mixed purposes can help you create your own highly effective media messages.

YOUR TURN 9 Distinguishing Media Purposes

Select three different types of media messages. For example, you might choose a billboard, a radio talk show, and an Internet Web site. For each message, identify the media form used to deliver the message, the message's genre, and the purposes you believe the message is meant to fulfill. To identify purposes, ask yourself

- what the message's creators hope to gain
- what action the creators want you to take
- why the creators chose this media form for their message

From those purposes, identify the message's primary purpose and one or more secondary purposes. Be prepared to discuss your findings with the rest of your class and to explain your conclusions.

Comparing and Contrasting Media Coverage

WHAT'S AHEAD?

In this section, you will compare and contrast media messages. You will also learn to

■ analyze how news stories are put together

■ compare and contrast different media coverage of the same event

A sk two friends to tell you what happened in geometry class when you were absent, and chances are you will hear two different **accounts,** or retellings, of what happened. "We talked about how to calculate the area of a circle and then reviewed yesterday's homework," one friend tells you. "First, Ms. Garcia passed back yesterday's homework for a class review," another says. Although your friends start with the same basic facts, they construct different accounts by focusing on different details. The truth is people rarely retell events in exactly the same way.

Looking at the News

How They Put It Together   Just as people rarely retell events in the same way, media sources often give differing accounts of a news event. This is because all news stories—on TV, on the radio, in magazines, in newspapers, and on the Internet—are *constructions* of events. Just as your friends decide which details to include when they retell a story, news writers and editors make **editorial decisions** about how news stories are put together. It is important to be aware of these editorial decisions because, whether intentional or not, the news you see, read, or hear may present only one side of the story and may carry personal or political bias.

Perception or Reality?   The editorial decisions writers and editors make shape your view of events. Compare your reactions to the following headlines describing the same event:

Files Missing from Government Office

FBI Officials Say Top-Secret Files Lost

Did you react more strongly to one of the headlines? Did the headlines cause you to picture the same event differently? The second headline was probably more attention getting. It mentions the FBI, an important government agency, and labels the missing files as "top-secret." The first headline is less specific and, therefore, less interesting.

By comparing how different media sources present the same story, you can see the types of editorial decisions media professionals make to affect your perception of events. Two aspects of news stories that vary depending on editorial decisions are **attention getters**—how words, images, and sounds are arranged to get an audience's attention—and **point of view**—the writer's angle, or viewpoint, on the subject. When you view or read a news story, be aware of how the writers or producers handle both aspects.

Attention Getters   Media sources compete for your attention. To get you to pay more attention to *its own* media messages, each media source uses its own unique blend of three common **attention-getting techniques:**

- **Controversy—focusing on an issue that stirs opposing views in readers or viewers.** (For example, a source might use a quotation or a sound bite from someone blaming damages on some person or group.)

- **Suspense—designing the narrative to create curiosity in viewers or readers about the outcome of an event.** (For example, a news article or TV news report might begin with, "Yesterday this family had a home. Today, they're living with nearby relatives.")

- **Juxtaposition—placing opposing images or words near each other to create tension.** (For example, a media source might show "before" and "after" photos or video of a town devastated by a tornado.)

Media professionals make key editorial decisions about how to arrange words, sounds, and images for the greatest impact. Depending on the form of the message, news stories usually include one or more of the following **attention-getting elements** to draw you in. Watch for these elements, and use them to make predictions about the content of news stories.

- **Headlines** are brief summaries printed in larger type at the top of a newspaper, magazine, or Internet news article. Some TV news programs begin with summary descriptions of the top stories.

- **Startling images** include shocking photographs (newspapers, magazines, or Internet) or video images (television or Internet) of an event.

- **Teasers** are promotional messages for news stories that will appear in an upcoming broadcast, often including startling images (see above) and brief, often alarming, statements designed to entice you into watching an

TIP   Keep in mind these other aspects of news stories also determined by editorial decisions:

- **Complexity**—the level of detail given about the subject, including background information and details from multiple sources

- **Sequence of information**—the order in which the story is presented

- **Emotional impact**—the story's appeal to its audience's feelings rather than reason

upcoming news broadscast. Newspapers, magazines, and Internet news sites occasionally include teasers about articles in future editions.

Point of View: Not Just the Facts   Most of us assume that news stories are objective accounts that contain only the facts about an event. Honest media professionals try to avoid distorting the facts with personal interpretations and subjective statements. However, they must also make choices about what angle—or **point of view**—to use in a news story. By identifying the point of view that a news report is taking, you can keep your mind open to, and possibly search for, alternative points of view. When you examine more than one point of view, you are better able to make your own informed decisions about the news being presented. To explore a media source's point of view, answer the following questions about a news story.

- **What terms are used to describe the main subject? Are these terms positive or negative?** For example, a politician might be described in one article as a rabble-rouser but as a statesman in another article.

- **How is the main subject shown in visual images?** Is the photograph or video of the subject flattering, or is it unfavorable? How is the subject dressed? What is in the background? Is the lighting bright or dark?

- **What kinds of sources are used in the story?** Does the story include statements only from people on one side of the issue?

YOUR TURN 10 Comparing and Contrasting Media Coverage of an Event

Find a news story that was covered in at least two different news media—newspapers, magazines, TV, or the Internet. Choose two of the news sources, and find examples of attention-getting techniques and elements in each one. Identify the point of view in each story. Then, compare and contrast each media source's coverage of the event by writing answers to the following questions. Be prepared to share your answers with the class.

- How did the attention-getting techniques in each story shape your impression of the event? How would your view of the event be different if your knowledge of it came from only one of these stories?

- Did the stories have similar points of view, or did they differ? Give evidence to support your answer.

- Do you think one media source did a better job of covering the event? Why do you think so?

2 *Choices*

Choose one of the following activities to complete.

▶ **CAREERS**

1. Chart Your Future Like most students your age, you are probably facing decisions about what you will do when you graduate from high school. Perhaps you are comparing schools to attend or jobs to pursue. To help you make your decisions, use what you know about comparison and contrast. Make a chart like the Relevant Features chart you created in the prewriting section of the Writing Workshop (page 70). In it, list all of the relevant features of the subjects (careers, for example, or different colleges) you are comparing. Then, write a **paragraph** that synthesizes the information in the chart.

▶ **LITERATURE**

2. Movie *vs.* Book Think of a movie you have seen that is based on a book. Select a scene from the movie, and read or re-read the corresponding portion of the book. Then, create a **chart** or other graphic that shows the similarities and differences between the movie version and the book. Post your chart or graphic in your classroom or somewhere else at your school.

▶ **SPEAKING AND LISTENING**

3. People Are Talking Imagine that you are a news reporter, perhaps for your school newspaper. Think of an event that happened in your community or school recently, making sure that it is an event you did not witness. Ask two friends separately to tell you their accounts of the event. With your friends' permission, create a two-column list to compare and contrast their accounts and viewpoints. Then, integrate your two friends' stories into your own retelling of the event. Make a **tape-recording** of your story.

▶ **CROSSING THE CURRICULUM: SCIENCE**

4. Concentrate on Comparisons Many chemical compounds that look similar are actually very different. For instance, it might be difficult to tell the difference between an unlabeled bottle of ammonia and an unlabeled bottle of water just by looking at them. Choose two chemical compounds that look very similar, and write a short **explanation** of how to tell them apart.

PORTFOLIO

CHAPTER

3

Examining Causes and Effects

Reading Workshop

Reading a Cause-and-Effect Article

Writing Workshop

Writing a Cause-and-Effect Explanation

Viewing and Representing

Analyzing the Effects of TV

Curiosity is a basic human characteristic. From the time you began to talk, "Why?" was probably one of your favorite questions: "Why does it get dark?" or "Why do I have blue eyes while my friend has brown eyes?" As you grew older you probably began to ask "What-if" questions. For example, you might have wondered "What if I become a lawyer?" "What if I take Spanish class instead of French?" or "What if my parents really *are* space aliens?"

When you began to ask yourself these questions, you started to develop the skill of examining **cause-and-effect relationships**—a process also known as **causal analysis.** Curiosity about causes and effects accounts for much of the human knowledge in the world. People have searched for the causes of diseases, tidal currents, blue skies, and rainbows. People have also wondered about the effects of sailing west to India, earthquakes, and pet ownership.

Informational Text

Exposition

YOUR TURN 1 Considering Causes and Effects

To gain a better understanding of the importance of causes and effects in the world around you, write down at least five inventions that are part of the world in which you live. With a classmate, make a list of the possible **causes** that drove each inventor to come up with the idea for each invention. Think about how the world has changed because of these inventions. Then, write down a few of the positive and a few of the negative **effects** of these inventions.

internet**connect**

go. hrw .com

GO TO: go.hrw.com
KEYWORD: EOLang 10-3

Reading a Cause-and-Effect Article

WHAT'S AHEAD?

In this section, you will read a newspaper article and learn how to

■ infer causes and effects

■ analyze cause-and-effect patterns

"**F**ire! Fire!" someone yells. What do you do? You move fast because you know that fires can be dangerous and destructive. You have seen, in newspapers and on television, dramatic images of raging fires destroying buildings or forests. Keep in mind, however, that although news stories typically focus on the negative effects of fire, fires can also have positive effects. The article on the next page, "Yellowstone Makes a Triumphant Return Ten Years After Fires," describes the positive effects that the massive forest fires of 1988 had on Yellowstone National Park.

Preparing to Read

READING SKILL

Inferring Causes and Effects   Often when you read, you recognize a cause-and-effect relationship because the writer directly states that relationship. At other times, the relationships are less obvious, and you have to make an **inference**—an educated guess based on your own knowledge and experience—about the causes or the effects. The article on the next page deals with several cause-and-effect relationships. The writer directly states some; others are not as obvious.

READING FOCUS

Cause-and-Effect Structure   Writers organize their explanations of cause-and-effect relationships by focusing on **causes,** on **effects,** or on **causal chains.** (Causal chains begin with the first cause and follow with a series of intermediate actions or events to the final effect.) For example, an essay focusing on causes identifies and explains several causes of one effect. An essay focusing on effects identifies and explains several effects resulting from one cause. An essay focusing on a casual chain identifies and explains multiple causes and effects. As you read the following article, see if you can tell whether the author focuses on causes, on effects, or on a causal chain.

The following article from the *Austin American-Statesman* describes the effects that the immense forest fires of 1988 had on the wild lands of Yellowstone National Park. As you read, jot down answers to the numbered active-reading questions.

Yellowstone Makes a Triumphant Return Ten Years After Fires

BY BRUCE BABBITT

What a difference a decade makes. Ten years ago this month, Yellowstone National Park was a sea of flames. Some of the largest wildfires in U.S. history swept restlessly across the park's magnificent terrain, incinerating forests, threatening historic buildings. The news media and politicians fanned the flames even higher. Yellowstone, they said, was devastated.

Night after night, horrific images of ash and flame flashed across America's TV screens. One evening, after showing an enormous expanse of blackened forest, network news anchor Tom Brokaw solemnly concluded: "This is what's left of Yellowstone tonight."

But guess what? Fire didn't destroy Yellowstone. Ten years later, we realize fire had the opposite effect. Fire rejuvenated Yellowstone. Elk and other wildlife are healthy. Tourism is thriving. Biodiversity is booming. New forests are rising from the ashes of old ones. The recovery is so dramatic it deserves a closer look.

First, a bit of background: The 1988 fires were gigantic. They swept over roughly 793,000 of Yellowstone's 2.2 million acres—one third of the park. Some were lightning-caused; others were of human origin. The $120 million firefighting effort amassed against them has been called the largest in U.S. history. The heroic work saved many key structures. But in the wild lands, it made almost no difference. What put Yellowstone's fires out was not retardant-dropping planes or armies of firefighters on the ground. It was a quarter inch of autumn rain.

In July and August, as fires raged across the park, business owners fumed. Our future is ruined, they said. Tourism is dead. But today, tourism is very much alive. Yellowstone has set numerous visitation records since 1988. Fire has not repelled tourists; it has attracted them—just as it attracts many species of wildlife. Ten years later, the number one question asked of Yellowstone naturalists remains "What are the effects of the fires?"

The answer is simple: The fires were therapeutic. Since 1988, some seventy scientific research projects have looked

1. As the fires raged, what long-term consequences did people expect?

2. What caused the fires?

at various aspects of the Yellowstone fires. Not one has concluded the fires were harmful. That sounds too good to be true. But it is. The science is there to prove it.

Come to Yellowstone this summer and see for yourself. Pull off the road near Ice Lake, east of the Norris Geyser Basin. Here the fire burned especially savagely. Hundreds of thousands, perhaps millions, of mature lodgepole pine trees were destroyed. But today, the forest floor is a sea of green—knee-high lodgepoles planted, literally, by the fires of 1988.

Yellowstone's lodgepole forest is a place of mystery. In order to live, it must first die. It must burn. The fire that swept through here worked an ancient magic: It scorched lodgepole cones, melted their sticky resin, and freed the seeds locked inside. Within minutes, a new forest was planted.

By suppressing wildfire, as Smokey Bear has taught us to do, we interrupt nature's cycles. We rob our western forests of something they need desperately. We steal their season of rebirth. Without fire, pine forests grow senile, prone to disease, and unnaturally thick. There are lessons in these lodgepoles. Too much protection is no virtue. We can harm what we try to save. I'm not suggesting that we worship fire—that we let it run wild outside of natural parks and wilderness areas. But we can respect its wisdom. We can treat it, when possible, as an ally, not an enemy, and use it more frequently under controlled conditions to protect communities and make forests healthier.

Look closely around Ice Lake and you will almost surely see something else: wildlife. Bison, elk, mule deer, white-tailed deer, bighorn sheep, and mountain goats have all prospered since 1988. Just as fire rejuvenated lodgepoles, so, too, did it revitalize plants that grazing animals eat. Walt Disney got it wrong: Bambi and his forest friends have nothing to fear—and much to gain—from fire.

If you're lucky, you may also see Yellowstone's king of beasts: the grizzly bear. To a grizzly, wildfire is a meal ticket. Fires kill trees, which fall to the ground and fill up with insects: grizzly sushi. Others enjoy the feast, too. Before 1988, three-toed woodpeckers were almost nonexistent in Yellowstone. After 1988, one ornithologist spotted thirty in one day. But dead lodgepoles are more than lunch counters; they are housing opportunities, home sites for mountain bluebirds, tree swallows, and other "cavity-nesting" birds and mammals.

Ten years ago, the news media said fire "blackened" Yellowstone. Today, we know the reverse is true. Fire has painted the park brighter, added color and texture to its ecosystem, and increased the diversity and abundance of its species. As Yellowstone scientist John Varley put it recently, "The biodiversity story over the past ten years has been fascinating. Biodiversity has gone through a revolution at Yellowstone."

3. What is one effect of the Yellowstone fires?

4. What conclusion does the writer draw about forest fires?

5. What animals benefit from fallen trees?

Inferring Causes and Effects

READING SKILL

Making a Connection When you read that one action or event is the result of another action or event, you are reading about a cause-and-effect relationship. A **cause** makes something happen; an **effect** is what happens as a result of that cause. The link between cause and effect can sometimes be very obvious; at other times you may be required to make an educated guess about the connection.

When writers want to make cause-and-effect relationships very obvious for the reader, they do so with clue words that signal the cause-and-effect relationship. The Yellowstone article, for example, notes that some of the fires were "lightning-*caused*." The relationship between lightning and the fires is very clearly signaled by the word *caused*. A few more words and phrases that can signal cause-and-effect relationships are

accordingly	because	effect	in order that	since
affect	cause	for	reason	therefore
as a result	consequently	if . . . then	results in	why

TIP Be careful. Sometimes clue words and phrases have uses unrelated to cause-and-effect relationships, as in the sentences, "His **cause** is just" or "She has not visited **since** she was a baby."

At times a writer only hints at a cause-and-effect relationship. In such cases, you will have to combine details in the text with your own knowledge and experience to make an educated guess about a cause-and-effect relationship. When you make an educated guess about probable causes or probable effects, you are **inferring** the presence of a cause-and-effect relationship that the writer has **implied.** For example, in "Yellowstone Makes a

Triumphant Return Ten Years After Fires," the writer states that though some fires were caused by lightning, "others were of human origin." The writer assumes that you are familiar enough with forest fires to infer what the "human" causes might have been: campers leaving a campfire unattended or out of control, or children playing with matches, for example.

THINKING IT THROUGH   Inferring Causes and Effects

You can use the following steps to infer, or make an educated guess about, implied cause-and-effect relationships. The process is modeled for you using a sentence from the article about the Yellowstone fires.

Example:
"Without fire, pine forests grow senile, prone to disease, and unnaturally thick."

▶ **STEP 1 Ask yourself, "What happens in the passage?"** (What is the effect?) *Forests become physically deteriorated, likely to contract diseases, and denser than they would naturally.*

▶ **STEP 2 Ask, "Why does it happen?"** (What is the cause?) *The lack of fire.*

▶ **STEP 3 Rewrite the passage using an explicit cause-and-effect signal word like *cause, effect,* or *because*.** Notice that the *cause* is lack of fire; the *effect* is that the pine forests grow senile, prone to disease, and unnaturally thick. *I can infer that the lack of fires causes pine forests to grow senile, prone to disease, and unnaturally thick.*

You can also discover cause-and-effect relationships by paying careful attention to the verbs the writer uses. Certain verbs are **causative verbs**—verbs that express cause-and-effect relationships. For example, here is a sentence from the Yellowstone article: *Fire rejuvenated Yellowstone.* In this sentence, *rejuvenated* is a causative verb meaning "to make seem new or fresh again." The cause-and-effect relationship is built into the verb *rejuvenated*. Fire is the cause; making Yellowstone seem new or fresh again is the effect of fire. If you are unsure whether a verb is a causative verb, look it up in a dictionary to see whether the verb describes an effect one thing has on another. Here are some other common causative verbs:

contract	destroy	expand	make
create	dissolve	inflate	produce
darken	energize	lighten	sharpen

Identifying Implied Causes and Effects

Using the steps in Thinking It Through, identify the cause-and-effect relationships in the following passages from the reading selection. It may not be necessary to go through every step for every passage.

1. But today, the forest floor is a sea of green—knee-high lodgepoles planted, literally, by the fires of 1988.

2. What put Yellowstone's fires out was not retardant-dropping planes or armies of firefighters on the ground. It was a quarter inch of autumn rain.

3. Fire has not repelled tourists; it has attracted them—just as it attracts many species of wildlife.

4. Before 1988, three-toed woodpeckers were almost nonexistent in Yellowstone. After 1988, one ornithologist spotted thirty in one day.

5. Just as fire rejuvenated lodgepoles, so, too, did it revitalize plants that grazing animals eat.

Cause-and-Effect Structure

READING FOCUS

I'm Beginning to Sense a Pattern . . . Newton's third law of motion says that for every action there is an equal and opposite reaction. The "butterfly" effect, an example of the chaos theory of physics, states that the movement of a butterfly wing somewhere in China can cause a chain reaction of events that affects the weather in California weeks later. With all the actions and "equal and opposite" reactions going on in the world, how can anyone keep up with them? How can you, as a reader, make sense of it all?

Here is one way: try to determine the writer's **organizational pattern.** For causal analysis, writers generally start with one of three patterns:

- **patterns that emphasize causes**

- **patterns that emphasize effects**

- **patterns that trace a causal chain**

From these simple organizational patterns, writers often develop more complex patterns to describe more complex cause-and-effect relationships. These **composite patterns** show a mixture of two or more of the simple patterns. By identifying the organizational pattern a writer uses, you will be better able to understand and follow the cause-and-effect relationships the writer explains.

Pattern 1: **Focus on Causes** Some pieces of writing focus on explaining what has caused a certain event to happen. Writers usually begin these pieces by presenting a clearly observed effect; then, they proceed to analyze the causes that have led to the effect. Sometimes these causes are obvious and easily explained. At other times, a writer will present only *possible* causes, because no one is certain of the exact reasons for the effect.

If a piece you are reading focuses on causes, you are likely to find an effect presented in the introductory paragraph as part of the thesis statement. Then, the body paragraphs will explain the causes of the effect.

The following diagram illustrates an example of a "focus on causes" organizational pattern. One cause, drought conditions, is inferred.

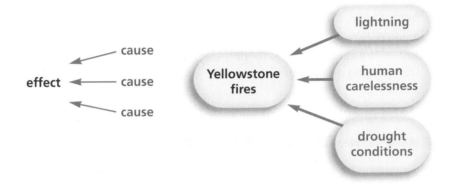

Pattern 2: **Focus on Effects** Sometimes a writer describes a cause and analyzes its effects. If the writer is discussing a recent situation, with effects not yet observed, the writer may speculate about *possible* effects.

In a piece that focuses on effects, you will likely find the cause presented as part of the thesis statement. The effects that result from the cause will be the topics of the piece's body paragraphs. Much of the Yellowstone article's focus was on the effects of the fire. The following illustration shows the pattern in which some of the effects are presented in the article.

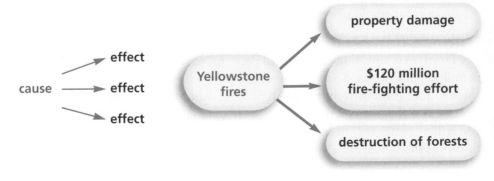

It is important for you as a reader to pay close attention to whether the writer of an article has pointed out both long-term and short-term causes and effects. **Short-term effects** are usually the most immediately identifiable, but **long-term effects** are often the most important. For example, as the article on the Yellowstone fires points out, most people recognized only the short-term destruction caused by the fires. Some saw a once beautiful Yellowstone National Park devastated by fire. Others saw an end to businesses that thrived on tourism. However, the long-term *positive* effects of rejuvenation turned out to be more important (and more surprising), although several years passed before they became obvious. The diagram below illustrates both the long- and short-term effects.

Pattern 3: **Causal Chain**   A causal chain is like a row of toppling dominoes—one event causing another, repeated until a final effect is reached. The event that begins a causal chain—known as the **initial cause**—is followed by an effect that becomes the cause of another effect. This process is repeated until the **final effect**—the effect that ends the chain—is reached. Each **intermediate** (in-between) **cause** or **effect** is like a link in a chain. Though one link may not be as important or as strong as the other links, they are all necessary to the chain. If just one of these intermediate causes were absent, the final effect would not be reached.

Typically, you will find an initial cause stated in the thesis of an article. Within the body of the article, you will then read explanations of each link in the chain of events through the final effect. In the Yellowstone article, you probably noticed that the writer discussed a few causal chains. This diagram shows part of a causal chain from that article.

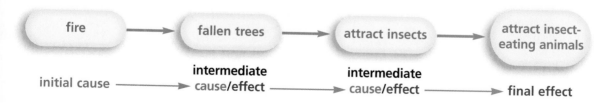

> **Pattern 4: The Composite Pattern**   When you read a causal analysis, you may not always find a single organizational pattern that covers all the information given. A situation or process may be too complicated to be effectively described using a simple pattern. The following diagram illustrates a composite cause-and-effect pattern that explains the relationship between causes and effects in a volcanic eruption.

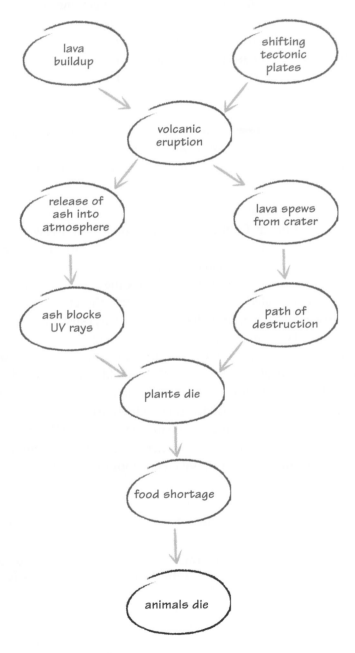

Analyzing Cause-and-Effect Structure

To analyze the complex cause-and-effect relationships in "Yellowstone Makes a Triumphant Return," redraw and fill in the causal-chain diagram below. Draw a red circle around the initial cause, green circles around the intermediate causes, and a blue circle around the final effect. Identify at least one long-term and one short-term effect.

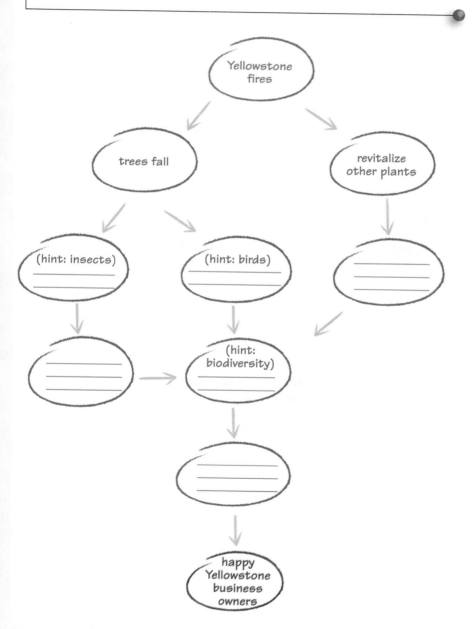

Suffixes

When you read complicated cause-and-effect explanations like Bruce Babbitt's article on the Yellowstone fires of 1988, you might run into some unfamiliar words. One way to prepare yourself to identify the meanings of unfamiliar words is to learn some basic suffixes. A **suffix,** a word part of one or more syllables, is added to the end of a word to alter its meaning or to change its part of speech. The suffixes in the chart at right often act as indicators of changes, causes, or effects.

Suffix	Meaning	Example
–ate	become, cause	activate
–ation	the result of _____ing	summation
–en	cause to be, become	cheapen
–fic	making, causing	horrific
–ic	caused by	acidic; choleric
–ize	make, cause to be	terrorize

THINKING IT THROUGH   **Using Suffixes**

Use these steps to figure out the meanings of many words with suffixes.

▶ **STEP 1 Write the word down, but put a long dash between the root and the suffix.** Suppose you needed to figure out the meaning of the word *compilation.* compil—ation

▶ **STEP 2 Write down a known word that has the same suffix.** relaxation

▶ **STEP 3 Write down everything you know about the known word and about the suffix.** Relaxation means taking a break, or relaxing. Based on the meaning of the suffix –ation, it means "the result of relaxing."

▶ **STEP 4 Now, use what you know to make an inference—an educated guess—about the definition of the unfamiliar word.** If relaxation is the result of relaxing, then compilation must be the result of compiling. For example, when a music group puts out a compilation disc, it must be the result of compiling, or gathering together, all their best songs.

Be careful, though; many suffixes have multiple meanings. For example, –ic can also mean "like," as in the word *angelic.*

PRACTICE

Using the steps in Thinking It Through, above, write definitions for the words at right. Then, look up the words in a dictionary to check the accuracy of your definitions.

1. horrific
2. revitalize
3. rejuvenate
4. terrific
5. blacken

Inferring Causes and Effects

Reading tests often measure your ability to infer, or make an educated guess about, causes or effects not directly stated in a reading passage. Because inference reading passages will not include clue words or phrases such as *because* or *as a result*, you must figure out the cause-and-effect relationship within them yourself.

Here is a typical reading passage and test question:

Damage by pollution to ecosystems can be slow but sure. Acid rain, for instance, changes the quality of the water in ponds and streams. When frogs and toads lay eggs in acidic water, fewer of their offspring reach maturity. When there are fewer frogs and toads, the insect population explodes. The insects, in turn, feed on plants and crops, which may prompt farmers and gardeners to use more pesticides. These pesticides can eventually get washed by rain into waterways, where they might create further problems.

1. From this paragraph, what can you infer about the effects of frogs and toads on their ecosystems?

   A. American factories are the largest cause of acid rain.

   B. Frogs and toads help to keep insect populations down.

   C. Fish, which eat tadpoles, suffer when frog and toad populations decline.

   D. Frogs and toads eat plants and crops.

THINKING IT THROUGH   **Inferring Causes and Effects**

Use the following steps to answer cause-and-effect inference test questions like the sample question above.

▶ **STEP 1 Skim the passage once for a general understanding; then re-read it carefully.** Keep in mind that most of these questions are designed to measure your reading comprehension, not your reading speed.

▶ **STEP 2 Locate key words and phrases in the sample answers that match similar words and phrases in the reading passage.** Answers **A** and **C** share few key words with the reading passage. The reading passage does not mention *factories* or *fish*. Answers **B** and **D** contain key words which are in the reading passage.

▶ **STEP 3 Apply your knowledge to the remaining answers.** The passage states that *insects* (not frogs and toads) eat plants and crops, so **D** is wrong. Your knowledge that frogs and toads eat large numbers of insects confirms that **B** is correct.

Writing a Cause-and-Effect Explanation

WHAT'S AHEAD?

In this workshop, you will write a cause-and-effect essay. You will also learn to

■ narrow your topic effectively

■ write a thesis statement

■ recognize oversimplification and false cause and effect

■ use infinitives to vary sentence beginnings

■ correct dangling modifiers

Imagine that you and your friends are on the way to play basketball at a local park when you see a bulldozer tearing up the court. You have been playing there for years, and now, without any notice, it is being destroyed. You decide to send letters to the newspaper and the city council to express your concern. However, before you put pen to paper, you will want to consider two questions: *What caused this event to happen?* and *What will the effects of this event be?*

These are typical questions to ask yourself when you are preparing a **cause-and-effect explanation,** or a **causal analysis,** such as the one you will write in this Writing Workshop. By following the steps in this workshop, you will learn how to examine both the causes and effects of an event or situation and how to create an effective, well-supported essay on any cause-and-effect topic that you choose.

Prewriting

Choose a Situation or Event

Pulling Order from Chaos The world around you is an immensely complex cause-and-effect system—an almost infinite number of actions and reactions are constantly taking place. With so many cause-and-effect topics to choose from, focusing in on one good topic for a cause-and-effect essay can be difficult. Here are a few good ways to narrow the list.

■ **Create an If-Then Log.** Look at the world around you and jot down if-then situations or events. Ask yourself, "**If** (a certain event or situation) occurred, **then** what effects would it cause?" Some areas where you might search for events and situations are local and professional sports, grades, and driving. For example, **if** your school's star quarterback were injured, **then** what effect would it have on the rest of the team?

- **Investigate news sources,** including radio and TV programs or newspaper and magazine articles. Look for thought-provoking stories about important political events or recent scientific discoveries. Ask yourself "Why did that happen?" or "What will happen because of this?"

- **Write about what you know.** Use your personal experiences or collaborate with other writers and use their experiences as a source of cause-and-effect topics. For example, you may know firsthand the causes of soil erosion or the effects of exercise on appetite.

Make a list of promising topics. Then, review the list and choose the one topic you find most interesting.

Narrow Your Topic

Sharpen the Focus   Once you have found an interesting topic, you must decide whether it is too general or too specific to cover in the amount of space you have for your essay. For example, if you chose to write on the effects of the invention of the personal computer, you could easily have a book-length project on your hands—a short paper would not do justice to the topic. However, if you narrowed the topic to the effects that the personal computer has had on writing school essays, you might be able to cover the subject adequately.

In a short paper, plan to discuss only the most important or most immediate causes or effects associated with your topic. Trying to cover too many causes or effects or trying to discuss a chain of causes and events with too many links would be overwhelming for you and your readers.

TIP   Cause and effect may also be used as an **elaboration technique in a persuasive essay.** For example, if you were writing to persuade the school board to devote more of its budget to school music programs, you might stress the positive effects of music education.

Consider Purpose, Audience, and Tone

Who Wants to Know?   The main **purpose** of your essay is to explain clearly a causal relationship to your **audience,** or readers. You will be giving your readers information that you think will be useful or interesting to them. Knowing your audience can help you decide what information to include in your essay. If your readers are already familiar with your cause-and-effect topic, how will you maintain their interest? Do you have new information that they do not know? If your readers are unfamiliar with your topic, how much background detail will you need to give them so that your explanation makes sense? Will you need to explain technical terms? Often it is best to think of a broad audience composed of some readers who are familiar with your topic and some readers who are unfamiliar with it. Provide enough background information for readers to understand your topic, but not so much that you will bore readers who are already familiar with it.

Knowing your audience will also help you determine what tone you should use in your writing. **Tone** is the reflection of your attitude toward your subject and your audience. Your tone can be happy, angry, serious, lighthearted, disgusted, or any other feeling. **You express tone in writing through your style—your choice of words, details, and sentence structure.** You might be tempted to write your causal analysis in a serious, conservative tone—but you do not have to. You should adjust your tone to your subject and your audience. For example, if you are writing a humorous essay for your class or a club to which you belong, your tone can be informal and breezy. If you are writing to the school board requesting that new courses be added to the curriculum, your tone should be formal and respectful.

KEY CONCEPT

A word closely associated with tone is **voice.** Your speaking voice is recognizable to people who know you; similarly, your writing **style** should reflect your uniqueness. Even though a causal analysis may be on a serious topic, this does not mean that your language has to be stuffy and overly formal. You are much more likely to impress people by sounding natural than you are by using unnecessarily big words or complex sentence structures. Still, you should avoid being too informal or colloquial—don't use slang or other words that might put off your audience.

Write Your Thesis

Focus the Vision   A **thesis statement** is a precise statement of the main idea of your essay as a whole. Creating a thesis statement is like focusing a camera lens to get the clearest possible view of a photographic subject. **To write a thesis statement for a causal analysis, take all of your thoughts and ideas about your topic and focus them into one clear main idea**—stating whether you are focusing on causes, on effects, on causes and effects, or on a chain of causes and effects. Remember that your thesis statement can change. You might discover a better approach to your topic as you develop your paper. Refining your thesis is part of the writing process. Begin by using the following Thinking It Through steps to determine the focus of your essay.

KEY CONCEPT

Focusing on Causes or Effects

Use the following steps to form a thesis statement for your essay. Model student responses are based on an essay written about the causes and effects of falling asleep in class.

▶ **STEP 1** Write your topic on a piece of paper. Fold the paper in half lengthwise. On one half of the paper, write the question *Why did (or does) it happen?,* and then, under the question, list the probable cause or causes associated with your topic.

▶ **STEP 2** On the other half of the paper, write the question *What are the results?* Then, list all the effects associated with your topic.

TOPIC: FALLING ASLEEP IN CLASS

Why does it happen? (causes)	What are the results? (effects)
after-school jobs	disrupts class
extracurricular activities	miss important class information
physical problems	detention
lack of sleep	embarrassing
	grounded by parents

▶ **STEP 3** Compare the number of items on each side of the page. Did you end up listing more causes or more effects? Which seem more significant—the causes you listed, or the effects—or do they seem equally significant? Based on your responses, decide whether to write about causes, effects, or both. There are nearly the same number of significant causes and effects. My essay will focus on both.

▶ **STEP 4** Write a thesis statement that clearly indicates the approach you will take in your essay: a cause-centered approach, an effects-centered approach, or an approach that involves discussing both causes *and* effects. A thesis can be written as a formula:

thesis = topic + your focus on causes, effects, or both

Example:

topic   causes
Teenagers fall asleep in class for many reasons, and as a

                        effects
consequence, suffer many negative results.

CRITICAL THINKING

Oversimplification and False Cause and Effect

You must think critically about causal relationships—how causes and effects are connected. For example, in looking at a friend's wilted houseplant you might assume that the owner had neglected the plant. However, a critical investigation might reveal that the owner in fact overwatered the plant in an effort to take care of it. By making a thorough investigation of causes and effects, you can avoid two common fallacies, or errors in thinking, in cause-and-effect explanations: **oversimplifying** and **false cause and effect.**

■ **Oversimplifying:** Most events have more than one cause. When you identify a single major cause but ignore all other causes, you are oversimplifying. Clues to oversimplification are words such as *only, never,* and *always* or phrases such as *the cause is* or *the effect is.* To remedy many oversimplification problems, you can limit, or qualify, your cause-and-effect statement with such phrases as *an*

important factor, the three major effects, or *one of the main reasons.*

Oversimplification: Human overpopulation is responsible for the decline in the African cheetah population.

Revised: Human overpopulation is *one of many contributing factors* in the decline in the African cheetah population.

■ **False Cause and Effect:** This error in thinking is made when you incorrectly assume that just because one event follows another in time, the first event caused the second.

False Cause and Effect: Every time I attend a school soccer game, the team wins. The team must win because I am there.

Revised: *Although I'd like to think that* I cause our school soccer team to win whenever I attend a game, *there are other causes for* the wins.

PRACTICE

Identify each of the following statements as an oversimplification, a false cause-and-effect statement, or a valid cause-and-effect statement. Be prepared to explain your answers.

1. Our parrot squawks whenever my sister's boyfriend comes in the room. It must not like him.

2. Stress causes sleeplessness.

3. Many people with perfect eyesight begin to experience some vision problems as they age.

4. Practicing a sport every day will guarantee you a position on a pro team.

5. Taxation without representation was the cause of the American Revolution.

6. An apple a day keeps the doctor away.

7. Freezing rain caused the cancellation of the football game.

8. Carolyn's improved energy probably comes from her new habits: regular exercise and proper eating.

9. If I forget my umbrella today, it will rain.

10. Hearing loss is caused by listening to too much loud music.

Gather and Organize Support

Find and Assemble Your Essentials   To make your essay convincing, you will need to include details that support your points. These supporting details come from **facts, statistics, real-life examples,** and **expert opinions.** Where do you find this support?

- To locate facts and statistics, look at **reference materials** such as encyclopedias, newspapers, magazines, and Web pages and newsgroups.

- **Some details may even come from personal experiences** or the experiences of those you know. Depending on your topic, you might also interview friends, neighbors, or relatives for real-life examples.

- **Interviewing people who are knowledgeable about your topic** is often very helpful. Appropriate people to interview for expert opinions may include professors, government officials, or law officers.

A Balancing Act   A well-supported cause-and-effect essay relies on a variety of supporting details. How well you organize these supporting details determines the effectiveness of your explanation. Well-balanced and well-organized support presented in a **coherent, logical progression** makes your essay easier to write and easier for your audience to read.

Your causal analysis may involve a clear causal chain—beginning with the first cause and following a series of intermediate actions or events to the final effect. For explanations of causal chains, you should consider arranging your information in **chronological order,** beginning your explanation with the initial cause and working through subsequent events to end your explanation with the final effect. If your focus is primarily on causes or on effects rather than on a causal chain, consider arranging your information in **order of importance**—moving from the least important to the most important factor, or vice versa.

> **TIP**   Reverse chronological order starts with an effect or series of effects and then traces them back to the original cause.

YOUR TURN 4   Preparing to Write

Review each of these prewriting steps before you begin your essay.

- Choose a cause-and-effect situation to write about and narrow it down to a manageable topic.

- Remember your purpose for writing this essay. Keep your audience in mind and write with an appropriate voice and tone.

- Write a clear thesis statement.

- Gather and organize your supporting evidence.

Cause-and-Effect Essay

Framework	Directions and Explanations

Introduction

- Get your readers interested.
- Provide background information.
- Include a clear thesis.

Listen Up   Like the opening scene of a movie, your introduction should hook your audience and make them want to see what comes next. Surprise your readers: Make a bold statement. Present an interesting statistic, fact, or example. Surprise them with what they don't know.

The Background   Give information to set the stage for your cause-and-effect explanations. Show your readers why your explanation is important and worth reading.

Announce the Main Event   Clarify your purpose for your readers by providing them with a well-focused thesis statement at the end of your introduction.

Body

- Present the causes and/or effects of your topic in a clear sequence.
- Support the causes and/or effects with adequate detail.

Telling the Tale   If your essay involves an analysis of a **causal chain,** consider using **chronological order.** Otherwise, use **order of importance.** Whatever order you choose, be sure there is a logical progression of ideas. Make sure that you back up each of your cause-and-effect statements with supporting details such as statistics, facts, examples, and expert opinions.

Conclusion

- Remind your readers of your thesis and bring your essay to a close.

The Curtain Call   Summarize your essay's main points completely but concisely. Consider ending with a question, prediction, or thought-provoking statement.

YOUR TURN 5   Writing a First Draft

Write the first draft of your cause-and-effect essay, using the framework above and the Writer's Model on the next page as guides.

A Writer's Model

The following short essay, which is a final draft, closely follows the framework on the previous page. As you read the essay, notice how the highlighted words—cause-effect clue words— help communicate the writer's explanation of the causes and effects of sleeping in class.

School Daze

In the middle of presenting a lesson to the class, your teacher unexpectedly stops speaking. Everyone in the class becomes expectantly silent—nothing is heard except a faint sound from somewhere in the back of the room, a noise that sounds like . . . snoring? Suddenly, with a loud *thwack!*, your teacher claps a book shut, and the snoring culprit is jarred from his sleep, lifting his head from his desk with a startled, bleary-eyed look on his face. Read old comic strips or watch really old TV shows, and you will see a similar scene. There is a history of schooltime dozing. You would think times have changed. Unfortunately, though, falling asleep in class is actually an all-too-common occurrence among today's active teenagers—one which has both complex causes and serious consequences.

Why do students sometimes fall asleep in class? An obvious reason is lack of sleep. However, there are also causes for getting too little sleep. Homework is a daily occurrence for most students, one that can take three to four hours per night. A teenager who wants to be able to participate in any activity besides homework must frequently stay up late in order to fit everything in. Club activities, sports, computer-game playing, and TV viewing, for example, all contribute to teens having less time for both homework and sleep. Sometimes teens lack sleep because of after-school jobs that are taken on to earn extra money for college, family expenses, or simply for clothes and recreation. For students with jobs, losing sleep is often preferable to quitting their jobs or even cutting back on their hours.

Physical problems are another factor that can cause students to fall asleep in class. For example, insomnia—the inability to sleep—may keep a student up at night, causing exhaustion during class hours. Insomnia, which may be triggered by stress and

INTRODUCTION
Interesting opener

Background information

Thesis

BODY
Cause 1
Support for cause 1

Facts

Cause 2
Support for cause 2

(continued)

(continued)

anxiety, is a serious problem that may require medical attention. Medical evidence also supports the idea that each person has an internal clock that helps to determine his or her individual sleep pattern. Unfortunately, these internal clocks are not always synchronized with school class schedules.

Effects

The effects of falling asleep in class can be quite serious. First of all, sleeping in class is not a good way to endear your-self to teachers, who are not likely to tolerate it for very long. (It is extremely embarrassing to awaken from a blissful nap to find your teacher standing next to your desk, glowering at you.) In addition, napping students run the risk of becoming the target of jokes and disparaging comments—not to mention the occasional paper wad—leveled by classmates. However, the most detrimental effect of sleeping in class is missing out on important instruction and suffering the consequences. In the long run, chronic sleepers may end up serving a great deal of detention time and, in serious cases, failing classes. These students might also wind up being grounded by their parents for long periods of time.

Causal chain: fall asleep in class→miss instruction→fail classes→get grounded

CONCLUSION Restatement of thesis

Prediction

To stay more alert in class, teens should think about these effects and do something to deal with the causes. Since teens are probably not going to address the problem, falling asleep in class will probably remain an all-too-common occurrence. It will likely continue until more teens find a way to balance their personal and social lives with school and work, while still finding enough time for those precious *z*'s.

HI & LOIS reprinted with special permission of King Features Syndicate, Inc.

A Student's Model

The following excerpt from a cause-and-effect essay is by student writer Gwen Miller of Fairmont Junior High School in Boise, Idaho. Her parenthetical citations refer to the sources she used as support for her essay.

TV Baby Sitters: Help or Hindrance?

The TV blaring disrupts the peace of the apartment complex. A child's eyes are glued to the character dancing on the screen. He has been sitting there for hours. The child's father sits exhausted, not sure what to do when the children's shows are replaced with the evening news. His built-in baby sitter is about to quit its job, so he makes the decision to buy a video machine. However, is feeding his child a diet of nothing but TV really good for his child? Along with the many reasons parents leave their children to be baby-sat by the TV, there are also many negative effects of this electronic caregiver.

TV is the only way many parents know to keep their children entertained. They are not aware of the many dangerous sides of television. For example, according to the Center for Media Education, children who watch an abundance of TV have a greater chance of obesity and increased alcohol and drug use (Jones 22). The Center also states that the American Medical Association, the American Psychological Association, and others believe that viewing TV violence can have lifelong harmful effects on children's health (Jones 33). A 1999 policy statement from the American Academy of Pediatrics suggests parents avoid all television for children under two. The statement says, "While certain television programs may be promoted to this age group, research on early brain development shows that babies and toddlers have a critical need for direct interactions with parents and other significant caregivers for healthy brain growth and the development of appropriate social, emotional, and cognitive skills" (26). Instead of turning on the TV for entertainment, parents can do other fun activities with their children. . . .

INTRODUCTION
Interesting opening

Hypothetical scenario to set the stage

Thesis statement

BODY
Major support for thesis statement

Expert testimony as support

More expert testimony as support

Alternatives to negative effects

Revising

Evaluate and Revise Your Draft

Take Two   There are two key areas to consider when you set out to evaluate and revise your paper: the first is content and organization; the second is style. Work collaboratively with a peer to review your essay once, using the content and organization guidelines on this page, and then review it a second time, using the style guidelines on page 115.

➤ **First Reading: Content and Organization**   What have you done especially well in your draft? Where might you make improvements? Use the following chart to find out. Ask yourself the questions in the left-hand column of the chart. The tips in the middle column will help you answer the questions. If you identify a problem in your paper, use the revision technique suggested in the right-hand column to fix it.

Cause-and-Effect Essay: Content and Organization Guidelines for Peer and Self-Evaluation

Evaluation Questions	▶ Tips	▶ Revision Techniques
❶ Will the introductory paragraph make a reader want to keep reading?	▶ **Highlight** attention-getting phrases or sentences. If there are none, revise.	▶ **Add** an anecdote, fact, question, or example that will get readers interested in your topic.
❷ Does the introduction contain a clear thesis statement?	▶ **Underline** the cause-and-effect thesis statement. If there is not one, or if it is not very clear, revise.	▶ **Add** a sentence that clearly states the essay's main idea and focus.
❸ Are the cause-and-effect statements adequately developed?	▶ **Draw arrows** between each cause or effect and the sentences used as support for each one. If there are not at least two arrows pointing to sentences supporting each cause and effect, revise.	▶ **Elaborate** on cause-and-effect statements by supporting them with facts, statistics, examples, and expert opinions.
❹ Does the paper present information in an organized format?	▶ **Number** the causes and effects in your paper. If the numbers do not seem to reflect an ordering strategy such as order of importance or chronological order, revise.	▶ **Rearrange** your causes and effects. Consider using order of importance or chronological order.
❺ Does the essay have a reasonable and logical conclusion?	▶ **Double underline** the sentence in the conclusion that restates the thesis of your essay. If you cannot find one, revise.	▶ **Add** a sentence that restates the focus of your essay.

ONE WRITER'S REVISIONS Here is how one writer used the content and organization guidelines to revise some sentences from the cause-and-effect essay on page 111. Study the revisions and answer the questions that follow.

> In the long run, chronic sleepers ~~might~~ *These students might also* wind up being
>
> grounded by their parents for long periods of time ~~and these~~
>
> ~~students~~ may ~~also~~ end up serving a great deal of detention time *and, in serious cases, failing classes.*

reorder

elaborate

Analyzing the Revision Process

1. Why did the writer add "failing classes" to her list of effects?
2. Why did the writer switch the order of effects? In your opinion, is this order better? Why or why not?

YOUR TURN 6   Focusing on Content and Organization

Revise your essay using the content and organization guidelines on page 114. Use the example revisions shown above as a model.

Second Reading: Style   In your first reading, you focused on content and organization. In the second reading, you will look at how you *express* your ideas—your style. Unless you revise for style, you may develop habits that make your writing monotonous. For example, when writing your causal analysis, you might start many of your sentences with "The cause is . . ." or "The effect is . . ." To avoid such repetitive sentence structure, you might try to vary some of your sentence beginnings by using **infinitives** and **infinitive phrases**.

PEER REVIEW

Ask a classmate to read your essay and to answer the following questions:

1. Does the thesis statement prepare you for the rest of the paper?
2. What is the most significant cause or effect in the paper? Why do you think so?

COMPUTER TIP

Most word-processing programs have an Undo command. The Undo command lets you revert to material that you prefer to your revision.

Style Guidelines

Evaluation Question	Tip	Revision Technique
Do many of the sentences begin the same way? Are some structures overused?	▶ **Put parentheses around** the first six words of each sentence. Revise half of the sentences that have both a subject and a verb in the first six words.	▶ **Reword** sentences to begin with infinitives or infinitive phrases.

Focus on Sentences

Reference Note

For more information and practice on **infinitives** and **infinitive phrases,** see page 479.

Using Infinitives and Infinitive Phrases as Openers

Good writers, like good chefs, know that making their work appealing requires excellent presentation. One way to clarify *why* an action is performed is to use an infinitive or infinitive phrase. To vary sentence beginnings, use an infinitive or infinitive phrase as the opener of the sentence. Look at the following examples.

He had the car's engine checked **to ensure a safe trip**. [*To ensure a safe trip* is the infinitive phrase that tells *why*.]

To ensure a safe trip, he had the car's engine checked. [The infinitive phrase opens the sentence, but still tells *why*.]

ONE WRITER'S REVISIONS Here is how the writer of the model cause-and-effect essay on page 111 used the guidelines on page 115 to revise some sentence beginnings.

BEFORE REVISION

(Teens should think about these effects) and do something

to deal with the causes to stay more alert in class. (Falling

asleep in class will probably remain) an all-too-common

occurrence, since teens are probably not going to address

the problem. (It will likely continue until more) teens find

a way to balance their personal and social lives . . .

The subject and the verb appear within the first several words of these sentences.

reword

AFTER REVISION

To stay more alert in class, teens should think about these effects and do something to deal with the causes. Since teens are probably not going to address the problem, falling asleep in class will probably remain an all-too-common occurrence. It will likely continue until more teens find a way to balance their personal and social lives . . .

Analyzing the Revision Process

1. Why did the writer move the infinitive phrase to the beginning of the first sentence? Does it change the sentence's meaning?

2. Why did the writer not revise the final sentence?

 Focusing on Style

Revise your essay using the style guidelines on page 115. Use the example revision shown on page 116 as a model.

Designing Your Writing

Flowcharts and Diagrams   Two types of visuals commonly used in causal analysis are *flowcharts* and *diagrams*. A **flowchart** illustrates a series of causes and effects, using geometric shapes (such as squares, circles, and triangles) connected by lines or arrows to indicate movement in a cause-and-effect chain. **Diagrams** use illustrations also with lines or arrows to indicate the relationship between causes and effects.

Whether you create graphics on a computer or draw them by hand, the following tips will help you make your graphics effective illustrations of your cause-and-effect essay.

- Include only graphics that are explained or reinforced by information in your text. Graphics never *replace* information from your text.

- Your graphics should read left to right, top to bottom. The initial cause should be on the far left and the end result to the farthest right.

- When you illustrate a causal chain, clearly indicate the starting or initial cause in the chain and the ending effect in the chain.

- Use dark, thick arrows to ensure that the connections between causes and effects are easy to see.

- Briefly and clearly state only essential details. Do not try to fit all the details from your essay into your graphic. Instead, use only the important details that will help your reader understand the information in your essay.

- Use consistent sizes and shapes for similar types of information.

Reference Note

For more on **flowcharts** and **diagrams,** see pages 857 and 858 of the Quick Reference Handbook.

Publishing

Proofread Your Essay

Getting It Right Before you prepare a final copy of your essay, work collaboratively with a peer to make sure that the essay is free of errors in grammar, spelling, and punctuation. As you proofread, check your essay for **dangling modifiers**—modifying words, phrases, or clauses that do not clearly and sensibly modify a word or a group of words in a sentence. Dangling modifiers confuse your reader and muddle your explanation.

Grammar Link

Dangling Modifiers

In a causal analysis, the relationships between causes and effects must be clear. This connection can be confusing if your reader cannot understand to which word each modifier refers.

When you use **verbal phrases,** be careful to avoid creating **dangling modifiers.** Be sure that the noun immediately after the verbal phrase is the one the phrase modifies. You may correct a dangling modifier by adding a word or words that the dangling phrase can sensibly modify or by adding a word or words to the dangling phrase.

Dangling **To earn extra spending money, the summer** was spent working for her father. [Did the summer earn money?]

Correct **To earn extra spending money, Sachi** spent the summer working for her father. [adds a word (*Sachi*) that the dangling phrase can sensibly modify]

Dangling **While reaching into my pocket for change,** my **car** rolled into the tollbooth. [Was the car reaching?]

Correct **While I was reaching into my pocket for change,** my car rolled into the tollbooth. [adds words (*I was*) to the dangling phrase]

Reference Note

For more information and practice on **dangling modifiers,** see page 626. For more information on **verbal phrases,** see page 472.

PRACTICE

Revise the following sentences to correct their dangling modifiers. Write your answers on your own paper.

1. While driving to school, flashing lights appeared in the road.
2. Running to catch the bus, Kara's shoestrings tripped her up.
3. Having selected a college, a trip to the campus was planned.
4. To be a good ballplayer, daily practice is extremely important.
5. When hosting a dinner party, a variety of food should be provided.

Publish Your Essay

Your Name in Lights   Try reaching an audience for your cause-and-effect essay through one of these publishing ideas.

- **Submit your local sports-related or school-related essay to your school's newspaper and to club or sports newsletters.** For example, fellow students might want to read an essay discussing how recent school board decisions will affect their daily lives.

- **If your topic relates to a historical event, try submitting your essay to a historical society newsletter.** For example, an essay on the impact of the railroad on your town's development might interest members of a local historical society.

- **Showcase your illustrated science-related cause-and-effect essay by participating in a science fair.** For example, you might explain the causes and effects of damage to the earth's ozone layer.

Reflect on Your Essay

PORTFOLIO

A Job Well Done   To think about the writing skills you gained while working on your essay and the decisions you made along the way, write responses to these questions.

- Did you have trouble finding enough causes or effects to discuss, or were there too many? Could you have broadened or narrowed your topic? Explain your answer.

- How did you choose whether to focus on causes, on effects, on both causes and effects, or on a causal chain?

- Did you find any dangling modifiers in your essay? How will you remember to check for dangling modifiers in future essays?

   If this essay will be part of a writing portfolio, be sure to include your answers to these questions along with your essay.

YOUR TURN 8   Proofreading, Publishing, and Reflecting

Before you turn in your essay, make sure to

- proofread it carefully
- consider how you might publish it
- reflect on your essay by considering the writing process you went through to create it

Connections to Life

Participating in Group Discussions

One good way to share your causal analysis with an audience is through a group discussion. A **group discussion** involves face-to-face communication among a small number of people who meet **for a specific purpose, such as to brainstorm ideas, share information, solve a problem, or arrive at a decision.** By taking part in a group discussion, you can receive feedback on your ideas—and learn about other people's ideas at the same time.

Playing a Part Effective group discussions require that each participant have a role: either leader, recorder, or participant. Each role is defined by its key responsibilities, summarized in the following chart.

Leader	• announces the discussion topic
	• keeps the discussion moving and on the topic
	• encourages each member to participate
	• manages group interaction
Recorder (secretary)	• records significant information, such as all major points of agreement and disagreement, and any decisions made
	• prepares a final report
Participant	• contributes to the discussion
	• cooperates, asks clear questions, and shares information
	• listens carefully to others
	• responds appropriately

Be aware that you may be called upon to play any of these roles in a discussion. Also, make sure that each role and its responsibilities are clear to every group member before the discussion begins.

Being Prepared All members of a group discussion should be well prepared. If there is an outline, or **agenda,** that the discussion will follow, you should look it over and be ready to ask questions or provide information on each item listed. Being prepared may involve doing some research if you do not know much about a particular item on the agenda. Allow yourself ample time to research topics before the discussion takes place.

Listening During a discussion, concentrate on what other participants are saying, instead of on what you want to say next. Make sure you **ask questions to clarify** anything that you do not understand. Take notes on what other participants have to say, and keep the following questions and ideas in mind while others are speaking.

- **What is the source of the speaker's information?** Is the source reliable? Focus your attention on the speaker's message.

- **Do the speaker's details support his or her message?** Are any facts or ideas contradictory? Interpret what the speaker is saying.

- **Does the speaker's conclusion follow logically from the details presented?** Does the speaker avoid logical errors, such as over-simplification and false cause and effect? Evaluate how well the speaker has presented the message.

Speaking Speak loudly enough to be heard and clearly enough to be understood. Be sure that your **tone of voice** is appropriate for your **audience** and the topic being discussed. For group discussions among your peers, a relaxed "be yourself" tone is usually fine. However, even in informal situations you should follow these guidelines:

- Be considerate of other participants.
- Let others finish talking before you comment on their ideas.
- Ask appropriate questions.
- If you want to disagree with the ideas of a participant, do so with courtesy and tact.
- Focus your own comments on the facts and issues of the discussion.
- Respect others' opinions.

Feedback A final factor in developing group discussion skills is **feedback**—offering others an evaluation of the strengths and weaknesses of their discussion points and accepting their evaluation of yours. You can ask the following questions after a group discussion to evaluate the success of the discussion and the participants' discussion skills. Be sure to consider the individual participants (including yourself) and the group as a whole.

- Was the group goal clearly stated at the beginning of the discussion?
- Did the group have a discussion agenda or outline? If so, was it followed?
- Was everyone prepared?
- Did each participant perform the key responsibilities of his or her role as leader, recorder, or participant?
- Did all group members participate?
- Were all participants listening actively and speaking clearly?
- Was there any conflict? Was it resolved respectfully?

YOUR TURN 9 Participating in Group Discussions

- Form a small group of five to six students to discuss the topic of one or more of the causal analysis essays you and your classmates wrote for the Writing Workshop (or another topic, if your teacher prefers).
- Before beginning the discussion, be sure to determine who will be the leader, who will be the recorder, and who will be participants.
- Decide among yourselves whether or not you will have an agenda to follow for your discussion. If you decide to have an agenda, follow it.
- Be prepared to take notes during your discussion and to write evaluations of yourself and your peers to hand in to your teacher.

Analyzing the Effects of TV

No one would deny that television is a powerful medium. Indeed, since the 1950s, television has been recognized as a very influential form of mass media. Television has had an impact on the educational, political, and economic systems of countries around the world. Television has also reshaped the patterns of family life. Some critics believe that television has weakened personal and community relationships by isolating people in their living rooms. Others believe there is a definite cause-and-effect relationship between television and practically every malady of modern society.

Television and the Real World

Mold or Mirror?   From one point of view, the reason television is such a powerful medium is that television programs are reflections of the world. According to this point of view, the psychiatrist in a sitcom and the detective in a police drama **represent,** or portray, real-life people going about the business of real life. Television, then, is seen as a mirror that reflects a true image of life in our society.

Another point of view is that television molds—at least partially—the way that people see the world around them. Many media critics argue that television shapes people's values and attitudes, especially those of children. For example, some believe that a child who regularly watches a television program in which violence is the ultimate solution to problems will accept, perhaps even use, violence as a solution to his or her own problems.

The truth is that both points of view—television as mirror and television as mold—are partially true. To some degree, **television reflects the real world,** and, to some degree, **television molds people's views of the real world.** The important question for you to ask yourself is "To what extent does television influence *my* view of the world?" To answer this question, you must become a critical viewer—an analyzer of television.

True Lies?   One way television mirrors the real world is in the number of careers and walks of life that are depicted in entertainment programming. On any given night of television programming, you might see

- a doctor performing an emergency operation
- a lawyer defending a murder suspect
- a sportscaster preparing for a broadcast
- a parent giving advice to a teenager

People of these types exist in the real world, of course—and all of the scenarios occur in the real world. The question is "How realistic and accurate are television's **representations,** or depictions, of these people and scenarios?" To find out, you must do a **comparative analysis.** For example, you might first analyze, or **deconstruct,** programs that show a particular career as it is represented on television. Then, you could find out how realistic that representation is by talking to people who actually work in that field.

Through Rose-Colored Glasses   Imagine that your favorite television series is about a nurse in a big-city hospital. You watch the hour-long series every week. In fact, you like the main character, Lucinda, so much that you watch re-runs, refuse to answer the phone during the broadcast, and dream of a career as a nurse. How would you answer someone who asked you why being a nurse is so appealing to you? The chart below lists some reasons and examples you might provide to answer such a question.

Reasons that a career as a nurse appeals to me	Examples from the TV program
Nurses are highly trained, well-paid professionals.	In one episode, Lucinda saved a patient's life because she recognized unusual symptoms in the patient. She refused to give the patient medicine that would have proved fatal. She has a fabulous apartment in the city, so she must make a lot of money.
Nurses are compassionate people who care about all of their patients and their co-workers, too.	In last week's episode, Lucinda took great care of one really rude patient. She also covered a mistake that another nurse had made.
Nurses lead very exciting, full lives.	In every episode, Lucinda has to deal with emergencies that are a matter of life and death. She has a glamorous life outside of work, too.
Nurses are respected by the people they work with and the patients they serve.	The medical staff and the patients look up to Lucinda. They all think she is great.

Reality Check   Now, suppose that you talk about your dream of a career in nursing to your best friend. Your friend responds with surprising news: Her uncle is a veteran nurse at Megalopolis Memorial Hospital. With your friend's help, you call her uncle to find out what being a nurse is *really* like.

Reasons that a career as a nurse appeals to me	What a real nurse told me
Nurses are highly trained, well-paid professionals.	Lou said that while it is true that nurses are highly trained, the pay is not as good as it should be. Nurses often have to "struggle to make ends meet, like everybody else."
Nurses are compassionate people who care about all of their patients and co-workers.	Lou said that as a rule nurses are compassionate people who want their patients to get better, but that patients and co-workers are not always easy to like.
Nurses lead very exciting, full lives.	Lou said that this is so true that he "stays at the point of exhaustion all the time." He also said that the pressures on a nurse make for a lot of "wear and tear on the nerves."
Nurses are respected by the people they work with and the patients they serve.	Lou said that most health care professionals treat nurses with respect, although some don't. Patients, he said, often are more demanding than respectful, though the appreciative patients more than make up for the unappreciative ones.

As the example shows, the difference between "TV life" and real life can be great. Therefore, a critical viewer of television should never lose sight of the fact that what he or she sees on television is just a *representation* of something that exists in real life, and that some TV *representations* of the real world are not very accurate or realistic at all.

YOUR TURN 10   Checking TV Representations of Reality

Working in groups of three or four, brainstorm a list of three prominent careers that are commonly depicted on prime-time television. Then, brainstorm a list of characteristics of each career as television represents it. Contact people who actually practice each career and ask them to comment on your list of career characteristics. Finally, create a third list of the information often omitted from TV representations of these careers. Share your group's results with the rest of the class.

Choices

Choose one of the following activities to complete.

►CAREERS

1. To Be or Not to Be
Choose a career that interests you. List three positive and three negative effects this career choice might have on your life. For example, if you decided to become a doctor, you might list "opportunity to help people" as a positive effect. Under negative effects you might list "possibly being on call at all hours." Create a **poster** for your classmates highlighting the pros and cons of this career choice.

►VIEWING AND REPRESENTING

2. A Double Take Videotape a nightly news report. As you review it, take notes on news stories that involve cause and effect. For example, you might see a news report on the effects of new medical research, or the causes of reading problems among high school students. Look carefully for examples of oversimplification or false cause and effect. Use your notes to prepare a short **oral presentation** for your class about the news story.

►CROSSING THE CURRICULUM: ARTS & SCIENCE

3. Make It Work! Rube Goldberg (1883–1970) was a cartoonist famous for dreaming up complex cause-and-effect inventions to accomplish simple tasks. With a small group of peers, draw your own **Rube Goldberg machine** to perform a simple task such as turning on a radio, feeding a pet, or emptying the garbage. Include at least five steps between start and finish. Be prepared to explain your causal chain to your classmates.

►CROSSING THE CURRICULUM: LITERATURE

4. Motivations and Consequences Writers of fiction often shape their characters and plots around cause and effect. Choose a character from a work of fiction and write a **short analysis** of the causes, or motives, of the character's behavior. What effects do his or her actions have on fellow characters or the plot? For example, in Shakespeare's *Julius Caesar*, what are the *causes* and *effects* of Brutus's betrayal of Caesar?

PORTFOLIO

4 Analyzing Problems

Reading Workshop

Reading a Problem-Analysis Article

Writing Workshop

Writing a Problem-Analysis Essay

Speaking and Listening

Giving an Informative Speech

Viewing and Representing

Recognizing News Genres

Analyzing Problems

- There are traffic jams every afternoon at a traffic light near your school.

- Your dog keeps discovering new ways to get out of the yard, costing you time and aggravation in trying to find him.

- Your grades are falling. Between your part-time job and extracurricular activities, you have less and less time for homework.

> **Informational Text**
>
> Exposition

A good way to deal with problems like these is to analyze the **factors** (conditions or situations) that help cause them. By **analyzing** (looking at all the parts that contribute to the whole) you can better understand what causes a problem and maybe how to solve it. Problem analysis helps to create an awareness of problems and, through awareness, to motivate others to find solutions. News media, community meetings, and governmental assemblies are only a few of the many public forums where people exchange ideas and seek ways to make the world a better place.

YOUR TURN 1 Analyzing Problems

With a partner, brainstorm a list of problems that affect not just you personally, but others as well. Make a two-column chart. In the first column, list three or four problems, and in the second column, list some of the factors that you think cause or contribute to each problem. Next, discuss the problems with your partner. Be prepared to share your chart and discussion notes with your class.

GO TO: go.hrw.com
KEYWORD: EOLang 10-4

Reading a Problem-Analysis Article

WHAT'S AHEAD?

In this section, you will read a problem-analysis article and learn how to

- **make and evaluate generalizations**
- **analyze problem-solution structure**

Have you ever been told, "Be careful what you wish for. You just might get it"? Often, when people make wishes, they fail to anticipate the consequences that their wishes might have. For example, we wish for technological advances to make our lives easier, but we fail to foresee some of the problems these advances can cause. The following article, "Danger Beneath the Dash," examines an unintended problem created by cellular phone use and discusses some of the factors that contribute to the problem.

Preparing to Read

READING SKILL

Making Generalizations   You make a **generalization** whenever you combine information in a text with what you already know to make a statement or judgment that applies to the world in general. For example, if you read an article stating that late out-of-town games leave your school's volleyball team ill-prepared for the next school day, you might make the generalization that athletes in other sports may be similarly affected. From the specific case of the volleyball team, you generalize about *all* school athletes.

READING FOCUS

Problem-Solution Structure   When you read about problems, pay special attention to the way the writer has organized the information. You will find that although the following elements are present, writers arrange them in different ways.

- a clear statement of the problem
- evidence (facts, statistics, and anecdotes) of the problem
- discussion of contributing factors—situations that help cause the problem
- suggested ways to solve the problem

As you read the following article, notice how the writer raises your awareness of a problem and the factors that contribute to it. Jot down answers to the numbered active-reading questions as you read.

from Reader's Digest

DANGER BENEATH THE DASH

BY STEVEN LEVINGSTON

Sharon Fultz, 38, had her mind on the future as she drove her car south on Morgan Ross Road in Morgan Township, Ohio. It was July 1, 1997, and she was chatting on her hand-held phone with her fiancé, Christopher Congdon, about their wedding plans. Apparently engrossed in her conversation, she sailed through a stop sign. Congdon heard his fiancée cry out . . . as a truck broad-sided her car at about 50 miles an hour.

The car's fuel tank ruptured, and flames engulfed the car and the truck's front end. The truck driver, who couldn't avoid the collision, escaped and tried to rescue Fultz, but the flames pushed him back. Sharon Fultz, who was to be married later in the month, died at the scene.

This tragic accident is a searing reminder of a growing danger: distracting electronic gadgetry in our cars. It's no surprise that we love cellular phones, which now are used by more than 62 million Americans. We're a society on the run, and to save time, we conduct business, chat with friends, make our arrangements—all from the car.

Experts warn, however, that cell phones and other devices in a car can drive us straight to disaster if we're not careful. In a study published in 1997, University of Toronto researchers Donald Redelmeier and Robert Tibshirani analyzed data from Toronto drivers with cell phones who were involved in crashes. Their shocking conclusion: Drivers talking on a cell phone were *four* times as likely to have an accident as those not on the phone. That's similar to the risk of driving with a blood-alcohol level at the legal limit.

"Nothing's quite as wonderful as

1. Why do you think the article begins with a real-life example instead of first stating the problem?

2. Why do so many people use cell phones?

3. What specific details raise your awareness of the dangers of cell phone use?

a cell phone if you have a traffic problem," says Stephanie Faul, communications director for the AAA Foundation for Traffic Safety. "But there's no question they contribute to crashes."

To remain safe, experts suggest applying these new rules of the road:

Don't dial and drive

Just the mechanics of dialing or answering the phone can prove dangerous. A twenty-six-year-old tow-truck driver was heading to work in his truck on a Sunday morning in June 1997, according to police. After he entered Cedar Lake, Indiana, he drove along U.S. 41 toward 133rd Avenue. Realizing he was late, he picked up his cell phone and looked down to punch in his work number, police said.

In front of him, Richard and Barbara Francis were heading to church when the light turned red at 133rd Avenue. Richard glanced in his rearview mirror and spotted the truck bearing down on him.

"Barb, we're going to get hit," he yelled after realizing he couldn't get out of the way. The truck plowed into the car's rear, devouring the entire back end, according to police. Barbara, cut and bruised, had to be extricated from the wreck. (Charges of speeding against the driver were later dismissed.)

> **4. What possible solution does the subhead above suggest?**

The Insurance Institute for Highway Safety says the safest way to make calls from your car is just before or after your trip. Others suggest using your cell phone while stopped at a traffic light, or asking a passenger to field the call.

Some experts say that cautiously pulling over to the side of the road and finding a place to park before making a call is a safe way to use your cell phone. This may seem inconvenient, but "when your conversation is over," says James Solomon of the National Safety Council, "you can focus on driving again."

Don't think dialing is the only problem

Initially experts believed that the problems with car phones lay mostly with its mechanical use—dialing, holding the phone, putting it back—and that hands-free speakerphones might offer an advantage. But a bigger problem is the mental distraction caused by talking on the phone.

> **5. What evidence of mental distractions is given in the next three paragraphs?**

"I've been run off the road by people on a car phone," says Alvin Yamaguchi, a motorcycle officer with the California Highway Patrol. "When you're on the phone, you're thinking about your conversation—not about the road."

Talking on a car phone is often more distracting than listening to the

A sign in Brooklyn, Ohio, where it is a misdemeanor to use a cell phone while driving unless both hands are on the steering wheel

often tend to be suppressed," he says.

Beware of more high-tech distractions

Sophisticated communication and navigation devices are now showing up in rental cars and in high-end luxury models. They help us pinpoint our location, browse the Internet, check e-mail, receive and send faxes by voice command all while seated behind the wheel.

In 1997, one automaker demonstrated a prototype car with Internet access, complete with a computer screen in the center of the dashboard. "Companies are creating these devices because people want them," says Julie Rochman of the Insurance Institute for Highway Safety. "We know that more and more will be coming on the market, and they can be very distracting. These items can be beneficial in reporting impaired drivers to law enforcement, calling for help, keeping you from getting lost. But these new technologies have to be used responsibly."

"Driving is a full-time job," concludes National Safety Council's James Solomon. "You should not be doing anything else behind the wheel."

radio or the tape deck. Moreover, it's a greater drain on our mental faculties than chatting with a passenger, experts say. A voice on a cell phone is usually not as distinct and requires more concentration to comprehend. What's more, a passenger can alert you to road dangers. The person in the car with you is aware of traffic, whereas the person not in the car isn't," says Roger Koppa of the Texas Transportation Institute.

Walter Wierville, a fellow at Virginia Tech's Center for Transportation Research, says that a driver may be looking at the road while talking on the phone, but still miss important cues. "In particular, objects in your peripheral vision

6. Does Dr. Rochman see similarities between cell phones and other electronic gadgets? Why do you think so?

| READING SKILL ➤

Making Generalizations

Beyond Specifics   A **generalization** goes way beyond a specific case to make a general statement about a whole group of cases. You make generalizations all the time—combining your **prior knowledge** (what you already know) with details from your reading, observations, and experiences to make a statement that applies to an entire classification of things or people. For instance, what statement could you make about the following sentences that would apply to all of them?

> One auto company decided to name its new pickup truck the Mountain Lion. Their new four-door sedan is called the Stallion. Another company named its new sports utility vehicle the Grizzly and its new sports car the Cheetah.

If you said, "It seems that automobile companies are basing the names of their new vehicles on animals," then you would be making a generalization. You have created a general statement based on the key words and the pattern in the passage's details—animals' names and new automobiles. As a reader, you use generalizations in two ways.

- **You identify writers' generalizations.** In "Danger Beneath the Dash," for instance, the writer provides real-world examples, facts, statistics, and quotes from experts. From all this specific information, the writer makes generalizations about *all* drivers who talk on cell phones. Determining what generalizations a writer makes helps you evaluate the accuracy of his or her writing. If a writer bases generalizations on insufficient evidence or faulty logic, then you should be skeptical about what the writer presents. When you read a problem analysis, consider also whether the writer's own opinions (bias) about the problem affect the generalizations he or she makes.

■ **You make your own generalizations** based on information in your reading to help you discover the essential meaning of a passage.

True or Not? Just because a statement sounds like a generalization doesn't make it valid, or true. "All pigs have wings" and "Every sun has nine planets" are invalid, or unsound, generalizations. To evaluate a writer's generalization and your own, use these questions:

■ **Is the generalization based on sufficient information?** Generalizations require support—a great many facts, statistics, and real-life experiences. A generalization based on only one example or a single experience is a **fallacy** (error in thinking) known as a **hasty generalization.** Beware of making your own hasty generalizations and watch out for writers who fail to support their generalizations with sufficient information.

■ **Is the generalization relevant?** Stick to the point. For instance, a generalization about the cost of cell phone service would not be relevant to the problem discussed in "Danger Beneath the Dash."

■ **Does the generalization contain qualifying words?** Words like *many, most, usually,* and *often* limit the claim a generalization makes. Since most generalizations do not apply to every single situation, these qualifying words often signal a valid generalization. Be suspicious of too-broad statements that contain words like *every, all, always,* and *never*; most generalizations have exceptions.

TIP When you are asked to make a generalization about a reading passage on a test, base your generalization *only* on the information given in the passage.

THINKING IT THROUGH   **Making Valid Generalizations**

Use the following steps to make valid generalizations based on a reading passage. The example responses are based on another article about safe cellular phone use.

▶ **STEP 1 List key details (facts, statistics, and other evidence) from the reading passage.** Each day, fifty thousand highway and neighborhood emergencies are reported with cellular phones. Dialing 911 on a cellular phone is a free call with most service providers. The use of cellular phones can reduce emergency response times in many situations.

▶ **STEP 2 Consider your own knowledge or experience that relates to what you have read.** I once had a flat tire and had to walk two miles to find a phone. A cellular phone would have been helpful then. Imagine my trouble if I had been in a serious accident. My parents once used their cellular phone to report a reckless driver to the police.

▶ **STEP 3 Combine your prior knowledge with the text information to make a generalization.** In many situations, cellular phones are helpful, possibly even life saving.

▶ **STEP 4 Evaluate your generalization. Is it valid? Is it based on sufficient information? Is it relevant?** There are two facts, a statistic, and two examples from my own life. The generalization is related to the data and observations about cell phone use. Many and possibly are words that qualify, or limit, the statement. This is a valid generalization.

YOUR TURN 2 Making Generalizations

Use the Thinking It Through steps above and information from "Danger Beneath the Dash" to evaluate the three generalizations below. Is each generalization valid, relevant, and based on sufficient evidence? Be prepared to discuss each generalization with the class.

1. Traffic safety professionals are very concerned about improper cell phone use.
2. People should never use a car phone while driving.
3. It can be dangerous for people to read a map while driving.

READING FOCUS

Problem-Solution Structure

One Step at a Time   One good way to work through an analysis of a problem is to examine how the writer organizes his or her explanation. When you look closely at the organizational structure, you may discover that it follows one of the patterns common to problem-analysis articles. Once you recognize a pattern, then you can map the organizational structure, either in writing or in your head. Knowing the pattern is like having a map of the text that helps you see and understand the writer's main points and important supporting details.

There are several ways writers organize an analysis of a problem. The focus may be either on the problem or on its possible solutions—or sometimes both. "Danger Beneath the Dash" focuses more on evidence and contributing factors and less on solutions because the solution to the problem is obvious: Don't talk on the phone while you are driving.

The chart on the next page shows the organization of "Danger Beneath the Dash." Notice how many sections of the essay focus on the problem.

Focus on the Problem	
1. State the problem.	The increasing use of cellular phones while driving is a growing problem.
2. Give evidence.	The article provides many different warnings and statistics from experts.
3. Examine contributing factors.	Drivers look away from the road to dial or pick up the phone.
4. Propose a solution.	Don't talk on a cell phone while driving.

Imagine an article that, unlike "Danger Beneath the Dash," is about a problem with a less-obvious solution: hunger in developing countries. Few people would argue that hunger in developing countries is not a problem; therefore, the article would focus more on the solution and less on the problem. By focusing on solutions, a writer draws your attention to thinking about what is most important—finding answers.

Focus on the Solution	
1. State the problem.	While industrialized countries have plenty of food, many people in developing countries do not have enough.
2. Give evidence.	Statistics show the prevalence of starvation and malnutrition in developing countries.
3. Propose and examine solutions.	Governments and charities could direct aid in the form of food supplies.
	Governments and charities could create programs to develop business and industry.
	Governments could institute reforms to eliminate blocks to distribution of food.

TIP Although problem-analysis articles primarily explain a problem, they can also have a secondary persuasive purpose. For example, "Danger Beneath the Dash" is trying to persuade drivers to stay off the phone while they are driving.

YOUR TURN 3 **Analyzing Problem-Solution Structure**

The chart at the top of the page does not list all the ideas and information in the "Danger Beneath the Dash" article. Copy the chart onto your own paper and fill it in with more evidence, contributing factors, and proposed solutions discussed in the article.

Context Clues: Definitions and Restatements

When you read problem-analysis articles, you may encounter unfamiliar words—technical terms, for example. A good way to find the meanings of these terms is to look for **definition and restatement context clues.** These are words or phrases defining an unfamiliar term or restating it. Commas or dashes that set off a definition or restatement from the rest of the sentence can signal these context clues. Words or phrases like *are, is, or, that is, also known as,* *which is to say, sometimes called,* and *meaning* can also signal a definition or restatement:

Airtime, actual time spent talking on a cell phone, often determines the billing rate for cellular phone users. [The definition is underlined; the commas signal a context clue.]

You will often find that both clue words and punctuation signals appear together in a sentence.

THINKING IT THROUGH **Using Context Clues**

Use the steps below to apply definition and restatement context clues. The sample responses are based on the following sentence.

Cell phone use while driving is an *impediment,* or obstacle, to safe driving.

1. **Find a word or phrase that restates the unfamiliar word.** Check for signal words or for commas or dashes that set off the definition or restatement from the unfamiliar word. The word obstacle is set off from the rest of the sentence with commas; the clue word or also signals a restatement.

2. **Try replacing the unfamiliar word with the definition or restatement to see if the sentence still makes sense.** Cell phone use while driving is an obstacle to safe driving.

3. **Write your best guess about the meaning of the unfamiliar word.** The meaning of impediment must be similar to obstacle—a hindrance or obstruction.

PRACTICE

Use the steps above to find the meanings of the italicized words in the following sentences. Write answers on your own paper.

1. The very thought of surfing the Internet while driving seems *ludicrous*—that is, absurd—to some people.

2. Sharon Fultz was *engrossed*—totally absorbed—in a conversation.

3. The truck driver made *futile* attempts to avoid the collision, which is to say he tried unsuccessfully to miss her car.

4. Her car was completely *engulfed* in flames. Fire quickly swallowed the entire car.

5. Barbara was carefully *extricated* from the wreck, meaning that she was freed by rescue workers using special equipment.

Answering Logic Questions

Reading tests often test your ability to see how the relationship of two or more details in a passage fit logically into an overall pattern. These patterns include comparisons, contrasts, and chronologies (time orders). Below are clue words and phrases that signal each of these patterns.

- comparison—*equally*, *like*, and *similar*
- contrast—*but*, *however*, and *nonetheless*
- chronological—*after*, *before*, *later*, and *next*

Matching the same clue words in the passage with those in an answer choice indicates the best answer. Here is a typical reading passage and a logic question.

In the past few years, approximately thirty-five out of every 100,000 sixteen-year-old drivers have died. Some states are tackling this problem head-on by adopting graduated licensing programs for new teen drivers. Most plans begin with an ordinary learner's permit and then progress to daytime-only driver's licenses before granting unrestricted licenses. By adopting a similar graduated licensing program, the country of New Zealand reduced teen driving deaths nearly 13 percent.

1. The writer provides information about New Zealand in order to

   A. contrast driving in New Zealand with driving in the U.S.

   B. show that New Zealand had graduated licensing programs before the U.S.

   C. point out that teen driving is a problem

   D. show that graduated licensing programs like those in New Zealand can effectively reduce teen driving deaths

THINKING IT THROUGH   Answering Logic Questions

Keep the following steps in mind as you answer a logic question.

1. **Read the question carefully, and then locate specific details in the passage.** *Information about New Zealand is in the last sentence of the paragraph.*

2. **Look for clue words that signal what kind of relationship the details have with the rest of the passage. Then, look for clue words that show the same relationship.** *The sentence about New Zealand uses the clue word similar, which indicates that this detail is making a comparison. Only answer D uses a clue word that indicates a comparison—like.*

3. **Eliminate answers that show inaccurate relationships.** Remember, even though the statement made in a possible answer may be true, it may not show the same relationship indicated in the passage. *Answer A uses the word contrast, which is a contrast clue, making it an incorrect choice. B uses the chronology clue word before, making it incorrect. C doesn't have any clue word and is clearly wrong. Only D has a comparison clue word, so D is the correct answer.*

Writing a Problem-Analysis Essay

WHAT'S AHEAD?

In this workshop, you will write an analysis of a problem. You will also learn how to

- **investigate the factors that contribute to a problem**
- **gather and organize support for an analysis of a problem**
- **coordinate and subordinate ideas**
- **eliminate "word wasters"**
- **recognize and correct sentence fragments**

What makes some problems so difficult to solve? Often it is their complexity. Complex problems are usually made up of several different parts. When you **analyze** a problem, you break it into its parts in order to understand it better. For example, imagine that your school has recently adopted the baboon as its mascot. You know this adoption is a problem, but in order to understand this problem fully and explain it to others, you will need to analyze it. What factors make this situation—having the baboon as the school mascot—problematic? An analysis of the problem might reveal that

- a majority of students are unhappy with the choice
- it makes the school vulnerable to ridicule
- it is unlikely that a baboon suit can be found or that anyone would be willing to wear it if it were

In this Writing Workshop, you will learn how to analyze a problem by identifying and discussing the parts that make up the problem.

Prewriting

Find a Problem to Analyze

The Needs of the Many   Everyone has problems, but not every problem will interest a general audience of readers. You need to choose a problem that will. For example, you would probably not want to write a detailed analysis of your Aunt Bertha's battle with the tomato worms that have invaded her garden. "Who cares?" your readers would say. Instead, choose a problem that matters both to you and to your readers.

For instance, one writer, whose essay you will read later in this chapter, chose to write about the high rate of traffic accidents involving teenage drivers—a problem that will certainly interest many readers. To begin looking for an interesting problem to analyze and discuss in your essay, try the following suggestions.

- **Read a weekly newsmagazine or watch the national and local news on TV each evening for a week.** Keep on the lookout for stories about ongoing problems that will interest you and your readers.

- **Browse the Web.** Find information about government and community groups devoted to raising awareness of specific problems.

- **Check your local and school newspapers.** Look at the editorials and letters to the editor. Check items about school board and city council meetings to identify problems your community is currently facing.

After using one or more of these suggestions, list two or three problems that you think might be good topics for an analysis. Share your list of problems with your classmates. Then, choose one problem that you would like to analyze.

TIP You might want to work collaboratively on this problem-analysis essay. If so, work with your teacher so that you and your fellow students are sure of your individual responsibilities.

Consider Purpose, Occasion, Audience, and Tone

The Right Style   How can you show readers that the problem you are writing about is significant and that your analysis of it is sensible? Start by considering your **purpose** (goal for writing), **occasion** (opportunity for writing), **audience** (readers), and **tone** (your feelings toward the problem).

Purpose and Occasion   Generally, **the purpose for writing an analysis of a problem is to raise readers' awareness of the problem and to explain the problem so that readers have a better understanding of it.** In addition, you may have **occasion,** or a real-life reason, to write about the particular problem you chose. For instance, if you are about to get your driver's license, you might have occasion to analyze the high rate of accidents among teenage drivers.

KEY CONCEPT

Audience and Tone   You need to tailor your writing to your particular audience—that includes both what you say to them and how you say it. To help you tune in to your audience's needs, ask yourself the questions in the following Thinking It Through.

▶ **Who is my audience?** Figure out who might be interested in learning about the problem you have chosen. What do you know about the concerns and interests of those readers? Which aspects of the problem will interest them most?

▶ **What do my readers already know about this problem?** Some readers will need background information; others may want to know more about certain aspects of the problem. For example, if you are writing about the high rate of auto accidents involving teenagers (the problem) and parents are your audience, you might assume that they are painfully aware of the high cost of insuring teenage drivers.

▶ **What tone is appropriate for addressing my audience?** Remember, your **tone** reveals your attitude toward your topic and your readers. You achieve a particular tone through word choice and sentence style. For your analysis of a problem, use a tone formal enough so that you will be taken seriously, but informal enough to avoid seeming stuffy and dry. If you were writing to your state representatives, for example, your tone would be more formal than if you were writing for your classmates.

TIP   A word closely related to tone is *voice.* **Voice** is the identifiable characteristics of your writing that make it sound like you. What voice will you want to show through your writing? Do not write long, complicated sentences or use certain words just because you think they sound important or intelligent. The best words to use are the ones you are most comfortable using—words that sound like you, not like someone else. Be careful, however, to maintain a voice that is appropriate to your audience. In classroom writing, you should avoid slang and other overly informal language.

Investigate Your Problem

First Things First   Before you can explain your problem to an audience, you need to get a better understanding of it yourself. Do some initial research or investigation into the problem, keeping these two goals in mind:

■ getting a better understanding of the problem you have chosen

■ gathering specific facts, quotations, and examples you can include in your essay to support your ideas

To find sources, look at the suggestions below. Use at least two types of sources to obtain information.

- **Visit a library.** Check current magazines, journals, newspapers, or books to get up-to-date information on your problem.

- **Conduct interviews.** If you know or can find someone who is knowledgeable about your problem, make an appointment with him or her for an interview. Be sure to prepare a list of questions ahead of time and to take detailed notes during the interview. You might also want to tape-record the interview.

- **Search the Internet.** You can find ongoing—even *endless*—discussions of specific problems posted on Internet newsgroups and on mailing lists. Remember, though, that anyone can post a comment on the Internet. Make sure you use information only from reputable individuals or organizations—information that can be verified in other sources.

- **Observe directly.** If your problem is local, go out and do some direct observations to gather information. For example, if you are writing about stray dogs and cats, visit a local animal shelter or an organization that helps stray pets. Take notes on where and when stray animals gather and who is feeding them.

Reference Note

For more on **interviewing,** see page 902 in the Quick Reference Handbook.

TIP As you do your research, keep track of your sources of information; you may need to cite them in your essay. For information on **citing sources,** see page 237.

Analyze Your Problem

Questions and Answers After gathering information, you can begin to analyze the problem. One of the best ways to begin analyzing a problem is to ask yourself the *5W-How?* questions (*Who, What, When, Why, Where,* and *How?*). The chart below shows how one writer used the *5W-How?* questions to analyze the problem of teenage auto accidents.

Problem: The high rate of traffic accidents involving teenage drivers	
Who is affected by the problem?	Parents, teenagers, police, insurance companies, doctors, and the general public
Why are they concerned?	Everybody wants to save lives and money, but teenage drivers want to retain their freedom.
When did this problem become evident?	The problem has probably been around as long as teenagers have been driving. Maybe it seems worse now because more teens are driving.

(continued)

(continued)

Where is this a problem—locally, statewide, nationally, or globally?	It is a national problem—maybe even a world-wide problem. I have heard that some other countries have much better teenage-driver safety records than the United States does.
What are the causes of the problem?	Inexperienced drivers, peer pressure to take risks while driving, the perception that accidents only happen to other people
How does this problem affect me and my audience?	Bad driving puts everyone at risk, and makes adults view teenagers as irresponsible. Teenagers and their parents pay high insurance rates.

Choose Key Points Look through your notes and your answers to the *5W-How?* questions and select three to five key points to cover in your essay. These should be the ideas that you think are the most important for your readers to know. The writer who created the chart above chose these three key points (the answers to the *How?* question).

> **TIP** When drafting your essay you will most likely revise these key points for content and style and then use them as topic sentences for your body paragraphs.

Key Points:

Bad driving puts everyone at risk

Unsafe driving makes adults view teens as irresponsible.

Teenagers and their parents pay high insurance rates.

YOUR TURN 4 Choosing and Analyzing a Problem

Use the guidelines above to choose, investigate, and analyze a problem for a problem-analysis essay.

Provide Support

Legs to Stand On You pick up your newspaper one morning and find the following headline on the front page: "Local Penguins Attack Again." Unless you live in Antarctica or in the far reaches of the Southern Hemisphere, you are going to have a hard time believing that headline. You read on. Aha! The news story explains that your local zoo had five penguin handlers roughed up by the little tuxedo-wearing birds in the last three weeks. Now you understand that there really is a local penguin problem.

What changed your mind was that the news story provided **supporting details** for the headline. You, too, will need to provide a variety of supporting details for your key points in order to explain your problem to readers. Here are four types of support you can use.

- **Facts** (objective statements that can be checked) and **statistics** (number facts) give strong support. The student writing about teenage auto accidents found that in the United States more than six thousand teenagers die in auto accidents every year. Be sure that your facts are accurate and up-to-date. Record the original sources of your facts since most teachers will require you to cite them.

- **Expert testimony** (quotations and comments) carries weight because it comes from someone who has already studied or experienced the problem. For example, if you were writing about fire safety problems, you might quote a representative of your local fire department. Whenever you use quotations, make sure they are accurate—a person's exact words.

- **Examples** (specific cases that illustrate a point) can come from your personal knowledge or from research. The student writing about teenage auto accidents found examples of ways that teenagers can lower their car insurance rates.

- **Anecdotes** (brief stories about a real person or event) provide a human element and add interest to your essay. An anecdote about a student from your high school who crashed her car makes the topic of teenage auto accidents more personal and compelling.

To find facts, expert testimony, examples, and anecdotes that support your key points, look carefully at the information you gathered during your initial research. If these sources do not provide enough supporting details, do more research—and keep looking until you find what you need.

Write Your Thesis Statement

Make a Statement After gathering support for your key points, your next step is to generate a preliminary **thesis statement**—a sentence stating your topic plus your controlling (main) idea about the topic. Your thesis statement should state your problem and alert your readers to its seriousness, and it should relate directly to the key points you have chosen as your focus. Here is one writer's preliminary thesis statement.

> The distressing safety record of teenage drivers is still a real problem in the United States today.

TIP If you find as you write that you need to change or add to your key points, you can go back and revise your thesis statement to reflect the changes or additions you make.

Coordinating and Subordinating Ideas

As you look through your notes you may ask yourself, "How can I distinguish the problem from its contributing factors?" or "Which of these ideas should I choose to include in my essay?" One way to begin making sense of your ideas is to group related ideas and then classify them as either *coordinate* or *subordinate*.

Coordinate ideas are equal in importance to one another. These are often your key points that become the main ideas of your body paragraphs. These ideas, for example, are coordinates: *Kerry plays the guitar. Marcus creates computer games. Ann is a talented dancer.*

Subordinate ideas are less important ideas. They are supporting details that elaborate on broader or more important points. With the preceding statements about Kerry, Marcus, and Ann, the following would be a subordinate point: *Ann specializes in bolero and flamenco styles.*

Your first step in organizing your ideas should be to try to find the relationship between them. That is, you need to look at each idea and ask, "Is this idea equal in importance to other ideas on the list, or is it a less important point that supports another idea?"

PRACTICE

For each item, write *S* (for *subordinate*) for every statement that is subordinate to the boldface statement. Write *C* (for *coordinate*) for every statement that is coordinate to the boldface statement.

Write your answers on your own paper.

1. **Crowded classrooms are a major problem.**

   A. There are as many as forty students in some classrooms.

   B. New legislation may alleviate most of the class-size problems through increased state funding of teacher certification programs.

   C. Some classrooms present a fire hazard because of overcrowding.

   D. One in five teachers says she feels overwhelmed by the number of students in each class.

2. **Construction of the new elementary school has fallen behind schedule.**

   A. Severe weather conditions have caused many delays.

   B. The school board had trouble choosing a final design.

   C. The old building was poorly designed.

   D. Obtaining permits took longer than originally estimated.

3. **The price of movie tickets keeps increasing.**

   A. Video rental prices also are rising.

   B. Theaters must continually pay to upgrade their sound systems.

   C. Theater owners' taxes increase yearly.

   D. Distributors charge theater owners more money to rent films.

Organize Your Essay

Put Things in Order   In your essay, **your key points and supporting details should follow a logical progression so that your readers can easily comprehend your explanation.** To make sure that your essay follows a logical progression, use one of these three organizational patterns:

KEY CONCEPT

- **Order of importance**   Begin with the least important point and build up to the most important one, or the reverse.
- **Chronological order**   Present your problem as it has developed over time.
- **Cause-and-effect order**   Choose this order to show what caused your problem or to indicate what the effects of the problem are.

For her essay on the high rate of auto accidents among teenage drivers, this writer arranged her key points by order of importance, from least to most important. She created the following chart to reflect that plan.

> **TIP**   You may use more than one order in your essay, but choose one as the dominant, overall pattern. If a detail does not fit the pattern, ask yourself whether it is worth keeping. If your answer is yes, find a place to fit it in.

Initial thesis	The distressing safety record of teenage drivers is still a real problem in the United States today.
Key point 1 (least important)	Unsafe driving makes adults view teens as irresponsible.
Key point 2 (next important)	Teenagers and their parents pay high insurance rates.
Key point 3 (most important)	Bad driving puts everyone at risk.

YOUR TURN 5   Getting Ready to Write

Make sure that you have completed each of the following prewriting steps before drafting your essay.

- Provide facts and statistics, expert testimony, examples, and anecdotes to support your key points.
- Write a thesis statement that states your problem and alerts readers to its seriousness.
- Organize your essay by order of importance, chronological order, or cause-and-effect order.

Problem-Analysis Essay

Framework

Directions and Explanations

Introduction

- Catch your audience's attention.
- State the problem in your thesis.

Start with Something Interesting   A good way to get an audience's attention is to start with an intriguing question or with an anecdote to which an audience can relate on a personal level.

Make Yourself Clear   The key to your entire essay is your thesis statement. It should clearly and concisely outline the problem you discuss in the essay.

Body

- State the key points in your analysis of the problem.
- Provide support for your key points.
- Organize ideas in a way that makes sense.

Close to Home   One way to help your readers recognize the seriousness of your problem is to help them realize how the problem affects them. If you can show that the problem has an impact on your readers' lives, they are more likely to be interested in what you are saying.

Do Not Confuse the Issue   Focus on only one key point in each body paragraph of your essay. Provide enough supporting details—facts, statistics, quotations, examples, and anecdotes—to create a well-developed paragraph. Use transitions to help coherence.

Conclusion

- Restate your thesis.
- Emphasize the seriousness of the problem and its importance to your audience.

Repeat Yourself   Do not simply copy the thesis sentence from your introduction and insert it in your conclusion. Restate the thesis in terms that will remind your audience how the problem should matter to them.

 Writing a First Draft

Using the framework above, write a first draft of your own problem analysis. Before you begin, read the Writer's Model that follows.

A Writer's Model

This first draft of an essay closely follows the framework on the previous page.

Licensed—but Safe?

How safe on the road are today's teenage drivers? Few people will deny that the safety features built into today's cars are more advanced than ever. Driver's education students today graduate with a greater awareness of road dangers thanks to the efforts of their teachers, to public service announcements in the media, and to student groups such as Students Against Drunk Driving (SADD) and Youth Against Road Rage (YARR). Some states have even enacted graduated licensing programs that ease teenagers into driving privileges and responsibilities. Therefore, teenage drivers today *should* be safer on the road than they have ever been, right? Well, it may be too early for congratulations. To tell the truth, the distressing safety record of teenage drivers is still a real problem in the United States today.

Part of the problem is that teenagers' bad driving record creates a negative image of teens. How often are words like *irresponsible* and *reckless* used to describe teenagers? Comments like the following, from a recent poll taken at the East Towne Mall, are common from adults. "What do you expect when you give a kid the keys? Trouble, that's what." "It's not a matter of if a sixteen-year-old will have an accident; it's a question of when." Never mind that many teenagers drive perfectly well—some adults still expect the worst.

Insurance companies know that teenage drivers are a greater risk, so they charge them higher premiums. Parents who add a teenager to their policy may find that their insurance premiums double, because insurance companies know that half of all teenage drivers have an accident within a year of getting a license. Not all teenagers have a bad record, but teenagers are the group with the highest accident rate among American drivers. Taking driver's education, having good grades and a good driving record, and driving a less-expensive car bring down the premiums a little, but the high rates still make things tough for whoever makes the payments.

INTRODUCTION

Facts

Thought-provoking question

Thesis

BODY
Point 1

Quotations

Point 2

Statistic

Fact

Fact

(continued)

(continued)

Point 3

However, the greatest cost associated with poor teenage driving is not monetary—it is the cost in human lives. Car crashes are a leading killer of American teenagers—more than

Statistics

six thousand teenagers die in auto accidents every year. That is like having everyone in three high school homerooms die every week. Although teenagers make up only 7 percent of the American driving population, they are involved in an

Fact

astonishing 14 percent of all fatal auto accidents. Even crashes that do not kill can cause long-term problems for both drivers

Anecdote

and victims. For example, when she was sixteen, Tara Davis (not her real name) crashed her mother's car head-on into a pickup truck, seriously injuring two people. Though she was not injured physically, the accident devastated Tara emotionally. In fact, she was unable to move on with her life and her plans for her future until she asked for and received forgiveness from the people she injured. "I've never tried to forget what I caused to happen," she says, "because I don't want to cause something like that again."

CONCLUSION

Every teenager looks forward to a driver's license and the freedom associated with driving. Even so, teenagers need to realize that along with that freedom come responsibilities and

Restatement of thesis

some significant risks. Those risks will be reduced only when teenagers realize that the high rate of accidents among teenage drivers is a serious but preventable problem.

FOR BETTER OR FOR WORSE © Lynn Johnston Productions Inc./Dist. by United Feature Syndicate, Inc.

A Student's Model

The following passage from a problem-analysis essay was written by David Thompson, a student from McNeil High School in Austin, Texas. It focuses on a problem he is concerned about—eating disorders in athletes his own age.

Athletes Trying to Be Too Perfect

The gymnast's vault scores a 9.5! She is a successful athlete, so obviously she is in great physical condition, the picture of health, right? Incredibly, this gymnast is extremely unhealthy and, in fact, is at high risk for cardiac arrest. She is secretly fighting bulimia, an eating disorder that is characterized by a cycle of binge eating followed by purging to try ridding the body of calories. This girl is not alone, either; eating disorders are on the rise for both male and female athletes.

Two of the most prevalent eating disorders affecting athletes are anorexia nervosa and bulimia nervosa. People with anorexia lose enormous amounts of weight from excessive dieting. These people usually do not know or admit they have a problem, and they consider themselves fat no matter what their real weight is. Anorexics will often do anything not to eat, and even when they weigh as little as eighty pounds will continue to say they are fat. Medical complications from anorexia include hair loss, irregular heartbeats, constipation, loss of bone mass, kidney and liver damage, and finally cardiac arrest and death. According to the Harvard Eating Disorder Center, "a young woman with anorexia is twelve times more likely to die than other women her age without anorexia." (www.hedc.com) Victims with bulimia nervosa indulge in a cycle of binge eating and then purging to get rid of unwanted calories. Bingeing, though, does not have to mean eating thousands of calories. To many bulimics, eating just one cookie could be considered bingeing. Purging is accomplished in several ways, including self-induced vomiting, excessive exercise, fasting, diuretics, and diet pills. Unlike anorexia, bulimics usually realize they have a health problem. . . .

INTRODUCTION
Attention-getting opening

Thesis

BODY
Point 1

Facts

Statistic

Facts

Revising

Evaluate and Revise Your Draft

Take a Second Look   Before you share your problem-analysis essay with readers, read through it at least twice: One reading should focus on your content (have you clearly and thoroughly discussed the problem?) and organization (does your analysis follow a logical progression?). The second reading should focus on your style, or how you express your ideas. Then, revise your essay to make it the best it can be.

➤ **First Reading: Content and Organization**   By yourself or with a partner, use the chart below to evaluate the content and organization of your essay.

Problem Analysis: Content and Organization Guidelines for Peer and Self-Evaluation		
Evaluation Questions	▶ **Tips**	▶ **Revision Techniques**
❶ Does the introduction get readers interested in the problem discussed in the essay?	▶ **Circle** any sentence in the introduction that grabs a reader's attention. If you do not find one, revise.	▶ **Add** an attention-getting opener; **cut** any material that does not build up to the thesis of the essay.
❷ Does the thesis state the problem clearly?	▶ **Double underline** the thesis statement. If it does not clearly state the problem, revise.	▶ **Add** a thesis statement that presents the problem clearly.
❸ Does the writer present a reasoned analysis of the problem that includes at least three key points?	▶ **Bracket** the sections in each body paragraph that introduce a key point. If you do not see at least three sets of brackets or if each bracketed section does not focus on one aspect of the problem, revise.	▶ **Add** key points so that at least three points discuss each different part of the problem.
❹ Does each body paragraph include support for the key point?	▶ **Put a star** beside each fact, statistic, example, and so forth that supports a key point. If there are not at least two stars for each key point, revise.	▶ **Elaborate** by supplying facts, statistics, expert testimony, examples, and anecdotes to support each key point.
❺ Does the conclusion restate the thesis of the essay?	▶ **Highlight** any sentence in the conclusion that restates the thesis. If you do not find one, revise.	▶ **Add** a sentence that clearly restates—but does not repeat word-for-word—the thesis.

ONE WRITER'S REVISIONS Below is a passage from an early draft of the essay on page 147. The handwritten revisions show how the writer revised the passage based on the guidelines from the previous page.

Parents who add a teenager to their policy may find that their

insurance premiums ~~rise~~, _double_ because insurance companies know that

half of all ~~many~~ teenage drivers have _an_ ~~accidents~~. _within a year of getting a license._

replace

elaborate

Analyzing the Revision Process

1. What key point does the writer seem to be making in this passage?
2. How do the revisions strengthen this point?

YOUR TURN 7 **Focusing on Content and Organization**

Evaluate and revise your problem-analysis essay using the content and organization guidelines on the previous page.

PEER REVIEW

Have a classmate read your essay and answer the questions below.

1. For what audience was this essay intended?
2. Are there any aspects of the problem that have not been considered?

> **Second Reading: Style** An analysis of a complex problem can be hard for readers to follow—even without unnecessary words and phrases such as "at the present period of time" and "in my opinion I think." In fact, faced with these "word wasters," some readers may decide it is just not worth the time and trouble needed to read your analysis. Hold your readers' attention by eliminating unnecessary repetition and padding. Say what you mean clearly and directly. Use the following guidelines to eliminate "word wasters" from your writing.

COMPUTER TIP

E-mail copies of your essay to peer reviewers. Ask them to review the essay and return the copies and their comments to you by e-mail.

Style Guidelines		
Evaluation Question	▶ **Tip**	▶ **Revision Technique**
Do sentences contain redundant phrases or flabby phrases and clauses?	▶ **Underline** words or phrases that add length but not meaning. **Circle** the words _which_ and _that,_ and check to see if the clauses they introduce can be revised.	▶ **Cut** or **replace** any underlined words or phrases that dilute the meaning of a sentence. **Replace** unnecessary clauses and phrases.

Focus on

Word Choice

Eliminating "Word Wasters"

Do you want to know a great way to frustrate your readers? Load your essay with unnecessary phrases and clauses. On the other hand, if you want your readers to understand your ideas, try this instead: Make every word in the essay count. Take a look at the examples of "word wasters" below—phrases or clauses that add length to sentences but no substance. All these "word wasters" can be reduced so that a reader does not have to wade through extra words to get to the message.

Redundant Phrases: *in the morning about nine o'clock A.M., repeat again, but nevertheless, because of the fact that, and moreover, surrounding circumstances, few in number* [The underlined words can be omitted without changing the meaning of the phrase.]

Flabby Phrases: *at the present time (now), for the reason that (because), with regard to (about), with the result that (so that)* [The words or phrases within parentheses can replace the flabby phrase.]

Flabby *Which* and *That* Clauses: *problems, which are frequent (frequent problems), solutions that require creative thinking (solutions requiring creative thinking), examples that were worthwhile (worthwhile examples)* [The phrase in parentheses can replace the *which* or *that* clause.]

ONE WRITER'S REVISIONS   Below is a sentence from an early draft of the problem-analysis essay on page 147, along with a revised version of the same sentence. Study the sentences, and then answer the questions that follow them.

BEFORE REVISION

How safe on the road are today's teenage drivers? Few

flabby *that* clause   people will deny that the safety features (that) people build into

redundant phrase   the present cars of today are more advanced than ever.

AFTER REVISION

> How safe on the road are today's teenage drivers? Few people will deny that the safety features built into today's cars are more advanced than ever.

"Word wasters" have been cut or replaced.

Analyzing the Revision Process

1. Why do you think the writer replaced the phrase "the present cars of today"?

2. How did reducing the *that* clause to a phrase help the sentence?

YOUR TURN 8 **Focusing on Style**

Using what you have learned about "word wasters," search your essay for phrases or clauses that dilute your writing. Cut "word wasters" to create a more effective essay.

Designing Your Writing

Using Color   Now that color printers and color copiers are widely available, color can be used to clarify messages and to speed up readers' comprehension—both things that are especially important in an essay that analyzes a complex, potentially confusing problem. You can use color to

- highlight a point
- tell the reader where to look first
- group related items

   Should you make your essay a rainbow of color? You shouldn't if you want your audience to be able to read it. Here are some guidelines for using color.

- **Use color for clarity and emphasis, not decoration.** Color attracts the eye—you want readers to be drawn to your content, not to the decoration.

- **Remember that bright colors attract the eye more strongly than dull colors.**

- **Use colors that strongly contrast with the background.** Contrast is the reason black letters on white are the easiest to read. Yellow on white is nearly impossible to read. On the other hand, **yellow** is effective against a dark background—for example, in a magazine print advertisement or on a Web page.
- **Stick to a few colors.** Using too many colors can confuse readers—the last thing you want to do.
- **Use color to unify your essay.** If you begin highlighting your subheads in green, do not switch to blue later in the essay.

Here is how one writer used color to emphasize an attention-getting sentence.

> No more helium-filled balloons! Environmentalists and animal rights groups are boycotting balloons because they are concerned about wild animals that die from eating such balloons.

Another student writer used color to differentiate heads from subheads in this way:

Crowded Classrooms
Not Enough Teachers   One major factor in the problem of overcrowded classrooms is that there are not enough teachers to go around. The ratio of students to teachers worsens with the start of each new school year. . . .

Here is how one writer used color to liven up a chart and to make the lines clearly distinguishable.

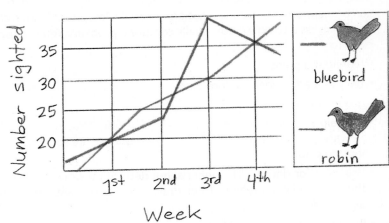

Proofread Your Essay

A Real Fixer Upper   Who will enjoy reading your essay if it is full of errors? You want your audience to focus on what you say—not on spelling and grammar errors. Work with a peer to proofread your essay carefully to eliminate errors. Use the guidelines in the following Grammar Link to deal with one all-too-common error: sentence fragments.

Reference Note

For more on **sentence fragments,** see page 340.

Grammar Link

Sentence Fragments

A group of words may begin with a capital letter and end with a period, but that is no guarantee that it forms a sentence. **Sentence fragments** are groups of words that look like sentences but are not. To decide whether a particular group of words is a sentence or a fragment, use these tests:

1. Does the group of words have a subject?

2. Does it have a verb?

3. Does it express a complete thought?

If the group of words fails to meet even one of the tests, it is not a complete sentence.

Most fragments occur in writing when an explanation, example, or some other addition is added to the main statement. Many fragments can be corrected just by joining them to a sentence. If not, you may have to add words to make a complete sentence.

Here are examples of two types of fragments.

Prepositional Phrase Fragment	In the other room. Ray yawned.
Sentence	In the other room, Ray yawned. [The fragment is joined to the sentence.]
Verbal Phrase Fragment	Using creative thinking.
Sentence	Burke's greatest skill is using creative thinking. [A subject and a verb are added.]

PRACTICE

Correct any sentence fragments in each of the following items. If an item does not contain a fragment, write C for *correct*. Write your answers on your own paper.

1. Having more accidents. Teenagers must pay more for insurance.

2. Police enforcing the speed limit.

3. It was especially difficult for me. Learning to drive can be difficult.

4. Before having a flat tire myself. I didn't realize how important it was to carry a spare.

5. Studying more. I made better grades.

Publish Your Essay

Put the Gears in Motion   You want others to recognize the seriousness of the problem you have analyzed and to begin working toward solutions. Try one or more of the ideas listed below to share your essay with an appropriate audience.

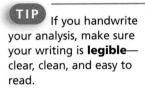

TIP   If you handwrite your analysis, make sure your writing is **legible**—clear, clean, and easy to read.

- **Create a problem bank.** Gather copies of your class's problem-analysis essays, put them into a binder, and ask your school librarian to place the binder in the library for use as a "problem bank." Other students at your school who are interested in problem solving and problem analysis may use the problem bank as a resource.

- **Schedule a debate.** If your school has a debate team, share your essay with the debate coach and ask him or her to consider using your problem as the topic for a schoolwide debate.

- **Form a task force if your problem is school related.** Does your problem directly affect students at your school? Is it something your school, as a community, may be able to solve? If so, submit your problem-analysis essay to your school newspaper and invite students, teachers, and parents to form a task force to discuss possible solutions to the problem.

PORTFOLIO

Reflect on Your Essay

Look Back   After you have completed your essay, take a moment to answer the following questions and find out what you have learned from this experience.

- What new ideas or information did you discover about your problem?

- What was the most helpful skill you learned from writing an analysis of a problem?

- What, if anything, do you think you will do differently when you next write a problem analysis?

YOUR TURN 9   Proofreading, Publishing, and Reflecting

Why write an essay if no one is going to read it? Proofread your essay carefully, and then share it with an audience. Finally, use the questions above to reflect on what you learned.

Analyzing the Problems of a Literary Character

Daily life seems to be full of problems. You read about them in the newspaper, hear about them on the radio, and watch them on the television. Like real life, literary works also present readers and audiences with a variety of problems that characters must confront and resolve by the end of the story. These problems are called **conflicts**. When you analyze a problem in literature, you are examining the story's **plot** elements.

The following chart analyzes the problems of the title character in the play *Antigone* by Sophocles. The plot elements are listed in the left column, with key terms shown in boldface, and examples provided from the play are given in the right column.

The **basic situation** (the major characters and the circumstances in which they find themselves)	A man named Polyneices is killed while leading an attack on the city of Thebes (from which he has been exiled). Creon, the city's king, decrees that anyone who attempts to bury Polyneices will be punished with execution.
The **conflict** (the major problem between opposing forces, characters, or emotions)	The conflict in *Antigone* is between the law of conscience and the law of the land. Antigone (Polyneices' sister) faces a difficult choice: leave her brother's body unburied (a terrible sacrilege in ancient Greek religion) or defy Creon's decree and risk execution.
Complications (developments that take place because of the existing conflict, or any elements that intensify the conflict)	Antigone's personality complicates the problem. She makes her choices because she is a brash, outspoken person who will follow her beliefs—no matter the consequences.
The **climax** (the moment of greatest suspense or tension)	Creon sentences Antigone to death for sprinkling earth over her brother's body. She tragically chooses to take her own life.
The **resolution** (the final solution to the problem or conflict)	Creon's son (who loves Antigone) kills himself in grief, an act that causes Creon to realize that he was wrong.

YOUR TURN 10 Analyzing the Problems of a Literary Character

Analyze the problems of a main character in one of your favorite literary works. Make a chart like the one above for your character; then, present your findings to your classmates in a brief oral presentation.

Talk   Listen

WHAT'S AHEAD?

In this section, you will learn how to

■ **prepare a memorable speech**

■ **deliver your speech in an interesting way**

■ **conduct a question-and-answer session**

■ **listen actively to a speech**

Giving an Informative Speech

Suppose that you have analyzed the problem of pollution in a neighborhood creek, and you want to alert local businesspeople, homeowners, and elected officials to the problem. One way you can share your information is to write an informative speech and deliver it during a community meeting.

In this section, you will learn how to create and deliver an informative speech. Creating a speech is in many ways like writing an essay. You choose a subject, determine your audience, and then gather and organize your information in an interesting and logical way. Informative speeches and informative essays share these characteristics:

■ a clearly defined purpose

■ language appropriate for the audience

■ an engaging introduction

■ a well-supported thesis statement

■ a logical progression of ideas

■ a conclusion that summarizes the main points

Prepare a Memorable Speech

Zoom In   The topic for your speech should interest you and be something you already know about. However, it must have a narrow focus so that you can cover it adequately in a limited amount of time. For example, "pollution" is much too broad a topic for a speech, but "pollution in Brushy Creek" is manageable. Gather information you may need from interviews, surveys, books, reference works, periodicals, or Web sites. Once you have chosen a topic and researched it (if needed), write a **thesis statement** that expresses your most important idea about your topic. Think also about **occasion,** the setting for your speech and what motivated you to give it. Will it be a city council chamber, where strict, formal procedures must be followed or will it be an informal classroom setting? Are you giving the speech because you are passionate about the topic and wish to share this interest with others? Consider the **task** you are trying to accomplish with your speech. If your speech is on a problem you have researched, your task is to help your audience become aware of the problem and understand the seriousness of the problem.

TIP To maintain your audience's attention, adapt your speech to suit their interests and knowledge. If your audience is your classmates, you might consider polling them to find out what they already know about your topic.

Who's Out There?   Consider your **audience**—the people who will be listening to your speech. If you are lucky, they are ready and willing to learn something new. Sometimes, though, they are a captive audience, present only because they are required to be there. Part of your goal is to make sure that audience members go away from your speech feeling that they have learned something interesting and important.

Good Form!   The structure of your speech is very similar to the three-part structure of an essay. Use the following framework as a guide.

Introduction	• Get your audience's attention. Begin with a startling statement, an interesting story, or a thought-provoking question. • Gain your audience's goodwill. If your audience likes or respects you, they will be more likely to listen to and think about what you say.
Body	• Give supporting information for your main points. • Organize the main points of your speech in one of the following ways: **Chronological Order**—Arrange events and details as they developed over time. **Order of Importance**—Arrange information from least important to most important. **Cause-and-Effect Order**—Arrange information to show causes and effects (results of those causes). **Comparison-and-Contrast Order**—Arrange details to show similarities or differences.
Conclusion	• Summarize and emphasize the main points of your speech. • Leave your audience with a greater interest in your topic.

Watch Your Language   Make sure that what you say is immediately understandable. Because this is a formal speech, be sure to choose **standard language,** that is, standard English, to communicate your ideas. Standard language is the kind of English people are expected to use in school and business situations.

TIP When you speak to an audience that is familiar with your subject, you can use **technical language** your audience will recognize. On the other hand, define any technical terms when an audience is unfamiliar with your subject.

Deliver Your Speech in an Interesting Way

Here are some tips that will help you make the presentation of your speech more interesting.

- **Be enthusiastic.** If you show genuine interest in your topic, it will be easier for you to get your audience interested in it.
- **Know your speech well.** Before you deliver your speech, practice it several times. Be sure of the pronunciation of key terms, and note places where you might add verbal emphasis.
- **Speak from notes.** Once you know your speech well, write notes to use as you speak. Don't try to memorize your speech (you may get stuck) or read it word for word. Know your general points and details, and glance at your note cards whenever you need reminding.
- **Maintain eye contact.** Do not keep your head down and your eyes locked on your notes. Look out at your audience and use eye contact to keep your listeners involved in your speech.
- **Say it with feeling.** Speak loudly enough so everyone can hear you, and vary your **rate of speaking, volume,** and **pitch.**

Think Visually Readers can read and re-read a written paper as many times as they want until they feel they understand it. However, listeners must actively listen and try to understand and remember your speech the first time through, because they cannot ask you to give it a second time. You can help your listeners remember your speech by making use of **visuals**—materials that an audience can see, such as charts, graphs, slides, transparencies, and films. If you use visuals with your speech,

- clearly explain the content of the visual to your audience and connect the visuals to your speech
- don't overdo—use only as many visuals as you need to illustrate or emphasize the most important points of your speech
- test audio or video equipment before your speech to be sure it is working properly

Conduct a Question-and-Answer Session

If possible, end your speech with a question-and-answer period. Listeners will have a chance to become more actively involved, and you will have a chance to clear up any misunderstandings. The **feedback** you get from your audience can help you to **set goals** for improving future speeches or other presentations. Use the following suggestions to make your question-and-answer period more productive.

TIP **Feedback** from your audience, such as smiles, nods of agreement, fidgeting, or confused looks, can help you know how to adjust your presentation. If your audience seems confused, slow your pace or repeat key ideas. If they seem bored, try varying your rate of speaking, volume, and pitch.

Feedback also helps you to evaluate your effectiveness and to set goals for future presentations.

- **Call on people from all over the audience.** Try to involve everyone—including those at the back and on the sides of the audience.

- **Respond to questions clearly and succinctly.** Instead of responding with words repeated directly from your speech, give short, clear responses that build on points you have already made.

- **Don't worry if you can't answer every question.** Rather than try to bluff your way through an answer, tell your audience that you will try to locate the information and forward it later to anyone who is interested.

Listen Actively to a Speech

When it is your turn to be a listener, pay careful attention to what the speaker is saying. Even if you are already a good listener, these tips will help improve your critical-listening skills.

TIP Part of your task as a listener is to analyze, evaluate, and appreciate the presentation. As you actively listen to a speech, you may want to use what you have learned about purpose, audience, tone, and delivery to create your own criteria (standards of judgement) to analyze, evaluate, and appreciate.

- **Take notes.** As the speaker talks, jot down notes about each key point.

- **Think ahead.** To stay actively involved, you should try to anticipate the points the speaker might make next and then confirm and adjust your predictions as you listen. Jot down questions you want to ask the speaker later.

- **Relate what the speaker is saying to your own life.** For example, if the speaker is talking about the importance of wearing bicycle helmets, you might briefly recall a bicycle accident you had as a child and relate what the speaker is saying to that experience.

- **Participate in the question-and-answer period.** Ask the speaker to clarify anything you found confusing. You can also use the time to give the speaker positive comments, telling him or her about specific parts of the speech that you found particularly informative.

YOUR TURN 11 **Creating and Delivering an Informative Speech**

Follow the guidelines in the previous section to create and deliver an informative speech. Make sure to follow each of these steps:

- Deliver your speech in an interesting way, using eye contact and variations in your rate of speech, volume, and pitch.

- Plan appropriate visuals and demonstrations that will make your speech memorable.

- Conduct a question-and-answer session after your speech, if possible.

Recognizing News Genres

WHAT'S AHEAD?

In this section, you will learn how to

- **recognize three common news genres**
- **analyze the coverage of individual news programs**

What kind of news would there be if the world had no problems? Consider how much of the news you receive is about local, national, and global problems. One of the main ways this "problem news" and other kinds of news reaches you is through television news programs, many of which fit into the three genres described below.

What Are News Genres?

National nightly news broadcasts mostly present breaking news stories about events that have happened since the previous evening. Within a half-hour broadcast (including commercials), each news item may receive less than a minute of airtime, so the depth of coverage is limited.

Newsmagazines are often broadcast once a week (sometimes more). They provide more detailed coverage of topics, not just breaking news. A weekly newsmagazine will generally present only a handful of stories—four or five at the most—in the space of an hour, so the depth of coverage is greater than that on the nightly news. Many of the stories presented on weekly newsmagazines are **human-interest** stories, stories that are designed to evoke emotional responses, such as joy, compassion, outrage, and sympathy. Human-interest stories may or may not actually provide much factual information about a topic.

Documentaries are creatively constructed *interpretations* of actual events, people, or groups. They are often broadcast as "specials"—not according to a daily or weekly schedule. Like newsmagazines, documentaries usually do not deal with breaking news. Instead, a one-hour (sometimes less) news-related documentary generally deals with a single topic, and therefore treats that topic in much greater depth than either a nightly news broadcast or a multiple-story newsmagazine can. Keep in mind that documentaries often reflect the filmmaker's bias or point of view. Documentaries have been made on such varied topics as the music of India, the Battle of Gettysburg, the rain forests of Peru, presidential campaigns, Michael Jordan, Michelangelo, and the *Titanic*. Most news-related documentaries are about historical events or people or are about news items that are still developing or that show possible long-lasting consequences.

Why Do They Do It?   Sometimes it is easy to forget that a news program does anything more than inform, but nonfiction TV can serve one or more of a **variety of purposes**: to inform, to educate, to entertain, to persuade, for self-expression, and for profit. For example, a newsmagazine program about the latest record-breaking multiple birth can inform you by showing you the problems parents go through when an event like this happens. The program can also entertain you by showing cute videotape of the adorable babies, and it may additionally attempt to persuade you by interviewing doctors about the risks associated with fertility drugs.

Also, when watching news programs, consider who the **target audience**—the people to whom the programs are designed to appeal—might be. To remain on the air, any television program must attract enough viewers to encourage advertisers to sponsor the show. To attract viewers, producers must shape the content of their programs to suit the interests and desires of their target audience. Oftentimes, the commercials that are shown during the program will give you some clue about who the producer expects will be watching.

When you watch nightly news programs, newsmagazines, and documentaries, you may begin to notice that each can have purposes and target audiences that are very specific to its genre.

Knowing What You Are Getting

To help you analyze the news genres that you see on television, use the following questions whenever you conduct a focused news-viewing session. Not all questions will be relevant to each news genre, since, for example, documentaries focus specifically on one news item instead of on several. Remember, too, to record pertinent information, such as the program's name, the topics it covers, its length, and the number of news items it includes.

■ How much of the program is devoted to breaking news? What other kinds of stories are presented?

■ What aspects of the topic (or topics) were *not* covered at all?

■ Does the program provide factual information, or does it just leave you with an emotional reaction? Explain your answers.

■ Which purpose or purposes do you think the news stories serve? Explain your response.

TIP   To spot stories designed to manipulate your feelings, be on the lookout for emotional background music, an overdose of stirring images, and a narrow focus on individual people and their problems. Stories with these characteristics often fail to provide enough facts or statistics to give a big-picture view of the problem and the number of people it affects.

- What advertisements aired during the broadcast? What target audience is reflected in the commercials? Why?
- What unanswered questions do you have after watching the program?

The following is an example portion of an analysis one student made using the questions that begin on page 163 as a guide.

	Does the program provide factual information, or does it just leave you with a feeling? Explain.
National Nightly News **Name:** Nightly World News **Topic(s):** forest fire, Senate budget deadlock, former baseball commissioner passed away, floods in Asia, latest election campaign news **Length:** 21 minutes **Number of news items:** 18	Most of the program seemed factual. The political coverage seemed fair—neither side was being blamed in the budget negotiations. However, there were some upsetting images of the results of a forest fire and of the Asian floods. I am not sure how the producers could really present information on these two topics without some sort of emotional impact.
Newsmagazine **Name:** In Focus	

YOUR TURN 12 Analyzing the Content and Depth of Coverage in News Programs

Watch three types of news programs: a national nightly news broadcast, a newsmagazine, and a news-related documentary. Using the questions on page 163 and above, analyze the programs. Then, use your notes to answer the following questions. Explain all your answers.

- Which type of news program leaves you with the most factual information? The most emotional reactions?
- Which type of news program shows the least bias?
- Does each genre have the same purposes? The same target audience?
- In your judgment, does each of these programs provide more than enough, enough, or not enough coverage for each news item?

Choices

Choose one of the following activities to complete.

▶ CAREERS

1. Give a Checkup Conduct an interview with a health professional (a nurse, doctor, or dentist, for example). Ask about the health problems he or she treats: What kinds of problems are typical, how are they treated, and what research needs to be done to treat them? After completing the interview, present a brief **oral report—** a short profile of the health professional and of the methods he or she uses to research and treat problems.

▶ CROSSING THE CURRICULUM: LITERATURE

2. Hatch a Plot Make some trouble for a fictional character. Think of a problem that interests you, and write a **summary** of a short-story plot based on the problem. Remember that the main character's responses to the problem should create a conflict to be resolved in the story.

▶ SPEAKING AND LISTENING

3. Join the Debate Go to your school's drama or debate coach and ask to sit in on a debate class or competition. Take notes on how the debaters discuss the problems they have researched. What rules do they follow? How do they argue a point without erupting in anger? If debaters present a solution to the problem, how do they convince you that their solution is a good one? Create a **"how-to" booklet** about debate that you can share with others.

▶ MEDIA AND TECHNOLOGY

4. Tune It In Some TV and radio stations show the government in action with live or taped broadcasts of trials, hearings, city council meetings, school board meetings, and so on. Watch or listen to one of these broadcasts and make notes on

- problems discussed
- people discussing the problems
- any solutions discussed

Use your findings to write a **profile** of how governmental officials try to solve problems. Consider including this profile in your portfolio.

PORTFOLIO

5

Analyzing a Short Story

character
PLOT
setting
theme STYLE

Reading Workshop

Reading a Literary Analysis

Writing Workshop

Writing a Literary Analysis

Viewing and Representing

Critiquing a Film

Speaking and Listening

Presenting an Oral Interpretation

Analysis

■ An automobile mechanic working on a car uses the process of elimination to confirm her initial diagnosis of an engine malfunction.

■ A book reviewer closely examines a new thriller to determine how its author builds suspense.

> **Informational Text**
>
> **Exposition**

What do these scenarios have in common? Both involve **analysis:** the process of breaking something into parts and then examining the parts to discover how they work together. For example, during the telecast of a diving competition, commentators might play back each dive in slow motion, discussing every twist and turn. Their analysis would help viewers understand what made each dive successful or unsuccessful.

A writer of a **literary analysis** uses a similar process to explore the techniques an author uses to create memorable characters or to convey meaningful themes throughout a work. That is, the writer might focus on certain *literary elements* to better understand the work as a whole. In turn, readers use literary analyses to increase their understanding of a work and to form opinions about it.

YOUR TURN 1 Analyzing Literature

Think about one of your favorite novels as a whole. Then, jot down notes about the characters, scenes, and other parts of the novel that you enjoyed most. Finally, discuss your notes with a small group.

internet**connect**

go. hrw .com

GO TO: go.hrw.com
KEYWORD: EOLang 10-5

Reading a Literary Analysis

Consider this scene: A dark room in an old house whose sole human occupant hears the sound of clanking chains as someone—or something—climbs the stairs. Could this ominous scene appear in some Christmas story? Indeed it does, and the story has become a classic: *A Christmas Carol*, by Charles Dickens. In the essay you will read next, the contemporary American novelist John Irving analyzes how Dickens crafted this haunting holiday tale.

Preparing to Read

READING SKILL

Drawing Conclusions When you read a literary analysis, you are presented with a wealth of information about a work. To understand this information, you must **draw conclusions** as you read. A conclusion is a type of **inference,** an educated guess that you make by combining details from the text with your own knowledge and experience.

You draw conclusions all the time. For example, when you try to find an address in an unfamiliar city, you take in details from a map and from street signs. You combine these details with what you already know about street-numbering systems. From all of this, you can decide if you are on the right track. As you read Irving's analysis, begin to draw some conclusions about his overall opinion of *A Christmas Carol*.

READING FOCUS

Literary Elements Many things can be broken into parts. For example, the elements of the game of tennis include a court, two players, and rackets. Likewise, stories all have certain basic elements:

plot	character	theme
setting	point of view	language

As you read John Irving's introduction to *A Christmas Carol*, see if you notice which of these elements he focuses on in his analysis.

A Christmas Carol is a novella, a fictional work longer than a short story but shorter than a novel. In this excerpt from Irving's introduction, he analyzes how Dickens uses some key literary elements. As you read the excerpt, write down answers to the numbered active-reading questions.

from An Introduction to Charles Dickens's

A Christmas Carol

by John Irving

A Christmas Carol was originally subtitled "Ghost Story of Christmas"; the accent on the ghostly (*not* the Christmas-y) elements of the tale was further emphasized in Dickens's Preface to the 1843 edition. "I have endeavoured in this Ghostly little book, to raise the Ghost of an Idea, which shall not put my readers out of humour with themselves, with each other, with the season, or with me."

If that doesn't alert his readers sufficiently, Dickens titles the first stave[1] of his carol "Marley's Ghost," *and* the author states no less than four times in the first four paragraphs that Marley is dead. "Marley was dead: to begin with"—the first sentence of the first paragraph. "Old Marley was as dead as a door-nail"—the last sentence of the first paragraph. "You will therefore permit me to repeat, emphatically, that Marley was as dead as a door-nail"—the last sentence of the second paragraph. And, finally: "There is no doubt that Marley was dead. This must be distinctly understood, or nothing wonderful can come of the story I am going to relate"—the second and third sentences of the fourth paragraph. I think we get the idea. An editor of today's less-is-more school of fiction would doubtless have found this repetitious, but Dickens never suffered a minimalist's[2] sensibilities; in Dickens's prose, the refrain is as common as the semicolon.

From the beginning, Scrooge's cantankerous character is unsparing with his cynicism; his miserliness—more so, his utter shunning of humanity—

> **1.** What point about Dickens's writing style do you think Irving is trying to make in this paragraph?

---

1. Dickens divided *A Christmas Carol* into five sections called staves.

2. A minimalist uses simple structures and forms, often repetitiously.

makes him seem a fair match for any ghost. "The cold within him froze his old features," as Dickens describes him. "He carried his own low temperature always about with him; he iced his office in the dog-days; and didn't thaw it one degree at Christmas." Beggars don't dare to approach him. "Even the blindmen's dogs" give Scrooge a wide berth. "It was the very thing he liked. To edge his way along the crowded paths of life, warning all human sympathy to keep its distance"—Ebenezer Scrooge is the original Bah-Humbug man. "If I could work my will," Scrooge declares, "every idiot who goes about with 'Merry Christmas,' on his lips, should be boiled with his own pudding, and buried with a stake of holly through his heart."

> **2. After reading this paragraph, what can you quickly determine about Ebenezer Scrooge?**

Scrooge is such a pillar of skepticism, he at first resists believing in Marley's Ghost. "You may be an undigested bit of beef, a blot of mustard, a crumb of cheese, a fragment of an underdone potato. There's more of gravy than of grave about you, whatever you are!" Yet Scrooge is converted; beyond the seasonal lessons of Christian charity, *A Christmas Carol* teaches us that a man—even a man as hard as Ebenezer Scrooge—can change. What is heartening about the change in Scrooge is that he learns to love his fellowman; in the politically correct language of our insipid times, Scrooge learns to be *more caring*. But, typical of Dickens, Scrooge has undergone a deeper transformation; that he is persuaded to believe in ghosts, for example, means that Scrooge has been miraculously returned to his childhood—and to a child's powers of imagination and make-believe.

> **3. What theme, or underlying message, from *A Christmas Carol* does Irving seem to be discussing in this paragraph?**

Dickens's celebration of ghosts, and of Christmas, is but a small part of the author's abiding faith in the innocence and magic of children; Dickens believed that his own imagination—in fact, his overall well-being— depended on the contact he kept with his childhood. Furthermore, his popularity with his fellow Victorians, which is reflected by the ongoing interest of young readers today, is rooted in Dickens's remarkable ability for rendering *realistically* what many adults condescendingly call "fantasy." . . .

> **4. What aspect of Dickens's writing does Irving discuss in this paragraph?**

This is a Christmas story, yes; as such, it has a happy ending. But, as Marley's Ghost tells Scrooge, the tale is truly a warning. We had best improve our capacity for human sympathy—or else! We must love one another or die unloved.

Most of us have seen so many renditions of *A Christmas Carol* that we imagine we know the story, but how long has it been since we've actually *read* it? Each Christmas, we are assaulted with a new carol; indeed, we're fortunate if all we see is the delightful Alastair Sim.[3] One year, we suffer through some treacle[4] in a western setting; Scrooge is a grizzled cattle baron, tediously unkind to his cows. Another year, poor Tiny Tim hobbles about in the Bronx or in Brooklyn; old Ebenezer is an unrepentant slum landlord. In a few years, I'll be old enough to play the role of Scrooge in one of those countless amateur theatrical events which commemorate (and ruin) *A Christmas Carol* every season. We should spare ourselves these sentimentalized enactments and reread the original—or read it for the first time, as the case may be.

It may surprise us to learn that there is not one scene of Scrooge interacting with Tiny Tim, although that is a cherished moment in many made-for-television versions; it is also surprising that, in the epilogue, Dickens anticipates his own detractors. Of Scrooge, the author writes: "Some people laughed to see the alteration in him, but he let them laugh, and little heeded them; for he was wise enough to know that nothing ever happened on this globe, for good, at which some people did not have their fill of laughter in the outset; and knowing that such as these would be blind anyway, he thought it quite as well that they should wrinkle up their eyes in grins, as have the malady in less attractive forms. His own heart laughed: and that was quite enough for him." . . .

5. By making this statement, what objections about the character of Scrooge do you think Dickens may have been anticipating?

To his readers, Charles Dickens called himself "Their faithful Friend and Servant." In his Preface to the 1843 edition of *A Christmas Carol*, Dickens bestowed a generous benediction; he confessed his hopes for his "Ghostly little book" *and* for his readers—"May it haunt their houses pleasantly." In truth, . . . 150 years after the carol was written—Dickens's "Ghost Story of Christmas" continues to haunt us pleasantly. "And so, as Tiny Tim observed, God bless Us, Every One!"

---

3. An actor who played Scrooge in a 1951 film version of *A Christmas Carol*.

4. treacle: anything excessively sweet.

READING SKILL

Drawing Conclusions

Put Two and Two Together   As you read John Irving's essay, you probably drew some conclusions about the story and about Irving's view of it. To draw those conclusions, you had to "put two and two together"—to combine what you read with what you already know. When you draw a conclusion from your own reading, you use information from the text along with your prior knowledge to make a judgment about the text.

When you read fiction or nonfiction, drawing conclusions helps you more fully understand the author's meaning. Often, especially in fiction, authors "show" rather than "tell." For example, a writer might describe a single tear coming from a character's eye instead of directly stating, "He suddenly felt sad." In his essay, Irving says of Scrooge that "Beggars don't dare to approach him." From that detail, he expects you to understand—to draw the conclusion—that Scrooge is stingy.

The following Thinking It Through provides a general set of steps that you can use to draw conclusions as you read.

THINKING IT THROUGH   Drawing Conclusions

Read through the passage below, and then use the steps on the following page to draw some conclusions about it.

Dickens's *A Christmas Carol* was a great success with the readers of his day, and it remains a very popular story even now. The idea of a ghost story in which a seemingly unredeemable man is transformed for the better will continue to intrigue readers around the world for many years to come.

STEP 1 Identify the topic of the passage. The phrases <u>remains very</u> <u>popular</u> and <u>will continue to intrigue readers</u> suggest that the topic may be the lasting popularity of <u>A Christmas Carol</u>.

STEP 2 Relate the topic and contents of the passage to your own knowledge and experiences. I know that <u>A Christmas Carol</u> is a ghost story and that it is performed every year at my school. I also know that several movie versions are shown each year. I have no doubts that it is still very popular.

STEP 3 Use your knowledge and experiences to draw a conclusion about the topic of the passage. The writer never directly states, "The lasting popularity of <u>A Christmas Carol</u> is due to the idea behind it: a ghost story about a bad man who becomes good." However, based on my knowledge and experiences, I think that is the conclusion the writer wants readers to make.

YOUR TURN 2 Drawing Conclusions

Use the steps above to answer each of the following questions about John Irving's essay. Write your answers on your own paper.

1. Based on the last sentence of the fifth paragraph, what conclusions can you draw about Irving's opinion of "fantasy" and about the differences in the attitudes of adults and young readers toward it? Support your answer with quotations from this reading.

2. Based on Irving's statements in the seventh paragraph, what conclusion can you draw about his attitude toward recent versions of *A Christmas Carol*? Support your answer with quotations from this reading.

Literary Elements

READING FOCUS

Building Blocks **Plot, setting, character, point of view, theme,** and **language** are the most important elements an author uses to create the overall effect of a story. As a reader of a literary analysis, you must be familiar with these elements so that you can decide whether you agree with the writer's analysis of them. The chart on the following page explains the most important of these elements and provides important questions to ask about each.

Literary Elements	Questions
Plot is the term used to describe the actions and events in a story. Key terms related to plot include **conflict**—the problems a character faces in a story, and **climax**—the high point of a plot, the scene that settles the story's main conflict and determines how the story turns out.	Does the analysis contain a detailed discussion of the sequence of events in the story, or of the problems or difficulties the main character faces?
Setting is the time and place in which a story takes place. It may provide background for understanding characters and events in the story or for creating a particular mood or atmosphere.	Is there much discussion of the time or place in which the story happens?
Characters are the individuals in a story. **Characterization** is the way that an author reveals the qualities and traits of these individuals—either directly through description, thoughts, or feelings or indirectly through dialogue.	Is much of the analysis devoted to discussing the traits or qualities of the main character, or of another character in the story?
Point of view is the vantage point or "angle" from which a story is told. In **first-person point of view** the narrator is a character in the story and speaks using the pronoun *I*. A first-person narrator can tell only what he or she sees, hears, is told, or believes—but not what any other character sees, hears, is told, or believes. In **third-person point of view,** the narrator speaks from outside the story—not as a character—and uses third-person pronouns such as *he, she,* and *them.* A ***third-person omniscient*** narrator can reveal the thoughts of all characters or describe any event. A *limited third-person* narrator reveals the thoughts of just one character; that is, the story's events are filtered through the mind of that one person.	Does the writer of the analysis seem to spend much time discussing the "angle" or vantage point from which the story is told?
Theme is an important idea about life or human nature revealed in a story. It is not just a subject, like "war," but an insight, such as "war wounds are not only physical." (Authors usually don't state their themes directly, so readers have to draw their own conclusions about theme by analyzing the characters, events, setting, and dialogue the author uses.)	Is much of the analysis given over to discussing the story's message—an important idea about life or about people that the story reveals?
Authors of fiction, just like poets, use **language** to achieve certain effects. For example, an author may use *alliteration* (repeated consonant sounds) or *assonance* (repeated vowel sounds) to create a particular mood in a story. Another author may use a *refrain* (a repeated word or phrase) to try to drive home an important point.	Does the writer of the analysis seem especially interested in the writing style (word choices, figurative language, and so on) used by the author of the story?

Elements at Work   A literary analysis can enhance even the most critical reader's appreciation of a story by explaining how a writer uses various elements to create certain effects. Just as a tennis commentator might discuss a player's agility, endurance, and great backhand return, a literary analysis can explain each story element's

- **function** (how the element works in the story; what its purpose is)

- **effect** (what the reader feels or understands because of the presence of the element)
- **development** (how the writer creates or builds on the element—to set a mood or emphasize a theme, for instance)

For example, Irving begins with Dickens's use of language—specifically, Dickens's use of repetition—as the following quotation shows.

> ". . . Dickens titles the first stave of his carol 'Marley's Ghost,' *and* the author states no less than four times in the first four paragraphs that Marley is dead."

Irving then supports this statement by quoting four passages from the story that repeat the same idea: Marley is dead. However, he does not just *identify* the repetition—he actually begins by explaining its function: to emphasize that Marley is a ghost, and that the story is therefore a ghost story, something a reader might otherwise not have noticed right away.

YOUR TURN 3 — Analyzing Literary Elements

Read each of the following passages from the reading selection. Think about the specific literary element Irving discusses in each passage. Then, for each passage, write an answer to the following questions.

- Which literary element does Irving focus on in this passage?
- Does he discuss the element's function, effect, or development? Why?

Compare your responses with those of two or three other students. Keep in mind that you may not come to exactly the same conclusions because readers respond to texts differently.

1. "But, typical of Dickens, Scrooge has undergone a deeper transformation; that he is persuaded to believe in ghosts, for example, means that Scrooge has been miraculously returned to his childhood—and to a child's powers of imagination and make-believe."

2. "This is a Christmas story, yes; as such, it has a happy ending. But, as Marley's Ghost tells Scrooge, the tale is truly a warning. We had best improve our capacity for human sympathy—or else!"

3. "From the beginning, Scrooge's cantankerous character is unsparing with his cynicism; his miserliness—more so, his utter shunning of humanity—makes him seem a fair match for any ghost."

MINI-LESSON VOCABULARY

Using Roots

One way to deal with unfamiliar words is to study **word roots,** the basic blocks of meaning on which words are built. For example, knowing that the root *–ject* means "to cast or throw" will help you to understand words such as *dejected,* which means "cast down; discouraged." In this word, the root *–ject–* is combined with the prefix *de–* (meaning "down") to create the word's meaning. Here are three common roots and their definitions:

1. *–dict–, –dictat–* to say, command, or speak
2. *–vert–, –verse–, –verg–* to turn
3. *–pend–, –pens–* to hang or weigh

THINKING IT THROUGH   Using Word Roots

Use these steps to strengthen your vocabulary using root words.

1. **Remember the root meaning by associating it with a word you already know.** To remember *–dict–,* meaning "to say, command, talk, or speak," you might associate it with *contradict,* which means "to speak against."

2. **Keep in mind that some roots have alternative spellings.** For example, *–dict–* can also appear as *–dictat–,* as in the word *dictate,* meaning "to speak or read for a person to transcribe."

3. **When you recognize the root in a word you do not know, see if you can figure out its meaning.** If the word can be divided into roots and prefixes and suffixes, you will have to put the meanings of parts together. For example, the word *edict* is made up of the prefix *e–,* meaning "out," and the root *–dict–.* You can conclude that the word means "a speech or command given out."

4. **Test your meaning to see if it fits the context of the sentence.** For example, in the sentence *The officer's **edict** was obeyed by all,* you could say that "a speech or command given out" fits well with something that is obeyed.

PRACTICE

Using the steps above, choose the correct meanings of the boldface words. Put your answers on your own paper.

1. They resented his **dictatorial** methods. **(a)** very childish **(b)** controlling **(c)** extremely difficult **(d)** obviously untrustworthy

2. The last day of summer camp caused my sister's **pensive** mood. **(a)** joyous **(b)** indifferent **(c)** excited **(d)** sad

3. The rebels tried to **subvert** the movement toward peace. **(a)** overturn **(b)** instigate **(c)** support **(d)** create

4. They discussed the novelist's **diction. (a)** use of character **(b)** thematic ideas **(c)** plot complication **(d)** word choice

Literary Elements

Reading tests often include questions that ask you to describe certain literary elements in reading passages of literary selections. Below is a sample reading passage and a multiple-choice question about it that might appear on a test. Following the question is a set of steps you can use to find the correct answer.

> To Dr. Kresta's query about how they were doing, Mr. Barrow replied, "So far, so good, as long as the weather holds."
>
> Suddenly, unpredictable gusts of wind threatened to rip apart the hot-air balloon they had been riding in as they tried to com- plete their around-the-world flight. High-altitude temperatures froze the controls, increasing the chance for a potentially fatal crash landing. Below the balloonists, vast stretches of sparsely populated terrain— deserts and mountains—offered scant hope for rescue should they be forced to land.

1. Based on the passage above, the setting could be described as
   A. a mountain range
   B. thousands of feet in the air
   C. the desert
   D. a cold rain forest

THINKING IT THROUGH   **Describing Literary Elements**

The following steps will help you answer test questions about literary elements.

▶ **STEP 1 Read the question and choices *before* you read the passage** so you know exactly what to look for in the passage. The question clearly asks about the setting of the passage. I know I must look for details of setting.

▶ **STEP 2 Be sure you understand the literary element you are asked to find.** Setting involves *when* and *where* the story takes place.

▶ **STEP 3 Look for information in the passage that relates to the literary element you are asked to find.** I see from the passage that the two people are in a "hot-air balloon" at a "high altitude." The passage says nothing about when the story takes place.

▶ **STEP 4 Choose the answer that most correctly relates to the details in the passage.** Choice **A** is incorrect; mountains are mentioned, but the balloon is high above them. Choice **B** could be correct; hot-air balloons are usually found high in the air. Choice **C** is incorrect; the desert is mentioned but lies far below the balloon. Choice **D** is incorrect because a rain forest is not even mentioned in the passage. The answer must be **B**.

Writing a Literary Analysis

In this workshop, you will write a literary analysis. You will also learn how to

- **focus your analysis and develop a thesis**
- **collect, elaborate on, and organize details**
- **use complex sentences**
- **use quotation marks**

You have just read the last page of a book that you really enjoyed. In fact, several days later you are still thinking about it. You begin to wonder where you can read a discussion about the workings of the story or about the author. One place is in an **analysis**—a literary analysis.

A **literary analysis** is an in-depth look at a work of literature. In this Writing Workshop you will plan, organize, and write a literary analysis of a short story of your choice. Your goal as you write should be to create something that you would be proud to share.

Prewriting

Choose a Story

The Choice Is Yours   What kinds of stories do you like to read? Your personal taste in reading is a good place to start when choosing a story to analyze. You might also think about authors whose stories you have enjoyed. The chances are that other stories by the same authors will interest you.

Read and Respond Personally to Your Story

Dig In   As you read, it is a good idea to respond personally to what you are reading. When you involve yourself in what you read, you become an active reader. An active reader of a story

- **forms opinions** by asking, "How do I feel about the story?"
- **judges or measures** the characters and plot by asking, "How do I feel about the characters, events, and situations in the story?"
- **questions things** by asking, "What about the story is confusing?"
- **predicts** by asking, "What will happen next?"

TIP   Remember that personal responses to stories are neither right nor wrong. Two people can read the same story and come away with completely different views of it. Your response is unique to you.

Consider Purpose, Audience, and Tone

Get Things Straight When you write an analysis of a short story, your **purpose** is to provide a clear and detailed explanation of how the author uses literary elements to shape the entire piece. Because you can assume that your **audience** has already read your story, you do not need to retell the plot.

You should maintain a formal tone in your literary analysis. **Tone** is your attitude toward your subject; it is conveyed through your use of language. Writing in the third person (using the pronouns *he, she,* and *they*) and avoiding the contractions and colloquialisms of conversational expressions will help you achieve a formal tone.

> **TIP** A literary analysis, like many other forms of nonfiction, is meant to be somewhat persuasive. To some degree, writers of literary analyses want their readers to agree with their opinions of the story and of the story's author.

Analyze Your Story

Take a Closer Look Authors manipulate literary elements—the components of stories—to achieve different effects. You analyze a short story to discover the important elements in a story and how the author uses them. Analyze the elements in a story by answering the questions below.

Literary Element	Analysis Questions
Plot—the action or series of events in a story. Conflicts are the problems the characters face. These conflicts can be internal or external. The **climax** is the point in the story at which the main conflict is resolved.	• What important problems or difficulties do the characters face? • How are the characters' problems resolved? • Do the events happen logically?
Setting—the time and place in which the story occurs. The setting provides important background for understanding people and events in the story.	• Where and when does the story take place? • Do the time and place affect characters and events, cause a conflict, or set a mood?
Characters—the individuals in a short story. *Characterization* is how the characters' qualities are revealed: *directly* through description, thoughts, or feelings, or *indirectly* through dialogue.	• What is the main character like? • How are the characters' qualities revealed? • What motivates the characters? • Does the main character change? If so, how and why?

(continued)

(continued)

Point of view—the angle from which the story is told. The angle can be from a character in the story (signaled by first-person pronouns such as *I*) or from an outside person (signaled by third-person pronouns such as *he* or *she*). In some short stories the point of view shifts.	• How does point of view affect your response? • Does the narrator speak with the pronoun *I*? (This point of view is called **first person.**) • Can the narrator reveal the thoughts of any character? (This point of view is called **third-person omniscient.**) • Does the narrator relate events from the view of just one character? (This point of view is called **third-person limited.**)
Foreshadowing—a hint or suggestion of coming events.	• Does the author hint at events that might take place later? If so, where and how?
Irony—a surprising contrast between appearance or expectation and reality. Irony can be humorous or bitter, but it always makes us think.	• Do the author or characters ever say one thing, but mean something different? (This contrast is **verbal irony.**) • Do characters face situations surprisingly unlike their expectations? (This contrast is called **situational irony.**) • At any point, do you know more than the characters do? (This contrast is called **dramatic irony.**)
Theme—an important idea about life or human nature. Rather than stating a theme directly, writers often expect readers to figure out the theme.	• What important idea about life or human nature does the story reveal? • How is this theme developed?

Here is part of an analysis log one writer created to record information about literary elements in a story titled "A Man Called Horse."

Analysis Log: "A Man Called Horse"

Literary Element	Responses
Plot	Main character has problems with his feelings of self-worth. These problems are resolved when he moves to the West and is captured by Crow Indians—with whom he "earns" his future.
Setting	The story takes place on the northern plains of the American frontier near the middle of the nineteenth century. The location gives the story a feeling of danger and adventure.
Characters	The main character is a New England man who eventually calls himself Horse. His traits are revealed by direct and indirect characterization. He is motivated by a need for a sense of self-worth.
Theme	The theme of this story is that a person has to earn a sense of self-worth. The author develops this theme by describing the events Horse goes through to gain self-worth.

Find a Focus and Develop a Thesis

Pick Your Target Once you have analyzed how literary elements are used in your story, you can decide which elements will serve as the focus of your analysis. You can zero in on a single element, or you can discuss how two elements work together. For example, the student writing about "A Man Called Horse" might choose to discuss the way the author shows how the man's character changes through events in the story.

Next, draft a preliminary **thesis statement. Your thesis statement is important because it identifies the element or elements on which you will focus,** *and* **it states your main idea about those elements.**

KEY CONCEPT

THINKING IT THROUGH   Finding a Focus and Developing a Thesis

Use the following steps to find a focus and construct a thesis statement for your analysis. The example responses are based on "A Man Called Horse."

▶ **STEP 1 Recall what went through your mind after you first read the story.** Your initial reaction to the story is often a clue to insights you might want to share with your readers. *The main character changed a lot from the beginning to the end of the story.*

▶ **STEP 2 Review your answers to the analysis questions about story elements on pages 179 and 180.** Think about the literary element for which you seem to have the most interesting information. *The most interesting information in my answers concerns the story's main character.*

▶ **STEP 3 Compare your response in step 1 to your response in step 2.** It is likely that your most interesting answers to the analysis questions will support your overall reaction to the story. *Since my first reaction was to the main character and I have a lot of notes about the main character, I'll focus on characterization.*

▶ **STEP 4 Decide what you want to say about the element or elements you find most important.** Your thoughts about these elements will be your **main idea, or thesis.** *The author's use of characterization shows how the main character changes through the story.*

▶ **STEP 5 Form your thesis statement by joining the literary element(s) with your main idea about them.** Write a sentence that includes the story's title, the author, the literary element(s) on which you will focus, and your main idea. *In the short story "A Man Called Horse," Dorothy M. Johnson traces the changes that one nineteenth-century young man undergoes in his search for self-worth.*

YOUR TURN 5 **Laying the Groundwork for Your Analysis**

Delve into your short story by using the preceding steps. Remember to consider your purpose, audience, and tone, analyze your story, and find a focus and develop your thesis.

Gather Support

Focusing In   Your readers are not likely to accept your ideas if you do not support them. In a literary analysis, support consists of **key points** to support your thesis, **details** from the story to support key points, and **elaboration** that explains the details and ties them to the key points.

KEY CONCEPT ➤

Key Points   **The key points you make should relate directly to your thesis.** There are several techniques you can use to determine your key points.

- **Try asking questions about the thesis.** Consider the example thesis about "A Man Called Horse" in the Thinking It Through on page 181. A student writer could ask, "What has to be in this essay to reflect Horse's change? What does Horse say or do that shows the change?"

TIP   When discussing events from a story, always use the **literary present tense.** That is, always refer to the events in the story as if they were happening in the present—not in the past.

- **Set up contrasts and freewrite about them.** Seeing contrasts often helps you discover ideas. *At the beginning of the story, Horse is discontented and longing. At the end of the story, Horse is content, proud, and confident.*

- **Create a map showing how the main idea develops through the story.** This technique works well when writing about characterization.

In the beginning of the story, Horse is discontented and feels no self-worth. → In the middle of the story, Horse begins to experience things that change him personally. → By the end of the story, Horse is a man with a sense of honor and self-worth.

Supporting Details   Supporting details are the evidence you include to support your key points. When you establish the points you want to make about a story, you will discover supporting details in the text. You can include supporting details by using three methods:

- **paraphrasing,** or restating a passage in your own words
- **summarizing** the main points of a passage in a condensed form
- **direct quotations,** or using the exact words from a story

TIP Use strong, active verbs in your literary analysis. Replace words such as *show* and *use* with more descriptive ones such as *mirror* and *trace.* Make passive sentences active whenever possible.

Elaboration   Supporting a key point with a detail from the story is not enough. You must elaborate on details to explain *how* they support your key points. The following portion of a chart shows the three key points that a writer makes to support a thesis statement about "A Man Called Horse."

Thesis: In the short story "A Man Called Horse," Dorothy M. Johnson traces the changes that one nineteenth-century young man undergoes in his search for self-worth.

Key Point	Story Detail	Elaboration
Johnson first characterizes her main character as a person discontented with a life others might envy.	**Quotation:** . . . the man has "every comfort and privilege his father's wealth could provide."	This description mirrors his casual acceptance of a privileged life.
Later on, when this man is captured by Indians, Johnson uses the man's thoughts and feelings to show his personal growth.	**Summary:** After months of hearing an unfamiliar language, one day he is surprised to discover that he understands a phrase he overhears.	This boost to his spirits is shown by his decision to try to marry into the family he serves.
As Horse takes his final steps from alienation to self-worth, Johnson shifts her focus to Horse's outer life.	**Paraphrase:** Unexpectedly, Horse decides to stay and care for his destitute mother-in-law.	His unselfish decision to stay and care for her shows just how much he has changed.

Organize Your Analysis

Get It in Order   Often, your topic and your ideas will suggest a natural way to arrange your points and supporting details. For example, to address how an author uses plot to build suspense, you might discuss the events in **chronological order.** You can also order information by **order of importance.**

 6 Collecting and Organizing Your Ideas

Use the preceding steps to collect and organize details. Remember to collect details (quotations, paraphrases, or summaries) that support your key points and elaborate on each detail you provide.

Writing

Literary Analysis

Framework   **Directions and Explanations**

Introduction

■ Open with an interesting comment on the story.

■ Include a thesis statement.

A Good Start   Use an observation, a question, or a quotation related to your thesis to describe a connection you made to the story.

Set Your Focus   Your thesis statement should include the title and author of the story, the literary element or elements on which you will focus, and your main idea about the element or elements.

Body

■ State first key point with support and elaboration.

■ State second key point with support and so on.

Make Your Point   Develop a paragraph for each of your other key points. Arrange them in a logical order.

Back It Up   Support each point by quoting, paraphrasing, or summarizing details from the story. Elaborate by explaining how the details connect to each point.

Conclusion

■ Restate your thesis.

■ Summarize your key points.

Finish with a Flourish   Leave your readers with something to consider. One good way to close your essay is with a general comment about the story that relates to your thesis.

YOUR TURN 7   Writing a First Draft

Using the framework and the directions and explanations above as a guide, write a first draft of your literary analysis. Read the Writer's Model on the next page to see how one writer developed a thesis.

A Writer's Model

The following literary analysis closely follows the framework on the previous page.

Characterization in "A Man Called Horse"

INTRODUCTION

Thesis

"Who am I?" and "Where do I belong?" are questions people have always asked themselves as they approach adulthood. In the short story "A Man Called Horse," Dorothy M. Johnson traces the changes that one nineteenth-century young man undergoes as he finds answers to those questions in his search for self-worth.

BODY
First key point

Johnson first characterizes her main character, an unnamed young man, as a person discontented with a life others might envy. The author tells readers that living in a "gracious old Boston home," the man has "every comfort and privilege his father's wealth could provide." This description mirrors his casual acceptance of a privileged life. The author goes on to explain that the man knows himself so little that he does not even know why he is unhappy. Vaguely sensing that he does not belong and hoping to find his "equals," he moves to the West, where he believes "all white men" are "kings." His money allows him to surround himself with men he respects, but who show no interest in being his friends.

Support and elaboration

Later on, when this man is taken captive by a band of Crow Indians, Johnson uses the man's thoughts and feelings to show his first steps toward personal growth. She first displays the character's humiliation by describing how he is tethered and forced into servitude: "They took him along in a matter-of-fact way, as they took the captured horses." The man knows he is being treated as a nonperson, but he is too afraid for his life to fight against his captors. Johnson reveals the man's growing ingenuity when she describes how he pretends to be a horse, a meek "bearer of burdens." The man knows that it is shrewd to do so, because it helps him fare much better. Then, Johnson shows a spark of happiness in him: After months of being ordered around in an unfamiliar language, one day he is surprised to discover that he understands a phrase he overhears. This boost to his spirits is shown by his decision to try to marry into the family he serves. He reasons

Second key point

Support and elaboration

(continued)

(continued)

Third key point

Support and elaboration

that doing so will help him to escape. Thus, Horse, as he now calls himself, sets out to win the Crows' respect.

As Horse takes his final steps away from alienation toward self-worth, Johnson shifts her focus to Horse's outer life. He kills a member of an enemy tribe and steals two horses—actions the Crows view as brave. Then, by gaining a wife and wealth, he wins the respect he sought from the Crows and the sense of worth he sought for himself. His hard-won self-respect is tested, however, when he loses all his possessions, the entire camp moves away, and his wife dies in childbirth. Unexpectedly, Horse decides to stay and care for his destitute mother-in-law. His unselfish decision to stay and care for her shows just how much he has changed: "He could afford to be magnanimous, for he knew he was a man."

CONCLUSION

Summary of key points

General comment related to the thesis

Johnson's characterization of Horse parallels his personal growth. By describing his life in Boston, she underscores his sense of alienation, even though he has all the material things he could want. She then shifts to reveal the thoughts and feelings behind his actions as he takes the initiative to secure a future as a more giving, noble man. Perhaps her story suggests that for many people, the path to self-worth ultimately lies in taking action to achieve it.

Crow Warriors

A Student's Model

The following is an excerpt from a literary analysis written by Jeremy Schmidt, a student from University High, University of Chicago Lab Schools in Chicago, Illinois.

Number One

Everybody strives to be recognized as an individual, but this is often a difficult task. This idea is illustrated in Kurt Vonnegut's short story, "The Lie." At the beginning of the story, Sylvia thinks of her son Eli only as one of many Remenzels; by the end, she begins to think of him as an individual. The change that occurs in Eli's mother has an important effect on their relationship and on Eli himself.

Throughout the early part of the story Sylvia Remenzel thinks of her son as the next Remenzel to attend Whitehill, not as a distinct individual. While they are driving to school Sylvia says to Eli, "If I were you, I'd be so excited I could hardly stand it." She is pressuring Eli to feel "excited" or happy about his entrance into high school. She then tells him that his four years at the Whitehill school will be the "best" years of his life. Rather than inquiring about his feelings, she is telling him how to feel. Sylvia assumes that since all the Remenzel men have attended, been successful at, and enjoyed Whitehill, Eli will also. She fails to even consider the possibility that Eli is not "excited" about going to Whitehill or that this school is not right for Eli because of his individual character. . . .

Sylvia eventually recognizes her own misconception of her son. During the Remenzels' talk with the headmaster of Whitehill, he explains that Eli was not accepted to the school due to his previous grades and his poor score on the entrance exam. He tells them that "to expect him to do Whitehill work would be both unrealistic and cruel." Sylvia's mind momentarily goes "blank." This suggests that Sylvia has been shocked into completely reassessing her son's life and needs.

INTRODUCTION

Thesis

BODY: First key point

Support and elaboration

Second key point
Support and elaboration

Revising

Evaluate and Revise Your Draft

Check It Twice   Carefully read your whole paper at least twice. First, examine content and organization using the guidelines below. Then, use the guidelines on the next page to help you focus on sentence style.

➤ **First Reading: Content and Organization**   The following chart will help you evaluate and revise the content and organization of your analysis. First, answer the questions in the left-hand column. If you need help, use the tips in the middle column. Then, use the revision techniques in the right-hand column to make any needed changes.

Literary Analysis: Content and Organization Guidelines for Peer and Self-Evaluation

Evaluation Questions	▶ Tips	▶ Revision Techniques
❶ Does the opening capture the reader's attention?	▶ **Underline** the sentences that hook the reader. If no sentences are underlined, revise.	▶ **Add** a quotation, a question, or a personal connection you made to the story.
❷ Does the thesis statement provide the title of the story, the author, the literary element(s) discussed, and the main idea about the element(s)?	▶ **Put a 1** over the title, a **2** over the author, a **3** over key words that signal the literary element(s) discussed, and a **4** over the main idea. If any number is missing, revise.	▶ **Add** any missing parts to the thesis statement.
❸ Do details from the story support each key point? Is sufficient elaboration provided for each story detail?	▶ **Put an A** next to the sentence that states the key point in each body paragraph. **Put a B** next to details that support the key points. **Put a C** next to any sentence that explains how a detail connects to the key point. If an **A**, **B**, or **C** is missing from a body paragraph, revise.	▶ **Add** one or more sentences that quote, summarize, or paraphrase story details to support your key points. **Elaborate** by explaining how the details connect to the paragraph's key point. **Cut** any sentences that are not connected to the key point of a paragraph.
❹ Is the language in the analysis appropriate for the intended audience, purpose, and tone?	▶ **Draw a box** around any contractions, colloquial expressions, or other informal language. Revise the boxed parts.	▶ **Replace** informal expressions with words that set a more formal tone. For sentences not in the third person, **rewrite** them from the third-person point of view.
❺ Does the conclusion restate the thesis and summarize the key points? Does it leave readers with something to consider?	▶ **Highlight** the restatement of the thesis and **circle** the summary of the key points. If any of these parts is missing, revise.	▶ **Add** a restatement of the thesis and a summary of the key points. **Add** a thought that applies the thesis to a more general world.

ONE WRITER'S REVISIONS Here is how one writer used the content and organization guidelines to revise part of the literary analysis on page 185. Study the revisions carefully, and then answer the questions that follow.

> Johnson first characterizes her main character, an unnamed young man, as a person discontented with a life others might envy. The author tells readers that living in a ~~ritzy house~~ the *"gracious old Boston home,"* man has "every comfort and privilege his father's wealth could provide." *This description mirrors his casual acceptance of a privileged life.*

replace

elaborate

Analyzing the Revision Process

1. Why did the writer revise her description of the house?
2. Why did the writer add a sentence after the quoted material?

YOUR TURN 8 Focusing on Content and Organization

Using the guidelines on page 188, revise the content and organization of your literary analysis. Use the example revisions above as a model.

> **Second Reading: Style** An engaging literary analysis should not use too many short, choppy sentences. Instead, combine such sentences into **complex sentences** by using **adjective clauses**—subordinate clauses introduced by **relative pronouns** (such as *who, whom, which,* and *that*) that modify a noun or pronoun. Use the following guidelines to incorporate more of these kinds of complex sentences into your paper.

PEER REVIEW

Ask a classmate to read your analysis and answer these questions.

1. Which quotations, summaries, or paraphrases from the story most effectively support the writer's key points? Why?

2. What is the writer's thesis? Does the writer close with a final thought about this thesis? What is that thought?

Style Guidelines

Evaluation Question	▶ Tip	▶ Revision Technique
Does the paper include too many short, choppy sentences?	▶ **Underline** repeated nouns in back-to-back sentences. Consider revising these sentences.	▶ **Eliminate** choppy sentences by using adjective clauses to combine sentences. **Replace** a repeated noun with the relative pronoun of the adjective clause.

Focus on Sentences

Using Complex Sentences

When you are writing about specific key ideas from a short story, you will sometimes write short sentences whose ideas are so closely related that you use some of the same words in each sentence. Because these short sentences are logically connected, you can combine them by using adjective clauses. The examples below show how two sentences containing a repeated noun can be combined into a single complex sentence by using an adjective clause. In combining sentences this way, you embed one sentence inside the other by replacing the repeated noun with a relative pronoun.

> **Sentences containing a repeated noun (*Poe*):** Edgar Allan **Poe** was a writer. **Poe** was born in Boston.

> **Sentences combined using an adjective clause that is introduced with a relative pronoun (*who*):** Edgar Allan Poe, **who** was born in Boston, was a writer.

ONE WRITER'S REVISIONS Here is how the writer of the model literary analysis on page 185 used a relative pronoun to combine two simple sentences into a complex sentence.

BEFORE REVISION

    In the short story "A Man Called Horse," one nineteenth-century young man undergoes <u>changes</u>. He experiences <u>changes</u> as he finds answers to those questions in his search for self-worth. Dorothy M. Johnson traces those <u>changes</u>.

The word changes is repeated unnecessarily.

AFTER REVISION

    In the short story "A Man Called Horse," Dorothy M. Johnson traces the changes **that** one nineteenth-century young man undergoes as he finds answers to those questions in his search for self-worth.

Sentences are combined using a relative pronoun.

Analyzing the Revision Process

1. What did the writer accomplish by combining the sentences?
2. Is there any advantage of not combining the sentences? If so, what is it?

 **Focusing on Style**

Use the style guidelines on page 189 to locate repetition in your paper and to eliminate it by creating complex sentences.

Designing Your Writing

Formatting Your Essay   Your teacher will probably give you specific directions about formatting your literary analysis. If not, you can use the following MLA guidelines.

- **Use one-inch margins** all around so that your pages are easy to read.
- **Double-space** lines of text, and **indent the first line of paragraphs** five spaces. **Align text** on the left, but **leave the right margins ragged.**
- **Center the title** of your essay at the top of the first page. In the upper left-hand corner, **include your name, the course name, your teacher's name,** and **the date. Number the pages** (except the first page) in the top right-hand corner.
- If your teacher requires a title page, **center the title, your name, the course name, the teacher's name,** and **the date** on a separate page.

TIP   These guidelines specifically address essays written with word-processing software, but several apply also to handwritten essays.

Essay Without Title Page

Name
Course
Teacher
Date

Title

_____
_____
_____
_____
_____
_____.

Title Page

Title
Name

Course
Teacher
Date

Weaving Quotations into Your Essay

You know one way to support a key idea in your analysis is to include supporting quotations from the story. However, if you fail to integrate these quotations skillfully, you will affect the communication of your ideas. An effective way to use short quotations is to weave them into your sentences, at the beginning, middle, or end. Look at the following examples:

Beginning: "He was envious still, even among the horses," which are capable of fending for themselves.

Middle: Because he amused the Crows "like a strange pet," they gave him food in the winter.

End: Forced into servitude, he is filled with rage, "although anger was an emotion he knew he could not afford."

When you integrate a quotation into a sentence, be sure that the quoted material fits grammatically into the sentence. For example,

be sure that what you end up with is a complete sentence and not a sentence fragment.

Sentence Fragment	"A future," he realizes, "something to be earned." [lacks a verb]
Complete Sentence	"A future," he realizes, is "something to be earned."

You can also use a short phrase to introduce a quotation into a sentence, as in the following example:

According to Johnson, "One of the customs of courtship involved sending a gift of horses to a girl's older brother and bestowing much buffalo meat upon her mother."

TIP When the material you quote takes up more than four lines in your analysis, create a **block quotation.** In MLA style, block quotations begin on a new line; each line of the quotation is indented one inch (about ten spaces). When you set off a quotation this way, do not enclose it in quotation marks.

PRACTICE

For each practice item below, weave the quotation into the sentence. You do not have to use all the words in a quotation, and you may add or revise words in the sentence.

1. **Sentence** Poe uses sensory details to create a feeling of terror.

   Quotation "His room was as black as pitch with the thick darkness. . . ."

2. **Sentence** Edgar Allan Poe uses comparisons for description.

   Quotation "old man's heart" and

"sound, such as a watch makes when enveloped in cotton"

3. **Sentence** In "The Tell-Tale Heart," Poe immediately establishes the narrator as troubled.

   Quotation "nervous—very, very dreadfully nervous"

4. **Sentence** Poe's use of personification reinforces the atmosphere of terror.

   Quotation "when all the world slept"

Proofread Your Analysis

A Last Look   Before publishing your analysis, work collaboratively to proofread it at least twice for errors in grammar, spelling, and punctuation. In a literary analysis, it is important to pay particular attention to your punctuation of the title of the story and of direct quotations.

Reference Note

For more information on **quotation marks,** see page 743.

Grammar Link

Using Quotation Marks in a Literary Analysis

In a literary analysis it is particularly important that quotation marks be used correctly.

- **Enclose titles of short stories in quotation marks.**

  I read the story "The Cold Equations."

- **Use quotation marks at the beginning and the end of material quoted directly from a story.** Place commas and periods inside closing quotation marks; place semicolons and colons outside closing quotation marks. Exclamation points and question marks are placed inside the closing quotation marks only when they are part of the quoted material.

  Godwin reinforces the stowaway's innocence by saying she "belonged in that world of soft winds and a warm sun, music, and moonlight."

  At one point in the story, Barton says, "You're afraid, but you're not a coward"; this statement reflects Barton's admiration of his stowaway.

  Marilyn says, "I've caused everyone I love to be hurt, haven't I?"

- **Use single quotation marks to enclose a quotation within a quotation.**

To reinforce the idea that technology is frightening and cold, Godwin includes Marilyn's comments on the spaceship, "'Isn't it—' She stopped, and he looked at her questioningly. 'Isn't it cold in here?'"

PRACTICE

On your own paper, correct errors in the punctuation of story titles and quotations in the following sentences.

1. In Leslie Marmon Silko's The Man to Send Rain Clouds," imagery reinforces the story's conflict: The wind pulled at the priest's brown Franciscan robe and swirled away the cornmeal and pollen".

2. Louise wants to be sure that Teofilo 'won't be thirsty.'

3. The priest asks, What brings you here?

4. Leon "took a piece of string out of his pocket and tied a small gray feather in the old man's long white hair;' here he observes tradition.

5. Why does Leon say "now the old man could send big thunder-clouds for sure?"

Point of View Stories are told from some-body's perspective. The literary term for this is **point of view**—who is telling the story. You have several points of view to pick from for your story, and each has its advantages. After deciding which one is right for your story, be sure that you use it consistently; carelessly shifting points of view can confuse readers. Here are three basic points of view:

- **First-person point of view:** One of the characters tells the story (using the first-person pronoun *I*). This character can reveal only his or her own thoughts and feelings.

- **Third-person omniscient (all-knowing) point of view:** The narrator, who is not a character, can tell what all characters are thinking and feeling and what is happening in other places in the story.

- **Third-person limited point of view:** The narrator, who is not a character, tells the story through the mind of one character.

Setting Once you have determined plot and point of view, you can consider the **setting:** the time, place, and **mood** (the atmosphere or feeling a story conveys). The more detailed your descriptions of setting are, the more interesting the setting will be to readers.

What's the Big Idea? Many stories are built around a **theme**—a meaning an author tries to convey about life or human nature. You can convey a theme in your story by hinting at it in the story's title or through dialogue spoken by characters.

Learn by Example Read the following excerpts from "The Bride Comes to Yellow Sky" by Stephen Crane. Note that some of the excerpts illustrate more than one literary element. The annotations explain how the literary elements function in the excerpt.

Setting—Crane includes specific descriptions of the setting—the plains of Texas.

> The great Pullman was whirling onward with such dignity of motion that a glance from the window seemed simply to prove that the plains of Texas were pouring eastward. Vast flats of green grass, dull-hued spaces of mesquite and cactus, little groups of frame houses, woods of light and tender trees, all were sweeping into the east, sweeping over the horizon, a precipice.

Plot (conflict), Point of view—Internal conflict begins with the town marshal returning with his new bride to Yellow Sky, afraid of how the people will react. The story is told from the third-person omniscient point of view.

> He, the town marshal of Yellow Sky, a man known, liked, and feared in his corner, a prominent person, had gone to San Antonio to meet a girl he believed he loved, and there, after the usual prayers, had actually induced her to marry him, without consulting Yellow Sky for any part of the transaction. He was now bringing his bride before an innocent and unsuspecting community.

The California Express on the Southern Railway was due at Yellow Sky in twenty-one minutes. There were six men at the . . . "Weary Gentleman." . . . A young man . . . suddenly appeared in the open door. He cried: "Scratchy Wilson's . . . turned loose with both hands."

"Don't know whether there'll be a fight or not," answered one man grimly. "But there'll be some shootin'—some good shootin.'"

Plot (complication), Character— The plot becomes more complicated when Scratchy Wilson, the town troublemaker, starts a fight. The one man who handles him is the marshal. Scratchy is characterized as a troublemaker who often goes wild and looks for a gunfight with Marshal Potter. This is the story's external conflict.

Presently they heard from a distance the sound of a shot, followed by three wild yowls. It instantly removed a bond from the men in the darkened saloon. There was a shuffling of feet. They looked at each other. "Here he comes," they said.

Plot (suspense)—Crane builds suspense by describing how the men in the saloon wait for Scratchy to come.

Potter and his bride walked sheepishly and with speed. . . . As they circled the corner, they came face to face with a man in a maroon-colored shirt who was feverishly pushing cartridges into a large revolver. Upon the instant the man dropped his revolver to the ground, and, like lightning, whipped another from its holster.

Plot (climax)—The climax of the story comes when Jack Potter and his new wife are making their way to Potter's house and bump into Scratchy Wilson as he is loading his gun.

"Married!" said Scratchy, not at all comprehending. . . . "Well," said Wilson at last, slowly, "I s'pose it's all off now." . . . He was not a student of chivalry; it was merely that in the presence of this foreign condition he was a simple child of the earlier plains. He picked up his starboard revolver, and placing both weapons in their holsters, he went away.

Character (development), Plot (resolution)—Upon noticing the marshal's new wife, Scratchy Wilson no longer wants to fight him. Crane reveals another side of this villain—his simplicity. This scene is also the plot's resolution. Potter's new status as a married man ends Wilson's torment of the town.

YOUR TURN 11 **Writing Your Short Story**

Using the guidelines above, write the story you would like to tell. Once you have finished your first draft, give your story a title. Then, revise, proofread, and publish the story.

Critiquing a Film

WHAT'S AHEAD?

In this section you will learn to

■ identify and critique literary elements in a film

■ identify and critique technical elements in a film

Critiquing a film is much like analyzing a story. In both cases, you evaluate how the creator conveys thoughts, ideas, images, and events. The writer of a story has only one way to do this: words. A filmmaker uses many elements to tell a story—dialogue, action, visual images, music, and other elements. These elements must combine seamlessly to contribute to the overall effect. This seamlessness makes a good movie difficult to analyze. It is hard to pay attention to the separate elements when you are holding your breath to see if the heroine escapes!

Watching and Forming an Opinion

Presenting the Elements   Stories you see on the big screen contain the same elements as stories you read—point of view, setting, character, plot, theme, and so on. Although many movies are based on stories previously published in books or magazines, filmmakers must handle these literary elements differently because film itself is different. Aside from presenting literary elements through spoken dialogue and occasional narration, a filmmaker must *show* the literary elements of a story.

Point of View   One key difference between stories in books and stories on film is that most films lack a narrator. That is, in most films, the camera becomes the narrator, the point of view from which the story is told. The filmmaker uses the camera to show the audience what he or she wants them to see. Of course, there are exceptions. Some movies have a narrator that tells part of the film's story in a ***voice-over***—that is, the narrator is heard but not seen.

Setting   You can identify a film's setting by watching, listening, and noting details, such as clothing styles. For instance, if a film opens with a character wearing clothes that were in style twenty years ago, you quickly get an idea of the time in which the story occurs. One way that place is often conveyed is through the depiction of landmarks, such as the New York City skyline.

A filmmaker can also convey a setting directly by superimposing a temporary title on the screen at a film's beginning or at scene changes. For example, a film or a scene in a film might open with the words *London, 1602* temporarily shown at the bottom of the screen.

Character   Characters in a film are not usually described through ***direct characterization*** (descriptions provided by a narrator). Instead, their appearance and actions are depicted by actors for viewers to see with their own eyes. Sometimes a character's thoughts will be heard in a voice-over so the audience can get a more direct understanding of the character.

Plot   Plot development in a film works very much as it does in stories in books. There is a conflict with complications that build to a climax. Of course, as a film viewer, you actually see events and characters' actions instead of reading descriptions of them.

Theme   A theme of a film is also similar to a theme of a story in a book. However, instead of inferring a story's theme from written words, a viewer must determine a movie's theme based on what is seen and heard.

Evaluating the Elements   To critique a film well, you must work from a set of **evaluation criteria:** standards for judging the effectiveness of individual elements of the film. Just as you have to meet standards to get an A in a course or to qualify for one of your school's teams, a film should measure up to certain standards to be judged a good film. The following chart lists some basic criteria you can use to evaluate the use of literary elements in film.

Element	Criteria
Point of View	• The film presents the story from a point of view that helps the characters seem real.
Setting	• The filmmaker creates a setting that is realistic, believable, and consistent.
Characters and Actors	• The characters seem like real people. • The characters/actors interact well with each other.
Plot	• The story holds a viewer's interest. • The story presents believable problems or conflicts for characters to resolve.

Of course, this list of criteria is just a starting point. When you critique a film, you will also have to consider your specific personal preferences about what makes a movie good or bad and use those preferences as additional criteria.

Identifying and Critiquing Technical Elements

When reading a story in a book, you must picture the setting, characters, and events in your mind. However, in a film, all story elements are displayed, portrayed, and acted for you under the direction of a filmmaker.

To present these story elements in a movie, a filmmaker must manage many **technical elements** (lighting, sound, and camera techniques) specific to movies. Therefore, in addition to identifying and critiquing the literary elements in a film, you should identify and critique how effectively a filmmaker deals with some common technical elements. The following chart presents just some of the basics. There are many more specific technical elements that you can evaluate in a film. However, for a film critique intended for a general audience (not for filmmakers or film students), the elements and criteria below are a good starting point.

Element	Criteria
Lighting—the way in which each scene is lit (bright or dark or soft or harsh, for example)	• Lighting should help the filmmaker create a mood, tone, or atmosphere. • It may enhance the aesthetic (artistic) experience of watching the film; some scenes may take on the qualities of fine paintings.
Sound—the sound effects, music, and dialogue that accompany the images in the film	• Sound should be appropriate to each scene; for example, lighthearted music and comical sound effects should not accompany a solemn scene (unless the filmmaker intends to create a contrast to achieve a certain effect).
Camera Techniques—the techniques used by the filmmaker to alter the audience's view of the characters and scenes. These include adjustments in camera angles and movement, zooms, and close-ups.	• Camera techniques should help to keep viewers involved and interested in the characters and scenes. • They should not distract from the story the filmmaker is telling. • They may be used for a variety of effects: to depict visual confusion, for example, or to help create a humorous mood.

A Model Critique

Below is a model critique built from the lists of criteria on pages 199 and 200. The writer begins with a one-sentence description of the film, then comments on the filmmaker's use of literary and technical elements, and closes with a one-sentence summary of his overall opinion of the movie. (The film the writer discusses is an imaginary one, not a real movie.)

Young Guinevere

As you might guess from the title, *Young Guinevere* tells the story of the young woman who became queen to the legendary King Arthur. However, this Arthurian story is told in a unique way—not from the vantage point of Arthur or his knights, but from that of the woman who eventually stood with Arthur at the center of the legends. This point of view adds a new dimension to the tales, making the characters seem more genuine and lively than they have in any other film version of the story. The plot the characters find themselves in (a retelling of Guinevere's young life up to and including her courting by Arthur) drifts into silliness at times but never leaves viewers bored. The principal actors the film brings together always keep things interesting, playing off each other for both comic and tragic effects. The one exception is Jenny Osgood, who plays a wildly over-the-top older sister to the title character. However, Allison Harvey's brilliant performance as a smart, self-confident, completely charming Guinevere more than makes up for any shortcomings in the rest of the cast. With some minor lapses, the film's director and crew also make the setting come alive; the costumes, sets, and other details all help to create a world that is at the same time both fantastic and believable.

(continued)

One-sentence description

Point of view
Characters

Plot

Actors

(continued)

Lighting

Sound

Camera techniques

Summary of overall opinion

The director handles the film's technical elements nicely. In the festive scenes, the lighting often brings out the brilliant colors of the period costumes. In the grittier scenes (such as the battle scenes) the director makes appropriate use of darkness to remind viewers of the misery and terror that lurked in the shadows of the legends. A great deal of thought also went into the film's soundtrack; the music heard in many scenes fits the world of the film perfectly. However, the film has one flaw that is hard to ignore: the director sometimes slips into using "stylish" camera techniques that have no real purpose and only serve to distract viewers from the characters and the story.

Overall, though, *Young Guinevere* is a fascinating visit to Guinevere's world and its people, skillfully crafted by a director who shows a great love for the subject.

YOUR TURN 12 **Critiquing a Film**

Choose a film to critique, and watch it (either on video or at a theater). Make sure the film is one you would be comfortable discussing aloud with your teacher and classmates at school.

When watching the film, take notes about the filmmaker's use of literary and technical elements. Be sure to

- indicate how the film's setting is conveyed
- write down character names and descriptions
- note any special uses of camera techniques, lighting, or sound

After you have watched the film, use the lists of criteria on pages 199 and 200 to evaluate it. You may need to watch the film a second time to focus on how the story is told. Then, using the model on page 201 as a guide, write your critique. Make sure to share it with classmates or others who have seen the same film, and discuss similarities and differences in your opinions of the film. Try to publish your review on a class Web page or school Web site, or add your review to a class book of movie reviews.

Presenting an Oral Interpretation

An **oral interpretation** of a short story is a dramatic reading that communicates the story's meaning and artistry to a group of listeners. In this workshop you will sharpen your analytic and acting skills by crafting and performing an oral interpretation of a short story.

WHAT'S AHEAD?

In this section you will learn to

■ select and analyze a short story for oral interpretation

■ present and evaluate an oral interpretation

Select and Analyze a Short Story

You Choose   Select a short story that you like. The more a story interests you, the better able you will be to communicate its meaning and **mood,** or atmosphere, to others. Consider these factors in choosing a selection.

■ The story should have **technical quality**—it should be well written.

■ Stories that deal with **universal themes** appeal to a wide range of listeners.

■ The **length** of the short story is important. If you do not have time to read the entire story, you might use an excerpt or choose a shorter work.

Pick It Apart   To present the **meaning,** or message, of a short story to others, you must first understand it yourself. To discover the story's meaning, analyze its literary elements, such as plot, characters, theme, point of view, and mood. These last two elements are discussed below.

Point of view   In adapting a short story for an oral interpretation, the **point of view**—the vantage point from which a writer tells a story—will determine what reading voice you use.

■ In stories told from the **first-person point of view,** an "I" tells the story. Tell first-person stories as though you were the main character.

■ Many stories are told from the **omniscient,** or "all-knowing," **point of view.** The omniscient narrator can reveal the thoughts and feelings of all the characters. Use your own voice to present this point of view.

Mood   Writers create **mood,** or atmosphere, through descriptive details and evocative language. Adapt your tone of voice to the story's mood.

TIP   Even if you present an excerpt of a short story, you should shorten the story by cutting **dialogue tags,** such as "Jose stated." You can also eliminate references to characters or events that are not part of the passage you are reading.

Create, Practice, and Evaluate

Begin with an Introduction In your introduction, name the author and the title of the piece you will present. If you are presenting an excerpt, describe the characters and the action preceding the passage.

Put It All Together After you have analyzed your selection, marked the manuscript, and planned an introduction, use the following tips to craft and practice your performance.

TIP To mark your manuscript:

- Use commas, semicolons, periods, and dashes for pauses.
- Use underlining for louder volume.
- Use question marks for rising inflection.

For more on oral interpretation, see page 905 in the Quick Reference Handbook.

- **Know your text well.** Read your story aloud several times so that you are very familiar with it. Find out how to pronounce difficult words.

- **Use your voice to convey meaning.** Portray different characters by changing the pitch of your voice, and vary your rate of speech to indicate changes in the story's action.

- **Use gestures and facial expression to aid communication.** Use your body, hands, and facial expressions to convey meaning and mood.

Be an Appreciative Listener These questions are for evaluating your own and your peers' oral interpretations. Use your peers' feedback to set goals for future presentations.

Evaluation Questions	Yes	No
1. Does the reader's introduction prepare the listener for the story?		
2. Does the reader speak clearly and smoothly and change his or her voice as necessary to portray the story's narrator and characters?		
3. Does the reader vary his or her volume, pitch, and rate of speech to help convey the story's meaning and mood?		
4. Does the reader use gestures and facial expressions to help convey the story's meaning and mood?		
5. Does the reader make frequent eye contact with the audience?		

YOUR TURN 13 Presenting and Evaluating an Oral Interpretation

Choose a short story, and analyze it carefully. Create and practice an oral interpretation of the story, and then present it to the class. Evaluate your peers' performances, and be prepared to share your evaluations with your classmates.

Choices

Choose one of the following activities to complete.

▶ LITERATURE

1. A True Review Develop a **review**—either written or oral—of a literary work. Your review should summarize significant events and details and should note important images or ideas for audience members who have not read the work. Evaluate the work by using critical analysis of its elements, and support your conclusions with relevant examples and accurate references to the text. Defend your point of view about the work with precise language.

▶ CAREERS

2. Discover Strategies
Writers often give readings of their works at bookstores. Attend one of these readings, and ask the writer some specific questions about the writing strategies he or she uses. Combine the writer's responses with your own writing strategies to form a **writing checklist.** Share your checklist with classmates. If you cannot attend a reading, send your questions to the writer in care of his or her publisher.

▶ MEDIA AND TECHNOLOGY

3. Analyze an Analysis Find a review to analyze. You might choose a movie review or a magazine article reviewing a new software program. Then, create a **graphic organizer** by dividing a piece of paper into three columns, and labeling them "Strengths," "Weaknesses," and "Other." As you read the review, jot down strengths and weaknesses in the appropriate columns. If any of your responses do not fit either of these categories, write them in the third column. Finally, discuss your organizer with other students.

▶ VIEWING AND REPRESENTING

4. Illustrate a Children's Book Create an **illustrated children's book.** Focus on these four literary elements: plot, character, setting, and point of view. Once you have written the story, draw or paint illustrations of the more interesting characters and events in the plot. Be sure your story is appropriate for children. When finished, share your story with students in a local elementary school.

PORTFOLIO

6

Sharing Research
Results

Reading Workshop

Reading a Research Article

Writing Workshop

Writing a Research Paper

Viewing and Representing

Evaluating Web Sites

Investigation

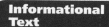

Informational Text

Exposition

- A screenwriter is writing a screenplay for a movie about Michelangelo. In order for the movie to be historically accurate, she must gather information for the story's events, setting, costumes, and so on.

- On a family vacation, you read a roadside historical marker. You discover you are at the site of a famous battle in which one of the participants has the same last name as you. You become curious about whether you may be related.

- One day during lunch, you stop and think about the name of your school. Until now, you have never wondered why your school is named for a person or even who the person was. You decide to find out.

    Research is used all around you. People research when they want to explore, discover, or learn about something or when they just want to satisfy their curiosity. People do research to learn about another culture or time period and to understand the world we live in.

YOUR TURN 1 Brainstorming About Research and Investigation

With two or three classmates, make a two-column chart. In the first column, list people or professionals who you think would use research in their lives or in their work. In the second column, provide reasons you think they would use research. Share your results with your class.

internet**connect**

go. hrw .com

GO TO: go.hrw.com
KEYWORD: EOLang 10-6

Reading a Research Article

WHAT'S AHEAD?

In this section, you will read a research article and learn how to

- **paraphrase what you have read**
- **identify primary and secondary sources**

Suppose you are preparing for an around-the-world trip, but you know nothing about the countries to which you are traveling. Your only clues are the spending money you obtained ahead of time. When you look at this money, you notice that each country has its own uniquely designed currency. What can you learn about each country by looking at the artwork on the currency? Who are the people on the bills? The research article on the following pages, "The Art of Money," can help you answer these questions.

Preparing to Read

READING SKILL

Paraphrasing A **paraphrase** is a restatement of someone's ideas or words in your own words. Paraphrasing is a valuable tool when you read. You can paraphrase to check your comprehension of the main ideas and details of a piece. A paraphrase can also help you explain ideas expressed in complicated or unusual terms, as in a poem or in a symbolic piece of writing such as a myth or fable. After you have read "The Art of Money" and answered some questions about it, you will have a chance to go back and paraphrase parts of it in order to check your understanding of the piece.

READING FOCUS

Primary and Secondary Sources A researcher may include both primary and secondary sources in a report. A **primary source** is firsthand, original information. For example, the letters John Adams wrote to his wife during the drafting of the Declaration of Independence are a primary source of information about that time period. A **secondary source** is information derived from or about a primary source. Books (such as history books) written by authors who read and interpreted Adams's letters are secondary sources. Both types of sources can be valuable when doing research. As you read "The Art of Money," see if you can determine which sources the writer mentions are primary and which are secondary.

The writer of the following article researched the images found on paper money from around the world. As you read the article, jot down answers to the numbered active-reading questions.

1. Based on the title and subtitle, what do you think the article will be about?

from Smithsonian

The Art of Money

BY DAVID STANDISH

Across the globe, the images on a country's currency offer a window on its culture

When I'm traveling outside the country, I generally think about the local currency only in terms of how many—or how few—pounds, francs, kroner, yen, or pesos constitute one U.S. dollar. Even with a calculator, I'm usually too confused or flustered to pay much attention to what the money looks like. Compared with our own currency, most foreign notes seem too colorful and too cute, anyway. Haven't we all referred to exotic dough as "play money" at least once? Since you know you'll be coming back to good old greenbacks, foreign money is hard to take seriously—beyond figuring out the exchange rate, that is. But the images and designs on paper money say a lot about the country that issues it.

Money and National Self-Image

Through their money, countries project their self-image—to themselves and to foreigners—and reveal what's important to them, and how they want to be seen by the rest of the world. I first began noticing this on a trip to China some years

ago. This wasn't too long after Richard Nixon's presidential visit [1972], and the Chinese had come up with two separate currencies, one for regular folks and one for the new influx of tourists. The tourist yuan bills were new and crisp and looked like cigarette coupons from the '50s. Engraved on the front were tranquil bucolic scenes, while on the back were instructions in English on the currency's proper use. The other notes were worn, dingy, somewhat smaller than the tourist yuan, and emblazoned with images not of the Chinese landscape but of socialism and industrialization on the march: happy workers bearing hoes, a mighty freighter steaming along. China was supposed to evoke images of waterfalls for us, but happy, communal socialist work for the Chinese people.

The dual Chinese currencies reminded me of the vast difference between most Caribbean island currencies and

2. What is the author's source for the information in this paragraph?

Jamaican money. The face of the Cayman Islands' dollar bill, for instance, bears a portrait of Queen Elizabeth II. To her left, there's an open undersea pirate treasure chest filled with gold coins (which could be taken as a subliminal advertisement for Cayman banking practices, I guess), while the back depicts a coral reef scene of serene tropical fish.

Bermuda's turquoise two-dollar bill bears a familial resemblance, too: Queen Elizabeth on the front, flanked by a sea horse and an anemone. And most of the Netherlands Antilles' bills feature adorable engravings of birds, the only exceptions being the nostalgic port view on the one-gulden note, and an airliner in flight (presumably whisking in tourists) on the 2½-gulden note. But Jamaican money offers nowhere near as much soothing escapism.

One of the appealing things about Jamaica is that it's a country, not just a beach; you can see this on the money. I happen to love the place, and have read Jamaican history, so I know about the guys on the two-dollar bill and the ten—Paul Bogle and George William Gordon, respectively. Both were leaders of the failed Morant Bay Rebellion of 1865—a movement to give greater rights to newly freed slaves—and both were executed for their trouble. True, the two-dollar bill (no longer printed but still legal tender) does have a lovely emerald streamertail hummingbird (also called the "doctor bird") hovering next to Bogle. But on the back is a happy, racially mixed group of kids, a shining sun, and the words "Out of Many, One People." . . .

3. How does the author know so much about Jamaica?

4. In your own words, explain the differences between the currencies of Jamaica and of the Caribbean islands.

Plastic and Op Art

A new wrinkle in money—or maybe the absence thereof—is plastic. Australia no longer prints its notes on paper. They're now made of a polymer that looks and feels fairly paperish, but has a certain slipperiness to it that seems somehow untrustworthy. The notes also have a clever new anticounterfeiting device: little see-through cellophane-like windows with hologram designs embedded in them. The overall look of the bills is eye-catchingly busy. On the front of the ten, for instance, is emblazoned the central head shot of A. B. "Banjo" Paterson (the poet who wrote the lyrics to "Waltzing Matilda") wearing an understated Western hat. To Paterson's left, a cowboy gallops on horseback, flicking a whip at a group of wild horses that seem to be racing out of Banjo's right neck and shoulder like spooked equine[1] Athenas.[2] These images are superimposed on a profusion[3] of op-art circles and curves, in a smear of colors including blue, yellow, green, and violet, plus the see-through window with a windmill in it. Little danger of nodding off while handling Australian money.

5. Based on this subhead, what do you think this section will be about?

6. How does the author feel about the new Australian money?

---

1. **equine:** of, like, or characteristic of a horse.
2. **Athena:** the Greek goddess of wisdom, skills, and warfare.
3. **profusion:** an abundance.

National Heroes

Something else that's interesting about various currencies is that the national heroes depicted on the bills generally don't mean anything two doors away. Banjo Paterson, for instance, was certainly somebody I'd never heard of before I began looking into this. Also J. Abelardo Quiñones. As someone who takes a certain pride in blabbing out quiz show answers in front of my kids, to prove I'm not as completely dumb as they think I am, encountering these famous unknowns was a seriously humbling experience.

I figured the people pictured on the most common bills would generally be those best known or most important to a particular country. (I based this assumption on our choice of George Washington for the one-dollar bill.)

Given the standard cultural bias in what has passed for my education, I didn't feel too bad about not knowing who D. Sukhbaatar was on the Mongolian fifty-tugrik note, say, or Alhaji Sir Abubakar Tafawa Balewa (who gets the prize for the longest name I encountered) on Nigeria's five-naira bill. I was relieved to find that my *Encyclopaedia Britannica* knew them both. Sukhbaatar was a revolutionary leader in the Mongolian war of independence from China after World War I, and Balewa was Nigeria's first federal prime minister, killed in an army coup in 1966.

> **7. What is the author saying about the national heroes depicted on bills?**

> **8. How did the author find out the identities of Sukhbaatar and Balewa?**

But I felt I ought to know who the distinguished gent in the stiff white collar on Canada's five-dollar bill is. Sir W. Laurier? I didn't have a clue. But then I didn't know who J. A. Macdonald on the ten-dollar bill was either. You probably do. Laurier was prime minister between 1896 and 1911, and Macdonald was Canada's first prime minister, serving two terms between 1867 and 1891. "Though accused of devious and unscrupulous methods," the *Britannica* says, "he is remembered for his achievements." Not by me, until now. I'm proof of why our neighbors to the north think we're arrogant and ignorant when it comes to them. . . .

Favorite and Not-So-Favorite Bills

I am not alone in liking [my favorite bill] best. Several people I talked to at an international travel agency, who spend their working lives shuffling 164 various currencies, agreed. It's the face of the Netherlands' fifty-gulden note, to me the prettiest of them all. The image is a close-up of a bee on a single sunflower, colored a cheery yellow with some orange and green, and detailed with quintessential Northern Renaissance precision. It is money fit for framing.

Which is something that can't be said for our own money, which gets my vote as the world's most boring. I think it is the only national currency that's based on a dreary green color. If that isn't emblematic[4] of our puritan past, in which money

> **9. Why was it a good idea for the author to consult an international travel agency?**

---

4. **emblematic:** symbolic.

was viewed as a necessary evil instead of something that should be colorful and beautiful, I don't know what is. Our money is also fairly weird. I mean, what must people of other countries think when they see that enigmatic, glowing eye, balanced on a pyramid on the back of the one-dollar bill? That the United States traces its origins back to visitors from outer space who purportedly founded Egypt?

And what sort of country would put Salmon P. Chase on what was its largest circulating bill—now outmoded but still legal tender—the ten thousand dollar note? Civil War buffs will recall that Chase was Secretary of the Treasury under Lincoln, but really, wouldn't W.C. Fields or Marilyn Monroe or William Faulkner or Mickey Mouse have been better?

The new fifties and hundreds aren't much of an improvement. They have buildings on the back—the Capitol and Independence Hall, respectively—and the portraits on the front are still U. S. Grant and Ben Franklin, but the heads, well, they're too big. And with the new, bigger print to go with them, as a friend of mine noted, they seem to have been designed by aging baby boomers for aging baby boomers—all of us who can no longer read without our glasses. MONEY: THE LARGE-PRINT EDITION.

Actually, the weirdest picture is on the back of the ten-dollar bill. Stare at it for a while sometime. In the first place, it's an etching of the U.S. Treasury Building, which is an institutional narcissism[5] that a number of other currencies

also indulge in. (It would be more forgivable if the backs of most of our U.S. bills didn't also feature representations of buildings. More of our uptightness about money, if you ask me.)

> **10. What does the author think about the United States' money?**

The ten-dollar bill is also one of our few notes with ordinary citizens on it. I count seven tiny figures standing in front of the imposing neoclassical[6] Treasury Building, which is the star of the etching. Except for a single 1920s-vintage vehicle, the street in the foreground is empty.

> **11. How does the author know about the figures on the United States' ten-dollar bill?**

I look at this and wonder: What does this say about America? For one thing, in this driving-besotted[7] land, it's disturbingly appropriate that we felt compelled to depict an automobile. There's an everyday bleakness to the scene, which might have been painted by Edward Hopper[8] or photographed by Walker Evans.[9] There's a lonely, nondemocratic feeling to it that I'm sure no one ever intended—but it's there.

But unlike the Netherlands' lovely fifty-gulden note, at least this bleak scene will pay our bills.

---

5. **narcissism:** self-love; excessive interest in one's own importance.

6. **neoclassical:** of a revival of classic style and form in art, literature, and so on.
7. **besotted:** silly.
8. **Edward Hopper** (1882–1967): an American realist painter known for his bleak depictions of everyday American big-city life.
9. **Walker Evans** (1903–1975): an American photographer best known for his photographs of poverty in the rural South during the Great Depression.

Paraphrasing

READING SKILL

Telling It Your Way   "The Art of Money" is an informational article describing the images on paper money from many countries. If you wanted to explain the article to a friend, one way would be to *paraphrase* the writer's words. When you **paraphrase,** you retell information in your own words, making sure to keep the meaning of the original text. Thus, paraphrasing is a good way to check your understanding of what you are reading. If you can retell someone's words or ideas in your own words, you have a good understanding of what you have read.

Keep in mind that a paraphrase is somewhat different from a *summary.* In a **summary,** you retell only the most important information or details of a text, a fact that makes a summary almost always shorter than the original text. On the other hand, a paraphrase is more detailed, often includes your interpretation, and is usually as long as the original piece. The chart below shows how one student paraphrased a sentence from "The Art of Money." Notice that the paraphrase is about as long as the original; the ideas are just expressed in simpler terms.

TIP   Whether you use a paraphrase or a summary, you can include a direct quotation. Just make sure to set it off with quotation marks and to give credit to the original source.

Original	Paraphrase
Through their money, countries project their self-image—to themselves and to foreigners—and reveal what's important to them, and how they want to be seen by the rest of the world.	The money that different countries use reveals three things about them: their identities, their values and their philosophies.

Paraphrasing a Passage

Use the following steps to paraphrase a reading passage.

▶ **STEP 1 Re-read the passage to make sure you get the overall meaning.** You might have to look up unfamiliar words to understand the entire passage.

▶ **STEP 2 Identify the main ideas of the passage.** Look for topic sentences and thesis statements. Make sure the ideas in your paraphrase are the same as those in the original passage.

▶ **STEP 3 Restate the ideas in your own words.** You can use synonyms in place of key words from the passage. Stick closely to the original, using your own sentence structure to follow the passage point by point.

▶ **STEP 4 Compare the original passage with your paraphrase to make sure you have kept the original ideas but explained them in your words.** Your restatement should be about the same length as the original passage but phrased in your own words.

YOUR TURN 2 **Paraphrasing**

Using the steps above, paraphrase paragraphs three ("The dual Chinese currencies . . .") through five ("One of the appealing things . . .") of "The Art of Money."

| READING FOCUS ➤

Primary and Secondary Sources

First- or Secondhand News?   It is important for readers to recognize the sources a writer uses in a research paper or article; when you know the sources of information, you can judge whether the information is reliable and accurate. You can also judge whether a source is current or outdated. For example, a 1980 edition of an encyclopedia would not be a current source for an article about today's space exploration. Sources of information in research articles are divided into two types: *primary sources* and *secondary sources*.

A **primary source** is the first recording of the information. Primary sources include historical documents, letters, transcripts or tapes of interviews or speeches, lab reports, eyewitness accounts, and statistical surveys. If you were reading an article about the Declaration of Independence, and the writer cited a passage from Thomas Jefferson's own journal, then the passage would be a primary source. Primary sources usually carry more weight since they come directly from an authority. Just remember that a primary source could be mistaken or could show bias.

On the other hand, if the writer cited an article about Jefferson written by someone else, the article would be a **secondary source.** Secondary sources include encyclopedias, documentaries, biographies, and history books. You will use secondary sources on virtually any research project.

It is easier to identify sources in **formal research** articles than in **informal research** articles. In a formal research article, the writer includes clear documentation of where he or she obtained the information in the article. This documentation usually appears as footnotes or as a list of works cited in the piece. (A **list of works cited** includes print and nonprint sources, unlike a bibliography, which lists only print sources.) The sources may also be cited in parentheses immediately after the information in the article.

An informal research article, on the other hand, contains no footnotes or detailed list of the works cited. Instead, a sentence might begin with a short introductory phrase such as "According to the president of the company."

If a research article includes a list of works cited, use the information there to determine which sources are primary and which are secondary.

YOUR TURN 3 Identifying Primary and Secondary Sources

The following sentences from "The Art of Money" contain references to primary and secondary sources. Identify the type of source cited in each sentence, and write a short explanation of why the source is primary or secondary.

1. I first began noticing this on a trip to China some years ago. (page 209, paragraph 2)

2. I happen to love the place, and have read Jamaican history, so I know about the guys on the two-dollar bill and the ten—Paul Bogle and George William Gordon, respectively. (page 210, paragraph 2)

3. I was relieved to find that my *Encyclopaedia Britannica* knew them both. (page 211, paragraph 3)

4. Several people I talked to at an international travel agency, who spend their working lives shuffling 164 various currencies, agreed. (page 211, paragraph 5)

5. I count seven tiny figures standing in front of the imposing neo-classical Treasury Building. . . . (page 212, paragraph 4)

Specialized and Technical Terms

Knowing the meanings of the specialized and technical terms related to the topic of a research paper will increase your understanding of the piece. For instance, in "The Art of Money," the writer uses the word *note* to mean "a piece of paper money or a bill." This use of *note* is called jargon. **Jargon** refers to language that has a special meaning for a particular group of people. People working in money-related fields refer to paper money as *notes*. To a musician, however, the word *note* would more commonly mean "a tone with a certain pitch."

THINKING IT THROUGH

Understanding the Meanings of Specialized and Technical Terms

Use the guidelines below to determine the meanings of jargon.

1. **Use context clues.** Examine the context—the way the term is used in a sentence. Good writers will usually give readers a short explanation of technical terms within a sentence or paragraph.

2. **Look for the terms in reference books.** Dictionaries, encyclopedias, or other reference books provide information on particular subjects. Pay special attention to technical terms that have other meanings in popular use.

3. **Ask someone who is familiar with the subject.** A club or professional organization might be another good source of information.

4. **Use online sources.** You could use a search engine on the Internet to find sites where the specialized terms might be used, discussed, or defined.

PRACTICE

Using the methods described above, determine the meanings of the italicized words in each of the following sentences. Put your answers on your own paper.

1. The museum had over 400,000 coins in its *numismatics* exhibition.

2. On the front of the Australian ten, the images of Banjo Paterson and the group of wild horses are *superimposed* over the op-art circles and curves.

3. The back of the American ten-dollar bill contains an *etching* of the U.S. Treasury Building.

4. The *greenback* was issued in the U.S. during the Civil War.

5. The Netherlands' fifty-*gulden* note features a bee on a sunflower.

Using Context to Understand Specialized or Technical Terms

On many reading tests, you may be asked to find the meaning of a specialized or technical term in a reading passage in order to test your vocabulary and ability to reason. If you do not already have the word in your vocabulary, consider its **context**—that is, look at how the word is used in the sentence in order to figure out the meaning.

Read the following passage, and use the Thinking It Through steps below to figure out the answer to the reading question.

The Bureau of Engraving and Printing, an agency of the U.S. Treasury Department, issues all of the paper money for the United States. The money is printed by pressing paper between felt pads and metal plates that have been cut, or engraved, with special designs and brushed with ink. Money printed with this *intaglio* process is the most difficult to counterfeit.

1. In the passage, *intaglio* is another name for
   A. an agency of the U.S. Treasury Department
   B. a printing technique
   C. paper money
   D. a method of counterfeiting

THINKING IT THROUGH

Using Context to Understand Specialized or Technical Terms

Use the following steps to find the meanings of specialized terms.

1. **Read the question and the answer choices, and then read the passage again.** Re-reading the passage with the question and answer choices in mind might help you find the writer's explanation of the specialized or technical term.

2. **Look at the word's context for clues to the word's meaning.** In the last sentence of the passage above, *intaglio* refers to a kind of process for making money. Much of the passage describes how the money is made.

3. **Cross out the answers that do not seem correct.** You could eliminate choice **A** and choice **C** because neither an agency nor paper money are processes.

4. **Review the context of the specialized or technical term again, and make an educated guess at the word's meaning.** Choices **B** and **D** are both possibilities. However, the passage says the intaglio process is the most difficult to counterfeit. Choice **B** must be the correct answer.

Writing a Research Paper

WHAT'S AHEAD?

In this workshop, you will write a research paper and you will

- gather and document sources on a topic
- create a thesis and an outline
- evaluate sources
- revise for variety in sentence length
- correct misplaced modifiers

Does a person's handwriting really reflect his or her personality? What food sources will eventually be grown on the bottom of the ocean? Will computers someday have artificial intelligence? What kinds of breakthroughs have been found to halt the aging process?

To find the answers to these questions you would probably have to research—or, as some people put it, explore. In fact, research is a way of exploring your world, of learning what information is out there waiting to be discovered. Like explorers, researchers delight in digging up and sharing their finds. That is exactly what you will be doing in this workshop—exploring to discover information and sharing it with others in a research paper.

Prewriting

Choose a Subject

The Right Foot You have probably heard the expression "starting off on the right foot." In writing a research paper, the "right foot" is an interesting subject that you can develop into a suitable topic. Start with your interests. Below are some places for finding possible subjects to research.

- **Hit the books.** Browse through your textbooks, as well as the nonfiction section of your school's library or media center, a bookstore, or a video store. What subjects intrigue you more than others?

- **Skim the media.** Skim current newspapers and magazines, and watch news programs and public television shows. What issues or subjects catch and hold your attention?

- **Surf the Web.** Pick a search engine and search a subject or term related to one of your interests. Which results of the search would you be interested in pursuing further?

- **Talk to the experts.** Talk to your neighbors and relatives about their jobs and hobbies. What are your questions, and what are their answers? Which answers inspire more questions?

- **Pound the pavement.** Observe your surroundings, noting the sights and sounds (for example, the old radio collecting dust in your basement) that might be interesting subjects to research.

Before moving on, use one or more of the ideas above to list at least three possible research subjects.

Narrow Your Subject to Refine Your Topic

Approach and Landing   In orbit, space shuttle astronauts gain a truly global view of the planet. However, as the shuttle descends toward Earth, they begin to see the planet in increasingly greater detail.

Similarly, as you begin a research paper, you first identify a subject and gain an overview of it. Then, you make your "approach," examining the subject in greater detail until you "land" on a suitable topic. Here are some ways you can move from an overview of your subject to a more specific, manageable research subject.

- **Read two or three general articles about your subject in reference books such as encyclopedias.** Notice headings and subheadings in the articles, and consider using one as the topic of your paper.

- **Search the World Wide Web** for pages or sites containing key words related to your subject.

- **Look up your subject in the *Readers' Guide to Periodical Literature*** or in your library's card catalog or online catalog. Note the topics listed under the subject headings.

- **Discuss your subject with someone** (a teacher, neighbor, parent, or friend, for example) who has expert knowledge about it. Ask for help with narrowing your subject down to a workable topic.

Once you have arrived at a suitable topic, jot down a short description of it. For example, a writer who began with radio as a subject might decide to narrow his topic to "the effects of early radio on life in the United States."

The questions in the Thinking It Through on the next page will help you evaluate whether topics you are considering are suitable for a research paper. The student responses show how the same writer used the questions to evaluate his topic.

▶ **Does this topic interest you enough that you will be able to interest others in it?** The more a topic interests you, the more likely you will be able to bring it to life for your readers. Most people take the radio for granted, but I can't imagine life without it. Readers would probably be surprised to learn how much early radio changed people's lives.

▶ **Is the topic objective rather than subjective?** Your experiences and opinions are not suitable for a research paper because they are personal, subjective topics. For example, "my trip to Mexico" would not be a good choice, because *you* would be the only source of information. Your topic should be one you can research in information sources. "The effects of early radio on life in the United States" is an objective topic, one that I can research in print and nonprint sources.

▶ **Are enough different sources of information on the topic readily accessible?** What kinds of books, articles, and nonprint sources might have information on your topic? You may have trouble gathering enough information on your topic if it is too recent or too technical or if the source material is not available locally. Encyclopedias and books about radio history would probably have information on the development of radio, and business and entertainment magazines of the early radio days likely covered it, too. The Internet might also be a good source for material on how radio changed people's lives.

Think About Purpose, Audience, and Tone

| KEY CONCEPT ⟶

Your Mission Is . . . The basic **purpose** of a research paper is to inform. As you research your topic, you will **uncover information and develop your own ideas about the topic.** When you write your paper, you will inform your readers about what you have learned.

Think, too, about the needs and interests of your potential **audience**—your readers. Readers expect to come away from a research paper with a better understanding of the topic or a new way of looking at it. The following questions will help you consider your readers' needs and interests.

■ **What aspects of the topic might interest my readers?** How does the topic relate to their lives?

■ **What do my readers probably already know about the topic?** What background information might they need?

■ **How might I increase my readers' understanding of the topic** or give them a new way to think about it? What would they like to learn?

Think about your **tone**—your attitude toward your topic and readers. The typical academic research paper, like the one you will write for this chapter, and the typical professional research report, like the ones you may do for your job someday, are *formal* in tone. A formal tone usually has the following characteristics of style.

- **Third-person point of view.** Use third-person pronouns, such as *he, she,* and *they,* to reflect your objective stance. First-person pronouns, such as *I* and *we,* reflect a subjective stance. Your purpose in a research paper is to convey information, not a personal opinion.
- **Relatively formal language.** Avoid casual and informal language, such as slang, colloquial expressions, and contractions.

Your **voice**—the unique sound and rhythm of a writer's language—can still sound natural although you are writing in a serious, formal tone. Through your choice of words, sentence structure, and punctuation, you can strike a balance by sounding authoritative and informed without being dry and boring.

Develop Research Questions

What Was the Question?   Remember that a research paper should ask and answer good questions. Before you consult sources on your topic, jot down some specific questions to explore. Your natural curiosity will suggest some questions, and the ones in the following chart will help you round out your investigation. Working with a list of research questions will make it easier for you to sort through the information you find.

General Questions	Specific Questions on Your Topic
What is the topic, and how can you define it?	What was life in the United States like when radio was introduced?
What are the topic's parts, and how do they work together?	How did early radio affect entertainment, information delivery, and the economy?
How has the topic changed over time?	How has the impact of radio changed over time?
How is the topic similar to or different from related topics?	How do the effects of early radio compare to the effects of other, more recent technological innovations?
What are the topic's advantages or disadvantages?	What advantages did early radio have over existing media?

Use the steps on pages 218–21 to choose and refine a topic; to consider your purpose, audience, and tone; and to compile a list of research questions.

Find Sources

Inquiring Minds   The first step in finding information on your topic is knowing where to look. You will need to analyze and synthesize information from a variety of print and nonprint sources. The following chart lists some library and community resources you can use for your research. **Remember that some sources are primary (firsthand information, such as a copy of a historical document) and others are secondary (information derived from or about a primary source, such as an encyclopedia article about a histori-cal document).** In addition to the sources below, look for information in unexpected places, such as maps, presentations, and public documents.

| KEY CONCEPT

Reference Note

For more information on **using the library**, including online cata-logs, online databases, and the Internet, see page 866 of the Quick Reference Handbook.

Library and Community Resources	
Resource	**Source or Information**
Card catalog or online catalog	Books listed by title, author, and subject (most libraries also list audiovisual materials)
Readers' Guide to Periodical Literature or *National Newspaper Index*	Subject and author index to magazine and journal articles, index to major newspapers
Microfilm or microfiche	Indexes to major newspapers such as *The New York Times* and *The Washington Post*, back issues of newspapers and magazines
General reference books or CD-ROMs	Encyclopedias, encyclopedia yearbooks, dictionaries
Specialized reference books or CD-ROMs	Biographical reference sources, encyclope-dias of special subjects (sports, arts, and so on), atlases, almanacs
Videotapes and audiotapes	Movies, documentaries, filmstrips, audio-tapes of books
The librarian	Help in finding and using sources
World Wide Web and online services	Articles, interviews, bibliographies, pictures, videos, sound recordings

Local government offices	Facts and statistics, information on local government policies, experts on government
Local offices of state and federal officials	Voting records of government officials, recent or pending legislation, experts on state and federal government
Museums and historical societies	Special exhibits, libraries and bookstores, experts on various subjects
Schools and colleges	Libraries, experts on various subjects
Local newspaper offices	Clippings, files on local events and history

Create Source Cards

Keeping Track   Before you take notes *from* a source, record information *about* the source. That way, you will not find yourself with a great quotation you really want to use but have no idea where you found it. Keeping track of your sources is essential for giving credit within your paper as well as for preparing the Works Cited list that accompanies your final version.

For each of your sources, record the author, title, and publication information on an index card or sheet of paper or in a computer file. Then, assign each source a number. (Source cards are sometimes called *bibliography cards*.)

Here is an example of a source card for a book with a single author. Notice that along with the source information, the card includes a **source number,** the **location** where the source was found, and the book's **call number.**

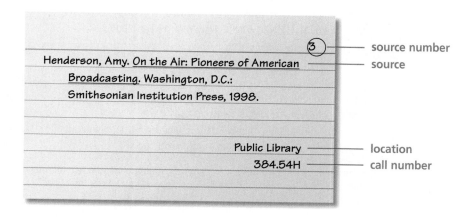

source number

Henderson, Amy. <u>On the Air: Pioneers of American</u> — source
     <u>Broadcasting</u>. Washington, D.C.:
     Smithsonian Institution Press, 1998.

Public Library — location
      384.54H — call number

The following guidelines tell you how to record the necessary information for different types of sources. As you fill out your source cards, refer to these guidelines and note the special uses of punctuation.

Reference Note

For more on **capitalizing and punctuating titles,** see page 682.

Guidelines for Recording Source Information

1. **Book with One Author.** Write the author's or editor's name, last name first (follow the names of editors with a comma and the abbreviation *ed.*); the title of the book; the place of publication; the publishing company's name; and the year of publication. (To make it easier to locate a book later, put its call number in the lower right-hand part of the index card, paper, or computer file.)

   Collins, Philip. Radios: The Golden Age. San Francisco: Chronicle Books, 1987.

2. **Source with More Than One Author.** For the first listed author, write the last name first. For all other authors, write the first name first. Then, follow the format for books with one author to complete the record.

   Buxton, Frank, and Bill Owen. Radio's Golden Age: The Programs and Personalities. New York: Easton Valley Press, 1966.

3. **Magazine or Newspaper Article.** Write the author's name (if given), last name first; the title of the article; the name of the magazine or newspaper; the day (if given), month, and year of publication; and page numbers on which the article begins and ends. For an article in a newspaper that has different editions or multiple sections, specify the editions (use *ed.*) and/or sections before the page number.

   Stark, Phyllis. "On the Air." Billboard 1 Nov. 1994: 120–124.

4. **Encyclopedia Article.** Write the author's name (if given), last name first; the title of the article; the name of the encyclopedia; the edition (if given); and the year of publication. (Use the abbreviation *ed.* for *edition.*)

   "Radio as a Medium of Communication." The Encyclopedia Americana. International ed. 1998.

5. **Radio or TV Program.** Write the program title; the name of the network; the call letters and city of the local station (if any); and the broadcast date.

   NBC Nightly News. NBC. WNBC, New York. 13 Feb. 2000.

6. **Movie or Video Recording.** Write the title of the work and the director or producer's name (use *Dir.* for *Director* and *Prod.* for *Producer;*) for movies, write the original distributor's name (for movies not available on video) and the year of release; for video recordings, write the word *Videocassette* or *Videodisc*, the distributor's name, and the year the video recording was released.

   A Brief History of Time. Dir. Errol Morris. Videocassette. Paramount Studios, 1992.

7. **Interview.** Write the interviewee's name, last name first; the type of interview (personal or telephone); and the day, month, and year of the interview.

   Strohmer, Joseph. Telephone interview. 12 Dec. 2000.

8. **CD-ROM.** Write the author's name (if given), last name first; title (include print publisher, date, and page numbers if material was first in a print source); type of CD-ROM or database; the word *CD-ROM;* city (if given); distributor; date of publication.

Foote-Greenwell, Victoria. "The Life and Resurrection of Alexandre Dumas." Smithsonian July 1996: 110+. Middle Search. CD-ROM. EBSCO Publishing. Nov. 1996.

9. **Online Source.** Write the author's name (if given), last name first; title of the work; title of the site; volume number, issue number, or other identifying number; posting date; name of any institution or organization associated with the site; date of access; and internet address.

Baker, Robert T. "100 Years of Radio." CyberProfile Journal. 16 Mar. 1997. RTB Web Design. 30 Nov. 1998 <http://rtb.home.texas.net/history.htm>.

FOR BETTER OR FOR WORSE © Lynn Johnston Productions Inc./Dist. by United Feature Syndicate, Inc.

TIP The format for recording source information shown on these pages is the one recommended by the **Modern Language Association of America (MLA).** Your teacher may ask you to use a different format, such as that of the **American Psychological Association (APA).** Be sure you know which format your teacher requires.

YOUR TURN 5 Gathering Sources

Review the prewriting steps related to finding sources and creating source cards. Find at least five possible sources for your topic and create a source card for each.

MINI-LESSON CRITICAL THINKING

Evaluating Sources

GIGO—garbage in, garbage out—is as true for a research paper as it is for the output from a computer. The quality of your research paper will be only as good as the sources you use. Before you decide whether to use a particular source, evaluate it carefully. Putting your sources to the **4R** test will help you judge whether a source is worth using.

- **Relevant**   Does the source have information that directly relates to your research questions? For a print source, check the table of contents and the index. For a non-print source, read a review or a summary. For example, the table of contents entry "The Rise of Broadcast Journalism" indicates that the book *On the Air* contains information about radio news shows.

- **Reliable**   Can you trust the source to be accurate and objective? Well-respected magazines and newspapers, such as *Smithsonian* and *National Geographic,* have earned the trust of their readers.

- **Recent**   Is the copyright date of the source recent? Even for a history topic, you should have some up-to-date sources that present modern perspectives.

- **Representative**   If your topic is controversial, you need to find sources that address more than one side of the issue so that you can take an objective, balanced approach. For example, if some scientists say that exercise lengthens life span and others say that it does not, report both theories.

PRACTICE

Use the 4R test to evaluate the items listed below. They are potential sources for the topic "the effects of early radio on life in the United States." Compare and discuss your results with those of three or four classmates.

1. A book titled *History of Radio to 1926,* published by the American Historical Society in 1938

2. A Web page titled "Stories from Early Radio," first published on the Internet in 1998

3. A magazine article titled "The latest fashions in designer radio equipment," published in 1999

4. A book titled *Radio: The Only Useful Mass Medium*, published in 1985

5. A book titled *Demographic Vistas: Television in American Culture,* published in 1984

6. A play script titled *The Fall of the City: A Verse Play for Radio*, published in 1937

7. An article titled "Radio as a Medium of Communication," published in *Encyclopedia Americana* in 1994

8. A Web page titled "My Favorite Radio Programs," first published on the Internet in 2000

9. A book titled *Growing Up with the Radio: A Journey Through the Tunes of the 1960s,* published in 1998

10. A novel titled *Radio Life,* published in 1962

Prepare to Take Notes

Plan Your Route   Before you begin taking notes, take some time to create an **early plan,** which might take the form of a **list** or a **conceptual map,** to guide the rest of your research. This plan is tentative and will probably change as you read and learn more. Your early plan should include

- your refined topic
- headings that are suggested by your reading
- subdivisions that you think you might pursue

Refer to your early plan as you take notes, using its headings to decide what information to record. Remember, though, that you are free to add, delete, or rearrange parts of your early plan at any time. As you create your plan, be sure to consider the **relative value** of significant facts. Here is the early plan the writer made for the research paper on the effects of radio.

Early Plan

The Effects of Radio on Life in the United States

    Background

    Effects on entertainment

    Original types of programs

    Later types of programs

       News events

       Politics

    Effects on information delivery

    Effects on the economy

       Manufacturers of sets

       Other segments of the economy

TIP   To help you revise your plan, keep these points in mind.

- If you have too little information about a major heading, delete that heading and substitute another heading for which you have more information.
- If you have too much information about a major topic, subdivide that topic into two.
- If you have new information, alter or replace a major heading to include the new information.

Take Notes

TIP As you take notes, refine your topic and ask additional questions based on the information you gather.

Bookmarks and Key Words Begin gathering information by skimming a source. Use self-sticking notes or slips of paper to mark pages with information on your topic. (Bookmark Web sites that look promising.) After deciding what information you want to use from the source, think about how that information fits into your early plan. Then, take notes from the source by **quoting, paraphrasing,** or **summarizing** it. Be sure to distinguish your own ideas from those of your sources. The chart below shows how one writer used the three techniques to take notes from Neil Weiner's "Early Internet Business—Stories from Early Radio."

Technique	Example
Quote only when the author's exact words, as well as the ideas, are important. Copy the material word for word, and put quotation marks around it.	"The big taboo, the unthinkable moral violation in this new, pure instrument of democracy, was blatant paid advertising."
Paraphrase when you need to explain an idea in detail. A **paraphrase** is a restatement in your own words—your own sentence structure and vocabulary—that allows for more detail.	Because radio was seen as a tool of democracy, paid advertising was considered improper.
Summarize when you have to remember only the main idea of what you read or hear. A **summary** is a highly condensed version—one-fourth to one-third the length of the original—in your own words.	Paid advertising was considered distasteful.

TIP When taking notes, be sure that you distinguish information that is **fact** from information that is **opinion** by using phrases such as "Mr. Honeyton says" or "according to Mr. Honeyton."

TIP Try color-coding your note cards. For example, you could put all the sources of information for one book on blue cards and all the citations for another book on yellow cards.

Follow these steps to ensure that your notes are clear and easy to use.

- **Use a separate 4" × 6" note card, sheet of paper, or computer file for each item of information.**
- **In the upper left corner, write a key word or key phrase** (perhaps a heading from your early plan) so that you can tell at a glance what the note is about.
- **In the upper right corner, write the source card number** (see page 223).
- **Write the text of the note** (a quotation, a summary, or a paraphrase).
- **Write the page number** on which you found the information.

After you have completed a note card, double-check to make sure that you have recorded quotations exactly and that you have correctly interpreted the information. Below is an example of a properly formatted note card.

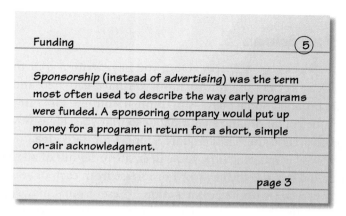

Funding	⑤

Sponsorship (instead of advertising) was the term most often used to describe the way early programs were funded. A sponsoring company would put up money for a program in return for a short, simple on-air acknowledgment.

page 3

TIP Unless you quote a source directly, always take notes in your own words. Change the sentence structure, too. When you use someone else's words *or* ideas without giving proper credit, you commit *plagiarism,* a serious academic offense. Avoid plagiarism by always crediting your sources—even when restating the author's ideas.

Write a Thesis Statement

The Driving Force The thesis statement for a research paper states your main idea about your topic, and it lets your readers know what you plan to cover. Drafting a preliminary thesis statement will help you identify which aspects of the topic you want to emphasize. It will also help you organize the information you have collected. These three steps will help you draft your thesis statement:

- **Review the information you have gathered,** especially the main ideas you put on each note card.

- **Think about what possible approaches your notes suggest.** Will your paper explore new information? examine how the topic has changed over time? demonstrate a cause-and-effect relationship? demonstrate a comparison-contrast relationship?

- **Draw conclusions by writing a sentence that concisely illustrates the approach supported by the information in your notes.** The writer who chose "the effects of early radio" for a topic drafted this preliminary thesis statement: *Early radio dramatically affected American entertainment, information delivery, and business.*

Reference Note

For more on **writing thesis statements,** see page 386.

Remember that your preliminary thesis statement will serve as a *working* main idea. Think of it as a guidepost, not as a predetermined road. You may decide to revise it, perhaps more than once, as you continue shaping your paper.

Organize Ideas

Put Your Ducks in a Row   Once you have written your thesis statement, you can review the information you have gathered and begin to develop an **organizational plan**—a preliminary outline for your paper. It is important for you to **organize your paper so that your ideas flow in a logical progression and there is adequate support for each idea.**

KEY CONCEPT

You may be wondering how you will create order out of all the sources you collected. First, use the key word or phrase from each of your notes to group all notes with similar information. These groups may suggest the main sections or ideas of your paper. Then, you can decide how best to order the ideas within each group of cards and which supporting details to use. Although you may be able to order your information exclusively in one of the following ways, you will probably find a combination of the orders necessary.

Reference Note

For more on **orders of organization,** see page 374.

- **Chronological order** gives events in the order they happen.
- **Logical order** groups related ideas together.
- **Order of importance** begins with the most important detail and moves to the least important (or the reverse).

Create a Formal Outline

Where's the Map?   If you were planning to visit a number of sites in each of several different states, a map would help you plan your trip. You might change your itinerary along the way, but at least you would have a clear idea about where you planned to go.

An **outline** is like the plan for such a trip. Once you have chosen an order for your information, you can begin creating your *working outline*. A **working outline** is a plan that allows you to arrange details in groups without using numbers or letters. To do this, you first must group the notes you have made under the major headings in your early plan. Then, subdivide the notes under each heading into smaller sets and give each set a subheading.

You may be asked to create a formal outline for your research paper. Here is the beginning of the outline one writer prepared after researching early radio. (A complete outline would contain more specific details under each capital letter.) A *formal* outline like this, with Roman numerals and capital letters, can also be made after a report is written to serve as a table of contents for the research paper.

Reference Note

For more on **creating outlines,** see page 950 in the Quick Reference Handbook.

Thesis: Early radio dramatically affected American entertainment, information delivery, and business.

  I. The invention of radio
    A. Earlier developments
      1. Discovery of radio waves
      2. Wireless transmission of Morse code signals
      3. Wireless transmission of sounds
    B. Early equipment

  II. Effects on entertainment
    A. Duplication of existing forms
    B. Creation of new forms

  III. Effects on information delivery

TIP In organizing your ideas, it may help to work collaboratively with another student. Discuss which order you each think will be most effective for your paper and why. Listening to others' ideas can help to clarify your own ideas.

TIP Outline entries may be words, word phrases, or complete sentences. Another way to determine the organization of your research paper is to **map your ideas.** For more on **mapping,** see page 955 of the Quick Reference Handbook.

YOUR TURN 6 **Preparing to Write**

Before you begin to draft your research paper, make sure to

- create an early plan
- take notes from the sources you have identified
- review the information you find
- write a thesis statement that expresses your main idea and suggests your approach
- organize your notes and prepare an outline

Research Paper

Framework   **Directions and Explanations**

Introduction ——————
- Arouse interest with an attention getter.
- Include your thesis statement.
- Suggest which aspects of the topic your paper covers.

Make a Good First Impression   Begin with an informative title that gives a clue to the controlling idea of your thesis statement. Then, get your readers' attention right away, perhaps by using an interesting detail you found in your research.

Create a Thesis to Remember   Your thesis sentence may open your paper, or it may work well as the last sentence of your introductory paragraph.

Guide Your Readers   Prepare readers by indicating in the thesis the main points of the paper.

Body ——————
- Develop your first main point with related supporting details.
- Develop each of your additional main points with related supporting details.

Develop Your Information   Create one or more paragraphs for each of the main points in your outline. Each paragraph should include a topic sentence and supporting details such as summaries, paraphrases, or quotations. Don't forget to show how your research information connects to your topic sentences.

Conclusion ——————
- Restate your thesis.
- Leave readers with an insight.

Final Impression   To close your paper, remind your readers of your thesis. Also, leave your readers with an insight or a question or thought to ponder.

YOUR TURN 7 **Writing a First Draft**

Using the framework, write the first draft of your research paper. Also, look at the Writer's Model on the next page.

A Writer's Model

The following final draft of a research paper closely follows the framework on the preceding page. Note the use of parentheses to show sources of information. These parenthetical citations are explained on page 237.

The Rise of Radio

It nestles on your night stand, occupies a prominent place in your entertainment center, and rules the road from the dashboard of your car: the radio. This simple appliance is so common that most people take it for granted, yet radio is a relatively new invention. In fact, the first commercial radio station, KDKA in Pittsburgh, did not go on the air until 1920 (Stark 120). Before long, however, the new medium dramatically affected the nation's entertainment, information delivery, and economy.

The invention of radio was made possible by a number of earlier developments. German physicist Heinrich Hertz, drawing on established mathematical principles, discovered the existence of radio waves in 1887. Eight years later, in Italy, Guglielmo Marconi successfully completed the first wireless transmission of Morse code signals. An American invention helped move radio closer to reality: Lee De Forest's 1907 Audion, which made it possible to transmit sounds, not just signals. A full decade before KDKA debuted, De Forest broadcast a live performance by famed Italian tenor Enrico Caruso from New York City's Metropolitan Opera House (Yenne 77).

Few people were equipped to hear that landmark broadcast, however, because radio was still very much a do-it-yourself project; most people built their own receivers. In 1921, one such "tinkerer," twenty-eight-year-old Franklin Malcolm Doolittle of New Haven, Connecticut, even used his home-made transmitter to broadcast the Yale-Princeton football game from his home (Gelman 80). The first commercially produced receivers became available in 1920, when a Pittsburgh department store began offering sets for ten dollars. The response was so enthusiastic that Westinghouse began mass producing the appliances (Baker).

When radio found its way into the majority of American households, it brought the nation together in an

(continued)

INTRODUCTION
Attention getter

Source with one author

Thesis

Background information

Paraphrase

Background information

Paraphrase

Summary
Online Source

BODY: First main point

Phrase/clause
quotation
Supporting details

Source with no
author given
Author's name in text

Second main point

Indirect source
Summary

Third main point
Supporting details

Short quotation

Additional supporting
details

Additional supporting
details

unprecedented way. Radio reached into "once dreary homes, reducing the isolation of the hinterlands and leveling class distinctions" (Henderson 44). At first radio programming simply duplicated existing forms of entertainment: singers, musicians, comedians, lecturers. Coping with technical difficulties left little time for creating new types of shows. Later, as the technical problems were resolved, programmers began adapting existing formats and experimenting with new types of shows, including variety shows, serials, game shows, and amateur hours ("Radio as a Medium of Communication"). As programming expanded, radio truly became, in researcher Amy Henderson's words, "a theater of the mind" (144).

The introduction of radio also radically altered the way people learned about events in the outside world. For the first time in history, everyone could receive the same information simultaneously. As sociologists Robert and Helen Lynd, writing in the 1920s, noted, "With but little equipment one can call the life of the rest of the world from the air . . ." (qtd. in Monk 173). Live coverage gave news events an immediacy far greater than newspapers or newsreels could provide. In fact, most people first learned of such historic events as the 1941 Japanese attack on Pearl Harbor from the radio (Stark 120).

Equally important was radio's impact on the economy. The first, and most noticeable, effect was to add a new consumer product to people's wish lists. Most early sets were strictly functional—"a box, some wire, and headphones" (Baker). Once the initial demand was satisfied, however, manufacturers began stimulating repeat sales by offering new models each year, with the goal of placing a "radio in every room" (Collins 10).

The demand for sets was a boon to manufacturers, but it struck fear into some other segments of the economy. Newspapers worried that radio would drive them out of business (Henderson 90). Similarly, members of the traditional entertainment industry feared that the new technology would cut into the sales of tickets and recordings (Stark 120).

Surprisingly, advertisers were slow to realize the opportunities radio offered. At first, most business people assumed that profits would come solely from the sale of sets and replacement parts. In addition, paid advertising was

(continued)

considered improper for what was initially viewed as a "new, pure instrument of democracy" (Weiner). Instead, early programs were underwritten by "sponsors," with companies receiving only a brief, discreet acknowledgment in return for their support (Weiner). Eventually, however, this approach gave way to the direct advertising that is familiar today.

Reviewing the rise of radio makes clear how instrumental the medium was in shaping the nation's entertainment, information delivery, and economy. Today, with the advent of television and the Internet, radio is no longer the primary source of news and entertainment for most people, nor is its impact on the economy as far-reaching. Still, each day millions of listeners wake, work, and play to the rhythms of radio, and many would be lost without it. The radio may have been muted, but it has not been unplugged.

Works Cited

Baker, Robert T. "100 Years of Radio." CyberProfile Journal. 16 Mar. 1997. RTB Web Design. 30 Nov. 1998 <http://rtb.home.texas.net/history.htm>.

Collins, Philip. Radios: The Golden Age. San Francisco: Chronicle Books, 1987.

Gelman, Morrie. "75 Years of Pioneers." Broadcasting and Cable 6 Nov. 1995: 80–92.

Henderson, Amy. On the Air. Washington, DC: Smithsonian Institution Press, 1988.

Monk, Linda R., ed. Ordinary Americans. Alexandria, VA: Close Up, 1994.

"Radio as a Medium of Communication." The Encyclopedia Americana. International ed. 1998.

Stark, Phyllis. "On the Air." Billboard 1 Nov. 1994: 120–124.

Weiner, Neil. "Stories from Early Radio." Background Briefing. 14 April 1996. 28 Mar. 1999 <http://www.backgroundbriefing.com/radio.html>.

Yenne, Bill. 100 Events That Shaped World History. San Francisco: Bluewood, 1993.

Summary

CONCLUSION
Restatement of thesis

Concluding thought

TIP Research papers and their *Works Cited* lists are normally double-spaced. Because of limited space on these pages, A Writer's Model and A Student's Model are single-spaced. The *Elements of Language* Internet site provides a model of a research paper in the double-spaced format. To see this interactive model, go to **go.hrw.com** and enter the keyword **EOLang 10-6.**

A Student's Model

The following passages are excerpted from a research paper written by Yen Co of Independence High School in San Jose, California, about her state's Teenage Driving Act.

<table>
<tr><td>

Background

Thesis statement

Main point

Source with one author

Supporting statistics

Summary

</td><td>

An Indecisive Conclusion

. . . The Teenage Driving Act regulates the actions of teenagers by limiting the allowable number of passengers, the hours during which a teenager can drive, and the driving experience needed before the issuance of a license. Although the new Teenage Driving Act contributes to road safety and saves the state money, its efficiency is questionable.

. . . Statistics show that motor collisions are the leading cause of death among teenagers, responsible for nearly one-third of teenage deaths (Smith). Teenagers account for 17 percent of the driving population, but are involved in 14 percent of all fatal traffic accidents and nearly 20 percent of total crashes. More than 6,300 drivers and passengers aged fifteen to twenty died in traffic crashes in 1996—an average of more than seventeen deaths each day ("Seeking to Reduce"). Since most accidents involving teenagers happen between the hours of 9 P.M. and 6 A.M. (Willis), the new regulations aim to decrease accidents in this range of time by requiring first-year drivers to be accompanied by a parent, guardian, or licensed driver over the age of twenty-five when driving between midnight and 5 A.M. . . .

Works Cited

"Seeking to Reduce Teen Driver Deaths." USA Today. Dec. 1997. Apr. 1999 <http://www.elibrary.com/s/edumark>.

Smith, Donna. "Graduated Licensing." Parents Against Speeding Teens. Aug. 1996. Apr. 1999 <http://www.pastnh.org/grad.htm>.

</td></tr>
</table>

Credit Your Sources

Credit Where Credit Is Due You need to give credit to any writer from whose work you have gathered specific information. The challenge is in deciding *when* and *how* to do this.

- **When?** Give credit for specific data (facts, statistics, numbers, dates, and so on), original ideas, opinions, insights, or any other information that you found in the work of another writer.

  The only instances when you do not need to give credit are **common knowledge,** information the average person should know (such as "Television is a more recent invention than radio"); **familiar proverbs** ("A fool and his money are soon parted"); and **well-known quotations** ("Ask not what your country can do for you . . .").

- **How?** Give credit within the body of your paper using MLA-style parenthetical citations, unless your teacher gives you other directions. **Parenthetical citations** are simply credits given within parentheses immediately following borrowed information. You need to give only enough information in the parenthetical citation to aid the reader in finding the full citation on the Works Cited page and to show exactly where in that source you found the information. Be sure you include a Works Cited list at the end listing all of the works you have cited. (See the example on page 235.)

  This sentence from the Writer's Model on page 233 includes a parenthetical citation: "The first radio station, KDKA in Pittsburgh, did not go on the air until 1920 (Stark 120)." A reader then could consult the Works Cited list to learn that the information was taken from an article written by Phyllis Stark in the November 1, 1994, issue of *Billboard* magazine.

  The following chart provides specific guidelines for citing sources within your report, using MLA-style parenthetical citations.

Guidelines for Giving Credit Within a Paper

Place the information in parentheses at the end of the sentence in which you used someone else's words or ideas. Examples taken from the research paper on page 233 are indicated with an asterisk (*).

1. **Source with one author.** Author's last name followed by page number(s). (Stark 120)*

2. **Sources by authors with the same last name.** First and last names of each author followed by the page number(s). (Jackson Smith 38), (Leslie Smith 78)

3. **Source with more than one author.** All authors' last names followed by page number(s). (Burton and Owen 3)

(continued)

(continued)

4. **Source with no author given.** Title or a shortened form of it and the page number(s). ("Radio Daze" 152)

5. **One-page source, unpaginated source, CD-ROM or online source, or article from an encyclopedia or other work arranged alphabetically.** Author's name only. If no author's name is given, title only. (Weiner)*

6. **More than one source by the same author.** Author's last name and the title or a shortened form of it followed by the page number(s). (Allen, "Only Yesterday" 7), (Allen, "Since Yesterday" 19)

7. **Author's name given in paragraph.** Page number only. (144)

8. **Indirect source.** *Qtd. in* ("quoted in") before the source and a page number. (qtd. in Monk 173)*

The next chart provides specific guidelines on how to correctly cite sources in a Works Cited list at **the end of your report.** Readers can turn to this list when they want complete publication information about the sources you have cited in your report.

Guidelines for Preparing the List of Works Cited

1. On a separate sheet of paper, center the words *Works Cited* (or *Bibliography* if all of your sources are print sources) one inch from the top.

2. For each entry on the list, follow the format you used for your source cards (page 223).

3. Organize your list using the following conventions.

   - List your sources in alphabetical order by the authors' last names.

   - If no author is given, alphabetize by the first important word in the title.

   - If you use two or more sources by the same author, write the author's name in the first entry only. For all other entries, use three hyphens where the author's name would be, followed by a period. Then, give the title, publication information, and page number(s). Arrange multiple entries alphabetically by the first important word in the title.

   Example:

   Allen, Frederick Lewis. Only Yesterday: An Informal History of the 1920's. New York: Harper, 1951.

   ---. Since Yesterday: The 1930's in America. New York: Harper, 1939.

4. Begin each listing at the left margin. If a listing is longer than one line, indent all the following lines five spaces.

   Example:

   Henderson, Amy. On the Air. Washington, DC: Smithsonian Institution Press, 1988.

Integrate Direct Quotations into Your Paper

And I Quote . . .   Using direct quotations in your research paper adds credibility to your writing. Just be sure to avoid using too many long quotations, and vary the pattern of your sentences to make your writing read smoothly. Also, make sure you do not use quotations just to fill out your paper. If you overuse quotations, your paper will look like a cut-and-paste version of other authors' works. The chart below shows some examples of ways to weave quotations from the book *On the Air* by Amy Henderson (Smithsonian Institution Press, 1988) into a paper.

Type of Quotation	Directions	Example
phrase or clause	Place the quotation within your own sentence and enclose it in quotation marks.	Researcher Amy Henderson states that radio became "a theater of the mind" as people experimented with imaginative new formats (144).
short quotation (four lines or less)	Introduce the quotation in your own words and enclose it in quotation marks.	According to Henderson, "The dramatic works of Norman Corwin, Orson Welles, and Archibald MacLeish showcased radio as a theater of the mind, with an imaginative scope beyond that of any other arena" (144).
long quotation (more than four lines)	Set off the quotation by indenting each line ten spaces from the left margin. Introduce it in your own words, followed by a colon. Do not use quotation marks.	Once the technical challenges involved with radio broadcasting were under control, new forms could be explored: The dramatic works of Norman Corwin, Orson Welles, and Archibald MacLeish showcased radio as a theater of the mind, with an imaginative scope beyond that of any other arena. Made possible by network willingness to experiment with creative programming on a sustained (that is, unsponsored) basis, these dramas proved that radio—though a mass commercial enterprise—was capable of producing eloquence. (Henderson 144)

WALNUT COVE reprinted with special permission of King Features Syndicate, Inc.

Revising

Evaluate and Revise Your Draft

Read and Read Again   Read your draft at least twice. The first time, focus on content and organization. The second time, concentrate on style.

TIP   You may also want to ask a classmate to use the chart below to review your essay and give you feedback.

▶ **First Reading: Content and Organization**   The content and organization guidelines below will help you examine your paper and consider possible changes. First, answer the questions on the left. Next, use the tips in the middle to mark changes. Finally, use the suggestions in the column on the right to make revisions to your writing.

Research Paper: Content and Organization Guidelines for Peer and Self-Evaluation

Evaluation Questions	▶ Tips	▶ Revision Techniques
❶ Does the opening grab the reader's attention?	**Put brackets** around the sentence(s) intended to hook the reader's interest. If no sentences are bracketed, revise.	**Add** an interesting fact, question, or observation.
❷ Does the thesis statement appear early in paper? Does it identify the topic and main idea and suggest which aspects of the topic are covered?	**Underline** the thesis statement. **Double underline** the words that suggest which aspects of the topic the paper covers. If any part is missing, revise.	**Add** a sentence identifying your topic and main idea. **Elaborate** by mentioning the aspects of the topic covered in your paper.
❸ Is each main point supported with relevant information—summaries, paraphrases, or quotations?	**Put a capital _A_** by the first main point. **Put a lowercase _a_** at the beginning of each sentence that supports that point. Continue this pattern with each point. If any capital letters are not followed by lowercase ones, revise.	**Elaborate** by adding your own ideas or information and summaries, paraphrases, or quotations. **Rearrange** information so that it clearly supports the appropriate main point.
❹ Is proper credit given for each source of information?	**Put a number** at the end of each sentence that uses information from an outside source. **Put the same number** over the corresponding citation. If any numbered sentence has no citation, revise.	**Add** citations for any information (other than common knowledge) summarized, paraphrased, or quoted from an outside source. **Delete** citations for any information that is common knowledge.
❺ Does the conclusion restate the paper's thesis?	**Put a wavy line** under the restatement of the thesis. If no sentence has a wavy line, revise.	**Add** a paraphrase of the thesis.

ONE WRITER'S REVISIONS The following example shows how one writer used the content and organization guidelines to revise a part of the research report on page 233. Examine the revisions carefully, and then answer the questions that follow.

> The invention of radio was made possible by a number of
> earlier developments. *, drawing on established mathematical principles,* German physicist Heinrich Hertz discov-
> ered the existence of radio waves in 1887. Eight years later, in
> Italy, Guglielmo Marconi successfully completed the first wire-
> less transmission of Morse code signals. An American invention
> helped move radio closer to reality: Lee De Forest's 1907
> Audion, *, which made it possible to transmit sounds, not just signals.* A full decade before KDKA debuted, De Forest broad-
> cast a live performance by famed Italian tenor Enrico Caruso
> from New York City's Metropolitan Opera House (Yenne 77).

add

elaborate

Analyzing the Revision Process

Use the following questions to help you consider the reasons for the author's revisions.

1. Why did the writer add the phrase to the second sentence?
2. How does the elaboration in the fourth sentence help the reader understand the paragraph's main points?

YOUR TURN 8   Focusing on Content and Organization

Use the guidelines on page 240 and the model furnished by One Writer's Revisions above to revise the content and organization of your research paper.

PEER REVIEW

Ask a classmate to read your research paper and to answer the following questions:

1. After reading the introduction, were you clear about the paper's topic and approach? Why or why not?
2. Which main point was developed most completely? Why do you think so?
3. What new information did you learn by reading this paper?

Second Reading: Style   Research reports are packed with information, much of it new to the audience. To make your report as "reader friendly" as possible, you need to make sure the information is presented in a manner that will retain your reader's interest. One way to accomplish this goal is to vary the length of your sentences.

Evaluation Question	▶ Tip	▶ Revision Technique
Are too many sentences in the research paper long and complicated?	▶ **Underline** every other sentence with a colored marker. Use a different colored marker to underline the remaining sentences. If there are several long sentences in succession (longer than twenty to twenty-five words), revise.	▶ **Rearrange** overly long sentences to create two or more shorter sentences.

Focus on Sentences

Varying Sentence Length

When you include quotations and paraphrases in your first draft, you may find yourself using too many long sentences. Long sentences can be a good way to emphasize a point by building up to it, as a sort of climax. However, using *only* long sentences can make your writing monotonous for readers. Long sentences also demand closer attention on the part of the reader and can produce confusion.

ONE WRITER'S REVISIONS Here is how the writer of the model research paper on page 233 used the Style Guidelines to vary sentence length.

Reference Note

For more on **varying sentence length,** see page 352.

BEFORE REVISION

one 35-word sentence

> When radio found its way into the majority of American households, it brought the nation together in an unprecedented way, reaching into "once dreary homes, reducing the isolation of the hinterlands and leveling class distinctions" (Henderson 44).

AFTER REVISION

two sentences created from one

> When radio found its way into the majority of American households, it brought the nation together in an unprecedented **way. Radio reached** into "once dreary homes, reducing the isolation of the hinterlands and leveling class distinctions" (Henderson 44).

Analyzing the Revision Process

1. How did the writer divide one sentence into two?
2. How did breaking the long sentence into two shorter sentences improve the paragraph?

COMPUTER TIP

You can use a word-processing program's save-as command to save alternate versions of your paper while experimenting with changes. That way, you will always have a copy of the original in case you want to revert to it.

YOUR TURN 9 Varying Sentence Length

Use the style guidelines on page 242 to evaluate the length of sentences in your research paper and to divide sentences if necessary.

Designing Your Writing

Site Maps   Another way to share your research is to transform the information into a Web site. The **home page,** the first page of information in your Web document, should introduce your research topic. If you decide to publish your research this way, remember that a well-constructed Web site often starts with a *site map* to help site visitors understand what information is included. A **site map** is a visual depiction of the general structure and organization of a Web site. A site map usually lists every page on the site that includes a *hyperlink* to the home page. (A **hyperlink** is an image or highlighted section of text that takes you to another Web page when you click on it.) Site maps can be simple listings or more complicated image maps. To create your site map, list your ideas and organize them into four or five main sections; you can use the major points in the outline for your research paper. These points then become the main pages of your site. Organize your specific or detailed information under these pages. Here is an example of how to set up a site map with just the home page and main pages.

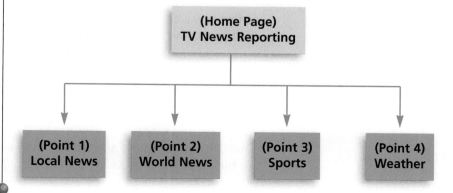

(Home Page)
TV News Reporting

| **(Point 1)** Local News | **(Point 2)** World News | **(Point 3)** Sports | **(Point 4)** Weather |

Publishing

Proofread Your Essay

Reference Note

For more information and practice on avoiding **misplaced modifers,** see page 627.

Perfect It   So that your work looks polished and credible, work collaboratively with a peer to read your paper at least twice more, checking for grammar, spelling, and punctuation errors. Be sure to notice, for instance, whether you have misplaced any modifiers. Remember that modifying words, phrases, and clauses should be placed as close as possible to the words they modify.

Grammar Link

Correcting Misplaced Modifiers

When you are informing your readers about the results of your research, a **misplaced modifier** can muddle your meaning. This mistake also might be taken as carelessness and undermine your credibility. **A modifier (a word, phrase, or clause that makes the meaning of another word or word group more specific) should be placed as near as possible to the word or group of words it modifies.** Otherwise, you may confuse or mislead a reader. To understand how to correct misplaced modifiers, review these examples.

Misplaced Word	Most families almost listened to the radio daily. [The adverb *almost* seems to modify *listened.*]
Clear	Most families listened to the radio almost daily.
Misplaced Phrase	Some people had problems with reception living in remote areas. [The participial phrase *living in remote areas* seems to modify *reception.*]
Clear	Some people living in remote areas had problems with reception.
Misplaced Clause	Entire families that dominated the living room would gather around the device. [The adjective clause *that dominated the living room* seems to modify *families.*]
Clear	Entire families would gather around the device that dominated the living room.

PRACTICE

Revise each of the following sentences by correcting the misplaced modifier. You may need to add words and punctuation to make the meaning of a sentence clear.

1. Television is common today, which was a novelty when it first came out.
2. At first it was thought that television for most people would be too expensive.
3. Television was demonstrated to many people attending a World's Fair for the first time.
4. Many people thought that television would do away with radio when it came along.
5. Entertainers found new audiences showcasing their talents on television.

Publish Your Essay

Spread the Word   Here are some ways to share the results of your research with an audience, using a variety of formats.

■ Show your paper to content-area teachers who are knowledgeable about your topic. They may have some helpful comments or suggestions about your research.

■ Ask a media specialist in your school if you can set up a display of research reports written by your peers and yourself. Other students will be able to use the display as sources of ideas for research subjects.

■ Record a reading of your report and offer the audiotape to your school's media specialist. He or she might be able to play it for other students.

■ Publish your paper on the Web so that others interested in the topic can use it as a resource.

TIP   If you have written your essay for a general audience and now wish to publish it for a more specific audience—local experts on the topic, for example—you may need to refine your essay a bit. Always keep in mind what your audience already knows about the topic and how you might further inform them.

Reflect on Your Essay

PORTFOLIO

Learning from Experience   You are nearing the end of a complex project requiring persistence and skill. Take a moment to reflect on your experience with the research paper by answering the following questions in writing.

■ How did researching and writing about your topic (as opposed to other ways of learning about it, such as hearing a lecture) affect what and how much you learned?

■ The next time you research and write about a topic, which parts of the process will you definitely use? What will you do differently?

   If you add your report to your portfolio or learning log, date your responses to these questions and include them in your portfolio or learning log as well.

YOUR TURN 10   Proofreading, Publishing, and Reflecting

Review each of the steps explained in this section. Before you turn in your research paper, be sure to

■ proofread it carefully
■ consider publishing options
■ record reflections on your writing experience

Research in the Media

Research skills come in handy for more than just writing research papers. People who create various kinds of media messages must do research. Here are just two examples of the ways research is used in the media.

- A television news reporter must research the background of an investigative story.
- A Web site designer must research information on her topic to create accurate hyperlinks for sites.

Often, many pieces of factual information—information that can be proven or verified—in a media message have been researched by someone.

Stay for the Credits   Not only must creators of many media messages do research, but they must also, just like you, give credit to their sources. Often, sources are acknowledged during the credits at the end of a film or television show. Sometimes, however, credit is given in a way that is a little harder to spot. For instance, a reporter might say, "According to meteorologist Joe Whitey, this was the first tornado ever to hit New Hampshire." Who is the source of the information about tornadoes? Joe Whitey, the meteorologist, is.

Seeing Is Believing?   You've probably heard the expression "Don't believe everything you read." Well, don't believe everything you see, either. To be a critical media viewer, try to identify the source of any information given. Always consider the reliability of the information, whether or not a source is given.

YOUR TURN 11   Identifying Research in Media Messages

With one or two classmates, consider two different kinds of media messages. For example, you might consider a nightly news report and a Web site, or a newsmagazine and a documentary film. As you view or read each media message, try to identify at least three pieces of researched information. Then, see if you can identify the sources used. Make a chart like the one below to organize your findings.

Medium	Fact	Source
Newspaper article	Sixty percent of Americans agree with the recent Supreme Court decision.	The Gallup Poll

Evaluating Web Sites

Searching on the World Wide Web is like opening a floodgate: Waves of information come surging into your computer. Sometimes the amount of information can be overwhelming. How can you navigate the hundreds of Web pages on your topic without an online librarian to help you? Once you find a site that seems helpful, how can you determine whether the site gives reliable, accurate, and up-to-date information? By using the techniques described in this section, you can ride these waves of information without going under.

WHAT'S AHEAD?

In this section, you will learn to
- find Web sites related to a topic
- evaluate Web sites for reliability and validity

The World Wide Web

Getting What You Want   When you type keywords about a research topic into a search engine, you often get results that seem overwhelming. Many times the search engine will produce hundreds or thousands of matches or near matches to a search. Where do you begin? Instead of visiting the sites one at a time, there are a couple of simple ways to determine whether a site will be useful to you.

Check the Meter   Many search engines will tell you how useful a Web site will be by placing a number or other indicator alongside the site's address. This number signifies the percentage of the Web site that matches your research topic. If you were researching the history of animation, for instance, and you found a site devoted entirely to the history of animation, the number alongside the address might be *98*. On the other hand, if you found a site that is devoted to animation in the last decade, the number might be somewhat smaller. To save time and to keep your research on track, choose only the sites with the highest percentages. All search engines will list the highest percentages (the closest matches) first.

Be Specific   Whittle your search down by being as specific as possible. If you were searching for the history of a certain cartoon character, the keyword *animation* might be too broad and would produce results related to *all* animation. Searching for the character's name, however, probably would produce the best results.

What Can You Depend On?   There are a couple of ways to make sure that a Web site is a reliable source of information. You can choose a site from a university (indicated by the abbreviation *edu* in the Web address, which is also called the URL, or uniform resource locator) or a library. These sites usually are more reliable than others. The suffix *org* in the URL also indicates a more reliable source. Many national magazines and newspapers will reference these sites. You can also visit individual home pages (those that are personal and not affiliated with any organization), but always double-check them against at least one other source since the individual may not be an expert or part of a respected and trusted organization.

A Whale of a Resource   Ultimately, it will be up to you to determine whether a site is valid. A site is valid to your research if the site is relevant, meaningful, and appropriate to the topic. To check the validity of a Web site, remember the acronym ORCCCA:

Objective: Make sure the site is objective and not overly biased toward one side of an issue. If a site is sponsored by a single corporation, for instance, determine whether personal interests influence the information.

Reliable: Verify that the site is produced by a reliable source—an expert in the field, a respected organization, or a trusted publication.

Complete: Make sure that the information is detailed and complete. Points should be supported with sufficient evidence, such as examples. All points of view (all views on the topic) should be presented.

Clear: Consider whether the information is readable, easy to navigate, and well organized. Remember, though, that clarity usually is a matter of opinion.

Current: Confirm that the information is up-to-date. Check for dates when the information was updated, added, or otherwise modified.

Accurate: Determine whether the information is correct. Names and dates should be included for all sources cited. If no citations are provided, confirm the information with another source.

YOUR TURN 12   Evaluating Web Sites

Working with a partner, think of a name, word, or phrase related to each of your research topics and type it into a search engine. Once the search engine produces a list of sites, select three or four of them by applying the guidelines above. Determine which site is the most reliable and valid, and provide your reasons. Share your results, explaining how you applied the guidelines, with the rest of the class.

Choices

Choose one of the following activities to complete.

▶ CAREERS

1. Research Your Future
Pick a career, or field, you think might match your interests and talents, and brainstorm some questions about it. In a media center or bookstore, find some resources that contain information about research strategies used in that field. Skim the materials, and **take notes** about the answers you find. Present your findings in an **oral or video presentation.**

▶ LITERATURE

2. Your Very Own Book Club
Select an author whose work you admire. Then, research the author's life to discover how it might have influenced his or her writing. Are there any events, themes, or character types that are present in both? Why might this be true? Share your discoveries in a **letter** to a friend or classmate who also enjoys the author's work.

▶ CROSSING THE CURRICULUM: THE ARTS

3. Your Art Form Think of an art form—modern dance, sculpture, hip-hop—that appeals to you, and write a sentence explaining how you feel about the art form and why. For example, "The blues cheer me up, because I let go of sad feelings when I listen to them." Then, use keywords to locate Web sites related to your topic, and search for other people's views on it. Using your original statement (or a revised version of it) as the topic sentence, write a **paragraph** about your art form, incorporating some of the views you found on the Internet.

▶ MEDIA AND TECHNOLOGY

4. One Research Report Leads to Another A research paper can serve as a source of inspiration. After reading your classmates' research reports, you may have questions that could be clarified by further research. Work collaboratively in small groups to compile a set of research questions suggested by each group member's report. Then, choose one topic, conduct an online search, and create an **early plan** for a possible group research report.

 **PORTFOLIO**

 7 Persuading Others

With all the milk I drink, my name might as well be Calcium Ripken, Jr. Really, I'm a huge milk fan. Besides being loaded with calcium, there's nothing like it when it's ice cold. Which is why I drink the recommended 3 glasses a day. And as you'd probably guess, I'm not one to miss a day.

got milk?

Reading Workshop

Reading a Persuasive Newspaper Article

Writing Workshop

Writing a Persuasive Essay

Viewing and Representing

Analyzing Editorial Cartoons

Speaking and Listening

Giving a Persuasive Speech

Choosing Sides

- The high school four miles up the road is the same size as yours but has four times as many computers. Is that fair?

- Advertisers spend about $700 million annually on TV ads aimed at young people. Do you think that is right?

- The state legislature is proposing to raise the legal driving age in your state. Do you think it would be a good idea?

Like many students, you probably have opinions on these and other issues concerning the world, the nation, your community, and your personal life. Maybe you have read articles or heard speeches in which writers or speakers voiced opinions on issues ranging from world peace to whether there is enough parking space for students at your school.

When people try to convince you to agree with their opinions, they are trying to **persuade** you. Advertisers, politicians, teachers, parents, and friends all use persuasion. You also persuade others when you take a stand on something important to you.

Informational Text

Persuasion

 Talking About Persuasion

In a small group of classmates, share recent experiences in which you have tried to persuade someone to do or believe something. Note whether the attempts at persuasion were successful. Keep a list of everyone's contributions. Be ready to share your list with the class.

internet**connect**

GO TO: go.hrw.com
KEYWORD: EOLang 10-7

Reading a Persuasive Newspaper Article

WHAT'S AHEAD?

In this section you will read a persuasive newspaper article and learn how to

- **distinguish facts from opinions**
- **identify the elements of persuasion**

You probably read newspaper articles and magazine articles that are informative, entertaining, or both. Some articles, however, serve another purpose—persuasion. The writer of a persuasive article is trying to convince you to agree with his or her position on some issue. For instance, maybe you have noticed that television sets seem to be everywhere, in places where you never expected to see them—in a grocery store, for example. The author of the following article, "Force-Fed Television," expresses a very definite opinion on this abundance of television sets. As you read the article, think about what the author's position is and whether you agree with it.

Preparing to Read

| READING SKILL | **Distinguishing Facts from Opinions**   When deciding whether you agree with a writer's position, you must consider the facts he or she provides. Since persuasive writing includes both *facts* and *opinions*, it is important to distinguish between the two. A **fact** is information that can be proven true; an **opinion** is a judgment or belief that cannot be proven true. As you read the article on the next page, look for points that are facts and for statements that are opinions.

| READING FOCUS | **Elements of Persuasion**   Persuasive pieces always contain certain techniques that are intended to persuade you to agree with a position and, sometimes, to take action for or against something. Persuasive techniques include **opinion statements** that directly state or imply a position, **reasons** and **evidence** that support a position, and **emotional appeals** that engage your feelings. As you read "Force-Fed Television," see if you can spot any of these persuasive techniques.

See if you can determine the writer's position in the following article. As you read, write down answers to the numbered active-reading questions.

from We The Media

FORCE-FED TELEVISION

by Adam Hochschild

Some friends from Moscow once introduced me to a lovely Russian custom. Before embarking on a trip, you "sit for the journey." Sitting quietly for a few minutes, you guarantee yourself a safe return by getting into the right, meditative frame of mind as you begin a major voyage.

Anyone looking for a few quiet moments in the place where most Americans begin longer voyages these days— an airport departure gate—is in for big trouble. Besides all the other distractions, there's often a new one: a flickering TV set. I first began encountering these TVs some months ago, and did some research to find out how widespread they are. It turns out that TVs are now installed at more than a thousand gates in more than twenty-five major American airports. The number is growing rapidly.

These TVs usually hang from the ceiling, exasperatingly out of reach of an angry foot or a hand trying to turn the sound off. Woe to the traveler who has an extra hour or two and hopes to read a book. You can't escape. And surely many people want to. At gates cursed with these TVs, most passengers are trying to talk, work, or read. But with little luck, for that penetrating TV sound relentlessly needles its way into a conversation or onto the page.

Nobody can claim that this is a service that travelers have asked for. They haven't. The TVs are there because there's big money to be made from them. Last year, Nielsen Media Research reported that 8.4 million people a month saw airport TV ads. Many millions in advertising dollars get divided between three parties to a deal: the airport, the airline whose gate it is, and the CNN Airport Network, which provides the programming. CNN employs retired baseball home run king Hank Aaron to sign up new airlines and airports.

> **1. What does the author do in this paragraph to capture your interest?**

> **2. What information does the author provide to convince you that there is a problem with television in public places?**

A TV set in a public place is different from one in your home. You can't turn it off. This force-fed TV is proliferating in part precisely because advertisers know that air travelers are likely to be working-age professionals—who usually watch less TV than children, housewives, retired people, and the poor. Furthermore, at home, everybody is more likely to turn off the sound during commercials. But airport TV is zap proof.

Not only in airports is television busy finding captive audiences, a phenomenon known in the advertising business as "place-based media." Despite strenuous opposition from parent and teacher groups, Channel One carries its commercials into thousands of school classrooms. Café USA is a TV network aimed at shopping-mall food courts. The Commuter Channel's silent screens hang above many cities' subway platforms. Happily, a recent Turner empire attempt aimed at supermarket shoppers, the Checkout Channel, failed. (NBC has been test-marketing the idea, however. "Our mission is to sell eyeballs to advertisers," the executive running the program has said.) Specially tailored TV programming is already creeping into doctors' waiting rooms. What sort of captive audience will they find next? Watch out for the Traffic Jam & Toll Plaza Network.

What is to be done the next time you fly? It won't work to courteously ask airport ticket agents to turn the TV off. They can't. Inadvisable for different reasons is using a sledgehammer or wire cutters to do the job yourself: This could land you in a place where you'd *really* be a captive audience, with nothing to do except watch TV all day long.

But there are other things you can do. You can support one of the organizations working to reduce the noxious effects of TV on American life, like UNPLUG or TV-Free America. And you can complain to the public authority that runs your local airport. What is a public place if not a spot where you can carry on an uninterrupted conversation?

In public places, TV is a form of pollution, like cigarette smoke. Smoke can at least be partly sucked away by a good ventilation system. The noise of an unwanted TV can't be. Regulation of unwanted noise is nothing new: many communities place restrictions on jet skis, leaf blowers, and snowmobiles. Thirty years ago people would have laughed at the idea of limiting smoking in public, but today, in the airport in my home city of San Francisco and in many others, smokers have to go to a special room. Why not a room for TV watchers?

3. How does the author try to stir your emotions in this paragraph?

4. What does the author want his readers to do?

5. What sentence in this paragraph seems to sum up the author's opinion, or point of view?

First Thoughts on Your Reading

Get together with a partner or small group to answer the following questions about "Force-Fed Television." Write your answers on your own paper.

1. Why do you think the author decided to put his opinion statement in the final paragraph instead of in the introduction?

2. What words and images did the author use to appeal to some of your emotions?

3. Did the author convince you to agree with his position? Why or why not?

Distinguishing Facts from Opinions

READING SKILL

The Facts About Facts and Opinions "Force-Fed Television" includes some of the author's **opinions** on the problem of television in public places. Opinions cannot be proven true because they are simply judgments, beliefs, or interpretations based on emotions or speculations. The following statement is an example of an opinion in the article:

> In public places, TV is a form of pollution, like cigarette smoke.

There is no way to prove this statement right or wrong; it is just the author's opinion.

TIP   Keep in mind that writers sometimes disguise opinions by stating them with authority as if they were facts.

Example:
It is a well-known fact that all students' test scores will rise when students spend less time watching television.

Putting the phrase "It is a well-known fact" in a sentence does not make the content of the sentence factual. Obviously, there is no way to prove that *every* student's scores will rise. Therefore, this statement is not a fact; it is an opinion.

If the author of the article had stated his opinion that TVs in public places are a form of pollution and had stopped there, the article would not be very convincing. However, good authors realize that in order to convince you, they have to back up their opinions with relevant **facts.** For example, the author of "Force-Fed Television" includes the following fact about TVs in airports:

> It turns out that TVs are now installed at more than a thousand gates in more than twenty-five major American airports.

What makes this statement a fact? It is a fact because it can be proven true. Some facts, as in the example above, are **statistics,** which are simply facts based on numbers. Your job as a reader of a persuasive piece of writing is to determine which statements are opinions and which are facts. Making this distinction will help you to understand the writer's motivation and to evaluate how credible, or believable, the writer is. If you are not sure whether a particular statement is an opinion or a fact, you can use the following Thinking It Through steps to find out.

THINKING IT THROUGH — Distinguishing Facts from Opinions

Use the following steps to determine whether this statement from "Force-Fed Television" is a fact or an opinion.

> CNN employs retired baseball home run king Hank Aaron to sign up new airlines and airports.

▶ **STEP 1 Read the statement carefully.**

▶ **STEP 2 Use the following checklist to make an initial decision about whether the statement is a fact or an opinion.**

Fact	Opinion
_X_ Gives information such as statistics or specific examples that can be proven true	___ Gives information that cannot be proven true
_X_ Cannot be argued	___ Can be argued
___ May tell source of information	___ May include indefinite terms, such as *lots* or *many*
	___ May include generalization clue words, such as *all*, *every*, *always*, or *never*
	___ May include opinion clue words, such as *should* or *must*
	___ May include "value" clue words, such as *good*, *bad*, *worst*, or *best*

The information about Hank Aaron can be proven true: He works for CNN; he hit a record 755 home runs; and he is signing up new airlines and airports for the CNN Airport Network. The statement is a fact.

▶ **STEP 3** **To confirm that a statement is a fact, double-check by asking yourself, "How and where could I find proof for this statement?"**

A source at CNN could probably confirm the statement about Hank Aaron, or you might find the information in a news article.

YOUR TURN 2 Identifying Facts and Opinions

Use the steps in Thinking It Through to decide which of the following sentences from "Force-Fed Television" are opinions and which are facts. Write **O** for opinion and **F** for fact. Put your answers on your own paper, and be prepared to explain your answers.

1. Anyone looking for a few quiet moments in . . . an airport departure gate—is in for big trouble.
2. Café USA is a TV network aimed at shopping-mall food courts.
3. Last year, Nielsen Media Research reported that 8.4 million people a month saw airport TV ads.
4. Furthermore, at home, everybody is more likely to turn off the sound during commercials.
5. Regulation of unwanted noise is nothing new; many communities place restrictions on jet skis, leaf blowers, and snowmobiles.

Elements of Persuasion

READING FOCUS

The Main Ingredients   "Force-Fed Television" contains many elements that clearly identify it as a persuasive piece of writing. Many readers of persuasive writing do not notice these separate elements. On your first reading, you will probably be aware only of your immediate response to the piece—agreement or disagreement. Critical readers go further by asking themselves why they responded as they did. They know that what they are really responding to are the three key elements of persuasive writing:

- **a strong opinion (or main idea)**—a directly stated or implied opinion about an issue on which people might disagree

- **logical appeals**—convincing reasons and evidence that support the writer's opinion

- **emotional appeals**—anecdotes and words with strong connotations that are intended to stir feelings in a reader

Writers do not always directly state their opinions; instead, they **imply,** or suggest, them. In these cases, readers must analyze the text and **infer,** or figure out, the writers' opinions.

Opinion An opinion is the main idea of a persuasive piece of writing. It can be stated directly in a single sentence, or it can be implied throughout the piece or even by the title. An opinion also can be the topic sentence of an individual paragraph within a longer piece. When you are trying to recognize opinion statements, it might help to know that they can be worded in several ways, as shown in the following chart:

Judgment Opinion	Teenagers can improve their lives by watching less television.
"Why" Opinion	The concert tour failed because of a lack of advertising funds.
Prediction Opinion	TV advertisements soon will be seen in every building in America.
"Should" Opinion	City governments should restrict the number of TV sets in airports.

Logical appeals Writers must also provide support for an opinion in order for it to be considered seriously. The main way that writers of persuasive pieces support their opinions is through **logical appeals.** Logical appeals are the convincing **reasons** (common-sense statements that appeal to a reader's sense of logic) and the **evidence** (facts, statistics, expert opinions, examples, and anecdotes) that supports those reasons. The evidence an author provides can make or break a persuasive piece of writing. Without evidence, a writer's opinion would not be considered seriously.

The following chart contains a reason that might be used to support the opinion statement, "Teenagers can improve their lives by watching less television," and five forms of evidence that might be used to support the reason.

Reason: Even though most teenagers think they need television in their lives, they really do not.	
Fact	TV is by far the favored medium for advertising to children.
Statistic	In a study by CNN, 28 percent of teens reported that they could manage without a television.
Expert Opinion	Dr. Victor Strasburger, Director of Adolescent Medicine and Professor of Pediatrics at the University of New Mexico School of Medicine, says that American children and adolescents spend more time watching TV than in any other activity except sleeping.

Example	Instead of watching TV, teenagers could read more books.
Anecdote	Some parents on my street have completely removed television sets from their homes.

Emotional appeals   **Emotional appeals** stir feelings like happiness, sadness, or anger in a reader. You might say that they are techniques that writers use to "tug at your heartstrings."

One of the ways writers appeal to readers' emotions is to include words with strong **connotative meanings**—sometimes referred to as **loaded language**. These words have undertones that link attitudes or feelings with the words and, in this way, heighten the seriousness of the issue for readers. As a reader, be aware, though, of too much loaded language in persuasive writing. Overuse of loaded language might also signal a lack of solid logical appeals in support of the opinion statement. Another technique writers of persuasion often use is to include an **anecdote,** or brief story, in which they describe experiences or events that appeal to a reader's emotions.

Unlike opinion statements and logical appeals, which are essential to almost any piece of persuasive writing, emotional appeals are not used by every writer of persuasive pieces. However, they do appear very often. Look at the following examples of emotional appeals.

Emotional Appeals		
Type	**Examples**	**Explanation**
Loaded Language (Connotative Words)	Will you be an *unsuspecting victim* of this electronic mall the next time you are unlucky enough to *stumble,* however briefly, on a shopping channel while channel-surfing?	*Unsuspecting victim* has strong connotations of mistreatment or suffering. *Stumble* suggests an accidental event.
Anecdote	Last year, a man reportedly spent his entire savings on items he purchased from a shopping channel.	This anecdote might make you feel sorry for the man.

It is important for you to recognize emotional appeals when you read. While they are a valid tool for persuading readers, you must be sure to form your response to a writer's opinion based on the logic of his or her reasons and evidence, not just on emotions. Sometimes, though, you will find that a writer has used evidence that appeals to *both* logic and emotions, as in the example on the next page.

Example:
American young people waste 15,000 hours watching television by the time they graduate from high school.

In the example above, the details about how much time children spend watching television is factual but also might touch people's feelings about the future of today's youth. This kind of evidence packs a double persuasive punch. It convinces readers that the writer's opinion is valid, and at the same time it involves readers' emotions. As a reader, it is important to note both the logical and emotional appeal of such statements.

YOUR TURN 3 — Identifying Elements of Persuasion

Copy the chart below on your own paper. Then, get together with two or three of your classmates to complete the chart. First, write down the opinion expressed in "Force-Fed Television" on page 253. Remember that a writer's opinion, or main idea, can be implied by the title of a piece of writing. Then, examine the essay for an example of one reason and of each type of support listed in the chart. Put an *E* beside each emotional appeal; put an *L* beside each logical appeal. If the support is both, put both letters. Be aware that you might not find every kind of support listed in the chart. For effective persuasion, writers must include logical appeals, but they need not include all types.

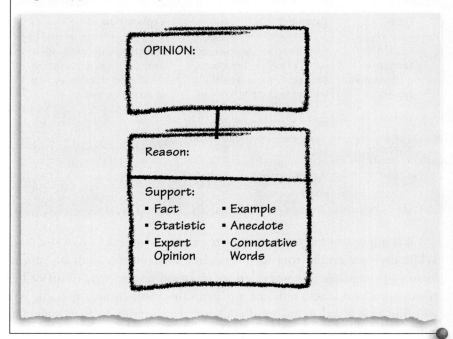

OPINION:

Reason:

Support:
- Fact
- Statistic
- Expert Opinion
- Example
- Anecdote
- Connotative Words

VOCABULARY

Understanding Connotations and Denotations

An effective persuasive writer chooses words not only for their **denotations** (meanings found in the dictionary) but also for their **connotations** (the feelings and emotions associated with words). In the following examples, note how the second sentence reads quite differently from the first when the italicized words are replaced with more neutral words.

1. The *penetrating* sound from the TV *needled* its way into the room.

2. The *noticeable* sound from the TV *made* its way into the room.

THINKING IT THROUGH — Understanding Connotations and Denotations

Use the following steps to understand the connotations of *creeping* in this sentence from "Force-Fed Television."

> Specially tailored TV programming is already *creeping* into doctors' waiting rooms.

1. Be sure you understand the denotation of the word by checking its definition in a dictionary. Creeping means "to advance gradually."

2. Using a dictionary or thesaurus, if needed, brainstorm words or phrases that could replace the word. entering, sneaking, slinking.

3. Categorize the replacement words as negative, positive, or neutral by determining if they have any associations or feelings for you. Neutral: entering. Negative: sneaking, slinking. Both negative words seem threatening, like snakes and bugs moving.

4. Decide if the original word is more like the neutral, the negative, or the positive synonyms. Creeping seems more like the negative words. It has a threatening feeling (connotation).

PRACTICE

Use the steps above to identify the connotations of each italicized word.

1. Woe to the traveler who has an extra hour or two and hopes to read a book. You can't *escape.*

2. This force-fed TV is *proliferating* in part precisely because advertisers know that air travelers are likely to be working-age professionals . . .

3. Not only in airports is television busy finding *captive* audiences . . .

4. Happily, a recent Turner *empire* attempt aimed at supermarket shoppers, the Checkout Channel, failed.

5. You can support one of the organizations working to reduce the *noxious* effects of TV on American life . . .

Fact-and-Opinion Questions

Standardized tests often include questions designed to check your ability to distinguish between facts and opinions. Here is a typical reading passage and multiple-choice question.

People with children should keep the family's television sets under lock and key. The concern over children and television comes from the constant bombardment of violent behavior on TV.

A recent study showed that 44 percent of network television and 85 percent of premium cable programming contains violence. The amount of violence on TV continues to grow each year. Over three years, the number of prime time shows depicting violence rose from just over a half to well over two thirds.

Parental monitoring of what children and teens view is not the complete answer. Only 38 percent of parents say they watch television with their children on a fairly regular basis. The best way to avoid the damaging effects of TV violence is to remove televisions from the reach of vulnerable children and young adults.

Which statement from the selection is an opinion?

A. The amount of violence on TV continues to grow each year.

B. Only 38 percent of parents say they watch television with their children on a fairly regular basis.

C. Violence on TV is always damaging to children and teens.

D. People with children should keep the family's TV sets under lock and key.

THINKING IT THROUGH   Answering Fact-and-Opinion Questions

Use the following steps to answer fact-and-opinion questions.

▶ **STEP 1 Read each statement carefully.**

▶ **STEP 2 Ask yourself, "Can the statement be proved true?"** Cross out the statements that can be proven true. **A** is a fact that is clearly proven in the selection. **B** is a statistical fact signaled by the use of the word *percent.*

▶ **STEP 3 Look for clue words that signal an opinion.** Words such as *should, must, always,* and *never* signal an opinion. **C** makes a judgment that violence on TV is *always* damaging. **D** states something the author thinks *should* be done.

▶ **STEP 4 Continue through all the answer choices.** When you think you have found the correct answer, check to see that the fact or opinion is actually stated in the passage. Do not settle on the first fact or opinion you find. In this case **C** is an opinion; however, it does not appear in the passage. Therefore, **D** is the correct answer.

Writing a Persuasive Essay

Imagine this situation: City officials plan to decrease traffic on the street in front of your high school by making the street one-way. This means that you and many of your friends would have to drive several blocks out of your way before turning around toward home. You believe that the city should find another way to decrease traffic on the street, but how can you share your views? One way is to express and support them in a persuasive essay.

In this Writing Workshop, you will learn how to do just that—create a persuasive essay on a topic about which you have a strong opinion. Your goal in the essay will be to state your opinion clearly and to support it with reasons and evidence.

WHAT'S AHEAD?

In this workshop, you will write a persuasive essay and learn how to

- form an opinion statement
- gather support for your opinion
- evaluate your reasoning
- avoid overusing the passive voice
- find and correct double negatives

Prewriting

Choose an Issue

A Powerful Issue   A good topic for a persuasive essay is an issue that brings up strong feelings in you and in others. Be on the lookout for these issues in your everyday life. Consider what sets off your "unfairness meter." Think about situations or events that make you feel angry, sad, or enthusiastic, for example. Once you have come up with a few possible issues for your persuasive essay, ask yourself the following questions.

- **Is the issue important to me?** If the issue is one that matters deeply to you, it will be easier to persuade your readers to care about it.

- **Do I have an opinion on the issue?** Just being able to say you do or do not like a situation is not enough. You have to describe in detail how things would be different or better if you had the power to do something about the issue.

- **Do people have different opinions on the issue?** If everyone agrees with your views on the issue, there is no one to persuade. Remember the saying "There are two sides to every story," and pick an issue about which people disagree.

- **Is my opinion supportable?** Will you be able to gather enough facts and examples to make a case that your audience will consider seriously? Will you be able to respond effectively to any **opposing arguments** (objections to your opinion)?

After you have chosen and considered a few possible issues, write down the one that you think you can deal with best in a persuasive essay.

Write an Opinion Statement

Get on Your Soapbox When you write a persuasive essay, your first job is to create a preliminary opinion statement (sometimes called a thesis). You can always revise your opinion statement later. This statement should clearly state your issue and your opinion on it. The following chart shows that good opinion statements contain both elements.

TIP Avoid using words such as *all, every, never, worst,* or *best* in opinion statements. Statements that include these words are often **broad generalizations,** as opposed to **valid opinions** that can be supported with facts.

Issue	Opinion
The proposed one-way street	would cause problems for many students.
Recycling	is something good that people can do for the earth.
The preservation of natural resources	is a very important benefit of recycling.

Consider Your Purpose, Audience, and Tone

Your Readers Await You As the writer of a persuasive essay, your **purpose** is to persuade your readers. More specifically, you want to convince them to think differently about an issue or to follow the course of action you suggest. To persuade your readers effectively, you must understand them well. To get a better understanding of your audience, ask yourself the following questions.

- **What will my readers already know about the issue?** Consider how much background information you will have to provide in order for your readers to understand your position on the issue.

- **What will make my readers care about this issue?** Think about how the topic affects the lives of your readers.

- **What objections might my readers raise to my opinion?** Anticipate opposing arguments so you can respond to readers' concerns and persuade them to see things your way.

- **What will they want to know more about?** Consider aspects of the issue about which readers might want more information.

The writer who created the Writer's Model that begins on page 273 used the following chart to organize his responses to the preceding questions. After you have identified the audience for your persuasive essay, create a chart like this one and fill it out.

TIP Before you start to analyze your audience, you have to know who the members of that audience will be. To identify your audience, ask yourself, "Who is affected by this issue?" and "Who has power to take action on this issue?"

ISSUE: RECYCLING

Audience	Responses to Questions
Readers of my local newspaper	**What they know:** They probably know about the need to recycle—about the amount of garbage that we all produce.
	What will make them care: Help them recognize just how serious the garbage problem is and how recycling can help.
	What objections they might raise: They might think that recycling costs too much—but I could counter with details about how it saves money in the long run.
	What they will want to know more about: They will probably expect specific facts and statistics about how much garbage we produce and the problems it creates.

TIP Your writing **voice** (the unique style with which you express your ideas) should further the goal of the essay: to present your opinion and to support it with convincing reasons and evidence.

KEY CONCEPT

Your choice and arrangement of words determines your tone—your attitude and feelings about your issue. Choose your words to suit your audience and your purpose for writing (in this case, persuasion). If your readers are put off by your tone, they may not take your opinion seriously. In a persuasive essay, your tone should be as serious and as carefully considered as your opinion.

Gather Support for Your Opinion

Getting Your Facts Together   You must support your opinion in a persuasive essay, or you won't convince readers. To be convincing, you must use **logical appeals,** which include **reasons** and **evidence.** As the diagram below shows, reasons support your opinion, and evidence supports your reasons.

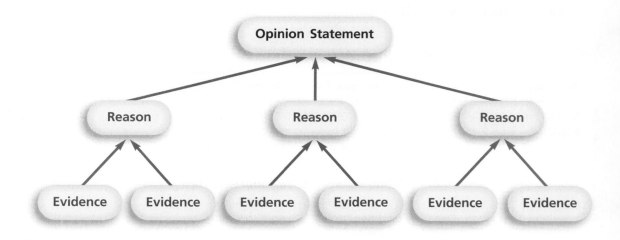

Reasons   These are logical statements that answer the question *Why?*

Opinion	People should recycle.
Reasons that answer the question *Why?*	1. Recycling reduces the mountains of garbage we produce. 2. Recycling saves water and energy. 3. Much of the garbage we throw away could be recycled with very little effort.

Finding Your Reasons

Use the following strategies to help you think of supporting reasons for your opinion.

▶ **STEP 1 Ask yourself, "What are the advantages of agreeing with my opinion?"** Think of ways that agreeing with your opinion will **help** the people in your audience—for example, by making them healthier or happier. *Advantage of recycling: It helps to make people healthier by reducing the waste that ends up in ground water.*

▶ **STEP 2 Ask yourself, "What are the disadvantages of agreeing with my opinion?"** Think of ways that agreeing with your opinion might **make things more difficult** for the people in your audience—for example, by requiring them to sacrifice time or money. *Disadvantage of recycling: It takes too much time for people to separate recyclable materials from the rest of the garbage they throw out.*

▶ **STEP 3 Turn your responses about advantages and disadvantages into reasons that support your opinion.** An advantage becomes a reason when you simply state the advantage. A disadvantage becomes a reason when you refute (prove wrong through argument) the disadvantage as you would an opposing argument. *Advantage as a reason: Recycling helps to make people healthier by reducing the waste that ends up in ground water. Disadvantage as a reason: The small amount of personal time each of us takes to recycle can save all of us time by reducing the amount of garbage that we, as a society, must take time to process.*

TIP A persuasive essay differs from a **formal logical argument**—a line of reasoning that attempts to explain or to prove by logic. Formal logical arguments include research reports, business proposals, and some school essays.

Evidence Evidence includes the facts, statistics, expert opinions, anecdotes, and examples that support your reasons.

TIP You might have to do some research in order to gather support for your opinion. Besides traditional sources, you could contact local resources, such as a recycling center. You could find expert opinions in news articles. You could search on Web sites.

Types of Evidence	Examples
Facts statements that can be checked by testing, observation, or research	In older landfills, toxins leached into the soil and eventually into the ground water.
Statistics facts that are numerical and are tabulated to present information about a subject	People in the United States throw away 40 percent of all the garbage in the world.

(continued)

(continued)

Expert Opinions statements made by a recognized authority on the subject	The Environmental Protection Agency estimates that in the next decade 10 percent of our cities will run out of landfill space.
Anecdotes extended examples, or stories, used to support a main idea	While driving to a relative's house yesterday, I noticed that mountaintops once covered by beautiful pine trees were now completely bare.
Examples specific instances, or illustrations, of a general idea	Recycling paper instead of making paper from trees reduces water use and energy use.

Use a chart like the one below to collect support for your opinion. In the left column, the student listed reasons. In the right-hand column, the student showed specific evidence to support each reason.

OPINION: People really need to throw away less by recycling more.	
Reasons (Why?)	**Supporting facts, statistics, expert opinions, anecdotes, and examples**
Much of the garbage that is now tossed out could be recycled.	• Statistic: Government officials estimate that 60 percent of all this trash could be recycled. • Statistic: Environmentalists suggest a much higher figure—as much as 70 to 90 percent.
Recycling more of our garbage can also save precious resources.	• Example: Every week, for example, 50,000 trees are sacrificed to produce Sunday newspapers in the United States. • Fact: By recycling newspapers we can rescue trees from destruction.
Recycling more can reduce the mountains of garbage produced—and reduce the costs associated with all the landfills where the garbage is dumped.	• Fact: Garbage, unfortunately, does not just disappear like magic after it is hauled away. • Fact: Garbage usually goes into landfills—many of which have created toxic pollution problems and monumental cleanup costs. • Expert Opinion: The Environmental Protection Agency estimates that in the next decade 10 percent of our cities will run out of landfill space.

Emotional Impact   An **emotional appeal** is support that targets readers' feelings and emotions. Persuasive writers appeal to their readers' feelings and emotions by using **examples, anecdotes,** and, most commonly, **words with strong connotations.**

Examples pack emotional power because they show the impact of your issue on a specific place, situation, or person. Look at the general statement and the specific example below.

General Statement   Runoff from landfills pollutes creeks.

Specific Example   Dog Run Creek, once a favorite community swimming and fishing spot, is now a lifeless, weed-choked gully marked with large signs warning the unwary not to swim in or eat fish from the cloudy water.

The specific example might have a strong impact on a reader who calls to mind his or her own favorite creek and who might, therefore, be alarmed at the idea of landfill runoff polluting this creek.

Anecdotes are brief stories that illustrate a point. They can affect readers' emotions by showing how your issue affects people like them. Look at the following anecdote about the use of trees for paper products.

Anecdote   Ed Chafee recently visited his old hometown. He looked forward to seeing some familiar faces, but most of all he wanted once again to wander through the forests he had loved as a boy. When he got there, the forests were gone, replaced by evenly spaced saplings. The entire forest had been turned into paper towels.

Words with strong connotations (loaded language) can also affect readers' emotions. Words such as *grimy, rotten, fresh,* and *clear* can make your reader feel disgusted by or attracted to what you are describing. In the chart below, notice how the italicized words in the right-hand column add emotional impact to the original sentences in the left-hand column.

Original Sentences	Revised Sentences with Connotative Words Added
People can help save a forest.	People can help *rescue priceless* forests *from destruction.*
People can help just by recycling newspapers.	People can *have a far-reaching impact* just by recycling newspapers.

TIP Use connotative words carefully. If you use too many of them, you risk overstating the importance of your issue so much that your readers might not take it, or you, seriously.

CRITICAL THINKING

Evaluating Your Reasoning

As you gather the reasons and evidence that support your opinion, it is important to find and correct statements that contain faulty reasoning—statements that sound like logical reasons but really are not. If readers detect faulty reasoning in your essay, they might decide that your support is not valid or that you are trying to fool them. Consider the two following common errors in reasoning— errors you could make if you are not careful. Both of these errors result from oversimplifying a complicated situation, that is, from failing to take all the facts and alternatives into account.

Hasty Generalizations Don't fall into the trap of basing conclusions on inadequate evidence. Make sure that you consider all the facts before you generalize. Also, keep in mind that there may be exceptions to your generalization; therefore, you should use qualifying words such as *many, most, generally,* and *some*

where needed to turn a hasty generalization into a valid one.

> **Inadequate Evidence:** The first time I played baseball, I hit a home run.
>
> **Hasty Generalization:** Baseball is an easy game that I can play well without having to practice.

The fact that someone hits a home run once does not mean he or she can play baseball well without practicing.

Either-Or Reasoning This error involves describing a situation in terms of two extreme alternatives and suggesting that there is only one correct choice. Usually there are several choices between the two extremes.

> **Either-Or Reasoning:** If you do not call me every night, you do not love me.

Obviously, there can be several reasons why someone does not call every night.

PRACTICE

Identify the type of faulty reasoning used in each of the numbered items below. On your own paper, write *H* if the item is a hasty generalization. Write *E* if it uses either-or reasoning.

1. People cannot save forests if people do not recycle paper.

2. Loads of glass for recycling are often contaminated by unrecyclable glass. Therefore, it is not worthwhile to recycle glass.

3. If people do not recycle, the earth will become completely polluted.

4. Recycling a stack of newspaper piled one meter high saves a ten-meter-tall evergreen tree. People should not be allowed to subscribe to daily newspapers.

5. More landfill space is saved by recycling paper than by recycling any other material. Recycling materials other than paper does not accomplish anything.

Organize Your Support

Get Your Information in Order Before writing, you should decide how to order the reasons for your opinion logically. Keep in mind that the parts of your essay that readers will remember the most—the high-profile parts—are at the end of the essay and at the beginning. Therefore, one way to show a **logical progression** of your reasons is to put your strongest reason last, where it is most likely to be remembered by your readers, and your second strongest reason first—in the beginning of the essay. Place remaining reasons in the middle of the essay.

To determine the strength of your reasons, think about the impact each will have on your readers. The strongest reason will have the most impact. Use a chart like the one below to organize your reasons. As you add to your chart, add numbers to show the strength for each reason. Use the number *1* to show the strongest, the number *2* for the next strongest, and so on.

KEY CONCEPT

OPINION: *People really need to throw away less by recycling more.*

Reasons:

2   Much of the garbage that is now tossed out could be recycled.

3   Recycling more of our garbage can save precious resources.

1   Recycling more can reduce the mountains of garbage produced—and reduce the costs associated with all the landfills where the garbage is dumped.

YOUR TURN 4   Planning Your Persuasive Essay

Review each of the prewriting steps; before you start writing your persuasive essay, remember to

- choose an issue that stirs strong feelings in you and that is likely to capture the interest of your readers
- create a clear opinion statement (thesis)
- consider your audience, purpose, and tone
- determine the reasons for your opinion, anticipate opposing arguments, and gather support for each reason
- organize reasons and evidence for your opinion

Writing

Persuasive Essay

Framework

Directions and Explanations

Introduction
- Open with an attention-getter.
- Give background information.
- Present your opinion statement.

Body
- Provide reasons and support.
- Refute opposing arguments.

Conclusion
- Restate your opinion.
- Include a call to action.

Interest Earning   Start with a statement, statistic, story, or question that will draw your readers into the issue. The author of the Writer's Model on page 273 uses *Garbage!* to hook readers.

Looking Back   Give your readers whatever background information you think they will need in order to understand the issue.

Your Two Cents   Near the beginning of your paper, provide a clear, powerful opinion statement expressing your position.

Sound Reasoning, Good Support   Focus each body paragraph on a different reason. Provide facts, statistics, expert opinions, anecdotes, or examples to support each reason. Strive for three reasons.

The Other Side   Predict and respond to any opposing arguments your readers might have.

Emotions in Motion   Use language that will inspire strong feelings in your readers, or provide an example or anecdote that will appeal to their emotions.

Your Opinion (Re)statement   Restate what you are trying to convince your readers to think, believe, or do—or just summarize your reasons.

Get Busy!   The conclusion of a persuasive essay often asks the audience to do something or suggests ways they can get involved. The author of the Writer's Model makes a call to action when he asks, "Do you care enough to do your part by recycling?"

 Writing a First Draft

Follow the framework and the directions and explanations above as you write a first draft of your persuasive essay. Also, read through the Writer's Model on the next page.

A Writer's Model

The following is a final draft of a persuasive essay that closely follows the framework on the previous page.

Do Something Good for the Earth

Garbage! It smells bad and looks disgusting. Most people prefer not to think about trash more than once a day, and that is only when they take it out. People in the United States should be thinking about garbage more, however, because they throw away 40 percent of all the garbage in the world. People really need to throw away less by recycling more.

Much of the garbage that is now tossed out could be recycled. Of the 200 million tons of garbage that U.S. citizens produce yearly, about 42 percent is paper (from trees), 8 percent is glass, 9 percent is metal (from ore, a natural resource), 7 percent is plastic (from petroleum, a natural resource), 8 percent is rubber (mostly from rain forests), 8 percent is food waste, and 18 percent is yard waste. Government officials estimate that 60 percent of all this trash could be recycled. Environmentalists suggest a much higher figure—as much as 70 to 90 percent.

Recycling more of our garbage can also save precious resources. Every week, for example, fifty thousand trees are sacrificed to produce Sunday newspapers in the United States. By recycling newspapers, we can rescue trees from destruction. We can also save water and energy by recycling. Recycling paper instead of making paper from trees reduces the amount of water used to make the paper by 60 percent and the amount of energy by 70 percent. Aluminum cans show the biggest savings from recycling. To produce a can from recycled aluminum takes 95 percent less energy than from ore.

Recycling more can reduce the mountains of garbage produced—and reduce the costs associated with all the landfills where the garbage is dumped. Garbage, unfortunately, does not just disappear like magic after it is hauled away. It usually goes into landfills—many of which have created toxic pollution problems and monumental cleanup costs. People often object to recycling by saying that it costs too much. What they need to understand is that recycling actually <u>saves</u> money by reducing waste and by eliminating the costs that go along

(continued)

INTRODUCTION
Attention grabber

Background

Opinion statement
BODY: Reason 1
Evidence—facts and statistics

Reason 2
Emotional appeal—connotative words

Reason 3

Evidence—facts

Opposing argument

Response to opposing argument

(continued)

with solid-waste disposal and landfill cleanup.

CONCLUSION
Restatement of opinion/summary of reasons

Much of what is thrown away now <u>can</u> be recycled—and recycling is the best way to preserve natural resources and to reduce the costs of processing all the garbage. Anyone who loves the earth can help make it a better place by recycling.

Emotional appeal

Garbage makes our shared home, this planet, less livable for the people of today and for the children of tomorrow. People have caused this garbage crisis, and only people can solve it.

Call to action

Do you care enough to do your part by recycling?

A Student's Model

The following persuasive essay is by Katie Baker of Holmes High School in Covington, Kentucky. She begins the essay by stating her opinion and listing three reasons for it in the introduction. Notice how she then focuses each body paragraph on one of the reasons.

Uniforms Reduce Problems

Students enrolled in a public high school should be required to wear a school uniform. Many studies show that when school-uniform policies are put into place, there is an improvement in both attitude and school-work. Wearing uniforms would also reduce clothing costs and many problems related to competition in dress.

Mrs. Chung, a principal at a high school, conducted research on the results of wearing uniforms. She said, "In the past two or three years, several schools in the nation have begun to require a school uniform. All of these schools are reporting improved student grades and improved student behavior."

Uniforms are also less expensive than regular clothing. An outfit for a student can easily cost sixty dollars. A uniform would cost fifty-four dollars or less and would save money. This would be especially helpful to families on a low budget.

Last, uniforms would reduce the competition in dress among students. Students who do not have as much money as others would not have to be embarrassed about their parents' income.

Uniforms would not cause a threat to a student's individual freedom because there are lots of other things that make you "you" besides clothing. Wearing uniforms would reduce many problems and would improve grades and behavior. Therefore, students enrolled in public high school should be required to wear a school uniform.

Statement of opinion (thesis)

Overview of 3 reasons

Support for reason 1

Support for reason 2

Support for reason 3

Response to opposing arguments

Restatement of opinion

Revising

Evaluate and Revise Your Draft

Perfecting Your Persuasive Essay Read your whole essay carefully at least twice. During the first reading, use the guidelines below to evaluate and revise **content** and **organization.** When you read the second time, use the guidelines on page 277 to evaluate and revise for **style.**

➤ First Reading: **Content and Organization** The chart below will help you evaluate and revise your writing. First, work collaboratively to answer the questions in the left-hand column. If you need help in answering, refer to the tips in the middle column. Then, make the changes suggested in the right-hand column.

Persuasive Essay: Content and Organization Guidelines for Peer and Self-Evaluation

Evaluation Questions	▶ Tips	▶ Revision Techniques
❶ Does the beginning grab the reader's attention, include necessary background information, and provide a clear opinion statement?	▶ **Put brackets** around any sentence that is intended to get the reader interested. **Put a check mark** by any background information. **Circle** the writer's opinion. If any of these parts is missing, revise.	▶ **Add** an interesting statement, question, or anecdote. **Add** background facts the reader would need to understand the issue. **Elaborate** on background. **Add** an opinion statement.
❷ Are there adequate reasons and sufficient evidence to support the opinion statement?	▶ **Underline** each reason. **Number** the sentences that provide evidence for each reason. If underlining or numbers are missing, revise.	▶ **Add** reasons or **elaborate** on existing reasons. **Add** evidence (facts, statistics, expert opinions, anecdotes, and examples) that supports them. **Cut** any unnecessary sentences.
❸ Are opposing arguments addressed?	▶ **Put a plus sign** by any sentence that anticipates and responds to an opposing argument. If a plus sign is missing, revise.	▶ **Add** sentences that identify and convincingly respond to opposing arguments. **Elaborate** on existing responses.
❹ If appropriate, does the paper contain any emotional appeals?	▶ **Put the letter *E*** by emotional appeals. If you have none, revise— only if appropriate.	▶ **Add** connotative words and examples that will appeal to the reader's emotions.
❺ Is the writer's opinion restated in an effective conclusion? If appropriate, does the conclusion include a call to action?	▶ **Put a box** around the sentence that restates the writer's opinion. **Highlight** any call to action. If either part is missing, revise.	▶ **Add** a sentence that restates your position. **Rewrite** your conclusion to make it effective. **Add** a call to action (if appropriate).

ONE WRITER'S REVISIONS Here is how one writer used the guidelines to revise part of the persuasive essay on page 273. Look over the revisions and answer the questions that follow.

> Recycling more of our garbage can also save precious
> *fifty thousand*   *sacrificed*
> resources. Every week, for example, trees are ~~used~~ to produce
>
> Sunday newspapers in the United States. By recycling news-
> *rescue trees from destruction.*
> papers, we can ~~make a difference.~~

add, replace

replace

Analyzing the Revision Process

1. Why did the writer add information to the second sentence?

2. Why do you think the writer replaced the word *used* and the phrase *make a difference*?

YOUR TURN 6 Focusing on Content and Organization

Revise your persuasive essay using the content and organization guidelines on the previous page. Use the revisions above as a model.

PEER REVIEW

Work collaboratively to peer edit. Ask a classmate to read your persuasive essay and to answer the following questions:

1. What was convincing about the way the writer supported his or her opinion?

2. How did the writer appeal to your emotions?

Second Reading: Style Your first reading focused on your content and organization. Your second reading will focus on style. One common stylistic error that writers often make is overuse of **passive-voice verbs.** The way to correct this error is to replace passive-voice verbs with their **active-voice** counterparts (verbs expressing action done by the subject). Using the active voice in a persuasive essay makes your writing direct, forceful, and authoritative—in short, more persuasive. Use the following style guidelines to replace passive-voice verbs in your writing.

Style Guidelines

Evaluation Question	▶ Tip	▶ Revision Technique
Does the essay contain too many passive-voice verbs?	▶ **Underline** each *be* verb (*am, is, are, was, were, be, being, been*) in the essay. Do not underline *be* verbs used to express a state of being. Do not underline *be* verbs in quotations.	▶ **Reword** two thirds of your passive-voice verbs so that the subject of the sentence performs the verb.

Focus on Sentences

TIP You do not have to use the active voice all of the time. You might use the passive voice when

■ you do not know who performed the action
■ you do not want to reveal the performer
■ you want to emphasize the receiver of the action

Active and Passive Voice

A verb in the **active voice** expresses an action performed *by* the subject of the sentence. A verb in the **passive voice** expresses an action done *to* the subject of the sentence. In the passive voice, the verb always contains a form of *be* (such as *am, is, are, was,* or *were*) and a past participle form of the main verb (such as *flooded* or *estimated*). As the examples below show, the active voice is generally more compelling, while the passive voice often seems weak.

Passive Voice The earth **is polluted** by people.
[This sentence seems weak because it fails to emphasize who does the polluting.]

Active Voice People **pollute** the earth.
[This sentence is more compelling because it clearly emphasizes who pollutes—people.]

ONE WRITER'S REVISIONS Here is how the writer of the model persuasive essay on page 273 revised a part of his draft.

BEFORE REVISION

Our shared home, this planet, <u>is</u> made less livable for people and for the children of tomorrow by garbage. This garbage crisis <u>was</u> caused by people, and it can <u>be</u> solved only by people.

The underlined *be* verbs could signal the use of passive voice.

AFTER REVISION

Garbage makes our shared home less livable for the people of today and for the children of tomorrow. People caused this garbage crisis, and only people can solve it.

Both sentences now are in the active voice.

Reference Note

For more on **active voice,** see page 601.

Analyzing the Revision Process

1. Why are the sentences with active-voice verbs more effective?

2. Why might these revisions be especially important in the conclusion of a persuasive essay?

YOUR TURN 7 **Focusing on Style**

Revise the style of your essay. Use the guidelines on page 277 to eliminate any overuse of passive-voice verbs.

Designing Your Writing

Using Visuals You know that support is essential to any persuasive essay: Readers will more likely agree with a writer's position if opinions are supported by plenty of relevant reasons and evidence. To make your support more appealing and clearer to readers, you could present this information in visuals such as graphs, charts, tables, or pictures. These tools might make it easier for readers to grasp statistics and other factual information. Here are some suggestions to make your support stand out:

- **Put statistical information in a chart or table.** Sometimes numbers and other statistical information are easier to read and to compare when presented in a chart or table.

- **Use pie charts and bar graphs to illustrate compared amounts, times, or dates.** You could clearly illustrate, for instance, the proportions of waste products produced by Americans every year. Most word-processing programs include a tool for creating graphs.

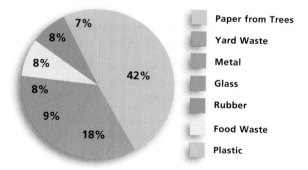

7% | Paper from Trees
8% | Yard Waste
8% | Metal
42% | Glass
8% | Rubber
9% | Food Waste
18% | Plastic

- **If appropriate, include photographs or drawings to support an opinion and possibly to appeal to readers' emotions.** For instance, a picture of mountains of garbage would be appropriate to illustrate the results of not recycling.

Publishing

Proofread Your Persuasive Essay

Reference Note

For more on finding and correcting **double negatives,** see page 656.

Last Look Now that you have polished the content, organization, and style of your essay, proofread it to be sure it conforms to the **conventions of written language**—in other words, that it is free of grammar, spelling, and punctuation errors. Take special note of whether you have included any double negatives.

Grammar Link

Double Negatives

A **double negative** is the use of two negative words in one sentence when one will do. If you use double negatives, you end up delivering a message that is the opposite of what you intend—which could be disastrous in persuasive writing. Here are two simple rules that will help you find and correct double negatives.

1. **Do not use *no, none, nothing, not,* or *–n't* with another negative word.**

Nonstandard	There is not no reason to close the beach. (If there is not *no* reason, then there must be *some* reason.)
Standard	There is no reason to close the beach.
Standard	There is not any reason to close the beach.

2. **Do not use the words *hardly* or *scarcely* with another negative word.**

Nonstandard	The swimmer could not hardly finish the race.
Standard	The swimmer could hardly finish the race.

Nonstandard	There is not scarcely enough in this glass to cover the bottom.
Standard	There is scarcely enough in this glass to cover the bottom.

PRACTICE

Each of the following sentences contains a double negative. Rewrite each sentence to correct the double negative, being careful not to change the intended meaning. Write your answers on your own paper.

1. The school library does not have no computers for student use.
2. The football team was so muddy that you could not see none of the numbers on their uniforms.
3. The bus had a flat tire, and the driver could not do nothing about it.
4. When school is out for the summer, there is not scarcely anyone on the campus.
5. Most high school seniors cannot hardly wait for college.

Publish Your Persuasive Essay

Have Your Say Persuasive writing is meant to be shared. Here are some ways you might share your persuasive essay with an audience.

- Send your persuasive essay to an organization interested in your issue or empowered to make the changes called for in your essay.
- Submit your persuasive essay to your school newspaper or to a newspaper or magazine that publishes articles on issues like yours.
- If possible, try to get your essay published on a Web page.

TIP If you wish to publish your essay for a more specific audience (a local organization, for example) than you originally intended, you may need to refine your essay a bit. Keep in mind what your audience knows and how they might be convinced.

PORTFOLIO

Reflect on Your Persuasive Essay

Taking a Deeper Look Every time you write and reflect on your writing, you can learn something new. To reflect on what you have learned in this workshop, provide short responses to these questions.

- What difficulties did you have finding reasons to support your opinion, or evidence to support your reasons? How did you solve these problems?
- What revisions do you think strengthened your essay the most? Why?

Use your responses to these questions to help you **evaluate your writing** and **set future goals as a writer.**

YOUR TURN 8 Proofreading, Publishing, and Reflecting

Review each of the steps discussed in this section. Before you turn in your persuasive essay, remember to

- proofread it carefully, looking for double negatives
- consider publishing options
- reflect on the skills you used to create your persuasive essay

...AND THAT, IN ESSENCE, GENTLEMEN, IS MY STUDIED OPINION!

INTERESTING THEORY, RW!

OH, HE PRESENTS A CONVINCING ARGUMENT...

...UNHAMPERED AS HE IS BY FACTS AND INFORMATION

BORN LOSER reprinted by permission of Newspaper Enterprise Association, Inc.

Analyzing a Writing Prompt

Many writing tests begin with a set of directions, called a **prompt,** for which you are asked to write a response. A prompt usually specifies the topic and form you should use, along with the audience and purpose for which you should write.

In order to be successful on a writing test, you must analyze the prompt to understand *exactly* what you are being asked to write. If you misread or misunderstand a prompt, your score will not be as high as it could be—no matter how well written your response is. Looking for key words or phrases in the prompt—such as *write* or *explain*—will help you be successful. Also, be aware that words and phrases such as *think about* and *include* are actually clues to the required information. Here is an example of a typical writing prompt.

> You have a new principal in your school. She has asked for input about changes to make the school better. Think about the change you want to suggest, and write a letter to persuade your principal to make the change at your school. Remember to include the reasons for the change and the supporting evidence for your reasons.

THINKING IT THROUGH   **Analyzing a Prompt**

The following steps will help you analyze writing prompts.

1. **Read through the entire prompt.** Start by getting a general idea of what is being asked of you.

2. **Re-read the prompt, noticing key words and phrases that signal four specific requirements for your writing:**

   - the *topic:* the specific subject you are asked to address
   - the *form:* the shape and structure of the writing—for example, a letter or an essay
   - the *purpose:* the reason for writing—for example, to inform or to persuade
   - the *audience:* the intended reader of your writing—for example, another student, a reader of a local newspaper, or a teacher

   Example:
   Then, write a letter [**form**] to persuade [**purpose**] your principal [**audience**] to make the change at your school [**topic**].

3. **Jot down, underline, or highlight the required elements signaled by the key words or phrases you discovered.**

   Topic: the change that I think should be made at the school

   Form: a letter

   Purpose: to persuade

   Audience: the school principal

Writing Letters of Application

One practical form of persuasive writing is a letter of application. Here are some guidelines for effective letters of application.

Opinion State why you think you are the best person to choose.

Reasons Provide reasons why you believe you are the right person.

Evidence Back up your reasons with details about your education and experience. You might also include a professional recommendation.

The model letter below is in response to a classified job ad in a city newspaper.

6523 Farley Road
Duluth, MN 55807
January 23, 2001

Michael Chumchal
Michael's Photography
1371 Gault Street
Duluth, MN 55805

Dear Mr. Chumchal:

    I believe that I am an ideal candidate for the job of photographer's assistant you recently advertised in *The City Gazette*.   **Opinion Statement**

    I have academic qualifications. I take photography classes at Jackson High School, and I am president of the school photography club.   **Reason and evidence**

    I completed a work/study program last semester with Superior Photography and am a photographer for the school newspaper.   **Reason and evidence**

    Please let me know if you need more information.

              Sincerely yours,

              Isabel Tovar

              Isabel Tovar

YOUR TURN 9   **Writing a Letter of Application**

Choose a classified job ad from a local newspaper. Then, use the information at the top of the page to write a letter of application for the job.

Analyzing Editorial Cartoons

WHAT'S AHEAD?

In this section, you will analyze an editorial cartoon. You will also learn how to

- identify symbolism
- understand exaggeration and caricature
- find and interpret analogies
- recognize irony

Here is a riddle for you: When are cartoons not funny? Answer: When they are editorial cartoons that you don't understand. On the comics page of your newspaper, the cartoons are meant only to entertain, and the humor is easy to recognize. However, editorial cartoons, sometimes called political cartoons, can be completely different.

What Is an Editorial Cartoon?

Editorial cartoons are illustrations. Located in the editorial section, sometimes called the Op-Ed section, of newspapers, they are designed to make you think about current issues and to sway you toward the cartoonist's point of view. If you understand the techniques used to create them, you will have a better chance of getting the point and appreciating the humor. Here are some common elements of editorial cartoons:

- **Symbolism:** Using a picture to stand for a more abstract concept
- **Exaggeration/Caricature:** Overstating an aspect of a problem or exaggerating a person's physical features
- **Analogy:** Comparing two things; for instance, directly or indirectly comparing a situation or event with a historical or fictional event
- **Irony:** Contrasting (often humorously) between appearance or expectation and reality

Symbolism   Instead of using several words or sentences to convey an idea, editorial cartoonists often use symbolism. They use pictures as symbols for larger ideas, people, organizations, and so on.

Exaggeration/Caricature   Exaggeration and caricature are tools that editorial cartoonists use to make their opinions clear. Without exaggeration and caricature, the cartoonist's opinion might not be clear enough, or the problem might not be obvious. In the example that appears to the right, Mr. Spock from the *Star Trek* series is made to have ears that extend above his head. The cartoonist does this to exaggerate the fact that Mr. Spock has large ears.

Analogy   Like symbolism, an analogy can often express an idea that might otherwise take many words to describe or explain. It is sometimes easier to describe a situation or event by comparing it to a historical or fictional situation or event.

Irony   Cartoonists often use irony to emphasize a point because it suggests the absurdity of a problem.

Other Elements   Editorial cartoons may include **dialogue bubbles** (bubbles in which the characters' speech appears), **captions,** and **labels** to make clear to the reader what people and objects are being represented. For instance, the camera-toting monkeys in the cartoon on page 287 would look confusing if the evil castle were not labeled "Tabloids."

Personal freedom and civil rights are two of the concepts often treated in editorial cartoons. In the cartoon above, the cartoonist **exaggerates** the security worker's job by having him confiscate the man's freedom. Here, the word *freedom* **symbolizes** the idea of personal freedom. The cartoonist is suggesting that airport security measures have gone too far and that travelers' personal freedoms are being taken away.

Courtesy of Clay Bennett, North America Syndicate.

The man in the cartoon above is seeking clean air in a world filled with smog. It is **ironic** that the only source for this clean air is at a gas station that fuels the cars that cause the pollution in the first place. It is also **ironic** that the air is intended to fill the tires of cars and not the lungs of people. The cartoonist **exaggerates** the problem of air pollution by filling the frame with smog and by suggesting that the man's only source for clean air is from a gas station air machine.

Courtesy of Craig Macintosh, Minneapolis Star-Tribune.

This cartoon on academics and sports recruiting also uses **exaggeration** to illustrate its point that colleges recruiting athletes do not care enough about the education an athlete receives. Notice that the cartoonist uses a **label** on the recruiter's briefcase to tell readers who is being represented in the cartoon.

FLY, MY PRETTIES!

TABLOIDS

© 1997 Steve Breen, Asbury Park Press. Reprinted by permission.

The cartoon above **exaggerates** the problem of privacy-invading photographers sent out by tabloid newspapers (the kind you find at supermarket checkouts) by making an **analogy** between them and the flying monkeys from the movie *The Wizard of Oz*. In the movie, the monkeys are portrayed as evil and menacing, which is how many people view tabloid photographers.

YOUR TURN 10
Analyzing an Editorial Cartoon

Find an example of an editorial cartoon in a newspaper, and briefly analyze it by answering the following questions on your own paper. Then, share and discuss your cartoon and analysis with a group of two or three classmates.

■ What is the issue addressed in the cartoon? What do you think is the cartoonist's opinion about the issue?

■ Which techniques (symbolism, exaggeration/caricature, analogy, or irony) are used in the cartoon?

■ Is the cartoon humorous? What makes it humorous?

■ What is another opinion a person could have about the issue treated in the cartoon? How could the cartoon be revised to communicate that opinion?

WHAT'S AHEAD?

In this section, you will give a persuasive speech. You will also learn how to

■ use logical and emotional appeals

■ improve your speaking style

■ evaluate a persuasive speech

Giving a Persuasive Speech

Cellular phones, e-mail, satellite dishes; no matter how many advancements are made in communications technology, the spoken word remains the most powerful persuasive force of all. Whether they come from a politician making a campaign speech at your local community center or from a news anchor hosting a televised round-table debate on a hot issue, spoken words have enormous impact. Although making a speech can be scary, it does not have to be. Giving a speech is a way to make your words come alive and give color and depth to an issue.

Persuasive Speech

Match Topic to Task   When you are faced with giving a persuasive speech, your first consideration must be your **task**. Your task might be to give a speech assigned by your teacher or to speak as a candidate for student council. You need to know the exact requirements of the task set forth by your teacher or required by the **occasion** of your speech. Occasion refers not only to such physical considerations as time, location, availability of audiovisuals, and time limits, but also to real-life events that might prompt your speech, such as a serious accident prompting you to speak on the need for a new traffic light. Once you have considered task and occasion you can select a topic to match, preferably one about which you have definite opinions. You might wish to adapt material from the persuasive essay you wrote in the Writer's Workshop for your persuasive speech.

A Recipe for Success   Because the purpose of your speech is to convince the members of your audience to think or do something, it is important that you tailor your speech to them. You need to decide upon your **thesis, support,** and **tone** with them in mind.

Thesis   The **thesis** of your speech states your position on the issue. How you state this position depends on your audience. For instance, here are two thesis statements for a speech adapted to two different audiences.

Bikers: Motorcycle helmets save your lives and should be required by law.

Lawmakers: You are helping to make streets safer by passing a law to require bikers to wear motorcycle helmets.

Support   No one is going to be convinced if you don't back up your thesis with convincing claims or arguments. You can use two persuasive techniques to support your thesis:

- **Logical appeals.** Even a skeptical audience will be convinced when you support your thesis with solid reasons and support those reasons with **valid proofs** from **reliable sources**.

- **Emotional appeals.** To affect the audience's feelings so that they will agree with you, use statements, images, and sensory details that arouse strong feelings—pleasure, anger, joy, sadness, and so forth.

No matter how you choose to support your thesis, your presentation should demonstrate that you are informed and concerned. Your purpose is to persuade, but your obligation is to be accurate, truthful, and ethical.

Tone   The tone of your speech reflects your attitude toward your topic and your audience. You indicate tone in speech not only by your choice of words, but by facial expressions, physical gestures, and your **tone of voice**. Depending upon your audience and your topic, your tone might be dignified, respectful, ironic, or a combination of these and more. For example, if you are trying to persuade your city council of the need for a recreation center for teenagers, you would probably want to use objective, mature language and a dignified, sincere, and respectful tone of voice.

Once you decide upon your thesis, support, and tone, you must organize your speech. Persuasive speeches are usually organized according to one of two approaches. With the **deductive** approach, you state your thesis first, then deliver your reasons and support. With the **inductive** approach, you present reasons and support first, building to a thesis statement.

Practice Makes Perfect   To ensure that your speech runs smoothly and to avoid embarrassment, you will need to be well rehearsed. If you are prepared, you will be less likely to be unnerved. In addition, thorough rehearsal will help you to develop the best nonverbal behavior and vocal skills for your particular speech and audience. Just be sure to practice in front of an audience so that you can get used to speaking in front of a group and to use your visuals as you practice delivering your speech. If you will use them during your speech, practice using your note cards. Also, experiment with a timer or watch as you practice to ensure that you stay within a certain time limit.

TIP To make your speech as persuasive as possible, you should use **effective language,** language that is appropriate for your topic and your audience. To emphasize particular points, you can use **rhetorical strategies** such as **repetition** (saying exact words more than once), **restatement** (using different words to repeat an idea or point), **parallelism** (rhythmically repeating words, phrases, clauses, or sentences to emphasize a point), and **announcement** or **sign-posting** (emphasizing a point by announcing its importance).

TIP Avoid making unjust attacks or exaggerations about the opposing side, as the audience will rapidly lose faith in your ethics, or moral standards.

Seeing and Hearing Nonverbal behavior can affect the impact you have on your audience as much as your words can. **Nonverbal behavior** includes eye contact, facial expressions, gestures, and posture. The chart below shows the important points to keep in mind for nonverbal behavior.

Appearance	Good appearance, in both your clothing and your grooming, is not going to guarantee a good speech, but poor appearance can lessen your chances of achieving your goal.
Eye Contact	Eye contact means direct visual contact with the eyes of the people in your audience. The key is to look at someone or some group at all times—for instance, for a few seconds talk to people on the left side of the front row; then talk to people at the right rear, and so on.
Facial Expressions	Concentrate on what you are saying, not on the fact that you are giving a speech. Avoid the deadpan expression—an expressionless facial appearance, and avoid a conflicting expression—a facial expression that does not match your words or actual feelings.
Effective Gestures	Use the same natural gestures that you use in ordinary conversation.
Good Posture	Stand up straight with both feet firmly on the ground. Good posture creates an impression of confidence and authority.

Verbal behavior, or your speaking skill, is another factor that can determine how persuasive you are. The way you use your voice plays a major role in your success as a speaker. The chart below shows important elements of good verbal behavior.

Enthusiasm	You should show **enthusiasm**—a strong positive feeling for your topic—through your voice. Listeners who believe that a speaker is enthusiastic will become enthusiastic themselves.
Vocalized Pauses	**Vocalized pauses**—the meaningless sounds speakers use to fill time—weaken your effectiveness. Some common pauses are *uh, well uh, um,* and *you know.*
Enunciation	**Enunciation** refers to the distinctness of the sounds you make. Be sure your enunciation is clear and precise. Sloppy enunciation, such as saying *gunna* for *going to,* causes problems for the audience.
Vocalization	Speak at the **pitch** (highness or lowness of sound) at which you feel the least strain and have the best resonance. Practice controlling your speaking **volume,** the loudness or intensity of speech. Don't speak too softly or too loudly. Practice speaking at a steady **rate,** neither too quickly nor too slowly. Your audience should not have to struggle to keep up with you; neither should they seem to be impatient for you to speed up.

Becoming the Listener

Evaluation Time To evaluate the quality and effectiveness of a speech, you must analyze not only words but also a speaker. To decide if a classmate's persuasive speech (or your own) is effective, you must consider the **message** and **delivery.**

Get the Goods In order to evaluate a speech's **content,** you must become a **critical listener.** It is easy to focus on a speaker's voice or mannerisms and miss what the person actually says. It is also important to remember that a polished delivery does not guarantee good content, and a poor delivery can mask valid thoughts and ideas. As you focus your attention to listen, use the following questions to analyze the content of a speech.

- What is the speaker's message—his or her opinion? Was it stated clearly?
- Does the speaker adequately support this opinion or claim with relevant points and evidence?
- Does the speaker use valid logical appeals or arguments?
- Does the speaker use emotional appeals appropriately?
- Is the speaker's message **coherent** and clearly organized?
- Are the speaker's word choices precise and appropriate to the audience?
- Does the speaker use the **conventions of oral language,** including syntax, effectively?

Special Delivery Is a clearly stated, well-supported opinion all it takes to convince you? Probably not. A speech must also be delivered well to be effective. Your reaction to a speaker's **delivery** is probably immediate and instinctive. You stifle a yawn or sit up and take notice. Many elements of delivery combine to have this effect. To evaluate a speaker's delivery, ask yourself the following questions as you listen.

- Does the speaker make eye contact with the audience and use natural facial expressions?
- Does the speaker show enthusiasm?
- Does the speaker avoid vocalized pauses and enunciate words distinctly?
- Are the pitch and volume of the speech appropriate?
- Does the speaker have a good pace?

Is critical listening just a classroom skill? Of course not. In addition to evaluating your classmates' speeches, you can also use the preceding questions about content and delivery to evaluate media presentations and live speeches by public figures.

TIP To analyze a historically significant speech from the past, use the criteria on this page and also think about the impact the speech would have had on its audience. Especially consider rhetorical devices used by the speaker, including repetition, analogies, and rhetorical questions.

Fair Play A special problem in evaluating a persuasive speech is judging the speech based on the opinion it expresses. Imagine that you are an active member of a community group that promotes the spaying and neutering of pets. One of your classmates gives a persuasive speech titled "Neuter or Spay—It's the Only Way." You obviously agree with the speech before the speaker has even opened her mouth. You might also be tempted to say that she gave a good speech because you agree with it. Try to put aside your opinion and focus on the speech itself to make a fair evaluation.

Support Your Local Speaker When you evaluate a speech, put yourself in the speaker's shoes. Be aware that the speaker and audience are constantly sending one another signals. Do you think that a speaker can give exactly the same speech to a polite, interested audience and a rude, bored audience? Chances are that the better audience will hear the better speech. Here are some things you can do to give speakers a better chance of success.

■ Welcome each speaker with enthusiasm.

■ Focus your attention to look at the speaker and be willing to make eye contact.

■ Let your natural reactions to the speech show on your face and in your body language. If you look puzzled, then the speaker will have a chance to clarify the point.

■ Note any questions that occur to you, and save them for the question and answer period.

Feedback Loop Use feedback from your classmates to evaluate the effectiveness of your speech. What parts of your speech worked well? What needed improvement? In addition to improving presentations through collaborating or conferring with peers, use the criteria on page 900 to refine your rehearsals or to reflect on your final presentation. Then set goals for the content and delivery of your next speech.

YOUR TURN 11 — **Practicing, Delivering, and Evaluating a Persuasive Speech**

Create and deliver a persuasive speech. Practice your speech in front of a few classmates before presenting it to your entire class. When it is time to deliver the speeches, use the preceding questions to help you evaluate your own and others' speech presentations.

Choices

Choose one of the following activities to complete.

▶ **CAREERS**

1. Persuasion That Pays
Interview a professional whose career involves persuasive writing, such as a salesperson, fund-raiser, or speech writer. Then, write a **paragraph** about the specific writing strategies and persuasive skills that are involved in his or her daily work.

▶ **LITERATURE**

2. Poetically Persuasive
Not all persuasive pieces have to take the form of a formal persuasive essay or letter. Some forms of persuasion can be very creative. Using the opinion from the persuasive essay you wrote, draft a **poem** or **song lyric** that expresses your position and the reasons for it.

▶ **MEDIA AND TECHNOLOGY**

3. Web of Persuasion Using the opinion from the persuasive essay you wrote, create a **Web page** that might convince others to take a stand on the issue. Think about what would make the Web page persuasive. Should your page have a persuasive title? persuasive pictures? In deciding how to approach this task, you may want to visit some existing persuasive Web pages to see what kinds of elements they use.

▶ **CROSSING THE CURRICULUM: JOURNALISM**

4. Editorially Yours Write an **editorial** that expresses your views on an issue. You may choose an entirely different issue from the subject of your essay. For instance, there may be a social, technological, or environmental situation that stirs a strong reaction in you. If you need to, do research on the issue to form a stronger opinion about it. Look at editorials in your local newspaper and notice their content and tone.

▶ **ART**

5. In Your Opinion Convert your persuasive essay into an **editorial cartoon.** Keep the basic elements of editorial cartoons in mind: symbolism, exaggeration/caricature, analogy, and irony. (For more on **editorial cartoons,** see page 284.)

PORTFOLIO

8 Using Persuasion in Advertising

Reading Workshop

Reading a Persuasive Brochure

Writing Workshop

Creating a Persuasive Brochure

Viewing and Representing

Creating a Documentary on Print Advertising

Persuading Others

- Island Mini-Cars puts your life into the fast lane!

- Aggressor Athletics gear is for you. Take your game to the next level.

- Give a gift from the heart: Donate to your local blood bank today.

Informational Text

Persuasion

It is easy to find enticements like these printed on brightly colored brochures in the lobbies of hotels and restaurants, in airport kiosks, in racks at the travel agency, or on bulletin boards around your community. **Brochures**—print advertisements that fold to create several pages—use both words and images to persuade you to buy a product or a service or to support an organization or a cause. Most brochures catch your eye with exciting images, then draw you into in-depth information. Brochures have one great advantage over other forms of advertising: their portable size makes them easy for their maker to distribute and for an audience to read at its convenience.

YOUR TURN 1 Brainstorming About Brochures

With a few of your classmates, discuss any brochures you have seen. List the products, services, or causes advertised, along with the places you found the brochures. What do you remember most about them? What types of goods or services do you think are most commonly advertised through brochures? Take notes on your discussion and be prepared to discuss your findings with your class.

internet **connect**

go. hrw .com

GO TO: go.hrw.com
KEYWORD: EOLang 10-8

Reading a Persuasive Brochure

Fun parks, athletic wear, and blood banks are just some of the many products, services, and organizations that are advertised in brochures. Since brochures can present much information in a small space, they are used to advertise a wide variety of interesting and surprising things. For example, the brochure on the following page, "Adopt-A-Bison," will try to gain your support for a program that is rebuilding bison herds in the prairies of Oklahoma.

Preparing to Read

READING SKILL

Identifying Persuasive Techniques   Advertising works to persuade you to buy products and services or to support causes. How do advertisements like brochures convince you to take action? They use **persuasive techniques,** including logical and emotional appeals. Some advertisements, however, rely very heavily on emotion and not as much on logic and evidence. If you are not aware of the emotional appeals used to get your attention—and your money—you might be misled into paying for or supporting something without really knowing why. As you read the following brochure, think about the techniques it uses to accomplish its purpose—to convince you to adopt a bison.

READING FOCUS

Analyzing Persuasive Visual Elements   Unlike persuasive articles, brochures use **persuasive visual elements**—columns, graphics, headings, and colors—to convince readers. Besides being tools for persuasion, these elements attract readers' attention, help make reading easier, and emphasize the points that their creators believe deserve special attention. As you read the brochure that begins on the next page, notice which items first catch your attention. These items probably highlight key ideas that the writer wants you to remember.

In the following persuasive brochure, The Nature Conservancy tries to convince you to protect America's native bison. As you read, answer the numbered active-reading questions on your own paper.

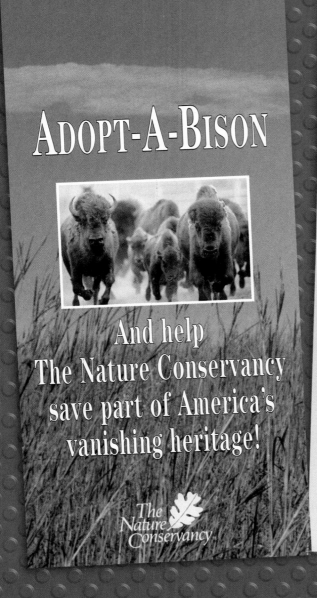

ADOPT-A-BISON

And help
The Nature Conservancy
save part of America's
vanishing heritage!

The Nature Conservancy

Here's how to adopt a bison and what you get when you do:

By adopting a bison, you're playing a vital role in restoring and preserving one of the last great expanses of tallgrass prairie. It's easy and inexpensive to do.

Simply choose the animal you prefer. Then, mail your contribution of $25 or more. Or call 1-800-555-BISON toll-free.

You will receive a handsome adoption certificate, suitable for framing, complete with your name along with the name and photo of your bison. We'll keep you updated on The Nature Conservancy's Tallgrass Prairie Preserve throughout the year with our lively quarterly newsletter, *Prairie Thunder.*

"Oh give me a home . . ."

1. Why do you think the writer chose this headline?

The Tallgrass Prairie Preserve: Restoring a Lost Ecosystem.

As settlers turned the prairie into the nation's breadbasket, an entire ecosystem that supported hundreds of plants and animals disappeared.

It could have been gone forever, if it weren't for The Nature Conservancy and its 37,000-acre Tallgrass Prairie Preserve in Osage County, Oklahoma. Here you can journey back in time and experience the prairie as our ancestors did with 8-foot-tall grasses, breathtaking wildflower displays, and roaming bison.

Why the bison must graze for the prairie to bloom.

The prairie depends on climate, fire, and bison to survive.

The fire—which The Nature Conservancy manages through controlled burns—prevents trees and brush from overwhelming the prairie and removes dead vegetation, allowing new plants to sprout.

The bison, attracted by this new growth, graze it and then move on, giving the land time to recover. They also wallow in the grasses and rub against the trees and boulders. This in turn affects the growth of plants and the patterns of fires.

But while nature will take care of the 30 to 50 pounds of forage a bison consumes each day, there are many other expenses the Conservancy must cover to ensure that the tallgrass prairie is not just a legend, but a reality.

Adopt a bison—and help keep the legend alive.

Your tax-deductible gift of $25 will give you a personal stake in the future of the tallgrass prairie:

2. How do the brochure's photographs help you understand its message?

- It will help us track the herd and research its role in sustaining the prairie.
- It will let us re-create the "wide open spaces" of yesteryear and secure the perimeter with fencing that can stand up to a one-ton charge.
- It will help make sure the herd remains disease-free.

Act today—make a lasting mark on tomorrow!

You're the key to our success at the Tallgrass Prairie Preserve. Because the prairie depends on the bison. The bison depend on us. And we depend on *you.*

3. Why do you think the brochure includes this section?

So please act now. Adopt a bison, and help us to restore this precious legacy, so that it will be here for our children . . . and their children . . . and their great-great-grandchildren.

Which bison will be your bison?

4. Why did the writer give contributors a choice of bison to support?

Prairie Chief.
Weighing close to a ton and boasting a massive mane, this mature bull likes to spend most of his

time alone, wallowing in the prairie dust or shining up his horns by rubbing them on trees. In July and August, however, he can be found fighting with the other bulls as they compete for females in their annual courtship ritual called rutting.

Wildfire. A young bull just hitting his prime. He enjoys hanging out with his pals, and it's always a contest to prove who's the strongest and toughest. He's also proving to be quite a flirt with the heifers.

Buster. He's just cutting his horns and going through that awkward adolescent stage. Poor Buster is easily recognizable by his "spotted" face, dark legs, and fur now the dark brown of an adult. Sometimes it's tough growing up— even for a bison!

Sweet Pea. This two-year-old pregnant female is about to become a first-time mother.

After a 9 1/2-month gestation period, she will give birth to a 50-pound baby. During her pregnancy, you will find her spending most of her time with her own mother and the other mature females. And of course, she's also busy "eating for two."

Penny. She is a lovable little newborn who spends most of her day at Mom's side. Her cute voice is a squeaky grunt,

and she'll remain the coppery red color of a penny until she's three months old.

Pick your favorite, and mail your gift. Or call toll-free: 1-800-555-BISON.

ADOPT-A-BISON

5. What impression of Penny do words such as *lovable*, *cute*, and *squeaky* give you?

First Thoughts on Your Reading

With a partner or on your own, answer the following questions about "Adopt-A-Bison." Write your answers on your own paper.

1. **What part of the brochure's design first attracted your attention? Why?**
2. **What feelings did the descriptions of different bison give you as you read the brochure?**

READING SKILL

Identifying Persuasive Techniques

Act Now! All advertisements use **persuasive techniques**—methods used to convince you to purchase a product or service or to support a cause. Have you ever seen a commercial that made you feel that you could be more attractive by using a particular cologne, shampoo, or deodorant? If so, you have experienced persuasive techniques that play on your emotions or on your perceptions of the product to make the sale. These kinds of persuasive techniques are not all necessarily bad. However, some advertisements rely too much on emotional persuasive techniques to convince you and do not provide enough facts or evidence.

In order to make good choices about what you do with your money and time, you need to be able to distinguish between real evidence and persuasion aimed purely at your emotions. Look for the reasons and evidence, and make your decisions based on those elements. The persuasive techniques that follow are based solely on emotion.

TIP A critical reader or viewer will not simply accept a persuasive message at face value. Be careful to distinguish among fact, opinion, and fiction in print and nonprint advertisements as well as in electronic media, such as Web sites.

- **The bandwagon technique attempts to persuade the reader to do something because everyone else is doing it.** The bandwagon technique invites readers to "join the crowd" or "join the winning side," and it reinforces people's natural desire to be accepted and admired. Its opposite is **plain folks,** which promotes a product or service because it is effective and sensible rather than popular—the sort of thing plain folks (regular people like you) use or buy.

    Bandwagon: Join the stampede to save the bison.

    Plain folks: Bison are down-to-earth, just like you.

- **Transfer projects the positive or negative qualities of one person, entity, object, or value onto another. Transfer is used to make the second item in a comparison more acceptable or to discredit it.** For example, a car ad may show a cheetah, trying to draw a connection between the car and the cheetah's grace and speed. A **testimonial** is one kind of transfer in which famous people endorse a product or cause. The positive qualities of the famous person are transferred to the product or cause they endorse.

> **Testimonial:** "Show your support for nature today by contributing to the Homes for Wildlife fund."—Koko Markelli, star of TV's *Mother Nature*.

- **Emotional words attempt to create a strong feeling in the reader.** Their connotations evoke either positive or negative emotions about someone or something. Value words, such as *love, happiness, security,* and *wisdom* call up positive emotions because of their association with the readers' beliefs.

> **Emotional words: Cute, furry** prairie dogs once **frolicked** on the open plains. Now, colonies of these **playful** animals are scarce.

- **Glittering generalities focus on highly valued concepts and beliefs such as patriotism, peace, freedom, glory, and honor.** The "glitter" and positive emotional appeal of these concepts sometimes cause readers to lower their guards and to accept information that is not adequately supported. **Name-calling** is the counterpoint to glittering generalities. This technique uses words with intense negative emotional appeal to make readers condemn a product or idea without examining the evidence.

> **Glittering generality:** The gray wolf is a hero of the American wilderness. It roams freely, evading the fenced-in areas provided for it by well-meaning supporters. Help the wolf stay free.
>
> **Name-calling:** The gray wolf is a sneak thief and scavenger that preys upon the helpless stock of hard-working families.

TIP Two or more persuasive techniques can be used at the same time. For example, *transfer* is used if an advertisement portrays Uncle Sam—the positive qualities of this fictional character would be transferred to a product, service, or cause. However, the advertisement would also be using *glittering generalities,* because Uncle Sam symbolizes the highly valued concepts of patriotism, freedom, and democracy.

THINKING IT THROUGH

Recognizing Emotional Persuasive Techniques

The steps on the next page will help you recognize emotional persuasive techniques in a brochure or in other advertisements. The sample responses are based on the following excerpt from "Adopt-A-Bison."

Penny. She is a lovable little newborn who spends most of her day at Mom's side. Her cute voice is a squeaky grunt, and she'll remain the coppery red color of a penny until she's three months old.

▶ **STEP 1 Read the passage carefully.**

▶ **STEP 2 To analyze the passage for emotional persuasive techniques, ask yourself the following questions:**

- Does this passage make you think that everyone else is supporting the cause (bandwagon)? No.

- Does it project the qualities of one person, group, or object onto another (transfer)? No.

- Does it use emotional words to create a strong feeling in you? Yes. The section uses words like "lovable little newborn," "cute," and "squeaky grunt."

- Does it refer to highly valued, abstract ideas, such as freedom and democracy (glittering generalities)? No.

▶ **STEP 3 Decide which emotional persuasive techniques are being used and what reaction the passage is trying to evoke.** This passage uses emotional words that make me feel as if I should protect this "baby."

YOUR TURN 2   Identifying Persuasive Techniques

Using the steps in Thinking It Through above, identify the persuasive techniques used in the examples below. Write your answers on your own paper.

1. Adopt-A-Bison—And help The Nature Conservancy save part of America's vanishing heritage!

2. **Buster.** He's just cutting his horns and going through that awkward adolescent stage. Poor Buster is easily recognizable by his "spotted" face, dark legs, and fur now the dark brown of an adult. Sometimes it's tough growing up—even for a bison!

3. School classes, community organizations, and business associations from across the country: These are some of the people who have already adopted their own bison. Won't you and your organization be next?

4. Like another of America's symbols, the bald eagle, the bison rely on us to limit our encroachment into their environment.

Analyzing Persuasive Visual Elements

Designed to Grab You You may have had an experience like this one. You are on vacation with your family. While your parents are checking into your hotel, you spot a stand full of brochures. Maybe you can find an interesting museum or park to visit, or a fun shopping district. As you pause in front of the stand, there is much competition for your attention. **Visual elements** such as headlines, graphics, colors, and type style most likely will determine which brochure you choose to pick up and read. Once the brochure is in your hands, the same visual elements reinforce the brochure's message, making you more interested in buying the product, visiting the place, or joining the cause. The following chart lists some of these visual elements and their uses.

Persuasive Visual Elements	
Headings and subheadings	• divide up, or group, related information • contain key words that instantly identify each section • help readers predict what information is contained in the brochure and locate the information that interests them
Warm colors (reds, yellows, and oranges)	• give readers a sense of warmth and good feeling • work well for brochures that urge readers to get involved, take action, or make an impulsive decision
Cool colors (blues, purples, and greens)	• give readers a feeling of distance and professionalism • can help a brochure seem more factual and informative
Graphics	• emphasize major points • provide images of unfamiliar places, animals, objects, or people • combine with captions to reinforce text • draw readers to any text that wraps around the graphic
Type sizes and fonts	• can encourage the reader's eye to slow down when type is small—slow reading pace helps a reader absorb complex ideas or persuasive points • can catch the reader's attention with headings in large type

YOUR TURN 3 Analyzing Visual Elements

Working with a partner, find in the "Adopt-A-Bison" brochure on page 297 an example of each of the visual elements explained above. Then, explain how each of the examples you found makes the brochure more persuasive.

MINI-LESSON VOCABULARY

Synonym and Antonym Context Clues

To make sure their messages come through clearly, ad writers often use **synonyms**—words with similar meanings to those of other words—and **antonyms**—words with opposite meanings to those of other words. Look for synonym or antonym context clues when you encounter unfamiliar words. Signals for synonym context clues are *be* verbs and words like *or* and *and*. Signals for antonym context clues are words such as *different, unlike, though,*

opposite, contrast, or *but.*

Synonym Context Clue: The Citizens' *Coalition* **is** an alliance of neighborhood groups.

Antonym Context Clue: Our new dog is not *ornery,* **but** easygoing.

If no clues are given, sometimes common sense will lead you to a familiar word that is a synonym or antonym of the unfamiliar word.

THINKING IT THROUGH — Using Synonyms and Antonyms

Use the steps below to help you define unknown words using synonyms and antonyms. The sample responses are based on the following example sentence.

> . . . there are many other expenses the Conservancy must cover to ensure that the tallgrass prairie is not just a *legend,* but a reality.

1. **Find clue words that might signal a synonym or antonym.** The word <u>but</u> may indicate that an antonym follows.

2. **Find a word you think may be the synonym or antonym.** The word <u>reality</u> could be an antonym for <u>legend</u>.

3. **Replace the unfamiliar word with the familiar synonym or with a word or**

phrase that expresses the familiar word's opposite. ". . . to ensure that the tallgrass prairie is not just <u>the opposite of reality</u>."

4. **Use the meaning of the synonym or antonym to come up with your own definition.** A <u>legend</u> is <u>the opposite of reality</u>—<u>imaginary</u> or <u>a fantasy</u>.

PRACTICE

Use the steps above to define the italicized words in the sentences below. Write your definitions on your own paper.

1. The prairie provides plenty of *forage* for the bison, whose need for food is provided for by grasses and other plants.

2. Fire is not a curse, but a *boon* to the prairie.

3. Unlike the boundless prairies of old, today's prairies have a *perimeter.*

4. Bison are part of America's *heritage.* With careful planning, though, they can be part of our future, too.

5. To the early settlers, the *vast* tallgrass prairie was as large as the sea.

Persuasive Devices

Because the ability to recognize persuasive devices is so important in making informed decisions, this ability is often tested on standardized reading tests. Read the passage and the question below, and then use the Thinking It Through steps to determine the correct answer.

> The bison, or buffalo, which once provided food and clothing to many American Indians, should be the symbol of America. This animal, like the American spirit, reflects the strength to survive against enormous odds. Bison numbered nearly 50 million prior to European colonization; but hunters had almost wiped them out by the late 1800s—leaving only 835 alive in 1885. However, with the help of conservationists like zoologist William Temple Hornaday, this animal now numbers as many as 200,000. Thus, because it was nurtured and has survived in the freedom of our vast western plains, the untamable bison best embodies American perseverance.

1. The writer tries to convince the reader that the bison should be the American symbol by

  A. relating that bison provided food and clothing for American Indians

  B. explaining that even though hunters nearly wiped out the bison, it survived

  C. stating that William Temple Hornaday helped save the bison from extinction

  D. showing that the bison once numbered 50 million

THINKING IT THROUGH   **Recognizing Persuasive Devices**

1. Rephrase the statement as a question to be answered with one of the possible choices. Which choice supports the idea that the bison should be the American symbol?

2. Read each answer choice to see if it supports the question.

- "A" says that American Indians relied on bison for food and clothing. This is true for some American Indians, but it does not support the idea that bison would make a good American symbol. "A" must be incorrect.

- "B" states that bison are survivors. The passage says that the bison, "like the American spirit, reflects the strength to survive." "B" is probably correct.

- "C" is a supporting fact about how the bison survived, but does not directly support the writer's idea. "C" is incorrect.

- "D" shows that there were great numbers of bison once, but it is illogical to think that great numbers reflect the spirit of America. "D" must be incorrect.

3. Decide which is the best answer. Choice "B" is correct.

Creating a Persuasive Brochure

Imagine that you have been making a little extra money mowing lawns in your neighborhood. The school year is almost over, and you would love to make enough money to go on the class trip. Maybe you could create a brochure to get more customers.

Perhaps you and a friend volunteer at the local animal shelter. Every day, you see pets that need a loving home. Surely more people would adopt a lovable dog or cat if they knew how important and affordable adoption is. Maybe you could create a brochure to help your fuzzy friends.

These examples are only two of the many practical uses for a persuasive brochure that you could create. In this workshop, you will learn how to create a brochure that persuades readers to take action or change their ways of thinking.

WHAT'S AHEAD?

In this workshop you will write a persuasive brochure and learn how to

- **determine a primary idea**
- **create an eye-catching design**
- **evaluate reasoning in advertising**
- **eliminate clichés**
- **use consistent verb tenses**

Prewriting

Choose a Product, Service, or Cause

What's Your Angle? Considering all the products, services, or causes that you could advertise, how will you decide which one to choose? Try these tips to find a good topic for your brochure:

- **Think about your hobbies and interests.** Could any of them be the basis for your own part-time business? Lawn work, baby-sitting, painting, and car washing are all services that could earn you some extra entertainment (or college) money. Advertise your own service.

- **Consider your community's unique attractions.** Does your town boast an old frontier fort, a great boating lake, or the world's largest chicken statue? Persuade people to visit your local attractions.

- **Think about school festivals, celebrations, or events.** Check with your school office for upcoming events such as science fairs, dances, or special presentations. Spur your community's interest in these events.

- **Close your eyes and think of the perfect world.** What problems would you solve? Would litter disappear overnight? Maybe you could convince people to stop running yellow traffic lights. Convince readers of a problem and prompt them to help solve it.

Here is what one student wrote after considering her hobbies.

> My friends and I enjoy working on computers. Our computer club has talked about fund-raising through setting up and maintaining computers. I will create a brochure for our computer service.

Consider Your Purpose, Audience, and Tone

Give the People What They Want The **purpose** of your brochure is to persuade its readers that your product, service, or cause meets their needs or is something they want to support. To begin doing that, you must identify your audience. Your **audience** consists of the people whom you expect to read your brochure. To identify your audience, you must ask the following questions about your product, service, or cause: Who needs it? Who wants it? Who has the time and money for it?

Here is how the computer club student determined her audience.

> **Who needs our service?** anyone who has trouble understanding computers, software, the Internet
>
> **Who wants our service?** people who want to improve their computer skills—people who cannot get help through work or school. Adults who are not in college might find that help is hard to find.
>
> **Who has the time and money for our service?**
>
>   **Time**—would be determined a lot by when we are available: nights and weekends. That is when most students and people with 9–5 jobs would more likely also have free time.
>
>   **Money**—Since most people in school can get free assistance with computers, they might not pay for the service. Adults who are not in college should be able to pay for our help.
>
> **My audience:** adults who are not familiar with computers and do not have access to training at work or school

TIP The audience of an advertisement is often referred to as a **target market,** a name that makes sense if you think of the ad as "aimed" at a very specific group of people.

Once you have determined your audience, or target market, then you must analyze what they want and need from your product, service, or cause, and how you can meet those wants and needs. The following Thinking It Through can help you analyze your audience.

THINKING IT THROUGH — Analyzing Audience

Use the following Thinking It Through steps to analyze your brochure's audience. The examples provided are responses one student had when making a brochure for a computer service.

▶ **STEP 1 Write a statement defining your audience.** My audience is adults who are not familiar with computers and do not have access to training at work or at school.

▶ **STEP 2 List your audience's wants and needs.**
1. staying in touch with family and friends
2. overcoming difficulty getting computers set up
3. contacting people with similar interests
4. staying current with technology for the workplace

▶ **STEP 3 Explain how your product, service, or cause can address each of your audience's wants or needs.**
1. staying in touch: teach the use of e-mail
2. getting computers set up: help set up computer systems and software
3. contacting people: teach about the Internet, chat rooms, and newsgroups
4. staying current with technology for the workplace: help develop up-to-date computer skills

TIP Keep in mind that your audience's wants include emotional desires, such as the desire to feel intelligent, attractive, or compassionate.

TIP Sometimes you will find **contractions** and sentence fragments in advertisements. Some advertisers feel this informal style choice is very effective. However, remember that these grammatical choices are unacceptable in most business and academic writing.

The **tone** of your brochure (the attitude or feeling that you express about the subject and your readers) is very important in persuading your readers that your product, service, or cause is worthwhile. Choose words and phrases that have a positive tone to make your audience feel good about themselves and what you are promoting. Avoid negative words and phrases that might make your audience feel uncomfortable. For example, the student trying to raise money for her computer club wants to make sure her tone is proper for adults. She should choose her words to make her readers feel good about the service but not bad about their own lack of skills. She must also decide on a proper balance of formal and informal language—informal enough to make the readers feel relaxed and comfortable, but not so informal as to make them feel that she and her friends are unprofessional. Formal and informal language choices include those of vocabulary, pronunciation, spelling, and grammar.

> **TIP** Always keep in mind your **occasion**—the motivating force behind your writing. Often there is more than one motivating factor. For example, the student from the computer club was motivated both by being given a classroom assignment *and* by her club's need to raise funds.

YOUR TURN 4   Designing Your Brochure

> Choose a product, service, or cause that you would like to advertise or promote in a brochure. Answer the questions on page 307 to identify your audience. Then, follow the Thinking It Through steps to analyze your audience's wants and needs. Lastly, determine the tone you will use to persuade your audience.

Consider Your Style

Point Fingers The whole purpose of your brochure is to get your reader to act or think in a certain way. Your **style,** or word choice, has an effect on your reader. Use your text to address your audience directly. You are probably familiar with the classic Uncle Sam image shown in the margin. Notice how it directly addresses *you,* asking for *your* personal involvement. You, too, should use the personal pronouns *you* and *our* to establish a person-to-person connection with your readers. Here is an example of how one writer changed a sentence to be more inclusive of her audience and to establish a person-to-person connection.

> **Before:** Whenever the customer needs help, the Tech Teens will be there.
>
> **After:** Whenever you need us, the Tech Teens will be there.

> **TIP** In most of your classroom writing, second-person pronouns are not appropriate. However, brochures present a unique exception to this rule.

Short and Sweet The message in your brochure should be concise and to the point. Your reader should be able to find and understand the important information about your product, service, or cause quickly. To avoid cramming too much information into your brochure, thereby making it difficult to read, consider the guidelines on the next page.

- **Limit your sentences to fifteen words or fewer.** Short sentences help readers to read the information rapidly and to hold onto ideas more easily.

- **Write paragraphs of only two to four sentences.** Readers can then find the information they want more quickly.

- **Use strong, action-oriented verbs.** They encourage readers to take action.

Determine the Primary Idea

What's the Big Idea? Your brochure should have one main point, or **primary idea.** For example, the main point for a beach-vacation brochure is that the audience should go to the beach. A brochure for highway litter control focuses on the fact that drivers should not litter our roadways. **Think about the one primary idea, suggestion, or recommendation on which you want the readers of your brochure to act.** All of your writing should focus on that one main idea. For example, the primary idea for the computer club service was "We help customers solve their computer problems."

| KEY CONCEPT

To express their primary idea, most brochures use a *slogan*, which is similar to the thesis statement of an essay. **Slogans** are short, catchy phrases that are designed to be remembered. Good slogans show the audience how the product or service can fulfill their wants and needs. For example, the slogan "Bananas equal energy" appeals to its audience's desire to be energized.

Teaser slogans grab an audience's attention and make the audience want to know more. The slogan "Share the power of reading with a friend" is intriguing because it makes readers wonder, "How can I share it?" Once curiosity is aroused, readers will probably want to read more of the brochure to find out how they can do their part.

Some slogans use **repeated words or phrases** to catch our attention, as in the slogan "Eat right. Eat rice." Other slogans include **rhymes,** such as "Great advice: Rice is nice!" Some writers use **alliteration,** the repetition of consonant sounds, to make their slogans memorable. For instance, the following slogan uses the sound of alliterative *t*'s to create a memorable slogan for a roller coaster: "The untamable tornado—Can you take it?"

To come up with a catchy slogan, consider your primary idea and then look at the most important parts of that idea—the key focus. For the computer service brochure, the student thought her key focus should be that she and her friends would *help* their customers and not just do things *for* them, and, of course, that their expertise is in computers. Once you have the key focus in mind, brainstorm some catchy words that relate to it. Combine these catchy words with strategies such as repeated words or phrases, rhyme, and alliteration to create a memorable slogan.

Here is how the student working on the computer service brochure came up with some slogan ideas.

Primary Idea: We help customers solve their computer problems.

Audience's Most Important Desire or Need: They want to use computers in work or hobbies but need help or guidance in setting up, operating, and maintaining computers.

Key Focus: <u>help</u> and <u>computers</u>

Catchy Words: guiding, leading, helping, technology, future, troubles

Possible Slogans: "Tackling Technology Troubles," "Guiding You into the Future," "Leading You Toward Future Technology"

Provide Support for Your Primary Idea

Back It Up   Once you have a slogan, you need to consider what the rest of your brochure will say. One way to start is by reviewing the responses you made to the Thinking It Through on page 308. This information on how your product, service, or cause meets the wants and needs of your audience will provide the content of your brochure. Follow the guidelines below to elaborate on your ideas for this persuasive brochure.

- **Use one idea for one paragraph.** Focus on a single idea in each paragraph to help your readers focus on and understand your message. Use **subheadings**—section titles that state or hint at the main idea for each section.

- **Support your claims.** Just claiming that your product meets readers' needs is not persuasive. As in any persuasive writing, you need to support your claims and declarations with concrete examples or statistics. Brainstorm a list of examples that support your claims about your product. Use your local library or the Internet to research facts, statistics, and other information to support your claims.

- **Anticipate your audience's questions.** Good persuasive brochures should anticipate and answer questions that many readers will probably have. Try to put yourself in your audience's place to brainstorm a list of questions. Then, be sure to answer them in your brochure.

- **Include a call for action.** Once your readers are persuaded, they will be ready to take action. Include a section in your brochure that tells readers what specific actions they need to take to purchase the product or service or to get involved with the cause.

Know Your Format

InFORMATion It should be obvious at first sight that brochures are different from essays. Brochures have an easily recognizable **format,** or physical design, created through the use of shapes, sizes, and folds. The most common brochures are tri-fold or quad-fold designs, in which a sheet of paper is folded into three or four parts. The brochure you create for this workshop will be a tri-fold design. Below is a diagram of how this design works.

TIP When visualizing your final tri-fold brochure, remember that as you look at the inside spread, the middle panel will fold over from the back of the right side of the paper, and the front panel will fold in from the left.

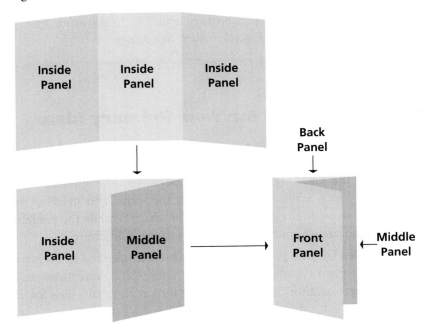

COMPUTER TIP

If you are using a word-processing program, you can create a professional-looking brochure. First, change your page orientation from portrait (8.5 x 11 inches) to landscape (11 x 8.5 inches). Then, use the column-formatting features to create a tri-fold brochure.

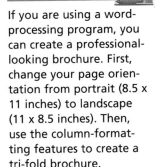

Brochure Panels The front and back panels are very important for selling your product, service, or cause. The **front panel** is likely to be the first part of your brochure that your readers will see. Imagine a potential customer or supporter picking up your brochure. How will you capture that person's attention and draw him or her into reading further? Be sure to identify your intended audience and the product, service, or cause, so that your audience will keep reading for more information.

Commonly, after looking at the front panel, a reader will flip the brochure over and look at the **back panel**—where many *5W-How?* questions are answered: *How can I contact a representative for this cause? When is this business open? Where can I find this festival?*

The **middle panel** is often a transitional space between the alluring front panel and the *inside spread,* which provides the bulk of the information in the brochure. The middle panel can begin to provide more substantial information while continuing to provide a visually persuasive element to draw readers into the inside spread. The degree to which information and enticement are mixed depends on the writer.

The **inside spread** (made of three panels) is where you will provide the majority of information on your product, service, or cause. You will need to persuade through valid, logical arguments supported with facts and evidence. You will still want to use visuals, mainly as supports for the claims you make in persuading your audience. For example, the writer of the brochure promoting teen help for computer users thought this would be a good place for a chart showing the increase in the number of local homes with Internet access—something that would have been more difficult using only text. At the same time, she also thought a cartoon might add a lighthearted element to the inside spread of her brochure. She thought her audience would appreciate the blend of serious information and informality, rather than a straightforward, serious brochure.

Plan Your Visual Elements

Picture This   Brochures combine visual and textual elements to make persuasive points and grab a reader's attention. As you create your brochure, think about how its *look* will achieve these goals. **Graphics such as graphs, charts, photos, and drawings emphasize the strong selling points of your product or service.** Each panel of your brochure should contain at least one graphic to keep it from becoming too **text-heavy.** You can find graphics in old magazines or books, on the Internet, or possibly in computer software you or your school own. You can also draw your own graphics or create them with a computer to jazz up your brochure or give it a personal touch. Remember, though, that all your graphics should be clearly connected to the text around them.

Graphics in persuasion can play different roles: They can capture attention and visually support ideas or descriptions in your text. Keep your audience and product, service, or cause in mind as you choose graphics. For some audiences and products, bold graphics work well; for others, more subdued, practical graphics are best. Good visual elements make readers think, feel, and wonder.

KEY CONCEPT

Reference Note
For more on **graphics and visual design,** see page 855 of the Quick Reference Handbook.

> **TIP**   Remember that you must get permission to reproduce any copyright materials (like most visuals from magazines and books).

Location, Location, Location   **Page layout,** also called **visual** or **graphic design,** is how the elements of your brochure are arranged on the page. The positions of your visual and textual elements are nearly as important as their content. Too little or too much visual design can make your brochure either too dull or too busy, respectively. Here are some guidelines to help you make decisions about your page layout.

- **Identify the purpose of your brochure by placing your slogan on the front panel.** Write the slogan in a font sized eighteen points or larger. If you create your brochure by hand, letters should be 1/2 to 3/4 inches high.

- **Use a readable type size of ten or twelve points** in the brochure's body. Ten to twelve points for letters will be about 1/4 inch for handwritten text.

- **Insert headings that identify each major section of your brochure** to help your audience quickly find the information they want.

- **Use section headings, also known as subheadings,** above each section. These act as titles to the sections and state or hint at the main idea for each section. Section headings guide readers to the information that is most important to them. For example, the student creating the computer service brochure put section headings over each section that discusses an individual service. Readers, then, are able to quickly find and read about the services they desire and skip over the services they don't need.

- **Use single spacing between lines in your paragraphs and double-space between paragraphs to organize support for your primary idea and help readability.** You do not have to indent new paragraphs because you are using a block format.

- **Align your type only to the left-hand side of the page.** By leaving the right margin unjustified, or free from rigid alignment, you will reduce eyestrain for your reader.

- **Balance your text and visuals with white space (the unprinted portions of the page).** Brochures without white space look cluttered and are difficult to read.

YOUR TURN 5 Designing Your Brochure

Decide on one primary idea for your brochure and formulate a slogan before gathering support for your primary idea. Then, decide on the visual elements of your brochure, such as graphics and page layout. Create a **mock-up**, or rough sketch, of your brochure to help you make sure it will fold and look the way you want it to.

CRITICAL THINKING

Evaluating Reasoning in Advertising

Persuasive advertising, like all persuasion, should include sound reasons and factual evidence. However, advertisers also use certain persuasive techniques to encourage target audiences to believe in something or to do something to benefit the advertiser, not necessarily the consumer. It is possible for an advertiser to go too far in trying to show a product, service, or cause in the best light and actually to deceive the public. However, informed, critical readers want to feel that advertisements appeal to their honest judgment and will resent any writing that merely manipulates them. If you use any of the following persuasive techniques in your brochure, keep in mind that if you do not also include sound reasons and factual evidence, you risk discrediting yourself and your product, service, or cause.

Technique	Example
Assertion is presenting statements as facts without any supporting evidence. True or not, assertions imply that what is stated needs no further proof.	It goes without saying: Baseball is the greatest American sport. So who would turn down a chance to bring a Class AA team to town?
Attacking the person is name-calling that criticizes the person who holds an opinion, rather than the opinion itself. It does not deal with the real issues.	No one as unpatriotic as Bob Jones deserves to be our congressman.
Card-stacking is providing only those facts that support your case, hoping that the audience will not notice the facts that have been left out.	The debate boils down to just one inescapable fact: The adoption of school uniforms would deny teens their personal freedom.
Circular reasoning is restating an opinion or conclusion in different words and trying to pass it off as a reason or supporting evidence.	Sheika is the best choice for class president because she would make the best leader.
Either-or reasoning is describing a situation as if there are only two choices.	If you really care, you should buy your sweetheart roses for Valentine's Day.

PRACTICE

Identify each statement below as attacking the person, circular reasoning, either-or reasoning, card-stacking, or assertion.

1. Xlurp: For your thirst, it's either this or nothing at all.

2. Xlurp is the best thirst quencher because nothing else satisfies your thirst so well.

3. Victory sports drink is for people from Dullsville.

4. Xlurp puts you on top of your game. Period.

5. Comparing Xlurp to Victory, you'll find that Xlurp has the vitamin C, electrolytes, and carbohydrates your body needs.

Writing

Framework

Front Panel

- Open with a catchy slogan.
- Identify the product, service or cause and its intended audience.
- Use eye-catching visual elements.

Directions and Explanations

Send Up a Flare Catch your reader's attention by using a memorable slogan. Make your slogan 18-point type or larger.

Take Aim Your intended audience should know this brochure is aimed at them. Some brochures use illustrations or photos to identify the intended audience.

Bait Your Hook Use persuasive techniques to draw your readers into reading further.

A Writer's Model

Eye-catching visual

Guiding You into the Future
Slogan

Computers are not always user-friendly. When you need reliable help with your computer, call the Tech Teens.

555-TECH

How Can We

√ **Internet and E-mail Tutoring**

Isn't it time to get connected? Discover what the World Wide Web has to offer you. Take the bold step toward utilizing connectivity to make your business hum—or just jot a note to a Navy buddy!

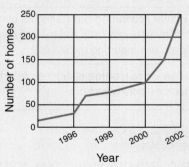

Local Homes with Internet Access

Visual element (chart)

√ **Computer and Printer Maintenance**

Tech Teens can keep your computer system in top order. Call us if your system fails, and we will get things running again.

Whenever you need us, we will be there.

Inside Spread

- Include sections that sell the primary idea.
- Include section headings.
- Emphasize major points visually.

Directions and Explanations

One and Only Each paragraph or section should contain one idea that supports the primary idea expressed in your slogan.

Use Your Head(ings) Each section should have a heading that identifies it. Headings help readers predict the content of each section and locate the information they want.

A Solid Center Use facts, concrete examples, and statistics to support each point. Supporting evidence makes your brochure more persuasive.

Visualize It Use graphics to catch the reader's eye and to help explain your message.

Help You?

Heading

√ **Software Tutoring**

Subheading

Let Tech Teens help you learn that new software program in a few simple lessons. We can teach you in your home or office or in our classroom lab.

√ **Computer System Setups**

Don't waste your precious time with wires, cords, and packing bubbles—call the Tech Teens. We can set up a new system or add hardware such as printers and scanners to existing systems. Tech Teens can even install new software.

Visual element (illustration)

Hey, You're Just a Bunch of Kids!

Don't feel bad if that's the first thing that comes to your mind! We get that often! Sure, we don't have degrees, but together we do have experience.

Among us we have:

- 50 years of experience on computers
- Expertise in over 40 different programs
- 1000s of hours logged in online
- 75 operational Web pages on the Internet

Visual element (photo)

All proceeds from Tech Teens go to fund the Marshall High School Computer Club for further education and equipment.

(continued)

Middle Panel

- Continue drawing your readers' attention.
- Use additional eye-catching graphics.
- Begin providing information.

Back Panel

- Provide necessary contact information.
- Tell readers what actions to take.

Reel Them In You have caught the attention of your readers; now, continue to draw them into your brochure by using persuasive graphics and text.

Be a Spark The back of your brochure tells readers what action to take to acquire the product or service or to contribute to the cause.

Call, Write, or Visit Provide necessary contact information, such as addresses, telephone numbers, maps, or directions.

Translator, Please!

Learning to use computers can feel like a trip to another planet. Every day you hear a new phrase connected with computers or the Internet. We translate and bring you into the tech community faster than you can double-click!

Information on service

Call Us for Home/Office Consultation, or Visit Us at Marshall High

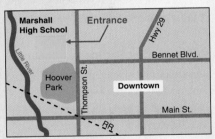

Tech Teens are the Marshall High School Computer Club. You can find us at Marshall High School, 1234 Thompson St., Smith, Idaho.

Call Tech Teens for

- Internet and E-mail Tutoring
- Software Tutoring
- Computer System Setup
- Computer and Printer Maintenance

Contact information

Tech Teens are available:
Monday–Friday, 3–7 P.M.
Saturday, 9 A.M.–2 P.M.

Call 555-TECH

A Student's Model

The following are the front and back panels, followed by the first two panels of the inside spread, of a brochure created by Jason Potterf, a student at Communications Arts High School in San Antonio, Texas. Notice how the front panel directly addresses his readers and tempts them with the image of delicious food. He uses rhyme to make his slogan catchy and memorable.

Visual element (eye-catching photo)

Turn Your Cafeteria into a **Slogan**

Gourmet Cafe

Tired of the same cafeteria food every day? Let **Direct address** **Gourmet School Lunch** deliver the best to your school. **Identification of audience**

Call Today!
1-555-GOURMET

Visual element (color)

How Can I Contact You?

Contact information

Write, call, or e-mail us at:

12345 W. Main

Anytown, USA 90210

1-555-GOURMET

info@scholasticgourmet.com

Writing Workshop   **319**

Subheading

Hungry for a Change?

Visual element (photo)

Tired of the same choices every day in your school's cafeteria? We are the solution to your problem.

Gourmet School Lunch

delivers delectable meals to local schools every day, bringing you the very best in midday cuisine.

We offer a broad selection of deli sandwiches for your dining pleasure. We also offer real Italian calzones and even pizza!

The best part of our service is the price. We offer superior food at affordable prices. This way you can eat like a king and not end up in the poorhouse.

Subheading

Delectable Midday Dining

Visual element (photo)

Order one of our many classic sandwiches, or create your own. We stock a wide variety of lunch meats, vegetables, and quality hand-baked bread to satisfy any sandwich craving.

YOUR TURN 6 **Writing a First Draft**

Use the framework beginning on page 316 to help you write a first draft of your persuasive brochure. The Writer's Model that begins on the same page is an example of a brochure.

Revising

Evaluate and Revise Your Draft

Give It the Once-Over   You would never participate in a sports tournament or give a musical performance without practicing, would you? Even the best performers practice constantly, working toward perfection. Writing a brochure is no different. Your first draft is not ready for an audience yet. You should read over your brochure at least twice before publishing it. In the first reading, use the guidelines below to evaluate content and organization. The second time through, use the guidelines on page 322 to revise for style.

First Reading: Content and Organization   The chart below will help you evaluate and revise your persuasive brochure. Answer the questions in the left-hand column. If you need help answering the questions, refer to the tips in the middle column. Finally, if you need to revise, use the techniques in the right-hand column.

Persuasive Brochure: Content and Organization Guidelines for Peer and Self-Evaluation

Evaluation Questions	▶ Tips	▶ Revision Techniques
❶ Does the front panel contain a catchy slogan?	**Put brackets** around the slogan. If there is no slogan, revise.	**Add** a slogan or **replace** ordinary words and phrases with catchier ones.
❷ Does the front panel identify the intended audience and product, service, or cause?	**Circle** the sentence, phrase, or graphic that identifies the audience. **Underline** the product, service, or cause. If you do not find both, revise.	**Add** sentences, phrases, or graphics that identify the audience and the product, service, or cause.
❸ Does each section include headings or subheadings?	**Put the letter *H*** by each heading or subheading. If a section does not have an *H*, revise.	**Add** a heading or subheading to any section that does not have one.
❹ Does each section contain concrete facts, examples, and statistics?	**Put a star** next to each fact, example, or statistic in each section. If there are no stars in a section, revise.	**Elaborate** by using facts, examples, or statistics to support claims made in sections with no stars.
❺ Does the brochure use graphics, such as illustrations and charts?	**Put a check mark** next to each graphic. If each panel does not have a graphic, revise.	**Replace** text-heavy sections with a balance of graphics and text.
❻ Does the back panel contain a call to action?	**Highlight** the specific actions that the reader is to take. If you do not find any, revise.	**Cut** any text that does not encourage action. **Add** specific actions for your reader to take.

ONE WRITER'S REVISIONS Below are the revisions one writer made using the content and organization guidelines on page 321. Read the revisions and then answer the questions below.

add

elaborate

> ✔ *Computer System Setups*
> Don't waste your precious time with wires, cords, and packing
>
> bubbles—call the Tech Teens. We can set up a new system or
>
> *such as printers and scanners*
> add hardware ∧ to existing systems.

PEER REVIEW

Revise collaboratively by asking a classmate to review your brochure and answer the following questions:

1. What element of the brochure first grabbed your attention?

2. Which support did you find most convincing? Which did you find least convincing? Why?

Analyzing the Revision Process

1. What does adding a heading to the beginning of the section do for the reader?

2. How did adding the two examples improve the brochure?

YOUR TURN 7 **Focusing on Content and Organization**

Revise your essay using the content and organization guidelines on page 321. Use the example revisions shown above as a model.

▷ **Second Reading: Style** The first time you read through your brochure, you focused on content and organization. Your second reading should focus on style. Style is an important part of persuasion because the words you use can get readers' attention, help them feel comfortable, and encourage them to trust you. Advertising writers sometimes use common phrases to make their writing more familiar or folksy. However, some of these phrases (called **clichés**) have been used so much that readers do not even notice them. Do not run the risk of boring and turning off your reader—avoid using clichés in your persuasive brochure.

Style Guidelines

Evaluation Question	▶ Tip	▶ Revision Technique
Does the brochure include clichés?	▶ **Double underline** any sayings you have heard often before. Revise any underlined phrases.	▶ **Replace** each cliché with a fresh, original saying.

Eliminating Clichés

A **cliché** is a tired expression that once was fresh and original but over time has become stale through overuse. The first person to compare an upset stomach to a stomach "full of butterflies" had a fresh and original thought. By now, though, that phrase has been repeated so many times that it has become a cliché. Here are some clichés that seem to sneak into writing.

believe it or not	the last straw	sink or swim
crying shame	let's face it	too good to pass up

If an advertisement uses a cliché, its audience may think that the product or service is as stale and unimaginative as the cliché.

ONE WRITER'S REVISIONS The writer of the persuasive brochure on page 316 used the style guidelines on page 322 to eliminate clichés.

BEFORE REVISION

We translate and bring you into the tech community <u>faster than the blink of an eye.</u>

cliché

AFTER REVISION

We translate and bring you into the tech community faster than you can double-click!

reword

Analyzing the Revision Process

1. How does the revision change your image of the service?
2. What other original expressions can you think of to replace the cliché in the Before Revision example?

YOUR TURN 8 **Focusing on Style**

Revise your brochure to eliminate clichés by using the style guidelines on page 322. Use the example revisions shown above as a model.

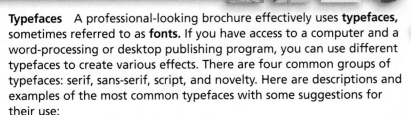
Typefaces A professional-looking brochure effectively uses **typefaces,** sometimes referred to as **fonts.** If you have access to a computer and a word-processing or desktop publishing program, you can use different typefaces to create various effects. There are four common groups of typefaces: serif, sans-serif, script, and novelty. Here are descriptions and examples of the most common typefaces with some suggestions for their use:

a serif —

serif

- A **serif** typeface has lines or curves (called serifs) at the ends of its letters. For some people, a serif typeface is easier to read because the serifs create a visual base line for reading, making them the best choice for body text. Common serif typefaces include Garamond, Palatino, and Times.

sans-serif

- **Sans-serif** typefaces do not have fine lines on the ends of each letter. This simplicity of style can make words seem bold and eye-catching, which is why they are often used in headings, slogans, and captions. Common sans-serif typefaces include Arial, Futura, and Helvetica.

script

- **Script** typefaces, which imitate cursive handwriting with the letters connected to each other, are more difficult to read. They are more suitable for items such as invitations or menus. Some common script typefaces are Brush, Chaucer, and Zapf Chancery.

H
novelty

- **Novelty,** or display, typefaces are very "showy" and expressive. They capture the reader's attention. However, they should not be used in body text since they are very difficult to read at length. Novelty typeface names often reflect the mood of the type; for example, Daisy, Neon, Salsa, and Stencil.

Notice that the Tech Teens brochure on page 316 effectively mixes both serif and sans-serif typefaces. A sans-serif typeface is used in the headings and subheadings, making them seem bolder, while a serif typeface is used in the body text to aid readability and text flow. The student model on page 319 makes good use of a script typeface on the front panel to draw an implied, natural connection between the brochure and a menu.

Remember these tips while you design your writing using typefaces:

- Too many typefaces will make your brochure look busy and disjointed. **Use only one or two in your finished product.**
- **Text set in all capital letters can slow down reading speed;** use all caps only in headings or subheadings.

Publishing

Proofread Your Brochure

The Final Run-Through   Once you have revised the content, organization, and style of your brochure, you still need to proofread it. Proofreading helps you make sure that your brochure is free from grammar, spelling, and punctuation errors. Readers tend to assume that an error-filled brochure advertises a low-quality product or service.

Reference Note

For more information and practice on **consistent verb tenses,** see page 597.

Grammar Link

Consistent Verb Tenses

An advertisement that catches your eye reads "Everything must go! Our district manager saw our prices and says they are too high—so he marked everything down 20%!" You might wonder "He *says* the prices are too high? Does that mean they are *still* too high?" Persuasive advertising must communicate clearly and make a good first impression. Grammatically incorrect or awkward writing can confuse the reader and spoil this impression. Make sure your writing is the best it can be by maintaining **consistent verb tenses.** Verb tense indicates the time of the action or state of being expressed in the verb.

Do not change from one verb tense to another unless you need to show a change in the time of the action or state of being you are describing.

Incorrect	The Lawn King **cut** my grass, **waters** my plants, and **took** care of all my lawn and garden maintenance. [Was the work done in the past or present?]
Correct	The Lawn King **cut** my grass, **watered** my plants, and **took** care of all my lawn and garden maintenance. [past tense]
Correct	The Lawn King **cuts** my grass, **waters** my plants, and **takes** care of all my lawn and garden maintenance. [present tense]

PRACTICE

Rewrite each of the following sentences to correct verb tense problems. Write your answers on your own paper.

1. Super Software organized your files and stores your documents.

2. Software Co. sells Super Software and offered all products through mail order.

3. Customers say Super Software makes computing fun. They also said it is the best software on the market.

4. Super Software was developed by the same people who brought you Simple Spreadsheets and who collaborate on the Winning Word-Processing Program.

5. If Super Software did not meet your standards, send it back for a full refund.

Publish Your Brochure

Show It Off   If you have an actual product, service, or cause you are promoting, try one of these ideas to get your brochure into the hands of your intended audience:

- Hand out copies of your brochure around your neighborhood or at a local store.
- Display your brochure on public bulletin boards in your neighborhood.
- If your brochure is for a cause, send it to an organization involved with that cause. Perhaps they will use your brochure to help the cause.
- If your brochure is for a product or service that might interest your classmates, share your brochure with them. Be sure to get permission from school officials to do this.

PORTFOLIO

Reflect on Your Brochure

Looking Back   Every chance to write is a chance to learn something you did not know before. To make the most of this opportunity, think about the process you went through to write your persuasive brochure. Then, write answers to the questions below on your own paper.

- Do the visual elements you chose make your brochure more persuasive? If so, how? If not, what other visual elements might you have chosen?
- Are you satisfied with the tone of your brochure? If so, why? If not, how might you have set a more engaging, persuasive tone?
- What did you like about writing a brochure as opposed to an essay? What did you find more difficult?

 YOUR TURN 9   Proofreading, Publishing, and Reflecting

Use the information above to help you

- proofread your brochure, paying close attention to clichés
- eliminate unnecessary shifts in verb tense
- choose a way to publish your brochure
- reflect on the writing process used to create your brochure to help you become a more thoughtful writer

Analyzing Persuasion in the Media

Thirty seconds or less—that is all it takes to sell a brand-new car, a cereal, or a video game. In spite of their time limits, television commercials are one of the most dominant forms of advertising used today. Unlike a brochure, which can be picked up and taken along by a reader, a commercial must get the message across to its audience in one minute or less. Good commercials have to be creative and attention-grabbing to get their messages across to viewers in this short time span.

Why? Why? Why? Every year, companies pay millions of dollars to have their products or services broadcast on local or national television. Why?

The main reason is that commercials are effective. They combine some of the best elements of all forms of advertising—the audio of a radio spot and the best visual elements from a print ad. The ability of the commercial to tell a story or to present intriguing scenarios has made it an art form. In short, commercials work at two levels: selling a product, service, or cause and enhancing the image of a product through creative storytelling.

Make It Quick In a commercial's short time, it first must get the viewer's attention. Some commercials rely on a story line or the familiar faces of actors, sports celebrities, or animated characters to hook viewers. Other commercials grab viewers by quickly cutting scenes into a montage of fast-paced video and music. You can even find commercials that rely on an "anti-" appeal. Instead of creating an attention-grabbing beginning, they rely on quiet music or even silence—hoping that the absence of sound will attract the viewer.

Once a commercial has a viewer's attention, it must convey information or create a feeling. Some commercials focus on presenting as much information as possible—leaving viewers with a thorough knowledge of what they are promoting. Other commercials convey only an emotional feeling that can override any logical consideration.

Who's the Target? Every ad has a **target audience** for whom the ad is especially created—the people who are most likely to purchase the product or service or to support the cause. Advertisers try to broadcast commercials when the target audience will be watching. For example, cars and trucks are usually advertised at different times than toys.

The target audience is also crucial in determining the content of the commercial. Products likely to be used or purchased by one age group, for example, may be advertised as part of an adventurous or glamorous lifestyle, while products that appeal to another age group may focus more on a prosperous, safe life. Note that the same kind of product can be advertised in two very different ways, depending on the target audience. For example, think of how differently an economy car is advertised compared to a luxury car.

To determine the target audience for a commercial, pay attention to these elements:

- **the age and gender of the actors**—a commercial showing only 40-year-old men is probably targeted at 40-year-old men

- **the music played either in the background or foreground**—music from the 1960s or 1970s appeals to people who grew up during those decades

- **the cost of the product or service being advertised**—the more expensive the item, the more likely the commercial will target an audience of above-average income

- **slogans or catch phrases that may identify the target audience**—a commercial that states "your children are your number one concern" is obviously targeting parents

Also, consider who wants or needs the product being advertised. For example, an advertisement for diapers would be targeted at parents with young children.

Logging On   Here is part of a chart one student made to log his observations on television commercials.

Commercial	Time of Broadcast	Target Audience	How the Advertisement Appeals to the Target Audience
1. Toughie Toy Trucks	9 A.M. Saturday	young children	The trucks are driving around without any help. My brother has one of these trucks, and they do not operate that way. They look more fun in the commercial, even to someone older like me.
2. Smile Juice	3 P.M. Tuesday (videotaped)	parents—The mother in the ad addresses the viewer as if he or she is a peer.	There are four happy preschool-aged children playing while the mother makes them juice. Most of the message is about the vitamins and how healthy the juice is for "growing children."

YOUR TURN 10 Analyzing Persuasion in the Media

Over the period of a week, make a log of the television commercials you see. Pay attention to differences in kinds of commercials that appear at different times of the day and on different days of the week.

Then, draw conclusions about the effect a target audience has on an advertisement's content. What was used in the commercials to address the target audience? Why were the commercials broadcast at this specific time? Share your findings with your classmates.

Creating a Documentary on Print Advertising

With thirty-one million teens in the United States spending about $140 billion annually, there is no question that teenagers are an appealing target for advertisers. Money is not the only thing such a large group has to offer. Advertisers also target teens to support causes, follow certain career paths, and adopt certain lifestyles. As a member of this **target audience**—people for whom certain ads are especially created—you should use your knowledge of persuasive techniques to spend your money wisely, to support worthy causes, and to make informed decisions. In this workshop you and a group of classmates will use the information you have gained in this chapter to create your own **documentary**—an informative nonfiction film or video that explores and analyzes the real world. Your documentary's topic will be the persuasive methods used in a print advertisement targeted specifically at teenagers.

WHAT'S AHEAD?

In this section you will make a documentary that analyzes and evaluates persuasive techniques in advertising. You will also learn how to

■ set limits on time and topic for a video production

■ plan text, visuals, and music

■ get feedback on your documentary

Preproduction

In Search of . . . The first steps in creating your video are similar to the steps of prewriting an essay. You need to determine an approach to covering your topic. Beginning your research could be as simple as sitting down and flipping through some magazines or newspapers to look for advertisements you feel are specifically aimed at you and your peers. Another approach is to look at what brand names are popular around your school or neighborhood; then, you can investigate what role advertising has had in the choices you and your peers have made. Look not only in magazines and newspapers that are popular with your friends, but also in magazines read by your parents, teachers, or other adult friends and

Reference Note

For more on **persuasive techniques,** see page 300.

relatives. Looking at advertisements aimed at another target audience gives you a comparative basis for seeing how you and your peers are targeted.

Know Your Limits It is tempting to try to do too much when you make your first documentary. Although you may have movie-length dreams, your first documentary should have a more limited scope. By limiting the time and narrowing your topic, you can make your focus more in-depth.

Limit Your Time Focus your documentary so that it takes *five to seven minutes*. Do not, however, overpack those few minutes with too much information. You want to create memorable impressions of a select few main points rather than overload your audience.

Narrow Your Topic Narrow your topic so that you can cover it in a short time period. One way to do this is to find one specific print advertisement and look at the many persuasive techniques that ad uses. Another approach is to choose a persuasive technique and show many ads that illustrate that technique. Here is how one student narrowed his topic:

> As I looked through several magazines and newspapers, one advertisement really grabbed my attention because of how different it was from the others. Instead of bright colors or images of people having fun, it was toned down and had a serious-looking guy up front. It was an advertisement for the Navy. My documentary will examine how different persuasive techniques are used in this one ad.

The Audience Is Listening Before you proceed, ask yourself questions about your **audience.** Who would best benefit from seeing your video? How will you make your information appealing to them? Your program content will also vary depending on the **gender, economic status, education,** and **age** of the members of your intended audience. Keep the following guidelines in mind—they apply to all audiences.

- **Engage your audience's emotions.** Logical evaluations can often grow from initial emotional reactions. Consider how you want your audience to feel after viewing your documentary.

- **Make your audience care about the subject.** Your documentary should relate to the lives of the audience, or else why would they care? Allow your audience to share in your experience as you search for answers to questions. People enjoy learning about new and interesting things.

    Here is what the student who found the Navy advertisement wrote down about his audience.

> The audience for my documentary will most likely be my class-mates and teacher; but if I like the final product, I might show it to my other friends and family—a pretty diverse group.

Talk the Talk   As with any special area of knowledge, video making and filmmaking have a vocabulary all their own. **Technical language,** or **jargon,** can be useful when you are writing or speaking to a group of peers who share the same profession, field of study, or hobby. When properly used, technical language compresses complex information into a precise word or two. Learn and use the following terms when writing or speaking with your peers as you make your documentary.

Term	Definition
Close-up	a camera shot (see below) in which the camera is perceived to be very close to the subject
Cover shot	a long camera shot that establishes the setting of the scene
Fade-in	a technique for beginning a scene in which the scene begins as black, then slowly appears
Fade-out	a technique for ending a scene in which the scene slowly disappears to a black screen
Full shot	a camera shot that shows a person from head to toe
Shot	the frame of a video; a shot can be wide (far away from the subject), medium (closer to the subject), or close-up
Sound effects	a sound added to a video to enhance actions in the video
Stills	photographs used in a video
Voice-over	narration that is dubbed over live action or stills
Zoom	a movement toward or away from the subject, usually through use of a zoom lens

A Show-and-Tell Agenda   Before you begin taping your documentary, plan exactly what you want to show and tell your audience. The more planning you do before taping, the better your final project will come out. Begin by writing a scene-by-scene outline of your documentary that lists the main points you want to present and the order in which you will present them. On the next page is the script outline for the documentary on the Navy ad.

Reference Note
For more on **outlining,** see page 230.

TIP Planning is especially important if you do not have editing equipment and must tape your documentary in the sequence in which it will be shown. This technique is known as **in-camera editing**.

Scene 1: Introduction: hook. Student in class reading magazine, sees the advertisement, and then has a daydream about it.

Scene 2: The daydream: student dressed as sailor, saluting.

Scene 3: Focus in on brochure. Voice-over explains how persuasive advertising can be and explains some common persuasive techniques.

Scene 4: Voice-over explains that one target audience for this advertisement is young adults. "Person-on-the-Street" interviews: We ask students passing by what they think of the advertisement. See how many of the persuasive techniques catch their attention. Prompt them to give initial reactions first, and then to look more closely at the techniques. (For example, "What do you think of the slogan 'Navy. Let the journey begin'?" or "What impression does the image make on you?")

Scene 5: Voice-over explains that we will talk in depth with an advertising professional about persuasive techniques.

Scene 6: Final commentary on the research done. Has the research shown that the persuasive techniques used in this ad are effective for the target audience?

TIP As you plan your documentary production, take a few minutes to examine how media affects your own and others' perceptions of reality. Specifically, think about how viewing your documentary will affect audience's perception of reality and how creating your documentary will affect your own views.

Sound and Vision   Next, add details to your **script** outline to describe exactly how and where **words, visual elements,** and **music** will be included in the documentary. Keep in mind that you want to give your scenes variety. Who is going to want to watch a video screen showing a magazine or newspaper ad for five minutes? Use the chart below to incorporate effectively words, visual elements, and music into your documentary.

Words	• Use a conversational style with short, concise sentences.
	• Identify the subject for the audience: for example, the advertisement you are analyzing, the product or service advertised, or the people you interview.
	• Explain on-screen action that is not readily obvious to the viewer.
	• Use words to ease transitions between scenes.
	• Provide background information that can't be shown on-screen.
Visual elements	• Show any speakers to establish identification.
	• Combine wide shots of whole scenes with close-ups.
	• Signal scene transitions through use of zoom or fade features.

Music	• Signal scene transitions.
	• Add moods to scenes.

Keep the following facts in mind as you create your script.

- Normally, scenes are about five to ten seconds long.

- The two most important segments of your documentary are the beginning, which captures your audience's attention, and the ending, which should leave a positive impression.

People Power   A golden rule of documentary writing is that you *must* use people to convey ideas to the audience. A great documentary about Mount Everest chronicles *people* climbing Mount Everest. Great documentaries about war have focused on tales of *human* suffering or triumph. Your documentary should also have a human face to it. Instead of saying that ads for Brand-X athletic shoes have strong emotional appeal, show how emotionally attached teens who wear Brand-X are to their shoes.

Face to Face   Another way to put human faces behind your facts is to interview your peers, your parents, or experts in your community. See what opinions or special knowledge they have that might prove useful. For example, an advertising expert could help you analyze your advertisement. Consider the following questions when selecting people to interview.

- **Is the person knowledgeable about the topic of your documentary?** You might consider people who are associated with the product, service, or cause advertised. You could interview people who have used the product or service, or who have supported the cause advertised.

- **Does the person have primary or secondary knowledge of your topic?** That is, will the person give you information from personal experience or information gained through study?

- **Is the person a reliable source?** What sort of qualifications does this person have—years of experience or a degree, perhaps? Keep in mind that although experience often comes with age, some younger people may have more up-to-date information. Also, consider that your source may have a biased point of view on your topic, that is, a partiality for or against the product, service, or cause in your documentary.

TIP   Firsthand knowledge often adds to an interviewee's credibility; however, in some cases, people with secondary knowledge may be more objective.

Make an appointment by phone or mail with your interviewee. Keep your appointment and be sure to call in advance if you need to reschedule. If it is not practical for you to arrange an in-person interview (for example, if the person lives too far away), try conducting your interview over the phone.

Here are some tips for conducting interviews.

- **Prepare a list of questions ahead of time for the interview.** Include a variety of **open questions,** which encourage the interviewee to talk at length, and **closed questions,** which can be answered with "yes" or "no."

- **Ask only one question at a time and allow the interviewee time to answer without interruption.**

- **Listen carefully and paraphrase (state in your own words) any answers you find to be unclear.** This will give the interviewee a chance to clear up any confusion.

Avoid having one person talking on-screen any longer than is necessary to establish who is speaking. Instead, show what the person is discussing—for example, the product or service—and use the speaker's comments as narration.

Putting It All Together Here is the script of the first two scenes of the documentary on the Navy advertisement. Directions for the scene are in italic print, and narration and dialogue are in regular print. Technical terms are in italic bold. If you handwrite your script, substitute underlining for italic print, and use all capital letters for italic bold print.

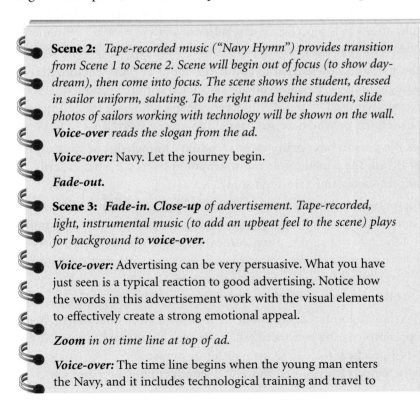

Scene 2: *Tape-recorded music ("Navy Hymn") provides transition from Scene 1 to Scene 2. Scene will begin out of focus (to show daydream), then come into focus. The scene shows the student, dressed in sailor uniform, saluting. To the right and behind student, slide photos of sailors working with technology will be shown on the wall.* **Voice-over** *reads the slogan from the ad.*

Voice-over: Navy. Let the journey begin.

Fade-out.

Scene 3: **Fade-in.** *Close-up of advertisement. Tape-recorded, light, instrumental music (to add an upbeat feel to the scene) plays for background to* **voice-over.**

Voice-over: Advertising can be very persuasive. What you have just seen is a typical reaction to good advertising. Notice how the words in this advertisement work with the visual elements to effectively create a strong emotional appeal.

Zoom *in on time line at top of ad.*

Voice-over: The time line begins when the young man enters the Navy, and it includes technological training and travel to exotic places. It concludes with the young man leaving the Navy for a high-tech career in the civilian world—continuing his journey.

Zoom out to focus on the young man and satellite dishes.

Voice-over: The words and image combine to appeal to some teenagers' desire to work in a cutting-edge, high-tech career. Also, the serious-looking young man would appeal to teenagers who have a sense of personal maturity.

Now Boarding . . .   After writing a script, create a **storyboard**—a series of sketches of key scenes with notes on visuals, narration, dialogue, and music. Your storyboard will show the progression of your documentary from the first scene to the final closing credits. Each segment of the storyboard should have a picture to represent the visuals, as well as annotations to the side that indicate key dialogue, narration, or music. Do not worry if you are not a great artist—storyboards are meant to be rough sketches. Like all forms of writing, your storyboard probably will not be perfect on your first try.

Reference Note
For more on **story-boarding,** see page 50.

Production

Get Your Gear   To tape your documentary, you will need equipment, such as a handheld video camera, videotapes, and microphones. Make sure every member of your group knows how to use the equipment. You may want to have one member of your group take care of all of the equipment and make sure it is in working order.

TIP If one member of your group is especially proficient with the camera, you may want him or her to tape the entire documentary.

Talking Pictures   Once you have finalized your script and gathered your equipment, it is time to tape. Take advantage of areas around your school or neighborhood. Vary your shots to include live action and still, close-up, medium, and wide shots. Your visuals should be easy to see, to identify, and to understand. This may mean you will need to add voice-overs to explain. For example, you may need to point out where a specific persuasive technique appears in an ad. At other times, you should let your visuals speak for themselves. Whenever possible, use a tripod to ensure that your camera is steady during taping.

Make sure your documentary includes credits. Your credits should show the names of each member of your group and how each contributed to the documentary (for example, narrator, cameraperson, set designer).

Postproduction

High Polish, or Diamond in the Rough?   Even after you have shot your documentary, you still may be able to make changes if your school or your community has editing facilities. Preview your finished documentary, and use the questions below to help you revise and edit.

- What is the main point of your documentary? Does every scene relate to that main point?

- Does any of the narration seem too obvious? Is there too much narration or too little?

- Are all of the shots clear and easy to follow? Are any jerky or out of focus?

   Once you have reviewed your video with the questions above in mind, redo any of the scenes that are unclear or confusing.

Opening Night   Once your documentary is finished, you will want to show it off. Consider arranging a showing for your class or invite the whole school to a screening before or after school. Finally, you may want to consider asking classmates to join with you in hosting a film festival at your school.

The Reviews Are In   After your documentary has debuted, get feedback from your audience. Ask viewers to answer a few questions to determine how clearly you communicated your information. You might give out a questionnaire or ask a few audience members to stay behind for brief interviews. Ask your viewers questions such as the ones below.

- What is the strongest point of the video?

- What is the weakest point of the video?

- What is the overall quality of the taping?

- Are any sections of the narration unclear?

- In one sentence or phrase, what is the main point of the video?

Use the answers to these questions to evaluate your effectiveness, revise your documentary, and to set goals for your next documentary project.

YOUR TURN 11   Creating Your Documentary

Using the above instruction, create a documentary on persuasive techniques in print advertising. Pay as careful attention to the preproduction and postproduction processes as you do to the actual taping.

Choices

Choose one of the following activities to complete.

▶ CAREERS

1. In the Ad Game Contact a local advertising firm to learn about strategies people in advertising careers use to compose their writing. To analyze these strategies, ask an interviewee how he or she approaches the three stages of the writing process: prewriting, writing, and revision. Also ask about the special challenges and rewards of this kind of writing career and what a typical day is like. Share your findings with your classmates in an **oral presentation,** or invite the interviewee to come speak to your class.

▶ LITERATURE

2. Come to Sunny Mars Think of your favorite book's setting—possibly another planet, an imaginary world, a desert island, or a real place. Create a **print advertisement** for that place, convincing vacationers that this is the ideal place to visit. Use compelling visual elements such as graphics and color to catch your reader's attention. Then, continue the appeal with tempting descriptions of your place. Share your advertisement with other fans of the book or people you think might be interested in reading the book.

▶ CROSSING THE CURRICULUM: HISTORY

3. Rabble-Rousing Many of the great movements in world history occurred because a person with an idea persuaded more people, who persuaded even more, and so on. Pick a major event or movement in history, such as the Boston Tea Party or the women's movement. Then, write a **brochure** persuading your audience to join in your movement.

▶ MEDIA AND TECHNOLOGY

4. Apples vs. Oranges Pick a product that is widely advertised. Then, find a print advertisement, television commercial, radio spot, and brochure for that product. You might even check to see if there is a Web site for the product. Finally, create a chart in which you compare and contrast the persuasive elements of the advertisements. Which form of advertisement do you think is the most effective? Why? Share your findings in a **group discussion** or in a **multimedia presentation.**

PORTFOLIO

Sentences and Paragraphs

9 Writing Complete Sentences

10 Writing Effective Sentences

11 Understanding Paragraphs and Compositions

Writing Complete Sentences

Sentence Fragments

internet connect

go.
hrw
.com

GO TO: go.hrw.com
KEYWORD: EOLang

A *sentence fragment* is a group of words that is only a part of a sentence. Since a fragment of something is not the whole thing, it will not be as useful to you as it could be. Just as a fragment of a bowl cannot hold much food, a fragment of a sentence may not communicate what you want to say. To communicate clearly, whether at school or in the workplace, you must write complete sentences.

To be complete, a sentence must (1) have a subject, (2) have a verb, and (3) express a complete thought. If any of these requirements is not met, the group of words is a fragment rather than a complete sentence.

FRAGMENT   Is a large, hairy spider. [The subject is missing. *What* is a large, hairy spider?]

SENTENCE   The tarantula is a large, hairy spider.

FRAGMENT   Some tarantulas of South America to a body length of 3 1/2 inches. [The verb is missing. *What* do they do to a length of 3 1/2 inches?]

SENTENCE   Some tarantulas of South America can grow to a body length of 3 1/2 inches.

FRAGMENT   Although tarantulas of the United States are feared. [The word group has a subject and a verb, but it does not express a complete thought.]

SENTENCE   Although tarantulas of the United States are feared, their bite is only as dangerous as a bee sting.

Fragments usually occur when you are writing in a hurry or when you are a little careless. For example, you might create a fragment by leaving out an important word or two. Also, you might chop off part of a sentence by putting in a period too soon.

To find out if what you have written is a fragment, you can use the following simple three-part test:

1. Does the group of words have a subject?

2. Does it have a verb?

3. Does it express a complete thought?

If even one of your answers is no, then you have a fragment.

> **NOTE** By itself, a sentence fragment does not express a complete thought. However, a fragment can be used for effect in writing if it is clearly related to a sentence that comes before or after it. Read the following groups of words:
>
> ```
> The stark mountains. The lush valley.
> The quiet lake.
> ```
>
> By themselves, these fragments do not make sense because we do not know to what they relate. Now, read them along with a sentence placed before them:
>
> ```
> When he reached the peak, the hiker
> stopped to take in the beauty. The stark
> mountains. The lush valley. The quiet lake.
> ```
>
> As you can see, the sentence gives the fragments meaning. It fills in the missing parts.
>
> Experienced writers sometimes use sentence fragments for effect. In most of your formal writing, however, you should avoid using fragments. As you gain more experience as a writer, you may feel comfortable enough to experiment in your informal writing. Still, it is important to master the basics first.

Exercise 1 Identifying Sentence Fragments

Try the three-part test on each group of words on the next page. In each case, identify what, if anything, is missing. If the group of words is missing a subject, write *S*. If it is missing a verb, write *V*. If the group of words has both a subject and a verb but does not express a complete thought, write *I* for incomplete. Write *C* if the words form a complete sentence.

1. Vampire bats only in the tropics of Central and South America.
2. Most horror tales about vampire bats are not true.
3. Vampire bats very small mammals.
4. Although they do bite other animals.
5. That they do not drain their victims of blood.
6. Their small teeth are as sharp as needles.
7. While animals are sleeping.
8. But can be dangerous.
9. Some vampire bats carriers of rabies.
10. The greatest danger to victims is infection.

"What was it like back in the days when people talked and wrote in complete sentences?"

BERRY'S WORLD reprinted by permission of Newspaper Enterprise Association, Inc.

Phrase Fragments

A *phrase* is a group of words that does not contain a subject and a verb. Because it does not have all the basic parts of a sentence, a phrase by itself is a fragment. Three kinds of phrases are often mistaken for sentences: *verbal phrases*, *appositive phrases*, and *prepositional phrases*.

Verbal Phrases

A *verbal* is a word that is formed from a verb but is used as another part of speech. Because verbs and verbals are look-alikes, it is sometimes hard to tell the difference between them. That is why *verbal phrases* (phrases that contain verbals) are easily mistaken for sentences—they can appear to have verbs in them when they really don't.

Watch for verbals in phrases. Some verbals have endings such as *–ing*, *–d*, or *–ed*. Another kind of verbal often has the word *to* in front of it (*to run, to look*). A verbal phrase alone does not express a complete thought.

FRAGMENT Our class interested in deserts.
SENTENCE Our class was interested in deserts.

FRAGMENT Found in hot and cold climates.
SENTENCE Found in hot and cold climates, deserts are created when the earth's surface receives little or no rain.

FRAGMENT Learning about the Gobi Desert.
SENTENCE Learning about the Gobi Desert made me interested in studying deserts.

FRAGMENT To find information about deserts.
SENTENCE We went to the library to find information about deserts.

Reference Note

For more on **verbal phrases,** such as **participial phrases, gerund phrases** and **infinitive phrases,** see page 472.

NOTE When a verbal phrase modifies, or describes, another word in a sentence, it is usually best to place the phrase as close as possible to the word it modifies. However, some verbal phrases make sense either at the beginning or at the end of the sentence.

Appositive Phrases

An *appositive* is a noun or pronoun that identifies or describes a nearby word in the sentence. An *appositive phrase* consists of an appositive and its modifiers. Because an appositive phrase does not express a complete thought, it cannot stand alone as a complete sentence.

FRAGMENT   A strange rock formation.

SENTENCE   Devils Tower, a strange rock formation, has sage moss and grass on its flat top.

Prepositional Phrases

A *prepositional phrase* is a group of words that contains a preposition, a noun or pronoun called the object of the preposition, and any modifiers of the object.

FRAGMENT   Of volcanic rock.

SENTENCE   Devils Tower is an 865-foot-tall tower of volcanic rock.

Exercise 2   Revising Phrase Fragments

Using the photograph on the next page to help spark your imagination, create a sentence from each of the following phrase fragments. You may (1) add the fragment to a complete sentence or (2) develop the fragment into a complete sentence by adding a subject, a verb, or both.

1. moving slowly and deliberately on the surface of Mars
     1. *Moving slowly and deliberately on the surface of Mars, the space vehicle* Sojourner *looked like a large bug.*

or

The space vehicle Sojourner *was moving slowly and deliberately on the surface of Mars.*

1. in outer space
2. through asteroid fields
3. to discover the unknown
4. sampling rocks and soil
5. excited and surprised
6. a remote-controlled vehicle
7. fueled by scientists' imaginations
8. on the planet's horizon
9. shattered by asteroids
10. to probe the surface of Mars

Reference Note

For more on **independent and subordinate clauses,** see pages 492 and 493.

Subordinate Clause Fragments

A *clause* is a group of words that has a subject and a verb. One kind of clause, an *independent clause,* expresses a complete thought and can stand alone as a sentence. For example, the independent clause *I missed the bus* is a complete sentence. However, another kind of clause, the *subordinate clause,* does not express a complete thought and cannot stand alone as a sentence. A subordinate clause fragment is easy to identify because it suggests a question that it does not answer.

FRAGMENT When flocks of scarlet ibises come to roost in the mangrove trees of the Caroni Swamp. [*What* happens when the ibises roost in the mangrove trees?]

SENTENCE When flocks of scarlet ibises come to roost in the mangrove trees of the Caroni Swamp, the trees seem to blossom in bright red.

FRAGMENT Which is the national bird of Trinidad. [Note that this group of words would be a complete sentence if it ended with a question mark. However, as a statement, it does not express a complete thought. It does not tell *which* is the national bird of Trinidad.]

SENTENCE The scarlet ibis, which is the national bird of Trinidad, begins its flight at sunset.

FRAGMENT   That was established by the government. [*What* was established by the government?]

SENTENCE   Part of the Caroni Swamp is a bird sanctuary that was established by the government.

NOTE   A subordinate clause telling *why, where, when,* or *how* (an adverb clause) generally may be placed before or after the independent clause. When you combine sentences by inserting an adverb clause, try the clause in both positions to see which reads better to you.

EXAMPLES   **Because it wanted to protect the beautiful bird,** the government of Trinidad established the Caroni Bird Sanctuary.

or

The government of Trinidad established the Caroni Bird Sanctuary **because it wanted to protect the beautiful bird.**

When the adverb clause comes first, remember to separate it from the independent clause with a comma.

Exercise 3 Revising Subordinate Clause Fragments

Use what you have learned about subordinate clause fragments to correct the following paragraph. First, find the clause fragments. Then, revise the paragraph by combining the subordinate clauses with independent clauses. (There may be more than one way to combine them.) Change the punctuation and capitalization as necessary.

Before and during the Civil War, the Underground Railroad helped hundreds of slaves to escape to the North. The Underground Railroad was a system of travel. That moved the slaves from one house to another. Until they reached the North and freedom. "Conductors" on the Underground Railroad would plan the slaves' journey to the next "station." One conductor on the Underground Railroad was Harriet Tubman. Who was born a slave in 1821. After she escaped from the South in 1849. She dedicated herself to helping other slaves escape. Because Harriet Tubman was brave. More than three hundred people were able to reach freedom.

Exercise 4 — Using Subordinate Clauses in Sentences

Use your skills and your imagination to make a complete sentence from each of the following subordinate clauses. To make a complete sentence, add an independent clause at the beginning or end of the subordinate clause. Add capitalization and punctuation wherever necessary.

EXAMPLE
1. because she is a versatile performer

1. *Because she is a versatile performer, the actor Rita Moreno has had a long, successful career on stage, in films, and on television.*

1. who inspires me
2. when I rented the movie
3. because I enjoy her acting
4. if the performance is good
5. that wins the award
6. whose singing is wonderful
7. once I controlled my excitement
8. as if she were dancing on air
9. although I never saw her in person
10. which she portrayed with great skill

NOTE You have seen that it is easy to mistake phrases and subordinate clauses for complete sentences. It is also easy to mistake a series of items for a complete sentence. In the following example, the series of items in boldface type is a fragment. It may make sense along with the sentence that comes before it, but it cannot stand on its own because it does not express a complete thought.

FRAGMENT My brother enjoys different types of science. **Biology, chemistry, and astronomy.**

To correct the series fragment, you can

- **make it into a complete sentence**

- **link it to the previous sentence with a colon**

Corrections appear in boldface type.

SENTENCE My brother enjoys different types of science. **He enjoys** biology, chemistry, and astronomy.

or

My brother enjoys different types of science**:** biology, chemistry, and astronomy.

Exercise 5 Identifying and Revising Fragments

The writer of the following paragraph is explaining why she wants to be an oceanographer. However, the sentence fragments in the paragraph make the meaning unclear. Help make the paragraph clearer by finding and revising the fragments. To correct each fragment, you can (1) link it to an independent clause or (2) develop it into a complete sentence.

```
        Whenever I am at the beach. I think
about the vast world that exists beneath
the ocean's surface.  Though the marine
life is interesting. The ocean floor is what
really interests me. The deepest known spot
in the Pacific Ocean is the Mariana Trench.
Which is the deepest known spot in any
ocean. It lies 36,198 feet below sea level.
In 1960, the bathyscaph Trieste dove to a
record depth in the trench. Plunging 35,810
feet. The Atlantic Ocean is the shallowest
ocean. With an average depth of 11,700
feet. The deepest known spot in the
Atlantic Ocean is the Milwaukee Depth. It
lies 27,493 feet below the surface. In the
Puerto Rico Trench. These trenches exceed
the average depth of the ocean floor.
Reaching deep into the earth's surface.
```

Run-on Sentences

A **run-on sentence** is two or more complete sentences that are written as one sentence. Because run-on sentences do not show where one idea ends and another begins, they can confuse readers. There are two kinds of run-on sentences: the *fused sentence* and the *comma splice*.

In a **fused sentence,** the writer has joined two or more sentences with no punctuation between them.

RUN-ON   Measurements originally were related to the sizes of people's hands, arms, and feet an inch was once defined as the width of a thumb.

CORRECT   Measurements originally were related to the sizes of people's hands, arms, and feet. **A**n inch was once defined as the width of a thumb.

TIPS & TRICKS

To identify run-on sentences, try reading your writing aloud. A natural, distinct pause in your voice usually means that you have come to the end of a thought. If your voice pauses, but your sentence keeps going, you may have a run-on.

Another way to spot run-ons is to look for subjects and verbs. This strategy will help you see where one complete thought ends and another one begins.

In a *comma splice,* the writer has joined two or more sentences with only a comma to separate them.

RUN-ON A foot was the length of a person's foot, a yard was the distance from a person's nose to the end of his thumb when his arm was outstretched.

CORRECT A foot was the length of a person's foot. **A** yard was the distance from a person's nose to the end of his thumb when his arm was outstretched.

Revising Run-on Sentences

There are several ways to revise a run-on sentence. As shown in the previous examples, you can always make two separate sentences. However, you can also make a compound sentence if the independent clauses in the run-on are closely related.

Reference Note

For more on **forming compound sentences,** see page 358.

1. You can make a compound sentence by adding a comma and a coordinating conjunction (*and, but, for, nor, or, so,* or *yet*).

RUN-ON In photography, an aperture controls the amount of light exposing the film a shutter controls how long the film is exposed to the light.

REVISED In photography, an aperture controls the amount of light exposing the film**, and** a shutter controls how long the film is exposed to the light.

2. You can make a compound sentence by adding a semicolon.

RUN-ON A slower shutter speed allows more light to expose the film a faster shutter speed allows less light to expose the film.

REVISED A slower shutter speed allows more light to expose the film**;** a faster shutter speed allows less light to expose the film.

3. You can make a compound sentence by adding a semicolon and a *conjunctive adverb*—a word such as *therefore, instead, meanwhile, still, also, nevertheless,* or *however.* A conjunctive adverb should be followed by a comma.

Reference Note

For a list of **conjunctive adverbs,** see page 724.

RUN-ON   Cameras have been greatly improved over time, controlling exposure with the aperture and shutter has remained the same.

REVISED   Cameras have been greatly improved over time**;** **nevertheless,** controlling exposure with the aperture and shutter has remained the same.

Exercise 6 **Revising by Correcting Run-ons**

The following items are confusing because they are run-on sentences. Using the method of revision indicated in parentheses, correct each run-on sentence.

1. Cambodia is a Southeast Asian country it is bordered by Thailand, Laos, and Vietnam. (Make into two sentences.)
2. Most of the people living in Cambodia belong to the Khmer ethnic group, people belonging to other ethnic groups also live there. (Use a semicolon and a conjunctive adverb.)
3. Cambodia has a famous river called the Mekong it also has a large lake called Tonle Sap. (Use a comma and a coordinating conjunction.)
4. Like many other Asian countries, Cambodia has a climate that is good for growing rice, no one should be surprised to find out that rice is the country's principal crop. (Use a semicolon and a conjunctive adverb.)
5. More than 200,000 people from other countries visit Cambodia each year most of them are tourists. (Make into two sentences.)
6. In the northwestern part of Cambodia, there is an area known as Angkor it is now a popular site for visitors to the country. (Use a semicolon.)

7. Some of the structures in Angkor are more than eight hundred years old they are world renowned for their beautifully carved details. (Make into two sentences.)

8. Angkor, an area in the northwestern part of the country, is the most popular tourist destination in Cambodia many people visit the country just to see it. (Use a semicolon.)

9. Angkor Wat, the most famous monument at Angkor, was originally built as a temple it also served as an astronomical observatory. (Use a comma and a coordinating conjunction.)

10. Another monument, called Angkor Thom, features a structure called the Bayon two hundred stone faces decorate its surface. (Use a semicolon.)

Review A **Correcting Fragments and Run-on Sentences**

Most of the items below contain fragments or run-on sentences. Correct the fragments and run-on sentences in any of the ways you have learned. If an item is correct, write *C*. Change the punctuation and capitalization wherever necessary.

1. Many kinds of forests in the world, including tropical rain forests, temperate forests, and evergreen forests.

2. In rain forests, trees form a dense canopy. Which shuts out much of the sunlight.

3. After falling to the warm, damp forest floor, plants decay and release nutrients.

4. Animals need forests in order to live forests provide places to live and sources of nourishment.

5. The carefully balanced food chain in forests nourishing all forest creatures.

6. Although some countries that cut down rain forests institute programs to help maintain the forest as a resource.

7. Some forests have been damaged by acid rain, a product of air pollution mixing with rain to develop sulfuric acid.

8. Forests perform several vital functions for other living things, among them are cleaning carbon dioxide from the air and preventing soil erosion.

9. People clearing forests for thousands of years but increased deforestation as the earth's population has increased.

10. In order to help save our forests, people have set aside national parks and have replaced felled trees with new ones.

Review B · Revising Fragments and Run-on Sentences

When you read the following paragraphs, you will notice several sentence fragments and run-on sentences. First, identify each fragment and run-on. Then, rewrite the passage correctly. Change the punctuation and capitalization wherever necessary.

Heroes come in all shapes and sizes. Women and men, adults and children. However, one hero looked quite different from what you might imagine. Living in Czechoslovakia after World War II and named Antis. This hero was a German shepherd dog.

Shortly before World War II, Antis was adopted by a man named Jan Bozdech. Bozdech served in the British Air Force during the war, afterwards, he returned to his homeland, Czechoslovakia. Because the Soviet Union controlled his country. Bozdech eventually decided to escape to Austria with his dog. During the journey, Antis alerted his master to the presence of police and border patrols, when Bozdech almost drowned trying to cross a fast-flowing river in the dark, Antis grabbed his master's jacket and pulled him to safety.

Near the end of their journey to freedom. A border guard began to walk toward Bozdech. Who was sleeping. Antis diverted the guard's attention by leaping around and distracting him. The guard did not find Bozdech, he and his faithful dog made it to safety.

Writing Effective Sentences

Combining Sentences

Whether you are writing a school or workplace assignment or a personal letter, your goal is to communicate your ideas. Therefore, you want your writing to be clear, effective, and interesting. Short sentences can be effective, but too many of them make writing sound choppy. For example, notice how the many short sentences in the following paragraph make it boring to read.

> A geyser is a spring. A geyser shoots
> hot water into the air with great force.
> Some geysers erupt continually. Some gey-
> sers remain inactive for long periods.
> The water seeps into the earth's surface
> through cracks. The water expands into
> steam when it reaches extremely hot rocks.

Sentence combining is a way to improve choppy writing. Below and on the next page, you can see how the paragraph about geysers can be improved by combining the short sentences into longer, smoother sentences.

Notice that even though the sentences are longer, the revised paragraph is shorter and more precise. That is because sentence combining has helped to eliminate repeated words and ideas.

> A geyser is a spring that shoots hot
> water into the air with great force. Some
> geysers erupt continually, while some remain

inactive for long periods. The water seeps into the earth's surface through cracks and expands into steam when it reaches extremely hot rocks.

Inserting Words

You can combine short sentences by taking a key word from one sentence and inserting it into another sentence. When you do this, you may have to delete one or more words. You may also have to change the form of the word you insert.

Using the Same Form	
ORIGINAL	Andrew Lloyd-Webber composed the music for several Broadway musicals. The musicals were popular.
COMBINED	Andrew Lloyd-Webber composed the music for several **popular** Broadway musicals.
Changing the Form	
ORIGINAL	Lloyd-Webber is best known for his melodic scores. The scores flow.
COMBINED	Lloyd-Webber is best known for his **flowing** melodic scores.

NOTE When you change the form of a word before inserting it into a sentence, you often add an ending that makes the word an adjective or an adverb. The endings you will use most frequently are –ed, –ful, –ing, and –ly.

Exercise 1 Combining Sentences by Inserting Words

On the next page are ten sets of sentences about the many uses of common plants. Combine each set into one sentence by inserting the italicized word(s) from the second sentence into the first sentence. The directions in parentheses will tell you how to change the form of a word if it is necessary to do so.

EXAMPLE 1. You can find books that describe the uses of herbs. These books describe the *many* uses that herbs have.

1. *You can find books that describe the many uses of herbs.*

1. Plants have always been valued for their properties. These properties are *medicinal*.
2. Digitalis, a medicine for heart failure, is extracted from the foxglove plant. Digitalis is an *effective* medicine.
3. The recipes for many old-fashioned herbal remedies have been lost. The loss of these recipes is *unfortunate*. (Add –*ly*.)
4. Some herbal remedies have been passed down through many generations of families. The families *trust* these remedies. (Add –*ed*.)
5. Plants are still used to make products such as shampoos and hair dyes. These products are *beauty* products.
6. The ancient Egyptians used dill in healing. This healing was *herbal*.
7. Research shows that dill helps relax the muscles of the digestive tract. These muscles are the *smooth* muscles.
8. Another herb, echinacea, was adopted by plains settlers as a remedy for stings and snakebites. This was a *folk* remedy.
9. Many recent European studies show that echinacea has remarkable properties. These properties can *heal*. (Add –*ing*.)
10. Did you know that cinnamon was used by the Ancient Chinese as a treatment for digestive problems? The cinnamon was a *powder*. (Add –*ed*.)

Exercise 2   Combining Sentences by Inserting Words

In Exercise 1, the key words were italicized for you. Now it is up to you to decide which words to insert. There may be more than one way to combine each set of sentences; choose the combination you think is best. Change the forms of words wherever necessary.

1. The Statue of Liberty, a copper sculpture on Liberty Island, towers over a bay. The bay is Upper New York Bay.
2. In 1884, France gave the statue to the United States as a gift of friendship. The statue is massive.
3. The people of France donated the money to construct the statue. Their donation was generous.
4. French sculptor Frederic Auguste Bartholdi tried to complete the statue in time for the centennial celebration of the Declaration of Independence. He was not successful.
5. In 1986, a restoration of the Statue of Liberty was completed. The restoration was extensive.

Inserting Phrases

You can also combine closely related sentences by reducing one sentence to a phrase and inserting it into the other sentence. When it is inserted, the phrase gives additional information about an idea expressed in the sentence.

Reference Note

For more on **the different kinds of phrases**, see page 467.

Prepositional Phrases

A *prepositional phrase* contains a preposition, its object, and any modifiers of the object. Usually, you can move a prepositional phrase from one sentence into another without changing the phrase in any way.

ORIGINAL   Great Salt Lake is an inland body of saltwater. The lake is in northwestern Utah.

REVISED   Great Salt Lake is an inland body of saltwater **in northwestern Utah.**

Participial Phrases

A *participle* is a word that is formed from a verb and that can be used as an adjective. A participle usually ends in *–ing* or *–ed*. A *participial phrase* contains a participle and any modifiers or complements the participle has. The whole participial phrase acts as an adjective in a sentence.

Sometimes you can combine sentences by reducing one sentence to a participial phrase. When you insert the participial phrase into the other sentence, place it close to the noun or pronoun it modifies. Otherwise, you may confuse your reader.

ORIGINAL   Juanita Platero describes the conflict between old and new ideas. She does this as she writes about Navajo culture.

REVISED   **Writing about Navajo culture,** Juanita Platero describes the conflict between old and new ideas.

Appositive Phrases

An *appositive phrase* is made up of an appositive and its modifiers. It identifies or describes a noun or pronoun in a sentence. Sometimes you can change one sentence into an appositive phrase and insert it into another sentence. Like a participial phrase, an appositive phrase should be placed directly before or after the noun or pronoun it modifies. The phrase should be separated from the rest of the sentence by a comma (or two commas if you place the phrase in the middle of the sentence).

	ORIGINAL	Neil Armstrong is best known for his historic first steps on the moon. Neil Armstrong is a former U.S. astronaut.
	REVISED	Neil Armstrong, **a former U.S. astronaut,** is best known for his historic first steps on the moon.

Exercise 3 Combining Sentences by Inserting Phrases

Insert phrases to combine each of the following pairs of sentences into one sentence. (There may be more than one way to combine each pair.) For some of the sentence pairs, the hints in parentheses will tell you when to change the forms of words and when to add commas. To help you get started, the words you need to insert are italicized in the first five sentence pairs.

EXAMPLE
1. Migrant farmworkers move from region to region. They *follow the seasonal crop harvests.* (Change *follow* to *following,* and add a comma.)

1. *Following the seasonal crop harvests, migrant farmworkers move from region to region.*

1. Migrant laborers move constantly. They *search for work.* (Change *search* to *searching,* and add a comma.)
2. Many live in extreme poverty. They live *without adequate food, shelter, and medical care.*
3. Many migrant laborers are unable to find other kinds of work. They *lack education.* (Change *lack* to *lacking,* and add a comma.)
4. Cesar Chavez championed the rights of migrant farmworkers. He was *a labor union organizer.* (Add two commas.)
5. Chavez was born in Arizona. He was born *on a farm.*
6. His family became migrant workers. They became migrant workers after losing their farm.
7. Chavez helped make the voices of farmworkers heard. He organized grape pickers in the 1960s. (Change *organized* to *organizing,* and add a comma.)
8. He established a union. It was called the National Farm Workers Association.
9. Chavez organized strikes and boycotts. He was committed to non-violent protest. (Add a comma.)
10. He helped to improve working conditions for migrant laborers. He did this through his organizing efforts.

Using Compound Subjects and Verbs

You can also combine sentences by using compound subjects and verbs. Just look for sentences that have the same subject or the same verb. Then, use coordinating conjunctions (such as *and, but, for, nor, or, so,* and *yet*) to make a compound subject, a compound verb, or both.

ORIGINAL	Jaguars are large, spotted cats. Leopards are large, spotted cats.
REVISED	**Jaguars and leopards** are large, spotted cats. [compound subject with the same verb]
ORIGINAL	Jaguars live in the Americas. Jaguars hunt in the Americas.
REVISED	Jaguars **live and hunt** in the Americas. [compound verb with the same subject]
ORIGINAL	Jaguars hunt and attack other animals. Leopards hunt and attack other animals. These cats rarely attack humans.
REVISED	**Jaguars and leopards hunt and attack** other animals **but** rarely **attack** humans. [compound subject and compound verb]

STYLE TIP

So is often overworked in writing. Think twice before using it.

NOTE When you combine sentences by using compound subjects and compound verbs, make sure your subjects and verbs agree in number.

ORIGINAL	Asia is home to the leopard. Africa is home to the leopard.
REVISED	Asia and Africa **are** home to the leopard.

Reference Note

For more on **subject-verb agreement,** see page 512.

Exercise 4 **Combining Sentences by Using Compound Subjects and Verbs**

Here are five pairs of short, choppy sentences. Combine each pair into one sentence by using a compound subject, a compound verb, or both.

1. Glaciers shape landforms over time. Volcanoes also shape landforms over time.
2. Antarctica is mostly covered by glaciers. Greenland is mostly covered by glaciers.
3. Glaciers move slowly. Glaciers shape the land as they flow across it.
4. A volcano begins as molten rock beneath the earth's surface. It gradually rises upward.
5. Volcanoes can create land area. Glaciers can also create land area. They both can destroy land area.

Creating a Compound Sentence

If the thoughts in two sentences are related to one another and are equal in importance, you can combine the sentences to form a *compound sentence.* A compound sentence is two or more independent clauses joined by

- a comma and a coordinating conjunction

  or

- a semicolon

  or

- a semicolon and a conjunctive adverb

Reference Note

For a list of **common conjunctive adverbs,** see page 724.

ORIGINAL	Veins carry blood to the heart. Arteries carry blood away from the heart.
REVISED	Veins carry blood to the heart**, but** arteries carry blood away from the heart. [comma and coordinating conjunction]

or

Veins carry blood to the heart**;** arteries carry blood away from the heart. [semicolon]

or

Veins carry blood to the heart**; however,** arteries carry blood away from the heart. [semicolon and conjunctive adverb]

Exercise 5 Combining Sentences into Compound Sentences

The following sentences are fine by themselves, but together they would make a choppy paragraph. Using the above methods, combine each pair of sentences into a compound sentence. Try to use each method at least once. Be sure to use the correct punctuation.

1. In 1881, a French company began building a canal through the Isthmus of Panama. The United States took over construction of the canal in 1903.
2. Workers labored for ten years to complete the canal. One of the toughest obstacles was disease.
3. The Panama Canal is a valuable engineering achievement. Ships using the canal can shorten their journeys by thousands of miles.
4. The canal is about 50 miles long. Because of its winding course, ships come out only 27 miles east or west of their entrance point.
5. The United States controlled the Panama Canal Zone after 1914. On January 1, 2000, the Republic of Panama assumed complete control of the canal.

Creating a Complex Sentence

If two sentences are unequal in importance, you can combine them into a *complex sentence.* Just turn the less important idea into a subordinate clause, and attach it to the other sentence (the independent clause).

Reference Note

For more on **independent** and **subordinate clauses,** see pages 492 and 493.

Adjective Clauses

You can make a sentence into an adjective clause by replacing its subject with *who, whom, whose, which,* or *that.* Then you can use the adjective clause to give information about a noun or pronoun in another clause.

ORIGINAL   Christopher Columbus noted the unusual quantity of floating seaweed. He crossed the Sargasso Sea.

REVISED   Christopher Columbus, **who crossed the Sargasso Sea,** noted the unusual quantity of floating seaweed.

ORIGINAL   The Sargasso Sea is a strange, still area. It is part of the Atlantic Ocean.

REVISED   The Sargasso Sea is a strange, still area **that is part of the Atlantic Ocean.**

NOTE   If an adjective clause is not essential to the meaning of the sentence, set it off with commas. If it is essential to the meaning, no commas are necessary.

NONESSENTIAL   This fireplace, **which my brother built,** is a replica of one in Williamsburg, Virginia.

ESSENTIAL   The fireplace **that my brother built** is a replica of one in Williamsburg, Virginia.

Adverb Clauses

You can also combine sentences by turning one sentence into an adverb clause. The adverb clause modifies a verb, an adjective, or another adverb in another clause.

To make a sentence into an adverb clause, add a subordinating conjunction (*although, after, because, if, when, while*) at the beginning. The conjunction shows the relationship between the ideas in the adverb clause and the ideas in the independent clause. If the adverb clause comes first, set it off from the independent clause with a comma.

Reference Note

For a list of **common subordinating conjunctions,** see page 499.

ORIGINAL	Sailing ships were sometimes trapped in the Sargasso Sea. There wasn't enough wind to sail.
REVISED	Sailing ships were sometimes trapped in the Sargasso Sea **when there wasn't enough wind to sail.**

ORIGINAL	Sailors used to fear the Sargasso Sea. They heard strange tales about it.
REVISED	**Because they heard strange tales about it,** sailors used to fear the Sargasso Sea.

Noun Clauses

You can make a sentence into a noun clause by adding a word like *that, how, what, whatever, who,* or *whoever.* Then you can insert the clause into another clause. When you combine the sentences, you may need to change or delete some words.

ORIGINAL	Someone will arrive first. That person will get the best seat.
REVISED	**Whoever arrives first** will get the best seat.

ORIGINAL	The players were informed. The game had been forfeited.
REVISED	The players were informed **that the game had been forfeited.**

> **Exercise 6** **Combining Sentences into a Complex Sentence**

┌HELP┐

Before you begin Exercise 6, review the words that can be used to introduce subordinate clauses. These words are included in the explanations on pages 359 and 360.

Here are ten pairs of sentences about Napoleon I. Combine each pair by turning the second sentence into a subordinate clause and inserting it into the first sentence. For the first six pairs, you are given hints about how to create the subordinate clauses. For the last four, you will have to use your own judgment. You may have to add or delete some words in the sentences. Add commas where necessary.

1. Napoleon I conquered much of Europe. He crowned himself emperor of France in 1804. (Use *who.*)
2. In 1769, Napoleon was born on the French island of Corsica. The island had been purchased from Italy the year before. (Use *which.*)
3. Napoleon gained control of the French government in 1799. The French people had lost faith in the five-member Directory. (Use *because.*)
4. Napoleon married Marie Louise, daughter of the emperor of Austria, in 1810. France's principal enemy by 1796 was Austria. (Use *although.*)
5. After Paris was captured in 1814, Napoleon was exiled to the small island of Elba. Napoleon gave up the throne. (Use *who.*)

6. Troops praised Napoleon as their emperor on his march back to Paris. The troops had been sent to arrest Napoleon. (Use *that*.)

7. French troops and combined forces from several countries soon clashed in Belgium, although Napoleon had assured his enemies of something. He would not make war.

8. Napoleon was defeated on June 18, 1815, at the Battle of Waterloo. He had won many military battles.

9. Napoleon was captured by a British battleship. At the time, Napoleon was trying to escape to the United States.

10. Napoleon was exiled to the British island of St. Helena in the Atlantic Ocean. Napoleon was considered a threat to peace.

Review A **Revising Sentences by Combining**

Using all the sentence-combining skills you have learned, revise and rewrite each of the following sets of sentences into one sentence. You may combine by inserting words or phrases, by creating compounds, or by creating complex sentences. You may have to add or delete some words. Add punctuation where necessary.

1. Espionage is the secret collection of intelligence information. The history of espionage goes back over two thousand years.

2. Around 500 B.C., Sun Tzu wrote a book giving instructions on organizing an espionage system. Sun Tzu was a Chinese military theorist.

3. In the nineteenth century, Joseph Fouché, duc d'Otrante, worked to create a network of police agents and spies. Fouché was the French minister of police.

4. In World War I, one of the most famous German spies was Mata Hari. She posed as an Indian dancer in Paris.

5. World War II saw an enormous growth in worldwide espionage. Countries needed quick, accurate information about their enemies.

6. One of the most remarkable intelligence operations in World War II was Operation Double Cross. In Operation Double Cross, almost all the German spies in Great Britain were captured. These German spies were turned into double agents.

7. Japan's most successful espionage led to the attack on the U.S. naval base at Pearl Harbor. This attack was a surprise, and it happened in World War II.

8. Today in the United States, the Central Intelligence Agency gathers secret information. This information is about national security. The Central Intelligence Agency is also called the CIA.

9. The Federal Bureau of Investigation is responsible for counter-espionage within the United States. The FBI was formed in 1908.
10. It is difficult to know the exact number of espionage agents in the world today. Espionage agents work to keep information about themselves hidden.

Review B **Revising a Paragraph by Combining Sentences**

Using all the sentence-combining skills you have learned, revise and rewrite the following paragraph. Use your judgment about which sentences to combine and how to combine them. Try for smooth, varied sentences that are easy to understand, but do not change the original meaning of the paragraph.

```
    Prairie dogs are very sociable. They
live in communities called towns. The towns
can be large. The towns consist of numerous
burrows. The word dog is part of this ani-
mal's name. The prairie dog is actually a
rodent. It gets its name from the sound it
makes. The sound is similar to a dog's
bark. Livestock might step into the burrows
that prairie dogs make. Some ranchers fear
this. However, horses usually do not step
into prairie dog burrows. Cows do not usu-
ally step into prairie dog burrows.
```

Improving Sentence Style

In the first part of this chapter, you learned how to reduce choppiness in your writing by combining sentences. Now you will learn more ways to polish your sentence style and make your writing more effective.

Using Parallel Structure

TIPS & TRICKS

Begin to look for parallel structure in sentences when you combine words, phrases, and clauses by using the coordinating conjunction *and*.

When you join several equal or related ideas in a sentence, it is important that you express these ideas in a similar way. You can do this by balancing the structure of your sentence parts. For example, you should balance an adjective with an adjective, a phrase with a phrase, and a clause with a clause. This kind of balance in writing is called *parallel structure.*

NOT PARALLEL	He learned three things: shooting, passing, and how to dribble. [two gerunds and a phrase]
PARALLEL	He learned three things: **shooting, passing,** and **dribbling.** [three gerunds]

NOT PARALLEL	A good coach must learn to communicate with players, to organize a schedule, and adversity. [two phrases and a noun]
PARALLEL	A good coach must learn **to communicate with players, to organize a schedule,** and **to handle adversity.** [three phrases]

NOT PARALLEL	My sister decided that she would study coaching techniques and to work with the youth basketball league. [a clause and a phrase]
PARALLEL	My sister decided **that she would study coaching techniques** and **that she would work with the youth basketball league.** [two clauses]

Exercise 7 Revising Sentences to Create Parallelism

Some of the following sentences are out of balance. Bring balance to them by using parallel structure. You may have to delete or add some words. If a sentence is already correct, write *C*.

1. Athens, the capital of Greece, is known for its ancient ruins, busy lifestyle, and enjoying fine Greek food.
2. Because it is nearly three thousand years old and its rich history, Athens attracts many visitors.
3. Athens attracts artists and historians and is attractive to tourists.
4. People often drive very fast in Athens and scare the pedestrians.
5. I like seeing the sights in Athens to learn about its history.

Revising Stringy Sentences

What is a *stringy sentence*? Read this one:

I was going on a fishing trip with my uncle, and I knew I would need a lot of luck, and I always fish in the same spot that my uncle does, but he always catches more than I do, but this time I brought all of my fishing lures so that I would be prepared.

BLOOM COUNTY reprinted by permission of International Creative Management, Inc. Copyright © 1984 Berkely Breathed.

The ***stringy sentence*** on the previous page has too many independent clauses strung together with coordinating conjunctions like *and* or *but*. Because the ideas are all treated equally, it is difficult to see how they are related to one another. To fix a stringy sentence, you can

- **break the sentence into two or more shorter sentences**
- **turn some of the independent clauses into subordinate clauses or phrases**

Now read the following sentences aloud and hear the difference. Notice how the writer has broken up the stringy sentence into three shorter sentences and turned an independent clause into a subordinate clause.

```
I was going on a fishing trip with my
uncle, and I knew I would need a lot of
luck. Although I always fish in the same spot
that my uncle does, he always catches more
than I do. This time I brought all of my
fishing lures so that I would be prepared.
```

There are usually several ways to revise a stringy sentence. The most important thing is to make the meaning clear for your reader.

Exercise 8 Revising Stringy Sentences

Revise each of the following stringy sentences. For some items, you can just break the stringy sentence into two or more shorter sentences. For others, you will have to turn an independent clause into a subordinate clause or a phrase to show the relationship between the ideas. Change the punctuation wherever necessary.

1. Music is used for entertainment, relaxation, and self-expression, and it is used in every culture, and it is a very important part of our lives.
2. Music is an ancient art, and people learned to make flutes around 10,000 B.C., and they began to write music around 2500 B.C.
3. Today, much popular music is electronically produced, and many musicians play electric guitars and synthesizers, and some even play electric violins.
4. Different countries have different kinds of music, but some kinds of music are internationally popular, and those kinds include rock music and rap music.
5. Rock music first became popular in the 1950s, and it was inspired by blues and jazz music, but its sound was different from anything people had heard.

Revising Wordy Sentences

Read the following sentence.

```
    Anticipating that tomorrow's forthcoming
examination may be perplexing, I have made
the astute conclusion that we should dili-
gently scrutinize our scholarly tomes at
the decline of day.
```

When you read sentences like this, you probably wonder what language the writer is using. How much easier and clearer it is to say "The test tomorrow may be hard, so let's study tonight." Here are three tips for creating sentences that are not too wordy:

- **Do not use more words than you need.**
- **Do not use fancy, difficult words where plain, simple ones will do.**
- **Do not repeat words or ideas unless it is absolutely necessary.**

WORDY	Our sofa has a lot of weight to it.
IMPROVED	Our sofa is heavy.

WORDY	The reason I am undertaking the task of photographing the exteriors of these abandoned buildings is that I have an interest in architecture.
IMPROVED	I am taking pictures of these abandoned buildings because I am interested in architecture.

WORDY	Greg speaks Spanish well, and his Spanish is clear and fluent.
IMPROVED	Greg speaks clear, fluent Spanish.

Exercise 9 **Revising Wordy Sentences**

Some of the following sentences are wordy. For each sentence, ask the following questions: Does it have unnecessary words? Does it have fancy words that can be replaced with simple ones? Does it repeat ideas? If you answer yes to any question, revise the sentence to reduce the wordiness. If a sentence doesn't need improvement, write *C*.

1. Caves are dark, damp areas that don't have any light.
2. Many caves have beautiful, icicle-like mineral formations called speleothems.
3. Luray Caverns, which is a cave system that is situated in the area of northern Virginia, is famous for its colorful speleothems.

4. Lascaux Cave, a famous cave in southwestern France, has many ancient, prehistoric wall paintings.
5. Cavefish are small, cave-dwelling fish that are not equipped with optical organs.

Varying Sentence Beginnings

You would probably get bored if you ate the same food at every meal. Variety is as important in your writing as it is in your diet. The basic subject-verb sentence pattern is fine sometimes, but if it is all you ever use, your writing will be monotonous.

Read the following paragraph. Notice that while the paragraph is correct, it is boring because every sentence follows the same subject-verb pattern.

```
    The pool was nearly empty on an early
weekend morning. Dedicated swimmers swam
multiple laps. A few sunbathers and parents
with small children sat on the grass at the
edge of the pool and watched. The day grew
hotter, and the sun rose higher. The pool
became more crowded. The pool was soon
filled with young people. They laughed as
they played games and splashed each other.
```

Now read a revised version of the paragraph. Notice how the varied sentence beginnings break the monotony of the subject-verb pattern.

```
    On an early weekend morning, the pool
was nearly empty. Dedicated swimmers swam
multiple laps. A few sunbathers and parents
with small children sat on the grass at the
edge of the pool and watched. As the day
grew hotter and the sun rose higher, the
pool became more crowded. Soon the pool was
filled with young people. Laughing, they
played games and splashed each other.
```

Instead of starting all your sentences with subjects, try opening sentences in a variety of ways. Begin with single-word modifiers, with phrases, and with subordinate clauses. Remember to add commas as necessary after introductory words, phrases, or clauses.

Varying Sentence Beginnings	
Single-Word Modifiers	**Grotesquely,** Dr. Frankenstein's monster began to rise from the table. [adverb] **Frightened,** Dr. Frankenstein jumped back. [participle] **Cackling,** Igor ran from the room. [participle]
Phrases	**With little hope,** Sam entered the writing contest. [prepositional phrase] **Excited that he had won,** Sam accepted the award. [participial phrase]
Subordinate Clauses	**Because Manuel was tall,** people expected him to play basketball. **Although Manuel wasn't interested in playing basketball,** he always went to the games.

Exercise 10 **Varying Sentence Beginnings**

Using what you have learned about varying sentence beginnings, revise each of the following sentences. The hint in parentheses will tell you whether to begin with a phrase, a clause, or a single-word modifier.

EXAMPLE 1. Astronomy is one of the oldest of the sciences, and it still intrigues scientists today. (phrase)

1. *Still intriguing scientists today, astronomy is one of the oldest of the sciences.*

1. Maps of the heavens were first drawn on stone or parchment, and they were created by the ancient Chinese. (phrase)
2. Early humans started watching the sun, moon, and stars when they learned that understanding the heavens could help their harvests. (subordinate clause)
3. Astronomers work with large radio and optical telescopes and space probes today. (single-word modifier)
4. The moon lacks wind, atmosphere, and weather and would be an ideal location for an observatory. (phrase)
5. The early Egyptians planned their festivals and events by studying the heavens, but the ancient Greeks were the first to study the sky scientifically. (subordinate clause)
6. Galileo supported Ptolemy's idea that the sun was the center of the universe and was threatened with punishment. (phrase)

7. William Herschel discovered the planet Uranus by using a home-made telescope. (phrase)
8. Astronomers have been able to predict the paths of planets because Newton proved that gravity rules the universe. (subordinate clause)
9. The Hubble Space Telescope was placed in orbit in 1990. (phrase)
10. The Hubble Space Telescope's vision was initially blurry, but it was repaired in 1993 by astronauts. (single-word modifier)

Varying Sentence Structure

Reference Note

For more on **types of sentence structures,** see page 504.

You have learned to create different kinds of sentences by combining sentences and varying sentence beginnings. Now you can use this skill to create a better writing style. For varied, interesting paragraphs, it sometimes is not enough just to create sentences of different lengths. You also need to use a variety of sentence structures. That means using a mix of simple, compound, and complex (and sometimes even compound-complex) sentences in your writing.

Read the following short paragraph, which is made up of only simple sentences.

```
    My sister went to college. She was ner-
vous at first. She was determined to be a
success. She worked hard every day. She
graduated at the top of her class. I was
proud of her. We celebrated after the cere-
monies. We ate a big meal. My mother took
pictures of the whole family.
```

Now read the revised version of the paragraph. The writer has included a variety of sentence structures to break the monotony of the first version.

```
    Although she was nervous at first, my
sister went to college. Because she was
determined to be a success and because
she worked hard, she graduated at the top
of her class. I was proud of her. We cel-
ebrated after the ceremonies as we ate a
big meal, and my mother took pictures of
the whole family.
```

Notice how the use of subordinate clauses improved some sentences and made the paragraph clearer. Besides adding variety, subordinate clauses help show how the ideas in a sentence are related.

Be sure you understand the type of relationship each subordinating conjunction expresses.

CONTRAST *although, even though, though,* and *while*

REASON *as, because, considering that, if, since,* and *so that*

TIME *after, as, as long as, as soon as, before, when,* and *while*

COMPUTER TIP

You can use a word-processing program's cut and paste functions to move subordinate clauses within a document. If you change your mind, you can always move the text again.

Exercise 11 **Revising a Paragraph to Create a Variety of Sentence Structures**

Using what you have learned about combining sentences and varying structure, revise the following paragraph to make it smoother and more varied. A combination of different kinds of sentences will make the paragraph much more fun to read.

> My friends and I had lunch. We ate at a food court on the second floor of a mall. The food court has food from different countries. About twenty restaurants are there. Lin had soup and salad. I had a burrito. It was delicious. Joe and Debbie split a pizza. Then we walked around and looked at the people. We all imagined what they were thinking. There was a fashion show on the main floor. Debbie and I admired the clothes. Lin and Joe liked estimating the costs of the outfits. We looked at a display of new cars. We talked about the kinds of cars we would like to have.

Review C **Writing a Paragraph Using a Variety of Sentence Structures**

You are the director of a music video for a new song called "The Edge of Dreams." Write a paragraph explaining which singers, dancers, and musicians you will cast in your video. Their names may be real or fictional. If you want your reader to understand and be interested in your casting choices, you will need to make your paragraph lively and clear. Capture your reader's attention by using a variety of interesting sentence structures. Avoid wordy and stringy sentences, and be sure to check for parallel structure as you revise.

TIPS & TRICKS

Use the strategies you have learned in this chapter to revise your own writing. Look for opportunities to better your work by combining sentences and improving sentence style.

Understanding Paragraphs and Compositions

How Paragraphs and Compositions Fit Together

A paragraph is made up of sentences grouped together for a reason—usually to present and support a single *main idea.* In the same way, a composition is made up of a group of paragraphs. The paragraphs in a composition are a bit like the players on a football team. Each player on a football team is assigned a position, and each has an individual contribution to make. However, it is teamwork—the players working together—that usually wins the game. Similarly, each paragraph in a composition expresses a main idea of its own, but the paragraphs also work together to develop and support a *thesis,* or controlling idea, that makes the composition work as a whole.

The Parts of a Body Paragraph

While paragraphs in narrative writing do not always have a central focus, paragraphs in most other types of compositions do usually emphasize a main idea. These paragraphs, often called *body paragraphs*, usually have three major parts: a *topic sentence, supporting sentences*, and (sometimes, but not always) a *clincher sentence.* The table that follows provides more details about each of these parts.

Parts of Paragraphs	
Main Idea	• provides the central focus of the paragraph
Topic Sentence	• directly states the paragraph's main idea • often is the first sentence in the paragraph • may be found at the end of the paragraph, for emphasis or variety

Supporting Sentences	• support the main idea of the paragraph
	• use the following kinds of details:
	    sensory details: information collected using the five senses (sight, hearing, smell, touch, and taste)
	    facts: information that can be proven
	    statistics: facts based on numbers
	    examples: specific instances or illustrations of a general idea
	    anecdotes: an extended example or brief story, often entertaining or amusing

Clincher Sentence	• sometimes (but not always) is found at the end of longer paragraphs • emphasizes or summarizes the main idea of a paragraph • adds zing to a paragraph • often includes a transitional phrase • most often is used with longer, complicated paragraphs to reinforce the main idea

STYLE TIP

Clincher sentences should not be overused. Weak clinchers like "Those are the reasons I dislike snow" make your writing dull. They lack the punch that effective clinchers have.

Keep in mind that paragraphs may be developed by using either one kind of supporting detail or by combining several kinds together. For example, if you were writing an autobiographical narrative, you might use a combination of sensory details, anecdotes, and examples.

NOTE Some paragraphs lack topic sentences. Instead of being directly stated, the main idea of these paragraphs is said to be *implied,* or unstated. For example, paragraphs in fiction rarely contain topic sentences. However, in your school essays, using topic sentences helps you focus on your topic and helps your readers easily identify and understand your main ideas.

Putting the Parts Together

The following passage shows how the parts of a paragraph work together to support a main idea.

Topic
Sentence

Supporting
Sentences

(Facts and
Statistics)

Clincher
Sentence

Electric insect traps, or "bug zappers," are effective killing machines, but they kill the wrong kind of insects, claims University of Delaware entomologist Doug Tallamy. Over the course of a summer, Tallamy and a high school student, Tim Frick, analyzed the victims of the electric traps installed in six yards in Newark, Delaware. Of the 13,789 insects killed, just 31—less than one-quarter of one percent—were biting insects. Tallamy and Frick estimate that the millions of traps employed in the U.S. needlessly kill 71 billion to 350 billion "nontarget insects" each year, causing untold damage to ecosystems. Bug zappers, they conclude, are "worthless" as well as "counter-productive."

Steve Nadis, "Bug Zappers Miss Their Mark,"
Omni magazine Web site

TIPS & TRICKS

Often a paragraph that describes a sequence of events or actions has no topic sentence. To identify the main idea and create a topic sentence for such a paragraph, think of a one-sentence summary of what happens in the paragraph.

Notice that the topic sentence immediately calls the reader's attention to the paragraph's main idea: These traps kill the wrong insects. Each supporting sentence contains information that supports this main idea, with the writer using facts and statistics to provide more detailed support. The final sentence, a clincher sentence, emphasizes the main idea by presenting a judgment based on the facts and statistics in the supporting sentences.

Exercise 1 Identifying Parts of Paragraphs

See if you can identify the parts of paragraphs in the three paragraphs that begin on the following page. First, locate the topic sentence in each paragraph. Then, identify each supporting sentence as either a sensory detail, a fact, a statistic, an example, or an anecdote. Finally, determine whether any of the paragraphs have a clincher sentence.

1.   Animals bitten by some snakes bleed internally, because the venom contains an anticoagulant. For the past decade researchers have studied snake venom in search of a drug that would prevent blood clots that can trigger heart attacks. Robert Gould of Merck Research Laboratories thinks his company has found one: "We tested eleven kinds of vipers and found proteins in their venom that keep human blood platelets from sticking together." Merck synthesized one of the proteins of the saw-scaled viper's venom and used the knowledge gained to design a drug called Aggrastat. It may save thousands of lives a year.

John L. Eliot, "Snake Venom Strikes at Heart Attacks," *National Geographic*

2.   On Prince Edward Island [Canada] change has often come slowly. Some parts of the island got paved roads and "the lights," as electricity was called, only in the early sixties. The 1970s finally saw the demise of the one-room schoolhouse, and even more recently small family farms have given way to agribusinesses—operations of up to 3,000 acres that grow potatoes to feed the North American appetite for french fries. How islanders come to accept this newest—and potentially most far-reaching—form of change remains to be seen.

Ian Darragh, "Prince Edward Island: A World Apart No More," *National Geographic*

3.   Prairie dogs are talented linguists. "They possess the most sophisticated natural animal language so far decoded," says Con Slobodchikoff of Northern Arizona University. Researching alarm calls of Gunnison's [a species of prairie dog], he found that they discriminated among predators—humans, hawks, coyotes, and dogs. Moreover, the prairie dogs

(continued)

(continued)
distinguished between people of different sizes, and when they gave the same call for a man—wearing the same clothes—after not seeing him for two months, "that blew me away," says Slobodchikoff.

Michael E. Long, "The Vanishing Prairie Dog," *National Geographic*

Qualities of Paragraphs

Having the parts of a paragraph in place is just the beginning of developing a good paragraph. The next step is to consider the three qualities of any well-written paragraph: *unity, coherence,* and *elaboration.* You can think of these qualities as the strong glue that holds the parts of a paragraph together.

Unity

Unity is the quality achieved when all of the sentences in a paragraph work together as a unit to express or support one main idea. Unrelated ideas spoil unity and distract the reader. Unity is present in a paragraph when at least one of the following is true:

- **All sentences in a paragraph relate to the main idea stated in the topic sentence.**

- **All sentences in a paragraph relate to an implied main idea.** When there is no stated topic sentence, all the sentences support the paragraph's unstated main idea, or **implied main idea.**

- **All sentences in a paragraph relate to a sequence of events.** In a narrative paragraph, unity is achieved when all the sentences work together to narrate the event.

TIPS & TRICKS

To identify an implied main idea of a paragraph, determine the topic of the first sentence, and then refine and adjust this idea as you continue reading the supporting sentences of the paragraph.

Coherence

Along with unity, good paragraphs have *coherence.* Coherence is achieved when all of the details and ideas in a paragraph are logically arranged and clearly connected. To ensure that the ideas in a paragraph are arranged in a way that makes sense, pay attention to the **logical**

progression or **organizational pattern,** of the ideas. Use one of the orders described in the chart below.

Building Coherence: Types of Order		
Order	**When To Use**	**How It Works**
Chronological	• to tell a story • to explain a process	• presents actions and events according to the order in which they occur
Spatial	• to describe a place or object	• arranges details or ideas according to their location in space
Logical	• to explain or classify (by defining, dividing a subject into parts, or comparing and contrasting)	• groups related details or ideas together to show their relationship
Order of Importance	• to inform or to persuade	• arranges details or ideas from most important to least important, or vice versa

STYLE TIP

At times, multiple orders may be used to add variety to writing. For example, within a narration (which typically follows chronological order) a description of a scene or place may follow a spatial order.

In addition to presenting details in an order that makes sense, a paragraph that has coherence should also show *how* these details are connected. You can show connections by using **direct references** or **transitional expressions.**

Building Coherence: Connecting Ideas	
Connecting Strategy	**How It Works**
Direct References	• use a noun or pronoun that refers to a noun or pronoun used earlier • repeat a word used earlier • use a word or phrase that means the same thing as one used earlier

(continued)

(continued)

Building Coherence: Connecting Ideas	
Transitional Expressions (including prepositions that show chronological or spatial order and conjunctions)	• compare ideas (*also, and, besides, in addition, similarly, too*) • contrast ideas (*although, but, however, instead, nevertheless, otherwise, yet*) • show cause and effect (*as a result, because, consequently, so, therefore, thus*) • show time (*after, before, eventually, finally, first, meanwhile, then, when*) • show place (*above, across, around, beyond, from, here, in, on, over, there, to, under*) • show importance (*first, last, mainly, then, to begin with*)

Elaboration

STYLE **TIP**

There are many types of information you can provide as elaboration: examples, descriptions, expert opinions, reasons, evidence, personal experience, statistics. You should use a combination of these to give your writing variety.

Along with unity and coherence, a good paragraph should have *elaboration.* A paragraph has elaboration when it contains supporting sentences (supporting details) that thoroughly develop its main idea. A paragraph lacks elaboration when it does not contain enough supporting sentences, or when its supporting sentences do not sufficiently develop a paragraph's main idea. A lack of elaboration can confuse readers and cause them to doubt whether the writer understands what he or she is trying to say.

To help you think of ideas to use for elaboration, try one of the following strategies. For the examples provided, the writer's topic was the clean-up of a neighborhood vacant lot.

Purpose: Description
Strategy: Freewrite a list of details based on the five senses

---

Smell: garbage
rotting fruit

Sight: rusty old cans
broken glass
old shoes

Taste: smelled so bad I thought
I could taste the trash

Touch: cold to start, warm sun
came out eventually

Hearing: chatter about what
we would do with area
once cleaned up

Purpose: Exposition
Strategy: Use *5W-How?* questions

Who was involved?
    neighborhood association
    Councilmember White
    my family

What was changed?
    neighborhood lot was cleaned up

When was it changed?
    last October

Where did it happen?
    corner lot on Fifth and Willow streets

Why did it happen?
    citizens were concerned

How did it happen?
    neighborhood association arranged clean-up day
    city provided dumpsters, gloves

┌ TIPS & TRICKS ┐

The 5*W-How?* questions are especially useful for generating ideas to answer questions on an essay test. Just use the topic of the question as the basis for each of the six questions.

Purpose: Persuasion
Strategy: Cluster

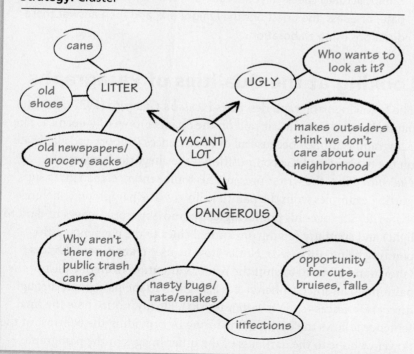

(continued)

(continued)

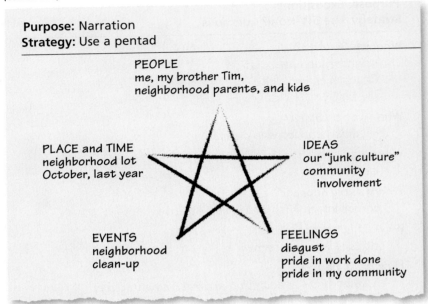

Purpose: Narration
Strategy: Use a pentad

PEOPLE
me, my brother Tim,
neighborhood parents, and kids

PLACE and TIME
neighborhood lot
October, last year

IDEAS
our "junk culture"
community
involvement

EVENTS
neighborhood
clean-up

FEELINGS
disgust
pride in work done
pride in my community

> **NOTE** When you speak with someone face-to-face, you are able to respond directly to questions from that person. When you write, you cannot actually speak to your readers. However, you can try to anticipate, or guess, the questions they might ask, and then answer these questions using elaboration.

Looking at the Qualities of Paragraphs

The following paragraph describes Picasso's *Guernica* (1937), a mural painted after a German air raid on the Spanish town of Guernica. The paragraph is unified because all of its sentences support and elaborate on the main idea of the composition—the allegorical nature of *Guernica*. First, the writer presents his topic sentence, then gives supporting examples from the painting. To give the paragraph coherence, the writer arranges his points **logically** (moving from images of dark to light) and **spatially** (giving directional clues to the elements of the painting being discussed). Notice how he uses **transitional devices** (shown in boldface) to shift the reader's attention from one part of the painting to another. Coherence is also given to the paragraph through **direct references** (shown with asterisks). Finally, notice how the final sentence follows the cue of the painting by providing the contrast of the flower of hope to the darkness of the other images of the paragraph.

According to Picasso, *Guernica* is allegorical.* He* explained some of the symbolism.* The horse with the spear in its back, the inevitable victim* of bullfights, signifies* victimized* humanity overwhelmed by brute* force. The motif of the shrieking mouth is repeated in that of the screaming woman with her dead child **at the left**, the face of the soldier **below**, and the victim* of the flames **at the right**. The bull, standing* for brutality,* is the only triumphant figure in this symbolic* struggle between the forces of darkness and those of light, between barbarism and civilization. **Above**, an arm reaches forward to hold the lamp of truth over the whole gruesome scene. **Amid** the general havoc and gloom the artist sounds one soft note* of optimism. **Above** the victim's* severed arm and broken sword **in the bottom center** is a tiny plant in bloom to signify* the force of renewal.

William Fleming, *Arts and Ideas*

Topic Sentence

Example 1

Example 2

Example 3

Example 4

Example 5

Example 6

TIPS & TRICKS

Notice the direct references indicated with asterisks. For example, *He,* in the second sentence, refers back to *Picasso,* in the first sentence. *Allegorical,* in the first sentence, is repeatedly referred to by similar-meaning words and phrases such as *symbolism, standing for, symbolic,* and *signify.* Variations of *victim* and *brutality* are also repeated throughout the paragraph.

Pablo Picasso. *Guernica*, 1937, oil on canvas, 11' 5½" x 25' 5¾". Museo del Prado, Madrid.

NOTE To check your own writing for elaboration, coherence, and unity, ask whether your writing is "on **TOP**":

- **T = Topic** Are all points and sentences about the topic? This ensures **elaboration.**

- **O = Order** Is there a logical/clear order of ideas? This ensures **coherence.**

- **P = Points of development** Is there sufficient development of ideas? This ensures **unity.**

Exercise 2 Improving the Qualities of Paragraphs

In the following three paragraphs, the ideas are poorly arranged, making it difficult to make sense of what the writers are saying. Also, some of the information in each paragraph may detract from that paragraph's unity. After you determine which type of order would make sense for each paragraph, revise each paragraph by rearranging sentences into that order. Eliminate any sentences that are unrelated to the main idea and incorporate direct references and transitions. Finally, decide whether there is sufficient elaboration to support the main idea. Be prepared to explain your revisions.

1. Pre-treat all fabric by soaking it in a solution of soda ash and water. Allow the dye to react with the fabric by placing the items in a plastic bag for twenty-four hours. Squirt dyes on tied material. Use only 100% cotton material. Protect your eyes, skin, clothes, and work area from spills. Twist your fabric in spirals or fold it into interesting patterns. Mix dyes in glass jars, then place in squirt bottles. Tie, using either rubber bands or string. Rinse first in cool, then warmer water until the water runs clear.

2. Politics and entertainment seem strangely intertwined. Early in life, Ronald Reagan appeared in a total of fifty-two feature movies. Minnesota even elected a former professional wrestler and actor, Jesse "The Body" Ventura, to the office of governor in 1998. Singer/actor Sonny Bono was half of the Sonny and Cher variety team before entering into politics. Cher continued in music and film, even earning an Academy Award. Starting as mayor of Palm Springs, California, in 1988, Bono eventually became the U.S. Representative from California's 44th District in 1994. Ronald Reagan's political career went from Republican governor of California (1967–75) to fortieth president of the United States (1981–89). Australian

Peter Garrett, lead singer of Midnight Oil, is active in his country's politics. Whether in politics or entertainment, some people seem destined for the spotlight.

3.   Only ten percent of visitors to the Grand Canyon actually hike into the canyon. The first sight of the Grand Canyon is enough to make your heart leap into your mouth. A trip to the Grand Canyon is not the same without a hike down into the canyon itself. Gift shops, food concessions, and a hotel all have been run by the famous Fred Harvey Company since 1876. Do not even try to hike down to the river and back in one day. Tours into the canyon on the backs of mules are conducted daily. The Grand Canyon is approximately one mile deep, 277 miles long, and up to eighteen miles across. The Colorado River snakes across the bottom of the canyon. Reservations are always recommended. Las Vegas is in nearby Nevada. The mules are sure-footed and they provide an excellent photo opportunity for the brave adventurer.

Review A   Analyzing Paragraphs

With two or three classmates, look through a variety of sources to find four different kinds of paragraphs—one that explains, one that describes, one that persuades, and one that narrates. You might look in magazine and newspaper articles and advertisements, instruction manuals, and reviews of movies, CDs, or books. After you have found the paragraphs, identify their **parts** (topic, support, and clincher sentences) and **qualities** (coherence, unity, and elaboration). Then, identify which paragraphs are particularly weak or strong. If you decide that a paragraph is weak, explain why. For example, write "fails to provide support" or "lacks unity."

Paragraphs Within Compositions

Just as individual sentences function as parts of a paragraph, paragraphs function as parts of longer pieces of writing called *compositions*. Within a composition, paragraphs are used for a variety of reasons:

- to explain another step in a process or another part of a subject
- to introduce another kind of support for an opinion
- to show movement in time or place
- to indicate a change in speaker in dialogue
- to break up unusually long sections of text

What Makes a Composition?

In much the same way that paragraphs are built from different types of sentences, compositions are built from different types of paragraphs. Some complex main ideas require more detailed elaboration than one paragraph can supply. **Compositions** consist of paragraphs that individually elaborate on specific points of a complex main idea, which is the main focus of the composition. You will remember that a paragraph has three parts: a topic sentence, supporting sentences, and (sometimes) a clincher sentence. Compositions may also have three parts: an *introduction*, a *body*, and a *conclusion*. Paragraphs and compositions are also similar in that they both require unity, coherence, and elaboration to support their main ideas.

The Introduction

STYLE TIP

Introductions can vary in length from one short sentence to several paragraphs. Length is determined by the scope of the thesis.

Because the **introduction** is the first thing your readers see, you will want to be sure it creates a good impression. This means that the time you take in writing an introduction is well spent. After all, if an introduction is not well written, your reader might not bother reading the rest of your composition. You will write good introductions if you keep in mind that an introduction should do these three things:

- catch the *reader's interest*
- set the *tone of the composition*
- present the *thesis statement*

Catching the Reader's Interest

To understand the importance of good introductory sentences, think about TV commercials. The first few seconds of a good commercial will quickly grab your attention and make you want to watch the rest. Similarly, the first few sentences of a good introduction will immediately attract your readers and give them a reason for reading more.

Techniques for Writing Introductions

If you have trouble beginning a composition, try using one of the following six techniques. Each is illustrated by a sample introduction about roadside attractions throughout the United States. You can also try combining techniques for variety.

1. **Begin with a question.** Some introductions begin with a question that contradicts the thesis. Others use a rhetorical question—one with no answer expected. Any question that applies to the reader can be intriguing, as in this introduction:

> What would possess a man to dig giant holes in the ground, and then plunge ten vintage Cadillacs nose-first into the holes, burying them with just the back ends sticking out? Would you believe it was done for "artistic" purposes? Stanley Marsh III claims that is why he created his "Cadillac Ranch" in 1973 just west of Amarillo, Texas, on Interstate 40. His creation has led many people to question: *Is it art?*

COMPUTER TIP

Experiment with different types of introductions for the same composition. Type several different introductions in a separate file, then cut-and-paste your best one into your first draft. Be sure to save the others in case you change your mind or think of ways to improve one to make it fit better.

2. **Begin with an anecdote or example.** An *anecdote* is a little story, or real-life incident, that may be humorous or just intriguing. An *example* is a specific instance or illustration of a general idea. Going to a concert is an example of a good time you might have with a group of your friends. An introduction to a composition on tornadoes could begin with an example describing a place where a tornado has struck. The following introduction begins with an anecdote.

> I remember when I was in kindergarten and my parents bought me my first yo-yo. To me, it was like magic the way my father, sister, mother—nearly everyone but me—could make it bob down, and then shoot right back up where it started. If you could do tricks with it, then you were definitely some sort of genius. After I had gained a modest amount of skill with the yo-yo, I grew bored with it. Now, though, after visiting the National Yo-Yo Museum in Chico, California, and seeing the world's largest yo-yo (256 pounds!), a little bit of that magic has come back.

3. **State a startling fact or an unusual opinion.** This method will grab your readers' attention: They will want to see how you will support your main idea or defend your opinion.

> It is not the Statue of Liberty, the Liberty Bell, or even Mount Rushmore that best exemplifies the true spirit of America. Instead, it is the monument to the boll weevil in Enterprise, Alabama. Built in 1919, this monument is dedicated to the swarm of insects that destroyed this cotton town's main crop. It symbolizes the town's turning its attention to other crops that eventually brought prosperity. This is an example of the true spirit of America—facing adversity and triumphing while maintaining a sense of humor.

4. **Begin with background information.** Facts and other specific details not only help your reader understand your main idea but also may create interest in your topic.

For years Kissimmee, Florida, could boast having the world's largest alligator. Standing adjacent to the Gator Motel, this roadside attraction was a full 126 feet long. However, the reptile had to give up its title in 1992, when 200-foot-long (and one-inch-thick) "Swampy" appeared in Christmas, Florida. Of course, these are not real alligators—just human-made tributes to the creatures that are a part of so many Floridians' lives.

5. **Set the scene.** Just as a short story may begin with a description of the setting (when and where the events take place), you might describe the setting of your topic.

Driving across a seemingly endless North Dakota highway, with fields of rye blowing in the wind, weary travelers may not quite believe their eyes. Off in the horizon, starting as barely a speck, comes in to view what appears to be a cow—a very BIG cow. Travelers are drawn to her like a magnet. She is known as "Salem Sue." Standing thirty-eight feet tall, she is the proud symbol of the small dairy town of New Salem.

6. **Begin with a simple statement of your thesis.** You do not always have to be clever. You can be direct and get right to your main idea.

Roadside attractions are a time-honored tradition of American culture, reflecting our big attitudes and sense of humor.

Setting the Tone

As you introduce the topic of your composition, the words you choose, the details you include, and the rhythm of your sentences all set the composition's *tone*—your attitude toward your audience and topic. The tone of a composition may be serious, humorous, formal, informal, critical—even outraged. For example, the author of the paragraph about the painting *Guernica* (page 379) discusses a serious subject, and his tone remains formal.

Vinnie Ream

The Thesis Statement

The *thesis statement* is a sentence or two in the introduction that announces your topic and what you want to say about it. Your entire composition will support the ideas presented in this statement.

Some thesis statements simply state the topic, for example: *Vinnie Ream was commissioned by Congress in 1866 to sculpt a memorial statue of Abraham Lincoln.* This introduces the topic of the sculptor commissioned to do the Lincoln sculpture, which stands in the rotunda of the U.S. Capitol in Washington, D.C.

Other thesis statements, including the ones you are often asked to write, do more. They also identify a main idea the writer is trying to prove in the composition. Here is one example of this kind of thesis statement:

> Congress's 1866 decision to award a $10,000 commission to 18-year-old Vinnie Ream for a marble statue memorializing the nation's recently assassinated president, Abraham Lincoln, vaulted the young sculptor into the center of a storm of controversy.
>
> Ethel Yari, "Teenage Lincoln Sculptor," *American History*

In this thesis sentence we are introduced to the topic *and* the main idea of the composition, which is about the controversy that Ream's commission caused.

Hints for Writing and Using a Thesis Statement

1. **Develop your thesis statement from information you have gathered.** Review your prewriting material—the many facts and details you have gathered. Ask yourself: *What main idea do the facts and details suggest?*

2. **Include both a topic and your main idea about it.** Most thesis statements answer these two questions: *What is my topic? What am I saying about my topic?* To make sure you have included both parts, underline the topic and circle the main idea.

   For example, read this thesis statement: *"If you take sensible precautions with clothing, equipment, and safety, you can enjoy bicycling all year long."* It is clear that this writer is going to discuss year-round bicycling (topic) and specific precautions you need to make with clothing, equipment, and safety (main idea).

Hints for Writing and Using a Thesis Statement

3. **Be clear and specific.** Keep your language and ideas sharp and definite. Compare this vague thesis statement with the actual one you have just read: "If you want to continue bicycling, you need to take care of a lot of things."

4. **Keep your thesis statement in front of you as you plan and write.** It will help keep you on track. Every idea and detail should directly support your thesis statement, so be focused and get rid of any that do not.

NOTE Your **preliminary thesis statement,** the first one you develop before you actually write your composition, is probably direct and straightforward. You may even think it is a little dull. Later on, you can revise it to give it more zing, as professional writers do. Here is an example of how one writer revised a thesis statement.

PRELIMINARY   Although rain seldom comes to the Sonoran Desert, when it does, flash flooding often accompanies it, creating major changes in the lives of animals, plants, and landscape of the region.

REVISED   "Flash flood!" That wall of water racing down the dry creek bed is the first rain to come to the Sonoran Desert in months—and whether beast, plant, or the very landscape itself, life is about to change in an instant.

Exercise 3 **Analyzing Thesis Statements**

On your own paper, identify the specific topic and the main idea of each of the following thesis statements.

EXAMPLE   1. The habitat of the Cuban bee hummingbird—the world's smallest bird—must maintain its perfect balance to support such a fragile creature.

1. *Topic: Cuban bee hummingbird habitat*
    Main idea: The bird's habitat must be maintained.

1. Professional sports lost three greats to retirement in 1999: basketball's Michael Jordan, hockey's Wayne Gretzky, and football's John Elway.

2. Pet owners seem to come in two antagonistic species: cat people and dog people; but, members of both sides should recognize that the two species of pet actually do share many characteristics.

STYLE **TIP**

Sometimes in longer papers, of five hundred or more words, it is a good idea to use a **multipoint thesis,** in which you list the main point of each body paragraph. Here is a multipoint thesis with the three points underlined:

The introduction of printing <u>encouraged writing,</u> <u>furthered literacy,</u> and <u>expanded the flow of information.</u>

Generally, a multipoint thesis promotes good organization and coherence, because it gives the framework for the body of your composition.

3. When you consider buying your first car, keep in mind the factors that can cause it to depreciate, or lose value, over just the first year.
4. With the advent of the printing press, cheap books became readily available in England and the English language was forever changed.
5. While CDs have virtually replaced LPs, think twice before you chuck that turntable into the trash.
6. Although humans may believe that they are the only ones on the planet who have rhythm, many living things use some form of rhythmic movement in their everyday patterns.
7. Designed to protect sheep from a highly destructive predator, the 1553-mile long Dingo Fence of Australia has had a greater ecological impact than originally imagined.
8. The formulas that languages use to create their words for greeting and leave-taking are odd.
9. Exploring the history of many words for food and dining reveals the story of exploration during the Renaissance.
10. In order to understand wildlife conservation, people must first understand the relationship between an animal and its habitat.

The Structure of Introductions

Reference Note

For more on **writing introductions,** see page 943 in the Quick Reference Handbook.

To shape introductions in both formal and informal writing, writers often follow a common format: They move from general information to a more specific statement—often a thesis statement. Think of a funnel. The wide opening at the top of the funnel is like the general opening of an introduction. The slender end of the funnel is like the precise thesis to which the introduction narrows.

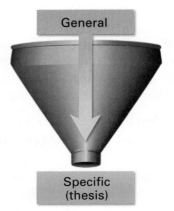

General

Specific
(thesis)

In the following example introduction, notice how the sentences grow increasingly more specific, with the last statement serving as a thesis.

> Human civilizations are always questioning and changing the requirements they have for the people who lead and represent them. William Shakespeare, the great Elizabethan dramatist, recognized this tendency in himself and in his audience and explored the nature of leadership in a great majority of his plays. The characters he portrays as leaders or aspiring leaders often are models for the strengths and weaknesses of particular leadership types. In *Julius Caesar,* he focuses his attention upon three types of revolutionary leaders represented by the idealistic Brutus, the self-serving Cassius, and the popular Antony.

Another type of introduction is one that you might think of as a "twist." It begins by stating commonly accepted knowledge, but adds a twist that calls this knowledge into question. This kind of introduction is known as a **"But" introduction,** because the thesis begins with a word or phrase indicating an opposite, such as *but, however,* or *on the other hand.* "But" introductions can be very effective in capturing a reader's attention. For example, in the following paragraph, the thesis twist begins with "But no."

TIPS & TRICKS

In formal writing, you should avoid beginning a sentence with a conjunction such as *but.* Instead, choose one of the synonym forms *however* or *on the other hand* to begin a "But" introduction.

> With all the advances toward equality for women, you've got to assume there are lots of women programmers, right? After all, it's not as though computer science is a discipline that requires more brawn than brains. But no: According to statistics compiled by Tracy K. Camp, then an assistant professor of computer science at the University of Alabama, the number of undergraduate degrees in computer science that is awarded to women has been shrinking steadily, both in real numbers and as a percentage of degrees awarded.
>
> Wendy M. Grossman, "Access Denied,"
> *Scientific American*

For each of the two published introductions below, answer the following questions.

- What technique does the writer use in the beginning of the introduction? (Look back over the techniques on pages 383–385.)
- How well do you think the technique works? Would you continue reading the article?
- How would you describe the tone—the writer's attitude toward the topic? What words and details in the introduction reveal the tone?
- Does the introduction follow the structure you learned about on page 388? If not, how does it differ?

1. Entomophagy, or bug eating, writes David George Gordon in *The Eat a Bug Cookbook,* is good for the planet. It takes only a quarter as much feed to raise a pound of roach meat as it does to raise a pound of beef. "And consider this: Many of our common garden pests are edible. If everyone served rapacious critters such as vine weevils and tomato hornworms at the dinner table, we'd have little need for most over-the-counter pesticide[s]."

    Kim Hubbard, Review of *The Eat a Bug Cookbook, Discover*

2. Since the space age began four decades ago, rockets have lifted more than 20,000 metric tons of material into orbit. Today 4,500 tons remain in the form of nearly 10,000 "resident space objects," only five percent of which are functioning spacecraft. These objects are just the large ones that military radars and telescopes can track. Of increasing interest to spacecraft operators are the millions of smaller, untrackable scraps scattered into orbits throughout near-Earth space, from only a few hundred kilometers to more than 40,000 kilometers (25,000 miles) above the surface of the planet.

    Nicholas L. Johnson, "Monitoring and Controlling Debris in Space," *Scientific American*

The Body

Your composition would read like a telegram if you simply stated your main ideas without supporting them. To have an effective composition you need to include a *body* of supporting paragraphs. These paragraphs, which are the core of your composition, support, or prove, the thesis or main idea by developing it with supporting details. All body paragraphs should relate directly to the thesis statement and should connect smoothly with one another. In other words, the body of a composition should have the qualities of unity, coherence and elaboration.

Unity

It is a strain to try to listen to someone whose thoughts leap illogically from one idea to another. A composition has *unity* when instead of leaping between ideas, its paragraphs work smoothly together to support a single main idea—your thesis. Unity is lost when any detail or statement detracts from the sense of "oneness" in the composition.

Coherence

Coherence means that ideas within the composition are strongly connected. In a coherent composition, the ideas are easy to follow from paragraph to paragraph and the writing seems to flow smoothly from beginning to end. The reader does not have to agonize over what something means; nothing sounds awkward or disjointed. You can make your composition coherent by arranging ideas sensibly and by using *direct references* and *transitional expressions* to show how ideas are connected.

Direct References   One way to connect ideas from paragraph to paragraph is to make *direct references* to something you have already mentioned. Here are three ways to use direct references.

1. Use pronouns to refer to nouns or ideas in previous paragraphs. For example, by using the pronouns *she, they,* or *this,* you can avoid awkwardly repeating nouns.
2. Repeat key words or phrases. Tie paragraphs together by reminding the reader of what is important.
3. Use synonyms or slight rewordings of ideas and key words introduced in previous paragraphs. Too much repetition sounds awkward.

Reference Note

When you write the body of a composition, it is often helpful to draft a plan, whether an **early plan** (sometimes called a **rough outline**), or a **formal outline.** For more information about early plans and formal outlines, see pages 950 and 951 of the Quick Reference Handbook.

Reference Note

For more on **direct references** and **transitional words and phrases,** see pages 375 and 376.

Transitional Expressions You can also use *transitional expressions*—words and phrases like *for example, therefore, of course,* or *on the other hand*—to connect ideas and make relationships clear.

Elaboration

Elaboration, the third element of good compositions, is the technique of supporting and explaining the thesis of a composition completely. This is achieved by including details, reasons, and evidence. Without proper elaboration, readers will be left confused or unconvinced. In some cases, such as in scientific reports, several paragraphs of elaboration may be needed to explain a certain point completely. In other cases, just a few paragraphs of elaboration may be sufficient. The amount of elaboration that you need depends on what you are trying to show. However, you should always strive to develop your thesis thoroughly and convincingly.

Exercise 5 **Analyzing Body Paragraphs**

Analyze the following pair of body paragraphs by answering these questions. Be prepared to explain your answers.

1. Identify the main idea that creates unity between the paragraphs.
2. Write a thesis statement that summarizes the main idea.
3. Identify examples of direct references and transitional expressions that the writer uses to show coherence between the two paragraphs.
4. Identify sentences in the second paragraph that elaborate on the main idea.

> I had come to the Science Center because I'd heard of its booming popularity and wondered what it was doing right. L.A. is, after all, a place of many diversions. It's got amusement parks galore, it's got beaches, it's got mountains, it's got celebrities out and about, along with year-round SPF-15 sun. In addition, there is the dismal 1996 report from the National Science Foundation, which states that "only 49 percent of Americans know that the Earth revolves around the sun once each year."
>
> *(continued)*

(continued)
So I wondered just what it takes these days to propel people . . . to visit, of all things, a science museum.

First off is free admission, although you do have to pony up five dollars for parking. There's the appeal of a big, airy, and all-around impressive brand-new building. Most important, presumably, are all the interactive exhibits that the museum hopes will generate some wonder about science in all these potential [National Science Foundation] grant applicants.

Mark Wheeler, "Science Friction," *Discover*

The Conclusion

The third element of compositions, the **conclusion,** is just as important as the introduction. Take advantage of the fact that the conclusion is the last thing your reader will see in your composition, and write a solid conclusion that completes the work of your introduction and body paragraphs. A strong conclusion should give the reader a sense that all of your ideas have been properly tied together and explained thoroughly. A composition that lacks a strong conclusion can leave the reader feeling puzzled. The following are some techniques that you can use to create effective conclusions.

1. **Restate the main idea.** Say it again, but use different words. This is probably the easiest kind of conclusion to write. When you use this technique, it works well to put the reworded version of your thesis statement at the beginning of the last paragraph. The following conclusion restates the thesis illustrated in the first model introduction on page 383.

   Is the Cadillac Ranch art? That is not for any one person to decide yes or no. However, if you are ever passing through Amarillo, Texas, why not make a stop at this roadside attraction and let your own eyes, mind, and heart continue the debate for yourself? Just watch your step for cacti and rattlers.

STYLE TIP

Oftentimes, descriptive and narrative compositions do not need distinctive conclusions separate from and following the body paragraphs. The description or experience is self-contained and does not require further elaboration or summarization.

2. **Refer to the introduction.** Bring the reader back full circle by referring to something in your introduction other than just the thesis.

> Returning home from my trip to the National Yo-Yo Museum, I searched in the attic, under the bed, and at the back of the closet, but found no yo-yos. Like fairies in Peter Pan, maybe yo-yos disappear when we stop believing in them. A 256-pound yo-yo demands attention and belief. Thanks to the people in Chico, California, though, this American treasure will continue to spark magic in all those who see it.

3. **End with a thoughtful comment, a personal reaction, or a look to the future.** Think of this kind of conclusion as a way to "extend" your thesis.

> Like Swampy the Gator in Christmas, Florida, or Salem Sue the cow in New Salem, North Dakota, roadside attractions are more than just humorous attempts at being "the biggest and the best." They are icons of pride in community. While they may not have the longevity of the pyramids or Stonehenge, they should stand as reminders to future generations of who we were and what we considered important.

4. **Use a quotation.** A quotation that is startling or moving works well to end a composition. Be sure to show how the quotation is relevant to your composition.

> Romain Gary wrote in *Promise at Dawn* that "humor is an affirmation of dignity, a declaration of man's superiority to all that befalls him." The dignity of Enterprise, Alabama, is evident in the Boll Weevil Monument, which remains the centerpiece of the downtown district. Through humor, the people of Enterprise have shown their superiority to the 1915 agricultural disaster that befell them.

5. **End with a call to action.** Persuasive essays often end by asking the reader to take a specific action. This method can make an effective ending for other kinds of compositions, too.

> Do not let America's proud tradition of roadside attractions fade into the past like its drive-in movie theaters and Burma Shave signs. Do your part to maintain any giant fiberglass animals or balls of twine in your town. Support retailers with colossal Muffler Men and anyone with the audacity to place giant pink inflatable gorillas in bikinis anywhere on their establishment. If your community does not have a "world's largest," don't you think perhaps it is time it did?

6. **Summarize the main points developed in the body.** Rephrase the topic sentences of each of your body paragraphs.

> Roadside attractions serve a purpose in asking the motorist speeding by at seventy-plus mph to slow down, stop by, and take a moment to see that our communities are more than just highway markers, gas stations, and blurs on the periphery. Giant yo-yos invite you to learn the history of this popular toy. Salem Sue and Swampy the Gator tell of the local economy or wildlife. Boll Weevil monuments tell the tale of perseverance in the face of adversity. However, behind it all are the people of America you might not ordinarily meet. As you stop and share a laugh with a fellow traveler or listen to a local tell his or her story, you are enriched in ways you never could have been if that roadside attraction had not prompted you to stop.

In formal compositions, writers often conclude with a restatement of the thesis followed by summaries of their main points. The structure for a formal conclusion is similar to reversing the "funnel" approach you learned for introductions (see page 388). In these conclusions, writers move from the specifics of their composition into a general final statement.

Specific
(restated thesis)

General

(see page 388)

see page 388

<aside>
S T Y L E   T I P

Although conclusions can vary in length, the typical conclusion to an in-school essay will have 3–4 sentences. Longer conclusions may indicate that material was not adequately covered within the body paragraphs or that too lengthy a restatement of the points presented is being given.
</aside>

Exercise 6 Improving a Conclusion

Here are the first drafts of conclusions for two compositions. With a partner, decide what is wrong with each conclusion. How can it be improved? Then, write better conclusions. You will need to infer the main idea of the compositions from the details in the paragraphs. You can change the paragraphs any way you like, make up details, or even start over completely.

1. That is why I think there should be ramps for people in wheelchairs and some sort of help for people with other disabilities. That does not even mention the problems they have getting decent jobs. I hope you will agree.

2. In conclusion, it is obvious that scuba diving is a hobby that people of all ages can enjoy. As I said in my introduction, "Scuba diving is a relaxing and unusual pastime that parents and children can share." Plus, scuba diving can be less expensive if you buy used equipment.

Using a Basic Framework

The following framework shows in a general way how an introduction, body, and conclusion come together to form a complete composition. Each of the Writing Workshops in this book has a more specific framework that provides guidelines for a particular type of writing.

Framework for Composition	
Introduction	• catches the reader's interest • sets the tone for the composition • presents the thesis statement
Body	• states the main points • provides support for the main points
Conclusion	• reinforces the main idea stated in the thesis statement • ties together the main points of the body • leaves the reader with a sense that the composition has been "wrapped up"

The following is the final draft of a composition on bicycle touring. You might want to use this composition as a model for a composition of your own.

Two-Wheel Holidays

INTRODUCTION

Automobiles speed along highways at sixty-five miles an hour or more. Bullet trains rocket down their tracks at nearly two hundred miles an hour. If that is not fast enough for you, the Concorde jet carries passengers faster than the speed of sound! However, despite faster means of transportation, more and more people are choosing to take day trips, overnights, or extended tours the slow way—by bicycle. If you are interested in bicycle touring, you will need to make some specific preparations involving your bike, yourself, your clothing, and your route.

Thesis statement

BODY
Major point:
Your bike

The first thing to consider is your bicycle. With so many types to choose from (road bikes, off-road bikes, mountain bikes, and all-terrain bikes) you can pick one that is appropriate for the kind of terrain on which you will be traveling. Whichever bike you choose, it should be in excellent condition. Equip the bike with a map, a light, a bicycle-repair kit, a first-aid kit, saddlebags for food and clothing, and a water carrier.

Major point:
Your physical
condition

Your bike may be in good shape, but what about you? Whether your trip is a few miles to the next town or across country, you need to get yourself in good physical condition. Start an exercise program and build up your muscles and endurance gradually. You should be able to cycle ten to fifteen miles a day easily.

Major point:
Your clothing

Now think about clothing. What you pack will depend on the season, but always prepare for possible bad weather. Pack rain gear and clothing that allows freedom of movement as it protects you from strong winds, wet, and cold. In general, avoid clothing that might interfere with your mobility or comfort, and be sure to wear a helmet. Head injuries are a cyclist's biggest worry.

Major point:
Safety

Bicycle safety does not end when you put on your helmet. Helmets provide some protection in case of an accident, but you are still better off avoiding accidents altogether—especially when you are sharing the road with motorists. Remember to ride to the right, on the shoulder or far in the right lane. Avoid busy roads if at all possible. Use lights, reflectors, and bright or light-colored clothing to make yourself visible to motorists. Finally, remember, always use hand signals to indicate turns or lane changes, just as you would use turn signals when driving a car.

Finally, talk to experienced cyclists and read books and magazines to plan your route. You may want to join the American Youth Hostels (AYH), which offers its members inexpensive lodging and group rides. Bicycling magazines appear each month with information and special features about bicycle touring. An organization called the Adventure Cycling Association publishes guidebooks, maps of the U.S. National Bicycle Trails Network, and a list of bicycle tour operators.

Major point: Planning your route

If you plan your trip well, you will discover that bicycle touring—alone or with a group—is more fun than faster ways of travel. Before you go, give yourself time to get your bike, your body, your clothing, and your route in top condition. Careful advance planning practically guarantees a safe trip.

CONCLUSION

Restatement of thesis

NOTE First-person (I) and second-person (you) points of view are typically used only in informal writing. Formal writing requires a sense of objectivity toward the topic and distance from the reader. For this type of writing, the third person (he, she, it, they) is the most acceptable. Consider your audience when deciding the level of formality you will be required to achieve.

COMPUTER TIP

While composing on the computer, remember to save your work every ten to fifteen minutes as you write, and keep backup copies of all your work.

Review B **Writing an Informative Composition**

You have learned that a composition has three parts:

introduction + body + conclusion = composition

You can use this structure for many **writing purposes**—to inform, to persuade, to describe, and to narrate. Use the facts below and on the following page to write a short informative composition about the Crazy Horse Memorial in South Dakota. You do not have to use all the information provided, but use as much as you need to make a complete composition. You may also add any information you can find through research or your own knowledge. Begin by developing a thesis statement. Then, create a good introduction and conclusion for the main points and elaboration in the body. Review the framework on page 397 to see how the parts should come together. Finally, evaluate and revise your composition to make sure that it demonstrates unity, coherence, and elaboration.

The Warrior, the Sculptor, and
the Crazy Horse Memorial

1. Crazy Horse signed no treaties and refused to move to a reservation.
2. Crazy Horse began an armed uprising when the U.S. government did not comply with the Treaty of 1868.
3. Crazy Horse, of the Lakota (Sioux) people, died in 1877 at age thirty-four.
4. When asked, "Where are your lands now," Chief Crazy Horse responded, "My lands are where my dead lie buried."
5. Korczak Ziolkowski assisted Gutzon Borglum in the carving of Mount Rushmore in the summer of 1939.
6. Interestingly, Mr. Ziolkowski is often referred to simply as Korczak.
7. In 1939, Sioux Chief Henry Standing Bear wrote to Korczak asking him to sculpt a mountain memorial: "My fellow chiefs and I would like the white man to know the red man has great heroes, too." This

was in reference to Mount Rushmore, on which work continued until 1941.

8. During early work on the memorial, Korczak had to climb up and down a 741-step staircase to deal with his gas-fueled compressor as many as nine times a day.

9. Korczak died in 1982, and his family continues working on the memorial to carry on his vision.

10. The fiftieth anniversary of the Crazy Horse Memorial was celebrated in 1998 with the unveiling and dedication of the completed face.

11. The completed memorial will be 563 feet tall and 641 feet long.

- The arm will be nearly the length of a football field.

- The head will be as big as all the Mount Rushmore heads combined.

- The completed head will be nearly seven stories tall.

- The horse's nostril will be large enough to hold a five-room house.

PART 3

Grammar, Usage, and Mechanics

internet connect

go.
hrw
.com

GO TO: go.hrw.com
KEYWORD: EOLang

Grammar

12 Parts of Speech Overview
13 The Parts of a Sentence
14 The Phrase
15 The Clause

Usage

16 Agreement
17 Using Pronouns Correctly
18 Using Verbs Correctly
19 Using Modifiers Correctly
20 A Glossary of Usage

Mechanics

21 Capitalization
22 Punctuation: End Marks and Commas
23 Punctuation: Semicolons and Colons
24 Punctuation: Italics, Quotation Marks, and Ellipsis Points
25 Punctuation: Apostrophes, Hyphens, Dashes, Parentheses, Brackets
26 Spelling
27 Correcting Common Errors

Parts of Speech Overview
Identification and Function

Diagnostic Preview

Determining the Parts of Speech of Words

Identify the part of speech of each italicized word or word group in the following paragraphs.

EXAMPLES   What were the **[1]** *most* common forms of transportation **[2]** *between* **[3]** *colonial* times and the twentieth **[4]** *century*?

　　1. adverb

　　2. preposition

　　3. adjective

　　4. noun

Since the [1] *condition* of the roads prevented [2] *extensive* use of wheeled vehicles, the most reliable means of transportation in colonial times was the [3] *saddle horse*. Some [4] *exceptionally* wealthy people kept carriages, but [5] *these* were usually heavy vehicles [6] *that* were pulled by two or more horses. Such carriages were [7] *satisfactory* for short trips, [8] *but* they were not practical for long journeys.

Stagecoaches were introduced in [9] *America* in about 1750. [10] *By* this time roads ran between such major cities as New York and

Boston. Although these roads [11] *were* little more than muddy tracks, [12] *most* were wide enough for a four-wheeled coach. [13] *Three* or four pairs of horses [14] *were harnessed* to a coach. Generally, however, the vehicles were so heavy that [15] *coach* horses tired [16] *quite* [17] *rapidly* [18] *and* had to be either rested frequently [19] *or* changed at post houses along the route. The design of horse-drawn vehicles soon improved, and until the early years of the twentieth century, buggies and wagons remained a common [20] *form* of transportation.

Nouns

12a. A *noun* names a person, a place, a thing, or an idea.

Persons	hero	teachers	audience	Mai Ling
Places	museum	countries	rain forest	San Diego
Things	stereo	songs	fences	Pacific Ocean
Ideas	sympathy	fairness	generosity	Impressionism

Exercise 1 **Identifying Nouns in Sentences**

Identify the nouns in the following sentences. Treat as single nouns all capitalized names containing more than one word.

EXAMPLE
1. Elizabeth Cady Stanton was born in the state of New York in 1815.

1. *Elizabeth Cady Stanton, state, New York*

HELP

You do not need to include years, such as *1815*, in your answers for Exercise 1.

1. As a young woman, Elizabeth Cady Stanton studied mathematics and the classics both at home and at Troy Female Seminary, from which she graduated in 1832.
2. Beginning at an early age, she recognized the injustices suffered by women, especially in education and politics.
3. In 1840, she married Henry Stanton, a prominent abolitionist.
4. At an antislavery convention in London, England, Mrs. Stanton was outraged at the treatment of the female delegates.
5. She later helped to organize the first meeting to address the rights of women.
6. At that convention, she read her "Declaration of Sentiments," outlining the inferior status of women and calling for reforms.

7. Among these reforms, the most controversial one was giving wom-en the right to vote.
8. In 1850, Stanton began working with Susan B. Anthony.
9. These two women did much work for the suffrage movement.
10. Stanton remained adamant about effecting change for the remainder of her life.

Common Nouns and Proper Nouns

Reference Note

For more on **capitalizing proper nouns,** see page 669.

A *common noun* names any one of a group of persons, places, things, or ideas. A *proper noun* names a particular person, place, thing, or idea. Generally, common nouns are not capitalized; proper nouns are.

Common Nouns	Proper Nouns
mountain	Mount McKinley
novelist	Louisa May Alcott
museum	Museum of Fine Arts
ship	*Queen Elizabeth 2*
movie	*Casablanca*

Compound Nouns

Reference Note

For information about **capitalizing the parts of a compound noun,** see page 669.

A *compound noun* consists of two or more words that together name a person, a place, a thing, or an idea. The parts of a compound noun may be written as one word, as separate words, or as a hyphenated word.

One Word	Separate Words	Hyphenated Word
basketball	civil rights	no-hitter
newspaper	Arts and Crafts Club	sister-in-law

NOTE   If you are not sure how to write a compound noun, look it up in an up-to-date dictionary. Some dictionaries may give two correct forms for a word. For example, you may find the word *vice-president* written both with and without the hyphen. Generally, use the form the dictionary lists first.

Exercise 2 Replacing Common Nouns with Proper Nouns and Identifying Compound Nouns

For each of the following common nouns, give a proper noun. Then, write *compound* next to each compound noun that you write.

EXAMPLE **1.** river

    1. Mississippi River—compound

1. play	**6.** newspaper	**11.** planet	**16.** actor
2. state	**7.** ocean	**12.** poet	**17.** explorer
3. street	**8.** writer	**13.** country	**18.** scientist
4. song	**9.** poem	**14.** friend	**19.** religion
5. president	**10.** car	**15.** continent	**20.** document

Concrete Nouns and Abstract Nouns

A *concrete noun* names a person, a place, or a thing that can be perceived by one or more of the senses (sight, hearing, taste, touch, and smell). An *abstract noun* names an idea, a feeling, a quality, or a characteristic.

Concrete Nouns	Abstract Nouns
dog	liberty
sunset	beauty
thunder	kindness
silk	success
Nile River	Buddhism

Collective Nouns

A *collective noun* names a group of people, animals, or things.

Collective Nouns		
audience	crowd	orchestra
batch	flock	pride
bouquet	gaggle	set
bunch	jury	staff
cluster	litter	swarm

Reference Note

For information on **using verbs with collective nouns,** see page 522.

┌─HELP─

The singular form of a collective noun names a group. Other kinds of nouns must be made plural to name a group.

Identify each of the italicized nouns in the following paragraph as *proper* or *common* and as *concrete* or *abstract.* Also, if the noun is a *compound noun* or a *collective noun,* label it as such.

EXAMPLE   Doesn't the Cajun **[1]** *dish* in the picture look delicious?

   1. common, concrete

Cajuns are descended from a **[1]** *group* of French settlers who were expelled from Acadia by the British in 1755. When some of these displaced people settled in the **[2]** *Atchafalaya Basin* in southeastern

Louisiana, they had to invent **[3]** *ways* to use local foods in their traditional French recipes. If you've never tried Cajun food, the crawfish in this picture may be unfamiliar to you. In **[4]** *addition* to the plentiful crawfish, shrimp, oysters, and other seafood, freshwater fish, alligator meat, **[5]** *rice,* and many **[6]** *spices* find their way into Cajun cooking. Gumbos are soups flavored with **[7]** *filé,* which is powdered sassafras leaves. **[8]** *Gumbos* often contain okra and sausage, chicken, or seafood. The **[9]** *popularity* of these and other Cajun dishes has spread throughout the **[10]** *United States* in recent years.

Pronouns

12b. A *pronoun* **takes the place of one or more nouns or pronouns.**

EXAMPLES   Susan watched the monkey make faces at her little brother and sister. **She** laughed at **it** more than **they** did. [*She* is used in place of *Susan,* it in place of *monkey,* and *they* in place of *brother* and *sister.*]

When others saw the monkey, **they** began laughing, too. [*They* takes the place of the pronoun *others.*]

The word or word group that a pronoun stands for is called the ***antecedent*** of the pronoun. In the first example above, *Susan* is the antecedent of *she, monkey* is the antecedent of *it,* and *brother* and *sister* are the antecedents of *they.* In the second example, *others* is the antecedent of *they.*

Reference Note

For information about **choosing pronouns that agree with their antecedents,** see page 532.

Personal Pronouns

A **personal pronoun** refers to the one(s) speaking (*first person*), the one(s) spoken to (*second person*), or the one(s) spoken about (*third person*).

	Singular	Plural
First Person	I, me, my, mine	we, us, our, ours
Second Person	you, your, yours	you, your, yours
Third Person	he, him, his, she, her, hers, it, its	they, them, their, theirs

EXAMPLES **I** hope that **you** can help **me** with **my** homework.

He said that **they** would meet **us** outside the theater.

NOTE This textbook refers to the words *my, your, his, her, its, our,* and *their* as possessive pronouns. However, because these words can come before nouns and tell *which one* or *whose,* some authorities prefer to call them adjectives. Follow your teacher's instructions regarding these possessive forms.

Reflexive and Intensive Pronouns

First Person	myself, ourselves
Second Person	yourself, yourselves
Third Person	himself, herself, itself, themselves

A **reflexive pronoun** refers to the subject of a sentence and functions as a complement or as an object of a preposition.

EXAMPLES I'm not quite **myself** today. [*Myself* is a predicate nominative identifying *I*.]

Cecilia let **herself** in through a trapdoor. [*Herself* is the direct object of *let*.]

They chose costumes for **themselves.** [*Themselves* is the object of the preposition *for*.]

Reference Note

For more information about **complements,** see page 450. For more about **objects of prepositions,** see page 426.

TIPS & TRICKS

To tell whether a pronoun is reflexive or intensive, use this simple test: Read the sentence aloud, and omit the pronoun. If the meaning of the sentence stays the same, the pronoun is most likely intensive. If not, the pronoun is probably reflexive.

EXAMPLE
She changed the tire herself. [*She changed the tire* makes sense. The pronoun *herself* is intensive.]

An *intensive pronoun* emphasizes its antecedent and has no grammatical function in the sentence.

EXAMPLES   Ray painted the mural **himself.**

The children dyed the eggs **themselves.**

Demonstrative Pronouns

A *demonstrative pronoun* points out a person, a place, a thing, or an idea.

this	that	these	those

Reference Note

For more about **demonstrative adjectives,** see page 414.

EXAMPLES   **This** is our favorite campsite.

The tomatoes we grew in the garden taste better than **these.**

NOTE   The words that can be used as demonstrative pronouns can also be used as adjectives.

PRONOUN   **This** tastes good.
ADJECTIVE   **This** hummus tastes good.

Interrogative Pronouns

An *interrogative pronoun* introduces a question.

who	whom	which	what	whose

EXAMPLES   **What** is the address of this house?

Whose is the red truck parked outside?

Relative Pronouns

Reference Note

For more about **relative pronouns** and **subordinate clauses,** see page 496.

A *relative pronoun* introduces a subordinate clause.

that	which	who	whom	whose

EXAMPLES   The dog **that** you trained is very well behaved.

She is the candidate **who** promises to listen to the people.

Indefinite Pronouns

An *indefinite pronoun* refers to a person, place, idea, or thing that may or may not be specifically named.

all	each other	most	one another
another	either	much	other
any	everybody	neither	several
anybody	everyone	nobody	some
anyone	everything	none	somebody
anything	few	no one	someone
both	many	nothing	something
each	more	one	such

EXAMPLES   **Everything** we will need is packed in the trunk.

Has **anyone** called for Mr. Reynolds?

NOTE Many of the pronouns you have studied so far may also be used as adjectives.

EXAMPLES   **that** oyster   **whose** pearl   **some** shells

Reference Note

For information about **distinguishing between pronouns and adjectives,** see page 414.

Exercise 3 Identifying Pronouns in Sentences

Identify the pronouns in each of the following sentences.

EXAMPLE   1. Let me tell you about one of the camping trips that I took last summer.

1. *me, you, one, that, I*

1. All of the other members of my family like to go camping, but few of them enjoy the outdoors more than I do.
2. Last summer several of my cousins and I stayed at a rustic camp in the Rocky Mountains, which are not far from our hometown.
3. At camp we learned how to build a campfire and how to keep it going ourselves.
4. A group of us even went beyond that—we learned to cook meals over the open fire.
5. One of our counselors showed those who were interested how to cook themselves simple meals.
6. Each of his recipes was delicious and easy to follow, and everyone ate everything in sight.
7. All of us enjoy anything cooked over an open fire.

HELP—

In Exercise 3, if a pronoun is used more than once, note it each time it appears.

GRAMMAR

8. We also enjoy telling stories while sitting beside the fire.

9. Sometimes everybody tells ghost stories.

10. Who wants to go to sleep afterward?

COMPUTER TIP

Using a computer software program's thesaurus can help you choose appropriate adjectives. To make sure that an adjective has exactly the connotation you intend, look up the word in a dictionary.

Adjectives

12c. An *adjective* modifies a noun or a pronoun.

To modify means "to describe" or "to make the meaning of a word more specific." An adjective is a modifier that tells *what kind, which one, how many,* or *how much.*

What Kind?	Which One?	How Many?	How Much?
spilled ink	**this** park	**twenty** miles	**no** salt
English tea	**these** papers	**two** men	**enough** water
howling winds	**that** house	**several** apples	**some** food

An adjective may be separated from the word it modifies.

EXAMPLES   She is **clever.**

The sky had become **cloudy** suddenly.

NOTE   An adjective that is in the predicate and that modifies the subject of a clause or sentence is called a *predicate adjective.*

Reference Note

For more information on **predicate adjectives,** see page 454.

Articles

The most frequently used adjectives are *a, an,* and *the.* These words are usually called *articles.*

   A and *an* are called *indefinite articles* because they refer to any member of a general group. *A* is used before a word beginning with a consonant sound; *an* is used before a word beginning with a vowel sound.

EXAMPLES   **A** park ranger helped us.

Shady Lane is **a** one-way street. [*One-way* begins with a consonant sound.]

They planted **an** acre with corn.

We kept watch for **an** hour. [*Hour* begins with a vowel sound.]

The is called the **definite article** because it refers to someone or something in particular.

EXAMPLES   **The** park ranger helped us.

They planted **the** acre with corn.

The hour dragged by.

Exercise 4   Identifying Adjectives and the Words They Modify

For the following sentences, identify each adjective and the word it modifies. (Do not include the articles *a*, *an*, and *the*.)

EXAMPLE   **1.** In the latter part of the nineteenth century, bicycling became a popular sport in the United States.

     1. latter—part; nineteenth—century; popular—sport

1. By the 1890s, an extraordinary craze for bicycling had swept the nation.

2. Though bicycles had been available for years, the early versions made for an awkward ride.

3. Ungainly cycles like the one in the picture had a very large wheel in the front and a small wheel in the back.

4. In 1885, however, a more sensible model was introduced, one that resembled the modern cycle.

5. Energetic people everywhere took to this kind of bicycle.

6. Bicycling soon became a national sport.

7. Cyclists joined special clubs that took vigorous tours through the countryside.

8. A typical ride might cover twenty miles, with a welcome stop along the way for refreshments.

9. Races were also popular with enthusiastic spectators, who often outnumbered those at ballgames.

10. The fans enjoyed watching these tests of endurance, which sometimes lasted six days.

GRAMMAR

Pronoun or Adjective?

Some words may be used either as adjectives or as pronouns. In this book, demonstrative, interrogative, and indefinite terms are called pronouns when they stand for other nouns or pronouns. They are called adjectives when they modify nouns or pronouns.

PRONOUN	**Which** did you choose, Roberto?
ADJECTIVE	**Which** book did you choose to read, Alex?

PRONOUN	**Those** are excited fans.
ADJECTIVE	**Those** fans are excited.

> **NOTE** The words *this, that, these,* and *those* are called **demonstrative adjectives** when they modify nouns or pronouns and are called **demonstrative pronouns** when they take the place of nouns or other pronouns.

In this book, the words *my, your, his, her, its, our,* and *their* are considered possessive pronouns. However, some authorities consider them to be adjectives. Follow your teacher's instructions on labeling these words.

Exercise 5 **Identifying Words as Adjectives or Pronouns**

Tell whether each italicized word in the following paragraph is used as a *pronoun* or an *adjective.* For each adjective, give the word it modifies.

EXAMPLES Of ants and wasps, [1] *which* do you think are considered [2] *antisocial*?

1. pronoun
2. adjective—which

Although ants are related to wasps, there are [1] *many* differences between [2] *these* two kinds of insects. [3] *All* ants are social insects. They live together in colonies, [4] *each* made up of three castes: a queen, males, and workers. Unlike ants, [5] *most* wasps are solitary insects. [6] *Most* of the 20,000 known species of wasps are solitary. Of [7] *these,* [8] *many* are hunting wasps [9] *that* make individual nests. [10] *These* wasps usually build their nests in the ground. [11] *Some* nest in wood or mud. However, not all wasps are antisocial; [12] *some* behave more like their cousins the ants. [13] *These* wasps live in permanent colonies of adults and young. While [14] *most* wasps are solitary, there are about 1,000 species of social wasps. Among the best-known social wasps are [15] *those* within a group that, like ants, has a caste system in [16] *its* societies. The queen builds a small nest consisting of a [17] *few* cells, and then she lays eggs. [18] *These* hatch into workers. The workers enlarge the nest, [19] *which* is made of material that has been chewed, regurgitated, and mixed with saliva. [20] *Some* of the best-known social wasps are yellow jackets and hornets.

Noun or Adjective?

When a word that can be used as a noun modifies a noun or pronoun, it is called an adjective.

EXAMPLES   **salad** bowl   **chicken** dinner

                  New England states   **gold** medal

> **NOTE** Notice in the preceding examples that the proper noun *New England* remains capitalized when it is used as an adjective. An adjective that is formed from a proper noun is called a ***proper adjective.***

Some word groups are considered compound nouns.

EXAMPLES   salad dressing   chicken hawk   New England clam chowder

By checking an up-to-date dictionary, you can avoid mistaking a word that is part of a compound noun for a word that is considered a separate adjective.

Reference Note

For more information about capitalizing **proper adjectives,** see page 669. For more about **compound nouns,** see page 406.

Review B   **Identifying Nouns, Pronouns, and Adjectives**

Identify the nouns, pronouns, and adjectives in the following sentences. For each adjective, give the word it modifies. (Do not include the articles *a, an,* and *the.*)

EXAMPLE   **1.** Several different kinds of butterflies flew around us.

        1. nouns—kinds; butterflies

           pronoun—us

           adjectives—several (kinds); different (kinds)

1. Our teacher, Mr. López, identified the various trees along the nature trail.

2. Many people are working to clean up polluted rivers and streams to make them livable environments for wildlife again.

3. The flag over the hotel was a welcome sight to the two travelers.
4. The antique doll was dressed in a sailor hat and a blue suit.
5. A large cake sat in the center of the kitchen table.
6. Along the Hudson River, autumn leaves colored the highway with bright splashes of orange and red.
7. Someone has filled the fruit bowl with dates and walnuts.
8. As a young girl, Susan B. Anthony was taught Quaker religious tenets, which include the belief in the equality of all people.
9. The bird feeder in the elm tree in my yard attracts cardinals, robins, and chickadees.
10. The dust jacket of that literature anthology has certainly seen better days.

Review C **Identifying Nouns, Pronouns, and Adjectives**

Identify each numbered, underlined word in the following paragraph as a *noun*, a *pronoun*, or an *adjective*.

EXAMPLE The Spanish built the first *ranchos,* or ranches, that were in the [1] United States.

1. *noun*

Californians Catching Wild Horses with Riata by Hugo Wilhelm Arthur Nahl (1833–1889), Oil on canvas mounted on masonite $19\frac{5}{8}$ x $23\frac{3}{4}$″. Collection of the Oakland Museum, Kahn Collection.

The [1] man in this picture is a *vaquero,* but you can call [2] him a cowboy. *Vaqueros* got their name from the [3] Spanish word *vaca,* which means "cow." In fact, cowboys were at [4] home on the range in Mexico long before they gained [5] legendary status in the United States. Notice that this *vaquero* wears [6] leather chaps (*chaparejos*) to protect his legs and uses a [7] lariat (*la reata*) to rope the steer. [8] Many other words that we associate with cowboys came into the English language from [9] Spanish. [10] These include *rodeo, stampede,* and *bronco.*

Verbs

12d. A *verb* expresses action or a state of being.

In this textbook, verbs are classified in three ways: (1) as main or helping verbs, (2) as action or linking verbs, and (3) as transitive or intransitive verbs.

Main Verbs and Helping Verbs

A *verb phrase* consists of one *main verb* and one or more *helping verbs* (also called *auxiliary verbs*).

EXAMPLES   I **am reading** Thomas Hardy's novel *Under the Greenwood Tree*. [*Am* is a helping verb. *Reading* is the main verb.]

We **should have been listening** instead of talking. [*Should, have,* and *been* are helping verbs. *Listening* is the main verb.]

Commonly Used Helping Verbs				
Forms of *Be*	am	be	being	was
	are	been	is	were
Forms of *Have*	had	has	have	having
Forms of *Do*	did	do	does	
Modals	can	might	shall	would
	could	must	should	
	may	ought	will	

NOTE A *modal* is an auxiliary verb that is used to express an attitude toward the action or state of being of the main verb.

EXAMPLE   I **may** go to the concert after all. [The modal *may* expresses an attitude of possibility in relation to the main verb *go.*]

Helping verbs may be separated from the main verb.

EXAMPLE   **Did** she **paint** the house?

NOTE The word *not* and its contraction, *n't*, are never part of a verb phrase. Instead, they are adverbs telling *to what extent*.

Reference Note
For more about **modals,** see page 599.

Reference Note
For more about **adverbs,** see page 422.

GRAMMAR

Exercise 6 Identifying Verbs and Verb Phrases

Identify the verbs and verb phrases in the following sentences. Be sure to include all helping verbs.

EXAMPLE 1. The marching band would be performing during half time.

1. *would be performing*

1. Because of the cold weather, the members of the band worried about their half-time performance.
2. Marcia and the other saxophone players were clapping their hands vigorously so that their fingers wouldn't become even more numb in the raw, icy air.
3. They imagined what would happen if their fingers froze to the keys of their instruments.
4. Instead of music, harsh noise would blare out and probably startle the spectators.
5. The other band members would likely skip a beat, and chaos would soon spread across the field.
6. Out of step, the flute players might well stumble into the clarinet players, collide with the trombone players, or even trip over the drummers.
7. When half time was called, Marcia and her friends rolled their eyes and laughed about the dreadful scene they had just pictured.
8. Such a disaster couldn't possibly happen, could it?
9. As the band marched onto the field, large, white snowflakes swirled in the air and settled on the brand-new uniforms and shiny instruments.
10. Some people were leaving the stands when the principal announced over the loudspeaker: "Ladies and gentlemen, the band will now play 'Jingle Bells.'"

Action Verbs and Linking Verbs

An *action verb* expresses either physical or mental activity.

| PHYSICAL | bring | say | shout | jump | breathe |
| MENTAL | ponder | trust | review | evaluate | guess |

EXAMPLES Please **return** this book. [*Return* expresses physical action.]

Do you **know** Han? [*Do know* expresses mental action.]

A *linking verb* connects the subject to a word or word group that identifies or describes the subject. Such a word or word group is called a *subject complement.*

EXAMPLES   Kelp **is** the scientific name for seaweed. [The subject complement *name* identifies the subject *Kelp.*]

Kelp **has been** a good source of iodine. [The subject complement *source* identifies the subject *Kelp.*]

Kelp **tastes** good in salads. [The subject complement *good* describes the subject *Kelp.*]

As it ages, kelp **becomes** brown. [The subject complement *brown* describes the subject *kelp.*]

Reference Note

For more information about **subject complements,** see page 453.

GRAMMAR

Commonly Used Linking Verbs			
Forms of *Be*			
be	were	shall have been	should be
being	shall be	will have been	would be
am	will be	can be	could be
is	has been	may be	should have been
are	have been	might be	would have been
was	had been	must be	could have been
Others			
appear feel look seem sound taste			
become grow remain smell stay turn			

Some of the verbs listed as *Others* in the previous chart can be used as action verbs as well as linking verbs.

LINKING   Emilia **felt** calm at the seashore.
ACTION   Emilia **felt** the waving strands of kelp.

The forms of *be* are not always used as linking verbs. That is, they do not always link a subject to a subject complement. Instead of a subject complement, an adverb that tells *where* or *when* may follow the form of *be.* In such cases, the verb *be* is called a *state-of-being verb.*

EXAMPLE   My friends and I **were** there yesterday. [The verb *were* is followed not by a subject complement but by *there*, which tells *where*, and by *yesterday*, which tells *when*.]

TIPS & TRICKS

To determine whether a verb in a sentence is a linking verb, substitute a form of the verb *be.* If the sentence makes sense, the verb is most likely a linking verb.

LINKING

Emilia **felt** calm at the seashore. [The verb *was* can sensibly replace *felt: Emilia was calm at the seashore.*]

ACTION

Emilia **felt** the waving strands of kelp. [The verb *was* cannot sensibly replace *felt.*]

Exercise 7 Identifying Verbs as Action Verbs or Linking Verbs

Identify each italicized verb in the following sentences as an *action verb* or a *linking verb*.

EXAMPLE 1. The ancient Egyptians *built* a grand temple for Amon-Re, their chief deity.

1. action verb

1. Situated on the banks of the Nile River in Egypt, these ruins at Karnak *are* some of the most impressive sights in the world.
2. The largest structure there *is* the Great Temple of Amon-Re.
3. As you can see, its immense size *dwarfs* people.
4. The 42-meter-high gateway *amazes* visitors who follow the avenue of sphinxes that leads to the entrance.
5. The ceiling of the temple *rests* more than 23 meters above the floor.

6. Of course, the central columns that support the stone roof *look* enormous.
7. Carvings *decorate* the surfaces of these huge columns.
8. Even an amateur engineer *can appreciate* the tremendous efforts that must have gone into the completion of this temple.
9. We now *know* that inclined planes, combined with levers and blocking, enabled the ancient Egyptians to raise the large stones.
10. A remarkable technical achievement, the Great Temple of Amon-Re today *remains* a monument to the ancient builders' skills.

Exercise 8 Writing Sentences Using Verbs as Both Linking and Action Verbs

For each of the following verbs, write two sentences. In the first sentence, use the verb as a linking verb; in the second sentence, use it as an action verb.

EXAMPLE 1. become

1. *We become older by the day.*
   That hat becomes her.

1. appear	**3.** smell	**5.** look	**7.** remain	**9.** taste
2. sound	**4.** grow	**6.** feel	**8.** stay	**10.** turn

Transitive Verbs and Intransitive Verbs

A *transitive verb* has an *object*—a word that tells who or what receives the action of the verb.

EXAMPLES   She **trusts** her friend. [The object *friend* receives the action of the verb *trusts*.]

              Zora Neale Hurston **wrote** novels. [The object *novels* receives the action of the verb *wrote*.]

An *intransitive verb* does not have an object.

EXAMPLES   The audience **applauded.**

              The train **stops** here.

The same verb may be transitive in one sentence and intransitive in another.

TRANSITIVE   Elsa **swam** the channel. [The object *channel* receives the action of the verb *swam*.]

INTRANSITIVE   Elsa **swam** for many hours. [no object]

TRANSITIVE   Miss Castillo **weeds** the garden every day. [The object *garden* receives the action of the verb *weeds*.]

INTRANSITIVE   Miss Castillo **weeds** every day. [no object]

> **NOTE**   Action verbs can be transitive or intransitive. All linking verbs are intransitive.
>
> ACTION   I **studied** my geometry notes for an hour. [transitive]
>
>   Luis also **studied** for an hour. [intransitive]
>
> LINKING   We **are** ready for the quiz. [intransitive]

Like a one-word verb, a verb phrase may be classified as *transitive* or *intransitive* and as *action* or *linking*.

EXAMPLES   We **are planting** some cactus dahlias. [transitive action]

              They **should bloom** in about six weeks. [intransitive action]

              The flowers **will be** deep red. [intransitive linking]

Reference Note

For more about **objects of verbs,** see page 455.

GRAMMAR

"I MISS THE GOOD OLD DAYS WHEN ALL WE HAD TO WORRY ABOUT WAS NOUNS AND VERBS."

© 1984 by Sidney Harris-Punch.

─HELP─

If you are not sure whether a verb is transitive or intransitive, look in a dictionary. Most dictionaries group the definitions of verbs according to whether the verbs are used transitively (*v.t.*) or intransitively (*v.i.*).

Identifying Verbs as Transitive or Intransitive

Identify the verb in each of the following sentences, and tell whether it is *transitive* or *intransitive.*

EXAMPLE   1. We eagerly anticipated our trip to the seashore.

1. *anticipated—transitive*

1. The strong winds died down.
2. We quickly packed a lunch for our trip to the seashore.
3. The whitecaps on the ocean disappeared.
4. The sunlight sparkled on the splashing surf.
5. At low tide, Rosita suddenly spotted a starfish.
6. She noticed its five purplish arms.
7. She touched a soft, brown sponge floating nearby.
8. Three shore crabs swam in the tidal pool.
9. The beach was alive with interesting creatures.
10. Have you seen the ocean?

Adverbs

12e. An *adverb* modifies a verb, an adjective, or another adverb.

An adverb tells *how, when, where,* or *to what extent* (*how much, how long,* or *how often*).

Adverbs Modifying Verbs

EXAMPLES   The bird was chirping **outside.** [*where*]
The bird chirped **today.** [*when*]
The bird chirped **loudly.** [*how*]
The bird **never** chirped. [*to what extent*]

Identifying Adverbs and the Verbs They Modify

Identify the adverbs in the following sentences. For each adverb, give the verb that it modifies.

EXAMPLE   1. The Montgolfier brothers worked steadily and earnestly to build the first hot-air balloon.

1. *steadily—worked, earnestly—worked*

⎡TIPS ⅋ TRICKS⎤

Many adverbs end in *–ly.* However, not all words ending in *–ly* are adverbs. For instance, the following words are adjectives: *homely, kindly, lovely,* and *deadly.* To tell whether a word is an adverb, ask yourself these questions:

- Does the word modify a verb, an adjective, or an adverb?

- Does the word tell *when, where, how,* or *to what extent?*

1. Birds, bats, and bugs fly effortlessly.
2. During the eighteenth century, a few creatures involuntarily entered the skies.
3. In 1783, an unpiloted balloon was tested, and a hot-air balloon carrying a sheep, rooster, and duck was launched later in the year.
4. Humans successfully flew for the first time in November of 1783.
5. The first balloonists floated gently above Paris in a hot-air balloon that had been cleverly designed by the Montgolfier brothers.
6. Although their earlier attempts had failed, the Montgolfiers kept trying and finally settled on a balloon made of paper and linen.
7. Early balloons differed significantly from modern balloons like those pictured, which are sturdily constructed of coated nylon.
8. Despite their ingenuity, the Montgolfiers originally thought that smoke, rather than hot air, would effectively push their balloon skyward.
9. In their experiments, they initially produced hot smoke by burning straw and wool.
10. Balloonists greatly appreciated the discovery that dense smoke was not a requirement for flight.

Adverbs Modifying Adjectives

EXAMPLES   It was a **fiercely** competitive game. [The adverb *fiercely* modifies the adjective *competitive*.]

The **exceptionally** brave police officer was given an award. [The adverb *exceptionally* modifies the adjective *brave*.]

Exercise 11   Identifying Adverbs and the Adjectives They Modify

In each of the following sentences, an adverb modifies an adjective. Identify the adverb and the adjective it modifies.

EXAMPLE   1. A wagon train traveling to northern California carried a considerably large number of pioneers.

       1. *adverb—considerably; adjective—large*

1. The immensely long wagon train started out from Denver, Colorado.
2. Both oxen and mules were used to pull unusually large wagons.
3. Even in good weather, the long trail through the mountains was fairly hazardous.
4. A moderately hard rain could turn the trail into a swamp.
5. When the trail was too muddy, the heavier wagons became mired.

| STYLE   TIP |

Some of the most frequently used adverbs are *too, so, really,* and *very.* In your writing, try to avoid these overused words. Some adverbs that are less common are given below:
  completely
  dangerously
  definitely
  dreadfully
  entirely
  especially
  generally
  particularly
  rather
  surprisingly
  unusually

6. Wagons that were extremely heavy had to be unloaded before they could be moved.
7. Stopping for the night along the trail was a consistently welcome experience.
8. It offered relief to thoroughly tired bones and muscles.
9. Nights in the mountains could be quite cold.
10. On terribly cold nights, the travelers would roll up in blankets and sleep near their campfires.

Adverbs Modifying Other Adverbs

EXAMPLES The guide spoke **extremely** slowly. [The adverb *extremely* modifies the adverb *slowly,* telling *to what extent* the guide spoke *slowly.*]

We will go to the mall **later** today. [The adverb *later* modifies the adverb *today,* telling *when* today.]

Noun or Adverb?

Some words may be used as either nouns or adverbs. When identifying parts of speech, classify words that are used to modify verbs, adjectives, and adverbs as adverbs.

NOUN I was at **home.**
ADVERB "Be **home** by nine o'clock," Dad said.

NOUN **Tomorrow** is another day.
ADVERB Do you want to go to the zoo **tomorrow**?

Exercise 12 Identifying Adverbs and the Words They Modify

Identify the adverb or adverbs in each of the following sentences. After each adverb, give the word it modifies and the part of speech of that word.

EXAMPLE 1. My sister Juana and I often had talked about getting a houseplant for our room.
1. *often—had talked (verb)*

1. A couple of months ago, Juana and I finally decided to buy a houseplant for the kitchen.
2. The large ones we saw were too expensive for us.
3. Suddenly, Juana had a brainstorm.
4. "Let's buy some seeds and grow them indoors."

Reference Note
For information on adverbs used to join words or word groups, see **relative adverbs** on page 497 and **conjunctive adverbs** on page 492.

5. At the seed store, the owner, Mrs. Miller, greeted us cheerfully.
6. We explained that we wanted to grow a large plant but that our room never gets bright sunlight and that in the winter it can be especially chilly and dark.
7. "These are seeds of the bo tree, an unusually hardy member of the fig family native to India," said Mrs. Miller.
8. "There, this tree is sacred to Buddhists because it is said that the Buddha received enlightenment under a bo tree."
9. When we got back to our house, we planted the seeds.
10. In a short time, they sprouted, and we now have an unusual houseplant that is suited to our environment.

Exercise 13 Using Words as Adjectives and Adverbs

Write a pair of sentences for each word. In the first sentence, use the word as an adjective; in the second, use it as an adverb.

EXAMPLE   1. kindly
  1. *She had a kindly manner.—adjective*
    She spoke kindly.—adverb

1. daily	**3.** late	**5.** far	**7.** further	**9.** straight
2. fast	**4.** more	**6.** early	**8.** hard	**10.** right

Review D Identifying Parts of Speech

Identify the part of speech of each italicized word or word group in the following paragraphs. If the word is an adjective or an adverb, be prepared to tell what it modifies.

EXAMPLES   Without warning, the [1] *serenity* of the [2] *snow-covered* mountains is assaulted.
  1. *noun*
  2. *adjective*

With a [1] *thunderous* roar, a mighty avalanche [2] *crashes* [3] *headlong* down the mountainside. [4] *Some* of these slides travel at speeds of more than 200 miles an hour and pose a [5] *deadly* threat to skiers, mountain climbers, and the people [6] *who* live and work in the mountains.

One [7] *common* suggestion for surviving an avalanche is to make swimming motions to remain on top of the snow. However, people caught in avalanches [8] *rarely* can save [9] *themselves*. They are [10] *usually* immobilized, and the slide [11] *forces* snow into their nose and mouth.

HELP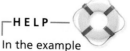

In the example for Review D, the adjective *snow-covered* modifies the noun *mountains*.

Avalanche workers in the [12] *United States* and abroad have [13] *long* realized the [14] *potential* [15] *destructiveness* of certain slide paths. The workers [16] *have concluded* that an avalanche can be [17] *greatly* reduced if [18] *explosives* [19] *are used* to trigger a [20] *series* of [21] *smaller* slides before [22] *one* large mass of snow can build up. [23] *Today,* the detonation of explosives has become a standard [24] *practice* for controlling avalanches in [25] *this* country.

Prepositions

12f. A *preposition* is a word that shows the relationship of a noun or a pronoun, called the ***object of the preposition,*** to another word.

Notice in the following examples how the prepositions show different relationships between the verb *rode* and *village*, the object of each preposition.

EXAMPLES   I rode **past** the village.   I rode **near** the village.

I rode **through** the village.   I rode **around** the village.

I rode **toward** the village.   I rode **beyond** the village.

NOTE   A preposition, its object, and any modifiers of the object form a ***prepositional phrase.***

STYLE TIP

In formal writing and speaking, you should avoid using a preposition at the end of a sentence when possible.

INFORMAL
Jaime asked me to name some people whom I look up to.

Sometimes rearranging such sentences results in an awkward or pretentious construction.

AWKWARD
Jaime asked me to name some people up to whom I look.

In formal situations, therefore, it is often best to reword sentences to avoid using such expressions.

FORMAL
Jaime asked me to name some people whom I **admire.**

Reference Note

For more about **prepositional phrases,** see page 467.

Commonly Used Prepositions			
aboard	below	for	past
about	beneath	from	since
above	beside	in	through
across	besides	inside	to
after	between	into	toward
against	beyond	like	under
along	but (meaning	near	underneath
amid	except)	of	until
among	by	off	up
around	concerning	on	upon
at	down	onto	with
before	during	outside	within
behind	except	over	without

A preposition that consists of two or more words is called a *compound preposition.*

EXAMPLES The soccer game was delayed **because of** rain.

Who is sitting **in front of** Arturo?

Commonly Used Compound Prepositions		
according to	in addition to	instead of
because of	in front of	on account of
by means of	in spite of	prior to

Preposition or Adverb?

Some words may be used as either prepositions or adverbs. Remember that an adverb is a modifier and does not have an object.

PREPOSITION Marge climbed **down** the ladder.
ADVERB Marge climbed **down** carefully.

PREPOSITION **Above** the dry riverbed, buzzards circled lazily.
ADVERB **Above,** buzzards circled lazily.

NOTE As a preposition, the word *to* precedes a noun or a pronoun to form a prepositional phrase. Do not confuse such a prepositional phrase with an *infinitive*—a verb form preceded by *to.*

PREPOSITIONAL PHRASES	to the library	to her	to Louisiana
INFINITIVES	to create	to play	to compare

Reference Note
For more information on **infinitives,** see page 479.

Exercise 14 **Writing Sentences Using Words as Prepositions and as Adverbs**

For each of the following words, write two sentences. In the first sentence, use the word as a preposition and underline the prepositional phrase. In the second sentence, use the word as an adverb. Be prepared to tell which word the adverb modifies.

HELP
In the second example sentence for Exercise 14, the adverb *in* modifies the verb phrase *are going.*

EXAMPLE 1. in
1. We are going <u>in the house</u> now.
We are going in now.

1. around 3. inside 5. up 7. outside 9. by
2. under 4. on 6. below 8. past 10. aboard

GRAMMAR

Reference Note

For a discussion of using **conjunctions in sentence combining,** see page 357. For the rules governing the use of **punctuation with conjunctions,** see pages 358, 703, and 724.

Conjunctions

12g. A *conjunction* joins words or word groups.

Coordinating Conjunctions

Coordinating conjunctions join words or word groups that are used in the same way.

Coordinating Conjunctions			
and	but	for	nor
or	so	yet	

TIPS & TRICKS

You can remember the coordinating conjunctions as FANBOYS:
For
And
Nor
But
Or
Yet
So

EXAMPLES   The orchestra played waltzes **and** polkas. [*And* joins two nouns.]

We can walk to the neighborhood pool **or** to the park. [*Or* joins two prepositional phrases.]

I looked for Hal, **but** he had already left. [*But* joins two clauses.]

Correlative Conjunctions

Correlative conjunctions are pairs of conjunctions that join words or word groups that are used in the same way.

Correlative Conjunctions	
both . . . and	not only . . . but also
either . . . or	whether . . . or
neither . . . nor	

Reference Note

Another kind of conjunction, the **subordinating conjunction,** is discussed with **subordinate clauses,** on page 498.

EXAMPLES   **Neither** the baseball team **nor** the soccer team has practice today.

Both the track team **and** the volleyball team enjoyed a winning season.

Their victories sparked the enthusiasm **not only** of students **but also** of teachers and townspeople.

Exercise 15 Identifying Coordinating and Correlative Conjunctions

Identify the coordinating conjunctions and correlative conjunctions in the following sentences.

EXAMPLE   **1.** When did whaling and the whaling industry begin to decline?

       1. and

1. Once, Nantucket and New Bedford, Massachusetts, were home ports of huge whaling fleets.
2. Whaling brought tremendous profits into these ports, but the golden days of whaling ended about the same time as the U.S. Civil War.
3. Even when it was successful, a whaling trip was no pleasure cruise for either the captain or the crew.
4. The living conditions were often quite dreadful, so maintaining order was no easy task on a long voyage.
5. Inevitably, the sailors had time on their hands, for they didn't encounter a whale every day.
6. To relieve the monotony and resulting boredom, the crews of whaling ships often would exchange visits.
7. Both the captains and their crew members looked forward to such visits.
8. The sailors enjoyed the opportunity not only to chat but also to exchange news.
9. The decline of whaling and of the whaling industry was signaled by the development of a new fuel.
10. By 1860, our country no longer needed large quantities of whale oil because kerosene, a cheaper and better fuel, had replaced it.

Interjections

12h. An *interjection* expresses emotion. An interjection has no grammatical relation to the rest of the sentence.

Interjections						
ah	ouch	ugh	wow	oops	hey	oh

STYLE **TIP**

Interjections are common in casual conversation. In writing, however, they are usually used only in informal notes and letters, in advertisements, and in dialogue.

An interjection is generally set off from the rest of the sentence by an exclamation point or by a comma or commas. Exclamation points indicate strong emotion. Commas indicate mild emotion.

EXAMPLES   **Whew!** What a day I've had!

            Well, I'm just not sure.

            There must be**, oh my,** a dozen snakes there.

Exercise 16   **Using Interjections**

Using the interjections from the list provided, complete the following sentences. Be sure to use the words as interjections and not as adjectives or adverbs.

EXAMPLE   **1.** ____ Wait for me!

        1. Hey!

excellent	well	whoa	ouch	wow
oops	whew	hey	cool	yow

  1. ____ that's hot!
  2. ____ I forgot to do my homework.
  3. ____ our teacher didn't collect the assignments today.
  4. ____ tomorrow is a holiday!
  5. ____ I can't decide; both puppies are adorable.
  6. ____ he didn't know you were an athlete.
  7. ____ she won the race!
  8. ____ what time are you going home?
  9. ____ my name was drawn in the raffle!
10. ____ our runner was passed inches away from the finish line!

Determining Parts of Speech

12i. The way a word is used in a sentence determines what part of speech the word is.

The same word may be used as different parts of speech. To figure out what part of speech the boldface word is in each of the following sentences, read the entire sentence. What you are doing is studying the **context**—the way the word is used in the sentence. From the context, you can identify the part of speech that *light* or *help* is in each of the following sentences.

EXAMPLES   Rich heard the **light** patter of raindrops. [adjective]

The flash of **light** hurt her eyes. [noun]

Use care when you **light** the fire. [verb]

Please **help** your sister with her homework. [verb]

I will provide **help,** but I won't do your work for you. [noun]

If you can't find the answer in the instruction manual, you may have to call the **help** desk. [adjective]

Exercise 17 Determining the Parts of Speech of Words

Determine the part of speech of the italicized word in each of the following sentences. Be prepared to explain your answers.

EXAMPLES   **1.** Marisa holds the school *record* for the 100-meter dash.

1. *noun*

2. Marisa ran the race in *record* time.

2. *adjective*

1. They decided that the hedge needed a *trim*.
2. Their hedges always look *trim* and neat.
3. We usually *trim* the tree with homemade ornaments.
4. Mom always *shears* a couple of inches off the top of the tree.
5. Later, she uses *shears* to cut straggling branches.
6. I wasn't thirsty, but I did *down* one glass of water before finishing my workout.
7. Dale ran *down* the stairs and hugged his sister.
8. "If heights bother you, don't look *down*," the guide warned.
9. I asked for Tuesday off, *but* my boss gave me Monday off instead.
10. All *but* two of the students voted in the class elections.

┌─**HELP**──

In the first example, *record* is a noun functioning as the direct object of the verb *holds*. In the second example, *record* functions as an adjective modifying *time*.

Review E Writing Sentences Using Words as Different Parts of Speech

Write two sentences for each of the following words, using the word as a different part of speech in each sentence. At the end of the sentence, write what part of speech the word is in that sentence.

EXAMPLE   **1.** hand

1. *Jesse hurt his hand. (noun)*
   Please hand me the biscuits. (verb)

1. long	**3.** back	**5.** iron	**7.** tie	**9.** outside
2. cut	**4.** fast	**6.** some	**8.** for	**10.** empty

Determining the Parts of Speech of Words

Identify the part of speech of each italicized word or word group in the following paragraph.

EXAMPLES   The **[1]** *homes* of many **[2]** *of* the early farmers on the Great Plains **[3]** *were* **[4]** *quite* **[5]** *primitive*.

1. noun   3. verb   5. adjective
2. preposition   4. adverb

[1] *Early* farmers on the [2] *Great Plains* eked out a rough existence, [3] *for* there were few towns, stores, or other signs of civilization. [4] *Many* farm homes were constructed mostly of sod bricks, [5] *which* were cut [6] *out of* the prairie. Trees were in short supply on these windswept lands, but the resourceful settler might find a few [7] *cottonwoods* growing [8] *along* a creek or river. [9] *These* [10] *could be used* to build a frame for the roof, which was then covered [11] *lightly* with grassy earth. Grass, both [12] *on* the roof [13] *and* in the sod, helped to hold

the house together. Some of [14] *these* rugged homes had a door made of timber, but [15] *quite* often a cowhide [16] *was draped* across the entrance. [17] *Inside* was a dirt floor covered with a bearskin [18] *or* a buffalo hide. As more settlers moved [19] *west*, bringing furnishings and [20] *building* materials, farmers eventually abandoned these first, primitive dwellings and built homes that were more conventional.

Writing Sentences with Words Used as Different Parts of Speech

Use each of the following words or groups of words in a sentence. Then, indicate what part of speech the word or word group is.

EXAMPLE   **1.** gold

1. *Tamisha bought a gold bracelet. (adjective)*

1. novel
2. Park Avenue
3. this
4. are laughing
5. yesterday
6. tomorrow
7. or
8. quietly
9. both . . . and
10. silver
11. hiked
12. oh
13. tasted
14. but
15. often
16. inside
17. underneath
18. appeared
19. whew
20. in

Chapter Review

A. Identifying the Parts of Speech in Sentences

For each of the following sentences, identify each italicized word as a *noun,* an *adjective,* a *verb,* an *adverb,* a *pronoun,* a *preposition,* a *conjunction,* or an *interjection.*

1. In the late nineteenth century, many men *worked* as cowboys on *cattle* drives.
2. There *were few* comforts on the trail.
3. Some *improvement* came after *Charles Goodnight* put together the first chuck wagon.
4. A hinged lid swung *down* from the wagon to reveal a simple *but* complete kitchen.
5. The *first* chuck wagons were pulled *by* oxen.
6. *These* were later replaced by mules *or* horses.
7. *Most* of the cowhands who took part in the historic cattle drives remain *nameless.*
8. Cowboys were *instrumental* in opening trails that were later used by the men and women who *settled* the frontier.
9. *Railroads soon* began to crisscross the country; the cowboy was no longer needed to drive cattle.
10. *Hey!* Did you know that ranchers still hire *cowboys* to brand and herd cattle, repair fences, and do many other jobs?

B. Identifying the Parts of Speech in a Paragraph

Identify the part of speech of the italicized word or words in each sentence in the following paragraph.

[11] In the *thirty* years following the Civil War, millions of long-horn cattle were driven *over* long trails from ranches in Texas to rail-roads in Kansas. [12] During this *period,* the cowboy *became* an American hero. [13] Novels *and* magazine articles *glorified* life on the range. [14] The men *who* rode this rugged land, however, had to endure *many* hardships. [15] Cowboys spent most of their *time* in the saddle, rounding up strays and moving the herd *along.* [16] Caring for sick animals, repairing fences, and, *well,* doing what had to be done *were* all part of a normal working day. [17] At the end of such a day, each cow-

boy *not only* had to look after his horse *but also* had to cook dinner for *himself* and do a host of other chores. [18] The quiet *evenings* gave cowboys a chance to relax by telling stories and singing *campfire* songs. [19] Such details of trail life are *realistically* portrayed in the *popular* paintings of Charles M. Russell. [20] *Because of* these images and our need for a *truly* American hero, cowboys have become a colorful part of our history.

C. Identifying Pronouns in Sentences

Identify the pronouns in each sentence as *personal, reflexive, intensive, demonstrative, interrogative, relative* or *indefinite.*

21. They delivered their supplies themselves.

22. One of their colleagues spent all summer teaching himself French.

23. A few pooled their resources and decided to send these to Aunt Joan.

24. Who has been raking the leaves in the backyard?

25. Anybody who has done the homework could do this exercise.

D. Identifying Words as Nouns, Pronouns, or Adjectives

Tell whether each italicized word in the following paragraph is used as a *noun,* a *pronoun,* or an *adjective.* For each adjective, give the word it modifies.

[26] Nearly *everybody* has heard a Strauss *waltz.* [27] The waltz is a form of *ballroom* dance that originated in *Germany* and *Austria* in the *eighteenth* century. [28] Johann Strauss was the most famous and, *some* say, the best *composer* of waltzes. [29] *He* was born in *Vienna,* the *capital* city of Austria, in 1825. [30] Strauss came from a *well-established* family of musicians. [31] *His* father and brothers Eduard and Josef were *respected* composers and conductors in *their* own right. [32] Johann toured with an *orchestra* for many years, but in 1870, when his *first* wife said *she* would like *him* to write operettas, he turned his attentions to writing *music.* [33] His most famous compositions are Die Fledermaus (The Bat), an *operetta,* and "The Blue Danube" waltz, which later became *famous* as one of the *themes* of the 1968 movie 2001: A Space Odyssey. [34] Johann Strauss wrote more than *five hundred* orchestral compositions. [35] When he died in Vienna in 1899, his *worldwide* reputation as the *"Waltz King"* was assured.

E. Classifying Nouns

Identify each italicized noun in the following sentences as *proper* or *common* and *concrete* or *abstract*. Also, tell if a noun is *compound*.

36. On *Sunday*, the neighbor's *dog* barked all night.

37. To our *surprise*, the *zebras* cantered noisily across the path.

38. A painting by *Monet* that always gives me a feeling of *serenity* hangs in the *Metropolitan Museum of Art* in New York.

39. "As you know," said *Mr. Cima* proudly, "*knowledge* is *power*."

40. Seeking *solitude*, Kathryn hiked across the hills of *Connemara*.

Writing Application
Using Adjectives in a Poem

Vivid Adjectives   The Czech author Franz Kafka wrote about a man who becomes an insect! Imagine that you are changed into an animal or an object. Using at least ten carefully chosen adjectives, write a poem describing yourself.

Prewriting   Select an object or an animal that you think you would like to be. Next, freewrite descriptive words about the object or animal. You may want to consult an article in an encyclopedia for additional details or pictures of your chosen topic.

Writing   As you write your first draft, concentrate on using the most vivid adjectives that you have listed.

Revising   Read through your first draft, and underline each adjective. For each one, ask yourself whether any other word more precisely describes the noun or pronoun. Be sure that you have used at least ten different adjectives.

Publishing   Check your poem to make sure that all words are spelled correctly, especially any adjectives that you do not use very often in writing. Proofread your poem for any errors in grammar, punctuation, and spelling. Your class may want to share your poems by reading them aloud or displaying them on a bulletin board.

The Parts of a Sentence

Subjects, Predicates, Complements

Diagnostic Preview

A. Identifying Subjects, Verbs, and Complements

Identify each of the italicized words and word groups in the following sentences as a *subject*, a *verb*, a *predicate adjective*, a *predicate nominative*, a *direct object*, or an *indirect object*.

EXAMPLE   1. Robotics is the *science* or *technology* of robots.
      *1. science—predicate nominative; technology—
       predicate nominative*

1. Have *you* ever met a robot?
2. In the field of robotics, scientists have built vastly complex *robots*.
3. Today, these machines *are put* to work in factories, laboratories, and outer space.
4. How were these complex *machines* first used?
5. There are a *number* of interesting early examples of robots at work.
6. One of the first robots was a mechanical *figure* in a clock tower.
7. It raised a hammer and struck a *bell* every hour.
8. At the 1939 New York World's Fair, Elektro and Sparko were very popular *attractions*.
9. Elektro was *tall*, more than seven feet high.
10. Electric motors gave *Elektro* power for a variety of amazing tricks.

11. Sparko was Elektro's *dog.*
12. Sparko *could bark* and even *wag* his tail.
13. Today, *some* of the simplest robots are the drones in laboratories.
14. Basically, drones are *extensions* of the human arm.
15. They can be *useful* in many different ways.

B. Classifying Sentences According to Purpose

Punctuate each of the following sentences with an appropriate end mark. Then, classify the sentence as *declarative, interrogative, imperative,* or *exclamatory.*

EXAMPLE   **1.** There's a twenty-five-foot robot named Beetle

     1. There's a twenty-five-foot robot named Beetle.—declarative

16. Can you picture a robot twenty-five feet tall
17. Step up and say hello to Beetle
18. Perhaps you have heard of CAM, an even more advanced robot
19. It can travel on long legs across rough terrain as rapidly as thirty-five miles per hour
20. What an amazing creation it is

What Is a Sentence?

In conversation, people can often leave out part of a sentence without confusing their listeners. In formal writing and speaking, though, it is usually better to use complete sentences. They help to make meaning clear to your audience.

13a. A *sentence* is a word group that contains a subject and a verb and that expresses a complete thought.

A *sentence fragment* is a word or word group that is capitalized and punctuated as a sentence but that does not contain both a subject and a verb or that does not express a complete thought.

SENTENCE FRAGMENT   The magazine's essay contest for tenth-grade American history students. [no verb]

SENTENCE   The magazine's essay contest for tenth-grade American history students ends Tuesday.

Reference Note

For information on how to correct **sentence fragments,** see page 340.

COMPUTER TIP

Many style-checking software programs can help you identify sentence fragments. If you have access to such a program, use it to help evaluate your writing.

Reference Note

For more about the **understood subject,** see page 447.

SENTENCE FRAGMENT	Was chosen as the best one from over two thousand entries. [no subject]
SENTENCE	Her essay was chosen as the best one from over two thousand entries.
SENTENCE FRAGMENT	When the judges announced the winner. [not a complete thought]
SENTENCE	When the judges announced the winner, everyone applauded.

NOTE Some sentences contain an understood subject (you).

EXAMPLES   [You] Wait!

[You] Hold on to the reins.

Exercise 1 **Identifying Sentences and Sentence Fragments**

Identify each of the following word groups as a *sentence* or a *sentence fragment*. Be prepared to explain your answers.

EXAMPLES   1. Willa Cather wrote poetry, fiction, and nonfiction.
1. *sentence*

2. Grew up in the Midwest.
2. *sentence fragment*

HELP

Example 1 of Exercise 1 contains a subject and verb and expresses a complete thought. Example 2 does not contain a subject and does not express a complete thought.

1. Willa Cather was born in Back Creek Valley in northern Virginia.
2. In 1883, when she was nine years old.
3. Her family moved to the treeless prairie of Nebraska.
4. She tracked buffalo and collected prairie flowers.
5. Fascinated by the wild and rolling plains.
6. Listening to the stories of neighboring settlers.
7. They told memorable tales about the harsh struggles of the homesteaders.
8. After she graduated from high school in the village of Red Cloud, Nebraska.

9. The picture of Red Cloud on the previous page shows shops and people that would have been familiar to Willa Cather.
10. And the Opera House at the end of the street where Cather and her classmates graduated in 1890.
11. In college, Willa Cather discovered her talent for writing.
12. Contributing stories and reviews to local newspapers.
13. At first, her writing failed to reach a wide audience.
14. She succeeded in establishing herself as a writer.
15. After years earning a living as a schoolteacher and an editor in New York City.
16. Although Cather enjoyed living in New York.
17. She never lost touch with the sights and sounds of her childhood.
18. She describes how farmers turned the open plains into orderly fields of wheat and corn.
19. In *O Pioneers!*, her second novel.
20. In a later novel, *My Ántonia,* the immigrant neighbors of her childhood play prominent roles.

Subjects and Predicates

13b. Sentences consist of two basic parts: subjects and predicates.

The *subject* tells whom or what the sentence or clause is about, and the *predicate* tells something about the subject.

   Notice in the following examples that the subject may come before or after the predicate or between parts of the predicate.

SUBJECT	PREDICATE
Some residents of the desert	can survive a long drought.

PREDICATE	SUBJECT
Particularly noteworthy is	the Australian frog.

PREDICATE	SUBJECT	PREDICATE
For up to three years	it	can live without rainfall.

PREDICATE	SUBJECT	PREDICATE
How can	an animal	survive that long?

In each example above, all the words labeled *subject* make up the *complete subject;* all the words labeled *predicate* make up the *complete predicate.*

HELP——

In Exercise 2,
the subject may appear
anywhere in a sentence.

Exercise 2 Identifying Subjects and Predicates

Identify the complete subject and the complete predicate in each of the
following sentences.

EXAMPLE   1. When was the precious metal platinum discovered?

   1. complete subject—the precious metal platinum
       complete predicate—When was discovered

1. People from a variety of countries have been credited with the
   discovery of platinum.
2. Spanish explorers in search of gold supposedly discovered this
   precious metal in the rivers of South America.
3. However, the explorers considered it a worthless, inferior form
   of silver.
4. Their name for platinum was *platina,* meaning "little silver."
5. Back into the river went the little balls of platinum!
6. The platinum might then become gold, according to one amazing
   theory.
7. Europeans later mixed platinum with gold.
8. This mixture encouraged the production of counterfeit gold bars
   and coins.
9. Platinum commands a high price today because of its resistance
   to corrosion.
10. Such diverse products as jet planes and jewelry include platinum
    in some form.

The Subject

**13c. The main word or word group that tells whom or what the
sentence is about is called the *simple subject*.**

The ***complete subject*** consists of the simple subject and any words or
word groups that modify the simple subject.

EXAMPLES   A dog with this pedigree is usually nervous.
              Complete subject   A dog with this pedigree
                Simple subject   dog

            Both of these cockatiels are for sale.
              Complete subject   Both of these cockatiels
                Simple subject   Both

The Taj Mahal in India is one of the most beautiful buildings in the world.

Complete subject	The Taj Mahal in India
Simple subject	Taj Mahal

> **NOTE** In this book, the term *subject* usually refers to the simple subject unless otherwise indicated.

Reference Note

A compound noun, such as *Taj Mahal*, functions as a single unit. For more about **compound nouns,** see page 406.

The Predicate

13d. The *simple predicate,* or *verb,* is the main word or word group that tells something about the subject.

The *complete predicate* consists of the verb and all the words that modify the verb and complete its meaning.

EXAMPLES   Spiders snare their prey in intricate webs.

Complete predicate	snare their prey in intricate webs
Simple predicate	snare

Rosa has been looking for you all morning.

Complete predicate	has been looking for you all morning
Simple predicate	has been looking

Have my keys been found?

Complete predicate	Have been found
Simple predicate	Have been found

Notice in the preceding examples that the simple predicate may be identical to the complete predicate. Also, the simple predicate may be a one-word verb or a *verb phrase* (a main verb and one or more helping verbs).

Reference Note

For more about **verbs** and **verb phrases,** see page 417.

Commonly Used Helping Verbs				
am	did	has	might	was
are	do	have	must	were
can	does	is	shall	will
could	had	may	should	would

> **NOTE** In this book, the term *verb* usually refers to the simple predicate unless otherwise indicated.

TIPS & TRICKS

When you are identifying the simple predicate in a sentence, be sure to include all parts of a verb phrase.

EXAMPLE
Should Dad have painted the walls light gray? [The simple predicate is the verb phrase *Should have painted.*]

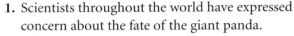

Exercise 3 Identifying Verbs and Verb Phrases in Sentences

Identify the verb in each of the following sentences. Be sure to include all parts of any verb phrases.

EXAMPLE 1. The giant panda of China is considered an endangered species.

1. *is considered*

1. Scientists throughout the world have expressed concern about the fate of the giant panda.
2. In recent years this animal's natural habitat has slowly become smaller.
3. Many forests of bamboo, the panda's favorite food, have died.
4. A panda like the one in the picture on this page may devour as much as forty pounds of bamboo daily.
5. However, each tender green shoot of bamboo contains only a very small amount of nutrients.
6. In addition, the large but sluggish panda is not known as a successful hunter.
7. In their concern for the panda's survival, scientists are now studying the habits of this animal.
8. A captured panda is held in a log trap for several hours.
9. During this time, scientists attach a radio to the panda's neck.
10. The radio sends the scientists valuable information about the animal's behavior in the wild.

Finding the Subject

To find the subject of a sentence, find the verb first. Then, ask "Who?" or "What?" before the verb.

EXAMPLES My cousin from Finland will arrive this afternoon. [The verb is *will arrive*. Who will arrive? *Cousin* will arrive. *Cousin* is the subject.]

On the other side of the brook stands a cabin. [The verb is *stands*. What stands? *Cabin* stands. *Cabin* is the subject.]

Exercise 4 Identifying Subjects and Verbs

Identify the subject and the verb in each of the following sentences. Be sure to include all parts of any verb phrases.

EXAMPLE
1. Our science class has been studying the migratory flights of different species of butterflies.

1. *subject—class; verb—has been studying*

1. Despite their fragile appearance, butterflies have a great deal of stamina.
2. They often fly more than one thousand miles during migration.
3. The painted lady butterfly, for example, has been seen in the middle of the Atlantic Ocean.
4. In fact, this species was once spotted over the Arctic Circle.
5. During the spring, millions of these insects flutter across North America.
6. Huge flocks of colorful butterflies fly from their winter home in New Mexico to places as far north as Newfoundland, Canada.
7. The brilliant orange-and-black monarch butterfly flies south each September from Canada toward Florida, Texas, and California.
8. The migratory flight of the monarch may cover a distance of close to two thousand miles.
9. Every winter for the past several decades, monarchs have gathered in a small forest not far from San Francisco.
10. The thick clusters of their blazing orange wings make this forest very popular with tourists.

13e. The subject of a verb is never in a prepositional phrase.

A *prepositional phrase* consists of a preposition, the object of the preposition, and any modifiers of that object.

EXAMPLES

| for the team | of mine | through the years |
| on the top shelf | at all times | along with my niece |

Do not mistake a noun or pronoun in a prepositional phrase for the subject of a sentence.

EXAMPLES   One of my cousins has visited Ghana. [Who has visited? *One* has visited. *Of my cousins* is a prepositional phrase.]

On top of the building is an up-to-date observatory. [What is? *Observatory* is. *On top* and *of the building* are prepositional phrases.]

Reference Note

For more information about **prepositional phrases,** see page 467.

─HELP─

Remember,
the subject is never in a
prepositional phrase.

Exercise 5 Identifying Subjects and Verbs

Identify the subject and the verb in each of the following sentences.

EXAMPLE
1. How much do you know about the Chinese experience in the United States?

1. *subject—you*
   verb—do know

1. The people in this picture are celebrating the arrival of the New Year in accordance with an ancient Chinese tradition.
2. These festivities, however, are occurring in the United States.
3. The Chinese New Year celebration, with its dragon parades and festive decorations, is a colorful addition to American culture.
4. In the 1850s the earliest Chinese immigrants came to the United States for jobs in the gold mines and on the railroads.
5. At first, only men could immigrate.
6. Not until much later could they send home to China for their wives and sweethearts.
7. As a result, not until the 1920s did the close-knit society of America's Chinatowns develop.
8. Have you read about the experience of Chinese immigrants in America?
9. I recommend the book *Longtime Californ': A Documentary Study of an American Chinatown.*
10. In this book, Victor G. Nee and Brett de Bary Nee trace the history of Chinese immigration to the United States and the development of the Chinese American community in San Francisco.

Exercise 6 Completing Sentences by Supplying Complete Predicates

Finish each of the following sentences by adding a complete predicate. Then, underline the simple subject once and the verb twice.

EXAMPLE
1. One of the horses _____.

1. One of the horses has escaped from the corral.

1. Those lions _____.
2. A white fence _____.
3. The surf _____.
4. The road by my house _____.
5. Students in our school _____.
6. The school bus _____.
7. The old, half-blind cat _____.
8. Sitting in innertubes, the tourists _____.
9. The stone wall _____.
10. Last month _____.

Review A Identifying Complete Subjects, Complete Predicates, Simple Subjects, and Verbs

Identify the complete subject and the complete predicate in each sentence in the following paragraph. Then, underline the simple subject once and the verb twice.

EXAMPLE
[1] For what is Benjamin Banneker best remembered?

1. complete subject—Benjamin Banneker
   complete predicate—For what is best remembered

[1] Benjamin Banneker (1731–1806) was born near Baltimore, Maryland, of a free mother and an enslaved father. [2] Considered free, Banneker could attend an integrated private school. [3] There he began his lifelong study of science and math. [4] Despite having only an eighth-grade education, this young man became a noteworthy astronomer and mathematician. [5] His astronomical research led to his acclaimed prediction of the solar eclipse of 1789. [6] A few years later, the first of his almanacs was published. [7] Banneker's almanacs contained tide tables and data on future eclipses. [8] Some bits of practical advice, as well as famous sayings, were also included. [9] These popular almanacs came out every year for more than a decade. [10] In addition to his scientific discoveries, Banneker is known for his work as a surveyor during the planning of Washington, D.C.

TIPS & TRICKS

In many sentences, you can find the subject and the verb more easily if you first cross out any prepositional phrases.

EXAMPLE
The team with the best record will play in the state tournament.
Subject   team
Verb   will play

Sentences Beginning with *There* or *Here*

The word *there* or *here* may begin a sentence, but it is almost never the subject. Often, *there* or *here* is used as an adverb telling *where*.

EXAMPLES   There are your **gloves.** [What are? *Gloves* are. *Gloves* is the subject. *There* tells where your gloves are.]

Here is my **nephew.** [Who is? *Nephew* is. *Nephew* is the subject. *Here* tells where my nephew is.]

NOTE Sometimes, *there* begins a sentence but does not tell *where*. In this use, *there* is not an adverb but an ***expletive***—a word that fills out the structure of a sentence but does not add to the meaning.

EXAMPLE   There is not much **time** left. [What is left? *Time* is left. *Time* is the subject. *There* does not add any meaning to the sentence, which may be rewritten without *there*: *Not much time is left.*]

Sentences Asking Questions

Questions usually begin with a verb, a helping verb, or a word such as *what, when, where, how,* or *why.* In most cases, the subject follows the verb or part of the verb phrase.

EXAMPLES   Where is your **parakeet**?

Did **you** make the team?

In a question that begins with a helping verb, such as the second example above, the subject generally comes between the helping verb and the main verb. To find the subject in any question, however, turn the question into a statement, find the verb, and then ask "Who?" or "What?" before the verb.

EXAMPLES   Were your friends early?
becomes
Your friends were early.
[Who were? *Friends* were.]

Where did the horses cross the river?
becomes
The horses did cross the river where.
[What did cross? *Horses* did.]

Exercise 7 Identifying Subjects and Verbs

Identify the subject and the verb in each of the following sentences.

EXAMPLE   1. There are several thousand asteroids in our solar system.
           1. subject—asteroids
              verb—are

1. There were three questions on the final exam.
2. Here is my topic for the term paper.
3. What did you choose for a topic?
4. Will everyone be ready at eleven o'clock?
5. There will be a study-group meeting tomorrow.
6. When should we go to the library?
7. There were very few books on the subject.
8. Have you outlined the next chapter?
9. Where will our conference be held?
10. Are there many magazine articles about Nelson Mandela?

The Understood Subject

In a request or a command, the subject is usually not stated. In such sentences, *you* is the **understood subject.**

REQUEST   [**You**] Please rake the yard.
COMMAND   [**You**] Pick up the fallen branches.

   When a request or command includes a name, the name is not the subject but a **noun of direct address.** *You* is still the understood subject.

EXAMPLE   Jason, [**you**] wash the dishes.

Compound Subjects and Compound Verbs

13f. A *compound subject* consists of two or more subjects that are joined by a conjunction and that have the same verb.

The parts of a compound subject are generally joined by the coordinating conjunction *and* or *or.*

EXAMPLES   **Mr. Olivero** and his **daughter** planted the garden. [Who planted? *Mr. Olivero* and *daughter* planted.]

            Either **Mr. Olivero** or his **daughter** planted the garden. [The two parts of the compound subject are *Mr. Olivero* and *daughter.*]

Reference Note

For information on using commas with **nouns of direct address,** see page 712.

13g. A *compound verb* consists of two or more verbs that are joined by a conjunction and that have the same subject.

The parts of a compound verb are usually joined by the coordinating conjunction *and*, *but*, or *or*.

EXAMPLES   At the street festival, we **danced** the rumba and **sampled** the meat pies.

I **have written** the letter and **addressed** the envelope but **have** not **gone** to the post office yet.

Both the subject and the verb of a sentence may be compound.

EXAMPLE   Yesterday, **Jamal** and **I built** a box kite and **painted** it bright yellow and green.

NOTE There are other cases in which a sentence may contain more than one subject and verb.

	S	V
COMPOUND SENTENCE	The unification of Italy in 1861 was a victory for Giuseppe Garibaldi,	

	S	V
	and the event ended centuries of civil strife.	

	S	V	S
COMPLEX SENTENCE	After the painter finished his self-portrait, he		

	V	V
	went out and ate dinner.	

Exercise 8 Identifying Subjects and Verbs

Identify the subject(s) and the verb(s) in each of the following sentences. If the subject is understood, write *(You)*.

EXAMPLE   1. Sarah, please return the overdue video and pay the late charges.

    1. *subject—(You)*
       verbs—return, pay

1. Jackets and ties are required in that restaurant.
2. Do any bears or wildcats live in these woods?
3. On our math test, Ann and Mark scored the highest.
4. Bring both a pencil and a pen to the history exam.
5. Miguel neither sings nor plays an instrument.
6. Where do you and Liz buy CDs?

STYLE   **TIP**

The helping verb may or may not be repeated if it is the same for all parts of the compound verb.

EXAMPLES
My aunt **will arrive** tomorrow and **will stay** with us for the holidays. [The helping verb *will* is repeated.]

My aunt **will arrive** tomorrow and **stay** with us for the holidays. [The helping verb *will* is not repeated.]

Reference Note

For more information on **compound sentences,** see page 504. For more information on **complex sentences,** see page 505.

7. The front and back tires are low and need air.
8. Play ball!
9. Humor and wisdom are often used in folk sayings.
10. Either Bill or Jan may stay and help us.

Exercise 9 **Completing Sentences by Supplying Subjects and Verbs**

Complete each of the sentences below with an appropriate complete subject or complete predicate. Underline the subject of each sentence once, and underline the verb twice.

EXAMPLE   1. Usually, the _____ leaves on time.

           1. *Usually, the northbound* <u>train</u> <u><u>leaves</u></u> *on time.*

1. _____ pull sleds through the snow.
2. Houseplants _____ sunlight.
3. Several of the football players _____ the sports drink.
4. After sunset, the neighbor's dog _____.
5. During daylight savings time, Don and Beth _____ their bikes after work.
6. _____ arrive every day.
7. The _____ of Congress voted against the bill.
8. _____ enjoyed the beautiful day.
9. Unsure of the correct direction, he _____ at the map.
10. _____ laughed.

Review B **Identifying Subjects and Verbs**

Identify the subject(s) and the verb(s) in each of the following sentences. If the subject is understood, write *(You)*.

EXAMPLE   1. Most birds and many insects can fly.

           1. *subjects—birds, insects*
              verb—can fly

1. How do birds fly?
2. Their wings lift and push them through the air.
3. Look carefully at an insect's wings.
4. Most have two sets of wings.
5. The pair in front covers the pair in back.
6. Other animals can move through the air without flying.
7. The flying fish swims fast and leaps out of the water.
8. How does the flying squirrel glide from tree to tree?

9. There are flaps of skin between its legs.
10. Because of its webbed feet, the flying frog can make long, gliding leaps through the air.

Complements

13h. A *complement* is a word or word group that completes the meaning of a verb.

A group of words may have a subject and a verb and still not express a complete thought. Notice how the boldface complements complete the meanings of the verbs in the following examples.

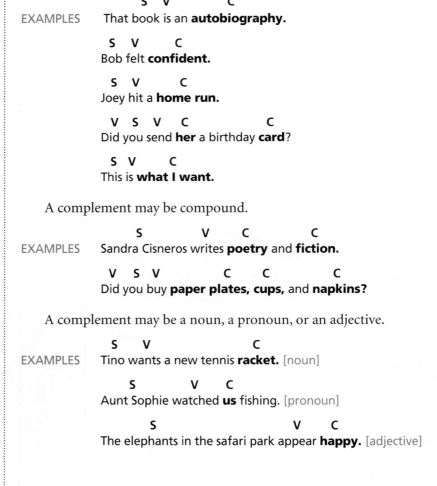

EXAMPLES
             S   V   C
           That book is an **autobiography.**

           S   V   C
           Bob felt **confident.**

           S   V   C
           Joey hit a **home run.**

          V   S   V C   C
          Did you send **her** a birthday **card**?

           S   V   C
           This is **what I want.**

A complement may be compound.

EXAMPLES
             S   V   C   C
          Sandra Cisneros writes **poetry** and **fiction.**

           V   S   V   C   C   C
          Did you buy **paper plates, cups,** and **napkins?**

A complement may be a noun, a pronoun, or an adjective.

EXAMPLES
            S   V   C
          Tino wants a new tennis **racket.** [noun]

            S   V   C
          Aunt Sophie watched **us** fishing. [pronoun]

              S   V   C
          The elephants in the safari park appear **happy.** [adjective]

Do not mistake an adverb for a complement.

ADVERBS   At the next intersection, should we turn right? [*Right* tells *where* we should turn.]

Lucy works hard. [*Hard* tells *how* Lucy works.]

COMPLEMENTS   You have the **right** to express your opinion. [*Right,* a noun, completes the meaning of the verb *have.*]

These pears are **hard.** [*Hard,* an adjective, completes the meaning of the verb *are.*]

Complements are never in prepositional phrases.

EXAMPLES   Christopher quoted from the poem. [*Poem* is part of the prepositional phrase *from the poem.*]

Christopher quoted the **poem.** [*Poem* is the complement.]

NOTE   Both independent and subordinate clauses contain subjects and verbs and may contain complements.

           S   V   C

EXAMPLES   Although **he appeared sluggish** at the start,

      S   V   C

Ricardo won the **race.**

     S   V   C   S   V   C

Josie is an **engineer who designs** computer **hardware.**

Exercise 10   **Writing Sentences with Subjects, Verbs, and Complements**

Construct ten sentences from the following groups of sentence parts. Add more than only a word or two to each group.

          SUBJECT   VERB   COMPLEMENT

EXAMPLES   **1.** pilot   flew   mission

1. The pilot flew a dangerous mission over Germany.

2. baby   became   sleepy

2. The baby became sleepy after her bath.

Subject	Verb	Complement
1. cyclists	planned	trip
2. musicians	performed	duet

(continued)

Reference Note
For more about **adverbs,** see page 614.

Reference Note
For more about **prepositional phrases,** see page 467.

Reference Note
For information about **independent** and **subordinate clauses,** see Chapter 15.

GRAMMAR

(continued)

Subject	Verb	Complement
3. speaker	looked	enthusiastic
4. dancer	tapped	rhythm
5. novel	is	suspenseful
6. Dennis	became	president
7. tambourine	sounds	funny
8. prime minister	gave	speech
9. raccoon	ate	banana peels
10. Girl Scout	built	fire

Exercise 11 Identifying Subjects, Verbs, and Complements

Identify the subject(s) and the verb(s) in the following sentences. Then, identify any complement(s) the sentence contains.

EXAMPLE   1. Have you ever seen a storm surge during a hurricane?

1. subject—you
   verb—Have seen
   complement—surge

1. A hurricane is a powerful storm, often measuring two or three hundred miles in diameter.
2. Such storms are notorious for their destructive power.
3. To be classified as a hurricane, a storm must have winds of at least seventy-four miles per hour.
4. These winds swirl around the *eye,* an area of calm in the center of the storm.
5. *Wall clouds* surround the eye of a hurricane.
6. Within these clouds the strongest winds and heaviest rain of the storm occur.
7. The winds and rain, along with the force of the sea, often produce enormous waves.
8. In a storm surge, tides rise well above normal.
9. Huge waves produce floods.
10. In fact, most hurricane-related deaths result from drowning in floods.

The Subject Complement

13i. A *subject complement* is a word or word group that completes the meaning of a linking verb and identifies or modifies the subject.

EXAMPLES We may be the only **ones** here. [*Ones,* a pronoun, completes the meaning of the linking verb *may be* and identifies the subject *We.*]

Roscoe seems **worried.** [*Worried,* an adjective, completes the meaning of the linking verb *seems* and modifies the subject *Roscoe.*]

Did you know that Lani is a soccer **player**? [*Player,* a noun, completes the meaning of the linking verb *is* and identifies the subject *Lani.*]

A subject complement may consist of more than one word.

EXAMPLES Michelangelo's full name was **Michelangelo di Lodovico Buonarroti Simoni.** [*Michelangelo di Lodovico Buonarroti Simoni,* a compound noun, completes the meaning of the linking verb *was* and identifies the subject *name.*]

A ring with her birthstone is **what she wants for her birthday.** [*What she wants for her birthday,* a noun clause, completes the meaning of the linking verb *is* and identifies the subject *ring.*]

NOTE Subject complements complete the meanings of linking verbs only. A word that completes the meaning of an action verb is generally a direct object or an indirect object.

There are two kinds of subject complements: the *predicate nominative* and the *predicate adjective.*

(1) A *predicate nominative* is a word or word group that is in the predicate and that identifies the subject or refers to it.

EXAMPLES Some caterpillars become **butterflies.** [*Butterflies* identifies the subject *caterpillars.*]

The winners should have been **they.** [*They* refers to the subject *winners.*]

She is the next **speaker.** [*Speaker* refers to the subject *She.*]

Reference Note

For lists of commonly used **linking verbs,** see page 419. For more about **compound nouns,** see page 406. For a discussion of **noun clauses,** see Chapter 15.

Reference Note

For more about **direct objects** and **indirect objects,** see page 456.

STYLE TIP

The use of the nominative case pronoun, as in the sentence *The winners should have been they,* is uncommon in everyday speech. You will often hear such expressions as *That's him* and *It is her.* In formal English, however, you should use the nominative case pronoun in such expressions: *That's **he*** and *It is **she.***

Reference Note

For more about the **cases of pronouns,** see Chapter 17.

A predicate nominative may be compound.

EXAMPLE   Our cats' names are **Wimpy** and **Henry.** [*Wimpy* and *Henry* identify the subject *names.*]

A predicate nominative may precede the subject and the verb.

EXAMPLE   What a fine **speaker** you are! [*Speaker* identifies the subject *you.*]

(2) A *predicate adjective* is an adjective that is in the predicate and that modifies the subject of a sentence or a clause.

EXAMPLES   You look **happy.** [*Happy* modifies the subject *You.*]

When she left, Norma appeared **calm.** [*Calm* modifies the subject *Norma.*]

A predicate adjective may be compound.

EXAMPLE   He said that the yogurt tasted **sweet** and **creamy.** [*Sweet* and *creamy* modify the subject *yogurt.*]

A predicate adjective may precede the subject and the verb.

EXAMPLE   How **silly** that commercial is! [*Silly* modifies the subject *commercial.*]

TIPS & TRICKS

Do not assume that every adjective in the predicate is a predicate adjective. Remember that a predicate adjective modifies only the subject.

EXAMPLES
This antique clock is **valuable.** [The adjective *valuable* is a predicate adjective because it modifies the subject *clock.*]

This antique clock is a valuable timepiece. [The adjective *valuable* is not a predicate adjective. It modifies the predicate nominative *timepiece,* not the subject *clock.*]

HELP

Some sentences in Exercise 12 have more than one subject complement.

Exercise 12 Identifying Predicate Nominatives and Predicate Adjectives

Identify the subject complements in the following sentences. Then, tell whether each complement is a *predicate nominative* or a *predicate adjective.*

EXAMPLE   1. Kimchi is a spicy Korean dish of pickled cabbage and peppers.

1. *dish—predicate nominative*

1. The last scene of the play is very intense.
2. Those two small birds are finches.
3. The music sounded lively.
4. It is difficult to choose a winner when each contestant's costume looks so elegant.
5. My goldfish Alonzo grows larger every day.
6. Andrea's report on digital recording is a highly detailed and technical one.
7. When did Uncas become a chief of the Mohegans?
8. Your solution to this algebra problem is clever.

9. We felt full after we had eaten Thanksgiving dinner.

10. The setting of the story is a Spanish castle that looks old and deserted.

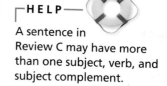

┌─HELP─
A sentence in Review C may have more than one subject, verb, and subject complement.

GRAMMAR

Review C Identifying Subjects, Verbs, and Subject Complements

Each of the following sentences contains at least one subject complement. Identify each subject, verb, and subject complement. Make a chart like the following one, and fill in the correct words.

EXAMPLE   **1.** Jazz was originally the music of African Americans.

	SUBJECT	VERB	SUBJECT COMPLEMENT
1.	Jazz	was	music

1. The style of 1920s musicians, such as Jelly Roll Morton, was smooth.

2. With the development of swing, the rhythm of jazz became more regular.

3. Practitioners of swing became known for their solo improvisation.

4. Billie Holiday was one of those practitioners.

5. She became the greatest singer in the history of jazz.

6. A typically American musical form, jazz was the sound of Louis Armstrong, "Count" Basie, Scott Joplin, and Ella Fitzgerald.

7. Created in the early twentieth century, jazz is a blend of elements from African and European music, but its irregular, or syncopated, rhythms are strictly African.

8. Early jazz was a combination of the cakewalk, a dance that was popular with many African Americans in the 1800s, and ragtime, which was mainly instrumental music.

9. After 1917, when jazz phonograph records became popular, the future of jazz appeared bright.

10. People remain fascinated by jazz, perhaps because it sounds new with each playing.

The Object of a Verb

An **object of a verb** is a complement that, unlike a subject complement, does not identify or modify the subject. An object of a verb is a noun, pronoun, or word group that completes the meaning of a *transitive verb*—a verb that expresses an action directed toward a person, a place, a thing, or an idea.

Reference Note

For more about **transitive verbs,** see page 421.

Reference Note
For more about **compound nouns,** see page 406. For more about **noun clauses,** see Chapter 15.

EXAMPLES   The cat was chasing a **moth.** [*Moth* completes the meaning of the transitive verb *was chasing.*]

Jeff's mother gave **him** some **grapes.** [*Him* and *grapes* complete the meaning of the transitive verb *gave.*]

Kevin and I enjoy **playing** chess. [*Playing,* a gerund, completes the meaning of the transitive verb *enjoy.*]

An object of a verb may consist of more than one word.

EXAMPLES   The journalist interviewed the **Secretary of State.** [*Secretary of State,* a compound noun, completes the meaning of the transitive verb *interviewed.*]

Do you know **what this is**? [*What this is,* a noun clause, completes the meaning of the transitive verb *Do know.*]

NOTE   Objects of verbs, like other kinds of complements, can appear in subordinate clauses as well as independent clauses.

EXAMPLE   After she had read **us** the **story,** the teacher gave **us** a **quiz** on it. [*Us* and *story* complete the meaning of *had read* in the subordinate clause. *Us* and *quiz* complete the meaning of *gave* in the independent clause.]

Two kinds of objects of verbs are *direct objects* and *indirect objects.*

13j. A *direct object* is a noun, pronoun, or word group that tells *who* or *what* receives the action of a transitive verb or shows the result of the action.

A direct object answers the question "Whom?" or "What?" after a transitive verb.

EXAMPLES   I took my little **sister** to the movie *Mulan.* [I took whom? *Sister.*]

She had already seen **it** four times. [She had seen what? *It.*]

A direct object may be compound.

EXAMPLE   The parrot said **"Good morning"** and **"Cat free to good home."** [The parrot said what? *"Good morning"* and *"Cat free to good home."*]

A direct object may precede the subject and verb.

EXAMPLE   What remarkable **tricks** the illusionist performed! [The illusionist performed what? *Tricks.*]

Direct objects are never found in prepositional phrases.

EXAMPLES   **Tom was driving in his car.** [*Car* is part of the prepositional phrase *in his car.* The sentence has no direct object.]

        Tom was driving his car. [*Car* is the direct object.]

Exercise 13   Identifying Verbs and Their Direct Objects

Identify the verbs and the direct objects in the following sentences.

EXAMPLE   **1.** My parents recently bought a 35-mm camera.

        1. verb—bought; direct object—camera

1. I borrowed my parents' new camera.
2. First, I loaded the film into the camera.
3. Then, I set the shutter speed.
4. I focused the camera on a distant object.
5. I could read the shutter speed in the viewfinder.
6. A flashing red light signals an incorrect setting.
7. Slowly and carefully, I pressed the button.
8. I then advanced the film for the next shot.
9. By the end of the day, I had snapped thirty-six pictures.
10. Have you ever taken photographs?

13k. An *indirect object* is a noun, pronoun, or word group that often appears in sentences containing direct objects. An indirect object tells *to whom* or *to what* (or *for whom* or *for what*) the action of a transitive verb is done.

EXAMPLES   **Meli read us her report.** [Meli read it to whom? *Us.*]

        They fed the horses some oats. [They fed oats to what? *Horses.*]

        Juan left you this message. [Juan left it for whom? *You.*]

        Carly knitted her pet dachshund a blanket. [Carly knitted it for what? *Dachshund.*]

If the word *to* or *for* is used, the noun or pronoun following it is part of a prepositional phrase and cannot be an indirect object.

PREPOSITIONAL PHRASE   Jeff wrote a note to me. [*Me* is part of the prepositional phrase *to me.*]

INDIRECT OBJECT   Jeff wrote **me** a note. [*Me* is the indirect object.]

┌HELP─

An indirect object generally comes between a verb and a direct object.

┌TIPS & TRICKS┐

When identifying complements, check first to see whether the verbs in the sentences are action or linking verbs. Remember that only action verbs may have direct objects and indirect objects and that only linking verbs may have predicate nominatives and predicate adjectives.

An indirect object may be compound.

EXAMPLE   The ski trip had given **Lucia** and **me** a wonderful vacation.
[The trip had given it to whom? *Lucia* and *me*.]

Exercise 14 Identifying Direct and Indirect Objects

Identify the direct objects and indirect objects in the following sentences. Not all sentences contain indirect objects.

EXAMPLE   1. His athleticism has earned Leroy many awards.
    1. *direct object—awards; indirect object—Leroy*

1. Last summer, Leroy told us his plans for the future.
2. He wants a place on the U.S. swim team in the next Olympic games.
3. Of course, this goal demands hours of hard practice.
4. Every day, Leroy swims one hundred laps in the college pool and works out with weights for an hour.
5. Such intense training could cost him his social life.
6. With his rigorous schedule, Leroy doesn't have much time to spend with friends.
7. However, we all understand and give him much encouragement and support.
8. We can't teach him the fine points of competitive swimming.
9. His coach does that.
10. Maybe we'll see Leroy at the next Olympics!

Review D Identifying Sentences, Fragments, Subjects, Verbs, and Complements

Identify each of the following word groups as a *sentence* or a *sentence fragment*. If a word group is a sentence, identify its subject(s) and verb(s). If a sentence has a complement, label the complement as a *predicate adjective*, a *predicate nominative*, a *direct object*, or an *indirect object*.

EXAMPLE   1. Will you be attending the Cinco de Mayo celebration?
    1. *sentence; subject—you; verb—will be attending; direct object—celebration*

1. Has the planning committee announced the date of the school carnival?
2. Perhaps next week.
3. Linda gave us a summary of her science project.
4. It was long and interesting.

5. Books and papers covered the desk and spilled onto the floor.

6. Although it was well written.

7. One of those dogs is not very obedient.

8. Ming Chin gave the children a handful of oatmeal cookies.

9. Kim, Juan, and Tracey were winners at the track meet last Saturday.

10. How happy they were!

Classifying Sentences by Purpose

13I. Depending on its purpose, a sentence may be classified as *declarative, imperative, interrogative,* or *exclamatory.*

(1) A *declarative sentence* makes a statement and ends with a period.

EXAMPLES   Toni Morrison won the Nobel Prize for literature in 1993.

          Although we were tired after working all day, we still wanted to go dancing.

(2) An *imperative sentence* gives a command or makes a request. Most imperative sentences end with a period. A strong command ends with an exclamation point.

EXAMPLES   Be careful. [mild command]

          Please open the window. [request]

          Wait! [strong command]

Notice in the examples above that a command or a request has the understood subject *you.*

(3) An *interrogative sentence* asks a question and ends with a question mark.

EXAMPLES   Can you speak Spanish?

          Did you say that you were taking French?

(4) An *exclamatory sentence* shows excitement or expresses strong feeling and ends with an exclamation point.

EXAMPLES   What a beautiful day this is!

          How I enjoy autumn!

Reference Note

For a discussion of how **sentences** are **classified by structure,** see page 504. For more on **end marks,** see Chapter 22.

S T Y L E   T I P

Sometimes a writer will use both a question mark and an exclamation point to express the combined emotions of disbelief and surprise.

EXAMPLE
"How could you have said that?!" she gasped.

You should limit the use of such combined punctuation to informal writing and dialogue.

NOTE Any sentence may be spoken so that it becomes exclamatory or interrogative. When writing dialogue, use an exclamation point or a question mark to show how you intend a sentence to be read.

EXAMPLES   "It's snowing." [declarative]

"It's snowing!" [exclamatory]

"It's snowing?" [interrogative]

Exercise 15 Classifying Sentences According to Purpose

Punctuate each of the following sentences with an appropriate end mark. Then, classify the sentence as *declarative, imperative, interrogative,* or *exclamatory.*

EXAMPLE   **1.** What kinds of music do you like

1. *What kinds of music do you like?—interrogative*

1. The loudspeakers in our living room are small yet powerful
2. Turn down the sound
3. How loud that is
4. Listening to loud music can damage a person's hearing
5. How many watts does your amplifier produce
6. Sound levels are measured in units called decibels
7. Do you know that an increase of ten decibels represents a doubling in the sound level
8. Do not blast your sound system
9. Keep it quiet
10. Music played softly is relaxing

Review E Understanding the Parts of a Sentence

In your own words, define each of the following terms, and write a sentence in which the term is illustrated.

EXAMPLE   **1.** a transitive verb

1. *A transitive verb is an action verb that takes an object. Babe Ruth played baseball.*

1. a sentence
2. a complete subject
3. a verb (simple predicate)
4. a verb phrase
5. a complete predicate
6. a simple subject

7. a subject complement
8. a direct object
9. an understood subject
10. an indirect object

Review F **Identifying Subjects, Verbs, and Complements**

Identify each italicized word or word group in the following paragraphs as a *subject*, a *verb*, a *predicate nominative*, a *predicate adjective*, a *direct object*, or an *indirect object*.

EXAMPLE   The photograph below shows the **[1]** *Great Pyramid of Khufu.*

1. *direct object*

The Great Pyramid of Khufu is **[1]** *one* of the wonders of the ancient world. **[2]** *It* was once encased with blocks of polished limestone. However, **[3]** *weather and thievery* **[4]** *have combined* to destroy the original structure. As you **[5]** *can see*, the pyramid **[6]** *looks* **[7]** *weather-beaten.* Still, it is an impressive **[8]** *sight.*

Hundreds of years ago, one invading Arab **[9]** *ruler* decided to rob the tomb of Khufu. With many workers at his disposal, he gave the **[10]** *men* his **[11]** *instructions.* The workers **[12]** *hacked* through the incredibly hard solid blocks of granite. Unexpectedly, **[13]** *they* broke into a tunnel. Imagine their **[14]** *excitement*! All too soon, however, they **[15]** *discovered* an enormous **[16]** *plug* of granite blocking their way. They cut around the plug and finally reached the inner **[17]** *chamber.*

Strangely enough, there was no **[18]** *gold.* No vast treasures **[19]** *sparkled* under the light of the torches. The tomb probably **[20]** *had been robbed* many centuries earlier by Egyptians familiar with its secret entrances.

Review G **Writing Sentences**

Write sentences according to the following guidelines. Underline the subject once and the verb twice in each sentence. If the subject is understood, write *(You)*.

EXAMPLES
  1. Write a sentence containing a direct object.
    1. *(You) Have another glass of milk.*

  2. Write a sentence beginning with *Here*.
    2. *Here are the missing puzzle pieces.*

1. Write a declarative sentence containing a verb phrase.
2. Write a sentence beginning with *There.*
3. Write an interrogative sentence.
4. Write an exclamatory sentence.
5. Write an imperative sentence.
6. Write a sentence containing a compound subject.
7. Write a sentence containing a predicate nominative.
8. Write a sentence containing a compound verb.
9. Write a sentence containing a predicate adjective.
10. Write a sentence containing an indirect object and a compound direct object.

GRAMMAR

Chapter Review

A. Identifying Subjects, Verbs, and Complements

Identify the italicized word or word group in each of the following sentences as a *subject*, a *verb*, a *predicate adjective*, a *predicate nominative*, a *direct object*, or an *indirect object*.

1. Native *cactuses* in the Southwest are in trouble.
2. Some species are already *vulnerable* to extinction.
3. Cactuses *are being threatened* by landscapers, tourists, and collectors.
4. Many people illegally harvest these wild *plants*.
5. There are many unique cactus *species* in Arizona.
6. Arizona is, therefore, an active *battlefield* in the war against the removal of these endangered species.
7. "Cactus cops" *patrol* the streets of Phoenix on the lookout for places with illegally acquired cactuses.
8. Authorized dealers must give *purchasers* permit tags as proof of legal sale.
9. First violations are *punishable* by a fine of five hundred dollars.
10. Illegally owned cactuses *may be confiscated* by the police.
11. What a thorny problem cactus *rustling* has become!
12. Why are illegal harvesters so *hard* to keep track of?
13. Many work at night and sometimes use permit *tags* over and over.
14. If you purchase a large cactus, always *examine* it for bruises.
15. A legally harvested cactus *should* not *show* any damage.

B. Identifying Subjects and Predicates

Identify the complete subjects and complete predicates in each of the following sentences.

16. The invention of motion pictures is attributed to many people.
17. Chief among the inventors are the French brothers Auguste and Louis Lumière.
18. A laboratory assistant of Thomas Edison named Dickson had invented a type of simple "peep-hole" viewing device called the Kinetoscope.
19. The Edison-Dickson Kinetoscope was displayed in Paris in 1894.

┌HELP─
A sentence in Part B may contain more than one subject and predicate.

20. Auguste and Louis were determined to improve upon it.
21. In 1895, their determination paid off, and the *cinématographe* was patented.
22. The *cinématographe* functioned as a camera and printer as well as a projector.
23. Everyday French life in the 1890s can be glimpsed in the Lumière brothers' first films.
24. Their 1895 film "Workers Leaving the Lumière Factory" is considered the first motion picture.
25. Ironically, *Lumière* means "light."

C. Completing Sentences by Supplying Subjects and Verbs

Complete each of the following sentences with an appropriate subject or verb. Identify your answer as a *subject* or a *verb*.

26. Greyhounds _____ races.
27. A few of the sophomores _____ after class.
28. Many _____ of the Great Plains were nomadic.
29. The audience _____ at the deathbed scene.
30. To get out of the maze, he _____ to where he had started.
31. _____ came tumbling down in the gale.
32. Dogs _____ to be walked regularly.
33. The wind _____ through the branches.
34. _____ smiled.
35. Every day after school, Maggie _____ pictures.

D. Identifying Predicate Nominatives and Predicate Adjectives

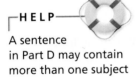

┌HELP┐

A sentence in Part D may contain more than one subject complement.

Write each subject complement in the following sentences, and then identify it as a *predicate nominative* or a *predicate adjective*.

36. We felt exhausted after the marathon.
37. Sitting in the shade was pleasant when the sunlight was so intense.
38. Those dogs are Dalmatians.
39. Your explanation is very clear.
40. My colleague Eric grows calmer every day.
41. Abdullah II became king of Jordan in February 1999.
42. Our neighbor Gary's new car is a very sleek and sporty model.

43. The painting looked somber.

44. The first part of the movie is very funny.

45. Their apartment is in a building that looks new and clean.

E. Classifying Sentences as Declarative, Interrogative, Imperative, or Exclamatory

Classify each of the following sentences as *declarative*, *interrogative*, *imperative*, or *exclamatory*.

46. Read this article about imperiled cactuses.

47. The author describes a trip into the desert with a legal hauler.

48. Can you imagine a saguaro worth three hundred dollars?

49. A crested saguaro is even rarer and can sell for thousands of dollars.

50. No wonder illegal harvesting is booming!

Writing Application
Using Varied Sentences in a Letter

Sentence Variety Your neighborhood Residents' Council would like to sponsor a dance for the teenagers in your area. However, the council is not sure what kind of dance teens would like. You have decided to write a short letter to the council to give your opinion.

Prewriting Decide how you feel about this issue. Then, jot down a few notes about what kind of dance you would like to have. Next, write some different opening sentences. Choose the opener that you think will be the most interesting and effective.

Writing As you write your letter, refer often to your prewriting notes. Use a variety of sentence structures.

Revising Ask an adult you know to listen to your letter. Does he or she think your opening sentence is interesting? Does he or she find your letter persuasive? Revise any sections that are unclear or that lack sentence variety.

Publishing Proofread your letter for any errors in grammar, punctuation, and spelling. You and your classmates may want to post the letter on the class bulletin board or Web page.

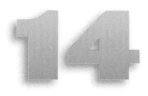
14

The Phrase

Prepositional, Verbal, and Appositive Phrases

Diagnostic Preview

Identifying Prepositional, Verbal, and Appositive Phrases

Identify each italicized phrase in the following paragraphs as a *prepositional phrase*, a *participial phrase*, a *gerund phrase*, an *infinitive phrase*, or an *appositive phrase*.

EXAMPLES   An interesting profession **[1]** *to consider as a career* is **[2]** *practicing law.*

1. to consider as a career—infinitive phrase
2. practicing law—gerund phrase

Susana, **[1]** *our next-door neighbor,* wanted **[2]** *to become an attorney.* After she earned a degree **[3]** *from a four-year college,* she took the Law School Admissions Test and was admitted **[4]** *to a prominent law school.* **[5]** *Having completed three full years of law school,* Susana was then awarded a J.D. degree. Before **[6]** *practicing law,* however, she took the state bar exam, **[7]** *a test required by the state board of bar examiners.* Only after **[8]** *passing this exam* had she completed the requirements **[9]** *to be admitted to the bar* and **[10]** *to practice law.*

[11] *Working as an attorney,* Susana provides service and advice **[12]** *relating to legal rights.* Even though she tries hard **[13]** *to keep cases out of court,* Susana enjoys the challenge **[14]** *of presenting cases*

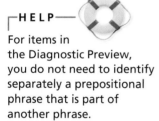

HELP

For items in the Diagnostic Preview, you do not need to identify separately a prepositional phrase that is part of another phrase.

to a jury. [15] *Representing a client in court,* however, is only part [16] *of* Susana's job. She devotes hours to [17] *gathering enough evidence* [18] *to defend a client.* She also spends time [19] *on research* and is required [20] *to write numerous reports.*

What Is a Phrase?

14a. A *phrase* is a group of related words that is used as a single part of speech and that does not contain both a verb and its subject.

PREPOSITIONAL PHRASE   for you and her [no subject or verb]
       INFINITIVE PHRASE   to be the best [no subject]

> **NOTE** A group of words that has both a subject and a verb is called a *clause.*
>
> EXAMPLES   They will be here soon. [*They* is the subject of *will be.*]
>
>   after she leaves [*She* is the subject of *leaves.*]

Reference Note
For more about **clauses,** see Chapter 15.

Prepositional Phrases

14b. A *prepositional phrase* includes a preposition, the object of the preposition, and any modifiers of that object.

EXAMPLES   A koala is a marsupial, a mammal **with an external abdominal pouch.** [The noun *pouch* is the object of the preposition *with.*]

               To me a koala looks **like a cuddly teddy bear.** [The pronoun *me* is the object of the preposition *To.* The compound noun *teddy bear* is the object of the preposition *like.*]

               Koalas, **along with several other marsupials,** are native **to Australia.** [The noun *marsupials* is the object of the compound preposition *along with.* The noun *Australia* is the object of the preposition *to.*]

Reference Note
For lists of **commonly used prepositions,** see page 426.

> **NOTE** Do not confuse a prepositional phrase beginning with *to*—as in *to me* or *to Australia*—with an infinitive, such as *to be* or *to learn.*

Reference Note
For more on **infinitives,** see page 479.

An object of a preposition may be compound.

EXAMPLE   Koalas feed **on only eucalyptus buds and leaves.** [The
           nouns *buds* and *leaves* are the compound object of the
           preposition *on.*]

Adjective Phrases

14c. **A prepositional phrase that modifies a noun or a pronoun is
called an *adjective phrase.***

An adjective phrase tells *what kind* or *which one.*

EXAMPLES   We ordered a dish **of salsa** and a basket **of tortilla chips.**
            [*Of salsa* modifies the noun *dish,* telling *what kind* of dish.
            Of tortilla chips modifies the noun *basket,* telling *what kind*
            of basket.]

            No one **in the class** has seen the movie yet. [*In the class*
            modifies the pronoun *no one,* telling *which one.*]

Two or more adjective phrases may modify the same noun
or pronoun.

EXAMPLE   The picture **of their candidate in today's newspaper** is
           not at all flattering. [Both *of their candidate* and *in today's
           newspaper* modify the noun *picture.*]

An adjective phrase may also modify the object of another prepositional phrase.

EXAMPLE   The coconut palms in the park **near the bay** were planted a
           long time ago. [*Near the bay* modifies *park,* the object of the
           preposition *in.*]

Exercise 1 **Identifying Adjective Phrases**

Identify the adjective phrase(s) in each of the following sentences.
After each adjective phrase, give the word it modifies.

EXAMPLE   1. Julius Caesar was one of the most successful generals in
               ancient Rome.

           1. *of the most successful generals—one*
               in ancient Rome—generals

TIPS & TRICKS

Unlike single-word adjec-
tives, adjective phrases
almost always follow the
noun or pronoun they
modify.

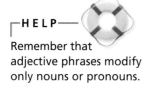

—HELP—
Remember that
adjective phrases modify
only nouns or pronouns.

1. Roman roads were one reason for Caesar's military successes.
2. The roads of ancient Rome linked the far corners of the empire.
3. Large blocks of hard stone provided a sound foundation for most major routes.
4. Caesar's interest in military roads showed his understanding of the vital importance of communication.
5. Close communication among the empire's provinces strengthened the power of the Roman rulers.
6. The need for roads was addressed in 312 B.C., when the 160-mile Via Appia was begun.
7. The curved surfaces of the road system facilitated drainage.
8. Heavy use of the highways lasted many centuries.
9. Some roads from the old empire still exist.
10. The Romans built nearly 50,000 miles of roads crossing Europe.

Adverb Phrases

14d. A prepositional phrase that modifies a verb, an adjective, or an adverb is called an *adverb phrase.*

EXAMPLES   The mole burrowed **under the lawn.** [*Under the lawn* modifies the verb *burrowed.*]

Althea Gibson was graceful **on the tennis court.** [*On the tennis court* modifies the adjective *graceful.*]

The child speaks quite clearly **for a two-year-old.** [*For a two-year-old* modifies the adverb *clearly.*]

Adverb phrases tell *when, where, why, how,* or *to what extent* (*how much, how long,* or *how far*).

EXAMPLES   **After the storm,** the town grew quiet. [*when*]

He glanced **out the window.** [*where*]

Most street musicians play **for tips.** [*why*]

This summer we're going **by car** to Kansas. [*how*]

She won the contest **by two points.** [*to what extent*]

STYLE   TIP

Be sure to place prepositional phrases carefully so that they express the meaning you intend.

MISPLACED
In its nest at the top of the tree, we could see the great blue heron with binoculars. [The sentence suggests that we are in the heron's nest at the top of the tree and that the heron has binoculars.]

IMPROVED
With binoculars, we could see the great blue heron **in its nest at the top of the tree.**

Reference Note

For more about **misplaced modifiers,** see page 627.

Adverb phrases may come before or after the words they modify, and more than one adverb phrase may modify the same word.

EXAMPLE **In the first inning** she pitched **with great control.** [*In the first inning* modifies the verb *pitched,* telling *when; with great control* modifies *pitched,* telling *how.*]

Exercise 2 Identifying Adverb Phrases

Identify the adverb phrases in the following sentences.

EXAMPLE 1. The plane taxied down the runway.
1. *down the runway*

1. The porters hiked toward the summit.
2. The chicken walked across the road.
3. During Ramadan, Muslims fast from sunrise to sunset.
4. Tamara and Dawn floated down the river on a raft.
5. We walked past many beautiful meadows and streams.
6. Beneath the waves, the ocean is calm.
7. We flew across the international date line.
8. After dinner, everyone slept.
9. Spinning out of control, we tumbled into the powdery snow and, laughing, brushed ourselves off.
10. The kayakers rested beside the river.

Exercise 3 Identifying Adverb Phrases

Identify the adverb phrase(s) in each of the following sentences. Then, give the word or word group the phrase modifies.

EXAMPLE 1. For several months no one has lived in the house next to ours.
1. *For several months—has lived in the house—has lived*

1. On Friday, Dad and I were alarmed by plaintive sounds that came from the abandoned house.
2. We searched inside the whole house, from the dusty attic to the cold, damp basement.
3. In the basement we found two stray kittens.
4. They were crying for food.

┌HELP
Some sentences in Exercise 2 contain more than one adverb phrase.

┌HELP
Remember that adverb phrases modify only verbs, adjectives, or adverbs. A prepositional phrase that modifies a noun or pronoun is an adjective phrase.

5. The noises we'd heard had been made by them.
6. I found an empty box in the corner and gently placed both of the kittens in it.
7. They seemed happy with their temporary home.
8. Then, we took the kittens to our house.
9. We lined the box with some soft, old towels and set it in the warm kitchen.
10. Now the plaintive sounds come from our house at all hours of the night and day.

Review A **Sentences with Prepositional Phrases**

Provide a prepositional phrase to complete each of the following sentences. After the sentence, identify the phrase as an *adjective phrase* or an *adverb phrase*.

EXAMPLE   **1.** _____ Mrs. Bowen reads the newspaper.

1. In the evening Mrs. Bowen reads the newspaper.—adverb phrase

1. I watched a spider climb _____.
2. _____ the children played hopscotch.
3. We planned a drive _____.
4. Her team played _____.
5. The sky divers jumped fearlessly _____.
6. Hundreds _____ stared.
7. _____ the cyclists unpacked their lunches.
8. There _____ winds a narrow road.
9. This movie will be playing _____.
10. _____ the dancers swayed with the music.
11. Katherine always finishes her homework _____.
12. _____, the children found some coins.
13. The beans _____ are very fresh.
14. Bao wrote a book _____.
15. The group was silent _____.
16. Alice went _____.
17. Everyone _____ was cheering.
18. We traveled _____ to the river.
19. The trees _____ are growing fast.
20. The children _____ are being very cautious.

Verbals and Verbal Phrases

Verbals are formed from verbs and are used as adjectives, nouns, or adverbs. The three kinds of verbals are the *participle*, the *gerund*, and the *infinitive*.

A **verbal phrase** consists of a verbal and its modifiers and complements. The three kinds of verbal phrases are the *participial phrase*, the *gerund phrase*, and the *infinitive phrase*.

The Participle

14e. A *participle* is a verb form that can be used as an adjective.

EXAMPLES   What is the temperature of the **boiling** water? [*Boiling*, formed from the verb *boil*, modifies the noun *water*.]

A **chipped** fingernail can be annoying. [*Chipped*, formed from the verb *chip*, modifies the noun *fingernail*.]

Your **chosen** topic is too broad, I think. [*Chosen*, formed from the verb *choose*, modifies the noun *topic*.]

Two kinds of participles are *present participles* and *past participles*.

(1) *Present participles* end in –*ing*.

EXAMPLES   The **smiling** graduates posed for the photographer. [*Smiling*, formed from the verb *smile*, modifies the noun *graduates*.]

For an hour we sat there **reminiscing.** [*Reminiscing*, formed from the verb *reminisce*, modifies the pronoun *we*.]

Standing and **applauding,** the audience cheered the cast of the musical *The Lion King*. [*Standing*, formed from the verb *stand*, and *applauding*, formed from the verb *applaud*, modify the noun *audience*.]

(2) Most *past participles* end in –*d* or –*ed*. Some are formed irregularly.

EXAMPLES   For dinner we prepared **grilled** salmon, **baked** potatoes, and **tossed** salad. [*Grilled*, formed from the verb *grill*, modifies the noun *salmon*; *baked*, formed from the verb *bake*, modifies the noun *potatoes*; and *tossed*, formed from the verb *toss*, modifies the noun *salad*.]

Reference Note

For lists of commonly used **irregular past participles,** see page 576.

For years the treasure had remained **hidden** under tons of **fallen** rock. [*Hidden,* formed from the verb *hide,* modifies the noun *treasure*; *fallen,* formed from the verb *fall,* modifies the noun *rock.*]

> **NOTE** Do not confuse a participle used as an adjective with a participle used as part of a verb phrase.
>
> ADJECTIVE   The shrimp gumbo, **simmering** on the stove, smelled delicious.
>
> VERB PHRASE   The shrimp gumbo **was simmering** on the stove.

Reference Note

For more about **verb phrases,** see pages 417 and 441.

Exercise 4   **Revising Sentences by Adding Participles**

After each of the following sentences is a participle in parentheses. Revise each sentence by inserting the participle next to the noun it modifies.

EXAMPLE   1. We collected funds for the restoration of the building. (*damaged*)

1. We collected funds for the restoration of the damaged building.

1. The space shuttle was greeted with loud cheers. (*returning*)
2. The parents named shows they found unacceptable. (*protesting*)
3. My sister did not hear the doorbell. (*ringing*)
4. The carpenter will show us how to fix this chair. (*broken*)
5. In 1949, Luis Muñoz Marín became Puerto Rico's first governor. (*elected*)
6. The stream crosses the farmer's land at three places. (*winding*)
7. We handed the envelope to the mail carrier. (*crumpled*)
8. This book includes many interesting facts about dinosaurs. (*illustrated*)
9. The Douglas fir behind our house has become a haven for several small creatures. (*fallen*)
10. The plane narrowly missed a radio antenna. (*circling*)

The Participial Phrase

14f. A *participial phrase* consists of a participle and any modifiers or complements the participle has. The entire phrase is used as an adjective.

STYLE ✏ TIP

When writing a sentence that contains a participial phrase, be sure to place the phrase as close as possible to the word or words it modifies.

MISPLACED
The Scouts spotted the white-tailed deer and her twin fawns gathering wood for a campfire. [The sentence suggests that the deer and her two fawns are gathering wood.]

IMPROVED
Gathering wood for a campfire, the Scouts spotted the white-tailed deer and her twin fawns.

Reference Note

For more information on the correct **placement of participial phrases,** see page 355. See page 707 for more on the **punctuation of participial phrases.**

Reference Note

For more information about **using commas with participial phrases,** see page 707.

In each of the following sentences, an arrow connects the participial phrase with the noun or pronoun the phrase modifies.

EXAMPLES   **Climbing the tree,** the monkey disappeared into the branches. [The participial phrase modifies the noun *monkey*. The noun *tree* is the direct object of the present participle *Climbing*.]

I heard him **whispering to his friend.** [The participial phrase modifies the pronoun *him*. The adverb phrase *to his friend* modifies the present participle *whispering*.]

We watched the storm **blowing eastward.** [The participial phrase modifies the noun *storm*. The adverb *eastward* modifies the present participle *blowing*.]

Voted back into office, the mayor thanked her supporters. [The participial phrase modifies the noun *mayor*. The adverb *back* and the adverb phrase *into office* modify the past participle *Voted*.]

The concert **scheduled for tomorrow at the park** has been postponed until next week. [The participial phrase modifies the noun *concert*. The adverb phrases *for tomorrow* and *at the park* modify the past participle *scheduled*.]

NOTE   When placed at the beginning of a sentence, a participial phrase is followed by a comma.

Exercise 5   Identifying Participial Phrases

Each of the following sentences contains at least one participial phrase. Identify each participial phrase and the word or words it modifies.

EXAMPLE   1. Robert Scott, commanding a British expedition to the South Pole, learned that another expedition was ahead of him.

     1. *commanding a British expedition to the South Pole—Robert Scott*

1. Hoping to be the first to reach the South Pole, Robert Scott (back row, center, in the photograph on the next page) took these four men with him on his final dash to the pole in November 1911.

2. Leading Scott, a British explorer, by sixty miles, a Norwegian expedition commanded by Roald Amundsen was moving swiftly, however.
3. Learning about Amundsen, Scott realized a race to the pole was on.
4. Plagued by bad weather and bad luck, Scott fell farther behind Amundsen.
5. Reaching the pole on January 17, the British found that the Norwegians had already been there.
6. Weakened by scurvy, frostbite, and exhaustion, the five explorers in the photograph set out on the eight-hundred-mile journey back to their base camp.
7. One member of the party, overcome by exhaustion and injuries, died before half the journey had been completed.
8. On March 15 another member, leaving the camp at night, crawled deliberately to his death in a violent blizzard.
9. Eight months later, a rescue mission, sent to find out what had happened, found the bodies of Scott and his companions.
10. Today, the ill-fated Scott expedition, acclaimed for its heroism, is more famous than the successful Amundsen expedition.

The Granger Collection, New York.

Review B Identifying Participles

Identify the participial phrases and the participles that are used as adjectives in the following sentences. Give the noun or pronoun each participle or participial phrase modifies.

EXAMPLE
1. We have been studying one of the most feared animals in the sea—the killer whale.

1. feared—animals

1. Killer whales, long known and feared as wolves of the sea, are not nearly as vicious as many people have thought.
2. Seeking to test the supposedly ferocious nature of the killer whale, scientists studied the whales' behavior.
3. After extensive study, scientists discovered that there is no proven case of an attack on a human by a killer whale.
4. In fact, scientists working with killer whales have confirmed that their charges are intelligent and can be quite gentle.
5. Most killer whales gathered in Johnstone Strait, which is a narrow channel between Vancouver Island and British Columbia in Canada, spend the summer and fall in large family groups.

┌HELP─
Sentences in Review B may contain more than one participle or participial phrase.

6. Choosing this spot to observe the mammals, researchers were able to identify more than one hundred whales.

7. The team of scientists, noting the unique shape of each whale's dorsal fin, named each whale in order to keep more accurate records.

8. Impressed by the long life span of killer whales, scientists have estimated that males may live fifty years and females may survive a century.

9. Cruising in groups called pods, most killer whales are highly social animals.

10. During the summer and fall in Johnstone Strait, many pods gather, splashing and playing in "superpods."

The Gerund

Reference Note

For more about **subjects,** see page 440. For more about **predicate nominatives,** see page 453. For more about **direct** and **indirect objects,** see page 456. For more about **objects of prepositions,** see page 467.

14g. A *gerund* is a verb form that ends in *–ing* and that is used as a noun.

A gerund can be used as a subject, a predicate nominative, a direct object, an indirect object, or an object of a preposition.

SUBJECT **Reading** will improve your vocabulary. [*Reading,* formed from the verb *read,* is the subject of the verb *will improve.*]

PREDICATE NOMINATIVE One popular summer sport is **swimming.** [*Swimming,* formed from the verb *swim,* is a predicate nominative identifying the subject *sport.*]

DIRECT OBJECT Both Dad and Mom enjoy **cooking** together. [*Cooking,* formed from the verb *cook,* is the direct object of the verb *enjoy.*]

INDIRECT OBJECT Before she decided to become a lawyer, she had given **teaching** thoughtful consideration. [*Teaching,* formed from the verb *teach,* is the indirect object of the verb *had given.*]

OBJECT OF A PREPOSITION After **studying,** how do you relax? [*Studying,* formed from the verb *study,* is the object of the preposition *After.*]

NOTE Gerunds, like present participles, end in *–ing*. Do not confuse a gerund, which is used as a noun, with a present participle, which may be used as an adjective or as part of a verb phrase.

GERUND	I have enjoyed **reading** about the different species of dinosaurs. [*Reading* is used as the direct object of the verb *have enjoyed*.]
PRESENT PARTICIPLE	I have spent several hours in the library, **reading** about different species of dinosaurs. [*Reading* is used as an adjective modifying the pronoun *I*.]
PRESENT PARTICIPLE	I have been **reading** about the different species of dinosaurs. [*Reading* is used as part of the verb phrase *have been reading*.]

Exercise 6 Identifying Gerunds and Participles

Identify the verbal in each of the following sentences, and tell whether it is a *gerund* or a *participle*. If the verbal is a gerund, tell how it is used: as a *subject*, a *predicate nominative*, a *direct object*, an *indirect object*, or an *object of a preposition*. If the verbal is a participle, tell which word it modifies.

EXAMPLES   1. Sleeping on the job is foolish.
            1. Sleeping, gerund—subject

          2. Let sleeping dogs lie.
            2. sleeping, participle—dogs

1. Their giggling annoyed the other viewers.
2. Virginia gave cycling a try.
3. Sneezing, the enemy scout revealed his location.
4. Fascinated, my sister asked to hear more about our wild plot.
5. Making friends in a new school can be difficult, but I am getting better at it.
6. The highlight of the season was watching our team win the regional tournament.
7. Spinning one full turn, the ballerina gracefully performed a pirouette.
8. During the summer, Carlota sometimes makes money by walking dogs for her neighbors.
9. My grandmother and I enjoy digging for clams.
10. Sensing the danger nearby, he shouted for help.

The Gerund Phrase

14h. A *gerund phrase* consists of a gerund and any modifiers or complements the gerund has. The entire phrase is used as a noun.

SUBJECT **The sudden shattering of glass** broke the silence. [The gerund phrase is the subject of the verb *broke.* The article *The,* the adjective *sudden,* and the adjective phrase *of glass* modify the gerund *shattering.*]

PREDICATE NOMINATIVE One of my chores in the summer is **mowing the lawn.** [The gerund phrase is a predicate nominative identifying the subject *One.* The noun *lawn* is the direct object of the gerund *mowing.*]

DIRECT OBJECT She enjoys **hiking in the mountains occasionally.** [The gerund phrase is the direct object of the verb *enjoys.* The adverb phrase *in the mountains* and the adverb *occasionally* modify the gerund *hiking.*]

INDIRECT OBJECT Ms. Yashima, a part-time reporter for the local newspaper, is giving **working full time** careful thought. [The gerund phrase is the indirect object of the verb *is giving.* The adverb *full time* modifies the gerund *working.*]

OBJECT OF THE PREPOSITION By **reading the works of Pat Mora,** I have learned much about Mexican culture. [The gerund phrase is the object of the preposition *By.* The noun *works* is the direct object of the gerund *reading.* The adjective phrase *of Pat Mora* modifies *works.*]

Reference Note

For more about the **possessive forms of nouns and pronouns,** see page 758.

NOTE   A noun or pronoun directly before a gerund should be in the possessive case.

EXAMPLES   **Eli's** dancing won him first prize in the contest.

His dancing has greatly improved since last year.

Exercise 7   Using Gerunds and Gerund Phrases

Use gerunds or gerund phrases to fill in the blanks of the following sentences.

EXAMPLE   1. The sign on the wall said "No ____."

1. *The sign on the wall said "No Smoking."*

1. ____ daily is a healthy hobby.

2. Fred Astaire was known for his ____.
3. ____ is advised for those who live in sensitive ecological zones.
4. After moving to England, Rick had to get used to many things, such as ____.
5. ____ is one of my claims to fame.
6. The ranger enjoys ____.
7. Most dentists recommend ____.
8. One way to increase your aerobic capacity is ____.
9. ____ helps me concentrate.
10. Give ____ your best effort.

The Infinitive

14i. An *infinitive* is a verb form that can be used as a noun, an adjective, or an adverb. Most infinitives begin with *to*.

Infinitives	
Used as	**Examples**
Nouns	**To err** is human. [*To err* is the subject of the verb *is*.]
	His dream is **to travel.** [*To travel* is a predicate nominative identifying the subject *dream*.]
	Betty wants **to act.** [*To act* is the direct object of the verb *wants*.]
Adjectives	The candidate **to believe** is Villegas. [*To believe* modifies the noun *candidate*.]
	She is the one **to ask.** [*To ask* modifies the pronoun *one*.]
Adverbs	Grandmother is coming **to visit.** [*To visit* modifies the verb *is coming*.]
	The favored team was slow **to score.** [*To score* modifies the adjective *slow*.]

NOTE The word *to* plus a noun or a pronoun (for example, *to Tokyo, to the movies, to her*) is a prepositional phrase, not an infinitive.

Reference Note
For more about **prepositional phrases,** see page 467.

┌─ H E L P ─┐

Some sentences in Exercise 8 contain more than one infinitive.

┌ S T Y L E   T I P ┐

Placing a word or word group between the sign of the infinitive, *to,* and the verb results in a **split infinitive.** Generally, you should avoid split infinitives in formal writing and speaking.

SPLIT
The director wants to, before rehearsal, speak with both the stage crew and the cast.

IMPROVED
The director wants **to speak** with both the stage crew and the cast before rehearsal.

Occasionally, however, you may need to use a split infinitive so that your meaning is clear.

UNCLEAR
He hoped to avoid carefully causing delays. [Does the adverb *carefully* modify the gerund *causing* or the infinitive *to avoid*?]

UNCLEAR
He hoped carefully to avoid causing delays. [Does the adverb *carefully* modify the verb *hoped* or the infinitive *to avoid*?]

CLEAR
He hoped **to carefully avoid** causing delays.

Exercise 8 Identifying and Classifying Infinitives

Identify the infinitives in the following sentences, and tell how each is used: as a *subject,* a *predicate nominative,* a *direct object,* an *adjective,* or an *adverb.*

EXAMPLE **1.** What do you want to do after you graduate from high school?

   1. *to do—direct object*

1. We are waiting to perform.
2. This summer she hopes to travel.
3. I am ready to leave.
4. Do you want to drive?
5. To forgive is sometimes difficult.
6. To excel, one must practice.
7. We are eager to go.
8. A good way to learn is to live.
9. The soup is still too hot to eat.
10. I said to Jo, "One way to improve is to practice."

The Infinitive Phrase

14j. An *infinitive phrase* consists of an infinitive and any modifiers or complements the infinitive has. The entire phrase can be used as a noun, an adjective, or an adverb.

NOUN **To hit a curveball solidly** is very difficult. [The infinitive phrase is the subject of the verb *is.* The noun *curveball* is the direct object of the infinitive *To hit,* and the adverb *solidly* modifies *To hit.*]

NOUN She wants **to study marine biology.** [The infinitive phrase is the direct object of the verb *wants.* The noun *biology* is the direct object of the infinitive *to study,* and the adjective *marine* modifies *biology.*]

ADJECTIVE His efforts **to trace his ancestry** led to greater appreciation of his heritage. [The infinitive phrase modifies the noun *efforts.* The noun *ancestry* is the direct object of the infinitive *to trace,* and the possessive pronoun *his* is used to modify *ancestry.*]

ADVERB I found his explanation difficult **to accept.** [The infinitive phrase modifies the adjective *difficult.*]

NOTE Unlike other verbals, an infinitive may have a subject. An *infinitive clause* consists of an infinitive with a subject and any modifiers or complements the infinitive has. The entire infinitive clause functions as a noun.

EXAMPLE   I wanted **him to come to our powwow.** [*Him* is the subject of the infinitive *to come.* The entire infinitive clause is the direct object of the verb *wanted.*]

GRAMMAR

Sometimes *to*, the sign of the infinitive, is omitted.

EXAMPLES   Did you watch her [to] **play** volleyball?

He will help us [to] **paddle** the canoe.

We don't dare [to] **go** outside during the storm.

COMPUTER TIP

Some style-checking software programs can identify and highlight split infinitives. Using such a program will help you eliminate unnecessary split infinitives from your writing.

Exercise 9 **Identifying and Classifying Infinitive Phrases and Infinitive Clauses**

Identify the infinitive phrases and infinitive clauses in the following sentences, and tell how each is used: as a *subject*, a *predicate nominative*, a *direct object*, an *adjective*, or an *adverb*.

EXAMPLE   1. Everyone in the class was eager to learn more about the life of Maya Angelou.

1. *to learn more about the life of Maya Angelou—adverb*

1. Our assignment was to read *I Know Why the Caged Bird Sings.*
2. I decided to write a report on Maya Angelou's descriptions of her childhood.
3. To grow up in Stamps, Arkansas, in the 1930s was to know great hardship.
4. Maya Angelou tried to show the everyday lives of African Americans during the Great Depression.
5. To accomplish this purpose meant including many descriptions; one such passage told about the process for curing pork sausage.
6. Angelou has an extraordinary ability to capture vivid details in her writing.
7. She helps us see her grandmother's store through the eyes of a fascinated child.
8. Angelou was eager to experience life beyond her hometown.

HELP

Some sentences in Exercise 9 contain more than one infinitive phrase or infinitive clause. Remember that the sign of the infinitive, *to*, may be omitted.

Link to **Literature**

9. Her talents and ambition enabled her to achieve success as a writer, a dancer, and an actress.

10. To dramatize her African American heritage was a dream she realized by writing a television series.

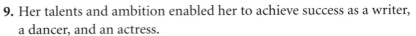
┌─HELP─┐
Remember
that *to,* the sign of the
infinitive, may be omitted.

Review C Identifying Types of Verbals and Verbal Phrases

Identify the verbal phrases in the following paragraph. Then, tell whether each verbal phrase is a *participial phrase,* a *gerund phrase,* or an *infinitive phrase.*

EXAMPLE [1] Looking at these control panels in the flight deck of a jumbo passenger jet, most of us feel completely lost.

1. *Looking at these control panels in the flight deck of a jumbo passenger jet—participial phrase*

[1] Intensive training is required for pilots. [2] Traveling the airways has become much easier because of modern technology. [3] Fortunately, in the flight deck sit people trained in the uses of these controls and instruments. [4] Sitting in front of identical control panels, both the captain and the first officer can fly the plane. [5] The captain, who uses the left-hand panel, operates a lever that controls the wing flaps and helps steer the plane. [6] Operating the brake panels is another one of the captain's jobs. [7] To the captain's right is the first officer, whose job is to help the captain. [8] The throttle, which governs the engines' ability to move the plane forward, is located between the captain and the first officer. [9] Some of the other instruments shown here are parts of the plane's navigation, autopilot, and communication systems. [10] At another station in the flight deck, the flight engineer monitors gauges and operates switches to control the plane's generators and the pressure and temperature in the cabin.

Review D Identifying Verbal Phrases

Identify the verbal phrases in the following paragraph. Then, tell whether each verbal phrase is a *participial phrase,* a *gerund phrase,* or an *infinitive phrase.*

EXAMPLE   **[1]** Would you like to have a summer job?

1. *to have a summer job—infinitive phrase*

[**1**] If you are not offered a job right away, remember that contacting a number of agencies and following up with phone calls and thank-you notes will increase your chances. [**2**] To persevere in the job hunt is very important. [**3**] Finding a summer job can be a difficult task. [**4**] The first step is to scan the classified ads listed in your local newspaper. [**5**] After discovering available opportunities, you can embark on the second step, which is matching your skills with the requirements of a specific job. [**6**] In most cases you can then contact a prospective employer by making a phone call or by writing a letter requesting an interview. [**7**] If you are asked to interview for a job, be sure to take care in preparing for the interview. [**8**] To make a good impression, be sure to arrive on time, to dress neatly, and to speak courteously. [**9**] Remember to avoid such nervous habits as constantly checking your watch or shuffling your feet. [**10**] By presenting yourself as calm, confident, and courteous, you may hear the magic words "We'd like you to work for us."

Appositives and Appositive Phrases

14k. An *appositive* is a noun or pronoun placed beside another noun or pronoun to identify or describe it.

EXAMPLES   My cousin **Bryan** is my best friend. [The appositive *Bryan* identifies the noun *cousin*.]

Our football team has won its first two games, **one** by three points and the **other** by six. [The appositives *one* and *other* identify the noun *games*.]

Soledad, a cautious **driver,** has never had an automobile accident. [The appositive *driver* describes the proper noun *Soledad*.]

14l. An *appositive phrase* consists of an appositive and any modifiers it has.

EXAMPLES   The Vescuzos live on Milner Lane, **a wide street lined with beech trees.** [The appositive phrase identifies the noun *Milner Lane*. Note that the participial phrase *lined with beech trees* is part of the appositive phrase because the participial phrase, like the adjectives *a* and *wide*, modifies the appositive *street*.]

Mount Kosciusko, **a part of the Australian Alps,** is the highest peak in Australia. [The appositive phrase describes the noun *Mount Kosciusko.* The prepositional phrase *of the Australian Alps* is an adjective phrase modifying the appositive *part.*]

An appositive phrase usually follows the noun or pronoun it identifies or describes. Sometimes, though, it precedes the noun or pronoun.

EXAMPLE   **A diligent and quick-witted student,** Mark always gets good grades. [The appositive phrase identifies the noun *Mark.*]

Appositives and appositive phrases that are not essential to the meaning of the sentence are set off by commas. However, an appositive that tells *which one of two or more* is essential to the meaning of the sentence and should not be set off by commas.

NONESSENTIAL   Is Karen's sister, **Marcia,** also a sophomore? [The appositive *Marcia* is not essential because Karen has only one sister.]

ESSENTIAL   Jorge's sister **Selena** is a sophomore. [The appositive *Selena* is essential because Jorge has more than one sister. Which one of the sisters is a sophomore? *Selena.*]

Exercise 10 **Identifying Appositives and Appositive Phrases**

Identify the appositive or appositive phrase in each of the following sentences, and give the word it identifies or describes.

EXAMPLE   1. Dr. Rosen, our family dentist, is a marathon runner.
1. *our family dentist—Dr. Rosen*

1. Soccer, my favorite sport, is very popular in South America and Europe.
2. The internationally famous soccer star Pelé is from Brazil.
3. Hausa, a Nigerian language, is widely used in western Africa.
4. Have you met my teacher Mr. Zolo?
5. Roseanne's youngest sister, Susan, speaks fluent Spanish.
6. Is your friend Greg getting married?
7. Cindy, a student at the community college, is studying computer-aided drafting.
8. The New York City Marathon, one of the largest spectator sports in the United States, is held each November.

Reference Note
For more information on **how to punctuate appositives and appositive phrases,** see page 711.

9. The Himalayas, the highest mountains on earth, are magnificent.
10. Always the one to object, Blair said, "Not on your life!"

Review E **Identifying Verbal and Appositive Phrases**

The following paragraph contains ten verbal and appositive phrases. Identify each phrase as a *participial phrase*, a *gerund phrase*, an *infinitive phrase*, or an *appositive phrase*.

EXAMPLE **[1]** Who was responsible for designing the Brooklyn Bridge?

1. *designing the Brooklyn Bridge—gerund phrase*

[1] The Brooklyn Bridge, a remarkable feat of design, spans the East River in New York City. [2] Linking the boroughs of Brooklyn and Manhattan, it was once the longest suspension bridge in the world. [3] Most of the pedestrians who cross the bridge are impressed by the grandeur of its graceful cables, a majesty that the postcard below cannot fully evoke. [4] To support the twin towers on the bridge, the brilliant John A. Roebling, its engineer, designed airtight caissons filled with concrete. [5] Working underwater on the caissons was painstakingly slow and extremely dangerous. [6] The workers also faced great danger when they had to spin the cables from one side of the river to the other. [7] Because of these hazards, the bridge is remembered not only for being a masterpiece of engineering but also for having cost the lives of many of its builders.

STYLE TIP

Using too many short sentences will make your writing choppy. By using prepositional, verbal, and appositive phrases, you can avoid the unnecessary repetition of words and can improve the flow of your ideas.

CHOPPY
The Appalachian National Scenic Trail is more than 2,000 miles long. The trail stretches from Mount Katahdin to Springer Mountain. Mount Katahdin is in Maine. Springer Mountain is in Georgia.

SMOOTH
Stretching from Mount Katahdin in Maine to Springer Mountain in Georgia, the Appalachian National Scenic Trail is more than 2,000 miles long.

Writing Sentences with Phrases

Write ten sentences, following the directions below for each sentence. Underline the given phrase in each sentence.

EXAMPLE   **1.** Use *to get there from here* as an infinitive phrase acting as an adjective.

         1. What is the fastest way <u>to get there from here</u>?

1. Use *in the garage* as an adjective phrase.
2. Use *for our English class* as an adverb phrase.
3. Use *from an encyclopedia* as an adjective phrase.
4. Use *by train* as an adverb phrase.
5. Use *walking by the lake* as a participial phrase.
6. Use *playing the piano* as a gerund phrase that is the subject of a verb.
7. Use *to hit a home run* as an infinitive phrase that is the direct object of a verb.
8. Use *to find the answer to that question* as an infinitive phrase acting as an adverb.
9. Use *the new student in our class* as an appositive phrase.
10. Use *my favorite writer* as an appositive phrase.

Chapter Review

A. Sentences with Prepositional Phrases

Provide a prepositional phrase for the blank in each of the following sentences. After writing the sentence, identify the phrase as an *adjective phrase* or an *adverb phrase*.

1. The tall building ＿＿＿ is the art museum.
2. *Brian's Song* is an inspiring story ＿＿＿.
3. The selection committee was impressed ＿＿＿.
4. ＿＿＿, we decided to spend the evening quietly at home.
5. I saw a raccoon ＿＿＿.
6. Early ＿＿＿, my family holds a big reunion for all of our relatives.
7. Last Christmas, Mother used a recipe similar to that ＿＿＿.
8. ＿＿＿, my father fought as a soldier in the U.S. Army during the Persian Gulf War.
9. After protesting that he wanted to stay up late, my young brother finally went ＿＿＿.
10. That rosebush ＿＿＿ had seen better days.

B. Identifying Participles and Participial Phrases

┌─**HELP**─
Some sentences in Part B contain more than one participle or participial phrase.

Identify the participial phrases and participles that are used as adjectives in the following sentences. Give the noun or pronoun each participle or participial phrase modifies.

11. She heard me sighing loudly.
12. Aided by good weather and clear skies, the sailors sailed into port a day early.
13. Searching through old clothes in a trunk, Ricardo found a map showing the location of a buried treasure.
14. Sparta and Athens, putting aside their own rivalry, joined forces to fight the Persians.
15. I would love to see it blooming; it must be quite a sight!
16. The cat hissed at the dog barking in the yard next door.
17. Waxing his car in the driveway, Joe overheard a bit of song from an open window nearby.

18. Known as Johnny Appleseed, John Chapman distributed apple seeds and saplings to families headed west.

19. Locked doors contradicted the "open" sign in the window.

20. Switching its tail, the leopard closed in on its prey.

┌HELP─

In Parts C and D, you do not need to identify separately a prepositional phrase or verbal phrase that is part of another phrase.

C. Identifying Phrases in Sentences

Identify each italicized phrase in the following sentences as a *prepositional*, *participial*, *gerund*, *infinitive*, or *appositive phrase*.

21. The sundial was one of the first instruments used for *telling time*.

22. *Regarded chiefly as garden ornaments,* sundials are still used in some areas *to tell time*.

23. The shadow-casting object *on a sundial* is called a gnomon.

24. Forerunners of the sundial include poles or upright stones *used as gnomons by early humans*.

25. *To improve the accuracy of the sundial,* the gnomon was set directly parallel to the earth's axis, *the imaginary line running through the planet's poles*.

26. The development of trigonometry permitted more precise calculations *in the construction* of sundials.

27. For everyday use, *owning a watch* has obvious advantages over using a sundial.

28. *In the past,* sundials were used *to set and check the accuracy of watches*.

29. The heliochronometer, *a sundial of great precision,* was used until 1900 *to set the watches of French railway workers*.

30. The difference *between solar time and clock time* is correlated by the use of tables *showing daily variations in solar time*.

D. Identifying Phrases in a Paragraph

Identify each italicized phrase in the following paragraph as a *prepositional*, *participial*, *gerund*, *infinitive*, or *appositive phrase*.

[**31**] A sundial is not difficult *to make with simple materials.* [**32**] First find a stick *to use as a gnomon.* [**33**] At high noon, plant the stick *in the ground,* tilting it slightly northward. [**34**] To mark the first hour, place a pebble at the tip of the shadow *made by the stick.* [**35**] An hour later, put another pebble at the tip *of the shadow.* [**36**] Continue this process *throughout the afternoon.* [**37**] *Starting the*

next morning, repeat the hourly process. **[38]** Be sure *to place the last pebble at high noon.* **[39]** Observing the completed sundial, you will note that the hour markers, *the pebbles,* are not equidistant. **[40]** *Your spacing of the markers* has demonstrated that shadows move faster in the morning and the evening than during the middle of the day.

Writing Application
Using Phrases in a Newspaper Article

Verbal and Appositive Phrases   As a reporter for the local newspaper, you have just attended the final contest of your community's annual dog show. Now, you have to write a short news article on the show. Be sure you use at least three verbal phrases and three appositive phrases.

Prewriting   First, make a list of the top dogs in the show. Give their names, their breeds, their owners, and their personalities. Interview the winner's owner for "the human perspective."

Writing   Newspaper articles usually present the most important information first, so be sure to include the *who, what, when,* and *where* of the dog show in the beginning of the article. Describe how the winners were chosen, and explain why each winner was judged to be the best in its class. You may also want to describe other features of the show, such as the setting, the size and enthusiasm of the crowd, or the owners' preshow grooming of contestants.

Revising   Read your first draft to a friend or family member, and ask for his or her reactions. Determine that you have given adequate information in as clear a manner as possible.

Publishing   Check to make sure that you have used at least three verbal phrases and three appositive phrases. Also, check your spelling, especially of the names of dog breeds with which you may not be familiar. Proofread your article for any errors in grammar, usage, and mechanics. You and your classmates may wish to read your finished articles aloud. Post the article on a class bulletin board or Web page.

The Clause
Independent Clauses and Subordinate Clauses

Diagnostic Preview

A. Identifying and Classifying Clauses

Identify the italicized clause in each of the following sentences as an *independent clause* or a *subordinate clause*. Then, identify each of the subordinate clauses as an *adjective clause*, an *adverb clause*, or a *noun clause*.

EXAMPLES
1. The New York bridge *that most people recognize* is the Brooklyn Bridge.
1. subordinate clause—adjective clause

2. Known around the world, *the Brooklyn Bridge may be the most famous bridge in the United States.*
2. independent clause

1. The Brooklyn Bridge, *which spans the East River between Brooklyn and Manhattan in New York City,* is one of the engineering wonders of the world.
2. *The bridge was designed and built by John Roebling and Washington Roebling, a father-and-son engineering team* who were pioneers in the use of steel-wire cables.
3. The steel-wire cables give the bridge a graceful appearance *that resembles a spider's web.*
4. *What impresses many people* who see the bridge is the strength and beauty of its design.
5. Massive granite towers *that are supported by concrete-filled shafts* are among its remarkable features.

6. *Although she was not an engineer,* Nora Roebling assisted in the efforts to complete the bridge.

7. The Roeblings discovered *that construction work could be both slow and dangerous.*

8. *Because they were required at times to work underwater in airtight chambers called caissons,* many workers, including the designer Washington Roebling, suffered from caisson disease, or decompression sickness.

9. *Since they were used to working in ships' rigging at great heights,* sailors were hired to string the miles of cable.

10. *John Roebling injured his foot at the work site,* and as a result, he died of tetanus shortly after construction began.

B. Classifying Sentences According to Structure

Classify each of the sentences in the following paragraph as *simple, compound, complex,* or *compound-complex.*

EXAMPLE   **[1]** Washington and Nora Roebling worked together to complete the project.

         1. *simple*

[11] After succeeding his father on the project, Washington Roebling was stricken by caisson disease; therefore, he was confined to bed. [12] The Roeblings lived in a house that was near the construction site, and Washington supervised the work through a telescope. [13] He dictated instructions to Nora, and she relayed them to the work crew. [14] Whether the work on the bridge could have continued without her assistance is doubtful. [15] When the bridge was finally completed in 1883, President Chester A. Arthur attended the dedication ceremony. [16] Because of his illness, Washington Roebling was unable to attend the ceremonies. [17] Instead, the President visited Roebling's home to honor the man who had struggled so valiantly to complete the bridge. [18] The bridge took thirteen years to build. [19] At the time of its completion, it was the world's longest suspension bridge. [20] The bridge is now more than a century old, and it still stands as a monument to the artistry, sacrifice, and determination of all the people who planned and built it.

Reference Note
For information about correcting **sentence fragments,** see page 340.

Reference Note
For more about **commas,** see page 700.

Reference Note
For more information on using **semicolons to join independent clauses,** see page 724.

What Is a Clause?

15a. A *clause* is a word group that contains a verb and its subject and that is used as a sentence or as part of a sentence.

Every clause has a subject and a verb, but not all clauses express complete thoughts. Those that do are called *independent clauses.* Those that do not are called *subordinate clauses.*

Independent Clauses

15b. An *independent* (or *main*) *clause* expresses a complete thought and can stand by itself as a sentence.

EXAMPLE
$$\text{S} \qquad \text{V}$$
The outfielders missed easy fly balls.

Independent clauses that express related ideas can be joined together in a single sentence. Often, the clauses are linked by a comma and one of the coordinating conjunctions (*and, but, or, nor, for, so,* or *yet*).

EXAMPLE
$$\text{S} \qquad \text{V} \qquad\qquad \text{S}$$
The outfielders missed easy fly balls**, and** the infielders

$$\text{V}$$
were throwing wildly.

Independent clauses can also be linked by a semicolon.

EXAMPLE
$$\text{S} \qquad \text{V} \qquad\qquad \text{S}$$
The outfielders missed easy fly balls**;** the infielders

$$\text{V}$$
were throwing wildly.

A conjunctive adverb or a transitional expression can be used after the semicolon to express the relationship between the independent clauses.

EXAMPLES
$$\text{S} \qquad \text{V}$$
The outfielders missed easy fly balls**; moreover,** the

$$\text{S} \qquad \text{V}$$
infielders were throwing wildly.

$$\text{S} \qquad \text{V}$$
The outfielders missed easy fly balls**; in addition,** the

$$\text{S} \qquad \text{V}$$
infielders were throwing wildly.

Common Conjunctive Adverbs		
also	however	nevertheless
anyway	instead	otherwise
besides	likewise	still
consequently	meanwhile	then
furthermore	moreover	therefore

Common Transitional Expressions		
as a result	for example	in other words
at any rate	in addition	on the contrary
by the way	in fact	on the other hand

Subordinate Clauses

15c. A *subordinate* (or *dependent*) *clause* does not express a complete thought and cannot stand alone as a sentence.

EXAMPLES   whom we spoke to yesterday

             because no students have applied for them

The thought expressed by a subordinate clause becomes part of a complete thought when the clause is combined with an independent clause.

EXAMPLES   The woman **whom we spoke to yesterday** told us about sources of financial aid for college applicants.

             Some scholarships are still available **because no students have applied for them.**

Exercise 1   Identifying Independent and Subordinate Clauses

For each of the following sentences, identify the italicized clause as *independent* or *subordinate*.

EXAMPLE   **1.** One of the guests *who spoke at the ceremony* was Barbara Jordan.

            1. subordinate

1. *Whenever I think of Barbara Jordan,* I imagine her as she looks in a picture taken at my mother's college graduation in 1986.

2. According to my mother, *Jordan spoke eloquently about the importance of values in our society.*

3. *Of course, her choice of subject matter surprised no one* since Jordan had long been known as an important ethical force in American politics.

4. *When Jordan began her public service career in 1966,* she became the first African American woman to serve in the Texas legislature.

5. In 1972, she won a seat in the U.S. House of Representatives, *where only one other black woman—Shirley Chisholm—had ever been a member.*

6. However, Jordan was still not widely recognized *until she gave the keynote speech at the 1976 Democratic National Convention.*

7. Seen on television by millions of people, *Jordan immediately gained national attention.*

8. Two years after the speech, Jordan decided *that she would retire from national politics.*

9. After she returned to Texas in 1978, *Jordan taught at the University of Texas at Austin.*

10. From 1991 until her death in 1996, she served on various government committees and used *what she had learned in her many years of public service* to fight corruption in politics.

Complements and Modifiers in Subordinate Clauses

Reference Note

For more about the different kinds of **complements,** see page 450. For more about **adjectives** and **adverbs,** see page 614. For more about **prepositional phrases,** see page 467.

A subordinate clause may contain complements and modifiers.

EXAMPLES   since she told **us the truth** [*Us* is the indirect object of the verb *told,* and *truth* is the direct object of *told. The* modifies *truth.*]

when I am **busy** [*Busy* is a predicate adjective modifying the subject *I.*]

after he had cooked **for us** [*For us* is a prepositional phrase modifying the verb *had cooked.*]

that he **recently** painted [*That* is the direct object of the verb *painted; recently* is an adverb modifying *painted.*]

who they were [*Who* is a predicate nominative identifying the subject *they.*]

Exercise 2 **Identifying Subjects, Verbs, and Complements in Subordinate Clauses**

Identify the subject and the verb in the italicized subordinate clause in each of the following sentences. Then, identify each complement in the clause as a *predicate adjective, predicate nominative, direct object,* or *indirect object.*

EXAMPLE   1. *After he shows us his new boat,* we will go swimming.

1. *he—subject; shows—verb; us—indirect object; boat—direct object*

1. We couldn't see *who had won the race.*
2. They couldn't tell *who the winner was.*
3. She is the celebrity *whom we saw at the restaurant.*
4. Kelly says *that her new house is beautiful.*
5. The horse *that you rode yesterday* was skittish.
6. *After we passed the test,* we celebrated.
7. Do you know *which country she is touring*?
8. *Because you had not given us the right address,* we missed the party.
9. Look for the mouse *that you heard last night.*
10. *Until Mike lent me this book,* I had never heard of the author Rudolfo A. Anaya.

Uses of Subordinate Clauses

Subordinate clauses can be used as adjectives, adverbs, or nouns.

The Adjective Clause

15d. An ***adjective clause*** is a subordinate clause that modifies a noun or a pronoun.

An adjective clause tells *what kind* or *which one* and generally follows the word or words it modifies.

EXAMPLES   I am now reading this book, **which is a historical novel about the Irish revolt of 1798.** [The adjective clause modifies the noun *book,* telling what kind of book.]

A photograph of those **who had participated in the school's Earth Day celebration** appeared on the front page of the local newspaper. [The adjective clause modifies the pronoun *those,* telling which ones.]

┌**HELP**─

Before doing Exercise 2, you may want to review **complements** in Chapter 13.

┌**S T Y L E**   **T I P**┐

Although a series of short, simple sentences can be effective, a variety of sentence structures is usually more effective. To make choppy sentences into smoother writing, combine shorter sentences by changing some into subordinate clauses. Also, avoid unnecessary repetition of subjects, verbs, and pronouns.

CHOPPY
    Ted runs every day. Ted is in training. He is training for a marathon.

SMOOTH
    Ted, who is in training for a marathon, runs every day.

In the example above, two of the short sentences are combined into a single subordinate clause.

Generally, an adjective clause that modifies a proper noun, such as *Emil* in the second example, is nonessential and is therefore set off by commas.

Reference Note

See page 704 for more about **essential** and **nonessential clauses.**

NOTE Depending on how it is used, an adjective clause is either *essential* or *nonessential*. An **essential** (or **restrictive**) **clause** contains information necessary to the sentence's meaning. A **nonessential** (or **nonrestrictive**) **clause** contains information that can be omitted without affecting the sentence's basic meaning. An essential clause is not set off by commas; a nonessential clause is set off by commas.

ESSENTIAL   The oboe is the only instrument **that I can play well.** [The adjective clause is essential because omitting it would change the basic meaning of the sentence.]

NONESSENTIAL   Emil, **who can play many instruments,** taught me how to play the oboe. [The adjective clause is nonessential because omitting it would not affect the basic meaning of the sentence.]

Relative Pronouns

An adjective clause is usually introduced by a *relative pronoun*.

Common Relative Pronouns				
who	whom	whose	which	that

These pronouns are called *relative pronouns* because they are used to relate an adjective clause to the word or word group the clause modifies. That word or word group is called the *antecedent* of the relative pronoun. Each relative pronoun also serves a grammatical function within the adjective clause.

EXAMPLES   Isabella Baumfree was an abolitionist **who is most often remembered as Sojourner Truth.** [*Who* relates the adjective clause to the noun *abolitionist. Who* also serves as the subject of the verb *is remembered* in the adjective clause.]

The topic **about which he is writing** is controversial. [*Which* relates the adjective clause to the noun *topic. Which* also serves as the object of the preposition *about* in the adjective clause.]

She is the person **whom I trust most.** [*Whom* relates the adjective clause to the noun *person. Whom* also serves as the direct object of the verb *trust* in the adjective clause.]

Do you know the name of the group **whose recording is number one on the charts**? [*Whose* relates the adjective clause to the noun *group. Whose* also serves as a possessive pronoun modifying *recording* in the adjective clause.]

Sometimes the relative pronoun is left out of a sentence. In such a sentence, the pronoun is understood and still serves a grammatical function within the adjective clause.

EXAMPLE   Ms. Chung is the legislator [**that** or **whom**] we met. [*That or whom* is understood. The understood relative pronoun relates the adjective clause to *legislator* and serves as the direct object of the verb *met* in the adjective clause.]

NOTE *Who* and *whom* refer to persons only; *which* refers to things only; *that* refers to persons or things.

Reference Note

For information on using **who** and **whom** correctly, see page 558.

Occasionally, an adjective clause is introduced by the word *where* or *when*. When used in such a way, these words are called **relative adverbs.**

EXAMPLES   Here is the spot **where we will have lunch.** [*Where* relates the adjective clause to the noun *spot.*]

This is the season **when it rains almost every day.** [*When* relates the adjective clause to the noun *season.*]

Exercise 3   Identifying Adjective Clauses

Identify the adjective clauses in the following sentences, and underline the relative pronoun or relative adverb in each clause. Then, give the word or words to which the relative pronoun or relative adverb relates. If a sentence contains an adjective clause from which the relative pronoun has been omitted, add the relative pronoun in parentheses and underline it.

HELP

Some sentences in Exercise 3 contain more than one adjective clause.

EXAMPLES   1. The topic that Melissa chose for her essay was difficult.

1. *that Melissa chose for her essay*—topic

2. The other topics she had considered were just as difficult.

2. *(that) she had considered*—topics

1. A speech community is a group of people who speak the same language.
2. There are speech communities that contain millions of people and some that have only a few people.
3. The first language you learn is called your native language.
4. People who master a second language are bilingual.
5. Those who conduct business internationally often need to know more than one language.
6. English, French, and Spanish, which many diplomats can speak, are among the six official languages of the United Nations.

7. Russian, Chinese, and Arabic are the other three languages that are used officially at the UN.
8. People for whom language study is important include telephone operators, hotel managers, and police officers.
9. Tourists traveling to countries where they do not know the local languages can find themselves at a disadvantage.
10. French is a language that is widely understood in parts of Europe, Africa, Southeast Asia, and the Middle East.

The Adverb Clause

15e. An *adverb clause* is a subordinate clause that modifies a verb, an adjective, or an adverb.

An adverb clause tells *how, when, where, why, to what extent,* or *under what condition.*

Reference Note

Introductory adverb clauses are usually set off by **commas.** See page 708.

EXAMPLES   Donna sounds **as if she has caught a cold.** [The adverb clause modifies the verb *sounds,* telling how Donna sounds.]

Before we left, we lowered the blinds. [The adverb clause modifies the verb *lowered,* telling when we lowered the blinds.]

You will see our house **where the road turns right.** [The adverb clause modifies the verb *will see,* telling where you will see our house.]

Will you move **so that I can see**? [The adverb clause modifies the verb *will move,* telling why you will move.]

Your stereo is louder **than it should be.** [The adverb clause modifies the adjective *louder,* telling to what extent the stereo is louder.]

André can type faster **than anyone else in his computer class can.** [The adverb clause modifies the adverb *faster,* telling to what extent Andre can type faster.]

As long as he starts early, he will arrive on time. [The adverb clause modifies the verb *will arrive,* telling under what condition he will arrive on time.]

Subordinating Conjunctions

An adverb clause is introduced by a *subordinating conjunction*—a word that shows the relationship between the adverb clause and the word or words that the clause modifies. Unlike a relative pronoun, which introduces an adjective clause, a subordinating conjunction does not serve a grammatical function in the clause it introduces.

Common Subordinating Conjunctions		
after	before	unless
although	even though	until
as	if	when
as if	in order that	whenever
as long as	provided that	where
as soon as	since	wherever
as though	so that	whether
as well as	than	while
because	though	why

Reference Note

Some of the words in this chart can be used as **adverbs** (see page 422) or **prepositions** (see page 426).

Exercise 4 Identifying Adverb Clauses and Subordinating Conjunctions

Identify the adverb clause in each of the following sentences, and circle the subordinating conjunction.

EXAMPLE
1. While the others worked inside the house, Ruth, Lou, and I worked in the yard.

   1. (While) the others worked inside the house

1. Because the house had been vacant for so long, the lawn and gardens were overgrown.
2. The grass in the front looked as if it hadn't been cut in months.
3. Ruth began mowing the lawn while Lou and I weeded the flower beds.
4. We decided to borrow some tools because the weeds were extremely thick.
5. We were unable to cut through the heavy undergrowth until we started using a machete.
6. Before we pulled out the weeds, we couldn't even see the roses.
7. We piled the debris in a huge mound so that it could be hauled away later.
8. After Ruth had mowed the lawn, she was exhausted.
9. We all stretched out in the shade when we stopped for a rest.
10. Long hours in the sun had made us feel as though the day would never end.

COMPUTER TIP

Because an adverb clause usually does not have a fixed location in a sentence, the writer must choose where to put the clause. The best place for it is usually a matter of personal taste and style, but often the placement is determined by the context.

If you use a computer, you can easily experiment with the placement of adverb clauses in sentences. Print out different versions of the same sentence containing the adverb clause along with the sentences that immediately precede and follow it. Read each version aloud to see how the placement of the clause affects the flow, rhythm, and overall meaning of the passage.

Exercise 5 Using Adverb Clauses

Complete the following sentences by adding adverb clauses.

EXAMPLE **1.** ____, I usually go straight home.

1. *When I finish work, I usually go straight home.*

1. ____, the show was canceled.
2. ____, the telephone rang.
3. The child was scared ____.
4. Constance will work ____.
5. ____, her dog goes with her.
6. Danny and Sandra plan to go biking ____.
7. Let me know ____.
8. Cindy is going to the bookstore ____.
9. I carry my passport ____.
10. ____, Hiroshi is an accomplished pianist.

Review A Identifying Adjective and Adverb Clauses

Identify the subordinate clauses in the following paragraph. Then, tell whether each is an *adjective clause* or an *adverb clause*.

EXAMPLE **[1]** Someone who pilots a balloon is an aeronaut.

1. *who pilots a balloon—adjective clause*

[1] In 1978, the aeronauts Ben Abruzzo, Max Anderson, and Larry Newman, whose home was Albuquerque, New Mexico, became the first people ever to pilot a balloon across the Atlantic Ocean. [2] Although Abruzzo and Anderson had been forced to land in the ocean in an

earlier attempt in *Double Eagle,* they had not given up. [**3**] Instead, they had acquired a new balloon, which they had named *Double Eagle II.* [**4**] Newman joined them because experience had shown the need for a third crew member. [**5**] On its journey from Maine to France, *Double Eagle II* was airborne for 137 hours, which is a little less than six days. [**6**] Although *Double Eagle II* relied on the wind's force, the balloon didn't just drift across the Atlantic; the aeronauts piloted it. [**7**] Abruzzo, Anderson, and Newman had to understand meteorology so that they could take advantage of favorable winds. [**8**] They also had to regulate their altitude constantly by adjusting their supply of helium and by losing ballast, as the balloonists shown on the previous page are doing. [**9**] When the balloon gained too much altitude, the crew lowered the aircraft by releasing some of the gas. [**10**] If the balloon lost altitude, the crew raised it by discarding ballast.

The Noun Clause

15f. A *noun clause* is a subordinate clause that is used as a noun.

A noun clause may be used as a subject, a predicate nominative, a direct object, an indirect object, or the object of a preposition.

SUBJECT	**What I need** is my own room.
PREDICATE NOMINATIVE	The happiest time in my life was **when we went to Costa Rica for the summer.**
DIRECT OBJECT	She believes **that lost time is never found again.**
INDIRECT OBJECT	We will give **whoever wins the contest** a prize.
OBJECT OF PREPOSITION	She has written an article about **how she was elected to the Senate.**

Reference Note

For more about **subjects,** see page 439. For more about **predicate nominatives,** see page 453. For more about **direct** and **indirect objects,** see page 456. For more about **objects of prepositions,** see page 426.

Common Introductory Words for Noun Clauses		
how	where	whoever
that	whether	whom
what	which	whomever
whatever	whichever	whose
when	who	why

Reference Note

Some of the words in this chart can be used to introduce **adjective clauses** (see page 495) and **adverb clauses** (see page 498).

Sometimes the introductory word serves a grammatical function within the noun clause, and sometimes it does not.

           PN   **S**   **V**

EXAMPLES   Do you know **what the problem is**? [The introductory word *what* is a predicate nominative of the subject *problem—the problem is what.*]

        S   **V**

                    I know **that she is worried.** [The introductory word *that* has no grammatical function in the clause.]

In some sentences the word *that* introduces a noun clause can be omitted.

EXAMPLES   He told us **[that] attendance is improving.** [The introductory word *that* is understood.]

                    The judge mentioned **[that] she was born in Guyana.** [The introductory word *that* is understood.]

Reference Note

For information about another kind of noun clause—**the infinitive clause**—see page 481.

┌─**H E L P**─

Some sentences in Exercise 6 have more than one noun clause.

Exercise 6 **Identifying and Classifying Noun Clauses**

Identify the noun clauses in the following sentences. Then, tell how each clause is used: as a *subject*, a *predicate nominative*, a *direct object*, an *indirect object*, or an *object of a preposition.*

EXAMPLE   1. Mr. Perkins, the band director, announced that we would play at half time this week.

           1. *that we would play at half time this week—direct object*

1. Mr. Perkins did not tell us, however, what we would be playing during the half-time show.
2. What we can never predict is whether he will choose a familiar march or a show tune.
3. He always gives whoever is asked to play each selection a chance to express an opinion about it.
4. He is genuinely interested in what we think of his sometimes unusual choices.
5. A drummer once told Mr. Perkins she did not like most show tunes.
6. How she could say that was a mystery to me.
7. Mr. Perkins told us we would play a medley of marches.
8. What everyone wanted to know immediately was who would play the solos.
9. He understands why that was our first question.
10. The crowd always applauds enthusiastically for whoever plays a solo.

Review B **Identifying Adjective, Adverb, and Noun Clauses**

Each sentence in the following paragraph contains at least one subordinate clause. Identify each subordinate clause, and tell whether it is an *adjective clause,* an *adverb clause,* or a *noun clause.*

EXAMPLE   **[1]** What's so special about the Blue Grotto, which the Italians call *Grotta Azzurra?*

     1. *which the Italians call* Grotta Azzurra—*adjective clause*

[1] In the painting below, you can see that the color and the hidden location of the Blue Grotto have made it famous. [2] The grotto is a cavern that can be entered only from the sea. [3] Do you know where the Blue Grotto is located? [4] It is on the west side of the Italian island of Capri, which lies at the entrance to the Bay of Naples. [5] Since the only opening to the cavern is approximately three feet high, visitors must lie down in a rowboat to enter the grotto. [6] The sapphire blue of the water inside the spacious, oval cavern is created by light that is refracted through the deep pool. [7] Although the calm, blue water looks inviting, the grotto is no longer a swimming hole. [8] In the past, however, people who lived in the area greatly enjoyed swimming there. [9] Tour guides tell whoever goes there that centuries ago Tiberius, a Roman emperor, used the Blue Grotto as his private swimming pool. [10] Seeing it today, you would agree that it's a pool fit for an emperor.

Sandro Chia, *Grotto azzurra* (1980). Oil on canvas (147 cm x 208 cm). Courtesy Galerie Bruno Bischofberger, Zurich, Switzerland. © 1998 Sandro Chia/Licensed by VAGA, New York.

Sentences Classified According to Structure

Reference Note

Sentences may also be **classified according to purpose.** See page 459.

The *structure* of a sentence is determined by the number and types of clauses it has.

15g. A sentence can be classified, depending on its structure, as *simple, compound, complex,* or *compound-complex.*

(1) A *simple sentence* contains one independent clause and no subordinate clauses.

A simple sentence may contain a compound subject, a compound verb, and any number of phrases.

EXAMPLES

            S   S   V

Cora and **Kareem bought** party supplies at the mall. [compound subject]

               S   V   V

Later, **they drove** to school and **decorated** the cafeteria for the Ecology Club's annual banquet. [compound verb]

(2) A *compound sentence* contains two or more independent clauses and no subordinate clauses.

A compound sentence is two or more independent clauses joined together by (1) a comma and a coordinating conjunction, (2) a semicolon, or (3) a semicolon and a conjunctive adverb such as *therefore, however,* or *consequently* followed by a comma.

Reference Note

See pages 703 and 724 for more information on **punctuating compound sentences.**

EXAMPLES

         S   V

Cora hung colorful streamers from the ceiling, **and**

         S   V

Kareem set party favors on the tables.

                   S   V   S

After an hour, they took a short break; then they

         V

went back to work.

         S   V

They agreed not to take any more breaks; **otherwise,**

         S   V

they would be late getting home.

NOTE Do not mistake a simple sentence with a compound subject or compound verb for a compound sentence.

	S V
SIMPLE SENTENCE	To pass the time, **they talked** about school and

 V
told stories about their families. [compound verb]

	S V
COMPOUND SENTENCE	To pass the time, **they talked** about school, and

 S V
they told stories about their families.

(3) A *complex sentence* contains one independent clause and at least one subordinate clause.

EXAMPLES
 S V S
When they had finished their work, they

 V
complimented each other on the results.

(4) A *compound-complex* sentence contains two or more independent clauses and at least one subordinate clause.

EXAMPLE
 S V
Cora waited for just the right moment to ask

 S V
Kareem to the banquet, and he promptly accepted her

 S V
invitation, adding that he had been planning to ask her.

Exercise 7 Classifying Sentences According to Structure

Classify each of the sentences in the following paragraph as *simple, compound, complex,* or *compound-complex.*

EXAMPLE
1. The Key Club decided to sponsor a rummage sale.
 1. *simple*

1. Organizing the rummage sale, the Key Club requested donations from everyone at school.
2. The club members accepted whatever was donated, but they welcomed housewares most.

STYLE TIP

Paragraphs in which all the sentences have the same structure can be monotonous to read. To keep your readers interested in your ideas, evaluate your writing to see whether you've used a variety of sentence structures. Then, use revising techniques—adding, cutting, replacing, and reordering—to enliven your writing by varying the structure of your sentences.

COMPUTER TIP

A word processor can help you check for varied sentence structure in your writing. Make a copy of your document. By inserting a return or a page break after every period, you can view the sentences in a vertical list and compare the structures of each sentence in a particular paragraph. Make any revisions on the properly formatted copy of your document.

3. The principal donated a vacuum cleaner; the soccer coach contributed a set of dishes; and several of the teachers provided towels and sheets.

4. The club sold almost everything that had been donated, and the members celebrated their success with pitchers of lemonade.

5. Afterward, they gave all the profits that they had made from the sale to the city's homeless shelter.

6. The shelter's employees were very grateful for the donations.

7. They offered the members of the Key Club the chance to tour the facility.

8. John took photos, and I interviewed both staff members and clients of the shelter.

9. After we had finished our article, we took it to the editor of the school newspaper.

10. The story was published in the next issue, and we received many compliments even though we hadn't expected any praise.

Review C **Writing Sentences with Varied Structures**

Write your own sentences according to the following guidelines.

EXAMPLE   1. Write a simple sentence containing a compound subject.
                 1. *My aunt and uncle live nearby.*

1. Write a simple sentence containing a compound verb.

2. Write a compound sentence containing two independent clauses joined by a comma and the conjunction *but*.

3. Write a compound sentence containing two independent clauses joined by a semicolon, a conjunctive adverb, and a comma.

4. Write a complex sentence containing an adjective clause.

5. Write a complex sentence beginning with an adverb clause.

6. Write a complex sentence ending with an adverb clause.

7. Write a complex sentence containing a noun clause used as the direct object.

8. Write a complex sentence containing a noun clause used as the subject.

9. Write a complex sentence containing a noun clause used as the object of a preposition.

10. Write a compound-complex sentence.

Chapter Review

A. Identifying and Classifying Clauses

For each of the following sentences, identify the italicized clause as *independent* or *subordinate*. Tell whether each subordinate clause functions in the sentence as an *adjective clause,* an *adverb clause,* or a *noun clause.*

1. Scientists have recently discovered *that chameleons are not masters of disguise.*
2. *Their changes of color are not attempts at camouflage;* they are responses to changes in light and temperature.
3. Chameleons, *which dislike any contact,* will tolerate it for the purpose of breeding.
4. *When two chameleons cross paths,* they do their best to frighten each other by hissing, snapping, and changing color.
5. Some scientists think *that such encounters control the chameleons' changes in color.*
6. Males occasionally fight, but *most chameleons try to avoid physical confrontation.*
7. Almost all of the species *that make up the chameleon family* live in trees.
8. *Because the chameleon moves slowly,* it would become an easy prey without its natural green and brown coloration.
9. *The chameleon's tongue is sticky and has numerous folds and furrows* that are lined with hooklike cells.
10. The tongue is propelled by a set of muscles *that can extend it as far as one and one-half times the length of the chameleon's body.*

B. Identifying and Classifying Subordinate Clauses

Identify each subordinate clause in the following sentences. Then, tell whether each subordinate clause is an *adjective clause,* an *adverb clause,* or a *noun clause.*

11. Before you buy the sweater, try it on.
12. Chang, whose mother is a dentist, just lost his retainer.

13. Do you know who won the speech contest?
14. The dog that scattered our garbage has annoyed all of us.
15. Don't agree to do the project if you don't like to paint.
16. Lisa said that she would provide food for the trip.
17. Until you pay back the money, I will charge you interest.
18. Reynaldo was thrilled with what you gave him for his birthday.
19. We saw a movie that scared even the bravest of us.
20. The CD that you borrowed yesterday belongs to my brother.
21. After we have dinner, let's remember to call Grandpa.
22. Do you know what the capital of Nigeria is?
23. Lilliput, which was invented by Jonathan Swift, is the land of tiny people in Swift's *Gulliver's Travels*.
24. Ariana was a bit worried about what you said about her.
25. The boy who climbed the tree to save the parakeet has endeared himself to everybody.
26. Our parents heard a song that moved them deeply.
27. Have you heard what happened at the intersection this morning?
28. If you don't like camping, don't go on the trip.
29. Tom and Phyllis said they would pay our dog's boarding costs.
30. We know exactly who is responsible, but we will point the finger at no one.

C. Classifying Sentences According to Structure

Classify each of the following sentences as *simple, compound, complex,* or *compound-complex.*

31. The Bugatti Motor Club hosted an exhibit of old motoring prints.
32. When our team finished the project, we all went out to lunch at the Mumbai Grill, and our friend Amrit met us there.
33. The hotel guests were surprised when the alarm went off.
34. Bill gave a speech, and I took notes.
35. Georges Bizet was the French composer who wrote *Carmen,* which is definitely my favorite opera.
36. The store employees decorated the storefront, the manager put on his best suit, and the customers arrived promptly at eight.
37. We students were very proud of our prize-winning principal.

38. The weather inland was unseasonably cold and frosty, but on the coast a mild wind was blowing from the south.

39. Our short film was shown in one of the theaters downtown; despite our dire predictions, it was fairly well received.

40. Under the foundations of many an old building in Rome, especially near the Forum and Colosseum, are even older foundations, some dating back to the late Empire.

Writing Application
Writing a Paragraph

Using Subordinate Clauses   The student council has decided to decorate your school with posters of popular artworks. To decide on the posters, the council has asked for recommendations, along with brief descriptions, for artworks that students would like to see. Write two paragraphs about two works (one paragraph on each work) that you would like to recommend. Use specific details and include at least five subordinate clauses.

Prewriting   Think of two paintings that you like, and find a picture of each one. If you do not know their titles, try looking in books or asking a librarian or art teacher. Think about why you particularly like these works, and jot down your reasons.

Writing   As you write, you may think of additional details and reasons. If you do, pause for a moment and consider how they fit in with the rest of your notes. Add to your rough draft any new information that fits in smoothly.

Revising   Read through your paragraphs to be sure they each have a topic sentence supported by your reasons for recommending each artwork. Check to see that you have used a total of at least five subordinate clauses in the two paragraphs. If you have not, try combining sentences by creating adjective, adverb, or noun clauses.

Publishing   Proofread your paragraphs for any errors in grammar, punctuation, and spelling. You and your classmates may want to present two or three of the class's recommendations to the school board or parent-teacher organization.

Agreement
Subject and Verb, Pronoun and Antecedent

Diagnostic Preview

A. Identifying Subject-Verb Agreement and Pronoun-Antecedent Agreement

In most of the following sentences, either a verb does not agree with its subject or a pronoun does not agree with its antecedent. For each incorrect verb or pronoun, write the correct form. If a sentence is already correct, write *C*.

EXAMPLES **1.** Every leaf, flower, and seedpod were glimmering with frost.

        1. was

      2. Were any tickets left at the box office for me?

        2. C

1. There was women, as well as men, who set out on the perilous journey into new territory.
2. The Morenos, I think, have the best chance of winning.
3. The store, the hotel, and the airport is all in a ten-mile radius of the beach.
4. *Bronzeville Boys and Girls* are a collection of poems by Gwendolyn Brooks.

5. Neither of the candidates has prepared their statement.
6. Mr. Ortega, along with other members of his firm, have established a scholarship fund for art students.
7. To apply for the scholarship, a student must submit at least four samples of their work.
8. The test results showed that about 80 percent of the respondents was in the average group.
9. A hostile crowd gathers outside the courtroom to show their disapproval of the verdict.
10. The committee was preparing their speeches for the meeting with the new governor.

B. Identifying Subject-Verb Agreement and Pronoun-Antecedent Agreement

For each sentence in the following paragraph, write the correct form of each incorrect verb or pronoun. If a sentence is already correct, write *C*.

EXAMPLE   **[1]** Aunt Bonnie, along with several other Peace Corps volunteers, are going to Kenya.

1. *is going*

[11] Neither my brothers nor my dad were surprised to hear that Aunt Bonnie is going to Kenya as a Peace Corps volunteer. [12] First, she and the other members of the Kenya group gathers in Philadelphia for a few days of orientation. [13] Their focus at this point are to meet one another and get acquainted. [14] Then the whole group travels together to Nairobi, Kenya, where everyone will have their last chance for months to enjoy hot running water! [15] After one night in Nairobi, half of them leaves for the town of Naivasha for eleven weeks of cultural sensitivity training. [16] Each of the volunteers get to live with a Kenyan family during this period of training. [17] The close daily contact will help them learn to converse in Swahili, one of the languages that is spoken in Kenya. [18] Bonnie don't know yet where exactly in Kenya she is going to be posted. [19] She, as well as the other members of her group, expects to be assigned to the area of greatest need. [20] No one in the group has been told their specific job assignment, but Bonnie says she will probably be helping Kenyans develop small businesses.

Agreement of Subject and Verb

16a. A verb should agree in number with its subject.

A word that refers to one person, place, thing, or idea is *singular* in number. A word that refers to more than one is *plural* in number.

Singular	video	child	I	thief	herself
Plural	videos	children	we	thieves	themselves

Reference Note
For more about forming the **plurals of nouns,** see page 787.

HELP

Most of the time, nouns ending in –s are plural (*aunts, bushes, cities, tacos, friends*); verbs ending in –s are generally singular (*gives, takes, does, has, is*). Note, though, that verbs used with the pronouns *I* and *you* do not end in *s*.

USAGE

> **Exercise 1** Identifying Words as Singular or Plural

Identify each of the following words as either *singular* or *plural*.

EXAMPLES
1. uncles
1. *plural*

2. leaf
2. *singular*

1. stories	6. mouse	11. he	16. pods
2. one	7. genius	12. has	17. donates
3. several	8. teeth	13. both	18. donation
4. applies	9. ability	14. toy	19. key
5. people	10. says	15. woman	20. many

(1) Singular subjects take singular verbs.

EXAMPLES   **Earline attends** college. [The singular verb *attends* agrees with the singular subject *Earline*.]

That **boy delivers** newspapers. [The singular verb *delivers* agrees with the singular subject *boy*.]

(2) Plural subjects take plural verbs.

EXAMPLES   **They attend** college. [The plural verb *attend* agrees with the plural subject *They*.]

Those **boys deliver** newspapers. [The plural verb *deliver* agrees with the plural subject *boys*.]

In a verb phrase, the first helping (auxiliary) verb agrees in number with the subject.

EXAMPLES   **Earline is attending** college.
They are attending college.

Reference Note
For more about **helping verbs,** see page 417.

A **boy** in my class **has been delivering** newspapers.

Two **boys** in my class **have been delivering** newspapers.

NOTE A gerund phrase or an infinitive phrase used as a complete subject takes a singular verb. Do not be misled by any particular noun or pronoun in the phrase. The gerund or infinitive serves as a singular simple subject.

EXAMPLES **Working with you and the others has been** a privilege. [The singular verb *has been* is used because the gerund *Working*, not the pronoun *you* or *others,* is the subject of the verb.]

To finish our science projects is our immediate goal. [The singular verb *is* is used because the infinitive *To finish*, not the noun *projects*, is the subject of the verb.]

Reference Note

For more about **gerund phrases** and **infinitive phrases,** see page 478 and page 480.

USAGE

Exercise 2 Selecting Verbs That Agree with Their Subjects

Choose the verb in parentheses that agrees with each subject given.

EXAMPLE 1. bells (*is ringing, are ringing*)

1. *are ringing*

1. people (*walks, walk*)
2. you (*is, are*)
3. house (*has stood, have stood*)
4. we (*talks, talk*)
5. Joan (*was, were*)
6. cattle (*is running, are running*)
7. result (*is, are*)
8. they (*believes, believe*)
9. crews (*sails, sail*)
10. women (*seems, seem*)
11. Lauren and Sierra (*laughs, laugh*)
12. everyone (*is, are*)
13. otters (*has swum, have swum*)
14. students (*graduates, graduate*)
15. boulder (*weighs, weigh*)
16. firefighting (*saves, save*)
17. Phoebe (*reads, read*)
18. jets (*flies, fly*)
19. children (*sings, sing*)
20. to whisper (*is, are*)

(3) The number of a subject usually is not determined by a word in a phrase or clause following the subject.

SINGULAR A **book** of poems **is** on the shelf. [The prepositional phrase *of poems* does not affect the number of the subject *book*.]

PLURAL The **dinosaurs** from the Jurassic Period **include** the Seismosaurus. [The prepositional phrase *from the Jurassic Period* does not affect the number of the subject *dinosaurs*.]

Reference Note

For more about **phrases,** see "Chapter 14: The Phrase." For more about **clauses,** see "Chapter 15: The Clause."

SINGULAR   The only **mammal** that has wings **is** the bat. [The subordinate clause *that has wings* does not affect the number of the subject *mammal*.]

PLURAL   **Frogs,** which live both on land and in water, **are** amphibians. [The subordinate clause *which live both on land and in water* does not affect the number of the subject *Frogs*.]

NOTE   *Together with, in addition to, as well as,* and *along with* are compound prepositions. Words in phrases beginning with compound prepositions do not affect the number of the subject or verb.

EXAMPLES   His technical **skills,** together with his delightful sense of humor, **have enabled** Enrique to become a successful computer consultant.

His delightful **sense** of humor, together with his technical skills, **has enabled** Enrique to become a successful computer consultant.

(4) A negative construction following the subject does not change the number of the subject.

EXAMPLE   **Carl,** not Juan and I, **is doing** the artwork.

Exercise 3 Choosing Verbs That Agree with Their Subjects

Identify the subject in each of the following sentences. Then, choose the verb in parentheses that agrees in number with the subject.

EXAMPLE   1. The price of haircuts (*has, have*) gone up.
1. price—has

1. A heaping basket of turnip greens (*was, were*) sitting on the counter.
2. The cost of two new snow tires (*was, were*) more than I had expected.
3. The community college course on collecting stamps always (*attracts, attract*) many people.
4. The members of the Pak family (*meets, meet*) for a reunion every year.
5. The carpeting you saw in the upstairs and downstairs rooms (*is, are*) going to be replaced.
6. The turquoise stones in this Navajo ring certainly (*is, are*) pretty.
7. One friend of my brothers (*says, say*) that I look a little like Whitney Houston.
8. The package sent by my cousins (*was, were*) smashed in the mail.

9. Not all the singers who tried out for the school choir (*sings, sing*) equally well.

10. Burt, not Anne and Laura, (*has, have*) borrowed the bicycle pump.

Review A **Completing Sentences That Demonstrate Agreement**

Anna Mary Robertson Moses (1860–1961), better known as "Grandma Moses," became famous for her paintings of rural America. Add words to the following word groups to complete ten sentences about this Grandma Moses painting, titled *The Barn Dance.* Make sure that all verbs agree with their subjects. Be prepared to identify the subject and verb in each sentence.

EXAMPLE
1. barn are
1. *The doors of the barn are wide open.*

1. clouds look
2. musician is playing
3. horse is drinking
4. barn dance are enjoying
5. buildings in the distance is
6. green wagon are waving
7. along with laughter and conversation, fills
8. guests have noticed the cloudy
9. who are at this barn dance
10. horses pulls

USAGE

The Barn Dance by Grandma Moses, 1860–1961, Copyright 1989. Grandma Moses Properties Co., New York.

Indefinite Pronouns

An ***indefinite pronoun*** refers to a person, a place, a thing, or an idea that may or may not be specifically named.

The words *one*, *thing*, and *body* are singular, and so are the indefinite pronouns that contain these words.

EXAMPLES
Was any**one** hurrying?

Every**body welcomes** the good weather.

No**thing has** been clarified.

EXAMPLES   Has **anyone** loaded the van?

Some of the campsites are vacant.

Please pack **everything** we will need for camping.

All of the space in the back seat is filled.

16b. Some indefinite pronouns are singular; others are plural. Certain indefinite pronouns may be either singular or plural, depending on how they are used.

(1) The following indefinite pronouns are singular: *anybody, anyone, anything, each, either, everybody, everyone, everything, neither, nobody, no one, nothing, one, somebody, someone,* and *something.*

EXAMPLES   **Neither** of the animals in the pen **has been fed** this morning.

Somebody is bringing a CD player to the birthday party on Saturday.

Was everyone on the volleyball team on time for the class picture at noon?

One of the puppies **has chewed** a hole in your tennis shoe.

NOTE *Either* and *neither* can be used as adjectives and correlative conjunctions as well as indefinite pronouns. When either word is used as an adjective or a correlative conjunction, it cannot be the subject of a sentence. Carefully identify the subject when you are deciding what form of a verb to use.

ADJECTIVE **Neither** animal has been fed. [The verb agrees with the subject *animal*. *Neither* modifies *animal*.]

CORRELATIVE CONJUNCTION **Neither** the cows nor the pigs have been fed yet. [The verb agrees with the subject that is nearer to it— *pigs*. *Neither* is part of the correlative conjunction *Neither . . . nor*.]

INDEFINITE PRONOUN **Neither** of the animals **has been fed.** [The verb agrees with the subject *Neither*.]

(2) The following indefinite pronouns are plural: *both, few, many,* and *several.*

EXAMPLES **Have both** of them **been** informed?

A **few** in the crowd **were** rowdy.

Many of the staff **write** and **edit** on word processors.

Several of the women **are** pilots.

(3) The following indefinite pronouns may be either singular or plural, depending on how they are used: *all, any, more, most, none,* and *some.*

These pronouns are singular when they refer to singular words and are plural when they refer to plural words.

SINGULAR **Most** of the job **was finished.** [*Most* refers to the singular noun *job.*]

PLURAL **Most** of the jobs **were finished.** [*Most* refers to the plural noun *jobs.*]

SINGULAR **Has any** of the shipment **arrived**? [*Any* refers to the singular noun *shipment.*]

PLURAL **Have any** of the shipments **arrived**? [*Any* refers to the plural noun *shipments.*]

SINGULAR **None** of the test **was** difficult. [*None* refers to the singular noun *test.*]

PLURAL **None** of the tests **were** difficult. [*None* refers to the plural noun *tests.*]

In each of the examples above, the object of the prepositional phrase following the indefinite pronoun provides a clue to the number of the pronoun.

NOTE In a sentence that does not include a phrase after the subject, you must find the number of the noun to which the pronoun refers. Make sure the verb has the same number as the antecedent.

EXAMPLES **Most was** interesting. [The pronoun *Most* may be referring to a portion of a book, of a movie, of a conversation, or some other thing.]

Most were interesting. [The pronoun *Most* may be referring to a number of books, photographs, ideas, or other things.]

HELP

Many of the words listed in Rule 16b, (1)–(3), can be used either as pronouns or as adjectives.

ADJECTIVES
One child is there.
Many children have left.
Some children remain.

PRONOUNS
One is there
Many have left.
Some remain.

USAGE

Read the following sentences aloud, stressing the italicized words.

1. *One* of those cups *is* broken.
2. Choose a bicycle; *either is* ready to go.
3. A *few* of the girls *are* experienced riders.
4. *Each* of the mariachi bands *has* performed one number.
5. *Some* of your mice *were* eating the cheese.
6. *Most* of the milk that I bought *is* gone.
7. *Neither* of these cars *has* a radio.
8. Here are the apples. *None are* ripe.

Exercise 4 Writing Sentences with Verbs That Agree
with Their Subjects

Rewrite each of the following sentences according to the directions in parentheses. Then, change the number of the verb to agree with the new subject.

EXAMPLE 1. Each of these books was written by Margaret Atwood.
(Change *Each* to *All*.)

1. *All of these books were written by Margaret Atwood.*

1. Everyone easily understands the rules of this game. (Change *Everyone* to *Most people*.)
2. Neither of the actresses was nominated. (Change *Neither* to *Both*.)
3. Has each of your cousins had a turn? (Change *each* to *both*.)
4. Some of the trees were destroyed. (Change *trees* to *crop*.)
5. Have any of the apples been harvested? (Change *apples* to *wheat*.)
6. Nobody has visited that "haunted" house. (Change *Nobody* to *Many of our neighbors*.)
7. Each is well trained. (Change *Each* to *Several*.)
8. One of the tires needs air. (Change *One* to *All*.)
9. All of the fruit was eaten. (Change *fruit* to *pears*.)
10. One of the puzzle pieces is missing. (Change *One* to *Some*.)

Exercise 5 Correcting Errors in Subject-Verb
Agreement

The subjects and verbs in some of the sentences on the next page do not agree. If a sentence is incorrect, write the correct form of the verb. If the sentence is already correct, write *C*.

EXAMPLE   1. Most of the world's diamonds comes from mines
                in Africa.

            1. *come*

1. Several of the forwards on the team was commended by
   the captain.
2. Neither of the coaches were happy with the decision.
3. Each of us are going to make a large poster for the upcoming
   election.
4. Some of the frozen yogurt have started to melt.
5. Does both of those games require special gear?
6. Either of Mr. Catalano's assistants have approval and can go.
7. None of the buildings were damaged by the hail.
8. None of the food have been frozen.
9. Neither of the book reports were finished on time.
10. Does anyone want to help me make gefilte fish for the
    Passover feast?

Review B Selecting Verbs That Agree with Their Subjects

For each of the following sentences, choose the verb in parentheses
that agrees with the subject.

EXAMPLE   1. How (*does, do*) astronauts on a space shuttle prepare
                their meals?

            1. *do*

1. (*Has, Have*) any of you ever wondered how meals are
   served to space-shuttle astronauts?
2. Each of the items for the day's menu (*comes, come*)
   sealed in its own container.
3. To help reduce weight on the spacecraft, many of the
   foods (*is, are*) dehydrated.
4. At mealtime, someone in the crew (*adds, add*) water
   to the scrambled eggs, vegetables, and puddings.
5. All of the water mixed with these foods (*is, are*) a
   byproduct of the fuel cells that provide the spacecraft's electricity.
6. Of course, because there is no gravity, not one of
   the beverages (*is, are*) pourable.
7. If a container is accidentally jolted, any uncovered liquid
   (*bounces, bounce*) into the air like a ball, as you can see.

8. Some of the food (*is, are*) covered in sauce so that surface tension will help to keep the food in dishes.
9. Amazingly, most of the foods (*tastes, taste*) delicious.
10. The menu for the astronauts even (*includes, include*) steaks and strawberries.

Compound Subjects

A *compound subject* consists of two or more subjects that are joined by a conjunction and that have the same verb.

16c. Subjects joined by *and* generally take a plural verb.

EXAMPLES   **Ramón** and **she like** hiking.

Her **brother,** her **uncle,** and her **cousin are** teachers.

Both the **scout** and the **counselor were** helpful guides.

NOTE Subjects joined by *and* that name only one person, place, thing, or idea take singular verbs. Singular compound nouns containing *and* also take singular verbs.

EXAMPLE   The club's **secretary and treasurer was** Eduardo. [one person]

Country and western has become our favorite kind of music. [one kind of music]

The **bed and breakfast** down the street **is** always reserved weeks in advance. [one place to stay]

16d. Singular subjects joined by *or* or *nor* take a singular verb. Plural subjects joined by *or* or *nor* take a plural verb.

EXAMPLES   **Marcelo** or **Donya knows** the address.

Neither our **phone** nor our **doorbell was working.**

Do the **Wilsons** or the **Campbells live** there?

Neither **cardinals** nor **finches come** to the birdfeeder.

16e. When a singular subject and a plural subject are joined by *or* or *nor,* the verb agrees with the subject nearer the verb.

EXAMPLES   Either **Harry** or his **aunts are planning** the activities for the beach party.

Neither the **potatoes** nor the **roast is** done.

Oral Practice 2 Using Verbs That Agree with Compound Subjects

Read the following sentences aloud, stressing the italicized words.

1. *Both* Steve *and* Edie *want* to be first chair violin.
2. You *and* I *are* in the same Spanish class.
3. *Neither* Gretchen *nor* Colleen *knows* the answer.
4. *Neither* Sam *nor* Miguel *likes* sports.
5. *Either* Judy *or* Bob *washes* the dishes tonight.
6. Roger *and* Carla *play* basketball every Saturday.
7. *Are* cats *or* dogs popular pets in the United States?
8. *Both* Marilyn *and* Marge *have* summer jobs.

Exercise 6 Choosing Verbs That Agree with Their Subjects

For each of the following sentences, choose the verb in parentheses that agrees with the subject of the sentence.

EXAMPLE
    1. The *pipa* and the *cheng* (*is, are*) the main instruments used in Chinese music.

    1. *are*

1. Neither my older brother Alexander nor my sister Elizabeth (*has, have*) a car.
2. Marlon and she (*is, are*) the dance champions.
3. Our relatives and yours (*is, are*) having a barbecue together next Saturday afternoon.
4. Both Michael Chang and Zina Garrison Jackson (*plays, play*) a good game of tennis.
5. Either the director or the actors (*is, are*) going to have to compromise.
6. Neither the grapes nor the cantaloupe (*was, were*) ripe enough for us to eat.
7. Both Hakeem Olajuwon and Reggie Miller (*is, are*) popular with fans.
8. Our class or theirs (*is, are*) going to sponsor the spring festival and dance.
9. Either the faucet or the shower head (*leaks, leak*).
10. Either a transistor or a capacitor (*has, have*) burned out in this receiver.

USAGE

Special Problems in Subject-Verb Agreement

Reference Note

For more about **nouns**, see page 405.

16f. Collective nouns may be either singular or plural, depending on their meaning in a sentence.

A *collective noun* is a noun whose singular form names a group.

Commonly Used Collective Nouns			
army	club	group	school
assembly	committee	herd	squad
audience	crowd	jury	staff
band	faculty	majority	swarm
choir	family	number	team
class	flock	public	troop

A collective noun is

- singular when it refers to the group as a unit
- plural when it refers to the individual members or parts of the group

SINGULAR	The **class has met** its substitute teacher. [the class as a unit]
PLURAL	The **class were disagreeing** with one another about the answers. [the class as individuals]

SINGULAR	The **team is** on the field. [the team as a unit]
PLURAL	The **team are working** together. [the team as individuals]

Exercise 7 Writing Sentences with Singular and Plural Collective Nouns

For each of the following collective nouns, write one sentence using the singular and one sentence using the plural.

EXAMPLE   **1.** cast

1. singular—The cast is having a wrap party.

plural—After the play, the cast are joining their friends and family for a wrap party.

1. squad	**3.** flock	**5.** group	**7.** troop	**9.** crowd
2. choir	**4.** jury	**6.** band	**8.** committee	**10.** family

USAGE

Review C Writing Sentences with Verbs That Agree with Their Subjects

Rewrite the following sentences according to the instructions in parentheses. Change the number of the verb if necessary.

EXAMPLE   **1.** The faculty are discussing their class schedules with the guidance counselors. (Change *discussing their class schedules* to *in a meeting*.)

    1. The faculty is in a meeting with the guidance counselors.

1. Both of the records are in the Top Forty. (Change *Both* to *Neither*.)

2. The choir has been rehearsing with the conductor. (Change *with the conductor* to *in small groups*.)

3. Everybody in the chorus is trying out for the school play. (Change *Everybody* to *No one*.)

4. Neither Carrie nor Jana is in the Pep Club this semester. (Change *Neither . . . nor* to *Both . . . and*.)

5. Gabriel García Márquez and Octavio Paz have won prizes in literature. (Change *and* to *or*.)

6. All of your papers were graded. (Change *All* to *Each*.)

7. Some of the wood burns. (Change *wood* to *logs*.)

8. The delighted team was waving and running around the stadium. (Change *waving and running around the stadium* to *assembling to accept their medals*.)

9. Either my cousins or Adrienne is bringing the pizza. (Reverse the order of the subjects.)

10. Macaroni and cheese always tastes good. (Change *and* to *or*.)

11. The archaeologist and the geologist are lecturing tomorrow. (Change *and* to *or*.)

12. They exercise regularly. (Change *They* to *She*.)

13. Either a banana or grapes are my favorite dessert. (Reverse the order of the subjects.)

14. Each of the flowers was beautiful. (Change *Each* to *All*.)

15. Tamisha and Heather's favorite pastime is jumping rope. (Change *Tamisha and Heather's* to *Tamisha's*.)

16. Neither of the flights is full. (Change *Neither* to *Both*.)

17. Most of the beans were gone. (Change *beans* to *bread*.)

18. The family was in the living room. (Change *in the living room* to *reading their favorite books*.)

19. The man or the woman is going to win. (Change *or* to *and*.)

20. All of us are happy. (Change *All* to *Not one*.)

USAGE

16g. A verb agrees with its subject but not necessarily with a predicate nominative.

EXAMPLES

               S   PN
The main **ingredient** in salsa **is tomatoes.**

      S   PN
Tomatoes are the main **ingredient** in salsa.

16h. When the subject follows the verb, find the subject and make sure that the verb agrees with it.

In sentences beginning with *here* or *there* and in questions, the subject generally follows the verb or part of the verb.

EXAMPLES

     Here **is** a **set** of keys.
     Here **are** the **keys.**

     Do they know the price?
     Does he know the price?

NOTE A contraction such as *here's, how's, there's, what's,* or *where's* includes the singular verb *is* or *has.* Use such a contraction only when a singular subject follows it.

INCORRECT   In an article in this magazine, there's several photos of the construction of the memorial to Chief Crazy Horse.

CORRECT   In an article in this magazine, there **are** several **photos** of the construction of the memorial to Chief Crazy Horse.

CORRECT   In this magazine, there**'s** an **article** with several photos of the construction of the memorial to Chief Crazy Horse.

Exercise 8   Proofreading for Subject-Verb Agreement

For each of the following sentences, if the subject and verb do not agree, write the correct form of the verb. If the verb already agrees with the subject, write *C*.

EXAMPLE   1. Sore muscles is a symptom of the flu.

                 1. *are*

1. When's your finals?
2. One requirement for becoming a pilot are quick reflexes.
3. Where's the nearest movie theater?
4. The highlight of the evening were the performances by the dance troupes.
5. Do the club meet Tuesday, Wednesday, and Thursday?

6. Methods for conserving energy is what the panel will discuss.
7. The most important component in this watch are the batteries.
8. Here's the books you reserved.
9. Maria Theresa's favorite part of the movie was the scenes in New England.
10. There's the keys that you misplaced.

Review D Identifying Sentences with Subject-Verb Agreement

For each of the following sentences, if the subject and verb do not agree, write the correct form of the verb. Be ready to explain your correction. If the verb already agrees with the subject, write *C*.

EXAMPLE   1. What's the typical ingredients of the soup called gazpacho?

            1. *are*

┌─HELP─

In the example for Review D, the verb is changed to agree with the plural subject, *ingredients*.

1. Steven and Maria is the first team to finish.
2. There's the boats I told you about.
3. Both my father and sister wants to see the Dodgers game.
4. Either the twins or Jamie are playing a practical joke.
5. How was the swimming and sailing at the beach?
6. Each of these old photos show your uncle Ahmad wearing a colorful, flowing dashiki.
7. Neither the windows nor the door is locked.
8. Contemporary rock-and-roll are rooted in ancient rhythms.
9. There's several football games on television on Sunday.
10. Where's my socks?

16i. An expression of an amount (a measurement, a percentage, or a fraction, for example) may be singular or plural, depending on how it is used.

An expression of an amount is

* singular when the amount is thought of as a unit

* plural when the amount is thought of as separate parts

SINGULAR   **Two years is** a long time. [one time]
PLURAL   Two **years** (1995 and 1998) **were** especially rainy. [separate years]

SINGULAR   **Fifteen dollars was** the price. [one price]
PLURAL   Fifteen **dollars were** torn. [separate dollar bills]

A fraction or a percentage is

- singular when it refers to a singular word
- plural when it refers to a plural word

SINGULAR   **Nine tenths** [*or* **Ninety percent**] of the student body **is** present today. [The fraction, or the percentage, refers to the singular noun *student body*.]

PLURAL   **Nine tenths** [*or* **Ninety percent**] of the students **are** present today. [The fraction, or the percentage, refers to the plural word *students*.]

Generally, a measurement (such as length, weight, capacity, or area) is singular.

EXAMPLES   **Nine square feet equals** one square yard.

Six hundred kilometers is the distance we traveled today.

Three cups of flour is what the recipe requires.

NOTE   In the expression *the number of, number* takes a singular verb. In the expression *a number of, number* takes a plural verb.

EXAMPLES   **The** number of female athletes **is growing.**

A number of girls **like** strenuous sports.

16j. When the relative pronoun *that, which,* or *who* is the subject in an adjective clause, the verb in the clause agrees with the word to which the relative pronoun refers.

EXAMPLE   A *corps de ballet* is a group of ballet dancers **that perform** together. [*That* refers to the plural noun *dancers* and therefore requires the plural verb *perform*.]

The Dutch painter Piet Mondrian, **who was** part of an art movement known as *de Stijl*, was fond of the colors red, yellow, and blue. [*Who* refers to the singular noun *Piet Mondrian* and therefore requires the singular verb *was*.]

NOTE   When preceded by *one of* + a plural word, the relative pronoun takes a plural verb. When preceded by *the only one of* + a plural word, the relative pronoun takes a singular verb.

PLURAL   Melba is **one of those players who** always **try** their best.

SINGULAR   Melba is **the only one of those players who** always **tries** her best.

16k. A subject preceded by *every* or *many a(n)* takes a singular verb.

EXAMPLE   **Every** parent and grandparent **is looking** on proudly.

           Many a hopeful performer **has gone** to Broadway in search of fame.

Exercise 9   Proofreading for Subject-Verb Agreement

For each of the following sentences, if the subject and verb do not agree, write the correct form of the verb. If the verb already agrees with the subject, write *C*.

EXAMPLES   **1.** Twenty-four dollars was scattered on the counter.

        1. were

        2. Every one of them have left.

        2. has

1. Many a sophomore and junior are participating.
2. Every takeoff and landing are cleared with the control tower.
3. Two thirds of my research paper have been typed.
4. Emilio has cousins who raise tropical fish.
5. Eight pounds were the baby's weight at birth.
6. Forty-eight percent of the seniors is planning to go to college.
7. Fifteen dollars is all we have raised so far.
8. Egypt is one of the nations that borders the Red Sea.
9. Silvia knows some people who owns a Christmas-tree farm.
10. Pluto is the only one of the planets that cross the orbit of another planet in our solar system.

16l. The contractions *don't* and *doesn't* should agree with their subjects.

Use *don't* (the contraction of *do not*) with the subjects *I* and *you* and with all plural subjects.

EXAMPLES   **I don't** have any paper.

        You don't need special permission.

        The **players don't** seem nervous.

Reference Note

For more information about **contractions,** see page 763.

USAGE

Use *doesn't* (the contraction of *does not*) with all singular subjects except *I* and *you*.

EXAMPLES   **Doesn't it** show up in this picture?

The **tire doesn't** have enough air.

Exercise 10 Using *Don't* and *Doesn't* Correctly in Sentences

Choose the correct form (*don't* or *doesn't*) for each of the following sentences.

EXAMPLES   1. _____ Lea speak several languages?

1. *Doesn't*

2. The birds _____ seem bothered by the wind.

2. *don't*

1. The calf _____ look very strong.
2. It _____ look good with that jacket.
3. We _____ play racquetball.
4. _____ these piñatas look colorful?
5. I _____ mind helping out.
6. You _____ have to watch the program.
7. Loretta _____ enjoy cleaning house.
8. A few of the contests _____ award cash prizes.
9. _____ it arrive tomorrow?
10. _____ they tinker with cars?

16m. Some nouns that are plural in form take singular verbs.

The following nouns take singular verbs.

civics	gymnastics	molasses
economics	linguistics	mumps
electronics	mathematics	news
genetics	measles	physics

EXAMPLES   **Linguistics is** the science of language.

News of the concert's cancellation **was** disappointing to the band members.

Has mathematics always **been** your best subject?

USAGE

NOTE Many nouns ending in *–ics,* such as *acoustics, athletics, ethics, politics, statistics,* and *tactics,* may be singular or plural, depending on how they are used. Generally, such a noun takes a singular verb when the noun names a science, system, or skill. The noun takes a plural verb when the noun names qualities, activities, or individual items.

EXAMPLES   **Acoustics deals** with the transmission of sound.

            The **acoustics** in the new auditorium **are** excellent.

Some nouns that are plural in form but that refer to single items take plural verbs.

binoculars	pants	shears
eyeglasses	pliers	shorts
Olympics	scissors	slacks

EXAMPLES   **Are** the **scissors** sharp enough?

            The **pliers seem** to be missing.

            Your gray **slacks are** in the laundry.

16n. Even when plural in form, the title of a creative work (such as a book, song, movie, or painting) generally takes a singular verb.

EXAMPLES   ***Majors and Minors* is** a collection of Paul Laurence Dunbar's poetry. [one book]

            ***The Gleaners* is** a famous painting by Jean-François Millet. [one work of art]

            Four Saints in Three Acts, with music by Virgil Thomson and words by Gertrude Stein, **was** first **produced** in 1934, with an African American cast. [one musical work]

16o. Even when plural in form, the name of a country, a city, or an organization generally takes a singular verb.

EXAMPLES   The **Solomon Islands has** a population of 350,000.

            Is Grand Rapids smaller than Detroit?

            Carrier Computers is having a sale on laptops.

┌**HELP**─

If you do not know whether a noun that is plural in form is singular or plural in meaning, look up the word in a dictionary.

│ **COMPUTER TIP**

Some word-processing programs can find problems in subject-verb agreement. You can use such a program to search for errors when you proofread your writing. If you are not sure that a usage that the program identifies as an error is truly an error, check this textbook.

USAGE

Proofreading for Subject-Verb Agreement

For each of the following sentences, if the subject and verb do not agree, write the correct form of the verb. If the verb already agrees with the subject, write *C*.

EXAMPLE
1. Mumps are a contagious disease.

1. *is*

1. Des Moines are the capital of Iowa.
2. The United Nations have its headquarters in New York City.
3. "Tales from the Vienna Woods" are one of Johann Strauss's most popular waltzes.
4. The Philippines comprise more than seven thousand islands.
5. Statistics are the collection of mathematical data.
6. The United Arab Emirates generate most of its revenue from the sale of oil.
7. Civics are definitely Alejandra's best subject.
8. When he is making alterations, the tailor's scissors usually hang around his neck on a leather band.
9. *Vermilion Lotuses* were among the paintings by Chinese artist Chang Dai-chien exhibited at the Smithsonian Institution.
10. Are the Olympics on television this afternoon?

Review E **Choosing Verbs That Agree with Their Subjects**

Choose the correct form of the verb given in parentheses in each of the following sentences.

EXAMPLE
1. (*Doesn't, Don't*) the French phrase *joie de vivre* mean "joy of living"?

1. *Doesn't*

1. Nguyen, along with her family, (*has, have*) invited me to the Vietnamese National Day celebration in the park.
2. They (*wasn't, weren't*) interested in learning how to play the accordion.
3. Carlos, not Martha or Jan, (*was, were*) answering all the letters.
4. Many of them (*has, have*) already read the novel.
5. *The Birds* (*was, were*) one of Alfred Hitchcock's great movies.
6. (*Doesn't, Don't*) Chuck intend to join the Air Force when he graduates?

USAGE

7. Caroline, like most of her classmates, (*wishes, wish*) vacation could last forever.
8. There (*is, are*) some good programs on educational television.
9. Neither of those books by Naguib Mahfouz (*is, are*) on our reading list.
10. The shears (*doesn't, don't*) need sharpening.

Review F — Choosing Verbs That Agree with Their Subjects

For each of the following sentences, choose the correct form of the verb in parentheses.

EXAMPLE
    1. The quills of a porcupine (*was, were*) used to make this pair of moccasins.

    1. were

1. (*Doesn't, Don't*) these quilled moccasins look as if they are beaded?
2. Quillwork, one of the traditional Plains Indians handicrafts, (*is, are*) an ancient and sophisticated art form.
3. The number of quills that grow on one porcupine (*is, are*) greater than you might think—about thirty thousand!
4. Five inches (*is, are*) the maximum length of these tubular spines.
5. Before being used in quillwork, every porcupine quill (*is, are*) dyed a bright color, softened in water, and flattened in an unusual way.
6. The quillworker, usually a woman, (*squeeze, squeezes*) each quill flat by pulling it between her teeth.
7. Among the Sioux, worn teeth were considered a badge of great honor because items decorated with the colorful quillwork (*was, were*) so important in tribal life.
8. Working the quills into complex geometric patterns (*require, requires*) great skill and coordination.
9. In quill weaving, each of the ribbonlike quills (*is, are*) passed tightly over and under threads of fiber or leather.
10. The finished quillwork (*is, are*) sewn onto clothing, saddlebags, or cradleboards as a decoration.

USAGE

Review G **Making Verbs Agree with Their Subjects**

For each of the following sentences, if the verb and the subject do not agree, supply the correct form of the verb. If the verb and subject already agree, write *C.*

EXAMPLE   1. *Sleeping Musicians* were painted by Rufino Tamayo.

          1. *was painted*

1. Gymnastics help keep me limber.
2. Few objections, besides the one about chartering the bus, was raised.
3. *Six Characters in Search of an Author* is a modern play that raises many interesting questions about art and reality.
4. Some of this land is far too hilly to farm.
5. In Maine, there's many miles of rocky coastline.
6. Four minutes were his time in that race.
7. Performing in front of a thousand people don't seem to bother the cellist Yo-Yo Ma.
8. Two thirds of a cup of milk is needed for this recipe.
9. Every three years my family have a reunion in Sierra Leone, the land from which our ancestors came.
10. Every student, teacher, and administrator are contributing to the fund-raising drive.

Agreement of Pronoun and Antecedent

The noun or pronoun that a pronoun refers to is called its *antecedent.*

16p. A pronoun should agree in both number and gender with its antecedent.

(1) Use singular pronouns to refer to singular antecedents. Use plural pronouns to refer to plural antecedents.

SINGULAR   **Richard Strauss** composed many operas. *Der Rosenkavalier* is perhaps **his** most famous.

PLURAL   The mountain **climbers** believe that **they** will reach the summit by Friday.

(2) Some singular pronouns indicate *gender*—*masculine, feminine,* or *neuter* (neither masculine nor feminine).

Masculine	he	him	his	himself
Feminine	she	her	hers	herself
Neuter	it	it	its	itself

EXAMPLES   Does **Margaret** like **her** dance class?

            Arturo is doing **his** homework.

            Because the **car** wouldn't start, **it** had to be towed.

Indefinite Pronouns

16q. Indefinite pronouns agree with their antecedents according to the following rules.

(1) The indefinite pronouns *anybody, anyone, anything, each, either, everybody, everyone, everything, neither, nobody, no one, nothing, one, somebody, someone,* and *something* are singular.

Notice that the use of a phrase or a clause after the antecedent does not change the number of the antecedent.

EXAMPLES   **Each** of the teams had **its** mascot at the game.

            One of the boys left **his** pen behind.

            Everybody in the girls' league has paid **her** dues.

When you do not know the gender of the antecedent, use both the masculine and the feminine pronoun forms, connected by *or.*

EXAMPLES   **Someone** left **his or her** pen behind.

            Everybody in the club has paid **his or her** dues.

NOTE When the meaning of *everyone* or *everybody* is clearly plural, it is common in informal speech and writing to use a plural pronoun to refer to it. In formal speech and writing, you should revise the sentence to eliminate the confusion rather than use the wrong pronoun form.

CONFUSING   When everyone arrives, explain the situation to him or her.

INFORMAL   When everyone arrives, explain the situation to them.

FORMAL   When **all** the people arrive, explain the situation to **them.**

S T Y L E   T I P

Some of the words listed in Rule 16q (1) can also be used as adjectives and as parts of correlative conjunctions.

ADJECTIVE
  Each flea hops.

CORRELATIVE CONJUNCTION
  Either Fido **or** the flea hops.

Reference Note

For more about **adjectives,** see page 412. For more about **correlative conjunctions,** see page 428.

STYLE TIP

You can often avoid the awkward *his or her* construction by substituting an article (*a*, *an*, or *the*) for the construction or by revising the sentence and using the plural forms of both the pronoun and its antecedent.

AWKWARD
Someone left his or her pen behind.

BETTER
Someone left **a** pen behind.

AWKWARD
Each of the club members has paid his or her dues.

BETTER
All of the club members have paid **their** dues.

(2) The indefinite pronouns *both*, *few*, *many*, and *several* are plural.

EXAMPLES **Both** of the candidates clearly stated **their** positions on the issue.

Many of the actors already know **their** lines.

(3) The indefinite pronouns *all, any, more, most, none,* and *some* may be singular or plural, depending on how they are used in a sentence.

Each of these pronouns is singular when it refers to a singular word and is plural when it refers to a plural word.

SINGULAR **Most** of this money belongs to Ms. Hayek. Would you take **it** to her, please? [*It* is used because *Most* refers to the singular noun *money*.]

PLURAL **Most** of these coins are rare, but I don't know what **they** are worth. [*They* is used because *Most* refers to the plural noun *coins*.]

Exercise 12 Choosing Pronouns That Agree with Their Antecedents

For the blanks in the following sentences, choose pronouns that agree with their antecedents.

EXAMPLE 1. Everyone on the boys' wrestling team did _____ best at practice today.

1. *his*

1. Some of the nations successfully defended _____ borders.
2. Neither of the sisters wanted to recite _____ lines.
3. Did any of the visitors forget _____ personal belongings?
4. One of the exhibits had _____ date changed from A.D. 1200 to A.D. 1350.
5. Each of the candidates bought _____ own TV air time.
6. Someone left _____ books behind.
7. Everyone who will need extra time should raise _____ hand.
8. Many of these blossoms were smaller than we had expected _____ to be.
9. If you find a few of the pieces, Sara said she could use _____.
10. Each of the dolphins displays _____ particular characteristics.

Compound Antecedents

16r. Pronouns agree with compound antecedents according to the following rules.

(1) Use a plural pronoun to refer to two or more antecedents joined by *and.*

EXAMPLE   The **guide** and the **ranger** wrapped **their** rain ponchos in **their** saddle rolls.

> **NOTE** Antecedents joined by *and* that name only one person, place, thing, or idea take singular pronouns.
>
> EXAMPLE   For dinner, I'm preparing **liver and onions.** I think you'll enjoy **it.**

(2) Use a singular pronoun to refer to two or more singular antecedents joined by *or* or *nor.*

EXAMPLE   Neither Heidi nor Beth took **her** umbrella with **her.**

Using a pronoun to refer to antecedents of different number may create an unclear or awkward sentence.

UNCLEAR   Neither the parrots nor the macaw has eaten its fruit. [*Its* agrees with the nearest antecedent, *macaw*, but the sentence is unclear. Does it mean that none of the birds have eaten their own fruit, that the parrots have not eaten the macaw's fruit, or that the macaw has not eaten its own fruit?]

Neither the macaw nor the parrots have eaten their fruit. [*Their* agrees with the nearest antecedent, *parrots*, but the sentence is unclear. Does it mean that none of the birds have eaten their own fruit, that the parrots have not eaten their own fruit, or that the macaw has not eaten the parrots' fruit?]

AWKWARD   Neither the macaw nor the parrots have eaten its or their fruit.

It is best to revise sentences to avoid unclear and awkward constructions like the ones above.

REVISED   Neither the macaw nor the parrots have eaten **the** fruit.
None of the birds have eaten **their** fruit.

STYLE TIP

Sentences with singular antecedents joined by *or* or *nor* can be misleading or may sound awkward when the antecedents are of different genders. Avoid using such sentences in your writing.

MISLEADING
Neither Karen nor Brian took his camera along. [Did Karen not take along Brian's camera, either?]

AWKWARD
Neither Karen nor Brian took her or his camera along. [Did Karen and Brian intend to take only one camera along—either hers or his?]

IMPROVED
Neither Karen nor Brian took **a** camera along. [The article *a* replaces the confusing pronoun.]

IMPROVED
Karen and Brian did not take **their** cameras along. [Antecedents joined by *and* require a plural pronoun, which does not indicate gender.]

USAGE

Special Problems in Pronoun-Antecedent Agreement

Reference Note

For a list of commonly used **collective nouns,** see page 522.

16s. A collective noun is singular when the noun refers to the group as a unit and plural when the noun refers to the individual members or parts of the group.

SINGULAR   The **orchestra** was looking forward to performing **its** rendition of Beethoven's *Pastoral Symphony*. [*Its* is used because the orchestra would perform the rendition as a unit.]

PLURAL   The **orchestra** were tuning **their** instruments when the conductor arrived. [*Their* is used because the members of the orchestra were tuning separate instruments.]

16t. An expression of an amount (a measurement, a percentage, or a fraction, for example) may take a singular or plural pronoun, depending on how it is used.

An expression of an amount is

- singular when the amount is thought of as a unit
- plural when the amount is thought of as separate parts

SINGULAR   **Two days** is a long time. **It** could seem like forever. [one time]
PLURAL   **Two days** (Monday and Friday) were especially cold and rainy. **They** were so wet that baseball practice was canceled. [two separate days]

SINGULAR   **Five dollars** was the price. I had **it** in my pocket. [one price]
PLURAL   **Five dollars** were torn. The vending machine would not accept **them.** [separate dollars]

A fraction or a percentage is

- singular when it refers to a singular word
- plural when it refers to a plural word

SINGULAR   **Nine tenths** [or **Ninety percent**] of the colony has returned to **its** usual routine. [The fraction, or the percentage, refers to the singular noun *colony.*]

PLURAL   **Three tenths** [or **Thirty percent**] of the ants have returned to **their** usual routines. [The fraction, or the percentage, refers to the plural word *ants.*]

Generally, a measurement (such as a length, weight, capacity, or area) is singular.

USAGE

EXAMPLES   **Nine square feet** equals one square yard. **This** is how much material you will need.

Six hundred kilometers is the distance we traveled today. How far is **that** in miles?

16u. Some nouns that are plural in form take singular pronouns.

(1) The following nouns take singular pronouns.

civics	genetics	mathematics	mumps
economics	gymnastics	measles	news
electronics	linguistics	molasses	physics

Reference Note
For information on when **to spell out numbers** and **when to use numerals,** see page 791.

EXAMPLE   I have good **news.** Would you like to hear **it**?

NOTE   Many nouns ending in –ics, such as *acoustics, athletics, ethics, politics, statistics,* and *tactics,* may take singular or plural pronouns, depending on how the nouns are used. Generally, when such a noun names a science, system, or skill, the noun takes a singular pronoun. When the noun names qualities, activities, or individual items, the noun takes a plural pronoun.

SINGULAR   The colonel explained **tactics** and how **it** differs from strategy.

PLURAL   The colonel outlined the **tactics,** and the general approved **them.**

HELP
Check a dictionary if you are not sure whether to use a singular or plural pronoun to refer to an antecedent ending in –ics.

Some nouns that are plural in form but that refer to single items take plural pronouns.

binoculars	shears	pants
Olympics	slacks	scissors
pliers	eyeglasses	shorts

EXAMPLE   Marissa is looking for the **scissors.** Do you know where **they** are?

(2) Even when plural in form, the title of a creative work (such as a book, song, movie, or painting) or the name of a country, a city, or an organization generally takes a singular pronoun.

EXAMPLES   Have you read **_Thousand Cranes_**? **It** was written by Yasunari Kawabata.

USAGE

My all-time favorite film is ***Dances with Wolves.*** One of **its** principal characters is played by the Canadian actor Graham Greene.

When we visited the **Philippines,** we spent most of our time on **its** chief island, Luzon.

I grew up near **Hot Springs,** Arkansas. **Its** claim to fame is **its** popular health resort.

Have you gone to **Sir Books–A–Lot?** **It** may have a copy of the book you need.

NOTE   The names of some teams, though plural in form, may take singular or plural pronouns. When the name refers to the organization as a unit, use a singular pronoun. When the name refers to the members of the organization, use a plural pronoun.

SINGULAR   The **St. Louis Cardinals** won **its** first World Series title in 1926. [*Its* is used because the St. Louis Cardinals won as a unit.]

PLURAL   Signing autographs, the **St. Louis Cardinals** thanked **their** fans for supporting **them** throughout the season. [*Their* and *them* are used because the individual players signed autographs and thanked the fans.]

16v. **The number of a relative pronoun (such as** *that, which,* **or** *who*) **is determined by the number of its antecedent.**

SINGULAR   Jessica, **who** always takes pride in **her** work, has been appointed editor of the school yearbook. [*Who* is singular because it refers to the singular noun *Jessica. Her* is used to agree with *who.*]

PLURAL   All **who** want to volunteer for the yearbook staff should raise **their** hands. [*Who* is plural because it refers to the plural pronoun *All. Their* is used to agree with *who.*]

Exercise 13   **Choosing Pronouns That Agree with Their Antecedents**

For the blanks in the following sentences, choose pronouns that agree with their antecedents.

EXAMPLE   1. I just read *Franny and Zooey;* have you read _____?

1. *it*

1. If I don't pack the binoculars now, I'll forget _____.

2. I'm looking for someone on the boys' swimming team who has parked _____ car in my space.

3. They have twelve dollars; is _____ enough?

4. Did the team scrimmage with _____ arch-rival?

5. Two thirds of the crew members have already had _____ turns standing watch.

6. The Millers and the Doyles had _____ windows broken by the hail last night.

7. All of the art class buy _____ own paper.

8. I could buy a bag of peanuts for sixty cents if I had _____ in correct change.

9. Either Stu or Mike will lend me _____ fishing gear.

10. The eyeglasses broke when _____ were dropped.

> **Review H** **Making Pronouns Agree with Their Antecedents**

Most of the following sentences contain pronouns that do not agree with their antecedents. If any pronoun does not agree with its antecedent, supply the correct pronoun or pronouns. If all of the pronouns in a sentence agree with their antecedents, write *C*.

EXAMPLE   **1.** Each of the girls is enjoying themselves.

           1. herself

1. All of these students at the Royal School of Dance in College Park, Florida, are learning traditional dances that come from her African heritage.

2. Some of the African and Caribbean dances have its roots in African folk tales.

3. At performances the members of the audience are often seen clapping its hands and swaying along with the music.

4. Before the last dance recital, I noticed either Carla or Shana practicing their steps.

5. Carla is one of those students who always know their steps ahead of time.

6. Angelique and Pamela moved her arms gracefully during the first dance.

7. Every authentic costume adds their color and movement to the dramatic spectacle.

8. Each of the girls brings their own personal style to the dances.

9. Many contemporary dancers and singers give a great deal of credit to the traditional sources of their art forms.
10. Both their hip-hop dancing and their clothing style have its origins in ancient African culture.

Review I **Identifying Subject-Verb Agreement and Pronoun-Antecedent Agreement**

Some of the following sentences contain an error in agreement. If a verb or pronoun is wrong, correct it. If the sentence is already correct, write *C*.

EXAMPLE   1. The gorilla, as well as many other mammals, are in danger of becoming extinct.

   1. *is*

1. Both Sid and Nikki like their new neighborhood and their new apartment.
2. Are either of you a member of the African American Cultural Society?
3. The computer camp lasts for five weeks. These are two weeks more than the tennis camp.
4. One of the police officers turned in their badge today.
5. Neither Fernando nor Bruce has brought all of their camping gear.
6. *All Dogs Go to Heaven* are my young nephews' favorite animated feature.
7. Which pair of these Navajo earrings were made by Narciso?
8. Where is the Athletics Department?
9. Just before the parade started, each of the eight men inside the gigantic dragon costume got their final instructions from Mr. Yee.
10. A few in the crowd was murmuring impatiently.
11. Is any of those peanuts left?
12. Either Tiger Woods or Se Ri Pak is Melinda's golf hero.
13. Every one of those stray cattle are going to have to be rounded up.
14. An additional feature of these models are the built-in stereo speakers.
15. Somebody has gone off and left their car running.
16. If anybody calls, tell them I'll be back by six o'clock this evening.
17. Each team has its own colors and symbol.
18. One of the goats were nibbling on a discarded popcorn box.
19. Are there no end to these questions?
20. Here's a pair of gloves for you.

Choosing Verbs That Agree with Their Subjects and Pronouns That Agree with Their Antecedents

For each of the following sentences, choose the correct verb or pronoun given in parentheses.

EXAMPLE   1. Not every one of the world's deserts (*is*, *are*) hot and sandy.

    1. *is*

1. Neither the manager nor the two salespeople (*was*, *were*) prepared for the number of customers.
2. Neither of the sets of barbells (*was*, *were*) easy to lift.
3. Where (*is*, *are*) the box of nails that came with this bookshelf kit?
4. The class have had (*it's*, *their*) individual portraits made.
5. The Harlem Globetrotters (*is*, *are*) surely one of the best-loved basketball teams in the world.
6. There (*is*, *are*) leftover macaroni and cheese in the refrigerator.
7. If anybody likes a spectacle, (*he or she*, *they*) will love seeing a drum corps competition.
8. Several members of the audience (*was*, *were*) waving wildly, hoping that Martin Yan would wave back.
9. Where (*has*, *have*) the sports section of today's newspaper gone?
10. Anyone who wants to get (*his or her*, *their*) program autographed by Jimmy Smits had better hurry.

Review K **Using Subject-Verb Agreement and Pronoun-Antecedent Agreement Correctly**

Revise each of the following sentences according to the directions given in parentheses. Be sure to change other words, especially verbs and pronouns, as necessary.

EXAMPLE   1. Both of the boys desperately want to go to the circus. (Change *Both* to *Each*.)

    1. *Each of the boys desperately wants to go to the circus.*

1. Both of their parents have agreed to the idea. (Change *Both* to *One*.)
2. To pay for the tickets, Jorge has to empty his piggy bank or his secret hiding place of all its money. (Change *his piggy bank or* to *both his piggy bank and*.)
3. Because of the excitement, none of the boys will eat much of their dinner tonight. (Change *none* to *neither*.)

4. Both of the boys want to bring their cameras. (Change *Both* to *One*.)

5. Each of them has earned an enjoyable evening of watching clowns, tigers, and elephants. (Change *Each* to *All*.)

6. Every one of the clowns has his or her own special tricks and stunts. (Change *Every one* to *All*.)

7. None of the people from town want to miss tonight's performance. (Change *None* to *Not one*.)

8. Not all of the families in town have money for tickets. (Change *Not all of the families* to *Not every family*.)

9. All but one of the free tickets to the circus have been picked up. (Change *All but* to *Only*.)

10. Much of the money the circus takes in will be given to the Children's Hospital; it will help pay for a new X-ray machine. (Change *Much of the money* to *Many of the donations*.)

Chapter Review

A. Identifying Subject-Verb Agreement

For each sentence, write the verb in parentheses that agrees with its subject.

1. Either the dog or the cat (*get, gets*) the party leftovers.
2. There (*is, are*) four herbs that almost any gardener can grow: basil, thyme, marjoram, and oregano.
3. All of these old letters (*was, were*) tied with ribbon and stored in a trunk in the attic.
4. Each of them (*is, are*) penned in bold, flowing handwriting.
5. Both Alicia and Isabel (*thinks, think*) that the former owner of the house put the letters in the attic.
6. Neither potatoes nor peanuts (*is, are*) grown on this farm anymore.
7. Two thirds of the electorate (*was, were*) at the polls in the last election.
8. Is it true that *Troilus and Cressida* (*is, are*) by Shakespeare?
9. Here (*is, are*) the latest scores of today's basketball games.
10. Most of the children on the island (*was, were*) not able to read very well.
11. Don't you think that five miles (*is, are*) too far to walk tonight?
12. A cool spring near the cottages (*supply, supplies*) them with water.
13. Politics (*is, are*) a popular topic of conversation during an election year.
14. Every man, woman, and child (*was, were*) frightened by the earthquake.
15. Neither of them (*knows, know*) for sure who wrote that message.
16. The jury (*has, have*) returned a verdict.
17. On the supervisors (*rest, rests*) the responsibility for implementing safe procedures.
18. The two songs we played at the Independence Day concert (*was, were*) written by Carly Simon.
19. There (*has, have*) been many visitors on the fairground today.
20. Everybody in the theater (*was, were*) thrilled by the rescue scene.

B. Choosing Pronouns That Agree with Their Antecedents

Provide personal pronouns to complete the following sentences correctly.

21. Either my sister Lavinia or my friend Millicent will let me borrow _____ camping equipment.
22. I looked in the cupboard for the scissors, but I couldn't find _____.
23. Three of the cars had _____ windows broken by thieves last night.
24. Not long ago, I saw *Romeo and Juliet;* have you seen _____ ?
25. I'm looking for Stan and Joel; do you know _____ ?
26. We visited Honduras and spent three days in _____ capital, Tegucigalpa.
27. Mothers Against Drunk Driving has _____ meeting in the conference room tonight.
28. Three quarters of the city's voters cast _____ ballots.
29. I need fifty cents; could you lend _____ to me?
30. The sunglasses had stains on _____ lenses.

C. Identifying Subject-Verb Agreement and Pronoun-Antecedent Agreement

In most of the following sentences, either a verb does not agree with its subject or a pronoun does not agree with its antecedent. Revise each incorrect sentence to correct the error. If a sentence is already correct, write *C*.

31. The meeting got out of hand when the discussion period began because everyone tried to express their opinion at the same time.
32. There on the corner of your desk are the package of books that I returned and that you claimed you never received.
33. Two students from each class is going to the state capital to attend a special conference on education.
34. Each of them are expected to bring back a report on the conference so that classmates can get firsthand information.
35. Since they will be on vacation next month, neither Miguel nor his sister are going to enter the mixed-doubles tennis tournament.
36. The audience expressed their admiration for the dancer's grace and skill by applauding wildly.

37. After the senator had read the proposed amendment, anyone who disagreed with the ruling was allowed to state their reason.

38. This collection of old Italian folk tales demonstrate the wisdom, humor, and creativity of my ancestors.

39. She is one of those competitive people who perform best under pressure.

40. Since neither of you have ever tasted fried plantains, my mother has invited you to eat a Cuban meal at our house tonight.

 Writing Application

Using Agreement in a Letter

Pronoun-Antecedent Agreement Your best friend moved away two months ago. You have just received a postcard from him or her, asking what's been happening recently in the old neighborhood. You answer the postcard by writing a short letter that brings your friend up to date. In your letter, include at least five pronouns that agree with their antecedents.

Prewriting Make a list of several interesting things to tell your friend. You may write about your real neighborhood or about one you have made up. Decide on the order in which you will tell about the items on your list. You may want to use time order (telling when things happened) or spatial order (telling where things happened).

Writing As you write, think about how to make your letter interesting to your friend. Use details that will help him or her picture the neighborhood and its people.

Revising Ask a classmate to read your letter. Are the events you describe interesting? Is it absolutely clear who did what and what belongs to whom? Use your reader's suggestions to revise your letter so that nothing in the letter is confusing.

Publishing Proofread your letter for any errors in grammar, usage, and mechanics. Be sure that all pronouns agree with their antecedents. The class may wish to post the completed letters on a class bulletin board or Web page.

Using Pronouns Correctly

Nominative, Objective, and Possessive Case; Clear Reference

Diagnostic Preview

A. Proofreading Sentences for Correct Pronoun Forms

Most of the following sentences contain an incorrect pronoun form. Revise each sentence by supplying the correct pronoun form. If a sentence is already correct, write *C*.

EXAMPLE
1. She and myself have different tai chi instructors.

1. She and I have different tai chi instructors.

1. Del is as good at math as her.
2. He's the sportscaster who irritates me with his pretentious talk.
3. Do you remember to who the letter was addressed?
4. Steve showed the negatives to Cecilia and I.
5. It can't be them; that's not their car.
6. Ben and you can come with they and me.
7. Leontyne Price's accomplishments were familiar to everyone in the class except him and I.
8. Us band members have to be at school early to practice marching.
9. There was some misunderstanding between he and his brother.
10. In front of the school stood two children, Charlene and he.

B. Proofreading Sentences for Correct Forms and Uses

Most of the following sentences contain at least one incorrect pronoun form or an unclear pronoun reference. Revise each sentence either by supplying the correct pronoun form(s) or by correcting the faulty pronoun reference. If a sentence is already correct, write *C*.

EXAMPLES   1. Dad and me went to the all-star basketball game.
1. *Dad and I went to the all-star basketball game.*

2. Many people outside the arena wanted to buy our tickets, which didn't surprise us.
2. *That many people outside the arena wanted to buy our tickets didn't surprise us.*

11. There's nothing like an action-packed all-star basketball game to give Dad and I a thrill!
12. Our team was only two points behind when Barkley's shot bounced off the rim, and Pippen and Robinson rushed for it.
13. As gravity pulled him and Robinson toward the floor, Pippen managed to tip the ball to Miller.
14. Miller saw Stockton coming, dribbled behind his own back, and eluded he and Malone.
15. When Stockton and Malone collided, nobody was more surprised than them.
16. If they made this, the score would be tied.
17. Miller looked for Hill and realized that the blur streaking up the court on the left was him.
18. He had to pass to whomever was open, and Hill was the one.
19. Hill took a shot and missed; four players struggled for the ball, which went in, which meant that Hill and his teammates won.
20. In the whirlwind action during the last couple of seconds, the frantic referee couldn't see whom had fouled who.

Case Forms of Personal Pronouns

Case is the form that a noun or pronoun takes to show its relationship to other words in a sentence. In English, there are three cases: *nominative*, *objective*, and *possessive*. Nouns have the same form in both the nominative and the objective cases. Nouns usually add an apostrophe and an *s* to form the possessive case.

STYLE **TIP**

Use the neuter pronoun *it* when referring to an animal unless the gender of the animal is made clear by another word in the sentence.

EXAMPLES

The sparrow was gathering twigs and taking them to **its** nest.

That bull was known for **his** bad temper. [The word *bull* indicates that the animal is male.]

Eric gave his poodle, Fifi, **her** squeaky toy. [The name *Fifi* indicates that the animal is female.]

Reference Note

For information on **forming the possessives of nouns,** see page 758.

Personal pronouns have different forms for the different cases.

Case Forms of Personal Pronouns		
Nominative Case		
	Singular	**Plural**
First Person	I	we
Second Person	you	you
Third Person	he, she, it	they
Objective Case		
	Singular	**Plural**
First Person	me	us
Second Person	you	you
Third Person	him, her, it	them
Possessive Case		
	Singular	**Plural**
First Person	my, mine	our, ours
Second Person	your, yours	your, yours
Third Person	his, her, hers, its	their, theirs

NOTE Notice that *you* and *it* have the same form in the nominative and objective cases. All other personal pronouns have different forms for each. Notice also that only third-person singular pronouns indicate gender (masculine, feminine, or neuter).

Exercise 1 **Identifying Personal Pronouns in a Paragraph**

Each sentence in the following paragraph contains at least one pronoun. Identify each personal pronoun. Then, give its person, number, case, and, if applicable, its gender.

EXAMPLE **1.** Jeffrey and I were chatting in front of his locker before the Art Club meeting.

1. *I—first person, singular, nominative case; his—third person, singular, possessive case, masculine*

1. Jeffrey mentioned your interest in African art and Francine's interest in modern art.

2. Did you and she know that African masks like the one below left influenced the development of the Modernist movement in art?

3. I've learned that African carvings inspired such twentieth-century artists as Pablo Picasso, who created this painting on the right.

4. The year 1905 was probably when he and his friends first saw African masks exhibited in Paris.

5. Amedeo Modigliani was especially affected by the stark masks, and he and Picasso created many works based on them.

6. Notice that the eyes in Modigliani's carving are very close together and that they and the lips look much like small knobs.

7. I used to think that Modigliani made his faces too long by mistake, but the error was mine.

8. Ms. Keller told me that he was copying the exaggerated shapes of Ivory Coast masks.

9. Picasso and Modigliani were only two of many European artists who got their inspiration from African art.

10. Obviously, we students weren't giving credit where credit was due!

The Nominative Case

Personal pronouns in the nominative case—*I, you, he, she, it, we,* and *they*—are used as subjects of verbs and as predicate nominatives.

17a. A subject of a verb should be in the nominative case.

A **subject of a verb** tells whom or what a sentence or a clause is about.

EXAMPLES   **I** solved the problem. [*I* is the subject of *solved.*]

     They know that **we** are going. [*They* is the subject of *know,* and *we* is the subject of *are going.*]

     Al and **she** cleaned the house. [*Al and she* is the compound subject of *cleaned.*]

—HELP—

Personal pronouns in the nominative case may also be used as **appositives.**

Reference Note

For information on **appositives,** see page 483.

TIPS & TRICKS

To help you determine which pronoun form(s) to use for a compound subject, try each form as the simple subject of the verb.

EXAMPLE
(*He, Him*) and (*I, me*) both studied for the test.

CHOICES
He studied or *Him studied*?

I studied or *me studied*?

ANSWER
He and **I** both studied for the test.

Reference Note

For information on **subjects of verbs,** see page 439.

For information on **subjects of verbs,** see page 439.

Oral Practice 1 **Using Pronouns as Subjects**

Read each of the following sentences aloud, stressing the italicized words.

1. *She* and *I* gave the dog a bath.
2. Terry and *he* plan to try out for the soccer team.
3. *We* sophomores organized the recycling campaign.
4. James Earl Jones and *she* are excellent role models for young actors.
5. Are *you* and *he* doing the report?
6. Either *we* or *they* may go to the championship finals.
7. The drill team and *we* took the bus.
8. The twins said that *they* go everywhere together.

Exercise 2 **Using Personal Pronouns in the Nominative Case to Complete Sentences**

Supply a personal pronoun for each blank in the following sentences. Vary your pronouns, but do not use *you* or *it*.

EXAMPLE   1. What part in the play does _____ have?
          1. *she*

1. The judge and _____ studied the evidence.
2. Ted and _____ took the wrong train.
3. Linda and _____ are planning a party.
4. _____ are having a science fair.
5. Either Julius or _____ will give you a ride.
6. _____ and _____ have been rivals for years.
7. I'm sure _____ knew about the meeting.
8. Soon _____ and _____ will be graduating.
9. Did you know that _____ and _____ saw Chita Rivera in a Broadway production of *West Side Story*?
10. _____ and _____ love the Asian dumplings served at restaurants.

Exercise 3 **Writing Sentences with Pronouns in the Nominative Case**

Use the following subjects in sentences of your own.

EXAMPLE   1. we and they
          1. *We and they are meeting after dinner.*

1. we teenagers
2. the other shoppers and I
3. he and his friends
4. Liz, Michelle, and she

5. they and their classmates

6. she and her mother

7. you and he

8. the children and I

9. we boys

10. they and their dogs

17b. A predicate nominative should be in the nominative case.

A *predicate nominative* completes the meaning of a linking verb and identifies or refers to the subject of the verb. A personal pronoun used as a predicate nominative generally completes the meaning of a form of the verb *be: am, is, are, was, were, be, been,* or *being.*

EXAMPLES

It was **I** who took the message.

The winner might be **he.**

Could the caller have been **she**?

Exercise 4 **Using Pronouns as Predicate Nominatives**

Complete each of the following sentences by supplying the personal pronoun called for in parentheses.

EXAMPLE

1. It was _____ who was the first emperor of China's Yuan dynasty. (*third person, singular, masculine*)

1. *he*

1. Do you think it was _____? (*third person, singular, feminine*)

2. It must have been _____. (*third person, singular, masculine*)

3. Good friends are _____. (*third person, plural*)

4. The pranksters were _____. (*first person, plural*)

5. It was _____ at the door. (*third person, plural*)

6. It is _____. (*first person singular*)

7. It may have been _____ on the phone. (*third person, singular, feminine*)

8. The winners should be _____. (*third person, plural*)

9. The best cook here is _____. (*third person, singular, masculine*)

10. The volunteers were _____. (*first person, plural*)

Review A **Using Pronouns in the Nominative Case Correctly in Sentences**

Supply a personal pronoun for the blank in each of the following sentences. Use a variety of different pronouns, but do not use *you* or *it.* Be ready to explain the reasons for your choices.

EXAMPLE

1. Are you and _____ going to the Fourth of July celebration?

1. *he*

TIPS & TRICKS

To help you determine which pronoun form to use as a predicate nominative, try each form as the simple subject of the verb.

EXAMPLE

The two teams in the final round were (*they, them*).

CHOICES

they were or *them were*?

ANSWER

The two teams in the final round were **they.**

Reference Note

For information on **predicate nominatives,** see page 453.

STYLE TIP

Expressions such as *It's me, This is her,* and *It was them* are examples of informal usage. Though common in everyday situations, such expressions should be avoided in formal speaking and writing. (The formal versions of the italicized expressions above are *It is I, This is she,* and *It was they.*)

HELP

In the example for Review A, the nominative-case pronoun *he* is correct because the pronoun is used as a subject.

HELP

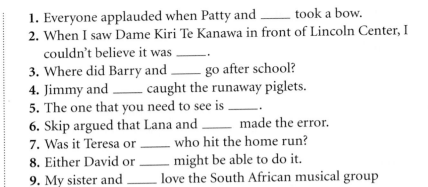

Personal pronouns in the objective case may also be used as **appositives.**

Reference Note

For information on **appositives,** see page 483. For more about **direct objects,** see page 456. For information on **transitive verbs,** see page 421. For more about **indirect objects,** see page 457.

1. Everyone applauded when Patty and _____ took a bow.
2. When I saw Dame Kiri Te Kanawa in front of Lincoln Center, I couldn't believe it was _____.
3. Where did Barry and _____ go after school?
4. Jimmy and _____ caught the runaway piglets.
5. The one that you need to see is _____.
6. Skip argued that Lana and _____ made the error.
7. Was it Teresa or _____ who hit the home run?
8. Either David or _____ might be able to do it.
9. My sister and _____ love the South African musical group Ladysmith Black Mambazo.
10. I believe that the Masked Marvel has to be _____.

Review B **Using Pronouns in the Nominative Case**

For each blank in the following paragraph, supply an appropriate personal pronoun. Do not use *you* or *it*.

EXAMPLE **[1]** _____ have learned from Mrs. Soto the value of recycling.
        1. *We*

HELP

Although more than one answer is possible for some items in Review B, you need to give only one response for each.

[1] _____ who are in Mrs. Soto's class are determined to win this year's "Save the Earth" trophy at our school. The two most enthusiastic people in our class are probably Pilar and [2] _____. I guess that's why Mrs. Soto asked whether [3] _____ and [4] _____ would organize the paper drive. Pilar explained to the class that if Americans recycled only their Sunday newspapers, half a million trees would be saved every Sunday! To illustrate her point, [5] _____ showed this photo. That is [6] _____ standing next to 580 pounds of paper—the amount the average American uses in one year. [7] _____ have gathered some other facts to inspire our classmates to recycle. Our friend Ben said that [8] _____ and his mother heard on the radio that the average American uses 1,500 aluminum drink cans every year. [9] _____ were amazed to learn that the energy saved from recycling just one aluminum can could keep a TV set running for three hours! No matter who wins the trophy, it will definitely be [10] _____ who share the prize of a cleaner, healthier planet.

The Objective Case

Personal pronouns in the objective case—*me, you, him, her, it, us,* and *them*—are used as direct objects, indirect objects, and objects of prepositions.

17c. A direct object should be in the objective case.

A *direct object* tells who or what either receives the action of a transitive verb or shows the result of the action.

EXAMPLES   Coach Johnson has been training **us.**

The coach has turned **them** into the best team in the state.

17d. An indirect object should be in the objective case.

An *indirect object* often appears in sentences containing direct objects. An indirect object tells *to whom* or *to what*, or *for whom* or *for what*, the action of a transitive verb is done.

EXAMPLES   Serena paid **him** a compliment.

Carlos saved **me** a seat in the first row.

NOTE Indirect objects do not follow prepositions. A pronoun preceded by a preposition is the object of a preposition.

17
c, d

Exercise 5 Using Pronouns in the Objective Case to Complete Sentences

Supply a personal pronoun for the blank in each of the following sentences. Use a variety of pronouns, but do not use *you* or *it*.

EXAMPLE   1. Donya sent Celie and _____ a postcard from Mexico City.

    1. *him*

1. The old sailor warned _____ about the danger.
2. The city awarded _____ its highest honor for their bravery.
3. You could ask Deborah or _____.
4. The crowd cheered _____ heartily.
5. Make sure that you ask _____ what her telephone number is.
6. The shark in that movie didn't scare _____ at all.
7. How can I recognize _____?
8. We saw Norman and _____ in their horse costume at the party.
9. Did you give Paula and _____ their assignments?
10. I bought my father and _____ identical birthday presents this year.

HELP

Although more than one answer is possible for some items in Exercise 5, you need to give only one response for each.

┌─ **H E L P** ─
In Review C,
the expression *Number 1*
indicates a first-person
singular pronoun.

Review C **Using Pronouns in the Nominative and Objective Cases**

The cheerleading squad is learning a new pyramid routine. To help organize the cheerleaders, the coach has assigned each one a number. In the following sentences, use a correct personal pronoun in place of each italicized expression.

EXAMPLES
1. Coach Welber tells Cara and *Number 5* where to position themselves.
   1. *her*

2. I asked whether *Number 8 and Number 1* can be in the pyramid next time.
   2. *we*

1. The three people forming the base of the pyramid are Harley, Michael, and *Number 5.*
2. Kimiko is the smallest, so it is *Number 6* who is at the top first.
3. *Number 8 and Number 1* give *Number 6* a boost.
4. After *Number 4* and Emilio have been in the middle row awhile, Rosie and *Number 1* ask for a turn.
5. Please show Luisa and *Number 6 and Number 3* their new positions.
6. Give Rosie or *Number 1* a signal when you are ready to jump down, Kimiko.
7. Next time, the ones in the middle row will be Harley and *Number 8.*
8. If anyone can support the person on top well, it's *Number 3.*
9. The winners of the next cheerleading meet will surely be *Numbers 1 through 8.*
10. Come here, and I'll tell you and *Number 4* about the next new formation.

17e. An object of a preposition should be in the objective case.

A noun or pronoun that follows a preposition is called an *object of the preposition.* Together, a preposition, its object, and any modifiers of that object make up a *prepositional phrase.*

EXAMPLES   to **them**   with **him**   for both **her** and **us**

             from **me**   next to **us**   between **you** and **me**

Reference Note

For lists of **commonly used prepositions,** see page 426. For more about **prepositional phrases,** see page 467.

Oral Practice 2 **Using Pronouns as Objects of Prepositions**

Read each of the following sentences aloud, stressing the italicized words.

1. There were calls for Walker and *us.*
2. This message is from Dolores and *her.*
3. With Arnie and *them* were the Malone twins.
4. Margo looked toward Francine and *me.*
5. They gave copies to *him* and *me.*
6. This drawing is by either Hector or *him.*
7. Don't hold this against Cho and *her.*
8. Between Vince and *him* sat an iguana.

TIPS & TRICKS

To help you determine which pronoun form(s) to use in a compound object of a preposition, try each form with the preposition.

EXAMPLE
  Gwen wrote to (*she, her*) and (*I, me*).

CHOICES
  to she or *to her*?

  to I or *to me*?

ANSWER
  Gwen wrote to **her** and **me.**

Exercise 6 **Selecting Pronoun Forms for Objects of Prepositions**

Choose the correct pronoun forms in parentheses in the following sentences.

EXAMPLE   1. Have you spoken to (*he, him*) or (*she, her*) recently?

           1. *him, her*

1. The referee called fouls on (*them, they*) and (*I, me*).
2. Fishing with Grandpa and (*he, him*) was fun.
3. We didn't want to leave without you and (*she, her*).
4. They assigned the same lab equipment to (*them, they*) and (*we, us*).
5. The duke directed a haughty sneer at the jester and (*he, him*).
6. After Carmen rolled the corn husks around the tamales, she handed them to Arturo and (*me, I*).
7. Everyone but Kevin and (*she, her*) thinks Ed Bradley is the best news commentator on television.
8. Between you and (*me, I*), I'd rather not.
9. The wary skunk circled around (*she, her*) and (*me, I*).
10. Uncle Vic will get the details from you and (*we, us*).

USAGE

USAGE

Exercise 7   **Writing Sentences Using Pronouns as Objects of Prepositions**

Write sentences of your own, using each of the following prepositions with a compound object. Use a personal pronoun for at least one of the objects in each sentence.

EXAMPLE   **1.** toward

       1. *The whooping crane stalked toward Mike and me.*

1. against	**3.** for	**5.** except	**7.** without	**9.** by
2. across	**4.** before	**6.** between	**8.** near	**10.** over

Review D   **Selecting Correct Forms of Pronouns**

For the numbered sentences, in the following paragraph, choose the correct pronoun forms in parentheses.

EXAMPLE   **[1]** Tina, Susan, and (*I, me*) are best friends.

       1. *I*

[**1**] Last fall, Tina talked Susan and (*I, me*) into going on a canoe trip with the Wilderness Club. [**2**] She warned (*we, us*) that we might get a good dunking before we were through. [**3**] When we set out, Susan and (*I, me*) could barely steer our canoe. [**4**] We watched another canoeist and saw how (*she, her*) and her partner maneuvered their craft. [**5**] Both they and (*we, us*) did well until we hit the rapids or, rather, until the rapids hit (*we, us*). [**6**] Susan grabbed our sleeping bags, and (*she, her*) and (*I, me*) both scrambled for our ice chest. [**7**] All of (*we, us*) were drenched, but no quitters were (*we, us*). [**8**] Tina's warning haunted all of (*we, us*) as (*we, us*) contemplated waterlogged sandwiches, soggy salads, and banana muffins with tadpoles in them. [**9**] Later, Susan and (*I, me*) discovered that our bedrolls had become portable water beds. [**10**] After a cold, squishy night, (*I, me*) concluded that wise are (*they, them*) who heed the voice of experience.

The Possessive Case

The personal pronouns in the possessive case—*my, mine, your, yours, his, her, hers, its, our, ours, their* and *theirs*—are used to show ownership or possession.

17f. The possessive pronouns *mine, yours, his, hers, its, ours,* and *theirs* can be used in the same way that the personal pronouns in the nominative and objective cases are used.

SUBJECT	**Mine** has a flat tire.
PREDICATE NOMINATIVE	This key is **yours.**
DIRECT OBJECT	Mrs. Fong takes **hers** for a walk twice a day.
INDIRECT OBJECT	Most teachers are not assigning **theirs** any homework for the holidays.
OBJECT OF PREPOSITION	Their coach spoke to **ours** about a possible rematch.

17g. The possessive pronouns *my, your, his, her, its, our,* and *their* are used to modify nouns and pronouns.

EXAMPLES　　**My** bicycle has a flat tire. [*My* modifies *bicycle.*]

　　　　　　This is **your** key. [*Your* modifies *key.*]

　　　　　　Mrs. Fong takes **her** dogs for a walk twice a day. [*Her* modifies *dogs.*]

　　　　　　Most teachers are not assigning **their** students any home-work for the holidays. [*Their* modifies *students.*]

　　　　　　Their coach spoke to **our** coach about a possible rematch. [*Their* and *our* each modify *coach.*]

NOTE　Some authorities prefer to call the possessive pronouns *my, your, his, her, its, our,* and *their* adjectives. Follow your teacher's instructions regarding these possessive forms.

17h. A noun or pronoun preceding a gerund generally should be in the possessive case.

A *gerund* is a verb form that ends in *–ing* and functions as a noun. Since a gerund serves as a noun, the noun or pronoun that precedes it should be in the possessive case in order to modify the gerund.

EXAMPLE　　They approved of the **students'** [or **their**] organizing a cleanup campaign.

　　Do not confuse a gerund with a *present participle,* which is also a verb form that ends in *–ing.* A gerund acts as a noun, whereas a present partici-ple serves as an adjective or as part of a verb phrase. The noun or pronoun preceding a present participle should generally not be in the possessive case.

EXAMPLE　　Every day after school, the principal saw the **students** [or **them**] working diligently.

USAGE

Reference Note

For more on **gerunds** and **present participles,** see pages 476 and 472.

NOTE Often the form of a noun or pronoun before an *–ing* word depends on the meaning you want to express. If you want to emphasize the *–ing* word, use the possessive form. If you want to emphasize the noun or pronoun preceding the *–ing* word, do not use the possessive form. Notice the difference in emphasis in the following sentences.

EXAMPLES   I can't imagine cousin **Liam's** [or **his**] driving. [emphasis on the gerund *driving*]

I can't imagine cousin **Liam** [or **him**] driving. [emphasis on the noun or pronoun preceding the present participle *driving*]

Special Problems in Pronoun Usage

The Relative Pronouns *Who* and *Whom*

17i. The use of *who* or *whom* in a subordinate clause depends on how the pronoun functions in the clause.

Nominative Case	who, whoever
Objective Case	whom, whomever

Follow these steps to decide whether to use *who* or *whom* in a subordinate clause.

STEP 1   Find the subordinate clause.

STEP 2   Decide how the pronoun is used in the clause—as subject, predicate nominative, direct object, indirect object, or object of a preposition.

STEP 3   Determine the case of the pronoun according to the rules of standard, formal English.

STEP 4   Select the correct form of the pronoun.

EXAMPLE   Roscoe is the only student (*who, whom*) earned a perfect score.

STEP 1   The subordinate clause is (*who, whom*) *earned a perfect score.*

STEP 2   In this clause the pronoun is the subject of the verb *earned.*

STEP 3   As a subject the pronoun should be in the nominative case.

STEP 4   The nominative form is *who.*

ANSWER   Roscoe is the only student **who** earned a perfect score.

STYLE   TIP

In informal English, the use of *whom* is becoming less common. However, in formal speech and writing, it is still important to distinguish between *who* and *whom.*

Reference Note

For information on **subordinate clauses,** see page 493.

EXAMPLE   Did they say (*who, whom*) the winner is?

STEP 1   The subordinate clause is (*who, whom*) *the winner is.*

STEP 2   In this clause the pronoun is the predicate nominative: *the winner is* (*who, whom*).

STEP 3   As a predicate nominative, the pronoun should be in the nominative case.

STEP 4   The nominative form is *who.*

ANSWER   Did they say **who** the winner is?

EXAMPLE   I saw Sabrina, (*who, whom*) I know from school.

STEP 1   The subordinate clause is (*who, whom*) *I know from school.*

STEP 2   In this clause the pronoun is the direct object of the verb *know: I know* (*who, whom*).

STEP 3   As a direct object, the pronoun should be in the objective case.

STEP 4   The objective form is *whom.*

ANSWER   I saw Sabrina, **whom** I know from school.

Remember that no words outside the subordinate clause affect the case of a pronoun in the clause. In the first example above, the whole clause *who the winner is* is the direct object of the verb *Did say* in the independent clause. In the subordinate clause, though, *who* is used as a predicate nominative, which takes the nominative case.

NOTE   The relative pronoun *whom* is often left out of a subordinate adjective clause but is nevertheless understood.

EXAMPLE   The man [*whom*] we saw on the elevator looked familiar.
[*Whom* is understood to be the direct object of *saw.*]

COMPUTER TIP

If you use a computer, you can use the search feature of a word-processing program to find each use of *who* or *whom* in a document. Then you can check to make sure that you have used the correct form of the pronoun in each instance.

USAGE

Exercise 8   Selecting *Who* or *Whom* to Complete Sentences Correctly

For each of the following sentences, choose the correct form, *who* or *whom*, in parentheses.

EXAMPLE   1. (*Who, Whom*) did you speak to yesterday?
           1. *Whom*

1. The student (*who, whom*) saw the eclipse is here.
2. (*Who, Whom*) did you vote for in the election?
3. Are you the person to (*who, whom*) I give my essay?

4. I don't know (*who, whom*) has my notebook.

5. (*Who, Whom*) is on the telephone?

6. To (*who, whom*) are you speaking?

7. They are the people about (*who, whom*) I was talking.

8. He is not (*who, whom*) won the award.

9. Jonathan saw (*who, whom*) you greeted.

10. I feel sometimes that I don't know (*who, whom*) you are anymore.

WHICH IS CORRECT, "WHO ARE WE KIDDING?" OR "WHOM ARE WE KIDDING?"

WELL, I SUPPOSE "WHOM" IS CORRECT ALTHOUGH MOST PEOPLE WOULD SAY "WHO"

WHAT DO YOU THINK OUR CHANCES ARE OF WINNING TODAY?

OH, I'D SAY ABOUT 'FIFTY-FIFTY...

WHOM ARE WE KIDDING?

PEANUTS reprinted by permission of United Feature Syndicate, Inc.

Exercise 9 **Determining the Use of *Who* and *Whom* in Subordinate Clauses**

Identify the subordinate clause containing *who* or *whom* in each of the following sentences. Then, tell how *who* or *whom* is used in the clause— as *subject*, *predicate nominative*, *direct object*, or *object of a preposition*.

EXAMPLES **1.** She is someone whom we all admire.

    1. whom we all admire—direct object

    2. He is the person about whom I wrote my report.

    2. about whom I wrote my report—object of a preposition

1. The people who are born in Puerto Rico live in a commonwealth, with its own Senate, Supreme Court, and Cabinet.

2. In 1969, the governor needed a secretary of labor on whom he could depend.

3. The person whom he appointed would occupy the most difficult and sensitive position in the Cabinet.

4. Do you know who the choice was?

5. The choice fell to Mrs. Julia Rivera De Vincenti, who became the first woman to occupy a Cabinet post in Puerto Rico.

6. De Vincenti, who had completed the requirements for a Ph.D. degree in management and collective bargaining at Cornell University, was a good choice.

7. De Vincenti, who was later appointed to the U.S. Mission to the United Nations, was the first Puerto Rican to serve in that capacity.

8. She addressed the General Assembly and showed that she was a person on whom they could rely.

9. She praised her compatriots, from whom new advances in agriculture had recently come.

10. I'm sure her compatriots appreciated her praise, for De Vincenti was someone who herself was worthy of praise.

USAGE

Appositives

17j. A pronoun used as an appositive should be in the same case as the word to which it refers.

An *appositive* appears next to another noun or pronoun to identify or describe that noun or pronoun.

EXAMPLES   The late arrivals—**she, he,** and **I**—missed the first act. [The pronouns are in the nominative case because they refer to the subject *arrivals.*]

The co-captains should be the best bowlers, **he** and **she.** [The pronouns are in the nominative case because they refer to the predicate nominative *bowlers.*]

The article you're reading mentions the winners, **her** and **me.** [The pronouns are in the objective case because they refer to the direct object *winners.*]

Ms. Lee gave the debaters, **them** and **us,** name tags. [The pronouns are in the objective case because they refer to the indirect object *debaters.*]

The contestants were narrowed to two finalists, **him** and **her.** [The pronouns are in the objective case because they refer to *finalists,* the object of the preposition *to.*]

The pronoun *we* or *us* is sometimes followed by a noun appositive.

EXAMPLES   **We** sophomores raised the most money for charity. [The pronoun is in the nominative case because it is the subject of the verb *raised.* The appositive *sophomores* identifies *We.*]

The judges awarded **us** members of the marching band a superior rating. [The pronoun is in the objective case because it is the indirect object of the verb *awarded.* The appositive *members* identifies *us.*]

> **Review E** **Selecting Pronouns to Complete Sentences Correctly**

Choose the correct pronoun form in parentheses in each of the following sentences. Then, tell whether the pronoun is used as a *subject,* a *predicate nominative,* a *direct object,* an *indirect object,* an *object of a preposition,* or an *appositive.*

EXAMPLE   **1.** Andre is giving Jena and (*I, me*) marimba lessons.
       1. me—indirect object

TIPS & TRICKS

To help you determine which pronoun form(s) to use as an appositive or with an appositive, read the sentence with only the pronoun.

AS AN APPOSITIVE
The coach congratulated the two starting forwards, Angela and (*I, me*).

CHOICES
The coach congratulated I or *The coach congratulated me*?

ANSWER
The coach congratulated the two starting forwards, Angela and **me.**

BEFORE A NOUN APPOSITIVE
(*We, Us*) girls made the playoffs!

CHOICES
We made the playoffs or *Us made the playoffs*?

ANSWER
We girls made the playoffs!

USAGE

Reference Note
For information on **appositives,** see page 483.

1. The two winners, Sean and (*she, her*), received huge green ribbons decorated with shamrocks.
2. Will Meg and (*she, her*) run the concession stand?
3. The coach asked you and (*I, me*) for help with the equipment.
4. Becky and (*she, her*) rode their bikes to the meeting.
5. The lighting crew for the play was Manuel and (*I, me*).
6. They treat very well (*whoever, whomever*) they hire.
7. I think that Denzel Washington and (*he, him*) starred in *Much Ado About Nothing*.
8. They met my cousins—Jennie and (*she, her*)—at the airport.
9. Joe Leaphorn and Jim Chee are the Navajo detectives (*who, whom*) Tony Hillerman writes about in his crime stories.
10. The people who were costumed as pirates are (*they, them*).

Review F Proofreading for Correct Pronoun Forms

Most of the sentences in the following paragraph contain at least one pronoun that is used incorrectly. Identify each incorrect pronoun, and write the correct form. If the sentence is already correct, write *C*.

EXAMPLE [1] Two of my cousins and me tried to determine how everyone else at the family reunion was related to we cousins.

1. *me—I; we—us*

Family Relationship Chart

grandparent

great-uncle or great-aunt

parent

uncle or aunt

first cousin once removed

SELF

brother or sister

first cousin

second cousin

child

nephew or niece

first cousin once removed

second cousin once removed

grandchild

great-nephew or great-niece

first cousin twice removed

second cousin twice removed

—— Red lines link siblings.   ↓ Blue arrows show descent.

[1] Us cousins were getting so confused at the family reunion that Rochelle, Darla, and me made the Family Relationship Chart shown at left. [2] Before long, the busiest people at the picnic were they and me! [3] Aunts and uncles consulted us to find out who they were related to and just how they were related. [4] It all started when Jules wanted to know the connection between him and Vicky. [5] We figured out that Vicky is the great-granddaughter of Jules's grandmother's brother, so her and Jules are second cousins once removed. [6] Looking at our chart, we could see that Vicky and Jules are in different generations, even though him and her are the same age. [7] All afternoon, curious relatives besieged Rochelle, Darla, and I with many questions. [8] We helped whomever asked us. [9] Grandmother said she was very proud of we girls. [10] Everyone learned something new about our family ties that day and gave the two other girls and I a big round of applause.

Determining Correct Pronoun Forms

Write the correct form of each incorrect pronoun in the following sentences. Write *C* if all of the pronouns in a sentence are in the correct case.

EXAMPLE   **1.** Nelson Mandela, whom shared the Nobel Peace Prize in 1993, was elected president of South Africa in 1994.

     1. who

1. Be careful who you tell.
2. May Marie and I cut a few pictures out of this old copy of *Ebony*?
3. My family goes to the dentist who Ms. Calhoun recommended.
4. Coretta said there would be other flag bearers in addition to Hugh and I.
5. At the head of the parade were us Girl Scouts.
6. The treaty gave them and the Ojibwa people the right to harvest wild rice there.
7. Nobody except Josh and him finished the marathon.
8. Joanne and us found a great beach.
9. Did your father and them reach an agreement about the boundary dispute?
10. We wish we had neighbors that were more like Sylvia and he.

Review H **Selecting Pronouns to Complete Sentences**

For each of the following sentences, choose the correct pronoun in parentheses. Be prepared to give a reason for your answer.

EXAMPLE   **1.** Jason and (I, me) attended the Golden Spurs horse show.

     1. I

1. Heather and (*he, him*) live on a blueberry farm.
2. Did the teacher give that assignment to (*whoever, whomever*) was absent yesterday?
3. We wondered (*who, whom*) started the rumor.
4. Do you intercept passes as well as Robin and (*she, her*) do?
5. The supporting players were Dina, Janelle, and (*she, her*).
6. I was standing in line behind Dave and (*he, him*).
7. You and (*I, me*) could write our biographical sketches on General Colin L. Powell, who was chairman of the Joint Chiefs of Staff under President George Bush.
8. The skit was written by Cy and (*he, him*).

┌─HELP─
In the example for Review H, the nominative-case pronoun *I* is correct because the pronoun is used as a subject.

USAGE

9. The electrician warned (*he, him*) and (*I, me*) about the frayed wires.

10. Amy Tan, (*who, whom*) the critics had praised, autographed a copy of her novel for me.

Reflexive and Intensive Pronouns

Reflexive and intensive pronouns (sometimes called *compound personal pronouns*) have the same forms.

Reflexive and Intensive Pronouns		
	Singular	**Plural**
First Person	myself	ourselves
Second Person	yourself	yourselves
Third Person	himself, herself, itself	themselves

A **reflexive pronoun** refers to the subject of a verb and may serve as a direct object, an indirect object, a predicate nominative, or an object of a preposition.

DIRECT OBJECT	Diners at this restaurant serve **themselves.**
INDIRECT OBJECT	I made **myself** a gyro sandwich.
PREDICATE NOMINATIVE	Dale is just not **himself** today.
OBJECT OF PREPOSITION	He suddenly remembered the promise he had made to **himself.**

An **intensive pronoun** has only one function: to emphasize its antecedent.

EXAMPLES Don't you think we can install the computer program **ourselves**?

Only you **yourself** can make that decision.

NOTE A pronoun ending in *–self* or *–selves* should not be used in place of a personal pronoun.

NONSTANDARD	Sonia and myself sang a duet in the talent show.
STANDARD	Sonia and **I** sang a duet in the talent show.
NONSTANDARD	Chad bought tickets for himself and myself.
STANDARD	Chad bought tickets for himself and **me.**

STYLE   TIP

The words *hisself, theirself,* and *theirselves* are non-standard English. Always use *himself* and *themselves* instead.

TIPS & TRICKS

To help you decide whether a pronoun ending in *–self* or *–selves* is reflexive or intensive, use this test: Omit the pronoun from the sentence. You can omit an intensive pronoun, but not a reflexive pronoun, from a sentence without significantly changing the meaning of the sentence.

INTENSIVE
Did you change the oil in the car **yourself**?
[*Yourself* can be omitted: *Did you change the oil in the car?*]

REFLEXIVE
Did you hurt **yourself**?
[*Yourself* is the direct object of *Did hurt* and cannot be omitted without changing the meaning of the sentence.]

USAGE

Exercise 10 Using Reflexive and Intensive Pronouns

For each blank in the following sentences, supply a pronoun ending in *–self* or *–selves* that correctly completes the sentence. Then, identify the pronoun as *reflexive* or *intensive*. If neither a reflexive nor an intensive pronoun would be correct, give a personal pronoun.

EXAMPLE   1. Did Jamal make this delicious stew _____ ?

1. *himself—intensive*

1. Working quickly and efficiently, we volunteers decorated the auditorium all by _____ .
2. Mona's cat cleans _____ right after it eats.
3. Did Julio and _____ have a good time at the concert?
4. Having gotten my braces off, I finally feel like _____ again.
5. The judges _____ could not reach a consensus.
6. How are Eric and _____ supposed to react in this scene?
7. Only time _____ will prove one of us right.
8. Give _____ a big pat on the back.
9. Where do you think they have hidden _____ ?
10. With her fever gone, Carla is _____ today.

┌HELP┐

Some sentences in Exercise 10 have more than one possible correct answer, but you need to give only one answer for each.

USAGE

Pronouns in Incomplete Constructions

17k. A pronoun following *than* or *as* in an incomplete construction should be in the same case as it would be if the construction were completed.

EXAMPLES   I know Mac better than **he** [knows Mac].
            I know Mac better than [I know] **him.**

            Do you visit Aunt Bessie as often as **we** [visit Aunt Bessie]?
            Do you visit Aunt Bessie as often as [you visit] **us**?

Exercise 11 Selecting Pronouns for Incomplete Constructions

For each of the sentences on the next page, choose the correct form of the pronoun in parentheses. Also, supply in parentheses the missing part of the incomplete construction. Then, give the use of the pronoun in its clause. If the construction may be completed in two different ways, provide both completions. Then, tell how the pronoun in each completion is used in the sentence.

1. I like Jay Leno better than (*she, her*).

   1. *she (likes Jay Leno)—subject; (I like) her—direct object*

 1. We played defense better than (*they, them*).
 2. When Andre Agassi won the men's singles title at the French Open, nobody was as pleased as (*I, me*).
 3. Nobody tried harder than (*she, her*).
 4. You are a month younger than (*he, him*).
 5. I know Millie better than (*she, her*).
 6. Did you walk as far in the walkathon as (*I, me*)?
 7. Richard bought more tickets than (*we, us*).
 8. Bianca lives farther away than (*we, us*).
 9. She visited Lisa more often than (*I, me*).
 10. Carlos plays classical guitar in the style of Andrés Segovia but, of course, not as well as (*he, him*).

┌HELP┐

Not all sentences in Exercise 11 can be completed in more than one way.

Reference Note

For information on **pronoun-antecedent agreement,** see page 532.

USAGE

Clear Pronoun Reference

Generally, a pronoun has no definite meaning by itself. Its meaning is clear only when the word or word group it stands for is known. This word or word group is called the ***antecedent*** of the pronoun.

17l. A pronoun should refer clearly to its antecedent.

(1) Avoid an ***ambiguous reference,*** which occurs when any one of two or more words can be a pronoun's antecedent.

AMBIGUOUS	Marissa called Yolanda while she was at the library last weekend. [Who was at the library, Marissa or Yolanda?]
CLEAR	While Marissa was at the library last weekend, **she** called Yolanda.

or

CLEAR	While Yolanda was at the library last weekend, Marissa called **her.**

AMBIGUOUS	After viewing Roy's paintings and Elton's sculpture, the judges awarded his work the blue ribbon. [Whose work was awarded the blue ribbon?]
CLEAR	The judges awarded Elton the blue ribbon after viewing **his** sculpture and Roy's paintings.

or

CLEAR	The judges awarded Roy the blue ribbon after viewing **his** paintings and Elton's sculpture.

(2) Avoid a *general reference,* which is the use of a pronoun that refers to a general idea rather than to a specific antecedent.

Most general reference errors are caused by the misuse of the pronouns *it, this, that, which,* and *such.*

GENERAL   Paul has a job interview after school today. That explains why he is wearing a suit. [*That* has no specific antecedent.]

CLEAR   Paul is wearing a suit because he has a job interview after school today.

or

CLEAR   The reason Paul is wearing a suit is that he has a job interview after school today.

GENERAL   My biology class is going to the coast this week, which should be fun. [*Which* has no specific antecedent.]

CLEAR   My biology class is going to the coast this week. The trip should be fun.

or

CLEAR   Going to the coast with my biology class this week should be fun.

(3) Avoid a *weak reference,* which occurs when a pronoun refers to an antecedent that has been suggested but not expressed.

WEAK   Ryan is multilingual. One of those that he speaks fluently is Mandarin. [The antecedent *languages* is suggested by the use of the pronoun *those* but is not expressed.]

CLEAR   Ryan speaks several languages. One of those that he speaks fluently is Mandarin.

or

CLEAR   Ryan is multilingual. One of the languages that he speaks fluently is Mandarin.

WEAK   Royale writes stories, and she hopes to make it her career. [The antecedent *writing* is suggested by the use of the pronoun *it* but is not expressed.]

CLEAR   Royale writes stories, and she hopes to make writing her career.

(4) Avoid an *indefinite reference,* which is the use of a pronoun that refers to no specific antecedent and that is unnecessary to the meaning of the sentence.

Most indefinite reference errors are caused by the misuse of the pronouns *it, they,* and *you.*

BLONDIE reprinted with special permission of King Features Syndicate, Inc.

Familiar expressions such as *it is raining, it's early,* and *it seems* are standard and acceptable, although they do not refer to definite antecedents.

INDEFINITE	In the newspaper, it reported that the robbers had been caught. [The pronoun *it* is not necessary to the meaning of the sentence.]
CLEAR	The newspaper reported that the robbers had been caught.
INDEFINITE	During the Middle Ages in Europe, you very likely would not live past the age of thirty. [The pronoun *you* does not truly refer to the reader and does not have any specific antecedent.]
CLEAR	During the Middle Ages in Europe, a person very likely would not live past the age of thirty.

Exercise 12 Revising Unclear Pronoun References

Most of the following sentences contain unclear pronoun references. Revise each faulty sentence.

EXAMPLE
1. In a brochure recently published by the Environmental Protection Agency (EPA), it promotes precycling to reduce waste.

1. *A brochure recently published by the Environmental Protection Agency (EPA) promotes precycling to reduce waste.*

If you use a computer, you can use the search feature to locate all occurrences of the pronoun *it* in a piece of your writing. Every time the pronoun appears, check its reference carefully. Is the reference clear?

If necessary, use the replace function to substitute a better word for the pronoun, or rewrite the sentence so that the pronoun clearly refers to a specific antecedent. Use the same procedure to check your uses of the pronouns *you, they, this, that, which,* and *such.*

1. The newest twist in recycling is *precycling*—cutting it off at its source.
2. Last month, after reading the EPA's brochure, my family decided to put its ideas into practice.
3. We now choose products that have less packaging; we carry groceries home in reusable cloth bags instead of paper or plastic ones; and we buy containers that can be refilled, which is easy.
4. Sara asked Mom if she could write to the Mail Preference Service, Direct Marketing Association and ask that our names not be sold to mailing-list companies.
5. That greatly reduced the amount of junk mail we get.
6. When we do have waste products, inventing new ways to use them becomes a challenge in creative thinking; one of them was mine.
7. Now we pack fragile objects in bits of plastic foam and other nonrecyclable materials so that they don't get broken in shipping.
8. We use plastic produce bags as sandwich wrappers or as liners for small trash cans, and it works just fine.
9. We also convert cottage cheese cartons and margarine tubs into food-storage containers, and we plan to make a habit of it.
10. In just a few short weeks, we've learned that by remembering the three *r*'s—*r*educe, *r*euse, and *r*ecycle—you can help to protect our precious environment.

Chapter Review

A. Using Pronouns Correctly in Sentences

For each sentence, choose the correct word in parentheses.

1. Francis said that in a few years he would give his stamp collection to his brother and (*I, me*).

2. Everyone was waiting impatiently to find out (*who, whom*) the new cheerleader would be.

3. My little sister is a much better basketball player than (*I, me*).

4. After the accident, the police questioned (*he, him*).

5. We found that (*she, her*) was the one who called twice last night.

6. At the self-service gas station, drivers must pump gasoline (*theirselves, themselves*).

7. Speaking of Ken Griffey, Jr., (*he, him*) and his dad are the first father and son ever to play professional baseball together on the same team.

8. Seeing a car with an out-of-state license plate in my driveway, I ran inside to see (*who, whom*) was there.

9. That trailer with the silver stripe is (*our, ours*).

10. Do you mind (*me, my*) eating while we walk?

B. Selecting Pronouns to Complete Sentences Correctly

Choose the correct pronoun form in parentheses. Then, tell whether the pronoun is used as a *subject*, a *predicate nominative*, a *direct object*, an *indirect object*, an *object of a preposition*, or an *appositive*.

11. The two Italian drivers, Dario and (*he, him*), came in first and second.

12. The entire cast in the first scene of the second act consisted of Beth and (*I, me*).

13. They met Stuart and (*he, him*) at the railroad station.

14. I thought the best soloists in the band were (*they, them*).

15. Teddy and (*she, her*) arrived with minutes to spare.

16. (*Whoever, Whomever*) wants to learn about good manners should listen to my Aunt Rita.

USAGE

17. The stars of that movie were Robert Duvall and *(he, him)*.

18. Edmond Dantès was the wronged prisoner about *(who, whom)* Alexandre Dumas wrote in *The Count of Monte Cristo*.

19. Will Colin and *(he, him)* help us with the painting?

20. Ms. Oliveira asked you and *(I, me)* about staying and helping with the decorations.

21. I asked my mother *(who, whom)* called last night.

22. The pair of ballad singers, Tommy and *(she, her)*, left the stage to great applause.

23. The person *(who, whom)* you spoke about will be the next leader of the expedition.

24. We gave Louis and *(he, him)* a ride to school.

25. She is a better swimmer than *(I, me)*, but the coach said he needed both of us on the team.

26. I will support *(whoever, whomever)* is selected for president.

27. It is not fair to give *(they, them)* extra responsibilities just because they are more responsible.

28. *(Who, Whom)* is supervising the drama festival this year?

29. To go on the field trip, you need written permission from your parents and *(I, me)*.

30. Everyone else finished the test earlier than *(they, them)*.

C. Proofreading Sentences for Correct Pronoun Usage

Most of the following sentences contain errors in pronoun usage. Write the correct pronoun form for each error. If a sentence is already correct, write *C*.

31. Us athletes have little time to spend watching television.

32. The one who organized the new filing system was she.

33. Ask Lorna and he about the outcome of the race.

34. Ramona had not decided who she would vote for in the election.

35. Between you and I, that painting is worth much more.

36. We are willing to help whoever is in need.

37. Edna said that you speak Spanish better than her.

38. We can only guess whom it was.

39. The package was sent to Rob and I.

40. The drama coaches are Mr. Rolando and she.

Writing Application
Using Pronouns Correctly in a Letter

Reference Note

For information on **writing letters,** see "Writing" in the Quick Reference Handbook.

Clear Pronoun Reference   Your favorite musical group isn't happy with the director of their latest video. As a result, they are sponsoring a "Be a Music Video Director" contest. To enter, you have to write a letter explaining your idea for a different video of the same song. Tell which singers, dancers, and musicians you would cast in your video. Include at least ten pronouns in your sentences. Be sure that no pronoun has an unclear antecedent.

Prewriting   Start by choosing the song for which you want to make a video. Then, list some ideas for three or four scenes in your video. Next to each scene idea, list the performers you would use in that scene and describe the action. In addition to actual people, you may want to have cartoon characters or other animated figures in your video.

Writing   As you write sentences about your music video, make the sequence of events clear. Make the spatial relationships clear, too, telling where the cast members are in relation to each other.

Revising   Check the rough draft of your letter to be sure that your explanation is clear. If you have included too many performers or too many details, eliminate the least interesting ones now.

Publishing   Read your letter, looking for inexact uses of the pronouns *it, this, that,* and *which.* If your sentences contain inexact pronoun references, revise those sentences. Proofread your letter to correct errors in grammar, punctuation, and spelling. Your class may wish to vote on the best music video idea in each of several categories, such as rock, country, and rap.

USAGE

CHAPTER

Using Verbs Correctly
Principal Parts, Tense, Voice, Mood

Diagnostic Preview

A. Writing the Past and Past Participle Forms of Irregular Verbs

For each of the following sentences, write the correct form (past or past participle) of the italicized verb.

EXAMPLES **1.** *know*   I have _____ Zoe since we were in kindergarten together.

      1. *known*

      2. *swim*   Has Samuel ever _____ out to the rocky island in the middle of the lake?

      2. *swum*

1. *ride*   Jeffrey and Lee have _____ their bikes fifty miles today.
2. *write*   I read the letters Grandpa _____ to Grandma in 1960.
3. *take*   Dad, I know that you've _____ us to two concerts this year, but please take us to just one more.
4. *fall*   All that winter day the snow _____, blanketing everything.
5. *see*   Rebecca soon _____ why the old house had sold so cheaply.
6. *drink*   The gerbil has _____ most of its water.
7. *begin*   As darkness fell and the children still had not returned, I _____ to worry.
8. *bring*   Margot has _____ popcorn and apples for the party.

9. *speak*   At the assembly yesterday, Sergeant Lewis _____ about
responsible driving.

10. *give*   The Nez Perce had _____ the starving fur traders food
and helped them repair their canoes.

B. Revising Sentences to Correct Problems in Verb Tense and Voice

Rewrite the following sentences, replacing verbs that are in the wrong tense or that are in an awkward voice. If a sentence is already correct, write *C*.

EXAMPLES   **[1]** Genna gave her report on Captain James Cook and shows us some maps and pictures of the areas he had explored.

1. *Genna gave her report on Captain James Cook and showed us some maps and pictures of the areas he had explored.*

[2] We were surprised to learn how many places were explored by him.

2. *We were surprised to learn how many places he had explored.*

[11] Captain Cook, one of the greatest explorers of all time, sailed large areas of the Pacific Ocean and makes accurate maps of the region. **[12]** Cook joins the navy as a seaman in 1755, and many promotions were received by him before he became the master of a ship in 1757. **[13]** Because of his knowledge of geography, astronomy, and mathematics, he is selected to lead a scientific expedition to the Pacific. **[14]** The purpose of Cook's expedition is to observe the passage of Venus between Earth and the sun, a very rare occurrence. **[15]** On the voyage, Cook wins a battle against scurvy, a serious disease caused by lack of vitamin C. **[16]** Raw cabbage, which contained vitamin C, was eaten by the sailors to prevent the disease. **[17]** By the time the voyage is over, the ship traveled around Cape Horn to Tahiti in the Pacific Ocean. **[18]** After he observes the passage of Venus, Cook sails off to explore the east coast of New Zealand, which was claimed by him for England. **[19]** The Hawaiian Islands were later explored by Cook on his final voyage to the Pacific and were named the Sandwich Islands by him. **[20]** In a dispute over a canoe, Cook was killed by island inhabitants, and in accordance with naval tradition, he was buried at sea in 1779.

USAGE

C. Determining Correct Uses of *Lie* and *Lay*, *Sit* and *Set*, and *Rise* and *Raise*

If a verb form in one of the following sentences is incorrect, write the correct form. If a sentence is already correct, write *C*.

EXAMPLE   1. Has Maurizio already risen the flag?

1. *raised*

21. You can sit the wastebasket in the corner.
22. Everyone rose when the judge entered the courtroom, and then everyone sat when she sat.
23. The mysterious shape suddenly raised from the shadows.
24. I like to lay out under the stars and just think.
25. The servant had lain out the emperor's robes of yellow, the color that only members of Chinese royalty were permitted to wear.

The Principal Parts of Verbs

Verbs have four basic forms called *principal parts.* All of a verb's other forms come from its principal parts.

18a. The four principal parts of a verb are the *base form,* the *present participle,* the *past,* and the *past participle.*

NOTE   Some authorities refer to the base form as the *infinitive.* Follow your teacher's instructions when labeling this verb form.

┌HELP┐

The words *is* and *have* are included in the chart to the right because helping verbs are used with the present participle and past participle to form some tenses.

Reference Note

For more about using **helping verbs with present participles and past participles,** see page 417.

Base Form	Present Participle	Past	Past Participle
believe	[is] believing	believed	[have] believed
walk	[is] walking	walked	[have] walked
teach	[is] teaching	taught	[have] taught
run	[is] running	ran	[have] run
do	[is] doing	did	[have] done
be	[is] being	was, were	[have] been
cost	[is] costing	cost	[have] cost

NOTE Sometimes a past participle is used with a form of *be*, as in *was chosen, are known, is being seen.* This use of the verb is called the **passive voice.**

EXAMPLES   A complete list of rules **is given** to all the contestants two weeks before the competition.

If a book is due on a Sunday, no fines **are charged** if the book **is returned** by the following Monday.

Reference Note

For more about **passive-voice verbs,** see page 601.

Regular Verbs

18b. A *regular verb* generally forms its past and past participle by adding *–d* or *–ed* to the base form.

Base Form	Present Participle	Past	Past Participle
receive	[is] receiving	received	[have] received
blame	[is] blaming	blamed	[have] blamed
work	[is] working	worked	[have] worked

One common error in the use of the past and the past participle forms of a regular verb is leaving off the *–d* or *–ed* ending.

NONSTANDARD   They use to live in Waco, Texas.
STANDARD   They **used** to live in Waco, Texas.

NONSTANDARD   Are you suppose to meet with them tomorrow?
STANDARD   Are you **supposed** to meet with them tomorrow?

NONSTANDARD   She ask me to go to the dance.
STANDARD   She **asked** me to go to the dance.

Reference Note

For a discussion of **standard** and **nonstandard usage,** see page 638.

NOTE Most regular verbs that end in *e* drop the *e* before adding *–ing.* Some regular verbs double the final consonant before adding *–ing* or *–ed.*

EXAMPLES   snore   snoring   snored

nap   napping   napped

Reference Note

For guidelines on spelling verbs when **adding *–d*, *–ed*, or *–ing*,** see page 784.

USAGE

A few regular verbs have alternative past and past participle forms ending in *t*.

Base Form	Present Participle	Past	Past Participle
burn	[is] burning	burned *or* burnt	[have] burned *or* burnt
leap	[is] leaping	leaped *or* leapt	[have] leaped *or* leapt
dream	[is] dreaming	dreamed *or* dreamt	[have] dreamed *or* dreamt

┌HELP─
The regular verbs *deal* and *mean* always form the past and the past participle by adding *t*: *dealt, (have) dealt; meant, (have) meant.*

> ### Exercise 1   Using the Past Form of Regular Verbs

Give the correct past form of each verb in parentheses.

EXAMPLE   1. With a mighty heave, the elephant (*push*) the log out of the river.

    1. *pushed*

1. Charlene (*answer*) all the questions correctly.
2. When Greg was in Ireland, he (*kiss*) the Blarney stone.
3. As I walked by, they (*smile*).
4. Melissa (*pull*) the wagon, which was full of rag dolls.
5. Denise (*watch*) the wildlife through her binoculars.
6. Spence and James (*play*) the trombone and the clarinet at the concert last night.
7. Mother Teresa (*help*) many people.
8. After receiving the postcard, Eduardo (*laugh*).
9. Last Saturday, my friends (*dance*) the polka at our school's international festival.
10. Tracy (*paint*) a powerful self-portrait that will appear in next month's exhibit.

Irregular Verbs

18c. An *irregular verb* forms its past and past participle in some way other than by adding *–d* or *–ed* to the base form.

An irregular verb forms its past and past participle in one of the following ways: (1) changing consonants, (2) changing vowels, (3) changing vowels *and* consonants, or (4) making no change.

	Base Form	Past	Past Participle
Consonant Change	bend	bent	[have] bent
	send	sent	[have] sent
Vowel Change	sing	sang	[have] sung
Vowel and Consonant Change	catch	caught	[have] caught
	go	went	[have] gone
	fly	flew	[have] flown
No Change	set	set	[have] set

Principal Parts of Common Irregular Verbs

Base Form	Present Participle	Past	Past Participle
become	[is] becoming	became	[have] become
begin	[is] beginning	began	[have] begun
blow	[is] blowing	blew	[have] blown
break	[is] breaking	broke	[have] broken
bring	[is] bringing	brought	[have] brought
build	[is] building	built	[have] built
burn	[is] burning	burned or burnt	[have] burned or burnt
burst	[is] bursting	burst	[have] burst
buy	[is] buying	bought	[have] bought
catch	[is] catching	caught	[have] caught
choose	[is] choosing	chose	[have] chosen
come	[is] coming	came	[have] come
cost	[is] costing	cost	[have] cost
cut	[is] cutting	cut	[have] cut
dive	[is] diving	dove or dived	[have] dived
do	[is] doing	did	[have] done
draw	[is] drawing	drew	[have] drawn
drink	[is] drinking	drank	[have] drunk
drive	[is] driving	drove	[have] driven

(continued)

USAGE

┌HELP─
Since most
English verbs are regular,
people sometimes try to
make irregular verbs fol-
low the regular pattern.
However, such verb forms
as *throwed, knowed,
shrinked,* and *choosed* are
considered nonstandard.

If you are not sure
whether a verb is regular
or irregular, look it up in a
dictionary. Entries for
irregular verbs list the principal parts. If an entry for a
verb does not list the principal parts, the verb is a
regular verb.

(continued)

\	\	\	\
Principal Parts of Common Irregular Verbs			
Base Form	Present Participle	Past	Past Participle
eat	[is] eating	ate	[have] eaten
fall	[is] falling	fell	[have] fallen
feel	[is] feeling	felt	[have] felt
fight	[is] fighting	fought	[have] fought
find	[is] finding	found	[have] found
fly	[is] flying	flew	[have] flown
forgive	[is] forgiving	forgave	[have] forgiven
freeze	[is] freezing	froze	[have] frozen
get	[is] getting	got	[have] got *or* gotten
give	[is] giving	gave	[have] given
go	[is] going	went	[have] gone
grow	[is] growing	grew	[have] grown
have	[is] having	had	[have] had
hear	[is] hearing	heard	[have] heard
hide	[is] hiding	hid	[have] hidden *or* hid
hit	[is] hitting	hit	[have] hit
know	[is] knowing	knew	[have] known
lead	[is] leading	led	[have] led
leave	[is] leaving	left	[have] left
let	[is] letting	let	[have] let
light	[is] lighting	lighted *or* lit	[have] lighted *or* lit
lose	[is] losing	lost	[have] lost
make	[is] making	made	[have] made
pay	[is] paying	paid	[have] paid
put	[is] putting	put	[have] put
read	[is] reading	read	[have] read
ride	[is] riding	rode	[have] ridden
ring	[is] ringing	rang	[have] rung
run	[is] running	ran	[have] run
say	[is] saying	said	[have] said

USAGE

┌─HELP───

Some verbs have two correct past or past participle forms. However, these forms are not always interchangeable.

EXAMPLES
He **shone** the candle into the cellar. [*Shined* would also be correct.]

I **shined** my shoes. [*Shone* would be incorrect in this usage.]

If you are unsure about which past participle to use, check an up-to-date dictionary.

Principal Parts of Common Irregular Verbs

Base Form	Present Participle	Past	Past Participle
see	[is] seeing	saw	[have] seen
seek	[is] seeking	sought	[have] sought
sell	[is] selling	sold	[have] sold
send	[is] sending	sent	[have] sent
sing	[is] singing	sang	[have] sung
sink	[is] sinking	sank or sunk	[have] sunk
sleep	[is] sleeping	slept	[have] slept
speak	[is] speaking	spoke	[have] spoken
spend	[is] spending	spent	[have] spent
stand	[is] standing	stood	[have] stood
steal	[is] stealing	stole	[have] stolen
swim	[is] swimming	swam	[have] swum
take	[is] taking	took	[have] taken
teach	[is] teaching	taught	[have] taught
tear	[is] tearing	tore	[have] torn
tell	[is] telling	told	[have] told
think	[is] thinking	thought	[have] thought
throw	[is] throwing	threw	[have] thrown
wear	[is] wearing	wore	[have] worn
win	[is] winning	won	[have] won
write	[is] writing	wrote	[have] written

Oral Practice 1 **Using Regular and Irregular Verbs**

Read each sentence aloud, stressing each italicized verb.

1. Keisha *is braiding* Tiffany's hair in cornrows.
2. Bob *read* the want ads today, just as he *has read* them all week.
3. Mom, I *am bringing* you breakfast, but I *have eaten* your toast!
4. Warren *drew* the designs for the posters.
5. Paloma Picasso, the jewelry designer, *has chosen* an artistic career different from her famous father's.
6. Carrie *went* to Penn State; Hector *is going* to Boston College.
7. Someone *ate* the spaghetti, but nobody *has touched* the baked beans.
8. If you *have* never *seen* a meteor shower, *run* outside right now!

Exercise 2 **Using the Past and Past Participle Forms of Irregular Verbs**

Give the correct form (past or past participle) of the verb given before each of the following sentences.

EXAMPLE   **1.** *write*   Diego has _____ a report on Pueblo culture.

1. *written*

1. *sing*   The rain fell after we had _____ the national anthem.
2. *begin*   I had already _____ my homework.
3. *freeze*   The subzero winds nearly _____ the Pawnee hunters as they tracked the herd of bison.
4. *fly*   Last summer we _____ in a lighter-than-air balloon.
5. *see*   During our visit to Hawaii, we _____ a group of performers do a traditional hula dance.
6. *take*   My sister has _____ that course.
7. *fall*   By the time Rolando finished carving the little figure, hundreds of tiny wood shavings had _____ to the floor.
8. *throw*   The horse had _____ its shoe.
9. *break*   We hoped we hadn't _____ the machine.
10. *speak*   Harley's grandmother _____ to our class about her parents' lives as sharecroppers in the early 1900s.

Exercise 3 **Using the Past and Past Participle Forms of Irregular Verbs**

Give the correct form (past or past participle) of each italicized verb in the following paragraph.

EXAMPLE   Have you **[1]** (*see*) any of the artwork by Henry Ossawa Tanner?

1. *seen*

We recently **[1]** (*see*) paintings by the African American artist Henry Ossawa Tanner. Tanner had **[2]** (*choose*) his lifelong career in art by the time he was thirteen years old. While walking in a park one day, he and his father had **[3]** (*come*) upon a landscape artist at work. Years later, Tanner **[4]** (*write*), "It was this simple event that . . . set me on fire." Young Henry **[5]** (*bring*) such eagerness to his work that, before long, he **[6]** (*teach*) himself to draw well enough to be admitted to one of the finest art schools in the country. His paintings were beautiful but did not sell well, so Tanner **[7]** (*go*) abroad. He **[8]** (*fall*) in love with the city of Paris and lived and worked there for the rest of his life, winning many important painting awards. Shown here is his best-known work, *The Banjo Lesson,* which he painted in Paris from sketches he had [**9**] (*draw*) years earlier in North Carolina. In 1969, long after Tanner's death, a touring exhibit finally [**10**] (*give*) Americans a look at the work of this gifted artist.

Henry Ossawa Tanner, *The Banjo Lesson* (1893). Hampton University Museum, Hampton, VA.

Exercise 4 **Choosing the Past and Past Participle Forms of Irregular Verbs**

Choose the correct verb form in parentheses in each of the following sentences.

EXAMPLE
    1. Frieda has (*gave, given*) much thought to pursuing a career in engineering.
    1. given

1. We (*did, done*) everything we could to help him.
2. Who has (*drank, drunk*) all the orange juice?
3. Someone has already (*tore, torn*) out the coupon.
4. I wish you had (*spoke, spoken*) to me about it sooner.
5. I dived off the board and (*swam, swum*) the length of the pool.
6. You must have (*rung, rang*) the doorbell while I was outside.
7. Nancy had never (*ate, eaten*) a tamale before.
8. Lois (*blowed, blew*) up the balloon.
9. Suddenly the balloon (*burst, bursted*).
10. We (*drove, driven*) to the train station in a hurry.

Six Troublesome Verbs

Lie and *Lay*

The verb *lie* means "to rest," "to recline," or "to be in a place." *Lie* does not take a direct object. The verb *lay* means "to put (something) in place." *Lay* generally takes a direct object.

Principal Parts of *Lie* and *Lay*			
Base Form	Present Participle	Past	Past Participle
lie	[is] lying	lay	[have] lain
lay	[is] laying	laid	[have] laid

EXAMPLES   Please **lie** down. [no direct object]

The packages **are lying** here. [no direct object]

The key **lay** on the shelf. [no direct object]

The old papers **had lain** on the desk for months. [no direct object]

Please **lay** the tools down. [*Tools* is the direct object.]

I **am laying** your packages here. [*Packages* is the direct object.]

The boy **laid** the key on the shelf. [*Key* is the direct object.]

He **had laid** the old papers on the desk. [*Papers* is the direct object.]

Oral Practice 2) **Using the Forms of *Lie* and *Lay* in Sentences**

Read each of the following sentences aloud, stressing the italicized verb.

1. The mason *is laying* the tiles on the patio.
2. A light haze *lay* over the hills.
3. The cat *laid* its toy on the doorsill.
4. Someone's books *are lying* in the hall.
5. She *had lain* down for a nap.
6. Where *could* I *have laid* the recipe?
7. *Lay* the material on the counter.
8. You *could lie* down and relax.

Exercise 5 Choosing the Forms of *Lie* and *Lay*

Choose the correct verb form in parentheses in each of the following sentences.

EXAMPLE   1. The sheet music is (*lying, laying*) on the piano.

            1. *lying*

1. Do not (*lay, lie*) the socks there.
2. Eduardo (*lay, laid*) in the sleeping bag and waited for sleep.
3. The pasture (*lies, lays*) in the valley.
4. A sheet (*lay, laid*) over the rug to catch paint spatters.
5. The clothing had (*lain, laid*) on the floor all week.
6. Kitty had (*lay, laid*) the book down.
7. Mrs. Nakamoto was (*lying, laying*) out everything necessary for the tea ceremony.
8. The theories developed by Albert Einstein have (*lay, laid*) the groundwork for many other scientific discoveries.
9. The cat has been (*lying, laying*) on my coat.
10. (*Lying, Laying*) the tip by my plate, I rose to leave the restaurant.

Exercise 6 Using the Forms of *Lie* and *Lay*

If a verb in the following sentences is incorrect, write the correct form. If the verb is already correct, write *C*.

EXAMPLES   1. On the bed laid the child's favorite kachina doll.

            1. *lay*

            2. Julia had lain rose petals along the stage.

            2. *laid*

1. The towels laying in the corner all need to be washed.
2. Yesterday, all we did was lie around and play CDs.
3. The runner crossed the finish line and laid down in the grass.
4. The fox had laid in the thicket until the hunters had passed.
5. After I had tripped, I sat there feeling embarrassed, my groceries laying all around me.
6. He was lying under the car, tinkering with the muffler.
7. The workers had lain down their tools and gone to lunch.
8. My gym bag was laying right where I had left it.
9. In his speech, Cesar Chavez lay the responsibility for social change on the shoulders of all citizens.
10. She sighed and lay down the phone receiver.

TIPS & TRICKS

To decide whether to use *lie* or *lay,* ask yourself the following questions:

QUESTION 1
What do I mean? (Is the meaning "to be in a place," or is it "to put in a place"?)

QUESTION 2
What time does the verb express?

QUESTION 3
Which principal part shows this time?

EXAMPLE
Feeling very drowsy, I (*lay, laid*) on the couch.

QUESTION 1
Here the meaning is "to be in place." Therefore, the verb should be a form of *lie*.

QUESTION 2
The time is past.

QUESTION 3
The past form of *lie* is *lay*.

ANSWER
Feeling very drowsy, I **lay** on the couch.

USAGE

In each of the following sentences, a form of *lie* or *lay* is used. If the wrong form is used, write the correct form. If a sentence is already correct, write *C*.

EXAMPLES

1. Oscar rarely spends the weekends laying on the couch.
1. *lying*

2. He had planned to spend his Saturday lying new tile in the kitchen.
2. *laying*

1. Several boxes of fired-clay tiles laid on the floor of the garage.
2. Before he started, he lay out all his materials and carefully read the directions on the container of adhesive.
3. At first, he made good progress and had lain sixteen rows of tile by lunch time.
4. Then he ate a sandwich and laid down on the sofa for a few minutes.
5. When he returned to the kitchen, Oscar found that his dog, Stanley, was laying where the next row of tiles was supposed to go.
6. Oscar had forgotten that Stanley liked to lay in that particular place on the kitchen floor.
7. In fact, Stanley had lain there for his morning nap ever since he was a puppy.
8. Oscar got a juicy meat scrap out of the refrigerator and laid it on the floor just beyond Stanley's snoring nose.
9. The wily Stanley had been laying in wait and, in a flash, grabbed the meat.
10. To Oscar's dismay, Stanley resumed his nap with a satisfied sigh, and Oscar learned that the worker isn't the only one who can lay down on the job!

Sit and *Set*

The verb *sit* means "to rest in a seated, upright position" or "to be in a place." *Sit* seldom takes a direct object. The verb *set* means "to put (something) in a place." *Set* generally takes a direct object. Notice that the past and the past participle of *set* are the same as the base form.

Principal Parts of *Sit* and *Set*			
Base Form	Present Participle	Past	Past Participle
sit	[is] sitting	sat	[have] sat
set	[is] setting	set	[have] set

EXAMPLES   You **may sit** here. [no direct object]

Where **are** Diana and Vince **sitting**? [no direct object]

The guest speaker **sat** between Eduardo and me. [no direct object]

His bicycle **has sat** in our driveway for a week. [no direct object]

You **may set** your books here. [*Books* is the direct object.]

Where **are** Diana and Vince **setting** the computer desk? [*Desk* is the direct object.]

The guest speaker **set** his briefcase between Eduardo and me. [*Briefcase* is the direct object.]

He **had set** his bicycle in our driveway last week. [*Bicycle* is the direct object.]

Oral Practice 3 **Using the Correct Forms of *Sit* and *Set* in Sentences**

Read each of the following sentences aloud, stressing the italicized verb.

1. *Set* the groceries on the counter.
2. The travelers *set* out early to avoid the midday heat.
3. Would you please *set* the chairs under the tree in the front yard?
4. The bird *sat* on the wire.
5. During Hanukkah, we always *set* the menorah in a place of honor.
6. We *had sat* in the lobby for an hour.
7. They *have been sitting* on the porch.
8. Rosa Parks made history when she chose to *sit* rather than to give up her seat to a white passenger.

STYLE **TIP**

You may know that the word *set* has more meanings than the one given here. Check in a dictionary to see if the meaning you intend requires an object.

EXAMPLE
The sun **sets** in the West.
[Here, *sets* does not take an object.]

USAGE

USAGE

Exercise 8 Selecting the Correct Forms of *Sit* and *Set*

Choose the correct verb form in parentheses in each of the following sentences.

EXAMPLE   1. He (*sat, set*) on the park bench and read the newspaper.

    1. *sat*

  1. A few of us were (*sitting, setting*) at our desks.
  2. He had (*sat, set*) in the rocker since dusk.
  3. He (*sat, set*) the package on the doorstep.
  4. Ida was (*sitting, setting*) out the chips and dip for the guests.
  5. We had been (*sitting, setting*) on a freshly painted bench.
  6. They (*sat, set*) the seedlings in the window boxes.
  7. He had (*sit, set*) his retainer on his lunch tray.
  8. (*Sit, Set*) this Pueblo pottery in the display case.
  9. I could (*sit, set*) and watch the birds all day.
  10. We patiently (*sat, set*) and waited for the travelers to arrive.

Exercise 9 Writing the Forms of *Sit* and *Set*

For each numbered blank in the following paragraph, write the correct form of *sit* or *set*.

EXAMPLE   Before **[1]** _____ down to rest, Meriwether Lewis and William Clark decided that the group should climb to the top of the bluff.

    1. *sitting*

   To gain a view of the surrounding land, Lewis and Clark's group climbed to an outcropping of gray rocks that **[1]** _____ atop the bluff. It was late afternoon, and the Shoshone guide Sacagawea **[2]** _____ her pack down beside the rocks and **[3]** _____ down in their shade to rest. Lewis saw her from where he was **[4]** _____ nearby and approached with a friendly "May I **[5]** _____ here with you?" Several other members of the expedition saw them **[6]** _____ together and wondered what they were discussing. In fact, Lewis was asking her in what direction she thought the party should **[7]** _____ out in the morning. Gazing westward from the bluff, Sacagawea saw that she was in familiar territory and soon **[8]** _____ her mind on heading down the mountainside toward the northwest. By the time the sun had **[9]** _____, Lewis agreed that the route she had chosen would be the easiest to follow. A wise leader, he realized that he had never **[10]** _____ foot in these lands, while she had passed this way before.

The Granger Collection, New York.

Review A **Choosing the Correct Forms of *Lie* and *Lay* and *Sit* and *Set***

Choose the correct verb form in parentheses in each of the following sentences.

EXAMPLE **1.** She (*set, sat*) at the computer, reading her e-mail.

1. *sat*

1. (*Setting, Sitting*) on the table was a pair of scissors.
2. Please (*sit, set*) the carton down carefully.
3. Sakura folded her kimono and (*lay, laid*) down to sleep.
4. (*Sit, Set*) all the way back in your seat.
5. The dirty dishes had (*laid, lain*) in the sink for hours.
6. Yesterday, Tom (*lay, laid*) the blame for his lateness on his clock.
7. The cat always (*sits, sets*) on the couch.
8. If only we could have (*laid, lain*) our hands on the treasure!
9. The tickets to the Wynton Marsalis concert were (*lying, laying*) right where I had left them.
10. King Tut's tomb (*lay, laid*) undisturbed for centuries.
11. Have you ever (*sat, set*) around with nothing to do?
12. She (*sat, set*) down at her desk with her checkbook and calculator in front of her.
13. Santa Anna, (*setting, sitting*) on his horse, ordered his troops to attack the Alamo.
14. The beached rowboat (*lay, laid*) on its side.

15. She (*sat, set*) looking toward the horizon.

16. Laura had just (*sat, set*) down when the phone rang.

17. Julie (*lay, laid*) her handbag on the counter.

18. Pieces of the jigsaw puzzle were (*lying, laying*) on the floor.

19. Jack was (*setting, sitting*) outside on the top step.

20. Were you (*lying, laying*) down for a while before dinner?

Rise and *Raise*

The verb *rise* means "to go up" or "to get up." *Rise* does not take a direct object. The verb *raise* means "to lift" or "to cause (something) to rise." *Raise* generally takes a direct object.

Principal Parts of *Rise* and *Raise*			
Base Form	Present Participle	Past	Past Participle
rise	[is] rising	rose	[have] risen
raise	[is] raising	raised	[have] raised

EXAMPLES

I usually **rise** at 6:00 A.M. [no direct object]

She **is rising** uncertainly. [no direct object]

The banner **rose** in the gust of wind. [no direct object]

Has the price of gasoline **risen**? [no direct object]

I usually **raise** the blinds at 6:00 A.M. [*Blinds* is the direct object.]

She **is raising** her hand uncertainly. [*Hand* is the direct object.]

The gust of wind **raised** the banner. [*Banner* is the direct object.]

The gas station **has raised** the price of gasoline. [*Price* is the direct object.]

Oral Practice 4   Using the Forms of *Rise* and *Raise*

Read each of the following sentences aloud, stressing the italicized verb.

1. *Has* the moon *risen* yet?

2. The builders *raised* the roof of the new house at noon.

3. The temperature *rose* as the sun climbed higher.

USAGE

4. Listening to "I Have a Dream," a speech by Dr. Martin Luther King, Jr., always *raises* my spirits.

5. Trails of mist *were rising* from the lake.

6. How much *did* the river *rise* during the flood?

7. The butterfly *rose* from the leaf and flitted away.

8. My baby sister *was raising* her head to look around.

Exercise 10 **Using the Correct Forms of *Rise* and *Raise***

For the blank in each of the following sentences, write the correct form of *rise* or *raise.*

EXAMPLE   **1.** Does the orderly _____ the flag every morning?

   1. raise

1. _____ the cards higher, please.

2. The gigantic Kodiak bear is _____ on its hind legs to look around.

3. The tide _____ and falls because of the moon.

4. Carlos and Pilar _____ the piñata above the heads of the children.

5. Up toward the clouds _____ the jet.

6. Many American Indian peoples have traditionally _____ corn as a staple food crop.

7. Prices have _____ in the last few years.

8. The traffic officer had _____ his hand to signal us.

9. My sister and I had _____ before the sun came up this morning.

10. Robert Kennedy _____ to fame in the 1960s.

Review B **Using the Correct Forms of *Lie* and *Lay,* *Sit* and *Set,* and *Rise* and *Raise***

If a verb in one of the following sentences is incorrect, write the correct form. If a sentence is already correct, write *C.*

EXAMPLE   **1.** The baby starlings were setting in the nest.

   1. sitting

1. Set the eggs down carefully.

2. The frog was setting on the lily pad and croaking loudly.

3. The judge studied the papers and then lay them beside her gavel.

4. The cattle were lying in the shade by the stream.

5. Do you think the temperature will raise much higher?

6. Wanda sat out the equipment for the experiment.

7. Why don't you lie those things down?

8. Instead of laying down, you should be getting some type of strenuous exercise.

9. The raccoon raised up on its hind legs.

10. Set down for a while and relax.

Tense

18d. The *tense* of a verb indicates the time of the action or the state of being expressed by the verb.

Verbs in English have six tenses: *present, past, future, present perfect, past perfect,* and *future perfect.* These tenses are formed from the four principal parts of verbs. The following time line shows how the six tenses are related to one another.

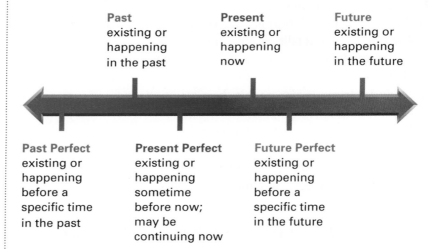

Past
existing or happening in the past

Present
existing or happening now

Future
existing or happening in the future

Past Perfect
existing or happening before a specific time in the past

Present Perfect
existing or happening sometime before now; may be continuing now

Future Perfect
existing or happening before a specific time in the future

Verb Conjugation

Listing all of the forms of a verb according to tense is called *conjugating* a verb. The following charts show all six tenses of a regular verb (*talk*) and of an irregular verb (*give*).

Principal Parts of the Regular Verb *Talk*			
Base Form	Present Participle	Past	Past Participle
talk	[is] talking	talked	[have] talked

Conjugation of the Regular Verb *Talk*

Present Tense

Singular	*Plural*
I talk	we talk
you talk	you talk
he, she, *or* it talks	they talk

Past Tense

Singular	*Plural*
I talked	we talked
you talked	you talked
he, she, *or* it talked	they talked

Future Tense

Singular	*Plural*
I will (shall) talk	we will (shall) talk
you will (shall) talk	you will (shall) talk
he, she, *or* it will (shall) talk	they will (shall) talk

Present Perfect Tense

Singular	*Plural*
I have talked	we have talked
you have talked	you have talked
he, she, *or* it has talked	they have talked

Past Perfect Tense

Singular	*Plural*
I had talked	we had talked
you had talked	you had talked
he, she, *or* it had talked	they had talked

Future Perfect Tense

Singular	*Plural*
I will (shall) have talked	we will (shall) have talked
you will (shall) have talked	you will (shall) have talked
he, she, *or* it will (shall) have talked	they will (shall) have talked

USAGE

STYLE   TIP

Traditionally, the helping verbs *shall* and *will* were used differently. Now, however, *shall* can be used almost interchangeably with *will*.

Reference Note

For information on **using shall and will,** see page 600.

Each tense has another form, called the ***progressive form,*** which is used to express continuing action or state of being. The progressive form consists of the appropriate tense of the verb *be* and the present participle of a verb.

Present Progressive	am, are, is talking
Past Progressive	was, were talking
Future Progressive	will (shall) be talking
Present Perfect Progressive	has, have been talking
Past Perfect Progressive	had been talking
Future Perfect Progressive	will (shall) have been talking

Only the present and the past tenses have another form, called the ***emphatic form,*** which is used to show emphasis. In the present tense, the emphatic form consists of the helping verb *do* or *does* and the base form of the verb. In the past tense, the emphatic form consists of the verb *did* and the base form of a verb.

Present Emphatic	do, does talk
Past Emphatic	did talk

NOTE The emphatic form is also used in questions and negative statements. These uses do not place any special emphasis on the verbs.

QUESTION   Why **do** snakes **shed** their skins?

NEGATIVE   If Uncle Pedro **does**n't **arrive** soon, we should
STATEMENT   call Aunt Lu.

Principal Parts of the Irregular Verb *Give*

Base Form	Present Participle	Past	Past Participle
give	[is] giving	gave	[have] given

Conjugation of the Irregular Verb *Give*

Present Tense

Singular	*Plural*
I give	we give
you give	you give
he, she, *or* it gives	they give

Present Progressive: *am, are, is giving*

Present Emphatic: *do, does give*

USAGE

Conjugation of the Irregular Verb *Give*

Past Tense

Singular
I gave
you gave
he, she, *or* it gave

Plural
we gave
you gave
they gave

Past Progressive: *was, were giving*
Past Emphatic: *did give*

Future Tense

Singular
I will (shall) give
you will (shall) give
he, she, *or* it will (shall) give

Plural
we will (shall) give
you will (shall) give
they will (shall) give

Future Progressive: *will (shall) be giving*

Present Perfect Tense

Singular
I have given
you have given
he, she, *or* it has given

Plural
we have given
you have given
they have given

Present Perfect Progressive: *has, have been giving*

Past Perfect Tense

Singular
I had given
you had given
he, she, *or* it had given

Plural
we had given
you had given
they had given

Past Perfect Progressive: *had been giving*

Future Perfect Tense

Singular
I will (shall) have given
you will (shall) have given
he, she, *or* it will (shall) have given

Plural
we will (shall) have given
you will (shall) have given
they will (shall) have given

Future Perfect Progressive: *will (shall) have been giving*

─HELP─

The conjugation of the verb *give* in the chart at left is in the active voice. Many verbs can be in either the active voice or the passive voice.

Reference Note

For a discussion of the uses of the **active voice** and the **passive voice**, see page 601. For the **conjugation of *give* in the passive voice**, see page 602.

USAGE

The Uses of the Tenses

18e. Each of the six tenses has its own uses.

(1) The *present tense* expresses an action or a state of being that is occurring now, at the present time.

EXAMPLES   Sonja **owns** a calculator. [present]

Larry **is** in the Chess Club. [present]

We **are rehearsing** the play. [present progressive]

I **do appreciate** your helping me. [present emphatic]

The present tense is also used

- to show customary or habitual action or state of being

EXAMPLE   He **runs** two miles a day.

- to state a general truth—something that is always true

EXAMPLE   The equator **divides** the earth's surface into the Northern and Southern Hemispheres.

- to summarize the plot or subject matter of a literary work (such use is called *literary present*)

EXAMPLE   In Act III of *The Tragedy of Julius Caesar*, the conspirators **assassinate** the Roman leader.

- to make a historical event seem current (such use is called *historical present*)

EXAMPLE   During the unstable years following the 1910 Mexican Revolution, Emiliano Zapata and his army **occupy** Mexico City three different times.

- to express future time

EXAMPLE   We **travel** abroad next month.

(2) The *past tense* expresses an action or a state of being that occurred in the past and did not continue into the present.

EXAMPLES   I **ran** toward the door. [past]

Tomás **was** the club's president last year. [past]

The boys **were playing** football. [past progressive]

We certainly **did enjoy** your performance. [past emphatic]

(3) The *future tense* expresses an action or a state of being that will occur. The future tense is usually formed with the helping verb *will* or *shall* and the base form of a verb.

EXAMPLES   I **will travel** this fall. [future]

        I **shall leave** soon. [future]

        Gia and I **will be** there at seven o'clock. [future]

        Will you **be waiting** for us? [future progressive]

A future action or state of being may also be expressed by using

- the present tense of *be* followed by *going to* and the base form of a verb

EXAMPLE   **Are** you **going to drive** her to the airport?

- the present tense of *be* followed by *about to* and the base form of the verb

EXAMPLE   They **are about to begin** the ceremony.

- the present tense of a verb with a word or word group that expresses future time

EXAMPLE   I **take** my driving test **next Friday.**

(4) The *present perfect tense* expresses an action or a state of being that occurred at an indefinite time in the past. The present perfect tense is usually formed with the helping verb *have* or *has* and the past participle of a verb.

EXAMPLES   She **has visited** Chicago. [present perfect]

        They **have been** to the office. [present perfect]

The present perfect tense may also be used to express an action or a state of being that began in the past and that continues into the present.

EXAMPLES   She **has worked** there several years. [present perfect]

        I **have been taking** guitar lessons for nearly six months. [present perfect progressive]

NOTE Use the past tense, not the present perfect tense, to express a specific time in the past.

EXAMPLE   We **saw** [*not* have seen] the movie last night.

USAGE

(5) The *past perfect tense* expresses an action or a state of being that ended before another past action or state of being occurred. The past perfect tense is usually formed with the helping verb *had* and the past participle of the verb.

EXAMPLES After Mary Anne **had revised** her essay, she handed it in. [past perfect]

Mr. Hahn told us that he **had been** a Peace Corps volunteer in Somalia. [past perfect]

The frustrated chemist finally realized that she **had been overlooking** an important step in the experiment. [past perfect progressive]

(6) The *future perfect tense* expresses an action or a state of being that will end before another future action or state of being. The future perfect tense is usually formed with the helping verbs *shall have* or *will have* and the past participle of a verb.

EXAMPLES By the time you receive this postcard, **I will have returned** home. [future perfect]

Before then, you and he **will have become** U.S. citizens by naturalization. [future perfect]

At the end of this year, I **will have been attending** school for ten years. [future perfect progressive]

─HELP─

In Exercise 11, the use of the past and present perfect verb tenses gives the example sentences different meanings.

My sister took piano lessons for two years. [The past tense *took* indicates that the piano lessons occurred in the past and did not continue into the present.]

My sister has been taking piano lessons for two years. [The progressive form of the present perfect tense *has been taking* indicates that the piano lessons began in the past and are continuing into the present.]

Exercise 11 Identifying the Tenses of Verbs

Identify the tenses of the verbs in each of the following pairs of sentences. Also tell whether the verbs are in progressive or emphatic form. Be prepared to explain the difference in meaning between the sentences in each pair.

EXAMPLE 1. My sister took piano lessons for two years.
My sister has been taking piano lessons for two years.

1. *took—past; has been taking—present perfect progressive*

1. I will start the assignment this afternoon.
I will have started the assignment by this afternoon.
2. What happened here?
What has been happening here?
3. She lived in Cleveland for four years.
She has lived in Cleveland for four years.

4. I do have an after-school job.
I did have an after-school job.
5. Some students were practicing karate during their lunch break.
Some students have been practicing karate during their lunch break.

Exercise 12 **Using the Different Tenses of Verbs**

Change the tense of the verb in each of the following sentences by following the directions given in the parentheses.

EXAMPLE 1. Have you done your homework? (Change to past emphatic.)

1. *Did you do your homework?*

1. Otto lived here for a year. (Change to future perfect.)
2. I leave for school at 7:00 A.M. (Change to future.)
3. Have you read Thomas Sowell's excellent how-to book *Choosing a College*? (Change to present perfect progressive.)
4. Will you go? (Change to past emphatic.)
5. Were they at the party? (Change to past perfect.)
6. Were you there? (Change to present perfect.)
7. The soloist sings well. (Change to present emphatic.)
8. The bus arrives on time. (Change to future.)
9. By then, Cammi had returned. (Change to future perfect.)
10. The klezmer band will play for an hour without a break. (Change to future perfect progressive.)

Consistency of Tense

18f. Do not change needlessly from one tense to another.

(1) When describing events that occur at the same time, use verbs in the same tense.

EXAMPLES Roy **looked** through his binoculars and **saw** a large bear as it **raced** back to the woods. [All of the verbs are in the past tense.]

Roy **looks** through his binoculars and **sees** a large bear as it **races** back to the woods. [All of the verbs are in the present tense.]

(2) When describing events that occur at different times, use verbs in different tenses to show the sequence of events.

EXAMPLES   Yesterday, Donald **told** us that his brother **works** part time at the animal shelter. [The past tense *told* is correct because the action of telling occurred at a specific time in the past. The present tense *works* is correct because the action of working occurs now.]

Sela's family **lives** next door but **will be moving** to Salinas, California, next month. [The present tense *lives* is correct because the action of living occurs now. The future tense *will be moving* is correct because the action of moving will be occurring in the future.]

Exercise 13 Proofreading for Consistency of Tense

Most of the sentences in the following passage contain at least one error in the use of tenses. Revise the incorrect sentences to correct each error. If a sentence is already correct, write *C*.

EXAMPLE   **[1]** The American Revolution began in 1775 and ends in 1783.

1. *The American Revolution began in 1775 and ended in 1783.*

[1] The painting below depicts the outcome of one of the most important battles of the American Revolution, a battle that took place in September and October 1777 at Saratoga, New York. [2] The leader of the British troops, General John Burgoyne, had set up camp near Saratoga and is planning to march south to Albany. [3] Burgoyne's

The Granger Collection, New York.

army has been weakened by a recent attack from an American militia, which had ambushed some of his troops at Bennington, Vermont. [4] Although the march to Albany is dangerous, Burgoyne decided to take the risk because he feels bound by orders from London.

[5] Meanwhile, also near Saratoga, the American troops under General Horatio Gates gather reinforcements and supplies. [6] The American forces outnumbered their British enemies by a margin of nearly two to one. [7] The Americans are much better equipped than the British, whose provisions are badly depleted.

[8] In spite of these disadvantages, the British launch an attack on the Americans on September 19, 1777. [9] After four hours of fierce fighting, the Americans, led by General Gates or General Benedict Arnold (who later became an infamous traitor to the American cause), withdraw. [10] The British, however, have suffered serious losses, including many officers. [11] Burgoyne urgently sends messages to the British command in New York and asked for new orders. [12] He never received a response, possibly because the messages are intercepted. [13] Burgoyne's tactics became desperate. [14] He boldly leads a fresh attack against the Americans on October 7. [15] This time, however, his troops endure even worse casualties, and the next day Burgoyne prepares to retreat.

[16] The Americans surround Burgoyne's army before it could leave Saratoga. [17] As the painting shows, Burgoyne had surrendered to Benedict Arnold. [18] The Convention of Saratoga, under which Burgoyne gave up his entire force of six thousand troops, is signed on October 17. [19] Saratoga becomes a turning point in the American Revolution. [20] Six years later, in 1783, the British signed a peace treaty with the Americans, and the American Revolution ended.

Modals

18g. A *modal* is a helping (or auxiliary) verb that is joined with a main verb or an infinitive to express an attitude toward the action or state of being of the main verb.

The helping verbs *can, could, may, might, must, ought, shall, should, will,* and *would* are used as modals.

(1) The modal *can* or *could* is used to express ability.

EXAMPLES   **Can** you **speak** French?

I **could have gone,** but I was too tired.

Reference Note

For more about **helping (auxiliary) verbs** and **main verbs,** see page 417.

USAGE

(2) The modal *may* is used to express permission or possibility.

EXAMPLES   You **may leave** the table. [permission]

It seems that her truck's struts **may be** defective. [possibility]

(3) The modal *might*, like *may*, is used to express possibility. Often, the possibility expressed by *might* is less likely than the possibility expressed by *may*.

EXAMPLE   Rumor has it that Mel Gibson **might be** there, but I doubt it.

(4) The modal *must* is used most often to express a requirement. Sometimes, *must* is used to express an explanation.

EXAMPLES   The hippopotamus **must spend** most of its time in the water, or its skin will become dry. [requirement]

He **must have been caught** in traffic. [explanation]

(5) The modal *ought* is used to express an obligation or a likelihood.

EXAMPLES   Does Ms. Garza think that she **ought to promote** Mr. Whitman? [obligation]

The tornado **ought to be gone** soon. [likelihood]

(6) The modal *will* or *shall* is used to express future time.

EXAMPLES   When **will** (or **shall**) we **leave** for lunch?

Tim **will take** a look at your car.

(7) The modal *should* is used to express a recommendation, an obligation, or a possibility.

EXAMPLES   Mom **should go** to the doctor for her sprain. [recommendation]

Students **should hand in** their homework on time. [obligation]

Should you **have** any complaints about the service, please do not hesitate to let us know. [possibility]

(8) The modal *would* is used to express the conditional form of a verb.

A conditional verb form usually appears in an independent clause that is joined with an "if" clause. The "if" clause explains *under what condition(s)* the action or state of being of the conditional verb takes place.

| STYLE 〰️ TIP |

In the past, careful writers and speakers of English made a distinction between the modals *shall* and *will*. Nowadays, however, writers and speakers tend to use *will* in most cases. Only in certain situations do they typically use *shall*.

EXAMPLE
  Shall we dance?

EXAMPLE   If the economy had been better, the president **would have won** reelection. [conditional]

Would is also used to express future time in a subordinate clause when the main verb in the independent clause is in the past tense.

EXAMPLE   They promised us that they **would bring** the music. [subordinate clause]

Additionally, *would* is used to express an action that was repeated in the past, an invitation or offer, or a polite request.

EXAMPLES   Every day I **would get up** early and **go** for a walk. [repeated past action]

Would you **like** some of this pie? [offer]

Would you please **tell** me the time? [polite request]

Exercise 14 **Writing Appropriate Modals**

For each of the following sentences, supply an appropriate modal.

EXAMPLE   **1.** If we are all agreed, I _____ write the final document.
          1. will

1. I _____ have forgotten to answer that question.
2. No, Jeff, you _____ not let your hamster out of its cage.
3. "I _____ try to finish by tomorrow," Maria said.
4. The weather report said it _____ snow, or it _____ not.
5. All participants _____ return the permission slips by Friday.
6. Colleen _____ almost reach the light bulb.
7. After reviewing the entries, the panel _____ announce its decision.
8. Even with the manual, I simply _____ not figure out this program.
9. Frank _____ be happy to help, if you ask him nicely.
10. As soon as you finish your part of the report, Sharon _____ write the conclusion.

Active Voice and Passive Voice

Voice is the form a transitive verb takes to indicate whether the subject of the verb performs or receives the action.

18h. When the subject of a verb performs the action, the verb is in the *active voice.* When the subject of a verb receives the action, the verb is in the *passive voice.*

Reference Note

For further discussion of **transitive verbs,** see page 421. For more information about **direct objects,** see page 456.

STYLE   **TIP**

Choosing between the active voice and the passive voice is a matter of style, not correctness. Be aware, however, that using the passive voice can sometimes produce an awkward or weak effect.

AWKWARD PASSIVE
The yardwork will be finished tomorrow by me.

ACTIVE
I **will finish** the yardwork tomorrow.

Reference Note

For the **conjugation** of the **verb give in the active voice,** see the chart on page 592.

USAGE

As the following examples show,

- a verb in the active voice has a direct object, which tells who or what receives the action; a verb in the passive voice does not have a direct object.

- a verb in the passive voice may or may not be followed by a prepositional phrase that begins with *by* and tells who or what performs the action.

	S	V		DO

ACTIVE VOICE   The blazing fire **destroyed** the outside walls. [The subject *fire* performs the action; the direct object *walls* receives the action.]

		S	V	

PASSIVE VOICE   The outside walls **were destroyed** by the blazing fire. [The subject *walls* receives the action; *fire,* the object of the preposition *by,* performs the action.]

		S	V	

PASSIVE VOICE   The outside walls **were destroyed.** [The subject *walls* receives the action; the performer of the action is not given.]

	S	V	DO

ACTIVE VOICE   She **grows** corn on her farm. [The subject *She* performs the action; the direct object *corn* receives the action.]

	S	V

PASSIVE VOICE   Corn **is grown** on her farm. [The subject *corn* receives the action; the performer of the action is not given.]

As shown above, a verb in the passive voice is always a verb phrase that consists of a form of the verb *be* and the past participle of a verb. The following chart shows the conjugation of the verb *give* in the passive voice.

Conjugation of the Irregular Verb *Give* in the Passive Voice	
Present Tense	
Singular	*Plural*
I am given	we are given
you are given	you are given
he, she, *or* it is given	they are given

Conjugation of the Irregular Verb *Give* in the Passive Voice

Past Tense

Singular	*Plural*
I was given	we were given
you were given	you were given
he, she, *or* it was given	they were given

Future Tense

Singular	*Plural*
I will (shall) be given	we will (shall) be given
you will (shall) be given	you will (shall) be given
he, she, *or* it will (shall) be given	they will (shall) be given

Present Perfect Tense

Singular	*Plural*
I have been given	we have been given
you have been given	you have been given
he, she, *or* it has been given	they have been given

Past Perfect Tense

Singular	*Plural*
I had been given	we had been given
you had been given	you had been given
he, she, *or* it had been given	they had been given

Future Perfect Tense

Singular	*Plural*
I will (shall) have been given	we will (shall) have been given
you will (shall) have been given	you will (shall) have been given
he, she, *or* it will (shall) have been given	they will (shall) have been given

USAGE

┌─ H E L P ─

Because the use of *be* or *been* with *being* is awkward, in the passive voice the progressive form is generally used only in the present tense and past tense.

EXAMPLES

My favorite teacher **is being given** an award. [present progressive, passive voice]

My favorite teacher **was being given** an award. [past progressive, passive voice]

Using the Passive Voice

18i. The passive voice should be used sparingly.

Use the passive voice

- when you want to emphasize the receiver of the action

EXAMPLE   The mayor **was reelected** by a landslide.

- when you do not know, or do not want to reveal, the performer of the action

EXAMPLE   Vicious rumors **have been spread** about the politician.

Exercise 15 Identifying Verbs in the Active and Passive Voices

Identify the verb in each of the following sentences as *active* or *passive*. If the verb is in the passive voice, revise the sentence so that the verb is in the active voice.

EXAMPLE   1. We were shown by our art teacher some prints of Lucia Wilcox's artwork.

1. *passive—Our art teacher showed us some prints of Lucia Wilcox's artwork.*

1. The paintings of Lucia Wilcox are admired by many artists around the world.
2. Her blindness during her last years made her final works particularly interesting.
3. She was befriended and taught by Raoul Dufy, Fernand Léger, Robert Motherwell, and Jackson Pollock.
4. Her paintings have been shown often in gallery exhibits around the world.
5. She lost her eyesight suddenly, though not unexpectedly.
6. Her blindness was caused by a tumor near the optic nerve.
7. According to Wilcox, after losing her vision, she had better sight than anyone else.
8. Her vision and her mind were described by her as free of "static" and "distractions."
9. Because of her blindness, her style and subject matter were altered from energetic silhouettes to larger canvases in lush colors.
10. Her style was imitated by many well-known artists.

Exercise 16 Using the Passive Voice

Rewrite any of the following sentences that contain awkward passive-voice constructions. If you think a sentence is best the way it is, write *C* and be prepared to explain your answer.

EXAMPLE   1. My car was serviced by Tom, my favorite mechanic.
         1. *Tom, my favorite mechanic, serviced my car.*

1. According to the editorial, the city's surplus money was wasted by inefficient politicians.
2. My home was damaged by a tornado recently.
3. The right-rear tire must have been punctured by a nail in the driveway.
4. The bridge was damaged by rushing water.
5. The classroom computer was stolen over the weekend.
6. While I was away visiting my cousins in Nebraska, my cat was fed by my neighbor.
7. My sleep was interrupted by loud, bass-heavy music from our neighbors' party.
8. The president's failure to be reelected was caused by sudden economic downturn.
9. The farmer's crops were destroyed by drought back in the 1980s.
10. The book was read by them.

┌HELP─
In the example for Exercise 16, the performer of the action is known, and there is no reason to emphasize the receiver of the action. The passive voice is unnecessary and awkward.

USAGE

Review C Choosing the Correct Forms of Verbs

Choose the correct verb form in parentheses in each of the following sentences.

EXAMPLE   1. Has the club (*risen, raised*) its membership dues?
         1. *raised*

1. Little Billy was (*lying, laying*) in wait for us.
2. He had accidentally (*thrown, throwed*) his homework away.
3. The spilled laundry (*laid, lay*) in a wet heap.
4. We ate until we almost (*burst, bursted*).
5. The kitten (*drank, drunk*) from the dog's bowl.
6. Haven't you ever (*swam, swum*) in a lake before?
7. When Chief Dan George walked to the podium, cheers (*rang, rung*) out.
8. Have you ever (*rode, ridden*) a roller coaster?
9. I knew I should have (*brought, brung*) my camera.
10. Uh-oh, I think this phone is (*broke, broken*).

Mood

18j. *Mood* is the form a verb takes to indicate the attitude of the person using the verb.

(1) The *indicative mood* is used to express a fact, an opinion, or a question.

EXAMPLES   Jose Saramago **is** the Portuguese writer who **won** the Nobel Prize in literature in 1998. [fact]

They **think** we **are** next in line. [opinion]

Can you **name** the first three presidents of the United States? [question]

(2) The *imperative mood* is used to express a direct command or request.

EXAMPLES   **Close** that window! [direct command]

Please **read** that paper aloud. [request]

(3) The *subjunctive mood* is used to express a suggestion, a necessity, a condition contrary to fact, or a wish.

EXAMPLES   Her parents recommend that Alison **try** cooking as a career. [suggestion]

It is essential that we **be** at the airport on time. [necessity]

If I **were** you, I would call them immediately. [condition contrary to fact]

I wish you **were** here. [wish]

Exercise 17   Identifying Mood Forms of Verbs

Identify the mood of the italicized verb in each of the following sentences as *indicative*, *imperative*, or *subjunctive*.

EXAMPLE   **1.** It is necessary that we *review* the safety instructions.

      1. subjunctive

1. What *is* Purnima's favorite book?
2. *Look* at my uncle's photos of Kenya.
3. It is required that we *take* a foreign language next year.
4. Mr. McEwan *toured* the Aran Islands last summer.
5. I suggest that you *put* on a life jacket before water-skiing.

6. I *think* Rosalinda's stereo will be perfect for the party.
7. Soon-hee wishes the camping trip *were* next Saturday.
8. *Try* out for the leading role, Eric.
9. Sri Lanka *is* off the southern coast of India.
10. My friend David teases me as though he *were* my brother.

Review D **Choosing the Correct Forms of Irregular Verbs**

Supply the correct form of each italicized verb in the following paragraph.

EXAMPLE   I liked this picture as soon as I **[1]** (*see*) it.
   1. *saw*

   Have you ever **[1]** (*see*) this fascinating picture of an impossible structure? It is called <u>Waterfall</u>, and it was **[2]** (*draw*) by the Dutch artist M. C. Escher. He **[3]** (*take*) the basic idea for this artwork from the optical illusion shown below. As you can see, a two-story waterfall has **[4]** (*set*) a miller's wheel in motion. Then, after the water has **[5]** (*leave*) the wheel, it zigzags through a channel until it **[6]** (*come*) to the top of the waterfall again. Wait, though—has the water **[7]** (*go*) uphill on its way back to the top of the waterfall? No, obviously the stream has **[8]** (*run*) away from the fall on the same level as the bottom of the fall. Then how can the water now be back at the top where it **[9]** (*begin*)? Escher never answered that question, but he once wrote that if the miller simply **[10]** (*throw*) in a bucket of water now and then to replace water that had evaporated, he would have a "perpetual motion" machine!

© Roger Penrose

Mood   **607**

Chapter Review

A. Writing the Past or Past Participle Form of Verbs

Write the correct past or past participle form of the italicized verb in parentheses in each of the following sentences.

1. Although Emily Dickinson (*write*) poetry most of her life, very little of her work was published until after her death.
2. When he saw that the animals had (*drink*) all the water, he gave them more.
3. Regarding weeds as unwanted intruders, she pulled them from the ground and (*throw*) them over the fence.
4. The water was cold and daylight was fading, so he (*swim*) only a short distance before turning back to shore.
5. The dew (*freeze*) during the night, covering each twig and blade of grass with a crisp, silvery coating.
6. After my brother had given his new puppy a bath, he (*seem*) to be wetter than the dog.
7. She (*speak*) in such a low, hushed voice that the people in the audience had to strain to hear her remarks.
8. Frightened by the traffic, the deer (*run*) back into the forest.
9. At the front of the parade was an officer who (*ride*) a prancing black horse.
10. When the church bell (*ring*) on Tuesday evening, the villagers became alarmed.

B. Revising Verb Tense or Voice

Revise the following paragraph, correcting verbs that are in the wrong tense or that use passive voice awkwardly. If a sentence is already correct, write *C*.

[11] Miguel de Cervantes was born in 1547 in Alcalá de Henares, near Madrid, Spain. [12] Unlike most other writers of his time, he does not attend a university. [13] Cervantes is acquiring a somewhat different form of education by serving as a soldier and being captured by pirates. [14] He is held captive by the pirates for five years until his

family ransoms him. [15] Little was written by him until he is in his late thirties. [16] In 1605, at the age of fifty-eight, Cervantes is publishing the first part of his masterwork, *Don Quixote;* then he wrote nothing significant for eight years. [17] In 1615, the second part of *Don Quixote* was published. [18] Cervantes' life has been continuing to have ups and downs, and a series of government jobs prevent him from writing full-time. [19] However, in the last three years of his life, many fine works were written by him. [20] Cervantes has lived a fascinating life, and world literature is richer because of it.

C. Determining Correct Use of *Lie* and *Lay, Sit* and *Set,* and *Rise* and *Raise* in Sentences

Most of the following sentences contain at least one error in the use of *lie* or *lay, sit* or *set,* or *rise* or *raise.* Identify each incorrect verb, and write the correct form. If a sentence is already correct, write *C.*

21. We left our lawn furniture setting on the patio.
22. Grandpa decided to sit the plates on the sideboard.
23. They lain the bricks next to where we set out the logs.
24. When the dough has raised for thirty minutes, turn it onto the floured board.
25. The sun has set and the moon is rising.
26. When we in America are rising from bed in the morning, people in China are laying down to sleep.
27. As the enemy patrol passed by, the parachutists laid quietly in the undergrowth.
28. Cadet Rojas rose the flag to the sound of reveille on the bugle.
29. I feel a little dizzy; I think I'll lay down for a while.
30. The architect raised to go find the blueprints.

D. Using the Different Tenses of Verbs

Change the tense of the verb in each of the following sentences by following the directions given in parentheses.

31. Pamela sat at her desk for an hour. (Change to *future perfect.*)
32. The lead actor changes costumes quickly. (Change to *present emphatic.*)

33. Have you watched the TV miniseries on Thomas Jefferson? (Change to *present perfect progressive*.)

34. Sean will speak for half an hour. (Change to *future perfect progressive*.)

35. Were you at the inauguration? (Change to *past perfect*.)

36. Were we ever informed? (Change to *present perfect*.)

37. Dad leaves for the office at 7:30 A.M. (Change to *future*.)

38. The plane arrives on time. (Change to *future*.)

39. By then, the Holts had checked in at the hotel. (Change to *future perfect*.)

40. They are talking to the police. (Change to *past emphatic*.)

E. Choosing the Correct Forms of Verbs

Write the correct form of each italicized verb in the following sentences. In some instances you will need to add *have, has,* or *had*.

41. The bed is unmade; he must (*lie*) down for a while before he went out.

42. During yesterday's storm, flying debris (*break*) most of the windows and littered the floors.

43. The car isn't in the garage; they must (*take*) it.

44. I was feeling very tired when I got home, so I (*lie*) down right away.

45. Hot and dusty from their long walk up the sloping road, the men seized the water jugs and (*drink*) every drop.

46. Several people (*rise*) to protest, but the presiding officer silenced their complaints at once.

47. That sweater didn't fit when I tried it on this morning; it must (*shrink*) in the wash yesterday.

48. After heavy rains had continued day after day, the water (*burst*) through the dam and flooded the fields.

49. So far, she (*take*) every opportunity to promote the plan.

50. After they (*ride*) several miles in silence, the leader suddenly started singing.

Writing Application
Using Verb Tense in an Essay

Establishing Time of Action   It's Cultural Appreciation Week at your school. Your teacher has asked you to write a short essay about your own cultural or ethnic group. In your essay, you should explore several ways in which people of your heritage have enriched life in your community. Use correct verb tenses to describe some of the contributions these people have made in the past, some activities they are currently involved in, and what you think they might offer in the future. Use at least five different verb tenses in your essay.

Prewriting   Brainstorm a list of your ethnic or cultural group's outstanding leaders, scholars, athletes, and artists, as well as activities, events, clubs, and community service projects. Select three or four of the group's main contributions to mention in your essay. Many people can claim more than one ethnic or cultural heritage. If you can, you may want to write about the group you know the best or the one in which you are most interested.

Writing   While you are writing your first draft, try to add details that show the uniqueness of your cultural heritage. Consider how you can use verb tenses to make the sequence of events in your essay clear.

Revising   Read through your essay to be sure that you have included at least one contribution from each different time period: the past, the present, and (speculatively) the future. Check to see that you have used at least five different tenses.

Publishing   Make sure that you have formed all verbs correctly, paying special attention to irregular verbs. Proofread your essay for any errors in grammar, usage, and mechanics. You might create a bulletin board display of all the essays your classmates have written; or your class may wish to prepare a cultural-appreciation presentation for another class or for the whole school. If one is available, you may also want to post your essay on a class Web site.

Using Modifiers Correctly

Forms, Comparison, and Placement

Diagnostic Preview

A. Revising Sentences to Correct Errors in the Use and Placement of Modifiers

Most of the following sentences contain an error in the use or placement of modifiers. Revise each incorrect sentence to correct the faulty modifier. If a sentence is already correct, write *C*.

EXAMPLE
1. The planets that are most farthest from the sun are Neptune and Pluto.

1. *The planets that are farthest from the sun are Neptune and Pluto.*

1. While building a fire in front of the hogan, Manaba's dog began to tug at the hem of her doeskin dress.
2. The greenhouse effect may be causing more higher temperatures worldwide.
3. Adrianne knows more about chemistry than anybody in her class.
4. Hank worked rather hasty so he could catch up with Nina.

5. Marian felt bad, but she knew things could be worser.

6. Millie can sing as well as Scott, but of the two, he's the best dancer.

7. By playing carefully, the game was won.

8. Steady and confident, a keen sense of balance enables Mohawk ironworkers to help build tall bridges and buildings.

9. Although Helen would be better in the leading role, Wenona will probably get the part because she is more reliable.

10. Because one carton of chemicals smelled badly, it was examined before being used in the laboratory.

B. Revising a Paragraph to Correct Errors in the Use and Placement of Modifiers

Most of the sentences in the following paragraph contain an error in the use or placement of modifiers. Revise each incorrect sentence. You may need to add or rearrange words for clarity. If a sentence is already correct, write *C*.

EXAMPLE   **[1]** My aunt Penny had enclosed a ticket in my birthday card for Bobby McFerrin's concert.

1. *My aunt Penny had enclosed in my birthday card a ticket for Bobby McFerrin's concert.*

[11] Hailed by many critics as one of today's greatest male vocalists, my aunt Penny took me to see Bobby McFerrin. [12] Waiting for the concert to start, the auditorium was filled with eager fans. [13] Wondering where the band was, I kept my eyes on the empty stage. [14] When it was time for the show to start, a slender, barefoot man walked out from the wings, carrying a cordless microphone dressed only in blue jeans. [15] Assuming he was a stagehand, he began to sing, and then I realized that this was Bobby McFerrin! [16] Instantly, the complex rhythm of the music fascinated the audience that he made up as he went along. [17] I suddenly understood why one of his popularest albums is called *Spontaneous Inventions*! [18] Alone in the spotlight with only his voice and no band at all, two thousand people sat spellbound until he took his final bow. [19] All his life, Bobby McFerrin has enjoyed listening to and performing jazz, pop, rock, soul, African, and classical music. [20] Bobby's parents are both classical musicians, and he thanks them for giving him a rich musical environment on the back of every album he makes.

What Is a Modifier?

A *modifier* is a word or word group that makes the meaning of another word or word group more specific. The two kinds of modifiers are *adjectives* and *adverbs*.

One-Word Modifiers

Adjectives make the meanings of nouns and pronouns more specific.

Reference Note

For more information on **adjectives,** see page 412.

ADJECTIVES   Etta has a **mischievous** smile. [The adjective *mischievous* makes the meaning of the noun *smile* more specific.]

Only he answered the letter. [The adjective *Only* makes the meaning of the pronoun *he* more specific.]

Isn't his dog **well-trained**? [The compound adjective *well-trained* makes the meaning of the noun *dog* more specific.]

Adverbs make the meanings of verbs, adjectives, and other adverbs more specific.

Reference Note

For information on **adverbs,** see page 422.

ADVERBS   Etta smiled **mischievously.** [The adverb *mischievously* makes the meaning of the verb *smiled* more specific.]

The tree is **quite** healthy. [The adverb *quite* makes the meaning of the adjective *healthy* more specific.]

The car went **surprisingly** fast. [The adverb *surprisingly* makes the meaning of the adverb *fast* more specific.]

Reference Note

For information on **subjects and predicates,** see page 439. For information on **predicate adjectives,** see page 454.

19a. If a word in the predicate modifies the subject of the verb, use the adjective form. If it modifies the verb, use the adverb form.

ADJECTIVE   The cantor's voice was **beautiful.** [*Beautiful* modifies *voice.*]

ADVERB   The cantor sang **beautifully.** [*Beautifully* modifies *sang.*]

ADJECTIVE   The corn grew **tall.** [*Tall* modifies *corn.*]

ADVERB   The corn grew **quickly.** [*Quickly* modifies *grew.*]

USAGE

Adjective or Adverb?

While many adverbs end in –*ly,* others do not. Furthermore, not all words with the –*ly* ending are adverbs. Some adjectives also end in –*ly.* Therefore, you cannot tell whether a word is an adjective or an adverb simply by looking for the –*ly* ending.

Adverbs Not Ending in –*ly*	
call **soon**	remain **here**
not concerned	let **loose**
arrive **home**	**very** tall

Adjectives Ending in –*ly*	
elderly dachshund	**holy** place
curly lettuce	**silly** remark
only time	**timely** event

Some words can be used as both adjectives and adverbs. To decide whether a word is an adjective or an adverb, determine how the word is used in the sentence.

Adjectives	Adverbs
She is an **only** child.	She has **only** one brother.
That fighter is a **fast** plane.	The plane goes **fast.**
He caught the **last** boat.	They left **last.**

Exercise 1 **Identifying Adjectives and Adverbs and the Words They Modify**

Identify the adjectives and adverbs in the paragraph on the following page, and give the words they modify.

EXAMPLE **[1]** First, get a craft knife and some stiff black paper.

1. *First—adverb—get; craft—adjective—knife; some— adjective—paper; stiff—adjective—paper; black— adjective—paper*

HELP

Include only one-word modifiers in Exercise 1. Also, do not include the articles *a, an,* and *the.*

[1] In many cultures, cutting paper to make pictures is a traditional art. [2] For example, Mexican artisans use a small, very sharp knife to cut designs in pieces of colored paper. [3] As the oddly shaped scraps fall away, an image is slowly revealed. [4] Planning the work is a challenge because each part of the picture must connect somehow to the border or to another part of the design. [5] As you can see in these designs, the artist sometimes leaves a background pattern of stripes or lines to support the main subject. [6] The knife must not be even slightly dull, or the artist might accidentally tear one of the tiny paper bridges! [7] The work is very intricate. [8] Artisans must be meticulous. [9] Visualizing the finished product before actually completing it is a necessary skill. [10] Sharpening the knives that are used is an important skill, too.

Phrases Used as Modifiers

Like one-word modifiers, phrases can also be used as adjectives and adverbs.

EXAMPLES   It is time **for departure.** [The prepositional phrase *for departure* acts as an adjective that modifies the noun *time*.]

Bringing tears to our eyes, the comedian told some of her best jokes. [The participial phrase *Bringing tears to our eyes* acts as an adjective that modifies the noun *comedian*.]

Dr. Makowski is the one **to ask next.** [The infinitive phrase *to ask next* acts as an adjective that modifies the pronoun *one*.]

Tina is becoming fluent **in Italian.** [The prepositional phrase *in Italian* acts as an adverb that modifies the adjective *fluent*.]

Speak **with clarity in debates.** [The prepositional phrases *with clarity* and *in debates* act as adverbs that modify the verb *Speak*.]

The truck driver swerved just quickly enough **to avoid a collision.** [The infinitive phrase *to avoid a collision* acts as an adverb that modifies the adverb *enough*.]

Reference Note

For information about **different kinds of phrases,** see page 467.

Clauses Used as Modifiers

Like words and phrases, clauses can also be used as adjectives and adverbs.

EXAMPLES   Raphael is the painter **that I like best.** [The adjective clause *that I like best* modifies the noun *painter.*]

       Before my great-grandfather left Russia, he sat in his kitchen one last time. [The adverb clause *Before my great-grandfather left Russia* modifies the verb *sat.*]

Reference Note
For information on **clauses,** see page 492.

Eight Troublesome Modifiers

Bad and *Badly*

Bad is an adjective. In most uses, *badly* is an adverb.

ADJECTIVE   Fido was **bad.**
ADVERB   Fido behaved **badly.**

Remember that a word that modifies the subject of a verb should be in adjective form.

NONSTANDARD   The cheese smelled badly.
STANDARD   The cheese smelled **bad.** [*Bad* modifies *cheese.*]

> **NOTE** In informal situations, *bad* or *badly* is acceptable after *feel.*
>
> INFORMAL   She feels **badly** about the mistake.
> FORMAL   She feels **bad** about the mistake.

Reference Note
For information on **using standard English,** see page 638.

Good and *Well*

Good is an adjective. It should not be used to modify a verb.

NONSTANDARD   She sings good.
STANDARD   She sings **well.**
STANDARD   Her singing sounds **good.** [*Good* is an adjective that modifies the noun *singing.*]

Well may be used either as an adjective or as an adverb. As an adjective, *well* has two meanings: "in good health" and "satisfactory."

EXAMPLES   Trish is **well.** [Trish is in good health.]

       All is **well.** [All is satisfactory.]

USAGE

As an adverb, *well* means "capably."

EXAMPLE   Pedro did **well** in the music competition.

Slow and *Slowly*

In informal situations, *slow* is used as both an adjective and an adverb.

EXAMPLES   We took a **slow** boat to China. [*Slow* is an adjective modifying *boat*.]

Please go **slow**. [*Slow* is an adverb modifying *go*.]

Slowly is always an adverb. In formal uses, you should use *slowly* rather than *slow*.

EXAMPLES   The train **slowly** came to a stop.

Drive **slowly** on slippery roads.

Real and *Really*

Real is an adjective meaning "actual" or "genuine." *Really* is an adverb meaning "actually" or "truly."

EXAMPLES   Tom is a **real** mountain climber. [*Real* is an adjective modifying *climber*.]

The flood victims **really** need assistance. [*Really* is an adverb modifying *need*.]

Although in everyday situations *real* is commonly used as an adverb meaning "very," avoid using it as an adverb in formal speaking and writing.

INFORMAL   He kicked **real** well in the game.
  FORMAL   He kicked **really** well in the game.

| STYLE   TIP |

Really is overused in everyday speech. When possible, use another more descriptive adverb in place of *really*.

Exercise 2   Choosing Correct Adjective and Adverb Forms

In each of the following sentences, choose the modifier that is correct according to the rules of formal, standard English.

EXAMPLE   1. Each of the gymnasts performed (*real, really*) well.
          1. *really*

1. I can't hear you (*good, well*) when the water is running.
2. The opening paragraph is written (*good, well*).
3. The situation looks (*bad, badly*).

4. Why does ketchup come out of the bottle so (*slow, slowly*)?

5. She certainly plays the marimba (*good, well*).

6. Can you dance (*real, really*) well?

7. These shoes don't fit (*bad, badly*) at all.

8. Our coach said that we should do the exercise (*slow, slowly*).

9. Did you do (*good, well*) on the last algebra test?

10. The chef at the corner cafe cooks (*real, really*) spicy food.

Exercise 3 Using Adjective and Adverb Forms Correctly

Each of the following sentences contains at least one italicized adjective or adverb. If the italicized word is incorrect according to the rules of formal, standard English, give the correct word. If the sentence is already correct, write *C*.

EXAMPLE   **1.** Soon after my brother Skipper opened his new shop, he grew *real* concerned about its future.

  1. *really*

1. My brother opened Skipper's Skate City last April 1, and as the graph below shows, the shop did not do *well* at first.

2. Skipper wondered whether business had started *slow* because he wasn't advertising enough or because his display window wasn't drawing in people.

3. He'd see people walking *slow* past the shop and pointing at the gear on display, but hardly anyone stopped.

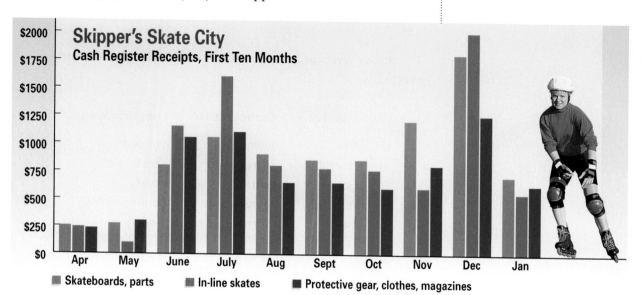

Skipper's Skate City
Cash Register Receipts, First Ten Months

■ Skateboards, parts   ■ In-line skates   ■ Protective gear, clothes, magazines

4. By the end of May, Skipper thought about giving up because he was doing so *bad.*

5. He would have felt *real* bad about failing, especially because Dad had lent him money to open the shop.

6. Then school let out, and within days, business was going *good.*

7. In-line skates and skateboards started selling *real* well; in fact, by the end of summer, Skipper was able to pay Dad back.

8. When school started, skateboards kept selling *good,* but total sales fell somewhat.

9. Skipper's receipts looked rather *badly* during the fall, but thanks to Christmas and Hanukkah, all went *good* in December.

10. By then, Skipper was a veteran of seasonal business cycles; he wasn't fazed when January's receipts weren't as *well* as those of other months.

Comparison of Modifiers

Modifiers—adjectives and adverbs—may be used to make comparisons.

ADJECTIVES	Juan is nearly as **tall** as I.
	Robert is **taller** than I.
	Of all the players, Antoine is the **tallest.**

ADVERBS	No other land animal can run as **fast** as the cheetah.
	The cheetah can run **faster** than any other land animal.
	Of all land animals, the cheetah can run the **fastest.**

19b. Modifiers change form to show comparison.

The three degrees of comparison are *positive, comparative,* and *superlative.*

Positive	Comparative	Superlative
low	lower	lowest
fearful	more fearful	most fearful
good	better	best
promptly	more promptly	most promptly
badly	worse	worst

Regular Comparison

(1) Most one-syllable modifiers form the comparative degree by adding *–er* and the superlative degree by adding *–est.*

Positive	Comparative	Superlative
thin	thin**ner**	thin**nest**
safe	saf**er**	saf**est**
dry	dri**er**	dri**est**
fast	fast**er**	fast**est**
soon	soon**er**	soon**est**

(2) Two-syllable modifiers may form the comparative degree by adding *–er* and the superlative degree by adding *–est*, or they may form the comparative degree by using *more* and the superlative degree by using *most*.

Positive	Comparative	Superlative
lovely	loveli**er**	loveli**est**
tricky	tricki**er**	tricki**est**
awkward	**more** awkward	**most** awkward
firmly	**more** firmly	**most** firmly
rapid	**more** rapid	**most** rapid

(3) Modifiers that have three or more syllables form the comparative degree by using *more* and the superlative degree by using *most.*

Positive	Comparative	Superlative
enthusiastic	**more** enthusiastic	**most** enthusiastic
fortunate	**more** fortunate	**most** fortunate
predictably	**more** predictably	**most** predictably
effectively	**more** effectively	**most** effectively
significantly	**more** significantly	**most** significantly

USAGE

STYLE TIP

Many two-syllable modifiers may correctly form the comparative and superlative degrees by either adding *–er* and *–est* or using *more* and *most.*

If adding *–er* or *–est* makes a word sound awkward, use *more* or *most* instead.

AWKWARD
  specialer

BETTER
  more special

HELP

A dictionary will tell you when a word forms its comparative or superlative form in some way other than by adding *–er* or *–est* or *more* or *most.* Look in a dictionary if you are not sure whether a word has irregular comparative or superlative forms or whether you need to change the spelling of a word before adding *–er* or *–est.*

(4) To show a decrease in the qualities they express, modifiers form the comparative degree by using *less* and the superlative degree by using *least*.

Positive	Comparative	Superlative
calm	**less** calm	**least** calm
frequent	**less** frequent	**least** frequent
helpful	**less** helpful	**least** helpful
slowly	**less** slowly	**least** slowly
courageously	**less** courageously	**least** courageously

Irregular Comparison

The comparative and superlative degrees of some modifiers are irregular in form.

Positive	Comparative	Superlative
bad	worse	worst
badly	worse	worst
ill	worse	worst
good	better	best
well	better	best
little	less	least
many	more	most
much	more	most
far	farther *or* further	farthest *or* furthest

The word *little* also has regular comparative and superlative forms: *littler, littlest.* These forms are used to describe physical size (the *littlest* toad). The forms *less* and *least* are used to describe an amount (*less* money).

NOTE Do not add *–er, –est* or *more, most* to irregularly compared forms. For example, use *worse,* not *worser* or *more worse.*

Exercise 4 **Writing the Comparative and Superlative Forms of Modifiers**

Write the comparative and superlative forms of each of the following modifiers.

EXAMPLE 1. skillful

1. *more (less) skillful; most (least) skillful*

USAGE

1. loudly
2. bad
3. humid
4. efficiently
5. silly
6. good
7. likely
8. well
9. fundamental
10. clearly

11. dark
12. wild
13. deep
14. heavy
15. pretty
16. healthy
17. attractive
18. intelligent
19. eccentric
20. friendly

Use of Comparative and Superlative Forms

19c. Use the comparative degree when comparing two things. Use the superlative degree when comparing more than two.

COMPARATIVE   Omaha is **larger** than Lincoln.
Roberto is a **better** typist than I am.
Which of these two shirts is **less expensive**?

SUPERLATIVE   Omaha is the **largest** city in Nebraska.
Roberto is the **best** typist in the class.
Which of these four shirts is **least expensive?**

19d. Include the word *other* or *else* when comparing one member of a group with the rest of the group.

ILLOGICAL   Rhode Island is smaller than any state in the Union. [Rhode Island is a state in the Union. Logically, Rhode Island cannot be smaller than itself.]
LOGICAL   Rhode Island is smaller than any **other** state in the Union.

ILLOGICAL   Stan is taller than anyone in his class. [Stan is a member of his class. Logically, Stan cannot be taller than himself.]
LOGICAL   Stan is taller than anyone **else** in his class.

19e. Avoid using double comparisons.

A *double comparison* is incorrect because it contains both *–er* and *more (less)* or both *–est* and *most (least)*.

| STYLE | TIP |

In informal situations, the superlative degree is commonly used to compare two things.

EXAMPLES
May the best team [of two] win.

Put your best foot forward.

In formal speaking and writing, however, the comparative degree should be used when two things are being compared.

Reference Note

For a discussion of **stand-ard** and **nonstandard English,** see page 638.

| NONSTANDARD | The second movie was more funnier than the first one. |
| STANDARD | The second movie was **funnier** than the first one. |

NONSTANDARD	What is the most deadliest snake?
STANDARD	What is the **deadliest** snake?
STANDARD	What is the **most deadly** snake?

| NONSTANDARD | Pancho is the least dullest debater. |
| STANDARD | Pancho is the **least dull** debater. |

19f. Be sure your comparisons are clear.

When making comparisons, indicate clearly what items are being compared.

UNCLEAR	The climate of Arizona is drier than South Carolina. [The sentence incorrectly compares a climate to a state.]
CLEAR	The climate of Arizona is drier than **the climate** of South Carolina.
CLEAR	The climate of Arizona is drier than **that** of South Carolina.

| UNCLEAR | Fresh vegetables at a farmers' market are sometimes lower in price than a grocery. [The sentence incorrectly compares vegetables to a grocery.] |
| CLEAR | Fresh vegetables at a farmers' market are sometimes lower in price than **those at** a grocery. |

State both parts of a comparison completely if there is any chance of misunderstanding.

UNCLEAR	We know her better than Dena.
CLEAR	We know her better than **we know** Dena.
CLEAR	We know her better than Dena **does.**

Reference Note

For information on **irregular comparisons,** see page 622.

> **Exercise 5** Using Modifiers Correctly

Most of the following sentences contain an error in the use of modifiers. Identify each error, and then write the correct form. If a sentence is already correct, write *C*.

EXAMPLE **1.** Of the Ganges and Amazon rivers, which is more longer?

1. *more longer—longer*

1. Laurie is more friendlier than she used to be.
2. Which of the four seasons do you like better?
3. I never saw a leader more stronger than Chief Billie of the Seminoles.

USAGE

4. Margaret Mead was one of the world's most famous anthropologists.
5. Of the two colleges that I am considering, Spelman College in Atlanta looks more interesting.
6. Anika arrived earlier than anyone in her family.
7. Muscles in the leg are stronger than the arm.
8. Denver's elevation is higher than that of any major city in the United States.
9. I wrote to Sally more often than Carlos.
10. This year's drought was much worse than last year.

Review A **Correcting Errors in the Use of Modifiers**

Each of the sentences in the following paragraph contains at least one error in the use of adjectives and adverbs. Find each error, and supply the necessary correction.

EXAMPLE **[1]** Of the four pots shown on this page, which do you think is the more delicate one?

1. *more delicate—most delicate*

[1] Among ceramic artists of the Southwest, perhaps the most famousest are the four women who made these coiled pots, using techniques handed down for more than 2,000 years. [2] Lucy Lewis's Acoma pottery is more delicate than any Southwest pottery. [3] Lewis used the most whitest clay. [4] Because this clay is scarce, the walls of her pots are the thinner of them all. [5] Maria Martinez's San Ildefonso pottery is more thicker and heavier than Lewis. [6] Of all the Southwest pottery styles, Martinez's black-on-black pottery may be the most best known. [7] No color is used, but the background areas of the black pot are burnished slowly with a small smooth stone until they become quite a bit more shinier than the main design. [8] Many of Margaret Tafoya's Santa Clara pots are also solid black, but of these two kinds of black pottery, the Santa Clara pots are the heaviest. [9] The bold, colorful Hopi pots of Fannie Nampeyo may be the more impressive achievement of all, because Nampeyo's family had to re-create the technique by studying shards of ancient pots found in 1895. [10] The pottery by these four women is beautifuller than many other artists.

Dangling Modifiers

19g. Avoid using dangling modifiers.

A modifying word, phrase, or clause that does not clearly and sensibly modify a word or word group in a sentence is a ***dangling modifier.*** To correct a dangling modifier, add or replace words to make the meaning clear and logical.

DANGLING	Frustrated, all of the scientists' data were reexamined. [Were the scientists' data frustrated?]
CLEAR	Frustrated, the **scientists** reexamined all of their data.
DANGLING	Looking back over my shoulder, the team went into a huddle. [Was the team looking back over my shoulder?]
CLEAR	Looking back over my shoulder, **I** saw the team going into a huddle.
DANGLING	While riding to the store, my front bicycle tire went flat. [Was the bicycle tire riding to the store?]
CLEAR	While **I** was riding to the store, my front bicycle tire went flat.
DANGLING	To qualify for the Olympics, many trial heats must be won. [Do trial heats qualify for the Olympics?]
CLEAR	To qualify for the Olympics, a **runner** must win many trial heats.

or

Before a runner may qualify for the Olympics, **he or she** must win many trial heats.

When a modifying participial or infinitive phrase or a clause comes at the beginning of a sentence as in the examples above, the phrase is followed by a comma. Immediately after that comma should come the word or word group that the phrase modifies.

NOTE A sentence may appear to have a dangling modifier when *you* is the understood subject. In such cases, the modifier is not dangling; it is modifying the understood subject.

EXAMPLE   To assemble the bookcase, (you) read the instructions.

Exercise 6 Correcting Dangling Modifiers

The following sentences contain dangling modifiers. Revise each sentence so that its meaning is clear and correct.

STYLE   TIP

A dangling modifier may occur when a sentence is in the passive voice. Rewriting sentences in the active voice not only eliminates many dangling modifiers but also makes your writing more interesting and lively. If you frequently find dangling modifiers in your writing, concentrate on staying in the active voice.

PASSIVE VOICE
Reaching as high as I could, the ball was caught just before it reached the fence. [*Reaching as high as I could* is a dangling modifier.]

ACTIVE VOICE
Reaching as high as I could, I caught the ball just before it reached the fence. [*Reaching as high as I could* modifies *I.*]

Reference Note

For information on the **understood subject,** see page 447.

EXAMPLE   **1.** Running through the park, the lake looked cool and inviting.

     1. *Running through the park, I thought the lake looked cool and inviting.*

or

     As I ran through the park, I thought the lake looked cool and inviting.

┌**HELP**┐

Although two revisions for the example in Exercise 6 are shown, you need to give only one for each item.

1. Hurrying through the last fifty pages, the book was fascinating.
2. Being a novice basketball player, my dribbling needs work.
3. When leaving the train, the station is on the right.
4. Exhausted by the hard work, a long nap sounded good.
5. Driving through the Rockies, the landscape was magnificent.
6. Having overslept, my exam results were poor.
7. Although excited, sleep came easily.
8. As a new student, it was difficult at first to find my way around.
9. To repair an appliance, experience is helpful.
10. Looking at recent consumer surveys, more Americans are working at home.

USAGE

Misplaced Modifiers

19h. Avoid using misplaced modifiers.

A word, phrase, or clause that seems to modify the wrong word or word group in a sentence is a *misplaced modifier.* Place modifying words, phrases, and clauses as near as possible to the words they modify.

Misplaced One-Word Modifiers

MISPLACED   Alone, thoughts of returning soon to earth comforted the astronaut living in the space station. [Were the thoughts alone?]

CLEAR   Thoughts of returning soon to earth comforted the astronaut living **alone** in the space station.

MISPLACED   Exhausted, a good night's rest was what the hikers needed. [Was a good night's rest exhausted?]

CLEAR   A good night's rest was what the **exhausted** hikers needed.

Be sure to place modifiers correctly to state clearly the meaning you intend.

EXAMPLES **Only** on Saturdays, my brother and I watch cartoons for an hour. [My brother and I watch on Saturdays, not on any other days.]

On Saturdays, my **only** brother and I watch cartoons for an hour. [I have no other brothers.]

On Saturdays, my brother and I watch **only** cartoons for an hour. [My brother and I watch nothing but cartoons.]

On Saturdays, my brother and I watch cartoons for **only** an hour. [My brother and I watch for no more than an hour.]

NOTE One-word modifiers such as *almost, even, hardly, just, merely, nearly, not,* and *only* generally should be placed directly before the words they modify.

MISPLACED According to the club's minutes, all of the members were not at the meeting on Friday.

CLEAR According to the club's minutes, **not** all of the members were at the meeting on Friday.

MISPLACED Before 6:00 P.M. a movie ticket only costs $3.50.

CLEAR Before 6:00 P.M. a movie ticket costs **only** $3.50.

Misplaced Phrase Modifiers

Adjective phrases, adverb phrases, and verbal phrases should be placed near the words they modify.

MISPLACED I'm lucky because I feel that I can always talk about my problems with my dad. [Does *with my dad* modify *talk* or *problems*?]

CLEAR I'm lucky because I feel that I can always talk **with my dad** about my problems.

MISPLACED Early Spanish explorers encountered a hostile environment searching for gold in the Americas. [Does *searching for gold in the Americas* modify *explorers* or *environment*?]

CLEAR **Searching for gold in the Americas,** early Spanish explorers encountered a hostile environment.

Reference Note

For a discussion of the different kinds of **phrases,** see "Chapter 14: The Phrase." For information on **using commas to set off modifying phrases,** see page 704.

MISPLACED	You will need a crescent wrench to assemble the bookshelf.
	[Does *to assemble the bookshelf* modify *You* or *wrench*?]
CLEAR	**To assemble the bookshelf,** you will need a crescent wrench.

Exercise 7 Revising Sentences by Correcting Misplaced One-Word and Phrase Modifiers

The following sentences contain misplaced one-word and phrase modifiers. Revise each sentence so that its meaning is clear and correct.

EXAMPLE

    1. Our cat was waiting on the front porch for us to come home patiently.

    1. *Our cat was waiting patiently on the front porch for us to come home.*

1. Rosa Parks calmly refused to move to the back of the bus with quiet dignity.
2. I found a huge boulder taking a shortcut through the woods.
3. On one of his fruit trees, Mr. Tate noticed some caterpillars.
4. Our ancestors hunted deer, bison, and other large animals with weapons made of wood and stone.
5. Flying over the bridge, Missie spotted a blue heron.
6. We noticed several signs advertising the new theme park riding down the highway.
7. We could see corn growing from our car window.
8. Barking wildly and straining at the chain, the letter carrier was forced to retreat from the dog.
9. The softball team almost practices every afternoon.
10. He recounted an incident about a nuclear chain reaction during his chemistry lecture.
11. Pierre saw a Great Dane cycling through the park.
12. Tired from their hiking, we offered shelter to the backpackers.
13. Stress has almost caused all of his hair to turn gray.
14. She had a raincoat over her arm with a blue lining.
15. The two women hurried before the bus's departure to get a snack from the vending machine.
16. I have nearly read all of his books.
17. The boy ate all the yogurt with red sneakers.
18. Jan watched a deer sitting in a chair on the porch.
19. They listened to the symphony standing in the mezzanine of the auditorium.
20. Running, the course seemed very long to the athlete.

Reference Note

For a discussion of the different kinds of **clauses,** see Chapter 15. For information on **using commas to set off modifying clauses,** see page 704.

COMPUTER TIP

A spell-checker can easily find nonstandard forms such as *baddest, expensiver,* and *mostest.* However, you will need to examine placement of modifiers yourself.

Misplaced Clause Modifiers

Adjective and adverb clauses should be placed near the words they modify.

MISPLACED	Each player on the team will receive a trophy that wins the tournament.
CLEAR	Each player on the team **that wins the tournament** will receive a trophy.
MISPLACED	The bowl slipped off the table, which was full of gravy, and broke.
CLEAR	The bowl, **which was full of gravy,** slipped off the table and broke.
MISPLACED	The spelunkers saw many bats hanging upside down from their roosts while they were exploring the cave.
CLEAR	**While they were exploring the cave,** the spelunkers saw many bats hanging upside down from their roosts.
MISPLACED	Kirstie couldn't attend the farewell party for her nephew who was moving to El Paso because she was ill.
CLEAR	**Because she was ill,** Kirstie couldn't attend the farewell party for her nephew who was moving to El Paso.

> **Exercise 8** **Revising Sentences by Correcting Misplaced Clause Modifiers**

The following sentences contain misplaced clause modifiers. Revise each sentence so that its meaning is clear and correct.

EXAMPLE 1. Because he has allergies, Dr. Crane gives our pet beagle a shot once a month.

1. *Because our pet beagle has allergies, Dr. Crane gives him a shot once a month.*

1. I gave some of the baseball cards to my cousin that I had acquired over the years.
2. The plane landed safely on the runway that had the engine trouble.
3. That picture was hanging on the wall, which we bought in Canada.
4. They took the backpack to the manager's office, which appeared to be lost.
5. Jan showed the rooms to her visitors that she had painted.
6. That is a good plan for meeting the deadline next Friday that you have proposed.

7. She sang a song titled "On the Shore" at the talent show, which she had written herself.
8. I adopted a kitten at the animal shelter that needed a home.
9. I served dinner to a friend that I cooked myself.
10. The plate fell on the floor that was full of baked beans.

Review B **Correcting Dangling and Misplaced Modifiers**

The following sentences contain dangling and misplaced modifiers. Revise each sentence so that its meaning is clear and correct.

EXAMPLE
1. Hurrying, my books slipped out of my hands and fell down the stairs.

1. *As I was hurrying, my books slipped out of my hands and fell down the stairs.*

1. Caught in the net, escape was impossible.
2. Looking through the telescope, the moon seemed enormous.
3. While out running, his mouth got dry.
4. The ocean came into view going around the bend.
5. Doing a few tap-dance steps, the wooden floor got scratched.
6. Built on a steep hillside overlooking the sea, we found the ocean view breathtaking.
7. I mentioned the book to my sister Roseanne that I recently read.
8. After finishing the housework, the room almost sparkled.
9. To make manicotti, pasta is stuffed with ricotta cheese.
10. Glenda sang a song about finding true love in a high, clear voice.
11. Looking at her passport, there was no visa stamp.
12. Running up and down the bungalow walls, she saw dozens of mice.
13. While standing in front of the fun-house mirror, her reflection was tall and thin.
14. Painted, we thought the house looked much better.
15. Singing in the shower, the hot water ran out.
16. Reaching for the telephone, the books toppled and fell to the floor.
17. Lauren told the interviewer about the time she performed for the president when she was interviewed.
18. While driving to work, the radio broke.
19. Songbirds have been coming to the birdfeeders, which migrate this time of year.
20. Sitting in the freezer, she saw two kinds of frozen yogurt.

┌HELP─┐

In Review C,
you may need to rearrange
or add words to make the
meaning clear.

Review C **Correcting Errors in the Use of Modifiers**

Most of the sentences in the following paragraph contain at least one error in the use of modifiers. Revise each sentence according to the rules of standard, formal English. If a sentence is already correct, write *C*.

EXAMPLE **[1]** Egyptian priests inscribed a decree on a black stone honoring Ptolemy V, a king of Egypt (203–181 B.C.).

1. *Egyptian priests inscribed on a black stone a decree honoring Ptolemy V, a king of Egypt (203–181 B.C.).*

[**1**] Much about life in ancient Egypt before the 1800s was unknown because nobody could read Egyptian hieroglyphics. [**2**] Then, this black stone found in the Nile Delta gave Egyptology the most publicity than it had ever had before. [**3**] Found in 1799 near a village called Rosetta, archaeologists called the slab the Rosetta Stone. [**4**] The slab was inscribed with three bands across its polished surface of writing, each in a different language: hieroglyphics on the top, another unknown language in the middle, and Greek on the bottom. [**5**] Scholars could read the Greek writing, which stated that each of the three bands contained the same decree in honor of Ptolemy V. [**6**] Full of excitement, it was hoped by archaeologists that they could use the Greek part to decipher the hieroglyphics. [**7**] Progress in translating the individual hieroglyphics, however, went real slowly. [**8**] It had been thought that each of the symbols stood for a whole word until this time. [**9**] However, a French scholar working on the Rosetta Stone named Jean François Champollion wondered why it took more hieroglyphic symbols than Greek words to write the same message. [**10**] He correctly guessed that certain symbols stand for parts of words, and after working hard for twenty years, many of the signs were proved to stand for sounds.

Chapter Review

A. Correcting Errors in the Use of the Comparative and Superlative Forms

Each of the following sentences contains an error in the use of modifiers. Identify each error, and then write the correct form.

1. I was more hungrier than I thought, so I ate three plums.
2. He was the more able and intelligent of the three job applicants.
3. Was Hitler notoriouser than Stalin?
4. John, Richard's twin brother, was the oldest by three minutes.
5. After Diego had started lifting weights, he bragged that he was stronger than anyone in town.
6. People who live along this road complain because it is the worse road in the entire township.
7. Both Floyd and his brother are landscape designers who are in demand throughout the state, but Floyd is best known in this area.
8. After the band practiced, it sounded more better.
9. When I had a choice of strawberry or vanilla, I took vanilla because I liked it best.
10. Looking across the water at sunset, you can see the beautifullest view you can imagine.

B. Revising Sentences by Correcting Dangling and Misplaced Modifiers

Each of the following sentences contains a dangling or misplaced modifier. Write each sentence, arranging the words so that the meaning is logical and clear.

11. Yipping and running in circles, they saw that the dogs could herd the sheep into the pen.
12. The winners marched off the platform carrying trophies.
13. A police officer warned students who drive too fast about accidents during the defensive-driving class.
14. After escaping from slavery, the importance of education was often stressed by Frederick Douglass.
15. We went to visit my grandmother, who used to be a history teacher at my school yesterday.

┌─ **HELP** ─
In Part B of the Chapter Review, you may have to add or delete some words. Be sure to use commas where they are needed to set off the introductory and interrupting modifiers.

USAGE

16. Climbing the stairs, his glasses fell off.
17. Maria took a close-up photograph of a lion with a telephoto lens.
18. Nesting in a tree outside my window, I see a small bird.
19. A young woman knocked on the door wearing a suit and hat.
20. Walking in the sunshine, it felt warm to us.

C. Revising Sentences by Correcting Unclear Comparisons and Incorrect, Misplaced, and Dangling Modifiers

Most of the following sentences contain an unclear comparison, an incorrect form of a modifier, a misplaced modifier, or a dangling modifier. Write each sentence, correcting the error. If a sentence is already correct, write *C*.

21. Seeing that no damage had been done, their cars drove away in opposite directions.
22. Working long hours and taking few vacations, the success that he had longed for came to him after many years.
23. The temperature in Houston is higher than Chicago.
24. Looking through a telescope, the Cliffs of Dover came into view.
25. The branches of the tree hung over the fence that we planted.
26. Walking very careful over the uneven cobblestones, the elderly woman made her way from one end of the lane to the other.
27. The gift was more costlier than I had expected it to be.
28. The glass fell onto the floor, which was full of cranberry juice.
29. Balking, I quickly grew frustrated with the mule.
30. Michael hoped that his time on the sprint was faster than Patrick.

Writing Application
Using Comparison in a Consumer Guide

Comparative and Superlative Degrees You and your sister Charlotte plan to buy a piece of audio equipment together. You have found a magazine article comparing several brands and showing the information in a big table. However, because Charlotte is visually impaired, the table can't help her decide. She asks you to narrow the choices to four brands, and then to write and record on audiotape a short comparison of their prices and features.

Prewriting Find a magazine article that contains a table comparing different kinds of audio equipment. Study the table, and list the features that you think would be most important. Then, choose four products that seem acceptable, and jot down some comparisons.

Writing As you write your first draft, carefully select comparative and superlative modifiers so that your explanation is not confusing. Tell why you would eliminate certain models from consideration. Include each of the degrees of comparison: positive, comparative, and superlative.

Revising Ask a classmate to evaluate the clarity of your comparison. Add or revise details of the comparison to eliminate confusion.

Publishing Using your textbook, check to be sure that you have used adjectives and adverbs correctly. Proofread your comparison for any errors in grammar, usage, and punctuation. Post the completed paragraphs on the class bulletin board or Web page, or you may want to collect them and bind them in a booklet titled *An Audio Equipment Consumer Guide.*

USAGE

20

A Glossary of Usage
Common Usage Problems

Diagnostic Preview

A. Revising Errors in Usage

In each of the following sets of word groups, one word group contains an error in the use of standard, formal English. Identify the word group that contains an error, and then write the word group correctly.

EXAMPLE   1. a. Her speech implies that a change is needed.
                b. Leave me have some oranges, too.
                c. This house is somewhat larger than our old one.

                1. b. *Let me have some oranges, too.*

1. **a.** wasn't no reason
   b. words had no effect
   c. can hardly wait

2. **a.** families that emigrated to New Zealand
   b. sail as far as the channel marker
   c. made allusions to classical literature

3. **a.** being that he was alone
   b. when the people accepted new ways
   c. the woman who was elected

4. **a.** what kind of frog
   b. overtime besides the regular work
   c. an hypnotic speaker

5. a. saw on TV that our team had won
   b. Lee Haney proudly excepted his Mr. Olympia trophy.
   c. the house beside the highway

6. a. that he is doing alright
   b. Let him have his own way.
   c. Leave the door open when you go.

7. a. Teach your dog this trick.
   b. I'm feeling kind of ill.
   c. might have been too late

8. a. Simira is taller than her sister.
   b. Dough will rise in a warm place.
   c. We read where the damage was extensive.

9. a. Try to be on time.
   b. They walked a long way.
   c. Them stairs are dangerous and need repairs.

10. a. The bag burst, spilling the rice.
   b. The Polynesian alphabet has less characters than the English alphabet does.
   c. Take those books off that shelf.

B. Proofreading Paragraphs to Correct Usage Errors

Revise each of the sentences in the following paragraphs to correct the error in the use of standard, formal English.

EXAMPLE   **[1]** The last time I visited my aunt and uncle in Florida, they told me about a interesting town.

   1. *The last time I visited my aunt and uncle in Florida, they told me about an interesting town.*

   [11] After the Civil War ended, Joseph E. Clarke decided that African Americans had ought to start a town of their own. [12] He wanted to build such a town, but no one would sell or donate land for this kind of an endeavor. [13] However, Joseph Clarke was a man who had great determination, and he wasn't hardly going to give up hope. [14] Finally, in 1877, with money what was donated by a New York philanthropist and with land offered by a Floridian named Josiah Eaton, Clarke obtained the first twelve acres of what would become Eatonville, Florida. [15] Eatonville, located just beside Orlando, is recognized as the oldest incorporated African American town anywheres in the United

States. [16] This here community has always been populated and governed entirely by black people. [17] The African Americans which flocked to Eatonville built homes, churches, and schools, and they cultivated gardens and orange groves. [18] The residents didn't lose no time in establishing a library, a post office, and a newspaper. [19] Today, after more than a hundred years of self-government, the citizens of Eatonville continue to feel the affects of Joseph Clarke's courage and vision. [20] With its light industry, new businesses, and booming real estate development, Eatonville enjoys economic growth, just like the rest of central Florida does.

Reference Note

For a list of **words often confused,** see page 793. Use the **index** at the back of the book to find information about other usage problems.

About the Glossary

This chapter provides a compact glossary of common problems in English usage. A *glossary* is an alphabetical list of special terms or expressions with definitions, explanations, and examples. You will notice that some examples in this glossary are labeled *nonstandard, standard, formal,* or *informal.*

The label ***nonstandard*** identifies usage that is suitable only in the most casual speaking situations and in writing that attempts to re-create casual speech. ***Standard*** English is language that is grammatically correct and appropriate in formal and informal situations. ***Formal*** identifies standard usage that is appropriate in serious speaking and writing situations (such as in speeches and in compositions for school). The label ***informal*** indicates standard usage common in conversation and in everyday writing such as personal letters. In doing the exercises in this chapter, be sure to use only standard English.

Formal	Informal
angry	steamed
unpleasant	yucky
agreeable	cool
very impressive	totally awesome
accelerate	step on it

Reference Note

For more information about **articles,** see page 412.

a, an   Each of these words, called an ***indefinite article,*** refers to a member of a general group. Use *a* before words beginning with a consonant sound; use *an* before words beginning with a vowel sound.

USAGE

EXAMPLES   In ancient Greece and Rome, **a** person would go to see **an** oracle to consult the gods.

Did Jimmy Lee have to buy **a** uniform for his new job? [*A* is used before *uniform* because *uniform* begins with a consonant sound.]

Several of the tourists searched for **a** hotel for more than **an** hour. [*A* is used before *hotel* because *hotel* begins with a consonant sound. *An* is used before *hour* because *hour* begins with a vowel sound.]

accept, except   *Accept* is a verb that means "to receive." *Except* may be either a verb or a preposition. As a verb, *except* means "to leave out." As a preposition, *except* means "excluding."

EXAMPLES   Gary did not **accept** the bribe.

Students who were absent last week will be **excepted** from the group of students taking today's test.

Everybody **except** me knew the answer.

affect, effect   *Affect* is generally used as a verb meaning "to influence." *Effect* used as a verb means "to accomplish" or "to bring about." Used as a noun, *effect* means "the result of some action."

EXAMPLES   Working part time did not seem to **affect** his study habits.

Did the medicine **effect** a cure?

Coach Cortez said that the weather had little **effect** on the teams' performances.

ain't   *Ain't* is nonstandard. Avoid using *ain't* in formal speaking and in all writing other than dialogue.

EXAMPLES   These **aren't** [not *ain't*] my shoes.

Chris **isn't** [not *ain't*] going to the concert.

all ready, already   See page 793.

all right   *All right* means "satisfactory"; "unhurt, safe"; "correct"; or, when used in reply to a question or to introduce a remark, "yes." Although the spelling *alright* is sometimes used, it has not become accepted as standard usage.

EXAMPLES   The storm is over, and everyone is **all right**.

All right, I'll call you later.

Reference Note

For more about **verbs,** see page 417. For more about **prepositions,** see page 426.

USAGE

all the farther, all the faster   These expressions are used informally in some parts of the United States. In formal situations, use *as far as* and *as fast as*.

INFORMAL   This is all the farther we can go.
FORMAL   This is **as far as** we can go.

allusion, illusion   An *allusion* is an indirect reference to something. An *illusion* is a mistaken idea or a misleading appearance.

EXAMPLES   The poem's title is an **allusion** to a Hopi folk tale.

The documentary shattered viewers' **illusions** about migrant workers.

The magician was a master of **illusion.**

a lot   Write the expression *a lot* as two words. *A lot* is often used informally as a noun meaning "a large number or amount" or as an adverb meaning "a great deal" or "very much."

INFORMAL   A lot of critics have praised the film.
FORMAL   **A large number** of critics have praised the film.

INFORMAL   Our guests arrived a lot earlier than we had expected.
FORMAL   Our guests arrived **much** earlier than we had expected.

among   See **between, among.**

and etc.   *Etc.* is the abbreviation of the Latin words *et cetera,* meaning "and others" or "and so forth." Therefore, *and* should not be used before *etc.*

EXAMPLE   I earn money by baby-sitting, running errands, mowing lawns, **etc.** [not *and etc.*]

anyways, anywheres, everywheres, nowheres, somewheres   Use these words without an *s* at the end.

EXAMPLE   **Anywhere** [not *Anywheres*] you travel, you see the same hotel chains.

as   See **like, as, as if, as though.**

as if, as though   See **like, as, as if, as though.**

at   Do not use *at* after *where.*

NONSTANDARD   Where did you see them at?
STANDARD   Where did you see them?

a while, awhile   The noun *while,* often preceded by the article *a,* means "a period of time." *Awhile* is an adverb meaning "for a short period of time."

EXAMPLES   I haven't heard from my pen pal for **a while.**

I usually read **awhile** before going to bed.

bad, badly   See page 617.

barely   See **The Double Negative** (page 656).

because   In formal situations, do not use the construction *reason . . . because.* Instead use *reason . . . that.*

INFORMAL   The reason we are holding the fund-raiser is because we want to buy new band uniforms.

FORMAL   The **reason** we are holding the fund-raiser is **that** we want to buy new band uniforms.

The sentence may also be revised without the use of *the reason.*

FORMAL   We are holding the fund-raiser because we want to buy new band uniforms.

being as, being that   Use *because* or *since* instead of these expressions.

NONSTANDARD   Being as her grades were so good, she got a scholarship.
STANDARD   **Because** her grades were so good, she got a scholarship.

NONSTANDARD   Being that he was late, he had to stand.
STANDARD   **Since** he was late, he had to stand.

beside, besides   *Beside* is a preposition meaning "by the side of." *Besides* as a preposition means "in addition to." As an adverb, *besides* means "moreover."

EXAMPLES   He glanced at the person **beside** him.

Did anybody **besides** you see what happened?

I liked the sweater; **besides,** I needed a new one.

between, among   Use *between* when referring to two things at a time, even if they are part of a larger group.

EXAMPLES   A strong bond exists **between** the twins.

I paused **between** chapters. [Although there are more than two chapters, I paused only between any two of them.]

Reference Note

For more about **nouns,** see page 405. For more about **adverbs,** see page 422.

USAGE

COMPUTER TIP

The spellchecker on a computer will catch misspelled words such as *anywheres* and *nowheres*. The grammar checker may catch errors such as double negatives. However, in the case of words often confused, such as *than* and *then* and *between* and *among*, you will need to check your work yourself for correct usage.

Use *among* when referring to all members of a group rather than to separate individuals in the group.

EXAMPLES   We distributed the pamphlets **among** the crowd.

There was some disagreement **among** the editorial staff.

borrow, lend, loan   The verb *borrow* means "to take [something] temporarily." The verb *lend* means "to give [something] temporarily."

EXAMPLES   May I **borrow** your binoculars?

I'll be glad to **lend** you my binoculars.

Loan, a noun in formal English, is sometimes used in place of the verb *lend* in informal situations.

INFORMAL   Will you **loan** me your umbrella?
FORMAL   Will you **lend** me your umbrella?

bring, take   *Bring* means "to come carrying something." *Take* means "to go away carrying something." Think of *bring* as related to *come* and *take* as related to *go.*

EXAMPLES   **Bring** your radio when you come over tomorrow.

Don't forget to **take** your coat when you go.

bust, busted   Avoid using these words as verbs. Instead, use a form of *break* or *burst* or *catch* or *arrest.*

EXAMPLES   I **broke** [not *busted*] the switch on the stereo.

The water main **burst** [not *busted*].

Did the police **arrest** [not *bust*] the suspects?

but, only   See **The Double Negative** (page 656).

Exercise 1 Identifying Standard Usage

For each of the following sentences, choose the correct word from the pair given in parentheses.

EXAMPLE   **1.** They stood there for (*a while, awhile*), gazing at the clear night sky.
    1. a while

1. The tasks were divided evenly (*among, between*) the two scouts.
2. The audience was deeply (*affected, effected*) by Simon Estes's powerful baritone voice.

USAGE

3. We were afraid the bull had (*busted, broken*) loose.

4. No one (*accept, except*) the sophomores will attend.

5. Please (*bring, take*) these papers when you leave.

6. Penicillin has had a profound (*affect, effect*) on modern medicine.

7. I couldn't find the cat (*anywhere, anywheres*).

8. Uncle Joe said that the crosslike rays radiating from the moon were an (*allusion, illusion*) caused by the screen door.

9. (*Beside, Besides*) Julie and Zack, who else has signed up for Saturday's 10K walk?

10. In his remarks about Dr. King, the speaker last night made an (*allusion, illusion*) to Gandhi, whose nonviolent protests paved the way for the civil rights movement in the United States.

Exercise 2 **Proofreading to Correct Usage Errors**

Revise each of the following sentences by correcting the error or errors in usage. If a sentence is already correct, write *C*.

EXAMPLE   **1.** Where was Frank Matsura's photography studio at?

        1. Where was Frank Matsura's photography studio?

1. In 1903, this young Japanese artist, Frank Matsura, arrived somewhere in the backwoods settlement of Conconully, Washington.

2. This was all the farther he would go, for he lived in or near this rough frontier settlement for the remaining ten years of his life.

3. When he came to town, Matsura was wearing a elegant formal suit and was carrying bulky camera equipment he had taken with him.

4. Back in Seattle, Matsura had excepted a job in Conconully as a helper and laundryman at the Elliott Hotel.

5. Soon he was living in a tiny room behind the kitchen and performing his menial job with alot of energy and cheer.

6. When he was off duty, he carried his camera everywheres he went, photographing the area's people, scenery, events, and etc.

7. After a while, he settled in nearby Okanogan and opened a small studio.

8. Being as Matsura was a warm, extroverted person, he made many friends between settlers and American Indians alike.

9. Oddly, though, he never told anyone about his past, even after he had lived there a while.

10. To this day, nobody knows who he really was, where he was born at, or why he chose to live and die so far from his home.

can, may   Use *can* to express ability. Use *may* to express possibility.

EXAMPLES   Do you think you **can** repair this camera?

Ethan has said that he **may** run for class president.

To express permission in formal situations, use *may*, not *can*.

INFORMAL   Can I sit here?

FORMAL   **May** I sit here?

can't hardly, can't scarcely   See **The Double Negative** (page 656).

could of   Do not use *of* in place of *have* after verbs such as *could, should, would, might, must,* and *ought.*

EXAMPLE   Muriel **could have** [not *could of*] gone with us.

discover, invent   *Discover* means "to find, see, or learn about something that already exists." *Invent* means "to be the first to make or do something."

EXAMPLES   Luis W. Alvarez **discovered** many subatomic particles.

Sarah Boone **invented** the ironing board.

Reference Note

For more information about **contractions,** see page 763.

don't, doesn't   *Don't* is the contraction of *do not. Doesn't* is the contraction of *does not.* Use *doesn't,* not *don't,* with singular subjects except *I* and *you.*

EXAMPLES   It **doesn't** [not *don't*] matter to me.

The poem **doesn't** [not *don't*] rhyme.

effect   See **affect, effect.**

emigrate, immigrate   *Emigrate* means "to leave a country to settle elsewhere." *Immigrate* means "to come into a country to settle there."

EXAMPLES   My great-grandfather **emigrated** from Mexico.

Much of Australia's population is composed of people who **immigrated** there in recent centuries.

everywheres   See **anyways,** etc.

except   See **accept, except.**

fewer, less   *Fewer* is used with plural nouns. It tells "how many." *Less* is used with singular nouns. It tells "how much."

EXAMPLES   There are **fewer** whales than there once were.

   We should have bought **less** meat and more vegetables.

good, well   See page 617.

had of   Do not use *had of* for *had.*

EXAMPLE   If I **had** [not *had of*] known that you wanted to read Forrest Carter's *The Education of Little Tree,* I would have lent you my copy.

had ought, hadn't ought   Do not use *had* or *hadn't* with *ought.*

NONSTANDARD   You hadn't ought to say such things.
STANDARD   You **ought** not to say such things.
STANDARD   You **shouldn't** say such things.

NONSTANDARD   They had ought to have left earlier.
STANDARD   They **ought** to have left earlier.
STANDARD   They **should** have left earlier.

hardly   See **The Double Negative** (page 656).

he, she, it, they   Do not use a pronoun along with its antecedent as the subject of a verb. Such an error is called the **double subject.**

NONSTANDARD   My father he works downtown.
STANDARD   My **father works** downtown.

hisself, theirself, theirselves   These words are nonstandard. Use *himself* instead of *hisself,* and use *themselves* instead of *theirself* or *theirselves.*

EXAMPLES   My uncle considers **himself** [not *hisself*] an average golfer.

   The members of the Ecology Club should be very proud of **themselves** [not *theirself* or *theirselves*].

hopefully   *Hopefully* is an adverb meaning "in a hopeful manner." In formal situations, avoid using *hopefully* for an expression such as *I hope* or *it is hoped.*

Reference Note
For more information about **pronouns,** see page 408.

INFORMAL	Hopefully, Gloria Estefan's next concert tour will include a performance in our city.
FORMAL	**I hope** Gloria Estefan's next concert tour will include a performance in our city.
FORMAL	We listened **hopefully** as the disc jockey gave the details of Gloria Estefan's next concert tour.

illusion   See **allusion, illusion.**

immigrate   See **emigrate, immigrate.**

imply, infer   *Imply* means "to suggest." *Infer* means "to interpret" or "to draw as a conclusion."

EXAMPLES   In her speech, the candidate **implied** that she is for tax reform.

From the candidate's speech, I **inferred** that she is for tax reform.

invent   See **discover, invent.**

it's, its   See page 796.

Exercise 3   **Identifying Standard Usage**

For each of the following sentences, choose the correct word from the pair given in parentheses.

EXAMPLE   **1.** (*Gary Soto, Gary Soto he*) is my favorite writer.

1. *Gary Soto*

1. Did he say that he had painted the mural (*himself, hisself*)?
2. From his letter, I (*implied, inferred*) he would be away all summer.
3. He (*don't, doesn't*) always say what he means.
4. (*Emigration, Immigration*) to Alaska was spurred by the gold rush.
5. The heat has affected the growing season; we'll harvest (*fewer, less*) olives this year.
6. You could (*have, of*) borrowed some paper and a pencil from me.
7. As beasts of burden, dogs served the Comanches (*good, well*), often pulling a travois laden with more than forty pounds of baggage.
8. Mary Beth Stearns (*discovered, invented*) a technique for studying electrons.
9. Many French Canadians (*emigrated, immigrated*) from Quebec to work in the industries of New England.
10. Audrey must (*have, of*) taken my jacket by mistake.

Revise the following sentences to correct each error in the use of standard, formal English. If a sentence is already correct, write *C*.

EXAMPLE
    1. Hopefully, the ambigrams shown here will motivate you to create similar designs.

    1. I hope the ambigrams shown here will motivate you to create similar designs.

1. A scientist, philosopher, and writer, Douglas R. Hofstadter he enjoys creating symmetrical designs from written words.

2. He and a friend discovered a new pastime; the resulting designs are called ambigrams.

3. Not every word lends itself to this method, but you might be surprised at how many words can be made into ambigrams.

4. As you might of known already, a *palindrome* is a word or expression that has the same letters in the same sequence both forward and backward—for example, *toot* or *Madam, I'm Adam.*

5. I don't mean to infer, though, that an ambigram has to be a palindrome—an ambigram simply has to look symmetrical.

6. Usually, ambigrams they can't be formed unless you tinker with the letter shapes and connect them in new ways.

7. You had ought to start with a word that has six letters or fewer.

8. For some good ideas, you may want to look below at the ambigrams for the words *Jamal, Steve, Chris, Felix, Wendy, Mexico,* and *dance.*

9. Don't forget that you can mix cursive, printed, capital, and lowercase letters to create affects like the ones in these ambigrams.

10. If you become stumped, you might find that you could of succeeded by adding some decorative flourishes.

USAGE

kind of, sort of   In formal situations, avoid using either of these expressions for the adverb *rather* or *somewhat*.

INFORMAL   The waves were sort of rough.

FORMAL   The waves were **rather** [or *somewhat*] rough.

kind of a(n), sort of a(n)   In formal situations, omit the *a* or *an*.

EXAMPLE   This bolt takes a special **kind of** [not *kind of a*] nut.

kinds, sorts, types   With the singular form of each of these words, use *this* or *that*. With the plural form, use *these* or *those*.

EXAMPLE   I know more about **that kind** of music than about any of **those** other **kinds.**

learn, teach   *Learn* means "to gain knowledge." *Teach* means "to provide with knowledge."

EXAMPLES   She **learned** how to saddle a horse.

The stable owner **taught** her how.

leave, let   *Leave* means "to go away." *Let* means "to allow" or "to permit." Avoid using *leave* for *let*.

EXAMPLES   We had to **leave** early to catch the plane.

Let [not *Leave*] them go first.

We **let** [not *left*] the trapped bird go free.

less   See **fewer, less.**

lie, lay   See page 582.

like, as, as if, as though   In formal situations, do not use the preposition *like* for the conjunction *as, as if,* or *as though* to introduce a subordinate clause.

INFORMAL   This animal sheds its skin like a snake does.

FORMAL   This animal sheds its skin **as** a snake does.

INFORMAL   This looks like it might be the right place.

FORMAL   This looks **as if** [or *as though*] it might be the right place.

might of, must of   See **could of.**

neither, never, no, nobody, no one, not (–n't), nothing, nowhere   See **The Double Negative** (page 656).

Reference Note

For more information about **subordinate clauses,** see Chapter 15. For more about **conjunctions,** see page 428.

nowheres   See **anyways,** etc.

a number of, the number of   *A number of* is generally plural and *the number of* is generally singular. Make sure that the verb agrees with the subject.

EXAMPLES   **A number of** job positions **are** open.

The number of job positions **is** limited.

of   See **could of.**

of   Do not use the preposition *of* after other prepositions such as *inside, off,* and *outside.*

EXAMPLES   The diver jumped **off** [not *off of*] the board.

Outside [not *Outside of*] the building was a patio.

off, off of   Do not use *off* or *off of* in place of *from.*

NONSTANDARD   Here's the money I borrowed off of you.

STANDARD   Here's the money I borrowed **from** you.

only   See **The Double Negative** (page 656).

ought to of   See **could of.**

> **Exercise 5**   **Identifying Standard Usage**

For each of the following sentences, choose from the choices given in parentheses the word or expression that is correct according to the rules of standard, formal English.

EXAMPLE   **1.** Who (*learned, taught*) you how to play mah-jongg?

1. *taught*

1. The total length of the Great Wall of China is about 4,000 miles, if branches (*off, off of*) the main wall are included.
2. Carlos was (*outside, outside of*) the house.
3. We went to the hardware store for a special (*kind of, kind of a*) wrench.
4. Rachel Carson's books (*learned, taught*) me to care about ecology.
5. (*Leave, Let*) us listen without any interruptions.
6. How many pamphlets did you get (*from, off of*) the sales representative?
7. Why did she feel (*like, as if*) she'd said something wrong?
8. T. J. said the number of unclaimed prizes (*was, were*) surprising.

9. Why didn't the U.S. government (*leave, let*) the Cherokee people stay in their Southeast homelands?
10. They didn't want to take the boat out because the waves looked (*kind of, rather*) choppy.

┌HELP─
Some sentences in Exercise 6 contain more than one error.

Exercise 6 Proofreading to Correct Usage Errors

Revise each of the following sentences by correcting the error or errors in the use of formal, standard English. If a sentence is already correct, write *C*.

EXAMPLE
1. My mother once tried to learn me how to do fancy needlework.

1. *My mother once tried to teach me how to do fancy needlework.*

1. Until recent times, most young girls learned to do fancy needlework.
2. Beginning when a girl was kind of young, her mother or another woman would learn her many embroidery stitches.
3. Then, at the age of nine or ten, the girl would be given the task of making a sampler like the one shown here, using every kind of a stitch she knew.
4. Usually, the girl's parents wouldn't leave her be idle.
5. She had to work on the sampler every day like her life depended on it!
6. When the sampler was finished, it didn't lie inside of a drawer.

7. Instead, it was left on display to show that the girl was industrious and well educated in homemaking skills.
8. Many people think these sort of sampler must have been popular in America and nowhere else.
9. However, a number of countries in Europe, Asia, and Africa have prized this kind of a needlework exercise for centuries.
10. Today, American girls aren't judged by their stitchery like they once were, and some never learn anything about needlework.

reason . . . because   See **because.**

rise, raise   See page 588.

scarcely   See **The Double Negative** (page 656).

she   See **he, she, it, they.**

should of   See **could of.**

sit, set   See page 585.

some, somewhat   In formal situations, avoid using *some* as an adverb meaning "to some extent." Use *somewhat.*

INFORMAL   This medicine should help your cough some.
  FORMAL   This medicine should help your cough **somewhat.**

somewheres   See **anyways,** etc.

sort of   See **kind of, sort of.**

sort of a   See **kind of a(n), sort of a(n).**

sorts   See **kinds, sorts, types.**

suppose to, supposed to   To express an intention or plan, use the verb form *supposed* before an infinitive.

EXAMPLE   We were **supposed to** [not *suppose to*] meet Wendy at eight o'clock.

Reference Note
For more information about **infinitives,** see page 479.

take, bring   See **bring, take.**

teach   See **learn, teach.**

than, then   *Than* is a subordinating conjunction used in comparisons. *Then* is an adverb meaning "at that time" or "next."

EXAMPLES   She is younger **than** you are.

            I swept the floor; **then** I emptied the trash.

Reference Note
For more information about **subordinating conjunctions,** see page 498.

USAGE

that See **who, which, that.**

their, there, they're See page 799.

theirself, theirselves See **hisself, theirself, theirselves.**

them Do not use *them* as an adjective. Use *those* instead.

EXAMPLE   It's one of **those** [not *them*] fancy show dogs.

they See **he, she, it, they.**

this here, that there Avoid using *here* or *there* after *this* or *that*.

EXAMPLE   Let's rent **this** [not *this here*] movie instead of **that** [not *that there*] one.

try and, try to Use *try to,* not *try and.*

EXAMPLE   When you're at bat, you must **try to** [not *try and*] relax.

types See **kinds, sorts, types.**

unless See **without, unless.**

use to, used to Do not leave off the *d* when you write *used to.*

EXAMPLE   Alicia **used to** [not *use to*] take tae kwon do lessons.

way, ways Use *way,* not *ways,* when referring to a distance.

EXAMPLE   She lives quite a **way** [not *ways*] from here.

well See page 617.

what Do not use *what* in place of *that* to introduce an adjective clause.

EXAMPLE   This is the book **that** [not *what*] I told you about.

when, where Do not use *when* or *where* incorrectly to begin a definition.

NONSTANDARD   *SRO* is when tickets for all the seats have been sold, leaving standing room only.

STANDARD   *SRO* means that tickets for all the seats have been sold, leaving standing room only.

STANDARD   *SRO* is the abbreviation for *standing room only;* it means that tickets for all the seats have been sold.

where Do not use *where* for *that.*

EXAMPLE   I read **that** [not *where*] the word *bayou* comes from the Choctaw word *bayuk,* meaning "small stream."

Reference Note

For more information about **adjective clauses,** see page 495.

where . . . at   See **at.**

who, which, that   *Who* refers to people only. *Which* refers to things only. *That* refers to either people or things.

EXAMPLES   Carlotta, **who** is a sophomore, won the gold medal.

Her medal, **which** is actually gold-plated, is quite heavy.

Carlotta is the runner **that** [or *who*] won the gold medal.

This medal is not the first one **that** she has won.

who, whom   See page 558.

who's, whose   See page 800.

without, unless   Do not use the preposition *without* in place of the conjunction *unless* to introduce a subordinate clause.

EXAMPLE   I can't use the car **unless** [not *without*] I ask Mom.

would of   See **could of.**

your, you're   See page 800.

> ### Exercise 7   Revising Errors in Usage

Revise each of the following sentences to correct the error in usage.

EXAMPLE   **1.** I am use to the noise.

1. I am used to the noise.

1. A solar eclipse is when the moon comes between the earth and the sun and blocks the light.
2. The workers which put up that new office building certainly finished it quickly.
3. Ronald E. McNair was aboard the space shuttle what exploded in January 1986.
4. Was the senator suppose to arrive this morning?
5. A run-on sentence is where two sentences are erroneously joined as a single sentence.
6. As soon as the rain lets up some, we'll leave.
7. Them mosquitoes can drive a person nearly crazy.
8. Antonio Freeman carried the ball a long ways down the field before he was tackled.
9. I think I read in the paper where Amy Tan has a new novel coming out next month.
10. I'm tired of trying to cut the grass with this here old lawn mower, which should be in an antique exhibit.

Review A Identifying Standard Usage

For each of the following sentences, choose the correct word or word group from the choices given in parentheses.

EXAMPLE 1. If it (*don't, doesn't*) rain tonight, we'll start harvesting the crop tomorrow.

1. *doesn't*

1. Thanks to modern medicine, there are (*fewer, less*) cases of tetanus and diphtheria nowadays.
2. I tried to (*learn, teach*) my dog to do tricks, but he just sat and stared at me.
3. I see (*where, that*) pandas are an endangered species.
4. Cape Porpoise is (*somewhere, somewheres*) near Portsmouth.
5. Priscilla wrote a longer paper (*than, then*) Tammy did.
6. To make American Indian fry bread, you need flour, baking powder, salt, (*and etc., etc.*)
7. We (*hadn't ought, ought not*) to decide until we are certain of all the facts.
8. Amy couldn't see the screen (*without, unless*) I took off my hat.
9. Someone must (*of, have*) left the door unlocked.
10. Lewis Latimer (*discovered, invented*) an improved filament for the earliest electric light bulbs.

Review B Identifying Standard Usage

For each of the following sentences, choose from the choices given in parentheses the word or word group that is correct according to the rules of formal, standard English.

EXAMPLE 1. The rear-view mirror fell (*off, off of*) Ted's bike.

1. *off*

1. Stevie Wonder has written a number of hit songs since the 1960s, and he (*don't, doesn't*) look (*as if, like*) he's ever going to stop.
2. (*Inside, Inside of*) the box was (*a, an*) heap of glittering gems.
3. May I (*imply, infer*) from your yawns that you are bored?
4. My great-grandmother (*emigrated, immigrated*) from Italy when she was a young woman.
5. (*Beside, Besides*) speaking Spanish, Vera can speak a little Portuguese.
6. Linda (*doesn't, don't*) enjoy doing (*them, those, that*) sort of exercise.
7. Ahead of us on the desert, a lake seemed to sparkle, but it was only an (*allusion, illusion*).

8. This prolonged water shortage will (*affect, effect*) the whole state (*accept, except*) for two counties.

9. I don't think my parents will (*leave, let*) me borrow the car in this kind of weather.

10. Because of the indiscriminate slaughter, each year there were (*fewer, less*) bison.

11. When Wilmer is very tired, he (*don't, doesn't*) talk much.

12. The disagreement (*between, among*) the two friends caused a number of problems.

13. When he goes to the next potluck dinner, he will (*bring, take*) potato salad.

14. We saw several puffins, eight sea lions, a humpback whale, and (*a, an*) eagle while we were on a daylong Alaskan cruise.

15. I felt as if I (*could have, could of*) run forever.

16. The mayor (*which, who*) used to wear running clothes has been reelected.

17. (*Them, Those*) Asian currencies are rising rapidly in value.

18. Rick wanted to (*try and, try to*) complete a painting each week.

19. The weary explorers traveled quite a (*way, ways*) during their three-week journey.

20. Did you read (*where, that*) the space shuttle someday may be going to the moon?

Review C **Proofreading a Paragraph to Correct Usage Errors**

Revise each of the sentences in the following paragraph by correcting the error or errors in the use of formal, standard English. If a sentence is already correct, write *C*.

EXAMPLE   [1] Sequoyah was the person which devised the Cherokee alphabet.

        1. *Sequoyah was the person who devised the Cherokee alphabet.*

[1] Imagine single-handedly discovering a system for writing a language that had never before been written! [2] In about 1809, the Cherokee scholar Sequoyah became aware of "talking leaves," the written pages that were used by white people to communicate with one another. [3] Being that Sequoyah he felt that the ability to write had greatly helped white people, he decided he had ought to create a similar system for his people. [4] Instead of making up an alphabet like the one used in English, he chose to create this here syllabary. [5] Each

The Granger Collection, New York

character in Sequoyah's syllabary stands for one of the eighty-five syllables what are used in speaking Cherokee. [6] Sequoyah copied some letters from a English book, but in his system they have different meanings. [7] During the twelve years that it took Sequoyah to complete his writing system, he was ridiculed by many Cherokees who thought his efforts were kind of foolish. [8] However, after the syllabary was finished and accepted by most Cherokees, they realized they should not of scoffed. [9] After a while, thousands learned how to read and write, and soon books and newspapers were being printed in Cherokee. [10] Sequoyah was honored by his people for learning them to read and write, and his writing method is still used today.

The Double Negative

A *double negative* is the use of two or more negative words to express a single negative idea. Before the 1700s, two or more negatives were often used in the same sentence for emphasis. In English, this usage is no longer considered correct, and a double negative is regarded as non-standard. Avoid using double negatives in your writing and speaking.

Common Negative Words			
barely	neither	none	nowhere
but (meaning "only")	never	no one	only
	no	not (–n't)	scarcely
hardly	nobody	nothing	

NONSTANDARD	Jade wasn't but a child then.
STANDARD	Jade **was but** a child then.
NONSTANDARD	We hadn't scarcely enough time to finish the test.
STANDARD	We **had scarcely** enough time to finish the test.
NONSTANDARD	There isn't no reason to be nervous.
STANDARD	There **is no** reason to be nervous.
STANDARD	There **isn't any** reason to be nervous.

NONSTANDARD	We searched for clues but didn't find none.
STANDARD	We searched for clues but **found none.**
STANDARD	We searched for clues but **didn't find any.**

NONSTANDARD	I didn't hear nothing.
STANDARD	I **heard nothing.**
STANDARD	I **didn't hear anything.**

Exercise 8   Revising Sentences That Contain Double Negatives

Each of the following sentences contains too many negative words. Revise each sentence. Be careful not to change the intended meaning.

EXAMPLE
1. Theo wanted some ancient Greek coins, but the coin dealer didn't have none.

1. *Theo wanted some ancient Greek coins, but the coin dealer had none.*

or

Theo wanted some ancient Greek coins, but the coin dealer didn't have any.

1. The boy hadn't never been in an airplane.
2. After a lazy summer, Pat can't hardly jog a mile.
3. She was sleeping so soundly she didn't hear nothing.
4. Angela looked for Easter eggs but she didn't see none.
5. Lee Ann has not never been to the Grand Canyon.
6. Char did not want no part of the childish plan.
7. Isn't there no milk left at the store?
8. The stranded motorist doesn't have no spare tire.
9. No one has never walked on the planet Mars.
10. There isn't scarcely any hope for that team to win.

─HELP─

The sentences in Exercise 8 may be correctly revised in more than one way. You need to give only one revision for each.

Revise each of the following sentences, correcting the error or errors in the use of formal, standard English. Practice saying aloud the corrected sentences.

EXAMPLE   **1.** Now a museum, the Imperial Palace (also called the Forbidden City) use to be the home of China's royal family.

     1. *Now a museum, the Imperial Palace (also called the Forbidden City) used to be the home of China's royal family.*

1. They don't have hardly any chance to score before the buzzer sounds; the situation looks sort of hopeless to me.
2. You ought to have seen how beautiful Santa Fe was at Christmas, with nearly every house surrounded by flickering *farolitos*— paper-bag lanterns that have candles inside of them.
3. I might of gone to the concert if I had of heard about it earlier.
4. Pam and her sister Stacey look so much alike that you can't hardly see the differences among them.
5. My cousins didn't hardly know how to swim, but they wouldn't of missed going to the lake.
6. Them reference books in the library are kept in some kind of a special section.
7. This here is the car what I told you about.
8. Hadn't you ought to try and help them?
9. Many of the American Indian leaders which visited Washington, D.C., in the late 1800s proudly wore their traditional clothing rather than dress like their white hosts did.
10. I wonder where them fishing poles are at.
11. We don't live in that there neighborhood no more.
12. We might of gone on the tour, but we wouldn't of had no camera to take pictures.
13. A foot fault in tennis is when the server steps over the base line before hitting the ball.
14. Since there wasn't scarcely any rainfall last spring, there are less mosquitoes this summer.
15. When the play was over, the audience seemed sort of subdued.
16. Shing searched for rice noodles in the grocery store but didn't find none.
17. I saw on the news where many manufacturers will install an improved security system in their new cars.

18. Miss Kim she likes to give those kind of surprise quizzes.

19. Let's try and finish early so we can relax some.

20. In the early 1500s, Ponce de León searched for the Fountain of Youth somewhere on the island of Bimini.

Nonsexist Language

Nonsexist language is language that applies to people in general, both male and female. For example, the nonsexist terms *humanity, human beings,* and *people* can substitute for the gender-specific term *mankind.*

In the past, many skills and occupations were generally closed to either men or women. Words like *seamstress, stewardess,* and *mailman* reflect those limitations. Since most jobs can now be held by both men and women, language is adjusting to reflect this change.

When you are referring generally to people, use nonsexist expressions rather than gender-specific ones. Following are some widely used nonsexist terms that you can use to replace gender-specific ones.

Gender-Specific	Nonsexist
businessman	executive, businessperson
chairman	chairperson, chair
common man	ordinary person
congressman	representative
deliveryman	delivery person
fireman	firefighter
foreman	supervisor
housewife	homemaker
mailman	mail carrier
male nurse	nurse
man-made	synthetic, manufactured
mankind	humanity
manpower	workers, human resources
May the best man win!	May the best person win!
policeman	police officer
salesman	salesperson, salesclerk
seamstress	needleworker
steward, stewardess	flight attendant
weatherman	meteorologist

If the antecedent of a pronoun may be either masculine or femi-nine, use both masculine and feminine pronouns to refer to it.

EXAMPLES   **Anyone** who wants to be considered should present **his or her** application to the office.

Any applicant may bring a résumé with **him or her** to the office.

Often, you can often avoid the awkward *his or her* construction (or the alternative *his/her*) by substituting an article (*a, an,* or *the*) for the construction. Another solution is to reword the sentence, using the plural forms of both the pronoun and its antecedent.

EXAMPLES   Any interested **applicant** may submit **a** proposal.

All interested **applicants** may submit **their** proposals.

| STYLE ✏ TIP |

Avoid using the awkward expressions *s/he* and *wo/man*.

Exercise 9 Using Nonsexist Language

Rewrite each of the following sentences to avoid using gender-specific terms and awkward expressions.

EXAMPLE   1. The factory is advertising for a night watchman.
           1. *The factory is advertising for a security guard.*

1. The weathermen predict sunny skies for the rest of the week.
2. The new chairman is in the office.
3. She was a published authoress and an admired public figure.
4. The male nurse in Grandma's ward was helpful and kind.
5. One of Suzi's ambitions is to become a congressman.
6. We wanted to find the address, so we looked for a mailman.
7. The research done aboard the space shuttle will benefit all mankind.
8. Senator Dupont's political platform was full of references to the common man.
9. The career of fireman is a noble one.
10. Aboard that airline, the stewardesses wear red.

PEANUTS reprinted by permission of United Feature Synndicate, Inc.

USAGE

Chapter Review

A. Revising Expressions by Correcting Errors in Usage

In each of the following sets of word groups, one word group contains an error in usage. Rewrite this word group correctly, using standard, formal usage.

1. **a.** anywheres you travel
   b. as fast as sound travels
   c. to learn Greek cooking from him

2. **a.** affect the outcome
   b. the candidate implied in his speech
   c. among his two opponents

3. **a.** made illusions to the Bible
   b. fewer participants in the contest
   c. asked what kind of car that is

4. **a.** family that emigrated from Germany
   b. should of gone yesterday
   c. discovered another planet

5. **a.** to try and win the game
   b. feeling all right
   c. that kind of car

6. **a.** letting the dog out
   b. an effect of cold weather
   c. books, pencils, papers, and etc.

7. **a.** ate everything accept the peas and dessert
   b. older than you
   c. bringing your records when you come over

8. **a.** I heard nothing.
   b. Lisa can hardly tell the difference.
   c. That cat ain't Samantha, is it?

9. **a.** picture that fell off the wall
   b. that kind of a dog
   c. larger than he is

USAGE

10. **a.** sitting beside the tree
    b. going a little ways
    c. not reality but illusion

11. **a.** whose coat doesn't fit well
    b. that fewer people learned to read back then
    c. inside of the cabinet

12. **a.** car looking like it had been wrecked
    b. chair that was blue
    c. water jug that burst

13. **a.** She effected an improvement.
    b. This is a problem that must be resolved.
    c. Less students joined the club this year.

14. **a.** Take the package to the mail room.
    b. Apples fell off of the tree.
    c. That will scarcely be enough food for all of them.

15. **a.** invented a better safety device
    b. if no one beside my aunt knows
    c. if you're feeling all right

16. **a.** Funds were allotted among six counties.
    b. Where is my hammer at?
    c. This is as far as the fence extends.

17. **a.** We are going nowhere, Mary Sue.
    b. Doesn't he know the way?
    c. He knows more then he reveals.

18. **a.** We were gone for a hour.
    b. Try to learn this poem.
    c. Leave the green grapes on the vine.

19. **a.** I have saved alot of money.
    b. Please stay awhile, John.
    c. One of the glasses broke.

20. **a.** It was an illusion caused by light on the surface.
    b. Their report implies a need for funds.
    c. That dog he limps.

21. **a.** no exception to this rule
    b. being that she is the oldest
    c. taking a torque wrench to Robin's garage

22. **a.** The reason he left is that he's upset.
    b. The crust looked like it had been burned.
    c. They ought to study before the test.

23. **a.** when the ice busted a pipe
    b. so he can lend me a dollar
    c. emigrate from their birthplace

24. **a.** and leave me have my turn
    b. the mechanic who worked on our car
    c. somewhat cold for swimming

25. **a.** haven't only three days of vacation
    b. the effects of smoking
    c. learned that the winner had been announced

26. **a.** Davenport, Iowa, was as far as we could go on a tank of gas.
    b. Name the borders between the three countries.
    c. Davy will learn the children good manners.

27. **a.** should have taken more time
    b. everywheres you go
    c. Uncle Mark and Aunt Zita taught themselves how to repair a computer.

28. **a.** A number of different kinds of birds nest there.
    b. I'm reporting on the invention of the internal-combustion engine.
    c. By calling me by my last name, the teacher infers disapproval.

29. **a.** outside of the assembly hall
    b. as if he had seen a ghost
    c. asking how much he borrowed from you

30. **a.** In the morning we let the raccoon go.
    b. Engine knock is when a car engine makes a pinging sound because of low-octane fuel.
    c. Kathryn is supposed to work late.

B. Proofreading a Paragraph to Correct Usage Errors

Revise the paragraph on the following page by rewriting each sentence to correct the error or errors in the use of formal, standard English. If a sentence is already correct, write *C*.

[**31**] I can't hardly believe what this book says about King Arthur. [**32**] It says that there wasn't no real King Arthur who ruled England during the Middle Ages. [**33**] Arthur was actually a powerful chieftain around A.D. 500, at the outset of the so-called Dark Ages. [**34**] The book infers that the legend of a noble king who introduced chivalry into England is the work of storytellers. [**35**] Most of the illusions to the Round Table are based on a fifteenth-century work called *Le Morte Darthur* by Sir Thomas Malory. [**36**] Some of the legends say that Arthur excepted more than a thousand knights for membership at the Round Table. [**37**] Although there might of been some truth to these legends, Malory's version says there were two hundred fifty knights who earned the right to sit at the Round Table; others say twelve. [**38**] Some of the most famous contests were among Modred, a wicked man, and Sir Lancelot, a brave defender of honor. [**39**] When Arthur lay dying, he was taken away to the magical isle of Avalon. [**40**] The story doesn't go no further, but it implies that Arthur will return someday to inspire noble deeds.

C. Identifying Standard Usage

For each of the following sentences, choose from the choices given in parentheses the word or word group that is correct according to the rules of standard, formal English.

41. With a little effort you (*could have, could of*) written a better report.
42. Shane's answer to my question was (*kind of, rather*) vague.
43. For the band trip I must remember to take my uniform, music, instrument, (*etc., and etc.*)
44. We wanted to go (*everywhere, everywheres*) on our one-week vacation.
45. It looked (*like, as if*) the fire had started in the hayloft.
46. Our team (*had ought, ought*) to win the championship.
47. (*This, This here*) store is having sales in all of its departments.
48. (*Whose, Who's*) briefcase is that?
49. Where should we (*meet, meet at*)?
50. I heard (*where, that*) the mayor would not run for reelection.

Writing Application
Creating a Flier

Using Formal, Standard English   Create a flier for an organization that will soon be providing a public service in your community. The organization you choose might provide health, recreation, or housing services, or it might do something else. In a one-page flier, describe the organization's goals and achievements and explain some of the services it offers. Include at least five examples of standard usage covered in this chapter, and underline each example.

Prewriting   Begin by listing services that your community needs, and note what kinds of organizations supply these services. You may write about a real service group, such as the American Heart Association, or you may wish to write about a fictitious group. Also, list some of the positive effects the group will likely have on your community. Organize your notes so that you can present your information in several coherent paragraphs.

Writing   As you write your first draft, you may think of points you would like to add or changes you would like to make in the presentation of your information. If so, look back over your prewriting notes and determine where your additions and changes will best fit.

Revising   Give your flier to a classmate to read, and use your partner's comments on the clarity of your writing to help you make any necessary revisions.

Publishing   Check your flier for errors in grammar, spelling, and usage. With your teacher's permission, you could post your flier on the class bulletin board or Web page.

Capitalization
Standard Uses of Capitalization

Diagnostic Preview

A. Capitalizing Sentences Correctly

For each of the following sentences, correctly write the words that should be capitalized.

EXAMPLE **1.** Renée searched everywhere in freeport, maine, until she found a gift at l. l. bean for her grandparents.

1. *Freeport; Maine; L. L. Bean*

1. Our september trip to ireland included a stay in kilkee, a coastal village.
2. At the end of class, ms. kwan said that friday's geology II exam will include questions about the appalachian mountains.
3. We should change our dollars to pesos before we board the flight to santiago, chile.
4. The thanksgiving day parade travelled from martin luther king, jr., boulevard to fifty-first street.
5. During their trip to colorado, the barreras hiked up pikes peak.
6. The title of her new television special is *one in a million*.
7. Both ernest hemingway and walt disney once worked for the *kansas city star*.
8. Every easter sunday, grandma penny sings "we praise thee, o god, our redeemer, creator," which was translated from german.
9. One of the cities of the incas, machu picchu, lay hidden among the andes mountains in southern peru and was never discovered by spanish conquerors.

10. In 1982, the colombian writer gabriel garcía márquez was awarded the nobel prize in literature.

11. The winner of the first kentucky derby, the annual race at churchill downs in louisville, was a horse named aristides.

12. In 1983, sally ride became the first american woman in space when the space shuttle *challenger* was launched from cape canaveral.

13. Frederick douglass was the first african american member of the department of justice's u.s. marshals service.

14. If Beth improves her grades in english and history II, her parents will let her apply for a job at the walgreens drugstore on forty-third street.

15. Our debate team argued in favor of pro-american economic policies as the best way to foster democracy in the developing countries of africa, asia, and south america.

B. Capitalizing a Paragraph Correctly

For each sentence in the following paragraph, correctly write the words that should be capitalized.

EXAMPLE   [1] Last summer we visited my uncle carlos, who lives in new york city.

1. Carlos; New York City

[16] One of new york city's most popular tourist attractions is the empire state building. [17] The building, at fifth avenue and thirty-fourth street, attracts 2,500,000 visitors a year. [18] Among them are troops of boy scouts and girl scouts, who camp out on the eighty-sixth floor. [19] The building was financed by john jakob raskob, the founder of general motors. [20] It opened in 1931, during the great depression. [21] At the time, it was the tallest building on earth (1,250 feet), but it's since been overshadowed by chicago's sears tower (1,450 feet) and others. [22] The observatory on the one hundred second floor accounts for much of the empire state building's continuing appeal; when the weather is clear, the observatory provides a view of five states: new york, new jersey, connecticut, pennsylvania, and massachusetts. [23] On may 1, 1991, publicists threw a party to mark the building's sixtieth birthday. [24] One of those who attended was the actress fay wray, who starred in the 1933 movie *king kong*, in which the building was featured. [25] Another attendee was jack brod, one of the original tenants, who proclaimed of the building, "it's got history woven into it."

Using Capital Letters Correctly

HELP

In your reading, you will notice variation in the use of capitalization. Most writers, however, follow the rules presented in this chapter. In your own writing, following these rules will help you communicate clearly with the widest possible audience.

Reference Note

For more about using **capital letters in quotations,** see page 743.

MECHANICS

STYLE   TIP

Some poets do not capitalize lines of poetry. When you quote from a writer's work, use capital letters as the writer uses them.

21a. Capitalize the first word in every sentence.

EXAMPLES   **T**he Second Seminole War lasted nearly eight years.

                      After the war many Seminoles remained in the Everglades and never officially made peace with the U.S. government.

The first word of a quoted sentence should begin with a capital letter, whether or not the quotation begins your sentence.

EXAMPLE   In *Walden,* Henry David Thoreau writes, "**I**f you have built castles in the air, your work need not be lost; that is where they should be."

When quoting only part of a sentence, capitalize the first word of the quotation if (1) the person you are quoting capitalized it or (2) it is the first word of your sentence.

EXAMPLES   What is suggested by the metaphor "**c**astles in the air"?

                    "**C**astles in the air" is a metaphor that suggests one's dreams, goals, or ambitions.

NOTE Capitalize the first word of a sentence fragment used in dialogue.

EXAMPLE   When he was asked whether he had read *Walden,* Mario answered, "**O**nly part of it."

Traditionally, the first word in a line of poetry is capitalized.

EXAMPLES   **S**torm, blow me from here
                    With your fiercest wind
                    Let me float across the sky
                    '**T**ill I can rest again.

                              Maya Angelou, "Woman Work"

21b. Capitalize the pronoun *I* and the interjection *O*.

The interjection *O,* usually used only for invocations, is followed by the name of the person or thing being addressed. Do not confuse *O* with the common interjection *oh,* which is capitalized only when it begins a sentence or is part of a title.

EXAMPLES   The first line **I** read in the poem was "Hear us, **O** Zeus."

                I finished the race, but **oh,** was **I** exhausted.

> **NOTE** *Oh*, unlike *O*, is followed by a mark of punctuation, usually a comma or an exclamation point.

21c. Capitalize the first word in both the salutation and the closing of a letter.

EXAMPLES   **D**ear Mr. Velazquez: **M**y dear Jennifer,

               Sincerely yours,   **Y**ours truly,

21d. Capitalize proper nouns and proper adjectives.

A *common noun* names one of a group of persons, places, things, or ideas. A *proper noun* names a particular person, place, thing, or idea. A *proper adjective* is formed from a proper noun.

A common noun is capitalized when it

* begins a sentence

         or

* begins a direct quotation

         or

* is part of a title

Common Nouns	Proper Nouns	Proper Adjectives
a **w**riter	**D**ickens	**D**ickensian character
a **r**eligion	**B**uddhism	**B**uddhist monk
a **c**ountry	**F**rance	**F**rench bread
a **q**ueen	**V**ictoria	**V**ictorian era
a **p**lanet	**V**enus	**V**enusian terrain
a **r**egion	the **M**idwest	**M**idwestern values

In a compound proper noun, articles, coordinating conjunctions, and short prepositions (those with fewer than five letters) are not capitalized.

EXAMPLES   Prince **o**f Wales

               National Association **f**or **t**he Advancement **o**f Colored People

               Girl Scouts **o**f **t**he United States **o**f America

Reference Note

For information on **commas and colons in salutations,** see pages 715 and 730.

Reference Note

For more information about **common nouns** and **proper nouns,** see page 406. For more about **proper adjectives,** see page 415.

MECHANICS

NOTE Proper nouns and proper adjectives may lose their capitals after long use.

EXAMPLES **d**iesel **b**ologna **b**raille **w**att

When you are not sure whether to capitalize a word, check a dictionary to see in which uses (if any) it is capitalized.

COMPUTER TIP

The range of correct spellings of personal names can foil even the best spell-checking software. One way to avoid this problem is to customize your spell-checker. If your software allows, add to it frequently used names that you have difficulty spelling or capitalizing correctly.

(1) Capitalize the names of persons and animals.

Persons	**N**olan **R**yan	**L**atrice **K**antor	**H. H. M**unro
	William the **C**onqueror	**D**r. **E**ileen **C**ruz	**J**erome **W**ilson, **J**r.
		Bill **G**ates	
Animals	**L**assie	**S**ocks	**W**hite **F**ang
	Babe	**R**over	**F**luff

NOTE Some names contain more than one capital letter. Usage varies in the capitalization of *van, von, du, de la,* and other parts of multiword names. When possible, verify the spelling of a name with the person with that name, or check in a reference source.

EXAMPLES **D**e **L**a **C**ruz **M**c**E**nroe **R**ed **C**loud **V**an **D**ongen

de **l**a **M**are **O'S**hea **W**ells-**B**arnett **v**an **G**ogh

Reference Note

For information about **capitalizing abbreviations** such as *Dr.* and *Jr.,* see page 686.

(2) Capitalize initials in names and abbreviations that come before or after names.

EXAMPLES **J. D.** Rockefeller Louis **J.** Halle **D**r. Suzi Cohen

Tom Taliaferro, **M.D.** **S**r. Garcia **M**s. Bradford

Exercise 1 **Proofreading Paragraphs for Correct Capitalization**

Most of the sentences in the following paragraphs contain errors in capitalization. Write the correct form of each incorrect word. If the capitalization of a sentence is already correct, write *C.*

EXAMPLE [1] These pictures capture only a few of the many sides of Gordon parks, renowned Photographer, film director, writer, and composer.

1. *Parks; photographer*

[1] A self-taught photographer, gordon Parks grew up in Fort Scott, Kansas. [2] after winning a rosenwald Fellowship for a series of pictures about life in Chicago's Slums, He got his first full-time photography job with the Farm Security Administration in Washington, D.C. [3] In 1949, he joined the staff of *Life* magazine. [4] During his nearly twenty years with *Life*, Parks covered assignments ranging from Junior High School science conventions to Paris Fashion Shows. [5] He also wrote many of the essays that accompanied his photographs, as well as two Volumes of autobiography, *A Choice of Weapons* and *Voices in the Mirror*.

[6] turning to a career in the movie industry in 1968, Parks moved to Hollywood, where his son Gordon Parks, jr., took this photograph of him preparing to direct a scene from the film version of *The Learning Tree*. [7] Parks also wrote the film's screenplay and, working at the grand piano in his Hollywood apartment, its musical score. [8] His success with the film led to other writing and directing projects, including *Leadbelly,* the story of the blues musician Huddie ledbetter.

[9] In September 1997, an exhibition of his photography opened at the Corcoran Gallery in Washington, D.C. [10] Some of his best-known projects have included *Voices in the Mirror* and the words and music for *Martin,* a classical Ballet honoring the late dr. martin luther king, jr.

(3) Capitalize geographical names.

Type of Name	Examples	
Countries	the **N**etherlands	**A**rgentina
	Ghana	**S**witzerland
Towns, Cities	**C**hicago	**L**aredo
	Stratford-on-**A**von	**B**erlin
	San **D**iego	**S**t. **P**etersburg
Counties, Townships, Parishes, Provinces	**O**range **C**ounty	**C**addo **P**arish
	Franklin **T**ownship	**Y**orkshire
	East **B**aton **R**ouge **P**arish	**C**ape of **G**ood **H**ope **P**rovince
States	**O**regon	**T**exas
	New **Y**ork	**S**outh **C**arolina
Regions	the **M**iddle **E**ast	**G**reat **P**lains
	the **W**est	**Y**ukon
	the **N**ortheast	**S**un **B**elt

NOTE Words such as *south, east,* and *northwest* are not capitalized when they indicate direction.

EXAMPLES **w**est of the bridge   heading **n**orth

Type of Name	Examples	
Continents	**S**outh **A**merica	**E**urope
	Asia	**A**frica
Islands	**G**alveston **I**sland	the **I**sle of **W**ight
	the **L**esser **A**ntilles	**K**ey **W**est
Mountains	**A**llegheny **M**ountains	**M**ount **S**t. **H**elens
	Sierra **M**adre	**P**ikes **P**eak
Other Geographical Names	**S**henandoah **V**alley	**K**alihari **D**esert
	Bryce **C**anyon	**T**impanogos **C**ave
	Cape **H**atteras	**S**inai **P**eninsula

Type of Name	Examples	
Bodies of Water	**A**tlantic **O**cean **R**ed **S**ea **P**ersian **G**ulf	**S**uwanee **R**iver **R**io **G**rande **L**ake of the **O**zarks
Parks, Forests	**R**edwood **S**tate **P**ark **N**orth **T**ongass **N**ational **F**orest	**B**ernheim **F**orest **S**tone **M**ountain **M**emorial **P**ark
Roads, Highways, Streets	**R**oute 41 **I**nterstate 10 **S**unshine **S**tate **P**arkway	**C**entral **A**venue **S**outh **F**iftieth **S**treet **P**leasant **H**ill **R**oad

NOTE The second word in a hyphenated street number begins with a lowercase letter.

EXAMPLE   Fifty-**t**hird Street

A word such as *city, island, river,* or *street* is generally not capitalized unless it is part of a proper noun.

Proper Nouns	Common Nouns
traffic in **M**exico **C**ity	traffic in a large **c**ity
visiting **C**aptiva **I**sland	visiting a barrier **i**sland
bridging the **O**hio **R**iver	bridging the **r**iver
across **D**elancey **S**treet	across a congested **s**treet

Exercise 2   Using Correct Capitalization

If one or more words in each of the following word groups should be capitalized, write the entire word group correctly. If a word group is already correct, write *C*.

EXAMPLE   **1.** atop granite peak
          1. atop Granite Peak

1. zion national park
2. gulf of tonkin
3. explored Mount ararat
4. hiking trails in a state park
5. at moon lake
6. a house on starve island
7. beside the ohio river
8. in lancaster county

STYLE   TIP

Since *rio* is Spanish for "river," *Rio Grande River* is redundant. Use only *Rio Grande.*

   Other terms to watch for are

- *sierra,* Spanish for "mountain range" [Use only *Sierra Nevada,* not *Sierra Nevada Mountains.*]

- *yama,* Japanese for "mountain" [Use only *Fuji-yama* or *Mount Fuji,* not *Mount Fuji-yama.*]

- *sahara,* Arabic for "desert" [Use only *Sahara,* not *Sahara Desert.*]

- *gobi,* Mongolian for "desert" [Use only *Gobi,* not *Gobi Desert.*]

MECHANICS

9. mekong delta
10. across baffin bay
11. ventura boulevard
12. the tides in the bay
13. new york skyline
14. forty-fifth street

15. near the isle of wight
16. the west side of the river
17. population of the north
18. near dundee mountain
19. coffee from brazil
20. coast of australia

> **Exercise 3** **Proofreading a Paragraph for Correct Capitalization**

Capitalize the words that should begin with a capital letter in the following paragraph. Do not include the words already capitalized. If a sentence is already correct, write *C*.

EXAMPLE **[1]** Until last year I'd never been farther from lawrenceburg, tennessee, than pulaski, which is only seventeen miles east.

1. *Lawrenceburg; Tennessee; Pulaski*

[1] Naturally, I was excited when our choir decided to have an international arts and crafts fair to raise money for a trip to washington, d.c. [2] Colleen O'Roark suggested that the fair feature crafts and food from countries in europe, africa, and asia. [3] Juana Santiago, whose family is from venezuela, pointed out that we should also include items from central america and south america. [4] Julian Moore, who recently returned from visiting relatives in Monrovia, said he'd bring a display of Liberian baskets. [5] Karen Cohen offered items from quebec, one of our neighbors to the north. [6] Maxine Hirano, who was born in tokyo, japan, promised to demonstrate paper folding. [7] Some of us met later at Paula Bowen's house, on the northeast

corner of columbus street and hickory lane, to choose items to represent the united states. [8] We selected American Indian artifacts from the southwest, country crafts from the appalachian mountains, and shell gifts from the states along the gulf of mexico. [9] Erin McCall, whose family moved to lexington avenue from phoenix, arizona, volunteered to bring rocks that she had bought at a gift shop in petrified forest national park. [10] When the fair was over, we had raised enough money to include on our trip to the nation's capital a tour of mammoth cave national park in kentucky.

(4) Capitalize the names of organizations, teams, institutions, and government bodies.

Type of Name	Examples
Organizations	**A**merican **M**edical **A**ssociation **N**ational **H**onor **S**ociety **L**eague of **W**omen **V**oters **O**rganization of **A**merican **S**tates
Teams	**E**astside **J**ets **H**arlem **G**lobetrotters **N**ew **Y**ork **R**angers **P**ortsmouth **C**hess **M**asters
Institutions	**G**ood **S**amaritan **H**ospital **R**idgemont **H**igh **S**chool **S**tanford **U**niversity
Government Bodies	**D**epartment of the **I**nterior **T**ampa **C**ity **C**ouncil the **N**uclear **R**egulatory **C**ommission

NOTE Do not capitalize words such as *democratic, republican,* and *socialist* when they refer to principles or forms of government. Capitalize these words only when they refer to specific political parties.

EXAMPLES   Voting is part of the **d**emocratic process.

Was George W. Bush the **R**epublican nominee?

(5) Capitalize the names of businesses and brand names of business products.

Type of Name	Examples	
Businesses	**T**hrifty **D**ry **C**leaners **S**ears, **R**oebuck and **C**o.	**F**irst **N**ational **B**ank **F**ields **D**epartment **S**tore
Business Products	**S**chwinn **M**esa **GMC** **J**immy	**C**allaway **B**ig **B**ertha **A**pple **M**acintosh

STYLE   TIP

The word *party* in the name of a political party may be capitalized or not; either way is correct.

EXAMPLE
Republican **P**arty
or
Republican **p**arty

Within a piece of writing, be consistent about using a capital or lowercase letter to begin the word *party*.

(6) Capitalize the names of buildings and other structures.

Type of Name	Examples	
Buildings and Other Structures	**D**etroit **W**estin **H**otel	**M**osque of **O**mar
	Fox **T**heater	**B**uckingham **P**alace
	Colosseum	**S**an **R**oque **D**am
	Washington **M**utual **T**ower	**Q**ueens-**M**idtown **T**unnel
	Natchez **T**race **P**arkway **B**ridge	**M**etropolitan **M**useum

(7) Capitalize the names of monuments, memorials, and awards.

Type of Name	Examples
Monuments, Memorials, and Awards	**D**inosaur **N**ational **M**onument
	Korean **W**ar **V**eterans **M**emorial
	Effigy **M**ounds **N**ational **M**onument
	Nobel **P**rize
	Perry's **V**ictory and **I**nternational **P**eace **M**emorial
	Heisman **T**rophy

Do not capitalize a word such as *building, monument,* or *award* unless it is part of a proper noun.

(8) Capitalize the names of historical events and periods, special events, and holidays and other calendar items.

Type of Name	Examples	
Historical Events and Periods	the **B**attle of **G**ettysburg	the **D**ark **A**ges
	the **Y**alta **C**onference	**G**reat **D**epression
	Children's **C**rusade	the **S**tone **A**ge

Type of Name	Examples	
Special Events	the **B**oston **M**arathon	the **A**ll-**S**tar **G**ame
	the **N**ational **M**inority **J**ob **E**xpo	the **I**owa **S**tate **F**air
		Special **O**lympics
Holidays and Other Calendar Items	**V**alentine's **D**ay	**F**riday
	Earth **D**ay	**M**arch
	Cinco de **M**ayo	**K**wanzaa

NOTE Do not capitalize the name of a season unless the season is being personified or is part of a proper name.

EXAMPLES   We looked forward to **s**pring after the long **w**inter.

Autumn in her russet garb followed green **S**ummer.

Are you going to the **W**inter Wonderland Dance?

Exercise 4   Identifying and Correcting Errors in Capitalization

Correct the capitalization errors in each of the following sentences by capitalizing letters as needed.

EXAMPLE   1.   Some Norse folk tales originated in the Dark ages.

1.   *Ages*

1. Dr. Bourgeois applied to his local branch of the American medical association.
2. Gary works in the afternoons at Ridgeway discount appliance mart.
3. The house of Representatives passed the bills, but they died in the senate.
4. One of Lena's ancestors was at the battle of the Argonne.
5. Did you say you were planning to run in the Boston marathon?
6. Thanksgiving day always falls on the fourth Thursday in november.
7. When it was completed in 1973, the Sears tower in Chicago was the tallest building in the world.
8. Aaron couldn't decide whether to cheer for his hometown team, the Wisconsin badgers, or his new favorite, the Texas longhorns.
9. Her ambition is to win a pulitzer Prize someday.
10. The library's new Apple macintosh is scheduled to be delivered next week.

(9) Capitalize the names of nationalities, races, and peoples.

Type of Name	Examples		
Nationalities, Races, and Peoples	**I**talian	**C**anadian	**C**aucasian
	African	**J**ewish	**H**ispanic
	Navajo	**M**icronesian	**I**ndo-**I**ranian

(10) Capitalize the names of religions and their followers, holy days and celebrations, sacred writings, and specific deities.

Type of Name	Examples	
Religions and Followers	**J**udaism	**M**uslim
	Buddhism	**C**onfucian
	Christianity	**M**ormon
Holy Days and Celebrations	**A**sh **W**ednesday	**H**anukkah
	Ramadan	**C**hristmas **E**ve
	Yom **K**ippur	**P**entecost
Holy Writings	the **B**ible	**R**ig-**V**eda
	the **T**almud	**E**xodus
	the **K**oran	**D**ead **S**ea **S**crolls
Specific Deities	**A**llah	**V**ishnu
	God	the **H**oly **S**pirit

NOTE The words *god* and *goddess* are not capitalized when they refer to the deities of ancient mythology. The names of specific mythological deities are capitalized, however.

EXAMPLE The Roman **g**oddess of grain was **C**eres.

(11) Capitalize the names of ships, trains, aircraft, and spacecraft.

Type of Name	Examples	
Ships, Trains, Aircraft, and Spacecraft	*Queen Mary*	*Spirit of St. Louis*
	R.M.S. *Titanic*	*Orient Express*
	Lake Shore Limited	*Enterprise*
	Electra	*Atlantis*

NOTE The names of the make and model of a vehicle also are capitalized.

EXAMPLES **M**itsubishi **E**clipse [car]

Kris **K**raft [boat]

(12) Capitalize the names of planets, stars, constellations, and other heavenly bodies.

EXAMPLES **P**luto [planet] **P**ollux [star]

Andromeda Galaxy [galaxy] **U**rsa **M**ajor [constellation]

Great **N**ebula [nebula] **T**itan [moon]

NOTE The word *earth* is not capitalized unless it is used along with the name of another heavenly body that is capitalized. The words *sun* and *moon* are generally not capitalized.

EXAMPLES Unlike **E**arth, neither **M**ercury nor **V**enus has a **m**oon.

The **s**un is a star.

The **m**oon is the **e**arth's only natural satellite.

21e. Do not capitalize the names of school subjects, except course names followed by a number and the names of language classes.

Type of Name	Examples		
School Subjects	**a**lgebra	**c**hemistry	**m**usic
	Algebra II	**C**hemistry I	**M**usic 101
	Latin	**G**erman	**M**andarin
	English	**S**panish	**D**utch

NOTE Do not capitalize the class name *freshman, sophomore, junior,* or *senior* unless it is part of a proper noun.

EXAMPLES A number of **s**ophomores attended this spring's **J**unior **P**rom.

The **S**ophomore **S**ingers performed for the **f**reshmen.

TIPS & TRICKS

Generally, a singular noun identified by a number or letter is capitalized.

EXAMPLES
Room 13   **F**igure C
Chapter 21   **E**xample D
Channel 32   **S**uite 4A

However, the word *page* is usually not capitalized, nor is a plural noun followed by two or more numbers or letters.

EXAMPLE
Look at **c**harts A and B on **p**age 273.

Correcting Capitalization Errors

Identify the words that should be capitalized in each of the following sentences. Do not include words that are already capitalized.

EXAMPLE
1. The spanish explorer juan ponce de león landed in florida in 1513.

1. *Spanish; Juan Ponce de León; Florida*

1. The area now known as florida was originally inhabited by native american peoples, including the apalachees, the creeks, and the seminoles.
2. The state is bounded on the north by alabama and georgia, on the east by the atlantic ocean, on the south by the straits of florida and the gulf of mexico, and on the west by alabama and the gulf of mexico.
3. The spanish founded st. augustine, the state's first permanent european settlement, in 1565, making it the oldest colonial city in the united states.
4. When spain ceded florida to the united states in 1821, the u.s. government demanded that the native peoples move west.
5. The strength and dignity of the seminole leader osceola, who led his people in the fight to retain their lands, are evident in this 1838 painting by george catlin.

6. Most of the seminoles eventually moved to present-day oklahoma, but a few hundred fled to the everglades, a huge wilderness area in southern florida that now includes everglades national park.
7. Founded in 1886, eatonville, florida, is the oldest incorporated african american town in the united states.
8. After the cuban revolution in the late 1950s, and again in the early 1980s, many cubans fled to miami.
9. Miami has also served as a major point of entry for haitian refugees who have braved the atlantic ocean in search of a better life.
10. Among the asians who have settled in the state are refugees from vietnam, many of whom make their living fishing along the northern coast of florida.

Osceola by George Catlin. Courtesy of the Department of Library Services. American Museum of National History.

Identify the words that should be capitalized in each sentence in the following paragraphs. Do not include words that are already capitalized.

EXAMPLES **[1]** Trivia games test your knowledge of subjects as diverse as american inventors, the korean war, and popular music.

1. *American, Korean War*

[2] my parents have played trivia games against my brother and me since we moved to cleveland four years ago.

2. *My, Cleveland*

[1] Last saturday, may 18, my brother Ted and i finally won our first trivia match against our parents. [2] Some of the courses Ted is taking this semester are history, political science, and french; mine include world literature I and geography II. [3] We surged into the lead when our parents couldn't remember that the first united states satellite, *explorer I,* followed the soviet union's *sputnik I* into space. [4] From my geography class, I remembered that mount McKinley is the highest point and death valley is the lowest point on the north american continent.

[5] Our parents rallied for the lead by knowing that the boy on the cracker jack box is named jack and that his dog's name is bingo. [6] Then Ted came up with the fact that the steel framework of the statue of liberty was designed by the frenchman alexandre gustave eiffel, who also designed the eiffel tower in paris. [7] None of us knew that john wilkes booth was only twenty-six years old when he shot abraham lincoln at ford's theater on good friday in 1865. [8] Mom, who has always been a loyal democrat, knew that *engine 1401*—the southern railways locomotive that carried franklin d. roosevelt's body from warm springs, georgia, to washington, D.C.—can now be seen in the smithsonian institution.

[9] Ted and I lost several points because I didn't know that kleenex tissues were first used as gas-mask filters during world war I. [10] However, Ted won the game for us by remembering that the white house was called the executive mansion before it was burned by the british during the war of 1812.

MECHANICS

Reference Note

For more information about **capitalizing and punctuating abbreviations,** see page 686.

| STYLE | TIP |

For special emphasis or clarity, writers sometimes capitalize a title used alone or following a person's name.

EXAMPLES
The **G**overnor firmly stated her opinion on the issue.

Her predecessor called the new **P**rincipal **C**hief "the best person for the job."

┌HELP─

Some titles are traditionally always capitalized. If you are unsure whether to capitalize a title, look it up in a dictionary.

21f. Capitalize titles.

(1) Capitalize a person's title when the title comes before the person's name.

Type of Name	Examples	
Titles	**G**eneral Powell	**D**r. Sakamoto
	President Kennedy	**M**arshal Foch
	Queen Margrethe	**A**rchbishop Tutu

Generally, a title used alone or following a person's name is not capitalized, especially if the title is preceded by *a* or *the*.

EXAMPLES   In 1991, Boris Yeltsin became the first freely elected **p**resident of the Russian Federation.

Who was the U.S. **p**resident during World War II?

Christine Todd Whitman served as **g**overnor of New Jersey in the 1990s.

A title used alone in direct address is generally capitalized.

EXAMPLES   Well, **M**ayor, will you please test the microphone?

Do you intend to visit the disaster area, **G**overnor?

Please be seated, **S**ir [*or* **s**ir].

(2) Capitalize a word showing family relationship when the word is used before or in place of a person's name, unless the word follows a possessive noun or pronoun.

EXAMPLES   **A**unt Edith   **U**ncle Fred   **G**randmother Bechtel

my **a**unt Edith   your **u**ncle Fred   Maria's **g**randmother

(3) Capitalize the first and last words and all other important words in titles and subtitles.

Unimportant words in a title include

- articles: *a, an, the*
- coordinating conjunctions: *and, but, for, nor, or, so,* and *yet*
- short prepositions (fewer than five letters): *of, to, in, for, from, with*

NOTE Capitalize an article (*a, an,* or *the*) at the beginning of a title or subtitle only if it is the first word of the official title or subtitle.

EXAMPLES Last summer, Joan read *The Outsiders* and *Harriet Beecher Stowe: A Life.*

Joan reads both *The Atlantic Monthly* and the *Rocky Mountain News.*

Type of Title	Examples	
Books	*Songs of the Tewa*	
	Silent Dancing: A Partial Remembrance of Puerto Rican Childhood	
Chapters and Other Parts of Books	"The Philippines: Its Land and Resources"	
	"Index of Literary Skills: A Writer's Guide"	
Periodicals	*U.S. News & World Report*	
	Chicago Sun-Times	
Poems	"Love Without Love"	
	"I Like to See It Lap the Miles"	
Short Stories	"The Man to Send Rain Clouds"	
	"The Woman Who Had No Eye for Small Details"	
Plays	*A Raisin in the Sun*	
	Sunday in the Park with George	
Historical Documents	Treaty of Versailles	
	Articles of Confederation	
Movies	*Antz*	*Ever After*
	The Parent Trap	*The Prince of Egypt*
Radio and TV Programs	*War of the Worlds*	
	Face the Nation	
	Hercules: The Legendary Journeys	
Works of Art	*Crossing the Brook*	
	Two Mexican Women and Child	

(continued)

HELP

The official title of a book is found on its title page. The official title of a newspaper or other periodical is found on its masthead, which usually appears on the editorial page or the table of contents.

Reference Note

For information about which **titles** should be **italicized** and which should be in **quotation marks,** see pages 740 and 747.

MECHANICS

(continued)

Type of Title	Examples	
Musical Works	"Blue Moon"	
	Amahl and the Night Visitors	
Audiotapes and CDs	*Echoes of Time and the River*	
	In Memory of a Summer Day	
Videos and Video Games	*Pocahontas II: Journey to a New World*	
	Fast Break	
Comic Strips	*Calvin and Hobbes*	*Dilbert*
	Cathy	*Jump Start*

Review C **Correcting Capitalization Errors**

Most of the following sentences contain errors in capitalization. Write the correct form of each word that contains an error. If the capitalization of a sentence is already correct, write *C*.

EXAMPLE
1. In 1995, a. leon higgenbotham, the jurist and civil rights advocate, was awarded the presidential medal of freedom.

1. *A. Leon Higgenbotham, Presidential Medal, Freedom*

1. At the hirshhorn museum in washington, d.c., Millicent and James saw one of georgia o'keeffe's finest paintings, *cow's skull: red, white and blue.*

2. In *people* magazine, Kim read about bill cosby's earlier television series *the cosby show.*

3. When I visited grandma Sánchez at white sparrow Hospital, I read to her from jimmy santiago baca's *martín & meditations on the south valley.*

4. In 1908, mary baker eddy founded the *christian science monitor.*

5. My cousin Judy's favorite statue is *indian hunter* by paul manship.

6. I enjoyed reading annie dillard's *pilgrim at tinker creek,* particularly the chapter "the horns of the altar."

7. The prize-winning journalist carl t. rowan was the first african american to serve on the National Security council.

8. The president addressed the american people in a television news broadcast after he had met with the president of France.

MECHANICS

9. Well, Governor, will Mayor Johnson and the county commissioners attend the groundbreaking ceremony for the new hospital?

10. Jane White, the president of the latin club, showed us a videotape of *julius caesar.*

Review D **Proofreading Paragraphs for Correct Capitalization**

The sentences in the following paragraphs contain errors in capitalization. Write the correct form of each incorrect word.

EXAMPLE **[1]** The energetic personality of montana's former state senator from the Fiftieth District is obvious in the Painting by Christopher Magadini below.

    1. *Montana's, painting*

[1] Bill Yellowtail, jr., the first member of the crow people to serve in the Montana State Senate, represented an area hit hard by drought and a decline in the demand for beef. [2] Yellowtail, a democrat, ran for office to help save the Area's remaining small family farms and ranches. [3] A Rancher himself, he raises cattle in the Lodge Grass valley in Southeastern Montana with his Mother, his brother, and his sister.

[4] Yellowtail supplements his income from ranching by outfitting fly-fishing trips on the Bighorn river. [5] In addition, he works as a Tour Guide on the Crow reservation and at the Custer battlefield national monument. [6] He has also served as a consultant for the Montana-wyoming Agriculture-Tourist Project, which is helping ranchers develop tourism as an industry; as a member of the Board of Directors of the Nature Conservancy; and as the director of the Environmental protection agency.

[7] After graduating from Lodge Grass high school at the head of his class, Yellowtail attended dartmouth College in hanover, New Hampshire. [8] Although Dartmouth was founded to educate american Indians, Yellowtail was the first american indian to enroll there in twenty years. [9] At first he was unprepared academically, but by the time he Graduated in 1971, he was on the dean's list. [10] Regarding his major subject, Geography, Yellowtail said, "the relationship between humanity and the environment is little understood; it's a Discipline we very much need today."

Abbreviations

21g. Generally, abbreviations are capitalized if the words that they stand for are capitalized.

An *abbreviation* is a shortened form of a word or word group.

EXAMPLE   The **G**en. Science I [General Science I] classes will be going to the planetarium on **F**ri. [Friday], **D**ec. [December] 15.

Abbreviations of most proper nouns and of titles used along with proper nouns are capitalized.

(1) Capitalize abbreviations that come before or after names of persons, such as *Mr., Mrs., Ms., Dr., Gen., Ph.D., Jr.,* and *Sr.*

EXAMPLES   **M**s. Christina O'Reilly   **G**en. Marcus Whitman

John H. Glenn, **J**r.   Sharon Roberts, **Ph.D.**

(2) Capitalize abbreviations of geographical names.

EXAMPLES   **M**t. **S**t. **H**elens   Madera **C**o.   **T**ex.

Ozark **M**ts.   Bahama **I**s.   **F**la.

Reference Note

For information on **punctuating abbreviations** that come before or after names in sentences, see page 696.

STYLE   TIP

Only a few abbreviations are appropriate in the regular text of a formal paper written for a general audience. In tables, notes, and bibliographies, abbreviations are used more freely in order to save space.

NOTE   A two-letter state code without periods is used when the abbreviation is followed by a ZIP Code. Each letter of the abbreviation is capitalized.

EXAMPLE   Atlanta, **GA** 30328-1647

(3) In addresses, capitalize abbreviations such as *St., Ave., Dr., Rd., P.O., Rm.,* and *Apt.*

EXAMPLES   531 Guadalupe **A**ve.   **P.O.** Box 1628

2414 Grand **S**t.   33 Hillside **D**r., **A**pt. 17A

Witte Hall, **R**m. 1018   658 Culver **C**t.

(4) Capitalize abbreviations of the names of organizations, government bodies, and businesses.

EXAMPLES   American Dental **A**ssn.   **U.S. D**ept. of Transportation

Motorola, **I**nc.   Digital Equipment **C**orp.

Some proper nouns are often abbreviated to a series of capital letters without periods.

National Aeronautics and Space Administration	**NASA**
Federal Communications Commission	**FCC**
General Motors	**GM**
Brigham Young University	**BYU**
Public Broadcasting Service	**PBS**

Some common nouns, too, are abbreviated to a series of capital letters without periods.

personal computer	**PC**	television	**TV**
chief executive officer	**CEO**	vice president	**VP**
central processing unit	**CPU**	deoxyribonucleic acid	**DNA**
frequency modulation	**FM**	videocassette recorder	**VCR**

However, the abbreviations of most common nouns, with or without periods, are not capitalized.

pages	**pp.**	pound	**lb**
lines	**ll**	tablespoon	**tbsp**
transitive verb	**vt.**	centimeter	**cm**
abbreviation	**abbr.**	kilogram	**kg**
inch(es)	**in.**	miles per hour	**mph**

NOTE The abbreviations of most units of measurement do not include periods. To prevent confusion with the word *in,* however, writers should include a period in the abbreviation of *inch* or *inches* (*in.*).

Exercise 5 Correctly Capitalizing Abbreviations

For the following word groups, correct any errors in the capitalization of abbreviations. If a word group is already correct, write *C.*

EXAMPLE
1. to get his teeth cleaned by dr. Larson
1. *Dr.*

1. 330 Farley rd.
2. two sources written by Herbert Hunter, ph.d.
3. 2904 Spring st., apt. 1501
4. that Widgets, inc., is hiring summer help

5. because ms. Lynch will be the interim ceo
6. visiting Tulsa, okla.; Wichita, kans.; and Omaha, neb.
7. the guest speaker maj. Felicia Payne
8. writing your research paper on a PC
9. ability to lift 50 lbs
10. sending entries to p.o. box 1770, San Antonio, Tx 78297-1770
11. the educational tape from Nasa that is stuck in the vcr
12. said mr. Wills wrote a book about st. Augustine
13. to contact dr. Tuomala by writing to rm. 302, 1403 Washtenaw ave., Ann Arbor, mi 48014-3177
14. reaching a speed of 250 MPH
15. the CPU in your new computer
16. a convention in ft. Worth, Texas
17. 1 Tbsp of oregano
18. Brian Donovan, Jr.
19. the film school at ucla
20. the u.s. dept. of the Treasury

Chapter Review

A. Using Capitalization Correctly

For each of the following sentences, identify the word or words containing an error in capitalization and correct each error. If a sentence is already correct, write *C*.

1. This year my easiest classes are geometry, spanish, and American history.
2. Mexico city is built on the site of tenochtitlán, the aztec capital.
3. We rent videotapes from the Grand Video company.
4. Colorado is located West of the Great Plains.
5. Lansing, Michigan, is in Ingham county.
6. She lives at 321 Maple boulevard, which is south of here.
7. My RCA Stereo is ten years old and still works well.
8. Maggie entered her poodle in the San Marcos Dog club's show.
9. They live half a block north of Twenty-first Street.
10. Our neighbors are alumni of Howard university in Washington, d.c.
11. Last Spring my stepsister Lisa joined the National Audubon society.
12. While we were in San Juan, puerto rico, we toured El Morro Castle.
13. The club members celebrated Bastille Day by having dinner at a French restaurant.
14. Has Ms. Davis written to the U.S. department of Agriculture for information on soybean cultivation in the Midwest?
15. Mars was the Roman God of war.
16. We're holding a car wash next Saturday to raise money for the Habans high school fall festival.
17. The Islands that make up the west indies separate the Atlantic ocean from the gulf of mexico and the Caribbean sea.
18. Would you like to be the first student to ride in a Spaceship to another planet?
19. The post–Civil war period known as reconstruction officially ended in 1877.
20. Erica wants to be secretary of the Shutterbug Club.

MECHANICS

B. Capitalizing Words in a Paragraph Correctly

For each sentence in the following paragraph, write correctly the words that should be capitalized or made lowercase. If a sentence is already correct, write *C*.

[21] Cartoons and Caricatures have been popular since at least the Eighteenth Century. [22] George cruikshank and William hogarth were two of the most famous cartoonists in england in the 1700s and 1800s. [23] In the early 1840s, the famous British satirical magazine *punch* was established. [24] *punch,* a weekly, ran a feature called *"punch's* cartoons," which became very popular. [25] However, the person who is sometimes considered the originator of modern cartooning was the french artist Honoré Daumier (1808–1879), who was once briefly imprisoned for creating a vicious caricature of king Louis-Philippe. [26] In the United States, Thomas nast gained Fame in 1874 by introducing the elephant into his cartoons as the symbol of the Republican party. [27] Nast also made the Donkey the symbol of the democratic party. [28] In the early twentieth century, other well-known american cartoonists included Charles Addams, peter arno, and James thurber. [29] More recently, Gary Larson, Scott Adams, and Garry Trudeau have been among the best-known U.S. cartoonists. [30] The next time you pick up the Comics page in your favorite paper, spare a thought for all the History behind those cartoons!

C. Using Capitalization Correctly

For each of the following items, write the entire word group, correcting the words that should be capitalized or made lowercase. If a word group is already correct, write *C*.

31. Forty-Second Street

32. cars from germany

33. interstate 35

34. hernandez high school

35. the Metropolitan museum of modern art

36. Thomas Jefferson State Park

37. african american artist

38. the *titanic*

39. andromeda galaxy

40. American History 101

D. Correcting Sentences by Capitalizing Words

Most of the following sentences contain errors in capitalization. Write the correct form of each word that contains an error. If the capitalization of a sentence is already correct, write *C*.

41. Mom and dad subscribe to *Newsweek* and *U.S. news & world report.*

42. Lotte enjoyed reading Mark Twain's *The Innocents Abroad* and has been asking for other Twain titles.

43. The speed of 100 MPH is roughly equivalent to 160 KPH (kilometers per hour).

44. Ramon is registered to take english, math II, and German.

45. Everyone was happy that Monday, columbus day, was a Holiday.

Writing Application
Writing a Guidebook

Using Capital Letters You have been asked to write a guidebook for a group of visitors from your town's sister city in Japan. Write an informative booklet that helps your visitors take a brief walking or driving tour through your town. Be sure to capitalize the proper nouns you use.

Prewriting List the sights you will include in your guidebook. (If you live in a large city, you may need to limit the tour to only one part of the city or to the city's main sights.) For information on the town's history, you may want to check the local library.

Writing As you write your first draft, keep in mind that this is your guests' first visit. Try to anticipate their questions without overwhelming them with details. You may want to make a map of your tour with the various sights labeled.

Revising Have you included enough information about each sight, and is the information correct? Add, delete, change, or rearrange details as necessary to make your guidebook clearer and more interesting.

Publishing Proofread your work carefully for errors in grammar, usage, and mechanics. Pay special attention to the correct use of capital letters. After sharing your guidebook with your classmates, you and they may want to compile a larger guidebook to give to new students.

MECHANICS

Punctuation
End Marks and Commas

Diagnostic Preview

A. Correcting Sentences by Adding Periods, Question Marks, Exclamation Points, and Commas

Rewrite the following sentences, adding periods, question marks, exclamation points, and commas where they are needed.

EXAMPLE   **1.** When is the bus coming or has it already left

               1. When is the bus coming, or has it already left?

1. On June 1 2000 I wrote to the Wisconsin Department of Development at 123 Washington Ave Madison WI 53702-0645
2. Federico Peña the mayor of Denver Colorado from 1983 to 1991 was born in Laredo Texas in 1947.
3. Wow Bill what a great save you made on the last play of last night's game
4. Water transports nutrients throughout the body aids in digestion and helps regulate body temperature
5. I M Pei who was born in China has designed many buildings in the United States for example City Hall in Dallas Texas and the Government Center in Boston Massachusetts
6. The chief crops grown in Trinidad an island in the Caribbean are sugar coffee cocoa citrus fruits and bananas

7. Did you know that Diné College located in Tsaile Arizona was founded in 1968

8. If I finish my report if I do the laundry and if I promise to be home by eleven may I go to the concert

9. After I stayed up very late I was exhausted of course yet I couldn't fall asleep right away

10. Along with the letters and magazines in our mailbox last Wednesday we found a large heavy package addressed to Phyllis M Saunders M D

B. Correcting Paragraphs by Adding Periods, Question Marks, Exclamation Points, and Commas

Rewrite each sentence in the following paragraphs, adding periods, question marks, exclamation points, and commas where they are needed.

EXAMPLE   [1] As soon as I got home I called my best friend Stephanie to tell her about my vacation

1. *As soon as I got home, I called my best friend, Stephanie, to tell her about my vacation.*

[11] Stephanie have you ever visited Cody Wyoming [12] Well if you do visit be sure to stop by the Buffalo Bill Historical Center [13] Opened in 1927 in memory of William "Buffalo Bill" Cody an army scout who later had his own Wild West show the center is actually four museums in one [14] The Buffalo Bill Museum the Whitney Gallery of Western Art the Cody Firearms Museum and the Plains Indian Museum are all under one roof.

[15] All of the museums are interesting but the best one I believe is the Plains Indian Museum which has artifacts from American Indian cowhands settlers and roving artists [16] Of all the treasures in the museum's collections the highlight is an exhibit on Tatanka Iyotake better known as Sitting Bull the mighty Sioux warrior holy man chief and statesman [17] The exhibit includes a dozen drawings that Sitting Bull who was born about 1831 and died in 1890 made while he was a prisoner at Fort Randall an army post in the Dakota Territory [18] Depicting some of his many battlefield conquests the drawings reveal his talent for design and composition

[19] Other displays show weapons clothing and accessories of the Cheyenne Shoshone Crow Arapaho Blackfoot and Gros Ventre peoples [20] What a journey back through time the museum offers

MECHANICS

End Marks

An **end mark**—a period, a question mark, or an exclamation point—is used to indicate the purpose of a sentence. A period is also used at the end of many abbreviations.

22a. **A statement (a declarative sentence) is followed by a period.**

EXAMPLES   Barb needed a ride home.

Margaret Walker's poems celebrate the trials and triumphs of African Americans.

22b. **A direct question (an interrogative sentence) is followed by a question mark.**

EXAMPLES   What score did you get on the road test?

Weren't you nervous?

A direct question should be followed by a question mark even if the word order is like that of a declarative sentence.

EXAMPLES   You got what score on the road test?

You weren't nervous?

> **NOTE** Be sure to distinguish between a declarative sentence that contains an indirect question and an interrogative sentence, which asks a direct question.
>
> INDIRECT QUESTION   She asked me who nominated him for class president. [declarative sentence]
>
> DIRECT QUESTION   Who nominated him for class president? [interrogative sentence]

22c. **An exclamation (an exclamatory sentence or a strong interjection) is followed by an exclamation point.**

EXAMPLES   What an exciting game that was! [exclamatory sentence]

Oh, no! Not again! [strong interjection]

A mild interjection is generally followed by a comma.

EXAMPLES   Well, what do you think I should do?

Oh, I suppose that would be acceptable.

Reference Note

For more information on **classifying sentences according to purpose,** see page 459.

STYLE **TIP**

In dialogue, a declarative or an interrogative sentence that expresses strong emotion may be followed by an exclamation point instead of a period or a question mark.

EXAMPLES
There you are!
Why are you always late!

MECHANICS

NOTE Instead of an exclamation point or a comma, another mark of punctuation—a period, a question mark, or a dash, for example—may be used after an interjection, depending on the meaning of the sentence.

EXAMPLES "Hmm. That's a difficult question," responded Alina.

"Well? What's the answer?" Roberto inquired.

"Oh—no, that's not right," Salvador said, changing his mind.

22d. A request or command (an imperative sentence) is followed by either a period or an exclamation point.

Generally, a request or a mild command is followed by a period; a strong command is followed by an exclamation point.

EXAMPLES Open the door, please. [request]

Open the door. [mild command]

Open the door right now! [strong command]

Exercise 1 **Using End Marks**

Rewrite the following sentences, adding or replacing end marks as needed. If a sentence is already correct, write *C*.

EXAMPLE 1. Ouch Please be more careful, Sarah

1. *Ouch! Please be more careful, Sarah.*

1. Did you know that Teresa is moving to Hammond
2. Yikes A rattlesnake.
3. Alexander the Great was born more than two thousand years ago.
4. I read an article about chuckwallas?
5. "Wow. Great shot?"
6. Can you tell me the way to Prater Park!
7. Generally, the green chile is spicier than the red
8. St. Stephen's Cathedral is certainly a beautiful sight?
9. Did you know that Paul McCartney is actually Sir Paul.
10. Gloria wakes up early every day to go for a walk
11. Irene asked whether the student named most likely to succeed was Phil Assad?
12. Will you be able to meet us at the Bristol Hotel!
13. The master of ceremonies was Joel Bourgeois
14. The author Laura Ingalls Wilder was born in Wisconsin
15. When did the Harts move to San Marcos

Reference Note

For more information about **dashes,** see page 770. For more about **interjections,** see page 429.

STYLE TIP

In dialogue, sometimes a command or request is expressed as if it were a question. The meaning, however, may be imperative, in which case a period or exclamation point is used.

EXAMPLES

May I have your full attention, please.

Will you pay attention!

STYLE TIP

Sometimes (most often in dialogue), a writer will use more than one end mark to express (1) intense emotion or (2) a combination of emotions.

EXAMPLES

"I will never—and I mean never—ride a roller coaster again!!" Barbara exclaimed. [intense emotion]

"You said what?!" Alejandro shouted. [combination of curiosity and surprise]

Although acceptable in informal or creative writing, the use of double end punctuation should be avoided in formal writing.

MECHANICS

16. Have you ever heard the music of Theseus Flatow.
17. Ask Tonya whether Kennedy is one of her favorite presidents.
18. How exciting the first moonwalk must have been.
19. Did you know that some of the world's most venomous snakes are found in Australia!
20. Boy I'd love to be a veterinarian.

Abbreviations

An *abbreviation* is a shortened form of a word or phrase.

22e. **Many abbreviations are followed by a period.**

Personal Names

Abbreviate given names only if the person is most commonly known by the abbreviated form of the name.

EXAMPLES	Louis **J.** Halle	**J. F.** Kennedy	**W.E.B.** DuBois
	Ida **B.** Wells	**M.F.K.** Fisher	**M. C.** Escher

Titles

You may abbreviate social titles whether used before the full name or before the last name alone.

EXAMPLES	**Mr.** Xavier Jackson	**Mrs.** Laval
	Dr. Beth Higgins	**Sr.** (Señor) Guzman

You may abbreviate civil and military titles used before full names or before initials and last names. Spell them out before last names alone.

EXAMPLES	**Sen.** John Glenn	**Senator** Glenn
	Gen. Colin Powell	**General** Powell

Abbreviate titles and academic degrees that follow proper names.

EXAMPLES	Harry Connick, **Jr.**	John H. Watson, **M.D.**

If a statement ends with an abbreviation, do not use an additional period as an end mark. However, do use a question mark or an exclamation point if one is needed.

EXAMPLES   This is Patrick Lewis, Jr.

Do you know Patrick Lewis, Jr.?

NOTE Do not include the titles *Mr., Mrs., Ms.,* or *Dr.* when you use a professional title or degree after a name.

EXAMPLE **Dr.** Peter Neibergall *or* Peter Neibergall, **M.D.** [not *Dr. Peter Neibergall, M.D.*]

Agencies and Organizations

An *acronym* is a word formed from the first (or first few) letters of a series of words. Acronyms are written without periods. The abbreviations for many agencies and organizations are written as acronyms.

AMA, American Medical Association USN, United States Navy
CIA, Central Intelligence Agency UN, United Nations

After spelling out the first use of the names of agencies and organizations, abbreviate these names and other things commonly known by their acronyms.

EXAMPLE After the fall of the Berlin Wall in 1989, most Eastern European nations applied to join the **North Atlantic Treaty Organization,** their former enemy. Poland, Hungary, and the Czech Republic subsequently joined **NATO** in 1999.

Geographical Terms

In regular text, spell out names of states and other political units whether they stand alone or follow other geographical terms. Abbreviate them in tables, notes, and bibliographies.

TEXT Frank McCourt spent his early years in Brooklyn, New York, and Limerick, Ireland.

On our vacation to Canada, we visited Québec City, the capital of the Province of Québec.

TABLE London, U.K. Dublin, Ire.
Québec City, P.Q. Oxnard, Calif.

FOOTNOTE ³The Public Library in New Castle, Del., has an entire collection of early Thomaston manuscripts.

BIBLIOGRAPHY ENTRY *The Great Law of Peace and the Constitution of the United States of America.* Akwesasne, **N.Y.**: Tree of Peace, 1988.

MECHANICS

In regular text, spell out every word in an address. Some words should be abbreviated in envelope addresses and may be abbreviated in tables and notes.

NOTE Two-letter state abbreviations without periods are used only when the ZIP Code is included.

EXAMPLE Stilwell, **KS** 66085-8808

COMPUTER TIP

Publishers usually print time abbreviations as small capitals, like this: A.M. Your word processor may offer small capitals as a style option. If it does not, or if you are writing by hand, you may use either uppercase or lowercase letters for time abbreviations, as long as you are consistent in each piece of writing.

STYLE TIP

In your reading, you may come across the abbreviations *C.E.* and *B.C.E.* These abbreviations stand for *Common Era* and *Before Common Era*. They are used instead of *A.D.* and *B.C.*, respectively, and are used after the date.

EXAMPLES
752 **C.E.**

3000 **B.C.E.**

Time

Abbreviate the two most frequently used era designations, *A.D.* and *B.C.* The abbreviation *A.D.* stands for the Latin phrase *anno Domini*, which means "in the year of the Lord." It is used with dates in the Christian era. When used with a specific year number, *A.D.* precedes the number. When used with the name of a century, it follows the name. The abbreviation *B.C.*, which stands for "before Christ," is used for dates before the Christian era. It follows either a specific year number or the name of a century.

EXAMPLES   In **A.D.** 1452, the Ottoman Turks invaded Constantinople.

By the end of the first century **A.D.**, the Romans had conquered much of Europe.

Cleopatra was a Greek-speaking queen of Egypt in the first century **B.C.**

In regular text, spell out the names of months and days whether they appear alone or in dates. Both types of names may be abbreviated in tables, notes, and bibliographies.

TEXT	Our next meeting will take place on the last **Tuesday** in **October.**
TABLE	Tues. afternoon Oct. 13, 2002
FOOTNOTE	"These authors first met on **Jan.** 16, 1887.
BIBLIOGRAPHY ENTRY	Ibata, David. "Information Highway to the Future," *Chicago Tribune*, 17 **Nov.** 1992, final **ed.**, **sec.** 1:8.

Abbreviate the designations for the two halves of the day measured by clock time. The abbreviation *A.M.* stands for the Latin phrase *ante meridiem*, meaning "before noon." The abbreviation *P.M.* stands for *post meridiem,* meaning "after noon." Both abbreviations follow the numerals designating the specific time.

EXAMPLES Andrew works five days a week from 8:00 **A.M.** until 5:00 **P.M.**

Units of Measurement

In regular text, spell out the names of units of measurement, whether they stand alone or follow a spelled-out number or a numeral. Such names may be abbreviated in tables and notes when they follow a numeral. Most such abbreviations are written without periods. However, do use a period after the abbreviation for *inch* (*in.*) to prevent confusion with the word *in.*

TEXT The speed limit here is sixty **miles per hour** [not *mph*]. The dorm room measured twenty **feet** [not *ft*] by fourteen.

TABLE

1 **tbsp** vinegar	75°**F**
6 **ft** 6 **in.**	5 **oz** cumin

Exercise 2 **Using Abbreviations**

Rewrite the following sentences, correcting errors in the use of abbreviations in formal writing.

EXAMPLE 1. I was born in Miami, FL.
1. *I was born in Miami, Florida.*

1. A. Lincoln was president of the United States from 1861 to 1865 and led the Union during the Civil War.
2. The flight for Santiago departs today at 4:30 P.M. in the afternoon.
3. Charlemagne ruled as emperor of the Romans until 814 A.D.
4. Duluth, MN, and Superior, WI, are two principal United States ports on Lake Superior.
5. The parcel was addressed to Mrs. Clare on Newcome Street in Ashburton Falls, MA.
6. Alexander the Great was born in Macedonia in B.C. 356.
7. The final speaker of the evening was Lt. Holden.
8. Please chew with your mouth closed, J. R..
9. Did that happen in 47 B.C?
10. The dogs were tired, as they had been playing since 6:00 A.M. in the morning.

Do not use *A.M.* or *P.M.* with numbers spelled out as words or as substitutes for the words *morning, afternoon,* or *evening.*

EXAMPLE
The festival will begin at **8:00 P.M.** (or **eight o'clock in the evening**) Saturday [not *eight P.M. Saturday*].

Also, do not use the words *morning, afternoon,* or *evening* with numerals followed by *A.M.* or *P.M.*

EXAMPLE
The next train for Greenwich leaves at **1:30 P.M.** (or **one-thirty in the afternoon**) [not *1:30 P.M. in the afternoon*].

MECHANICS

Review A **Using Periods, Question Marks, and Exclamation Points**

Insert periods, question marks, and exclamation points correctly in the following sentences. Use each type of end mark—period, question mark, and exclamation point—at least once.

EXAMPLE
1. Oh boy, it was a good thing we were friends?
1. *Oh boy, it was a good thing we were friends!*

1. Hey, Jo, my cousin Liz and I went hiking near Denver, Colorado
2. We carried our backpacks and slept in tents along the way
3. Each afternoon, we would make a cup of cocoa
4. Halfway through our trip, I wondered where the other box of instant cocoa was
5. Liz appeared puzzled
6. Which of us was responsible for packing all the food items
7. She thought I was, and I thought she was
8. Luckily, we have always gotten along well
9. At the end of the trip, Liz reached into her pack to get a jacket
10. Instead of a jacket, there was the other box of cocoa

Commas

Items in a Series

22f. Use commas to separate items in a series.

EXAMPLES
The camp counselor distributed baseballs, bats, volleyballs, tennis rackets, and bandages. [words in a series]

We have a government of the people, by the people, and for the people. [phrases in a series]

I know I will pass the test if I take good notes, if I study hard, and if I get a good night's sleep. [clauses in a series]

When the last two items in a series are joined by *and, or,* or *nor,* the comma before the conjunction is sometimes omitted when the comma is not needed to make the meaning of the sentence clear.

CLEAR WITHOUT COMMA   The entertainers sang, danced and juggled.

MECHANICS

NOT CLEAR	John, Sue and Marian went fishing.
WITHOUT COMMA	[Did John go fishing, or is he being addressed?]
CLEAR WITH COMMA	John, Sue, and Marian went fishing.

NOTE Words customarily used in pairs—such as *macaroni and cheese* and *law and order*—are set off as one item in a series.

EXAMPLE   We could order a sandwich, macaroni and cheese, or soup.

If all the items in a series are joined by *and, or,* or *nor,* do not use commas to separate them.

EXAMPLES   We ran **and** walked **and** even limped to the finish line.

He said that neither poverty **nor** discrimination **nor** discouragement prevented Derek Walcott from becoming an accomplished writer.

Independent clauses in a series are generally separated by semicolons. Short independent clauses, however, may be separated by commas.

EXAMPLES   We swam laps in the cool, refreshing pool; after that, we jogged around the lake; and we exercised with free weights, stationary bicycles, and rowing machines.

We swam, we jogged, and we exercised.

22g. Use commas to separate two or more adjectives preceding a noun.

EXAMPLE   I've had a long, hectic, tiring day.

When the last adjective in a series is thought of as part of the noun, the comma before the adjective is omitted.

EXAMPLES   I mailed the package at the main post office. [Together, *post* and *office* name a place.]

For lunch we had smooth, creamy broccoli soup. [Together, *broccoli* and *soup* name a thing.]

You can use two tests to determine whether an adjective and a noun form a unit.

TEST 1:   Insert the word *and* between the adjectives preceding the noun. If *and* fits sensibly between them, use a comma. In the first example above, *and* cannot be logically inserted: *main and post office.* In the second example, *and* sounds sensible between the first two adjectives (*smooth and creamy*) but not between the second and third adjectives (*creamy and broccoli*).

STYLE   TIP

For clarity, some writers prefer always to use the comma before the conjunction in a series. Follow your teacher's instructions on this point.

Reference Note

For more about using **semicolons,** see page 724.

MECHANICS

Reference Note

A word such as *post office* is called a **compound noun.** For more about **compound nouns,** see page 406.

TEST 2: Change the order of the adjectives. If the order of the adjectives can be reversed sensibly, use a comma. *Creamy, smooth broccoli soup* makes sense, but *broccoli creamy soup* and *post main office* do not.

NOTE If a word modifies one of the adjectives preceding the noun, the word is an adverb, not an adjective, and therefore should not be followed by a comma.

EXAMPLE   Which of these neckties looks best with this **light** green shirt? [*Light* modifies the adjective *green,* not the noun *shirt.*]

Exercise 3 Correcting Sentences by Adding Commas

For each of the following sentences, write each word that should be followed by a comma, and then add the comma. If a sentence is already correct, write *C.*

EXAMPLE   1. The king wore a thick warm luxurious robe.
           1. *thick, warm,*

1. One terrible summer when we were little, I had mumps you had measles and he had chickenpox.
2. The river overflowed again and filled our basement and drenched our neighbor's carpet.
3. Coriander cumin and saffron are three spices that are widely used in traditional Mexican cooking.
4. I took a flashlight a sleeping bag extra tennis shoes a rod and reel and a parka on our camping trip.
5. Magic Johnson Michael Jordan Larry Bird and Julius Erving have each received a Most Valuable Player award at least once for their achievements on the basketball court.
6. At the gymnastics meet, Les performed on the parallel bars the rings and the high bar.
7. With a quick powerful leap, the stunt double bounded over the burning balcony.
8. We looked in the sink on the floor and on Kim's clothing for her missing contact lens.
9. Have you read any of the novels by Jane Austen or the Brontë sisters or Virginia Woolf?
10. A little blond child in faded bluejeans emerged from the shrubbery to stare at the mail carrier.

Independent Clauses

22h. Use a comma before *and, but, for, nor, or, so,* or *yet* when the conjunction joins independent clauses.

EXAMPLES   Patrick brought the sandwiches, **and** Cindy brought the potato salad.

We got there on time, **but** Jeff and María were late.

> **NOTE** Always use a comma before *yet, so,* or *for* joining independent clauses. The comma is sometimes left out before *and, but, or,* or *nor* if the independent clauses are very short and the sentence will not be misunderstood without it.

EXAMPLES   He was apprehensive, **yet** he was also excited.

The bears failed to catch any salmon, **so** they went away.

I applied for the job **and** I got it.

Do not confuse a compound sentence with a simple sentence that has a compound verb. Generally, a comma does not precede the conjunction joining the parts of a compound verb.

COMPOUND SENTENCE   Han brought charcoal and lighter fluid, **but** she forgot matches. [two independent clauses]

SIMPLE SENTENCE   Han brought charcoal and lighter fluid **but** forgot matches. [one independent clause with a compound verb]

If the independent clauses contain commas, a semicolon may be required to separate them.

EXAMPLE   One of the cats had brown, black, and yellow spots; and the other, younger one was pure black.

Reference Note

For more about **simple sentences and compound sentences,** see page 504. For more about **compound subjects and compound verbs,** see page 447.

Reference Note

For more about **semicolons,** see page 724.

> **Exercise 4** Correcting Sentences by Adding Commas

For each of the following sentences, write the word that should be followed by a comma, and add the comma after it. If a sentence is already correct, write C.

EXAMPLE   1. Uncle Phil carefully steered the boat through the narrow channel and Lynn began baiting the hooks.

    1. channel,

1. All students must arrive on time for no one will be admitted late.

MECHANICS

2. The movie review complimented all the performers but the leading actress received the strongest praise.
3. A few rowdy spectators tried to grab the star so the bodyguards formed a ring around him.
4. The Japanese actors in Kabuki plays do not speak but they pantomime lines chanted by narrators on the stage.
5. Some people today work fewer hours than their grandparents did yet for many there never seem to be enough hours in a day.
6. The cost of living is rising for consumers pay higher prices than they did last year for gasoline and other products.
7. Our guide led and we followed closely.
8. Two groups of Hopi disagreed about how to run the town of Oraibi; they settled the matter with a tug of war and the losers moved away and founded the town of Hotevilla.
9. She did not like the story in the science fiction magazine nor did she enjoy the illustrations.
10. High school graduates may go on to college or may begin working immediately.

Nonessential Clauses and Phrases

22i. Use commas to set off nonessential subordinate clauses and nonessential participial phrases.

A *nonessential* (or *nonrestrictive*) subordinate clause or participial phrase contains information that is not necessary to the basic meaning of the sentence.

NONESSENTIAL CLAUSES	Emilia Ortiz, **who lives across the street from me,** won a scholarship to Stanford University.
	The capital of Massachusetts is Boston, **which is sometimes called the Athens of America.**
NONESSENTIAL PHRASES	Kelly, **waiting outside the stage door,** got the band leader's autograph.
	Born in Detroit, Robert Hayden was educated at the University of Michigan and later became a distinguished professor there.

The nonessential clause or phrase in each of the preceding examples can be left out without changing the main idea of the sentence.

TIPS & TRICKS

Generally, a subordinate clause or a participial phrase that modifies a proper noun is nonessential.

MECHANICS

EXAMPLES   Emilia Ortiz won a scholarship to Stanford University.

The capital of Massachusetts is Boston.

Kelly got the band leader's autograph.

Robert Hayden was educated at the University of Michigan and later became a distinguished professor there.

An *essential* (or *restrictive*) *subordinate clause* or *participial phrase* is not set off by commas because it contains information that is necessary to the meaning of the sentence.

ESSENTIAL CLAUSES   The sophomores **who made the Honor Roll** were listed in the school newspaper.

Library books **that are lost or damaged** must be replaced.

ESSENTIAL PHRASES   Students **planning to try out for a role in the play** should sign up no later than Friday afternoon.

Two poems **written by Lorna Dee Cervantes** are included in our literature book.

Notice how leaving out the essential clause or phrase affects the main idea of each of the examples above.

EXAMPLES   The sophomores were listed in the school newspaper. [Which sophomores?]

Library books must be replaced. [Which library books?]

Students should sign up no later than Friday afternoon. [Which students?]

Two poems are included in our literature book. [Which two poems?]

Some subordinate clauses and participial phrases may be either essential or nonessential. The presence or absence of commas tells the reader how the clause or phrase relates to the main idea of the sentence.

NONESSENTIAL CLAUSE   Marla's sister, **who attends Stanford University,** sent her a sweatshirt. [Marla has only one sister. That sister sent the sweatshirt.]

ESSENTIAL CLAUSE   Marla's sister **who attends Stanford University** sent her a sweatshirt. [Marla has more than one sister. The one attending Stanford University sent the sweatshirt.]

TIPS & TRICKS

Generally, a subordinate clause or a participial phrase that tells *which one(s)* of two or more is essential. Also, a subordinate clause beginning with *that* and modifying a noun or pronoun is generally essential.

MECHANICS

Reference Note

For more about **subordinate clauses,** see page 493. For more about **participial phrases,** see page 473.

NONESSENTIAL PHRASE	My former lab partner, **now living in Chicago,** visited me last week. [I have only one former lab partner. That person visited me last week.]
ESSENTIAL PHRASE	My former lab partner **now living in Chicago** visited me last week. [I have more than one former lab partner. The one living in Chicago visited me last week.]

Exercise 5 Correcting Sentences by Adding Commas

For each of the following sentences, write each word that should be followed by a comma and add the comma after it. If a sentence is already correct, write *C*.

EXAMPLE 1. Gigantic supermarkets which offer a stunning variety of goods and services developed from much smaller stores that first opened in the nineteenth century.

1. *supermarkets, services,*

1. The stores that became the world's first self-serve supermarkets were designed by Clarence Saunders who was an innovative entrepreneur.
2. Saunders who lived in Memphis, Tennessee named his stores Piggly Wiggly.
3. Some say that he got the idea for the name when he saw a fat pig wiggling under a fence.

4. The first Piggly Wiggly store which opened in 1916 had only one long aisle.

5. Customers shopping there saw all the products before they came to the exit.

6. Noticing that people often had difficulty finding products Albert Gerrard opened his own grocery store.

7. All of the items that were for sale were arranged alphabetically.

8. The name that Gerrard selected for his store was Alpha-Beta.

9. George Hartford who founded the Great Atlantic & Pacific Tea Company in 1859 nicknamed his stores A&P.

10. Developed by Michael Cullen the model for today's huge supermarkets opened in an abandoned garage in New York in 1930.

Introductory Elements

22j. Use a comma after certain introductory elements.

(1) Use a comma to set off a mild exclamation such as *well, oh,* or *why* at the beginning of a sentence. Other introductory words such as *yes* and *no* are also set off by commas.

EXAMPLES   **Sure,** I'll go with you.

            Oh, look at that car!

            No, I haven't taken the exam yet.

(2) Use a comma after an introductory participle or participial phrase.

EXAMPLES   **Shivering,** the couple hurried into the warm lobby of the movie theater.

            Calling for a timeout, the referee blew his whistle and signaled.

            Exhausted after a three-mile swim, Diana emerged from the water.

Reference Note

For more information about correcting **misplaced and dangling modifiers,** see page 626.

NOTE   When writing an introductory participial phrase, make sure that it modifies the subject in the sentence; otherwise, the phrase is a misplaced or dangling modifier.

MISPLACED	Swimming in the huge aquarium, visitors of all ages were fascinated by the rare species of tropical fish. [Were visitors swimming in the aquarium?]
REVISED	Swimming in the huge aquarium, the rare species of tropical fish fascinated visitors of all ages.
REVISED	Visitors of all ages were fascinated by the rare species of tropical fish swimming in the huge aquarium.
DANGLING	Looking through the magazine, a recipe for *fattoush,* a delicious Syrian bread salad, caught Chris's attention. [Was a recipe looking through the magazine?]
REVISED	Looking through the magazine, Chris spotted a recipe for *fattoush,* a delicious Syrian bread salad.

Reference Note

For more information about **prepositional phrases,** see page 467.

(3) Use a comma after an introductory prepositional phrase if the phrase is long or if two or more phrases appear together.

EXAMPLES   **During the long bus ride home,** we sang songs and told stories to amuse ourselves.

By the light of the harvest moon in September, we went on an old-fashioned hayride.

Reference Note

For more information about **parenthetical expressions,** see page 770.

A single, short introductory prepositional phrase is not followed by a comma unless the sentence is awkward to read without one or unless the phrase is parenthetical.

EXAMPLES   In the book the writer develops a clever plot. [The sentence is clear without the comma.]

In the book, review pages 236–290. [Without the comma, *book review* could be read as a compound noun.]

In the book review, the critic praised the writer's clever plot. [Without the comma, *review* could be read as a verb.]

By the way, do you have a copy of the book? [The phrase is parenthetical.]

(4) Use a comma after an introductory adverb clause.

An introductory adverb clause may appear at the beginning of a sentence or before any independent clause in the sentence.

EXAMPLES **When you've gone to this school for a while,** you'll know your way around, too.

The first game of the season is Friday; **after we claim our first victory,** we'll celebrate at Darcy's Deli.

Reference Note

For more about **adverb clauses,** see page 498.

NOTE Generally, an adverb clause that comes at the end of a sentence is not preceded by a comma.

EXAMPLE   Wolfgang Amadeus Mozart composed his first opera **when he was twelve years old.**

Exercise 6 Correcting Sentences with Introductory Elements by Adding Commas

For each of the following sentences, write the word that should be followed by a comma and add the comma after it. If a sentence is already correct, write *C*.

EXAMPLE   **1.** Trying to reduce the amount of fat in their diets many Americans are eating less meat.

    1. diets,

1. Yes for many people around the world, meat is not a daily food staple.
2. Serving as a main source of nutrition whole grains such as corn, oats, wheat, and rice feed millions.
3. In Mexico a favorite nutritious dish is a corn tortilla with beans.
4. Because the soybean is high in protein it has been a principal crop in Asian countries for more than five thousand years.
5. If you'd like more variety in your diet you may want to substitute unrefined whole grains for meat occasionally.
6. Offering healthful alternatives to meat whole grains contain nutrients such as vitamins, proteins, amino acids, and starches.
7. In the process of making spoilage-resistant products some food manufacturers refine whole grains.
8. Refined for commercial use the grains lose most of their food value because the nutritious outer hulls are stripped away.
9. If you take time in the supermarket you should be able to find whole grains.
10. Since many cookbooks now include recipes for grain dishes you can learn to use grains in many tasty snacks and meals.

MECHANICS

Review B Using Commas in a Paragraph

For the following sentences, write each word that should be followed by a comma. Then, add a comma after each word.

EXAMPLES [1] Throughout the ages around the world people have used weapons for hunting for fighting, and for defending themselves from wild animals.

1. world, hunting,

[2] According to archaeologists weapons were among the earliest tools.

2. archaeologists,

[1] Many weapons that were produced in early times were similar in appearance function and design. [2] The English word *weapon* is related to the Old English *wæpen* the Dutch *wapen* the German *Waffe* and an earlier common root. [3] Sticks stones and natural poisons such as the toxic sweat of these Central and South American frogs were probably the first weapons. [4] Among those varieties of weapons the stick thrown by hand became one of the most heavily specialized. [5] As you can see the dart the arrow the spear the lance and the javelin were all developed from the stick thrown by hand. [6] Another kind of weapon, the sling, was used all over the world for it was easy to make and not too difficult to master. [7] According to the Biblical account, when the Hebrew king David was just a boy he killed the Philistine giant Goliath with a simple hand-made sling. [8] An unusual weapon similar to the sling is the bola which is a cord with heavy weights of stone or wood or metal at the ends. [9] In some parts of South America gauchos still use bolas which can entangle cattle without inflicting pain injury or death. [10] Over the centuries these simple weapons have been developed into highly sophisticated and deadly artillery such as the missiles that were used in Operation Desert Storm.

Interrupters

22k. Use commas to set off an expression that interrupts a sentence.

(1) Use commas to set off nonessential appositives and nonessential appositive phrases.

An *appositive* is a noun or pronoun placed beside another noun or pronoun to identify or describe it. An *appositive phrase* consists of an appositive and its modifiers.

EXAMPLES   A senator from Kansas, **Nancy Landon Kassebaum,** was the principal speaker. [appositive]

Do you know him, **the boy wearing the blue shirt**? [appositive phrase]

A *nonessential* (or *nonrestrictive*) *appositive* or *appositive phrase* adds information that is unnecessary to the basic meaning of the sentence. In other words, the meaning of the sentence is clear and complete with or without the appositive or appositive phrase.

EXAMPLES   Have you read *At Home in India*, **a book by Cynthia Bowles**?

On July 20, 1969, Neil Armstrong, **one of the three astronauts on the Apollo 11 mission,** became the first person to walk on the moon.

Notice that the meaning of each of the examples above remains clear and complete without the appositive phrase.

EXAMPLES   Have you read *At Home in India*?

On July 20, 1969, Neil Armstrong became the first person to walk on the moon.

An *essential* (or *restrictive*) *appositive* or *appositive phrase* is not set off by commas because it adds information that makes the noun or pronoun it identifies or explains more specific. In other words, if you were to omit an essential appositive or appositive phrase, you would leave out key information or would change the intended meaning of the sentence.

EXAMPLES   My friend **James** helped me.

Speaking of movies, have you seen the animated film ***The Prince of Egypt***?

MECHANICS

TIPS & TRICKS

Generally, an appositive or appositive phrase that tells *which one(s)* of two or more is essential.

Reference Note

For more information about **appositives** and **appositive phrases,** see page 711.

Notice how omitting the appositive from each of the preceding examples changes the meaning of the sentence.

EXAMPLES   My friend helped me. [Which friend?]

Speaking of movies, have you seen the animated film? [Which animated film?]

> **Exercise 7** **Correcting Sentences with Appositives and Appositive Phrases by Adding Commas**

Correctly punctuate the appositives and appositive phrases in the following sentences. If a sentence is already correct, write *C*.

EXAMPLE   1. Leonardo da Vinci an Italian Renaissance artist is perhaps best remembered for painting *Mona Lisa.*

1. *Leonardo da Vinci, an Italian Renaissance artist, is perhaps best remembered for painting* Mona Lisa.

Mona Lisa by Leonardo da Vinci.

1. Between 1500 and 1506, Leonardo da Vinci a brilliant man created several major works.
2. My favorite painting *Mona Lisa* was painted then.
3. Leonardo's painting *Mona Lisa* is a prized possession of the Louvre in Paris.
4. The painting a portrait of a young Florentine woman is slightly cracked as a result of temperature changes.
5. The *Mona Lisa* an ideal type of portrait revolutionized portrait painting.
6. Leonardo's work influenced the young painter Raphael.
7. Raphael's painting *The Grand Duke's Madonna* was done in the style of *Mona Lisa.*
8. In 1911 an Italian house painter Vincenzo Perugia stole the *Mona Lisa* from its frame.
9. For two years members of the Paris police some of the world's cleverest detectives were baffled by the crime.
10. Since its recovery, the painting one of the most valuable portraits in the world has been closely guarded.

(2) Use commas to set off words used in direct address.

Reference Note

For information on **words of direct address,** see page 447.

EXAMPLES   **David,** please close the door.

Did you call me, **Mother**?

Yes, **Mr. Ramos,** I turned in my paper.

(3) Use commas to set off parenthetical expressions.

A *parenthetical expression* is a side remark that adds information or shows a relationship between ideas.

Common Parenthetical Expressions		
after all	however	nevertheless
at any rate	I believe	of course
consequently	in fact	on the contrary
for example	in the first place	on the other hand
for instance	meanwhile	that is
generally speaking	moreover	therefore

EXAMPLES   **In fact,** Emily Dickinson is my favorite poet.

You are, **I hope,** planning to arrive on time.

Sometimes such expressions are not used parenthetically and are not set off by commas.

PARENTHETICAL   Long-distance calls are a bargain, **at any rate.**
[meaning "in any case"]

NOT PARENTHETICAL   Long-distance calls are a bargain **at any rate.**
[meaning "at any cost"]

NOTE   A contrasting expression introduced by *not* is parenthetical and should be set off by commas.

EXAMPLE   Emily Brontë, **not her sister Charlotte,** wrote *Wuthering Heights.*

Review C   **Correcting Paragraphs by Adding Commas**

For the following paragraphs, write each word that should be followed by a comma and add the comma after it.

EXAMPLE   **[1]** The artist Faith Ringgold painstakingly hand-letters her beautiful unique story quilts.

1. *beautiful,*

[1] Continuing the ancient tradition of quilting Ringgold combines printed dyed and pieced fabric with acrylic paintings or photo etchings. [2] By placing the tradition in a new context the artist gives it new meaning.

Reference Note

Parentheses and **dashes** are sometimes used to set off parenthetical expressions. See page 770.

COMPUTER TIP

If you use a computer, you may want to create a file of the parenthetical expressions listed on this page. Refer to this file as you proofread your writing, and be sure that you have punctuated these expressions correctly. If your word-processing software has a search function, use the function to speed up your proofreading. The computer will search for and highlight each occurrence of whatever expression you select.

MECHANICS

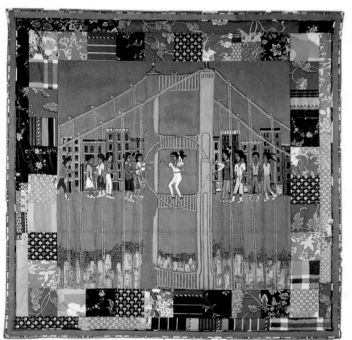

Faith Ringgold, *Double Dutch on the Golden Gate Bridge* (1988). Acrylic, canvas, painted, dyed, pieced fabric (68½″ × 68″). © 1988 Faith Ringgold Inc. Private Collection.

[3] Ringgold whose earlier works include landscapes murals masks and soft sculptures began making story quilts in 1980. [4] Titled *Echoes of Harlem* the first one was a collaboration between the artist and her mother the dress designer Willi Posey who learned quilting from her own grandmother who had learned it from her own mother a slave.

[5] Most of Ringgold's story quilts are designed to be viewed as parts of a series not as separate pieces and many include portions of a narrative linking the works in the series. [6] The work pictured here *Double Dutch on the Golden Gate Bridge* has no accompanying text and is from the *Woman on a Bridge* series which includes five works. [7] Capturing the excitement of a childhood game it depicts a pastime cherished by generations of African Americans. [8] The work speaks however to more than a single culture and appeals to all people who recognize in it joyful moments from their childhoods.

[9] Ringgold still lives and works in Harlem the section of New York City where she was born. [10] Did you know Amy that one of her story quilts sold for $40,000 and is in the permanent collection of the city's Guggenheim Museum a major gallery of modern art?

Conventional Uses of Commas

22l. Use commas in certain conventional situations.

(1) Use commas to separate items in dates and addresses.

EXAMPLES   On Saturday, June 21, 1999, Robert moved to Miami Beach, Florida, with his parents.

His new address is 814 Georgia Avenue, Miami Beach, FL 33139-0814.

Notice that a comma generally separates the last item in a date or an address from the words that follow it.

Do not use commas to set off the following items.

- the month from the day

EXAMPLE   My brother's birthday is **October 22**.

- the month from the year when the day is given before the month

EXAMPLE   Was the date of your graduation **20 May 2000**?

- the month from the year when no day is given

EXAMPLE   The hottest month on record here is **August 1996**.

- a house number from a street name

EXAMPLE   Ms. Lee lives at **531 Winchester Street**.

- a state abbreviation from a ZIP Code

EXAMPLE   Is the last part of your new address Richmond, **VA 23235-4766**?

- items preceded by prepositions

EXAMPLE   The McCaslins moved to 419 Cedar Avenue **in** Chicago **on** September 10 **of** 1998.

(2) Use a comma after the salutation of a personal letter and after the closing of any letter.

EXAMPLES   Dear Marcus**,**   Dear Aunt Meg**,**

                Affectionately yours**,**   Sincerely yours**,**

NOTE Use a colon after the salutation of a business letter.

EXAMPLES   Dear Dr. Cho**:**

                To whom it may concern**:**

(3) Use a comma to set off an abbreviation, such as *Jr.*, *Sr.*, or *M.D.*, that follows a person's name.

Notice that when words follow a person's title, a comma appears both before and after the title.

EXAMPLES   Elena Moreno**, M.D.**

                Russell E. Davis**, Jr.,** has been elected mayor.

Reference Note
For more about **colons**, see page 729. For more about writing **letters**, see "Writing" in the Quick Reference Handbook.

MECHANICS

Unnecessary Commas

22m. Do not use unnecessary commas.

Too many commas can be as confusing as too few. Do not use a comma unless a rule requires one or unless the meaning would be unclear without it.

CONFUSING On Friday, after school, my friend, Rita, and I played badminton at her house until her dog, Ruffles, a frisky, golden retriever, joined us and ran off with the shuttlecock, clenched in its teeth.

CLEAR On Friday after school, my friend Rita and I played badminton at her house until her dog Ruffles, a frisky golden retriever, joined us and ran off with the shuttlecock clenched in its teeth.

> **Exercise 8** **Correcting Sentences by Adding Commas**

For the following sentences, write each word that should be followed by a comma and add the comma after it.

EXAMPLE **1.** On our way to Birmingham Alabama we stayed overnight in Chattanooga Tennessee.

      1. Birmingham, Alabama, Chattanooga,

1. On August 1 1999 we moved from Eureka California to 220 Tuxford Place Thousand Oaks California.
2. We left Tampa Florida on Monday June 15 and arrived in Albuquerque New Mexico on June 17.
3. The hotel on Gulfport Road was destroyed by fire on Tuesday March 13 1984.
4. My brother received a letter that began, "Dear John There's something I've been meaning to tell you."
5. We interviewed Franklin R. Thomas M.D. at his emergency clinic on Wilson Road.
6. On July 11 2001 Christa and Jerry will join hundreds of other cyclists and ride from Minneapolis Minnesota to Chicago Illinois.
7. The party will take place October 9 at 2480 Hastings Road in Birmingham Alabama.
8. Raphael X. Gideon Sr. is our new police chief.
9. Marcia traveled to Tyler Texas and Orlando Florida last month.
10. Dr. Martin Luther King Jr. was born on January 15 1929.

Review D **Proofreading a Letter for Correct Comma Usage**

Proofread the following letter, adding or deleting commas as needed.

EXAMPLE   **[1]** Uncle Victor lives in a small white house.

　　　　　1. small,

[**1**] August 26 2001

[**2**] Dear Amy

　[**3**] I received your letter, and wanted to send a quick reply answering your questions. [**4**] Uncle Victor does in fact have a new address; he and Aunt Margo moved to a faraway, beautiful land of sunshine. [**5**] Their new address is 1300 Fairwood Drive San Diego CA 99069. [**6**] They moved last month and Uncle Victor started his new job last Wednesday, morning. [**7**] They plan to be back in town to tie up loose ends by selling their house picking up their dogs and visiting with friends on Friday September 4. [**8**] I will have a few friends over for dinner that night, and hope you can come. [**9**] I will by the way be cooking my famous Greek dinner.

　　　　　[**10**] Affectionately yours

　　　　　Roy

Review E **Revising Paragraphs by Adding Commas**

For the sentences in the following paragraphs, write each word that should be followed by a comma and add the comma after it. If a sentence is already correct, write *C*.

EXAMPLE   **[1]** In their study of the culture of the ancient Greeks the drama students read about the three playwrights Aeschylus Sophocles, and Aristophanes.

　　　　　1. Greeks, Aeschylus,

[**1**] As early as the sixth century B.C. plays were performed in Athens Greece in the amphitheater pictured on the next page the

┌HELP──
Some of the sentences in Review E need more than one comma.

Theater of Dionysus. [2] The Theater of Dionysus is located on the south slope of the Acropolis an elevated fortified section of Athens. [3] The plays presented in ancient Greece marked the beginning of drama in the Western world. [4] In fact the English word *theater* comes from the Greek word *theatron* which means "a place for seeing."

[5] Wearing masks to show which characters they were portraying the actors in ancient dramas often played several different roles. [6] In addition all roles including those of female characters were performed by men.

[7] Although records show that Greek playwrights wrote hundreds of tragedies fewer than thirty-five of these plays survive. [8] The earliest Greek dramatist Aeschylus wrote the *Oresteia* a powerful story of murder revenge and divine mercy. [9] Sophocles often regarded as the greatest dramatist of all time is credited with writing more than one hundred plays. [10] Among the surviving works of Aristophanes whom the ancient Greeks considered the greatest comic playwright are the three satires *The Clouds The Wasps* and *The Frogs.*

Chapter Review

A. Using End Marks

Add or replace end marks in the following sentences, as needed.

1. Have you heard of the Bengali writer Rabindranath Tagore
2. Wow Look at that sunset
3. Last week I saw the cartoon version of *Alice in Wonderland*?
4. The first speaker was the Reverend James Elliot
5. Will you be in town next Friday!
6. Will you turn the radio down a little!
7. When was the impressive Swedish golfer Eric Estlund born.
8. "Oh darn it" exclaimed Paul in exasperation.
9. Musical backup was provided by the J. L. Bourgeois Trio
10. What an absolutely marvelous exercise.

B. Correcting Sentences by Adding Punctuation

Add periods, question marks, exclamation points, and commas where they are needed in the following sentences. If a sentence is already punctuated correctly, write *C*.

11. Although scholars aren't certain about who was the first European printer to use movable type Johann Gutenberg is usually credited
12. The students who have signed up for the field trip may leave at noon but all the others must attend classes
13. Gloria did you notice where I left my bowling ball
14. Miriam Colón who was born in Puerto Rico founded the Puerto Rican Traveling Theatre
15. Was the Great Pyramid in Egypt built sometime between 2600 and 2500 B.C.?
16. Vendors sold T-shirts, buttons caps and pennants to the sports fans outside the stadium
17. Listening to the orchestra play "The Star-Spangled Banner" I realized that I'm proud to be American
18. The hikers munched on sunflower seeds and quenched their thirst with ice-cold refreshing spring water
19. Isn't their address 1042 Cleveland Avenue Enid Oklahoma 73703

20. Marian Anderson a contralto was the first African American to become a permanent member of the Metropolitan Opera Company

21. Wow That's amazing

22. We rushed to the airport stood in line bought our tickets and then heard that the flight had been delayed for three hours

23. Norm has had quite a run of bad luck yet he still says tomorrow will be a better day for he prides himself on being an optimist

24. That Ming vase wrapped in cotton and packed in a crate was delivered to the museum earlier today

25. If we're late for practice again however Ms Stubbs will drop us from the team

26. How lucky I was

27. At the beginning of the eighteenth century Chikamatsu Monzaemon wrote the first Japanese tragedies to focus on the lives of common ordinary people

28. Nowadays the Sioux generally speaking make their living as farmers and ranchers

29. Jan Matzeliger an inventor in Lynn Massachusetts revolutionized the shoe industry in 1883 with his machine that joined the top of a shoe to its sole

30. These four students should report to the auditorium after lunch: Jeff Malone Mary Holt Kathryn Rogers and Hartmut Boylan Barthzwinger Jr

C. Correcting Paragraphs by Adding Punctuation

For each sentence in the following paragraph, add periods, question marks, exclamation points, and commas where they are needed.

[31] Going to visit Uncle Ricky is one of my greatest pleasures for he owns and operates a semitrailer [32] His big rig an eighteen-wheeler affectionately named "Pug" is used to haul produce from coast to coast [33] One of Uncle Ricky's craziest experiences was the time he left Boston and drove to 2842 Beltline Drive Logan Virginia to deliver a load of oranges grapefruit and lemons [34] When he arrived at the address he was dumbfounded [35] As a matter of fact

the address turned out to be that of a citrus orchard **[36]** Obviously, the orchard had been producing Logan's finest fruit for years **[37]** Climbing back on board "Pug" Uncle Ricky checked his shipping order **[38]** He realized with dismay that he should have delivered the shipment to Logan Vermont instead of Logan Virginia **[39]** Fortunately it was a clear run up a couple of interstates for "Pug" and Uncle Ricky delivered his fruit only half a day late **[40]** Now he chuckles about it and says wryly, "Well I did wonder how I had managed to arrive a whole day early"

Writing Application
Using Commas in Instructions

Using Commas Correctly   Create an educational board game or computer game, and write instructions explaining how to play it. Include information from at least one of your school subjects, such as math, science, or history. Use commas to make your instructions as clear as possible.

Prewriting   Choose a subject area that interests you. Then, decide what the object of the game will be. Jot down notes about the number of players, the kinds of supplies or equipment needed, and other rules of the game. Give your game a catchy title, and then arrange the instructions in an order that will be easy for players to follow.

Writing   Keep in mind that your instructions will be the players' only source of information. Try to anticipate their questions, and aim for a conversational tone, as if you were explaining the game in person.

Revising   Ask some of your friends to play the game. As you watch, note any problems they have with understanding the instructions. Then, add, delete, replace, or rearrange information to make the instructions easier to understand.

Publishing   Proofread your instructions, paying special attention to your use of end marks and commas. Use a computer to make a clean printout, or photocopy a neatly handwritten copy. You might offer copies of your game to your school's media center or to one of the organizations that serve your community.

Punctuation
Semicolons and Colons

Diagnostic Preview

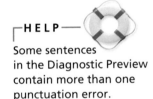
Correcting Sentences by Adding Semicolons and Colons

For each of the following sentences, write the word or numeral that precedes each punctuation error. Then, add the semicolon or colon needed.

EXAMPLE   1. Please bring the following items books, pencils, and newspapers.

　　　　　　1. *items:*

1. My aunt Pam loves to play backgammon and chess however, she rarely has time because she works at two jobs.
2. In 1904, Mary McLeod Bethune founded a school for girls in Daytona Beach, Florida that school is now Bethune-Cookman College.
3. Psalm 23 1–6 is one of the best-known passages in the Bible.
4. According to one book that I have read, *The Real McCoy The Life of an African-American Inventor,* an oil can used in railroad maintenance gave rise to the popular expression "the real McCoy."
5. If I had a million dollars, I would visit London, England Cairo, Egypt Buenos Aires, Argentina and Tokyo, Japan.
6. We have to write reports for gym class on one of the following athletes Jesse Owens, Sonja Henie, Jim Thorpe, Althea Gibson, or Babe Didrikson Zaharias.

7. Our neighbor's cocker spaniel barked all night long as a result, I did not sleep well.

8. Candace will have to take Sandra's place in tonight's performance unfortunately, Sandra sprained her ankle and cannot walk.

9. I have ridden bicycles, horses, and motorcycles and I have traveled in trains, buses, and planes.

10. Asia has both the highest and the lowest points on the earth's surface Mount Everest, the highest, soars 29,028 feet the Dead Sea, a salt lake, lies 1,300 feet below sea level.

11. Instructed to be prompt, we arrived at school at 7 15 A.M., but the doors were locked consequently, we had to wait until 7 30 A.M. to enter the building.

12. Indira Gandhi, who served for many years as the prime minister of India, grew up in the world of civic life, politics, and government for her father, Jawaharlal Nehru, was the first prime minister of India, from 1947 to 1964.

13. My friends Ruth and Cindy disagree about the role of fate in life Ruth believes that people can control their own destiny, but Cindy insists that people are simply pawns of fate.

14. I don't like to prepare outlines nevertheless, the highest grade I ever received was for a report that I wrote from an outline.

15. Mr. Kowalski has always regretted that he did not learn to speak Polish when he was a child now he is taking a conversational Polish class at the college.

16. The computer software business is an enormous, growing industry in fact, people can buy software that does everything from balancing budgets to plotting biorhythm charts.

17. Every morning Lonnie rises at 5 00, jogs until 5 30, showers, eats breakfast by 6 15, and catches the 6 35 bus.

18. Red Cloud, a leader of the Oglala Sioux, was a military genius he successfully defended Sioux lands against settlers who wanted to build a trail from Laramie, Wyoming, to Virginia City, Montana.

19. Gates of the Arctic National Park, which is located in northern Alaska, is known for its large populations of certain animals caribou, grizzly bears, moose, and wolves.

20. If you want to send fragile items through the mail, the post office recommends that you do the following pack them in fiberboard containers use foam, plastic, or padding to cushion them and then seal the package carefully, reinforcing it with filament tape.

Semicolons

Reference Note

For information on using a **comma** to **separate independent clauses that are joined by a coordinating conjunction,** see page 703.

23a. Use a semicolon between independent clauses that are closely related in thought and that are not joined by *and, but, for, nor, or, so,* or *yet.*

EXAMPLES
Everyone else in my family excels in a particular sport; I seem to be the only exception.

The river is rising rapidly; it is expected to crest by noon.

Reference Note

For information about **conjunctive adverbs,** see page 492.

23b. Use a semicolon between independent clauses joined by a conjunctive adverb or a transitional expression.

EXAMPLES
Leonor is planning to become an engineer; **however,** she is also interested in graphic design.

Only two people registered for the pottery lessons; **as a result,** the class was canceled.

Notice in the examples above that the conjunctive adverb and the transitional expression are each followed by a comma.

STYLE TIP

Use a semicolon to join independent clauses only if the ideas in the clauses are closely related.

INCORRECT
Greg likes Italian food; Marla prefers going to the beach.

CORRECT
Greg likes Italian food; Marla prefers Chinese food.

Commonly Used Conjunctive Adverbs			
accordingly	however	moreover	besides
also	nevertheless	consequently	instead
indeed	next	still	then
otherwise	furthermore	meanwhile	therefore

Commonly Used Transitional Expressions			
as a result	for example	for instance	in fact
in spite of	in conclusion	in other words	that is

NOTE When a conjunctive adverb or a transitional expression appears within one of the clauses instead of between the clauses, it is usually set off by commas. The two clauses may still be separated by a semicolon.

EXAMPLES
Ralph Ellison is best known for his 1952 novel, *Invisible Man*; he also, **however,** wrote short stories and essays.

Not all birds migrate south for the winter; cardinals, **for instance,** can stay in northern climates year round.

MECHANICS

Using conjunctive adverbs and transitional expressions can help you clearly show relationships between ideas. Notice in the examples below how these expressions clarify the relationship between the ideas expressed in the clauses.

EXAMPLES   The class has finished the nonfiction unit**; therefore,** we will begin the poetry unit on Monday. [Two ideas have a cause-and-effect relationship.]

The poems will be discussed in class**; meanwhile,** we will be working on our research papers on our own time. [Two ideas have a time relationship.]

Most students are studying poets from the distant past**; I, however,** am researching the poetic devices of a modern songwriter. [Two ideas have a contradictory relationship.]

Exercise 1   **Correcting Sentences by Adding Commas and Semicolons**

For the following sentences, write each word that should be followed by a semicolon or a comma. Add the needed punctuation mark after the word.

EXAMPLE   1. The clever carving shown here was handmade in Mexico today carvings like this are sold all over the world.

    1. *Mexico;*

1. The carvings come from the Oaxaca (pronounced wä•hä´•kä) Valley in fact 90 percent of the two hundred families who make them live in just three villages.
2. Carving has been a tradition among Oaxacans for hundreds of years only recently however have the artists sold their works outside the valley.
3. In many families, the fathers and older sons do the actual carving meanwhile the other family members sand and paint the figures.
4. The artists find inspiration for their creations in everyday life for example religion and nature are rich sources of ideas.
5. Even those carvers whose works have won worldwide acclaim have chosen to continue living in the valley their ties to their families and communities are very strong.

6. Art in Mexico is varied and distinctive and it exhibits a strong Spanish influence.

7. The Zapotec and Mixtec peoples of Puebla and Oaxaca have a long history of artistic craftsmanship the Mixtec were considered master goldsmiths.

8. The Mixtec built a tremendous pyramid in Cholula it was the largest pyramid of the ancient world.

9. During the thirteenth century, stone was a favorite medium of these peoples they also used bone, gold, jade, and wood.

10. Much of the art from southern Central America was destroyed during the years of the Spanish conquest but several historical manuscripts survive today.

23c. You may need to use a semicolon (rather than a comma) before a coordinating conjunction to join independent clauses that contain commas.

CONFUSING   June sat with Tony, Pat, and me, and Josh sat with Flora, Zack, and Geraldo.

CLEAR   June sat with Tony, Pat, and me; and Josh sat with Flora, Zack, and Geraldo.

CONFUSING   Searching for the house key, I found a dime, a nickel, and a penny, and John, my brother, found his lost watch.

CLEAR   Searching for the house key, I found a dime, a nickel, and a penny; and John, my brother, found his lost watch.

23d. Use a semicolon between items in a series if the items contain commas.

EXAMPLES   In 1990, the three largest cities in the United States were New York, New York; Los Angeles, California; and Chicago, Illinois.

You may turn in your book reports on Thursday, September 14; Friday, September 15; Monday, September 18; or Tuesday, September 19.

Exercise 2 **Correcting Sentences by Adding Semicolons**

For the following sentences, write each word that should be followed by a semicolon. Add the needed punctuation mark after the word. If a sentence is already correct, write *C*.

EXAMPLE 1. The winners of the regional science fair were Anya Garcia, who came in first, Jeff Ford, who came in second, and Alberto Robinson, who came in third.

  1. *first; second;*

1. The president of the student council has appointed the following members to chair committees: Anna Maria Chen, fundraising, Ben Cohen, volunteer services, and Donna Massad, event planning.

2. Fortunately, Candace remembered the address, or we would have been quite late, Roseanne.

3. Eli went to the matinee with Jae, Kerry, and Sung; but Josh, Taylor, and I preferred to go hiking.

4. After his concert in New York, my uncle Vittorio will come to visit on Thursday, March 25, Friday, March 26, or Saturday, March 27.

5. Would you prefer to live in Boston, Massachusetts, San Francisco, California, or Seattle, Washington?

6. Performers in the show were Tony Fernandez, trumpet and trombone, Donna Lee Bryant, clarinet and saxophone, and Danica Ward, drums and steel guitar.

7. I bought my sister several gifts, including a book, a skirt, and a tennis racket, but, unfortunately, I couldn't find a present for my mother, who wants an antique desk.

8. We admired the atrium's flowering vines, rock formations, and fountains, and then we stepped out into the courtyard, followed the flagstone path, and crossed the bridge over the goldfish pond.

9. To prepare for the performance we must set the stage, check the lights, and test the sound system; then, the dancers will take their places, the audience will be seated, and the curtain will rise.

10. On our backpacking trip to Eastern Europe, we hope to visit Prague, Czech Republic, Budapest, Hungary, Bucharest, Romania, and Krakow, Poland.

Review A   Correcting Sentences by Adding Commas and Semicolons

For the following sentences, write each word that should be followed by a semicolon or a comma. Add the needed punctuation mark after each word. If a sentence is already correct, write *C*.

EXAMPLE 1. The diagram on the next page shows the typical seating plan of a symphony orchestra a conductor occupies the podium.

  1. *orchestra;*

─HELP─
Some sentences in Review A may need more than one punctuation mark.

MECHANICS

1. All of the instruments in a symphony orchestra are divided into classes based on how they produce sound many musicians can play several instruments within a class.

2. The four classes are strings, woodwinds, brass, and percussion.

3. Some of the stringed instruments are played with a bow some are plucked with the fingers or with a pick still others are operated by means of a keyboard.

4. Woodwinds, which were once made mainly of wood, include the flute, the clarinet, and the saxophone but other materials, such as metal or plastic, are often used nowadays.

5. Most brass instruments, such as the trumpet, tuba, and cornet, have valves that regulate the pitch but the trombone, my favorite instrument, has a sliding section for this purpose.

6. Kettledrums, or timpani, are percussion instruments that can be tuned to a specific pitch most other kinds of drums, the cymbals, and the triangle however cannot be tuned.

7. A conductor's job is to coordinate the sounds produced by these different instruments however this task is only one of a conductor's responsibilities.

8. Conductors must study the theory of music for years furthermore they must be skilled at playing at least one instrument.

9. Many people think a conductor just establishes the tempo of the music they do not realize that he or she also selects the music, interprets the composer's meaning, and brings out the best performance in each musician.

10. The goal of many conductors is to lead a major orchestra such as one of those in London, England Mexico City, Mexico Boston, Massachusetts or Chicago, Illinois.

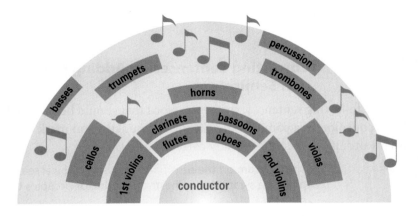

Colons

23e. Use a colon to mean "note what follows."

(1) Use a colon before a list of items, especially after expressions such as *the following* and *as follows*.

EXAMPLES   In Washington, D.C., we visited four important national sites**:** the White House, the Washington Monument, the Vietnam Veterans Memorial, and the Lincoln Memorial.

The only articles allowed in the examination area are **as follows:** pencils, compasses, rulers, and protractors.

During summer vacation, Juanita read biographies of **the following** people**:** John Ross and Annie Wauneka.

NOTE Do not use a colon between a verb and its complements or between a preposition and its objects.

INCORRECT   At the new amusement park we rode: the roller coaster, the Ferris wheel, the bumper cars, and the water slide.

CORRECT   At the amusement park we rode the roller coaster, the Ferris wheel, the bumper cars, and the water slide.
[The list serves as the direct object of the verb *rode*.]

INCORRECT   Our family has lived in: California, Arizona, and Texas.

CORRECT   Our family has lived in California, Arizona, and Texas.
[The list serves as the object of the preposition *in*.]

(2) Use a colon before a long, formal statement or quotation.

EXAMPLE   Thomas Paine's first pamphlet in the series *The American Crisis* starts with these famous words**:**

These are the times that try men's souls. The summer soldier and the sunshine patriot will, in this crisis, shrink from the service of their country; but he that stands it *now* deserves the love and thanks of man and woman.

23f. Use a colon before a statement that explains or clarifies a preceding statement.

EXAMPLES   He deserves a raise**:** He completed the project on schedule and under budget.

Preston slapped his forehead**:** He had forgotten to put oregano in the sauce.

HELP

When a list of words, phrases, or subordinate clauses follows a colon, the first word of the list is generally lowercase.

EXAMPLE
When you walk into class, you need to have the following with you: **y**our textbook, a pen and a pencil, writing paper, and a good attitude.

Reference Note
For information on **complements,** see page 450. For information on **objects of prepositions,** see page 467.

Reference Note
For information on using **long quotations,** see page 747.

HELP

When an independent clause follows a colon, the first word of the clause begins with a capital letter.

EXAMPLE
The current debate is still best summed up by Mark Twain: "**I**t is better to support schools than jails."

MECHANICS

23g. Use a colon in certain conventional situations.

(1) Use a colon between the hour and the minute.

EXAMPLES   6**:**15 P.M.   9**:**55 tomorrow morning

(2) Use a colon between chapter and verse in Biblical references.

EXAMPLES   Psalms 8**:**9   I Corinthians 13**:**1–13

(3) Use a colon between a title and a subtitle.

EXAMPLES   *I Like Jazz***:** *The Essence of Billie Holiday* [recording]

                  *Tilting Knights***:** *King Richard and Saladin* [painting]

(4) Use a colon after the salutation of a business letter.

EXAMPLES   Dear Ms. Weinberg**:**   Dear Sir or Madam**:**

┌─HELP──

Use a comma after the salutation of a personal letter.

EXAMPLE
  Dear Suzanne**,**

Reference Note

For more about writing **business letters** and **personal letters,** see "Writing" in the Quick Reference Handbook.

┌─HELP──

Some sentences in Exercise 3 may need more than one colon added.

Exercise 3   Correcting Sentences by Adding Colons

For the following sentences, write each word or numeral that should be followed by a colon, and add the colon. If a sentence is already correct, write *C.*

EXAMPLE   1.   I began my acceptance speech as follows "Fellow students, thank you for your votes!"

                1.   *follows:*

1. My little sister's favorite book is *The Great Kapok Tree A Tale of the Amazon Rain Forest* by Lynn Cherry.
2. Sometimes the paper comes at 7 15 A.M., but other times it doesn't hit the driveway until 8 00.
3. My niece has several items embossed with that logo a poster, a nightgown, a notebook, and a clock.
4. In William Shakespeare's play *Julius Caesar,* Caesar has this to say of courage "Cowards die many times before their deaths, /The valiant taste of death but once."
5. Sherry's favorite artists are Jacob Lawrence, Romare Bearden, and Margaret Burroughs.
6. I think the story of Moses and Pharaoh's daughter is told in Exodus 2 5–10.
7. The directions were as follows Cover with plastic wrap, place in microwave oven, and cook for at least ten minutes.
8. I prefer my bicycle to a car for three reasons I don't have to pay for gasoline, I don't need insurance, and I don't waste time looking for a place to park.

9. In Cuba, which is a Spanish-speaking country, most of the people are of Spanish, African, or Spanish-African descent.
10. We should buy a house Our taxes would be lower, and we'd have more space.

> **Review B** **Proofreading Sentences for Correct Use of Semicolons and Colons**

Each of the following sentences contains at least one error in the use of semicolons or colons. For each error, write the word or numeral that precedes the missing or incorrect punctuation and add the correct punctuation.

EXAMPLE   1. The electricity was out for three days, the phones were not working for a week.

         1. *days;*

1. I made a list so that I would remember everything we needed toothpaste, milk, wax paper, and cat food.
2. The entrance exam was finished, however, I would remain nervous until the results came back.
3. The carpet was green, black, and brown, so red, orange, and pink have been ruled out for the wall color.
4. The awards went to John, who read from *Evangeline,* Ann, who read from *The Bridge,* and Garrett, who read from *The Waste Land.*
5. The vacuum hose was brittle and cracked therefore, taping it was not going to be enough.
6. The bus to the game will be leaving at precisely 3 45.
7. Lupe was going to title her essay "Mary Had a Little Lamb; The Social and Personal Benefits of Pet Ownership."
8. The three-person teams will be as follows, Takara, Lani, and Nick, Jessica, Vince, and Tyrone, and Peter, Dolores, and Ruben.
9. Jeremy had this Mark Twain quote taped to his folder, "Man is the only animal that blushes. Or needs to."
10. Sue Ann thought she had all the homework she could handle: on the other hand, she still had two more classes in the afternoon.

> **Review C** **Correcting a Business Letter by Adding Semicolons and Colons**

For the numbered word groups in the letter on the following page, write each word that should be followed by a semicolon or a colon. Place the needed punctuation mark after each word.

COMPUTER TIP

Some software programs can evaluate your writing for common errors in the use of semicolons and colons. Such programs can help you as you proofread your drafts. Remember, however, that software cannot find every error. You will still need to proofread your writing carefully.

MECHANICS

HELP

Some word groups in Review C need more than one punctuation mark.

EXAMPLE   [1] Hampton University was founded in 1868 it was originally named Hampton Normal and Agricultural Institute.

1. *1868;*

[1] Dear Sir or Madam

[2] The media coordinator at Central High School suggested that I write to you she explained that Hampton has an extensive collection of materials on African American history. [3] For my history class I am preparing an oral report on the March on Washington of August 28, 1963, and if possible, I would like to display pictures of the march.

[4] I am particularly interested in pictures of the following speakers Floyd McKissick, John Lewis, Roy Wilkins, and Dr. Martin Luther King, Jr. [5] I would also like pictures showing the size and diversity of the crowd for example, a shot of the marchers filling the area around the Reflecting Pool between the Lincoln Memorial and the Washington Monument would be especially effective. [6] Either prints or slides will be useful however, I would prefer slides if they are available.

[7] My grandfather, who took part in the march, vividly remembers these words of Dr. King "Let us not seek to satisfy our thirst for freedom by drinking from the cup of bitterness and hatred." [8] Grandfather took several rolls of film himself that day unfortunately, the pictures were lost in a fire a few years ago.

[9] Please send me information on ordering copies of suitable pictures a stamped, self-addressed envelope is enclosed. [10] Thank you for your help I appreciate your attention to my request.

Sincerely,

Jesse Fletcher

Jesse Fletcher

MECHANICS

Chapter Review

A. Correcting Sentences by Using Semicolons and Colons

Most of the following sentences have a comma or no punctuation mark where a semicolon or a colon should be used. Write the word or numeral preceding each error; then, add the needed punctuation mark. If a sentence is already correct, write *C*.

1. American Indians inhabited North America long before any Europeans however, many Native Americans weren't recognized as citizens of the United States until 1924.

2. The planning committee meeting is scheduled for 3 15 this afternoon please don't be late.

3. The following committees will report at that time budget, membership, awards, and programs.

4. Every morning after I get up, I read a Bible verse this morning I read John 14 27.

5. We left some food out for the stray dog it looked so forlorn huddled in the doorway.

6. Our modern literature class has read these poems "Incident," by Countee Cullen, "The Love Song of J. Alfred Prufrock," by T. S. Eliot, and "Ars Poetica," by Archibald MacLeish.

7. When she transferred to Barton Academy, Millie joined several clubs, helped in planning the Spring Carnival, and worked at a food bank for the needy nevertheless, it took her months to make some new friends.

8. While campaigning to become mayor of San Antonio, Maria Antonieta Berriozabal summed up her point of view in these words: "Our greatest resource is our people. We have to deal with business interests and human needs simultaneously."

9. Conrad Aiken was a correspondent for *The New Yorker* and also wrote essays and short stories he is best known, however, for his narrative and philosophical poetry.

10. The Bering Strait links the Arctic Ocean with the Bering Sea both the strait and the sea are named for Vitus Bering, a Danish explorer of the eighteenth century.

11. The late S. I. Hayakawa once made this statement "It is not true that we have only one life to live; if we can read, we can live as many more lives and as many kinds of lives as we wish."

12. The winners in the Douglas Fun Run last Saturday morning were Otis Williams, a sophomore, Janice Hicks, a senior, and Rodrigo Campas, a junior.

13. They opposed every motion that came before the council meeting in addition, they said they would circulate petitions if any of the proposals passed.

14. At first the children were afraid, believing that they were lost only after their teacher reassured them that she knew the way did they settle down.

15. This design will be applied to the following types of machines commercial, manufacturing, military, and agricultural.

16. Uncle Ed became manager of Zaharias Cars and Trucks, Inc., he is a former Formula One racing driver.

17. In addition to her coming-of-age short stories, Doris Lessing, who grew up in Rhodesia (now Zimbabwe), has written several novels, one of which is *African Laughter Four Visits to Zimbabwe*.

18. In the past twelve years, Justin has lived in Tucson, Arizona, Dallas, Texas, Shreveport, Louisiana, and Tulsa, Oklahoma.

19. For the golf tournament, seasoned players were paired with players new to the game consequently, the experienced players were frustrated and the novices were confused.

20. When Hernando Cortes invaded Mexico in 1519, he burned his ships as a result, his troops were unable to desert, and there was little point in mutiny.

B. Correcting Sentences by Adding Colons

Correct the following sentences by writing each word or numeral that should be followed by a colon and then adding the colon. If a sentence is already correct, write *C*.

21. For the first time he could remember, the 6 52 train to Grand Central was late.

22. At his retirement dinner, Mr. Gonzalo had this to say "It was a long and rewarding career, but I'm glad it's over."

23. Dr. Duran's favorite dishes are spiced pork, Spanish rice, fried zucchini, and julienned King Edward potatoes.

24. In his office, Mr. McMurdo has various mementos of the war a German helmet, a recruiting poster, a bullet casing, a model of a tank, and a signed photograph of General Bradley.

25. In Rome, they visited three famous attractions St. Peter's Church, the Colosseum, and the Spanish Steps.

26. On the car ferry, signs were posted with the following directions Roll Up Your Windows, Turn Off Your Engine, No Smoking, and Stay in Your Car.

27. I live in the mountains for two reasons, The air is clean, and there aren't too many people.

28. Exodus 20 3 contains the following famous quote "Thou shalt have no other gods before me."

29. There are three countries I'd like to visit above all France, Japan, and Greece.

30. Ms. Lozano assigned us to write an essay on one of the following American leaders Franklin D. Roosevelt, Abraham Lincoln, or Susan B. Anthony.

C. Correcting Sentences by Adding Semicolons and Colons

For each of the following sentences, write the word or numeral preceding each punctuation error; then, write the missing semicolon or colon. If a sentence is already correct, write *C*.

31. The Bible reading began with John 14 27 and ended with Psalms 39 1–6.

32. Mr. Jackson's plane arrived twenty minutes late because of the dense fog, consequently, he missed the flight to Denver.

33. I have finally narrowed my choices for a housewarming gift a self-cleaning iron, a blender, some place mats and napkins, or casserole dishes.

34. You should start saving your money: Open a savings account, invest in stocks or bonds, or buy a certificate of deposit.

35. The following clubs will have their yearbook pictures taken at 2 15, the Pep Club, the Photography Club, and the Modern Dance Club.

36. At the airfield we saw two signs To the North Pole and To the South Pole.

37. Aunt Patty and my cousin Josh will be leaving with us fortunately, Mom and Dad should be able to join us later, after all.

HELP

Some items in Part C contain more than one punctuation error.

MECHANICS

38. Sandra, Dan, Gottlieb, and Pete nominated Latrice and Kris, Bertha and the Hobbs twins chose Jerry.

39. You need to get the following supplies at the store orange juice, laundry detergent, bread, and dog food.

40. The hideous painting had been taken down in its place someone had put up a poster.

41. Maria says she wants to go to a college in the Northeast however, she still has two years to decide.

42. Mrs. Patel's favorite colors are green, beige, and turquoise.

43. I quote from the introduction "The main purpose of this book is to educate, not to entertain."

44. She had two main objections to the film It was too long, and she could hardly understand a word the actors said.

45. Three days a week Mom is up by 6 30, but on the other days she sleeps until 7 15 or so.

46. Marquand's survey included the three most critical locations Mount Jefferson, Gurney Point, and Fort Rollerton.

47. Dr. Burkhardt loudly requested sesame oil, flour, vinegar, and caraway seeds.

48. Mario had forgotten his clarinet he was, therefore, prevented from practicing with the others.

49. Mr. Cahill assumed that everyone in the room had read his book he referred to it several times during his talk.

50. The membership of the international committee was as follows Japan, two, Italy, five, Mexico, three, France, five, Germany, four, United States, five.

Writing Application
Punctuating a Business Letter

Using Semicolons and Colons   You have just won the grand prize in Blue Star Airlines' Fly-by-Night Sweepstakes. For one week, you can travel free to anywhere Blue Star flies in the United States—just so long as your flights depart between 8:00 P.M. and 4:00 A.M. You can remain in one location for the whole week, or you can travel to as many places as you like. To use your prize, you must give Blue Star Airlines a detailed itinerary of your trip before you plan to take it. Write a letter, giving the information needed. Use semicolons and colons to make your information easy to understand.

Prewriting   First, decide where you would most like to go. (If you plan to include more than one destination, remember that the trip is to last only one week from start to finish.) Then, arrange the information in a clearly understandable order.

Writing   As you write your first draft, remember that the accuracy and completeness of your letter will affect how well the trip is planned and, therefore, how much you enjoy your trip.

Revising   Put yourself in the ticket agent's place as you evaluate the letter. Have you included all the necessary information? Have you arranged the details in a clearly understandable order?

Publishing   Make sure that you use the correct form for a business letter. Proofread your letter carefully, paying special attention to your use of semicolons and colons. Also, be sure that you correctly spell the names of your destinations. You might want to ask a classmate to play the part of the ticket agent. Ask him or her to read the letter. With your teacher's permission, post the completed letter on a class bulletin board or Web page.

MECHANICS

Reference Note
For more about **writing a business letter,** see "Writing" in the Quick Reference Handbook.

Punctuation
Italics, Quotation Marks, and Ellipsis Points

Diagnostic Preview

Correcting Sentences by Adding Italics (Underlining), Quotation Marks, and Ellipsis Points

Add or correct italics (underlining), quotation marks, and ellipsis points where they are needed in the following sentences. If a sentence is already correct, write *C*.

EXAMPLE   1. Have you read the Mayan folk tale The Hummingbird King? asked Soledad.

1. *"Have you read the Mayan folk tale 'The Hummingbird King'?" asked Soledad.*

1. Why did you buy another sleeping bag? she asked.
2. In his speech, Chief Joseph of the Nez Perce said that he would never fight again.
3. The dance company is performing Swan Lake, a ballet composed by Tchaikovsky.
4. Anita asked, Why did he say, I won't go to the game?
5. The Boston Cooking School Cookbook, now known as The Fannie Farmer Cookbook, was first published in 1891.
6. The first word my baby brother said was bird.
7. There's an article in this issue of Newsweek that I'd like you to read, said Joan.
8. Orson Welles wrote and directed the movie Citizen Kane.
9. Her street address has four 4's in it, said Rose. Did you know that?

10. Susan drove one hundred miles, he replied, to see you and your family on your birthday.

11. My art teacher subscribes to Godzilla, a periodical about Asian artists working in New York City.

12. Please write to me, Joyce requested. I want to keep in touch with you during your travels.

13. In my report on Dee Brown's book Bury My Heart at Wounded Knee, I almost forgot to cite the New Republic magazine as the source of one of the quotations I used.

14. As we ran down the street, Charles shouted, Faster! Faster!

15. Sally said, John just whispered, I'll be at the game tonight.

16. Mrs. Rivera said that our next history assignment is Chapter 14, Great Ideals in the Constitution.

17. Did you read the article The Costs of College Today?

18. My aunt asked, What did your friend mean when he said that you look rad in your new glasses?

19. The Novelist is in a collection of W. H. Auden's shorter poems.

20. You often use the French expression au revoir, said Hannah.

21. The editorial concluded with the statement "The end result . . . . . . will be a total breakdown of communications."

22. "I'll bring a cooler for the sandwiches," Jason said.

23. Isn't the song One Headlight on The Wallflowers' second album, Bringing Down the Horse?

24. Jaime said, "We need to get that finished before . . well, at least before the shop closes."

25. Maria is reading The Hobbit again; this will be the third time she's read the book.

Italics

Italics are printed letters that lean to the right, *like this*. When you are writing or typing, indicate italics by underlining. If your composition were printed, the typesetter would set the underlined words in italics. For instance, if you were to type

```
All sophomores in our school read The Good
Earth by Pearl Buck.
```

the sentence would be printed like this:

All sophomores in our school read *The Good Earth* by Pearl Buck.

COMPUTER TIP

If you use a computer, you can probably set words in italics yourself. Most word-processing software and printers are capable of producing italic type.

Reference Note

For information about **capitalizing titles,** see page 682.

TIPS & TRICKS

Generally, the title of an entire work (book, magazine, TV series) is italicized, and the title of a part (chapter, article, episode) is enclosed in quotation marks.

Reference Note

For examples of **titles that are not italicized but are enclosed in quotation marks,** see page 747.

HELP

Long musical works include operas, symphonies, ballets, oratorios, and concertos.

MECHANICS

24a. Use italics (underlining) for titles and subtitles of books, plays, long poems, periodicals, works of art, movies, TV series, and long musical works and recordings.

Type of Title	Examples	
Books	The Bean Trees	Summer Sisters
Plays	Hedda Gabler	Twelfth Night
Long Poems	Sundiata: An Epic of Old Mali	Evangeline
Periodicals	Kansas City Times	Sports Illustrated
Works of Art	Three Musicians	Hercules and Antaeus
Movies	The Return of Jafar	Jaws
TV Series	Touched by an Angel	Nova
Long Musical Works and Recordings	The Maid of Orleans The Magic Flute	The Nutcracker The Four Seasons

NOTE A long poem is one that is long enough to be published as a separate volume. Such poems are usually divided into titled or numbered sections, such as cantos, parts, or books. The titles of these sections should be enclosed in quotation marks.

EXAMPLE Alejandro's report is on "What the Thunder Said," the fifth stanza of T. S. Eliot's poem *The Waste Land.*

The articles *a, an,* and *the* written before a title are italicized (and capitalized) only when they are part of the official title. If you are not sure whether to include an article in a title, you can check the title page of a book or the masthead or table of contents of a periodical for the official title.

EXAMPLES Charles Dickens's book *A* Christmas Carol is a holiday favorite.

The article in *The* Wall Street Journal mentioned that among his other accomplishments, Frederick Douglass founded **the** North Star, a newspaper he published for seventeen years.

24b. Use italics (underlining) for the names of ships, trains, aircraft, and spacecraft.

Type of Name	Examples
Ships	*Lusitania*
Trains	*Orient-Express*
Aircraft	*Air Force One*
Spacecraft	*Pioneer 11*

24c. Use italics (underlining) for words, letters, symbols, and numerals referred to as such and for foreign words that have not been adopted into English.

EXAMPLES   The first **o** in **zoology** is pronounced with a long **o** sound.

In math, what does the **%** mean?

Sometimes his **3**'s look just like his **8**'s.

Montana's state motto is **Oro y Plata,** the Spanish phrase for "gold and silver."

NOTE   English has borrowed many words and expressions from other languages. Some of these words and expressions have become part of the English vocabulary and are no longer italicized.

EXAMPLES   hors d'oeuvre (French)   quesadilla (Spanish)

moccasin (Algonquian)   tae kwon do (Korean)

If you are not sure whether to italicize a word of foreign origin, look it up in a recent dictionary.

Exercise 1 **Correcting Sentences by Adding Italics (Underlining)**

Identify all the words and word groups that should be italicized in the following sentences.

EXAMPLE   **1.** In 1988, Toni Morrison won the Pulitzer Prize for her novel Beloved.

1. *Beloved*

1. Does the Vietnamese word chiao mean the same thing as the Italian word ciao?

STYLE   TIP

Generally, do not use italics for the title of your own paper. However, if your title contains a title that belongs in italics, you will need to use italics for that part of the title.

EXAMPLES

The Universal Appeal of the Works of Barbara Kingsolver [contains no title that belongs in italics]

The Allusions to Nature in ***The Education of Little Tree*** [contains a book title, which belongs in italics]

Be creative when giving your paper a title. Avoid using the title of another work as the complete title of your own work.

MECHANICS

2. The first full-length animated film, Snow White and the Seven Dwarfs, used two million drawings.

3. Among the items that the Pilgrims brought with them on the Mayflower were apple seeds.

4. James Earle Fraser, best known for his painting End of the Trail, designed the U.S. buffalo nickel.

5. In the eighteenth century, Edward Gibbon wrote the influential book History of the Decline and Fall of the Roman Empire.

6. In Voyage to the Bottom of the Sea, an old TV series, the submarine Seaview was commanded by Admiral Nelson.

7. Daktari is Swahili for the English word doctor.

8. The first U.S. space shuttle was named Columbia.

9. Richard Sears met Alvah Roebuck through an ad in the Chicago Daily News.

10. The three M's referred to in the company name 3M stand for Minnesota Mining and Manufacturing.

STYLE   TIP

Writers sometimes use italics (underlining) for emphasis, especially in written dialogue. The italic type shows how the sentence is supposed to be spoken. Read the following sentences aloud. Notice that by italicizing different words, the writer can change the meaning of a sentence.

EXAMPLES

"Are you going to buy the *green* shirt?" asked Ellen. [Will you buy the green shirt, not the blue one?]

"Are you going to buy the green *shirt*?" asked Ellen. [Will you buy the green shirt, not the green pants?]

"Are *you* going to buy the green shirt?" asked Ellen. [Will you, not your brother, buy it?]

Italicizing (underlining) words for emphasis is a handy technique that should not be overused. It can quickly lose its impact.

Exercise 2 Correcting Sentences by Adding Italics (Underlining)

Identify all the words and word groups that should be italicized in the following sentences.

EXAMPLE   1. Have you read The Wonderful Adventures of Nils by Selma Lagerlöf?

1. *The Wonderful Adventures of Nils*

1. I just finished reading Ellen Gilchrist's book The Courts of Love.

2. Kay enjoyed the movie Antz.

3. Occasionally, my cousins like to watch reruns of The Brady Bunch on television.

4. Antigone is a play by Sophocles.

5. Every morning while eating a bagel, she reads The New York Times.

6. My oldest brother's favorite painting is The Potato Eaters by Vincent van Gogh.

7. Europe's first transcontinental express train was the Orient-Express.

8. Charles Lindbergh flew across the Atlantic Ocean in the airplane Spirit of Saint Louis.

9. A poster of Salvador Dali's painting The Persistence of Memory hangs in our school library.

10. I subscribe to several magazines, including Escape and Entertainment Weekly.

Quotation Marks

24d. Use quotation marks to enclose a *direct quotation*—a person's exact words.

DIRECT QUOTATION	Joan said, "My legs are sore from jogging."

Remember to place quotation marks at both the beginning and the end of a direct quotation.

INCORRECT	"I'm taking the road test tomorrow, said Reed.
CORRECT	"I'm taking the road test tomorrow," said Reed.

Do not use quotation marks to enclose an *indirect quotation*—a rewording of a person's exact words.

INDIRECT QUOTATION	Joan said that her legs were sore from jogging. [a rewording of Joan's exact words]

(1) A directly quoted sentence begins with a capital letter.

EXAMPLE   Bianca asked, "**W**hen do we get our uniforms?"

Captialize a directly quoted remark, even if the remark is not a complete sentence.

EXAMPLE   Mr. Lozano answered, "**O**n Friday, of course."

> NOTE If a direct quotation is obviously a fragment of the original quotation, it may begin with a lowercase letter.
>
> EXAMPLE   Christine promised to be here "**a**s soon as possible."

(2) When an interrupting expression divides a quoted sentence into two parts, the second part begins with a lowercase letter.

EXAMPLES   "I hope," said Diego, "**t**hat it doesn't rain during the fiesta."

"I'm not sure," remarked Annette, "**w**hether I'll be able to attend the meeting."

If the second part of a quotation is a complete sentence, a period (not a comma) follows the interrupting expression, and the second part begins with a capital letter.

EXAMPLE   "The date has been set," said Greg. "**W**e can't change it."

MECHANICS

┌HELP┐

An expression identifying the speaker is not part of a direct quotation and should not appear inside the quotation marks.

INCORRECT
"Where, I inquired, have I seen you before?"

CORRECT
"Where," I inquired, "have I seen you before?"

When a direct quotation of two or more sentences by the same speaker is not divided, only one set of quotation marks is used.

| INCORRECT | Tamisha suggested, "Let's donate the profits from the car wash to Project Day Care." "It provides help for many low-income working parents in this area." |
| CORRECT | Tamisha suggested, "Let's donate the profits from the car wash to Project Day Care. It provides help for many low-income working parents in this area." |

(3) A direct quotation can be set off from the rest of the sentence by a comma, a question mark, or an exclamation point, but not by a period.

EXAMPLES   "Remember that your research reports are due Monday," Mrs. Castañeda announced.

"On what date does the Ides of March fall?" Elwyn asked.

"That's easy! It's March 15!" Dot exclaimed.

(4) When used with quotation marks, other marks of punctuation are placed according to the following rules:

- Commas and periods are placed inside the closing quotation marks.

EXAMPLE   "The concert tickets are sold out," Mary said, "and I had really hoped to go."

- Colons and semicolons are placed outside the closing quotation marks.

EXAMPLES   The following students have been named "most likely to succeed": Corey Brown and Sally Ling.

Paka quoted a Cameroonian proverb, "By trying often, the monkey learns to jump from the tree"; it reminded me of the expression "If at first you don't succeed, try, try again."

- A question mark or an exclamation point is placed inside the closing quotation marks if the quotation itself is a question or an exclamation. Otherwise, a question mark or exclamation point is placed outside the closing quotation marks.

EXAMPLES   "What time is the game tomorrow?" Maria asked.

Why did you shout, "It doesn't matter"?

While I was at bat, Vicky kept shouting, "Hit it over the fence!"

Don't say "I'd rather not"!

NOTE When both the sentence and the quotation at the end of the sentence are questions (or exclamations), only one question mark (or exclamation point) is used. It is placed inside the closing quotation marks.

EXAMPLE   Who asked "What time is it?"

Exercise 3 Writing Sentences with Direct and Indirect Quotations

Add quotation marks where they are needed in the following sentences. If a sentence is already correct, write *C*.

EXAMPLE   **1.** When I saw this ad in the paper, I said to Grandmother Hsu, *T'ai chi* is Chinese, isn't it?

　　　　　 1. *When I saw this ad in the paper, I said to Grandmother Hsu,* "T'ai chi *is Chinese, isn't it?"*

1. She seemed pleased that I'd asked and replied, Yes, it's short for *t'ai chi ch'uan.*

2. She explained that t'ai chi ch'uan was developed in ancient China as a system of self-defense and as an aid to meditation.

3. The ad says that it's for health and relaxation, I said.

4. Yes, she agreed, it's that, too; it improves coordination and flexibility. In fact, in China, people of all ages practice it.

5. You see, she went on, its postures and movements are all based on those of animals such as monkeys, birds, and snakes.

6. Snakes! I exclaimed.

7. Why do you twist your face so? Grandmother asked. If you observe a snake closely, you'll see how gracefully it moves.

8. That's true, I admitted.

9. Maybe, I said, thinking aloud, I'll check out this grand opening.

10. Imagine my surprise when Grandmother replied with a wide smile, I'll see you there. I'm one of the instructors.

ANNOUNCING

The Grand Opening of

Pathway T'ai Chi Studio
for health and relaxation

604 49th St.
Sunday, November 10
1:00 P.M.–5:00 P.M.

Complimentary refreshments will be served.
All Ages Welcome

24e. When you write dialogue (a conversation), begin a new paragraph every time the speaker changes, and enclose each speaker's words in quotation marks.

EXAMPLE

A man of Merv, well known as the home of complicated thinkers, ran shouting one night through the city's streets. "Thief, Thief!" he cried.

The people surrounded him, and when he was a little calmer, asked: "Where was the thief?"

"In my house."

"Did you see him?"

"No."

"Was anything missing?"

"No."

"How do you know there was a thief then?"

"I was lying in bed when I remembered that thieves break into houses without a sound, and move very quietly. I could hear nothing, so I knew that there was a thief in the house, you fool!"

Niamat Khan, "The Thief"

NOTE A long passage quoted from a book or another printed source is usually set off from the rest of the text. The entire passage is usually indented and double-spaced. When a quoted passage has been set off in one of these ways, no quotation marks are necessary unless the passage contains dialogue.

EXAMPLE

In his speech after his last battle against the whites, the Sauk chief Black Hawk displayed pride and honor in the face of defeat:

The bullets flew like birds in the air, and whizzed by our ears like the wind through the trees in winter. My warriors fell around me; it began to look dismal. I saw my evil day at hand. The sun rose dim on us in the morning, and at night it sank in a dark cloud, and looked like a ball of fire. That was the last sun that shone on Black Hawk.

24f. When a quoted passage consists of more than one paragraph, put quotation marks at the beginning of each paragraph and at the end of the entire passage. Do not put quotation marks after any paragraph but the last.

EXAMPLE   "Now, this car is one of our hottest sellers. It has bucket seats, a CD player, and alloy wheels.

        "It's also one of the safest cars on the road because of its heavy suspension and antilock brake system. It gets good gas mileage, too.

        "All in all, I think this would be the perfect car for you."

24g. Use quotation marks to enclose titles (including subtitles) of short works such as short stories, poems, essays, articles, songs, episodes of TV series, and chapters and other parts of books and periodicals.

Type of Title	Examples
Short Stories	"The Unicorn in the Garden" "The Gift of the Magi"
Poems	"Fire and Ice" "I Am of the Earth"
Essays	"Choice: A Tribute to Dr. Martin Luther King, Jr." "Marco Polo: Journey to China"
Articles	"The Ghost Dance" "Searching for Freedom"
Songs	"What's Going On" "I Will Remember You"
Episodes of TV Series	"Jerry's High School Reunion"
Chapters and Other Parts of Books, Periodicals	"Twentieth-Century Playwrights" "In Search of a New Frontier"

24h. Use single quotation marks to enclose a quotation or title within a quotation.

EXAMPLES   Ron said, "Dad yelled, 'No way!'"

           Val asked, "Did you like my rendition of 'America the Beautiful'?"

Reference Note

For examples of **titles that are italicized, not enclosed in quotation marks,** see page 740.

HELP

The titles of long poems are italicized.

STYLE   TIP

Generally, do not use quotation marks for the title of your own paper. However, if your title contains a title that belongs in quotation marks, you will need to use quotation marks for that part of your title.

EXAMPLES

Aesop: A Master Storyteller [contains no title that belongs in quotation marks]

Cassie in "Song of the Trees": A Character Analysis [contains a short-story title, which belongs in quotation marks]

MECHANICS

24i. Use quotation marks to enclose slang words, technical terms, and unusual uses of words.

S T Y L E   T I P

Avoid using slang words in formal writing and speaking. When using technical terms, be sure to explain their meanings. If you are using a technical term throughout a piece of writing, you will need to enclose in quotation marks only your first use of the term.

If you are not sure whether a word is appropriate or its meaning is clear, consult a recent dictionary.

EXAMPLES   My oldest brother said my new shoes look very "fly."

Is there now a computer that can perform more than fifteen "gigaflops" (that is, fifteen billion operations) a second?

Fire burns oxygen quickly; my chemistry teacher says flame is a "gas-guzzler."

Review A   **Correcting Sentences by Adding Italics (Underlining) or Quotation Marks**

For each of the following sentences, correctly write all the words that should be italicized (underlined) or enclosed in quotation marks.

EXAMPLE   1. He read aloud The Tell-Tale Heart from The Collected Stories of Edgar Allan Poe.

1. "The Tell-Tale Heart"; The Collected Stories of Edgar Allan Poe

1. Mr. Croce used the word denouement when he was discussing Rudolfo Anaya's novel Bless Me, Ultima.
2. By next Thursday I have to read the following works: The Medicine Bag, a short story by Virginia Driving Hawk Sneve; Crown of Shadows, a play by Rodolfo Usigli; and Daisy Bates: First Lady of Little Rock, an article by Lerone Bennett, Jr.
3. Have you read the newspaper article El Niño, Global Weather Disaster? asked Ewan.
4. While we were working on our essays, Karen asked me how many m's are in the word accommodate.
5. Oswald Rivera's novel Fire and Rain is about the Vietnam War.
6. Kim said her report, titled The Wit of Oscar Wilde, includes quotes from the short story titled The Happy Prince as well as the play The Importance of Being Earnest.
7. We had risotto alla milanese for dinner.
8. Mr. Guerra explained that the short story Luke Baldwin's Vow deals with conflicts in values.
9. Wouldn't Words to Live By be an excellent title for our song? Tomás asked.
10. She crossed the t with such a flourish that she obscured the letters above it.

MECHANICS

Review B Correcting Sentences by Adding Italics (Underlining) and Quotation Marks

Rewrite the following dialogue, and add italics (underlining), quotation marks, and paragraph breaks and indentations where they are needed in the following sentences.

EXAMPLE **[1]** Look at this intriguing painting, said Marshall.

1. *"Look at this intriguing painting," said Marshall.*

[1] He told us that he'd found the painting in Mexican American Artists, a book by Jacinto Quirate; the painting is in the chapter called The Third Decade.

[2] The painting is by the man in the photograph below, Emilio Aguirre, he explained, who titled it Alpha 1.

[3] What do you see when you look at it? he asked.

[4] You can't miss the Y on the left and the T on the right, he said.

[5] He went on, Can you make out the profile of a person sitting on the ground to the left of the T?

[6] Laura said, Yes, the head is an O; but I objected, saying that it looked more like a Q to me.

[7] I guess you're right, she said. Anyway, the G outlines the front of the body.

[8] Ben asked, Is the little b on the big O supposed to be the person's glasses? Also, he added, isn't that an M in the background, behind the T?

[9] Look at this! exclaimed Marlene. If you turn the painting ninety degrees to the left, the body looks like a question mark.

[10] Can you see why we all agreed when she said, Intriguing really is the word for Alpha 1?

Ellipsis Points

24j. Use ellipsis points (. . .) to mark omissions from quoted material.

ORIGINAL   The room overlooking the square had an ornate stone balcony with a view of the chateau. That building was an early-Renaissance confection of towers and turrets, partly encircled by the old city walls. I remember that next to the chateau was the town hall, a handsome, square Second Empire structure. A stand of plane trees and a parking lot full of cars adjoined the main gate. Beyond the city walls lay the yellow mustard fields rolling into the hazy distance.

(1) When you omit words from the middle of a sentence, use three spaced ellipsis points.

EXAMPLE   "The room overlooking the square had • • • a view of the chateau."

NOTE Be sure to include a space before the first ellipsis point and after the last one.

┌H E L P┐
Notice that in the example under Rule 24j(2), the word *next* is capitalized, even though it was not capitalized in the original. *Next* is capitalized in the example because it is being used as the first word of the sentence. The capital *N* is in brackets to show that the capital was added by the person quoting the material—that *next* was lowercased in the original.

(2) When you omit words from the beginning of a sentence within a quoted passage, keep the previous sentence's end punctuation and follow it with the points of ellipsis.

EXAMPLE   "That building was an early-Renaissance confection of towers and turrets, partly encircled by the old city walls• • • • [N]ext to the chateau was the town hall, a handsome, square Second Empire structure."

(3) When you omit words at the end of a sentence within a quoted passage, keep the sentence's end punctuation and follow it with the points of ellipsis.

EXAMPLE   "That building was an early-Renaissance confection of towers and turrets• • • • I remember that next to the chateau was the town hall, a handsome, square Second Empire structure."

(4) When you omit one or more complete sentences from within a quoted passage, keep the previous sentence's end punctuation and follow it with the points of ellipsis.

EXAMPLE   "That building was an early-Renaissance confection of towers and turrets, partly encircled by the old city walls**. . .** Beyond the city walls lay the yellow mustard fields rolling into the hazy distance."

To show that one or more lines of poetry have been omitted, use an entire line of spaced periods.

COMPLETE
POEM

Loveliest of trees, the cherry now
Is hung with bloom along the bough,
And stands about the woodland ride
Wearing white for Eastertide.

Now, of my threescore years and ten,
Twenty will not come again,
And take from seventy springs a score,
It only leaves me fifty more.

And since to look at things in bloom
Fifty springs are little room,
About the woodlands I will go
To see the cherry hung with snow.

A. E. Housman, "Loveliest of Trees"

POEM WITH
OMISSION

Loveliest of trees, the cherry now
Is hung with bloom along the bough,
And stands about the woodland ride
Wearing white for Eastertide.

• • • • • • • • • •

And since to look at things in bloom
Fifty springs are little room,
About the woodlands I will go
To see the cherry hung with snow.

Notice that the line of periods here marks the omission of four lines of poetry. Also, notice that the line of ellipses is as long as the preceding line of poetry.

24k. Use three ellipsis points (. . .) to indicate a pause in written dialogue.

EXAMPLE   "Yes, but • • • oh well, all right," she said.

HELP

Do not begin a quoted passage with points of ellipsis.

INCORRECT
". . . That building was an early-Renaissance confection of towers and turrets, partly encircled by the old city walls."

CORRECT
"That building was an early-Renaissance con-fection of towers and turrets, partly encircled by the old city walls."

MECHANICS

Omit the underscored parts of the following passages. Use ellipsis points and end marks to punctuate each omission correctly.

EXAMPLE   1. The old twin-gabled house, which my aunt had intended to sell, was struck by lightning.

1. *The old twin-gabled house . . . was struck by lightning.*

1. Santa Fe is one of the most popular vacation destinations in the United States. Why is a small city in the mountains of northern New Mexico, more than an hour's drive from the nearest airport, such a top tourist draw? The climate is superb, the cuisine is outstanding, and the combination of cultures is unique.

2. Senator McRory, a key figure in state politics for most of his fifty-four years, has decided to run for governor in the next election.

3. According to the newspaper article, "Master Gardener Yamamoto won the top award in the international bonsai competition, the first such event of the season. He plans to use the money to build an addition to his nursery."

4. A mature bull elephant, huge yet graceful, charged toward the water hole and scared the lions away.

5. The path curves onward and up,
   Shining like a scimitar's blade
   In the early morning rain,
   Guiding us to higher things.

6. Ambition and duty are the twin motives of the character of Teng in this movie, as they frequently are in the lives of real people.

7. The new airport, which will greatly increase the city's commercial and cultural ties to the outside world, will open next May.

8. "This novel is well-written but is quite unsatisfactory as a thriller. Its young author is known and deservedly respected for his realistic short stories set along the coast of Oregon and northern California, but he has much to learn before he can master the subtleties of plot and atmosphere," the book review said.

9. Mr. Sánchez arrived early from his long journey and promised he would show us his slides as soon as he had fully recovered the use of his voice.

10. "Was it true? Was it even possible? A complete reversal, her decision seems to contradict everything I know about her character," May thought aloud.

MECHANICS

Chapter Review

A. Correcting Sentences by Adding Italics (Underlining) and Quotation Marks

Write each letter, word, title, or word group that should be italicized (underlined) or in quotation marks. Then, supply the needed underlining or quotation marks.

1. Carlos Chavez, a Mexican composer and conductor, wrote the Sinfonìa de Antígona in 1933.
2. We have subscribed to the Orlando Sentinel for two years.
3. Are you going to help me, he asked, or shall I look for someone else?
4. Michael Crichton wrote the book Jurassic Park, which was made into a movie by Steven Spielberg.
5. Grandma's favorite expression is Mind your p's and q's!
6. Carla served a delicious Mediterranean appetizer called pulpo; when I asked her what it was, she told me it was octopus.
7. For our homework assignment we have to define ionization, electrolyte, quark, and neutrino.
8. During the Civil War, the Merrimack, on the Confederate side, and the Monitor, on the Union side, fought to a draw in the first battle between ironclad ships.
9. I never should have agreed to be on that committee, wailed Ellie. When I asked Mary to help, she said, Not on your life! Now I'm stuck doing all the work!
10. Where have you been, Ron? asked Leroy. The bus is leaving.
11. These students are Elwood High's finest scholars, the principal said, announcing the following scholarship winners: Daphne Johnson, Michael Lewis, Ruben Perez, and Winnie Chung.
12. One of my favorite TV shows, Disaster Chronicles, ran an episode called Volcanoes in Italy.
13. Sam, who's from Boston, drops the r's from the ends of words.
14. Politicians still quote Abraham Lincoln's expression government of the people, by the people, for the people.
15. We discussed Ann Bank's magazine article Rafting with Kids.
16. Indians Today, the Real and the Unreal is the opening chapter in Vine Deloria's book Custer Died for Your Sins.

17. My mother has never liked the term baby boomer.
18. Many articles about Emily Dickinson's poems contain the term paradox.
19. When the players came onto the field, the fans shouted, Go for it!
20. Have you seen Louise Nevelson's sculpture Young Shadows?

B. Correcting Sentences by Adding Italics (Underlining)

Write all the words and word groups that should be italicized in the following sentences.

21. Have you seen the movie A Bug's Life?
22. One of Claude Monet's first paintings was called Impression: Sunrise.
23. One of Bernard Shaw's best-known plays is Pygmalion, on which the musical My Fair Lady was based.
24. My cousins Suzi and Désirée, happy to be on vacation, took the train California Zephyr to Los Angeles last summer.
25. One of Dad's favorite TV programs is The X-Files.
26. I read an article in Sports Illustrated while I waited.
27. One of the fastest locomotives of its time was the Flying Scotsman, built in Britain in 1923.
28. Was Enola Gay the plane that dropped the atomic bomb on Hiroshima?
29. A Clergyman's Daughter is a novel by George Orwell.
30. Last night we all watched Star Trek: The Next Generation; one of my favorite episodes was showing.

C. Using Ellipsis Points Correctly

Omit the underscored parts of the following passages. Use ellipsis points and end marks to punctuate each omission correctly.

31. Our cousin Carlos, one of his college's star baseball players, is going to training camp in Arizona this spring.
32. The man was tall, in his mid-thirties, with a full mustache and short brown hair. His hair was combed straight back. He spoke with what I thought was a slight Midwestern accent.

33. Here, take my hand and follow me
<u>Thou eager one, dreamer of dreams,</u>
<u>Singer of life's oldest song,</u>
And together we will find the golden crown.

34. Dr. Bustamante, <u>a widely admired personality in the Chilean emigrant community,</u> is almost certain to be chosen as deputy mayor.

35. The film <u>is atmospheric and well acted but it</u> is too long by at least half an hour.

Writing Application

Writing an Interior Dialogue

Using Punctuation   You are scheduled to give an oral report on a short story of your own choosing. Write an interior dialogue recording your thoughts as you decide which of two stories to use. Use the marks of punctuation covered in this chapter in your interior dialogue.

Prewriting   List the titles of several short stories you have read. Then, choose the two about which you feel most strongly. Next, determine how you will distinguish between your different points of view as you decide which story to choose. For example, you could use your first name for one side, your middle name for another, and other names for as many different points of view as you have.

Writing   Write down your thoughts as you consider the pros and cons of using the two stories, presenting each thought in a correctly punctuated dialogue spoken from each point of view. Keep writing until you reach a decision. Try to keep track of where you are in the decision-making process.

Revising   Read over your dialogue and check whether your diction (word choice) and sentence structure sound authentic to you. Can you tell at all times to which story you're referring? Is it clear which one you decided to report on, and why?

Publishing   Check your dialogue for errors in grammar, spelling, and punctuation. Then, photocopy your dialogue, or post it on a class bulletin board or Web page. You and your classmates could record your dialogues on audiotape or act them out for one another in person or on film.

Punctuation
Apostrophes, Hyphens, Dashes, Parentheses, Brackets

Diagnostic Preview

A. Correcting Sentences by Using Apostrophes and Hyphens

For each of the following sentences, write the word or words that should have an apostrophe or a hyphen, and add the appropriate punctuation mark. If a sentence is already correct, write *C*.

EXAMPLE   1. Michaels stamp collection contains thirty two rare stamps.

  1. *Michael's*

     thirty-two

1. Because of the sudden blizzard, the armies supplies were cut off.
2. Its frustrating when the car wont start because its battery is dead.
3. After hours of discussion, we decided that we need a two thirds majority to pass new rules in the student council.
4. Even though Li moved here from Korea just last year and is still learning English, shes making As in most of her classes.
5. If you go to the game on Saturday, whos going to watch the children at home?
6. Miranda had the flu this past week, and now she has five days worth of homework to do this weekend.
7. Rodney interviewed the treasurer elect of the honor society for the "Personality Profile" column in the school newspaper.

8. James Berry, who was born in Jamaica, wrote the well received collection of short stories *A Thief in the Village and Other Stories.*

9. You should know that my aunts favorite expression is "Never let the sun set on your anger."

10. My brother in law Murray has worked at a resort in New Yorks Catskill Mountains for twenty one years.

11. The store clerk said she would refund our deposit if we return the tape recorder by five oclock.

12. The alarm clock hasnt worked since the morning I knocked it off the shelf.

13. Last week at the trial in New York City, the senator presented as evidence the anti American pamphlets distributed by the terror ist group.

14. You have such a wonderful singing voice that I'm sure youll get a part in the childrens summer theater production.

15. Dont be alarmed, Brian; the red +s on your history paper indicate correct answers.

B. Correcting Sentences by Using Dashes, Parentheses, and Brackets

Rewrite the following sentences, adding dashes, parentheses, and brackets where they are needed.

EXAMPLE
    1. The books on that table they are all nonfiction are on sale today.

    1. *The books on that table—they are all nonfiction—are on sale today.*

16. The discovery of gold at Sutter's Mill brought floods of people settlers, miners, prospectors, and merchants to California in their covered wagons.

17. The old white house on Tenth Street it was once a governor's mansion is a landmark in our town.

18. Answer the ten questions on this English quiz be careful, they're tricky! and then write a couplet or a limerick for extra credit.

19. John Steinbeck 1902–1968 won the Nobel Prize in literature in 1962.

20. According to O'Neal, Satchmo (the great jazz musician Louis Armstrong 1900–1971) profoundly influenced American music.

┌HELP──
Although some of the sentences in Part B of the Diagnostic Preview may be correctly revised in more than one way, you need to give only one revision for each sentence.

MECHANICS

Apostrophes

Possessive Case

The possessive case of a noun or a pronoun shows ownership or possession.

EXAMPLES   **Jorge's** calculator has a solar battery.

Where did you buy **yours**?

Pam's aunt is a plumber.

The birds had fed **their** young.

Nouns in the Possessive Case

25a. To form the possessive of most singular nouns, add an apostrophe and an *s*.

EXAMPLES   Barbara**'s** house   one boy**'s** uniform

a week**'s** salary   that stereo**'s** speakers

When forming the possessive of a singular noun ending in an *s* or a *z* sound, add only an apostrophe if

- the noun has more than one syllable

        and

- the addition of *s* would make the noun awkward to pronounce

EXAMPLES   Odysseus**'** adventures   for goodness**'** sake

Buenos Aires**'** citizens   the species**'** characteristics

Xerxes**'** army   each of that TV series**'** characters

If a singular noun ending in an *s* or a *z* sound does not satisfy both of these conditions, add an apostrophe and an *s*.

EXAMPLES   Carlos**'s** bicycle   a bus**'s** tires

Charles Dickens**'s** novels   my boss**'s** orders

25b. To form the possessive case of a plural noun ending in *s*, add only the apostrophe.

EXAMPLES   cats**'** owners   cities**'** problems

coaches**'** records   princesses**'** duties

MECHANICS

The few plural nouns that do not end in *s* form the possessive case by adding an apostrophe and an *s*.

EXAMPLES   geese**'s** migration   children**'s** stories

> **NOTE** In most cases, you should not use an apostrophe to form the plural of a noun.
>
> INCORRECT   The four horse's pulled the wagon.
>   CORRECT   The four **horses** pulled the wagon.

Exercise 1 **Writing the Possessive Forms of Nouns**

Make four columns headed *Singular*, *Singular Possessive*, *Plural*, and *Plural Possessive*. Write those forms of each of the following nouns.

EXAMPLE

	Singular	Singular Possessive	Plural	Plural Possessive
1.	temple	temple's	temples	temples'

1. governor
2. secretary
3. bird
4. spacecraft
5. woman
6. picture
7. pencil
8. class
9. chief
10. mouse
11. stereo
12. president
13. bear
14. photograph
15. grandmother
16. jacket
17. dress
18. novel
19. cup
20. lapse

Pronouns in the Possessive Case

25c. Do not use an apostrophe with possessive personal pronouns or with the possessive pronoun *whose*.

Possessive Personal Pronouns	
Singular	**Plural**
my, mine	our, ours
your, yours	your, yours
his, her, hers, its	their, theirs

Reference Note

For more examples of **plural nouns that do not end in s,** see page 787.

Reference Note

For information on using an apostrophe and an *s* to form the **plurals of letters, numerals, symbols, and words referred to as words,** see page 789.

HELP

If you do not know how to spell a plural form, look up the word in a dictionary.

25
a–c

MECHANICS

Reference Note

Do not confuse the possessive personal pronouns **your, their, theirs, its** and **whose** with the contractions **you're, they're, there's, it's,** and **who's.** See page 764.

My, your, his, her, its, our, and their are generally used before nouns. Mine, yours, his, hers, ours, and theirs are used as subjects, complements, or objects of prepositions. Note that his may be used either way.

EXAMPLES

This is **my** desk.	This desk is **mine.**
I borrowed **your** pencil.	I borrowed a pencil of **yours.**
His work is excellent.	**His** is the best work.

25d. To form the possessive of an indefinite pronoun, add an apostrophe and an *s.*

EXAMPLES   anyone**'s** choice   either**'s** idea

Reference Note

See pages 533–534 for a list of **indefinite pronouns.**

NOTE   The correct possessive forms of *someone else* and *each other* are *someone else's* and *each other's.*

Compounds in the Possessive Case

25e. Form the possessive of only the last word in a compound noun, such as the name of an organization or a business, and in a word group showing joint possession.

Compound Nouns	Urban League**'s** office Acosta and Rivera**'s** law firm sister-in-law**'s** office
Joint Possession	Bob and Jim**'s** canoe my aunt and uncle**'s** photograph

When a possessive pronoun is part of a word group showing joint possession, each noun in the word group is also possessive in form.

EXAMPLE   Sean**'s** and **her** conversation

Reference Note

For more about **acronyms** and **initialisms,** see page 687.

NOTE   The possessive of an **acronym** (a word formed from the first—or first few—letters of a series of words) or of an **initialism** (an abbreviation pronounced letter by letter) is formed by adding an apostrophe and an *s.*

ACRONYM   NATO**'s** member nations

INITIALISM   NBC**'s** new television program

25f. Form the possessive of each noun in a word group that expresses individual possession of similar items.

EXAMPLES   Michael's and Lila's wallets

                Denise's and Mark's books

25
d–f

STYLE   TIP

To avoid forming a possessive that sounds awkward, use a phrase beginning with *of* or *for* instead.

AWKWARD
  the Samuel H. Scripps American Dance Festival Award's winner

IMPROVED
  the winner **of** the Samuel H. Scripps American Dance Festival Award

Exercise 2   Using Apostrophes Correctly

Rewrite the following word groups, adding and deleting apostrophes where needed. If a word group is already correct, write *C*.

EXAMPLE   **1.** the cameras lens

           1. *the camera's lens*

1. one of your's
2. Anns and my project
3. their tennis shoes
4. my father-in-laws boat
5. each others books
6. Joe and Roys room
7. Lynns and Mikes shoes
8. someones art
9. whose feats
10. PBSs' fundraiser
11. a Jazz Festivals end
12. anyone elses pizza
13. Jims and Debs parents
14. the UNs general assembly
15. my loaves of bread
16. Sallys and his' horses
17. any of their's
18. neithers hope
19. Jeremiahs and Josephs toys
20. Ross' and Reeds team

Review A   Correcting Paragraphs by Adding Apostrophes

For the sentences in the following paragraphs, write each word that should be in the possessive case, and add the missing apostrophe.

EXAMPLE   **[1]** Last week I followed my parents suggestion and enrolled in an amateur photography class offered by our citys art center.

          1. *parents'; city's*

[1] I shared my mom and dads exasperation when, once again, I spent a whole weeks allowance on disappointing pictures. [2] I had borrowed Uncle Freds expensive camera, but even with the cameras extra features, my photographs looked like childrens smudged finger paintings. [3] My pictures of Bob and Ruths wedding reception, our familys social event of the year, were destroyed when I fell into the pool with

my camera. [4] Last summer I also took pictures during our week-long visit to Arizonas famous Painted Desert. [5] Unfortunately, I did not understand enough about the suns strong light at midday; consequently, most of my photographs had a washed-out look.

[6] My lifes most embarrassing moment occurred when I took a picture of my class for the schools yearbook and then discovered that I had forgotten to put film in the camera. [7] Another time, I took my camera to Toms party but could not get anyones attention long enough to set up the shots that I wanted. [8] As a result, I gave up on people and tried to take my two pets pictures; however, a parakeets wings and a dogs will are hard to control. [9] After all these bad experiences, I knew that I needed a professionals advice. [10] I'm pleased to report that during the first meeting of the photography class, the instructor raised all the students confidence, including mine.

Review B   **Proofreading for Errors in Possessive Forms**

Most of the following sentences contain an incorrect possessive form. For each error, give the correct form of the word. If a sentence is already correct, write *C*.

EXAMPLE   1. The island nation of the Philippines shows signs of both Spains and the United States occupations.

1. *Spain's; United States'*

1. The countrys national languages are Pilipino and English, but its people also speak Spanish and various regional languages.
2. Did you know that the yo-yos earliest use was as a weapon in the Philippine jungles?
3. My mothers boss was visiting the Philippines when Joseph Estrada became president in 1998.
4. President Estrada's previous career was that of film actor.
5. Tina's and Phil's plan to visit the Philippines was postponed when their baby was born.
6. The Philippines capital and largest city is Manila, which is on the big island of Luzon.
7. Both Kim and Marta's lunches came with delicious Filipino custard.
8. It's anyones guess how many islands actually make up the Philippines, though there are certainly more than seven thousand islands.

9. The Spanish monarch who's soldiers named the Philippines was King Philip II.
10. Childrens pastimes in the Philippines include kite flying and swimming.

Contractions

25g. Use an apostrophe to show where letters, words, or numerals have been omitted in a contraction.

A *contraction* is a shortened form of a word, a group of words, or a numeral. The apostrophes in contractions show where letters, words, or numerals have been left out.

Common Contractions			
who is	who's	she will	she'll
there is	there's	I am	I'm
could have	could've	you are	you're
1999	'99	we had	we'd
of the clock	o'clock	she has	she's
let us	let's	Lisa is	Lisa's
I would	I'd	they are	they're

S T Y L E   T I P
Many people consider contractions informal. Therefore, it is generally best to avoid using them in formal writing and speech.

Generally, the adverb *not* can be shortened to *n't* and added to a verb without any change in the spelling of the verb.

EXAMPLES	is not	isn't	were not	weren't
	are not	aren't	has not	hasn't
	does not	doesn't	have not	haven't
	do not	don't	had not	hadn't
	did not	didn't	would not	wouldn't
	was not	wasn't	should not	shouldn't
EXCEPTIONS	cannot	can't	will not	won't

Do not confuse contractions with possessive pronouns.

Contractions	Possessive Pronouns
Who's [Who is] next? **Who's** [Who has] helped you?	**Whose** turn is next?
It's [It is] purring. **It's** [It has] been asleep.	Listen to **its** purr.
You're [You are] late.	**Your** report is late.
There's [There is] a mule. **They're** [They are] healthy pets.	That mule is **theirs.** **Their** pets are healthy.

Exercise 3 **Using Contractions**

Provide appropriate contractions that correctly complete the following sentences.

EXAMPLE   **1.** We tried to call Beth and Jennifer, but they _____ answer their phone.

     1. didn't

1. _____ he going to the awards ceremony?
2. I fed the fish, but they _____ eating.
3. Marla has two cats, and _____ beautiful.
4. _____ bring me her notes tonight so I can study them.
5. _____ go to a movie.
6. Mom said _____ one apple in the basket.
7. He is sick, so he _____ coming with us.
8. I _____ believe the summer is already over.
9. You _____ read a scary book when you're home alone.
10. I _____ gotten the mail yet.

Exercise 4 **Recognizing the Correct Uses of Contractions and Possessives**

Choose the correct word in parentheses in each of the following sentences.

EXAMPLE   **1.** (*It's, Its*) never too late to learn something new.

     1. It's

1. (*You're, Your*) sure that (*you're, your*) allowed to bring (*you're, your*) book to the exam?

MECHANICS

2. (*Whose, Who's*) idea was it to visit the National Civil Rights Museum in Memphis during (*you're, your*) trip?

3. (*They're, Their*) trying to sell (*they're, their*) house.

4. (*It's, Its*) the best one of (*it's, its*) kind.

5. Do you know (*who's, whose*) responsible for (*they're, their*) confusion?

6. I hope the dog can find (*it's, its*) way (*they're, there*).

7. (*It's, Its*) Philip (*who's, whose*) always late.

8. Although (*it's, its*) been snowing all day, they're still planning to go.

9. (*Who's, Whose*) the designer of (*they're, their*) float in Galveston's Mardi Gras parade?

10. I know (*you're, your*) upset with the plan, but (*it's, its*) the only way to solve the problem.

Review C **Correcting Sentences by Adding Apostrophes**

Identify each word that needs an apostrophe in the following sentences. Then, correctly write the word.

EXAMPLE   **1.** Werent you the one who said you didnt like eggplant?

   1. Weren't; didn't

1. Whos going to be at Leon and Joshs party?

2. Lets hide and see whether theyll look for us.

3. I cant find the calamata olives and the feta cheese for the Greek salad.

4. Is the doctors appointment at nine oclock?

5. Cleve doesnt have time to mow both David's and Rays lawns.

6. The parents faces brightened as their children crossed the stage.

7. Were lucky that that dogs howls didn't awaken them.

8. Im trying to follow Pauls map to Jeans house.

9. Its extremely cold; therefore, I dont think you should go skiing.

10. Elise couldnt remember the characteristics of the tiger in the Chinese zodiac.

11. After track practice, hes going to record his best times.

12. It doesnt matter to me, but shes adamant about making her point.

13. We dont know whos batting next.

14. Im going to the dance with my best friend.

15. The Salvation Armys office is organizing the benefit concert.

16. Nothings going to stop them from playing volleyball after school.

17. You must stir the ingredients until theyre well blended.

18. After spending two weeks in Italy, Mary didnt want to come home.

19. Mom, please hang Teds jacket next to yours.

20. Youre responsible for counting the money.

Plurals

25h. Use an apostrophe and an *s* to form the plurals of numerals, symbols, all lowercase letters, some uppercase letters, and some words referred to as words.

EXAMPLES   Most of your cursive *u*'s and *U*'s are the same size.

Mr. Carr suggested that I replace some of the *so*'s in my paper with other words.

These *2*'s look like *7*'s.

It appears that the author has confused *@*'s and *&*'s.

Note that in the first example, the plurals of *u* and *U* could be misread as *us* and *Us* if the apostrophes were omitted. In the second example, the plural of *so* could be misread as the acronym *sos* if the apostrophe were omitted.

 Review D   **Correcting Sentences by Adding Apostrophes**

For each of the following sentences, write all the items needing apostrophes, and add the apostrophes.

EXAMPLE   **1.** You may agree with the school boards decision, but I dont.

1. *school board's; don't*

1. Are these *&*s or *8*s?
2. You forgot that there are two *as* at the beginning of *aardvark*.
3. My stepsister graduated from high school in 97 and graduated from college in 01.
4. Lewis Carrolls novel *Alices Adventures in Wonderland* was originally called *Alices Adventures Underground.*
5. Whos going to change the babies diapers?
6. After school were going to visit his sister; shes in St. Marys Hospital.
7. Did you write *os* or *0*s in the margin?
8. Its been six weeks since I checked the cars oil and its tires.
9. Your story would be better if youd remove about ten *very*s.
10. She learned the Hawaiian alphabets twelve letters, but Max didnt.

Reference Note

For more on forming the **plurals of numerals, symbols, letters, and words referred to as words,** see page 789.

 S T Y L E   T I P

Many writers add only an *s* to some of the kinds of plurals listed in Rule 25h. However, using both an apostrophe and *s* is not wrong and may be necessary to make your meaning clear. Therefore, it is a good idea always to include the apostrophe.

Be sure to use apostrophes consistently.

EXAMPLE
Are those *I*'s or *L*'s?
[Without an apostrophe, the plural of *I* would spell the word *Is.* Since an apostrophe and s are used to form the plural of one letter, an apostrophe and *s* are used with the other letter for consistency.]

MECHANICS

Hyphens

Word Division

25i. Use a hyphen to divide a word at the end of a line.

EXAMPLE   How long had the new museum been under construction before it was opened?

When dividing a word at the end of a line, keep in mind the following rules:

(1) Do not divide a one-syllable word.

INCORRECT   After a long journey the Spanish explorers reached their destination.

CORRECT   After a long journey the Spanish explorers reached
their destination.

CORRECT   After a long journey the Spanish explorers
reached their destination.

(2) Divide a word only between syllables.

INCORRECT   The fans stood and cheered while the band was playing the victory song.

CORRECT   The fans stood and cheered while the band was playing the victory song.

(3) Divide an already hyphenated word only at the hyphen.

INCORRECT   My stepsister Melissa plans to take a course in self-defense.

CORRECT   My stepsister Melissa plans to take a course in self-
defense.

INCORRECT   Ms. Malamud always seems to have such a hap-
py-go-lucky attitude.

CORRECT   Ms. Malamud always seems to have such a happy-
go-lucky attitude.

CORRECT   Ms. Malamud always seems to have such a happy-go-
lucky attitude.

(4) Do not divide a word so that one letter stands alone.

INCORRECT   In the gloomy twilight, we had caught a momentar-
y glimpse of them.

CORRECT   In the gloomy twilight, we had caught a momen-
tary glimpse of them.

─HELP─

If you are not entirely sure about the **syllabication** of a word—that is, the division of a word into syllables—look up the word in a dictionary.

MECHANICS

TIPS & TRICKS

Generally, a word containing double consonants may be divided between the double consonants.

EXAMPLES
 cor-rect   begin-ning

Generally, a word with a prefix or suffix made up of more than one letter may be divided between the prefix and the base word (or root) or between the base word and the suffix.

EXAMPLES
 semi-circle   pro-mote
 peace-ful   sign-ing

Write each of the following words, adding hyphens in each place where you could divide the word at the end of a line. If a word should not be divided, write *no hyphen*. If you are unsure where to divide a word, look in a dictionary.

EXAMPLE   1. harmonious

           1. *har-mo-ni-ous*

1. Olympic
2. algebra
3. toast
4. pemmican
5. drummer
6. alert
7. someone
8. Honduras
9. reservation
10. ditch
11. circle
12. traveling
13. kudzu
14. satisfaction
15. donation
16. mansion
17. topography
18. greet
19. self-esteem
20. Johnny-come-lately

Compound Words

Some compound words are written as one word (*blueberry*); some are hyphenated (*blue-collar*); and some are written as two or more words (*blue jay, Blue Ridge Mountains*).

Whenever you are not sure about the spelling of a compound word, look up the word in an up-to-date dictionary.

25j. Use a hyphen with compound numbers from *twenty-one* to *ninety-nine* and with fractions used as modifiers.

EXAMPLES   **twenty-seven** students

              a **two-thirds** majority [but *two thirds of the class*]

25k. Use a hyphen with the prefixes *all–*, *ex–*, *great–*, and *self–*; with the suffixes *–elect* and *–free*; and with all prefixes before a proper noun or proper adjective.

EXAMPLES   **all-**purpose   detergent**-free**

              ex-president   **anti-**Stalinist

              great-grandmother   **mid-**December

              self-control   **non-**Francophile

              secretary**-elect**   **pro-**American

STYLE	TIP

The prefix *half* often requires a hyphen, as in *half-life, half-moon,* and *half-truth.* However, sometimes *half* is used without a hyphen, either as part of a single word (*halftone, halfway, halfback*) or as a separate word (*half shell, half pint, half note*). If you are not sure how to spell a compound containing *half*, look up the word in a dictionary.

25l. Hyphenate a compound adjective when it precedes the noun it modifies.

EXAMPLES   a **well-organized** trip [but *a trip that was well organized*]

           an **after-school** job

Do not use a hyphen if one of the modifiers is an adverb ending in *ly*.

EXAMPLE   a **perfectly good** answer

NOTE Some compound adjectives are always hyphenated, whether they precede or follow the nouns they modify.

EXAMPLES   a **down-to-earth** person

           a person who is **down-to-earth**

If you have any doubt about whether a compound adjective is hyphenated, look up the word in an up-to-date dictionary.

Exercise 6 **Hyphenating Words Correctly**

For each of the following sentences, write and hyphenate the compound words that should be hyphenated.

EXAMPLE   1. The host of that late night show interviewed an expert on Italy's pre Renaissance years.

        1. *late-night; pre-Renaissance*

1. Ex students were not allowed at the festively decorated prom party.
2. His self confidence faded when he forgot his well planned speech.
3. Twenty five students said they had never heard of the well traveled Overland Trail to California.
4. Three fourths of the class voted, and the proposal was defeated by a seven tenths majority.
5. Our governor elect was once an all American football player.
6. In our debate on the United Nations, the pro UN side defeated the anti UN side.
7. General Colin Powell, who is a former resident of the Bronx, spoke quite eloquently about the importance of self determination.
8. Christopher's test scores ranked in the eighty eighth percentile.
9. You must turn in your reports by mid November.
10. My uncle's recipe for halftime nachos calls for fat free cheese and spicy salsa.

STYLE TIP

Although you may see a variety of spellings for some words with prefixes (*reelect, re-elect*), the preferred style today is to use no hyphen between most prefixes (except those indicated in Rule 25k) and the base word.

EXAMPLES
bimonthly   reexamine
antihero   nonessential

Be sure to include the hyphen, however, when one is necessary to prevent confusion or awkwardness.

EXAMPLES
re-creation [to prevent confusion with *recreation*]

pro-offshore drilling [to prevent awkwardness of *prooffshore*]

MECHANICS

Dashes

Sometimes a word, phrase, or sentence is used parenthetically; that is, it breaks into the main thought of a sentence. Most parenthetical elements are set off by commas or by parentheses.

EXAMPLES   Felipe, **however,** had a better idea.

Her suggestion **(that we serve fruit and cheese instead of junk food)** was approved unanimously.

Sometimes, though, such elements call for a sharper separation from the rest of the sentence. In such cases, dashes are used.

25m. Use a dash to indicate the beginning and the end of an abrupt break in thought or speech or to indicate an unfinished thought.

EXAMPLES   The party—I'm sorry I forgot to tell you—was not changed to next week.

"What I meant was—" Vonda began as the doorbell rang.

COMPUTER TIP

When you use a word processor, you can indicate a dash with two hyphens. Do not leave a space before, between, or after the hyphens. When you write by hand, use an unbroken line about as long as two hyphens.

25n. Use a dash to mean *namely, that is,* or *in other words,* or to otherwise introduce an explanation. Also, use a dash after the explanation if the sentence continues.

EXAMPLES   Our family owns two vehicles—a station wagon and a pickup truck. [*namely*]

The weather was unseasonably warm—in the low eighties—for February. [*that is*]

NOTE   Either a dash or colon is acceptable in the first example for 25n.

STYLE   TIP

Dates in parentheses after a person's name indicate the years of that person's birth and death. If the person is still alive, put the closing parenthesis immediately after the dash.

EXAMPLE
George Lucas (1944–) was born in Modesto, California.

Parentheses

25o. Use parentheses to enclose informative or explanatory material of minor importance.

EXAMPLES   The Temple of the Magician **(**I never thought I'd actually see it**)** rose majestically against the purple sky of Uxmal, in the Mexican Yucatán.

Eleanor Roosevelt **(**1884–1962**)** helped draft the Universal Declaration of Human Rights.

Be sure that the material enclosed in parentheses can be omitted without affecting the intended meaning or basic structure of the sentence.

| INCORRECT | When my six-year-old cousin said ("It's the first inning"), the rest of us watching the football game started laughing. |
| CORRECT | When my six-year-old cousin said, **"It's the first inning,"** the rest of us watching the football game started laughing. |

| INCORRECT | I sent the package on October 12 (that was ten days ago via express mail.) |
| CORRECT | I sent the package on October 12 **(that was ten days ago)** via express mail. |

A sentence enclosed in parentheses may fall within another sentence or may stand by itself.

(1) A parenthetical sentence that falls within another sentence

- does not begin with a capital letter unless it begins with a word that should be capitalized
- does not end with a period but may end with a question mark or exclamation point

EXAMPLES   When we reached Shaker Heights **(it's just outside Cleveland),** we met our cousins for dinner.

The John Hancock Tower **(isn't it in Boston?)** was designed by I. M. Pei.

NOTE   Generally, when parenthetical material falls within a sentence, punctuation does not precede the opening parenthesis but may follow the closing parenthesis.

| INCORRECT | Reading the novel by Samuel Clemens, (better known as Mark Twain) I learned much about American society in the nineteenth century. |
| CORRECT | Reading the novel by Samuel Clemens (better known as Mark Twain), I learned much about American society in the nineteenth century. [The comma following the closing parenthesis is used to set off the introductory participial phrase.] |

(2) A parenthetical sentence that stands by itself

- begins with a capital letter
- ends with a period, a question mark, or an exclamation point

STYLE   TIP

Too many parenthetical expressions in a piece of writing can distract the reader from the main idea. Keep your meaning clear by limiting the number of parenthetical expressions you use.

MECHANICS

EXAMPLES On the scoring sheet, mark your answers with a lead pencil. **(Do not use ink.)**

In 1996 he won another gold medal for the high dive. **(That was his ninth!)**

Follow these guidelines for determining when to use commas, dashes, and parentheses to enclose parenthetical material:

1. Remember that only material that can be omitted without changing the basic meaning or structure of the sentence is considered parenthetical.
2. Use commas to set off parenthetical material that is closely related to the rest of the sentence.

EXAMPLE We rehearsed for the show, a wonderful musical comedy.

3. Use a dash to indicate the beginning and the end of an abrupt change in thought or to indicate an unfinished thought.

EXAMPLE We rehearsed for the show—which many called the musical event of the year!

4. Use parentheses to indicate that the parenthetical material is of minor importance.

EXAMPLE We rehearsed for the show (at least those of us who could remember our lines did).

5. Don't overuse parenthetical material, or you may confuse your readers.

COMPUTER TIP

With the search-and-replace function of a word-processing program, you can check your writing for the incorrect or inappropriate uses of apostrophes, hyphens, dashes, and parentheses. Take full advantage of such a program when you are proofreading your work.

MECHANICS

Brackets

25p. Use brackets to enclose an explanation or added information within quoted or parenthetical material.

EXAMPLES The secretary of state, in her speech, said: "Diplomatic efforts seek to establish talks between the two nations [North and South Korea]." [The words are enclosed in brackets to show that they have been inserted into the quotation and are not the speaker's words.]

The faltering performance of the Russian economy in recent years has caused fluctuations in the world's financial markets. (See page 15 [Graph 1A] for a chronology.)

Exercise 7 Correcting Sentences by Using Dashes, Parentheses, and Brackets

Rewrite the following sentences, adding dashes, parentheses, and brackets where they are needed. If a sentence is already correct, write *C*.

┌─HELP─
Some sentences
in Exercise 7 have more
than one possible answer.
You need to give only one
answer for each sentence.

EXAMPLE   1. Garth Brooks and Shania Twain I have every one of their albums have won many awards.

     1. *Garth Brooks and Shania Twain (I have every one of their albums) have won many awards.*

1. "Yankee Doodle" it was the unofficial United States anthem at the time was played after the signing of the Treaty of Ghent.
2. While standing at the top of Pikes Peak, Katherine Lee Bates wrote the words to the song "America the Beautiful."
3. Lauryn Hill I love her songs! gave a concert here, and it sold out.
4. There were three original members of the Sons of the Pioneers Roy Rogers his real name was Leonard Slye, Bob Nolan, and Tim Spencer.
5. Linda Ronstadt has recorded many kinds of music, including rock, songs from the 1930's and 1940's, and Mexican tunes.
6. The Beatles used several names Foreverly Brothers, the Cavemen, the Moondogs, and the Quarrymen before they became the Beatles.
7. Last night's concert was about average the songs were good, but the singers were uninspired.
8. Cathy said, "I will listen to one of your CDs Mozart's *Requiem*, perhaps if you will listen to one of Lenny Kravitz's CDs."
9. Bob Dylan (1941– born Robert Allen Zimmerman) wrote "Blowin' in the Wind."
10. Whitney Houston's version of "The Star-Spangled Banner" have you heard it? wouldn't Francis Scott Key be pleased? was a hit.

Review E Proofreading for Errors in Punctuation

Each of the following sentences contains at least one error in punctuation. Correct the errors by adding apostrophes, hyphens, dashes, parentheses, and brackets where they are needed.

┌─HELP─
Although two
possible answers are given
for the example in Review
E, you need to give only
one answer for each
sentence.

EXAMPLE   1. Dont you ever wonder I frequently do about who invented different kinds of machines and tools?

     1. *Don't you ever wonder—I frequently do—about who invented different kinds of machines and tools?*

or

Don't you ever wonder (I frequently do) about who invented different kinds of machines and tools?

MECHANICS

1. Both Trishs and Roberts reports the ones required for social studies were about the shoe industry.

2. Trish said that she chose the subject because at least seventy five percent of the world's students wear shoes.

3. I thought the other report the one Robert gave on the invention of the lasting machine was more interesting, though.

4. Robert wrote, "The lasting machine (its parts are numbered in the patent drawing provided see the picture below) changed the shoe industrys future."

5. The machines inventor the distinguished looking young man pictured below was Jan Matzeliger.

6. He came to the United States from Dutch Guiana now Suriname before 1880 and found work as a shoemakers apprentice.

7. Matzeliger wasnt happy with how much of the workers time was spent putting shoes together.

8. Within ten years time he perfected a machine that shaped leather for the upper shoe and attached it to the sole.

9. Matzeligers patent for this much needed machine was granted in 1883.

10. The United Shoe Manufacturing Companys decision to buy the machine ultimately gave that company control of the United States shoe market.

The Granger Collection, New York.

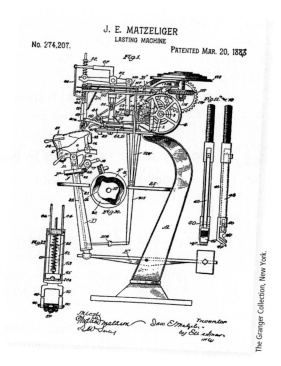

The Granger Collection, New York.

Chapter Review

A. Using Apostrophes and Hyphens Correctly

Add or delete apostrophes and hyphens as necessary in the following sentences.

┌─HELP─┐
Some sentences in the Chapter Review contain more than one error.

1. The towns record on supporting youth projects has been good.

2. The wet, muddy boots were lined up outside the door to the house.

3. Only fifty three people went to our ballet recital, and thirty of them were our relatives.

4. Everyones favorite performer was certainly the man in the turtleneck.

5. Christophers writing is hard to read because his *a*s look like *o*s.

6. The womens basketball team, which is coached by an ex Laker, has run up quite an impressive string of victories.

7. Sampson and Smiths French Bakery, which displays its pas tries in the window, is around the corner from my house.

8. Mr. Millers watercolors dont appeal to me, but they were given the jurys highest award.

9. Approximately twenty out of twenty five students agree that self esteem is among the most important personal qualities.

10. To verify safety standards, we have compared twenty-seven sport utility vehicles.

11. Theres someone at the door, and were already late for school!

12. Hes used too many *therefore*s in his sentences to get an A on his composition.

13. There are three 5s and four 8s missing from your answer's.

14. My sister in laws job is selling childrens sportswear.

15. The Jameses address contains four 7s.

B. Using Dashes, Brackets, and Parentheses Correctly

Add dashes, brackets, and parentheses where they are needed in each of the following sentences. Do not add commas or colons.

16. My cousins like many of Charley Pride's songs his "Crystal Chandeliers" is their favorite.

17. This report contains information about agriculture in those three South American countries Brazil, Argentina, and Colombia see Graph 3A on pp. 24–25.

18. I read the wrong chapter for my homework a disastrous mistake!

19. Mary Ellen Jefferson, a former district attorney, will speak at Thursday's assembly I'll have to miss gym class and will address the topic of student rights.

20. Bessie Coleman I read an article about her was the first licensed African American pilot.

C. Writing the Possessive Forms of Nouns

Write the singular possessive and plural possessive form of each of the following nouns.

21. house
22. computer
23. uncle
24. coach

25. cow
26. president
27. trellis

28. goose
29. wife
30. theory

D. Proofreading a Paragraph for Errors in Punctuation

Each sentence in the following paragraph contains at least one error in punctuation. Correct the errors by adding or deleting apostrophes, hyphens, dashes, and parentheses.

[31] The kangaroo, possibly Australias most famous indigenous animal, is a marsupial, a kind of mammal. [32] Marsupial's offspring are born extremely undeveloped. [33] A newborn joey a baby kangaroo measures only about one inch long. [34] A kangaroos pouch the pocket like opening in the mother's belly where the joey completes its development is one of the animal kingdoms' most unusual features. [35] With their huge hind feet, long tails, and small, deer like heads, kangaroos are among the worlds' most distinctive creatures. [36] Kangaroos and wallabies their smaller cousins both belong to an animal family called macropods the name means "big foot" in Latin which includes other animals such as the so called hare wallaby, the bettong, and the potoroo. [37] Kangaroo's life spans vary from six to eight years, on average. [38] They have few enemies and are protected by Australias no poaching laws. [39] Theyre fast, too; large specimens top speed is as

high as 30 miles per hour. **[40]** So closely are they bound up with Australias identity that the symbol of Qantas, the national airline, is yes, you guessed it a leaping "roo."

Writing Application
Punctuating a Poem

Using Dashes   You have decided to enter a local poetry contest for high school students. All the poems must reflect students' ideas about current events. For the contest, write a poem that uses at least four dashes.

Prewriting   Start by making a list of subjects that interest you. Then, choose a subject from your list, and freewrite about it. List as many sensory details as you can to describe your subject. Then, start grouping the details to create a loose structure for your poem.

Writing   Use your freewriting notes to write your first draft. As you form your ideas into lines of poetry, choose words and punctuation carefully, paying attention to both the images and the rhythms they create.

Revising   Read your poem silently to be sure that it says what you want it to say. Add, cut, or rearrange details to express your ideas more effectively. Then, read your poem aloud and listen to the rhythm of the words you have used. Make any changes that you feel will improve the rhythm, keeping in mind that you must include at least four dashes in the poem.

Publishing   Be sure to check the spelling and punctuation in your poem. If you have typed your poem or are using a word processor, check to see that the spacing around hyphens and dashes is correct. If your class has a Web page, you may want to collect your poems and publish them on the Internet.

Spelling
Improving Your Spelling

Diagnostic Preview

Correcting Misspelled and Misused Words and Numerals

Proofread the following sentences, and correctly write any misspelled or misused words or numerals.

EXAMPLE   **1.** Our parents will be dineing out tonight.

1. dining

1. When I went to the barn, the cows and calfs were eating hay.
2. Do you know weather Mars was a Roman diety?
3. I don't know whether the relay team won 1st or 2nd place.
4. Our Thanksgiving meal consists of turkey, stuffing, beans, cranberries, and potatos.
5. The principle's name is Mr. Goodson.
6. The child carried the turtle carefuly across the road.
7. Jill didn't mispell any words on the test.
8. The basketball team missed the bus, so they had to forfiet the game.
9. If I've told you once, I've told you 1,000 times: Don't exaggerate!
10. We decieved Janice so that she would not know we were throwing a surprise birthday party for her.
11. The affects of this weather system were completly unexpected.
12. I felt that the emergency team was quite couragous.
13. The director said two hundred seventeen people applied for the job.
14. If you excede the speed limit, you might get a ticket.

15. I was grateful to be offerred the lead in the play.
16. My parents' dog, an enormous Great Dane, is scarred of thunder and lightning.
17. Arguement is useless in this situation.
18. A Japanese animated cartoon will preceed the action movie.
19. Ed wants to write playes for a living.
20. Lauren ate 6 pieces of kiwi fruit.

Good Spelling Habits

26a. To learn the spelling of a word, pronounce it, study it, and write it.

(1) Pronounce words carefully.

EXAMPLES   a**thl**etic [not *athaletic*]

es**cape** [not *excape*]

heigh**t** [not *heighth*]

(2) Spell by syllables.

A *syllable* is a word part that can be pronounced as one uninterrupted sound.

EXAMPLES   pul • sate [two syllables]

bul • le • tin [three syllables]

en • vi • ron • ment [four syllables]

(3) Use a dictionary.

Do not guess about correct spelling. Look up any words you do not know how to spell. In the dictionary, you can often find other, related words that may help you remember the correct spelling. For example, you may find *denomination* easier to spell after you see its kinship with the words *nominate* and *denominator*.

(4) Proofread for careless spelling errors.

Always proofread what you have written so that you can eliminate careless spelling errors, such as typos (*thier* for *their*), missing letters (*temperture* for *temperature*), and the misuse of words that sound similar (*principal* for *principle*).

┌HELP──

If you are not sure about the correct pronunciation of a word, look it up in a current dictionary. The pronunciation of the word will usually be given in parentheses after the main entry. Use the pronunciation key in the dictionary to help you pronounce the word correctly.

MECHANICS

COMPUTER TIP

Spellcheckers can help you proofread your writing. Even the best spellcheckers are not foolproof, however. Some accept British spellings, obsolete words, archaic spellings, and words that are spelled correctly but are used incorrectly (such as *affect* for *effect*). Always double-check your writing to make sure that your spelling is error-free.

(5) Keep a spelling notebook.

Divide each page into four columns:

COLUMN 1   Correctly write any word you find troublesome.

COLUMN 2   Write the word again, dividing it into syllables and marking the stressed syllable(s). (You may need to use a dictionary.)

COLUMN 3   Write the word again, circling the difficult part(s).

COLUMN 4   Write down any comments that might help you remember the correct spelling.

Correct Spelling	Syllables and Accents	Trouble Spot	Comments
February	Feb'·ru·ar·y	Feb(ru)ary	Pronounce correctly.
disapproval	dis'·ap·prov'·al	di(sa)pprov(al)	Study Rules 26e and 26g.

Spelling Rules

ie and *ei*

26b. Write *ie* when the sound is long *e*, except after *c*.

EXAMPLES   ch**ie**f, bel**ie**ve, n**ie**ce, ach**ie**ve, perc**ei**ve, rec**ei**pt

EXCEPTIONS   **ei**ther, l**ei**sure, n**ei**ther, prot**ei**n

26c. Write *ei* when the sound is not long *e*.

EXAMPLES   forf**ei**t, fr**ei**ght, h**ei**ght, n**ei**ghbor, v**ei**l, w**ei**gh

EXCEPTIONS   anc**ie**nt, misch**ie**f, pat**ie**nce

–cede, –ceed, and *–sede*

26d. The only English word ending in *–sede* is *supersede.* The only words ending in *–ceed* are *exceed, proceed,* and *succeed.* Most other words with this sound end in *–cede.*

EXAMPLES   con**cede**, pre**cede**, re**cede**, ac**cede**

TIPS & TRICKS

Remember this rhyme:
i before *e*
except after *c*
or when sounded like *a*
as in *neighbor* and *weigh.*

HELP

Rules 26b and
26c apply only when the *i*
and the *e* are in the same
syllable.

EXAMPLES
sci • ence   de • i • ty

Exercise 1   Proofreading Sentences to Correct Spelling Errors

Proofread each of the following sentences, and correctly write the misspelled word or words.

EXAMPLE   1. Niether my neice nor I have tried bungee jumping.

   1. *Neither, niece*

1. During the 1920s, one craze superceded another, each one weirder than the one that preceeded it.
2. Pictured at right is fifteen-year-old Avon Foreman, who acheived fame in Baltimore for his bizarre liesure-time activity.
3. In 1929, he spent ten days, ten hours, ten minutes, and ten seconds perched atop a hickory sapling, at a hieght of eighteen feet.
4. Freinds and neighbors crowded around to give encouragement.
5. He even succeded in attracting the attention of the mayor, William F. Broening, who wrote to him that his "grit and stamina . . . show that the old pioneer spirit of early America is being kept alive by the youth of today."
6. The mayor beleived that Avon was indeed someone to look up to, evidently.
7. People continue to participate in and succede at a number of curious endeavors.
8. There are attempts to cross Antarctica using only dog sleds, leaps from great hieghts, and contests to see how many people will fit into a small car.
9. It seems that humans will always try to acheive unusual goals.
10. Undoubtedly, many people have recieved great entertainment from these occasionally ridiculous activities.

Adding Prefixes

A *prefix* is one or more letters or syllables added to the beginning of a word to create a new word that has a different meaning.

26e. When adding a prefix, do not change the spelling of the original word.

Reference Note
For a list of **prefixes,** see page 892.

EXAMPLES   mis + spell = mis**spell**   dis + advantage = dis**advantage**

   un + likely = un**likely**   il + legible = il**legible**

MECHANICS

Adding Suffixes

A *suffix* is one or more letters or syllables added to the end of a word to create a new word with a different meaning.

Reference Note

For a list of **suffixes,** see page 893.

26f. When adding the suffix *–ly* or *–ness,* do not change the spelling of the original word.

EXAMPLES	nice + ly = **nice**ly	mean + ness = **mean**ness
	usual + ly = **usual**ly	same + ness = **same**ness

Words ending in *y* usually change the *y* to *i* before *–ness* and *–ly:*

EXAMPLES   empty—empt**i**ness; easy—eas**i**ly

However, most one-syllable adjectives ending in *y* follow Rule 26f:

EXAMPLES   shy—**shy**ly; dry—**dry**ness

True, due, and *whole* drop the final *e* before *–ly:*

EXAMPLES   true—**tru**ly; due—**du**ly; whole—**whol**ly

Exercise 2 **Spelling Words with Prefixes and Suffixes**

Write each of the following words, adding the prefix or suffix given.

EXAMPLE   **1.** il + legible

       1. illegible

1. heavy + ness
2. dis + satisfied
3. il + legal
4. un + nerve
5. sincere + ly
6. whole + ly
7. mis + understood
8. ready + ness
9. un + likely
10. happy + ly
11. ordinary + ly
12. im + mature
13. sudden + ness
14. special + ly
15. over + rate
16. il + logical
17. un + flattering
18. dis + illusion
19. stubborn + ness
20. shy + ness

26g. Drop the final silent *e* before adding a suffix beginning with a vowel.

EXAMPLES	dine + ing = **din**ing	safe + er = **saf**er
	use + able = **us**able	nice + est = **nic**est

EXCEPTIONS   Keep the final silent *e*

- in a word ending in *ce* or *ge* before a suffix beginning with *a* or *o*

    service + able = **service**able

    advantage + ous = **advantage**ous

- in *dye* and in *singe* before *–ing:* **dye**ing and **singe**ing [to avoid confusion with *dying* and *singing*]

- in *mile* before *–age:* **mile**age

26h. Keep the final silent *e* before adding a suffix beginning with a consonant.

EXAMPLES   use + ful = **use**ful   care + less = **care**less

pave + ment = **pave**ment   live + ly = **live**ly

hope + ful = **hope**ful   large + ly = **large**ly

EXCEPTIONS   true + ly = **tru**ly   nine + th = **nin**th

argue + ment = **argu**ment   awe + ful = **aw**ful

Exercise 3   Spelling Words with Suffixes

Write each of the following words, adding the suffix given.

EXAMPLES   1. amuse + ing
   1. *amusing*

   2. care + ful
   2. *careful*

1. courage + ous
2. nine + ty
3. advance + ing
4. hope + less
5. approve + al
6. note + able
7. ride + ing
8. outrage + ous
9. dye + ing
10. true + ly

26i. For words ending in *y* preceded by a consonant, change the *y* to *i* before adding any suffix that does not begin with *i*.

EXAMPLES   lively + ness = **liveli**ness   rely + ed = **reli**ed

bury + al = **buri**al   funny + er = **funni**er

hasty + est = **hasti**est   study + ing = **study**ing

┌HELP───
Some one-syllable words do not follow Rule 26i.

EXAMPLES
  dry—**dry**ness
  shy—**shy**ly

26j. For words ending in y preceded by a vowel, keep the y when adding a suffix.

EXAMPLES enjoy + able = **enjoy**able   play + ful = **play**ful

survey + or = **survey**or   delay + ing = **delay**ing

EXCEPTIONS lay—**lai**d   pay—**pai**d   say—**sai**d   day—**dai**ly

---

Exercise 4 **Spelling Words with Suffixes**

Write each of the following words, adding the suffix given.

EXAMPLES   **1.** ready + ly

   1. readily

   2. relay + ing

   2. relaying

1. happy + est   **6.** spy + ing
2. marry + ing   **7.** employ + ing
3. relay + ed   **8.** try + ed
4. shiny + er   **9.** day + ly
5. obey + ed   **10.** busy + ly

26k. Double the final consonant before adding a suffix that begins with a vowel if the word (1) has only one syllable or has the accent on the final syllable and (2) ends in a single consonant preceded by a single vowel.

EXAMPLES   drop + ed = dro**pped**   run + er = ru**nner**

   begin + ing = begi**nning**   regret + able = regre**ttable**

EXCEPTIONS   For words ending in *w* or *x*, do not double the final consonant.

   few + er = **few**er   throw + ing = **throw**ing

   fax + es = **fax**es   perplex + ed = **perplex**ed

When a word satisfies both conditions but the addition of the suffix causes the accent to shift, do not double the final consonant.

EXAMPLES   confer + ence = **confer**ence

   prefer + able = **prefer**able

EXCEPTIONS   excel—exce**llent,** exce**llence,** exce**llency**

┌HELP──
The final consonant of some words may or may not be doubled. Either spelling is acceptable.

EXAMPLES
travel + ed = trave**led**
or trave**lled**

cancel + ing = cance**ling**
or cance**lling**

Exercise 5 Spelling Words with Suffixes

Write each of the following words, adding the suffix given.

EXAMPLE   **1.** slip + ed

          1. slipped

1. sad + er   **11.** excel + ence

2. propel + er   **12.** run + ing

3. shovel + ing   **13.** wax + ed

4. refer + al   **14.** droop + ed

5. repel + ent   **15.** drop + ing

6. confer + ed   **16.** accept + ance

7. suffer + ance   **17.** refer + ence

8. hop + ing   **18.** beep + ing

9. shop + ed   **19.** endow + ing

10. remit + ance   **20.** mow + er

© John Caldwell 1986.

Review A Proofreading a Paragraph to Correct Spelling Errors

Proofread the following paragraph, correcting each misspelled word.

EXAMPLE   **[1]** In what battle were the Shawnee cheif Tecumseh, his brother, and thier followers defeatted by William Henry Harrison?

         1. chief; their; defeated

┌H E L P──

No proper nouns in Review A are misspelled.

MECHANICS

George Catlin, *The Open Door, Known as the Prophet, Brother of Tecumseh.* National Museum of American Art, Washington, DC/ Art Resource, New York.

[**1**] The Shawnee war chief Tecumseh was commited to the goal of uniting American Indians. [**2**] He believed that unification was the only way to prevent white settlers from siezing the land on which his people lived. [**3**] Opposed to treaties that forced Native Americans to forfiet their land, Tecumseh believed that the land was owned by no one. [**4**] After much hard work, he succeded in convincing some midwestern American Indian peoples to join together. [**5**] With his brother, known as the Shawnee Prophet, Tecumseh urged his people to preserve their traditional ways of liveing and not to surrender the land. [**6**] Tecumseh and the Shawnee Prophet at left led thier followers in building Prophetstown at the location indicated on the map of Indiana below. [**7**] In 1811, while Tecumseh was delivering a speech in a neighboring village, the governor of the Indiana Territory, William Henry Harrison, and his forces easly attacked Prophetstown. [**8**] Against Tecumseh's wishes, the Shawnee Prophet and his followers proceeded to counterattack and finally had to consede defeat in the Battle of Tippecanoe. [**9**] Overun by Harrison, Tecumseh's people scattered, leaving the town in ruins and bringing to an end twenty years of Tecumseh's work. [**10**] Tecumseh had planed to start over, but his death in 1813 at the Battle of the Thames ended all hopes of uniting the various Native American nations.

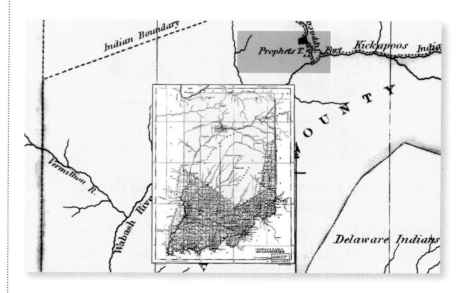

Forming Plurals of Nouns

26l. The singular form of a noun names one person, place, thing, or idea. The plural form names more than one. Remembering the following rules will help you spell the plural forms of nouns.

(1) For most nouns, add *s*.

SINGULAR	dog	kite	pencil	video	club	McGregor
PLURAL	dog**s**	kite**s**	pencil**s**	video**s**	club**s**	McGregor**s**

(2) For nouns ending in *s, x, z, ch,* or *sh,* add *es*.

SINGULAR	glass	suffix	waltz	trench	bush	Gomez
PLURAL	glass**es**	suffix**es**	waltz**es**	trench**es**	bush**es**	Gomez**es**

(3) For nouns ending in *y* preceded by a vowel, add *s*.

SINGULAR	alloy	turkey	essay	attorney	decoy	Sunday
PLURAL	alloy**s**	turkey**s**	essay**s**	attorney**s**	decoy**s**	Sunday**s**

(4) For nouns ending in *y* preceded by a consonant, change the *y* to *i* and add *es*.

SINGULAR	city	enemy	spy	penny	country
PLURAL	cit**ies**	enem**ies**	sp**ies**	penn**ies**	countr**ies**

> **NOTE** For most proper nouns ending in *y* preceded by a consonant, add *s*.
>
> EXAMPLES   Murphy—Murphy**s**
>   Brody—Brody**s**

(5) For some nouns ending in *f* or *fe*, add *s*. For others, change the *f* or *fe* to *v* and add *es*.

SINGULAR	belief	roof	fife	wolf	knife	leaf
PLURAL	belief**s**	roof**s**	fife**s**	wol**ves**	kni**ves**	lea**ves**

(6) For nouns ending in *o* preceded by a vowel, add *s*.

SINGULAR	patio	rodeo	ratio	barrio	kangaroo	Valerio
PLURAL	patio**s**	rodeo**s**	ratio**s**	barrio**s**	kangaroo**s**	Valerio**s**

(7) For most nouns ending in *o* preceded by a consonant, add *es*.

SINGULAR	tomato	potato	hero	echo	torpedo
PLURAL	tomato**es**	potato**es**	hero**es**	echo**es**	torpedo**es**

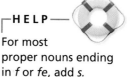

┌─**HELP**──

Some one-syllable words ending in *z* double the final consonant when forming plurals.

EXAMPLES
quiz   fez
qui**zz**es   fe**zz**es

MECHANICS

┌─**HELP**──

For most proper nouns ending in *f* or *fe*, add *s*.

EXAMPLES
van Cleef—van Cleef**s**
Radcliffe—Radcliffe**s**

┌ **TIPS** & **TRICKS** ┐

Noticing how the plural is pronounced will help you remember whether to change the *f* or *fe* to *v*.

For some common nouns ending in *o* preceded by a consonant (especially those referring to music) and for proper nouns, add *s*.

SINGULAR	taco	dojo	soprano	allegro	Sato
PLURAL	taco**s**	dojo**s**	soprano**s**	allegro**s**	Sato**s**

NOTE For some nouns ending in *o* preceded by a consonant, you may add either *s* or *es*.

SINGULAR	cargo	mosquito	motto	zero
PLURAL	cargo**s**	mosquito**s**	motto**s**	zero**s**
	or	*or*	*or*	*or*
	cargo**es**	mosquito**es**	motto**es**	zero**es**

(8) **The plurals of a few nouns are formed irregularly.**

SINGULAR	child	ox	woman	tooth	mouse	foot
PLURAL	child**ren**	ox**en**	wom**e**n	t**ee**th	m**ice**	f**ee**t

(9) **For a few nouns, the singular and the plural forms are the same.**

SINGULAR AND PLURAL	Chinese	scissors	salmon
	sheep	aircraft	binoculars

Compound Nouns

(10) **For most compound nouns, form the plural of only the last word of the compound.**

SINGULAR	bookkeeper	stepchild	two-year-old	grand jury
PLURAL	bookkeeper**s**	stepchild**ren**	two-year-old**s**	grand jur**ies**

(11) **For compound nouns in which one of the words is modified by the other word or words, form the plural of the word modified.**

SINGULAR	editor in chief	son-in-law	chief of staff	runner-up
PLURAL	editor**s** in chief	son**s**-in-law	chief**s** of staff	runner**s**-up

NOTE Some compound nouns have two acceptable plural forms.

SINGULAR	surgeon general	court-martial
PLURAL	surgeon**s** general	court**s**-martial
	or	*or*
	surgeon general**s**	court-martial**s**

MECHANICS

Words Borrowed from Other Languages

(12) For some nouns borrowed from other languages, plurals are formed as in the original languages.

Singular	Plural
alumnus [male]	alumni [male]
alumna [female]	alumnae [female]
phenomenon	phenomena
parenthesis	parentheses
datum	data

> **NOTE** A few nouns borrowed from other languages have two acceptable plural forms. For each of the following nouns, the plural form preferred in English is given first.

SINGULAR	formula	index	cactus	seraph
PLURAL	formulas	indexes	cactuses	seraphs
	or	or	or	or
	formulae	indices	cacti	seraphim

If you are ever in doubt about which spelling to use, remember that a dictionary generally lists the preferred spelling first.

Numerals, Letters, Symbols, and Words Used as Words

(13) To form the plurals of numerals, most capital letters, symbols, and most words referred to as words, add an *s* or both an apostrophe and an *s*.

SINGULAR	8	1700	T	&	and
PLURAL	8s	1700s	Ts	&s	ands
	or	or	or	or	or
	8's	1700's	T's	&'s	and's

EXAMPLES His *7*s [or *7*'s] look like *T*s [or *T*'s].

Do not write *&*s [or *&*'s] for *and*s [or *and*'s].

Phillis Wheatley wrote during the 1700s [or 1700's].

┌HELP┐
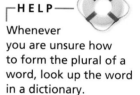
Whenever you are unsure how to form the plural of a word, look up the word in a dictionary.

MECHANICS

To prevent confusion, add both an apostrophe and an *s* to form the plurals of all lowercase letters, certain capital letters, and some words referred to as words.

EXAMPLES   The word *accommodate* has two *a*'s, two *c*'s, two *o*'s, and two *m*'s.

His essay is filled with *I*'s. [Without an apostrophe, the plural of the pronoun *I* could be confused with the word *Is*.]

Make sure that each one of your *her*'s has a clear antecedent. [Without an apostrophe, the plural of the word *her* could be confused with the possessive pronoun *hers*.]

Exercise 6 **Spelling the Plurals of Nouns**

Write the plural form of each of the following nouns.

EXAMPLES   **1.** piano

   1. pianos

   2. curriculum

   2. curricula

1. girl   **11.** cafeteria
2. valley   **12.** dormitory
3. sky   **13.** goose
4. coach   **14.** parenthesis
5. Japanese   **15.** diary
6. sister-in-law   **16.** blizzard
7. solo   **17.** patio
8. self   **18.** deer
9. notebook   **19.** abolitionist
10. stereo   **20.** 1900

Review B **Applying Spelling Rules**

Use Rules 26b–26l to explain the spellings of the following words.

EXAMPLE   **1.** boxes

   1. Add es *to form the plural of a noun ending in* x.

1. crises   **6.** misstep
2. deceive   **7.** meanness
3. proceed   **8.** noticeable
4. placement   **9.** referred
5. sopranos   **10.** countries

Writing Numbers

26m. Spell out a number that begins a sentence.

EXAMPLE **Two thousand** students attend Shawnee High School, I believe.

If a number appears awkward when spelled out, revise the sentence so that it does not begin with the number.

EXAMPLE I believe the number of students who attend Shawnee High School is **2,103.**

26n. Spell out a *cardinal number*—a number that states how many—that can be expressed in one or two words. Otherwise, use numerals.

EXAMPLES **fourteen** dogs **thirty-one** days **one thousand** votes

514 dogs **331** days **2,670** votes

Generally, do not spell out some numbers and use numerals for others in the same context. If numerals are required for any of the numbers, be consistent by using numerals for all of the numbers.

INCONSISTENT In the election, Lou Ann received ninety votes, and Darla received 103.

CONSISTENT In the election, Lou Ann received **90** votes, and Darla received **103.**

However, to distinguish between numbers that appear beside each other but that count different things, spell out one number and use numerals for the other.

EXAMPLE They bought **two 25**-pound bags of dog food.

26o. Spell out an *ordinal number*—a number that expresses order.

EXAMPLE My brother placed **third** [not 3rd] in the **first** [not 1st] race.

26p. Use numerals to express numbers in conventional situations.

Conventional situations include

* identification numbers

EXAMPLES Room **16**   pages **359–407**   Chapter **3**

Channel **32**   Interstate **10**   Rule **26k**

STYLE TIP

For large round numbers, you may use words only, numerals only, or a combination of words and numerals.

EXAMPLES
eight million dollars
or
$8 million

32,800,000,000
or
32.8 billion

Reference Note

Compound cardinal numbers from twenty-one to ninety-nine are hyphenated. For more about **hyphenated numbers,** see page 768.

MECHANICS

HELP

Compound ordinal numbers from twenty-first to ninety-ninth are hyphenated.

- measurements/statistics

| EXAMPLES | **68** degrees | **4½** feet | **14.5** pounds |
| | **20** percent | **16** years old | score of **32** to **18** |

- addresses

EXAMPLES   **18** Kresge Way   Charlotte, NC **28243-0018**

- dates

EXAMPLES   May **5, 2000**   **44** B.C.   A.D. **893**

- times of day

EXAMPLES   **6:30** A.M.   **11:15** P.M.

NOTE   Spell out a number used with *o'clock.*

EXAMPLE   **five o'clock** in the morning

Review C **Proofreading a Paragraph to Correct Spelling Errors**

Proofread the following paragraph, correcting the misspelled or misused words or expressions.

EXAMPLE   **[1]** 5 days ago, all of the members of my family except one joined my grandparentes in a lovly celebration of their wedding anniversary.

1. *Five; grandparents; lovely*

[1] Last Saturday my mom's parents, Grandma and Grandpa Reyes, celebrated their fortyeth anniversary by repeating their wedding vows in a beautiful ceremony at St. Teresa's Church. [2] Since I have my learnner's permit now and it was light out when we went to the church, Mom let me drive. [3] My aunts and uncles on Mom's side of the family were there with their husbands and wifes. [4] In addition, all of my cousins except Ernesto, whom I had been especially hopeing to see, attended the ceremony. [5] Unfortunately, the flights from Denver, where Ernesto goes to college, had been canceled because it had snowed heavyly there the night before. [6] Although I missed Ernesto, I enjoyed visiting with many of the 85 friends and family members who had come to the celebration. [7] Grandma and Grandpa had insisted that anniversary gifts were unecessary, but this time they were over-ruled. [8] You could tell that they were truely stunned when they

opened the gift from their children. [**9**] Mom and her sisters and brothers had chiped in to buy them plane tickets to Mexico City, where they were born. [**10**] Everyone had such a good time that we have already started planing for Grandma and Grandpa's 50th anniversary.

Words Often Confused

You can prevent many spelling errors by learning the difference between the words grouped together in this section. Some of them are confusing because they are *homonyms*—that is, they are pronounced alike. Others are confusing because they are spelled the same or nearly the same.

Reference Note

In the Glossary of Usage, Chapter 20, you can find many other words that are often confused or misused. You can also look the words up in a dictionary.

affect	[verb] *to influence* How did that sad movie *affect* you?
effect	[verb] *to accomplish, to bring about;* [noun] *a consequence; a result* Head Start centers can *effect* an improvement in the lives of many children. What *effect* did the rain have on the crops?
all ready	[adjective] *all prepared* We were *all ready* to leave.
already	[adverb] *previously* We had *already* painted the sets.
all right	[adjective] *satisfactory;* [adverb] *satisfactorily* The match was difficult, but your playing was *all right.* I think I did *all right,* too. [This is the only acceptable spelling. Although the spelling *alright* is in some dictionaries, it has not become standard usage.]
all together	[adjective] *in the same place;* [adverb] *at the same time* The players were *all together* in the gym. Sing *all together,* now.
altogether	[adverb] *entirely* I am not *altogether* convinced.
altar	[noun] *a table or stand at which religious rites are performed* When you reach the *altar,* you must kneel.
alter	[verb] *to change* When did you *alter* the schedule?

(continued)

brake	[verb] *to slow down or to stop;* [noun] *a device used to slow down or to stop* She tried to *brake* the bicycle with the hand *brake.*
break	[verb] *to cause to come apart, to fracture;* [noun] *a fracture* I did not *break* my wrist; I sprained it. The doctor said it is not a *break,* but a sprain.
capital	[noun] *center of government; money or property used in business;* [adjective] *punishable by death; of major importance; excellent; uppercase* What is the *capital* of Zimbabwe? You need *capital* to start a business. Do you support *capital* punishment? Begin every sentence with a *capital* letter.
capitol	[noun] *a building where a legislature meets* We could see the *capitol* from our hotel.
choose	[verb, rhymes with *shoes*] *to select* We *choose* partners today.
chose	[verb, past form of *choose,* rhymes with *nose*] *selected* Each of us *chose* a partner yesterday.
coarse	[adjective] *rough, crude* Burlap is a *coarse* fabric.
course	[noun] *a part of a meal; a series of studies; a playing field; a path of action;* [also used after *of* to mean *naturally* or *certainly*] She skipped the first *course* at dinner. The speech *course* helped my diction. A new golf *course* opened last week. What *course* will resolve the conflict? Of *course,* you are always welcome.
complement	[noun] *that which makes whole or complete;* [verb] *to make whole or complete* Without a *complement,* the sentence is incomplete. That scarf *complements* your outfit nicely.
compliment	[noun] *praise, a courteous act or statement;* [verb] *to express praise or respect* He received many *compliments* on his cooking. I *complimented* her on her success.

TIPS & TRICKS

Here is an easy way to remember the difference between *capital* and *capitol.* There is a d**o**me on the capit**o**l building.

TIPS & TRICKS

Here is an easy way to remember the difference between *complement* and *compliment.* A compl**e**ment is something that compl**e**tes.

MECHANICS

consul	[noun] *a person appointed by a government to serve its citizens in a foreign country* The United States *consul* in Tokyo met with a group of tourists.
council	[noun] *a group called together to accomplish a job* Members of the *council* voted on the resolution.
counsel	[noun] *advice;* [verb] *to advise* Sue followed her aunt's *counsel.* Sue's aunt *counseled* her to take judo lessons.
councilor	[noun] *a member of a council* The majority of the *councilors* voted for the resolution.
counselor	[noun] *an advisor* Ask your guidance *counselor.*
desert	[noun, pronounced des′•ert] *a dry region* The caravan crossed the *desert* at night.
desert	[verb, pronounced de•sert′] *to leave or abandon* They did not *desert* the sinking ship.
dessert	[noun, pronounced des•sert′] *the final, sweet course of a meal* For *dessert* we had fresh fruit.

Exercise 7 **Distinguishing Between Words Often Confused**

From the choices in parentheses, select the correct word or word group for each of the following sentences.

EXAMPLE   **1.** Is the Kalahari (*Desert, Dessert*) in Africa?

    1. Desert

1. They were (*all together, altogether*) in favor of the party.
2. The illness has had a strange (*affect, effect*) on everyone.
3. My cousin knows the (*capitol, capital*) city of every state.
4. Have you had your car's (*brakes, breaks*) inspected?
5. The British (*council, consul*) (*counciled, counseled*) the reporter to leave the country.
6. After all his worry, everything turned out (*all right, alright*).
7. Christopher said that the two new players for the guard position will (*compliment, complement*) our basketball team.
8. The actors were (*all ready, already*) for the audition.
9. My uncle will serve either flan or sopapillas for (*desert, dessert*).
10. Did you (*choose, chose*) that topic for your essay?

formally	[adverb] *in a proper or dignified manner, according to strict rules* Do you plan to dress *formally* for the party?
formerly	[adverb] *previously, in the past* This lake was *formerly* a valley.
hear	[verb] *to receive sounds through the ears* Please speak up; I can't *hear* you.
here	[adverb] *at this place* Let's sit *here*.
its	[possessive form of *it*] *belonging to it* The town has not raised *its* tax rate in years.
it's	[contraction of *it is* or *it has*] *It's* cold, and *it's* started to snow.
lead	[verb, rhymes with *need*] *to go first; to guide* Who will *lead* the Juneteenth parade?
led	[verb, past form of *lead*] He *led* us five miles out of the way.
lead	[noun, rhymes with *red*] *graphite in a pencil; a heavy metal* A pencil *lead* is not made of the metal *lead*.
loose	[adjective, rhymes with *goose*] *free; not close together; not firmly fastened* I forgot to lock the gate, and now the pigs are *loose*. Put all your *loose* papers in a folder. My little brother has two *loose* teeth.
lose	[verb, rhymes with *snooze*] *to suffer loss of* Don't *lose* your tickets.
miner	[noun] *a worker in a mine* The trapped *miners* were finally rescued.
minor	[noun] *a person under legal age;* [adjective] *less important* The curfew applies only to *minors*. He suffered *minor* injuries in the accident.
moral	[adjective] *good, virtuous;* [noun] *a lesson of conduct* We admire a *moral* person. The story's *moral* is "Look before you leap."
morale	[noun] *mental condition, spirit* After three defeats, the team's *morale* was low.

MECHANICS

RUBES by Leigh Rubin. By permission of Leigh Rubin and Creators Syndicate.

Miner surgery.

passed	[verb, past form of *pass*] *went by, beyond, over, or through*
	The tortoise *passed* the hare and won the race.
past	[noun] *time gone by;* [adjective] *of a former time;* [preposition] *beyond*
	Sitting Bull told many stories about the *past.*
	Adele read the minutes of the *past* meeting.
	The dog walked right *past* the cat.
peace	[noun] *calmness (as opposed to strife or war)*
	All hoped that the treaty would bring *peace.*
piece	[noun] *a part of something*
	We found the missing *piece* of the puzzle.

TIPS & TRICKS

Here is a way to remember the difference between *peace* and *piece.* You eat a **pie**ce of **pie.**

Exercise 8 **Distinguishing Between Words Often Confused**

From the choices in parentheses, select the correct word for each of the following sentences.

EXAMPLE   1. Marcy would like a (*peace, piece*) of pumpkin bread.
            1. *piece*

1. Where did you (*here, hear*) that Kiowa legend?
2. If you (*lose, loose*) the directions, we will never get there.
3. The mail from home improved the troops' (*moral, morale*).
4. The estate is being held in trust until the heir is no longer a (*minor, miner*).
5. My horse (*lead, led*) the parade.
6. In only a few minutes, the guest speaker will be (*hear, here*).
7. After he went on a diet, his clothes were too (*lose, loose*).
8. (*Formerly, Formally*), Lauryn Hill performed with the Fugees.
9. (*It's, Its*) not every day that her parents let her use the car.
10. On the tour, we (*past, passed*) the homes of many celebrities.

Review D **Proofreading an Article for Errors in the Use of Words Often Confused**

Proofread the article on the next page, correcting each incorrectly used word. If all words in a sentence are already used correctly, write *C.*

EXAMPLE   [1] The state legislature was not in session when the NHS members toured the capital.
            1. *capitol*

HELP

Some sentences in Review D contain more than one error.

NHS MEMBERS MEET GOVERNOR
by Cornelia Charnes, Staff Writer

[1] One of the advantages of living in the state capitol is having the opportunity to see state government up close. [2] Last Friday, twenty-seven members of our school's National Honor Society chapter toured the nearby capital building. [3] Tour guide Floyd Welty, who lead the group, outlined the workings of the government's three branches and pointed out many of the building's architectural features. [4] The students ate lunch in the underground cafeteria and even got to meet Governor (formally State Senator) Iola Jones.

[5] The group met Governor Jones just as they were already to leave the building. [6] Said student Botan Park, "Governor Jones shook hands with each of us and complimented us on being honor students. [7] Even though we're still miners, she told us, 'I want to here from you whenever you have a concern with my administration's policies.'"
[8] "Of course," added student Elena Cruz, "its her first term as governor, and we will be eligible to vote when she comes up for reelection."

[9] The group's sponsor, guidance councilor Diego Vargas, said, "I have been taking groups there for the passed ten years, but I have never met a governor before. [10] Meeting Governor Jones had a big effect on the students and on me."

TIPS & TRICKS

Here is an easy way to remember the difference between *principal* and *principle*. The princi**pal** is your **pal**.

personal	[adjective] *individual, private* The store manager gave us her *personal* attention.
personnel	[noun] *a group of people employed in the same work or service* The management added *personnel* to handle the increased workload.
principal	[noun] *the head of a school;* [adjective] *main or most important* The *principal* of our school is Mr. Osaka. The *principal* export of Brazil is coffee.
principle	[noun] *a rule of conduct; a fact or a general truth* Her *principles* are very high. Dr. Martin Luther King, Jr., supported the *principle* of nonviolence.
quiet	[adjective] *silent, still* The library is a *quiet* place to study.
quite	[adverb] *completely, rather, very* Are you *quite* sure this is the right path?

shone	[verb, past form of *shine*] *gave off light* The stars *shone* brightly last night.
shown	[verb, past participle form of *show*] *put or brought into view* The slides were *shown* after dinner.
stationary	[adjective] *in a fixed position* Are these desks movable or *stationary*?
stationery	[noun] *writing paper* Colored *stationery* is not appropriate for business letters.
than	[conjunction, used for comparisons] She arrived earlier *than* I did.
then	[adverb] *at that time; next* I didn't know you *then*. We swam for an hour; *then* we ate.
their	[possessive of *they*] *belonging to them* *Their* apartment has a view of the river.
there	[adverb] *at that place;* [also used as an expletive to begin a sentence] I have not been *there* in a long time. *There* is too much pepper in my soup.
they're	[contraction of *they are*] *They're* reading a book by Virginia Driving Hawk Sneve.

┌─────────────────┐
│ TIPS & TRICKS │
└─────────────────┘

Here is an easy way to remember the difference between *stationary* and *stationery*. You write a lett**er** on station**ery**.

Reference Note

For information on **possessive pronouns,** see page 556. For information on **adverbs,** see page 422. For information on **forming contractions,** see page 763.

MECHANICS

Exercise 9 Distinguishing Between Words Often Confused

From the choices in parentheses, select the correct word for each of the following sentences.

EXAMPLE
    1. We stayed in San Juan longer (*than, then*) we had planned.

    1. than

1. I am learning some of the (*principals, principles*) of physics.
2. The gold ring (*shone, shown*) with a warm glow.
3. He acts much older (*than, then*) he is.
4. The bookstore is having a big sale on (*stationery, stationary*).
5. You ask too many (*personnel, personal*) questions.
6. Soon after the strange uproar, all became (*quite, quiet*) again.
7. The *pad thai* they serve here is (*quite, quiet*) good.

8. Several Pueblo artists are displaying (*there, their, they're*) work.
9. If you see the (*principle, principal*) in the hall, tell her she's wanted in the main office.
10. (*Their, They're, There*) parents may not let them go.

to	[preposition; also part of the infinitive form of a verb] Please return these books *to* the library. He began *to* whistle.
too	[adverb] *also; more than enough* Rubén Blades is a musician and an attorney, *too.* You are *too* young to drive.
two	[adjective] *the sum of one + one;* [noun] *the number between one and three* I will graduate in *two* years. *Two* of my friends and I have great tickets for the Yo-Yo Ma concert.
waist	[noun] *the midsection of the body* At the Japanese restaurant, the server wore an obi around her *waist.*
waste	[noun] *a needless expense; unused material;* [verb] *to use foolishly* Waiting in line was a *waste* of time. *Waste* not; want not.
weather	[noun] *conditions outdoors* As the meteorologist predicted, the *weather* has been perfect all week.
whether	[conjunction; indicates alternative or doubt] They don't know *whether* or not they will go to the concert next weekend.
who's	[contraction of *who is* or *who has*] *Who's* there? *Who's* been coaching them?
whose	[possessive form of *who*] *belonging to whom* *Whose* book is this?
your	[possessive form of *you*] *belonging to you* *Your* coat is in the closet.
you're	[contraction of *you are*] *You're* always on time.

Exercise 10 Distinguishing Between Words Often Confused

From the choices in parentheses, select the correct word for each of the following sentences.

EXAMPLE 1. Are you planning (*to, too, two*) go (*to, too, two*) the dance, (*to, too, two*)?

1. *to; to; too*

1. Around his (*waste, waist*) he wore a handmade leather belt.
2. (*You're, Your*) mother made a delicious Korean dinner of *bulgogi*.
3. There was (*too, to, two*) much traffic on the interstate for us (*too, to, two*) enjoy the ride.
4. (*Whose, Who's*) going to use that ticket now?
5. It really doesn't matter (*whose, who's*) fault it is this time.
6. You, (*to, two, too*), can be a better speller if you try.
7. (*Weather, Whether*) or not it rains, we will be there.
8. Don't you agree that this is fine (*whether, weather*) for a softball game, Ivory?
9. (*Your, You're*) sure Ms. Thompson wanted to see me?
10. I don't know (*whose, who's*) taller, Hakeem Olajuwon or Reggie Miller.

Exercise 11 Proofreading a Paragraph to Correct Errors in the Use of Words Often Confused

Proofread the following paragraph, correcting errors in the use of words often confused.

EXAMPLE [1] Who's face is on this postage stamp?

1. *Whose*

[1] The face on the postage stamp on the next page is that of Benjamin Banneker, considered too be the first African American man of science. [2] First issued on February 15, 1980, this stamp honors a man who's contributions in the areas of mathematics and astronomy are impressive. [3] Banneker grew up on a farm in Maryland in the 1700s, a time when life was particularly difficult for African American people weather they were slaves or not. [4] Although free, Banneker, to, faced prejudice and discrimination. [5] However, a neighbor who was interested in science gave some astronomy equipment too Banneker.

The Granger Collection, New York.

[6] Banneker waisted no time in using it to determine when the sun and moon rose and set, when the brightest stars set, and when eclipses occurred. [7] All of this information was very helpful to a variety of people, including sailors who needed to chart courses and farmers who needed to know the whether. [8] Banneker compiled his data into an almanac, and after to or three attempts, he succeeded in getting his almanacs published each year for several years. [9] These popular books received widespread attention, and Benjamin Banneker became a symbol of what African Americans could do when their lives were not waisted in slavery. [10] If your someone who collects commemorative postage stamps, you will likely want this one, which celebrates the achievements of this gifted scientist.

Review E **Proofreading an Essay to Correct Errors in Spelling and in the Use of Words Often Confused**

Proofread the following paragraphs, correcting errors in spelling and in the use of words often confused. If all the words in a sentence are correct, write *C*.

EXAMPLE   [1] When you take the road test for your driver's license, I hope that you're expereince will be better then mine was.

    1. your; experience; than

[1] One of my most embarrassing moments occured the day I took the road test too get my driver's license. [2] Since one of the branches of the Motor Vehicle Department is near my dad's office, I met Dad their after school. [3] He tried to calm me down by telling me that the world would not end if I did not pass the first time. [4] Still, my hands were shakeing noticably when I got behind the wheel.

[5] The examiner, Mrs. Ferro, was very patient. [6] She assured me that the coarse was "a peice of cake" and that she would not ask me to do anything ilegal to try to trick me. [7] She said I would be fine if I just proceded steadyly and did not overeact to her instructions.

[8] Everything went surprisingly well until we reached the end of the course and Mrs. Ferro told me to stop the car and turn off the ignition. [9] I stopped, alright; I accidentaly slamed on the breaks so hard that we both went lurching forward against our seat belts. [10] Luckily, niether of us sustainned any injurys, and I succeeded in passing the test, despite mistakeing the end of the course for a cliff.

Chapter Review

A. Proofreading Sentences to Correct Spelling Errors

Proofread the following sentences, and correctly write the misspelled words. If a sentence is already correct, write *C*.

1. The new model with two sliding doors will supercede the old model with only one.
2. We had to wait for a long time at the level crossing for the frieght train to pass.
3. The restaurants of New Orleans are known for their atmosphere and fine dineing.
4. On the long drive through the Australian outback, we saw several kangaroos hoping alongside the road.
5. When nations are enemys, they send spys to gather information about one another.
6. Last Saturday we felt tired, so we decided to stay home and rent a couple of videoes.
7. Timothy Grant is actually one of my brother-in-laws; the other is Sammy Dunn.
8. Dot your *i*'s and cross your *t*'s, as my aunt Edna always used to say.
9. Do we put those figures inside brackets, or should we use parenthesises?
10. 245 people signed the petition.
11. The great French writer Voltaire lived during the 1700s.
12. The best-looking horses at the ranch were a pair of three-years-old.
13. Is this word mispelled?
14. People should be considerate of each other and not display meaness or hostility.
15. The first impression of the cathedral interior was one of great, echoing emptyness.
16. As Mr. Spock would say, their decision was ilogical.
17. Dad impulsively sent away for a set of Japanese steak knifes.
18. On the sewing table there were a sewing kit, a bolt of cloth, and Mom's and Grandma's scissorses.

HELP

None of the proper nouns in the Chapter Review are misspelled. Some sentences in the Chapter Review contain more than one error.

MECHANICS

19. When he writes, his eights look like threes.

20. My brother Walter wieghs one hundred and forty pounds and stands six feet tall.

B. Proofreading a Paragraph to Correct Spelling Errors

Proofread the following paragraph, and correctly write the misspelled words. If a sentence is already correct, write *C*.

[**21**] If I had to chose my favorite animal, it might be the Florida manatee, or sea cow. [**22**] Of coarse, I like dogs, cats, and elephants, but I have heard that manatees are extremly gentle and pateint. [**23**] I also read somewhere that manatees are more closely related to elephants than to seals or whales. [**24**] Normaly, manatees live near the shore in swamps or near the banks of canals. [**25**] A hungry sea cow can eat two hundred pounds of grass. [**26**] Unlike many other animals, manatees never run out of teath. [**27**] Manatees are very useful in clearing vegetation from the canals, so there often protected by law. [**28**] However, boat propelers often injure the animals. [**29**] Also, manatees and there cousins the dugongs have been hunted, especialy as sources of meat and oil. [**30**] Weather these beautyful creatures manage to survive as a species depends largely on us humans.

C. Distinguishing Between Words Often Confused

For each of the following sentences, write the correct word or words in parentheses.

31. That organization is growing; it is (*there, they're, their*) belief that society should devote more resources to the poor.

32. The sky is (*quite, quiet*) clear this evening, so we should be able to see the constellations.

33. The tiger slowly made (*its, it's*) way through the underbrush and then disappeared from view.

34. The gardener gave me a (*personal, personnel*) tour of the center's famous rose garden.

35. "Don't (*waste, waist*) your money on that CD; the songs are terrible," Luis warned us.

36. The mayor welcomed the new Swedish (*council, consul, counsel*) and her staff at a special reception.

37. I'm not sure what is meant by a (*capitol, capital*) offense.

38. The stock market crash in 1929 (*affected, effected*) the economy.

39. Do you know if the movie will be (*shone, shown*) at the children's film series?

40. Working conditions for coal (*minors, miners*) in the United States improved significantly during the twentieth century.

41. (*Your, You're*) coat is lying on the sofa.

42. We went out after dinner, but there were (*two, to, too*) many people in the street, so we came home.

43. What is the (*capitol, capital*) of Portugal?

44. Put on the emergency (*brake, break*) when you park on a hill.

45. Sometimes it's hard to know the (*moral, morale*) thing to do, but we must try.

46. She was so considerate that we (*complimented, complemented*) her on her kindness.

47. Striding off into the fields, Archie (*led, lead*) his troupe toward the mountains.

48. It was remarkable to watch the space shuttle land at great speed and for it to be completely (*stationery, stationary*) minutes later.

49. Uncle Ruben never eats junk food; he worries about his (*waste, waist*).

50. When you apply for a job, your application is forwarded to the (*personal, personnel*) department.

Writing Application

Using Correct Spelling in an Application Letter

Spelling Words   Imagine the best job you could have. Then, write the letter of application that will get you that job. The letter should be short—no longer than two paragraphs—and should be as clear as possible. In your letter use ten words from the spelling list on the following pages.

Prewriting   Start by making a list of five jobs that might interest you. Do some research in specialist publications or on the Internet to find the major requirements of your dream job so that you can use professional terms authoritatively in your letter. Once you have drawn up a list of dream jobs, choose one job and freewrite about it. Write down as many details as you can to describe the job, its responsibilities, and where you see the job taking you in the future.

Writing   Use your freewriting notes to help you write the first draft of your letter. You may want to begin your letter by stating how you learned of the job opening. Then, go on to explain how your training and experience make you suited for this particular job.

Revising   Ask a classmate to play the part of a personnel officer, and read your letter to him or her. Rearrange or cut details to make the letter more effective.

Publishing   Proofread your letter for any errors in grammar, usage, and mechanics. Be sure that all words are spelled correctly. With your teacher's approval, you might suggest a contest among your classmates to determine which students get their dream jobs. Post the completed letters on the class bulletin board or Web page, and follow up with the announcement of the successful applicants.

100 Commonly Misspelled Words

ache
again
always
among
answered
any
been
beginning
believe
break
built
business
busy
buy
can't
chief
choose
color
coming
cough

could
country
dear
doctor
does
don't
done
early
easy
enemy
enough
every
existence
February
finally
forty
friend
grammar
guess
half

happiness
having
hear
here
hoarse
hour
instead
knew
know
laid
loose
lose
making
meant
minute
none
often
once
piece
probably

raise
read
ready
said
says
scene
seems
separate
shoes
similar
since
straight
sugar
sure
tear
their
there
though
through
tired

tonight
too
trouble
truly
Tuesday
two
very
wear
Wednesday
week
where
whether
which
whole
women
won't
would
write
writing
wrote

300 Spelling Words

absence
absorption
abundant
acceptable
accidentally
accommodation
accompaniment
accurate
accustomed
achievement
acquaintance
actuality
adequately
administration
adolescent
aggressive

agriculture
amateur
ambassador
analysis
analyze
angel
annual
apparatus
appearance
application
appropriate
approximately
arousing
arrangement
ascend
association

athlete

bankruptcy
basically
beneficial
benefited
bicycle
breathe
brilliant
bulletin

calendar
category
changeable
characteristic
chemistry
circumstance

civilization
cocoon
commencement
commissioner
committed
comparative
comparison
competition
conceivable
confidential
confirmation
conscientious
consciousness
consequently
considerable
consistency

continuous
controlled
controversial
cordially
corps
correspondence
criticize
curiosity
curriculum

definition
delegate
denied
develop
difference
disastrous
disciple
dissatisfied
distinction
distinguished
dividend
dominant
dormitory

earnest
easily
ecstasy
eighth
eliminate
embroidery
endeavor
enormous
equipment
especially
essential
estimation
etiquette
exaggeration
examination
exceedingly
exceptional
excitable
executive
exercise
exhaustion

exhibition
expense
experience
extension
extraordinary

fallacy
fantasies
favorably
fiery
financial
foreigner
forfeit
fragile
fulfill
fundamentally

gasoline
gentleman
grammatically
grateful
guidance
gymnasium

handkerchief
heroic
hindrance
humorist
hygiene
hypocrisy

illustrate
imitation
immense
inability
incidentally
indispensable
influential
innocence
inquiry
institute
intellect
interference
interpretation
interruption
interval

irrelevant
irresistible
island

jealousy
journal

laborious
liability
lightning
likelihood
liveliest
locally
luxury
magnificence
maintenance
maneuver
mansion
martyr
maturity
medical
merchandise
merit
miniature
mischievous
missile
misspelled
monotony
mortgage
municipal

narrative
naturally
neighbor
noticeable
nuisance

obstacle
occasionally
occupy
odor
offensive
omitted
opinion
opposition
optimism

ordinary
organization
ornament

pageant
pamphlet
parachute
parallel
pastime
peaceable
peasant
peril
permanent
persistent
perspiration
pertain
phase
picnic
pigeon
playwright
pleasant
poison
politician
positively
possibility
practically
practice
precede
precisely
predominant
preferred
prejudice
preliminary
preparation
primitive
priority
prisoner
procedure
proceedings
procession
prominent
proposition
prosperous
prove

psychology
publicity
purposes

qualities
quantities
questionnaire

readily
reference
referring
regard
register
rehearsal
religious
remembrance
representative
requirement
resistance

resolution
responsibility
restaurant
ridiculous

satisfactorily
security
senator
sensibility
sheer
sheriff
significance
simile
situated
solution
sophomore
souvenir
specific
specimen

spiritual
strenuous
stretch
substantial
subtle
successful
sufficient
summarize
superintendent
suppress
surgeon
suspense
syllable
symbol
symphony

technique
temperature
tendency

tournament
traffic
twelfth
tying
tyranny

unanimous
undoubtedly
unforgettable
unpleasant
unusually

vacancies
varies
vengeance
villain

Correcting Common Errors

Key Language Skills Review

This chapter reviews key skills and concepts that pose special problems for writers.

- **Sentence Fragments and Run-on Sentences**
- **Subject-Verb and Pronoun-Antecedent Agreement**
- **Pronoun Usage**
- **Verb Forms**
- **Comparison of Modifiers**
- **Misplaced and Dangling Modifiers**
- **Standard Usage**
- **Capitalization**
- **Punctuation**
- **Spelling**

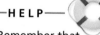

HELP

Remember that all of the exercises in Chapter 27 are testing your knowledge of the rules of standard, formal English. These are the rules you should use in your schoolwork.

Reference Note

For more about **standard** and **nonstandard English** and **formal** and **informal English,** see page 638.

Most of the exercises in this chapter follow the same format as the exercises found throughout the grammar, usage, and mechanics sections of this book. You will notice, however, that two sets of review exercises are presented in standardized test formats. These exercises are designed to provide you with practice not only in solving usage and mechanics problems but also in dealing with these kinds of problems on standardized tests.

Exercise 1 Identifying Sentences and Sentence Fragments

Identify each of the following word groups as either a *sentence fragment* or a *sentence*.

Reference Note

For information about **sentence fragments,** see page 437.

EXAMPLE   1. Running along the bank of the shallow creek.

            1. *sentence fragment*

 1. Science Technology Associates creating multimedia science products.
 2. Claudia needs a new ink cartridge for her printer.
 3. A new art exhibit from January 1 until March 15.
 4. When he went to the new restaurant, Marchel ordered chicken satay.
 5. A line of cars miles long.
 6. The tadpoles under the log when the rain began.
 7. We played checkers first; then we played chess.
 8. Because there is an expiration date.
 9. The rocks on the beach were very smooth.
10. Otters swimming and playing in the river.

Exercise 2 Identifying Sentences and Run-on Sentences

Identify each of the following word groups as either a *run-on sentence* or a *sentence*.

Reference Note

For information about **run-on sentences,** see page 347.

EXAMPLE   1. On Saturday I went to the park to walk my dog and play soccer with my friends, they were visiting from out of town for the weekend.

            1. *run-on sentence*

 1. All of my friends went to the concert last Saturday, I couldn't go.
 2. The triathletes swam, biked, and ran, I bet they slept well that night.
 3. The villagers work together when it is time to harvest the crops.
 4. After the storm, the porch was covered with leaves and sticks.
 5. It was a hot summer day, Joshua played in the pool.
 6. The telephone repairman rang the doorbell our dog barked.
 7. If we don't hurry, we'll be late for the play, we won't be allowed to enter until the first intermission.
 8. Vincent van Gogh, who is famous for paintings such as *Starry Night,* was born in the Netherlands.
 9. Tom realized he had no pen he asked Bob if he could borrow one.
10. After falling asleep on the sofa, the children were carried to bed by their parents.

COMMON ERRORS

Reference Note

For information about **sentence fragments,** see page 437.

Exercise 3 Identifying Sentences and Correcting Sentence Fragments

Most of the following word groups are sentence fragments. If a word group is a sentence fragment, write it correctly, making it a complete sentence. You may need to change the punctuation and capitalization. If the word group is already a complete sentence, write *S*.

EXAMPLE
1. When we left the soccer field.
1. *It was still morning when we left the soccer field.*

1. Fixed the smoke detector in the hall.
2. A new picture taken for his passport.
3. Born in Cleveland, Ohio, in the autumn of 1991.
4. Ruth tried out her new in-line skates today.
5. Playing basketball with friends from the neighborhood.
6. Wasn't that an exciting and pleasant surprise?
7. Because that high school has a new athletic program for students with disabilities.
8. The new movie about dinosaurs on Tuesday.
9. By the time the clowns arrived, the party was almost over.
10. Is a good role model?

Reference Note

For information about **run-on sentences,** see page 347.

Exercise 4 Correcting Run-on Sentences

Correctly write each of the following run-on sentences.

EXAMPLE
1. Thunder roared and rumbled lightning flashed across the dark skies.
1. *Thunder roared and rumbled, and lightning flashed across the dark skies.*

or

Thunder roared and rumbled; lightning flashed across the dark skies.

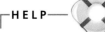

┌HELP──

Although sentences in Exercise 4 can be corrected in more than one way, you need to give only one revision for each sentence.

1. David Diaz has captured many honors for his artwork he won the 1995 Caldecott Medal for the picture book *Smoky Night.*
2. Jeremy wants to ask Iris to the dance, he doesn't know if she already has a date.
3. Rabindranath Tagore wrote the national anthems of two countries, India and Bangladesh, I wonder if anyone else has written two national anthems.
4. The math problems in the homework assignment were easy there were too many of them.

5. Five golfers from Madison High School were chosen for the tournament, this will be the first tournament for three of them.

6. Radio waves travel at the speed of light they can go through many solid objects, including the walls of most buildings.

7. My mother supports the incumbent candidate for treasurer my father will vote for the challenger.

8. Socrates was not afraid to die, he faced his own death sentence with bravery and self-assurance.

9. The largest province in Canada is Quebec, the capital of the province is Quebec City.

10. Lena wanted to learn how to stencil, she enrolled in a stenciling course at the library.

Exercise 5 **Correcting Sentence Fragments and Run-on Sentences**

Each of the following word groups is a sentence fragment, a run-on sentence, or a complete sentence. First, identify each by writing *F* for a sentence fragment, *R* for a run-on sentence, or *S* for a complete sentence. Then, correct each sentence fragment or run-on sentence.

Reference Note

For information about **sentence fragments,** see page 437. For information on **run-on sentences,** see page 347.

EXAMPLE
    1. Nearly all cultures having traditional folk dances.

     1. *F—Nearly all cultures have traditional folk dances.*

1. Most folk dances start as celebrations or religious rituals, such dances are often passed down from generation to generation.

2. Certain dances to bring good fortune to the dancers.

3. Some communities developed dances that they believed cured diseases, for instance, the tarantella developed in Italy as a ritual antidote for the bite of the tarantula.

4. Other dances celebrating birth, marriage, harvests, success in battle, and even death.

5. Over time, most folk dances change.

6. That some dances originally having religious or ritual significance have come to be danced purely for recreation.

7. Anyone who knows the origins of "Ring-Around-the-Rosy"?

8. In the United States, the square dance may be the most popular kind of folk dance clogging is common, too.

9. The do-si-do is a movement in square dancing in which two dancers start out facing one another, circle each other back-to-back, and then return to a facing position.

10. The term *do-si-do* from *dos à dos,* which, I believe, is French for "back-to-back."

COMMON ERRORS

Exercise 6 Identifying Verbs That Agree with Their Subjects

Reference Note
For information about **subject-verb agreement,** see page 512.

For each of the following sentences, choose the form of the verb in parentheses that agrees with the subject.

EXAMPLE   1. The cultural heritage of New Mexico's cities (*is, are*) reflected in their architecture, food, and customs.

    1. *is*

1. Many of the people who visit New Mexico (*spend, spends*) time in Albuquerque.
2. The architecture of the buildings (*represent, represents*) various periods in the city's history.
3. (*Has, Have*) anyone here ever read about or seen Albuquerque's Old Town?
4. One of the books Ana read (*identify, identifies*) Old Town as the site of the city's original settlement, founded by Spanish settlers in 1706.
5. Arts, crafts, and food now (*fill, fills*) the shops around the Old Town Plaza.
6. Amy's family (*has, have*) its annual reunion in Albuquerque.
7. Near Albuquerque (*is, are*) a number of American Indian reservations.
8. The pictures we took of the Rio Grande gorge (*give, gives*) you an idea of what the landscape is like in central New Mexico.
9. Neither Juan nor his parents (*was, were*) aware that near Albuquerque are mountains that often have snow on them.
10. Just to the east of the city (*is, are*) the Sandia Mountains.

Exercise 7 Proofreading Sentences for Correct Subject-Verb Agreement

Reference Note
For information about **subject-verb agreement,** see page 512.

Most of the following sentences contain errors in subject-verb agreement. If a verb does not agree with its subject, write that subject and the correct form of the verb. If a sentence is already correct, write *C.*

EXAMPLE   1. Each of them repeat the chorus after the soloist finishes.

    1. *Each repeats*

1. Someone I know drop in every time I try to finish my work.
2. News of his accomplishments have spread in recent years.

3. Here's the articles about Buck Ramsey that Han said she would lend you.
4. Has everybody signed up for a service project?
5. The picture of Nanci, Lyle, and Michelle are on the bulletin board.
6. St. Elmo's fire, which has been seen around the masts of ships, the propellers and wingtips of planes, and even the horns of cattle, is an odd glow that sometimes accompanies a steady electric discharge.
7. Under some rocks in the woods were a small box.
8. Tornadoes that occur in the Northern Hemisphere whirls in a counterclockwise direction.
9. The herd of cattle belong to Ms. Tallerud.
10. Singing and playing the guitar is also among Jan's talents.

Exercise 8 Selecting Pronouns That Agree with Their Antecedents

For each blank in the following sentences, select a pronoun that agrees with its antecedent.

EXAMPLE   1. One of the boys left _____ report card in the gym today.

　　　　　　　1. *his*

1. Each member of the women's soccer team had played _____ best during the game.
2. All of the students in my biology class have planted _____ seeds along the school's front entrance.
3. Nicholas or Benjamin will demonstrate _____ favorite drawing technique in class today.
4. Mr. Williams told us that anyone who wants to go on the field trip should turn in _____ permission slip on Monday.
5. Each of the novels has _____ own significance in the trilogy.
6. If someone wants to use the computer in the library, _____ should do so this afternoon.
7. Neither Karen nor Susan has finished researching _____ topic.
8. Any one of the passengers could have left _____ jacket on the train.
9. If Ricky and Joe are ready at 7:45 A.M., _____ will be able to ride the bus to school.
10. If we're going to go hiking, everyone should bring _____ own lunch and wear a comfortable pair of shoes.

Reference Note

For information about **pronoun-antecedent agreement,** see page 532.

COMMON ERRORS

For information about **pronoun-antecedent agreement,** see page 532.

COMMON ERRORS

Exercise 9 **Proofreading Sentences for Correct Pronoun-Antecedent Agreement**

Most of the following sentences contain pronouns that do not agree with their antecedents. If a sentence contains an error, rewrite the sentence to correct the error. If a sentence is already correct, write *C*.

EXAMPLE   1. Almost everybody I know has their favorite comic strips.

1. *Almost everybody I know has his or her favorite comic strips.*

1. Sara, one of my friends in the fourth-period art class, raised their hand and asked Mrs. Seymour about the history of comic strips.
2. Mrs. Seymour asked everyone to bring a sketchpad, their drawing pencils, and the Sunday comics to class the following day so that we could begin designing a class comic strip.
3. I can't remember whether it was Sara or Gillian who showed me a copy of the *Calvin and Hobbes* collection titled *Scientific Progress Goes "Boink,"* which they had bought at the mall.
4. The vivid colors and elaborate artistry of a comic strip like *Prince Valiant* or *Calvin and Hobbes* often help make them a popular Sunday strip.
5. Today, about 100 million people in the United States spend some of his or her time each day reading comics.
6. Juan and Robert offered to show the class their collections of adventure comics from the 1940s; each of them will give his presentation on Thursday.
7. Are you familiar with Linus and Lucy Van Pelt and his or her friends Charlie Brown and Snoopy?
8. In 1894, Joseph Pulitzer, one of the most famous newspaper publishers in the United States, introduced the first newspaper comic strip in their paper, *New York World.*
9. The magazine-style comic book first appeared in the 1930s; they usually feature serialized stories about the same group of characters.
10. If anyone wants to learn more about the history of comics, they could research the topic at a library.

Exercise 10 **Identifying Correct Forms of Pronouns**

Choose the correct pronoun in parentheses in each of the following sentences.

EXAMPLE 1. Jesse and (*I, me*) will compete at the track meet.

1. *I*

1. The police officer gave (*them, they*) tickets for speeding in a school zone.
2. The state's best hockey coach is (*he, him*).
3. The soloists in tonight's choir concert will be accompanied on piano by (*she, her*) and Paul.
4. Mr. Fishburn wondered (*who, whom*) had left a gift on his front doorstep.
5. The next president of the debate team will likely be (*she, her*).
6. Yes, the university has offered (*us, we*) scholarships.
7. Three volunteers, Hester, Kim, and (*I, me*), will help paint the mural in the gym.
8. Mrs. Murphy paid my sister and (*I, me*) ten dollars to shovel snow from her driveway.
9. "Are you going with Christy and (*him, he*) to tomorrow's soccer game?" Janet asked.
10. Carl Lewis and Michael Johnson are the two athletes (*who, whom*) I watched most closely during the 1996 Olympics.

Reference Note

For information about **using pronouns correctly,** see page 546.

Exercise 11 **Proofreading Sentences for Correct Forms of Pronouns**

Identify each incorrect pronoun in the following sentences, and write the correct form. If a sentence is already correct, write *C*.

EXAMPLE 1. The new neighbors thought that we and them should have a picnic.

1. *them—they*

1. Are you going to ride with him or I?
2. Us girls are tutoring students this summer.
3. The new exchange students are here; do you know them?
4. The most talented artist in our class is her.
5. When I was raising money for charity, the executives who I contacted were very generous.
6. My father and me plan to drive to New York this summer.

Reference Note

For information about **using pronouns correctly,** see page 546.

COMMON ERRORS

7. Did the teacher give them an assignment different from the one she gave us?
8. The boy thanked she and Paula for buying some of his lemonade.
9. It would be nice if they would bring our friends and we a pitcher of water.
10. He is the author who everyone adores.

Reference Note
For information about **inexact pronoun reference,** see page 566.

Link to Literature

Exercise **12** **Rewriting Sentences to Correct Inexact Pronoun References**

Rewrite each of the following sentences to correct the inexact pronoun reference.

EXAMPLE
1. Domingo first read about Tomás Rivera when he was in the school library.

1. *When Domingo was in the school library, he read about Tomás Rivera for the first time.*

1. In the catalog, they tell about Tomás Rivera's novel, which is titled . . . *y no se lo tragó la tierra.*
2. As a boy, Rivera worked as a migrant field hand. That may partly explain why he wrote so vividly about migrant workers in his book.
3. Rivera worked long hours in the fields, and it interrupted his formal education.
4. In the novel, it focuses on a Mexican American family of migrant workers.
5. The family follows crops and the work they provide; it means that they have to move often.
6. Rivera's novel is about the migrant workers' search for justice, and it is inspiring.
7. After reading a novel by Tomás Rivera and short stories by Reuben Sánchez, I decided to read more of his works.
8. Mandy talked to Adrianne about the conflicts in Rivera's novel after she had read it.
9. In the biography of Rivera, it states that in his later life he became the first Mexican American chancellor in the University of California system.
10. After he said that the film *And the Earth Did Not Swallow Him* was based on Rivera's novel, Todd went with Rajiv to the library to check out the video.

COMMON ERRORS

Exercise 13 Writing the Forms of Irregular Verbs

For each of the following sentences, provide the correct past or past participle form of the verb in italics.

Reference Note

For information about **using verbs correctly,** see page 572.

EXAMPLE   **1.** *write*   Joyce Carol Thomas _____ *Brown Honey in Broomwheat Tea.*

         1. *wrote*

1. *become* During the Cenozoic era, South America and North America _____ linked by a land bridge.

2. *speak* I had _____ to Jim before he left.

3. *bring* Geraldine has _____ me her new copy of *A Gathering of Flowers: Stories About Being Young in America.*

4. *give* Yesterday, Teresa _____ flowers to her grandmother.

5. *know* We _____ that the first czar of Russia was known as Ivan the Terrible.

6. *hear* Jonas had _____ that the picnic was postponed.

7. *choose* I wonder what subject Celeste _____ for her world history presentation last week.

8. *drive* My aunt Judy has _____ me to my ballet lessons every week this year.

9. *teach* Who _____ Jorge to play the clarinet?

10. *ride* I once _____ a bus across Oklahoma.

11. *break* Two hundred million years ago, the land mass known as Pangaea _____ apart.

12. *forget* Danny _____ to leave the front door unlocked so that I could get in.

13. *sing* Sandra _____ a ballad, which she dedicated to her mother and grandmother.

14. *fall* When I stepped on the patch of ice, I almost _____.

15. *leave* They _____ hours ago.

16. *begin* The Paleozoic era _____ 540 million years ago.

17. *think* Conrad _____ he had money in his checking account, but he didn't.

18. *do* How many times _____ you have to work that math problem before you got it right?

19. *freeze* When Chris and Michael were hiking in Colorado, their water _____ overnight.

20. *go* Last year, her family _____ to Asia.

COMMON ERRORS

Exercise 14 Proofreading Sentences for Correct Verb Forms

Reference Note

For information about **verb forms,** see page 592.

Identify each incorrect verb form in the following sentences, and write the correct form. If a sentence is already correct, write *C*.

EXAMPLE 1. From the 1920s through the 1940s, people in the United States listened to radio programs and gone to the movies more than they do now.

1. *gone—went*

1. The popularity of TV programs brung about the end of many radio shows.
2. It has not took very long for television to become one of the most popular forms of entertainment in the United States.
3. I use to think television had always been around, but the first regular TV broadcasts in the United States weren't until 1939.
4. Demonstrations of televisions drawed big crowds at the New York World's Fair in 1939.
5. In 1941, when the United States begun fighting in World War II, television broadcasting was suspended, but it resumed in 1945.
6. The sales of television sets soared after World War II, and by 1951, telecasts reached viewers from coast to coast.
7. Color programs weren't showed until 1953.
8. Of course, I've seen old black-and-white TV programs.
9. I also have heared some of the old radio shows from before the days of television.
10. Have you ever thought about how television has changed the way people in the United States spend their leisure time?

Exercise 15 Using the Different Tenses of Verbs in Sentences

Reference Note

For information on **verb tenses,** see page 590.

Change the tense of the verb in each of the following sentences according to the directions given after the sentence.

EXAMPLE 1. Ingrid studied French for two years. (Change *studied* to a present perfect form.)

1. *Ingrid has studied French for two years.*

1. Will's brother will graduate from college in the spring. (Change *will graduate* to a future perfect form.)
2. Adrian purchased new glasses before he went on vacation. (Change *purchased* to a past perfect form.)

3. Have you read any of Naomi Shihab Nye's poems? (Change *Have read* to a present perfect progressive form.)

4. The twins will play the same kind of instrument at the talent show. (Change *will play* to a past emphatic form.)

5. The acrobats are performing this evening. (Change *are performing* to a present perfect form.)

6. Will you work in your uncle's blacksmith shop this summer? (Change *will work* to a past progressive form.)

7. Bianca and Charles asked whether the building has an emergency evacuation plan. (Change *asked* to a future form.)

8. The new amusement park gives discounts to groups every day of the week. (Change *gives* to a past perfect form.)

9. Scott had hoped to take the driving test on Tuesday. (Change *had hoped* to a present emphatic form.)

10. The jugglers demonstrated their talent all afternoon. (Change *demonstrated* to a future form.)

<hr/>

Exercise 16 **Revising a Paragraph to Make the Tenses of the Verbs Consistent**

Read the following paragraph, and decide whether to rewrite it in the present or past tense. Then, rewrite it, changing the verb forms to correct any unnecessary changes in tense.

EXAMPLE **[1]** The children were eager to hear a story, so I begin to tell them the Navajo legend of Eagle Boy.

1. *The children are eager to hear a story, so I begin to tell them the Navajo legend of Eagle Boy.*

or

The children were eager to hear a story, so I began to tell them the Navajo legend of Eagle Boy.

[1] A young Navajo boy who lives with his parents often dreamed of eagles flying overhead. [2] One day, Father Eagle flew down to the boy, caught hold of his shirt, and carries him to a nest high on a cliff. [3] Father and Mother Eagle feed the boy cornmeal and then took him to the eagle people at the top of the sky. [4] Eventually, the boy goes to the home of Eagle Chief, who told him to remain there. [5] After Eagle Chief leaves, the boy became curious about an animal that he sees outside. [6] When the boy opens the door slightly to look more closely, Big Wind blew it completely open, pulling the boy outside, where the trickster Coyote is waiting. [7] The boy was soon tricked into touching Coyote's fur and turns into a coyote himself. [8] When Eagle Chief

Reference Note

For information about **consistent verb tense,** see page 597.

HELP

Although the example in Exercise 16 gives two possible revisions, you need to give only one revision for each sentence.

COMMON ERRORS

returns, he restored the boy. [9] Afterward, Eagle Chief names him Eagle Boy and gave him an eagle feather. [10] Eagle Boy then returns home to his parents, and he eventually became a great medicine man.

Exercise 17 Proofreading for Correct Comparative and Superlative Forms

Reference Note

For information about **using modifiers correctly,** see page 612.

Most of the following sentences contain errors in the use of comparative and superlative forms of modifiers. If a modifier is incorrect, give the correct form. If a sentence is already correct, write *C*.

EXAMPLE
    1. The second time I made lasagna, I prepared it most quickly.

    1. *more quickly*

1. I planted lantana and petunias next to each other; the lantana grew best because it could withstand heat and drought.
2. The more exciting field trip of any this year is scheduled for this fall.
3. I wonder which of the two mountain peaks is tallest.
4. Of the club's many members, he is less likely to run for president because he is so shy.
5. The more suspenseful chapter in the novel told of a violent storm that damaged the sails of the pirate ship and drove the ship off course.
6. Which is most fun for you, painting with watercolors or sketching?
7. Watching the two dogs dig in the ground, Carl laughed as the more younger one retrieved a small toy.
8. The colorfulest sunset I ever saw in Montana was near Billings.
9. Outside the theater, we all agreed that the movie was the least satisfying sequel that we had ever seen.
10. Of all the mailboxes in the neighborhood, ours is the more unusual.

Exercise 18 Proofreading Sentences for Correct Use of Modifiers and Comparisons

Reference Note

For information about **using modifiers correctly,** see page 612.

Revise the following sentences to correct each error in the use of modifiers and comparisons.

EXAMPLE
    1. In most areas, daisies are more easier to grow than orchids.

    1. *In most areas, daisies are easier to grow than orchids.*

1. Termites work in the dark and are less likelier to be seen than many other insects.
2. Raphael types faster than any student in his class.

3. Fortunately, no one was injured bad when the boats collided.
4. Although elephants are the largest land mammals, blue whales are the most largest mammals of all.
5. My friend Tim is more creative than anyone in his school.
6. The lion is more bigger than the lioness.
7. Aunt Gloria is more resilient than anyone I know.
8. I don't see good without my glasses.
9. The trekkers walked careful up the hill.
10. Kilimanjaro is the more magnificent mountain of any in Africa.

Exercise 19 Correcting Misplaced Modifiers

Each of the following sentences contains a misplaced modifier. Rewrite each sentence to correct the placement of the modifier.

Reference Note
For information about **misplaced modifiers,** see page 627.

EXAMPLE   1. Flying in close formation, the crowd watched the squadron of small biplanes overhead.

1. *The crowd watched the squadron of small biplanes flying in close formation overhead.*

1. Gathered into a heap, Nathan looked at the stalks of sugar cane.
2. I have always enjoyed listening to stories about my mother's childhood with my sister.
3. We watched the sun rise from our front porch.
4. Frank listened to music climbing the mountain.
5. We watched a film about how comets are formed in science class.
6. I saw a deer going to check the mail.
7. About six inches long, the *Tyrannosaurus rex* had sharp teeth.
8. They noticed a turtle on a log wading across the river.
9. We learned that the bridge had once collapsed as we rode over it.
10. Mr. Spinoza saw many earthworms planting his garden.

Exercise 20 Correcting Dangling Modifiers

Each of the following sentences contains a dangling modifier. Rewrite each sentence so that the modifier clearly and sensibly modifies a word in the sentence.

Reference Note
For information about **dangling modifiers,** see page 626.

EXAMPLE   1. Looking through the binoculars, the bird was brightly colored.

1. *Looking through the binoculars, I saw that the bird was brightly colored.*

1. While practicing the piano, the music fell off the music rack.

COMMON ERRORS

2. The people below looked like ants, peering down from the top of the Empire State Building.
3. Unable to complete the assignment on time, Bob's report had to be turned in late.
4. Perched on a high stool by the kitchen counter, the potatoes were easy to peel.
5. After stretching to warm up, the running shoes were tightly laced on my feet.
6. My telephone rang right after walking in the front door.
7. Determined to reach the finish line, the marathon seemed endless.
8. Looking overgrown and scraggly, the McKinneys decided to spend the weekend doing yardwork.
9. Studying fossil oysters found in Kansas, it was hypothesized that a shallow sea once covered at least part of that state.
10. All alone, the dark woods were mysterious and silent.

Exercise 21 Correcting Double Negatives and Other Errors in Usage

Eliminate the double negatives and other errors in formal, standard usage in the following sentences.

EXAMPLE   1. Karen should of brought her delicious chow mein to the potluck dinner yesterday.

1. *Karen should have brought her delicious chow mein to the potluck dinner yesterday.*

1. I went to the beach yesterday to look for driftwood and shells but couldn't find none.
2. Just try and imagine a city without vehicles of any sort!
3. I would rather go to the county park on this beautiful afternoon then stay indoors.
4. Our track team practiced until we weren't able to run no more.
5. The engine sounds like it is ready to fall out of the old truck.
6. We didn't want to see neither of the movies that were showing at the theater.
7. At breakfast this morning, my little brother found a small toy inside of that box of cereal.
8. Joel drove a long ways across town just to trade one football card.
9. Unfortunately, my science experiment didn't work as good as I thought it would.
10. This long stretch of highway has hardly no curves in it.

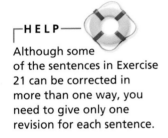

┌HELP──

Although some of the sentences in Exercise 21 can be corrected in more than one way, you need to give only one revision for each sentence.

Reference Note

For information about **double negatives,** see page 656. For information about **common usage errors,** see page 636.

Exercise 22 Correcting Errors in Usage

Identify and correct each error in the use of formal, standard English in the following sentences.

Reference Note

For information about **common usage errors,** see page 636.

EXAMPLE
1. Young people with inventive minds had ought to be encouraged!

1. *had ought—ought*

1. People from five to nineteen years old have discovered some new and important products and processes.
2. As a teenager, young Jerrald Spencer use to take apart electronic appliances just to see how they worked.
3. In 1977, at the age of fifteen, Spencer created his first marketed invention, a kind of an electronic toy.
4. That there toy led to a whole series of specialty toys sold in major department stores.
5. In 1895, the teenager Cathy Evans invented an unique process known as "tufting" for decorating bedspreads.
6. Her invention had a tremendous affect on the carpet industry; in fact, most carpet made today involves the process she developed.
7. In 1922, eighteen-year-old Ralph Samuelson decided to try and use snow skis to ski on water.
8. He didn't think that skiing on water would be much harder then skiing on snow.
9. Like he thought, after many tries his skis worked!
10. If you want to be an inventor, you won't succeed without you try.

Exercise 23 Proofreading Sentences to Correct Errors in Usage

Each of the following sentences contains an error in the use of formal, standard English. Identify each error. Then, write the correct usage.

Reference Note

For information about **common usage errors,** see page 636.

EXAMPLE
1. The tour guide last summer learned us much about the Lincoln Memorial.

1. *learned—taught*

1. This memorial, who was dedicated in 1922, is a popular attraction in Washington, D.C.
2. No less than 150 million people have visited the monument.
3. I was kind of amazed to hear that the memorial was built on what used to be marshland.
4. The architect Henry Bacon he designed the memorial.

COMMON ERRORS

5. I implied from our guide's talk that the Parthenon in Greece inspired Bacon's design.
6. It is not an allusion that the massive columns of both the Parthenon and the Lincoln Memorial tilt slightly inward.
7. The architects designed the columns this way because rows of truly straight columns give buildings the affect of bulging at the top.
8. I read where Daniel Chester French interviewed Lincoln's son Robert before sculpting the memorial's statue of Lincoln.
9. The spectacular 175-ton statue was carved in sections by the Piccirilli brothers, whose family had immigrated from Italy and settled in the United States.
10. The Gettysburg Address is inscribed on a wall inside of the memorial's hall.

Grammar and Usage Test: Section 1

DIRECTIONS   In the following sentences, either part or all of each sentence is underlined. Using the rules of formal, standard English, choose the answer that most clearly expresses the meaning of the sentence. If there is no error, choose A. Indicate your response by shading in the appropriate oval on your answer sheet.

EXAMPLE   **1.** Has everyone <u>chosen a topic for their</u> essay?

     (A) chosen a topic for their
     (B) chose a topic for their
     (C) choosed a topic for their
     (D) chosen a topic for his or her
     (E) chosen a topic for his and her

ANSWER   **1.**

1. <u>In the 1936 Olympic Games, I read that Jesse Owens won four gold medals.</u>

     (A) In the 1936 Olympic Games, I read that Jesse Owens won four gold medals.
     (B) In the 1936 Olympic Games, I read that four gold medals were won by Jesse Owens.
     (C) I read where Jesse Owens won four gold medals in the 1936 Olympic Games.
     (D) I read in the 1936 Olympic Games that Jesse Owens won four gold medals.
     (E) I read that Jesse Owens won four gold medals in the 1936 Olympic Games.

2. In some sports, a "goose egg" is <u>when a player has a score of zero.</u>

     (A) when a player has a score of zero
     (B) where a player has a score of zero
     (C) a score of zero
     (D) scoring a zero
     (E) that a player has a score of zero

3. <u>I can't hardly remember a time when the temperature was lower than it is today.</u>

     (A) I can't hardly remember a time when the temperature was lower than it is today.
     (B) I can't hardly remember a time when the temperature was lower then it is today.
     (C) I can hardly remember a time when the temperature was more lower than it is today.
     (D) I can hardly remember a time when the temperature was lower then it is today.
     (E) I can hardly remember a time when the temperature was lower than it is today.

COMMON ERRORS

4. This evening <u>less people will be driving</u> cars to the parade because there is less space available for parking.

(A) less people will be driving

(B) fewer people will be driving

(C) less people will have been driving

(D) fewer people will have been driving

(E) fewer people driven

5. The first tennis match was <u>between she and I.</u>

(A) between she and I

(B) between her and I

(C) between her and me

(D) between she and me

(E) among her and me

6. <u>While running to the bus stop this morning, some books fell out of my backpack.</u>

(A) While running to the bus stop this morning, some books fell out of my backpack.

(B) While running this morning, some books fell out of my backpack at the bus stop.

(C) While I was running to the bus stop this morning, some books fell out of my backpack.

(D) Some books fell out of my backpack while running to the bus stop this morning.

(E) I was running to the bus stop this morning while some of my books fell out of my backpack.

7. Raymond knows how to repair lawn mowers, <u>and he plans to make it his summer job.</u>

(A) and he plans to make it his summer job

(B) and he plans to make that his summer job

(C) and that is his plan for a summer job

(D) and he plans to make repairing lawn mowers his summer job

(E) which is his plan for a summer job

8. Creole dishes, the origins of which can be traced to Spanish, African, and Caribbean cooking.

   (A) Creole dishes, the origins of which can be traced to Spanish, African, and Caribbean cooking.

   (B) The origins of Creole dishes, which can be traced to Spanish, African, and Caribbean cooking.

   (C) Tracing the origins of Creole dishes to Spanish, African, and Caribbean cooking.

   (D) Spanish, African, and Caribbean cooking, which are the origins of Creole dishes.

   (E) The origins of Creole dishes can be traced to Spanish, African, and Caribbean cooking.

9. The coach doesn't think that him and I have practiced free throws enough today.

   (A) doesn't think that him and I

   (B) don't think that him and me

   (C) doesn't think that he and I

   (D) don't think that he and me

   (E) doesn't think that him and me

10. Some of the people who are standing in line have all ready bought their tickets.

   (A) who are standing in line have all ready

   (B) who are standing in line have already

   (C) whom are standing in line have all ready

   (D) whom are standing in line have already

   (E) which are standing in line have already

THE GRIZZWELLS reprinted by permission of Newspaper Enterprise Association, Inc.

Grammar and Usage Test: Section 2

DIRECTIONS   Read the paragraph below. For each numbered blank, select the word or group of words on the next page that best completes the sentence. Indicate your response by shading in the appropriate oval on your answer sheet.

EXAMPLE   __(1)__ you ever heard of sick building syndrome?

         1. **(A)** Has
              (B) Have
              (C) Did
              (D) Were
              (E) Hasn't

ANSWER   1.   (A)   (B)   (C)   (D)   (E)

In the early 1980s, a number of health problems suffered by office workers __(1)__ for the first time as symptoms of a single ailment called sick building syndrome. In addition to fatigue and eye irritation, __(2)__ symptoms included headaches, sore throats, colds, and flu. Studies indicate that sick building syndrome, __(3)__ has been responsible for a 30 percent rise in absenteeism in some businesses, can cause as much as a 40 percent drop in productivity. The problems resulting from this syndrome __(4)__ are caused by such indoor pollutants as formaldehyde, benzene, and trichloroethylene. These substances, which are found in furniture, insulation, and paint, __(5)__ trapped in climate-controlled buildings. Even though these pollutants are so widespread, the situation __(6)__ hopeless. Research originally conducted to help astronauts __(7)__ to a simple, effective solution—houseplants. Microorganisms in the roots of a potted plant __(8)__ with the plant to remove harmful substances from the air. The __(9)__ plants include chrysanthemums, which remove benzene, and spider plants, which remove formaldehyde. In addition, both peace lilies and English ivy __(10)__ trichloroethylene.

---

1. **(A)** identified
   (B) was identified
   (C) were identified
   (D) being identified
   (E) was being identified

2. **(A)** these
   (B) them
   (C) these here
   (D) these kind of
   (E) them kind of

3. **(A)** they
   (B) which
   (C) who
   (D) what
   (E) it

4. **(A)** more likely
   (B) more likelier
   (C) likelier
   (D) most likely
   (E) most likeliest

5. **(A)** becomes
   (B) becomed
   (C) becoming
   (D) become
   (E) is becoming

6. **(A)** is in no way
   (B) is not in no way
   (C) aren't in no way
   (D) it isn't hardly
   (E) isn't hardly

7. **(A)** have led
   (B) has led
   (C) has lead
   (D) leads
   (E) have lead

8. **(A)** they interact
   (B) it interacts
   (C) interact
   (D) interacts
   (E) is interacting

9. **(A)** most useful
   (B) usefullest
   (C) most usefullest
   (D) more usefuller
   (E) usefuller

10. **(A)** removes
    (B) they remove
    (C) removed
    (D) were removing
    (E) remove

COMMON ERRORS

Exercise 24 Correcting Errors in Capitalization

Each of the following word groups contains at least one error in capitalization. Correct the errors either by changing capital letters to lowercase letters or by changing lowercase letters to capital letters. Some capital letters are already correctly used.

EXAMPLE   1. Robert Burns's poem "a red, red rose"

        1. *Robert Burns's poem "A Red, Red Rose"*

1. my aunt elizabeth
2. growing up in the midwest
3. *the middle passage* by V. S. Naipaul
4. kansas city royals
5. west of sixty-fifth street
6. winter in denver
7. grandma's brother
8. senator Ann Greene
9. latin, art, and geometry II
10. a buddhist temple
11. the battle Of vicksburg
12. dr. l. f. livingstone
13. the book *a room with a view*
14. American indian pictographs
15. french-Speaking countries
16. a xerox® photocopier
17. Father's day
18. A vietnamese festival
19. orbiting mars or earth
20. Grand teton national park
21. the archaeology of greece and the aegean
22. a jewish synagogue
23. toni Morrison's book *jazz*
24. 7926 broadway boulevard
25. William Shakespeare's play *twelfth night*

Exercise 25 Correcting Errors in Capitalization

Each of the following sentences contains errors in capitalization. Correct the errors either by changing capital letters to lowercase letters or by changing lowercase letters to capital letters. Some capital letters are already used correctly.

1. oren lyons's formal title is faith keeper of the turtle clan.

1. *Oren Lyons's formal title is Faith Keeper of the Turtle Clan.*

1. i recently read about oren lyons, an Influential onondaga chief.
2. he is an american indian leader featured in *The Encyclopedia Of Native America,* which is a reference we use in our American History class.
3. the onondaga are an iroquois people.
4. before assuming this important position, mr. lyons was a successful commercial artist in new york city.
5. the iroquois tradition of having faith keepers dates back to hundreds of years before the pilgrims landed at plymouth rock.
6. mr. lyons edits a publication called *daybreak,* which is dedicated to the seventh generation to come.
7. as faith keeper, mr. lyons is responsible for making decisions that will ensure that the earth is habitable for another seven generations.
8. He also has many other responsibilities, including speaking before the united nations.
9. mr. lyons, other members of the iroquois league, and a group of lakota sioux addressed the united nations in geneva, switzerland.
10. Faith keepers work to uphold the traditions of their people as well as the principles of Democracy, community, and reverence for the Natural World.

Exercise 26 Proofreading Sentences for the Correct Use of Commas

Each of the following sentences needs at least one comma. Write the word or numeral that comes before each missing comma, and add the comma.

EXAMPLE
1. After separating the clear glass from the colored glass we collected paper for recycling.

1. *colored glass,*

1. Orb weavers are spiders that create beautiful complicated round webs.
2. We had planned to climb the mountain but the trail was closed because mountain lions had been sighted in the area.
3. Cheeky the neighbor's dog that chewed up my athletic shoes is now kept in his own yard.
4. Oh when will I stop worrying about things that will never happen?

Reference Note
For information about **using commas,** see page 700.

COMMON ERRORS

5. Italy in my opinion is the most beautiful country in the world.
6. On July 20 1969 the *Apollo 2* lunar module landed on the moon.
7. I wasn't chosen for the track team but I am trying out for soccer next week.
8. The American painter Charles Russell who is famous for his scenes of life in the West is my favorite artist.
9. The Perseid meteor shower which occurs annually appears to originate in the constellation Perseus.
10. Tired of waiting for the movie to start the audience began to murmur and fidget.

Exercise 27 Using Commas Correctly

Each of the following sentences needs at least one comma. Write the word or numeral that comes before each missing comma, and add the comma.

EXAMPLE   1. Tony have you ever heard of Dr. Percy L. Julian?
           1. *Tony,*

1. Julian born in Montgomery Alabama in 1899 grew up to become a renowned scientist.
2. After studying at DePauw University he graduated with highest honors; in fact he received a Phi Beta Kappa key and delivered the valedictory address.
3. Julian went on to Harvard where he earned a master's degree and then traveled to Austria to earn a Ph.D. at the University of Vienna.
4. As Ahmed says Dr. Julian must have been a brilliant man.
5. Dr. Julian taught at Howard University and West Virginia University but his fame began after he went to work as a research chemist for Glidden a paint company in Chicago Illinois.
6. During World War II Dr. Julian created a firefighting foam which by the way was made from soybean protein.
7. He received the 1947 Spingarn Medal which is the NAACP's highest award.
8. Interested in finding other uses for soybeans Dr. Julian established Julian Laboratories and its subsidiaries.
9. Over the course of his lifetime he developed an inexpensive cortisone for arthritis sufferers drugs to relieve glaucoma drugs to help victims of rheumatic fever and many other helpful medicines.
10. Dr. Julian died in 1975 but his impressive achievements live on.

Reference Note

For information about **using commas,** see page 700.

COMMON ERRORS

Exercise 28 Using Semicolons and Colons Correctly

The following sentences need semicolons and colons. Write the word or numeral preceding and the word or numeral following the needed punctuation, and add the proper punctuation. In some instances you will need to replace commas with either semicolons or colons.

Reference Note

For information about **semicolons and colons,** see page 722.

EXAMPLE   1. My brother likes to read adventure novels I prefer autobiographies of sports figures.

      1. *novels; I*

1. We both signed up for field hockey, however, the heavy snow has prevented practice all month.
2. In art class Juanna, Elaine, and Jim used acrylics and Todd, Tonya, and Jasper used oils.
3. We missed the 4 15 bus and had to wait for the 5 30 one.
4. The movie she recommended was *Geronimo An American Legend.*
5. From this airport there are direct flights to Frankfurt, Germany, Rome, Italy, London, England, and Paris, France.
6. Our choir is singing a song based on Psalm 19 14.
7. Our neighborhood has fiestas for various holidays for example, we have a piñata party on Cinco de Mayo each year.
8. I walk to school each day with Darla, Gene, and Greg and Sven, Petra, and Arnold join us on the walk home.
9. I have several postcards that my stepsister sent me from towns with unusual names, for instance, here are ones from Cut and Shoot, Texas, and Truth or Consequences, New Mexico.
10. The Ecology Club has adopted the following projects this semester setting out recycling bins, planting trees in the schoolyard, and adopting two miles of highway to keep clean.

Exercise 29 Punctuating Dialogue

Add paragraph indentions and insert quotation marks and other punctuation where needed in the dialogue on the following page.

Reference Note

For information about **punctuating dialogue,** see page 743.

EXAMPLES   [1] Hey, Sarah, I hear you've become a vegetarian Colin said. Won't you get tired of eating just vegetables?

      1.   *"Hey, Sarah, I hear you've become a vegetarian," Colin said. "Won't you get tired of eating just vegetables?"*

      [2] You've got some things to learn about vegetarians! Sarah said.

      2.   *"You've got some things to learn about vegetarians!" Sarah said.*

COMMON ERRORS

[1] Well, teach me Colin said. What is a vegetarian?

[2] You know that a vegetarian is a person who doesn't eat meat Sarah said but you don't know what a vegetarian does eat.

[3] Your mistake is one that many people make. They think that a vegetarian eats only vegetables, but vegetarians eat quite a variety of foods.

[4] Colin replied Okay, what else do vegetarians eat?

[5] Well, Sarah answered I eat whatever I want that isn't meat, and I try to eat healthful foods. I eat vegetables, of course, but also grains, breads, pastas, beans, nuts, soups, cereals, and fruit.

[6] Do you eat eggs and dairy products?

[7] Yes, Sarah replied I do, but some vegetarians don't. For instance, I sometimes eat quiche, cheese and vegetable enchiladas, and bowls of cereal with milk.

[8] Colin said, I guess you aren't having any trouble finding things to eat. I'm wondering, though, why you decided to become a vegetarian.

[9] I just wanted to feel better. Studies show that being a vegetarian is very healthful Sarah said.

[10] Colin said I remember learning that a diet without any animal products is cholesterol-free. You'll have to tell me about other health benefits of vegetarianism.

Exercise 30 Punctuating and Capitalizing Quotations and Titles

Reference Note

For information about **punctuating quotations and titles,** see page 743.

For each of the following sentences, insert quotation marks and other marks of punctuation where needed, and change lowercase letters to capital letters as necessary.

EXAMPLE   1. Should the U.S. flag be flown at the same level as or higher than a state flag asked Earl

1. *"Should the U.S. flag be flown at the same level as or higher than a state flag?" asked Earl.*

1. Megan's note says, The electrician at the repair shop said that our VCR would be ready by 5:00 P.M.

2. Physical therapy Karen said is really strengthening my brother's legs.

3. Leiningen Versus the Ants, by Carl Stephenson, is a frightening short story Bob said.

4. That's right, Victoria he replied You will want to plant the azaleas in partial sunlight.

5. Sean asked why did Paul yell Get off the porch! at the dog?

6. The following graduates have been named "most likely to succeed: Alexandra, Michael, and Jim.

7. When she hit her finger with the hammer while repairing the roof, Hannah yelled that does it!

8. What I asked the doctor is the patella?

9. The song Long Distance Call was one of the hits of the Chicago blues singer Muddy Waters.

10. No! Paula exclaimed I didn't say to use the green paint!

Exercise 31 Using Apostrophes Correctly

Revise the following word groups, adding apostrophes where they are needed. If a word group is already correct, write *C*.

EXAMPLE 1. giving to United Ways fund

1. giving to United Way's fund

1. somebodys hat

2. Are these Kims poems?

3. Judys and his show

4. ten oclock

5. both planes engines

6. The box was theirs.

7. How many *as* are in *aardvark*?

8. womens sizes

9. Anya and Tonis team

10. hadnt finished

11. that canoes hull

12. no one elses parents

13. Its memory capacity is huge.

14. that clubs newsletter

15. Mr. Harriss Irish setter

16. neithers fault

17. Howards and Marilyns tests

18. because Im sleepy

19. whose ring

20. Its going to rain.

Reference Note

For information about **apostrophes,** see page 758.

Exercise 32 Using Punctuation Correctly

The following sentences contain errors in the use of end marks, commas, semicolons, colons, quotation marks, apostrophes, and hyphens. Rewrite each sentence correctly.

EXAMPLE 1. When Mr Andrews finished painting the hall we asked him to paint the front porch

1. When Mr. Andrews finished painting the hall, we asked him to paint the front porch.

1. While she was in Hades Persephone ate the seed's of a pomegranate, in Greek mythology this fruit symbolizes marriage.

2. Someones father works on Royal Street but I cant remember whose.

3. The cities that I have most enjoyed visiting are the following New Orleans Louisiana Seattle Washington and Philadelphia Pennsylvania

4. Yes I have been to Guadalajara said Liza but not recently however I would like to go there again soon.

5. Twenty nine crows are cackling in the front yard and the noise is driving me crazy exclaimed Cathy.

6. Werent you nervous when the lizards snakes and scorpions started crawling around the two actors legs

7. Davids and Marys houses are both near the new shopping center which was completed in mid February.

8. You can give those posters to Margaret, Zack, and Greta and Phillip, Craig, and Matthew will give theirs to me.

9. Bobby yelled The dogs dish is gone said Suzu

10. That beautiful well known song is Over the Rainbow its my sister-in-laws favorite song.

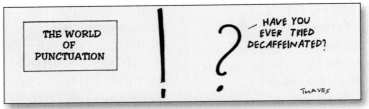

FRANK & ERNEST reprinted by permission of Newspaper Enterprise Association, Inc.

Exercise 33 Correcting Spelling Errors

Each of the following sentences contains spelling errors. Correctly write each misspelled word.

EXAMPLE   1. We forfieted the free vacation and enjoied our leisure time at home.

1. *forfeited, enjoyed*

1. The dog reacted in a wierd way, stareing straight ahead.
2. The pityful wailing of the kitten helped us find it.
3. We traveled on the route maped out for us and proceded at a steady pace.
4. They finally conceeded that the new system would cost a 3rd less to run than the old one did.
5. When the paper we collected for recycling was wieghed, we were gratifyed to learn that the amount exceeded one ton.

Reference Note

For information about **spelling rules,** see page 778.

6. Cleanlyness of the work space is especialy important when food is being handled.

7. 40 people signed up for the dance classes to learn waltzs, polkas, and line dances.

8. All the puppys at the animal shelter were cute, but the 1st one they showed us was the one we adopted.

9. My cousin drives 30 miles each way to her job at a wildlife park, where she takes care of the lions, tigers, and wolfs.

10. Both of the monkies are likely to throw tomatos.

Exercise 34 **Choosing Between Words Often Confused**

From each pair of words in parentheses, choose the word or word group that correctly completes the sentence.

EXAMPLE   **1.** (*You're, Your*) endangering the pedestrians by skating too fast.

     1. You're

1. When I applied for work at the restaurant, I spoke with the (*personal, personnel*) manager.

2. It is important to check the (*breaks, brakes*) on any vehicle before you start driving.

3. We had (*already, all ready*) opened the windows in the art room before Ms. Wong asked us.

4. What theme should we (*choose, chose*) for the prom?

5. Eleanor and Lupita said we could use (*they're, their*) binoculars when we go on the Audubon Society field trip.

6. What (*effect, affect*) will all the rain have on the mown hay?

7. The elephant returned to (*its, it's*) enclosure at feeding time.

8. What did the members of the (*counsel, council*) decide?

9. The (*lose, loose*) wing nut created a rattle in the trunk.

10. Use very fine, not (*course, coarse*), sandpaper for the finishing work on wood furniture or toys.

Reference Note

For information about **words often confused,** see page 793.

COMMON ERRORS

Mechanics Test: Section 1

DIRECTIONS   Each of the following sentences contains an underlined word or word group. Choose the answer that shows the correct capitalization, punctuation, and spelling of the underlined part. If there is no error, choose answer E (Correct as is). Indicate your response by shading in the appropriate oval on your answer sheet.

EXAMPLE   1. Please post these announcements for <u>the Columbus winter Carnival</u>.

        (A) the Columbus Winter Carnival

        (B) the columbus winter carnival

        (C) The Columbus Winter carnival

        (D) the Columbus Winter carnival

        (E) Correct as is

ANSWER   1.

1. "Can you tell us the <u>moral of the fable, Josh</u>"? asked Ms. Chen.

    (A) moral of the fable, Josh?"

    (B) morale of the fable, Josh?

    (C) moral of the fable," Josh?

    (D) moral of the fable, Josh?,"

    (E) Correct as is

2. We'll need <u>streamers balloons</u> and confetti to decorate for the baby shower.

    (A) Well, need streamers, balloons,

    (B) We'll need streamers, balloons,

    (C) We'll need: streamers, balloons,

    (D) We'll need streamers balloons,

    (E) Correct as is

3. The words of <u>Dr. Martin Luther King, Jr.,</u> are engraved on the Civil Rights Memorial.

    (A) Dr Martin Luther King, Jr.,

    (B) Dr. Martin Luther King Jr.,

    (C) Dr. Martin Luther King, Jr,

    (D) Dr. Martin Luther King, jr.,

    (E) Correct as is

4. "Did Coach really say, 'Run another <u>mile?'"</u> gasped Carla.

    (A) mile?"

    (B) mile,"

    (C) mile'?"

    (D) mile,'"

    (E) Correct as is

5. Choose a free subscription to one of these <u>magazines *Time*, *Newsweek*,</u> *Scientific American*, or *Harper's*.

    (A) magazines *Time*

    (B) magazines; *Time*,

    (C) magazines: "*Time*,"

    (D) magazines: *Time*,

    (E) Correct as is

6. The <u>men's and womens</u> shoe departments and the housewares department are having sales now.

    (A) mens and women's

    (B) men's and women's

    (C) mens' and womens'

    (D) mens and womens

    (E) Correct as is

7. The bus driver <u>said "that we should be quiet."</u>

    (A) said, "That we should be quiet."

    (B) said "That we should be quiet."

    (C) said, that we should be quiet.

    (D) said that we should be quiet.

    (E) Correct as is

8. I've visited three state <u>capitals: Boise, Idaho, Tallahassee, Florida; and</u> Montpelier, Vermont.

    (A) capitals: Boise, Idaho, Tallahassee, Florida,

    (B) capitols: Boise, Idaho; Tallahassee, Florida;

    (C) capitols: Boise; Idaho; Tallahassee; Florida;

    (D) capitals: Boise, Idaho; Tallahassee, Florida;

    (E) Correct as is

9. <u>The weather will not effect their plans</u> for this weekend.

    (A) The weather will not affect their plans

    (B) The whether will not affect their plans

    (C) The weather will not affect they're plans

    (D) The weather will not effect they're plans

    (E) Correct as is

10. <u>Its not John whose</u> left his papers in the library.

    (A) Its not John who's

    (B) It's not John whose

    (C) Its' not John who's

    (D) It's not John who's

    (E) Correct as is

Mechanics Test: Section 2

DIRECTIONS   Each numbered item below contains an underlined word group. Choose the answer that shows the correct capitalization, punctuation, and spelling of the underlined part. If there is no error, choose answer E (Correct as is). Indicate your response by shading in the appropriate oval on your answer sheet.

EXAMPLE   [1] February 9 2001

    (**A**) Febuary 9 2001

    (**B**) Febuary 9, 2001

    (**C**) February 9th 2001

    (**D**) February 9, 2001

    (**E**) Correct as is

ANSWER   1. Ⓐ Ⓑ Ⓒ ⬤Ⓓ Ⓔ

---

327 Hickory Lane
[1] Ankeny Iowa 50021
February 9, 2001

[2] Susan Washington DVM
49-A Johnson Circle
Des Moines, IA 51219

[3] Dear Dr. Washington:

Thank you for [4] agreing to lead the discussion at our club's next meeting. We members of [5] Future Farmers of America know how important the practice of veterinary medicine is to agriculture. [6] 39 students have already signed up to attend. As I mentioned on the phone last [7] week, our meeting will take place in Healy Lecture hall. We will begin at [8] 3:00 P.M, and if things go as planned, I will introduce you soon thereafter. We look forward to hearing [9] your views on veterinary medicine, and hope that you will stay for refreshments after the meeting.

[10] yours sincerely,

Michael Yoder

Michael Yoder
President, FFA
Ankeny High School

1. **(A)** Ankeny, Ia. 50021
   (B) Ankeny, IA 50021
   (C) Ankeny IA, 50021
   (D) Ankeny I.A., 50021
   (E) Correct as is

2. **(A)** Susan Washington DVM.
   (B) Susan Washington; DVM
   (C) Susan Washington, DVM
   (D) Susan Washington: DVM
   (E) Correct as is

3. **(A)** Dear Dr Washington:
   (B) Dear Dr. Washington,
   (C) Dear dr. Washington,
   (D) Dear Dr. Washington;
   (E) Correct as is

4. **(A)** agreing to led
   (B) agreeing, to lead
   (C) agreeing to lead
   (D) agreeing too lead
   (E) Correct as is

5. **(A)** Future Farmers Of America
   (B) future farmers of america
   (C) future farmers of America
   (D) future Farmers of America
   (E) Correct as is

6. **(A)** Thirty nine students
   (B) Thirty-nine students
   (C) Thirty-nine student's
   (D) Thirty-nine students'
   (E) Correct as is

7. **(A)** week: our meeting will take place in Healy lecture hall
   (B) week: our meeting will take place in Healy Lecture Hall
   (C) week, our meeting will take place in Healy lecture hall
   (D) week, our meeting will take place in Healy Lecture Hall
   (E) Correct as is

8. **(A)** 3:00 P M and if things go as planned,
   (B) 3:00 P M., and if things go as planed,
   (C) 3:00 P.M. and if things go as planned,
   (D) 3:00 P.M., and if things go as planned,
   (E) Correct as is

9. **(A)** your'e views on veterinary medicine, and
   (B) you're views on veterinary medicine; and
   (C) your views on veterinary medicine and
   (D) your views on veterinary medicine: and
   (E) Correct as is

10. **(A)** Yours sincerely,
    (B) Yours Sincerely
    (C) Your's sincerely,
    (D) Yours sincerely:
    (E) Correct as is

PART 4

Quick Reference Handbook

■ **The Dictionary** 846
■ **Document Design** 849
■ **The History of English** 861
■ **The Library/Media Center** 866
■ **Reading and Vocabulary** 876
■ **Speaking and Listening** 896
■ **Studying and Test Taking** 911
■ **Viewing and Representing** 928
■ **Writing** 939
■ **Grammar at a Glance** 960

The Dictionary

Information About Words

Dictionaries record how words are used in language. A dictionary of the English language shows how most English speakers say or spell a word and what the word means in different contexts. In a dictionary, you will also find information such as word histories and the various forms in which a word may appear.

Dictionary Entry

A dictionary entry gives the word and information about it. Each part of the following entry from an abridged dictionary is labeled and explained below.

1. **Entry word.** The boldface entry word shows how the word is spelled and divides it into

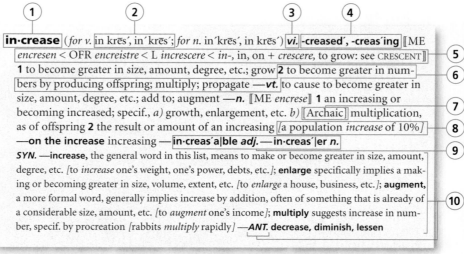

1 2 3 4

in·crease (*for v.* in krēs´, in´krēs´; *for n.* in´krēs´, in krēs´) **vi.** **-creased´, -creas´ing** ⟦ME *encresen* < OFR *encreistre* < L *increscere* < *in-*, in, on + *crescere*, to grow: see CRESCENT⟧ **1** to become greater in size, amount, degree, etc.; grow **2** to become greater in numbers by producing offspring; multiply; propagate **—vt.** to cause to become greater in size, amount, degree, etc.; add to; augment **—n.** ⟦ME *encrese*⟧ **1** an increasing or becoming increased; specif., *a)* growth, enlargement, etc. *b)* ⟦Archaic⟧ multiplication, as of offspring **2** the result or amount of an increasing *[a population increase of 10%]* **—on the increase** increasing **—in·creas´a|ble adj.—in·creas´er n.**
SYN. **—increase,** the general word in this list, means to make or become greater in size, amount, degree, etc. *[to increase one's weight, one's power, debts, etc.];* **enlarge** specifically implies a making or becoming greater in size, volume, extent, etc. *[to enlarge a house, business, etc.];* **augment,** a more formal word, generally implies increase by addition, often of something that is already of a considerable size, amount, etc. *[to augment one's income];* **multiply** suggests increase in number, specif. by procreation *[rabbits multiply rapidly]* **—ANT. decrease, diminish, lessen**

5 6 7 8 9 10

syllables. The entry word may also show capitalization and alternate spellings.

2. **Pronunciation.** The pronunciation is shown by the use of accent marks and either phonetic spellings or *diacritical marks*, the marks added to letters to indicate a change in their sound. A pronunciation key explains the meaning of diacritical marks or phonetic symbols.

3. **Part-of-speech labels.** The part-of-speech labels, which are generally abbreviated, indicate how the entry word should be used in a sentence. In cases where a word can be used as more than one part of speech, a part-of-speech label is given in front of each numbered or lettered series of definitions.

4. **Other forms.** To clarify spelling and usage, a dictionary may list plural forms of nouns, tenses of verbs, or the comparative forms of adjectives and adverbs.

5. **Etymology.** The etymology is the origin and history of a word. It shows how a word or part of a word passed into English from another language.

6. **Definitions.** Definitions are numbered or lettered when a word has more than one meaning.

7. **Special usage labels.** These labels identify words that have special meanings or are used in special ways in certain situations.

8. **Examples.** A simple phrase or sentence using the entry word may be included to clarify how the word is used.

9. **Related word forms.** These are various forms of the entry word, usually created by adding suffixes or prefixes.

10. **Synonyms and antonyms.** A list of synonyms and antonyms may appear at the end of some word entries. Sometimes synonyms, printed in capital letters, may also be included within the list of definitions.

Other Parts of a Dictionary

In addition to entry words, most dictionaries also include the following parts that provide additional information.

Abbreviations   Many dictionaries include a chart of common *abbreviations*. The chart may include abbreviations for weights, measurements, governmental agencies, and the names of states or geographical regions.

Biographical and Geographical Entries

Many dictionaries include a section that identifies famous historical figures, including important writers, musicians, politicians, scientists, inventors, and explorers. The entries identify each person's profession and provide the dates of his or her birth and death. The geographical section lists most of the populated places in the world, the pronunciation of their place names, and the size of their populations.

Colleges and Universities   The names of all the colleges and universities in the United States and Canada appear in many dictionaries, particularly school or college editions. The entries provide the school's location, the date of its establishment, and the number of students attending at the time of the dictionary's publication.

Copyright   The *copyright* indicates when a dictionary was published. When looking up the meaning of a word, use the latest edition of a dictionary to make sure that new words and new meanings of old words are included.

Guide to the Dictionary   Most dictionaries have a few pages near the beginning that give helpful hints about using the dictionary. The guide usually explains how the material is organized and what the abbreviations and fonts mean.

Index   Some dictionaries have an *index* that indicates where to find various dictionary features, including the pronunciation key, the section with word entries, and the biographical and geographical entries.

Pronunciation Key   A *pronunciation key* appears at the front of any dictionary and at the bottom of each page or pair of pages.

Scholarly Essays   The *scholarly essays* are written by language experts and provide information about subjects such as the history and growth of the English language, the way a new edition of the dictionary is different from a previous one, and how the dictionary was researched and prepared.

Types of Dictionaries

Different types of dictionaries provide different types and amounts of information. The dictionary you choose should be determined by the kind of information that you need.

Abridged   An *abridged* dictionary is the most common type of dictionary. It contains most of the words the average person uses or encounters in writing or reading. One advantage of abridged dictionaries is that they are frequently updated, so they can provide the most up-to-date information on meanings and uses of words. Abridged dictionaries are arranged in alphabetical order and include basic information, such as the spelling, definition, pronunciation, part of speech, and source of a word. They also include tables of commonly used abbreviations, selected biographical entries, and tables of signs and symbols.

Online   *Online dictionaries* are accessible on the Internet and may be abridged, unabridged, or specialized. You can often search for a word in this type of dictionary by entering not only the word itself, but also the word's part of speech or etymology. Some online dictionaries have audio features that allow you to hear a word's pronunciation. You can usually find online dictionaries under the reference section of a search engine's subject catalog. (See also **World Wide Web, Searching** on page 873.)

Specialized   *Specialized dictionaries* contain entries that relate to a specific subject or field. For example, there are specialized dictionaries for terms used in art, music, sports, gardening, mythology, as well as other subjects. Specialized dictionaries will include information that an abridged dictionary might not have. (See also the **Reference Sources** chart on page 870.)

Unabridged   An *unabridged dictionary* contains nearly all the words in use in a language. For example, the present twenty-volume edition of the *Oxford English Dictionary* contains over 500,000 entries. Each entry in the *OED* gives detailed descriptions of a word's source, its first appearance in the language, its various forms, and the way its meaning has changed over the last millennium. Each word's meanings and usage are illustrated with quotations from historical and literary sources that date back as far as the year 1150.

Document Design

Manuscript Style

The following chart provides guidelines for preparing handwritten or typed papers. (See also **Writing** on page 939.)

Guidelines for Submitting Papers

1. Use only one side of a sheet of paper.

2. Write in blue or black ink, or type your paper.

3. If you write by hand, do not skip lines, unless your teacher directs you otherwise. If you type, double-space the lines.

4. Leave one-inch margins at the top, sides, and bottom of each page.

5. Indent the first line of each paragraph (about five letter spaces).

6. Number all the pages except the first page. Place the number in the upper right-hand corner of the page.

7. Keep all pages neat and clean. You may make a few corrections with correction fluid. If you have several errors on a page and the page is difficult to read, write out or type the page again.

8. Follow your teacher's instructions for placing your name, the date, your class, and the title of your paper on a cover sheet or on the first page of your paper.

Desktop Publishing

Desktop publishing is the production of professional-looking documents, such as reports or newsletters, on a personal computer. Desktop publishers set words (text) on a page with images and graphics in a way that communicates a message and attracts readers' attention.

Page Design or Layout

Before computers changed the printing industry, documents were designed by hand. Page designers worked page by page, cutting up, arranging, and pasting strips of text, illustrations, headings, and captions. Now anyone with a computer can design an entire document. This section explains key concepts for designing pages that contain text. (Remember that the principles of effective page design also apply to pages that you write and lay out by hand.)

Alignment *Alignment* refers to how lines of text are arranged on a page. Text can be aligned in several ways.

■ **Left aligned** Text that is *left aligned* is set so each line forms a neat edge against the left margin. Most printed documents are set left aligned to facilitate reading from left to right.

EXAMPLE

This text is left aligned.
The lines form a straight
edge along the left margin.

■ **Right aligned** Text that is *right aligned,* such as pull-quotes and poetry, has lines that end against the right margin. Use right-aligned text sparingly because it is not easy to read. (See also **Pull-quote** on page 852.)

EXAMPLE

This text is right-aligned.
Notice how it forms a straight
edge along the right margin.

■ **Center aligned** Text that is *center aligned,* or *centered,* is set in the middle of the page. Center-aligned text usually appears in invitations, posters, or advertisements.

EXAMPLE

This text is center-aligned.
Each line is evenly spaced
on both sides of an invisible, vertical line
in the center of this column.

■ **Justified alignment** With *justified alignment,* both ends of each line of text form a straight edge. Extra spaces added between words ensure that the lines are even.

EXAMPLE

This sample text is justified. The
lines of text form neat edges
along the right and left margins.

■ **Ragged alignment** *Ragged alignment* means that the lines of text do not create a straight edge on both sides. Usually the right-hand side of the text is ragged in alignment.

EXAMPLE

This sample text is left-aligned and also ragged. Notice how the lines form a neat edge on the left but not on the right.

Bullet A *bullet* (•) is a symbol used to make information in a text stand out. Bullets are often used to separate information into lists. They attract attention and help readers remember the information included in the lists.

1. **Always indent a bulleted list** from the body of the text.
2. **Use plain bullets in formal documents.** Other, decorative symbols (such as ¶, $, or +) may be used as bullets in less formal forms of writing, such as journal entries and advertisements.
3. **Make sure that the items in your list are parallel in construction.** For example, use all nouns or all imperative sentences.

Call out A *call out* is a line or phrase of text that describes some aspect of a graphic image. Usually the call-out text is connected to the graphic by an arrow or line. Notice in the following diagram how the call outs identify the various parts of the illustration.

EXAMPLE

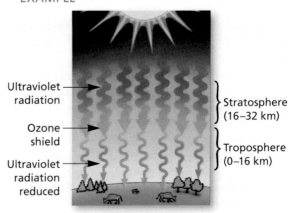

Ultraviolet radiation
Ozone shield
Ultraviolet radiation reduced
Stratosphere (16–32 km)
Troposphere (0–16 km)

Columns and Blocks of Text   Text is easier to read when it is contained in rectangular-shaped areas, such as in *columns* or *blocks*. The width of a column or block of text varies, depending on the size of the text and the format of the document. The text in posters, advertisements, and fliers, for example, is usually set in blocks so that it may be read quickly. Text in textbooks, reference books, and newspapers, which contain large quantities of information, usually appears in columns. (See also **Line Length** on page 852.)

Contrast   *Contrast* refers to the balance of light and dark areas on a page. Dark areas are those that contain blocks of text or graphics. Light areas have little type. A page with high contrast, or roughly balanced light and dark areas, is easier to read than a page with low contrast, such as one that is mostly light or one that is filled with text and images. (See also **Contrast** on page 854 and on page 856.)

Emphasis   *Emphasis* is how a page designer indicates to a reader which information on a page is most important. For example, the front page of a newspaper uses photographs and bold or large headlines to place emphasis on a particular story. Because readers' eyes are drawn naturally to color, large and bold print, and graphics, these elements are commonly used to create emphasis.

Graphic   A *graphic* is a picture, chart, illustration, or piece of artwork that is used to convey information visually. Short sections of text, such as headings, subheadings, titles, headers, and footers, may also be considered graphics because they serve a visual function. (See also **Graphics** on page 855 and **Headings and Subheadings** on this page.)

Gray Page   A *gray page* contains text almost exclusively. It has few or no graphics to indicate visually the organization or structure of the material on the page. As a result, reading and understanding the information on a gray page may be more difficult and time-consuming than reading information on a page that uses some graphics.

Grid Lines   *Grid lines* are vertical and horizontal intersecting lines that provide structure to a page by dividing it into neat sections. Grid lines are often used to plan the design or layout of a page but do not appear in the final printed document.

Gutter   A *gutter* is the crevice or margin of space between two pages in a bound book. For example, there is a gutter between this page and page 850.

Headers and Footers   *Headers* and *footers* provide information about a printed document. A header appears in the top margin of a page, and a footer appears in the bottom margin. Headers and footers may include

- the name of the author
- the name of the publication
- the date of the publication
- chapter or section titles
- page numbers

Headings and Subheadings   *Headings* and *subheadings* (also called *heads* and *subheads*) are used to give readers clues about the content and organization of a document.

- **Headings**   Headings give readers a general idea what a section of text, such as a chapter, will be about. Headings appear at the beginning of a section of text and are often set in larger or heavier letters or in a different style of letters from the rest of the text.

- **Subheadings**   Subheadings are more descriptive than headings and are used to indicate a new section or idea in the text. Several subheadings often appear under one heading. Like headings, subheadings are often set in larger or heavier letters or in a different style of letters from the rest of the text.

EXAMPLE

Goats Used in ———— heading
Park Beautification
Goats take on weeds ——— subheading
the old-fashioned way;
they eat them

In a move to combat the invasion of ——— text
nonnative weeds to Denver's city
parks, the city has arranged for a
herd of one hundred cashmere goats
to graze in the city parks.

Indentation   An *indentation* is the space skipped over from the left margin to indicate the beginning of a new paragraph in a text. An indentation should be about one-half inch. If you are preparing text on a computer or typewriter, one-half inch is equivalent to about five letter spaces.

Line Length   *Line length* is the number of characters (letters, spaces between words, and punctuation marks) a line contains. (Remember, a line is not a sentence; it is a single line of text that may or may not form a complete thought.) The best line length for a document depends on the size of the type and the format of the document. In general, limit line length to nine or ten words, or sixty-five characters. This makes the text easier to read.

Margins   *Margins* are the space that surrounds the text on a page. Most word-processing programs automatically set the side margins at 1.25 inches and the top and bottom margins at one inch. Margins are flexible, however. If your teacher recommends a different set of measurements for the margins of your papers, use them instead. (See also **White space** on page 853.)

Pull-quote   A *pull-quote* is a quotation from a text, such as a magazine article or story, that has been turned into an eye-catching graphic. Pull-quotes should be short and concise; often they are excerpts of a longer thought from the text. The purpose of the pull-quote is to catch the reader's interest.

EXAMPLE

There were once three brothers who had fallen deeper and deeper into poverty, and at last their need was so great that they had to endure hunger, and had nothing to eat or drink. Then said they: "It cannot go on like this, we had better go into the world and seek our fortune." They therefore set out.

"We had better go seek our fortune."

Rule Lines   *Rule lines* are lines used to create visual effects on a page. Rule lines may be thick or thin, vertical or horizontal, and they may set text off from a headline or caption, separate columns, or draw your eye to something on the page.

Title and Subtitle   A *title* is the name of an entire document. *Subtitles* are longer and more descriptive than titles. Often subtitles are attached to a title by a colon and appear in smaller letters.

In books, titles (and sometimes also subtitles) appear alone on a separate page, called the title page, at the very beginning of the book.

EXAMPLE

The Timetables of Women's History
A Chronology of the Most Important People and Events in Women's History

Visuals   *Visuals,* like *graphics,* are pictures, charts, illustrations, or artwork that convey information. (See also **Graphics** on page 855.)

White Space   *White space* is any area on a page where there is little or no text or graphics. White space provides a contrast to the dark ink on a page and makes the print more readable. Usually, white space is limited to the margins, the gutter, and the spaces between words, lines, and columns. (See also **Contrast** on page 851.)

Type

Type refers to the letters and markings used in printing and publishing. When Johannes Gutenberg introduced his printing press over 500 years ago, each letter of type was cut out of wood. Today, computers make printing considerably easier. The following section provides basic information about type and how to use it effectively. (See also **Font** on page 854.)

Capital Letters   *Capital* (or *uppercase*) *letters* help readers identify the beginning of a new sentence or idea. Capital letters command readers' attention and may be used in the following ways to create emphasis in a document.

■ **Dropped cap**   A *dropped cap* is an artistic use of a capital letter in the first word of a first paragraph of a text or section of a text. Dropped caps imitate medieval illuminated manuscripts in which the first letter of a section or chapter was enlarged and transformed into a colorful drawing.

EXAMPLE

Once upon a time there lived a young boy named Oliver.

■ **Headings or titles**   When headings or titles appear in the same typeface as the text, setting them in all capital letters helps them stand out from the rest of the document.

EXAMPLES

LOCAL RUNNER WINS NEW YORK CITY MARATHON

KEEPING AN EYE ON STUDENTS' NUTRITION

■ **Small caps**   *Small caps* are uppercase letters that are reduced in size. Usually they appear in abbreviations of time, such as 9:00 A.M. and A.D. 1500, or in the names of organizations, such as in NASA or NATO. Small caps may also be combined with true capital letters for an artful effect.

NOTE   Long sections of capital letters can be difficult to read. Use capital letters for contrast or emphasis, not for large bodies of text.

Captions   *Captions* are lines of text that appear under photographs or illustrations. They explain the meaning or importance of the graphic and connect it to the text. Because readers tend to look first at the graphics on a page, captions are often the first text they read. Therefore, captions should be concise, accurate, and interesting. Captions may appear in a smaller size type (usually two point sizes smaller) than the text, or they may appear in the same type size but italicized. (See also **Font** and **Font size** on page 854.)

Contrast   In terms of type, *contrast* refers to the visual effect of using different fonts in a document. As a general rule, use only two different fonts in a single document—one for the body of your text and captions and one for the headings and subheadings.

Font   A *font* is one complete set of characters (such as letters, numbers, and punctuation marks) of a given size and design. (The terms *font* and *typeface* are often used interchangeably, although those in the printing industry make a distinction between the two.) Thanks to computer technology, there are now more than ten thousand fonts available.

Font, Categories of   Thousands of fonts are available, each with its own name and unique appearance. In general, though, all fonts belong to one of the three following categories.

■ **Decorative, or script**   Decorative fonts are elaborately designed characters that convey a distinct mood or feeling. Script fonts, in which the letters touch each other, simulate handwriting. Because decorative fonts are too difficult to read as regular text, they should be used in small amounts for an artistic effect. They are most commonly used in wedding invitations or graduation announcements.

EXAMPLES
This is an example of the Zapf Chancery font.
This is an example of the Linoscript font.
This is an example of the Fresh Script font.

■ **Sans-serif**   The characters in *sans-serif* fonts are formed by neat straight lines, with no small strokes at the ends of the letters. (*Sans serif* means "without serifs, or strokes.") Sans-serif typefaces work well as headings and subheadings, pull-quotes, and captions because they have clean edges and are easy to read.

EXAMPLES
Helvetica is a sans-serif font.
Franklin Gothic is a sans-serif font.
Futura is a sans-serif font.

■ **Serif**   The characters in *serif* fonts have little strokes (serifs) attached at each end. The serifs are modeled on the connectors between letters in handwriting. As in handwriting, the little strokes help guide the reader's eyes from letter to letter and word to word. Serif type is commonly used to set large bodies of type because of its readable quality. (See also **Readability** on page 855.)

EXAMPLES
Palatino is a serif font.
New Century Schoolbook is a serif font.
Times is a serif font.

NOTE   Mixing types of fonts on a page creates high contrast; however, you should not use more than one font from each category. Too many fonts on a page confuses readers.

Font Size or Point Size   The size of the type in any document is called the *font size* or *point size*. Word-processing software provides many options for sizing text. In general, newspapers and textbooks use type measured at 12 points. Type for headings and headlines may range anywhere from 18 to 48 points. Captions usually appear in 9- to 11-point type.

Fonts, Styles of   In addition to the three categories of fonts, there are also several different *font styles*. Most text is set in *roman* font (in this case, "roman" means "not slanted"). *Italic* font has special uses, as for captions or book titles. Desktop publishing software has made available more elaborate font styles. Look at the following examples of eye-catching fonts. (See also **Font, Categories of** on page 854.)

EXAMPLES

roman boldface   *italic boldface*
<u>roman underscored</u>   r o m a n   e x p a n d e d
roman condensed   ROMAN CAPITALS
italic lowercase   *ITALIC CAPITALS*

NOTE Select your font styles carefully, and avoid using too many font styles in one document. Be consistent, as your reader may be confused if you change styles in the middle of your text.

Knockout Type   *Knockout,* or *reversed type,* is light type set against a contrasting, dark background.

EXAMPLES

Here is dark type set against a light background.
Here is knockout, or reversed, type.

Leading or Line Spacing   *Leading* (rhymes with *sledding*), or *line spacing,* is the distance between lines of text. Most word processors and typewriters allow you to adjust the amount of line spacing to single-, double-, or even triple-space measurements. For formal documents, use double-spacing.

Lowercase   *Lowercase* type is the set of letters that are not capital letters. Lowercase letters are characterized by *ascenders* (rising strokes, as in the letters *b* and *h*) and *descenders* (dropping strokes, as in the letters *g* and *y*). Most text is set in lowercase type because it is easy to read.

Readability   *Readability* refers to how easy a text is to read. Text with high readability is set in simple fonts and appropriate font sizes and has high contrast. (See also **Font size** and **Font, Styles of** on page 854.)

Graphics

Graphics organize and communicate information visually. They may be used to

- display data or information
- explain a process
- illustrate how something looks, works, or is organized
- show trends or relationships over time

Whether you use a computer to generate your graphics or prepare them by hand, you should select and design your graphics carefully. They must always convey information clearly and support the text that appears on the page. Text and graphics should fit together like the pieces of a jigsaw puzzle, so that readers will understand the overall goal and design of your document.

Arrangement and Design

The challenge of designing a document that contains text and graphics is to arrange all the components in a balanced and organized way. Consider the following elements when you design a document with graphics.

Accessibility   *Accessibility* refers to the ease with which readers can find information in a document. Increase a document's accessibility by using bulleted lists, headers, headings, footers, and subheadings.

Accuracy   All graphics or visuals must contain true information. Never manipulate or change images or the data shown in charts, graphs, or tables. Readers must be able to trust the information in the graphics you use in your document.

Color   *Color* naturally attracts a reader's eye, especially when it contrasts with the black and white of text and white space. Color may be used to attract the reader's attention, highlight a piece of information, indicate that certain items on a page belong together, or show the organization of the parts of a document or page.

- **Choosing color**   When choosing colors for graphics, remember the following guidelines.
  1. **Colors are for emphasis, not for text.** Text may look nicer in color, but readers will find it more difficult to read and won't remember it as well.
  2. **Colors should be used in pairs or schemes.** Color schemes provide contrast. A single color in a document will simply look out of place.
  3. **Choose colors that complement each other.** The colors that appear opposite one another on the color wheel on this page are always complements.
  4. **Use warm colors, such as red and orange, sparingly.** These colors appear to expand or "jump off" the page.
  5. **Use cool colors, such as blue and green, as background.** Because of their calming effect, blue and green will not compete with your text for the reader's attention.

- **Color Wheel**   The *color wheel* shows the relationships colors have to one another. The primary colors are yellow, red, and blue; all other colors are the result of combining these colors or mixing them with white or black. Colors that complement each other appear opposite each other on the wheel.

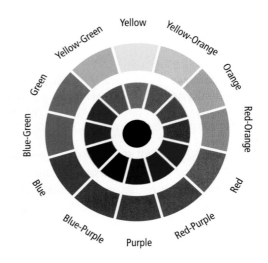

Contrast   *Contrast* is the effect of a striking difference between two things. Create contrast within graphics by using different visual cues for different kinds of information. For example, set important terms in boldface type or in bulleted lists and set chart labels in boldface or capital letters. Use color in your charts, graphs, and tables to make it easy to distinguish columns or bits of information. Contrast makes it easier for your reader to visualize your text and remember its content.

Emphasis   *Emphasis* refers to the use of visual cues such as color, capital letters, boldface or italic fonts, and large type size to draw attention to what you want readers to see. Graphics provide emphasis because they usually attract readers' attention first.

Focus   *Focus* refers to the most important part of an illustration or photograph—what the reader looks at first. Usually, photographs and illustrations depict a subject as seen through the photographer's or artist's eyes. When you design or select an image to include in your document, ask yourself the following questions about its focus.

- **Is the subject of the graphic clear?** Choose a graphic whose subject is immediately recognizable. Be sure that important parts of the subject are not covered or hidden from view.

- **Is the subject shown at the angle that you intend?** If you wish to emphasize a subject's height, show it from a low angle; if you want to show how small a subject is, show it from above. Always ask, "Will this graphic give readers a clear sense of what the text describes?"

- **Does the graphic include any distracting details?** Cut or trim the graphic so that its focus is clear.

- **Will you need to add labels to the graphic so readers will understand?** If the meaning of the graphic is unclear, add labels or captions. Remember, however, that too many labels make a graphic hard to understand. If the graphic becomes too cluttered, group labels into larger categories or find a simpler graphic.

Integration   *Integration* refers to the way the content of graphics and text fit together on the page. Place graphics and text that are related or cover the same material close together on the page. In addition, the text should direct the reader's attention to the visual and explain its content.

Labels or Captions   To help readers understand them, many graphics need *labels* or *captions*. Labels identify the content of charts, tables, and diagrams. Usually labels appear within the body of the graphic or visual, but sometimes they are attached to the visual or graphic by thin rule lines. Captions are usually full sentences that describe a photograph or illustration. They appear directly under, beside, or above the graphic. (See also **Captions** on page 853.)

Organization   *Organization,* or arrangement, refers to the placement or grouping of the text and graphics on a page. All the text and graphics that deal with a similar subject should be grouped together. Use visual cues such as headings and subheadings, similar fonts, color, and rule lines to show that certain elements are related. (See also **Integration** on this page.)

Voice   *Voice* refers to the unique sound and rhythm of a writer's language. Because the text and the graphics support one another, they should have a similar voice. For example, if a text is about a serious topic, then the graphics that accompany it should be serious and straightforward.

Types of Graphics

Graphics can add to the effectiveness and appeal of a document. Designing or selecting the right kind of graphic to support your text can be a challenge. However, the following list will help you decide from among some of the most common and helpful types.

Chart   A *chart* shows relationships among ideas or data. Two types of charts you are likely to use are *flowcharts* and *pie charts*.

- **Flowcharts**   *Flowcharts* use geometric shapes linked by arrows to show a sequence of events in a process. Notice how the following boxes on page 858 are set so that you read them from left to right and from top to bottom. In flow charts, all text is contained inside the shapes, and direction arrows indicate the direction of movement between boxes.

How to Make Lasagna

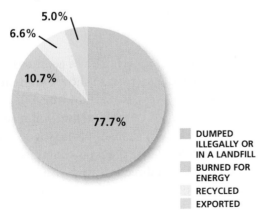

Preheat the oven to 375°. → Spread a thick layer of tomato sauce on the bottom of a 9" x 13" pan.

Cover with a layer of lasagna noodles. → Spoon ricotta or cottage cheese on the noodles.

Add tomato sauce to cheese. → Spread grated mozzarella cheese on the top.

Repeat the layers until ingredients are gone. → Sprinkle with Parmesan cheese and bake for forty-five minutes.

■ **Pie charts** *Pie charts* are circles that are divided into wedges like slices of a pie. Each wedge represents a certain amount of the total, depending on its size.

Where Old Tires Go

What happens to the 242 million scrap tires that are disposed of each year?

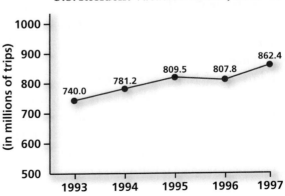

5.0%
6.6%
10.7%
77.7%

DUMPED ILLEGALLY OR IN A LANDFILL
BURNED FOR ENERGY
RECYCLED
EXPORTED

Diagram *Diagrams* use symbols or pictures to compare abstract ideas, show a process, or provide instruction. Diagrams may be hand drawn, computer generated, or photographed. They tend to be simple, showing only the important details of their subjects. The diagram below illustrates the circular movement of water in an ocean swell.

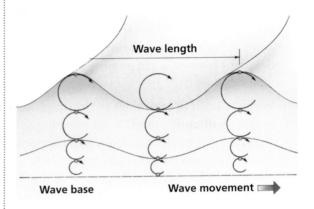

Wave length
Wave base   Wave movement ➡

Graph A *graph* can either show a comparison of quantities or display changes or trends over time. Notice in the following examples that the horizontal axis in a line or bar graph indicates points in time or categories of things, while the vertical axis shows quantities.

Line Graph

U.S. Resident Vacation Travel, 1993–97

(in millions of trips)

1000
900
800   781.2   809.5   807.8   862.4
700   740.0
600
500

1993   1994   1995   1996   1997

Bar Graph

Top Five Longest North American Rivers

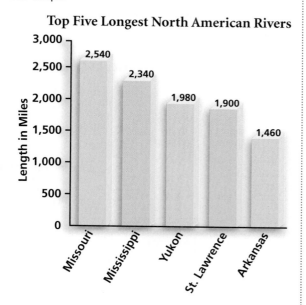

River	Length in Miles
Missouri	2,540
Mississippi	2,340
Yukon	1,980
St. Lawrence	1,900
Arkansas	1,460

Illustration *Illustrations,* such as drawings, photographs, and other artwork, may be used to show readers something new, unfamiliar, or indescribable; what something or someone looks like; or how something works. Illustrations differ from diagrams in that illustrations usually have more detail and are often in color. (See also **Diagram** on page 858.)

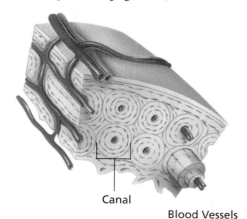

Canal

Blood Vessels

Storyboard *Storyboards* illustrate the course of an event or the scenes of a story. Storyboards may be used to plan a video or to map out the events in a story. The boxes in a storyboard contain drawings as well as text; text may also appear outside or under the boxes.

A boy finds a bottle on the beach. He sees a slip of paper inside the bottle.

He pulls out the slip of paper and reads what is written on it.

Table *Tables* provide detailed information arranged, using rows and columns, in an accessible, organized way. In the following example, notice that the information is logically organized and clearly labeled.

EXAMPLES

Two-Column Table

Top Five Travel Destinations, 1997	
Country	Number of Visitors (in millions)
France	66.8
United States	48.9
Spain	43.4
Italy	34.0
United Kingdom	26.0

Three-Column Table

Spending by International Visitors to the U.S. in 1996		
Country	Number of Visitors (in thousands)	Amount of Money Spent (in millions)
Canada	15,301	$ 6,763.00
Mexico	8,530	$ 3,001.00
Japan	5,047	$13,163.00
United Kingdom	3,105	$ 7,306.00
Germany	1,973	$ 4,573.00
France	990	$ 2,255.00

Time Line   Time lines identify events that have occurred over a given period of time. Usually, events are identified or described above the time line, and the time demarcations can be indicated above or below it. Some time lines are illustrated.

Time Line of Discoveries in Chemistry

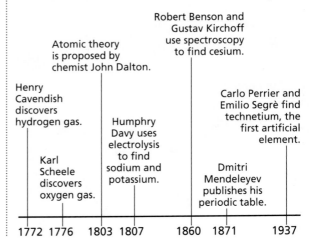

The History of English: Origins and Uses

The History of English

The oldest English-language documents still in existence were first written about 1,300 years ago, but the English language was spoken long before that. Over the centuries, English has evolved into the very different but equally rich and expressive language that it is today. The history of this development is a story of people, places, and times.

Beginnings of English

Many of the world's languages come from an ancient language called **Proto-Indo-European.** There are no records of this parent language, but it was probably spoken by peoples who lived in southeast Europe or Asia Minor six or seven thousand years ago. Tribes of these people slowly migrated throughout Europe and as far east as India. As they wandered in different directions, each tribe developed its own **dialect,** or distinct version of the language. The dialects eventually developed into separate languages. English, French, German, Italian, and Spanish are just a few of the languages that eventually developed through many stages from Proto-Indo-European. The kinship is obvious in the similarities of many words. The word *north* is an example.

EXAMPLE

ENGLISH: *north*
FRENCH: *nord*
GERMAN: *norden*
ITALIAN: *nord*
SPANISH: *norte*

Old English

Around A.D. 450, three Germanic tribes from northern Europe—the Angles, Saxons, and Jutes—began to invade, conquer, and settle parts of Britain. They took over land that had been settled centuries earlier by the Celts and later conquered, settled, then abandoned by the Romans. The separate dialects of the Germanic language the Angles, Saxons, and Jutes spoke eventually blended into one language, which was called *Englisc.* Today this language is referred to as **Old English.** Many Old English words have come down to us only slightly altered. Here are some examples:

EXAMPLES

Old English	Modern English
etan	eat
drincan	drink
daeg	day
niht	night

The structure of Old English, however, was very different from English today. Old English relied on word endings, or **inflections,** to indicate a word's gender, number, case, and person. For example, the noun *hund* ("hound" or "dog") was written *hund, hundes, hunde, hundas, hunda,* or *hundum,* depending on its use in a sentence. In contrast, Modern English relies on a word's position in a sentence to show the word's role in that sentence.

As Old English speakers came into contact with speakers of other languages, particularly Latin-speaking missionaries and Norse invaders, new words, or **loanwords,** entered the language. As English speakers learned Latin, they borrowed words such as *school, altar, candle,* and *paper* and made them part of English. Similarly, as Nordic Vikings settled in Britain, Norse words such as *skalpr (scalp), skrap (scrap),* *skith (ski),* and *sky* became part of the English language. In fact, most English words that begin with *sc* or *sk* are of Norse origin.

Middle English

In 1066, the Normans from France seized control of England. For the next 150–200 years, French was used for almost all written communication. It was the language of government, business, law, and literature in England. The common people of England, however, still spoke English—a form gradually changing into the language now called **Middle English.**

Why did the English language not die out under French rule? Several factors weighed in favor of English. For one thing, the English-speaking people—the common people, such as farmers, herders, servants, and craftspeople—outnumbered their French-speaking rulers. For another, the French rulers in England gradually lost contact with their French culture and language. As a result, three hundred years after the French invasion, English was once again the language of government, business, literature, and law in England. By this time, however, its grammar was becoming simpler as many of the complicated word endings disappeared. Both the grammar and structure were more like the English spoken today, as you can see from the following passage by the fourteenth-century poet Geoffrey Chaucer.

Bifel that in that sesoun on a day
In Southwerk at the Tabard, as I lay
Redy to wenden on my pilgrymage
To Caunterbury with ful devout corage,

Modern English

By 1500, almost everyone in England spoke English. However, because speakers and writers in different parts of England used different versions of the language, they often had trouble understanding each other. Gradually, the version spoken in London—the center of English culture, business, and trade—became the most widely used. When William Caxton brought the first printing press to London in 1476, he printed books in the London dialect. As printed books began to spread across England, spelling and grammar began to be "fixed" in print, and London English became the standard throughout England. The availability of cheap books meant that more people were reading and using the new standardized language. Handbooks of proper English usage, spelling, and pronunciation were soon published, along with the first dictionaries.

Although it had been standardized, the English language did not stop growing. As the Renaissance revived interest in classical languages, thousands of Greek and Latin words entered English. At the same time, English expanded into an international language. From the sixteenth century to the nineteenth century, English merchants, explorers, and settlers spread English to other parts of the globe. They also learned new words from other languages, enriching English with imports such as the following:

EXAMPLES

AFRICAN: marimba
DUTCH: cruise
HINDI: jungle
SPANISH: fiesta
TURKISH: yogurt

American English

Immigration to the American colonies in the late seventeenth and early eighteenth centuries brought about a new version of the language—*American English.* Over time, English colonists in America invented new words and changed the pronunciations and uses of some old words. They also borrowed words, such as *squash*, from American Indian languages. By 1776, the version of English spoken in America was distinct enough from that spoken in England to be called American English.

Like the United States itself, American English represents a variety of cultures and peoples. American Indians, Africans, and immigrants from countries around the world have enriched the language with words from their native tongues. Here are some examples:

EXAMPLES

AFRICAN: gumbo, okra
AMERICAN INDIAN: coyote, toboggan
CHINESE: yen, chop suey
GERMAN: kindergarten, frankfurter
SPANISH: canyon, patio

English in the Twenty-First Century

English has become the most widely used language in the world. It is an official language in more than eighty-seven nations and territories. About one third of the world's population speaks English. Diplomats frequently use it to communicate, and it is the world language of science, technology, aviation, and international trade. As people around the world contribute to the language, the word count continues to grow; the last count was over 600,000 words.

Varieties of American English

American English is a rich and flexible language that offers many choices. To speak and write effectively—at home, at school, and on the job—you need to know what the varieties of American English are and how to choose among them.

Dialects of American English

Like all languages, American English has many distinct versions, called *dialects*. Each has unique features of grammar, vocabulary, and pronunciation.

Ethnic Dialects An *ethnic dialect* is often used by people who share the same cultural heritage. Because Americans come from many different cultures, American English includes many different ethnic dialects. These dialects include, among others, Irish English, Yiddish English, and the Hispanic English of people from Puerto Rico, Cuba, Mexico, and Latin America. African American Vernacular English, one of the largest dialects, has elements of African languages and the dialect of the American South.

Regional Dialects The United States has four major regional dialects: the *Northern,* the *Midland,* the *Southern,* and the *Western.* The pronunciations of words often vary from one dialect to another. For example, some Southerners pronounce the words *ten* and *tin* the same way—as "tin." Some Midlanders and Southerners add an *r* sound to words, so that *wash* sounds like "warsh."

Similarly, regional dialects differ in vocabulary and grammar. For example, someone from New England might call a soft drink *tonic,* while people in other parts of the country might call it *soda* or *pop.* Someone from the South might say "sick *at* my stomach," while someone from the North might say "sick *to* my stomach."

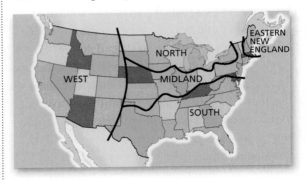

Standard American English

No variety of English is better or more correct than another. However, ***standard American English*** is the variety of English that is more widely used and accepted than any other in the United States. Because it is commonly understood, it allows people from different regions and cultures to communicate with one another clearly. It is the variety of English you read and hear most often in books and magazines and on radio, television, and the Internet. People are expected to use standard English in most school and business situations. This textbook presents rules and guidelines for using standard American English. To distinguish between standard American English and other varieties, this book uses the labels *standard* and *nonstandard.* Nonstandard language is not "wrong" language—it is language that is inappropriate in situations where standard English is expected.

Standard English—Formal to Informal

Your use of standard English can be formal, informal or anywhere in between. Which type you choose for communication will depend on many factors, including the occasion and purpose for which you are writing or speaking and your intended audience. The following chart shows some of the appropriate uses of formal and informal standard English.

Uses of Formal and Informal Standard English

Formal

Speaking formal classroom presentations, banquets, dedication ceremonies, and interviews

Writing serious papers and reports, tests, business letters, and job or college applications

Informal

Speaking everyday conversations, group discussions, informal speeches and telephone conversations

Writing personal letters, many types of classroom writing, and many newspaper and magazine articles

Standard English gives you the freedom to say the same things in many different ways. For example, in a formal setting you might say, "I'm pleased to meet you." On a less formal occasion you might choose to say, "Hi, how are you?" or "How's it going?" The differences between formal and informal English are mainly in sentence structure, word choice, and tone.

Features of Formal and Informal Standard English

Formal

Sentence Structure longer and more complex

Word Choice more precise and refined, sometimes technical or scientific

Tone serious and dignified

Informal

Sentence Structure shorter and simpler

Word Choice simple and ordinary, often includes contractions, colloquialisms, and slang

Tone conversational

Colloquialisms The word *colloquial* comes from a Latin word that means "conversation." *Colloquialisms* are the informal words and phrases of conversational language. They bring flavor and color to everyday speech and a friendly tone to writing. Many colloquialisms are figures of speech.

EXAMPLES She told me to quit **making such a racket.**

Since quitting her high-paying job, Pat has been **living hand-to-mouth.**

Slang *Slang* is highly informal English consisting of made-up words or old words used in new ways. It is often used by specific groups of people, such as students, musicians, or military personnel.

EXAMPLES **bad:** good, excellent

make like: imitate

scarf down: eat greedily

Although some slang words become accepted parts of the language, most have a relatively short life span.

The Library/ Media Center

Using Print and Electronic Sources

Consult the library/media center in your school or community to find information sources for classroom assignments and your personal interests. *Print sources* include books, periodicals (magazines, newspapers, and journals), and specialized forms (such as microforms or vertical files). *Electronic sources* include CD-ROMs, the Internet, DVDs, and online databases.

TIP Real-world documents not found in libraries can be excellent information sources for certain purposes. Such documents include

- consumer materials, such as user manuals, warranties, contracts, and technical directions
- business documents, such as memos and directories
- public materials, such as maps, schedules, and government records

Call Number A *call number* is a unique code assigned to a library book. It indicates how a book is classified and where it can be found in the library. Call numbers may be based on the Dewey decimal system or the Library of Congress system.

- **Dewey decimal system** The *Dewey decimal system* assigns nonfiction books to ten general subject categories. Each area is assigned a range of numbers, and within each range, subgroups of numbers identify more specific categories. Novels and short stories are grouped together under the category *Fiction* and are arranged by the author's last name. Biographies and autobiographies are arranged by the subject's last name.

- **Library of Congress System** The *Library of Congress system* uses code letters to identify subject categories. The first letter of a book's call number identifies its general category (such as history), and the second identifies the subcategory (such as American). The numbers beside each pair of letters identify a specific book within a category.

Card Catalog For each book in a library, the card catalog contains a *title card* and an *author card.* Nonfiction books also have a third card, a *subject card. Cross-reference cards,* which contain the words *see* or *see also,* may advise you where to look for additional information.

Catalog cards are arranged in alphabetical order in a cabinet of drawers, and each card contains the following information:

- the **call number** assigned to a book by the Dewey decimal or Library of Congress classification system
- the **author's full name,** last name first
- the full **title** and **subtitle** of a book
- the place and date of **publication**
- the general **subject** of a book (a subject card may show specific headings)
- a **description** of the book, such as its size and number of pages, and whether it is illustrated
- **cross-references** to other headings or related topics under which a book is listed

Many libraries have replaced or supplemented traditional card catalogs in drawers with electronic or online card catalogs. (See also **Online Card Catalog** on this page.)

CD-ROMs   A *CD-ROM* (*C*ompact *D*isc-*R*ead *O*nly *M*emory) is a digitally encoded compact disc that is designed to hold visual as well as audio information. A single CD-ROM may contain the equivalent of 250,000 pages of printed text. Many reference tools, such as encyclopedias, dictionaries, and indexes, are now available on CD-ROMs. CD-ROMs contain the same text as the printed versions but have the added attractions of searching capabilities, interactive graphics, and audio. The data can be accessed only by a computer with a CD-ROM drive, and the information can be printed out or downloaded directly to a disk. (See also the **Reference Sources** chart on page 870.)

Internet   The *Internet* is a global network of computers that enables a computer user to access information from other computers or networks anywhere in the world. Created in the late 1960s, the Internet was originally used by research scientists to share data electronically, but today the Internet has grown far beyond its beginnings and contains information on thousands of topics, scientific and nonscientific. Almost anyone who has a computer equipped with a modem can use the Internet, and there are many ways to view Internet material, including FTP (File Transfer Protocol), Gopher, Telnet, and *World Wide Web browsers,* which provide access to files and documents, news and discussion groups, bulletin boards, e-mail, and the *World Wide Web* (see page 871). The World Wide Web is the place on the Internet you are most likely to go for your research.

Microforms   *Microforms* are photographically reduced articles from newspapers and magazines. The two most common kinds of microforms are *microfilm* (a roll or reel of film) and *microfiche* (a small sheet of film). Special machines are needed in order to enlarge microfilm and microfiche images and project them onto a screen for viewing or reading. Libraries with documents on microfilm or microfiche typically provide these machines.

Online Card Catalog   An *online card catalog* is an electronic or computerized version of the card catalog. Instead of searching through individual cards, you may find a book by typing in a book's *title, author,* or *subject,* or you can use the *key words* command to find all the books that contain a certain word or words in their titles or descriptions. The computer quickly retrieves information based on your request and provides you with a screen similar to the one on the next page.

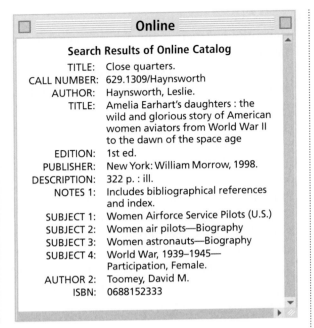

Online

Search Results of Online Catalog

TITLE:	Close quarters.
CALL NUMBER:	629.1309/Haynsworth
AUTHOR:	Haynsworth, Leslie.
TITLE:	Amelia Earhart's daughters : the wild and glorious story of American women aviators from World War II to the dawn of the space age
EDITION:	1st ed.
PUBLISHER:	New York: William Morrow, 1998.
DESCRIPTION:	322 p. : ill.
NOTES 1:	Includes bibliographical references and index.
SUBJECT 1:	Women Airforce Service Pilots (U.S.)
SUBJECT 2:	Women air pilots—Biography
SUBJECT 3:	Women astronauts—Biography
SUBJECT 4:	World War, 1939–1945—Participation, Female.
AUTHOR 2:	Toomey, David M.
ISBN:	0688152333

One advantage of using an online catalog is that the computer can tell you the *status* of a book—whether it is checked out, on loan to another library, or available at another library. Some online card catalogs even tell when a book that has been checked out is due back at your library.

Online Databases

An *online database* is a contained system of electronic information that may be accessed only by computer. In most cases, organizations such as universities, libraries, or businesses create or subscribe to databases that are of specific interest to the people in those organizations. *LEXIS–NEXIS* is an example of a subscription-only database. Users must have an identification number that allows them to read the information. Other databases are public and may be accessed through the World Wide Web.

Online Sources

Information that is *online* is information that may be located and accessed by using computers. Computers that are online are able to communicate with each other over telecommunication lines, such as telephone lines and fiber-optic cables, and via satellite. When computers are linked, they form a *network*. Computer networks are what make the Internet and the World Wide Web possible.

Radio, Television, and Film

A large portion of the programming on *radio* and *television* is made up of newscasts, newsmagazines, and documentaries, which are all important sources of information. Documentaries and educational materials are also produced on *film* or *video.* Descriptive listings of radio and television programs appear in newspapers and, in some cases, on the Internet. Indexes of educational films and videos, such as *The Video Source Book* (Gale, 1998), are available at libraries and book stores. Be sure to check the ratings provided for the films and videos before viewing them.

Readers' Guide to Periodical Literature

The *Readers' Guide to Periodical Literature* is an index of articles, poems, and stories from more than two hundred magazines and journals (periodicals). The articles are listed alphabetically by author and by subject, but not by title, and the headings are set in boldface type. A key located in the front of the *Readers' Guide* explains the meanings of the abbreviations used in the entries.

In addition to maintaining an updated bound set of the *Readers' Guide,* some libraries subscribe to an online version. To use this version, enter a search word or phrase into the computer and choose the records that interest you from the search results.

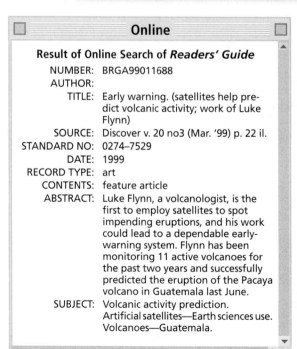

Printed *Readers' Guide*

(1) VOLCANIC ACTIVITY PREDICTION

(2) Early warning [satellites help predict volcanic activity; work of Luke Flynn] il *Discover* v20 no3 p22 Mr '99

(3) VOLCANIC SEA CHIMNEYS *See* Hydrothermal vents

VOLCANO PREDICTION *See* Volcanic activity prediction

VOLCANOES

    See also

    Volcanic activity prediction

Mounds of evidence support active sand dunes and ancient lava lakes on Mars [Mars Global Surveyor images] (4) J. Kross *Ad Astra* v11 no1 p11 Ja/F '99

    Argentina

    See also

    Mount Llullaillaco (Argentina and Chile)

    Chile

    See also

    Mount Llullaillaco (Argentina and Chile)

    Guatemala

(5) Early warning [satellites help predict volcanic activity; work of Luke Flynn] il *Discover* (6) v20 no3 p22 Mr '99

    Pacific Northwest

In search of the elusive megaplume [submarine volcanoes along the Pacific seafloor; research by E. Baker] J. Fischman. il map *Discover* v20 no3 (7) p108–15 (8) Mr '99

- (1) Subject entry
- (2) Title of article
- (3) Subject cross-reference
- (4) Author of article
- (5) Name of periodical
- (6) Volume number of periodical
- (7) Page references
- (8) Date of periodical

Online

Result of Online Search of *Readers' Guide*

NUMBER: BRGA99011688
AUTHOR:
TITLE: Early warning. (satellites help predict volcanic activity; work of Luke Flynn)
SOURCE: Discover v. 20 no3 (Mar. '99) p. 22 il.
STANDARD NO: 0274–7529
DATE: 1999
RECORD TYPE: art
CONTENTS: feature article
ABSTRACT: Luke Flynn, a volcanologist, is the first to employ satellites to spot impending eruptions, and his work could lead to a dependable early-warning system. Flynn has been monitoring 11 active volcanoes for the past two years and successfully predicted the eruption of the Pacaya volcano in Guatemala last June.
SUBJECT: Volcanic activity prediction. Artificial satellites—Earth sciences use. Volcanoes—Guatemala.

Reference Books Reference books are books of specialized information that are set aside in a separate section of any library. Reference books contain facts and information organized in a logical way, such as by alphabetical or chronological order or by category. Examples of reference books include encyclopedias, dictionaries, thesauruses, indexes, books of quotations, atlases, and almanacs. (See also the **Reference Sources** chart on page 870.)

Reference Sources There are many different kinds of reference sources that you can use to find specific kinds of information. The chart on the next page identifies and describes common reference sources and provides examples of print and electronic reference sources.

QUICK REFERENCE HANDBOOK

Reference Sources

Types of Reference Sources	Description	Examples
ALMANACS	Up-to-date information about current events, facts, statistics, and dates	• *Information Please Almanac* • *TIME Almanac- The Reference Edition* CD-ROM
ATLASES	Maps and geographical information	• *Hammond Atlas of the World* • *Microsoft Encarta World Atlas* CD-ROM
BIOGRAPHICAL REFERENCES (GENERAL)	Information about birth, nationality, and major accomplishments of prominent people, past and present	• *Biography Index* • *The International Who's Who* • *Biography Index* CD-ROM • *Dictionary of American Biography on CD-ROM*
BIOGRAPHICAL REFERENCES (SPECIALIZED)	Information about people noted for accomplishments in a specific field or for membership in a specific group	• *American Men and Women of Science 1998–9* (Bowker) • *Who's Who Among African Americans* • *The Multimedia Encyclopedia of the American Indian* CD-ROM
BOOKS OF QUOTATIONS	Famous quotations indexed or grouped together by subject	• *American Heritage Dictionary of American Quotations* • *The Oxford Dictionary of Quotations*
BOOKS OF SYNONYMS	Lists of exact or more interesting words to express ideas	• *Roget's International Thesaurus* • *Oxford Thesaurus on CD-ROM*
ENCYCLOPEDIAS	Articles of general information arranged alphabetically by subject in a single volume or in several volumes	• *The Columbia Encyclopedia* • *New Encyclopaedia Britannica* • The *World Book Encyclopedia* • *The Columbia Encyclopedia on CD-ROM*
INDEXES	Information in list form of articles found in periodicals or other information sources	• *Biography Index* • *New York Times Index* • *Art Index* CD-ROM • *Book Review Index on CD-ROM*
LITERARY REFERENCES	Information about where to locate various works of literature; information about authors and about individual literary works	• *Columbia Granger's Index to Poetry* • *Contemporary Authors* series • *Columbia Granger's World of Poetry on CD-ROM* • *Masterplots Nonfiction, Drama, Poetry CD-ROM*

Reference Sources		
Types of Reference Sources	**Description**	**Examples**
SPECIAL REFERENCE SOURCES FOR SPECIFIC SUBJECTS	Information related to specific subjects or topics of interest to researchers in specific fields	• *Encyclopedia of North American Sports History* (Facts on File) • *The Lives of the Artists* • *History of Music CD-ROMs* • *The Dictionary of Science and Technology CD-ROM*
STYLE AND WRITING MANUALS	Information about proper writing style and preparation of research papers	• *The Chicago Manual of Style* • *MLA Style Manual and Guide to Scholarly Publishing,* Second Edition • *Harbrace College Handbook* CD-ROM

Vertical File   A *vertical file* is a set of file drawers containing materials that are not likely to be cataloged anywhere else, such as pamphlets, newspaper clippings, and photographs. As the use of electronic or online resources increases, vertical files are less likely to be maintained by libraries.

World Wide Web   (*WWW* or the *Web*) Perhaps the best-known part of the Internet, the *World Wide Web* is an enormous system of linked, or connected, documents that contain text, graphics, sounds, and even video. The Web can be navigated only by computer users who have *browser* software installed on their computers. Documents (*Web sites* or *Web pages*) on the World Wide Web are connected by *hyperlinks,* which are specially coded parts of each document. When you click on a hyperlink, the computer accesses a new site and makes it appear on screen so it can be viewed, printed, or downloaded.

World Wide Web, Key Terms   The following terms will help you understand the workings of the World Wide Web.

■ **Browser**   A *browser* is a software application that allows you to access, save, and download documents, images, sounds, and videos from the Web. Searching the Web in this way is called *browsing* (See also **World Wide Web** on this page and **Web Site** on page 872.)

■ **Domain**   A *domain* is the name of a computer or server on the Internet from which you may access information. Every Web address specifies a domain, or particular computer.

■ **Home page**   A *home page* is the first screen or page of a Web site, and it usually functions as a guide to the rest of the site. Usually, the home page identifies the person or organization that sponsored or created the site and provides an index or table of contents for the site. Often a home page includes hyperlinks to related sites on the Web. (See also **Web Site** on page 872.)

■ **Hyperlink**   A *hyperlink,* or *link,* is a "button" or code word that allows a user to move from one place or page on the World Wide Web to another. On screen, hyperlinks usually appear in a contrasting color and are underlined. (See also **Hypertext Markup Language** on this page.)

■ **Hypertext**   A *hypertext* program allows a user to find and open related files and documents on the Web without having to quit or close the original file. It allows a user to move to and from one document to another via hyperlinks.

■ **Hypertext Markup Language**   *Hypertext Markup Language (HTML)* is the language used to create documents on the World Wide Web.

■ **Hypertext Transfer Protocol**   *Hypertext Transfer Protocol (HTTP)* is the language used by browser software to connect to different sites or documents on the World Wide Web.

■ **Search engine**   A search engine is a tool for finding specific information on the Web. (See also **World Wide Web, Searching** on page 873.)

■ **URL** (*U*niform *R*esource *L*ocator)   A *URL* is the address of a specific document on the Web. A typical URL includes words, abbreviations, numbers, and punctuation. The URL shown below would connect you to newspapers from around the world, organized by country and region, that can be read online through the Internet Public Library. The parts of the address are explained below.

```
   1       2        3
http://www.ipl.org/reading/news
```

1. The **protocol,** or how the site is formatted
2. The **domain name.** Domain names have at least two parts. The part on the left is the name of the company, institution, or other organization. The part on the right is a

general domain. Here are the abbreviations of the most common general domains. (see also **Domain** on page 871.)

Common Domains on the World Wide Web	
com	commercial
edu	educational
gov	governmental
net	administrative
org	nonprofit organization

3. The **subdirectory name** that shows where the specific piece of information you want is stored. (Each word following a slash requests a narrower search into the site.) Not all addresses will have this part.

■ **Web Site** (or **Web Page**)   A *Web site* or *Web page* is a document or location on the Web that is linked to other locations on the Web. A site may contain several Web pages. The screen on page 873 shows the most important parts of a browser and a typical Web site.

World Wide Web, Plagiarism   To take another person's idea or work and present it as your own is called *plagiarism*. Because the World Wide Web is such a vast source of information and because it is easy to download or copy information, plagiarism of electronic material has become a serious concern. Treat any information you find on the World Wide Web as if it were from a printed or published source. Avoid plagiarism by **paraphrasing** information you find on the Web, and **be sure to cite the sources of your information**. (See also page 237.)

1. **Toolbar** The buttons on the toolbar allow you to complete different functions such as moving to different pages, printing out information, searching, and seeing or hiding images.

2. **Location Window** This box shows you the URL, or address, of the site you are viewing.

3. **Content area** The area of the screen where the text, images, hyperlinks, and other parts of a Web page appear.

4. **Hyperlinks** Clicking on internal hyperlinks takes you to other parts of the same Web site. External hyperlinks take you to other Web sites.

5. **Scroll bar** Clicking along the horizontal or vertical scroll bar (or on the arrows at either end) allows you to move left to right or up and down in the image area.

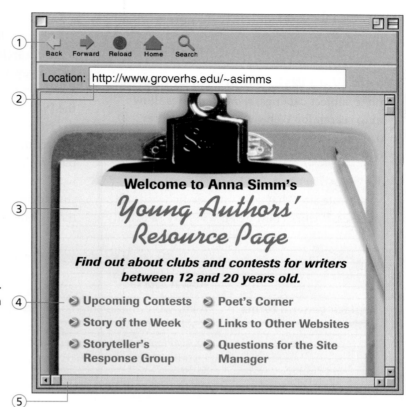

World Wide Web, Searching Computer users can locate information on the World Wide Web by using three different search methods: *direct address, search engines,* and *subject catalogs.* A combination of all three types of searches usually works best. Most search services on the Web allow you to use all three.

- **Direct address** The easiest way to find a Web site is to enter its address, or URL, in the location box. Type the address exactly, since the Internet will only identify it if the case and punctuation are correct. Of course, this search method does not work unless you have an exact address for the site you want to find.

- **Search engines** Search engines allow you to search *databases* that contain information about the millions of sites available on the Web. These databases are compiled automatically by computer programs called *robots.* (See also **World Wide Web, Using Search Engines** on page 874.)

- **Subject catalogs** A *subject catalog* provides an extensively organized table of contents of the World Wide Web. Unlike search engines, subject catalogs are organized by humans, not by machines. Information from Web sites is organized in broad categories, such as *Education* and *Entertainment,* which contain many specific subcategories. These subcategories in turn break down into even more specific sub-subcategories. To research a topic using a subject catalog, users identify a broad category and keep narrowing their focus through the subcategories and sub-subcategories until they find the specific information they need.

World Wide Web, Using Search Engines

Unlike subject catalogs, *search engines* allow you to search for Web sites that contain key words or phrases. These search tools also allow you to refine your searches.

■ **Key word search** A *key word search* helps you locate sites that contain specific words or phrases. It works best when you have selected a very clear topic to research. To begin a search, type key words in the space provided on the search engine screen and press the return key or the search or find button. The search engine checks the key words against the Web sites indexed in its database, noting the frequency and importance of the words you requested. When the comparison is completed, the results appear in the form of a list. The sites that contain all your key words should appear at the top of the list, and sites that contain fewer appear later, in descending

Refining a Key Word Search	
Tip	**How It Works**
Replace general terms with more specific ones.	A key word that is common or used in ways you do not expect can result in irrelevant matches. EXAMPLE If you are interested in classical dance, enter *ballet* instead of *dance*.
Use quotation marks.	By placing your key words or phrases in quotation marks, the search engine will find sites that use the words exactly as you have typed them. EXAMPLE Enter "Irish dance" to find sites specific to traditional Irish dancing rather than sites about Irish culture or ballet.
Use *and* and *not*.	Narrow your search by putting the word *and* between your key words. The search engine will find only Web sites that contain all words connected by *and*. EXAMPLE For sites that mention either form of entertainment, enter *Irish dance and Irish music*. Use *not* between key words to make sure that the search engine does not pull up sites that deal with topics that are similar but unrelated. EXAMPLE Enter *Celtic not Boston* to find information about Irish history and culture and avoid sites about the basketball team.
Use *or*.	To broaden your search, use *or* to let the search engine know that you would accept sites that contain any of your key words. EXAMPLE If you want sites that discuss either Irish dance or Irish music, enter *Irish dance or Irish music*.

order of relevant matches. Most search engines assign the items on the list a percentage or rank number to indicate how well the site matched your request.

- **Refining a key word search** Because search engines may identify hundreds or thousands of Web sites—or none at all—that contain your key words, you may find it useful to refine or focus your search to get good results. The chart on page 874 suggests some strategies that may help you. Keep in mind, however, that different search engines may require slightly different commands than

those listed here. The Help section of your search engine should tell you the specific commands that limit searches on it.

World Wide Web, Web Site Evaluation

The content of the World Wide Web is not monitored for accuracy in the way most newspapers, books, or magazines are. Consequently, you must think critically about the information you find there to make sure it is authoritative and reliable. Here are questions to help you to *evaluate* a Web site's value as a source of information.

Evaluating Web Sites	
Questions to Ask	**Why You Should Ask**
Who created or sponsored the Web site?	The information on a Web site is selected by the site's creator or sponsor, which the Web site's home page should identify. To make sure the information you get from the Web is reliable, use only Web sites that are affiliated with reputable organizations, such as government agencies, universities, and museums. The Web sites for these organizations will usually belong in the *edu, gov,* or *org* domains.
When was the page first posted and is it frequently updated?	This information usually appears at the end of a home page. Most often, it includes a copyright notice, the date of the most recent update, and a link to the creator's e-mail address. Since you want your information to be up-to-date, only use sites that have been updated recently.
What other Web pages is the site linked to?	Looking at the links provided in a Web site can help you determine how legitimate it is. If a site is a source of accurate information, it will have links to other reputable Web sites.
Does the Web site present information objectively?	Look for signs of bias, such as strong language or statements of opinion. An objective site will present ideas from both sides of an issue or debate clearly and fairly.
Is the Web site well designed?	A well-designed Web site has legible type, clear graphics, and working links and is easily searched or navigated. The written content of the site should be well organized and use proper spelling, punctuation, and grammar.

Reading and Vocabulary

Reading

Skills and Strategies

You can use the following skills and strategies to become a more effective reader.

Author's Purpose and Point of View, Determining   An author has a reason or *purpose* for writing a selection—to inform, to persuade, to entertain, or to express feelings. Some forms (such as business writing, policy statements, and user manuals) are suited to specific purposes, while other forms (such as Web sites) can be used for any purpose. In addition, authors have *points of view;* that is, they express their opinions or attitudes about their subjects. If an author's information seems unclear or inaccurate, consider whether his or her point of view might be strongly biased. To better understand a text, read carefully to determine an author's purpose and point of view.

> EXAMPLE   Using the Heimlich maneuver, you can dislodge an object from the throat of a choking victim. First, stand behind the victim and place your closed fist just below the victim's rib cage. Then pull your fist upward in a short thrust. In two quick steps you may save a life.

> Author's purpose: To inform about the steps of the Heimlich maneuver

> Author's point of view: The Heimlich maneuver can save lives and is therefore good to know.

Cause-and-Effect Relationships, Analyzing   A *cause* is the reason something happens. An *effect* is the result of that cause. By asking the questions "Why did this happen?" and "What are the effects?" as you read, you are analyzing cause-and-effect relationships in a text.

> EXAMPLE   We find fossils—the remains, preserved in rock, of plant and animal organisms—because of the conditions in which the organism died. If an organism died in a soft, wet place, such as a riverbed, its soft tissue soon dissolved or was eaten, and its plant remains or its skeleton was covered by sediment. Minerals in the watery sediment then reacted with the plant remains or with the animal's shell and hardened it. More sediment covered the remains or the hardened shell, thus preserving it in stone.

> Analysis: Fossilization is caused by an organism that died and decomposed in a watery environment. The effects of the moist climate were that the moisture and sediment preserved the dead organism's remains.

Clue Words				
Cause-Effect	Chronological Order	Comparison-Contrast	Listing	Problem-Solution
as a result	after	although	also	as a result
because	as	as well as	for example	nevertheless
consequently	before	but	in fact	therefore
if . . . then	finally	either . . . or	most important	this led to
nevertheless	first	however	to begin with	thus
since	not long after	not only . . . but also	such as	consequently
so that	now	on the other hand	finally	otherwise
therefore	second	similarly		
this led to	then	unless		
thus	when	yet		

Clue Words, Using   Writers use certain *clue words* to connect their ideas or to show relationships between ideas. Readers can use these clue words to identify the text's structure or organizational pattern. Common clue words are listed in the chart above. (See also **Text Structures** on page 885.)

Conclusions, Drawing   When you *draw conclusions,* you combine the information in a text with information you already know. As you read, you interpret and evaluate the information from a text, connect it to your experiences, and then draw conclusions that are logical yet specific to the text. (See also page 172.)

> EXAMPLE   I must admit that writing is not an easy job nor is it one that lets you socialize much. Often I have spent my vacations and weekends in the library or at the computer trying to finish an article or a paper before a deadline. Still, when you finally see your name in print, the effort seems worth it.
>
> Conclusion: The writer is a professional writer.

Fact and Opinion, Distinguishing   A *fact* is information that can be proven true or false. An *opinion* expresses a belief or point of view. You cannot prove that an opinion is true or false. Facts, however, are statements which can be checked in other reference works for accuracy. Facts are often used to support opinions. A reader who can distinguish between a fact and an opinion will not be easily misled. (See also page 255.)

> EXAMPLE
>
> Fact: Wolfgang Amadeus Mozart was a composer who lived from 1756–1791. [Reference works support this as a true statement.]
>
> Opinion: Mozart was the greatest composer who ever lived. [This statement cannot be proved true or false; it represents what one writer believes about Mozart.]

Generalizations, Forming   A reader forms a *generalization* by combining information in a text with personal experience to make a judgment that applies to the world beyond the text. (See also page 132.)

EXAMPLE   The Antarctic continent, the south-ernmost landmass, is buried under more than a mile of ice and surrounded by oceans and seas that are partly frozen and filled with icebergs. In summer, the temperatures rarely climb above freezing. On land, there are very few plants or animals that can withstand the cold, especially the deep cold (as low as –112°F) of winter.

Generalization: The Antarctic continent is not a place many creatures can or would want to live because it is so cold.

Graphics, Interpreting

Graphics convey information by using pictures or symbols. Writers use them to provide supporting evidence for their ideas. The most common forms of graphics used in informational writing are **charts, diagrams, graphs, tables,** and **time lines.** Graphics illustrate complex information in a simple, visual format. Most often, they provide a clear comparison of different but related points of information. As a reader, your job is to interpret the information presented in a graphic and to draw your own conclusions. You will most likely encounter the following types of graphics in your reading.

- **Charts** show the relationships of the parts of a whole to each other. Some charts are rectangular, but a pie chart is circular. The point of a pie chart is usually to show the proportions of the sections, not to show the specific amounts of each section or the value of the whole pie. The following pie chart shows the percentage of people in each class of Malory High School that regularly wear athletic shoes. Notice how the segments of the pie chart are identified as percentages.

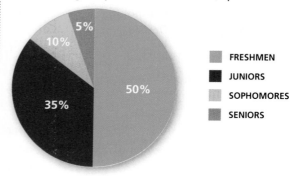

Percentage of Malory High School Population
That Regularly Wears Athletic Shoes, by Class

FRESHMEN
JUNIORS
SOPHOMORES
SENIORS

- **Diagrams** use pictures or symbols, such as circles or arrows, to illustrate a process, to compare abstract ideas, or to provide instruction. Diagrams should not be used to present numerical data because the shapes and forms used in diagrams do not accurately represent amounts. Look, for example, at the following diagram illustrating one octave (eight notes) of the C-major scale. These notes would correspond to the white keys on a piano keyboard.

A **Venn Diagram** uses intersecting circles to show how two ideas or things compare. The section of the diagram where the circles overlap contains the elements shared by the two things being compared. The remaining area in each circle contains the elements that are unique to each thing being compared. The Venn diagram on the next page illustrates the similarities and differences between the games of tennis and squash.

Venn Diagram

Tennis **Similarities** **Squash**

- Outdoor court; court surface may be clay or grass
- Ball hit over a net between opposing players
- Sets of games make up matches; men play up to five sets; women play up to three

- Equipment includes a racket and small, rubber-ized ball
- Ball must be hit by oppo-nent before it bounces twice on the floor or ground

- Indoor, enclosed court; walls are part of the playing court
- Ball hit onto any of the walls by players alternating shots
- Games played to nine points; best of three or five games makes a match

■ **Line and Bar Graphs** show changes or trends over time. Usually the horizontal axis in a line or bar graph indicates points in time, and the vertical axis shows quantities. The line and bar graphs below illustrate the sales trends of two brands of athletic shoes.

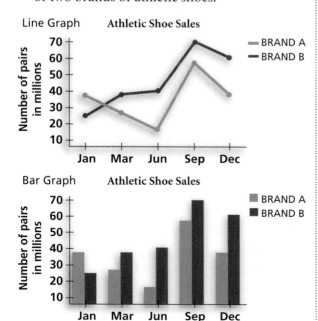

Notice that the vertical axes on both graphs begin at zero. Beginning a vertical axis with zero ensures that the data will be plotted accurately. Check for this when reading line or bar graphs. Also, be wary of any graph that switches the vertical and horizontal axes. If the vertical axis indicates the passing of time, the resulting peaks and valleys shown on the graph may be misleading. In the line graph below, the vertical axis indicates time. Notice how difficult it is to draw any conclusions from the graph.

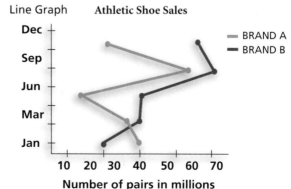

Sales of Three Brands of Athletic Shoes in Units of Millions					
Athletic Shoes	January	March	June	September	December
Brand A	40	33	20	57	41
Brand B	27	40	39	71	60
Brand C	11	15	19	21	25

- **Tables, like the one above,** provide information in an easy-to-read format. Tables do not show trends and patterns in data. Readers must draw their own conclusions about any relationships among the data.

- **Time lines** identify events that take place over the course of time. A time line is basically the horizontal axis of a graph. Usually, events are identified or described above the time line and the time demarcations are indicated below it. The time line below outlines important literary events in early Persian and Arabic literature.

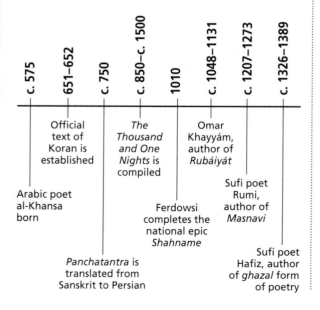

Effective graphics contain the following elements:

- a **body** that presents information in the form of a chart, diagram, graph, table, or time line; the body is specific to the type of information or data that is presented
- **labels** that identify and give meaning to the information shown in the graphic
- a **legend** that identifies special symbols, color coding, scale, or other features you need to understand the graphic; the legend appears as a small box placed near the body
- a **source** that tells where the information contained in the graphic was found; knowing the source helps you evaluate the accuracy of the graphic
- a **title** that identifies the subject or main idea of the graphic

As a reader, you should always read graphics carefully and with a critical eye. Keep in mind the following tips.

1. **Always read the title, labels, and legend** of any graphic before analyzing its data.
2. **Draw your own conclusions** and compare them to those of the writer.
3. **Think about what information is *not* included in the graphic.** Important information is sometimes left out because it does not support the author's conclusions.

4. **Watch out for optical illusions in graphs.** For example, bar graphs and pie charts that are shown in three dimensions are easily misread because some sections look more dense than others. Also, pie charts are often "exploded," with one segment pulled away from the others. Your eye naturally will be drawn to the exploded piece, but you should still pay attention to the whole picture.

5. **Look for manipulated data** by making sure that the horizontal axis of any graph indicates time, not amount. Also, make sure that the axes of a graph or sections of a pie chart are clearly labeled and consistently marked.

Implied Main Idea, Identifying Some writers do not directly state the main idea of their writing; instead, they choose to *imply*, or suggest, it. In this case, as a reader, you must analyze the meaning of the details you are given and decide what overall meaning these details combine to express. (See also **Stated Main Idea** on page 884.)

EXAMPLE   Every Thursday Lila Martinez spends a few hours at the senior citizens' center. Her activities vary from week to week. Sometimes she reads aloud; other times she plays checkers; but mostly she listens to stories the older people tell. Occasionally, she hears a story more than once, but she does not mind because listening to the older folks reminds Lila of her own grandmother.

Implied main idea: Lila Martinez's Thursday sessions at the senior citizens' center are important to her because the residents remind her of her own grandmother.

Inferences, Making An *inference* is a conclusion that a reader reaches based on information in a text and on the reader's prior knowledge and experience. As you read, you analyze the text to interpret what writers do not state directly and come to a decision. (See also **Conclusions, Drawing** on page 877.)

EXAMPLE   Garrett Morgan, an African American inventor, received a patent in 1914 for his invention of the Safety Hood. The hood, which was like a helmet connected by tubing to a clean air source, allowed its wearer, including firefighters and miners, to enter poisoned atmospheres and breathe safely. The Safety Hood was updated during World War I, becoming the modern gas mask.

Inference: Fires, mines, and battlefields are all dangerous situations in which a person might benefit from wearing a Safety Hood.

Memorizing *Memorizing* is the ability to read material and learn the exact words or the general concepts by heart. To develop your memorization skills, follow the tips in the chart below.

How to Memorize

1. Condense the information, if possible. Information can often be summarized or condensed in your notes.

2. Rehearse the material in several different ways. Using different senses often helps you to commit the material to memory. For example, write your notes, and then silently read them, remembering what they look like. Next, read the notes aloud into a tape recorder. Finally, listen to the recording. After some practice, you will learn which way or combination of ways helps you remember best.

3. Use memory tricks. Use the first letter of each word in a series to form a new word. Make a rhyme to help you remember facts. Associate information with a mental image.

4. Repeat the material. Review the material frequently in short, focused sessions. Try reading the material aloud, over and over again.

Paraphrasing A *paraphrase* is a type of summary in which you restate an author's ideas in your own words. Paraphrasing is a good way to check your understanding of the original text. To develop your paraphrasing skills, follow the tips in the chart below. Then, look at the example and paraphrase that follow the chart.

How to Paraphrase
1. Read the entire selection. Get the overall meaning before you begin writing your paraphrase.
2. Identify the main idea of the selection. Keep it in mind while you write your paraphrase.
3. Identify the speaker in fictional material. Is it the poet or author who is speaking or is a character speaking?
4. Write your paraphrase in your own words. Use complete sentences and standard paragraph form.
5. Review the selection. Be sure that your paraphrase expresses the same ideas as the original.

EXAMPLE   A camera is actually a simple mechanism. Images are made on film by aiming a camera at an object. Light reflected off the object travels toward the camera. Pushing the camera's shutter-release button opens and closes a tiny window in front of the camera, allowing the light to pass through a curved lens and reach the film. The shutter speed may be adjusted to allow for more or less light to shine through onto the film, varying the film exposure.

Paraphrase: A camera is a simple mechanism that works by aiming at an object. The reflection of the object enters the camera when you push the shutter button, which opens a tiny window in the front of the camera and lets the light reach the film. The speed of the shutter can be changed to allow more or less light into the camera, varying the film exposure.

Persuasive Techniques, Analyzing
An author uses **persuasive techniques** to convince readers to think or act in a certain way. As you read persuasive writing, look for logical reasoning and facts; don't be misled by an overemphasis on emotional appeals or faulty reasoning. (See also page 257.)

EXAMPLE   Nick Moseley is the best choice for the tenth-grade student council representative. Nick is an honors student, plays trumpet in the school band, serves as the goalie on the soccer team, and is active in his church. He knows how to be a team member and wants the tenth-grade class to have fun and to make a difference in the community this year. Do the right thing and vote for Nick on Thursday.

Analysis: The first sentence is the opinion, which is supported by evidence in the second and third sentences. The last sentence, however, appeals to emotions.

Predicting   *Predicting* is making an educated guess about what will happen next in a narrative or about the main idea of an expository or persuasive composition. To make predictions, use information from the text—including headlines, subheadings, and illustrations or graphics—plus your own knowledge and experience.

EXAMPLE   In the past, family gatherings always turned into tense showdowns between us kids and Great-uncle Leo, the oldest member of the family. At the end of the meal, he would lean back in his chair and work his way down the table, telling each of us how we had disappointed him. This year, however, Leo was weakened from illness. His fierce blue eyes seemed faded, and he ate little.

Prediction: The younger members of the family may not get a lecture from Great-uncle Leo because he has been ill.

Problem-Solution Relationships, Analyzing

When you read about a *problem,* you are dealing with an unanswered question. A *solution* is an attempt to answer the question. Writers will usually discuss a problem and then offer one or more solutions. Think about the problem as you read by asking questions such as "What is the problem?", "Who has the problem?" and "Why is it a problem?" Consider the offered solutions by asking "What is the outcome of each proposed solution?" and "What is the final result of the solution?" (See also page 134.)

EXAMPLE The only way for most students at Langley High to get to school is to take the bus. There is only one bus, however, and if students miss it, they miss the day. The student council proposed adding another bus to the route or asking students old enough to drive to form a car pool for the stragglers. The principal explained that the solutions were expensive or unfair to other students and suggested instead that students call each other to make sure they got to the bus. Now there is less absenteeism due to missing the bus.

Analysis: *What is the problem?* Students who miss the bus have no way to get to school. *Who has the problem?* Students who miss the bus. *Why is it a problem?* Students who miss the bus miss school. *What is the outcome of each proposed solution?* The student council proposals were too expensive or unfair to students who could drive. The principal's idea seemed easy and effective. *What is the final result?* Students call each other and get to school on time.

Reading Log, Using a

A *reading log* is simply a place where you write about reading. As you read, write down your honest reactions to the text: Ask questions, make associations, and note especially important passages. You can also use a reading log to record any prereading predictions or postreading reflections. Because readers have different experiences, interests, beliefs, and opinions, no two reading logs will be alike.

Reading Rate, Adjusting

Your *reading rate* is the speed at which you read a text. How quickly or how slowly you read depends upon why you are reading—your purpose. Your reading rate also depends on your background and experience with the material and the text's difficulty. Adjusting your reading rate to suit your purpose helps you to read more efficiently.

Reading Rates According to Purpose		
Reading Rate	**Purpose**	**Example**
Scanning	Reading for specific details	Hunting for the scenes with the main character in them
Skimming	Reading for main points	Reviewing a textbook's chapter headings, subheadings, and illustrations in preparation for a test
Reading for mastery	Reading to understand and remember	Taking notes and outlining a section in a textbook before beginning an assignment
Reading for enjoyment	Reading at the speed you find most comfortable	Reading a magazine article about an interest or hobby

SQ3R *SQ3R* is a popular reading and study strategy. SQ3R stands for the five steps in the reading process:

S *Survey* the entire text. Look briefly at each page—the headings, titles, illustrations, charts, and the material in boldface and italics.

Q *Question* yourself as you do your survey. What should you know after completing your reading? Make a list of questions to be answered.

R *Read* the entire selection. Think of answers to your questions as you read.

R *Recite* in your own words answers to each question.

R *Review* the material by re-reading quickly, looking over the questions, and recalling the answers.

Stated Main Idea and Supporting Details, Identifying

A *main idea* is the focus or key idea in a piece of writing. Main ideas often appear as topic sentences of paragraphs or in an introductory or concluding paragraph of a longer work. *Supporting details* support or explain the main idea.

NOTE A stated main idea is also called an **explicit main idea. (See also Implied Main Idea, Identifying** on page 881.)

EXAMPLE Professional journalism as a career for women began as early as 1828, when Sarah Hale, a noted advocate of women's rights, published the first magazine created by and for women. Women writers often reported on fashion and domestic issues. However, some women reporters went beyond those topics and wrote headline stories, went undercover for assign-ments, corresponded from abroad, or set up their own newspapers and magazines.

Main idea: Professional journalism as a career for women began in the early nineteenth century.

Supporting details: Sarah Hale published the first magazine for women. Some women reporters moved beyond fashion and domestic issues to cover national and international news or to set up their own newspapers.

Summarizing

A *summary* is a short restatement of the main points of a selection. When you summarize, you try to present a complete picture using as few words as possible. To practice your summarizing skills, follow the tips in the chart below. Then, look at the following example and its summary.

How to Summarize

1. Review the material carefully. Identify the main ideas and supporting details.

2. Condense the material. Focus only on key ideas, removing unnecessary details, examples, or repetitions. Write a sentence in your own words about each main idea.

3. Use your list of sentences to write your summary in paragraph form. Add transitional words to show how the ideas are related, if necessary.

4. Revise your summary. Be sure that it covers the most important points, that the information is expressed clearly, and that your words remain faithful to the author's intent.

EXAMPLE A sonnet is a fourteen-line poem, usually written in iambic pentameter. The Petrarchan sonnet has two parts: an octave (the first eight lines) and a sestet (the remaining six lines). Often the octave raises a question that is answered by the sestet. The Shakespearean sonnet has three quatrains (groups of four lines) and a concluding couplet (two lines). Both forms also have traditional rhyme schemes.

Summary: A sonnet is a fourteen-line poem set in iambic pentameter. The type of sonnet depends on how the lines are arranged. The Petrarchan sonnet has an octave and a sestet, while the Shakespearean sonnet has three quatrains and a couplet. Both forms have their own rhyme schemes.

Text Structures, Analyzing   A *text structure* is the pattern a writer uses to organize ideas or events. Writers commonly use five major patterns of organization: *cause-effect, chronological order, comparison-contrast, listing,* and *problem-solution*. Being able to recognize the way people, things, events, and ideas are related will help you to better understand a text. Use the following guidelines in your analysis.

1. **Search the text for the main idea.** Look for clue words that signal a specific pattern of organization (See also **Clue Words, Using** on page 877).

2. **Study the text for other important ideas.** Think about how the ideas connect, and look for an obvious pattern.

3. **Remember that a writer might use one organizational pattern throughout an entire text or might combine patterns.**

4. **Use a graphic organizer to map the relationships among the ideas.** The four common text structures, or organizational patterns, are illustrated below.

   ■ *Cause-effect pattern* shows the relationship between results and the ideas or events that made the results happen. (See also page 95.) The example in the next column shows the effects of low body temperature during surgery.

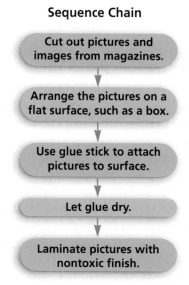

Causal Chain

Low body temperature during surgery

→ Reduced blood flow carrying oxygen

→ Inhibited immune system

→ Increased chance of infection

→ Prolonged hospital stays

→ Increased medical costs

■ *Chronological order* shows events or ideas happening in sequence. The following example shows the sequence for making a decoupage project.

Sequence Chain

Cut out pictures and images from magazines.

↓ Arrange the pictures on a flat surface, such as a box.

↓ Use glue stick to attach pictures to surface.

↓ Let glue dry.

↓ Laminate pictures with nontoxic finish.

■ *Comparison-Contrast pattern* points out similarities and differences in two or more topics. (See also page 62.) The following example compares two eighteenth-century African American women writers, Phillis Wheatley and Jarena Lee.

Phillis Wheatley   Similarities   Jarena Lee

(1753?–1784)   **(1783–?)**

- Born into slavery
- Pursued vocation as poet
- Published poetry

- First African American women writers to publish in United States
- Avid readers of the Bible

- Born a free woman
- Pursued vocation as preacher
- Published auto-biography

- *Listing pattern* presents material according to certain criteria such as size or importance. The following example lists the levels of a food chain.

List

1. Producers (Green plants that make food from sunlight)

2. Primary consumers (Plant eaters)

3. Secondary consumers (Carnivores that eat plant eaters and other carnivores)

4. Decomposers (Bacteria and fungi that decompose dead organisms)

- *Problem-Solution pattern* presents a problem and explains attempted solutions, their outcomes, and the final or end result. (See also **Problem-Solution Relationships, Analyzing** on page 883.) The following example illustrates the problem of stage fright for an inexperienced performer and lists solutions. The chart shows the ques-

tions asked about the problem, the analysis of the proposed solutions and their outcomes, and the final result.

Problem

What is the problem? A performer experiences extreme nervousness, or stage fright, before going on stage.

Who has the problem? Inexperienced performers suffer from stage fright before a performance.

Why is it a problem? The thought of performing in front of people seriously frightens the performer.

Proposed Solutions

- Deep breathing
- Stretching tense neck muscles
- Making positive statements

Outcomes

- Deep breathing can help the performer.
- Stretching tense neck muscles can relax the performer.
- Making positive statements, such as *I am calm* or *I am prepared,* can boost the performer's confidence.

Results

The combined solutions of deep breathing, muscle relaxation, and positive statements can help combat stage fright.

Transitional Words and Phrases, Using   *Transitions* are used by writers to connect ideas and create coherence. Recognizing transitions will help you to understand how the ideas in a selection fit together. (See also **Clue Words** on page 877.)

Vocabulary

Context Clues   Frequently, you may be able to figure out the meaning of an unfamiliar word by examining its *context,* or the group of words or sentences surrounding the unfamiliar word. Determining the meaning of new words in this way is called using *context clues.* The following chart shows examples of some of the common types of context clues. (See also pages 64, 136, and 304.)

How to Use Context Clues

Antonyms: Look for clues indicating that an unfamiliar word is opposite in meaning to a familiar word or phrase.

*After the **erratic** results of the first test, a second test was ordered in which the patient's heartbeat appeared to be regular and normal.*

Cause and Effect: Look for clues indicating that an unfamiliar word is related to the cause or is the result of an action, feeling, or idea.

*Because of Lara's **affinity** for animals, she will make an excellent veterinarian.*

Comparisons: Sometimes an unknown word may be compared with a more familiar word.

*The expression "Just say 'No'" is so overused that it has become a **cliché.***

Contrasts: An unfamiliar word may sometimes be contrasted with a more familiar word.

*The team's uniforms were **immaculate** before the game, but by the end of the first inning, they were filthy.*

Definition and Restatements: Look for words that define the term or restate it in other words.

*The **rift,** or break, between the two sisters had upset the entire family.*

Examples: Look for examples used in context that reveal the meaning of an unfamiliar word.

*The scientist was accused of several acts of **espionage,** including photographing secret documents and taping private conversations.*

Synonyms: Look for familiar words that may be synonyms for unfamiliar words.

*The club's **coffers** were so low that the members had to raise new funds in order to buy new uniforms.*

Word Bank   One method of increasing your vocabulary is to make a habit of collecting words in a *word bank,* a list of words gathered from your reading, listening, and viewing. Consult your dictionary for the definition of each new word. You may want to compile your personal word bank in a notebook or on a computer file.

Word Formations   Many English words are made up of word parts that come from other languages or that have been inherited from earlier forms of English. A complete word, one that can stand independently, is called a *base word,* or *root.* Word parts, such as prefixes and suffixes, may be added to base words to form new words. Look at the examples in the chart on the next page. They show how word parts can be combined with base words to create new words. (See also **Word Parts** on page 891.)

Word Formations

Prefix	Base Word	Suffix	New Word
dis–	continue	–ous	discontinuous
in–	compare	–able	incomparable
mis–	judge	–ment	misjudgment

Word Meanings   Words have many layers of meanings. Their meanings can change depending on the time, the place, and the situation in which they are used. Whether you are speaking or writing, it is very important that the words you choose match your purpose. Most words in the English language have a number of different meanings. Use the following definitions and examples to help you choose words that say what you want them to say.

■ **Analogies**   *Analogies* provide a special type of context in which you are asked to analyze the relationship between two words and then identify another pair of words with that same relationship. Analogy questions usually appear on standardized tests in multiple-choice form because they measure your knowledge of vocabulary as well as your ability to identify relationships and patterns among words.

EXAMPLE
1. SOUR : VINEGAR : __B__
A. sugar : sweet   C. loyal : faithful
B. hot : fire   D. chef : cooking

■ **Clichés**   A *cliché* is a tired expression whose overuse has made its message weak and boring. Some clichés began as vivid expressions or figurative language, but then became trite and lifeless.

EXAMPLES   blanket of snow, easier said than done, butterflies in my stomach, fit for a king, the long arm of the law, the dog ate my homework

■ **Colloquialisms**   *Colloquialisms* are words and phrases characteristic of conversational language. In fact, *colloquial* derives from a Latin word meaning "conversation." Used appropriately and sparingly, colloquialisms can give your informal writing and speaking a lively, personal tone. Avoid colloquialisms in formal writing and speaking.

Informal: What's going on?
Formal: How are you today?

■ **Denotation and connotation**   The *denotation* of a word is its literal meaning, or the definition given in a dictionary. The *connotation* includes the emotional ideas and feelings that people may connect to the word. Because connotations often stir people's feelings, they can have powerful effects on the listener or reader.

EXAMPLE   The words *persistence* and *stubbornness* have similar denotations, "the quality of not relenting, or continuing even in the face of opposition." Their connotations suggest different ideas, however. *Persistence* has a positive connotation of following a task through to the very end. *Stubbornness* has a negative connotation of being unreasonable or unwilling to listen to others.

■ **Euphemisms**   A *euphemism* is an indirect, agreeable term that is substituted for a more direct, less appealing one. Some euphemisms are used as a courtesy to avoid offending people; others, however, are used to mislead people—to hide unpleasant truths or misrepresent the facts.

Euphemism	More Direct Term
memorial park	cemetery
facilities	restrooms
previously owned	used
passed on	died

■ **Figurative language** *Figurative language* goes beyond the literal meaning of the words to create a special effect or feeling. The following chart shows the most common types of figurative language.

Type of Figurative Language	Example
A **metaphor** says that something *is* something else.	*The sun is a giant glowing ball.*
Personification gives human characteristics to nonhuman things.	*The cold drink of water offered in friendship spoke volumes to the tired, thirsty traveler.*
A **simile** compares two basically unlike things, using the words *like* or *as*.	*Her mouth snapped shut like a purse.*

■ **Idioms** *Idioms* are conversational phrases that mean something different from the literal meanings of the words they contain. Idioms often cannot be explained grammatically, and they make no sense if translated word-for-word into another language.

EXAMPLES

I did not want to go to the museum, but Shelly *talked me into it*.

Nora will be late because she couldn't *get out of* choir practice.

I asked her, *"What's up with that?"*

■ **Jargon** *Jargon* is a special language used by people in a particular profession, occupation, hobby, or field of study. Jargon is effective only if the reader or listener is familiar with its special meaning. Note in the following example how the single word *set* can mean different things to different groups.

EXAMPLE **Set**

Theater and film—the scenery of a production
Library—a complete series of a book or periodical
Mathematics—a collection of distinct elements, such as negative integers
Surfing—a group of waves (usually three)

■ **Loaded words** Words that have very strong connotations, either positive or negative, are said to be *loaded words*. Loaded words appeal to our emotions. They may influence us positively or negatively because of the feelings they arouse.

EXAMPLES

The diner serves *cheap, greasy food*.
The diner serves *inexpensive, home-style* food.
The *mob* of protesters *shouted their demands*.
The *group* of protesters *made their opinions heard*.

■ **Multiple meanings** Many English words have more than one meaning and may function as more than one part of speech. When using a dictionary to find a word's meaning, look at all the definitions given. Keep in mind the context in which you read or heard the word. Then, try the various definitions in that context until you find the one that fits.

EXAMPLE

When I asked Melba about her plans, she replied with a *blank* stare. [The third definition below best fits the meaning of *blank* in this context.]

blank (blank) *adj.* **1.** not covered by writing, print, or other markings **2.** not filled in **3.** expressionless **4.** lacking or unproductive

■ **Nonsexist language**   *Nonsexist language* is language that applies to people in general, both male and female. For many years it was acceptable practice to use English gender-specific terms, such as *man* or *mankind,* to describe groups that included both men and women. In recent years, writers have begun to use nonsexist terms instead, using, for example, *humanity* and *humankind* in place of the gender-specific *mankind.* In addition, many occupations that once were limited only to men or only to women are now open to both. As a result, many job titles have been adjusted to reflect the change. Below are some widely used nonsexist terms that you may use to replace older, gender-specific ones.

Gender-specific Terms	Nonsexist Terms
chairman	chairperson (or chair)
deliveryman	delivery person
fireman	firefighter
mailman	mail carrier
man-made	synthetic
policeman	police officer
salesman	sales representative
steward, stewardess	flight attendant
watchman	security guard

■ **Slang**   *Slang* is highly informal language. It consists of made-up words or of old words used in new ways. Slang is usually lively and colorful, and it can make the user seem up-to-date. Slang words are often a special vocabulary for close-knit groups such as students, musicians, and surfers. For example, in the 1980s the word *tubular* was surfer's slang for "pleasing, fine." Like *tubular,* most slang words have a short life.

■ **Synonyms**   *Synonyms* are words that have the same or nearly the same meaning. However, synonyms often have subtly different meanings. Use a dictionary or thesaurus to make sure that you understand the exact differences in meaning between synonyms. Often the difference between two synonyms is a matter of connotation. In the following sentences, it is clear that *stared* and *gazed* are synonyms for *looked,* but while *looked* is a general verb, *stared* and *gazed* describe specific ways of looking. (See also **Denotation and connotation** on page 888.)

EXAMPLES
The child on the bus *looked* at the bus driver.
The child on the bus *stared* at the bus driver.
[*Stared* suggests the child finds the bus driver's appearance startling or unusual.]
The child on the bus *gazed* at the bus driver.
[*Gazed* suggests the child finds the bus driver's appearance appealing or interesting.]

■ **Tired words**   A *tired word* is a word that once was clear and forceful but has now become vague and weak. The word has been used so often and so carelessly that it has become worn-out and almost meaningless.

EXAMPLES   *nice, fine, pretty, wonderful, terrific, great*

Word Origins   The *origin* of a word is the way it came into existence in a language. The origin and history of a word—its etymology—often appear in brackets along with its dictionary definition. The following etymology indicates that the origin of the word *eleven* is Middle English (ME) from Old English (OE).

EXAMPLE   eleven [ME *elleven* < OE *endleofan*]

Word Parts English words are made up of units called *word parts.* The three types of word parts are *roots, prefixes,* and *suffixes.* Knowing the meanings of roots, prefixes, and suffixes can help you determine the meanings of many unfamiliar words.

■ **Roots** The main part of a word is called the *root,* or *base word.* The root carries the word's basic meaning. Other word parts can be added to a root to create many different words. For example, the root –*port*– means "to carry." This root can be combined with other word parts to make new words, such as *portable, transportation,* or *import.* This root and many others come from Latin and ancient Greek.

Commonly Used Roots		
Root	**Meaning**	**Example**
Greek		
–anthrop–	human	anthropology, misanthrope
–chrono–	time	chronology, chronometer
–cycl–	circle	cyclone, bicycle
–dem–	people	democracy, demography
–graph–	write, writing	autograph, biography
–hydr–	water	hydrant, hydrate
–log–, –logy–	study, word	biology, monologue
–morph–	form	metamorphosis, polymorph
–phon–	sound	phonograph, symphony
Latin		
–cis–	cut	decision, concise
–cred–	believe	incredible, discredit
–dic–, –dict–	say, speak	dictate, predict
–fac–, –fact–, –fec–, –fic–	do, make	deface, manufacture, defective, efficient
–fid–	belief, faith	confident, fidelity
–frag–, –fract–	break	fragment, fracture
–ject–	throw	eject, trajectory
–junct–	join	conjunction, juncture
–magn–	large, grand	magnate, magnificent
–mal–	bad	malice, dismal
–mit–, –miss–	send	missionary, transmit
–ped–	foot	biped, pedestrian
–pend–, –pens–	hang, weigh	pendant, pensive
–pon–, –pos–	place, put	exponent, position

(continued)

Commonly Used Roots		
Root	**Meaning**	**Example**
–scrib–, –script–	write	inscribe, postscript
–solv–	loosen, accomplish	solvent, resolve
–ven–, –vent–	come	convention, prevent
-vers–, –vert–	turn	reverse, convertible
–voc–, –vok–	call	vocal, provoke
–volv–	roll, turn around	revolve, evolve

■ **Prefixes**   A *prefix* is a word part that is added before a root or base word. The word that is created from a prefix and a root combines the meanings of both its parts. Prefixes come from other languages and other forms of English.

Commonly Used Prefixes		
Prefixes	**Meanings**	**Examples**
Greek		
anti–	against, opposing	antimissile, antisocial
hyper–	over, above, excessive	hyperactive, hyperventilate
mon–, mono–	one	monarch, monologue
para–	beside, beyond	parallel, paralegal
psych–, psycho–	mind	psychiatry, psychology
Latin and French		
contra–	against	contradict, contravene
de–	away, from, off, down	deflect, defrost
dif–, dis–	away, not, opposing	differ, disappoint
e–, ef–, ex–	away from, out	emigrate, efface, extract
il–, im–, in–, ir–	not in	illogical, impolite, incite, irrational
post–	after, following	postpaid, postwar
pre–	before	prejudge, preview
pro–	forward, favoring	proceed, pro-American
re–	back, backward, again	return, reflect, reforest
Old English		
be–	around, about	beset, behind
mis–	badly, not, wrongly	misbehave, misfire, mispronounce
un–	not, reverse of	unhappy, unlock

■ **Suffixes** A *suffix* is a word part that is added at the end of a base or root word. Often, adding a suffix changes both a word's part of speech and its meaning. The following suffixes are primarily those that change a root word's part of speech and meaning.

Commonly Used Suffixes		
Suffixes	**Meanings**	**Examples**
Greek, Latin, and French		
Nouns		
–ance, –ence	act, condition	forbearance, excellence
–cy	state, condition	accuracy, normalcy
–er, –or	doer, actor	singer, conductor
–ion	action, result, state	union, fusion, confusion
–ism	act, doctrine, manner	baptism, patriotism, barbarism
–tude	quality, state	fortitude, magnitude
–ty, –y	quality, state, action	novelty, enmity, jealousy
Adjectives		
–able, –ible	able, likely	washable, divisible
–ate	having, characteristic of	desolate, collegiate
–ive	tending to, given to	reflective, pensive
–ous	marked by, full of	glorious, nervous
–ulent	full of, characterized by	turbulent, fraudulent
Adjectives or Nouns		
–al	doer, pertaining to	rival, autumnal
–ary	belonging to, one connected with	primary, adversary, auxiliary
–ent	doing, actor	confident, adherent
–ic	dealing with, caused by, person or thing showing	classic, choleric, workaholic
–ite	native, product, formed	Hittite, vulcanite, favorite
Verbs		
–ate	become, cause	animate, sublimate
–esce	become, grow, continue	convalesce, acquiesce
–ize	cause to be, subject to	jeopardize, oxidize
Old English		
Nouns		
–dom	state, rank, condition	kingdom, wisdom
–hood	state, condition	statehood, falsehood
–ness	quality, state	kindness, tenderness

(continued)

Commonly Used Suffixes

Suffixes	Meanings	Examples
Adjectives or Adverbs		
–ly	like, characteristic of	yearly, positively
–ward	in the direction of	downward, outward
Verbs		
–en	cause to be	blacken, weaken

Words to Learn The three hundred words in the list below may be used as the basis of your vocabulary study this year. Make it a habit to study unfamiliar words from this list regularly.

abdicate
abound
acquittal
admirably
aesthetic
affidavit
affiliate
amiable
amnesty
analogy
annihilate
antiquity
apex
appease
apprehensive
aptitude
arbiter
archaic
assert
astute
atrocious
aura
autonomy
axiom

balmy
bayou
bedlam
beguile
besiege

bestride
bias
botch
bourgeois
breach
buffet

callous
canine
cant
carp
casement
caustic
censure
charisma
clangor
clemency
cliché
clientele
closure
coffer
coincidental
colloquial
commence
commendable
compassion
compatible
compliance
composure
conceive

concession
condescend
condole
conducive
consolidate
constituent
contemptuous
contend
convene
crony
curtail

daunt
debase
debut
decimate
decrepit
defunct
delectable
demure
destitute
deteriorate
detonate
devastation
diminutive
discern
disconcerting
dissent
diversion
documentary

edifice
edify
effervescent
eject

electorate
elite
emancipate
emphatically
encompass
encumber
enjoin
ensue
episode
equilibrium
erratic
espionage
ethical
evade
evolve
exalted
excerpt
expedient
explicate
exultant

fabricate
facilitate
facsimile
farce
flagrant
fluctuate
fortitude

gloat
grimace

heresy
hieroglyphic
hors d'oeuvre

immaculate
impartial
impediment
implacable
imposition
inaccessible
inadvertent
inalienable
inanimate
inarticulate
incendiary
incentive
inclement
inconsistent
indestructible
indict
indifferent
indignant
indomitable
ineffectual
infallible
influx
inhibition
innate
innovation
insipid
insolence
intermittent
intuition
invariably
invincible
irksome
irrational
irrelevant
itinerary

jargon
jostle
judicious
juncture

lament
lapse
latitude
legacy
lexicon
livid

loathe

malignant
malleable
mandatory
mannerism
martial
meager
mediocre
melancholy
melodramatic
mentor
meticulous
militant
moderation
momentum
mortify
mosque
mull
mutable
mystic

naive
negligible
notoriety

obligatory
obliterate
oblivious
odious
opportune
ornate
ossify

pacifist
painstaking
palatable
pallid
paradox
paraphrase
parody
pastoral
patent
paternal
patriarch
pauper
perceive
perception

perseverance
personification
pertinent
pivotal
plausible
pompous
portly
posthumous
postulate
precarious
prelude
pretext
prevalent
prolific
prone
prophetic
protocol
protrude
proximity
purge

qualm
quantitative
quibble

rankle
ravage
reactionary
rebuke
recipient
recourse
rectify
recur
redundant
rejuvenate
reminiscent
rendezvous
repress
reprieve
requiem
requisite
resonant
retainer
retribution
rift
rivulet

sardonic
scenario
sequel
simulate
sordid
sporadic
stamina
steppe
stimulant
stipulate
stratagem
stringent
submission
subsidiary
subsidize
substantially
succulent
succumb
synopsis
synthesis

tawny
theoretical
throng
timorous
transcend
transition
transitory
translucent

ultimatum
unprecedented

vehement
verbatim
vibrant
vigilant
visage
vulnerable

wan
wane
wheedle
whimsical
wreak

zealous
zenith
zephyr

Speaking and Listening

Speaking

Casual conversations with family and friends account for most of your speaking. At times, however, you will be required to speak in situations that are not so casual. **Conventions of oral language** are those generally agreed-upon rules and regulations covering the grammar, vocabulary, and style of oral communication, and based upon the audience, occasion, purpose, and task of the communication. For example, the word choice and style of speech used in informal conversations between peers would not be the same as that used for job interviews or formal speeches. No matter what the occasion, you can use certain strategies and techniques to become a better speaker.

Debate

In a formal *debate* two teams (or sides) engage in a systematic discussion of a *proposition,* the issue being debated. The team that argues against the proposition is the *negative* team. The team that argues for the proposition is the *affirmative* team.

Features of a Debate   All debate formats share certain features.

- **Debate Proposition**   The proposition, or issue of the debate, is stated as a resolution and limited to a specific idea. The proposition should be debatable; that is, it should give the affirmative and negative sides the opportunity to build a reasonable case. For example, a debatable proposition is "Resolved: That four years of a foreign language be required for graduation from public high schools."

- **Debate Etiquette**   Debaters are required to show proper etiquette and good manners, and avoid ridicule, sarcasm, and personal attacks. A debate should be won or lost only on the basis of a well-prepared case delivered convincingly. Referring to participants in a debate with polite terms such as "the first affirmative speaker," "my worthy opponent," or "my teammates," is customary.

- **Debate Officials**   Often a chairperson decides on questions of debate rules raised by either side. Usually three appointed judges determine the winner of a debate, but the winning team is sometimes decided by a vote of the audience.

Formats of Debate   In the first part of most debates, both sides build their cases with constructive speeches. The affirmative side argues for the proposition and against anticipated arguments of the negative side. The negative side does just the opposite. The two sides take a break before making **rebuttal speeches,** in which they respond to the most effective arguments of the opposition. Debaters are given specific time limits for each speech. These time limits vary according to the debate format.

■ **Traditional or Formal Debate**   In this format, two teams of two speakers each debate. Each member of the affirmative and negative teams speaks twice. Each speech must be completed within a set time limit.

■ **Cross-examination Debate**   In this format, two members of each team can question their opponents. During cross-examination, speakers clarify issues and try to bring out the weaknesses in their opponents' case.

■ **Lincoln-Douglas Debate**   This type of debate commemorates the famous debates between Abraham Lincoln and Stephen A. Douglas, candidates for senator from Illinois in 1858. This format pits one affirmative speaker against one negative speaker.

Preparing for Debate   Effective debaters prepare their cases carefully by researching their sides of the debate proposition thoroughly. To prepare for a debate, you first identify the **issues,** or main differences between your position and the position of the opposing team. Then, you organize support for your arguments by gathering examples, expert testimony, statistics, and logical reasons. Your arguments and supporting evidence are put into a **brief,** or outline of your team's position in the debate. Next, you prepare to **refute,** or disprove, the argu-

ments of your opponents with logical reasons, facts, statistics, and the like. Last, you prepare for **rebuttal,** rebuilding your case by answering the points your opponents made in refuting your arguments; in addition, you anticipate weaknesses your opponents might find in your case.

Formal Speaking Occasions

Formal speaking is done at a specific time and for a specific reason. There are steps you can take to prepare for every formal speaking occasion.

Formal Speeches   Formal speeches require thoughtful preparation. The process of preparing a formal speech is similar to the process of writing a paper. To prepare a formal speech, follow the steps explained below.

1. **Identify purpose and task**   Your general purpose is the overall reason you have for giving the speech. The most common purposes of a speech are to inform and to persuade. Common purposes for giving speeches are described in the chart on page 898.

2. **Select a topic**   If you may choose the topic of your speech, be sure to select one that you find interesting. It will be difficult to interest your audience in your topic if you are not interested in it yourself. As you select a topic, keep the following questions in mind.

   ■ **What is the occasion of your speech?** What task prompts you to speak? For example, have you been asked to speak on behalf of your friend's candidacy for class treasurer? Your topic should fit the occasion.

   ■ **How much time will you have to deliver your speech?** Limit the scope of your speech to fit the time you are given.

General Types of Speeches

General Purpose for Speech	Purpose	Examples
Informative Speech	To present new information to an audience or to provide a new view of old information	• Lecture • News broadcast • Orientation • Instruction
Persuasive Speech	To change an attitude or belief or to move an audience to action	• Campaign speech • Advertisement • Debate
Special Occasion Speech	To entertain or amuse an audience or to acknowledge a special reason for the audience's presence	• After-dinner speech • Anecdote • Oral interpretation of a piece of literature • Campaign speech for student council • Speech honoring a retiring teacher

3. **Analyze the audience** After selecting a topic, consider how you can appeal to your audience's needs or interests. Use the following questions for adapting material to a particular audience.

- *Are the people in your audience mostly younger or older than you?* For a younger audience, use simple language, age-specific examples, and clear explanations. For an older audience, adopt a respectful tone, avoid slang, and use general examples an adult audience will understand.

- *What does the audience already know about the topic?* Provide enough background information for your audience to understand your speech. If you feel your audience will have some knowledge of your topic, provide an appropriate amount of background information. For the audience that knows a good deal, provide an advanced discussion that focuses on interesting issues or aspects of the topic.

- *How interested will the audience be in your topic?* The degree of the audience's interest in your topic should influence the content of your speech. An uninterested audience needs to be convinced that the topic is worthwhile. An interested audience needs to hear information that will justify and maintain its interest.

4. **Gather material and organize content** The next step in preparing a speech is to research the topic you have selected. Your school or community library can be a valuable resource in conducting your research. (See also **Library/ Media Center** on page 866 and the **How to Take Study Notes** chart on page 912.)

5. **Write the speech** The structure, language, and techniques you use to involve your audi-

ence in your topic are the three main factors to consider when you write your speech. The chart below gives guidelines for each of the basic features of a formal speech.

Features of a Formal Speech

Structure

The speech should be composed of three parts:

- an *introduction* with a thesis statement or main idea
- a *body*
- a *conclusion*

Language

The language you use should be appropriate for your audience. Keep in mind the following points.

- Use formal, standard English.
- Use technical terms sparingly and be sure to define them.
- Avoid slang, jargon, and euphemisms in your speech.

Audience Involvement

It is important to remember that written English sounds different when it is delivered orally. Make your speech more "listener-friendly" by doing the following.

- Use personal pronouns. For example, say "you may think" or "we believe" instead of "one may think" or "people believe."
- Ask rhetorical questions instead of making statements. For example, instead of telling the audience a fact or statistic, ask them "Did you know that . . . ?"

---

6. **Determine method of delivery** Now you need to decide how you will deliver your speech. There are several methods, each of which has advantages and disadvantages.

- The *manuscript speech* is read word-for-word from your written manuscript. This method allows little chance for omissions and mistakes, but it does not permit you to respond to audience feedback and often sounds dull and lifeless.

- The *memorized speech* is memorized word-for-word from your written manuscript. This method does give you the freedom to move around and to maintain eye contact with the audience, but it may sound stiff and unnatural. With this method, you also run the risk of forgetting parts of the speech.

- The *extemporaneous speech* is carefully outlined and rehearsed but not memorized. You can use notes to help you stay organized. This method sounds natural and allows you to respond to the audience, but requires much rehearsal time.

The extemporaneous speech is the most common type of speech. When you organize your materials for an extemporaneous speech, first write a complete outline. Then, prepare note cards to refer to as you present your speech.

Guidelines for Extemporaneous Speech Note Cards

1. Put only one key idea, possibly accompanied by a brief example or detail, on each card.

2. Make a special note card for material that you plan to read word-for-word, such as a quotation, a series of dates, or a list of statistics.

3. Make a special note card to indicate when you should pause to show a visual, such as a chart, diagram, graph, picture, or model.

4. Number your completed cards to keep them in order.

7. Rehearse the speech You will be a more effective speaker if you rehearse your speech beforehand, including your use of *nonverbal* and *verbal signals.* You use these signals whenever you speak, but they stand out very clearly when you are making a formal speech to a live audience.

- *Nonverbal Signals* You can communicate effectively with nonverbal signals like those described in the following chart.

Communicating with Nonverbal Signals

Nonverbal Signals	Tips and Effects
Eye contact	▪ Look directly into the eyes of as many members of the audience as you can. Eye contact communicates honesty and sincerity. It makes the audience feel as if you are speaking *with* them rather than *to* them.
Facial expression	▪ Facial expressions—smiling, frowning, raising an eyebrow, and so on—can reveal your feelings and add to or even take the place of a verbal message.
Gesture	▪ Making relaxed and natural gestures with your head, hands, or arms as you speak emphasizes verbal messages. Nodding the head for "yes" or shaking it for "no" or pointing with the index finger can effectively punctuate your speech.
Posture	▪ Stand up straight and look alert to communicate an air of confidence to your audience.

- *Verbal Signals* The expressiveness of your voice is a major factor in the effectiveness of your speech. The following verbal signals will help you communicate your message to an audience.

Communicating with Verbal Signals

Verbal Signals	Tips
Diction (the clarity of your pronunciation)	▪ Always speak clearly so that your listeners can understand you.
Emphasis (the stress put on a word or phrase)	▪ Emphasize key ideas or points in your speech by saying those words a little more loudly.
Pause (small silences in your speech)	▪ Use pauses to help listeners catch up or to suggest that what you have said or are about to say is important.
Pitch (how your voice sounds)	▪ When speakers are nervous, the pitch in their voices tends to become higher. Take a deep breath and relax before you speak to keep your voice's pitch at its most natural.
Rate (the speed with which you talk)	▪ Normal speed is about 120 to 160 words per minute. When delivering a speech, speak at a slower rate.
Volume (the level of sound you create)	▪ When giving a speech, speak more loudly than usual. Be sure to ask listeners if they can hear you before you begin your speech.

8. **Deliver the speech** No matter how much you have practiced your speech, you face a challenge when you stand in front of your audience. If you are like most people, you will be nervous. Here are some tips for overcoming your nerves and delivering an effective speech.

- *Be prepared.* Avoid excessive nervousness by organizing and being familiar with your speech notes and any audiovisual devices you plan to use.

- *Practice your speech.* Rehearse as if you are actually delivering your speech.

- *Focus on your purpose for speaking.* Think about what you want your listeners to do, believe, or feel as a result of your speech.

- *Pay attention to audience feedback.* Audiences send messages to speakers. Pay attention to them. Are people in the audience alert or are they yawning? Are they shaking their heads in disagreement or nodding in agreement? Depending upon the feedback you receive from the audience, you might need to adjust your pace, use more gestures, or speak more loudly.

9. **Use audiovisual devices (if appropriate).** You might want to use audiovisual devices to clarify or enhance your presentation by making it a multimedia presentation. Following are several types of audiovisual devices often used in multimedia presentations.

- audio recordings (such as cassettes or compact discs)

- images, audio files, and text stored and presented on a computer

- videotapes or videodiscs

- short films

- slides or filmstrips

- graphics such as charts, graphs, illustrations, diagrams

Use the following questions to determine if your presentation will benefit from the use of audiovisual devices.

- *Will audiovisual devices help you clarify a point?* Some ideas are easily explained verbally, but others need a visual to help clarify them. In those cases, using a chart or a poster will save you time and keep the audience on track.

- *Will the audiovisual devices help the audience remember a point?* Not every point in your speech is equally important. Decide which points will benefit from the emphasis given by an audiovisual.

- *Will the audiovisuals or multimedia distract the audience while you are speaking?* Make sure that the audiovisual devices are essential to your talk and can be displayed without taking the audience's attention away from what you are saying.

NOTE Make certain your audience can see or hear the audiovisual device you have chosen. Audio materials should be cued up and ready to play. Visuals should be large and clear enough to be seen from the back of the audience. (See also **Graphics** on page 855.)

Group Discussion *Formal group discussions* take place when clubs, organizations, and other groups meet on a regular basis to discuss important issues. Formal groups often follow an established set of rules known as *parliamentary procedure.* The basic principles of parliamentary procedure, listed below, protect the rights of the individual members of the group while providing a system for dealing with issues that come before the group.

- The majority decides.

- The minority has the right to be heard.

- Decisions are made by voting.
- Only one issue is decided at a time.
- Everyone is assured of the chance to be heard and has the right to vote.
- All votes are counted as equal.
- All sides of an issue are debated in open discussion.

A good source for information about parliamentary procedure is *Robert's Rules of Order, Newly Revised,* by Henry Robert. According to *Robert's Rules,* formal meetings should follow the procedure set forth in the following chart.

Order of Business

A formal meeting usually follows the standard order of business suggested in *Robert's Rules of Order:*

1. Call to order: The chairperson says, "The meeting will come to order."

2. Reading and approval of the minutes: The chairperson says, "The secretary (or recorder) will read the minutes from our previous meeting." The secretary reads the minutes, and the chairperson inquires, "Are there any additions or corrections to the minutes?" The minutes are then approved, or they are corrected and then approved.

3. Officers' reports: The chairperson calls for a report from other officers who need to report by saying, for example, "Will the treasurer please give us a report?"

4. Committee reports: The chairperson may ask the presiding officers of standing committees to make reports to the group.

5. Old business: Any issues that have not been fully resolved at the last meeting may now be discussed. The chairperson may ask the group, "Is there any old business to be discussed?"

6. New business: Any new issues that have not been previously discussed may now be addressed.

7. Announcements: The chairperson may ask the members, "Are there any announcements?"

8. Adjournment: The chairperson ends the meeting by saying, "The meeting is now adjourned."

Interviewing *Interviews* are communication situations in which one person, the *interviewer,* gathers ideas or information from another person, the *interviewee.* You may need to be an interviewer when you want to obtain firsthand information from people for a research project or report. When a potential employer questions you about your personal habits and work skills, you become the interviewee.

- **Conducting an Interview** Successful interviews require careful planning. The following chart provides useful suggestions for planning and conducting an interview.

Conducting an Interview

Preparing for the Interview
- Identify the person you want to interview. Select a reliable source—someone who is knowledgeable about your subject and who can be depended upon to give accurate information.
- Make arrangements well in advance. Set up a time that is convenient for the other person to meet with you.
- Gather background information about your subject, and about the person you will be interviewing. Then, make a list of questions to ask. Make sure the questions are arranged in a logical order and require more than yes or no answers.

Participating in the Interview
- Arrive on time, and be polite and patient.
- Ask the other person's permission to take notes or use a tape recorder.

Conducting an Interview

- Avoid argument. Be tactful and courteous. Remember that the interview was granted at your request.
- Be aware of your nonverbal communication—your facial expressions and your gestures. Keep good eye contact and nod to show understanding.
- Listen carefully, and ask follow-up questions if you do not understand an answer or if you think you need more information.

Following up on the Interview

- Review your notes to refresh your memory, and then make a summary of the material you have gathered.
- Send a note expressing your appreciation for the interview.

■ **Interviewing for a Job** Most people approach a job interview with a certain amount of nervousness. Such nervousness is understandable because most people do not often practice their interviewing skills before they need them. Being thoroughly prepared to be interviewed, however, can help relieve some of the anxiety. The suggestions in the following chart can help you prepare to be a successful interviewee.

NOTE The more you know about the company or job before you interview, the more confident you will feel. Your knowledge will also impress the interviewer with your interest, initiative, and responsibility. Do research in the library as part of your preparation for the interview.

How to Interview for a Position

1. Arrange an appointment. Write a business letter of application in which you request an interview for the job. If you are granted an interview, be prompt for your appointment.

2. Bring a résumé. If you have not already submitted a résumé, take one to the interview and give it to the interviewer. (See also **Résumé** on page 957.)

3. Be neat and well-groomed. It is important to look your best when you are interviewing to apply for any type of job.

4. Answer questions clearly and honestly. Answer the questions the interviewer asks, adding any additional information that might inform the employer that you are the right person for the job.

5. Ask questions. Questions that job applicants usually ask include requests for information about work hours, salary, or chances for advancement. By your questions, you show that you are interested in the company or business.

6. Be prepared to be tested. The employer may require you to take tests that demonstrate your skills, intelligence, or personality.

7. Follow up the interview. After the interview, write a short thank-you note. Tell the interviewer that you appreciated the opportunity for the interview and that you look forward to hearing from the company in the near future.

Informal Speaking Situations		
Situation	Purpose	Preparation and Presentation
Directions	To explain how to get to a particular place (Informational situation)	• Choose easiest route. • Divide the route into logical steps. • Use terms that are accurate or visual. If necessary, draw a map. • Repeat any steps if necessary.
Impromptu Speech	To speak for five minutes on a particular topic without any previous preparation (Informational situation)	• If you must choose the topic, think of one that is appropriate for your audience. • Think of a main idea, an attention-getting beginning, and some supporting ideas. • Speak clearly and in a confident voice. • Use a tone that is appropriate to the topic.
Instructions	To give information on how to do a particular task (Informational situation)	• Divide the information into clear, logical steps. • Give the steps in order. • Make sure your listener understands your instructions.

Introductions	To introduce yourself or another person to a person or group (Social situation)	• Take the initiative and introduce yourself if no one else does.
		• When introducing another person, identify the person by name.
		• When introducing another person, it is customary to address first
		  • a person of higher status
		  • an older person before a younger one
		  • the person you know better

Telephone Conversations	To communicate via telephone (Social situation)	• Call people at appropriate times of day. • Identify yourself and state the reason for your call. • Be polite and patient. • Keep your call to an appropriate length.

Informal Speaking Occasions

Informal speaking occasions are more personal and casual than formal occasions. Informal speaking situations tend to be either informative or social in nature. The chart above describes some common informal speaking situations.

Informal Group Discussion *Informal group discussions* usually involve a small number of people discussing items of interest to the group as a whole. The following section explains two elements of group discussion.

■ **Identifying a Purpose** Most group discussions have an announced specific purpose or goal. The following are typical purposes for group discussion.

Purposes for Discussion

- to brainstorm ideas
- to learn cooperatively
- to make a decision, evaluation, or recommendation
- to make plans
- to negotiate agreements
- to resolve conflicts
- to solve a problem

- **Participating in Discussion** Every member of a group involved in a discussion has certain responsibilities.

All group members: All members of a group discussion are responsible for paying attention to the discussion, respecting all group members' opinions, and offering thoughtful comments.

Chairperson: If a group has chosen a discussion leader or chairperson, he or she is responsible for introducing, guiding, moderating, and closing the discussion. The chairperson helps resolve any conflicts between members and makes sure that the group stays focused on its purpose or goal.

Group secretary or recorder: One person from the group is usually asked to take notes on important points or decisions made during a discussion. The group secretary or recorder is responsible for these notes and for reading them aloud at the beginning of the next group discussion.

Oral Interpretation

In **oral interpretation** you read a work of literature aloud, using acting as well as speaking skills—vocal techniques, facial expressions, body language, and gestures—to express your interpretation of the work. Following are the steps for preparing an oral interpretation.

1. **Find and cut material.** You usually have a specific purpose and audience in mind before you select and prepare material for an oral interpretation. You can, therefore, select material interesting to and appropriate for your audience. Consider, also, how much time you have for your presentation. For your oral interpretation, you will need to make an abbreviated version or **cutting** of a work of fiction, nonfiction, poetry, or drama. Use the following guidelines:
   - Follow the story line of the literary work in time order.
   - Delete tag lines such as "he said slowly." Instead, use these clues to tell you how to interpret the character's words as you express them.
   - Delete passages that do not contribute to the overall effect or impression you intend to create with your oral interpretation.

2. **Prepare the reading script.** You can type (double-spaced) and mark your reading script to help you in your interpretive reading. Underline words you want to give special emphasis, or use a slash mark (/) to indicate where you would like a dramatic pause.

3. **Rehearse your interpretation.** Rehearse different readings of your script until you find the one that expresses your interpretation. Use your voice in a manner that suits your presentation, and pronounce words carefully. Practice using your body and your voice to portray different characters.

4. **Deliver your presentation.** Begin your presentation by introducing the work of literature you are interpreting. Introduce the author, set the scene, and provide the necessary background for your audience to understand your interpretation. Then, deliver your interpretation.

Listening

Good listening takes more than good hearing. Listening is an active process. When you listen actively, you receive verbal and nonverbal messages, construct meanings for those messages, and respond to those meanings.

Basics of the Listening Process

Listening is as important to the communication process as speaking. The stages in the listening process are explained in the following chart.

The Three Stages of the Listening Process	
Before you listen	• **Be physically and mentally prepared to listen.** To be an effective listener, you should be physically comfortable and free of mental distractions that will interfere with your ability to focus.
	• **Determine your reason for listening.** Are you listening to be entertained? To be informed? To provide support or understanding? To receive instructions or directions? Identifying a reason for listening sets you up as an active listener.
	• **Decide what you already know about the speaker and the subject.** Bringing your prior knowledge of a subject or of a speaker to the surface can make your listening experience more productive.
	• **Add to your prior knowledge of the speaker and the subject.** Brainstorming with others or doing individual research to increase your knowledge of speaker and subject will improve your ability to understand and evaluate both.
	• **Keep an open mind.** Set aside any biases, prejudices, or preconceived notions you might have concerning the speaker or the topic of the speech. Make your judgments after listening to what the speaker has to say.
As you listen	• **Make connections to prior knowledge and experience.** Try to relate what the speaker is saying to what you know from any source—experience, books and magazines, television, school, and so on.
	• **Think of questions you would like to ask the speaker.** You may not have an opportunity to ask the speaker to clarify a point or expand upon an idea, but thinking of questions helps you to focus on the speaker's meaning.
	• **Make educated guesses about what a speaker will say next.** If you are wrong, try to determine what misled you.
	• **Find meaning behind what the speaker says directly.** Make inferences about a speaker's attitudes or opinions by paying attention to what he or she does not say.
After you listen	• **Discuss the speaker and the message with others.** Get together with others to exchange ideas, agree or disagree with the speaker's opinions, and relate what the speaker has said to what you have experienced, seen, and read.
	• **Write a summary and evaluation of the speaker and the presentation.** Writing about a presentation while it is fresh in your mind can help you clarify and solidify your thoughts and opinions.

Evaluating Yourself as a Listener

In order for oral communication to be effective, the listener must take as much of the responsibility for clear communication as the speaker. Therefore, it is important for you to be able to evaluate yourself as a listener. The following chart suggests points you should consider.

Evaluating Yourself as a Listener
A good listener should
■ be mentally and physically prepared to listen
■ be able to ignore distracting behavior by the speaker and members of the audience
■ focus on the speaker throughout the presentation
■ follow the organization of the speaker's presentation
■ distinguish between facts and opinions
■ think of questions to ask the speaker
■ determine the speaker's main idea and primary supporting details
■ withhold judgment until the presentation is over
■ listen for and detect bias or prejudice on the speaker's part
■ reflect upon the presentation after it is over
■ discuss the presentation with others
■ ask questions of the speaker if given the opportunity
■ write a summary or evaluation of the presentation

Four Types of Listening

There are four basic types of listening and a number of purposes or reasons for listening associated with each type.

Appreciative (or Aesthetic) Listening

When you listen for pleasure, such as hearing someone read a story or a poem, for example, you are engaged in appreciative listening. Certain strategies can make this type of listening experience more rewarding.

■ **Before Listening** Before you listen, ask (and use your prior knowledge to answer) as many questions as you can about the material you are going to hear. What is it about? What is the title of the piece? What kind of literature is it? Who is the author? **Make predictions based on your questions and answers.** You might predict, for example, that a poem entitled "Dawn" will involve a sunrise. **Based on the type of literature you will hear— poetry, fiction, drama—recall or research some of its basic elements.** If you are to listen to a poetry reading, for example, you might recall the kinds of figurative language or the importance of imagery.

■ **While Listening** As you listen, visualize what you are hearing. Jot down notes on any reactions, questions, or ideas you have while listening. Does the presentation remind you of a personal experience or something you have read? **Make personal connections** to the literature.

■ **After Listening** After you listen, confirm or correct the predictions you made before listening. Were your predictions correct, or did they require adjusting as you listened? Why did your predictions need to change? **Evaluate your response to the literature.** What did you like or learn or feel while listening? **Identify and discuss any artistic or literary elements that appeared in the literature, such as rhyme scheme, rhythm, imagery, theme, and so on.** What or how did these elements add to your listening experience? **Write a short evaluation of the presentation.**

Critical Listening When you listen to understand, analyze, and evaluate a speaker's message, you engage in critical listening—the type of listening you should apply to messages you hear in school, in the workplace, or in the media. You can use the strategies in the following chart to analyze and evaluate media presentations as well as live presentations.

How to Listen Critically	
What to do	**What to listen for**
Identify the speaker's purpose.	• Does the speaker make clear why he or she is giving the speech?
Distinguish between facts and opinions.	• Does the speaker make statements with which you agree or disagree? Ask yourself why you disagree. (Such statements are opinions. An *opinion* is a belief or a judgment about something that cannot be proved. A *fact* is a statement that can be proved true.)
Identify main ideas.	• What are the most important points? (Listen for clue words or phrases, such as *major, main,* and *most important.*)
Identify significant or supporting details.	• What dates, names, or facts does the speaker use to support the main points of the speech? What kinds of examples or explanations are used to support the main ideas?
Identify the order of organization.	• What kind of order does the speaker use to present the information—time sequence, spatial order, order of importance?
Listen to detect bias.	• Is the speaker biased, or prejudiced, toward one point of view? Does the speaker use extreme or all-inclusive words such as *never* or *always*? Does the speaker acknowledge other points of view?
Evaluate the speaker's credibility.	• Does the speaker refer to sources of information? Are the sources respectable or credible, such as newspaper and journal articles or reference materials?
Note comparisons and contrasts.	• Are some details compared or contrasted with others?
Predict outcomes and draw conclusions.	• What can you reasonably conclude from the facts and evidence presented in the speech?
Look for logic.	• Does the speaker build arguments in a logical way? Does the speaker use false logic, such as hasty generalization, false cause and effect, or circular reasoning?
Look for emotional appeals.	• Does the speaker use the bandwagon appeal? The glittering generality? Snob appeal? Plain folks appeal? The veiled threat?
Understand cause and effect.	• Do some events described by the speaker relate to or affect others? Does the speaker make the logical connections between cause and effect?

Comprehensive Listening This type of listening is sometimes called *informational listening* because you listen for the content of a message. Much of the listening you do in school, for example, is comprehensive listening. There are several instances in which you use comprehensive listening:

- **Listening for Information** You are often in situations where you listen to acquire information. When a veterinarian explains the required treatment of a problem your pet is having, for example, he or she is delivering information you need to understand, not attempting to persuade or entertain you. The following strategies are helpful in these situations.

  1. **The LQ2R Method** helps you when you listen for information from a speaker. The steps are described below.

     L Listen carefully to material as it is being presented.

     Q Question yourself as you listen. Mentally, or in your notes, make a list of questions as they occur to you.

     R Recite in your own words the information as it is being presented. Summarize the material in your mind.

     R Review the whole presentation. You should restate or reemphasize major points.

  2. **Note Taking** One method of keeping track of a speaker's ideas is to take notes. Because you cannot write down every word a speaker says, you need to develop an effective way to jot down a speaker's main points and supporting details as well as your own thoughts, questions, or comments. You could use split-page notes: Divide your paper so that forty percent of the page lies to the left and sixty percent

lies to the right. Take brief notes on the left-hand side only, leaving the right-hand side for reorganizing and expanding your notes after listening. (See also the **How to Take Study Notes** chart on page 912.)

- **Listening to Instructions** Because instructions are usually made up of a series of steps, you can easily misunderstand them. The following steps can help you make sense of instructions.

  1. **Listen for the order of the steps.** Listen for words such as *first, second, next, then,* and *last* to tell you when one step ends and the next one begins.
  2. **Identify the number of steps in the process.** Take notes if the instructions are long or complicated. Do not hesitate to ask for clarification or for the speaker to slow down as you take notes.
  3. **Visualize each step.** Imagine yourself actually performing each step. Try to get a mental image of what you should be doing at every step in the process.
  4. **Review the steps.** When the speaker is finished, be sure you understand the process from beginning to end. Ask questions if you are unsure.

NOTE When you take a message on the telephone, you are listening for information that answers the basic *5W-How?* questions—*Who? What? When? Where? Why?* and *How?* For example, you should take down details that answer questions such as *Who* is calling? *What* is the message or purpose for the call? *Where* can the caller be reached? *When* can the caller be reached? and *How* may you help the caller?

Empathic (or Reflective) Listening

When you want to help a friend understand a

difficult problem or when you want to show someone your understanding and acceptance, you engage in empathic listening. You indicate your empathy through your facial expressions and body language and through your responses to the speaker. Here are some strategies to use.

- Do much more listening than talking.
- Show genuine warmth and concern.
- Paraphrase what the speaker says to show your understanding.
- Respond to the speaker's feelings rather than analyzing the facts.
- Keep your opinions to yourself.

Special Listening Situations

Group discussions and *interviews* are situations that require that you participate not only as a careful listener, but also as a speaker.

Listening in a Group Discussion   Being a member of a group discussion is a little different from being a member of a large audience. The following tips should help you participate effectively in a group discussion.

- Maintain nonverbal communication by sitting up, looking at each speaker, and nodding to show agreement or understanding.
- Demonstrate respect for the other group members by paying attention and not making comments while they are speaking or listening.
- Take notes on each speaker's points and list your questions or comments.
- When you are ready to speak, raise your hand and be recognized.
- Concentrate on what the speaker is saying, not on what you intend to say when it is your turn to speak.

Listening in an Interview   An interview is a unique listening situation that takes place between two people: the interviewer and the interviewee. Here are some listening techniques you can use to make the most of an interview. (See also **Conducting an Interview** on page 902 and **Interviewing for a Job** on page 903.)

- **As interviewer**

1. **When you ask a question, listen to the complete answer.** Be courteous and patient as your interviewee answers. Think of follow-up questions as he or she responds.
2. **Respect the interviewee's opinions, even if you do not agree with him or her.** You may state your disagreement politely only if your comment will prompt the interviewee to clarify, expand, or provide support for a statement or claim. Do not express your disagreement if it is likely to upset your interviewee and disrupt the interview.
3. **Monitor your nonverbal communication.** Make sure that your nonverbal reactions, such as your facial expressions and your gestures, reflect a respectful tone. Maintain good eye contact, nod to show understanding, and smile to indicate your interest.
4. **Always thank the interviewee at the end of your interview.**

- **As interviewee**

1. **Listen to the interviewer's complete question before answering.** If you start answering the question before the interviewer finishes asking it, you might answer the wrong question.
2. **Answer the question.** Stick to the point the interviewer is addressing. Do not simply ignore the question and respond with something totally off track.

Studying and Test Taking

Study Skills and Strategies

To be successful in your high school studies, you need to develop skills and strategies for efficient studying. The methods on the following pages will help you get better grades and give you practical ways to approach the task of studying so you can understand and remember information you may need later.

Making a Study Plan

The following suggestions may help you make effective use of your study time.

1. **Know your assignments.** Keep an assignment calendar or planner for recording your assignments and their due dates. Make sure that you understand all the instructions for each assignment.
2. **Create a study plan.** Break your large assignments into small steps. Schedule deadlines for completing each step.
3. **Focus your attention.** Set aside a specific time and place for studying. Find out what study environment works best for you. Avoid distractions.

Organizing and Remembering Information

The strategies listed below can help you organize and remember information as you study.

Classifying   *Classification* is organizing information by arranging items into categories. You use classification when you make an outline, deciding which supporting ideas fit together under a major heading. In order to group things, you need to identify relationships among them.

> EXAMPLE   What do the following people have in common?
>
> Steven Spielberg, James Cameron, John Ford, Frank Capra
>
> ANSWER   They are all Academy Award-winning film directors.

You can also use classification to identify patterns in data. For example, look at the following chart.

What would be the heights of columns 6 and 7?

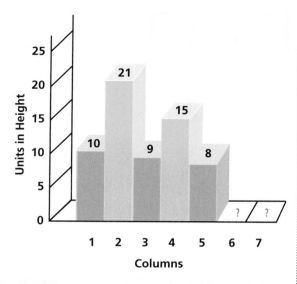

ANSWER The height of column 4 is six units less than the height of the preceding even-numbered column (column 2). Based on this pattern, column 6 would be <u>nine units high</u>. The heights of columns 3 and 5 are each one unit less than the height of the preceding odd-numbered columns (columns 1 and 3). Based on this pattern, column 7 would be <u>seven units high</u>.

Graphic Organizers

Using maps, diagrams, charts, and other graphic organizers can help you visually arrange information and understand it more easily. (See also **Types of Graphics** on page 857.)

Memorization

Frequent, short, focused sessions of practice are best when you are trying to memorize and retain material. Cramming for a test is not very efficient since you will not retain the information well.

Notes on Reading or Lectures

When reading or listening to a lecture, take notes that will help you organize and remember information later when you are studying or writing. The following steps explain how to take notes.

How to Take Notes

1. Recognize and record main points.

In a lecture, listen for clues such as **key words** and **phrases** used by the speaker. Repeated or stressed words and phrases such as *most importantly* or *pay close attention* usually indicate points that you should remember.

In a textbook, look for clues such as chapter headings or subheadings, lists, or graphic organizers like charts, time lines, and illustrations.

2. Make summaries of information you read or hear. Instead of recording every detail, put the ideas into your own words. Abbreviate and condense information about key ideas. Distinguish supporting points from the main points by indenting them in your notes.

3. Pay close attention to examples. The main points of lectures or lessons are often illustrated through examples. Sketching a simple diagram of the example in your notes—for instance, a diagram of a human nerve cell—may later help to jog your memory.

In the following notes, important details are arranged in groups. Each group is then given a heading that indicates the key idea that unifies the details in each group.

Rosa Parks

<u>Biography</u>
- African American, born Feb. 4, 1913—Tuskegee, Ala.
- grew up in Montgomery, Ala.
- despised injustice in treatment of blacks
- incident in Dec. 1955 started bus boycott
- fired from her tailoring job because of boycott
- sat in the front of a city bus on Dec. 21, 1956 after a Supreme Court ruling
- hired by congressman in Michigan—worked for him for more than 20 years
- 1987—founded Rosa and Raymond Parks Inst. for Self-Development

<u>Examples of Inequality in Treatment</u>
- had to sit at back of shoe stores
- had to sit at back of buses
- had to stand if white person wanted seat on bus

<u>Details of Montgomery Bus Boycott</u>
- Ms. Parks refused to give up seat to white man
- Ms. Parks said, "My only concern was to get home after a hard day's work."
- Ms. Parks arrested for her refusal
- Ms. Parks stopped using the bus
- Ms. Parks helped form the Montgomery Improvement Association with Dr. Martin Luther King, Jr.
- thousands joined her boycott of bus system
- many risked jobs
- many employers gave rides instead of losing workers
- boycott lasted 382 days
- sparked American civil rights movement

Outlines   An *outline* organizes the most important ideas and information from a passage. To create an outline, group ideas and information in an organized pattern that identifies their order and relationship to one another.

To sort and group items, ask yourself, *Which details belong together? What do they have in common?* Also think of a heading—a word or a phrase—that identifies what the details do have in common. For example, the words *bicycle helmet, water bottle,* and *tire repair kit* may all be grouped under the heading *Safety Items.*

To define the order of your organizational pattern, first decide upon the relationship between the groups. Sometimes the topic itself suggests a clear order. One type of order is **chronological (time),** or a step-by-step process. Another type is **spatial order,** which describes the layout of something. A third type of order is **order of importance,** which arranges ideas from the least important to the most important, or vice versa. (See also **Outlines** on page 950.)

Paraphrasing   When you *paraphrase,* you restate someone else's words in your own words. When you restate an idea in your own words, you are not just switching around words, but actually concentrating on the idea expressed in those words. Paraphrasing is a good way to check your understanding of what you read, especially if the original is written in poetic or elaborate language. A written paraphrase is usually approximately the same length as the original, so the technique of paraphrasing is generally not used for long pieces of writing. (See also **Paraphrasing** on page 882.)

SQ3R   *SQ3R* is a strategy designed to help you study from a book or textbook. The letters stand for:

   Survey the chapter.
   Question while you are surveying.
   Read actively.
   Recite after you have read a section.
   Review what you have studied.
(See also **SQ3R** on page 884.)

Summarizing A *summary* restates the main points from a lecture, book, or notes in a condensed way. A summary helps you identify and remember the most important points of the material you are studying. When you write a summary, you analyze the material, determining the most important points of the passage and deciding what information should be included or omitted in the summary. Making these decisions helps you remember the information in a passage. (See also **Summarizing** on page 884.)

Writing to Learn Writing is useful as a study tool with which you may focus your thoughts, respond to ideas, record your observations, plan your work, and restate ideas in your own words. Writing about what you have read or heard helps you see relationships among ideas and to comprehend the text. Use the following different forms of writing as you study.

Type of Writing	Purpose	Example
Diary	• helps you recall your impressions and express your feelings for class	Write about your reactions to a play you have seen or an article you read.
Freewriting	• helps you focus your thoughts on an assignment or after listening to a lecture to focus on the most important points	Write for three minutes after reading.
Journal	• helps you record your observations, descriptions, solutions, and questions	Write about problems or successes you had in solving word problems in math.
Learning Log	• helps you present a problem, analyze it, and propose a solution	Write about the way you will incorporate a source or piece of information into a research paper for your social studies class.

Test-Taking Skills and Strategies

There are two types of tests you are likely to encounter in school: *classroom tests* and *standardized tests*. You will need to learn new skills and consider different strategies for approaching the different kinds of questions you will be asked on each of these different types of tests.

Classroom Tests

The typical *classroom test* measures your ability to use key academic skills or to demonstrate your knowledge of specific academic subjects. In your student career, you have probably seen several types of test questions—essay questions, matching questions, multiple-choice questions, and true/false questions—used in various combinations through the years. The best way to prepare for classroom tests is by familiarizing yourself with the material on which you will be tested or by practicing the skill or skills you will be asked to demonstrate at the time of testing. Also, make sure that you are prepared for each kind of question that can appear on a classroom test by reading the following descriptions, tips, and examples.

Essay Tests ask you to demonstrate two things:

- that you can think critically about material you have learned

- that you are able to express your understanding in one or more well-written and organized paragraphs.

Essay questions provide different challenges than the other kinds of test questions since an essay question may ask you to con-sider several ideas in your answer. Also, an essay question requires you to do more than just know details such as dates and definitions; often you must know how these details relate to one another. To study for an essay test, follow these steps:

1. **Read your textbook, class notes, or other study materials carefully.**

2. **Make an outline** that identifies the main points and important details from material being covered.

3. **Create a set of possible questions and practice writing out answers.**

4. **Evaluate and revise your practice answers.** Check your notes and textbook for accuracy.

How to Answer Essay Questions

1. **Scan the questions on the test.** Make sure you know how many answers you are expected to write. If you have a choice of several items, decide which ones you think you can answer best. Then, plan how much time to spend on preparing and writing each answer.

2. **Read the questions carefully.** Highlight or circle the key terms in the question to be sure you have covered all the parts of the question. Familiarize yourself with the key verbs that commonly appear on essay tests. (See also the **Key Verbs That Appear in Essay Questions** chart on page 916.)

3. **Use prewriting techniques to plan your answer.** Make notes or create an outline to help you decide what you want to say. (See also **Prewriting Techniques** on page 952.)

4. **Evaluate and revise your answer as you write.** You probably won't have time to redraft your entire essay. Instead, leave yourself a little time to re-read your answer and correct any spelling, punctuation, or grammar errors.

Essay questions usually ask you to perform specific tasks that are expressed with action verbs. You can prepare to complete each task by familiarizing yourself with the key verbs and the kinds of information they request.

Key Verbs That Appear in Essay Questions		
Key Verb	**Task**	**Sample Question**
Analyze	Look carefully at the parts of a situation or issue to see how each part works.	**Analyze** the U.S. government's role in Operation Desert Storm.
Argue	Take a stand on an issue and give reasons to support your viewpoint or opinion.	**Argue** whether your school should require all students to participate in extracurricular activities.
Compare or Contrast	Point out similarities between things, people, or ideas.	**Compare** the lives and inventions of George Washington Carver and Thomas Edison.
Define	Give specific details that make something or some idea unique.	**Define** the term *imperialism* as it applies to early U.S. history.
Demonstrate	Provide examples to support a point.	**Demonstrate** that a line intersecting parallel lines produces equivalent angles.
Describe	Give a picture in words, presenting explicit details.	**Describe** your childhood home.
Discuss	Examine in detail.	**Discuss** the term *Manifest Destiny*.
Explain	Give reasons or make the meaning clear.	**Explain** why the United States entered World War II.
Identify	Point out specific persons, places, things, or characteristics.	**Identify** the leaders of the Confederacy and their importance in the Civil War.
Interpret	Explain the meaning or significance of an event, idea, or quotation.	**Interpret** the role of Cesar Chavez in organizing the farm labor movement.
List	Give the steps in order or provide certain details about a subject.	**List** the events leading up to the Montgomery bus boycott.
Summarize	Give a brief overview of the main points.	**Summarize** the effects of ozone depletion in the atmosphere.

Although there are a wide variety of essay questions, nearly all good answers contain the same qualities.

- The essay is well organized.
- The essay clearly presents main ideas and supporting points.
- The sentences are complete and well written.
- There are no errors in spelling, punctuation, or grammar.

Matching Questions
In matching questions, you must match each item on one list to a logically related item on another list.

EXAMPLE

Directions: Match each term in the first column to a description in the second column.

_D_	**1.** Shakespearean sonnet	**A.** group of eight rhymed lines
_C_	**2.** couplet	**B.** Italian sonnet
_A_	**3.** octave	**C.** group of two rhymed lines
_B_	**4.** Petrarchan sonnet	**D.** English sonnet
_E_	**5.** sestet	**E.** group of six lines

How to Answer Matching Questions

1. Carefully read all directions. Be sure you know whether answers can be used only once or more than once.

2. Match the items that you are sure of first. This will narrow the possible choices for the items of which you are less sure.

3. Guess intelligently on any remaining items. In the previous example, if the items remaining to be matched were 1 and 4, and B and D, you might guess that 1 matches D—because Shakespeare was English—leaving you with 4 matching B.

Multiple-Choice Questions
A multiple-choice question asks you to choose a correct answer from a given number of possible answers.

EXAMPLE

1. After she was arrested for refusing to yield her seat on a bus, Rosa Parks
   A. decided to stop using the bus system.
   B. was elected to Congress.
   C. moved to Tuskegee, Alabama.
   D. avoided the American civil rights movement.

How to Answer Multiple-Choice Questions

1. Read the initial statement carefully. Make sure you understand the statement completely before looking at your choices. Look for qualifiers, such as *not, always,* or *never,* because these words limit or affect the answer. In the example, you must choose the answer that best completes the sentence.

2. Read all the answers before making a choice. Sometimes the answer includes two or more choices, such as "Both A and B" or "All of the above."

3. Narrow your choices by eliminating the incorrect answers. Some answers are clearly wrong, such as D, while others may be only somewhat related to the correct answer. Looking at the example, you know that Rosa Parks was not elected to Congress, so you can rule out B.

4. From the remaining choices, select the answer that makes the most sense. The answer is A.

Short-Answer Questions
Short-answer questions ask you to show your knowledge about a subject in a brief, written reply. In general, short-answer questions require a

specific answer of one or two sentences. Some short-answer questions, such as a map, diagram, or fill-in-the-blank questions, can be answered with one or a few words. Usually, short-answer questions have only one correct answer; however, you are not given possible answers from which to choose.

EXAMPLE

1. What famous reason did explorer George Mallory give in 1924 for climbing Mt. Everest?

1. "Because it is there."

True/False Questions

True/False questions ask you to determine whether a given statement is correct.

EXAMPLE

1. T (F) The percentage of school-age children in the United States increased over the course of the twentieth century.

How to Answer True/False Questions

1. Read the statement carefully.

2. Check for qualifiers. Words such as *always* or *never* qualify or limit a statement's meaning.

3. Choose the correct answer based on the following principles:
- If any part of the statement is false, the entire statement is false.
- A statement is true only if it is entirely and always true.

Standardized Tests

Standardized tests evaluate your score according to a "standard" compiled from the scores of many other students who have taken the same test. The best-known tests of this type, such as the Scholastic Aptitude Test (SAT) and the American College Testing Program (ACT), are given to students across the entire United States;

however, other standardized tests may be developed by states or school districts. The two basic types of standardized tests are **aptitude** tests (intended to evaluate basic skills or reasoning abilities needed in various *general* areas of study) and **achievement** tests (intended to measure knowledge of *specific* subjects such as history, literature, sciences, mathematics, or foreign languages.) To prepare for both kinds of standardized tests, keep in mind the three tips in the following chart.

How to Prepare for Standardized Tests

1. Learn what skills will be tested. Your school may provide information booklets that tell you about the types of questions and how the test is scored. Practice with these or with published study guides available through bookstores and libraries.

2. Know what materials you need for the test. You may need to bring specific materials, such as your official test registration card, number-two pencils, or lined paper for writing an essay.

3. Determine how the test is evaluated. If there is no penalty for wrong answers, make your best educated guess on all questions possible. If wrong answers are penalized, however, make guesses only if you are fairly sure of your answers.

Finally, you should familiarize yourself with the different kinds of questions that standardized tests ask as well as the writing prompts that they include.

Analogy Questions

Analogy questions ask you to analyze the relationship between one pair of words and to identify or supply a second pair of words that has the same relationship.

Analogy questions usually appear on standardized tests in multiple-choice form.

EXAMPLE

1. Directions: Select the appropriate pair of words to complete the analogy.

   SHIRT : CLOTHING :: ___C___

   A. wheel : car
   B. page : read
   C. bicycle : vehicle
   D. globe : round

Sometimes, however, analogies are written as fill-in-the-blank questions, and you will need to fill in the missing item.

EXAMPLE

2. Complete the following analogy.

   DRIZZLE : DOWNPOUR :: dime : ___fortune___

How to Answer Analogy Questions

1. Identify the relationship between the first pair of words. In Example 1, a *shirt* is a type of *clothing;* the relationship is one of classification. (See also the **Types of Analogies** chart on page 920.)

2. Express the analogy in sentence or question form. Example 1 could be expressed as, "A *shirt* is a kind of *clothing,* just as a _____ is a kind of _____." Fill the blanks with each of the possible answers and see which makes sense. For example, "Is a *wheel* a kind of *car*?" It is not, so A is not the answer.

3. Find the best available choice to complete the analogy. If multiple-choice answers are provided, select the pair of words that shares the same relationship as the pair of words in the question. If you must fill in a word, select a word that has the same relationship to the word to the right of the double colons (::) as the two words in the question to the left of the colons. Example 2 shows a relationship of degree—a *drizzle* is a small amount of rain, and a *downpour* is a lot of rain. A *dime* is a small amount of money, and a *fortune* is a lot of money.

In addition to the three guidelines above, remember the following helpful tips.

- **Know the meanings of the symbols used in analogy questions.** The symbol : means "related to," while :: means "equals" or "is equivalent to."

- **Consider the parts of speech.** Some words may be used as more than one part of speech. Thinking about a word as a noun, a verb, or an adjective might help unlock the relationship in the analogy. If you cannot decipher the relationship between the words in the analogy, it may help to determine if one of the words can be another part of speech.

- **Become familiar with the types of analogy relationships.** Familiarize yourself with types of analogies typically found on standardized tests. Using the **Types of Analogies** chart on page 920, practice designing test questions of each type. Exchange with a peer and work through each other's questions.

- **Remember that it is the relationship between the words that is important, not the meanings of the individual words.** Look at Example 2. A *drizzle* and a *dime* have very little in common; but the relationship a *drizzle* has to a *downpour* is the same as the relationship a *dime* has to a *fortune:* degree. A downpour is more than a drizzle and a fortune is more than a dime.

Although there are many different relationships that can be represented in analogies, a smaller number of specific relationships are fairly common in standardized tests. Examples of these common types are shown in the chart on the following page.

Types of Analogies

Type	Example	Solution
Action to Performer or **Performer to Action**	TEACHING : PROFESSOR : : cleaning : housekeeper	*Teaching* is performed by a *professor,* just as *cleaning* is performed by a *housekeeper.*
Antonyms	PATRIOT : TRAITOR : : loyal : unfaithful	A *patriot* is the opposite of a *traitor,* just as *loyal* behavior is the opposite of *unfaithful* behavior.
Cause	GERM : SICKNESS : : water : dampness	A *germ* causes *sickness,* just as *water* causes *dampness.*
Characteristic	MAMMALS : FUR : : fish : scales	*Mammals* always have *fur,* just as *fish* always have *scales.*
Classification	BAGELS : BREAD : : pork : meat	A *bagel* is type of *bread,* just as *pork* is a type of *meat.*
Degree	COLOSSAL : LARGE : : microscopic : small	*Colossal* means very *large,* just as *microscopic* means very *small.*
Effect	TEARS : SORROW : : smiles : joy	*Tears* are the effect of *sorrow,* just as *smiles* are the effect of *joy.*
Measure	BAROMETER : AIR PRESSURE : : scale : weight	A *barometer* measures *air pressure,* just as a *scale* measures *weight.*
Part to Whole or **Whole to Part**	WATER : OCEAN : : sand : desert	*Water* makes up the *ocean,* just as *sand* makes up a *desert.*
Place	SPACE NEEDLE : SEATTLE : : Lincoln Memorial : Washington, D.C.	The *Space Needle* is located in *Seattle,* just as the *Lincoln Memorial* is located in *Washington, D.C.*
Synonyms	ROUND : CIRCULAR : : strong : muscular	*Round* is similar in meaning to *circular,* just as *strong* is similar in meaning to *muscular.*
Use	DESK : STUDY : : bed : sleep	A *desk* is used to *study,* just as a *bed* is used to *sleep.*

Critical-Reading Questions Standardized tests may include questions that require you to look critically at a reading passage and to find its organizational pattern, meaning, and purpose. These *critical-reading questions* (sometimes called *on-demand reading questions*) measure your ability to analyze and interpret a reading passage. In addition, these questions may ask you to decide if the passage effectively communicates the writer's intended meaning. Critical-reading test questions focus either on a particular approach to the passage or on one topic within the passage. The following chart shows types of critical-reading test questions and the actions you must take to answer them. For more information about and practice with some of the bulleted elements, see the page referred to in parentheses following the item.

Critical-Reading Test Questions

Rhetorical-strategy questions, or **evaluation questions,** ask you to judge the effectiveness of techniques used in a passage. These questions often ask you to identify and analyze

- the author's intended audience (page 264)
- the author's opinions (page 255)
- the author's purpose (page 876)
- the author's tone or point of view (page 876)

Inference questions, or **interpretation questions,** ask you to draw conclusions or make inferences about the meaning of information presented in a passage. These test items often ask you to identify

- ambiguities in information
- conclusions or inferences based on given material (page 27)

- specific conclusions or inferences that can be drawn about the author or the topic of a passage (page 172)

(See also page 27.)

Organization questions, or **main idea** or **detail questions,** ask you to identify the organizational techniques that the writer of a passage uses. You should be able to identify

- the main idea of a passage (page 65)
- arrangement of supporting details (page 60)
- the author's use of particular writing strategies (page 177)
- techniques used to conclude the passage
- transitional devices that make the passage coherent (page 375)

Style questions, or **tone questions,** ask you to evaluate the author's use of style in a passage. These test questions often ask you to identify

- the author's intended audience (page 264)
- the author's style
- the author's tone and voice (pages 958 and 959)

Synthesis questions test your knowledge of how parts of a passage fit together to form a whole. These questions ask you to interpret

- the cumulative meaning of details in a passage (page 24)
- techniques used to unify details

Vocabulary-in-context questions ask you to infer the meaning of an unfamiliar word by looking at its context. These test items ask you to determine the meaning of an unfamiliar word using context clues (page 217). (See also page 216.)

NOTE To help you make the best use of the time allotted, first scan the entire reading passage and the critical-reading questions that follow. Write notes in your test booklet as you are pre-reading both the passage and the questions. Then, read more slowly through the passage. Refer to your jotted notes as you answer the questions.

Here is a typical **reading passage** followed by sample test questions based on this passage.

> With the rise of capitalism, a new middle class emerged who wanted their children to speak the dialect of the "upper" classes. This desire led to the publication of many prescriptive grammars. In 1762 an influential grammar, *A Short Introduction to English Grammar with Critical Notes,* was written by Bishop Robert Lowth. Lowth, influenced by Latin grammar and by personal preference, prescribed a number of new rules for English. Before the publication of his grammar, practically everyone—upper-class, middle-class, and lower-class speakers of English—said *I don't have none, You was wrong about that,* and *Mathilda is fatter than me.* Lowth, however, decided that "two negatives make a positive" and therefore one should say *I don't have any;* that even when *you* is singular it should be followed by the plural *were;* and that *I* not *me, he* not *him, they* not *them,* and so forth should follow *than* in comparative constructions. Many of these "rules" were based on Latin grammar, which had already given way to different rules in languages that developed from Latin. Because Lowth was influential and because the rising new class wanted to speak "properly," many of these new rules were legislated into English grammar, at least for the "prestige" dialect.

Sample Critical-Reading Questions

1. According to the passage, in which order (from earliest to latest) did the following events occur?
   I. "Two negatives make a positive" became a rule of English grammar.
   II. New rules developed in languages that developed from Latin.
   III. Lowth wrote *A Short Introduction to English Grammar.*
   IV. A new middle class emerged.

   A. I, IV, III, II
   B. II, IV, III, I
   C. IV, III, II, I
   D. II, I, IV, III

[This is an organizational question; it requires you to identify the time sequence of these events and to arrange them in the correct historical time order.]

2. The word *prescribed* in the fourth sentence may be defined as
   A. claimed a right or title through long use
   B. advised as a medicine or treatment
   C. arose from long-standing usage or custom
   D. set down or imposed rules

[This is a vocabulary-in-context question; it requires you to determine the appropriate definition by examining the word's context in the passage.]

3. After reading the passage, one of your classmates wrote the following paragraph.

> Lowth's *A Short Introduction to English Grammar* did not help the English language as much as it caused a setback of hundreds upon hundreds of years. The book severely stunted the growth of a vibrant and living language. Grammar should be descriptive

rather than prescriptive. That is to say, it should attempt to describe linguistic knowledge rather than tell you how you should speak.

From this paragraph, you could assume that your classmate is critical of the idea that

A. grammar should describe language
B. grammar rules save our language from deteriorating
C. language changes with time
D. there is a no "correct" way to speak

[This is a rhetorical-strategy question; it requires you to identify the main points of the original passage and to recognize which of these points your classmate disputed.]

4. The new middle class wanted their children to speak "properly" so that

A. they could read and write better
B. they could be associated with the upper rather than the lower class
C. their language more closely followed its Latin roots
D. they could do better in the world of commerce

[This is an inference question; you are asked to draw a conclusion based on the material given in the passage.]

5. It can be inferred from the passage that Bishop Lowth was

A. a man who represented the eighteenth century
B. a pious man who strictly followed the rules of Latin grammar
C. a man who changed the English language significantly
D. a capitalist concerned with the welfare of his class

[This is a synthesis question; it requires you to read, in the passage as a whole, about the new rules applied to the English language. Then, adding up all the details, you might infer that Lowth and his book,

described as influential, prescribed rules that you know are still followed today.]

6. Readers of the reading passage are likely to describe it as

A. informal
B. historical
C. inspirational
D. biographical

[This is a question of style; it requires you to analyze the way the passage is written to determine the category or type of writing it represents.]

NOTE At times it will help you to compare the vocabulary and details in the prompt to those in the reading passage. If no vocabulary or details from the prompt appear in the reading passage, you must draw your own conclusions or come up with your own examples. For example, question 2 in the chart cites a word (*prescribed*) that is clearly present in the fourth sentence of the reading passage. Question 6, however, does not lead you to a specific section or detail in the passage. Instead you must draw your own conclusion about the passage as a whole.

Multiple-Choice Questions When you take a standardized test, you will probably find *multiple-choice questions* similar to those found on classroom tests. However, on standardized tests the multiple-choice questions will generally be easier at the beginning and become increasingly more difficult as you progress through the test. To tackle these questions, begin by answering all the easily answered questions first, then attempting the more difficult ones. Since each question, whether easy or difficult, is worth the same amount, this will help you make sure that all of the "guaranteed" points will already be in your pocket before you attempt the challenging ones. Do not spend too much time on any single question, though. Also, don't let time limits pressure you. Instead, stay calm and avoid making careless mistakes. (See also **Multiple-Choice Questions** on page 917.)

On-Demand Writing Questions Like essay questions, *on-demand writing questions* ask you to express yourself in one or more well-written and organized paragraphs in a limited amount of time. On-demand writing questions are different from essay questions, however, because you do not know the topic about which the prompt will require you to write. Usually these questions ask you to write a persuasive, informative, or descriptive essay in answer to a prompt that is broad but related to your general knowledge or experience. Because the ability to write on demand is such an important skill both in school and in the workplace, you will find that many states include on-demand writing questions as the core of their standardized testing.

EXAMPLES

Many high schools are now requiring students to participate in volunteer programs in order to graduate. Students receive credit for hours spent working for volunteer organizations in their communities. Write a persuasive essay in which you argue whether requiring students to volunteer is a good idea.

Most people have a favorite holiday, a time of the year or an occasion they like better than any other. Choose your favorite holiday and explain why you made that choice.

You may encounter a variation of the on-demand writing prompt in placement tests. The essays you write in response to placement test prompts will ask you to demonstrate your knowledge of a specific subject area. While the exact topic will not be known to you, you will

still be able to supply details for an answer from your educational background. For example, a prompt for an English-literature placement test may require you to know literary elements and pull details from certain plays, novels, or poems that you have studied in the past. Here is one example:

Define the term *poetic justice* and show how it applies to a major character in a literary work of your choice. Make sure that your essay is well organized and does not rely heavily on plot summary. Do not base your essay on an adaptation of a work, such as a movie or television program.

How to Answer an On-Demand Writing Question

1. Determine what the question is asking. By reading the passage carefully, you should be able to spot key verbs that indicate whether your answer should be persuasive, informative, or descriptive. (See also the **Key Verbs that Appear in Essay Questions** chart on page 916.)

2. Use prewriting techniques to plan your answer. On scratch paper or the inside cover of your test booklet, get your ideas flowing and begin determining how your answer will be organized. Freewriting, brainstorming, and clustering are some ways to get started. (See also **Prewriting Techniques** on page 952.)

3. Evaluate and revise your answer as you write. Make sure that your answer has a topic sentence, supporting details, transitions between ideas, and a clear conclusion.

Although you cannot study for the content of an on-demand writing test, you can still prepare yourself by following the steps below.

■ **Become familiar with the kinds of writing that on-demand writing questions often**

require. Read and learn to recognize the key qualities of persuasive, informative, and descriptive essays.

- **Practice writing answers to on-demand writing questions.** If possible, practice with questions that have appeared on state tests administered at your school in the past. Use a timer and the prewriting techniques to formulate answers. (See also **Prewriting Techniques** on page 952.)

- **Revise and proofread your answers.** If possible, share your answers with classmates. Have a discussion about which aspects of your answer are persuasive, informative, or descriptive.

Reasoning or Logic Questions   Some
questions test your reasoning abilities rather than your knowledge of a specific subject. *Reasoning or logic questions* may ask you to

- identify the relationship between two or more items, such as words, pictures, or numbers
- identify a pattern in a sequence of numbers
- predict the next item in a series of images

What comes next?

1. ●○ 2. ○● 3. ●● 4. ●●
  ○   ○   ●   ○
  ●●   ●●   ○●   ○●

How to Answer Reasoning or Logic Questions

1. Be sure that you understand the instructions. Reasoning or logic questions are usually multiple choice. However, sometimes you may need to write a word, phrase, or number or draw a picture for your answer. To answer the previous example, you will need to draw a pattern of shaded and unshaded circles.

2. Analyze the relationship implied in the question. Look carefully at the question to gather information about the relationship shared by the items. The two unshaded circles in the example are pointed outwards and moving in a counterclockwise direction.

3. Draw reasonable conclusions. Evaluate the relationship of the items to decide your answer. In the fourth frame of the example, the white dots should point toward the bottom right.

Verbal-Expression Questions   *Verbal-expression questions* assess how well you understand the meaning of written passages and grammatical correctness or clarity of written expression. The chart on page 927 shows the four standard types of verbal-expression questions. (For more information and practice with any of the **grammar, usage, and mechanics elements** indicated in the right-hand column, see the pages referred to in parentheses behind each item.)

Multiple-choice verbal-expression questions are not often asked in isolation. Instead, you find them within the context of a reading passage. Within a sample passage, usually a long paragraph, you will be given several words and phrases that are underlined and numbered. You are then asked to choose the answer that best expresses the meaning, is grammatically correct, or is consistent with the style and tone of the passage. Here is a typical verbal-expression test passage followed by sample questions:

> The young Williams sisters share a dream$_{(1)}$ of being ranked number one and number two in women's tennis. Their father, Richard Williams$_{(2)}$ has coached Venus and Serena since they were four and five years old. The girls began their professional careers as teens and soon caught people's attention. Venus played the U.S. Open in 1997.

She was the first African American woman to reach the U. S. Open finals in nearly forty years. About her <u>attitude that is sometimes overly confident</u>(3),

Venus has said, "You have to believe in yourself when no one else does—that makes you a winner right there."

Sample Verbal-Expression Questions

1. **A.** NO CHANGE
   B. shared
   C. has shared
   D. are sharing

[This is a question about grammar; it requires you to know the correct subject-verb agreement.]

2. **A.** NO CHANGE
   B. father (Richard Williams)
   C. father, Richard Williams,
   D. father Richard Williams,

[This is a question about punctuation; it requires you to know which mark of punctuation is appropriate here.]

3. Which is the best revision of this portion of the passage?
   A. NO CHANGE
   B. attitude, sometimes overly confident
   C. sometimes over-confident attitude
   D. sometimes overly confident attitude

[This is a revision-in-context question; it requires you to use revision skills to best express the ideas in the passage.]

4. How should sentences four and five be combined?
   A. Since Venus played the U.S. Open in 1997; she was the first African American woman to reach the U. S. Open finals in nearly forty years.
   B. Venus played the U.S. Open in 1997 and she was the first African American woman to reach the U. S. Open finals in nearly forty years.
   C. When Venus played the U.S. Open in 1997, she was the first African American woman to reach the finals in nearly forty years.
   D. Venus was the first African American woman to reach the U. S. Open finals in nearly forty years in 1997.

[This is a question about sentence structure; it requires you to know how to combine sentences effectively.]

Most current, best-known national tests contain only two basic types of test items used to test verbal expression. You should learn to recognize them as follows:

Most Common Types of Verbal-Expression Test Items

"NO CHANGE" Items

- give a list of suggested revisions of underlined, numbered portions of passage
- always contain one "NO CHANGE" choice (these words are often printed in capital letters) to be selected if the indicated part is correct as is

Critical-Thinking Items

- ask you to analyze and evaluate the passage as a whole
- ask you to make inferences about portions of a passage as related to the whole

Verbal-Expression Questions

Type of Question	What You Do
Grammar Questions	Identify the correct answer, using standard grammar and usage rules. These test items often cover use of • principal parts of verbs (page 574) • pronouns (page 467) • subject-verb agreement (page 512)
Punctuation Questions	Identify use of correct punctuation. These test items often cover correct use of • apostrophes and hyphens (pages 758 and 767) • end marks and commas (pages 694 and 700) • parentheses and quotation marks (pages 770 and 743) • semicolons, colons, and dashes (pages 724, 729, and 770)
Sentence-Structure Questions	Demonstrate knowledge of what is (and what is not) a complete sentence. These test items often cover • combining sentences (page 352) • fragments and run-ons (pages 340 and 347) • parallel structure (page 362) • transitional words (page 959) • verb usage (page 572)
Revision-in-Context Questions	Show appropriate revision to a part of or to an entire composition. These test items often cover • arranging ideas (page 945) • composition structure (page 943) • tone (page 958) • unity and coherence (page 391)

Viewing and Representing

Media Terms

Because media messages, such as advertisements, television programs, music videos, and movies, are a constant part of life, it is important to be able to understand, interpret, analyze, evaluate, and create media messages. With careful viewing, media messages can give you information or a fresh perspective, or they can help you define and solve problems. The terms defined below refer to many different areas of media communication, including television and film production, advertising, and journalism. The terms are grouped into three lists: **electronic media terms** (below), **general media terms** (page 932), and **print media terms** (page 936). (Terms relating to the Internet and the World Wide Web can be found in the **Library/Media Center** section on page 866; terms relating to use of type and graphics can be found in **Document Design** on page 849.)

Electronic Media Terms

Advertising   (See **Advertising** on page 936.)

Affiliate   An *affiliate* is a privately owned, local television or radio station that presents the programming of a national network. (See also **Network** on page 931.)

Animation   *Animation* is the film art of making drawings appear to move. An animated film may combine drawing, painting, sculpture, or other visual arts. Animators take film or video pictures of a scene at a rate of twenty-four frames per second, making small changes as they go. When viewed, the frames create the illusion of movement. Animation is used in many different types of media messages, including advertising and cartoons. (See also **Advertising** on page 936.)

Broadcasting   *Broadcasting* means using airwaves to send television or radio content over a wide area of potential viewers or listeners. **Commercial broadcasting** is for profit. Advertisers pay broadcasters for airtime in which to persuade the audience to buy their products or services. **Public broadcasting** is not-for-profit. In the United States, the Public Broadcasting Service (PBS) has more than three hundred affiliates, or member stations. The service is funded mostly by the federal government, corporations, and individual viewers and listeners. (See also **Affiliate** on this page.)

Cable Television   *Cable television* is a method of distributing TV signals using cables and wiring instead of airwaves to bring messages into people's homes. There are two principal types of cable TV companies. Some companies *create* original programming in the form of channels or networks, such as all-news networks or all-music channels. Other companies *distribute* packages, or groups, of many different channels into homes. (See also **Channel** on this page and **Network** on page 931.)

Camera Angle   The *camera angle* refers to the angle at which a camera is set when it is pointed at its subject. The angle may be low, high, or tilted. The effect of a low angle is to make the subject look tall and powerful. The high angle makes the subject look small. The tilted angle suggests that the subject is not balanced.

Camera Shots   A *camera shot* is what the viewer sees in a movie or video. Just as a written story needs many words, a film or video needs many shots in order to create a scene or story. Below are the most common shots used in film production.

- **Close-up shot**   A *close-up shot* is a shot of only the subject, usually a person's face.

- **Extreme close-up shot**   An *extreme close-up shot* is a very close shot, usually of only part of a person's face or part of the subject.

- **Medium shot**   A *medium shot* is a shot that shows the subject, usually a person from the waist up, and perhaps some of the background.

- **Long shot**   A *long shot* is a shot that shows a scene from far away, usually to show a place or setting of a scene.

- **Reverse angle shot**   A *reverse angle shot* is a view of the opposite side of a subject or of another person in the scene.

Channel   In general communication, a *channel* is the means by which a message is communicated. For example, if you are communicating verbally (such as by talking or singing), the channel is sound waves. If you communicate nonverbally (for instance, in pantomime), the channel is waves of light, because you see the facial expressions and exaggerated gestures of the pantomimist. In television and radio, the word *channel* means a fixed band of frequencies used for the transmitting of television or radio broadcasts. (See also **Medium** and **Message** on page 937.)

Copy   (See **Copy** on page 936.)

Credits   *Credits* refer to the list of names of people who worked to produce a program. This list usually appears at the end of a television program, film, or video or on the back of a compact disc case.

Demographics   (See **Demographics** on page 936.)

Digital Editing   (See **Digital Editing** on page 936.)

Docudrama   *Docudrama* is a type of documentary that blends elements of both documentary and drama to explore an actual historical, political, or social event. For example, docudramas may use actors, scripted dialogue, and special locations to re-create important events such as the signing of the Declaration of Independence.

Documentary   *Documentary* is a genre of film and television programming which uses language, sounds, and imagery to provide an interpretation of real-life events. Although documentaries attempt to relate factual information, they may only show one producer's perceptions or point of view. Documentaries often have informative, persuasive, and artistic purposes.

Drama   *Drama* is an art form that tells a story through the speech and actions of the characters in the story. Most dramas use actors who impersonate the characters. Some dramas are performed in a theater, while others are presented on film.

Editor   (See **Editor** on page 936.)

Electronic Media   The term *electronic media* refers to the forms of mass media products that are available to consumers through some type of electronic technology such as a computer or a television. Electronic media products can be found on the Internet, on the radio, and on television.

Feature News   (See **Feature News** on page 937.)

Hard News   (See **Hard News** on page 937.)

In-Camera Editing   *In-camera editing* refers to any editing that is performed through the operation of a video or film camera and not by the cutting and shaping of an editor. The sequence of shots and scenes remains exactly as they were gathered by the camera operator. In-camera editing is an effective method of creating video when editing is time-consuming or equipment is unavailable. To create an effective work using in-camera editing, a great deal of pre-production planning is required, including a complete shot list and storyboards. In most cameras, sound can be added after the images have been shot.

Internet   The *Internet* is a global network of computers. With the Internet and a computer equipped with a modem, a computer user may access information from another computer or a network of computers anywhere in the world.

Lead   (See **Lead** on page 937.)

Marketing   (See **Marketing** on page 937.)

Medium   (See **Medium** on page 937.)

Message   (See **Message** on page 937.)

Multimedia Presentation   A *multimedia presentation* is any presentation that involves two or more forms of media. For example, when you give an oral presentation and include a videotaped production or posters you have made, you are giving a multimedia presentation. One medium is your speaking voice, and the other medium is the videotape or the posters you use to support your presentation. A multimedia presentation that involves the use of presentation software or Web sites is sometimes called a **technology presentation.**

Nielsen Rating   *Nielsen rating* refers to the ratings system invented by the A. C. Nielsen Company, one of the largest marketing research companies in the United States. Nielsen ratings gather information about household television viewing choices from a sample of five thousand households selected to represent the population as a whole. Using a device called a peoplemeter, the firm gathers and distributes information including the program watched, the people watching it, and the amount of time each viewer spent watching. Nielsen ratings are used to measure a program's popularity and to pinpoint target audiences for shows. Advertisers make decisions about buying airtime for their commercials during specific shows based in part on Nielsen ratings.

Network   A *network* is a company that obtains and distributes programming to affiliated local stations or cable systems. Networks are not TV stations, but nearly 85 percent of all TV stations are affiliated with a network. Examples of networks include CBS, ABC, NBC, FOX, and WB. Each local station is responsible for its own programming, but a station that is affiliated with a network receives morning news programs, talk shows, soap operas, national news programs, sports programming, situation comedies, dramas, and late-night programming. The networks provide the programs free to stations in exchange for the right to sell advertising. (See also **Affiliate** on page 928.)

News   (See **News** on page 937.)

Newsmagazine   (See **Newsmagazine** on page 938.)

Photography   (See **Photography** on page 938.)

Political Advertising   (See **Political Advertising** on page 938.)

Producer   A *producer* is the person responsible for overseeing the creation of a movie or television or radio program. He or she is responsible for the following tasks:

- developing the overall message
- finding appropriate materials
- organizing a crew or staff
- finding and budgeting funding
- keeping the production on a timetable

Public Access   *Public access* refers to the channels on a cable television system set aside specifically for the public's use to create a variety of programs. These channels are often controlled by education officials or government leaders.

Ratings   *Ratings* are the system of categorizing films, TV programs, or video games by considering whether the content is appropriate for people of different ages. Ratings help adults and children evaluate the content of a message before viewing. (See also **Nielsen rating** on page 930.)

Reality TV   *Reality television* is the presentation of actual video footage taken by amateurs with police monitors and by surveillance cameras. Usually the footage is highly edited, but because reality TV is presented as an eyewitness account, people tend to find it believable.

Reporter   (See **Reporter** on page 938.)

Script   A *script* is the text or words of a film, play, or television or radio show. The format for film and TV scripts often includes information about the images to be shown. The script for news broadcasts is called *copy*. (See also **Copy** on page 936.)

Sequencing   *Sequencing* is the order in which scenes or images appear in a narrative. In television, film, and video, the editing process enhances sequencing by splicing together scenes, usually filmed separately and in different locations, to create a sense of flow or sequence.

Situation Comedy   A *situation comedy* is a television format that involves stories about a set of characters. The characters appear regularly each week in either a home, school, or work setting. Situation comedies involve humor and focus on life's ordinary problems and solutions. (See also **Genre** on page 934.)

Soft News   (See **Soft News** on page 938.)

Source   (See **Source** on page 938.)

Sponsorship   A *sponsorship* takes place when a business gives money to support a particular TV or radio program in return for commercial air time. Sponsorship is different from advertising because in sponsorship, a company's name is acknowledged but usually the product is not promoted. For example, public broadcasting may include sponsors' names and slogans. (See also **Broadcasting** on page 928.)

Storyboard   A *storyboard* is a visual script, or series of drawings, that indicates the appearance and order of shots and scenes in a script as well as audio and visual cues. (For an example of a **storyboard**, see page 51.)

Target Audience   (See **Target Audience** on page 938.)

Text   (See **Text** on page 938.)

General Media Terms

Audience   An *audience* is a group of receivers of a media message. Audiences may receive a message by listening, reading, or viewing. In the economics of the mass media business, advertisers pay to reach specific audiences when they place ads in newspapers, magazines, radio, television, or the Internet. Audiences are often identified by specific characteristics, or demographics. (See also **Demographics** on page 936.)

Authority   *Authority* refers to a quality of a message. A message that seems believable because it comes from a trustworthy and knowledgeable individual has authority. For example, a message about new regulations for teenage drivers would have more authority coming from a traffic safety instructor than from an outdated driver's handbook. (See also **Credibility** on this page and **Source** on page 938.)

Bias   A *bias* is a negative connotation or point of view. An editorial writer with a bias may present only one side of an issue or ignore information that does not support his or her position. (See also **Point of View** on page 935.)

Communicator   A *communicator* is a person involved in the act of communicating or sending messages to another person or persons (the audience). The receiver takes on the role of communicator when he or she returns the message.

Credibility   *Credibility* is the willingness to believe in or to trust what a person says and does. Credibility is not a characteristic of a speaker but a perception that exists in the minds of a listener or viewer. (See also **Authority** on this page.)

Critical Viewing   *Critical viewing* is the ability to use critical-thinking skills to view, question, analyze, and understand issues presented in visual media, including photography, film, television, and other mass media. Critical viewers use **media literacy** concepts to access, analyze, evaluate, and communicate media messages. On page 933 are five key concepts of media literacy and some questions to help you evaluate media messages.

Media Concepts	Evaluation Questions
1. All messages are made by someone. Every media message is written, edited, selected, illustrated, or composed by one or more individuals. Writers, photographers, artists, illustrators, and TV and radio producers all decide which elements (words, images, sounds) to include in a media message, which ones to leave out, and how to arrange and sequence the chosen elements. Knowing how media messages are constructed will help you better interpret the meaning of a message.	Ask yourself: "What words, images, or sounds are used to create the message?" and "What words, images, or sounds may have been left out of the message?"
2. Media messages are not reality. They are *representations* of reality that in turn shape people's ideas of the world. Fictional stories in the media can seem realistic if characters act in ways that seem authentic, but, of course, the stories are not real. An eyewitness news account of a natural disaster can seem real, but it usually reflects only one person's point of view, filtered through a TV camera and carefully edited down to a few images and words. Media messages can never match the complexity of the real world. Every media message also affects the way you think about the world. It is important that you judge the accuracy of media messages. Consider whether you think the messages reflect reality or show bias.	Ask yourself: "What is the point of view or experience of the message maker?" and "How does this message affect the way I think about a particular topic or idea?"
3. Each person interprets media messages differently. Your interpretation of a media message is based on your knowledge and experience. You can use your prior knowledge and experience to examine the many different stylistic features of a message and to evaluate the message within its context.	Ask yourself: "How does the message make me feel?" or "What does the message make me think of?"
4. People have a wide range of purposes for creating media messages. People create and share messages for many reasons; in modern culture making money is one of the most important. When people have political purposes, they use messages to gain power or authority over others. Understanding how messages operate in terms of their economic, political, social, and aesthetic purposes will help you better understand the context of a work.	Ask yourself: "Who created the message and why?" or "Is the producer's purpose to inform, to influence, to present ideas, to make money, to gain power, or to express ideas?"
5. Each mass medium—from TV to the newspaper to the Internet—has unique characteristics. Media messages come in different forms. A media producer makes choices about which kinds of media are most appropriate to convey a particular message. For example, TV news favors messages that are immediate and visual, while news photographs favor messages that have an emotional component. Knowing how the medium shapes the message will help you evaluate how image makers—news photographers or graphic artists, for example—represent meaning. Doing this can help you understand why the message makes you feel the way it does.	Ask yourself: "Through what medium is the message delivered?" and "How does the form affect the message?"

Decoding   *Decoding* is the making of meaning from verbal and nonverbal signals. For example, audiences decode symbols, such as words and pictures, when they watch TV or read a newspaper.

Deconstruction   *Deconstruction* is the process of analyzing, or taking apart, the pieces of a media message to understand its meaning. The process of deconstruction involves looking at both what is stated, such as the words printed on a newspaper page, and what is not directly stated, including elements of the historical, economic, and political context in which the newspaper was created.

Feedback   *Feedback* is a response from an audience to the sender of a message. It can be immediate or delayed. Applause, booing, and asking questions are typical forms of **immediate feedback** from an audience. Writing a letter to the editor to respond to a newspaper editorial and filling out a questionnaire on a Web page are forms of **delayed feedback.**

Formula   A *formula* is an established model or approach. In television and film, it refers to a typical combination of characters or presentation of material. In dramas which feature aliens from space, for example, the non-human characters are usually portrayed in grotesque make-up with physical features that produce terror and awe. The conventions of make-up for the alien characters is part of the formula.

Genre   A *genre* is a category of artistic forms or media products that share **conventions,** or commonly accepted ways of presenting messages. For example, before the opening commercials, prime-time TV news programs usually begin with a short, attention-grabbing segment that announces the day's headline events. Each genre has a particular audience and conventions. Some examples of genres within television are documentaries, dramas, and talk shows.

Interpretation   *Interpretation* is the process of creating meaning from exposure to a message through reading, viewing, or listening. People's interpretations of messages differ, depending on their life experiences, backgrounds, and points of view.

Media Law   Various government structures, laws, and policies regulate access, content, delivery, and use of the mass media. For example, the *First Amendment* to the Constitution forbids Congress to set up or in any way pass laws limiting speech or the press. *Copyright law* protects the rights of authors and other media owners against the unauthorized publishing, reproducing, and selling of their works. *Censorship* is any governmental attempt to suppress or control people's access to media messages. Some censorship, however, may be used to protect citizens against damage to their reputations (libel) or against invasions of their privacy.

News Values   *News values* are the set of criteria journalists use to determine whether information is newsworthy. News values include

- **timeliness**   events or issues that are happening now
- **conflict**   unresolved events or issues that are interesting to the public
- **novelty**   stories that contain unique, interesting elements
- **relevance**   stories that are of interest to local audiences
- **human interest**   stories that touch people's emotions

- **prominence** stories about celebrities, politicians, or other noteworthy people
- **impact** stories that make a difference in people's lives

If a news event has these features, it is more likely to be covered by the news media.

Newsworthiness *Newsworthiness* is the quality of an event that is worthy of being reported in a newspaper or news broadcast. An event must be of interest or importance to the public in order to be considered newsworthy. (See also **News Values** on page 934.)

Omission An *omission* is what is left out of a media message. All messages are selective and incomplete. For example, some films of historical events omit information or ignore historical figures in the events. Some news stories present only one side of a controversial issue, omitting information contrary to the slant of the story. Noticing what is not included in a message helps to identify the author's point of view. (See also **Point of View** below.)

Point of View *Point of view* can refer to the position or view of the person reporting a story or telling a tale in the mass media. Point of view is also a literary concept which can be used to interpret mass media texts ranging from docudramas to feature news stories. In the electronic media, point of view can be indicated by the type of narration used or by the type of camera shot used.

Propaganda *Propaganda* is any form of communication that uses persuasive techniques to reach a mass audience. Propaganda was originally defined as the spreading of biased ideas and opinions through lies and deception. This definition gave the concept of propaganda a negative connotation. However, as scholars began to study the topic in the 1940s, they came to realize that propaganda was everywhere. Over time, the concept of propaganda has lost some of its negative connotation. Propaganda is now thought of as the communication of a point of view with the goal of having audience members come to voluntarily accept this position as one of their beliefs. Advertising is one of the major forms of propaganda. (See also **Advertising** on page 936.)

Purpose The *purpose* of a media message is what its sender or creator intends to achieve. Usually, the purpose of a message is to inform, to educate, to persuade, to entertain, to express oneself, or to make money. A message may have both a primary and a secondary purpose.

Sensationalism *Sensationalism* is the media's use or portrayal of material that is intended to generate curiosity, fear, or other strong responses. The material can be exaggerated or shocking in content. Content that refers to romance, death, children, or animals is often sensational. (See also **Reality TV** on page 931 and **Tabloid** on page 938.)

Stereotypes *Stereotypes* are generalized beliefs based on misinformation or insufficient evidence about an entire group of individuals. A stereotype about teenagers, for example, would be that all teenagers are reckless drivers.

Visual Literacy *Visual literacy* is a person's awareness of how meaning is communicated through visual media, including the use of color, line, shape, and texture.

Print Media Terms

Advertising   *Advertising* is the use of images or text to promote or sell a product, service, image, or idea to a wide audience. Advertising is a marketing technique that is designed to persuade an audience. Typical advertising formats include print advertisements in newspapers and magazines, billboards, radio and television commercials, and electronic billboards on the World Wide Web. (See also **Marketing** on page 937 and **Sponsorship** on page 932.)

Byline   A *byline* is the name of the reporter or writer of a report published in a newspaper or magazine or presented on television or radio.

Circulation   *Circulation* is a measurement of the size of the audience for print media. It includes the total number of copies of a publication, such as a newspaper, that is delivered to subscribers, newsstands, and vendors.

Copy   *Copy* is the text in a media message.

Demographics   *Demographics* are the characteristics that define a particular audience. They include gender, age, educational background, cultural heritage, and income. Advertisers use demographics to target certain audiences. For example, advertisers know that many teenagers watch music videos, so in the commercial breaks they advertise items—such as special brands of clothing or food products—that they believe will especially appeal to teens.

Digital Editing   *Digital editing* is the use of computer technology to alter or change an image before it is presented to an audience. Photo editors often edit out distracting elements—such as telephone wires or shadows—from photo illustrations. However, large-scale digital editing of hard-news photographs is thought to be an unethical practice.

Editor   An *editor* supervises reporters. Editors decide what news stories will appear in print media or in broadcasting. They also check facts for accuracy and correct errors. (See also **News Values** on page 934.)

Elements of Design   *Elements of design* are the parts of an idea's visual representation—such as *color, line, shape,* and *texture*—that give meaning to the visual representation. The following list explains how each element communicates meaning. (See also **Document Design** on page 849.)

- **Color**   creates mood and adds realism with its eye appeal. Color designates areas of space by separating and emphasizing parts of a visual. Viewers also associate certain items with particular colors. For example, usually oranges and tangerines are associated with the color orange. (See also **Color** on page 856.)

- **Line**   determines the direction and speed of the viewer's eye movement. For example, straight lines suggest decisiveness, while curvy lines indicate gracefulness. Lines also communicate factual information in graphic organizers. (See also **Types of Graphics** on page 857.)

- **Shape**   emphasizes elements in the visual and adds interest. Often, shapes evoke emotional responses. For example, a square represents solidity, while a circle indicates completeness.

- **Texture**   is the manner in which the visual representation appeals to a viewer's sense of touch. Sometimes superficial texture in a visual may be created by cross-hatching, diagonal lines, or stippling.

Feature News *Feature news,* also called soft news, refers to news stories whose primary purpose is to entertain. Feature stories usually are not timely. Stories about celebrities and ordinary people, places, animals, events, and products are considered feature news because they generate sympathy, curiosity, or amazement in viewers, readers, or listeners. An example of feature news would be a profile of a high school principal who had shown effective leadership in a high risk, large, urban school district. (See also **Hard News** below and **Soft News** on page 938.)

Font A *font* is a style of lettering used for printing text. (For more on **Fonts,** see page 854.)

Hard News *Hard news* refers to fact-based reporting of breaking news stories. Hard news answers the basic *5W-How?* questions about timely subjects, such as national and international politics, economics, social issues, the environment, and scientific discoveries. An example of hard news would be a story reporting the results of a devastating natural disaster. (See also **Feature News** above and **Soft News** on page 938.)

Headline A *headline* is the title of a newspaper or magazine article, usually set in large or bold type. It has two purposes: to inform the reader of the content of the article and to get the reader's attention.

Lead A *lead* is the introduction to a newspaper article or a broadcast report. It ranges from one sentence to several paragraphs in length and contains information that motivates a reader or viewer to continue with the story. A lead usually contains the major facts of a story and may

also describe a curious or unusual situation to attract reader or viewer attention.

EXAMPLE

LONDON, August 20—The largest audience in history for a solar eclipse gathered Tuesday along a narrow arc of land running from the Isles of Scilly off England to eastern India, waiting for a celestial show that would last just a couple of minutes.

Marketing *Marketing* is the process of moving goods or services from the producer to the consumer. It includes identifying consumer wants or needs; designing, packaging, and pricing the product; and arranging for locations where the product will be sold. Marketing also includes promoting the product to a target audience through advertising or other means. (See also **Advertising** on page 936.)

Medium The *medium* of a message is the form in which it is presented or distributed, including film, video, radio, television, the Internet, and print.

Message A *message* is a combination of symbols that is communicated to one or more people. Messages are created by people who use symbols, including language, gesture, images, sounds, and electronic forms. Media messages are communicated through various mass media. (See also **Medium** above.)

News *News* is the presentation of current and interesting information that will interest or affect an audience. Local news is produced by local newspapers and radio and TV stations, which use their own equipment, reporters, and resources. The focus of local news is information that affects a small audience with regional interests. National news is produced by large newspapers and radio and TV stations. Because their resources are greater, national news organizations may cover more national and world issues or events.

Newsmagazine   A *newsmagazine* is a weekly, biweekly, monthly, or bimonthly printed journal that focuses on news issues. On TV, a newsmagazine is a news program divided into several news segments or stories.

Photography   *Photography* is a process of making pictures by using cameras to record patterns of light and images on film or on computer disks. Photography is both an art form and a major component of the mass media; it is used in making still photographs and motion pictures. People sometimes think that "a photograph never lies," but a photograph, like all media messages, is selective and incomplete. Photographers use a wide range of techniques to communicate their points of view, including the framing and composition of an image, the use of filters or digital editing, and the selection of what to include in the frame. (See also **Digital Editing** on page 936 and **Point of View** on page 935.)

Political Advertising   *Political advertising* is the use of the mass media to persuade listeners and viewers about a political candidate's ideas or opinions. Political candidates who use advertising must use techniques similar to those used to sell products. Their messages must be simple and attention-getting. (See also **Advertising** on page 936.)

Print Media   *Print media* refers to the hard copies of mass media products that are printed on paper to be read or looked at by consumers.

Examples of print media are newspapers, magazines, pamphlets, and flyers.

Reporter   A *reporter* is a journalist who is responsible for information gathering. Reporters gather information and work with editors to create TV and print news. (See also **Editor** on page 936.)

Soft News   *Soft news,* or feature news, is the presentation of general interest material, such as unusual pet stories, in a news format. Soft news is designed to entertain readers or viewers. (See also **Feature News** and **Hard News** on page 937.)

Source   A *source* is the person who first supplies information or ideas that are then shared with others. Journalists rely on sources for the information they report and select individuals that they believe are credible and have authority. (See also **Authority** on page 932.)

Tabloid   A *tabloid* is a publication with a newspaper format that provides sensational news items and photographs. Tabloids are highly dependent on stories and photographs of media celebrities. Tabloid producers often admit that the stories they report are either false or exaggerations of the truth.

Target Audience   A *target audience* is a segment of the population for which a product or presentation is designed. (See also **Demographics** on page 936.)

Text   *Text* refers to the symbols used to create a message, such as the language found in a book or the images and sound in a TV show.

Writing

Skills, Structures, and Techniques

You can use the following ideas and information to become a more effective writer.

Business Letters   A *business letter* is a formal way to share written information. Business letters may be used to request information, apply for a job, voice a complaint or express appreciation. Use the following guidelines to create professional-looking business letters.

■ **Parts of a business letter**   There are six parts of a business letter. They are usually arranged on the page in one of two styles. In **block form,** all six parts begin at the left margin, and paragraphs are not indented. In **modified block form,** the heading, the closing, and your signature begin to the right of the center of the page. All the other parts begin at the left margin, and all paragraphs are indented.

Business Letters

- Use white, unlined 8 1/2" x 11" paper.
- Type your letter or prepare your letter on a computer, using single-spacing and an extra line between paragraphs. If you write by hand, neatly write the letter, using black or blue ink. Check for typing errors and misspellings.
- Center your letter with equal margins on the sides and at the top and bottom.
- Use only one side of the paper. If your letter won't fit on one page, leave a one-inch margin at the bottom of the first page and carry over at least two lines onto the second page.
- Avoid mark-outs, erasures, or other careless marks.
- Use a polite, respectful, professional tone.
- Use formal, standard English. Avoid slang, contractions, and most abbreviations.
- Include all necessary information, but get to the point quickly. Be sure that your reader knows why you wrote and what you are asking.

Block Style

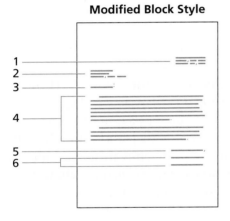

Modified Block Style

1. The *heading* usually has three lines:
   - your street address (or post office box number)
   - your city, state, and ZIP Code
   - the date the letter was written
2. The *inside address* gives the name and address of the person to whom you are writing. Use a courtesy title (such as *Mr.* , *Mrs.*, *Ms.*, or *Miss*) or a professional title (such as *Dr.* or *Professor*) in front of the person's name. Include the person's business title (such as *Director* or *Editor*) after the name. Finally, follow the name with the name of the company or organization and its address. If you do not know the name of the person who will read your letter—for example if you are writing to the service

department of a mail-order company from which you bought an item that was damaged in shipping—put the position title in the place of the name.

3. The *salutation* is your greeting. If you are writing to a specific person, begin with *Dear,* followed by the courtesy title or professional title, and the person's last name. End with a colon. If you don't have the name of a specific person, use a general salutation such as *Dear Sir or Madam:*. You can also use a department or a position title, with or without the word *Dear.*
4. The *body,* or main part of your letter, contains the message. If the body of the message requires more than one paragraph, leave a blank line between paragraphs.
5. The *closing* is your ending. Appropriate closings are *Yours truly, Sincerely,* or *Respectfully yours.* End the closing with a comma. Capitalize only the first word of the closing.
6. Your *signature* should be handwritten in ink, directly below the closing and above your typed or printed name. Always sign your full name with no titles.

> **NOTE** If you are including more in your envelope than just your letter, for example, a résumé, brochure, or writing sample, leave two lines blank after the signature, then type "encl." (for *enclosure*) plus the type of item or items you are enclosing.

■ **Types of business letters** There are four types of business letters.

1. **Appreciation or commendation letters** An *appreciation* or *commendation letter* is written to express appreciation or encouragement to a person, a group, or an organization. When you write an appreciation or commendation letter, it is important

to tell the person or organization exactly why you are pleased. Following is the body of a sample appreciation letter.

I am writing to congratulate all of you at WQBK on your change in format from top 40 to alternative music. Although I enjoy listening to popular music, I am more interested in hearing what musicians outside the mainstream are recording. My friends and I are tired of hearing the same twenty songs every day on the radio.

I hope that you succeed with your new format. I know that my friends listen to your station, and sometimes even my parents listen to you, too. Good luck!

2. **Complaint or adjustment letters** The purpose of a *complaint* or *adjustment letter* is to express your dissatisfaction with a service or product. In the letter, you should identify what is wrong and suggest a solution. Here is the body of a sample adjustment letter.

I have noticed that there are only two trash cans in Edgemont Park. I think that the litter situation would improve if the Parks Department would put more trash cans in the park. These cans should be convenient to the field, the picnic area, and the creek. More people would pick up their trash if there were containers close to where they are needed.

Please give your attention to this suggestion. I think Edgemont Park is a wonderful neighborhood resource that should be kept clean for everyone in our community to enjoy.

When you write a complaint or adjustment letter, remember to register your complaint as soon as possible after noticing the problem and explain exactly what is wrong. Include information such as

- what product or service you ordered or expected
- why you are not satisfied (for example, the item was sized incorrectly)
- how you were affected (for example, you lost time or money)
- how you think the problem may be solved

Keep the tone of your letter calm and courteous. Despite your frustration, your letter will be more effective if you are coolheaded and communicate the problem clearly.

3. **Letters of Application** *Letters of application* provide a selection committee or a possible employer with information about you. The information helps readers decide whether you are a good choice for a position or award such as a job or scholarship. (You might instead be asked to provide this information on a **form**, such as a standard job application.)

Guidelines for Letters of Application

1. Identify the position for which you are applying. Tell how you heard about it.

2. Depending on the position for which you are applying, you might mention
- your grade-point average
- your experience, or your activities, awards, and honors
- personal qualities or characteristics that make you a good choice for the position
- the date or times you are available to begin the position

3. Always offer to provide references. Your references should be responsible adults (usually not relatives) who have agreed to recommend you. Be prepared to supply their addresses and telephone numbers.

Below is an example of an application letter.

1437 Windy Ridge Road
Milwaukee, WI 53224
January 20, 2001

Mrs. Elaine Fong, Director
Spanish Student Exchange Program
P.O. Box 3001
New York, NY 10002

Dear Mrs. Fong:

I am writing to apply for the summer exchange program to Barcelona, Spain, as advertised in the January 13, 2001, edition of *Student Voices*.

I am a sophomore at Vince Lombardi High School in Milwaukee, Wisconsin. My grade-point average is 3.3, and I have studied Spanish for three years. Last semester I won an award for my work in this class.

I would be proud to be selected for this program. I am aware of the responsibility it involves. I would feel privileged to gain a new understanding of the Spanish culture, and, on my return, to share this information with others in my school and community.

I will gladly furnish references who can tell you more about my qualifications. My parents, too, are supportive of my interest.

Please let me know if there is any other information I need to give you before you may consider me as a candidate for this program.

Sincerely,

Taneesha Collins

Taneesha Collins

4. Request or order letters In a *request letter,* you are asking for something, such as information about a product or someone's time or services. In an *order letter,* you are asking for something specific. You might write an order letter to purchase a product by mail or request a brochure. In request or order letters, it is important to say clearly what you want.

Here is a sample request letter.

Shackelton High School
19 Brookside Drive
Latham, NY 12110
September 3, 2001

Mr. Stuart Reinhardt, Manager
Rollerama
2008 Route 9
Latham, NY 12110

Dear Mr. Reinhardt:

Shackelton High School's sophomore class has voted to hold a class party at Rollerama. As class secretary, I am writing to ask if we could plan this event for Saturday, November 12, from 7:30 P.M. to 10:30 P.M.

Could we rent the rink on the same terms as you gave the senior class last spring? The sophomore class can guarantee a minimum attendance of 75 students. Students will pay an admission price of $5.00. Skate rental will be an additional $2.50 charge.

Our class is looking forward to an enjoyable evening at Rollerama.

Yours truly,

Lindsey O'Donnell

Lindsey O'Donnell
Class Secretary
Class of 2003

When you are writing a request or order letter, remember the following points.

- State your request clearly.
- If you are asking someone to send you information, enclose a self-addressed, stamped envelope.
- If you are asking someone to do something for you, make your request well in advance.
- If you are ordering something, include all important information, such as the size, color, brand name, or any other specific information. If there are costs involved, add the amount correctly.

Compositions   A composition is a longer piece of writing that usually has three main parts: *introduction, body,* and *conclusion.* Each has a specific function, yet they all work together to communicate a main idea. The main idea is usually stated in the *thesis.* The three sections of a composition follow.

- **Introduction**   Your composition's *introduction* should do three things:
  1. **Catch the reader's attention.** The introduction may be the most important paragraph in your composition. If the introduction is not written well, your readers might not bother to read the rest of your paper.
  2. **Set the tone.** The words you choose and what you say about your topic set your composition's **tone.** The tone of a composition may be serious, humorous, formal, informal, critical, or even outraged.
  3. **Present the thesis.** A *thesis statement* is a sentence or two that identifies your topic and explains your main idea about it. A

Strategies for Writing a Thesis Statement	Example
1. **Review the facts and details in your prewriting notes. Identify the main idea and begin thinking about how your supporting ideas fit together.**	You notice that in your notes about homelessness in your city, there is little discussion about the problem. Your thesis might read: *The problem of homeless teens in our city needs more attention.*
2. **Check your thesis statement by asking both of the following questions: What is my topic? What am I trying to say about my topic?**	Topic: *teen homelessness* Main Idea: *People should be better informed about teen homelessness in the city.*
3. **Be clear and specific.**	You might make the thesis more specific by adding more information. Your thesis might read: *In our city alone, there are about a hundred kids without regular homes. The problem of teen homelessness is one that city leaders need to address.*
4. **Evaluate your thesis with your audience in mind. Will the reader care about what you are saying about your topic? About your arguments?**	You might think to yourself, "My classmates are the audience. They may not know much about the issue. They will probably be interested in it."

thesis statement works in a composition like a topic sentence works in a paragraph. The chart on page 943 shows some strategies for writing a thesis statement. Often, but not always, the thesis statement comes at the end of the introduction. When this is the case, the introduction moves from a general discussion of the topic to a narrower, more specific focus, as shown in the following graphic.

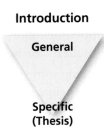

Introduction

General

Specific (Thesis)

To write an effective introduction, try beginning with one of the techniques in the chart below. The examples show how

Techniques for Beginning Introductions

Technique	Example
Begin with an anecdote or example.	*Suppose almost every morning you woke up in an unfamiliar place. Then suppose that you had to be able to pack everything you own into a suitcase or shopping bag. How would you feel in these situations? This is the experience of many teenagers who happen to be homeless.*
Begin with a startling fact or by adopting an unusual position.	*Mayor Ronnie Meyers attributes her career in politics to one thing —the six months that she, her two sisters, and her mother were homeless. Although she was only twelve at the time, she knew that the experience had changed her life. She decided that she would work to make sure other teens did not have to go through what she did.*
Use an appropriate quotation.	*"Being a teenager is hard enough without the added stress of being without a place to live," says Mario Ferrars, a social worker. "Too many kids are without a steady place to go to after school. It's a problem that is not recognized enough."*
Start with background information.	*In our city alone, there are more than two hundred people who are officially homeless. Half of these are under the age of fifteen. Only twenty percent of these young people are going to school five days a week. It is important to get all these students to school every day. The question is, how do we do that?*
Begin with a simple statement of your thesis.	*The homelessness situation is becoming an obvious problem in even the smallest cities and towns. What is less obvious is the way the problem is affecting teenagers.*
Begin with a question or a challenge to the reader.	*When you walk downtown, do you find yourself trying not to notice the people sleeping on the sidewalks or in stairwells? Or are you the kind of person who carries loose change so that you can donate it to people who really need it? Either way, have you noticed how young some of these homeless people are? You cannot deny that homelessness, especially of young people, is a problem in many cities.*

you might introduce a composition about homelessness.

NOTE Often you will have an occasion for writing, too. That means that you are writing because some recent event in the news or in your community prompted you to think about your topic. In other words, your problem has a context in the outer world. If possible, mention this occasion in your writing—it will make your paper relevant to your readers, too.

■ **Body** The *body* states and develops the composition's main points. Together, all the paragraphs in the body support one main idea—the thesis statement. When writing the body of your composition, keep in mind the following guidelines.

1. **Arrange your information** in a way that makes sense to your readers and is appropriate to your topic. This gives your composition *coherence*. The table below indicates four common ways to arrange ideas in a composition.

2. **Eliminate any details that do not support your thesis.** This gives your paper *unity*.

3. **Show how your ideas are connected** by using *direct references* and *transitional expressions*. (See also pages 375–376.)

■ **Conclusion** As the final part of your paper, the *conclusion* should do four things:

1. **Provide readers with a sense of completion.** Your readers have invested in your ideas by reading your entire composition. Be fair to readers by bringing together all the ideas you mentioned earlier.

2. **Restate your thesis.** Remember, your thesis statement was intended to show readers the direction your writing would take. Restating the thesis confirms that you have arrived at the place you wanted to be. Often a conclusion begins with a specific statement, such as a restatement of the thesis, and moves to general information. The following graphic may help you to visualize the organization.

Conclusion

Specific (Thesis)

General

Arranging Ideas		
Type of Order	**Definition**	**Example**
Chronological	order that presents events as they happen in time	explanation of a process; personal narrative; story
Spatial	order that describes objects according to their location	descriptions (near to far, left to right, top to bottom, and so on)
Importance	order that gives details from least to most important or the reverse	descriptions, evaluative writing; explanations (main idea and supporting details); persuasive writing
Logical	order that relates groups and items	comparison-contrast; explanations of cause and effect or problem-solution; definitions

3. **Summarize your major points.** By summarizing the main points of your composition, you allow your readers to review all that they have learned from you. Summarizing helps your readers remember what they read.

4. **Offer a solution or make a recommendation.** If you have taken a stand on an issue in your composition, you should stress your point in the conclusion by offering a solution or recommending an action to take. Including a stand or recommendation in the conclusion makes it more likely that the reader will remember and act on your opinion or idea.

To write an effective conclusion, try one of the following techniques:

Technique	Example
Restate your main idea.	*The problem of teenagers who are without homes is growing and will not resolve itself without more involvement of people in the community.*
Summarize your major points.	*Homelessness affects every part of a teenager's life—school work, social life, and involvement in sports, hobbies, and the community. Teens who might otherwise be active members of the community are too busy trying to hold their lives together. With more focused awareness on the part of the community, teen homelessness could be reduced, allowing teens to focus on the things that are important.*
Close with a final idea or example.	*The Spare Room program started by adults and teens in a neighboring city has reduced the number of homeless teens there by twenty percent in the last two years. The results speak for themselves—teen homelessness is a problem that can be solved in part by caring people with good ideas.*
End with a comment on the topic (a thoughtful observation, a personal reaction, or a look to the future).	*Look around your room and decide what you would put in a suitcase and carry with you. If it is not an easy choice, think of what it would be like to have no choice.*
Call on your readers to take action.	*If you and your family were to offer a homeless classmate a place to stay even one night a week, you would reduce the problem of teen homelessness in this city by a small but significant amount. Imagine how good it would feel to be able to say that you have done your part.*
Refer to your introduction.	*You don't have to have experienced homelessness, as Mayor Ronnie Meyers did, in order to get involved in the fight against homelessness.*

E-Mail Guidelines

- Always be polite in your messages—even if you know the person to whom you are writing. Being rude to someone in an e-mail is called *flaming*. Flaming often back-fires because there is always the chance that your angry message could be forwarded and read by someone you didn't intend to see it.

- Avoid using capital letters in your messages. CAPITAL LETTERS CONVEY SHOUTING. No one wants to be shouted at in cyberspace. (If you want to show emphasis, place asterisks (*) on either side of the important word or term. For example, "What do you think about the *metaphor* in chapter 2?")

- Use emoticons sparingly and never use them in formal e-mails. *Emoticons* are combinations of symbols that, when you tilt your head to the left, look like faces and suggest feelings. For example, the emoticon :-) suggests laughter or "I'm just kidding." Use them in informal e-mails only.

- Always pay attention to the addresses entered in your address line. Make sure that you are sending appropriate messages to the right people.

- Always fill in the subject line before you send a message. Providing a subject will help your readers prioritize your message, which could be only one of many they receive.

- Avoid forwarding an e-mail without asking the permission of the original sender. Private e-mails are usually intended for your eyes only.

- Keep your message concise and to the point. If possible, limit yourself to one full screen or less of text. Scrolling through long e-mail messages can be tedious.

- Use bulleted lists and indentation to make the document easy for your readers to read on-screen. Bulleted lists are especially helpful if you are raising more than one question or point.

- Always use standard English and make sure that your spelling, grammar, and punctuation are correct.

- Include salutations, such as "Dear Mr. Tate," if you are writing for the first time to someone you do not know. Also, ending with "Sincerely" or "Thank you" followed by your full name is always considered polite.

E-mail Electronic mail, or *e-mail,* is correspondence sent by the computer rather than through your local post office. You can use e-mail to write personal, informal letters or to send formal, business messages. Because e-mail is so easy to use, many people ignore the guidelines associated with writing letters when they are composing e-mail messages. Informal content and format are often acceptable when you write to someone you know well or send comments to a newsgroup or chat group where the discussions are clearly relaxed. However, if you are writing to someone you do not know well for business or research purposes, you should follow the guidelines listed above. Online etiquette, or "Netiquette," stresses that good manners and common sense are as important in cyberspace as they are in the real world.

Envelopes If you want a letter to arrive promptly at its destination, you must address its envelope correctly. Place the return address in the top left-hand corner of the envelope. In the center of the envelope, write the name and address of the person to whom you are writing. For a business letter, the addressee's name and address should exactly match the inside address. Use the proper two-letter state code rather than writing out the state name.

Forms   Printed forms vary, but the following techniques will help you fill out any form accurately and completely.

- Read all of the instructions carefully.
- Type or write neatly. Unless a pencil is specified, type or print your information in either blue or black ballpoint pen.
- Proofread your completed form and correct errors neatly.

Graphic Organizers   A *graphic organizer* is a visual device that helps you "see" what you are thinking. You can use graphic organizers to find a subject to write about, to gather information, and to organize your information. Following are some widely used types of graphic organizers.

- **Charts**   *Charts* are a practical, graphic way to arrange information. They help you see "blocks" of information, and their relationships, clearly. In the following chart, a writer has organized information about two minerals and their effects on health into three categories.

Mineral	Sources of Mineral	Uses by the Body	Deficiency Symptoms
Calcium	milk, cheese, whole grains, leafy vegetables, peas, and other legumes	bone and teeth development, muscular and nervous system functioning, blood clotting	soft bones, poor teeth, failure of blood to clot
Iron	liver, red meat, egg yolk, whole grains, prunes, nuts	healthy red blood cells	anemia

- **Clustering**   (See **Clustering** on page 953.)

- **Mapping**   (See **Mapping** on page 955.)

- **Sequence chain**   A *sequence chain* is a diagram that helps you see how one event leads to another. It works well when you are narrating or explaining a process. In the following example, the writer uses a sequence chain to show the steps of the water cycle.

Water in the oceans evaporates.

Airborne water, heated by the sun, evaporates into the atmosphere.

In the atmosphere, the water cools, condenses, and forms clouds.

Clouds release the water in the form of rain.

As rain, the water falls back to the surface of the earth and is absorbed.

Water that is not absorbed is caught up in rivers, streams, and creeks.

Water is transported back to the ocean.

- **Time line**   A *time line* organizes information chronologically on a horizontal line, with the first or earliest events on the left end and the most recent or latest events on the right end of the line.

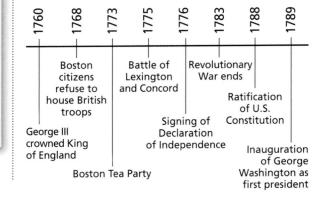

- **Formal outlines**   A *formal outline* is a highly structured, clearly labeled writing plan. It has a set pattern, using letters and numbers to label main headings, subheadings and details. An outline can use either topics (words and phrases) or complete sentences for each item. Here is a portion of a formal outline about bicycle touring.

> **Title:** Bicycle Touring
>
> **Thesis statement:** If you are interested in bicycle touring, you need to make some specific preparations involving your bike, yourself, your clothing, and your route.
>
> I. Your bike
>   A. Type of bike
>   B. Condition of the bike
>   C. Equipment
>   1. Map
>   2. Light
>   3. Kits
>   a. Bicycle-repair kit
>   b. First-aid kit
>   4. Saddlebags
>   5. Water container
> II. Your physical condition
>   A. Exercise program
>   1. Muscles
>   2. Endurance
>   B. Goal: 10-15 miles

Paragraphs   A paragraph is a group of sentences that presents and supports a main idea; it is also the primary building block in a composition. Although most of the paragraphs in a single composition are often of one major type, many compositions contain more than one type of paragraph. The four types of paragraphs vary by purpose.

- **Descriptive paragraphs**   A *descriptive paragraph* lets your readers visualize your subject, whether it is a person, an object, or a scene. Descriptive paragraphs are often organized according to spatial order and usually contain sensory details.

Sensory detail 1
Sensory detail 2
Sensory detail 3
Sensory detail 4

> The train pulled in, steaming and gasping, just as the sun came up. It had come from Dalian, 600 miles away, and it stopped everywhere. So it was sensationally littered with garbage—peanut shells, apple cores, chewed chicken bones, orange peels and greasy paper. It was very dirty and it was so cold inside the spit had frozen on the floor into misshapen yellow-green medallions of ice. The covering between coaches was a snow tunnel, the frost on the windows was an inch thick, the doors had no locks and so they banged and thumped as a freezing draft rushed through the carriages.
>
> Paul Theroux,
> *Riding the Iron Rooster*

- **Expository paragraphs**   Writers use *expository paragraphs* to explain and inform. Expository paragraphs are usually organized according to logical order and contain factual and statistical information. The facts and statistics in the following expository paragraph support and prove the main idea that the enormous amount of trash United States residents throw away today is a big problem.

Every year, the typical U.S. family throws out 2,460 pounds of paper, 540 pounds of metals, 480 pounds of glass, and 480 pounds of food scraps. All told, each of us throws away more than 1,200 pounds of trash per year, far more than people in most other countries. About 80 percent of that garbage ends up in landfills—dumps, as they are more commonly known. (Of the remaining 20 percent, about half is recycled and half is incinerated.) One big problem is that we are running out of landfill space—more than half of the nation's landfills will be full within ten years.

John Elkington, Julia Hailes, Douglas Hill, and Joel Makower, *Going Green*

- **Narrative paragraphs**   A *narrative paragraph* is used to tell a story or to illustrate an event or series of events, usually in chronological order.

In the radio room, Harold Bride was exhausted. The two operators were expected to keep the radio working twenty-four hours a day, and Bride lay down to take a much-needed nap. Phillips was so busy with the passenger messages that he actually brushed off the final ice warning of the night. It was from the *Californian*. Trapped in a field of ice, she had stopped for the night about nineteen miles north of the *Titanic*. She was so close that the message literally blasted in Phillips' ears. Annoyed by the loud interruption, he cut off the *Californian's* radio operator with the words "Shut up, shut up. I'm busy."

Robert D. Ballard, *Exploring the Titanic*

- **Persuasive paragraphs**   A writer uses a *persuasive paragraph* to express his or her opinion about a particular subject, for the purpose of convincing others to share the opinion or to take action. Writers of persuasive paragraphs usually use order of importance or logical order to organize their ideas.

Art history opens the child's imagination to other eras and cultures. If students of the next century are to work and live productively side by side with others from different cultures, they must respect and appreciate cultural differences and, at the same time, discern what they share in common with other peoples. The arts are one of the best ways of achieving this practical goal. Learning how to critique and judge art sharpens critical faculties by obliging the student to think independently, creatively, and to make reasoned judgments based on his or her knowledge and trained observations. Finally, consideration of aesthetic issues teaches them to be able to deal with the nature and meaning of art in their own lives.

Harold M. Williams, "Don't Ignore the Arts," *USA Today* magazine

Prewriting Techniques   The following techniques can help you find a subject about which to write and gather information about that subject. Although the prewriting techniques are presented separately, you may often use more than one technique at a time. You may also find that you prefer to use some techniques more than others.

- **Asking the *5W-How?* questions**   Ask yourself the reporter's questions—*Who?*

What? When? Where? Why? and *How?*—to find ideas for your writing.

EXAMPLE

> **Who** are some famous Creek leaders or chiefs?
>
> **What** was a Creek community like when Europeans first settled in North America?
>
> **When** did the Creeks first encounter Europeans?
>
> **Where** did they live at the time?
>
> **Why** are they called "Creeks"—an English word?
>
> **How** did Creeks react to the European settlers?

- **Asking *what if?* questions**   To stimulate your creative thinking, ask a variety of *What if?* questions about a subject. Imagine different everyday situations and see where these ideas take you.

> **What if** I could change one thing in the past?
>
> **What if** a familiar thing no longer existed?
>
> **What if** I could create something completely new?
>
> **What if** I could travel to another time?
>
> **What if** our society didn't use money?

- **Brainstorming**   Write down a subject, and then list all your ideas about that subject as quickly as you can. Resist the urge to evaluate your ideas; remember that you are trying to come up with as many ideas as possible. Keep going until you run out of ideas, and then evaluate the ideas as possible topics for writing. Brainstorming is also a good group activity.

EXAMPLE

> **Weather**
>
> | rain | heat | snow |
> | --- | --- | --- |
> | windchill | tornadoes | fog |
> | cloud formations | hurricanes | drought |

- **Chaining**   This technique uses questions and answers to help you make connections between ideas. It is a way to build new ideas from existing ones and often helps you to see subjects in a totally new light. Here are the steps for chaining.

  1. The first link in the chain is a question.
  2. The answer to that question becomes the next link.
  3. The third link is a question prompted by the answer in step 2. This process continues until you get the ideas you want.

EXAMPLE

Question: How will computers change our everyday world in the future?

Answer: It's possible that many people will work from their homes instead of in an office building.

Question: Won't this cause problems for the economy?

Answer: Possibly, but it could also open up the possibilities for new services and businesses.

Question: What kinds of new services would be needed?

Answer: Home offices, computer services for homes, and probably other businesses tied to home business needs.

- **Clustering**   Like brainstorming, *clustering* (also called *webbing* or *making connections*) is useful for generating creative ideas. First, write a subject in the middle of your paper. Circle the subject. Then, in the space around the subject, write whatever related ideas occur to you. Circle the new ideas and draw lines to connect the new ideas with the original subject. As you continue to think about the subject, write down your ideas and draw circles and lines to show connections among the ideas.

EXAMPLE

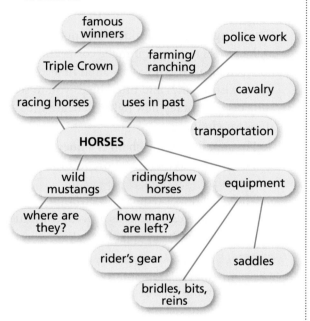

■ **Cubing** Investigate a subject by imagining a cube that has one of the following directions on each of its six sides: *Describe it. Compare it. Associate it. Analyze it. Apply it. Argue for or against it.* Write for three minutes about each side of the cube.

Electric Guitar

EXAMPLE

Describe it. The electric guitar has a solid body, usually of wood, that is a sort of figure-eight shape. Six metal strings are connected at the base of the body and at the top of the long straight neck. At the top of the neck are the machine heads that let you tune the strings by making them tighter or looser. A magnetic plate under the strings on the body translates the vibrations of the strings into electric signals that are turned back into sound by the amplifier. The tremolo arm is slender and silver and works by stretching and loosening the strings a little to make the sound bend.

■ **Freewriting** When you *freewrite,* you write whatever pops into your head. Think of a topic that interests you, and write about it for three to five minutes. Don't worry about using complete sentences or proper punctuation. Just write as much as you can, and stay focused on your topic. If you cannot think of anything new to write, copy the same word or phrase until something comes to mind.

EXAMPLE

RECYCLING: Using stuff again. Plastics, paper, glass, aluminum—in new products. Garbage landfills filling. Disposable diapers. Controversy. What's the right thing to do? And what's the use? Saving the Earth. OK, how? How can one person make a difference? Containers for collecting are great, and so is the fact that fast-food chains are using recycled sources. But still, there is so much stuff! Where will it all go in the end?

■ **Listening with a focus** Printed words are not your only source of information. You can also listen—to radio and television programs, to videotapes and audiotapes, and to experts during personal or telephone interviews. Before you listen, follow these steps:

1. Write down your topic, and then brainstorm or cluster what you already know.
2. Make a list of the information you need. Jot down questions that you would like to have answered as you listen. This list of questions should help guide and focus your listening.
3. Listen carefully with your questions in front of you. Take careful notes and pay close attention. Get the main points and supporting details by writing in phrases and using abbreviations.

■ **Looping**   Looping will help you to generate ideas that can be developed into an essay.

1. In this prewriting activity, you start with a subject and freewrite about the subject for a set period of time.
2. Include anything that comes into your mind on the subject. Even if you can't think of anything to say, continue writing for the specified period of time, even if all you write is "I can't think of anything to say." The important thing is to keep your pen or pencil moving.
3. After the time limit is up, read what you have written and pick out what seems to be most important or weighty in the loop. This is the center of gravity for that loop. You may have stated this center of gravity, or you may have to figure it out.
4. Finally, write your center of gravity sentence and begin the process again for two more loops.

■ **Mapping**   *Mapping* resembles clustering in form but is used to organize ideas rather than for generating ideas. It is a helpful visual way to determine whether you have enough support for each main idea. Notice how the following map groups main ideas and supporting details.

EXAMPLE

Getting there
passport photos
airlines
travel agency
French dictionary
luggage
prices?

Food to look forward to
baguettes
cheeses
fancy cooking that
   I can't afford

visiting France—
what to think about

Doing tourist things
Eiffel Tower
museums
riding the Métro
Notre Dame
Montmartre
Champs-Élysées

■ **Pentad**   A *pentad* is a star with five points, each of its points representing one of the following questions: *What is happening? Who is causing it to happen? How is it being done? Where and when is it being done? Why is it happening?* Think about your topic, and write an answer to each question. Then, read what you have written and determine a focus: Which points did you write the most about? Is there an interaction between those points? This focus will probably be your thesis statement. A pentad is a good prewriting technique to use when you are writing about literature.

EXAMPLE

What is happening?
Members of a family sit on their front porch to worry as they wait to hear from a bank about a loan that will let them keep their house.

Why is it happening?
The family needs a bank loan extension in order to keep the house and the family is not sure that it will receive it.

Short story: "Home" by Gwendolyn Brooks

Who is causing it to happen?
The women in the family are waiting while the father is at the bank.

When and where is it being done?
It is late afternoon on the front porch of the house.

How is it being done?
The women are sitting and talking, pretending that having to move will be a good thing.

■ **Reading with a focus**   You can get ideas for writing by reading books, newspapers, or magazines. When you read to find information, don't read everything. If there is an index or table of contents, use it to narrow your search. Skim the material, searching only for information about your topic. When you find relevant information, read carefully and take notes.

■ **Track Switching**   This technique takes advantage of the fact that people often think in a familiar track about subjects. You start by freewriting along the familiar track and then purposefully switch to another track. This technique often leads to fresh ideas. The steps for track switching are as follows.

1. Start by creating a statement about your subject, and freewrite about that statement for five minutes.
2. Create another statement about your subject that switches tracks—that is as different as possible from the first statement you made.

3. Write on this track for five minutes.
4. Repeat this process for five tracks. Remember that there are no rules about what you write for each track; just let the words flow along the track.

■ **Using your five senses**   Gather information about your topic through the use of all five senses: sight, hearing, smell, taste, and touch. If you stop to focus on all the sensory details around you, you will have a nearly endless supply of specific details for your writing.

EXAMPLE

Night football game

sight: dark green grass; funny yellowish lights and dark sky; players in maroon, orange-gold, muddy uniforms; referees in crisp black and white; fans a sea of every color, with red jumping out—blankets, gloves, coats

sound: chants of cheerleaders and fans; deep roar and shrieks of fans; bands—sounds fading in and out as they turn in formation on the field; airplanes faint overhead

smell: hot dogs and mustard; popcorn; newly cut grass

taste: cherry lip balm; stale, too-salty popcorn; tangy mustard

touch: cold air; sharp gusts of wind; hard bleacher seats; scratchy wool scarf against cheek

■ **Visualizing**   *Visualizing* means forming a mental image of something. Picture your subject in your "mind's eye." As you do so, use your imagination to write down details for each of the five senses.

The theater seems dark as you come in from the bright street. It is an old theater with a lobby carpeted in red. The walls have mirrors and old movie posters. The air smells of fresh popcorn that you know will taste like cardboard. We like to sit in the balcony, so we climb the curving staircase up two flights and find seats near the ceiling. The air is warmer than downstairs, and humid. Looking up, you can see the ceiling decorated with gold and with old-fashioned paintings. The seats are covered in red velour and feel squishy and uncomfortable and there is no place to put your bucket of popcorn.

■ **Writer's notebook or journal**   Use a special notebook or file folder to record your experiences and observations, feelings and questions. You can also collect print material that has special meaning to you, such as poems, songs, and newspaper articles. Try to write in your notebook daily, and date your entries. Soon your journal will be a sourcebook full of ideas about which you can write.

Résumé   A *résumé* is a summary of your background and experience. For many job positions, you are required to submit a résumé along with a letter of application. There are many ways to arrange the information on a résumé. Whatever style you select, be sure that your résumé looks neat and businesslike. (See also **Letters of Application** on page 941.)

```
                 TANEESHA COLLINS
               1437 Windy Ridge Road
                 Milwaukee, WI 53224
             Telephone: (414) 555-7023
             E-mail: taneesh@milwaukee.net

OBJECTIVE:
  Year abroad in Barcelona, Spain, as
  part of Spanish Student Exchange
  Program

WORK EXPERIENCE:
  June 1998           Recorder of read-
  to present          ings for blind in
                      English and in
                      Spanish
  September 2000      Organized Spanish
                      Club book and bake
                      sale
  January 2001        Helped design Spanish
                      Club Web page

EDUCATION:
  Sophomore, Vince Lombardi High
    School
  Grade-point average: 3.3

EXTRACURRICULAR ACTIVITIES:
  Spanish Club
  Chorale

ACHIEVEMENTS:
  Excellence in Spanish Award,
    December 2000

REFERENCES:
  Available on request
```

Revising and Proofreading Symbols

To some people, *editing* is simply making corrections, while to others, it includes both revising and proofreading. When you are revising or proofreading your own or a peer's work, use the following symbols to indicate any changes that should be made.

Symbols for Revising and Proofreading

Symbol	Example	Meaning of Symbol
≡	Maple High school	Capitalize a lowercase letter.
/	the First person	Lowercase a capital letter.
∧	on the fourth ^of^ May	Insert a missing word, letter, or punctuation mark.
∧	sep^a^erate	Change a letter.
⌐	in the ^West^ East—	Replace a word.
℘	tell me the the plan	Leave out a word, letter, or punctuation mark.
ᗡ	an unusšual idea	Leave out and close up.
◡	a water fall	Close up space.
∽	redieve	Change the order of letters.
(tr)	the last Saturday of September (in the month)	Transpose the circled words. (Write tr in nearby margin.)
¶	¶ "Help!" someone cried.	Begin a new paragraph.
⊙	Please don't go⊙	Add a period.
∧	Well∧what's the news?	Add a comma.
#	record#keeping	Add a space.
(:)	the following ideas(:)	Add a colon.
∧	Houston, Texas∧St. Louis, Missouri∧and Albany, New York	Add a semicolon.
=	typed in single=space	Add a hyphen.
∨	Sally∨s new job	Add an apostrophe.
(stet)	an extremely urgent message	Keep the crossed-out material. (Write stet in nearby margin.)

Tone   *Tone* refers to the feelings you convey through your writing. Your tone lets your readers know how you feel about them as well as how you feel about the subject of your writing. Tone is conveyed in three ways: by your choice of details, by the length and structure of your sentences, and by your choice of words.

- **Choice of details**   The *choice of details* in your writing lets your reader know what is important to you as a writer. For example, providing readers with lists of facts or statistics sets the tone as serious and objective, while writing about childhood memories of a place conveys a more intimate tone.

- **Sentence length and structure** The *length and structure* of the sentences in your writing also inform your tone. If your writing is full of long, convoluted sentences, then it is clear to readers that you are serious—perhaps even too serious—about the subject. Short, snappy sentences suggest a sense of playfulness.

- **Word choice** Your *word choice* lets your readers know how seriously you care about the subject. For example, the choice of formal language conveys a more serious, concerned tone than informal language. Conversely, the use of informal language, such as contractions and colloquialisms, suggests a more friendly, personal tone. The connotations of the words you use will also greatly inform your tone. For example, "that guy" is informal or casual, while "the gentleman" is polite and respectful.

Keep in mind that the *occasion* for which you are writing always affects your tone. The occasion is the reason for writing. Often the occasion is to fulfill an assignment for school, but it might also be to communicate with a friend or family member or to instruct someone younger than yourself. In thinking about occasion, ask yourself these three questions:

1. Why am I writing—for school? for fun? to brainstorm ideas?
2. Who will read my writing—a teacher, a friend, a stranger, or only me?
3. When or where will the reader read my writing—in front of the class, alone at home, somewhere else?

Transitions *Transitions,* or *transitional expressions,* are words and phrases that show readers how ideas and details fit together. (See also the **Transitional Expressions** chart on page 376.)

To connect your ideas within paragraphs and between paragraphs, learn to use transitional expressions such as the following ones.

time	at last, meanwhile, then, now, later, at first, by this time
place	here, there, beyond, farther, to the left, next, over, between
addition	and, besides, for example, furthermore
contrast	but, still, although, however, nevertheless
conclusion	thus, consequently, in conclusion, looking back, in review, finally

Voice The way a piece of writing "sounds," or its *voice,* is determined by sentence structure, word choice, and tone. Although audience and purpose influence your writing voice, always try to sound honest and natural.

Writing to Learn You can use writing for more than just an extension of a lesson (such as an essay). Writing can help you to understand the relationships of ideas in the texts that you read; for example, you can use mapping to see relationships between main ideas and details. Writing can also be a way of knowing. For example, if you freewrite about information from one of your classes, it will help you to see what you know.

Grammar at a Glance

┌─H E L P─┐

Grammar at a Glance is an alphabetical list of special terms and expressions with examples and references to further information. When you encounter a grammar or usage problem in the revising or proofreading stage of your writing, look for help in this section first. You may find all you need to know right here. If you need more information, **Grammar at a Glance** will show you where in the book to turn for a more complete explanation. If you do not find what you are looking for in **Grammar at a Glance,** turn to the index on page 1000.

abbreviation An abbreviation is a shortened form of a word or a phrase.

■ **capitalization of** (See page 686.)

TITLES USED WITH NAMES	**M**r.	**R**ev.	**J**r.	**E**sq.
KINDS OF ORGANIZATIONS	**C**o.	**I**nc.	**A**dmin.	**C**orp.
PARTS OF ADDRESSES	**B**lvd.	**R**d.	**P**kwy.	**P.O. B**ox
NAMES OF STATES	[without ZIP Codes]		**K**y.	**O**kla.
			Calif.	**S.C.**
	[with ZIP Codes]		**KY**	**OK**
			CA	**SC**
TIMES	**A.M.**	**P.M.**	**B.C.**	**A.D.**

■ **punctuation of** (See page 696.)

WITH PERIODS	(See preceding examples.)			
WITHOUT PERIODS	RN	IOU	EPA	UNICEF
	DC	(D.C. without ZIP Code)		
	mg	oz	yd	mph	km
	[Exception: in.]			

action verb An action verb expresses physical or mental activity. (See page 418.)

EXAMPLE   David **drove** from Vicksburg to Austin.

active voice Active voice is the voice a verb is in when it expresses an action done by its subject. (See page 601. See also **voice.**)

EXAMPLE   Ann **nailed** the planks together.

adjective An adjective modifies a noun or a pronoun. (See page 412.)

EXAMPLE   **An old** oak cast its **huge** shadow across **the front** yard.

adjective clause An adjective clause is a subordinate clause that modifies a noun or a pronoun. (See page 495.)

EXAMPLE   The poetry **that my aunt wrote** remains unpublished.

adjective phrase A prepositional phrase that modifies a noun or a pronoun is called an adjective phrase. (See page 468.)

EXAMPLE   Most **of the school** will be taking part in the fair.

adverb An adverb modifies a verb, an adjective, or another adverb. (See page 422.)

EXAMPLE   Is there **really** enough time for the play?

adverb clause An adverb clause is a subordinate clause that modifies a verb, an adjective, or an adverb. (See page 498.)

EXAMPLE   **Before I went home,** I thanked my hosts.

adverb phrase A prepositional phrase that modifies a verb, an adjective, or an adverb is called an adverb phrase. (See page 469.)

EXAMPLE   Sean and Henry stayed **after school** to help Ms. Gallogly **with the decorations.**

agreement Agreement is the correspondence, or match, between grammatical forms. Grammatical forms agree when they have the same number and gender.

 ■ **of pronouns and antecedents** (See page 532.)

SINGULAR   The teacher asked **Daniel** to name **his** favorite books, songs, and movies.

PLURAL   The teacher asked the **students** to name **their** favorite books, songs, and movies.

SINGULAR   I think Geraldo can name **each** of the countries and **its** capital city.

PLURAL   I think Geraldo can name **all** of the countries and **their** capital cities.

SINGULAR   Neither **Sue** nor **Christie** has **her** driver's license.

PLURAL   Both **Sue** and **Christie** have **their** driver's licenses.

■ **of subjects and verbs** (See page 512.)

SINGULAR   The **choreographer wants** to change some of the movements of the ballet.

SINGULAR   The **choreographer,** as well as the dancers, **wants** to change some of the movements of the ballet.

PLURAL   The **dancers want** to change some of the movements of the ballet.

PLURAL   The **dancers,** as well as the choreographer, **want** to change some of the movements of the ballet.

SINGULAR   **Each** of these beagle puppies **is** four weeks old.

PLURAL   **All** of these beagle puppies **are** four weeks old.

SINGULAR   **Either Paul or Sonia** usually **goes** fishing with me.

PLURAL   **Both Paul and Sonia** usually **go** fishing with me.

SINGULAR   Here **is** the **list** of sources I used to write my essay on the origins of jazz.

PLURAL   Here **are** the **sources** I used to write my essay on the origins of jazz.

SINGULAR   **Six days is** the length of time the astronauts will spend in space.

PLURAL   **Six days** of the school year **are reserved** for parent-teacher conferences.

SINGULAR   *The Adventures of Tom Sawyer* **includes** a hilarious scene in which Tom pretends to be sick.

PLURAL   Tom's **adventures include** some wild times.

SINGULAR   The principal **ingredient** in the Russian soup borscht **is** beets.

PLURAL   **Beets are** the principal ingredient in the Russian soup borscht.

SINGULAR   "For My People" is one poem **that was written** by Margaret Walker.

PLURAL   "For My People" is one of the poems **that were written** by Margaret Walker.

SINGULAR   "For My People" is the only one of the poems **that was written** by Margaret Walker.

ambiguous reference Ambiguous reference occurs when a pronoun incorrectly refers to either of two antecedents. (See page 566.)

AMBIGUOUS	One of the chief differences between the Seismosaurus and the Tyrannosaurus rex is that it did not eat meat. [Which dinosaur did not eat meat?]
CLEAR	One of the chief differences between the Seismosaurus and the Tyrannosaurus rex is that the Seismosaurus did not eat meat.

antecedent An antecedent is the word or words that a pronoun stands for. (See page 532.)

EXAMPLE   **Jim** and **Mimi** spent **their** summer traveling through New Mexico. [*Jim* and *Mimi* are the antecedents of *their.*]

apostrophe

- **to form contractions** (See page 763. See also **contraction.**)
  EXAMPLES   aren't   we'll   o'clock   '02

- **to form plurals of letters, numerals, symbols, and words used as words** (See page 766.)
  EXAMPLES   *v*'s and *w*'s   *A*'s, *I*'s, and *U*'s

                  1700's   PC's

                  $'s and ¢'s   replacing *so*'s with *therefore*'s

- **to show possession** (See page 758.)
  EXAMPLES   the student's test score

                  the students' test scores

                  children's tickets

                  somebody's gloves

                  Mother's and Aunt Shashona's story quilts

                  Philip and Nguyen's duet

                  one week's [*or* seven days'] vacation

appositive An appositive is a noun or a pronoun placed beside another noun or pronoun to identify or describe it. (See page 483.)

EXAMPLE   The Oscar-winning actor **Tom Hanks** was featured on that program.

appositive phrase An appositive phrase consists of an appositive and its modifiers. (See page 483.)

EXAMPLE   Mr. Trevelyan, **our new English teacher,** is from Maine.

article The articles, *a*, *an*, and *the*, are the most frequently used adjectives. (See page 412.)

EXAMPLE   **A** new car dealership rejuvenated **an** abandoned shopping center in **the** suburbs.

bad, badly (See page 617.)

NONSTANDARD   This salad dressing smells badly.
STANDARD   This salad dressing smells **bad.**

base form The base form, or infinitive, is one of the four principal parts of a verb. (See page 574.)

EXAMPLE   Dad is helping Stephanie **ride** her bike.

brackets (See page 772.)

EXAMPLES   The Ashanti proverb "What is bad luck for one man is good luck for another" reminds me of an expression I've often heard at rummage sales: "One man's trash **[**bad luck**]** is another man's treasure **[**good luck**].**"

The *Iliad* and the *Odyssey* (both attributed to Homer **[**some historians question this authorship**]**) are epic poems about events before, during, and after the Trojan War.

capitalization

■ **of abbreviations and acronyms** (See page 686. See also **abbreviation.**)

■ **of first words** (See page 668.)
EXAMPLES   **S**mall wooden dolls called kachinas represent spirits and ancestors revered by the Hopi.

Mr. Anaka told us, "**T**he publication of Rachel Carson's book *Silent Spring* in 1962 helped to launch our nation's environmental movement."

Dear Dr. Yamaguchi:

Best regards,

■ **of proper nouns and proper adjectives** (See page 669.)

Proper Noun	Common Noun
Dr. Martin Luther King, Jr.	minister
Prince Henry the Navigator	explorer
Antarctica	continent
Sierra Leone	country
Los Alamos County	county
New Brunswick Province	province
Marquesas Islands	islands
Lake Tanganyika	body of water
Mount Rainier	mountain
Pacific Rim National Park	park
Shoshone National Forest	forest
Ajanta Caves	cave
Great Salt Lake Desert	desert
Northeast	region
Fifty-sixth Street	street
Republican Party (or party)	political party
Battle of Seven Pines	historical event
Dark Ages	historical period
Cinco de Mayo	holiday
January, April, August, November	calendar items
Kiowa Apache	people
Christianity	religion
Muslim	religious follower
God (*but* the god Poseidon)	deity
Sukkot, or Feast of Tabernacles	holy days
Upanishads	sacred writing
Great Sand Dunes National Monument	monument
Wells Fargo Center	building
National Book Critics Circle Award	award
Saturn	planet
Polaris, or the North Star	star
Leo Minor, or the Lesser Lion	constellation
Empress of Ireland	ship
Challenger	spacecraft
Punjabi	language

■ **of titles** (See page 682.)

EXAMPLES **G**overnor Robert La Follette [preceding a name]

Robert La Follette, the former **g**overnor of Wisconsin [following a name]

Welcome, **G**overnor. [direct address]

Uncle Benjamin [*but* my **u**ncle Benjamin]

The People Could Fly: American Black Folktales [book]

Waterlilies in a Pond [work of art]

"**M**any **R**ivers to **C**ross" [song]

"**A V**isit to **G**randmother" [short story]

"**T**he **S**ky **I**s **J**ust **B**eyond the **R**oof" [poem]

Organic Gardening [magazine]

Shoe [comic strip]

case of pronouns Case is the form a pronoun takes to show how it is used in a sentence. (See page 547.)

NOMINATIVE My friend Justin and **I** are organizing a pet-sitting service.

The only sophomores on the school's debate team are Tyrone and **she.**

In my opinion, both gymnasts, Lori and **she,** deserved the first-place medal.

We student-council officers met with the principal to discuss the schedule of activities for Career Night.

Khufu was the Egyptian king **who** built the Great Pyramid at Giza.

Have you already heard **who** the winner is?

Do you think we should pay you more than **they**? [The pronoun is the subject of the incomplete adverb clause "than they pay you."]

OBJECTIVE The friendly park attendant directed **us** to the manatee aquarium.

Uncle Theo sent **me** his recipe for moussaka.

The chess match between Lucia and **him** was exciting.

A technical foul has been charged against both basketball players, Melinda and **her.**

Our art teacher showed **us** students some of the origami figures she had made.

Their supervisor wants **them** to learn to use different word-processing programs.

Michael Jordan, **whom** many consider the greatest basketball player of all time, retired from the sport in 1999.

"To **whom** do you wish to speak?" asked the secretary.

Do you think we should pay you as much as **them**? [The pronoun is the direct object of the verb *pay* in the incomplete adverb clause "as much as we pay them."]

POSSESSIVE **Your** stereo sounds better than **mine** does.

My parents don't approve of **my** watching television.

clause A clause is a group of words that contains a verb and its subject and that is used as part of a sentence. (See page 492.)

EXAMPLE While I sliced the onions [subordinate clause], Marcia peeled the avocado [independent clause].

colon (See page 729.)

■ **before lists**

EXAMPLES In a heptathlon, athletes compete in the following events: the 100-meter hurdles, the shot put, the high jump, the 200-meter dash, the long jump, the javelin throw, and the 800-meter run.

The United States government is divided into three branches: executive, judicial, and legislative.

■ **in conventional situations**

EXAMPLES 3:30 P.M.

Genesis 22:1–18

Lincoln at Gettysburg: The Words That Remade America

Dear Mrs. Wu:

comma (See page 700.)

■ **in a series**

EXAMPLE The principal ingredients of the traditional Navajo dish called *posole* are meat, hominy, and chili.

■ **in compound sentences**

EXAMPLE In our production of *Julius Caesar,* Saul portrayed the title character, and I played Brutus.

■ **with nonessential phrases and clauses**

EXAMPLES   The roving vehicle *Sojourner*, deployed during the Mars *Pathfinder* mission in 1997, provided scientists valuable data about the planet Mars. [nonessential phrase]

   Scott Joplin, who helped make ragtime music popular in the early 1900s, composed the ragtime opera *Treemonisha*. [nonessential clause]

■ **with introductory elements**

EXAMPLES   On his way to school this morning, Harold stopped at the post office to mail the invitations to his bar mitzvah.

   After we had read the poems by Gwendolyn Brooks, our teacher asked us to find examples of simile, metaphor, and personification.

■ **with interrupters**

EXAMPLES   That, in my opinion, is a most amusing comic strip.

   Citrus fruits, such as oranges and lemons, are good sources of vitamin C.

■ **in conventional situations**

EXAMPLES   On Tuesday, April 10, 2001, Mavis and I flew to Seattle, Washington, to attend a week-long computer seminar.

   She sent the job application to 345 Chestnut Street, Oshkosh, WI 54901-0345, on 15 May 2001.

comma splice A comma splice is a run-on sentence in which sentences have been joined with only a comma between them. (See page 348.) (See also **fused sentence, run-on sentence.**)

COMMA SPLICE   Usually the earth's moon is full only once each month, however, about every thirty-two months the moon is full twice in the same month, the second full moon is called a blue moon.

REVISED   Usually the earth's moon is full only once each month. However, about every thirty-two months the moon is full twice in the same month; the second full moon is called a blue moon.

REVISED   Usually the earth's moon is full only once each month. However, about every thirty-two months the moon is full twice in the same month. The second full moon is called a blue moon.

comparison of modifiers (See page 620.)

- ### comparison of adjectives and adverbs

Positive	Comparative	Superlative
young	young**er**	young**est**
tasty	tast**ier**	tast**iest**
persuasive	**more** persuasive	**most** persuasive
gracefully	**less** gracefully	**least** gracefully
good/well	**better**	**best**

- ### comparing two

EXAMPLES   Of the giant sequoia and the bristlecone pine, which species is **older**?

Which of these two computer models processes data **more quickly**?

I read that the diamond is **harder** than **any other** natural substance known.

- ### comparing more than two

EXAMPLES   Extending 6,529 feet (1,990 meters), the Akashi Kaikyo Bridge in Japan is one of the **longest** suspension bridges in the world.

Of all of us in the room, Jorge reacted **most calmly** to the news.

complement A complement is a word or word group that completes the meaning of a verb. (See page 450. See also **direct object, indirect object, predicate adjective,** and **predicate nominative.**)

EXAMPLES   Have you given **Dale** that **book**?

This book is a **favorite,** but that one is even **better.**

complex sentence A complex sentence has one independent clause and at least one subordinate clause. (See page 505.)

EXAMPLES   My neighbor Ms. Tanaka, who is a freelance photojournalist, is planning a trip to the Australian outback.

As Ms. Tanaka and I talked about her plans for her trip to the outback, she showed me photographs of her South American trip, which included a visit to the Galápagos Islands.

compound-complex sentence A compound-complex sentence has two or more independent clauses and at least one subordinate clause. (See page 505.)

EXAMPLES Hattie Caraway was the wife of the United States senator Thaddeus Caraway, and when he died in 1931, she was asked to serve out his term.

After she had completed her husband's term, Hattie Caraway ran for the Senate seat in the election of 1932 and won; as a result, she became the first woman elected to the United States Senate.

compound sentence A compound sentence has two or more independent clauses but no subordinate clauses. (See page 504.)

EXAMPLES In his spare time, Joshua enjoys painting; he especially likes to paint with watercolors.

The bat has wings and can fly, but it is not a bird; it is a mammal.

conjunction A conjunction joins words or groups of words. (See page 428.)

EXAMPLE **Both** Andrea **and** Walter were hoping to win **or** at least qualify for the contest, **but** they soon withdrew their names **because** so many people were ahead of them **and** it was late in the year.

contraction A contraction is a shortened form of a word, a numeral, or a group of words. Apostrophes in contractions indicate where letters or numerals have been omitted. (See page 763. See also **apostrophe**.)

EXAMPLES

I've [I have]	**here's** [here is or here has]
who's [who is or who has]	**they're** [they are]
couldn't [could not]	**it's** [it is or it has]
can't [cannot]	**don't** [do not]
'50–'51 school year [1950–1951]	**o'clock** [of the clock]

dangling modifier A dangling modifier is a modifying word, phrase, or clause that does not clearly and sensibly modify a word or word group in a sentence. (See page 626.)

| DANGLING | Leading us through the art museum, interesting anecdotes about the artists' lives were told. [Who is leading us through the art museum?] |
| REVISED | Leading us through the art museum, **the tour guide** told interesting anecdotes about the artists' lives. |

dash (See page 770.)

| EXAMPLE | Thousands of fans—23,764, to be exact—attended the championship game. |

declarative sentence A declarative sentence makes a statement and is followed by a period. (See page 459.)

| EXAMPLE | Ben Nevis is the highest mountain in Scotland and is higher than any other peak in Great Britain**.** |

direct object A direct object is a word or word group that receives the action of the verb or shows the result of the action. A direct object answers the question *Whom?* or *What?* after a transitive verb. (See page 456.)

| EXAMPLE | Tom painted the **mural** on the school wall. |

double comparison A double comparison is the nonstandard use of two comparative forms (usually *more* and *–er*) or two superlative forms (usually *most* and *–est*) to express comparison. In standard usage, the single comparative or superlative form is correct. (See page 623.)

| NONSTANDARD | Of Neptune's eight moons, the most largest is Triton. |
| STANDARD | Of Neptune's eight moons, the **largest** is Triton. |

double negative A double negative is the nonstandard use of two or more negative words to express a single negative idea. (See page 656.)

NONSTANDARD	Despite the inclement weather, the pilot didn't have no difficulty landing the plane.
STANDARD	Despite the inclement weather, the pilot **didn't have any** difficulty landing the plane.
STANDARD	Despite the inclement weather, the pilot **had no** difficulty landing the plane.

double subject A double subject occurs when an unnecessary pronoun is used after the subject of a sentence. (See page 645.)

NONSTANDARD	Most of the businesses in town they close by 6:00 P.M.
STANDARD	Most of the businesses in town close by 6:00 P.M.

end marks (See page 694.)

■ **with sentences**

EXAMPLES   For dessert, Grandmother served warm sopaipillas with honey. [declarative sentence]

Is the cedar waxwing, or cedarbird, indigenous to this area? [interrogative sentence]

Wow! [interjection] What a clever trick that was! [exclamatory sentence]

Please help your brother with his homework. [imperative sentence]

■ **with abbreviations** (See **abbreviation.**)

EXAMPLES   During spring break, we went to Washington, D.C.

When did you go to Washington, D.C.?

essential clause/essential phrase
An essential, or restrictive, clause or phrase is necessary to the meaning of a sentence and is not set off by commas. (See page 705.)

EXAMPLES   The woman **who helped us** is standing there. [clause]

The woman **standing there** helped us. [phrase]

exclamation point (See **end marks.**)

exclamatory sentence
An exclamatory sentence expresses strong feeling and is followed by an exclamation point. (See page 459.)

EXAMPLE   What a magnificent sight that is!

fragment (See **sentence fragment.**)

fused sentence
A fused sentence is a run-on sentence in which sentences have been joined together with no punctuation between them. (See page 347.) (See also **comma splice, run-on sentence.**)

FUSED   A tanka is a five-line poem that consists of thirty-one syllables the first and third lines contain five syllables each the other lines have seven each.

REVISED   A tanka is a five-line poem that consists of thirty-one syllables; the first and third lines contain five syllables each, **and** the other lines have seven each.

general reference A general reference is the incorrect use of a pronoun to refer to a general idea rather than to a specific noun. (See page 567.)

GENERAL   Misuko revised and proofread her rough draft on the French Revolution. That took her about three hours. [To what does *That* refer?]

REVISED   Revising and proofreading her rough draft on the French Revolution took Misuko about three hours.

gerund A gerund is a verb form ending in *–ing* that is used as a noun. (See page 476.)

EXAMPLES   **Painting** landscapes is Uncle Arthur's favorite hobby.

Some people say the best exercise is **swimming**.

gerund phrase A gerund phrase consists of a gerund and its modifiers and complements. (See page 478.)

EXAMPLE   By **leaving early,** Erica hoped to arrive before the others.

good, well (See page 617.)

EXAMPLES   Even a **good** bowler will occasionally roll a gutter ball.
I wish I could bowl as **well** [not *good*] as you.

hyphen (See page 767.)

■ **for division of words**

EXAMPLE   The words *hiss, sizzle, buzz,* and *roar* are good examples of the poetic device called onomatopoeia.

■ **in compound numbers**

EXAMPLE   The ratification of the Twenty-sixth Amendment in 1971 lowered the voting age from twenty-one to eighteen.

■ **with prefixes and suffixes**

EXAMPLES   In mid-December, the citizens of Mexico celebrate the Nine Days of Posada.

The guest speaker will be ex-Mayor Franklin Jackson.

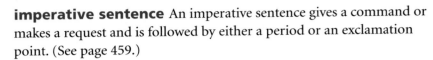

imperative sentence An imperative sentence gives a command or makes a request and is followed by either a period or an exclamation point. (See page 459.)

EXAMPLES   Please dry the dishes, Juan. [request]

Sit down! [command]

incomplete construction An incomplete construction is a clause from which words have been omitted. (See page 565.)

EXAMPLE   The study shows that we performed better **than they** [did].

indefinite reference An indefinite reference is the incorrect use of the pronoun *you, it,* or *they* to refer to no particular person or thing. (See page 567.)

INDEFINITE   In the newspaper, it says that the governor is planning to run for president.

REVISED   The newspaper says that the governor is planning to run for president.

independent clause An independent clause (also called a *main clause*) expresses a complete thought and can stand by itself as a sentence. (See page 492.)

EXAMPLE   After we had finished class, **Mr. Smith took us to the park.**

indirect object An indirect object is a noun, pronoun, or word group that often appears in sentences containing direct objects. An indirect object tells *to whom* or *to what* (or *for whom* or *for what*) the action of a transitive verb is done. Indirect objects generally precede direct objects. (See page 457.)

EXAMPLE   Pedro gave the **twins** a snack, and now they're ready to play all day.

infinitive An infinitive is a verb form, usually preceded by *to,* that is used as a noun, an adjective, or an adverb. (See page 479.)

EXAMPLE   Her dearest wish was **to participate** in the rafting trip.

infinitive phrase An infinitive phrase consists of an infinitive and its modifiers and complements. (See page 480.)

To welcome our new neighbors, we formed the commit-tee called Feel at Home.

interjection An interjection expresses emotion and has no gram-matical relation to the rest of the sentence. (See page 429.)

EXAMPLE **Well,** how long do we have to wait?

interrogative sentence An interrogative sentence asks a question and is followed by a question mark. (See page 459.)

EXAMPLE Would you like to come to Dr. Seymour's farewell dinner**?**

intransitive verb An intransitive verb is a verb that does not take an object. (See page 421.)

EXAMPLE The Shadwells **are sleeping.**

irregular verb An irregular verb is a verb that forms its past and past participle in some way other than by adding *d* or *ed* to the base form. (See page 576. See also **regular verb.**)

Base Form	Present Participle	Past	Past Participle
be	[is] being	was, were	[have] been
cast	[is] casting	cast	[have] cast
fall	[is] falling	fell	[have] fallen
find	[is] finding	found	[have] found
hit	[is] hitting	hit	[have] hit
make	[is] making	made	[have] made
ring	[is] ringing	rang	[have] rung
shake	[is] shaking	shook	[have] shaken
speak	[is] speaking	spoke	[have] spoken
think	[is] thinking	thought	[have] thought

italics (See page 739.)

■ **for titles** *The Once and Future King* [book]

Yahoo! Internet Life [periodical]

Gamera: The Guardian of the Universe [movie]

Perseus with the Head of Medusa [work of art]

Tales from the Vienna Woods [long musical composition]

■ **for words, letters, and symbols used as such and for foreign words**

EXAMPLES   Using the spellchecker, I discovered that I had transposed the letters **e** and **a** every time I had typed the word ***research.***

    The story ends with ***Requiescat in pace,*** the Latin phrase that means "Rest in peace."

its, it's (See page 796.)

EXAMPLES   **Its** [Mexico's] highest point is the volcanic mountain Citlaltépetl.

    It's [It is] more than 18,000 feet high.

    It's [It has] been a long time since the volcano has erupted.

lie, lay (See page 582.)

EXAMPLES   Weary from their hike, the scouts **lay** down and rested awhile. [past tense of *lie*]

    Weary from their hike, the scouts **laid** their backpacks down and rested awhile. [past tense of *lay*]

linking verb A linking verb connects the subject with a word that identifies or describes the subject. (See page 418.)

EXAMPLE   Italy **became** a republic in 1946.

misplaced modifier A misplaced modifier is a word, phrase, or clause that seems to modify the wrong word or words in a sentence. (See page 627.)

MISPLACED   The 4-H clubs throughout the United States, supported by the Department of Agriculture, strive to improve the head, heart, hands, and health of each of their members. [Is the United States supported by the Department of Agriculture?]

REVISED   **Supported by the Department of Agriculture,** the 4-H clubs throughout the United States strive to improve the head, heart, hands, and health of each of their members.

modifier A modifier is a word or word group that makes the meaning of another word or word group more specific. (See page 614.)

EXAMPLE   Gustav Mahler, **a major Austrian** composer **of the early twentieth century, often** used **the** idioms **of popular music in his compositions.**

nonessential clause/nonessential phrase A nonessential, or nonrestrictive, clause or phrase adds information not necessary to the main idea in the sentence and is generally set off by commas. (See page 704.)

EXAMPLES   The church on the corner, **in which the Reverend de Santis once preached,** is being renovated. [nonessential clause]

The top, **spinning wildly,** bounced down the steps. [nonessential phrase]

noun A noun names a person, place, thing, or idea. (See page 405.)

EXAMPLES   **Billie Holiday** sang beautifully.

We are vacationing in **Vermont.**

Please hand me the **scissors.**

Intelligence is difficult to measure.

noun clause A noun clause is a subordinate clause used as a noun. (See page 501.)

EXAMPLE   Tell me **what you did during the summer.**

number Number is the form a word takes to indicate whether the word is singular or plural. (See page 512.)

SINGULAR	tree	she	child	man
PLURAL	trees	they	children	men

object of a preposition An object of a preposition is the noun or pronoun that completes a prepositional phrase. (See page 426.)

EXAMPLE   One of the old **trees** was struck by **lightning.** *[Of the old trees and by lightning are prepositional phrases.]*

parallel structure Parallel structure is the use of the same grammatical forms or structures to balance related ideas in a sentence. (See page 362.)

NONPARALLEL The main duties of the receptionist are to greet callers, to take messages, and providing information.

PARALLEL The main duties of the receptionist are **to greet** callers, **to take** messages, and **to provide** information.

PARALLEL The main duties of the receptionist are **greeting** callers, **taking** messages, and **providing** information.

parentheses (See page 770.)

EXAMPLES The route traveled by the pony express riders **(**see the map on page 152**)** was dangerous.

The route traveled by the pony express riders was dangerous. **(**See the map on page 152.**)**

participial phrase A participial phrase consists of a participle and any complements and modifiers it has. (See page 473.)

EXAMPLE **Considered famous for its resorts,** the Yucatán is also a center of Mayan culture.

participle A participle is a verb form that can be used as an adjective. (See page 472.)

EXAMPLE I prefer to live in the South, where there are no **freezing** winters.

passive voice The passive voice is the voice a verb is in when it expresses an action done to its subject. (See page 601. See also **voice.**)

EXAMPLE Mr. Boylan's novel **has been translated** into German.

period (See **end marks.**)

phrase A phrase is a group of related words that does not contain a verb and its subject and that is used as a single part of speech. (See page 467.)

EXAMPLE Stacy, **Aunt Maeve's golden retriever,** probably **will place** first **in the sporting-dog category.** [*Aunt Maeve's golden retriever* is an appositive phrase. *Will place* is a verb phrase. *In the sporting-dog category* is a prepositional phrase.]

QUICK REFERENCE HANDBOOK

predicate The predicate is the part of a sentence that says something about the subject. (See page 441.)

EXAMPLE   She **wants to be a commercial airline pilot.**

predicate adjective A predicate adjective is an adjective that completes the meaning of a linking verb and that modifies the subject of the verb. (See page 454.)

EXAMPLE   Despite the heat, Bob and Beth appeared **fresh** and **alert.**

predicate nominative A predicate nominative is a noun or pronoun that completes the meaning of a linking verb and identifies or refers to the subject of the verb. (See page 453.)

EXAMPLE   The president of the company is **Francis McGuire, Ph.D.**

prefix A prefix is a word part that is added before a base word or root. (See page 781.)

EXAMPLES   un + fair = **un**fair   re + usable = **re**usable

mis + pronounce = **mis**pronounce   dis + qualified = **dis**qualified

mid + February = **mid**-February   ex + judge = **ex**-judge

preposition A preposition shows the relationship of a noun or a pronoun to some other word in a sentence. (See page 426.)

EXAMPLE   That novel **by** Joseph Conrad is **about** spies **in** nineteenth-century Geneva.

prepositional phrase A prepositional phrase includes a preposition, a noun or pronoun called the object of the preposition, and any modifiers of that object. (See page 426.)

EXAMPLE   **Before breakfast,** I like to watch the sun rise **over the rooftops.**

pronoun A pronoun is used in place of one or more nouns or pronouns. (See page 408.)

EXAMPLES   Paul and **I** wrote to Abigail and expressed **our** pleasure at **her** engagement.

All of the team members prepared **themselves** for the relay.

Who gave **you this?**

question mark (See **end marks.**)

quotation marks (See page 743.)

- **for direct quotations**

  EXAMPLE   "In class tomorrow," said Mr. McDermott, "we will begin studying the decline of the Mayan civilization."

- **with other marks of punctuation** (See also preceding example.)

  EXAMPLES   "In what country will the Summer Olympics of 2008 be held?" asked Katrina.

      Which poem by Dorothy Parker begins with the line "A single flow'r he sent me, since we met"?

      The teacher asked, "Who are the protagonist and the antagonist of Larry Woiwode's short story 'The Beginning of Grief'?"

- **for titles**

  EXAMPLES   "Tuesday Siesta" [short story]

      "My Mother Pieced Quilts" [short poem]

      "Wind Beneath My Wings" [song]

regular verb A regular verb is a verb that forms its past and past participle by adding *d* or *ed* to the base form. (See page 575. See also **irregular verb.**)

Base Form	Present Participle	Past	Past Participle
ask	[is] asking	asked	[have] asked
deceive	[is] deceiving	deceived	[have] deceived
drown	[is] drowning	drowned	[have] drowned
risk	[is] risking	risked	[have] risked
suppose	[is] supposing	supposed	[have] supposed
use	[is] using	used	[have] used

rise, raise (See page 588.)

EXAMPLES   Huge billows of smoke **rose** from the top of the mountain. [past tense of *rise*]

                They **raised** the window blinds to let in the light and warmth of the sun. [past tense of *raise*]

run-on sentence A run-on sentence is two or more complete sentences run together as one. (See page 347. See also **comma splice** and **fused sentence.**)

RUN-ON   Troy Menzies is a guitar player my father knew back in the 1960s and 1970s, they went to high school together.

REVISED   Troy Menzies is a guitar player my father knew back in the 1960s and 1970s. They went to high school together.

REVISED   Troy Menzies is a guitar player my father knew back in the 1960s and 1970s; they went to high school together.

semicolon (See page 724.)

- **in compound sentences with no conjunctions**

  EXAMPLE   Norman Rockwell was a prolific artist; he is perhaps best remembered for his cover illustrations for the *Saturday Evening Post.*

- **in compound sentences with conjunctive adverbs or transitional expressions**

  EXAMPLE   Many animals, such as frogs and alligators, are amphibious; **that is,** they can live both on land and in water.

- **between a series of items containing commas**

  EXAMPLE   In the famous Hindu epic *Ramayana,* the main characters are Prince Rama; Sita, his loyal wife; Lakshmana, his devoted brother; and Ravan, the ruler of the demons.

sentence A sentence is a group of words that contains a subject and a verb and expresses a complete thought. (See page 437.)

EXAMPLE   The swans glided low over the water before landing.

sentence fragment A sentence fragment is a group of words that is punctuated as if it were a complete sentence but that does not contain both a subject and a verb or that does not express a complete thought. (See pages 340 and 437.)

FRAGMENT	The samisen, a stringed instrument used in Japanese music.
SENTENCE	The samisen, a stringed instrument used in Japanese music, resembles a guitar.

FRAGMENT	Saying goodbye to our cousins.
SENTENCE	Outside, Mother was saying goodbye to our cousins.

simple sentence A simple sentence has one independent clause and no subordinate clauses. (See page 504.)

EXAMPLES	Chief Ta-sunko-witko (Crazy Horse) led the Sioux and Cheyenne forces to victory at the Battle of the Little Bighorn.
	Did Mike and Dana go with you to the Cherry Blossom Festival?

sit, set (See page 585.)

EXAMPLES	**Sitting** in his favorite chair, Grandfather told us a story about a talking camel named Yak-yak.
	Setting a bowl of popcorn in front of us, Grandfather began telling a story about a talking camel named Yak-yak.

slow, slowly (See page 618.)

EXAMPLES	The traffic was so **slow** on the highway that we decided to take a back road.
	The traffic moved so **slowly** on the highway that we decided to take a back road.

stringy sentence A stringy sentence is a sentence that has too many independent clauses. Usually, the clauses are strung together with coordinating conjunctions like *and* or *but*. (See page 363.)

STRINGY	The Greek hero Perseus went in search of the monster Medusa, and guiding the hero on his quest were the goddess Athena and the god Hermes, and in an effort to protect Perseus, Athena provided him with a mirrored shield.
REVISED	The Greek hero Perseus went in search of the monster Medusa. Guiding the hero on his quest were the goddess Athena and the god Hermes. In an effort to protect Perseus, Athena provided him with a mirrored shield.

subject The subject tells whom or what a sentence is about. (See page 439.)

EXAMPLES   **Doves** have always nested under the eaves of that old house.

              Where have **Harry and Lucas** gone?

subject complement A subject complement is a word or word group that completes the meaning of a linking verb and identifies or modifies the subject. (See page 453. See also **predicate adjective** and **predicate nominative.**)

EXAMPLES   Yellow is my least favorite **color.**

              Purple seems **richer.**

subjunctive mood The subjunctive mood is used to express a suggestion, a necessity, a condition contrary to fact, or a wish. (See page 606.)

EXAMPLES   Some of us recommended that Amy **be asked** to serve as the spokesperson for our group.

              If I **were** you, I would deposit the money in a savings account.

subordinate clause A subordinate clause (also called a *dependent clause*) does not express a complete thought and cannot stand alone as a sentence. (See page 493. See also **adjective clause, adverb clause,** and **noun clause.**)

EXAMPLES   The one **that I like** is on order.

              As soon as we get there, we will call you.

              Do you know **what you want?**

suffix A suffix is a word part that is added after a base word or root. (See page 782.)

EXAMPLES   usual + ly = usual**ly**   heavy + ly = heavi**ly**

              gentle + ness = gentle**ness**   employ + er = employ**er**

              admire + able = admir**able**   replace + able = replace**able**

              trap + ing = trapp**ing**   farm + ing = farm**ing**

QUICK REFERENCE HANDBOOK

tense of verbs The tense of verbs indicates the time of the action or state of being expressed by the verb. (See page 590.)

EXAMPLES   He and I **ride** the same bus to school. [present]

She **rode** a horse for the first time last weekend. [past]

Judy **will ride** with the Washingtons to next week's game. [future]

David **has ridden** in the parade for the last three years. [present perfect]

Kelley **had** always **ridden** to school with Dawn, but Dawn moved to another city. [past perfect]

By the time the carnival ends, I **will have ridden** on every ride. [future perfect]

transitive verb A transitive verb is an action verb that takes an object. (See page 421.)

EXAMPLE   Finally, Roderick **took** the step and **bought** the car.

underlining (See **Italics**)

verb A verb expresses an action or a state of being. (See page 417.)

EXAMPLES   He **carved** the figurine and **put** it on the windowsill.

They **are** very funny.

verbal A verbal is a form of a verb used as an adjective, an adverb, or a noun. (See page 472. See also **participle, gerund,** and **infinitive**.)

EXAMPLES   **Thrilled,** I said yes immediately. [participle]

I enjoy **playing** volleyball. [gerund]

The host asked us **to sit.** [infinitive]

verbal phrase A verbal phrase consists of a verbal and any modifiers and complements it has. (See page 472. See also **participial phrase, gerund phrase,** and **infinitive phrase**.)

EXAMPLE   Several large chicken hawks, **wheeling high in the sky,** were no threat to us.

verb phrase A verb phrase consists of a main verb and at least one helping verb. (See page 441.)

EXAMPLES **Had** he **met** her before?

Tony and Suzanne **are gardening.**

voice Voice is the form a transitive verb takes to indicate whether the subject of the verb performs or receives the action. (See page 601.)

ACTIVE VOICE Laotzu **founded** the Chinese philosophy of Taoism in the sixth century B.C.

PASSIVE VOICE The Chinese philosophy Taoism **was founded** by Laotzu in the sixth century B.C.

weak reference A weak reference is the incorrect use of a pronoun to refer to an antecedent that has not been expressed. (See page 567.)

WEAK Joan of Arc was a fearless soldier, and it inspired the French troops whom she led into battle. [To what does *it* refer?]

REVISED Joan of Arc was a fearless soldier, and **her courage** inspired the French troops whom she led into battle.

well (See *good, well.*)

who, whom (See page 558.)

EXAMPLES Ms. Guitterez, **who** teaches courses in accounting and computer science, has been voted Teacher of the Year.

Ms. Guitterez, **whom** the student body has voted Teacher of the Year, teaches courses in accounting and computer science.

wordiness Wordiness is the use of more words than necessary or the use of fancy words where simple ones will do. (See page 365.)

WORDY Sandra Cisneros, who is the author who wrote the book titled *The House on Mango Street,* which is a collection of short stories, was born in the city of Chicago in Illinois in the year 1954.

REVISED Sandra Cisneros, the author of the short-story collection *The House on Mango Street,* was born in Chicago, Illinois, in 1954.

QUICK REFERENCE HANDBOOK

Diagramming Appendix

Diagramming Sentences

A *sentence diagram* is a picture of how the parts of a sentence fit together and how the words in a sentence are related.

Subjects and Verbs

Reference Note

For more information about **subjects** and **verbs,** see page 439.

Every sentence diagram begins with a horizontal line intersected by a short vertical line, which divides the subject from the verb.

EXAMPLE   **Alice Walker wrote** *The Color Purple.*

Alice Walker	wrote

Understood Subjects

Reference Note

For more information about **understood subjects,** see page 447.

EXAMPLE   Answer the phone, please.

(you)	Answer

Nouns of Direct Address

Reference Note

For more information about **nouns of direct address,** see page 447.

EXAMPLE   Pass me the picante sauce, **Gina.**

Gina

(you)	Pass

Compound Subjects

EXAMPLE   **Arturo** and **Patsy** are dancing the conga.

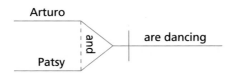

Reference Note

For more information about **compound subjects,** see page 447.

Compound Verbs

EXAMPLE   Roger **swims** and **dives.**

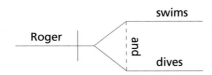

Reference Note

For more information about **compound verbs,** see page 448.

Compound Subjects and Compound Verbs

EXAMPLE   **Kittens** and **puppies can play** together and **become** friends.

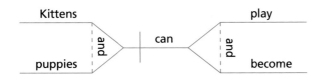

When the parts of a compound subject or a compound predicate are joined by a correlative conjunction, diagram the sentence this way:

EXAMPLE   **Both** Norma **and** Lisa will **not only** perform **but also** teach.

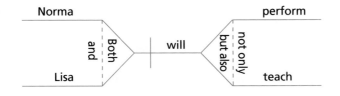

Reference Note

For more information about **correlative conjunctions,** see page 428.

Modifiers

Reference Note

For more information about **adjectives,** see page 412. For more about **adverbs,** see page 422.

Adjectives and Adverbs

Adjectives and adverbs are written on slanting lines beneath the words they modify.

EXAMPLE   **The blue** car **quickly** swerved **left.**

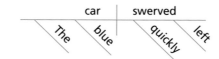

An adverb that modifies an adjective or an adverb is placed on a line connected to the word it modifies.

EXAMPLE   The Neville Brothers performed **exceptionally** well.

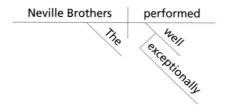

Reference Note

For more about questions and sentences beginning with **here** and **there,** see page 446.

Here, There, and *Where* as Modifiers

EXAMPLES   **Here** come the astronauts!

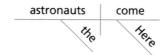

There goes the new Mohawk leader.

Where will the balloonists land?

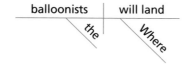

NOTE Sometimes *there* begins a sentence but does not modify the verb. When used in this way, *there* is called an *expletive.* It is diagrammed on a line by itself.

EXAMPLE   **There** are seven stars in the Pleiades.

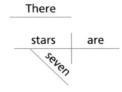

Subject Complements

A subject complement is placed after the verb on the same horizontal line as the simple subject and the verb. A line *slanting toward the subject* separates the subject complement from the verb.

Reference Note

For more information about **subject complements,** see page 453.

Predicate Nominatives

EXAMPLE   Some dogs are good **companions.**

Predicate Adjectives

EXAMPLE   That cockatiel is **friendly.**

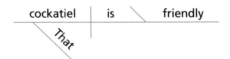

Compound Subject Complements

EXAMPLE   Martin Yan is both a **chef** and a **comedian.**

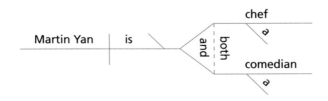

Objects

Reference Note

For more information about **direct objects,** see page 456.

Direct Objects

A direct object is placed after the verb on the same horizontal line as the simple subject and the verb. A *vertical* line separates the direct object from the verb.

EXAMPLE   Cathy led the **band.**

Compound Direct Objects

EXAMPLE   We heard **cheers** and **whistles.**

Indirect Objects

Reference Note

For more information about **indirect objects,** see page 457.

The indirect object is diagrammed on a horizontal line beneath the verb.

EXAMPLE   They gave **her** a present.

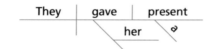

Compound Indirect Objects

EXAMPLE   Mr. Stephens lent **Karen** and **Shanna** *The Fire Next Time.*

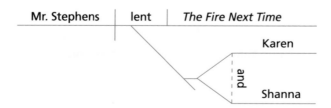

Phrases

Prepositional Phrases

The preposition is placed on a slanting line leading down from the word that the phrase modifies. The object of the preposition is placed on a horizontal line connected to the slanting line.

Reference Note

For more information about **prepositional phrases,** see page 467.

EXAMPLES The steep slopes **of the mountains** are covered **with forests.** [adjective phrase modifying the subject; adverb phrase modifying the verb]

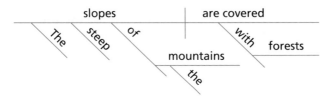

They sailed late **in the fall.** [adverb phrase modifying an adverb]

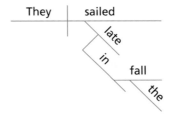

Nina read this Chinese folk tale to **Aaron** and **Joey.** [compound object of preposition]

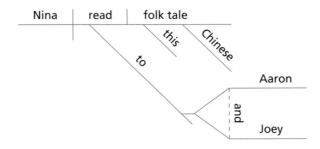

Down the valley and **across the plain** wanders the river.
[two phrases modifying the same word]

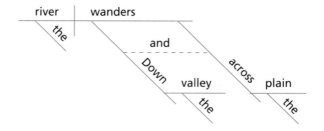

The princess lived **in a castle on the mountain.** [phrase modifying the object of another preposition]

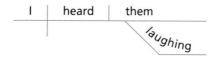

Reference Note

For more information about **participles** and **participial phrases,** see page 472.

Participles and Participial Phrases

Participles and participial phrases are diagrammed as follows.

EXAMPLES   I heard them **laughing.**

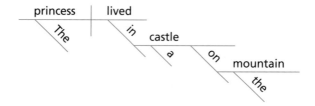

Waving her hat, Sara flagged the train **speeding down the track.**

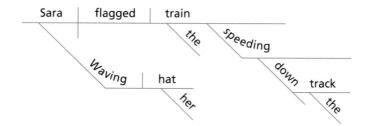

Notice above that the participle *Waving* has a direct object (*hat*), which is diagrammed in the same way that a direct object of a main verb is.

Gerunds and Gerund Phrases

Gerunds and gerund phrases are diagrammed as follows.

EXAMPLES   **Waiting** is not easy. [gerund used as subject]

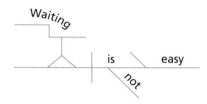

Waiting patiently for hours is often a sure means of **observing wild animals.** [gerund phrases used as subject and as object of a preposition]

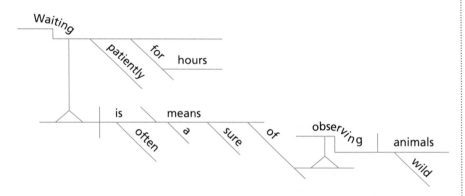

Notice above that the gerund *observing* has a direct object (*animals*).

Infinitives and Infinitive Phrases

Infinitives and infinitive phrases used as modifiers are diagrammed in the same way as prepositional phrases.

EXAMPLE   He plays **to win.** [infinitive used as adverb]

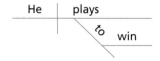

Reference Note

For more information about **gerunds** and **gerund phrases,** see page 476.

Reference Note

For more information about **infinitives** and **infinitive phrases,** see page 479.

Infinitives and infinitive phrases used as nouns are diagrammed as follows.

EXAMPLES **To choose the right career** takes careful consideration. [infinitive phrase used as subject]

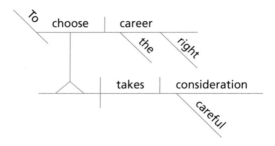

She is hoping **to visit Morocco soon.** [infinitive phrase used as direct object]

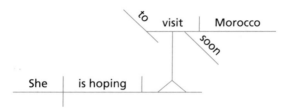

My brother watched **me prune the tree.** [infinitive clause with subject, *me,* and with *to* omitted]

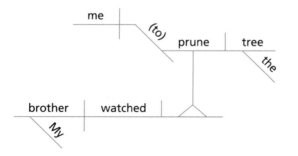

Reference Note

For more information about **appositives** and **appositive phrases,** see page 483.

Appositives and Appositive Phrases

Place the appositive in parentheses after the word it identifies or describes.

My cousin **Bryan** is a carpenter.

Mohammed Tahir comes from Yemen, **a country near Saudi Arabia.**

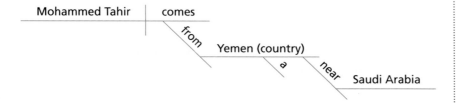

Subordinate Clauses

Adjective Clauses

An adjective clause is joined to the word it modifies by a broken line leading from the modified word to the relative pronoun.

EXAMPLES The coat **that I wanted** was too expensive.

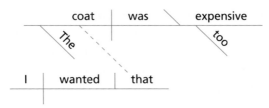

The box, **which contained the treasure,** was missing.

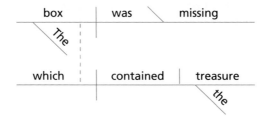

Reference Note

For more information about **adjective clauses,** see page 495.

She is the woman **from whom we bought the used car.**

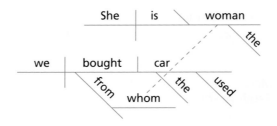

Adverb Clauses

Reference Note

For more information about **adverb clauses,** see page 498.

Place the subordinating conjunction that introduces the adverb clause on a broken line leading from the verb in the adverb clause to the word the clause modifies.

EXAMPLE   **Before a hurricane strikes,** ample warning is given.

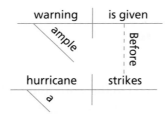

Noun Clauses

Reference Note

For more information about **noun clauses,** see page 501.

Noun clauses often begin with the word *that, what, who,* or *which.* These words may have a function within the subordinate clause or may simply connect the clause to the rest of the sentence. How a noun clause is diagrammed depends on how it is used in the sentence and whether or not the introductory word has a grammatical function in the noun clause.

EXAMPLES   **What she said** convinced me. [The noun clause is used as the subject of the independent clause. *What* functions as the direct object in the noun clause.]

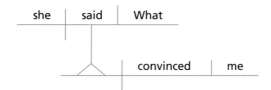

We know **that you won the prize.** [The noun clause is the direct object of the independent clause. *That* has no grammatical function in the noun clause.]

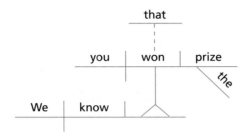

If the introductory word were omitted from the preceding sentence, the diagram would look like this.

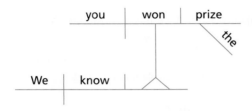

Sentences Classified According to Structure

Simple Sentences

EXAMPLES   The Hudson is a historic waterway. [one independent clause]

Denise hit a home run. [one independent clause]

Reference Note

For more information about **simple sentences,** see page 504.

Reference Note

For more information about **compound sentences,** see page 504.

Compound Sentences

EXAMPLE   A strange dog chased us, but the owner came to our rescue.
[two independent clauses]

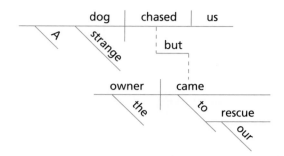

If the compound sentence has a semicolon and no conjunction, a straight broken line joins the two verbs.

EXAMPLE   Phillis Wheatley wrote poetry in the 1700s; she was the first published African American poet.

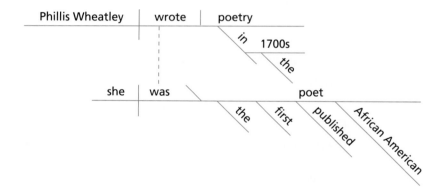

Notice above that the compound adjective *African American* is written on one slanted line.

    If the clauses of a compound sentence are joined by a semicolon and a conjunctive adverb (such as *consequently, therefore, nevertheless, however, moreover,* or *otherwise*), place the conjunctive adverb on a slanting line below the verb it modifies.

Reference Note

For more information about **conjunctive adverbs,** see page 492.

Dylan works part time after school**; consequently,** he can afford to buy a new bike.

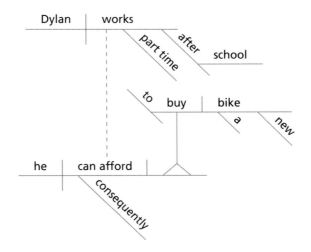

Complex Sentences

EXAMPLE   As night fell, the storm grew worse. [one independent clause and one subordinate clause]

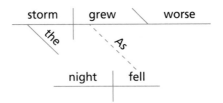

Reference Note
For more information about **complex sentences,** see page 505.

Compound-Complex Sentences

EXAMPLE   The room that Carrie painted had been white, but she changed the color. [two independent clauses and one subordinate clause]

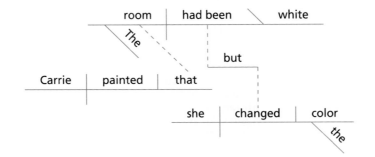

Reference Note
For more information about **compound-complex sentences,** see page 505.

A, an, 412, 638–39
A lot, 640
A number of, the number of, 649
A while, awhile, 641
Abbreviations
 of addresses, 698
 capitalization of, 670, 686–87, 697–98, 960
 in dictionaries, 847
 of geographical terms, 697–98
 of organizations, 697
 of personal names, 696
 punctuation of, 696–99, 715, 960
 of states, 697–98
 of time of day, 698–99
 of titles used with names, 696–97
 of units of measure, 699
Abridged dictionaries, 848
Abstract nouns, 407
Accept, except, 639
Accuracy, of sources, 226, 933
Acronyms, 760
Action verbs
 definition of, 418, 960
Active listening, 161
Active voice
 definition of, 601, 960
 writing in, 277–78
Addresses
 abbreviations and, 698
 commas and, 714–15
 envelope addressing, 947
 hyphenated street numbers in, 673
Adjective(s)
 articles, 412–13
 commas separating series of, 701–702
 comparison of, 620–24
 compound adjectives, 769
 definition of, 412, 614, 960–61
 demonstrative adjectives, 414
 diagramming and, 988
 nouns used as, 415
 placement of, 412
 possessive pronouns as, 409, 557
 predicate adjectives, 454
 pronouns distinguished from, 414
 proper adjectives, 415, 669–70
 punctuation of, 701–702
Adjective clauses, 495–97
 beginning with *that,* 705
 combining sentences and, 359

 definition of, 189, 495, 961
 diagramming and, 995–96
 as essential or nonessential clauses, 496
 placement of, 495
 punctuation of, 359
 relative adverbs and, 497
 relative pronouns and, 496–97
Adjective phrases
 definition of, 468, 961
 placement of, 468
Adjusting reading rate, 883
"Adopt-A-Bison," 297–99
Adverb(s)
 comparison of, 620–24
 conjunctive adverbs, 724–25
 definition of, 422, 614, 961
 diagramming and, 988
 modifying adjectives, 423
 modifying other adverbs, 424
 modifying verbs, 422
 overuse of, 79–80
 prepositions distinguished from, 427
 relative adverbs, 497
Adverb clauses
 combining sentences and, 345, 359–60
 definition of, 498, 961
 diagramming and, 996
 introductory adverb clauses, 359–60, 498, 708–709
 placement of, 345
 punctuation of, 359–60
 subordinating conjunctions and, 359–60, 498–99
Adverb phrases
 definition of, 469, 961
 placement of, 469–70
Advertising. *See also* headings beginning with
 Persuasive; Media; News; Television.
  compare/contrast persuasive elements of
   advertisements in oral presentation, 337
  creating documentary on print advertising, 329–36
  creating print advertisement about imaginary
   world, 337
  definition of, 936
  evaluating reasoning in advertising, 315
  oral presentation on advertising career, 337
  persuasive brochure, 306–26
  political advertising, 938
  write brochure about historical movement, 337
Aesthetic effects, in media, 87–88
Affect, effect, 639, 793
Affiliate, definition of, 928
Affixes. *See* Prefixes; Suffixes.
African American Vernacular English, 864
Agenda, for group discussions, 120
Agreement (pronoun-antecedent), 532–38
 collective nouns and, 536
 compound antecedents, 535
 definition of, 961

with expressions of amount and measurement, 536–37
gender, 532–33
indefinite pronouns and, 533–34
names of teams and, 538
nouns ending in *–ics,* 537
number and, 532–33, 538
personal pronouns and, 532–33
plural nouns taking singular pronouns, 537
special problems with, 536–38
titles of creative works and, 537–38
Agreement (subject-verb), 512–29, 962
collective nouns and, 522
combining sentences and, 357
compound prepositions and, 514
compound subjects and, 520
contractions and, 524, 527–28
definition of, 961
every or *many a,* 527
expressions of amount or measurement and, 525–26
geographic location and, 529
gerund phrases and, 513
indefinite pronouns and, 516–17
infinitive phrases and, 513
intervening words and phrases and, 46, 513–14
nouns plural in form with singular meaning, 528
number and, 512–14, 525–26
plural subjects and, 512–13
predicate nominative and, 524
singular subjects joined by *or* or *nor,* 520
subject following verb, 524
titles of work of art, music, literature, 529
verb agreeing with subject nearer verb, 520
verb with *I* or *you,* 512
Ain't, 639
Alignment, of text, 849–50
All, any, more, most, none, some, 534
All ready, already, 793
All right, 639, 793
All the farther, all the faster, 640
All together, altogether, 793
Allusion, illusion, 640
Almanacs, 870
Altar, alter, 793
Ambiguous reference, 566, 962–63
American English *See also* English language.
development of, 863.
dialects of, 864
standard American English, 864
Among, between, 641–42
An, a, 638–39
An American Childhood (Dillard), 19–20
Analogies
analogy questions on tests, 918–20
in editorial cartoons, 285, 287
meanings of words and, 888

types of analogies, 920
Analyzing
analysis questions for foreshadowing, 180
analyzing and writing about character's motivations, 125
audience, 140
comparative analysis, 123
definition of, 138, 167
editorial cartoons, 284–87
effects of television, 122–24
listing patterns, 886
news genres, 162–64
persuasive techniques, 327–28, 882
persuasive visual elements, 303
point of view analysis questions, 180
problem analysis, 128–56, 141–43, 150–53
problems of literary characters, 157
reviews of movies or software programs, 205
short story analysis, 167–94
writing prompts, 11, 282
And etc., 640
Anecdotes, 143, 258, 259, 269
Angelou, Maya, 668
Animation, definition of, 928
Announcements, as speaking situation, 902
Antecedent-pronoun agreement. *See* Agreement (pronoun-antecedent).
Antecedents
agreement with pronoun, 532–38
clear pronoun reference and, 566
definition of, 408, 532, 963
of relative pronouns, 496
Antigone (Sophocles), 157
Antonyms
analogies and, 920
context clues, 304, 887
in dictionaries, 847
Anyways, 640
Anywheres, 640
Apostrophe
with contractions, 763–64, 963
indefinite pronouns and, 760
plurals and, 766, 789–90, 963
possessive case and, 758–61, 963
Appearance, persuasive speaking and, 290
Application letter, 941–42
Appositive(s)
definition of, 343, 483, 561, 711, 963
diagramming and, 994–95
essential appositives, 711–12
nonessential appositives, 711
pronouns as, 561
punctuation of, 355–56, 484, 711–12
Appositive phrases, 483–84
combining sentences and, 355–56
definition of, 343, 483, 711, 963
diagramming and, 994–95

placement of, 355–56, 483–84
punctuation of, 484, 711–12
as sentence fragment, 343
Appreciative listening, 907
to an oral interpretation, 204
to a professional story reading, 205
Argument. *See* opinion statements *under* Persuasive
techniques.
Art activities
converting position papers into editorial cartoons,
293
drawing Rube Goldberg machine and explaining
its causal chain, 125
writing paragraphs about art forms after
researching them on World Wide Web, 249
"Art of Money, The" (Standish), 209–12
Articles, 412–13, 638–39, 964
Artistic oral performances, 203–204, 293, 337
As follows, **colon with,** 729
As if, like, 648
As, like, 648
As though, like, 648
Assertion, definition of, 315
At, 640
Atlases, 870
Attacking the person, definition of, 315
Attention getters, 87–88
Audience
analyzing audience, 140
cause-and-effect explanation, 105–106
comparison/contrast and, 68
formal speeches, 898
level of language, 400
literary analysis, 179
as media term, 932
persuasive brochure, 307–308
position paper, 264–65
problem-analysis essay, 139–40
research paper, 220
specific audience for personal reflection essay, 30
Audio reflection, of current event, 53
Audiovisual devices, for enhancing formal speeches,
901
Authority, as media term, 932
Auxiliary verbs. *See* Helping verbs.

Babbitt, Bruce, 93–94
Back panel, 312
Background information, providing, 68, 265, 272
Bad, badly, 617, 964
Bandwagon, 300
Bar graphs, 859, 879, 912
Base form, as principal part of verbs, 574, 964

Base words, 891–92
Be, forms of, 417, 419
as helping verb, 417
as linking verb, 419
passive voice and, 602
principal parts of, 574
progressive forms and, 592
Because, 641
Become, **principal parts of,** 577
Begin, **principal parts of,** 577
Being as, being that, 641
Believe, **principal parts of,** 574
Bend, **principal parts of,** 577
Berdichevsky, Norman, 57–59
Beside, besides, 641
Between, among, 641–42
Bias, 226, 876, 932, 933
Bibliographical references. *See* Works Cited.
Bibliography. *See* Works Cited list.
Biographical references, 847, 870
Blame, **principal parts of,** 575
Block method of comparison/contrast structure
definition of, 56, 62–63
organization diagram, 72
Block quotations, 192
Blow, **principal parts of,** 577
Body, coherence and, 391–92
of compositions, 391–92
elaboration and, 392
unity and, 391
Borrow, lend, loan, 642
Borrowed words. *See* Loanwords.
Both, few, many, several, 534
Brackets, 772, 964
Brainstorming
with a computer, 34
about brochures, 295
about research and investigation, 207
as prewriting technique, 953
Brake, break, 794
Break, **principal parts of,** 577
Bring, **principal parts of,** 577
Bring, take, 642
Broad generalizations, valid opinions and, 264
Broadcasting, definition of, 928
Brochures. *See also* Persuasive brochures.
definition of, 295
format of, 312–13
page layout, 313–14
panel design, 312–13
Browser, 871
Build, **principal parts of,** 577
Bullets, definition and uses of, 850
Burn, **principal parts of,** 576, 577
Burst, **principal parts of,** 577
Business letters
appreciation letters, 940–41

capitalization in, 669
closing, 715
complaint letters, 941
letters of application, 941–42
parts of, 939–40
punctuation of, 715
request letters, 942–43
types of, 940–43
Business texts
e-mail, 947
memos, 949–50
Bust, busted, 642
Buy, **principal parts of,** 577
Byline, definition of, 936

Cable television, 929
Caldwell, John, 785
Call numbers, 866
Callouts, 850
Camera techniques, in film, 200, 929
Can, could, 599
Can, may, 644
Capital, capitol, 794
Capitalization
of abbreviations, 670, 686–87, 697–98, 960
of building names, 676
of business names, 675
of businesses and brand names, 675–76
of comic strips, 684
common nouns and, 669, 965
of compass directions, 672
correct usage, 668–87
of dialogue, 668
direct quotations and, 743
of first words, 668, 964
of geographical names, 672–73
of historical events and periods, 676–77
of holidays and other calendar items, 676–77
of hyphenated numbers, 673
of interjection *O,* 668–69
of memorials, monuments, awards, 676
of musical works, 684
of names consisting of more than one word, 670
of nationalities, races, and peoples, 678
of organizations, teams, etc., 675
of planets and celestial bodies, 679
in poetry, 668
of political parties, 675
of pronoun *I,* 668
of proper adjectives, 669–70, 964
of proper nouns, 669–70, 964–65
in quotations, 668

of religions and their followers, holy days, sacred
writings, 678
of salutation and closing of letters, 669
of school subjects, 679
of seasons of year, 677
of ships, trains, aircraft, spacecraft, 678
of special events, 676–77
of specific deities, 678
of titles and subtitles, 682–84, 966
of titles of persons, 682
of words showing family relationship, 682
Capitol, capital, 794
Captions
document design and, 853
in editorial cartoons, 285
graphics and, 857
Card catalogs, 222, 866–67, 867–68
Card-stacking, definition of, 315
Career development activities
creating posters highlighting pros and cons of
career choice, 125
interviewing health professional and presenting
oral report, 165
interviewing professional and writing about
persuasive strategies and skills, 293
making relevant features chart of careers, 89
note-taking on research about particular careers,
249
oral presentation on advertising career, 337
oral response to interview question about personal
failure, 53
Cartoons. *See* Editorial cartoons.
Case forms of pronouns
definition of, 547
nominative case, 548, 549–51, 966
objective case, 548, 553–55, 966–67
possessive case, 548, 556–58, 967
Catch, **principal parts of,** 577
Causal chains
definition of, 92
diagram of, 99, 885
drawing Rube Goldberg machine and explaining
its causal chain, 125
Causative verbs, 96
Cause-and-effect article (reading)
cause-and-effect structure, 92, 97–100
inferring causes and effects, 92, 95–96
reading selection, 93–94
Cause-and-effect article (writing)
prewriting, 104–109
publishing (and proofreading), 118–19
revising, 114–15
writing, 110
Cause-and-effect relationships
causal analysis, 91
causal chains, 92, 99

causative verbs, 96
cause-and-effect order of ideas, 145
clue words, 95, 877
composite patterns for, 97, 100
context clues, 887
determining probable cause and probable effect, 22
false cause and effect, 108
implied cause-and-effect relationships, 95
inferring causes and effects, 92, 95–96
organizational patterns for, 97–100
oversimplification of, 108
patterns emphasizing causes, 97–98
patterns emphasizing effects, 97, 98–99
patterns tracing causal chains, 97–99
structure of, 92, 97–100, 101, 876, 885
Causes
    definition of, 95
    diagram of organizational pattern, 98
    focus on causes, 97–98
    inferring causes, 103
    initial causes, 99
    intermediate causes, 99
–cede, –ceed, –sede, **spelling rule for,** 780
Censorship, 934
Central ideas. *See* Main ideas.
Chaining, definition of, 953
Channel, definition of, 929
Characters
    analysis questions for, 180
    conflicts of characters in literary works, 157
    definition of, 174
    development of, 195
    direct characterization, 199
    in film, 199
    freewriting about, 195
    representation of television characters, 122–23
    writing analysis of character's motivations, 125
Charts
    flowcharts, 857–58
    interpreting charts, 912
    organizing information, 948
    pie charts, 858, 878
Children's books, writing and illustrating children's books, 205
Choose, **principal parts of,** 577
Choose, chose, 794
Choppy sentences, 352
Chronological order
    analyzing structure of, 885
    in cause-and-effect essay, 109
    clue words for, 877
    coherence and, 375
    definition of, 945
    in personal reflection essay, 36
    in problem-analysis essay, 145
Circular reasoning, definition of, 315
Circulation, as media term, 936

Clarity, color used for, 153
Classification, as study skill, 911–12
Clauses. *See also* Independent clauses; Subordinate clauses.
    adjective clauses, 189, 359, 495–97, 705, 961, 995–96
    adverb clauses, 345, 359–60, 498, 708–709, 961, 996
    definition of, 344, 492, 967
    essential (restrictive) clauses, 496, 705–706, 977
    infinitive clauses, 481
    as modifiers, 617
    nonessential (nonrestrictive) clauses, 496, 704–706, 977
    noun clauses, 360, 501–502, 977, 996–97
    placement of, 630
    punctuation of, 496
Clear reference, pronouns, 566–68
Clichés
    definition of, 37
    eliminating clichés in compositions, 322–23
    meanings of words and, 888
Clincher sentences, 371
Close-up, 331, 929
Clue words
    for cause-and-effect relationships, 877
    for chronological order, 877
    for comparison/contrast structure, 877
    for implied cause-and-effect relationships, 95
    for listing, 877
    for problem-solution structure, 877
Clustering, definition of, 953–54
Coarse, course, 794
Coherence. *See also* Order of ideas.
    connections between ideas and, 374–76
    definition of, 391
    direct references and, 375
    order of ideas and, 375
    transitional expressions, 376
Collaborating, to refine speeches, 292
Collaborative writing. *See* Peer review.
Collective nouns
    definition of, 407
    list of, 407
    pronoun-antecedent agreement and, 536
    subject-verb agreement and, 522
Colleges and universities, in dictionaries, 847
Colloquialisms
    definition of, 865
    meanings of words and, 888
Colons
    after salutation in business letter, 730
    before list of items, 729, 967
    before long, formal statement or quotation, 729
    between titles and subtitles, 730
    in Biblical references, 730
    in conventional situations, 730, 967

not before verb and complement or preposition and its object, 729
quotation marks and, 744

Colors
graphics design and, 153–54, 856
persuasive techniques and, 303

Combining sentences
with adjective clauses, 359
with adverb clauses, 345, 359–60
choppy sentences and, 352–53
with compound subject and compound verb, 357
inserting phrases and, 355–56
inserting words and, 353
into complex sentences, 359–60
with noun clauses, 360
subject-verb agreement and, 357

Come, principal parts of, 577

Comma(s)
abbreviations set off with, 715
adjective clauses and, 359
adjectives preceding noun and, 701–702
adverb clauses and, 359–60, 498
appositive phrases and, 355–56, 711–12
compound nouns and, 701
compound sentences and, 358, 701, 967
conjunctive adverbs and, 724–25
conventional uses of, 714–15, 968
direct address and, 712
interjections and, 430
interrupters and, 711–13, 968
introductory elements and, 707–709, 968
items in series and, 700–702, 967
letter salutations and closings and, 715
nonessential clauses and phrases and, 704–706, 968
parenthetical expressions and, 713, 772
quotation marks and, 744
transitional expressions and, 724–25
unnecessary use of, 716

Comma splices, 347, 348, 968

Common nouns
capitalization and, 669
definition of, 406, 669

Communicator, definition of, 932

Comparative analysis, 123

Comparative degree of comparison, 82, 620–24, 969

Comparing
as comparison/contrast, 67
context clues, 887

Comparison of modifiers
comparative degree, 620–24, 969
comparing two or more, 969
double comparison, 623–24, 971
irregular comparison, 622
positive degree, 620–22, 969
regular comparison, 621–22
superlative degree, 620–24, 969

Comparison/contrast article (reading)

comparison/contrast structure, 56
main idea and supporting details, 56
reading selection, 57–59

Comparison/contrast article (writing)
prewriting, 66–73
publishing (and proofreading), 82–83
revising, 78–81
writing first draft, 74

Comparison/contrast structure
analyzing comparison-contrast structure, 62–63, 885–86
block method, 56, 62–63
clue words for, 877
implied ideas and, 61
for persuasion, 67
point-by-point method, 56, 62–63
similarities and differences, 55
written explanation of comparison/contrast of two chemical compounds, 89

Complement, compliment, 794

Complements
compound complements, 450
definition of, 450, 969
direct objects as, 456–57
independent clauses and, 451
indirect objects as, 457–58
never in prepositional phrase, 451
predicate adjectives as, 454
predicate nominative as, 453–54
subject complements, 453–54
subordinate clauses and, 451, 494

Complete predicate, 439

Complete subject, 439

Complex sentences
combining sentences into, 189–90, 359–60
compound verbs and, 448
definition of, 505, 969
diagramming and, 999

Complexity, 87

Compositions. See also Writing process.
avoid beginning sentences with conjunctions in formal writing, 389
body of, 391–92, 945
conclusions of, 393–96, 945–46
definition of, 382
framework for, 397
function of paragraphs in, 382
introductions in, 382–89, 943–45
writer's model, 398–99

Compound adjectives, 769

Compound-complex sentences
definition of, 970

Compound direct objects, 456, 553, 990

Compound indirect objects, 458, 553, 990

Compound nouns, 406, 415, 441, 701
definition of, 406

Compound numbers, hyphen with, 768

Compound prepositions, 427, 514
Compound sentences
    combining sentences and, 358
    compound verbs and, 448
    conjunctive adverbs and, 349, 358
    coordinating conjunctions and, 348, 358
    definition of, 348–49, 358, 504–505, 970
    diagramming and, 998–99
    punctuation of, 348–49, 358
    run-on sentence revision of, 348–49
    simple sentences with compound elements
        distinguished from, 703
Compound subjects
    combining sentences and, 357
    definition of, 447, 520
    diagramming and, 987
Compound verbs
    combining sentences and, 357
    compound sentences and, 448
    definition of, 448
    diagramming and, 987
    helping verbs and, 448
Compound words, 760, 768–69
Compound-complex sentences
    definition of, 505, 970
    diagramming and, 999
Comprehensive listening, 909
Computers. *See also* Internet; World Wide Web.
    cut and paste commands and writing, 369, 383
    dimming the screen to brainstorm, 34
    grammar checking program, 341
    limitations of grammar checking programs, 80
    saving alternate versions of documents, 243, 400
    undo command, 115
    using FIND command to determine passive-voice
        construction, 279
Conclusions. *See also* Drawing conclusions.
    structure of, 396
    techniques for writing effective conclusions,
        393–96
    typical length of, 396
    in writing process, 393–96
Concrete nouns
    definition of, 407
    list of, 407
Conferencing. *See* Peer review.
Conflicts
    of characters in literary works, 157
    external conflicts, 195
    internal conflicts, 195
Conjunctions
    avoid beginning sentences with conjunctions in
        formal writing, 389
    coordinating conjunctions, 348, 357, 358, 428, 492
    correlative conjunctions, 428
    definition of, 428, 970
    subordinating conjunctions, 359–60, 498–99

Conjunctive adverbs
    compound sentences and, 349, 358
    independent clauses and, 492–93
    list of, 493, 724
    punctuation of, 724–25
Connections between ideas. *See* Direct references;
    Transitional expressions.
Connections to life
    analyzing persuasion in media, 327–28
    distinguishing purposes of media forms, 84–85
    participating in group discussions, 120–21
    research in media, 246
    writing letters of application, 283
Connections to literature
    analyzing problems of literary characters, 157
    writing free-verse poetry, 48–49
    writing short stories, 195–97
Connotations
    meanings of words and, 888
    overuse of, 269
    in persuasive writing, 259, 269
    understanding connotations, 261
Consistency of tense, 597–98
Consul, council, councilor, counsel, counselor, 795
Consumer materials, reading, 296–303, 866
Context clues
    antonyms and, 304, 887
    comparison/contrast, 64
    definitions and restatements, 136, 887
    synonyms and, 304, 887
    using context clues, 136
Contractions
    of adverb *not,* 763
    definition of, 763, 970
    list of, 763, 970
    possessive forms of pronouns distinguished from,
        760, 764
    subject-verb agreement and, 524, 527–28
Contrast
    context clues, 887
    in graphics, 856
    in page layout, 851
    type and, 854
Controversy, 87
Conventions of oral language. *See* Speaking.
Conventions of written language. *See* Compositions.
Conversation. *See* Dialogue.
Coordinate ideas, in essay writing, 144
Coordinating conjunctions
    compound sentences and, 348, 358
    compound subjects or verbs and, 357
    definition of, 428
    independent clauses and, 492
Copyright, of dictionaries, 847
Copyright law, 934
Correlative conjunctions, 428
***Cost,* principal parts of,** 574, 577

Could, can, 599
Could of, 644
Council, councilor, counsel, counselor, consul, 795
Course, coarse, 794
Cover shot, 331
Credibility, 226, 932, 933
Credits, definition of, 929
Critical listening, 908
    to a debate, 165
    to an informative speech, 161
    to a persuasive speech, 291
Critical reading questions on tests, 921–23
Critical thinking
    coordinating and subordinating ideas, 144
    evaluating reasoning, 270
    evaluating reasoning in advertising, 315
    evaluating sources, 226
    oversimplification and false cause and effect, 108
    synthesizing information into a thesis, 71
Critical viewing, definition of, 932
Critiquing, critiquing films, 198–202
Cross-examination debate, 897
Cubing, definition of, 954
Cut, **principal parts of,** 577

D

"Danger Beneath the Dash" (Levingston), 129–31
Dangling modifiers, 118, 626, 970
Dashes
    abrupt breaks in thought or speech and, 770
    example of usage, 971
    parenthetical elements and, 770
    to mean *namely, that is, in other words,* 770
    unfinished statements or questions and, 770
Databases, 868
Debate
    analyze the debate process, 165
    features of, 896
    formats of, 897
    preparing for, 897
Declarative sentences
    definition of, 459, 971
    punctuation of, 459, 694
Decoding, definition of, 934
Deconstruction, definition of, 934
Defining moments, definition of, 28
Definite articles, 413
Definition and restatement, context clues, 136, 887
Demographics, definition of, 936
Demonstrative adjectives, 414
Demonstrative pronouns
    definition of, 410
Denotation, 261, 888
Dependent clauses. *See* Subordinate clauses.

Descriptive details
    definition of, 18, 24
    factual details as, 24
    figurative details as, 24–25
    sensory details as, 24
Desert, dessert, 795
Designing your writing. *See* Document design.
Desktop publishing. *See also* Document design.
    page layout, 849–55
    type, 853–55
Details. *See also* Descriptive details; Factual details;
    Figurative details; Narrative details; Sensory details;
    Support.
    arranging details, 72–73
    chart for details, 33–34
    as expressing tone in writing, 106
    organizing details, 36
    supporting details, 56, 60–62
Dewey decimal system, 866
Diagramming sentences, 986–99
Diagrams, 858, 878, 912, 949
Dialects
    definition of, 861
    ethnic dialects, 864
    regional dialects, 864
Dialogue
    capitalization in, 668
    dialogue bubbles in editorial cartoons, 285
    fitting the speaker, 32
    as narrative detail, 24
    quotation marks and, 746
Diction, 900
Dictionaries
    antonyms in, 847
    definitions in, 847
    determining verbs as transitive and intransitive
        and, 421
    dictionary entries, 846–48
    entry words, 846–47
    etymology, 847
    examples in, 847
    guide to, 847–48
    part-of-speech labels in, 847
    pronunciation and, 847
    related word forms in, 847
    synonyms in, 847
    types of, 848
    usage labels, 847
Differences, comparison/contrast and, 68
"Digging the Past" (Lawrence), 7
Digital editing, definition of, 936
Dillard, Annie, 19–20
Direct address
    nouns of, 447, 986
    punctuation of, 712
Direct objects
    compound direct objects, 456

definition of, 456, 553, 971
diagramming and, 990
never in prepositional phrase, 457
pronouns in objective case and, 553
Direct quotations. *See also* Quotations.
integrating direct quotations, 239
paraphrasing and, 213
punctuation of, 193, 743–45, 980
summarizing and, 213
Direct references
connecting ideas in writing, 375, 391
examples of, 379
and transitions, 376
Directions, 672
Discover, invent, 644
Discussion. *See* Group discussions.
Dive, **principal parts of,** 577
Diversity (in language), 864–65
Divided quotation, 743
Do, **principal parts of,** 574, 577
Docudrama, definition of, 929
Document design. *See also* Desktop publishing; Page layout.
alignment, 849–50
bullets and, 850
callout, 850
color used for emphasis and clarity, 153–54, 856
color wheel, 856
contrast and emphasis, 851
designing Web pages, 45
desktop publishing, 849–55
fonts, 854
formatting an essay, 191
graphics, 857–60
grid lines, 851
guidelines for submitting papers, 849
gutters, 851
heading/subheading, 851–52
labels, 857
page layout, 849–53
persuasive brochure, 312–13
transforming information into Web site, 243
typefaces and fonts, 324, 853–55
using flowcharts, 117
using graphs, charts, tables, 279
using subheads, 81
Documentaries
creating a documentary on print advertising, 329–36
definition of, 929–30
as news genre, 162–63
postproduction, 336
preproduction, 329–35
production, 335
script writing, 331–35
terminology, 331
Don't, doesn't, 527–28, 644

Double comparisons, 623–24, 971
Double negatives, 280, 656–57, 971
Double subjects, 645, 971
Drama, definition of, 930
Draw, **principal parts of,** 577
Drawing conclusions. *See also* Conclusions.
definition of, 21, 168, 877
example of, 877
steps in, 172–73
Dream, **principal parts of,** 576
Drink, **principal parts of,** 577
Drive, **principal parts of,** 577

E-mail
guidelines for, 947
peer review by e-mail, 151
Eat, **principal parts of,** 578
Editing, first drafts. *See* Proofreading.
Editorial cartoons
analogy in, 285, 287
converting position paper into, 293
exaggeration/caricature in, 284–87
irony in, 285, 286
symbolism in, 284, 285
Editorials, writing editorials, 293
Editors, definition of, 936
Effect, affect, 639, 793
Effect. *See* Cause-and-effect essay.
Effects
definition of, 95
diagram of organizational pattern, 98
final effects, 99
focus on, 98–99
inferring effects, 103
intermediate effects, 99
long-term effects, 99
short-term effects, 99
ei **and** *ie,* **spelling rule for,** 780
Either, neither, 516
Either-or reasoning, 270, 315
Elaboration
in compositions, 42, 78, 114, 150, 188, 240, 276, 321, 376–78
example of, 379
on key points, 183
on main point, 376–78
Electronic media. *See also* Computers; Internet; Media; Television; World Wide Web.
definition of, 930
Elements of design, 936
Ellipsis points
never beginning quoted passages with, 751
for pause in dialogue, 751

for words omitted from quoted material, 750–51
Else, other, 623
Emigrate, immigrate, 644
Emotional appeals
    anecdotes and, 259, 269
    connotative words and, 259, 269
    as element of persuasion, 252, 257, 259, 301
    examples and, 269
    loaded language and, 259
Emotional impact
    news stories and, 87
    in persuasive writing, 269
Empathic listening, 31, 909–10. *See also* Reflective listening.
Emphasis
    color used for, 153–54
    in formal speeches, 900
    in graphics design, 856
    in page layout, 851
Emphatic form, verb tense, 592
Employment. *See* Jobs.
End marks, 694–95, 972
English language
    American English, 863–64
    clichés, 37, 322–23
    colloquialisms, 865
    connotations and, 259, 261, 269, 888
    denotation and, 261
    dialects, 861, 864
    formal, standard English, 865
    future of, 863
    history of, 861–63
    inflections, 862
    informal, standard English, 865
    jargon, 216
    loanwords, 741, 862
    Middle English, 862
    Modern English, 863
    nonsexist language, 659–60, 890
    nonstandard English, 638
    Old English, 862, 892, 893
    slang, 748, 865
    standard English, 638, 865
Enthusiasm, persuasive speaking and, 290
Enunciation, persuasive speaking and, 290
Envelopes, addressing, 947–48
–er, –est, 621
Essays
    comparison/contrast essay, 66–83
    personal reflection essay, 28–47
    problem-analysis essay, 138–56
Essential clauses and phrases, 496, 705–706, 972
Ethnic dialects, 864
Etymology, 847
Euphemisms, 888–89
Evaluating
    cause-and-effect essay, 114

    comparison/contrast essay, 78
    criteria for, 199
    personal reflection essay, 42–43
    persuasive speeches, 291
    problem-analysis essay, 150
    reasoning, 270, 315
    Web sites, 247–48
Events
    as narrative detail, 24
    sequence of, 597–98
Every, many a, 527
Everywheres, 640
Evidence. *See also* Reasons; Support.
    anecdotes, 268
    as element of persuasion, 252, 258
    expert opinions, 268
    facts, 267
    inadequate evidence, 270
    opinions, 268
    reasons why, 268
    statistics, 267
Exaggeration
    in editorial cartoons, 284–87
    persuasive speeches and, 290
Examples
    context clues for, 887
    in dictionaries, 847
    as support, 143, 258, 268
Except, accept, 639
Exclamation points
    exclamatory sentences and, 694–95
    interjections and, 430
    quotation marks and, 744–45
Exclamatory sentences
    definition of, 459, 694–95, 972
    punctuation of, 459–60
Expert testimony, 143, 258
Expletives, 446
Exposition. *See* Comparison/contrast essay; Informative writing; Research papers.
Extemporaneous speech
    definition of, 899
    guidelines for note cards, 899
Eye contact, during formal speeches, 290, 900

Facial expressions
    formal speeches and, 900
    persuasive speaking and, 290
Facts
    fact-and-opinion questions in test taking, 262
    opinion distinguished from, 228, 252, 255–57, 877
    as reasons in persuasive writing, 258
    relevant facts, 255–56

Factual details
  definition of, 24
  describing people and places, 31
  statistics, 143
Fade-in, 331
Fade-out, 331
Fall, **principal parts of,** 578
False cause and effect, 108
Feature news, definition of, 937
Feedback
  audience feedback during speeches, 160
  definition of, 934
  in group discussions, 121
Feel, **principal parts of,** 578
Fewer, less, 645
Fiction
  character conflict in, 157
  characters, 195
  climax, 195
  conflict in, 195
  elements of plot, 157
  meaning in, 203
  mood in, 203
  oral interpretation of, 203–204
  point of view in, 196, 203
  setting in, 196
  writing short stories, 195–97
Fight, **principal parts of,** 578
Figurative details
  definition of, 24
  describing people and places, 31
  metaphors, 25
  personification, 25
  similes, 25
Figurative language
  definition of, 37
  metaphors, 25, 37, 889
  personification, 25, 37, 889
  plot, 199
  in poetry, 49
  similes, 25, 37, 889
  using figurative language, 37
Figures of speech. *See* Figurative language.
Film
  character, 199
  critiquing films, 198–202
  model critique of, 201–202
  point of view, 198
  setting, 198–99
  theme, 199
Find, **principal parts of,** 578
First Amendment
  media law and, 934
First-person point of view, 196
First-person pronouns, 409, 548
  case forms, 548
5W-How? **questions,** 141–42, 952–53

Flier. *See* Brochure.
Flowcharts, 857–58
Fly, **principal parts of,** 577, 578
Focus, in graphics design, 856–57
Fonts, 854–55, 937
"Force-Fed Television" (Hochschild), 253–54
Foreshadowing, analysis questions for, 180
Forgive, **principal parts of,** 578
Formal debate, 897
Formal English, definition of, 638
Formal logical arguments, definition of 267
Formal outlines, 951
Formal research, 215
Formal speeches
  audiovisual devices and, 901
  avoiding contractions, 524
  avoiding slang, 748
  delivery, 899
  extemporaneous speech, 899
  features of, 899
  formal speeches, 897–901
  nonverbal signals, 900
  superlative degree and, 623
  topic selection, 897
  verbal signals, 900–901
  writing speeches, 898–99
Formal writing
  avoid beginning sentences with conjunctions, 389
  avoiding slang, 748
Formally, formerly, 796
Format
  of brochures, 312–13
  definition of, 312
Forms, completing, 948
Formula, as media term, 934
4R test for sources, 226
Fractions, hyphens and, 768
Fragments. *See* Sentence fragments.
Free-verse poem
  creating a, 48–49
  definition of, 48
  elements of, 48–49
  example of, 48
  literary devices in, 49
Freewriting, definition of, 914, 954
Freeze, **principal parts of,** 578
French loanwords, 893
Friendly letters, 949
"From an Introduction to Charles Dickens's *A Christmas Carol*" (Irving), 169–71
Front panel, 312
Full shot, 331
Fused sentences, 347, 972
Future perfect progressive tense, 592
Future perfect tense, 596, 984
Future progressive tense, 592
Future tense, 595, 984

Gender, agreement (pronoun-antecedent), 532–33, 548
General reference, pronouns and, 567, 973
Generalizations
broad generalizations, 264
fallacies, 133
forming generalizations, 877–78
glittering generalities, 301
hasty generalizations, 133, 270
making generalizations, 21, 128, 132–34
steps in making valid generalizations, 133–34
Generating ideas. *See* Brainstorming.
Genre, television genres, 934
Geographical terms, abbreviation of, 697–98
Gerund(s)
definition of, 476, 557, 973
diagramming and, 993
present participle distinguished from, 477
Gerund phrases
definition of, 478, 973
diagramming and, 993
Gesturing
formal speeches and, 900
persuasive speaking and, 290
Get, **principal parts of,** 578
Give
conjugation in passive voice, 602–603
conjugation of, 592–93
principal parts of, 578, 592
Glittering generalities, 301
Glossary, definition of, 638
Go, **principal parts of,** 577, 578
Good, well, 617–18, 973
Grammar Links
consistent verb tenses, 325
correcting misplaced modifiers, 244
dangling modifiers, 118
double negatives, 280
sentence fragments, 155
subject-verb agreement, 46
using comparative and superlative forms, 82
using quotation marks, 193
Graphic organizers, 912, 948
Graphics. *See also* Illustrations; Photography; Visuals.
arrangement and design of, 855–57
charts, 857–58
diagrams, 858
document design and, 855–60
elements of design, 936
graphs, 858–59
illustrations, 859
interpreting graphics, 878–81
in page layout, 851

storyboards, 859
tables, 859–60
time lines, 860
types of, 857–60
Graphs
definition of, 858–59
interpreting graphs, 912
Gray pages, in page layout, 851
Greek
prefixes, 892
roots, 891–92
suffixes, 893–94
Grid lines, in page layout, 851
Group discussions. *See also* Informal group discussions.
feedback in, 121
note taking and, 120
order of business, 902
parliamentary procedure and, 902
participating in, 120–21
purpose of, 901–902
roles in, 120
speaking in, 121
Grow, **principal parts of,** 578
Gutters, in page layout, 851

Had of, 645
Had ought, hadn't ought, 645
Handwritten papers, 194
Hard news, 937
Hardly, 656
Hasty generalizations, 133, 270
Have, **principal parts of,** 578
He, she, it, they, **as double subject,** 645
Headers and footers, in page layout, 851
Headings and subheadings, in page layout, 851–52
Headlines, definition of, 87, 937
Hear, here, 578, 796
Helping verbs
agreement with subjects, 512–13
compound verbs and, 448
list of, 417
with participles, 574
passive voice and, 602
Henderson, Amy, 239
Here, there, 446, 524, 988
Hide, **principal parts of,** 578
His or her **construction,** 533, 534
Hisself, theirself, theirselves, 645
Historical present tense, 594
History activities, writing brochure about historical movement, 337
Hit, **principal parts of,** 578

Hochschild, Adam, 253–54
Home page, 243, 871
Homographs, 26
Homonyms, 793–800
Hopefully, 645–46
Human-interest stories, 162
Hyperlink, 243, 871–72
Hypertext, 872
Hypertext Markup Language (HTML), 872
Hypertext Transfer Protocol (HTTP), 872
Hyphens
    compound numbers and, 768, 973
    compound words and, 768–69
    fractions used as adjectives and, 768
    prefixes and suffixes and, 768, 973
    word division at end of line and, 767, 973

Ideas for writing. *See* Brainstorming; Topics.
Idioms, 889
ie and *ei,* spelling rule for, 780
Illusion, allusion, 640
Illustrations, 205, 296, 859. *See also* Audiovisual devices; Graphics; Photography; Visuals.
Immigrate, emigrate, 644
Imperative mood, 606
Imperative sentences
    definition of, 459, 974
    punctuation of, 459, 695
Implied main ideas
    identifying implied main idea, 881
    lack of topic sentence and, 371
Imply, infer, 646
In-camera editing, definition of, 52, 332, 930
Incomplete construction, 974
Indefinite articles, 412, 638–39
Indefinite pronouns
    agreement with verb, 516–17
    definition of, 516
    list of, 411, 516
Indefinite reference, 567–68, 974
Indentation, in page layout, 852
Independent clauses
    commas and, 701, 703
    complements and, 451
    conjunctive adverbs and, 492–93
    coordinating conjunctions and, 492
    definition of, 344, 492, 974
    object of verbs and, 456
    semicolon and, 492, 701, 724–26
Index, in dictionaries, 848
Indicative mood, 606
Indirect objects
    compound indirect objects, 458, 553

    definition of, 457, 553, 974
    diagramming and, 990
    never following preposition, 553
    prepositional phrase distinguished from, 457
    pronouns in objective case and, 553
Indirect quotation, 743
Infer, imply, 646
Inferences. *See also* Making inferences.
    definition of, 18, 881
    inference questions on tests, 27, 921
    inferring causes and effects, 92, 95–96, 103
Infinitive(s)
    definition of, 479, 974
    diagramming and, 993–94
    prepositional phrases distinguished from, 479
    with *to* omitted, 481
    varying sentence beginnings with, 115–16
    as verbal, 479
Infinitive clauses, 481
Infinitive phrases
    definition of, 480, 974
    diagramming and, 993–94
    varying sentence beginnings with, 115–16
Inflection (speaking). *See* Emphasis.
Inflections, 862
Infomercial, 85
Informal English, definition of, 638
Informal group discussions. *See also* Group discussions.
    identifying purpose for, 904–905
    participating in, 905
Informal outlines, 950
Informal research, 215
Informal speaking
    giving/receiving directions and, 904
    giving/receiving instructions, 904
    impromptu speeches, 904
    making introductions, 904
    social situations and, 904
    superlative degree and, 623
    telephone conversations, 904
Information. *See also* Details; Facts; Support.
    gathering information, 68–70
    relevant information, 69
    synthesizing information into a thesis, 71
Informative oral messages
    interview health professional and present oral report, 165
    oral presentation on advertising career, 337
    videotape news program on cause-and-effect relationship and give oral presentation, 125
Informative speeches
    delivery, 160
    preparation, 158–59
    presentation, 158–61
    purpose, 898

question-and-answer session afterwards, 160–61
    structure, 159
    visuals for, 160
Informative writing. *See also* Analyzing.
    cause-and-effect explanation, 104–19
    literary analysis, 178–94
    position paper, 263–81
    problem-analysis essay, 138–56
    research article, 218–45
Infotainment programs, 85
Inside, 649
Inside addresses, business letters and, 940
Inside spread, 313
Instructions, 721, 904, 909
Intensive pronouns, definition of, 410, 564
Intent. *See* Purpose.
Interjections
    definition of, 429, 975
    punctuation of, 430, 695
Internet
    definition of, 930
    as reference source, 867
    writing online book review, 53
Interpretation, as media term, 934
Interpreting meaning, steps for, 35
Interrogative pronouns, 410
Interrogative sentences
    definition of, 459, 975
    punctuation of, 459, 460, 694
Intervening phrases
    definition of, 46
    subject-verb agreement and, 513
Interviewing
    conducting an interview, 902–903
    interviewing author about writing strategies, 205
    interviewing health professional and presenting
        oral report, 165
    people with shared experiences, 32
    preparing for, 902
Intransitive verbs, 421, 975
Introductions
    "but" introduction, 389
    in compositions, 382–89, 943–45
    as setting tone in a composition, 385
    structure of, 388–89
    techniques for writing, 383–85
    thesis statement, 386–87
    varying length of, 382
Introductory elements, punctuation of, 707–709
Invent, discover, 644
Invitations, 949
Irony
    analysis questions for, 180
    definition of, 180
    in editorial cartoons, 285
Irregular verbs, 576–79, 975–76

Irving, John, 169–71
Italics (underlining)
    for foreign words, 741
    for ships, trains, aircraft, etc., 741
    of titles and subtitles, 740, 975
    used for emphasis, 742
    of words, letters, symbols, and numerals, 741, 976
Items in series
    colons and, 729
    commas and, 700–702, 967
    semicolons and, 726
    as sentence fragment, 346
Its, it's, 796, 976

Jargon, definition of, 216, 889
Job applications, 941
Jobs
    application letters, 283
    interviewing for jobs, 903
    résumés and, 957
Journal, 914
Journalism activities, writing editorials, 293
Judgment opinions, 258
Juxtaposition, 87

Key points
    coordinate ideas as, 144
    as most important points, 142
    relating directly to thesis, 182
Key verbs in essay questions, 916
Keyboarding skills. *See* Computers.
Khan, Niamat, 746
Kind of a(n), sort of a(n), 648
Kind of, sort of, 648
Kinds, sorts, types, 648
Knockout type, 855
Know, **principal parts of,** 578

Labels, in editorial cartoons, 285, 287
"Land of the Giants" (Laycock), 4
Language. *See also* English language.
    nonsexist language, 659–60
    technical language, 159
Language skills, review of, 810–43
Latin

prefixes, 892
roots, 891–92
suffixes, 893
Lawrence, Jenny, 7
Lay, **principal parts of,** 582
Lay, lie, 582, 976–77
Laycock, George, 4
Lead, as media term, 937
Lead, **principal parts of,** 578
Lead, led, 796
Leader, in group discussions, 120
Leap, **principal parts of,** 576
Learn, teach, 648
Learning log, 914
Least, less, 622
Leave, let, 578, 648
Legibility, 194
Lend, borrow, loan, 642
Less, fewer, 645
Let, **principal parts of,** 578
Letters. *See also* Business letters.
    R.S.V.P. and, 949
Letters (correspondence)
    application letters, 283
    invitations, 949
    letters of regret, 949
    thank-you letters, 949
    writing letter after researching influences on
      writing of particular author, 249
Levingston, Steven, 129–31
Library of Congress classification system, 866
Library/media center
    call numbers, 866
    card catalogs, 222, 866–67
    Dewey decimal classification system and, 866
    Internet, 867
    microforms, 867
    online card catalog, 867–68
    Readers' Guide to Periodical Literature, 868–69
Lie, **principal parts of,** 582
Lie, lay, 582, 976
Light, **principal parts of,** 578
Lighting, film and, 200
Like, as, 648
Like, as if, as though, 648
Lincoln-Douglas debate, 897
Line graphs, 858, 879
Line length, in page layout, 852
Linking verbs
    definition of, 419, 976
    as intransitive, 421
    list of, 419
    subject complements and, 453
Listening
    active listening, 161
    in an interview, 903, 910
    appreciative listening, 907

barriers to effective listening, eliminating, 906, 907
comprehensive listening, 909
critical listening, 908
empathic listening, 909–10
evaluating self as listener, 907
evaluating speakers, 161, 204, 291–92, 908
    with focus, 954–55
    in group discussions, 910
    for information, 909
    to instructions, 909
    note taking and, 909
    process, 906
    purposes for, 908–910
    special listening situations, 910
    stages of, 906
    types of listening, 907–10
Listing patterns, analyzing listing patterns, 886
Literary analysis
    definition of, 167
    purpose of, 175
Literary analysis (reading)
    drawing conclusions, 168, 172–73
    literary elements, 168, 173–75
    reading selection, 169–71
Literary analysis (writing)
    prewriting, 178–83
    publishing (and proofreading), 193–94
    revising, 188–89
    writing first draft, 184
Literary present tense, 594
Literary texts
    children's book (illustrated), 205
    free verse poem, 48–49
    short story, 195
Literature. *See* Literature activities; Short story.
Literature activities
    analyzing problems of literary characters, 157
    charting comparison/contrast of movie and book,
      89
    conflicts of characters in literary works, 157
    creating print advertisement about imaginary
      world, 337
    describing literary elements on tests, 177
    development in, 175
    effects in literary texts, 175
    elements of literary texts, 168, 173–75, 179–80
    function in literary texts, 174
    literary analysis, 168–94
    summarizing short stories based on problems, 165
    writing analysis of character's motivations, 125
    writing letter after researching influences on
      writing of particular author, 249
    writing online book review, 53
    writing persuasive poetry and lyrics, 293
Loaded words, 889
Loan, borrow, lend, 642

Loanwords, 741, 789, 862
Logical appeals
    formal logical arguments, 266
    in persuasive writing, 257, 258–59
    reasons and evidence, 266
Logical arguments. *See* Logical appeals.
Logical order, 375, 945
Logical progression, 145. *See also* Coherence; Order of
    ideas.
Looping, definition of, 955
Loose, lose, 796
Lose, **principal parts of,** 578
LQ2R method, 908
–ly
    beginning sentences with words ending in *–ly,* 354
    parts of speech of words ending in *–ly,* 422
–ly, –ness, 782

M

Main clauses. *See* Independent clauses.
Main ideas. *See also* Thesis statement; Topic sentences.
    definition of, 56
    diagram of, 61
    elaboration in paragraphs, 376–78
    identifying main ideas and details, 22, 60–62, 372,
        884
    implied main idea, 371
    as main idea of persuasive writing, 257–58
    test taking and, 65
    as thesis, 60
Make, **principal parts of,** 578
Making generalizations. *See also* Generalizations.
    definition of, 21, 128
    methods of, 132–33
    prior knowledge and, 132
    steps in making valid generalizations, 133–34
Making inferences. *See also* Drawing conclusions.
    definition of, 21, 881
    difficulties with, 22
    drawing conclusions and, 21
    inference questions on tests, 27, 921
    making generalizations and, 21
    making predictions and, 22
    reading process and, 18
    three-step process of, 22–23
Manuscript speeches, 899
Many a, every, 527
Mapping
    definition of, 955
    ideas, 231
Maps (as source of information), 222
Margins, 852
Marketing, definition of, 937
Matching questions, 917

May, 600
May, can, 644
Meaning, in fiction, 203
Meaning of a word
    analogies, 888
    clichés, 888
    colloquialisms, 888
    connotations of, 888
    denotation, 888
    dictionary definitions, 847
    euphemisms, 888–89
    figurative language, 889
    idioms, 889
    jargon, 889
    loaded words, 889
    multiple meanings, 889–90
    nonsexist language, 890
    slang, 890
    synonyms, 890
    tired words, 890
Media
    analyzing persuasion in media, 327–28
    analyzing reviews of movies or software programs,
        205
    attention-getting elements, 87–88
    attention-getting techniques, 87
    comparison/contrast of media coverage, 86–88
    concepts, 933
    creating Web pages from position paper, 293
    docudramas, 85
    infomercials, 85
    infotainment programs, 85
    print media, 936–38
    purposes of media forms, 84–85
    research in, 246
    terminology, 51–52, 331, 928–38
    and the law, 934
    watch/listen to government procedure and make
        written profile of problem-solving techniques, 165
Medium, of media messages, 937
Memorandums. *See* Memos.
Memorized speeches, 899
Memorizing, steps in, 881
Memos, 949–50
Message, as media term, 937
Messages, taking messages, 950
Metaphors, definition of, 25, 37, 889
Microfilm/microfiche, 222, 867
Middle English, 862
Might, 600
Might of, 644
Miner, minor, 796
Mini-lesson (critical thinking)
    coordinating and subordinating ideas, 144
    evaluating reasoning, 270
    evaluating reasoning in advertising, 315
    evaluating sources, 226

oversimplification and false cause and effect, 108
synthesizing information into a thesis, 71
Mini-lesson (test taking)
analyzing writing prompts, 282
describing literary elements, 177
fact-and-opinion questions, 262
identifying main idea, 65
inference questions on reading tests, 27
inferring causes and effects, 103
logic questions, 137
recognizing persuasive devices, 305
using context to understand specialized or
technical terms, 217
Mini-lesson (vocabulary)
comparison/contrast context clues, 64
context clues: definitions and restatements, 136
multiple-meaning words, 26
specialized and technical terms, 216
suffixes, 102
synonym and antonym context clues, 304
understanding connotations and denotations, 261
using word roots, 176
Mini-lesson (writing)
using figurative language, 37
weaving quotations into essays, 192
Misplaced modifiers, 244, 627–30, 976
Modals
definition of, 417, 599
uses of, 599–601
Modern English, 863. *See also* English language.
Modifiers. *See also* Adjective(s); Adverb(s).
bad, badly, 617
clauses used as, 617
comparative degree of, 82, 620–24, 969
comparison of, 620–24, 969
dangling modifiers, 118, 626, 970
definition of, 244, 614, 977
diagramming and, 988–99
forms of, 614–17
irregular comparison, 622
misplaced modifiers, 244, 627–30, 976
one-word modifiers, 614–15
phrases used as, 616–17, 628–29
placement of, 627–30
positive degree, 620–22
possessive pronouns as, 557
real, really, 618
regular comparison, 621–22
slow, slowly, 618
superlative degree, 620–24
well, good, 617–18
Mood
creating mood, 203
definition of, 203
Mood (grammar)
imperative mood, 606
indicative mood, 606

subjunctive mood, 606
Moral, morale, 796
More, most, 621
Movie critique, 198–201
Movies. *See* Film.
Multimedia presentation
definition of, 930
formal speeches and, 901
Multiple-choice questions, 3–10, 14–15, 917, 923–24
Multiple-meaning words, 26, 889–90
Multipoint thesis, 387
Music, in documentaries, 333
Must, 600

Name-calling, persuasive techniques and, 301, 315
Narrative details
definition of, 18
people, things, places, dialogue, and events of
narratives, 24
National Audubon Society, 14
**Negative construction, agreement of subject and verb
and,** 514
Neither, either, 516
–ness, –ly, 782
Networks, definition of, 931
News
analyzing news genres, 162–64
controversy and, 87
definition of, 937
feature news, 937
hard news, 937
headlines and, 87, 937
identifying manipulative news stories, 163
juxtaposition and, 87
news values, 934–35
newsworthiness, 935
point of view and, 87, 88
soft news, 938
startling images and, 87
suspense and, 87
teasers and, 87–88
variety of purposes of, 163
News genres
feature news, 937
hard news, 937
soft news, 938
Newsmagazines, 162, 938
Nielsen ratings, 930
Nominative case, 549–51, 966. *See also* Predicate
nominative; Pronouns; Subjects of sentences.
Nonessential clauses and phrases, 496, 704–706, 977
Nonrestrictive clauses/phrases. *See* Nonessential
clauses and phrases.

Nonsexist language, 659–60, 890
Nonstandard English, 638
Nonverbal behavior
    appearance, 290
    eye contact, 290
    facial expressions, 290
    gesturing, 290
    posture, 290
Nonverbal communication. *See* Nonverbal behavior.
Note cards, for speech preparation, 899
Note taking
    during speeches, 161
    in group discussions, 120
    listening skills, 909
    note taking on research about careers, 249
    paraphrasing, 228
    quoting, 228
    researching and, 227–29
    as study skill, 912–13
    summarizing, 228
Noun(s)
    abstract nouns, 407
    collective nouns, 407, 522
    common nouns, 406, 669
    compound nouns, 406, 701
    concrete nouns, 407
    definition of, 405, 977
    of direct address, 447
    plural formation, 787–90
    in possessive case, 758–59
    proper nouns, 406, 669–70
    used as adjective, 415
Noun clauses
    combining sentences and, 360
    definition of, 501, 977
    diagramming and, 996–97
    introductory words, 501–502
Novella, definition of, 169
Nowheres, 640
Number (grammar). *See also* Plurals.
    agreement in number, 512–38
    definition of, 512, 977
    placement of subject and, 513–14
    plural in number, 512
    singular in number, 512
Numbers (numerals)
    cardinal numbers and ordinal numbers, 791
    forming plurals of, 789
    hyphenating compound numbers, 768
    spelling out, 791–92

***O, oh,* punctuation of,** 669

Object of preposition
    compound objects, 468
    definition of, 426, 555, 977
    pronouns, objective case, 555
Object of verb, 553. *See also* Direct objects; Indirect objects.
Objective case
    for direct object of verb, 553
    for indirect object of verb, 553
    for object of preposition, 555
    of personal pronouns, 548, 553–55
Occasion for writing
    definition of, 139, 945
    persuasive brochure, 309
Of, 649
Off, off of, 649
Old English, 862, 892–93. *See also* English language.
Omission, as media term, 935
Omniscient point of view, 203
On the Air (Henderson), 239
One-word modifiers, misplaced, 627–28
Online card catalog, 867–68
Online database, 868
Online dictionaries, 848. *See also* World Wide Web.
Opinions
    disguised opinions, 255
    fact-and-opinion questions in test taking, 262
    facts distinguished from, 228, 252, 255–57, 877
    judgment opinions, 258
    as main idea of persuasive writing, 257–58
    opinion statements, 252, 264, 266
    prediction opinions, 258
    "should" opinions, 258
    valid opinions, 264
    "why" opinions, 258
Oral interpretation
    considerations for, 203–204, 905
    definition of, 905
    evaluation of, 204
Oral performances and presentations
    compare/contrast persuasive elements of advertisements in oral presentation, 337
    interview health professional and present oral report, 165
    oral interpretation of short stories, 203–204
    oral presentation on advertising career, 337
    oral response to literature, 205
    two-minute oral response to interview question about personal failure, 53
    videotape news program on cause-and-effect relationship and give oral presentation, 125
Order of ideas. *See also* Organizing information.
    cause-and-effect order, 145
    chronological order, 36, 109, 145, 375, 945
    logical order, 145, 271, 375, 945
    multiple orders, 375
    order of importance, 109, 145, 375, 945

paragraph coherence and, 375
spatial order, 375, 945
Order of importance, 109, 146, 375, 945
Organizing information. *See also* Order of ideas.
diagram for block method, 72
diagram for point-by-point method, 73
ordered events list, 36
organizational plan, 230
organizational questions on tests, 921
Other, else, 623
Ought, 600
Ought to of, 644
Outlining
definition of, 231, 950
formal outlines, 951
informal outlines, 950
Outside, 649
Oversimplification, of cause and effect, 108

Page layout. *See also* Document design.
alignment of text, 849–50
bullets, 850
callouts, 850
columns/blocks of text, 851
contrast, 851
emphasis, 851
graphics, 851, 948–49
gray pages, 851
grid lines, 851
gutters, 851
headers and footers, 851
headings and subheadings, 851–52
indentation, 852
line length, 852
margins, 852
persuasive brochure, 313–14
pull-quotes, 852
rule lines, 852
titles and subtitles, 852–53
visuals, 853
white space, 853
Panel discussions. *See* Group discussions.
Paragraphs
clincher sentences of paragraphs, 371
coherence, 374–76
in compositions, 382
connecting ideas in, 375–76
descriptive paragraphs, 951
direct references and, 375
expository paragraphs, 951–52
implied main idea, 371, 881
main ideas, 371, 372
narrative paragraphs, 952

order of ideas, 375
paragraph main ideas, 60
parts of body of, 370–72
persuasive paragraphs, 952
supporting sentences, 371
topic sentences, 371
transitional expressions, 376
unity in, 374
Parallel structure, 362–63, 978
Paraphrasing
definition of, 213
direct quotations and, 213
for note taking, 228
steps in, 214, 882
as study skill, 913
Parentheses
examples of, 978
for material of minor importance, 770–71
for parenthetical elements, 772
punctuation within, 770–72
Parenthetical citations, 237
Parenthetical expressions
definition of, 713
list of, 713
punctuation of, 713, 770–72
Participants, in group discussions, 120
Participial phrases
combining sentences and, 355
definition of, 355, 473, 978
diagramming and, 992
placement of, 355, 474
punctuation of, 474, 707–708
reducing sentences to, 44
Participles
definition of, 44, 355, 472, 978
diagramming and, 992
helping verbs and, 574
past participles, 472–73
present participles, 472
as principal part of verbs, 574–79
as verbals, 472–73
Part-of-speech labels, 847
Parts of speech. *See also* Sentence parts.
adjectives, 412–15
adverbs, 422–24
conjunctions, 428
determined by use, 430–31
interjections, 429–30
labels in dictionaries, 847
nouns, 405–407
prepositions, 426–27
pronouns, 408–11
verbs, 417–21
Passed, past, 797
Passive voice
as awkward or weak, 602, 603
be and, 602

conjugation of verb *give*, 602–603
conjugation of verbs in, 602
definition of, 601, 978
helping verbs and, 602
past participles and, 602
uses of, 604
writing in, 277–78
Past participles
    passive voice and, 602
    as principal part of verb, 574–79
    as verbal, 472–73
Past perfect progressive tense, 592
Past perfect tense, 596, 984
Past progressive tense, 592
Past tense, 594, 984
Pay, **principal parts of,** 578
Peace, piece, 797
Peer review (evaluation)
    by e-mail, 151
    cause-and-effect essay, 114, 115
    comparison/contrast essay, 78, 79
    literary analysis, 188, 189
    personal reflection essay, 42, 43
    persuasive brochures, 321, 322
    position paper, 276, 277
    problem-analysis essay, 150, 151
    research paper, 240, 241
Pentad, definition of, 955–56
People
    describing people, 31
    interviewing people with shared experiences, 32
    as narrative detail, 24
    as sources in documentaries, 333–34
Periods
    after abbreviations, 696–99
    at end of sentences, 694
    quotation marks and, 744
Personal, personnel, 798
Personal pronouns
    case forms of, 547–58
    list of, 409
    possessive, 759–60
Personal reflection, definition of, 17
Personal reflection (reading)
    descriptive details, 18
    making inferences, 18
    narrative details, 18
    reading selection, 19–20
Personal reflection (writing)
    prewriting, 28–36
    publishing (and proofreading), 46–47
    revising, 42–43
    writing first draft, 38
Personal texts
    literary analysis, 178–94
    personal reflection essay, 28–47
Personification, definition of, 25, 37, 889

Persuasion. *See* headings beginning with Persuasive.
Persuasive brochures (reading)
    reading selection, 297–99
    visual elements for, 296
Persuasive brochure (writing)
    prewriting, 306–14
    publishing (and proofreading), 325–26
    revising, 321–24
    writing first draft, 316–18
Persuasive newspaper article (reading)
    distinguishing facts from opinions, 252, 255–57
    elements of persuasion, 252, 257–60
    reading selection, 253–54
Persuasive oral messages. *See* Persuasive speeches.
Persuasive speeches
    avoiding unjust attacks or exaggerations, 290
    evaluating persuasive speeches, 291
    nonverbal behavior, 290
    practice, 289–90
    purpose, 898
    support, 289
    thesis, 288–89
    topics, 288
    using visuals, 289
    verbal behavior, 290
Persuasive techniques
    analyzing persuasive techniques, 882
    analyzing persuasive visual elements, 303
    bandwagon, 300
    elements of, 252, 257–60
    emotional appeals, 252, 257, 259–60, 301
    evidence, 252, 258
    glittering generalities, 301
    identifying persuasive techniques, 300–302
    interview professional and write about persuasive strategies and skills, 293
    logical appeals, 257, 258
    name-calling, 301
    opinion statements, 252, 257
    plain folks, 300
    reasons, 252, 258
    test taking questions about, 305
    transfer, 300–301
Persuasive texts. *See* Advertising; Persuasive brochure (writing).
Photography, 938
Phrases
    adjective phrases, 468, 961
    adverb phrases, 469–70, 961
    appositive phrases, 355, 483–84
    definition of, 342, 467, 978
    diagramming and, 991–95
    gerund phrases, 478, 973, 993
    infinitive phrases, 115–16, 480, 974, 993–94
    intervening phrases, 46, 513
    as modifiers, 616–17

participial phrases, 44, 355, 473–74, 707–708, 978, 992

phrase fragments, 342–44

placement of, 628

prepositional phrases, 343, 355, 426–27, 443, 451, 457, 467–70, 468, 708, 979, 991–92

variety in beginning sentences and, 366–67

verb phrases, 417, 441, 985

verbal phrases, 118, 342–43, 472–81, 628, 984

Pie charts, 858, 878

Piece, peace, 797

Places

describing places, 31

as narrative detail, 24

Plagiarism, 872

Plain folks, 300

Planning, comparison/contrast essay, 73

Plot

analysis questions for, 180

definition of, 174

elements of, 157

in film, 199

Plurals

of compound nouns, 788

irregular plurals, 788

of letters, numerals, symbols, words referred to as words, 766, 789–90

of loanwords, 789

regular plurals, 787–88

Poetry

capitalization in, 668

figurative language, 49

sensory details, 49

sound elements, 49

writing free-verse poetry, 48–49

writing persuasive poetry, 293

Point of view

analysis questions for, 180

author's point of view, 876

definition of, 174, 876

in fiction, 203

first-person point of view, 196

in media, 198, 935

in news stories, 87, 88

omniscient point of view, 203

third-person point of view, 196

Point-by-point method of comparison/contrast structure

definition of, 56, 62–63

organization diagram, 73

Political advertising, 938

Position, definition of, 251

Position paper (writing)

prewriting, 263–71

publishing (and proofreading), 280–81

revising, 276–79

writing first draft, 272

Positive degree of comparison, 620–22

Possessive case

of acronyms, 760

apostrophes and, 758–61

of compound words, 760

compounds and, 760–61

contractions distinguished from, 760, 764

individual possession and, 761

joint possession and, 760

of nouns, 758–59

of organizations, businesses, 760

of personal pronouns, 548, 556–58

Posture

formal speeches and, 900

persuasive speaking and, 290

Predicate(s). *See also* Verb(s).

complete predicates, 411, 439

definition of, 439, 979

simple predicates, 441

Predicate adjectives, 454, 979, 989

definition of, 454

diagramming and, 989

Predicate nominative, 453–54

definition of, 551, 979

diagramming and, 989

pronoun as, 551

subject and verb agreement and, 524

Predicting

definition of, 22, 882

example of, 882

prediction opinions, 258

while viewing, 87

Prefixes

definition of, 781, 979

hyphens and, 768–69

list of, 892

spelling rule for, 781

as word parts, 892

Preposition(s)

adverbs distinguished from, 427

compound prepositions, 427, 514

definition of, 426, 979

list of, 426–27

objects of, 426, 467

Prepositional phrases

as adjective phrases, 468

as adverb phrases, 469–70

combining sentences and, 355

definition of, 343, 355, 426, 443, 467, 979

diagramming and, 991–92

indirect objects distinguished from, 457

infinitives distinguished from, 467

never contains complement, 451, 457

never contains subject, 443

objects of prepositions, 468

punctuation of, 708

as sentence fragment, 343

Preproduction, documentary, 329–35
Prereading, reading process and, xxxiv–xxxv
Prereading strategies, xxxiv–xxxv
Present participles
    as principal part of verb, 574–79
    progressive form and, 592
    as verbals, 472
Present perfect progressive tense, 592
Present perfect tense, 595, 985
Present progressive tense, 592
Present tense, 594, 984
Prewriting
    5W-How? questions, 141–42, 952–53
    chaining, 953
    comparison/contrast essay, 66–73
    literary analysis, 178–83
    looping, 955
    personal reflection, 28–36
    persuasive brochures, 306–14
    position paper, 263–71
    problem-analysis essay, 138–45
    research paper, 218–31
    techniques for, 952–57
    track switching, 956
    what if? questions, 953
    writing process and, xxxiv–xxxv
Primary purpose, of media forms, 85
Primary sources, 208, 214–15, 222–23
Principal, principle, 798
Print ads. *See also* Advertising; Persuasive brochure.
    creating a print ad, 337
Print media
    definition of, 938
    terminology of, 936–38
Problem-analysis article (reading)
    making generalizations, 128
    problem-solution structure, 128
    reading selection, 129–31
Problem-analysis article (writing)
    prewriting, 138–45
    publishing (and proofreading), 155–56
    revising, 150–53
    topic, 138–39
Problem-solution structure
    analyzing problem-solution pattern, 883, 886
    clue words for, 877
    focus on problems, 135
    focus on solutions, 135
    framework of, 128
    as persuasive, 135
Problems
    analyzing problems, 141–43
    focus on, 135
    watch/listen to government procedure and make
        written profile of problem-solving techniques, 165
Process explanation. *See* Cause-and-effect article

(writing).
Producers, definition of, 931
Progressive form of verbs, 592
Pronunciation, dictionaries and, 847
Pronoun-antecedent agreement. *See* Agreement
    (pronoun-antecedent).
Pronouns
    adjectives distinguished from, 414
    agreement with antecedent, 532–38
    as appositives, 561
    case forms of, 547–58
    definition of, 408, 979
    demonstrative pronouns, 410
    gender and, 532–33
    in incomplete constructions, 565
    indefinite pronouns, 411
    intensive pronouns, 410, 564
    interrogative pronouns, 410
    in nominative case, 548, 549–51
    number and, 532–33
    as object of preposition, 553, 555
    in objective case, 548, 553–55
    personal pronouns, 409
    in possessive case, 759–60
    in possessive case before gerunds, 557
    possessive case or contractions, 760, 764
    as predicate nominative, 551
    reference, 566–68
    reflexive pronouns, 409, 564
    relative pronouns, 410, 496–97, 526, 538
    special usage problems, 558–65
    third-person singular pronouns, 548
    unnecessary pronouns as double subject, 645
    using correctly, 547–68
    who, whom, 558–59
Pronunciation
    dictionaries and, 847
    as spelling aid, 779
Proofreading
    comparison/contrast essay, 82
    personal reflection essay, 46
    persuasive brochure, 325
    position paper, 280
    problem-analysis essay, 155
    research paper, 244
    short story, 193
    symbols for, 958
Proofs. *See* Support and Evidence.
Propaganda, definition of, 935
Proper adjectives
    capitalization of, 669–70
    definition of, 669
Proper nouns
    capitalization of, 669–70

definition of, 406, 669

Proposal. *See* headings beginning with Persuasive.

Proto-Indo-European language, 861

Public access, definition of, 931

Publishing
    cause-and-effect essay, 118–19
    comparison/contrast essay, 82–83
    literary analysis, 193–94
    personal reflection essay, 46–47
    persuasive brochure, 325–26
    position paper, 280–81
    problem-analysis essay, 155–56
    research paper, 244–45

Pull-quotes, 852

Punctuation
    apostrophes, 758–66
    brackets, 772
    colons, 729–30
    commas, 700–16
    dashes, 770
    ellipsis points, 750–51
    end marks, 694–95
    exclamation points, 694–95
    hyphens, 767–69
    italics (underlining), 739–41
    parentheses, 770–72
    periods, 694, 698–99, 744
    question marks, 694, 744–45
    quotation marks, 743–48
    semicolons, 724–26

Purpose
    author's purpose, 876
    cause-and-effect explanation, 105
    comparison/contrast essay, 67–68
    literary analysis, 179
    of media messages, 935
    personal reflection essay, 29–30
    persuasive brochure, 307
    position paper, 264–65
    problem-analysis essay, 139
    research paper, 220

***Put,* principal parts of,** 578

Question marks
    punctuating direct questions, 694
    quotation marks and, 744–45

Questions. *See also* Interrogative sentences; Test taking.
    5W-How? questions, 141–42, 952–53
    developing research questions, 221
    emphatic form of verbs in, 592
    indirect questions, 694

parts of speech in, 446
    question-and-answer sessions, 160–61
    subject-verb agreement and, 524
    using *there* or *here,* 446

Quiet, quite, 798

Quotation marks
    with colons, 744
    with commas, 744
    dialogue and, 746
    direct quotation and, 193, 743–45, 980
    enclosing titles of short stories, 193
    with exclamation points, 744–45
    interrupting expressions and, 743–44
    with other marks of punctuation, 193, 744–45, 980
    with periods, 744
    with question marks, 744–45
    with semicolons, 744
    single quotation marks to enclose quotation within quotation, 193, 747
    for slang words, technical terms, 748
    for titles of short stories, poems, essays, songs, television series, etc., 747, 980

Quotations. *See also* Direct quotations.
    block quotations, 192
    capitalization of, 668
    colons and, 729
    direct quotations, 743–45
    indirect quotations, 743
    long quotations set off from text, 746
    note taking and, 228
    pull-quotes, 852
    punctuation of, 193, 743–45, 980
    weaving quotations into essays, 192
    within quotations, 193, 747

Radio, watch/listen to government procedure and make written profile of problem-solving techniques, 165

***Raise,* principal parts of,** 588

Raise, rise, 588, 981

Ratings, definition of, 931

***Read,* principal parts of,** 578

Readers' Guide to Periodical Literature, 219, 222, 868–69

Reading aloud, to find run-on sentences, 242, 347

Reading logs, 883

Reading process, xxxiv–xxxv. *See also* Reading skills and focuses.
    adjusting reading rate, 883
    determining writer's intent, 876
    making connections, xxxiv–xxxv
    prereading, xxxiv–xxxv

reading with focus, 956
reading-writing connection, xxxiv–xxxv
Reading rate, adjusting reading rate, 883
Reading skills and focuses. *See also* Reading process.
    author's purpose and point of view, 876
    brochures, 296–303
    cause-and-effect article, 91–100
    cause-and-effect structure, 92, 97–100
    comparison/contrast article, 56–63
    comparison/contrast structure, 56, 62–63
    descriptive details, 18
    distinguishing facts from opinions, 255–57
    drawing conclusions, 168, 172–73
    elements of persuasion, 252, 257–60
    inferring causes and effects, 92, 95–96
    literary analysis, 168–75
    literary elements, 168, 173–75
    main idea and supporting details, 56, 60–62
    making generalizations, 128
    making inferences, 18
    narrative details, 18
    paraphrasing, 208, 213–14
    personal reflection essay, 18–25
    persuasive newspaper article, 252–60
    problem-analysis article, 128–35
    problem-solution structure, 128
    research article, 208–15
    visual elements, 296
Reading-writing connection, xxxiv–xxxv
Real, really, 618
Reality TV, definition of, 931
Reasoning
    either-or reasoning, 270
    evaluating reasoning, 270
Reasoning or logic questions, 925
Reasons. *See also* Evidence; Support.
    anecdotes, 259
    definition of, 266
    as element of persuasion, 252, 258
    examples, 259
    expert opinions, 258
    as facts, 258
    logical appeals and, 266
    statistics, 258
    steps in finding reasons, 267
Rebuttal speeches, 897
Receive, principal parts of, 575
Recorder, in group discussions, 120
Reference
    ambiguous pronoun reference, 566
    clear pronoun reference, 566–68
    general pronoun reference, 567
    indefinite pronoun reference, 567–68
    weak pronoun reference, 567
Reference books, 222, 869

Reference materials. *See also* Information;
    Library/media center; Sources.
    almanacs, 870
    atlases, 870
    biographical references, 847, 870
    database, 868
    geographical references, 847
    literature reference books, 222
    microfilm/microfiche, 222, 867
    Readers' Guide to Periodical Literature, 219, 222,
        868–69
    vertical file, 871
Refining style. *See* Revising.
Reflective listening, 909
Reflexive pronouns, definition of, 409, 564
Regional dialects, 864
Regular comparison of modifiers, 621–22
Regular verbs, 575–76, 980
Relative adverbs, adjective clauses and, 497
Relative pronouns
    adjective clauses and, 189, 496–97
    list of, 410, 496
    number and, 526, 538
    understood relative pronouns, 497
Relevant features
    chart for relevant features, 70
    definition of, 69
    making relevant features chart for careers, 89
    steps in discovering relevant features, 69
Reporters, definition of, 938
Reports, collaborate on compiling research questions
    and early plan for report writing, 249
Representation, of characters on television, 122–23
Request letters. *See* Invitations.
Research. *See also* Sources; World Wide Web.
    collaborate on compiling research questions and
        early plan for report writing, 249
    developing research questions, 221
    formal research, 215
    informal research, 215
    in media, 246
    note taking and, 227–29
    note taking on research about particular careers, 249
    for problem-analysis essay, 140–41
    research paper, 218–45
    writing letter after researching influences on
        writing of particular author, 249
    writing paragraphs about art forms after
        researching them on World Wide Web, 249
Research article (reading)
    paraphrasing, 208, 213–14
    primary sources, 208, 214–15
    reading selection, 209–12
    secondary sources, 208, 214–15
Research paper (writing)

prewriting, 218–31
publishing (and proofreading), 244–45
revising, 240–43
writing, 232
Restrictive appositives, 711–12
Restrictive clauses, phrases. *See* Essential clauses, phrases.
Résumé, definition of, 957
Revising
cause-and-effect essay, 114–15
comparison/contrast essay, 78–79
literary analysis, 188–89
personal reflection essay, 42–43
persuasive brochures, 321–24
position paper, 276–79
problem-analysis essay, 150–53
research paper, 240–43
symbols for, 958
writing process and, 9, 12
Ride, **principal parts of,** 578
Ring, **principal parts of,** 578
Rise, **principal parts of,** 588
Rise, raise, 588, 981
Roots, 176, 891–92
R.S.V.P., **please reply,** 949
Rule lines, 852
Run, **principal parts of,** 574, 578
Run-on sentences
comma splices and, 347, 348
definition of, 347, 981
fused sentences and, 347
revision of, 347–49

Salutation, of business letters, 940
Say, **principal parts of,** 578
Scarcely, 656
Science activities, written explanation of
comparison/contrast of two chemical compounds, 89
Scripts
definition of, 931
script outline, 331–35
Search engine, 872, 873, 874–75
Secondary purpose, of media forms, 85
Secondary sources, 208, 214–15
Second-person pronouns, 409, 548
–sede, –cede, **and** *–ceed,* **780**
See, **principal parts of,** 579
Seek, **principal parts of,** 579
Self– (prefix), 768
Sell, **principal parts of,** 579
Semicolons
compound sentences and, 348, 358, 981
conjunctive adverbs and, 348, 724–25, 981
independent clauses and, 492, 701, 724–26

for items in series containing commas, 726, 981
quotation marks and, 744
Send, **principal parts of,** 577, 579
Sensationalism, definition of, 935
Sensory details
definition of, 24
describing people and places, 31
in poetry, 49
Sentence. *See also* Sentence fragments; Sentence parts.
Sentence(s)
beginning with *there* or *here,* 446
capitalization of first word, 668
classified by purpose, 459–60
classified by structure, 504–505
clincher sentences, 371
combining sentences, 43–44, 352–60
complements and, 450–58
complex sentences, 189–90, 359–60, 448, 505, 969, 999
compound sentences, 348–49, 358, 448, 504–505, 703, 970, 998–99
compound-complex sentences, 505, 970, 999
declarative sentences, 459, 694, 971
definition of, 437, 981
diagramming sentences, 986–99
exclamatory sentences, 459–60, 694–95, 972
fused sentences, 347, 972
imperative sentences, 459, 695, 974
interrogative sentences, 459, 694, 975
punctuation of, 694–95
simple sentences, 504, 703, 982, 997
stringy sentences, 363–64, 982
supporting sentences, 371
varying sentence beginnings, 115–16, 366–67
varying sentence length, 241–42
wordy sentences, 365, 985
Sentence fragments
appositive phrases, 343
definition of, 340, 437, 981–82
identification of, 340–41
phrase fragments, 342–44
prepositional phrases, 343
series of items as, 346
subordinate clause fragment, 344–45
test for identifying, 155
used as writing style, 341
used for effect, 341
verbal phrases and, 342–43
Sentence parts.
complements, 450–58
predicates, 439–48
subjects, 439–48
Sentence structure, as expressing tone in writing, 106
Sentence style. *See also* Style.
improving sentence style, 362–69
Sequence chain, definition of, 948
Sequence of events, verb tense and, 597–98

Sequencing, definition of, 931
Series of items. *See* Items in series.
Set, principal parts of, 577, 585
Set, sit, 585, 982
Setting
    analysis questions for, 180
    definition of, 174
    in film, 198
    in short stories, 196
Shall, will, 600
She, it, they, he, 645
Shone, shown, 799
Short story
    characters, 195
    conflict and climax, 195
    example of structure of, 196–97
    meaning in, 203
    mood in, 203
    point of view, 196, 203
    setting, 196
    summarizing short stories based on problems, 165
    writing short stories, 195–97
Shot, camera, 331
Should, 600
Should of, 644
"Should" opinions, 258
Shown, shone, 799
Sibley Guide to Bird Life and Behavior, The, 14
Signature, business letter and, 940
Similarities, comparison/contrast and, 67
Similes, definition of, 25, 37, 889
Simple predicates, 441. *See also* Verb(s).
Simple sentences
    compound sentences distinguished from, 703
    definition of, 504, 982
    diagramming and, 997
Simple subjects, definition of, 440
Sing, principal parts of, 577, 579
Single quotation marks, 747
Single-word modifiers, varying sentence beginnings, 366–67
Sink, principal parts of, 579
Sit, principal parts of, 585
Sit, set, 585, 982
Site map, 243
Situation comedy, definition of, 931–32
Slang, 748, 865, 890
Sleep, principal parts of, 579
Slogans, 310
Slow, slowly, 618, 982
Social studies activities, audio reflection of current event, 53
Soft news, 938
Solutions, focus on, 135
Some, somewhat, 651
Somewheres, 640
Sophocles, 157

Sort of a(n), kind of a(n), 648
Sort of, kind of, 648
Sorts, types, kinds, 648
Sound effects, 331
Sound elements
    in film, 200
    in poetry, 49
Sources. *See also* Library/media center; World Wide Web.
    4R test for, 226
    card catalogs, 222, 866–67, 867–68
    crediting sources, 143, 237–38
    evaluating sources, 226
    general reference books, 222
    government sources, 223
    guidelines for giving credit within papers, 237
    guidelines for recording source information, 224–25
    in journalism, 938
    microfilm/microfiche, 222
    museums, 223
    newspapers, 223
    nonprint sources, 222, 867–68, 871–75
    online catalogs, 222
    people as source in documentaries, 333–34
    primary sources, 208, 214–15, 222–23
    print sources, 222, 869–871
    Readers' Guide to Periodical Literature, 219, 222; 868–69
    recent sources, 226
    relevant sources, 226
    reliable sources, 226
    representative sources, 226
    schools, 223
    secondary sources, 208, 214–15, 222–23
    source cards, 223
    videotapes and audiotapes, 222
    Works Cited list, 215, 238
Spatial order, definition of, 375, 945
Speak, principal parts of, 579
Speaking
    analyze the debate process, 165
    compare and contrast viewpoints, 89
    debate, 896–97
    extemporaneous speeches, 899
    formal speaking, 623, 748, 897–901
    in group discussions, 121, 901–902
    informative speeches, 158–61, 898
    interview author about writing strategies, 205
    manuscript speeches, 899
    memorized speeches, 899
    nonverbal behavior, 290, 900
    note cards for, 899
    oral interpretation, 203–204
    oral response to literature, 205
    persuasive speeches, 288–90, 898
    special occasion speeches, 898

tape-record story retelling an event, 89
verbal behavior, 290, 900–901
Special occasion speeches, 898
Specialized dictionaries, 848
Specialized terms
jargon and, 216
using context for understanding of, 217
Spelling
–cede, –ceed, –sede, 780
commonly misspelled words, 807
ie and *ei,* 780
–ly, –ness, 782
of numbers, 791–92
plurals of nouns, 787–90
prefixes, 781
pronunciation as aid to, 779
proofreading for errors, 779
rules for, 780–92
spelling notebook, 780
suffixes, 782–84
techniques for, 779–80
words often confused, 793–800
Spend, **principal parts of,** 579
Sponsorship, definition of, 932
SQ3R study method, 884, 913
Stand, **principal parts of,** 579
Standard English, 638, 865
Standardized tests, 918–27
Standish, David, 209–12
Startling images, 87
State-of-being verbs, 419
Stationary, stationery, 799
Statistics, 143, 258
Steal, **principal parts of,** 579
Stereotypes, definition of, 935
Stills, 331
Story. *See* Short story.
Storyboards
definition of, 50, 932
for documentaries, 335
example of, 51
as graphics, 859
Stringy sentences, 363–64, 982
Student's model
cause-and-effect essay, 113
comparison/contrast essay, 77
literary analysis, 187
personal reflection essay, 41
persuasive brochure, 319–20
position paper, 275
problem-analysis essay, 149
research paper, 236
Study skills, 911–14. *See also* Reading skills and focuses.
classification and, 911–12
graphic organizers, 912
interpreting graphics, 912
memorizing, 912

note taking, 912–13
organizing and remembering information, 911–14
outlining, 913
study plans, 911
Style. *See also* Sentence style.
combining sentences, 43–44, 352–60
eliminating clichés, 322–23
eliminating word-wasters, 152–53
overuse of adverbs, 79–80
revising stringy sentences, 363–64
revising wordy sentences, 365
sentence variety, 44
style questions on tests, 921
using active and passive voice, 277–78
using complex sentences, 189–90
using consistent verb tense, 325
using parallel structure, 362–63
varying sentence beginnings, 366–67
varying sentence beginning with infinitives, 115–16
varying sentence length, 241–42
varying sentence structure, 368–69
Subheadings, in page layout, 851–52
Subject complements
definition of, 453, 983
diagramming and, 989
linking verbs and, 453
placement of, 453–54
predicate adjectives, 454
predicate nominative, 454
Subjects of sentences, 439–48
complete subjects, 440
compound subjects, 447–48, 520
definition of, 439, 983
double subjects, 645
finding of, 442–43
nominative case and, 549–51
simple subjects, 440
understood subjects, 438, 447, 986
Subjects of verbs
definition of, 549
in nominative case, 549
pronoun form and, 550
Subject-verb agreement. *See* Agreement (subject-verb).
Subjunctive mood, 606, 983
Subordinate clauses
adjective clauses, 495–97
adverb clauses, 498–99
complements and, 451, 493
definition of, 493, 983
diagramming and, 995–96
noun clauses, 501–502
object of verbs and, 456
placement of, 345
as sentence fragment, 344–45
uses of, 494–502
variety of sentence beginnings and, 366–67
who, whom and, 558–59

Subordinate ideas, in essay writing, 144
Subordinating conjunctions, 359–60, 369, 498–99
Suffixes
definition of, 782, 983
hyphens and, 767
list of, 102, 893–94
meaning of, 102
spelling rules for, 782–84
using suffixes, 102
as word parts, 893–94
Summarizing
definition of, 213
direct quotations and, 213
example of, 884–85
how to summarize, 884
for note taking, 228
short stories based on problems, 165
as study skill, 914
Superlative degree of comparison, 82, 620–24
Support. *See also* Details; Facts.
arranging details, 72–73
cause-and-effect essay, 109
literary analysis, 183
persuasive newspaper article, 252, 257–60
persuasive brochure, 311
problem-analysis essay, 142–43
supporting details, 56, 60–62
Suppose to, supposed to, 651
Suspense, 87
Swim, **principal parts of,** 579
Syllable
as aid to spelling, 779
definition of, 779
word division at end of line and, 767
Symbolism, in editorial cartoons, 284
Synonyms
analogies and, 920
context clues for, 304, 887
dictionaries and, 847
meaning of a word and, 890
reference books and, 870
Syntax. *See* Clauses; Complements; Phrases;
Predicate(s); Sentence(s); Subjects of sentences.

T

Tables, 859–60, 880
Tabloids, 938
Take, **principal parts of,** 579
Take, bring, 642
Taking messages, 950
Taking notes. *See* Note taking.
Talk
conjugation of, 590–91
principal parts of, 590

Target audience
for advertisements, 327–28
definition of, 938
for documentary on print advertising, 329
for news programs, 163
Target market, persuasive brochure, 307
Teach, **principal parts of,** 574, 579
Teach, learn, 648
Tear, **principal parts of,** 579
Teaser, 87–88
Teaser slogans, 310
Technical directions, reading, 866
Technical elements, of film, 200
Technical language
in informative speeches, 159
media terminology, 51–52, 331, 928–38
Technical terms, 748
jargon and, 216
using context for understanding of, 217
Technology (and writing). *See* Computers.
Technology, analyzing reviews of movies or software programs, 205
Telephone communications, taking messages, 950
Television
analyzing effects of, 122–24
cable television, 929
purposes of nonfiction television, 163
watch/listen to government procedure and make written profile of problem-solving techniques, 165
Tell, **principal parts of,** 579
Tense
conjugation of verb *give,* 592–93
conjugation of verb *talk,* 590–91
consistency of, 597–98
definition of, 590, 984
progressive form and emphatic form, 592
sequence of events and, 597–98
uses of, 594–96
using consistent verb tense, 325
verb conjugation and, 590–93
Test taking
analogy questions, 918–20
classroom tests, 915–18
comparing reading passages, 4–10
critical reading questions, 3–10, 921–23
describing literary elements, 177
essay tests, 11–13, 915–16
fact-and-opinion questions, 262
identifying main idea, 65
inference questions on tests, 27, 921
inferring causes and effects, 103
logic questions, 137, 925
matching questions, 917
multiple-choice questions, 3–10, 14–15, 917, 923–24
on-demand writing questions, 11–15, 924–25
reasoning questions, 925

recognizing persuasive devices, 305
short-answer questions, 917–18
standardized tests, 3–15, 918–27
true/false questions, 918
verbal expression questions, 925–27
Text, as media term, 938
Text structures, analyzing text structures, 885–86
Than, then, 651, 799
Thank-you letter, 949
That there, this here, 652
That, who, which, 653
The, 413
Their, there, they're, 799
Theirself, theirselves, hisself, 645
Them, 652
Theme
analysis questions for, 180
definition of literary theme, 174
in film, 199
Themes, universal themes, 203
There, here, 446, 524, 988
Thesis, synthesizing information into a thesis, 71
Thesis statement. *See also* Main ideas; Topic sentences.
adjustment, 70
for causal analysis, 106–107
definition of, 143, 181, 386
hints for writing a, 386–87
literary analysis, 181–82
placement of, 60
preliminary thesis, 387
problem-analysis essay, 143
research paper, 229–30
steps in developing, 181
writing thesis statements, 70, 386–87
They, she, it, he, 645
Things, as narrative detail, 24
Think, principal parts of, 579
Third-person limited point of view, 196
Third-person point of view, 196
Third-person pronoun, 409, 548
This here, that there, 652
Thoughts and feelings, as narrative detail, 24, 32
Throw, conjugation of, 579
Time, abbreviation of elements of, 698–99
Time lines, 860, 880, 948
Time order. *See* Chronological order.
Tired words, 890
Titles
agreement of subject and verb in, 529
italics (underlining) and, 740
page layout and, 852–53
quotation marks and, 747
To, too, two, 800
Tone
cause-and-effect explanation, 106
choice of details and, 958
comparison/contrast and, 68

definition of, 30, 106, 179, 958
literary analysis, 179
personal reflection essay, 30
as personality of writing, 68
persuasive brochure, 308
position paper, 266
problem-analysis essay, 139
research paper, 221
sentence length and structure, 959
setting the tone in compositions, 385
word choices and, 959
Topic sentences. *See also* Main idea; Thesis statement.
main idea and, 371, 372
in a paragraph, 371, 372
Topics
cause-and-effect explanation, 104–105
comparison/contrast essay, 66–67
evaluating topics, 220
formal speeches, 897
literary analysis, 178
personal reflection essay, 28–29
persuasive brochure, 306–307
position paper, 263–64
problem-analysis essay, 138–39
research paper, 218–20
Track switching, 956
Traditional debate, 897
Transfer, persuasive techniques and, 300–301
Transitional expressions
definition of, 392, 886, 959
list of, 392, 493, 724
paragraph coherence and, 376
punctuation of, 724–25
signaling passage of time, 36
Transitive verbs
definition of, 455, 984
object of, 421
object of verbs, 455–57
True/false questions, 918
Try and, try to, 652
"Two Peoples Divided by Common Road Signs"
(Berdichevsky), 57–59
Two, to, too, 800
Type
capital letters, 853
captions and, 853
contrast and, 854
fonts, 854–55
knockout type, 855
leading or line spacing, 855
lowercase type, 855
Type sizes and fonts
limit use of, 324
persuasive techniques and, 303
Types, kinds, sorts, 648

Unabridged dictionaries, 848
Underlining (italics). *See* Italics (underlining).
Understood subject, definition of, 447
Unity
    in compositions, 391
    in paragraphs, 374
Unless, without, 653
URL (*Uniform Resource Locator***),** 872
Usage, 638–60. *See also* Agreement; English language;
    Modifiers; Pronouns; Verb(s).
Usage labels, in dictionaries, 847
Use to, used to, 652

Valid generalizations, 133–34
Valid opinions, 264
Venn diagram, 878, 912, 949
Verb(s)
    action verbs, 418–19
    active voice and, 601–602, 960
    agreement with subject, 512–29
    causative verbs, 96
    compound verbs, 448
    conjugation, 590–93
    definition of, 417, 984
    emphatic form, 592
    helping verbs, 417, 448, 602
    intransitive verbs, 421, 975
    irregular verbs, 576–79, 975
    lie, lay, 582
    linking verbs, 418–19
    main verbs, 417
    objects of, 421
    passive voice and, 601–604
    principal parts of, 574–79
    progressive form, 592
    regular verbs, 575–76, 980
    rise, raise, 588
    simple predicates, 441
    sit, set, 585
    tenses, 325, 590–98
    transitive verbs, 421
    troublesome verbs, 582–88
    verb phrases, 417
Verb mood. *See* Mood.
Verb phrases, 417, 441, 985
Verbal(s)
    definition of, 342, 472, 984
    gerunds, 476–77
    infinitives, 479

    participles, 472–73
Verbal behavior
    enthusiasm, 290
    enunciation, 290
    rate, 290
    vocalization, 290
    vocalized pauses, 290
Verbal-expression questions on tests, 925–27
Verbal irony. *See* Irony.
Verbal phrases
    commas and, 628
    dangling modifiers and, 118
    definition of, 342, 417, 472, 984
    gerund phrases, 478
    infinitive phrases, 480–81
    participial phrases, 473–74
    placement of, 343
    as sentence fragments, 342–43
Verb-subject agreement. *See* Agreement (subject-verb).
Vertical files, 871
Video reflection
    definition of, 50
    in-camera editing, 52
    planning, 50
    storyboard for, 50–51
    terminology for videotaping, 51–52
    videotaping, 52
Videotaping
    terminology for, 51–52
    video reflections, 50–52
    videotape news program and analyze cause-and-
        effect story for oral presentation, 125
Video techniques, 52
Viewing. *See* Listening.
Viewing and representing
    analyzing editorial cartoons, 284–87
    analyzing effects of television, 122–24
    comparison/contrast of media coverage (analysis),
        86–88
    creating documentary on print advertising, 329–36
    critiquing films, 198–202
    evaluating Web sites, 247–48
    genres, 162–64
    interpretation, 84, 122, 934
    making video reflections, 50–52
    media terminology, 928–38
    predicting while viewing, 87
    production, 85, 329–36
    videotape news program and analyze cause-and-
        effect story for oral presentation, 125
    writing and illustrating children's books, 205
Visual literacy, definition of, 935
Visualizing, definition of, 956
Visuals. *See also* Document design; Graphics;
    Illustrations; Photography.
    definition of, 853
    in documentaries, 332

persuasive brochure, 313–14
persuasive visual elements, 303
visual message for future archaeologists, 53
Vocabulary, 887–95. *See also* Word parts.
 antonyms, 304, 847, 887, 920
 connotation, 261, 269, 888
 context clues, 64, 136, 304, 887
 definitions and restatements of context clues, 136, 887
 denotation, 261, 888
 homographs, 26
 homonyms, 793–800
 jargon, 216, 889
 loanwords, 741, 789, 862
 media terminology, 928–38
 multiple-meaning words, 26, 889–90
 prefixes and, 781, 892, 979
 specialized and technical terms, 216
 suffixes and, 102, 782–84, 893, 983
 synonyms, 304, 847, 870, 887
 technical language, 159
 understanding connotations and denotations, 261
 vocabulary-in-context questions on tests, 921
 word roots, 176, 891–92
Vocalization, persuasive speaking and, 290
Vocalized pauses, persuasive speaking and, 290
Voice
 of graphics, 857
 in position paper, 266
 writing voice, 30, 959
Voice (grammar)
 active voice, 277–78, 601–602
 passive voice, 277–78, 601–603
 of verbs, 601–603, 985
Voice-over
 definition of, 52
 as narrator of film, 198, 331

Waist, waste, 800
***Walk,* principal parts of,** 574
Way, ways, 652
Weak reference pronouns and, 567, 985
***Wear,* principal parts of,** 579
Weather, whether, 800
Web sites
 creating Web sites from position paper, 293
 definition, 872
 evaluating Web sites, 247–48, 875
 transforming information into Web site, 243
Well, good, 617–18, 973
What, 652
***What if?* questions,** 953
When, where, 652

Where, 652
Where . . .at, 640
Which, 497
Which, that, who, 653
White space, in page layout, 853
Who, whom, 497, 558–59, 986
Who's, whose, 759, 800
"Why" opinions, 258
Will, shall, 600
***Win,* principal parts of,** 579
Without, unless, 653
"Woman Work," (Angelou), 668
Word bank, 887
Word division, rules of, 767
Word formations, 887–88
Word meanings, 888–90
Word origins, 890
Word parts. *See also* Vocabulary.
 base words, 891–92
 prefixes, 892
 roots, 891–92
 suffixes, 893
Word-processing tools, in writing process, 985–86. *See also* Computers.
Words
 changing form of, 353
 commonly misspelled words, 807
 compound words, 760, 768–69
 dividing at end of line, 767
 as expressing tone in writing, 106
 foreign words, 741
 hyphenated words, 768–69
 information about, 846–48
 multiple-meaning words, 26
 in scripts, 332
 spelling list, 807–809
 technical words, 748
 word roots, 176, 891–92
 words often confused, 793–800
 words to learn, 894–95
Wordy sentences, 365
***Work,* principal parts of,** 575
Working outline, 231
Workplace skills. *See* Career development activities; Interviewing; Jobs; Listening.
Works Cited List, 215, 238
World Wide Web
 common networks on, 872
 designing Web page, 45
 key terms of, 871–72
 plagiarism and, 872
 as research source, 219, 247, 867, 871–75
 searching on, 873–75
 Web site evaluation, 247–48, 875
 writing paragraphs about art forms after researching them on World Wide Web, 249

Would, 600
Would of, 644
Write, **principal parts of,** 579
Writer's intent, determining writer's intent, 876
Writer's model
    cause-and-effect essay, 111–12
    comparison/contrast essay, 75–76
    composition model, 398–99
    literary analysis, 185–86
    personal reflection essay, 39–40
    persuasive brochure, 316–18
    position paper, 273–74
    problem-analysis essay, 147–48
    research paper, 233–35
Writer's notebook, 957
Writing Application
    capitalization in a guidebook, 691
    comparative and superlative degrees of comparison in a consumer guide, 635
    punctuation of poetry, 777
    semicolons and colons in a business letter, 737
    using adjectives in poetry, 435
    using agreement (pronoun-antecedent) in letters, 545
    using commas in instructions, 721
    using correct spelling in an application, 805–806
    using formal, standard English in a flier, 665
    using pronouns correctly in correspondence, 571
    using subordinate clauses in a paragraph, 509
    using varied sentences in a letter, 465
    using verbal and appositive phrases in newspaper article, 489
    using verb tense in an essay, 611
    writing interior dialogue, 755
Writing a first draft
    cause-and-effect essay, 110
    comparison/contrast essay, 74
    literary analysis, 184
    position paper, 272
    problem-analysis essay, 146
    research paper, 232
Writing process. *See also* **Audience; Compositions; Evaluating; Prewriting; Proofreading; Publishing; Revising; Writing a first draft**
    form writing checklist from interviewing author about writing strategies, 205
    prewriting. *See* Writing workshop.
    publishing, 46, 82, 118, 155, 193, 244, 280, 325
    reading-writing connection, xxxiv–xxxv

    as recursive, xxxiv
    reflecting on, 47, 83, 119, 156, 194, 245, 281, 326
    revising drafts, 42, 78, 114, 150, 188, 240, 276, 321
    weaving quotations into essays, 192
    writing first draft, 38, 74, 110, 146, 184, 232, 272, 316
Writing to clarify and remember information, 959
Writing to learn. *See also* **Research paper,** 219, 221, 249
    about character's motivations, 125
    definition of, 959
    watch/listen to government procedure and make written profile of problem-solving techniques, 165
    writing paragraphs about using analysis skills in career, 205
Writing to reflect
    on cause-and-effect essays, 119
    on comparison/contrast essay, 83
    on literary analysis, 194
    personal reflection essay, 28–47
    on persuasive brochure, 326
    position paper, 281
    problem-analysis essay, 156
    research paper, 245
Writing workshop
    cause-and-effect explanation, 104–19
    comparison/contrast essay, 66–83
    literary analysis, 178–94
    personal reflection essay, 28–47
    persuasive brochure, 306–26
    position paper, 263–81
    problem-analysis essay, 138–56
    research paper, 218–45

You, **as understood subject,** 447
Your, you're, 800

Zoom, 331

SOURCES CITED:

From "Teenage Lincoln Sculptor" by Ethel Yari from *American History,* vol. 32, no. 3, August 1997. Published by Cowles History Group, a division of Cowles Enthusiast Media, Leesburg, VA, 1997.

From *A Man Called Horse* by Dorothy Johnson. Published by Crowell-Collier Publishing Company, New York, 1949.

From "Early 20th-Century Styles, Part II" from *Arts and Ideas,* Ninth Edition by William Fleming. Published by Harcourt Brace College Publishers, Fort Worth, 1995.

From "What Is Language?" from *An Introduction to Language,* Fourth Edition, by Victoria Fromkin and Robert Rodman. Published by Holt, Rinehart and Winston, Fort Worth, TX, 1988.

PHOTO CREDITS

Abbreviations used: (tl)top left, (tc)top center, (tr)top right, (l)left, (cl)center left, (c)center, (cr)center right, (r)right, (bl)bottom left, (bc)bottom center, (br)bottom right.

COVER: Scott Van Osdol/HRW Photo.

TABLE OF CONTENTS: Page vii (bl), John Langford/HRW Photo; ix, William Wegman, Tame Animals, 1987, Color Polaroid, 24 x 20 inches. Courtesy of William Wegman; x, Richard Megna/Fundamental Photographs; xi, Ron Colvin/ The Stock Illustration Source, Inc.; xiii, John Still/Photonica; xiv, National Fluid Milk Processor Promotion Board/Bozell Advertising Agency; xv, Victoria Smith/HRW Photo; xvi, ©1990 Robert A. Tyrrell; xvii, A & L Sinibaldi/Getty Images/Stone; xviii, Photo Edit; xix, Image Copyright ©2001 PhotoDisc, Inc.; xx, Peabody Essex Museum; xxi, Keren Su/Getty Images/Stone; xxii, Courtesy of McAllen International Museum/HRW photo by Eric Beggs; xxiii (tl), The Granger Collection, New York; xxiii (l), Clayton Fogie/Getty Images/Stone; xxiii (bl), Art Wolfe/Getty Images/Stone; xxiv, Jerry Jacka Photography/Courtesy of the Heard Museum, Phoenix, Arizona; xxv, SuperStock; xxvii, George Skene/Orlando Sentinel; xxviii, SuperStock.

PART OPENERS: Page xxxiv, 1, 338, 339, 402, 403, 844, 845, Dave Cutler/The Stock Illustration Source, Inc.

TAKING TESTS: Page 2, Digital Image copyright ©2004 EyeWire; 4, Johnathan/CORBIS; 8, Buddy Mays/CORBIS.

CHAPTER 1: Page 16, John Langford/HRW Photo; 20, Robert Dunne/Photo Researchers, Inc.; 40, Randal Alhadeff/HRW Photo; 45, Randal Alhadeff/HRW Photo.

CHAPTER 2: Page 54, William Wegman, Tame Animals, 1987, Color Polaroid, 24 x 20 inches. Courtesy of William Wegman.

CHAPTER 3: Page 90, Richard Megna/Fundamental Photographs.

CHAPTER 4: Page 126, Ron Colvin/The Stock Illustration Source, Inc.; 129, Sam Dudgeon/HRW Photo; 131, Photo by Jeremy Martin.

CHAPTER 5: Page 171, Hulton Archive/Getty Images; 186, Hulton Archive/Getty Images.

CHAPTER 6: Page 206, John Still/Photonica.

CHAPTER 7: Page 250, National Fluid Milk Processor Promotion Board/Bozell Advertising Agency; 274 (c), R. L. Kaylin/Getty Images/Stone; 274 (bc), Nick Gunderson/Getty Images/Stone; 285 (tr), Kasbohm & Company's You Can Draw!

CHAPTER 8: Page 294, Victoria Smith/HRW Photo; 297 (l), The Nature Conservancy; 297 (cl), Daryl Wilson/Tulsa World; 297 (bl), The Nature Conservancy; 298 (t), Michael Bisceglie/Animals Animals; 298 (cl), Ed Reschke/Peter Arnold, Inc.; 298 (bl), S. J. Krasemann/Peter Arnold, Inc.;

299 (tl), Renne Lynn/Photo Researchers, Inc.; 299 (cl), Jeff Lepore/Photo Researchers, Inc.; 299 (bl), Breck P. Kent/Animals Animals/Earth Scenes; 299 (tr), Robert P. Comport/Animals Animals/Earth Scenes; 299 (cr), Michael Bisceglie/Animals Animals/Earth Scenes; 299 (br), The Nature Conservancy; 309, Culver Pictures, Inc.; 317 (br), Sam Dudgeon/HRW Photo; 319, Sam Dudgeon/HRW Photo; 320 (tl), Sam Dudgeon/HRW Photo; 320 (cr), ©1998 Alan Krosnick/FoodPix; 330, United States Navy/BBDO, New York.

CHAPTER 9: Page 343, Joel Bennett/Getty Images/Stone; 344 (tl), Associated Press NASA TV; 344 (bl), Art Wolfe/Getty Images/Stone; 345, Library of Congress; 348 (bl), (br), Randal Alhadeff/HRW Photo; 349, John Elk III/Stock Boston.

CHAPTER 10: Page 352, John Lamb/Getty Images/Stone; 356, Bill Nation/Sygma; 358, Will and Dent McIntyre/Getty Images/Stone; 361, Giraudon/Art Resource, NY; 363, SuperStock; 365, Phil Degginger/Getty Images/Stone; 367, A & L Sinibaldi/Getty Images/Stone.

CHAPTER 11: Page 372, Sam Dudgeon/HRW Photo; 379, Centre de Arte Reina Sofia, Madrid, Spain/Art Resource, NY; 381, Tom Bean/Getty Images/Stone; 383, Wyatt McSpadden, Austin, TX; 384, Alabama Bureau of Tourism; 386 (tl), George Caleb Bingham portrait of Vinnie Ream. Courtesy of the State Historical Society of Missouri, Columbia; 386 (bl), Debbi Morello/Tom Keller & Associates; 387, ©1990 Robert A. Tyrrell; 394, Getty Images/FPG; 395, Roadsideamerica.com; 399, Hanson Carroll/Peter Arnold, Inc.; 400, 401, Courtesy of the Crazy Horse Memorial.

CHAPTER 12: Page 408, Ulf Sjostedt/Getty Images/FPG; 413, Getty Images/FPG; 416, Collection of the Oakland Museum, Kahn Collection; 420, Jose Fusta Raga/Corbis Stock Market; 423, SuperStock; 432, Nebraska State Historical Society.

CHAPTER 13: Page 438, Nebraska State Historical Society; 442, Keren Su/Getty Images/Stone; 443, Image Copyright ©2001 PhotoDisc, Inc.; 444, Martin A. Levick; 449, Corbis Images; 455, Digital Image copyright ©2002 EyeWire; 457, Image Copyright ©2001 PhotoDisc, Inc.; 461, Tibor Bognar/Corbis Stock Market.

CHAPTER 14: Page 469, Scala/Art Resource, NY; 471, Image Copyright ©2001 PhotoDisc, Inc.; 475, The Granger Collection, New York; 476, SuperStock; 481, AP/Wide World Photos; 482, Mark Wagner/Getty Images/Stone; 485, J. Greenberg/The Image Works.

CHAPTER 15: Page 494, Kennedy/TexaStock; 500 (bl), Alain DEJEAN/Sygma; 500 (br), Ron Behrmann.

CHAPTER 16: Page 519, NASA; 531, Peabody Essex Museum; 539, George Skene/Orlando Sentinel; 542, Robert Hynes/HRW Photo.

CHAPTER 17: Page 549 (tr), People's Republic of Congo, Northeast Region, Mahongwe Ethnic Group, Mask, Musee Barbier-Mueller, Geneva; 549 (c), Tate Gallery, London/Art Resource, NY; 549 (tr), Scala/Art Resource, NY; 552, Park Street Photography.

CHAPTER 18: Page 584, Peter Van Steen/HRW Photo; 598, The Granger Collection, New York.

CHAPTER 19: Page 616 (tl), (cl), Courtesy of McAllen International Museum/HRW photo by Eric Beggs; 619, Michelle Birdwell/HRW photo; 625 (cr), Jerry Jacka Photography/Courtesy of the Heard Museum, Phoenix, Arizona; 625 (r), Jerry Jacka Photography/Courtesy of the Faust Gallery, Scottsdale, Arizona; 625 (br), Jerry Jacka Photography; 625 (bc), Jerry Jacka Photography/Courtesy of Kathleen L. and William G. Howard; 632, (cl) (br), British Museum, London/Art Resource, NY.

CHAPTER 20: Page 643, Okanogan County Historical Society; 650, Cooper-Hewitt, National Design Museum, Smithsonian Institution/Art Resource, NY. Photo: Scott Hyde; 656, The Granger Collection, New York.

CHAPTER 21: Page 671 (cr), Gordon Parks/Hulton Archive/Getty Images; 671 (bl), John Dominis/LIFE Magazine ©Time Inc.; 674 (bl), James Holland/Stock Boston; 674 (bc), Photo Edit; 680, American History Museum; 685, Christopher Magadini/HRW photo by Eric Beggs.

CHAPTER 22: Page 706, Rex A. Butcher/Getty Images/Stone; 707, Dave Rosenberg/Getty Images/Stone; 709 (cr) (r) (br), Image Copyright ©2001 PhotoDisc, Inc.; 710 (tl), Clayton Fogie/Getty Images/Stone; 710 (tc), Art Wolfe/Getty Images/Stone; 712, Scala/Art Resource, NY; 718, Art Resource, NY.

CHAPTER 23: Page 725, Vicki Ragan.

CHAPTER 24: Page 749, Courtesy of Emilio Aguirre/HRW Photo by Eric Beggs; 774 (bl), (br), The Granger Collection, New York.

CHAPTER 25: Page 781, Bettmann/CORBIS; 786 (tl), National Museum of American Art, Washington DC/Art Resource, NY; 786 (br), Library of Congress; 801, The Granger Collection, New York.

CHAPTER 26: Page 813, Image Copyright ©2001 PhotoDisc, Inc.; 814, Museum of the American Indian, New York/HRW Photo Research Library; 820, Classic PIO Partners; 825, Digital Image Copyright ©2001 Artville; 826, Alan Schein/Corbis Stock Market; 836, Image Copyright ©2001 PhotoDisc, Inc.

ILLUSTRATION CREDITS

TABLE OF CONTENTS: Page vi (tl), Jim Chow.

CHAPTER 1: Page 45 (all), Leslie Kell; 51 (b), HRW.

CHAPTER 4: Page 154 (b), HRW.

CHAPTER 5: Page 166 (all), Jim Chow.

CHAPTER 6: Page 223 (b), 229 (t), Leslie Kell.

CHAPTER 8: Page 312 (c), Leslie Kell; 316 (all), 317 (bl), 318 (all), HRW; 334 (b), Leslie Kell.

CHAPTER 11: Page 373 (cr), Ortelius Design; 388 (bl), 396 (t), Leslie Kell.

CHAPTER 17: Page 554 (bl), Rondi Collette; 562 (bl), Leslie Kell.

CHAPTER 19: Page 619 (b), Leslie Kell.

CHAPTER 20: Page 647 (br), Jack Scott.

CHAPTER 22: Page 710 (br), Uhl Studios, Inc.

CHAPTER 23: Page 728 (br), Leslie Kell.

CHAPTER 24: Page 745 (br), HRW; 763 (tr), Ortelius Design.

CHAPTER 26: Page 780 (c), Leslie Kell.

QRH: Page 850 (bl), Barry Erikson; 859 (bl), Robert Margulies/Margulies Medical Art; 859 (tr), 861 (bl), HRW; 862 (br), Leslie Kell; 864 (tr), MapQuest.com, Inc.; 873 (tr), 878 (br), Leslie Kell; 954 (bl), HRW.